D1524950

Frontispiece. Diamond Jenness at Collinson Point, Alaska, April 10, 1914.
(Photo by G.H. Wilkins (later Sir Hubert Wilkins), CMC Photo No. 50806.)

Arctic Odyssey

The Diary of Diamond Jenness,
Ethnologist with the Canadian Arctic Expedition
In Northern Alaska and Canada, 1913-1916

Edited and annotated by
Stuart E. Jenness

With a Foreword by
William E. Taylor, Jr.

Canadian Museum of Civilization

To the memory of my father
DIAMOND JENNESS
1886 - 1969

Canadian Cataloguing in Publication Data

Jenness, Diamond, 1886-1969

Arctic Odyssey: the Diary of Diamond Jenness,
Ethnologist with the Canadian Arctic Expedition in Northern Alaska and Canada, 1913-1916

Includes bibliographical references.
ISBN 0-662-12905-1

1. Jenness, Diamond, 1886-1969 — Diaries.
2. Canadian Arctic Expedition (1913-1918)
I. Jenness, Stuart E. (Stuart Edward), 1925-
II. Canadian Museum of Civilization.
III. Title.
IV. Title: The Diary of Diamond Jenness,
Ethnologist with the Canadian Arctic Expedi-
tion in Northern Alaska and Canada, 1913-1916.

G635.J4A3 1991   917.19   C91-098504-9

Printed and bound in Canada

Published under exclusive license by:
Canadian Museum of Civilization
100 Laurier Street
P.O. Box 3100, Station "B"
Hull, Quebec
J8X 4H2

Cover Photographs:

Diamond Jenness (left) and William Laird McKinlay
exchanging anecdotes on board the Canadian Arctic
Expedition flagship *Karluk*, June 1913. (Photo NAC
C86412)

Inset. Diamond Jenness at Collinson Point, Alaska,
April 10, 1914. (Photo by G.H. Wilkins (later
Sir Hubert Wilkins), CMC Photo No. 50806.)

Contents

Illustrations

Foreword

The *Arctic Odyssey* of Diamond Jenness, presented here with the immediacy and humanity of a private journal, simply could not now happen. That Arctic world of 1913-16 no longer exists. Its climate and geography remain, but the people, their ways of living, feeling, thinking, believing, and behaving, vanished and are now only lost, vague memories in a few, very old minds. For such reasons, Jenness' Arctic journal holds vital content. It provides us insight at ground level of his long, tough voyage of discovery, so that anyone interested in Arctic America or Canadian studies will find this journal a rare and enriching experience. Further, for Arctic scholars, this journal presents the detailed context for those pioneer monographs that launched the career of young Jenness and led to his becoming Canada's pre-eminent anthropologist.

Who was this remarkably able beginner?[1] A young New Zealander, slim, light-boned, of modest height, certainly no husky, outdoor adventurer. I don't think Jenness ever weighed more than 125 pounds. He was soft-spoken, modest, unfailingly courteous, and almost diffident, and he had no previous Arctic experience. Jenness did his Oxford degree in classics and took a diploma in anthropology, then a new and struggling discipline. After a year's fieldwork in New Guinea he returned to New Zealand to convalesce from malaria, an exhausting disease that dogged him in the Arctic.

And then came the telegram from Ottawa inviting him to join the Canadian Arctic Expedition. One now works easily in the modern Arctic in a cosy network of logistics, food, gear, and communications. The Arctic is now so easy and so close we scarcely imagine the kinds of risks and demands encountered daily by Jenness and his C.A.E. co-workers. Arctic Canada was then far-distant, at the edge of imagination, a place where starvation, disaster, and death came easily and where hardship was commonplace. The young Jenness succeeded despite all that. Then with the early death of Henri Beuchat in the loss of the *Karluk* at the expedition's beginning, Diamond Jenness undertook all the anthropological work planned for the two anthropologists. Jenness, although the younger and less experienced of the two, managed to cover all one might have expected of both.

And the load was yet more. Unlike his colleagues who suffered seasonal restrictions to their work in botany, zoology, geography, and geology, Jenness pursued research all year round. Further, because he alone of the Southern Party became fully fluent in Inuktitut and understood the culture, he was often called upon as interpreter and liaison for his com-

---

1. A more detailed summary of the career and a bibliography of Diamond Jenness can be found in his obituary by Henry B. Collins and W.E. Taylor in the journal *Arctic* (Vol. 23, No. 2, June 1970), or in Taylor's foreword to the seventh edition of *Indians of Canada* (University of Toronto Press, 1977).

panions. During the winter of 1914-15 in Coronation Gulf, Jenness spent much time obtaining food and clothing from the Inuit. In addition he collected flora and fauna for his colleagues when in areas they did not visit.

Diamond Jenness came south to Ottawa in 1916, arranged his affairs, and volunteered for service overseas as a gunner in the Canadian field artillery. Returning to Ottawa in 1919 he took up his career as anthropologist in the Victoria Memorial Museum (a building now occupied by the Canadian Museum of Nature), married and began normal family life, undertook ethnographic fieldwork, and became eventually the museum's Chief Anthropologist. His five volumes of the 14 published for the Canadian Arctic Expedition constitute the largest individual contribution of any C.A.E. member and, remarkably, the five include linguistics, folklore, ethnomusicology, physical anthropology, material culture, and ethnography. His work also yielded two important collections, one of archaeological material from Barter Island and the other his superb Copper Inuit collection, both housed in the Canadian Museum of Civilization. In 1928 Jenness published his evocative *The People of the Twilight*, which stands, I think, as the best single book on the traditional Canadian Inuit. Then, in 1957, he published *Dawn in Arctic Alaska*, a vivid, retrospective account of his precarious first year on the Arctic coast, the winter of 1913-1914 in this journal.

These fundamental contributions to Arctic research earned Jenness a distinguished place in Canadian and international scholarship. Although today his successors properly look back in awe at these Arctic and museum research years, Jenness also did fieldwork and published on some of Canada's other native people, the Sarcee, Carrier, Sekani, Beothuk, Ojibwa, and Salish. His classic 1932 book *Indians of Canada* is so worthwhile as to require repeated re-publishing, most recently in 1989, as the seventh edition. Although he always denied being an archaeologist, Jenness first identified two very important prehistoric Eskimo cultures, the Dorset in Canada and Old Bering Sea culture in Alaska.

Diamond Jenness served as Deputy Director of Intelligence in the Royal Canadian Air Force during the second world war. Later, with his Arctic background and because of his enduring love for the Inuit, he completed five volumes on Arctic administration, published most commendably by the Arctic Institute of North America. Jenness had hoped these would help to improve governments' administrative policies and procedures for Arctic peoples.

Sadly, Diamond Jenness was never able to return to the Copper Inuit despite a yearning to do so.

Now, 75 years after the twilight of traditional Canadian Inuit life, the Jenness journal becomes available, thoroughly annotated by his son, Dr. Stuart Jenness. It is particularly gratifying that the Canadian Museum of Civilization, the present-day derivative of the National Museum of Canada in which Diamond Jenness carved his successful anthropological career, has elected to publish his remarkable Arctic journal, the first and yet the last of his outstanding scientific writings.

The pervasive and profound changes in Inuit life since 1916 have revitalized this journal as the rare record of an observer and participant in a vanished world. Diamond Jenness would have hoped, despite his modesty, that descendents of those Inuit whom he met on this odyssey would find this journal useful.

William E. Taylor, Jr., F.R.S.C.
Senior Scientist,
Canadian Museum of Civilization
October 5, 1990

Preface

I first became aware of (and interested in) my father's Arctic diary in 1955, when he asked if I would draw five maps and copy the music of a song for a book he was writing. This book, he told me, was based upon the daily diary he had kept while serving as ethnologist for the Canadian Government on the Canadian Arctic Expedition of 1913-1918. A year or so later his manuscript was rejected by the Canadian publisher to whom he sent it, possibly because it was solely about experiences in northern Alaska. At any rate, he quietly set the manuscript aside and turned his attention to other matters. When I learned of this I asked him if I might try to find a publisher for his manuscript in the United States, where its subject would probably receive a more favourable reception. He agreed, and to our mutual satisfaction, the first publisher approached was delighted with the manuscript, and it appeared in 1957 as *Dawn in Arctic Alaska*. Following its publication I asked my father what he planned to do with the original copy of the diary. As he had no further need for it, he replied, he would probably discard it. (He was never one to save things once he considered their usefulness ended.) Fortunately, I was able to persuade him to give it to me, and it resided in my office until 1962, when he asked for it back to send to the widow of Vilhjalmur Stefansson, at her request, in order that a copy of it could be added to the Stefansson Collection in Baker Library at Dartmouth College, Hanover, New Hampshire.

It was not until 1970, a year after my father's death, that I learned that his diary consisted of three volumes rather than one. The first volume, which was the one I knew, was somewhat larger in outside dimensions than the other two and contained entries from September 20, 1913, to July 26, 1914. The other two covered the periods July 27, 1914, to April 12, 1915, and April 13, 1915, to August 14, 1916, respectively. The first volume was, I believe, purchased in Barrow (or Cape Smythe as the small community was commonly called in 1913) to replace a small notebook my father took with him when he left the Expedition's flagship *Karluk*. The other two volumes, obtained after he rejoined the other scientists at Camden Bay in the spring of 1914, are similar to (though slightly larger and thicker than) the three diary volumes of his Expedition colleague K.G. Chipman. Hence they were probably part of the Expedition's stationary supplies, which were purchased in Victoria.

During the early 1970s I typed the contents of all three volumes. The edges of some pages in the first volume had become tattered by that time, but being familiar with my father's handwriting, I was able to interpret, I believe correctly, many words or parts of words that were difficult to identify and supply others that were missing entirely. The original three volumes were then donated by my mother to the National Archives of Canada, that they might be preserved and made available to future researchers. In return, the Archives provided our family with photocopies of the complete diary. The text on the following pages has been checked for accuracy against my photocopy of the handwritten original.

I have had two objects in mind in preparing my father's lengthy diary for publication: (1) to make its contents available for all persons interested in Eskimo activities, culture, and living conditions in northern Alaska and Canada early in this century; and (2) to offer a revealing glimpse of my father's personality and character, through his daily accounting of his adventures during the three years he was in the Arctic. Not simply a routine account of a series of chronological events, my father's daily entries also provide a view of the feelings and responses of an idealistic, sensitive, and dedicated young scientist thrust into dire living conditions in a culture totally foreign to any he had known previously. The three-volume diary is also, of course, an extraordinary account of a very modest man's industriousness and perseverance in carrying out far more than was expected of him, in spite of a multiplicity of delays, frustrations, perilous experiences, and recurring ailments. Although my father later drew considerably upon the diary's contents for his books (*Dawn in Arctic Alaska*, which deals with his experiences during his first winter in the north, and *People of the Twilight*, which deals with experiences he had during the next two years with the Copper Eskimos), for his five volumes in the Canadian Arctic Expedition Report Series (vol. 12 - 16), and for several articles, there remains sufficient valuable ethno-historical information to justify publication of the diary now in its entirety. To the basic writings I have added many notes, drawn from a wide range of sources, many of them hitherto unknown, to clarify and expand statements in the diary, providing thereby as complete a picture of my father's unique experiences as possible.

My interest in undertaking this project was augmented by the fact that I had known, in my younger days, most of the five other scientists with whom my father was associated during much of his Arctic experience. Dr. Anderson, Chipman, and Cox I recall quite vividly, and Johansen apparently visited our house on several occasions when I was very young. Stefansson too visited my father at our summer cottage near Ottawa in July 1931, though I do not recall the occasion and know of it only from the contents of a letter (Jenness, 1931) and several photographs taken at the time by R.S. Finnie (Finnie Collection, NAC Access No. 1987-154). O'Neill was the only one I did not meet; he resided in Montreal and his geological interests and activities took him in a different direction from that followed by my father. Nevertheless, I have felt a closeness to these men and the roles they played during their three years in the north, and it is highly probable that this personal familiarity has influenced my enthusiasm for, and perhaps obsession with, completing this literary undertaking.

The title for this ethno-historical treatise has been selected for two reasons: (1) The word "odyssey," as defined in *Webster's 3rd International Dictionary*, is "a series of adventurous journeys usually marked by many changes of fortune," which the author's account certainly is; and (2) the author was unusually fond of Homer's *The Odyssey*. In the summer of 1906, as one of only two students in a Greek class with Professor William von Zedlitz at Victoria University College, Wellington, New Zealand, he was invited to read *The Odyssey* each Friday evening in Greek at his professor's home, an activity he recalled nearly 60 years later with feelings of gratitude (Jenness, 1963). Again, during the seven months he wandered about southwestern Victoria Island with his Copper Eskimo friends in 1915, my father often found moments for reading passages in and obtaining spiritual comfort from a small copy of *The Odyssey* he carried with him. This book evidently had a special meaning to him, and he continued to extract both pleasure and comfort from it on later occasions, including a time two years later when he was in the muddy wartime trenches in France.

Regarding the material in the diary itself, I have deliberately reproduced as closely as possible its entire original wording. By adopting this approach, I have ensured not only the accuracy and completeness of the narrative contents but also the retention of the sheer poetic beauty of some of my father's passages. These occasional literary gems give a special insight into the influence his classical education had upon him, and are all the more awesome in view of the severity of the living circumstances during which they were sometimes written. Throughout the diary there is a genteelness of prose in his descriptions of the primitive living conditions he was experiencing and few expressions of complaint or criticism (although these would have been perfectly understandable considering his almost daily hardships, repetitious and often dreary routines, frustrations, and interpersonal irritations).

To render my father's chronological entries more readable, I have divided the entire work into four parts, each with many chapters, and have placed brief topical synopses at the start of each chapter, a practice that was common in publications of the diaries of several Arctic explorers in the 19th century. Part 1 and Part 2 coincide with the first two volumes of the original diary; Part 3 pertains to the seven months from April to November 1915 that my father spent with a small group of nomadic Copper Eskimos on Victoria Island. Part 4 covers the final nine months that he was in the Arctic, during which time he carried out a great deal of trading with the Copper Eskimos, recorded more than 120 of their songs, and conducted several brief forays to east and west to round out his ethnological knowledge of these stone-age native peoples who, within less than a decade, would experience radical changes to their way of life, brought on by the arrival of white traders, missionaries, mining prospectors, and others.

To complete this unusual story I have added a Prologue setting forth many of the events that led up to the first entries in the diary and an Epilogue setting forth what happened to some of the main characters after the diary ends. In addition I have added seven appendices with lists of various matters related to his work in the north. I have also supplied full references for the published books, reports, and articles and the many unpublished documents that I have cited.

In editing the diary I have retained my father's use of British (as distinct from American) spelling. I have also retained his spelling of the names of the many Eskimos he encountered, though some of them have several versions. I have chosen to do so because it has not been possible in most cases to determine which (if any) are the correct spellings. As writing was unknown to the people he met, my father had to rely upon his ear to catch the sounds of the spoken names and words and to relate them to the various sounds of the 26-letter English alphabet. Retention of his spelling of the Eskimo names and words, although perhaps somewhat confusing at times, will also provide some insight into the evolution of his comprehension of the Eskimo language. Stefansson (1921, pp. 440-442) years ago discussed this problem of translating Eskimo sounds into equivalent English sounds. Probably the most common spelling variations involve the interchange of 'k's' with 'q's' and 'j's' with 'y's'. Additionally, 'h' replaces 's' in a few names, a variant I am told reflects Copper Eskimo usage in contrast to that of the Mackenzie delta or northern Alaska. To circumvent the confusion the spelling variants may cause, I have included in Appendix 1 the variations in name spellings I have found in both his diary and his published works, in the writings of his colleagues, and those of some others as well.

I have also retained my father's use of the formal designations "Dr. Anderson" and "the Dr." whenever he refers to Rudolph Anderson, the leader of the Southern Party of the Expedition. Johansen likewise used the formal designation "Dr. Anderson" in his diary, and Chipman and O'Neill generally did so in their diaries. This usage, in my view, reflects the respect my father and his colleagues held for the knowledge, experience, and authority of their leader. It may also have been unconsciously encouraged by the latter, a quiet, soft-spoken, serious man, a former army officer, older by a decade than most of the others, and devoutly dedicated to achieving the successful completion of the work they had all been assigned. For consistency I have employed the same formal usage in my footnotes.

Two names that my father consistently misspelled throughout the diary were Stefánsson and Johansen; these he spelled Stefánnson and Johannsen. As there is no question on their proper spelling I have corrected them both throughout the diary, though I have deliberately omitted the accent over the 'a' following modern usage as well as that in Stefansson's own published work *The Friendly Arctic*. Several other non-Eskimo names are misspelled in the diary and where I have had proof of the correct spelling I have corrected them. They include Charles Thomsen, Andre Norem, Matt Andreasen, Daniel Blue, and Aarnout Castel, all of whom he encountered during his first year in the Arctic. The variants of these names given in the diary are included in Appendix 1.

I have also changed my father's spelling of a few geographic names, for which a correct form is now established. These include Wrangel Island (which was spelled Wrangell at that time but has since been changed to Wrangel in English writings) and Fort McPherson (which my father and others on the Expedition spelled Fort Macpherson at the time, but which was officially changed a few years later by the Canadian Board of Geographic Names). However, I have left unchanged my father's spelling of Cape Smythe (the spelling was changed to Cape Smyth by the U.S. Board of Geographic Names in 1978), which was used also for Charles Brower's trading post. The settlement is now known as Barrow, a name my father used occasionally in later parts of his diary.

I have retained my father's usage of the term *Eskimo* for the native people of northern Canada and Alaska, because the name *Inuit* came into common use in Canada only after his death in 1969. For consistency I have also retained the term in my footnotes. My father always regarded the word *Eskimo* as a completely acceptable and respectable ethnological term, and it has had long-established international usage. Early in the 1970s, following proposals from some Canadian native peoples, the term *Inuit* (= the people) rapidly replaced the term *Eskimo* in Canadian government documents, and in newspapers and magazines, and is now widely used in Canada, particularly in the northeastern part. The change was advocated, evidently, to get away from a commonly held perjorative connotation assigned the term *Eskimo* (= eaters of raw flesh) from its Indian derivation (see, for example, Gadacz, 1985, pp. 590-591). There remains, however, strong grounds for retaining the term *Eskimo* in professional treatises. Goddard (1984), for example, has refuted the perjorative connotation on derivational grounds, Sperry (1987) has expressed cultural and philosophical reasons for the retention of the word *Eskimo*, and the term is still in common use in the western Canadian Arctic (e.g. at Holman, Victoria Island, where the native handicrafts are still "hand made by Holman Eskimos") and in Alaska.

My father used many symbols and abbreviations throughout his diary, as one might expect. With few exceptions I have written these out — symbols such as '&', and words and geographic directions such as N.E. I have, however, retained his use of lbs (albeit technically incorrect) for pounds weight. Additionally I have changed many of his arabic numbers into words, identified times of the day as a.m. or p.m. to ensure clarity, inserted the year following the day and month at the start of each chapter, and added, deleted, or changed punctuation where I judged it to be necessary for a clear understanding of the text. Here and there, for completeness and/or clarity, I have also inserted one or more words in brackets in the text. In a few places I have formatted new paragraphs where these do not exist in the diary.

To the already lengthy daily account I have added many footnotes in order to clarify words or statements made by my father or to supply relevant supplementary information. His own footnotes, which occur in only a few places throughout the diary, are followed by his initials in brackets.

Apart from these editorial changes, however, which I consider to be of a minor nature, the core text of the diary remains as my father originally wrote it when he was in the Arctic. Unlike Dr. Anderson he did not prepare a typed copy (with changes and additions from the original version) after his return from the north. McConnell also typed his diary some years later, his original diary having been written in shorthand.

Copies of my father's many little sketches in his diary, though amateurish in appearance, have been included among the following pages because of the additional insight they provide into the direction of his interest in the culture he was studying. Most of them were drawn during the dark fall and winter months of his first year in the Arctic, when he did not have a camera. (Only Wilkins took a camera when Stefansson's little party left the *Karluk* on September 20, 1913. My father's personal camera was left behind on the *Karluk* and was therefore lost.) I have supplied captions to his sketches for identification purposes and in some instances to provide additional information. I have also included reproductions of three maps drawn by my father, one by his colleague John Cox, and one drawn by a middle-aged inland Eskimo woman in northern Alaska. To these I have added 25 maps showing the routes of his many journeys, to assist the reader in understanding and appreciating the extent of my father's travels. In preparing these maps I have utilized my early training as a field geologist to relate the descriptions of features he observed with features on aerial photographs and recent topographic maps, and am confident the results reproduce as closely as is now possible his actual routes.

My father was supplied with a Kodak 3A camera after he reached Camden Bay in March 1914 and took about 300 photographs during the next two years, of which 260 survive. There are in addition 18 photographs taken by G.H. Wilkins specifically for my father. These 278 photographs are listed in Appendix 6. The quality of many of his pictures is well below what today would be considered acceptable but is still remarkable considering the slowness of the film in 1914, the crude equipment and conditions available for their development at the time, and the fact that he developed most if not all of his pictures himself. Several of his photographs are included in the following pages, along with a few taken by other members of the Expedition because of their connection with his work and experiences. These are but a small part of the approximately 3000 photographs taken by the various members of the Canadian Arctic Expedition, the negatives of which are now stored by the National Archives of Canada in Ottawa. An almost complete duplicate set of negatives was until recently also stored in the Photo Retrieval and Microfilm Section of the National Museums of Canada (NMC) in Ottawa, where I was kindly given free access to view and order whatever photographs I desired. Photographs in this duplicate collection (now stored by the Canadian Museum of Civilization, Hull, Quebec) are identified in the figure captions and footnotes with a CMC Photo No. The photographs taken by the geologist, O'Neill, as well as four taken by my father but listed with O'Neill's photographs, are stored by the Library, Geological Survey of Canada, Ottawa.

Acknowledgments

For the initial impetus for this project I owe a large debt of gratitude to my father, who would find it rather amusing, I suspect, that I had so belatedly become studiously embroiled in his early endeavours. Additional early impetus was provided by William L. McKinlay, of Glasgow, Scotland, with whom I had the great pleasure of four stimulating and rewarding visits in the late 1970s and early 1980s prior to his death. His clarity of mind in recalling some of the events during the fateful last voyage on the *Karluk* so many years before provide me with a continuing sense of amazement and awe. Even after 70 years he recalled with warmth and much fondness his brief contact with my father, who was the first member of the Expedition he met on his arrival at Victoria late in May 1913.

During the preparation of the manuscript, I received much cooperation and assistance from personnel of the Canadian Museum of Civilization (Archaeological Survey of Canada, Canadian Ethnology Services, and Canadian Centre for Folk Culture Studies), the Canadian Museum of Nature (Vertebrate Zoology Division), and the National Archives of Canada (Manuscript Division), for which I am most grateful. Frequent encouragement from scientists interested in early activities in the Arctic and from many friends also provided much helpful stimulus.

Professor Roland Jeffreys, Chairman, Department of Classics, Carleton Univerity, Ottawa, kindly translated the Latin and Greek expressions my father included in the diary in entries for November 2, 1913, and June 6, 1914. Ms. Rosemarie Avrana Meyok, Innuinaqtun language specialist at Coppermine, N.W.T., gave me valuable assistance in the preparation of Appendix 2.

I acknowledge with pleasure the skillful drafting done by Victor Dohar and Jo-Anne Froescul on twenty-five maps and three ground plans in this book and also the careful and patient processing of my manuscript by the publishing staff at the Canadian Museum of Civilization.

Several individuals at the Baker Library (Stefansson Collection), Dartmouth College, Hanover, New Hampshire, most graciously ferreted out much material previously unknown to me pertaining to B. McConnell, G.H. Wilkins, and my father. The Archivist and Librarian of the Pitt Rivers Museum, University of Oxford, Oxford, England, supplied me with a copy of an almost unknown but important letter written in July 1913 by my father to one of his professors at Oxford, and steered me to several other letters, heretofore unknown but important, in the Bodleian Library at Oxford, written by my father between 1911 and 1919 to R.R. Marett, his Professor of Anthropology at the University of Oxford.

Encouragement to complete the manuscript came unexpectedly from many individuals I spoke to during a brief visit to Coronation Gulf and Victoria Island in July 1989 (aided partly by a travel grant from the "Arctic Awareness Program" of the Polar Continental Shelf Project, Department of Energy, Mines and Resources, Ottawa).

The contents of the diary are reproduced with the permission of the National Archives of Canada in Ottawa, and the photographs (with four exceptions) with the permission of the Canadian Museum of Civilization, Hull, Quebec, and the Geological Survey of Canada, Ottawa. The three aerial photographs (on page 297, copyright 1965, page 464, copyright 1957, and page 494, copyright 1949, Her Majesty the Queen in Right of Canada) are reproduced from the collection of the National Air-photo Library with permission of Energy, Mines and Resources, Ottawa. Figure 208 is reproduced with the permission of the *Ottawa Citizen.*

I am especially indebted to Dr. William E. Taylor, Jr., formerly Director of the National Museum of Man, Ottawa, and later President of the Social Sciences and Humanities Research Council of Canada, who offered professional encouragement to my undertaking over several years, arranged that I receive a Presidential grant from that Council to assist me in the completion of my research endeavours, graciously consented to write the Foreword for this book, and played a leading role in bringing my manuscript to the attention of the Publishing Director at the Canadian Museum of Civilization.

Throughout the five years I worked to get this diary into its present form I have been constantly encouraged and assisted by my wife Jean. She has spent hundreds of hours patiently reading and re-reading the typed manuscript against the photocopy of the original diary to ensure accuracy of reproduction and in reading several drafts and proofs of the manuscript as it evolved. For such wonderful support and constant encouragement I am deeply grateful.

Stuart E. Jenness
Ottawa, Ontario
September 28, 1990

Prologue

Initial Concept

The idea for a major scientific expedition into the Canadian Arctic came to Viljhalmur Stefansson (the Canadian-born but American-naturalized Arctic explorer) sometime between 1908 and 1912. He was then carrying out exploratory and ethnological investigations in the Arctic with the zoologist Dr. Rudolph M. Anderson, their Stefansson-Anderson Expedition of 1908-1912 being under the joint sponsorship of the American Museum of Natural History and the Geological Survey of Canada. The timing for his new expedition was almost ideal, for both Americans and Europeans were then contemplating exploratory expeditions into the region north of the Canadian mainland, and the question of sovereignty of whatever terrain was there became a heated political issue in Canada.

The expedition that assembled early in 1913 under Stefansson's command was the largest and most ambitious Canadian scientific undertaking to that day. It was also the most all-encompassing government scientific expedition into the Canadian Arctic prior to 1955, when the Geological Survey mounted the 28-man helicopter and fixed-wing aircraft-supported Operation Franklin to map 200,000 square miles of the high Arctic.

Sources of Information

Much has been written about the exciting achievements of the leader of the expedition, Viljhalmur Stefansson, who literally disappeared northward with a small group of men into the little-known Arctic islands in 1914 and reappeared finally in 1918, two years after he was supposed to conclude his expedition.[1]

In sharp contrast to the abundance of writings on Stefansson and his explorations, little of a narrative-type account has been published on the tireless daily efforts of the topographers, geologist, mammalogist, biologist, and ethnologist who formed what was known as the Southern Party of the Canadian Arctic Expedition. Their considerable scientific accomplishments, however, can be ascertained from fourteen scientific volumes on observations and collections in the C.A.E. Report Series, two popular books published by my father, a few published articles, the unpublished reports submitted to Ottawa between 1913 and 1916 by each of the scientists, published accounts in the hard-to-find annual reports of the Department of the Naval Service and the Department of Mines, Ottawa, between 1913 and 1919, and the unpublished letters[2] and diaries (or field notes) of the scientists who made up the Southern Party.

Diaries

All scientific members of the Expedition were under instructions from the Canadian Government to keep daily diaries of their activities throughout the duration of the Expedition (W.L. McKinlay, verbal communication, 1980). Several of these diaries, daily logs, or field notes still exist. During the preparation for publication of my father's diary I have had access to those of Stefansson, McConnell, McKinlay, Mamen, Wilkins, and Bartlett, of the Northern Party, and of Dr. Anderson, Chipman, Johansen, O'Neill, and my father of the Southern Party. The contents of these various documents proved highly variable in the usefulness to me of the information they included, reflecting in part differences in interests and personalities of the individual men. There can be little doubt, however, that the controversy in Victoria in June 1913, over the privacy of the diaries greatly inhibited the later inclusion of personal matters in any of them. "For several members of the Expedition, however, ... the proposed rule *re* diaries frosted any budding enthusiasm for keeping records, and as far as I know, most of the journals were later purposely kept as brief as possible ..." (Anderson, 1919b or later, p. 16). A few are especially brief, unfortunately, and offered me little information. The diaries of greatest value to me were those of the members of the Southern Party, for it was with them that my father was connected during most of the three years he spent in the Arctic.

The diary of Kenneth Chipman, the principal topographer with the Expedition, has provided considerable information to support, confirm, and augment the contents of my father's diary. As Chipman was apparently the least reticent in writing personal observations, his diary here and there provides a valuable insight into the relationships and general morale of the various members of the Expedition. His diary is in the National Archives of Canada, Ottawa.

The diary of Chipman's assistant, John Cox, has not been located. Early in the 1970s, however, Cox informed J.F. Kidd, an Arctic archivist with the National Archives in Ottawa, that as far as he could recollect he had left his diary in Ottawa after his return from the Expedition.[3] The results of the joint topographic activities of Chipman and Cox were published in 1924 in Volume 11 (Part 2) of the 15-volume C.A.E. Report Series.

Dr. Anderson's diary (or "field notes" as he entitled them) contains, in addition to many entries concerning the bird and mammal specimens he collected, much detail on the day-to-day activities of himself and other members of his Southern Party, plus copies of several letters from Stefansson, Wilkins, my father, and others. It lacks, however, the narrative form of my father's diary, and reflects through its largely impersonal tone Dr. Anderson's assumption that others (assumedly including Stefansson) might someday examine it. Nevertheless it has proven of great value in supplying supporting and additional information to my father's entries. Dr. Anderson's original handwritten field notes, along with a typed version he prepared himself (or had typed for him after his return from the Arctic), are in the Vertebrate Zoology Division of the Canadian Museum of Nature (CMN). Dr. Anderson (1917) published a brief account of the accomplishments of his Southern Party shortly after his return from the north, but did not write either his fuller official account of that party's accomplishments or his report on the extensive mammal and bird collections he made for the National Museum in Ottawa, though both were supposed to form volumes in the C.A.E. Report Series.

In 1987 after several years of searching I succeeded in locating, in the Arktisk Institut in Charlottenlund, Denmark, the personal diary and field notes of Frits Johansen, the marine biologist and naturalist with the Southern Party. The National Archives of Canada in Ottawa subsequently obtained photocopies of his diary and field notes and arranged to have the personal diary (which is written in Danish) translated into English, through the Translation Branch of the Department of the Secretary of State, Ottawa. Johansen's reports on Arctic insects, vegetation, fishes, and a kind of crustacean known as euphyllopods were published as parts of volumes 3, 5, 6, and 7 of the C.A.E. Report Series. From one or other of these reports I have obtained supplementary information on my father's contribution to the Expedition's insect collection (Appendix 4).

The diary of John J. O'Neill, the geologist with the Southern Party, was donated to the National Archives of Canada by his son in May 1989, after most of the work on the present manuscript had been completed. As its entries cover primarily those periods when O'Neill was conducting his field work, at which times he was always many miles away from where my father was working, it contains little information about my father's activities. In consequence, I have not cited it herein. I have, however, included several notes containing information from O'Neill's published report of his field work, which appeared in 1924 as the first half of volume 11 in the C.A.E. Report Series.

The remaining scientific member of the Southern Party was my father. As the Expedition's only ethnologist, following the death of his colleague H. Beuchat,[4] he carried out extensive studies of the northern Alaskan and Copper Eskimos, publishing several small articles on the former by the early 1920s, and lengthy reports on the latter in Volumes 12, 13, 14, 15, and 16 in the C.A.E. Report Series.[5] He intended to publish a report entitled "Contributions to the archaeology of western Arctic America" as the final volume of the C.A.E. Report Series, but did not complete it, though he submitted a preliminary draft manuscript of 106 pages on the subject late in 1914 (Jenness, 1914j). His original three-volume diary is in the National Archives of Canada in Ottawa.

Inception of the Expedition

Viljhalmur Stefansson initiated the Canadian Arctic Expedition 1913-18 through his desire to explore the vast areas north of Canada's mainland in search of unknown land. By late January 1913, barely weeks after his return from a 4-year expedition of exploration in the Arctic (the Stefansson-Anderson Expedition of 1908-12), Stefansson had obtained assurance of financial support for a new and bigger expedition — $22,500 from each of the National Geographic Society in Washington, D.C., and the American Museum of Natural History in New York City, and an additional $5000 from the Harvard Travellers' Club, to which he belonged (Stefansson, 1921, p. vi). Some time later the Geographical Society of Philadelphia promised him sufficient funds to purchase and provision a ship for the expedition, but by that time Stefansson had gone to Canada to seek additional financial backing.

Arriving in Ottawa in early February 1913, Stefansson promptly sought support from both the Geological Survey of Canada (which had co-sponsored his previous expedition) and the Canadian Prime Minister, Robert Borden. The latter and his government, concerned over the possible challenge that an American-sponsored exploration expedition might render to Canada's sovereignty over its uncharted northern regions, hastily decided to finance the entire expedition in order to ensure that the ships carrying the expedition into the northern waters flew the Canadian flag and that any new lands discovered were claimed in the name of Canada, not the United States.

Within but a few days of Stefansson's arrival in Ottawa the American-sponsored expedition (which was to have been called "The Second Stefansson-Anderson Expedition") became the "Canadian Arctic Expedition," with full sponsorship by the Government of Canada. Stefansson was placed in command of the Expedition provided that he became a British subject,[6] this requirement ostensibly for the sake of appearances. Dr. Anderson (an American citizen) was offered a continuing position as mammalogist with the Geological Survey of Canada in Ottawa and was placed in charge of the various scientific members of the Geological Survey who were to be sent north with the Expedition.

Division of Responsibilities

According to the official instructions issued to him in late May 1913, Stefansson was to be the overall commander of the Expedition but would specifically explore the Beaufort Sea and the unknown waters in that vicinity. Should he discover new islands or other lands he was to take possession of them for Canada. He was expected to go to Banks and Prince Patrick Islands and beyond seeking the new lands. His exploration party was called the Northern Party, and its scientific personnel came from several European countries.

Dr. Anderson, on the other hand, was to direct the work of the Geological Survey scientists in mapping the northern coast of Canada and adjoining islands near Coronation Gulf and evaluating the copper deposits in the region. He was also to direct the studies and collections of the two ethnologists recruited for the Expedition and the work of a marine biologist, and was himself to make extensive collections of mammals and birds for the National Museum of Canada. Known as the Southern Party, Anderson's group was to function entirely independently of the Northern Party once it left the staging base at Herschel Island.

Serious problems arose even before the Expedition sailed to the Arctic, stemming in part from the seemingly simple two-fold delegation of authority between Stefansson and Anderson, and these problems increasingly plagued the plans and careers of some members of the Southern Party during the course of the Expedition and for years thereafter.

My Father's Initial Involvement

My father first became involved in the Expedition late in February 1913, when he received the first of two cablegrams from Dr. Edward Sapir in Ottawa, Canada. This cablegram was worded something as follows: "Will you join Stefansson Arctic Expedition and study Eskimos for three years? Reply collect" (Jenness, 1957, p. 3). He was then at his parents' home near Wellington, New Zealand. Dr. Sapir was chief anthropologist with the Geological Survey of Canada and had evidently obtained my father's name from a member of his staff, Marius Barbeau, who, three years previously, had been a graduate student in anthropology with my father at the University of Oxford.[7]

A second cablegram from Dr. Sapir added "All expenses paid from New Zealand. $500 per year in field, salary when work up results. If acceptable, cable, sail Victoria B.C. Send instructions general delivery" (Sapir, 1913a).[8] My father cabled his acceptance of the offer and speedily prepared for the experiences recounted in the following pages.

When he joined the Canadian Arctic Expedition, my father was 27 years old and had had little acquaintance with snow, none whatsoever with sub-zero winters. He was to share ethnological studies of the little-known native people in the Coronation Gulf region (to whom Stefansson had a short while earlier given the name 'Copper Eskimos') with Henri Beuchat, a well-known anthropologist from France. Stefansson also regarded himself as an ethnologist, but his prime interest on this Expedition was the exploration for new land. In return for his scientific endeavours, my father was to receive from the Geological Survey the small annual salary quoted in the second cablegram to him in New Zealand ($500 per year) and living expenses during his three years in the Arctic. His salary and that of his colleague Beuchat (also offered $500 per year) were the lowest paid to any of the members on the Expedition (Beuchat, 1913b), excluding only the cook ($480 per year) and Stefansson himself, who asked no salary, having negotiated several exclusive publishing and lecturing contracts from which he expected to be hand-somely reimbursed. At the completion of the Expedition my father was expected to continue temporarily at a small salary with the Geological Survey in Ottawa (he was subsequently offered $140 per month) until he had completed writing up the reports of his field investigations. Once his reports were completed he was expected to return to New Zealand, though whether the Geological Survey was prepared to pay his fare home was not certain.[9]

First One on the Job

My father left Wellington for Auckland on April 8, 1913, travelling in all probability by boat. There he boarded the Union Steamship Co. liner *Makura* and sailed on April 11 for Vancouver, borrowing money from his father for his travelling expenses (he was eventually reimbursed for these expenses by the Geological Survey in Ottawa). Disembarking at Victoria on April 30 he stayed briefly at the Ritz Hotel, being the only scientific member of the Expedition in Victoria at the time. During the next four weeks he spent many hours at the Parliamentary library reading all he could find about the Arctic and about Eskimo studies in particular. When other members of the Expedition finally arrived in Victoria at the end of May, he moved into the James Bay Hotel where they were stay-ing, and for the next three weeks worked with some of them collecting and packing the Expedition's equipment on board the *Karluk*.

The *Karluk* was a California-built brigantine, launched in 1884, and used initially in the Alaskan salmon trade. In 1892 it was bought to operate in the newly opened whaling grounds near Herschel Island (northwestern Canada) and made 14 voyages into the Arctic before lying idle from 1911 to 1913 (Bockstoce, 1977, p. 99). Early in 1913 it was purchased at Stefansson's request from its owner Stabens and Friedman, a San Francisco outfitting firm, in order to provide sea transportation for the Northern Party under his command. Stefansson was acquainted with this vessel, having had passage on it along the northern coast of Alaska and Canada in 1908 and 1909. By the end of May 1913, it had been ex-tensively (and expensively) refitted at the Esquimalt shipyards near Vic-toria for the voyage north.

Duties Assigned My Father

Some of the duties my father was expected to undertake during the next three years were set forth in a letter of instruction (Sapir, 1913b) my father received upon his arrival at Victoria on April 30. According to this letter the main part of his work was to be the collection of ethnological material from the various groups of Eskimos he would encounter in the Arctic region for the National Museum of Canada in Ottawa. He was also to expend considerable effort in obtaining full information on the non-material side of Eskimo culture, such as religion, shamanism, social organization, beliefs, and customs, to obtain detailed data on the physical characteristics of the Eskimos, such as shapes and dimensions, face painting, and tattooing, and to report in detail on their methods of hunting and fishing and their technological capabilities. He was to be attached to the Southern Party of the Expedition, concentrating his ethnological and archeological work on the Copper Eskimos in the Coronation Gulf region (Jenness, 1922a, p. 9).

Evidence for Activities During the First Four Months

My father in all probability kept a detailed diary from the time he left his home in New Zealand until September 20, but if so it was left behind with his other personal effects when he left the *Karluk* and was therefore lost when that ship sank. The same fate befell early parts of the diaries of McConnell, Wilkins, and Stefansson. McKinlay's diary (a typed copy of which McKinlay gave to the National Archives of Canada in 1927) starts July 25, 1913, which suggests that his earlier notes also were lost.

Because we do not have the first part of my father's diary, his activities from the time he arrived in Victoria on April 30 until his departure from the *Karluk* on September 20 have had to be pieced together from bits of information in the diaries of other members of the Expedition and from scattered correspondence and unpublished material (saved largely by Dr. Anderson and McConnell) that relate to that period. Chipman's diary commences on June 15, 1913, and provides quite a lot of information about the voyage of the *Karluk* from Esquimalt to Nome, but from Nome Chipman travelled on the *Mary Sachs* to Camden Bay, so that his diary after July 13, 1913, does not mention my father's activities until they met again the following year. The diaries of McKinlay (1913-14), Captain Bartlett (1915), and Mamen (1913-14) contain a few details about my father's activities (or matters that relate to him directly) between July 13 (when the *Karluk* left Nome) and September 20. Dr. Anderson's field notes, though they commence on May 27, 1913, tell us little of my father's activities during the early period, for he had little contact with my father prior to the spring of 1914.

Discord at Victoria

On June 8 Stefansson called a meeting of all members of the Expedition to brief them on the official instructions they had just received from Ottawa and various other topics. Much concern was voiced over the food supplies, equipment, and general logistics of the Expedition at this meeting, and Stefansson's answers proved overly vague and non-reassuring. Further dissent and controversy arose when Stefansson informed them that all diaries (private as well as scientific), journals, and notes must be turned over to the government at the close of the Expedition. His given reason was that as an ethnologist he might find material of ethnological value in their notes (Anderson, 1924). Most of the gathered members expressed their strong disapproval, arguing that it would suppress their inclinations to write personal matters and limit their note taking to purely technical matters. My father was involved in this argument, showing Stefansson a letter from Dr. Sapir in Ottawa which stated that personal diaries need not be handed in to the government (Sapir, 1913c). Stefansson's reply was that he would "override" such instructions (Jenness, 1913b).

Several Expedition members also voiced their strong objections to two clauses that had been included in their contracts at the insistence of the Director of the Geological Survey of Canada, R.W. Brock (Sapir, 1913c). The first of these banned the giving out of news except by official reports to headquarters; the other one stipulated that all mail from Expedition members was to be sent to the Geological Survey in Ottawa to be forwarded from there. The news ban, they learned from Stefansson that day, was to protect his remunerative contracts for news items, articles, and a book on the Expedition. The direction of their personal mail through Ottawa, some of them suspected, could result in their letters being opened to prevent the leakage of news. There is no evidence, however, that any letters subsequently despatched from the Arctic through Ottawa were ever opened for inspection.

As a result of the general dissatisfaction with Stefansson's briefing on June 8, several members of the Expedition spoke of resigning immediately. Indeed, Dr. Anderson was so incensed he gave his resignation to Stefansson and sent a night telegram with his reasons for resigning to the Director of the Geological Survey (R.W. Brock). Stefansson finally persuaded him to continue with the Expedition, however, after pointing out that Dr. Anderson was the only member of the Southern Party with Arctic experience and repeatedly assuring him that the two divisions of the Expedition would operate entirely separately after leaving Nome and that Dr. Anderson would be totally in charge of the Southern Party thereafter (Anderson, 1924). Nevertheless several controversial matters remained unresolved that day, and the scientists' dissatisfactions and suspicions towards Stefansson continued to fester during the subsequent voyage north.

The Expedition Heads North

Renovations and loading finally completed, the *Karluk* steamed out of the harbour at Esquimalt on June 17, 1913, with the Expedition members and their equipment distributed in a highly disorganized manner on and below its deck. Her deck was piled high with 50 tons of bagged coal and sacks of fresh meat, vegetables, snow shoes and skiis, canoes, alcohol drums, and assorted wooden boxes. Stefansson remained behind briefly, attending to various matters including arranging the purchase of the 50-ton auxilliary schooner *Alaska* for the use of the Southern Party, before heading north from Seattle on July 1 with Dr. Anderson on the coastal steamer S.S. *Victoria* to catch up with the Expedition at Nome.

The *Karluk* steamed slowly northwards at a speed seldom exceeding 5 knots (it logged between 100 and 150 miles per day), through the Strait of Georgia, Queen Charlotte Strait and Sound, Fitz Hugh Sound, Tolmie

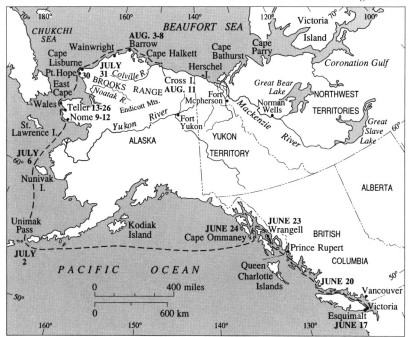

Figure 2. Map showing the route of the *Karluk* from Esquimalt, British Columbia to the Beaufort Sea, June 17 - August 12, 1913.

Channel, Grenville Channel, then past Prince Rupert, where it encountered heavy fog, and the Portland Canal at the southern border of Alaska. Musical concerts were given each evening on a Victrola that had been presented to the Expedition by Sir Richard MacBride, the Premier of British Columbia.

On the morning of the sixth day (June 23) the *Karluk* passed Ketchikan, encountered steering gear problems a few hours later, but managed to continue on past Stikine Strait and limped into Wrangell that night. There the pilot left the *Karluk* and returned to Victoria, and the ship's freshwater supply was replenished (it had been in short supply from the third day out of Esquimalt). Taking advantage of their first stop en route, the Expedition members went ashore, even though it was nearly midnight, to purchase and mail post cards to their friends. Later that night my father and Beuchat got into an extended discussion over the origin of an old totem pole they came upon in the town.

By the next evening (June 24) the *Karluk* passed Cape Ommaney and headed west across the Gulf of Alaska for Unimak Pass, encountering rolling seas, which put many of the men in their bunks. With sails hoisted to catch the tail wind the *Karluk* even managed to attain a speed of 7.5 knots part of the time. Engine trouble stopped the ship for several hours on one occasion, and a balky fireman refused to stoke the ship's fires even though threatened with imprisonment. By June 30 the ship's

Figure 3. Diamond Jenness (left) and William Laird McKinlay exchanging anecdotes on board the C.A.E. flagship *Karluk*, June 1913. (Photo NAC C86412)

freshwater supply was again low and the men were instructed to refrain from using it for washing. To while away the time many of the men resorted to rounds of boxing amidship, and on July 2 several matches were staged, one of them between Beuchat and my father (*Karluk Chronicle*).[10] In a rematch with Beuchat, my father reported ". . . the battle was stopped before I received mortal injuries" (Jenness, 1913c).

The same evening saw the *Karluk* sailing through Unimak Pass into the Bering Sea and fog. Four days later it sailed past Nunivak Island, only partly visible in the fog, and shortly after midnight on July 9 reached Nome, barely 4 hours ahead of the S.S. *Victoria*, on board which were Stefansson, Dr. and Mrs. Anderson, Dr. and Mrs. Murray, Miss Gertrude Allen (Stefansson's secretary), and Miss Bella Weitzner, of the American Museum of Natural History, who was helping Stefansson complete his 1908-12 report for that organization. At Nome the members of the Expedition were able to refresh themselves, both bodily (Chipman reported that the hot water was most welcome) and internally, while stationed at the Golden Gate Hotel. Most of them also received a good supply of mail, which had been brought north on the S.S. *Victoria*.

The Expedition's 'Naval Force' Increases

Shortly after their arrival at Nome, the Expedition members took possession of the 50-ton *Alaska*. It was supposed to be in first-class condition, but this proved not to be the case. Attempts were then made to divide the supplies shipped to Nome from Victoria and Seattle between the Northern and Southern Parties, to reduce the amount of this sort of activity originally scheduled for Herschel Island. After the *Karluk* steamed off on July 13 to Port Clarence, where it was to undergo engine repairs, it was realized that the *Alaska* was too small to carry all of the Southern Party's men and supplies. Using the authority granted him in the letter of instructions of May 29 from G.J. Desbarats, Deputy Minister of the Naval Service, Stefansson then purchased the 41-ton gasoline-powered schooner *Mary Sachs*, to carry the supplies and some men of the Southern Party to their destination.

This purchase necessitated renewed redistribution of the equipment, supplies, and personnel, which was once again accomplished in a rather haphazard fashion. My father's books and ethnological equipment, for example, were put on the *Mary Sachs*, which was the proper place for them, but he and his personal effects ended up on the *Karluk* because there was more passenger space there than on the two smaller schooners. Also, Stefansson expected the *Karluk* to reach Herschel Island before the other two ships, so the extra time there, he reasoned, would give both Beuchat and my father time to study the Eskimos around that little community and to do some archaeological excavations (Beuchat, 1913b).

The addition of the *Mary Sachs* brought the "Canadian Arctic Expedition Navy," as Chipman (1913-16, July 22, 1913) called it, to three schooners, five whaleboats (one with power), two other motor boats, three canoes, two dories, a dinghy, and several skin boats. By late July these were ready for their onslaught on the Arctic waters of northern Alaska and Canada.

Discord Again at Nome

While at Nome, several of the Expedition members arranged a meeting with Stefansson on the evening of July 10 to discuss several matters they found unsatisfactory and in need of resolution. Murray, Chipman, and my father were chief spokesmen (Jenness, 1913d), Murray speaking for the members of the Northern Party, Chipman for those of the Southern Party, and my father for himself and Beuchat. From all known accounts, Dr. Anderson was not at the meeting. The scientists sought planning details from Stefansson that he was largely unable to provide, with the result that the men got little more satisfaction from this meeting than they had received from the meeting in Victoria.

Stefansson (1921, p. 32) later wrote that this meeting was arranged because the men were concerned with the inadequacy of the freshwater supply of the *Karluk*. That matter was certainly one of their concerns, for the freshwater tanks on the *Karluk* had twice proven inadequate on the journey northwards. What troubled them even more, however, were the following seven technical matters (Chipman, 1913-16, July 10, 1913), none of which were mentioned in Stefansson's account of the meeting (1921, pp. 32-33): (1) the kinds of food supplies Stefansson had obtained in Seattle; (2) clothing; (3) the need for a proper base camp on land for the Northern Party; (4) information on where the Southern Party would make its base camp and what fuel supplies would be available there; (5) travelling equipment and dogs; (6) means of communications between the Northern and Southern parties; and (7) the availability of material for the two ethnologists to trade with the native peoples.

Stefansson's responses to these questions did not resolve the men's concerns, doubts, and suspicions, and at one point, in exasperation, he told them that they should have confidence in him and that their questions were impertinent. Murray, the oceanographer for the Northern Party, was so dissatisfied over the uncertainty of the arrangements, supplies, and delegation of authority that he almost resigned that same evening, but after some reflection wrote a strong letter to Stefansson stating his need for a shore base for his oceanographic work, and informing him that he would go no farther unless the matter of the shore base was settled (Beuchat, 1913b). Mackay wrote a similar letter to Stefansson. Stefansson's response was to try to get Johansen to replace Murray on the Northern Party, but Johansen refused. To appease Murray, Stefansson then promised him the use of the newly acquired schooner *Mary Sachs* for his oceanographic studies, but the following day he told Chipman that the ship would be put to other use (Chipman, 1913). My father's concern about having materials to trade with the natives was one of the few questions answered with any degree of adequacy, perhaps because that was a topic of more interest to Stefansson than the questions concerning the logistics of topographic mapping and oceanographic studies and collections.

The most serious question thrown at Stefansson at that meeting concerned leadership authority. The members of the Southern Party wanted Stefansson to put in writing that once the parties had separated Dr. Anderson was in full charge of the work of the Southern Party. Stefansson had agreed to such an arrangement in Victoria, but had not put it in writing as requested. At Nome he emphatically repeated that the Southern Party would operate entirely independently under the direction of Dr. Anderson, but again did not put it in writing, though asked to do so by Dr. Anderson sometime after the meeting (Jenness, 1914e). Later at Port Clarence he was once more asked by Dr. Anderson to state in writing that Dr. Anderson would have full charge of the Southern Party when the two parties separated (at Herschel Island), but he again failed to provide such a document (Jenness, 1914e), and the matter remained unsettled.

Northward from Nome

The *Karluk*, with my father and some of the other scientists on board, left Nome on July 13 for the more sheltered harbour at Port Clarence, while awaiting the completion of acquisitions and organization by Stefansson. The move may have been made "partly to get us out of the way and partly to avoid hotel expenses" (Jenness, 1914e). Upon arrival they anchored opposite the Lutheran Mission Station at Teller, where the water was deep enough for the ship, and where, according to Capt. Bartlett (Bartlett and Hale, 1916, p. 10), "we blew down the boiler, overhauled the engines, took on fresh water and rearranged our stores and equipment …"

While at Port Clarence, my father, McKinlay, and Beuchat went ashore in one of the canoes, heavily laden with instruments needed by McKinlay to undertake some magnetic work there. When a strong north wind came up in the afternoon, they signalled to the *Karluk* to send the motor dinghy for them. The dinghy's engine broke down while it was heading shoreward, and a whaleboat had to be manned to rescue it. It too ran into difficulties and had to return to the ship. Fortunately the three men were warmed and fed at the nearby Mission house, and after the wind died down were finally rescued by the whaleboat and returned to the *Karluk*. This was Beuchat's first canoe experience (Jenness, 1913b) and was also another example of trouble with the Expedition's boat equipment.

The *Karluk* and its men remained at Port Clarence until early morning, July 27, then headed for Barrow, along with the *Mary Sachs*, leaving the *Alaska* to follow after it had undergone extensive repairs, which delayed it until August 11. Around Cape Prince of Wales, the *Karluk* waited briefly for the *Mary Sachs*, which had fallen behind, and took Wilkins aboard, leaving Chipman and the geologist E. de K. Leffingwell to help Capt. Bernard navigate the smaller vessel around Point Barrow and on to Herschel Island. A short while later the two ships became separated in a dense fog and did not meet again.

The *Mary Sachs* and the *Alaska* subsequently made their way separately and with great difficulty along the north coast of Alaska as far east as Camden Bay, near the Canada-Alaska border, where they were forced by severe ice conditions to spend the winter.

Meanwhile the *Karluk*, with Stefansson (who had arrived belatedly from Nome), my father, Wilkins, McConnell, and five other scientific members of the Expedition, sailed alone northwards through the fog and rough Chukchi Sea waters, reaching Point Hope on July 30 for an overnight stop. There two young native men (Pauyuraq and Asecaq) were hired and came on board, and Stefansson was able to obtain an assortment of furs and skin boats. The *Karluk* left Point Hope the next day, passing Cape Lisburne a few hours later, and on August 1 encountered the ice pack, which halted its progress. By August 3 the ship was totally enclosed by ice, and Stefansson and Dr. Mackay took a dogsled to shore 2 miles distant, from where they walked to Cape Smythe, some 20 miles away. August 6 saw the *Karluk* a mile from Cape Smythe, and Dr. Mackay, Stefansson, and a friend of Stefansson's named John Hadley came aboard, together with several Eskimos (who were to hunt and sew clothing for the Northern Party), three skin boats, two kayaks, and three dogs. At the same time Expedition mail, including one of Wilkin's movie films, was left at Cape Smythe (Barrow) for forwarding. The *Karluk* got free of the ice on August 9 and steamed east of Point Barrow, close to shore and sounding constantly because of shallow water.

Decision to 'Put the Ship Into the Ice'

By August 11 the *Karluk* had worked its way east along the north shore of Alaska as far as Cross Island, where most of the Expedition members, including my father, went ashore. There they found traces of recent Eskimo habitation and a number of kinds of plants, including the Arctic poppy. They returned to the ship weary and wet (it had been raining) around 11:15 p.m. (Mamen, 1913-14, Aug. 11, 1913).

Faced with choosing between seeking a channel inside the offshore islands (which extend nearly 60 miles eastward from Cross Island to Flaxman Island), which was the route taken by most of the whaling ships at the time, or of trying to steam through leads in the ice outside the islands, Capt. Bartlett chose the latter course and headed the *Karluk* northward into the ice on the afternoon of August 12. His decision to do so may have been influenced by the knowledge that his heavily laden ship had grounded twice on the previous day (Bartlett, 1915, p. 25); he was also probably aware that the inside channel contained many shallow areas where the *Karluk* could run aground. Foggy conditions and the knowledge that his ship was greatly underpowered may have further influenced his decision.

Bartlett, as captain of the *Karluk*, was the rightful person to make the decision on the course his ship should follow on the afternoon of August 12, but he may have done so against Stefansson's wishes (see for example LeBourdais, 1963, p. 75; Diubaldo, 1978, p. 92; Hunt, 1986, p. 72). Stefansson was reportedly asleep at the time.

In any event, by 8 p.m. on the 12th, the *Karluk* became firmly entrapped some 20 miles northeast of Flaxman Island, not powerful enough to force its way any farther (Bartlett, 1915, p. 25), and this time it did not escape. Thereafter it drifted with the ice, first eastward for several days until it lay north of Camden Bay, then slowly westward until ultimately, in mid-January 1914, it was crushed by the ice and sank.

The Aborted Shore Trip

On the morning of August 29, after several days of confused preparation, my father and his fellow anthropologist Henri Beuchat set out from the *Karluk* for shore some 10 miles distant, accompanied by Wilkins, McConnell, Dr. Mackay, and three Eskimos (Kataktovik, Pauyuraq, and Asecaq) and with two heavily laden sledges pulled by seven dogs each, carrying a skin boat and provisions for three men and seven dogs for 30 days. Stefansson hoped that the two anthropologists and their Eskimo assistant would reach Flaxman Island, where they could leave a message at Leffingwell's cabin for the other two schooners, if they had not already passed, then push on east to Herschel Island to await or join Dr. Anderson and the others in the Southern Party. Stefansson gave them $100 in cash, cheques for $200 each, and another cheque for $500 with authority to act as an independent unit responsible to the Department of the Naval Service if the necessity arose, that is, if they did not soon make contact with the rest of the Southern Party. Stefansson also gave my father a pencilled note authorizing him to telegraph "such news as he considered interesting to the *New York Times*" (McKinlay, 1913-14, August 29). Both Beuchat and my father left letters with McKinlay in case anything should go amiss on their little expedition. The little group soon ran into nearly impassable ice conditions, which resulted in their *umiak* being badly damaged. Two hours after their departure from the ship Stefansson and Hadley started out with a sled to catch up with them to give them mail to send from Herschel Island. When he saw the condition of the men and their *umiak* Stefansson decided that they should cache some of their supplies and return to the ship. He hoped they might make a second attempt to get ashore, should ice conditions improve, but after waiting three days Stefansson ordered the return to the ship of the cached supplies.

Waiting Before the Action

During much of the next three weeks small parties of men went off hunting seals and birds to provide fresh meat for the men and food for the many dogs on the ship. Meanwhile the *Karluk* continued its slow westward drift within the ice mass. It was a dull and frustrating period for the men, and Stefansson urged them to exercise regularly on the ice to temper their spirits; Mamen even gave ski lessons on the ice for any

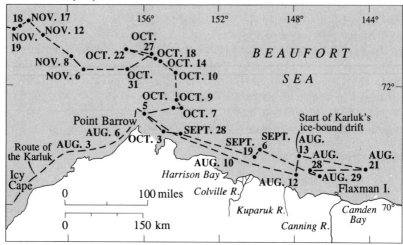

Figure 4. Map showing the course of the *Karluk* from August 3 - November 19, 1913 (Based on a map in Stefansson, 1921.)

who wished to benefit from them. By September 8 they had drifted west as far as Thetis Island, which they had passed on their way east on August 10. On September 17, at Stefansson's suggestion, my father, Dr. Mackay, and Mamen set off to the south to see if they could sight land, but returned unsuccessfully after travelling some 6 miles southwards. The next day Mamen and Dr. Mackay tried again to find land, but again returned without success. Snow, ice, and a low shoreline, together with the distance of the ship from shore, made it impossible to see land from the ship.

On the evening of September 19 Stefansson announced his intention of going ashore to hunt caribou in order to augment the ship's diminishing supply of fresh meat. In the past caribou had commonly summered just east of the Colville River, later migrating southwestward to winter southwest of Cape Smythe (Brower, 1944? p. 70). On this September day Stefansson decided to take 12 days' supplies, two sleds pulled by six dogs each, and Wilkins, McConnell, two Eskimos, and my father. He told McConnell that the sled experience would benefit my father later when he, McKinlay, Murray, and Beuchat would travel to Herschel Island to join Dr. Anderson and the rest of the Southern Party, and again after that when he lived among the Eskimos in the Coronation Gulf area. According to McConnell's diary, Wilkins and my father, then Bartlett and the ship's steward were called in turn to Stefansson's cabin for briefings about the hunting trip. Wilkins was very enthusiastic about the trip, but Jenness seemed to take it as a matter of course (McConnell, 1913-14, Sept. 19, 1913). Stefansson may have selected my father for this trip instead of Beuchat because my father was competent with a rifle and because Beuchat's health had been somewhat less than perfect during the previous month. Whatever the basis of his decision it may have saved my father's life, for Beuchat subsequently perished attempting to reach land after the *Karluk* sank. From this day onward, therefore, though he was unaware of it at the time, my father was to shoulder the full responsibility for all of the ethnological studies of the Copper Eskimos.

My Father's Diary

The first entry in my father's diary is September 20, 1913, recording the departure of Stefansson, Wilkins, McConnell, two young Eskimo men, and himself from the ice-bound *Karluk*. This date is also the starting date in Stefansson's diary. The diaries of Wilkins and McConnell commence on the previous day (September 19th), but both of these were typewritten later from their original notes. All previous diary entries recorded by these four men were left on the *Karluk* and were lost when that ship sank the following January. An entry dated October 14, 1913, in my father's diary reveals that he left the ship with a small notebook, from which he subsequently copied his account of the first weeks into what is now the first volume of his three surviving diary volumes. Unfortunately the whereabouts of this little notebook is unknown; it was probably discarded by my father.

The last entry in the diary is August 14, 1916 (erroneously recorded as July 14), a few hours before my father and his companions (Dr. Anderson, Cox, Johansen, Wilkins, and O'Neill) on the *Alaska* reached Nome, en route back to Ottawa. From Dr. Anderson's papers and diary and from Wilkins' diary it is possible to reconstruct a few details on the rest of the journey back to Ottawa. These are set forth in the Epilogue.

What follows now is the personal story of a young man, small of build, but large in determination to carry out the responsibilities that had befallen him to the fullness of his ability. The manner in which he carried out his responsibilities is given in considerable detail on the following pages.

Part 1

Unscheduled Sojourn in Northern Alaska

September 20, 1913 – July 26, 1914

Chapter 1. Stranded

Leaving the Karluk — *Provisions for 12 days — First night on the ice — Thetis Island — Foot injury — Shoreward progress blocked — Camp on Spy Island — Return to* Karluk *blocked — Ague attack —* Karluk *no longer visible — Fresh seal meat — Stefansson's views on Eskimo beliefs and customs — Move to Oliktok Point — Stefansson goes caribou hunting — More ague attacks — Ptarmigan for dinner — Old graves nearby — Stefansson returns without caribou — Decision to journey west to Cape Halkett*

Saturday, September 20th 1913

   The morning was fine and clear, with a mild easterly wind blowing. We were busy making preparations for our departure, Stefansson, Wilkins, McConnell, and myself, with the two Eskimos, Pauyuraq and Acicaq.[1] It was after dinner, about 1:30 p.m., when we got away, and we travelled continuously until 6:30 p.m. We have two sleds with six dogs each; two tents, both round, one of Burberry[2] with seven poles joined at the top, the other of drilling[2] [cloth] with a single centre pole; two stoves (one for alcohol, which can be lit quickly, but gives little heat, one for burning wood); an aluminum cooking set, provisions for 12 days, skis, rifles, and a few odds and ends. We expect to be away about a week, caribou-hunting on the mainland to obtain a little fresh meat. The *Karluk* has been stationary for a week, the ice in which she is beset being aground in 10 fathoms. The going on the first day was fairly good in spite of one or two rough places. In one of these the point of one of my skis was badly cracked through catching a ledge of ice. Possibly it can be mended. The dogs pulled well, but were visibly tired at the last. The leader of the second team[3] — a so-called Malemute named Watch — continually lay down in the track. He is the youngest dog of the team; the names of the others are Dock (or Ginger), Ham, Pudding, Jumbo, and Dub. The last two are splendid workers. Our camp is about 4 to 5 miles from the ship, slightly sheltered by a hummock of ice. McConnell,

Wilkins, and I have the drill tent, Stefansson and the two Eskimos, Pauy-uraq and Acicaq (Jerry and Jim) the other. Both of these Eskimos come from Point Hope. Stefansson heated some corned beef on the alcohol stove in his tent, then boiled tea (tabloid); this with five hard biscuits formed our meal. We turned in immediately afterwards. During the day we crossed a bear track and a few fox tracks, but did not see the animals themselves.

Sunday, September 21st

My feet became very cold in the early hours of the morning, and I had little sleep thereafter. My deerskin sleeping bag is both too long and too wide. We were up at 6 a.m. The weather outside was dull, but in the afternoon it cleared and the sun shone. The temperature is not very low apparently, though below freezing point; however, we have no thermometer. A moderate easterly blew all day. Breakfast — cooked on the alcohol stove — consisted of corned beef, biscuits, and tea. By 8 a.m. we were away. The going today was much the same as yesterday or rather better. There were several large ponds newly frozen over; the ice bent beneath the weight of the sleds and we had to rush them, and where it was too thin, make a detour round them. Soon after 11 a.m. we stopped for lunch — cold corned beef, chocolate, and biscuits, with a quart of tea we carried in a thermos flask. The dogs were as glad of the rest as we were. From the top of the large ice-hummock at the foot of which we rested, a low island could be descried to the south. We headed for this and landed about 2:30 p.m. It is the most westerly of the Jones or Thetis group, very low, of sandy gravel mostly covered with snow. Large quantities of driftwood were scattered all along the shore. While we cut up some firewood, erected the tents, and made all arrangements for the night, Stefansson walked over to the far side of the island to look for a passage to the mainland, for to the west of us there is open water. He saw some tracks of men[4] — one of whom was wearing European boots. Possibly they are Leffingwell's,[5] for their sled is of the Nansen type with wide runners, and Leffingwell, Stefansson says, is the only man who has this kind of sled about here. Our island[6] is the westernmost of the Thetis group — in the delta of the Colville River. On one of the islands of this group [Pingok Island] Stefansson dug on the site of some Eskimo ruins a few years ago. The depth of the sea from the *Karluk* south seems to decrease at a fairly uniform rate; at the *Karluk* it was 10 fathoms; sounding at lunch time today gave 6 fathoms, and half-way from our position then to the shore gave 3 1/2 fathoms. The bottom in each case was of mud. Two flocks of ducks flew over the island near our tents, the only bird or animal life of which we saw any signs. Plant life too appeared to be rather scarce. There were two or three kinds I noticed, of which one at least was the same as we gathered on Cross(?) Island.[7] The wood stove is a great improvement on the alcohol one – not only does it warm up the tent thoroughly, but we can dry our socks, mits, and *kamiks*[8] around it. The Burberry tent has no hole for the stove-pipes; our drill tent has, so the three of us (Wilkins, McConnell, and myself) have the benefit of the fire more than the others. Wilkins was chef tonight and gave us bacon, fried corned beef, rice with molasses, biscuits, and tea. I hurt my right foot today on a hard cake of ice — a bruised muscle, I think. It made me limp the rest of the day and was both painful and tiring. I hope it will be better tomorrow. It is now 8:30 p.m. and we are preparing to turn in. Under our deerskin sleeping bags we have two deerskins, fur side upward, and under them five sheepskins, wool downward. The latter are not very good, for snow and sand stick to the wool and keep them constantly wet.

Monday, September 22nd

We breakfasted at 6:30 a.m. in our drill tent. Wilkins lit the fire and warmed up together rice and corned beef, fried some bacon, made tea, and set out some biscuits. Near our tents was a large hummock of ice, from the top of which we could descry with the binoculars the masts of the *Karluk* some 12 miles to the north. Before 9 a.m. we started out southward over the young ice, but about 10 a.m. were brought to a stop by the ice becoming too thin. We took a sounding and the depth was only 1 fathom, while the water was nearly fresh. Turning northeast we made for another of the Thetis [Jones] Islands, some 4 miles east of the one we had just left. Presently we sighted a blue fox and almost simultaneously a white fox running over the glare ice. Several flocks of ducks flew by, but nothing came within range of our guns. On this second island [Spy Island] we found the debris of a recent camp[9] — empty tins, great numbers of bird skins, etc. Here we lunched — about 1:30 p.m. — frying some bacon and heating up the mixed rice and corned beef left over from breakfast; chocolate biscuits and tea completed the meal. Then we moved 300 or 400 yards further along the beach and pitched camp near a cached whaleboat, left apparently by the same people whose camp debris we observed earlier. Stefansson took his rifle and went out to examine the neighbourhood, and soon afterwards McConnell and Acicaq with shotguns went down to a pond of open water 1/4 mile away to try to obtain some ducks. Stefansson on his return announced that there was open water to the south and that it will be a week or so before we can cross to the mainland. Meanwhile we shall stay here, and tomorrow McConnell and Acicaq, with one sled will return to the *Karluk*.[10] McConnell and Acicaq brought back two eider ducks, three oldsquaw ducks, and a gull. Wilkins was cook again and gave us a mixture of crumbled biscuit and corn meat [corned beef] heated together, biscuits, and molasses, and tea. Stefansson sat in our tent until 9:45 p.m. writing a note for McConnell to take to the captain. While travelling today we saw a cutbank on the mainland, in the position where Cape Beechey is marked on the chart.[11] The chart, however, for this north coast is so inaccurate that it is impossible to identify with certainty many of the places that it marks. Leffingwell has been engaged for years in making an accurate survey from Demarcation Point to Cape Halkett and has almost

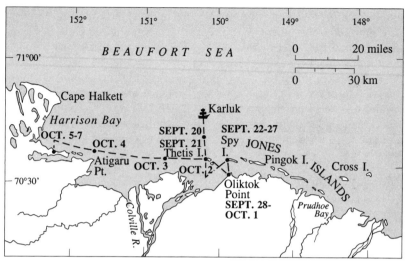

Figure 5. Map showing first week's travels.

finished the work. He gives the soundings all along the coast and in and out among the islands. At Nome he offered Capt. Bartlett a copy of his chart — Stefansson told me — but Bartlett refused.[12] A strong wind has been blowing all day from a little north of east and the air has felt very cold in consequence; probably the thermometer is not very low.

Tuesday, September 23rd

Wilkins, anticipating McConnell's departure for the ship, had breakfast ready by 5 a.m. — crumbled biscuit boiled, bacon, hard biscuit, and molasses. The wind, however, had increased during the night, creating small leads of open water to the north, so McConnell could not leave after all. Stefansson, feeling rather unwell, retired to his tent after breakfast and slept until 10 a.m. Wilkins and I skinned and cleaned the ducks and put them on the fire, while McConnell went down to the pool of open water to try and secure some more. The Eskimos reported a considerable crack to the north, consequently the wind must be driving the ice westward, and probably carrying the *Karluk* with it. She may drift beyond Point Barrow unless the ice is stopped by Cape Halkett. At present we are unable to reach either her or the mainland. McConnell returned about 8:30 a.m., and we had tea and biscuit, then he and Wilkins went off together after ducks. Stefansson turned out soon afterwards, and had tea also; to make the molasses go farther he made a mixture of lard and molasses (two parts lard to one of molasses) to be spread on the biscuits like butter; it certainly tastes well. McConnell and Wilkins and the Eskimos returning about noon, they with Stefansson set about making a wind-break with driftwood; I was officiating as cook for the day. Wilkins and Stefansson then went off to look for ducks, but returned empty-handed; I had equal ill-success as the result of an hour's watching beside a large pool — the ducks did not come close enough; and McConnell, who succeeded me, fared likewise. The bag for the day, therefore, was nil. At 4:30 p.m. we had an early dinner — ducks, biscuits, molasses mixed with lard, and tea. At 8 p.m. we had another meal — you can call it supper — comprising duck soup with rice, biscuits, compounded molasses, and tea. Finally we turned in about 9 p.m. The wind had changed about 5 p.m. to east-northeast and had diminished considerably in violence. A little later it almost died right away and a little snow fell. The thermometer, however, cannot be very far below freezing.

Wednesday, September 24th

McConnell was cook today, though Wilkins prepares breakfast as he sleeps nearest to the stove. We had breakfast at 7 a.m. — the rice soup of last night, bacon, biscuits, and compounded molasses, and tea. Wilkins immediately afterwards went out to look for ducks. Stefansson, McConnell, and I cleaned our rifles, while the [two] Eskimos also went off to look for ducks or seals. We have only two shotguns with us. The weather was calm and rather foggy. About a mile to the east of our island, Mr. Stefansson says, is the largest of the Thetis [Jones] Islands — [Pingok Island] about 7 miles long — where he did a little excavating some years ago. Towards noon all gathered for lunch — bacon, biscuits, and molasses compound, and tea. Our tabloid tea[13] is very good — it can be kept hot for a long time, and even reheated without tasting stale. In the afternoon McConnell skinned five birds for dinner (two oldsquaw ducks, an eider duck, and two gulls), while I gathered some drift wood and cut it up for firewood; sewing filled up the rest of my afternoon. My foot is still as painful as ever. Wilkins secured an oldsquaw duck; he saw a seal in the water but missed it. Stefansson sighted a seal lying on the ice about a mile from the tents, and sent the two Eskimos out after it. They used skis as the ice was thin, and worked up behind ice hummocks until within about 200 yards. The seal every minute or two raised its head, looked around, and dropped its head again. The Eskimos fired simultaneously, but missed, and the seal dived immediately into its hole. It was a common hair seal (*Phoca foetida*). For supper we had the birds boiled, with the water for soup, biscuits, compounded molasses, and tea; we turned in about 9 p.m. In the morning with the calm mild atmosphere the snow began to thaw a little, but in the afternoon the east wind sprang up again and increased towards evening, while the temperature fell appreciably.

Thursday, September 25th

The wind increased to a gale during the night, although in the morning the temperature seemed but little below freezing. For breakfast Wilkins heated up last night's soup and fried some bacon. McConnell immediately afterwards set about making a rucksack for himself. About 9:30 a.m. he and I took our guns and went west to a pool of open water to watch for ducks. We sat and waited behind a small hummock of ice, but an attack of ague (malarial)[14] overtook me, and I had to return to the tent. Inside the sleeping bag with a pile of clothes and sleeping bags on top, I recovered after an hour or so, though it left me somewhat slack and washed out. The rest of the day was spent in cleaning guns, mending clothes, etc. Wilkins cooked three oldsquaw ducks for dinner. Towards evening the wind subsided and a little sleet fell. This too passed over and the night was calm and mild.

Friday, September 26th

Breakfast at 7 a.m., after which Wilkins, McConnell, and the two Eskimos went off shooting; Stefansson retired to his tent, and I remained to cook. The air was calm, without a breath of wind, and the snow was thawing; it was true spring weather[15] in fact. I was mending my sleeping bag, which was torn down one seam, when Stefansson called me outside to observe the continuous band of black sky to the north, indicating a large body of open water in that direction. He thought it possible that the easterly gale we have just experienced may have cleared out the ice to the eastward, and that the *Karluk* may yet get free and reach Herschel Island.[16] There was great excitement towards noon. Stefansson had been searching the north with the binoculars and thought he saw the *Karluk* standing in towards us. He called the two Eskimos and McConnell, and proposed to kindle a large fire on the highest part of the island (about 10 feet above sea level). This, however, seemed useless, so they erected a kind of platform from which to watch the movements of the supposed vessel. Wilkins took a photograph of us gathered round it.[17] One after the other they returned to the tent for lunch, then went back to the platform. The dark spot, which seemed to be a vessel with its sails set, travelled rapidly eastward and by 3:30 p.m. was no longer visible. A light westerly breeze arose about noon, shifting round to the north towards evening; the temperature began to drop immediately. The bag [from our hunting efforts] today consisted of one gull, although a fox and three seals were observed. Consequently we had a tin of corned beef for dinner, boiled with rice, with biscuit[s] and molasses compound for dessert. Instead of tea we had chocolate, made by dissolving cake chocolate in boiling water and adding sugar. Pauyuraq, from a stump of red spruce (*ikiaq*), made two shotgun cleaning-rods. It is from red spruce that the Eskimos make their bows.

Saturday, September 27th

Wilkins' foot being painful (probably the effect of wearing skin boots) he elected to be cook today. McConnell has hurt his ancle and my foot is little better than it has been. We had breakfast at 6 a.m. and the [two] Eskimos went off to watch for seals beside a lead of open water. They missed several shots, but finally Acicaq killed a large hair seal (*Phoca foetida?*) and dragged it back to camp. I watched for an hour beside a lead which froze over last night, but had to return owing to another attack of malarial ague. Stefansson, McConnell, and the Eskimos went off again after lunch to try for more seals, but were unsuccessful. Lunch consisted of an enormous feast of boiled seal meat. Not having recovered from the ague I missed it, but was able to eat my share in the evening.[18] This seal will supply both the dogs and us with food for several days. Two days ago we found in the biscuit tin a piece of paper inserted by the girl who packed them. On it was written

Maud Rodgers	c/o Pophams [Biscuit Co.]
May 1913	Victoria, B.C.

"Please dear send me a p[icture] p[ost] card of the N[orth] Pole."[19]

The day has been almost windless and the air very mild, although a little snow fell this morning. The [two] Eskimos say that our mixture of lard and molasses resembles the half-digested vegetable food in the stomach of the caribou, which they call *nerukaq* (Point Hope).[20] Consequently we have christened it by that name too.

Stefansson gave me this expression

pisiksak.aqtilutik   *nuitkikpaqtut*
after they had been shot at they kept coming up again[21]

He told us the following regarding Eskimo beliefs and customs.[22] Every person has a soul (*nap.an*), which wanders about until the time of birth, when it enters the child and stays with it through life. But the *nap.an* is inexperienced and unable to look after the child. At birth, therefore, the child is called by the name of the last person — man or woman — who died in the neighbourhood, or if several have died since the last birth, by all their names. Now when a person dies the body is buried the following day, but the *nap.an* (or *nap.ata*) lingers in the house till the fourth day (if a man) or the fifth day if a woman. Then it is expelled, but remains at the grave until the next child is born in the neighbourhood. When the child receives the deceased's name, the deceased's *nap.an* at the same time enters the child and becomes its *atka* or guardian spirit (*kina atka* = what is his name). The child has now a double relation to the people in the neighbourhood. It embodies the *nap.an* of the deceased — so in addressing the child you address it as if it were the deceased. Thus a woman may call her own or another's child 'mother' or 'grandmother'. If, however, she is asked what relation of hers the child is, she will say it is her daughter, or brother's daughter or something of the kind. The child addresses its mother as mother, and if its mother is dead it addresses by that name the child that inherits its mother's name. The *atka* protects the child, guarding it from harm. A little child is wiser than an adult person, because its actions are inspired by its *atka* — the wise old man or woman who died. Consequently a child is never scolded or refused anything – even a knife or scissors. If it points to the mountain, the people look to see what there is there. They may see a caribou, in which case they say "See how much wiser the child is than we are; it could see the caribou when we couldn't." If they see nothing, they still say "The child saw caribou on the other side of the mountain, or perhaps it was a spirit." As the child grows older its *nap.an* becomes more experienced, and the protection of its *atka* becomes less necessary. Hence the parents are less afraid of offending the *atka* by punishing the child. They may, therefore, slap or scold the child when it is 10 years old or more — as soon as they consider its *nap.an* sufficiently developed. The *atka* does not leave the child, but its influence wanes as the years go by. At death the child's *nap.an* remains at the grave to be reincarnated in the first child born subsequently, but the *atka* disappears — no one knows what becomes of it. So the Eskimos believe in a future life, but it extends only through one generation; every man, that is to say, has two earthly lives. This belief extends from Cape Parry[23] to Nome.

The child calls anyone of whose relationship it is ignorant *arnakata* (= third person singular) (from *arnaq* = a woman, and *kata*). The word really means that the child's mother and the mother of the addressed person were sisters; in actual usage, however, it is used much more generally. It always implies, however, a certain degree of affection.

Stefansson told us a little about Eskimo surgery and medicine. For rheumatism they resort to bleeding and many Eskimos have scars all down their spines. Seal oil is used as a laxative, and with warm seal oil they extract stones from the ears. They believe that snow blindness is caused by the cold driving all the blood from the face into the head. As it returns it passes down the forehead into the eyes, making them red and producing blindness. A sure cure is to make two incisions, one above each eyebrow, to let out the blood as it is returning — if you can tell when that is.

A man may become an *angekok*[24] (= *añatkut*, Point Barrow) in two ways. The first is by purchase. Old *angekoks* have several familiar spirits, and are often willing to sell one or more of them when death is not far distant. The novice goes to him and bargains for one of these spirits — let us say his owl spirit. It will be very expensive — the old man may require a skin boat and many other things, but at last satisfactory terms are arranged. Then the old *angekok* goes into a house alone, beats his drum and conjures up the owl spirit. He tells it to attend henceforth the man who has bought it, if it is willing. Some days later the novice holds a similar seance and invokes the owl spirit. If it appears, all is well; he tells the people and thereafter is regarded as a full-fledged *angekok* to be called in whenever needed for sickness etc. If the owl spirit does not appear it is because the man is one of those unfortunate individuals who are disliked by the spirits. The old *angekok* will not restore the goods he has received, because the fault is not his; the people too despise the unfortunate object of the spirits' dislike. Consequently there is every inducement for the owl spirit to appear. The other method of becoming an *angekok* is by receiving a call. For example, a man may be building a snow house when he suddenly loses his knife. No living person is near, so it must have been a spirit who took it. Then the man rejoices, for he knows that one day, be it a few weeks or a few years hence, the spirit will come to him. Then one day it does come, perhaps while he is hunting, and gives him some task to do — it may be to make a horn spoon and leave it in a certain place. The man does so, and thereafter the spirit attends him and he is an *angekok*.

Sunday, September 28th

We breakfasted at 6:45 a.m. off seal meat, bacon, biscuit and *nerukaq*, and tea. Seal meat is much darker than other meat, but tastes all right. After breakfast Stefansson and Pauyuraq crossed over to the mainland on skis to find out if the ice was thick enough to bear the sleds. The rest of us remained in the tent, distracted with various petty occupations. I tried to repair my ski with a lashing of seal hide, Wilkins was cooking, McConnell sewing, and Acicaq studying English. Lunch was ready at 11:30 a.m., the piece de resistance being seal liver. Pauyuraq appeared while we were still eating, with instructions for us to strike camp and cross over to the mainland. Stefansson, he said, had gone to look for caribou. So as soon as lunch was over we loaded the sleds and set out. The ice was sticky and creaked ominously a few times, but an hour's travelling saw us safely over. We camped on the beach beside the remains of an old platform. McConnell soon afterwards took a shotgun and went off after an eider duck we had seen. He returned about an hour later with an oldsquaw duck and a yellow-billed loon. The yellow-billed loon, which is larger than the black-billed [common loon] (according to Stefansson), is about the size of a goose. Stefansson returned from hunting about dinner time — he had seen nothing. Near the camp were two or three small pools frozen over; from these we obtained drinking water by digging a hole with the axe. It was a little brackish and contained multitudes of tiny fish — copepods, I think. My foot has been rather painful the last two or three days and the fever has made me so weak that I find it very difficult to keep up with the sled, especially when I have to run ahead at times to check or disentangle the dogs. Our camp is at a place called Olektoq [Oliktok Point], at the eastern extremity of the Colville delta. It was here that the Eskimos of the west left their women when they went east to Barter Island to trade with the eastern Eskimos. It snowed all day, but though there was a slight breeze from the north the temperature did not seem very low. Last night our drill tent leaked badly, and our clothes and sleeping bags are wet.

Monday, September 29th

We had an early breakfast at 6 a.m. of seal meat, biscuits, *nerukaq*, and tea. Hardly was it over when the two Eskimos saw a flock of ptarmigan near the tents and shot three. Stefansson sent Wilkins and McConnell off, Wilkins to set up a notice on an old ruined house,[25] which we saw on the island next to that on which we were camped. McConnell was to travel along the chain of [Jones] islands to the easternmost, where two years ago there was an inhabited house; he was to return along the coast. Stefansson and the two Eskimos went caribou-hunting and I remained to cook. Two hours later Stefansson returned. McConnell and Wilkins had taken the wrong direction, he said. I made tea for him, but a sharp attack of ague came on while I was doing so, and I had to turn into my sleeping bag. Soon afterwards Stefansson went westward towards the mouth of the Colville River, and meeting Asicaq, sent him back to cook. Pauyuraq came back a few minutes before Acicaq, and not long afterwards McConnell — Wilkins had crossed over to the island. McConnell took over the cooking while the two Eskimos went shooting. Altogether their day's bag came to 17 ptarmigan. We boiled six for dinner — McConnell skinned four and I two. Wilkins returned soon after 5 p.m. with two large icicles hanging from his moustache like walrus-tusks. He had left the message at the ruin. He said that on one of the islands a few days previously he had noticed a miniature house made of tiny sticks planted in the ground thus:

Figure 6. Distribution of sticks in ground on one of the Jones Islands, to outline the shape of a house (top view on right).

Tuesday, September 30th

Breakfast at 7 a.m. Stefansson decided to go a day's journey inland to look for caribou, taking the two Eskimos, the Burberry tent, and one sled. The weather was fine and moderately clear. The morning was occupied in preparation, drying clothes, loading the sleds etc. About 1 p.m. they left and we three who remained settled down to lunch, biscuits, *nerukaq*, and chocolate. We have finished one biscuit tin and are now using the dog biscuits. After lunch I wandered round for an hour with the shotgun, but saw nothing in the way of game. Near our tent are several graves. In some the dead person was buried in the ground, logs were laid over the top, and a cross superposed (the result of Christianity); in others the corpse was merely laid on top of the ground and covered with driftwood. In a grave of the latter type Wilkins saw a skull half-burnt. Wilkins took the shotgun when I returned and wandered round, but saw nothing, and McConnell had the same ill-luck later. For dinner I fried some bacon and made chocolate. The atmosphere was foggy and the wind had sprung up again, so we drew the sled-cover round over the tent and turned in.

Wednesday, October 1st

We had an alarm last night at 9:45 p.m. The dogs began to bark furiously, and presently we heard something walking round the tent and sniffing. A loud scrunching noise followed, mingled with the tumult of dogs fighting. The tent was shaking violently and seemed as if it might collapse at any moment. We all jumped up, with thoughts of bear in our heads, but it proved to be only the dogs, which had broken loose and started to fight. Wilkins broke the butt of his rifle in restoring peace. At breakfast time, 7 a.m., a half-blizzard was blowing. We ate a ptarmigan apiece; biscuits, ptarmigan soup, and tea made up the rest of the meal. Then Wilkins set about repairing his rifle, while I washed the dishes and skinned a duck. A sharp attack of ague made me lie down,[26] but it had passed over by the time Stefansson and the two Eskimos returned — about 2:30 p.m. The weather rendered any attempt at caribou-hunting useless, so they had returned. For the rest of the day we remained in camp. A strong northeast wind blew uninterruptedly with snow in its train. We are almost out of dog-feed, so the ptarmigan must go to the dogs — an awful shame it seems. Pauyuraq skinned the loon and is to make a pair of slippers from it for me. It is useless remaining here any longer, so tomorrow we leave for Cape Halkett — about 70 miles away.

Chapter 2. Off to Barrow

McConnell off to investigate 'mast' — Return to Thetis Island — Heading west — Shortage of dog-feed — Another ague attack — Brief stay with Aksiatak and his family — Cape Halkett — Storage of equipment with Eskimo family — Another 20 miles covered — Cape Simpson — Tattoos on Eskimo women — News of the Karluk? *— Accommodation with Eskimo families — Crippled status of men — Arrival at Cape Smythe (Barrow) — News of other ships and men of the Expedition*

Thursday, October 2nd 1913

The morning was clear and calm with the snow melting a little. Our tent was half snowed in on one side; Wilkins took a photo of it. After breakfast the sleds were loaded, and everything was ready for starting when Stefannson saw something to the east, which might be either a post or the mast of a vessel. This delayed us for about an hour. Finally he sent McConnell with a pencilled note; if it proved to be a post he was to attach the note to it. Stefansson himself went south on snowshoes to look for caribou, while Wilkins, myself, and the two Eskimos with the sleds went nearly due north to the island on which we had first landed [Thetis Island]. We reached our old camping ground just before 4 p.m.,[1] and I resumed my duties as cook. Rice mixed with a tin of meat, biscuits, *nerukaq*, and tea, made up the evening meal. The molasses was finished so the *nerukaq* was made of lard and brown sugar. At 7:15 p.m. we lit a fire on top of an ice-hummock to guide McConnell and Stefansson. The latter turned up at 8:40 p.m. bringing a lump of whale meat (bowhead whale), which he had found. It weighed about 20 lb and had probably been used for trapping. McConnell did not turn up at all. Wilkins kept two fires burning until 3 a.m., one in the tent and the other on the ice-hummock. In the interval between dinner and Stefansson's arrival we had a kind of concert; the two Eskimos sang songs, using a box for a drum, and Wilkins and I responded.

Friday, October 3rd

The night was very cold and we all felt it. At breakfast time — 6 a.m. — the weather was clear and the sun shining. Wilkins and Pauyuraq went off to look for McConnell, taking a sled with them. They found him on his way to camp, about a mile off. He had arrived at our old camping ground 4 miles to the eastward about 6:30 p.m. The ice round the island was very thin, and he had fallen through up to his knees. Darkness coming on he decided to stay on the island for the night and dry his clothes. From the logs we had used for a wind-break he built up a huge fire, and though he did not sleep he did not suffer from the cold. The mast of a ship, he told us, had resolved itself into a stack of logs 6 inches or so in diameter. I cooked an early lunch, rice mixed with a tin of meat, biscuits, and *nerukaq*, and chocolate. By 1 p.m. we were packed up and set out westward, Stefansson going a short way out on the ice to the northward to look for the *Karluk*. We travelled due west about 10 miles and were pitching camp on a small ice-floe covered with deep snow when Stefansson turned up. The going was good, for we were travelling on bay ice. The dogs, however, are not so strong as they should be, because they are on short rations. We have only about 3 days dog-feed left. Wilkins' foot has been troubling him, but he found the skis a relief and used them most of the time, running ahead to make the track. My foot is rather painful and this, combined with the weakness which has resulted from the ague, caused me to ride on the sled most of the way.[2] For dinner we had pemmican, biscuits, and chocolate. Our food, too, is running low. The weather was good until 1:30 p.m., then it became foggy. The light easterly breeze of the morning increased during the afternoon, but we had it behind us. The temperature did not seem to be very low.

Saturday, October 4th

Breakfast at 6 a.m. — rice, a tin of meat, and chocolate. The wind during the night was fairly strong, but it died away towards morning, and when we started out at 8:10 a.m. the atmosphere was calm and very clear. Up till 10 a.m. the sun felt beautifully warm, then it became somewhat clouded. We travelled westward without a break until 11:30 a.m. when the Burberry tent was hoisted to boil some tea over the alcohol stove. This, with cold pemmican, made our lunch. I had been obliged to ride on the sled most of the time, being too weak to keep up, but the ice being good we made about 3 miles an hour. At lunch time a slight attack of ague came on, so I was wrapped inside my sleeping bag and lashed on top of the sled. Then we continued our journey westward, with two breaks, once for Asecaq to stalk a seal, once for Stefansson himself; both attempts were unsuccessful. Five or six seals were seen during the afternoon. At dusk we came to thin ice — a dog in each team fell through it — and were compelled to camp on a very small keg of ice. Two islands [the Eskimo Islands] lay to the south, apparently about 3 or 4 miles away. For dinner — which was cooked on the alcohol stove in the Burberry tent — we had bacon, cold pemmican, biscuits, and chocolate. The temperature has been very mild all day, with a very slight breeze from the east.

Sunday, October 5th

We had breakfast at 7 a.m.: pemmican, rice and biscuit all mixed together, with chocolate to drink. At 9 a.m. we set out. Just after noon we saw an Eskimo tent and rack to the south of our trail and directed our course towards it, reaching it at 1:40 p.m. It proved to be the home of Aksiatak and his family — a Colville River Eskimo who had just come down to the coast — five in all: the man, his wife, and three children, a girl about 8, another about 6, and a boy about 2 years of age. Stefansson had met him before, and each recognised the other. Aksiatak helped us to pitch camp, then invited us over to dinner. Here is the menu:

1st course	frozen fish, raw, with dried caribou fat (this latter is a very great delicacy and very expensive) and rancid seal oil
2nd course	– boiled ptarmigan
3rd course	– boiled fish (heads and all)
4th course	– tea

We changed our footgear in their tent and the lady of the house took charge of it all and hung the boots, etc. on the cords and sticks of the ceiling to dry. In blowing the fire the woman did not purse her lips as we did, but curled her tongue so as to make a kind of funnel. Both she and her husband smoked out of long pipes of the opium-pipe type, using imported tobacco. The children were very charming, especially the little girls. They appeared to be very fond of tea. The boy was allowed to play with the scissors or anything else that caught his fancy. He had his father's watch and began to hammer it on the floor; the father remonstrated very mildly. He dipped up snow-water from the pail; the mother waited until he had finished, then moved the pail behind the stove where he could not reach it. However, I saw her give him a slight push once. Before dinner the man produced a small bowl containing warm water, soap, and a towel. Our two Eskimos washed their faces and hands; we declined. Stefansson says it is a kind of sacrament among the Alaskan Eskimos, adopted with fervour from the whites; it has resulted in the rapid spread of many diseases, e.g., eye diseases, through the common use of a dirty towel. We used ptarmigan feathers for towels during the meal, and the woman used the same afterwards to wipe out the cups that we brought over. After dinner the man and his wife both smoked. These Eskimos gave us of their very best unstintingly. They are living themselves very largely on fish (caught with nets at a lake some distance away) and on ptarmigan, which the man shoots. The son [Itarklik] went to Point Barrow in a whaleboat to buy stores, but the early closing in of the ice prevented his return in the same way. He is expected every day now; we were mistaken for him. In the house there was flour, sugar, tobacco, and other white men's things. We gave them some tins of tabloid tea and a little tobacco that we had. To the children we gave a cake of chocolate, but they did not know what it was and seemed not to care for it. In addition we gave the family half a slab of bacon (= *tuktukiuk* = bad caribou); the man said he had tasted it before and could eat it if necessary, but was not keen on it; the woman knew it and liked it; the children had never seen it. On the platform beside the tent I saw a case of kerosene (coal oil) for the hurricane lamp. The boy was fed from a bottle containing diluted tinned milk! They buy their stores with foxskins. They were well provided with trade kettles, pans, cans, etc., but I saw no cutlery. The woman used a large and a small *ulo* [woman's knife] of iron; the man had a sheath knife. The man told us that during the summer he had shot only four caribou, and another man (his partner) only six. (According to Stefansson it takes at least 10 caribou to clothe a man for a year.) He had cached his sled at the mouth of the Colville River, and while he was inland about the time of the first ice (i.e., a month ago) five men came along and took it — white men, he thought, with one Eskimo; they had no dogs and had left their own sled — a rude structure of driftwood — in its place. We wonder whether the *Alaska* or the *Mary Sachs*[3] has been wrecked. His other sled, which he has here now, is shod with brass — very good in cold weather, Stefansson says. He [Aksiatak] told us further that Pedersen [captain of the *Elvira*] had put in at the mouth of the Sarvanaktok [Sagavanirktok] River this summer and traded with the Eskimos, but knew of no other vessel. Aksiatak's home here comprises the tent in which he is now living and a platform or rack on which he stores some of his goods. He is engaged in building a house for the winter, and has the framework already completed. It is made of driftwood logs set in the ground vertically side by side. His tent is a patchwork of cloth stretched over an oval frame of willow twigs — about 5 feet high, 9 feet long, and 7 feet wide. It was thus both roomy and comfortable. A flap of canvas hanging down formed the door. Inside, just to the right of the entrance, was a substantial wood stove — a trade article. The front half of the tent had a flooring of boards roughly cut out of driftwood; at the back were the skins, bedding, etc. The tent was clearly only a very temporary home, for it had an insufficient number of willow sticks, and driftwood was utilised instead. Neither the man nor his wife knew any English, so Stefansson translated for our benefit. We passed two islands about 11 a.m. which are called *Tigeragmiut*,[4] Aksiatak said, because long ago a war party of *Tigeragmiut* (Point Hope Eskimo) camped there. Their boats were stolen by the other Eskimos and all starved to death. Pauyuraq knew the story. I rode on the sled all day, being so weak that I have to stop and rest after walking 50 yards. Wilkins' foot troubled him somewhat. We made a bed of chips on which to stretch our skins and sleeping bags, all of which are very wet. The weather was fine all day, freezing, but not very cold; the air was perfectly calm. In the evening a brilliant band of carmine marked the sunset. Later there was a fine aurora — broad bands of white light extending roughly from northeast to southwest.

Monday, October 6th

Breakfast at 7 a.m. — bacon, cold pemmican, biscuits (Ramsay's dog biscuits), and chocolate. We had almost finished when we heard a shout from our Eskimo friend. According to Stefansson the custom in Eskimo settlements is that everyone goes to the house of the man who shouts first to eat. Each takes some contribution along with him if he has it, but if he has nothing he goes notwithstanding. The custom is fast breaking down now, Stefansson says, owing to missionary teaching. Our two Eskimos and Stefansson went over, the former taking half-a-dozen biscuits with them. When he returned Stefansson told me that Aksiatak had been brought up among the *Kañianergmiut*[5] Eskimo, but some of his relatives are living on the *Kuivuk* [Kobuk] River, which flows into Kotzebue Sound. His wife's father belonged to the *Kilermiut*,[5] her

mother to the *Utkeavigmiut* (Cape Smythe Eskimo). She herself was
brought up among the *Kagmalirmiut*.[5] (The *Kañianuq* [Kangianik] River
is at the headwaters of the Colville River, the *Kilerq* [Killik] is one of its
upper affluents, the *Kagmalik* a later affluent. There was a well-known
trade route formerly up the *Kuivuk* [Kobuk] and down the Colville
River.) About 10 a.m. Stefansson, Pauyuraq, and Aksiatak, with one of
our sleds, went inland to a lake where there is a great store of fish. They
expect to be back tomorrow. McConnell, Asecaq, and Wilkins went out
shooting at different times during the day, but were all alike unsuccessful. Asecaq saw a white fox. We sent three of our sheepskins over to the
Eskimo's tent to be dried, drying the other two sheepskins and our two
deerskins in our own tent. About 11 a.m. I had another attack of ague[6]
and had to turn into my sleeping bag. Wilkins in the afternoon made me
a special broth of chocolate and broken biscuit.[7] For dinner we had pemmican, bacon, and tea. Our food now is reduced to 30 lb pemmican, one
and a half slabs of bacon, three biscuits, two tins of tabloid tea, and eight
cakes of chocolate. We are perhaps 12 miles from Cape Halkett, according to Stefansson. The weather has been fine all day, the temperature
being very little below freezing. A strong wind sprang up last night but
died away in the morning. Sunrise was ushered in by a magnificent crimson glow in the east.

Tuesday, October 7th

The night was cold, probably below zero.[8] Wilkins found his skis
frozen in this morning. He left them on the ice yesterday; the tide rose
and covered them, then froze. It was necessary to dig them out. We had
breakfast at 8 a.m., the hors d'oeuvre being fried pemmican. We have
now tried this pemmican (Underwood's) cold, fried, and boiled, and are
all indifferent to it under any condition.[9] After breakfast Wilkins,
McConnell, and Asecaq went off shooting. McConnell returned about
11 a.m., unsuccessful, and we two had lunch — bacon, pemmican, and
tea. About 2 p.m. we saw Stefansson returning, and with him a stranger
woman and two children. We cooked some lunch for them — bacon,
pemmican, and tea — and they ate some frozen fish as well. Two families are living at the freshwater lake,[10] he said, engaged in fishing. They
were catching great numbers — about 600 the day he was there — and
throwing them into an icebox made of four rectangular pieces of ice. The
fish are a little over a foot long and very good eating. The Eskimos fed
his [Stefansson's] dogs well and gave him 258 fish besides. Stefansson
had not long returned when another sled with two men was sighted, who
turned out to be Aksiatak's son[11] and another man — the son-in-law of
the woman who came with Stefansson. She is the wife of Kunaluak, one
of the men at the fishing lake; one of her daughters married Ned Erie,[12] a
white man who has lived for some years at Barter Island, another
married a Japanese who owns a hotel on the Yukon River. She gave us
some sugar and a large piece of caribou meat. Aksiatak's wife presently
sent over a tinful of doughnuts (flour and baking powder mixed with

water and boiled in lard). Wilkins and Asecaq returned with 10 ptarmigan. Later Stefansson went over to the Eskimo's tent to learn the news, which he related to us on his return. Nothing was known of the *Karluk*, but three vessels — Lewie [Louis] Lane's [the *Polar Bear*], Captain Cottle's (the *Belvedere*), and Captain Pedersen's [the *Elvira*] — which were returning from Herschel Island, are all caught in the ice about 70 miles west of Herschel. It was a party from Cottle's ship which took Aksiatak's sled. Leffingwell was known to have reached Flaxman Island, and since he was travelling on the *Mary Sachs* that vessel must have got that far at least. C[harles] Brower's vessel with supplies reached Cape Smythe (near Point Barrow), but was crushed in the ice on its way back. Stefansson proposed to me this evening that I stay with Aksiatak and his family until he and the rest return from Point Barrow, then we would all go east to Herschel Island. Aksiatak today called a boy who came [back from the lake] with Stefansson *apan* (father), apparently on the 'atka' theory.[13]

The two women were tattooed thus:

Figure 7. Chin tattoos on Mrs. Aksiatak and Mrs. Kunaluak.

The weather all day has been gloriously fine. In the evening there was a splendid aurora, the streamers running approximately north and south.

Wednesday, October 8th

The arrangements are changed. I am to accompany the others to Point Barrow and stay there during the winter. There is more ethnological work to be done there than in the Mackenzie district, Stefansson says. Incidentally, it will be much more comfortable. We had breakfast in our tent — caribou and bacon, and later a second breakfast of doughnuts and tea in the Eskimo's tent. Aksiatak accompanied us on our journey today, and I rode on his sled — a small one with a team of four dogs. We started half an hour before the others, who left at 11 a.m. We stopped at 1 p.m. for lunch, raisins (given to us by the Eskimos), pemmican, and tea from the thermos flask. I had been extremely cold on Aksiatak's sled, being imperfectly clad for such travelling,[14] so Stefansson produced a pair of deerskin boots and deerskin trousers for me to wear, and I rode on top of one of our sleds [McConnell's], which was much more comfortable than the handlebars of Aksiatak's. It upset, though, three times, and deposited me in the snow. Our course was due west over the sea-ice, where the going was very good, and we travelled very fast. Then we crossed the neck of Cape Halkett, sped over two lagoons, issued again onto the sea-ice and reached a settlement of two houses[15] some 6 miles west of Cape Halkett about 5 p.m. In a cutbank beside one of the lagoons

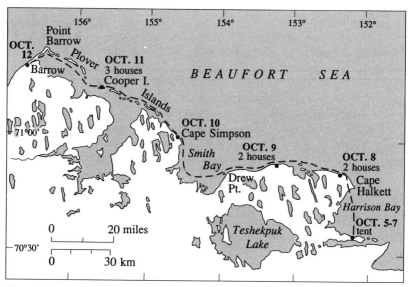

Figure 8. Map showing the author's route from Harrison Bay to Barrow, October 1913.

a young white fox had burrowed. The dogs of Wilkins' sled ran after it and Wilkins speared it. The Eskimos at [Cape] Halkett gave us [polar] bear meat (cold), scones, and tea. We stayed for some time in the first house, then adjourned (except Stefansson) to the other larger house where we were to sleep. Here the young wife, Aiva, baked scones, while the men played cards on the floor — a kind of poker[16] apparently. Aiva was so interested in the game that she allowed one batch of scones to burn. About 9:30 p.m. we had supper (tea and scones with a little butter and pemmican) then went to bed. Both the houses here are of wood covered with turf and snow. Under the platform in our house slept a large black dog; we three — Wilkins, McConnell, and myself — slept on the board floor in front with Asecaq and Pauyuraq, while the rest slept on the platform with their heads towards the door. The younger women and girls here are not tattooed ([though] one had a single short line on the chin), Stefansson says, because the missionaries forbade it. They appear to have very delicate hands. Primus stoves, sewing machines, and white men's apperterances of every kind we noticed among them. The small house differed from the larger [one] in having no wings and no sleeping platform. On top of the passage of our house were a sled and other things. When we arrived the men all came and shook hands, European fashion. Snow fell all day; it seemed like a foretaste of winter.

Thursday, October 9th

Aiva cooked more scones for breakfast, and we contributed frozen fish. Wilkins fried some bacon, and these with tea, coffee, and hard biscuits gave us a good breakfast, albeit a late one. The weather was

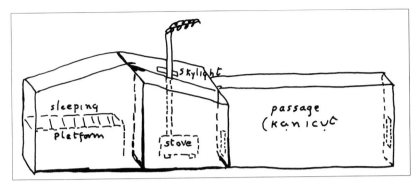

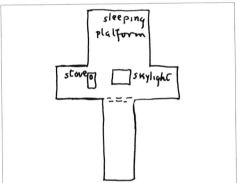

Figure 9. The larger of two houses about 6 miles west of Cape Halkett. It belonged to Samuel and Aiva. Plan view on left.[17]

foggy and cold, with a moderately strong wind blowing from the north-east. After breakfast, about 9 a.m., the Eskimo men went off in different directions over the ice with their guns; the bear of which we partook last night was shot by one of them the day before. The men no longer take off their upper garments in the house, as formerly, owing, Stefansson says, to missionary teaching; it is considered immodest. The women still carry the children naked in the hoods, apparently. Our hostess' little girl is named Josephine. The house is rather draughty now, but will be very warm when the snow piles over it. There were 10 of us sleeping here last night.[18] We left a good deal of stuff here to lighten the sleds. We seem to give our hosts a lot — bacon, pemmican, etc., each time. About 11 a.m. we started out, stopped at 2 p.m. to set up the Burberry tent, light the fire, and make chocolate, with which we ate pemmican and frozen meat. At 3:45 p.m. we started again and continued until 6 p.m., when we struck two empty Eskimo houses, built of wood, the timber set upright; both had boards on the floor. In one of these we decided to spend the night. The whole evening was taken up in cooking bread with a bag of flour and some baking powder the Eskimos gave us. Some was baked on the stove, some fried in bear's fat (they gave us some bear meat as well, which we boiled and ate). We must have travelled about 20 miles today, for the trail was good. Wilkins' foot troubled him badly and he was compelled to ride on the front sled most of the time.[19] I was on the back sled and the two Eskimos with me; they took it in turns to ride.

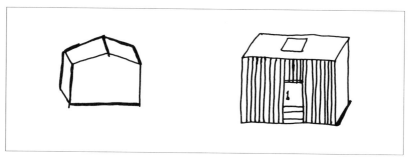

Figure 10. Two houses just west of Pitt Point.

Friday, October 10th

By daylight Wilkins was cooking bread for breakfast and lunch. We had also bear meat, bear soup, and tea. By 9:35 a.m. we got away, hoping to reach Point Barrow in 2 days. The houses[20] we slept in are not ruined places, but belong to certain Eskimos who are living elsewhere just now. The weather was dull, with a moderate northeast breeze. We travelled with three or four short stops until 2 o'clock. Our first stop was to enable Wilkins to take a photo or two of a cutbank,[21] and to give Stefansson an opportunity to expound his theory of their origin: the sea has forced its way under the soil, hence the layer of ice beneath the soil. Leffingwell[22] and others postulate a glacial epoch, he says. McConnell

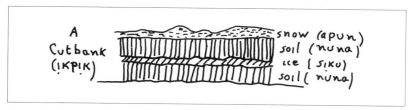

Figure 11. Cutbank west of Pitt Point.

hurt his ancle soon after we started and had to ride on the sled all day. All the others rode too at intervals, for the sleds were light. At 5:30 p.m. it was almost dark and we stopped for the day and made camp. We had gone too far inside Smith Bay[23] instead of straight across from point to point; consequently, although we had travelled perhaps 25 miles we were only about 1/2 mile beyond Cape Simpson. This means two more days to Barrow. Our two Eskimos are very careless and lazy; they intend to leave us at Barrow. Wilkins made some more bread, and this with caribou fat and tea furnished a dinner. We intended to have bear meat as well, but it took too long to boil. Not far behind the beach here, Pauyuraq says there is a pitch lake;[24] the first time he saw it an owl lay dead beside it. Stefansson says he has written a story about it.

Saturday, October 11th

We breakfasted at 7 a.m. on bear meat, bread, bear soup, and tea, and started out at 9 a.m. During the night a dog ate one of my sealskin boots and tore up the other. At 11 a.m. we reached some houses and racks, and stayed to lunch with some Eskimos there.[25] They gave us boiled fish,[26] a tin of Queensland boiled beef, hard-bread,[27] butter, and tea. They added to this two tins of meat, nearly 1 lb of butter, and 80 biscuits (hard-bread), and refilled our sugar bag; this was for us on the road. Stefansson, of course, repays them later. There were in the house four women, a man,[28] and a boy. One woman was very old.[29] Stefansson said that when she was a girl she visited McGuire's ship in 1852.[30] He obtained many stories from her. Now she has only three teeth left, the two upper incisors and the canini beside them. Stefansson said she had the rest drawn by a dentist at Barrow, out of mere caprici, not because there was anything wrong with them. One of the other women was blind, a third paralysed in the right leg below the knee and fore-arm.[31] She had a bandage round her

Figure 12. Chin tattoos on the three women at Añopkana's house.

head to relieve a headache. The fourth was apparently the manageress; she did the cooking. All four were tattooed with three bands, the middle one broad and made up apparently of four or five lines. The manageress had a few tattoo marks — mere blots — on the back of her hand. The man (Añopkana) had seen a vessel — the *Karluk* ? — out in the ice and had tried to reach it but could not.[32] It was drifting westward, but was too far off for him to see if anyone was on board. He had recently shot a polar bear. The houses (there were two) were of the usual wooden type. We started out again at 2 p.m. and after travelling an hour met a band of Eskimos 'trekking' from Point Barrow,[33] from whom we obtained an axe, as ours was broken. They told us that a vessel — the *Karluk* ? — had passed Point Barrow too far off to be recognised.[34] A young woman in the party had a short tattoo band on the chin, not quite in the middle. We stayed only 2 or 3 minutes then hurried on. I forgot to mention that the man Añopkana had a slight stammer, or rather an impediment, for he did not stammer, but seemed to be checked every few syllables in his utterance. Our route lay along the inside of a chain of islands, mere sandspits, and we had the trails of the other sleds to follow. In one or two places the ice was very thin and bent beneath the weight of the sleds.[35] We travelled at a fair speed till 7 p.m. when we reached three houses,[36] one of which was already occupied by a party of Eskimos who had come that day from Barrow. We occupied a second of the usual shape, i.e., rectangular and slightly gabled, built of wood covered first with turf then with snow, one hole being left for a skylight and another for the stove-pipe. The Eskimos lent us a fine primus stove, and sent us in a plate of current scones and a bag of oatmeal. We had porridge, bacon, scones, biscuits, butter, and chocolate, then turned in, Stefansson sleeping with the Eskimos. The weather all day was dull, a little snow falling most of the time. A very light breeze blew from the northeast.

Sunday, October 12th

We breakfasted at 7 a.m. and were away by 8:10. At this our last stop we left behind the wood and alcohol stoves, flour, oatmeal, and one or two other things, some in the house, some on top. In the night the dogs of one team got loose and started a fight. Stefansson and Pauyuraq turned out and tied them up again. In the morning they showed plenty of blood on their coats, but none were seriously hurt. We travelled rather slowly over lagoon ice until 12:30 p.m., when we stopped for [a] lunch [of] pemmican, hard-bread, and tea. Half an hour later we moved off again. Asecaq had a shot at a white fox, but missed it. About 3 p.m. we came to the tundra and by 4 p.m. were at Cape Smythe in Mr. Ch[arles] Brower's store[37] — our journey west was finished. Throughout we had been favoured with very good weather, considering the time of the year. Today a little snow fell, but there was no wind. Fox tracks were numerous all along the route and occasionally we had come upon the footmarks of bears. Ptarmigan also seemed to be plentiful until we neared Cape Smythe. The fish that were given to us at [Cape] Halkett are called 'white fish' by the whites. Mr. Brower says their native name is *ekalusaq*. Stefansson has suffered from a pain in the side during the last two days and consequently has ridden on the sleds a good deal. I have been able to do nothing else since the day we reached Aksiatak's house October 5th; and from [Cape] Halkett on, all of the others have ridden a great deal, the Eskimos from laziness, Wilkins and McConnell through being temporarily crippled. At Cape Smythe we learned that the *Alaska* and the *Mary Sachs* had been unable to get beyond Collinson Point,[38] and were passing the winter there, some 20 miles or so east of Flaxman Island. Further east three whalers were caught in the ice, one, the *Belvedere* close in to the shore, the other two — the *Polar Bear* and the *Elvira*[39] — some distance off shore. About 5 miles south of Cape Smythe the Norwegian 4-masted barque *Transit* was driven ashore on August 25th by the ice-floes, and most of her crew are now living at Cape Smythe. A vessel was seen rather more than a week ago drifting in the ice north of Point Barrow (about 9 miles northeast of Cape Smythe), but it was said to be a 2-masted schooner, so could not have been the *Karluk*.[40] Probably it was this vessel that was meant by the Eskimos who told us about the *Karluk*.

Chapter 3. Re-equipping at Barrow

Stefansson and Jenness ailing — New equipment ordered — Eskimo dance — Football game — Preference of dogs to reindeer for carrying mail to Kotzebue Sound — Skinning animals and associated Eskimo beliefs — Learning cat's-cradle figures — Eskimo tools and games — Visiting an Eskimo school — Letter writing — Completion of preparations for departure

Monday, October 13th 1913

Out-of-doors the weather was dull and foggy. We slept in Mr. Brower's store,[1] that is to say, Wilkins, McConnell, and I did; Stefansson slept over at his [Brower's] house a few yards away, and our [two] Eskimos with some of the Eskimos of the place. We dried our skins and cleaned our rifles, then for the rest of the day lay on some skins and read old newspapers and magazines. Stefansson is having an outfit prepared, buying dogs (he offers $25 for each), having a new tent made, and lining the Burberry tent.

Tuesday, October 14th

I had a sharp attack of ague this morning, which left me weak and washed out all day. Stefansson's side is no better; he thinks it is rheumatism. Pauyuraq was paid off yesterday; Asecaq is staying on with us. A northwest wind outside is blowing the ice floes in to the shore, although there is still a broad space of open water. Wilkins tested three varieties of primus stoves. Here are his equations:

Times

Variety of Stove	Lighting alcohol hr min	Water on hr min sec	Steam rising hr min sec	Boiling hr min sec	Boiling violently stove out hr min sec
1. Svea	7 16	7 19 30	7 24 30	7 27 10	7 28
2. Lovett	7 52	7 57	8 1 55	8 7	8 7 43
3. Primus	8 33	8 36 25	8 41 35	8 46 33	8 47 25

Quantity of water	= 1 pint
" " petroleum	= 1 "
No. strokes of pump	= 20
Wood alcohol	= 1 tablespoon full
Consumption of petroleum	= ?

Times from putting water on to boiling

Svea	7' 40"
Lovett	10'
Primus	10' 8"

[At this point in the diary the author inserted the following footnote:] "This is a copy of my diary, which was written in pencil in a small notebook. The copy was made partly at Cape Smythe, partly in Harrison Bay, when living with the Eskimos there, and finished Dec. 28th, 1913."

Figure 13. Cape Smythe Whaling and Trading Station, the store and living quarters at Cape Smythe managed by Charles Brower, when the author, McConnell, and Wilkins slept there. Photo by G.H. Wilkins, October 26, 1913 (CMC Photo No. 51454).

Wednesday, October 15th

The weather out-of-doors was fine and moderately clear. A little floe ice appeared on the horizon, but did not make its way to shore. I spent the morning and part of the afternoon in fixing sling-straps onto my rifle case. Wilkins passed the day in trying to fix up an old phonograph for Mr. Hopson.[2] McConnell acted as sous-chef — obtaining hints on cooking. Mr. Stefansson's side is no better — he has been trying to rest all day. Mrs. Brower[3] and one or two other Eskimo women are busy making footgear for us. Our friend Ikpik, whom we met at Cape Halkett [on October 8], turned up today. We are all trying to write letters. Mrs. Hopson taught me a cat's-cradle figure.[4]

Thursday, October 16th

The temperature was fairly high today, though a moderately strong west wind was blowing and snow fell part of the day. Mr. Brower's workmen are still pressing on with our outfit and the women with our clothing. A crutch was made for Mr. Stefansson to rest his foot. Wilkins has been making a box to contain a primus stove and a billy[5] on top, so that the primus can be lit and the water boiled without removing it from its case. I was rather seedy most of the day — I take capsule quinine 3(?) or 5(?) grains every other day now. However, with Wilkins' aid I tried to repair my broken ski. Mrs. Hopson is busy outfitting Alfred.[6] After tea I went over to an Eskimo house to see a dance. There were six men with drums sitting on the floor, and men, women, and children sitting indiscriminately round them. The house was square with a low gable and a ceiling. On each side was a window covered with the intestine of the big seal. At the back were two sleeping platforms, or rather one divided by a partition into two. Some of the drums appeared to be quite new. There were six, all of the same shape, though the sizes varied a little. A membrane is stretched over one side of a hoop of wood about a foot or 15 in-

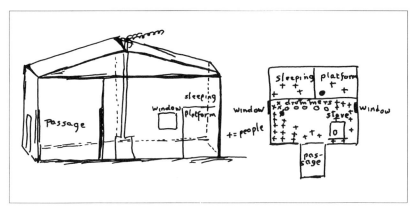

Figure 14. Sketch and plan of Eskimo house at Cape Smythe.

ches in diameter, and a short handle set in one end. With a thin stick a little longer than the diameter of the drum they strike the back or under side. (From time to time the membrane is moistened with water to keep it taut.) With a light stroke the membrane is hardly touched, the force of

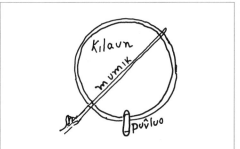

Figure 15. Cape Smythe drum.

the impact falling on the hoop. Harder strokes cause the stick to bend and to hit the membrane sharply, creating a deep bass note. When I went over first, with one of Hopson's children, the men were drumming and singing but no one was dancing. About 10 p.m., however, when I went over again a man was dancing, succeeded soon afterwards by another one. One of the drummers began to sing and to beat his drum. The others joined in, beating lightly, while the dancer made his preparations. Suddenly there came a sharp stroke on the drums and the dance proper began. One leg remained comparatively stiff and stationary on one spot, the other was bent and beat a tattoo on the floor. The arms and hands were waved about, in and out, and up and down, now under, now over the head, now crossing, now outstretched, every muscle in his limbs and body at full tension. From time to time he threw out broken exclamations, which sounded like "*ai ya ai ya.*" Each dance lasted about 2 minutes only. The second man we saw dancing executed five different dances, repeating two of them, with intervals of a minute or two.

Towards the end he was bathed in perspiration, although naked from the waist upward. It was noticeable that he put on a pair of gloves before he began to dance. Alfred Hopson says that often a man dances in a pair of gloves, then at the end hands them to some other man, who puts them on himself and dances. On the sleeping platform above the other four drummers on the floor (there were six drummers when we first went earlier in the evening) was an elderly man with a drum and a stick. He did not drum continuously like the rest, but occasionally patted the membrane with the palm of his hand or beat a few strokes with his stick. The audience joined in the singing. I noticed that some of the women, like some of the men, took off their upper garments and were naked to the waist — the room in fact was steaming. These women, however, seemed to hide themselves behind others when I appeared; Stefansson says the missionaries have condemned the custom. One of the drummers had a little boy about 1 1/2 years old, who fell asleep on his knees as he drummed. The membrane of the drums here at Point Barrow, Stefansson says, is generally the lining of the liver of the bowhead whale; next to

Figure 16. Chin tattoo, Cape Smythe woman.

that, thin caribou skin, and if not that the very thinnest sealskin; sometimes too it is of bladder. Some of the women I notice have one broad tattooed line from the middle of the mouth to the chin, composed of three or four lines close together. Only older women, as far as I have yet seen, have the narrower lines, one on each side. In sewing, the thimble is placed on the first finger and the needle pushed.

Friday, October 17th

The weather was fairly clear most of the day, although a very little snow fell in the afternoon. The temperature was comparatively mild. A moderate breeze blew from the eastward, with a touch of south. Wilkins finished his box for the primus lamp and outfit and made a darkroom lamp for Mr. Hopson. I spent most of the day writing and reading, and Mr. Stefansson in an armchair resting his side, which appears to be very little better. McConnell spent a short time sewing harness and the rest of the day pottering around reading and sleeping. My deerskin sleeping bag has been turned over to McConnell; his, which is larger, is being cut up to provide boots, and I am sleeping in Mr. Stefansson's wolfskin bag, which weighs about 25 lbs, and seems little if at all warmer than a deerskin bag a third of that weight. Our tents are nearly completed.

Mr. Hopson gave me the recipe for making slap-jacks or hot cakes: flour, baking powder (2 teaspoonfuls to a quart of flour), salt (1 teaspoonful), all sifted together — mix water, then an egg or two if possible, grease the frying pan and fry. Eat with butter, butter and sugar, treacle,[7] or molasses.

I saw an Eskimo today go out over the ice dragging his kayak, which was lashed to a small sled. He carried a spear and was going after seals in the leads of open water. Later I saw him return empty-handed. Wilkins took his photograph. The Eskimos here are rapidly losing the knowledge of their forefathers. They come to Mr. Brower to get him to make them *umiaks*, sleds, and snowshoes. At present he has two if not more native men in his employ.[8]

Saturday, October 18th

The temperature was lower today than it has yet been — -4°F at 8 a.m. However, there was very little wind, a slight breath from the east, and brilliant sunshine. At 7 a.m. the moon was on one side of the heavens and the sun the other, and each was producing its shadows. The colouring out of doors was very beautiful. The sea is still open along the shore, with here and there a small floe gleaming white on its sombre surface. Subdued orange and other tints gathered around the sun, and the water assumed a soft greenish tint such as I have seen nowhere else. It was pleasant to hear the lapping of the waves on the beach, and to see the tiny pebbles rolling to and fro. I spent the morning reading and writing; in the afternoon while the store was being cleaned up, I took a walk through the settlement. Some (the majority) of the Eskimos I notice are living in houses resembling white men's cottages — not covered with peat and snow to withstand the winter cold. I learned two new cat's-cradle figures this afternoon. Mr. Brower and one of his Eskimo workmen between them have nearly completed a ski to replace the ski of mine that was broken. They used a piece of hickory timber, of which a stock is kept to make sled-runners. The new tent is rectangular, with three poles, and an inner lining. It is very much larger than either of our old tents, and correspondingly heavy. I should guess that it weighs about 60 lbs. The lining for the Burberry tent is also nearly finished. Wilkins completed his dark-room lamp — an ingenious piece of work. McConnell spent the day in various odd jobs and in reading. He made the buckwheat and cornmeal cakes for breakfast this morning. They are made in exactly the same way as slap-jacks, except that a cupful of buckwheat flour or cornmeal is added to the ordinary flour. Mrs. Brower is making me a sleeping bag. I am much stronger now than when I arrived; after walking for more than an hour I did not feel tired in the least. Mr. Stefansson's side is rather better too. There was an aurora tonight of moderate brilliancy — streamers running north and south.

Sunday, October 19th

The weather, which was clear this morning, became cloudy this afternoon; the temperature was about zero and a moderate breeze was blowing from the northeast. The glass [barometer] is falling rapidly. The sea all around is open, with one or two small floes to the eastward. It is strange to see the vapour rising like smoke from the dark surface of the water — an effect of the difference in the temperatures of the sea and the atmosphere. We spent most of the day in reading and writing and playing cards. Two of the crew of the shipwrecked *Transit* came over in the afternoon, and the billiard table was brought into requisition. The Eskimos were playing football in the afternoon on the lagoon, and I went over to watch. The ball was half as large again as a cricket ball and was made of rags tied together. There appeared to be no rules — a player could kick the ball, run with it in his hands, throw it away, trip up opposing players, just as he pleased. Alfred Hopson, however, says that in the proper game the ball is kicked only, not carried or thrown; also that originally it was made of deer hair covered with deerskin.

Mr. Brower told me there are about 1000 reindeer in the neighbourhood, divided into two herds, known as No. 1 and No. 2. He himself owns some of the deer in herd No. 2; the rest are owned by a number of

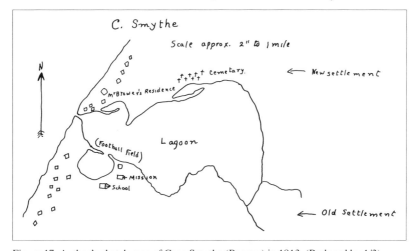

Figure 17. Author's sketch map of Cape Smythe (Barrow) in 1913. (Reduced by 1/3)

Eskimos. A reindeer is worth about $25. Recently they were used instead of dogs in the sled by the mail-carrier from Point Barrow to Kotzebue Sound, but they have been superseded by dogs again. With reindeer it is necessary to have relays every 100 miles or so, otherwise they starve, for on the trail they have no time to feed. Stefansson says that at Port Clarence many of the reindeer were afflicted with the tape-worm, which attacks either the brain or the liver. In the former case the deer becomes crazy and soon dies, in the latter it lingers on for a long time. It is said that human beings can incur the same disease by eating the liver of a deer afflicted with it. Roasting the meat does not kill the worm, but boiling does. The malady is contagious, and sometimes causes great depredations in a herd. I noticed today that the skins of some of the *umiaks* have already been removed. Mrs. Brower finished my sleeping bag yesterday; it is smaller and warmer than my old one. The gramophone was brought out this evening and we had a concert.

Monday, October 20th

The weather today was fine though foggy, the wind still from the east, but the temperature a little higher. The new ski Mr. Brower had made for me was finished this morning, all except the tarring. Several of us have tried it and it is very satisfactory. He is now making a pair of snowshoes for Alfred Hopson out of birch. Mr. Stefansson bought two seals today for dog meat, at a cost of $5 each. He has bought two new dogs, so apparently we shall have a third sled. His side is better; he believes it was rheumatism. Wilkins and McConnell tried the primus lamp in the Burberry tent, which is now provided with a red lining inside. The tent was erected outside on the snow and was heated very comfortably by the lamp. I went along to the hut of the shipwrecked *Transit* men — about 1/2 mile along the beach. The entrance to the passage was protected by large rectangular blocks of ice. Wilkins skinned his fox this afternoon. Formerly the Eskimos when they killed a fox, after it was skinned, cut the throat so that the head hung backwards.[9] The reason, Mr. Brower says, was that they believed that a fox wanted a knife, just as a male polar bear wanted a curved knife and a bow-drill (or its mouthpiece), whereas a female polar bear wanted an *ulo* and a needle case, and a seal, a whale, and a white fish all wanted fresh water because living in the salt sea they were thirsty.[10] For this reason when a bear is killed and its skin hung up in the house these articles are hung up beside it. On the fourth day (if a male), or the fifth (if a female) the spirit of the bear is drawn out and takes with it the spirits of the articles; the articles themselves can then be taken down and used again. Likewise when a seal or a whale is caught, fresh water is poured on their heads. Mr. Stefansson told me this. I learned another cat's-cradle figure today. My new sleeping bag is really too warm for the house. Stefansson is buying my rifle for the Expedition for $30.[11] The younger Eskimos appear not to possess the knowledge of cat's-cradle figures that their elders have.

Tuesday, October 21st

A foggy day with little wind and the air comparatively mild. The day passed in petty occupations, varied with reading and writing. Stefansson bought a couple of old kayak skin covers to put on the ground under the sleeping bags. Mrs. Brower is adding a piece of blanket to the mouth of my new sleeping bag in order to protect the shoulders. The tents are now finished, but Stefansson is trying to buy some more dogs. The Eskimo children here have learned some European games — e.g., oranges and lemons.[12]

I had a short run on skis this afternoon, but the country around here is not particularly suitable; there are small lumps of hard ice jutting up everywhere. The Eskimos taught me several cat's-cradle figures this afternoon.

Wednesday, October 22nd

The wind was southwest today — a moderate breeze, which blew the snow about a great deal. The current of the sea set northward, and much of the water is now ice-covered. The temperature must have been about zero. Stefansson bought a new sled today and is trying to obtain more dogs. Our outfit is practically complete, but Alfred Hopson will not be ready for two or three days. Mr. Brower is busy making him a pair of snowshoes. One of the Eskimos was drilling holes in the wood for the lashings and using for the purpose a bow-drill, which he had made espe-

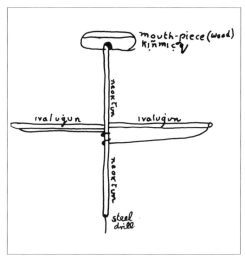

Figure 18. Eskimo bow-drill, Cape Smythe.

cially for the task. It was certainly very effective. Mr. Cram, the missionary schoolteacher, called this morning. He said that on June 1st there were 1666 reindeer in the two Point Barrow herds, but that about 300 had been killed during the summer slaughtering season. McConnell returned with him in order to use his typewriter and did not return until about 5 p.m. In the afternoon I went out for a stroll, but it was not pleasant walking against the wind. Mr. Brower tells me that the mouthpiece of the old bow-drill had a narrow flange to be held in the teeth and a wide body covering all round the mouth. In heavy drilling it was held against the chest. The cup into which the stem of the drill set was of stone — usually a kind of granite — which was let into the wooden mouthpiece. The bow was generally of bone or ivory and curved, while the point or drill itself was of stone (*sic*; see Fig. 18).

Two of the half-caste children were playing an Eskimo game last night. They sat on the floor facing each other and each curled his right (or left) wrist round the right (or left) wrist of the other and pulled. It is called *akamuktoaq*. When played with the elbows curled round each other it is called *kañermiksoaq*; with the little fingers interlocked *itiqoragmiksoaq*, the ring fingers *mikilyeragmiksoaq*, the middle fingers *kitixligmiksoaq*, the fore fingers *tikermiksoaq*. This evening Mr. Brower showed us three double skin shirts (one inside the other, the inner with the fur side in, the outer with the fur side out). They were of fawn-skin and were certainly very good. They cost him $48.50. The trimming was of wolverine's skin; one skin sufficed to trim the three. A wolverine's skin at the present time is worth about $25. The sky tonight was clear and the stars shining brightly. The moon is at the half, and there was a

Figure 19. Moonglow.

thin glow of light stretching from it nearly parallel to its flat side. About 9 p.m. the wind changed to the westward and the sky clouded over. The old man who was drilling the snowshoes had a long pipe with a very tiny ivory bowl lined inside with the metal casing of a cartridge. The part of the stem that fitted into the bowl was also of cartridge casing, the rest of wood with an ivory mouthpiece. The bowl was about 1/2 inch in diameter; the amount of tobacco it would contain was very small. Mrs. Hopson

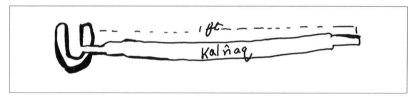

Figure 20. Eskimo pipe, Cape Smythe.

was using a skin-dressing knife made of stone (a chert?) set in horn (*iku.n*). It was jammed tight with a piece of white calico. The chipping of the stone was done with a piece of copper mounted in a groove cut in a handle of horn. Originally a pointed horn was used instead of copper, and the curve of the handle B was more pronounced to fit against the body, so Mr. Brower says. Mrs. Hopson used also a scraper (*iku.n*) of iron mounted on a piece of wood.

Thursday, October 23rd

The weather has been rather changeable, blue sky alternating with clouds. The clouds gained the supremacy in the afternoon. The wind — a light breeze — came from the southwest. The sea is closed in with ice except for a long lead about a mile from the shore and another on the horizon. The village Eskimos went seal hunting but secured nothing. It is reported that a polar bear has been shot between here and the schooner *Transit*. McConnell has been typing at the schoolhouse. Wilkins and I

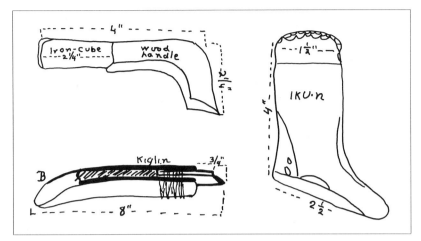

Figure 21. Mrs. Hopson's scraper (top), skin-dressing stone knife (right), and stone-chipping tool (bottom), Cape Smythe.

visited it this afternoon, and by way of preparation Wilkins cut my hair and clipped my beard this morning. We were introduced to Mrs. Cram,[13] who was conducting school, with a large class in one room under her own direction and another rather smaller class in an adjoining room supervised by an Eskimo young man. The children were put through some songs and action songs, and the elder ones made to work out sums and translate Eskimo words into English from dictation. We saw some of their drawings, and they seemed rather good. One child appeared to be half-Eskimo, half Polynesian, judging from its appearance. The girls all seemed to wear the hair long and parted in the middle, the boys clipped round without any parting. The schoolhouse, which was built by the U.S. government, is very comfortable within, though it looks like a large barn from without. It is a two-story place, with a number of rooms; in the private portion there is a dining room, kitchen, pantry, and three bedrooms. Coal for fuel is provided by the government. Leaving the school we visited the rival store to Mr. Brower's, kept by two officers from the wrecked [barque] *Transit*, and stocked with the goods which that vessel was carrying. Both officers are Norwegians, and they told me that my new ski was wrongly made. The toe, instead of being bent up with steam, should be worked up with tallow; this gives it a spring and pliancy, which steaming fails to do. On returning to Mr. Brower's I was taught some more cat's-cradle figures and this occupied the time until dinner. The days are rapidly growing shorter; the lamp has been lit about 3 p.m. for the last few days. The air today, however, was comparatively mild — Stefansson has engaged another Eskimo beside Asicaq to accompany us eastward.

Friday, October 24th

A dull day, with a strong breeze blowing from the south. It broke up the ice that had formed on the sea, and caused a swift current to run northward, piling up great blocks of ice to a height of 4 to 5 feet along the beach. Despite the fact that the wind had not abated in the least, the sea froze over again during the day, the current apparently having ceased. The day passed quietly in various occupations, with reading and writing whenever nothing else arose to be done. Stefansson was asking Mrs. Brower tonight how she addressed her children. Tommy, the eldest boy, she calls *acan* i.e., father's elder sister; David, the second boy,[14] she calls *atataruak*, i.e., grandfather. Both children, however, call her mother *aga*. My new footgear consists of a pair of sheepskin socks (wool inside) reaching to the ancles, a longer pair on top reaching to just below the knees, and a pair of sealskin boots outside of these, also with the fur inside, and with oakum insoles.

Saturday, October 25th

Another dull day with a moderate breeze from the west. The sea close in to the shore is covered with thick ice, but a mile or so out it is all open. Our outfit is practically complete and we are to leave on Monday. With Wilkins assistance I tarred the bottom of my new ski to keep it from becoming soaked with water. The tar had to be burnt in with a blow-lamp. Wilkins melted a tin of tallow (candle) to rub on the skis just before using them. McConnell was typing some of Stefansson's correspondence.[15] The day passed quietly. The atmosphere outside was very mild. We had a little excitement in the evening. Wilkins discovered to the northwest a light — presumably a vessel far out in the ice. All turned out to see, and various were the opinions — a ship, a star, an Eskimo with a lantern. A field-glass and finally a telescope was produced — it was the star Arcturus. There was a fine aurora — a bow stretching from the northwest round to the northeast and almost reaching the zenith.

Sunday, October 26th

The sun made one or two efforts to attain its old splendour, but the foggy atmosphere generally vanquished it. In the morning we finished off letters[16] and did various small tasks that remained to be done. After lunch we loaded one of the sleds, and Wilkins with four dogs drove off to the store with our lightest sled to pick up rice, etc. We shall have very heavy loads. Cape Smythe is an interesting place in the spring when the Eskimos engage in whaling on the ice off the shore.[17] There are very few places in the world where this is done. In this region Point Hope, Indian Point (on the Asiatic coast), and Point Barrow are the only three places. Probably the only other place that it occurs is in Hudson Bay. A strong current was running along in-shore this morning, but this afternoon the sea was closed for a mile or two out. The Eskimo men are leaving off their labrets.[18] With the younger men the corners of the mouth are not pierced at all, and the older men seem not to wear them normally.

Mr. Brower says that when he came here the Eskimos would not eat white men's food — flour, biscuits, etc. About 1882 when a vessel went ashore they emptied all the flour out of the sacks for the sake of the sacks. It was the inland Eskimos who first took to flour — one winter when they were nearly starving. In the evening Stefansson told Wilkins that he found himself unable to leave in the morning, having some business to do at Cape Smythe.[19] Consequently he, McConnell, and Alfred Hopson would stay some days longer, but Wilkins, myself, and the two Eskimos[20] were to take two sleds and leave the next morning as arranged. We were to go to the three families[21] at the fishing lake near Cape Halkett, and camp there and fish until Stefansson and the others arrived.[22] We half-loaded one of the sleds that night, and he distributed boots and mits to us. He gave me an order for $30 on the Department of Naval Service, Ottawa, in payment for my rifle.[23] It was late when we got to bed, Wilkins not until 1:30 a.m.[24]

Chapter 4. With Wilkins to the Fishing Lake

Blizzard in Smith Bay — Wilkins badly frost bitten — Eskimo hospitality — Sunday inactivity — Cramped sleeping quarters — Stocking up with whale meat — Reaching Aksiatak's house in Harrison Bay — On to the fishing lake — Netting the 'white fish' — To the coast for firewood — Description of fox-skinning — Dwindling food supply for men and dogs — Arrival of Stefansson and McConnell — Return to Aksiatak's house — Departure of Stefansson, McConnell, and Wilkins

Monday, October 27th 1913

Up at 4:30 a.m. (the local time is about an hour slow) and proceeded to load the sled. We had almost finished by breakfast time, 6 a.m., but after breakfast Stefansson examined the sleds, condemned the manner of loading, and reloaded them himself. The loads are very heavy, probably between 600 and 700 lbs on each sled. We got away finally about 7:45 a.m. Some of Mr. Brower's and Mr. Hopson's dogs were hitched to the sleds as well, and Alfred Hopson and McConnell, with a small empty sled, came with us part of the distance to show us the way.[1] The empty sled was to carry me going out[2] and themselves back to Cape Smythe again. Our route was different to the one we took when we came in, which would have been much more difficult. We went north about 5 miles then turned eastward across a big lagoon, hoping to strike the end of a sandspit on the other side. At 11:30 a.m. we sighted it, as we thought, and stopped for lunch, tea (we have two thermos flasks), biscuits, and *nerukaq*. Alf[red] Hopson and McConnell here turned back, taking with them the auxiliary dogs. We continued on, myself on foot henceforth, and finally reached the sandspit at 3:15 p.m., just as it was growing dark. Our old round drill tent was erected, the primus stove set going, and soon we were having dinner, bacon, biscuits, *nerukaq* and tea. At 6:30 p.m. (real time more nearly 7:30) we turned into our sleeping [bags], myself at least thoroughly tired. The weather was clear and calm till sunrise, which was ushered in by a brilliant crimson hue along the edge of the sky to the southeast. Then a light breeze arose from the south, changing soon after midday to north when a little snow fell. Stefansson is sending us on ahead to save the expense of our board at Cape Smythe, so he told us; it seems a very absurd reason, when he throws $1000 dollars away without second thought on things of little or no use.

Tuesday, October 28th

We slept well on the snow and were up early. For breakfast we had rice, biscuits, *nerukaq*, and tea. By 7:30 a.m. we were away, first northward along the sandspit to the point, a distance of 1 1/2 or 2 miles, then we struck east with nothing to guide us until we struck an old trail leading a little north of east, which led us to *Iglura*[3] at 10:30 a.m. *Iglura* is the name of the small settlement (three houses and a platform), where we stayed the night before we reached Cape Smythe [October 11th]. One of the houses was occupied when we arrived today, by a Point Hope man and his family, who are on their way eastward to trap during the winter. We picked up the alcohol stove, a can of alcohol, a small bag of oatmeal, and another of flour, which we had left on our way in, then continued on our way. At 12 noon we had lunch, biscuits, *nerukaq*, and tea, and reached another sandspit, with a platform but no house, at 2 p.m. following old trails. There was a little driftwood, so we set up our new wood stove. Boiled bear meat, biscuits (which we made of flour, baking powder, and water), hard-bread biscuits, butter, *nerukaq*, and tea formed a sumptuous dinner. The dogs have been very tired both today and yesterday. We make very slow progress, the loads being so heavy. This is fortunate for me, because I have not breath to travel fast, but can walk a medium pace for a good while.[4] It is very hard work, of course, for my limbs ache rather severely, but I don't have to ride any longer. Wilkins complained of his legs aching today. His foot is not well yet. Our new Eskimo [Añutisiak] seems more willing than Acicaq, but perhaps it is only a case of a new broom sweeping clean. Acicaq is a real professional at finding out ways of avoiding work of any kind, though perhaps not quite so expert as Pauyuraq was; the latter was a grumbler besides. Yesterday about 4 miles north of Cape Smythe we passed three or four mounds, in one of which (the largest) a *tornuaq* dwells, the Eskimos say. If anyone walks over his mound he causes the southwest wind to blow. Last year there was a long spell of southwest wind, and the Eskimos of Cape Smythe said it was because a woman had walked on this mound. Alfred Hopson told me this as we passed. The weather today has been dull with a little snow at times; the wind — a light breeze — changed its direction several times. There was a large mass of black sky to the north, indicating a great body of open water in that direction. Neither today nor yesterday has the air been very cold.

Wednesday, October 29th

We slept badly last night — at least Wilkins and I did, owing to the cold. All day today, though the sky has been cloudless, and the north breeze almost imperceptible, the temperature has been lower than any we have yet experienced — probably a number of degrees below zero. We had breakfast a little later than yesterday — bear-meat soup with a little rice and oatmeal in it, biscuits, butter, *nerukaq*, and tea — and were started by 8:30 a.m. For the first hour we travelled at a fair rate — probably a good 3 miles; then the dogs began to slack. About 10:30 a.m. we passed a house, which was in a very dilapidated condition. Half an hour previously we had passed two platforms or racks where we met a party of Eskimos when we were going into Cape Smythe. At that time there was a house there as well; now there was none. Travelling painfully on, along the outer edge of the chain of sandspits, we stopped at noon for lunch, biscuits, *nerukaq*, and tea, and discovered that one of our two thermos flasks was broken. An hour and a half later we reached Ekiuroq[5] — a place with three houses about 8 miles west of Cape Simpson, where we lunched before [October 11th] with a very old woman, a blind woman, and a cross-eyed man, etc. Another family has occupied the house, and intends to stay the winter. We were invited to dine with them and to sleep in their house also,[6] but preferred to sleep in one of the two empty houses, because we want to make a very early start tomorrow. However, they helped us unload our sleds and put the things in the house. Then we went over to their house, took off our boots, and had tea and biscuit, and later frozen fish. There was an elderly man and his wife, a young man and his wife with a baby about a week old, a boy of 8 or 9 years and another about 3. The last had gotten among some dogs that were fighting yesterday and received some nasty bites on the head and face. One eye was closed up entirely. The young wife was very good-looking — very different from the ordinary Eskimo type of flat broad face with thick lips. Her features were delicate, oval in outline, except that there was a slight broadening in the lower part. She resembled rather the Arab or North African type. Probably she has foreign blood in her. We sat in the house for a long time, then had tea and biscuits again, with our own butter. A new sled was coming from the east;[7] we could see the lantern-light. Almost certainly it is the family we saw at *Igloraq* yesterday. We thought we should be in the way, and as it was about 7 p.m., Wilkins and I retired to our house, lit the fire, and melted some ice ready for the morning, then turned into our sleeping bags. I have constantly re-marked the difference the sexes make in the manner of wearing the hair. The men have no parting, but wear the hair trimmed on all sides, as if it had been cut round the edge of a bowl; the women have the hair long be-hind and part it in the middle right down to the back of the head. The hair on each side is gathered into a single plait, and the two are some-times joined on the nape of the neck.

Thursday, October 30th

A light northeast breeze was blowing when we rose in the morning. We had an early breakfast of oatmeal, hard-bread, butter, *nerukaq*, and tea. Nevertheless it was 8 a.m. before we got away. One of the Eskimos of the place accompanied us with a light sled almost to Cape Simpson, which we reached about 10:30 a.m. The wind shifted to east-northeast and became much stronger. However, we struck out across Smith Bay, steering a trifle south of magnetic east. At noon we stopped for lunch, then continued on till 2:45 p.m., when we lit on a small keg of ice suit-able for water — the only one we had struck for some time — and de-cided to pitch camp. There was a mild blizzard at this time, and the dogs huddled together for shelter at the side of the tents. We did not take the harness off them or stop to feed them, but hurriedly erected the round tent and put the inner lining of the large rectangular tent round the out-side. Snow quickly drifted over it and held it secure. Both the primus stove and our old alcohol stove were set going, and soon we were eating caribou and hard-bread. We turned in immediately afterwards.

Friday, October 31st

Wilkins' birthday — 25th — [on] his last, his 24th, he was chased by Bulgarian cavalry. This one he was greeted by a blizzard in the middle of Smith Bay where two white men and an Eskimo were lost not many years ago, and after wandering aimlessly over the ice for some time froze to death. Snow was drifting about in the tent and covered everything — even our sleeping bags. Caribou, biscuits, and tea cheered us up a bit,[8] and then we began to load the sleds. First, however, they had to be dug out of the snow. As for the dogs, they were almost invisible. Everything was straightened out at last, and we set off at 5 minutes to 8, wondering whether the dogs would face the weather. Blizzards on this coast come only from the east, Stefansson says. Wilkins led the way and we struggled behind. About 9 a.m. we struck an old trail, and following this came unexpectedly to Pitt Point[9] about 11 a.m.; we were not anticipating it for another 2 hours at least. We stopped for lunch beside the cutbank, and gave the dogs some meat. Then off we started again. About 1 p.m. we reached a party of Eskimos living temporarily in rectangular drill tents while building their winter huts; they proposed to remain there during the winter. We exchanged greetings, were given a letter to be delivered to Leffingwell, and went on, greatly heartened by their cheerful faces. Following along the sea-ice just outside the cutbank we came at 3 p.m. to the three houses where we spent a night [Oct. 9th] on our way in [to Barrow]. The place is called *Okulik*.[10] At that time they were empty, now all three were occupied, but we put up at the largest, occupied by an elderly man with his wife and little girl (aged 4 or so), and a younger couple with a boy (about 18 months named Koruna). The older man's hair was just turning white. The younger man had a much thinner face than is usual with Eskimos — more hatchet-shaped — and his hair was curly in places. He is almost certainly of mixed blood. The younger woman was not tattooed, but the elder had five lines on her chin. The house was of the usual type, with a platform but no side wings. The old man [Akuvak] was attaching bone sinkers to his fishing net — one for every 15 meshes. He was a very cheerful, pleasant old fellow. The seal-gut skylight in these houses is ingeniously domed by wires, so that when it is not covered with snow or hoar-frost it catches every available particle of light from every direction. We were made very welcome and [were] soon feasting on home-made biscuits, tea, and walrus meat. Later in the evening we had tea and biscuits (hard-bread) before turning in. The evening passed in talking, stretched out on the floor or on the platform — a grateful relief after the blizzard. Wilkins is frost-bitten on the forehead, round one eye, and between the chin and the lips; I, very slightly on the side of the nose.[11] Both of us are full of aches and pains, especially in the limbs.

The first thing that happens as you approach a settlement is the rushing out of the people to greet you. They smile in your face, say hello perhaps, and shake hands, men and women alike. Then they help you unload your sled and take you into the house. In the passage you stop to brush the snow off your clothes, lest it should melt in the warm room and make everything wet. You take off your mits, boots, and outer coat, assisted perhaps by your hostess, who hangs them up to dry. Then with dry clothes on, you make yourself comfortable, while the lady of the house sets the stove aglow, and quickly makes biscuits of flour, baking powder, and water, all mixed and baked in the oven, and sets a meal before you to be washed down with unlimited draughts of tea. If you can, you add something to the stock, [such as] tea, hard-bread, butter, sugar, etc. Everyone is gay and happy and settles down to exchange news. When your things are dry your hostess examines them to see that they do not require mending; if they do, out comes her needle, sinew and thimble, and soon all is set to rights. Perhaps her pipe lies beside her during the operation, [one] of the long, small-bowled type before noticed,[12] with a small deerskin pouch to hold the tobacco.

Our old host (Asecaq translating) told us a story how that many years ago 20 schooners were caught in the ice up here one year, and only two escaped. The rest were never heard of again. Someone seems to have been drawing the long bow — either the old man, or his informant, or Asecaq — although it may possibly be true.[13]

Saturday, November 1st

The blizzard continued all day, so we stayed with our new friends. The Eskimos dug holes in the snow to shelter the dogs and set up ice blocks on the wind (east) side. The old lady put round patches on the toes and heels of Wilkins' boots, while the younger matron made biscuits, and the old man continued with his net. The younger man was carpentering and doing other work somewhere outside. We had breakfast at 7 a.m. — biscuits, hard-bread, walrus meat, tea, and coffee, and lunch about noon — biscuits and tea. Akuwa (our host) laid his net aside after lunch, and the rest too remained indoors idle for the most part. The old lady mended Asecaq's boots and made a fur covering to protect Wilkins' frozen forehead.[14] Another woman paid a short call and had a feast of walrus meat. About 4 p.m. the younger matron began to make biscuits and I to teach Akuwa to write the names of certain things, flour, butter, etc. Wilkins wrote a letter to leave for Stefansson. At 6 p.m. we were dining luxuriously on a tin of beef, boiled rice, biscuits, tea, and *nerukaq*. The beef, I fancy, was borrowed from a neighbour. A middle-aged man came in at the finish from one of the other houses, and later another younger man, and soon a pack of cards was produced and a set of four playing. The old lady had a pain in her stomach, so they gave her 11 drops of essence of peppermint (labelled 'artificial'). She was well enough to be interested in the game. The question of our leaving tomorrow gave rise to an animated discussion. "We should have our faces frozen again," they said, "and besides why should we leave seeing that they were glad for us to stay with them and it was pleasanter here than outside." To be sure the blizzard showed no signs of abating, and if the weather is no better early tomorrow morning we shall stay. This family says grace before every meal, and night and morning have public prayer. It is conducted in a very reverential manner, not gabbled through as quickly as possible like the grace the dame said at *Ikiuraq* [*Ekiuroq* or *Ikiak*] when we were going in to Cape Smythe [on October 11th].

Sunday, November 2nd

Being Sunday, no work was done today. Outside the blizzard seemed worse than ever, so we stayed indoors all day. Oatmeal, boiled potato-mash, and biscuits formed our breakfast. About 10 a.m. the families from the other two houses, each consisting of a man, his wife, and one child, came across to our house, and divine service was held, modelled somewhat on the Anglican form. There was no sermon, but a number of hymns (in Eskimo) of the familiar kind like 'Abide with me', and prayers by almost everyone present.[15] The children made considerable noise during the prayers, and from time to time the dogs in the passage raised their voices in an uninvited chorus. There were many comical features in the service,[16] but it seemed to me that one or two at least of the congregation displayed a real spirit of devotion, whatever their spiritual ideas of the Christian religion may be. The congregation dispersed after lunch (which consisted of hard-bread, *nerukaq*, and tea), and our younger matron set about baking more biscuits. The dogs live in the passage, *ubi homines feminaeque naturae necessitatem perficiunt. Heri cum quisquis inter ludendum eperdeto*[17] *statim omnes latera fregerunt cachinno; sic mores.*[18] Later in the afternoon two men came in; they are camped with others a little further along the coast, being the same that we passed on Friday. The old man was the stammerer (Añopkana) who told us [October 11th] he had seen the *Karluk*; the other was his son. We sat and talked for a long time, then dinner was served, a ptarmigan apiece for Wilkins and me, and eider ducks and seal meat for the rest. We had a little blubber to help it down, but neither of us appreciated the 'delicacy'. The two women and the children waited until we had finished, then had their dinner. An hour later the guests left, and our two Eskimos [Asecaq and Añutisiak] went over to one of the other houses. The old man [Akuwa] showed me his calendar for 1913, and I made him a new one for 1914. Tea and biscuits were furnished for supper, and we turned in soon after.

Monday, November 3rd

It was noticeable last night after we went to bed that the old man did not pray — at least not aloud. The night before, the prayer was comparatively short — the preceding night inordinately long. The weather when we got up did not seem very promising. However, we decided to leave and loaded the sleds before breakfast. The lady of the house cooked *mukpaurat*,[19] and as that always takes a long time on small stoves such as these Eskimos have, we did not get away until 9:30 a.m. It appears that there is no leave-taking among Eskimos — no saying goodbye, or thanking the host — you just go out of the house and set off. Sometimes some of the people turn out to see you go, sometimes not.[20] The weather was not so bad as it had seemed. The wind was still easterly, but not strong, so that very little snow was drifting. About 1/2 mile from Okulik [Oka-lik] was the tent of our visitors of the preceding afternoon, who are on their way to Cape Halkett to Kuraluk's[21] place, whither we are bound also. The dogs travelled fairly well, and at noon we reached a new settlement of three houses, as far as I can remember, but we did not stop except to speak for a moment to a man who came out to us. At 12:45 we stopped for lunch. Soon after we set off again, a sled passed us travelling in the opposite direction, but closer inshore. There were five dogs in front and one behind, and one man — the sled was empty. We had been following the trail of another sled all day, and about 2 p.m. we caught up to it. With it were three men, a woman, and two children, one about 4 years of age, sitting on the sled, the other about 8 months [old], she was carrying on her back while tramping with the sled. At 2:30 p.m. we came to a settlement of two houses, and here both we and the people of the other sled put up for the night. The latter unloaded their sled altogether, putting the things on a rack or platform such as one always finds beside an Eskimo house. On it are placed the kayak, stores, ropes, anything and everything, in fact, which is not required in the house. Sometimes the roof of the house is used instead or as well, but where a protracted stay is intended a platform appears always to be erected. It is soon made — merely a few posts and a few beams laid on top of them. It protects the things from everything except man and the polar bear, but more especially from the dogs, which are the scavengers of the place, seldom if ever fed. We spent the night in the largest of the two houses — a new place, which had been built since we passed this way.[22] Our hostess, who had one child, a boy about 8, was occupied from 3 till 9 p.m. in making *mukpaurat* for her numerous guests. Wilkins and I, as soon as we entered, were given a cup of tea and a large fried *mukpaurat*, i.e., a flap-jack. Even so the evening meal was a slender one — only about half the number of *mukpaurat* that was needed had been made. At odd moments our hostess attended to our boots and clothing — she put a patch over the soles and heels of Añutisiak (or Aikie), the new Eskimo we took on at Point Barrow. The poor lady was noticeably quite tired out. Not one of the many men present offered the least help, except that her husband brought in wood from outside, and once or twice ice also. The new lady, however, who had come with the sled was called on to help several times, and an old dame who was there once or twice examined the boots and put the insoles in them. The new lady made herself quite at home, cheerfully assisted when called on, and frequently took a leading part in the conversation. She was still young, with a voice less harsh and guttural, more nearly sweet and 'English' than that of any other Eskimo woman I have met. She had too, as Shakespeare would say, a merry humour, and her laugh rang out at every provocation. She must be exceedingly strong, for she showed not the faintest sign of fatigue. Our house was large and well constructed, notwithstanding the fact that it had taken only three days in the building, as they told us. It had no sleeping platform; the man and his people slept at each end, and visitors wherever they could find room. About 13 adults, besides three children, were in it with us, and yet the house was not crowded. The door, hinged with skin, was set back a little behind the line of the wall, and there was a corre-

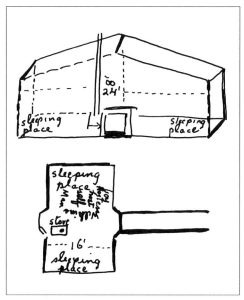

Figure 22. Side and plan views of Eskimo house east of Pitt Point.

sponding small alcove opposite just behind the stove. Altogether the room presented a very cheerful aspect; it was warm and comfortable, and everyone seemed bright and happy, even our hostess. Añutisiak was teaching her son a new trick. He laid seven or eight short sticks across his nose, balancing them; then he attempted to let them fall — one by one if possible — and catch them in his mouth. The game is called *aku-blagaq*. In making the beds a place was made for me next to the husband at one end of the house. In the corner was the boy, then our hostess, her husband next, myself, and finally an old man whom I took to be the father or father-in-law. Wilkins lay cross-wise at our heads. Neither the men nor the women have the least scruple about taking off their upper garments, unless perhaps occasionally in the presence of white strangers, due, Stefansson says, to missionary teaching. One or two of the men took off their trousers, I think merely to change them; I do not think they slept naked. I noticed, though, that in changing their trousers they were careful to expose as little of their persons as possible. One of the dogs slept in the house with us.

Tuesday, November 4th

Everyone was up very early — our hostess of necessity, because she had to cook more *mukpaurat* for breakfast. The new lady divided the task with her, and at one and the same moment some were baking in the oven, others frying, some on top of the stove, some on a primus lamp, and yet others being boiled in lard above another primus lamp. This time there was enough and [some] to spare; the evening before they were supplemented by a little rice boiled with seal oil — not a very tasty dish. The custom is for all to dip into the same bowl. Before breakfast we loaded our sleds. On re-entering [the house], a bowl with a little warm water [in it] was set before us, with a small piece of soap and a towel. I washed first, then Wilkins in the same water, then the old man; afterwards I don't know who used it, but I saw another bowl circulating at the same time, and all appeared to enjoy it. Stefansson says it is regarded as a religious rite preparatory to eating. We set off immediately after breakfast, at 7:00 a.m. (about 8 a.m. true time). (After our arrival at Cape Smythe we set our watches by Mr. Brower's time, which was about an hour behind the true time. From this place onwards I shall give the true time as near as we can judge it.) The sled of the other newcomers accompanied us, but [was] empty. They were going a little way east to dig up a stranded whale and obtain some whale meat. Apparently they propose settling about here for the winter. The going was rather heavy today, for the wind had piled up deep drifts of soft snow in which the dogs floundered and the sleds stuck. Once we tried to go further out from shore, but the ice became too rough. At 11:30 a.m. we passed a new house, but did not stop. The other sled had stayed behind shortly before. Travelling slowly we reached at last our destination, Kuraluk's place, the two houses about 6 miles west of Cape Halkett (*Isuk*), where we cached a lot of our things on our way to Point Barrow. One of the two houses, that in which we slept then, is now temporarily vacant; the other is double and occupied by two families, each consisting of a man, his wife, and one child of about 18 months or 2 years. One of the men [Ikpik] is a Point Hope man (*Tikeragmiut*). They put us up in their house. We entirely unloaded one sled, for tomorrow we have to go after whale meat. There are two stranded [bow-head] whales, one on either side of this place, both close. We have to set up about 1000 lbs of the meat on a platform ready for the sled or sleds that return from the *Alaska* to Point Barrow. Then [we] have to go on to the fishing village where Stefansson obtained so many fish before, and with our nets — we have two — we have to obtain more fish to furnish dog-feed for the journey to the *Alaska*. When we arrived at this place one of the men had just shot some

Figure 23. Eskimo shovel, Cape Halkett area.

ptarmigan, another was shovelling snow with a wood-shovel made from two planks, but with the blade thinned down and shod with iron. At the bottom of the handle, which was very broad and awkward looking, a rope loop for a grip was attached. Our hostesses, soon after we arrived, had tea and *mukpaurat* ready and gave us a good meal. We had another about 8 p.m., ptarmigan, *mukpaurat*, and tea.

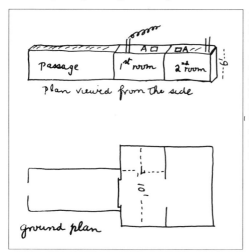

Figure 24. Double- room house, Cape Halkett area. Side view (top); ground plan (bottom). A,A = Skylights with a transparent covering made from the great intestine of the seal. The first room has a sleeping platform, the second not. There is no door between the two rooms, the whole structure, except of course the chimneys and the skylights, is covered with snow. [D.J.]

The Eskimos here are very thrifty with their tea. They are all great tea-drinkers. Any tea which may be left in a cup, together with the tea-leaves culled from each cup, they return to the tea-kettle; it makes the next brew stronger, and tea, to be good in their estimation must be strong. Most families appear to have a small 'table cloth' (more correctly perhaps 'food-cloth' for it is laid on the floor) of what we commonly call oil-cloth. It is kept very clean, as cleanliness goes here. So, too, is the floor where it is set, for it is constantly swept and washed with a floor-cloth (which by the way is used for a dozen other purposes). Two or three wing feathers of a bird, tied at one end, make a very servicable broom. Every family has plates, cups, pots, kettles, buckets, etc., and the majority apparently have primus stoves, and some [have] sewing-ma-

Figure 25. Eskimo woman's knife *uluraq*.

chines. The women are exceedingly skillful in the use of their peculiar knife — the *uluraq* — whether in disjointing meat, in cutting skins, or in ripping down a seam. All that I have seen in use have iron blades and wood, bone, or ivory handles. They are of various sizes; some have the blade about 2 inches long, others 6 inches. In the old days stone took the place of iron, and Stefansson has obtained a few rare specimens from here. In Victoria Land I believe copper is used. These Eskimos seem very fond of a joke. I was drinking my tea, and did not notice that our host, who had just filled Wilkins' cup, was waiting kettle in hand to fill mine. I was laying my empty cup down on the floor when I noticed him, and at once said "*naga*" (no). A roar of laughter followed, his own the loudest — the "no" was so unexpected. The affection of parents for their little children is very marked. They play with them, hug them, and in general behave towards them just as English parents do. I forgot to mention that in the house we stayed at last night was a man of middle age, whose body seemed whiter than that of an ordinary Eskimo, his hair too was slightly curled. A girl living in the other house of this settlement [last night] was very fair and quite European in her features, whereas the man's features were typically Eskimo. An old man came along with us part of the way and left us at the settlement we passed at 11:30 a.m. today.

Wednesday, November 5th

Our hosts gave up the inner room to us last night. There were no public prayers, and no grace said before any meal. In the first room is a fine clock of imitation marble. On the rack outside are a number of fox-traps, which resemble what are called rabbit-gins. The alarm went off at 6 a.m., but just as in civilized countries, everyone was a little late. We had porridge and *mukpaurat* for breakfast. Then Wilkins and our two Eskimos went off to dig out the whale (it was stranded 4 or 5 years ago), while I remained to repair two of the dog-harnesses, which were broken. Our hosts were occupied in cutting up some logs outside, and one went off with his gun, returning at noon with two or three ptarmigan and a snowy owl. Wilkins and our two Eskimos had not returned by lunch-time, which consisted of *mukpaurat* with currants in [them], and tea. Hardly had we finished when the old man Amakuk, who came part way with us yesterday, entered the house without warning and proceeded to take off his things. A few minutes afterwards Wilkins and the two Eskimos entered. They had been vainly digging at the tail of the whale when the old man came along, and showing them the head told them to dig there. Here in a short time they had cut out a large quantity of meat. After they had eaten we harnessed up a sled and set out to bring the whale meat in and store it in Kuraluk's house, which was already two-thirds full of it. We brought in all that was cut up,[23] in two trips; in the second one the sled was only half full. We saw a white fox running to and fro, but the season does not open until November 15th; consequently the Eskimos have not yet laid down their traps. In the distance a sled was approaching; we could see the light of the lantern. About 5 p.m. Anupkona [Añopkana] and his wife arrived with the aged dame who told Stefansson so many stories — we had lunch with them near Cape Simpson on our way in [to Cape Smythe, October 11th]. Anupkona's house is beside us here — for the one we are in is new. No fuss was made of them. Anupkona and the old lady came into our house and were given tea and biscuits, but the wife did not appear for more than an hour afterwards; probably she was fixing up their house. The old dame was very gay. She remarked that Wilkins had been quite a handsome man before he was frost-bitten, but that had spoilt his good looks.[24] One of the children was playing with his father's watch and knocked it several times against the wall. The father attempted two or three times to take it away, but the child cried so he let it be. Our fountain pens[25] had run dry, so Wilkins and I made a little ink in a cup from Walkden's Ink Powder, of which I have a tin. It is with this that I am writing now. One of the Eskimos showed me a new and rather intricate cat's-cradle figure this morning. One of our hostesses was smoking a cigarette (a made one, for they buy cigarette-paper at Cape Smythe) in the latest Parisian fashion — I observed the stranger lady at our last resting-house do the same. On the other hand, some of the men chew, but do not smoke. One man at our last rest-house had a pipe, which appeared to be of the usual type — a long stem with cartridge attachment where it should enter the bowl; but it had no bowl. He smoked it quite cheerfully nevertheless. The ancient dame helped to pluck the birds that were shot, our hostesses being diverted from time to time by the necessity of stoking the fire, baking *mukpaurat*, etc. The men, while dinner was being prepared, played cards. We had boiled ptarmigan, snowy owl, and the soup from it, and it tasted fine. The younger women almost all seem to wear a ring on the ring finger, but often on the wrong hand. Many of the younger men have a ring on the little finger — of silver or brass or something similar — it does not seem to matter what. One of our hostesses is remarkably good-looking for an Eskimo — judged from our standards of beauty. Wilkins says she reminds him of a girl he knew in the West Indies — to me she suggests the Madonna in one of Raphael's pictures. The weather today was rather foggy, with a light breeze from a little north of east, as yesterday. The temperature was low, and on first facing the wind it burned the parts

Figure 26. Circle and dot design (left) and side view of button and eye with rawhide cord.

of the face where we were frost-bitten. The ancient dame who turned up this evening ["Lady Maguire"] has a belt of deerskin about 2 inches wide, with the fur on one side. At one end is a bone button with a flat oval-shaped head, engraved with circle and dot designs set as closely as possible on the upper and under surfaces. The button is attached to the belt by means of a small 'eye', through which a rawhide cord passes. At the other end of the belt is a rawhide loop, which slips over the button.

Thursday, November 6th

It was nearly 8 a.m. before anyone rose this morning — why, I do not know. The old dame slept across our heads, and the old man Amatuk [Amakuk] in a similar position in the first room. Just before we turned in, these two were playing cat's cradles for our amusement. The stove we have in our room is of the same type as Mr. Brower made for us at Cape Smythe — we have it on the sled now. It does not seem very satisfactory, for it becomes choked with ashes. In consequence of our late rising it was 10 a.m. before we finished breakfast — *mukpaurat* and porridge — Wilkins and the two Eskimos then went off to dig out another load of whale meat. Yesterday we must have brought in about 800 lbs; another load of 500 or 600 lbs will be ample. I remained behind, only two men being able to work at once on the whale, and opened the coal-oil case and filled our primus lamp, hurricane lamp, and kerosene can (kerosene is known as coal oil along the American Pacific Coast). The Eskimo dogs have been eating the rawhide lashings of one of our sleds, but the damage is not very serious. Either one or two more families have turned up — there are three new sleds. Ikpik is here;[26] he stayed to help Wilkins and the Eskimos dig out the whale. There is a young married woman, too, who I think is called Aiva, our old [i.e. former] hostess here, and the lady paralysed down one side. Wilkins suddenly appeared at noon. Ikpik, he said, was doing all the work and our two Eskimos and himself looking on. So he came back to take lunch down for them, and the sled. I helped him harness up the dogs, then went inside for lunch. The weather outside was moderately clear, although the sun was not visible, and the temperature comparatively mild, with little or no wind. While our hostess — the Madonna-like one — was preparing breakfast this morning, she had occasion to go outside to bring in more firewood. Her child caught her 'skirt' as she passed. After waiting fully a minute for the child to let go she gently drew her skirt away. The child began to cry, so she turned at once, picked it up, and sat down with it until its attention was directed to something else, and she could go out unnoticed. On the other hand, I have seen them take things away from the child, but immediately soothe it in some other way — e.g., giving it something else. The old man Amakuk left this morning. As he was starting out his hosts gave him a present of a tin of baking powder, some seal blubber, and perhaps other things, which I did not see. We gave him a packet of 'English breakfast tea'. He lives a few miles further along the coast. The new arrivals made a rack this morning on which to set their three sleds. The four uprights were standing, they merely joined them by four cross-pieces. One sled was shod with steel runners, like ours, one with brass, which is said to slide very well on hard snow, but not so well on soft, and to stick badly on ice. The other was a much rougher sled, more heavily built, with very high and narrow wooden runners shod with steel. There hardly seems to be any typical shape for the sleds here, unless it be those with high narrow runners made from a single piece of wood, into which the uprights are morticed. Our hosts are making a sled of this type, and the runners are now hanging up over the stove to dry. One sled here has curiously shaped handle bars.

Figure 27. Sled handle bars (side view).

It is interesting to watch the water supply being brought in. A lad went off from the other house here dragging a small sled with an axe in it. About 200 yards away out on the sea-ice is a small ice-hummock. From this he chopped off several large blocks, loaded his sled, and dragged it back to the ice. When ice is not procurable, snow is used, but it requires a very large quantity of snow to make a little water. The best way is to melt a little snow first, and boil the water, then shovel the snow in.

Near the other house are a number of long sticks set upright in the ground. They are for the tent next summer and come, these people say, from a great river a long way off. I suppose they are willow sticks from the Colville River. Wilkins brought in a heavy load of whale meat this afternoon, probably about 600 lbs. We are taking a little of it along with us. Then we loaded both sleds as far as possible in preparation for an early start tomorrow morning for Aksiatak's house.[27] Aksiatak is the first Eskimo we met here [on October 5]; he was living in a tent at the time, but had a house nearby already constructed, but without any turf around it. From his place we make for the fishing lake. By 4 p.m. today it was becoming quite dark. One of the men here was out hunting on the ice today and fired three times at a polar bear, wounding but not killing it, so that it escaped. For dinner we had rice boiled with currants in it. Our hostesses made a double quantity of *mukpaurat* so that there should be no delay in the morning. I was taught seven new cat's cradles this evening by one of our hosts — he seems to know an extraordinary number; so does the lady of the next house, who arrived last night.

Friday, November 7th

We were all up at 5 a.m., had a breakfast of oatmeal and *mukpaurat*, and started out at 8:25 a.m. Niniyuk, the husband of the 'Madonna' hostess, accompanied us with his sled. Having a very light load he relieved one of our sleds of a little of its burden. Nevertheless one of our sleds was very heavily laden, and our progress was slow in consequence. We continued eastward on the sea-ice for a couple of miles or more, skirting a fine cutbank. Then we turned sharply south, crossed a narrow neck of land, and found ourselves on a lagoon. Another neck of land intervened, and then a second lagoon, apparently smaller, then over another isthmus we reached the sea-ice again. It was now 11:30 a.m. and the going had not been easy, especially over the land. So we stopped and had lunch — biscuits, molasses, and butter. The molasses can had been placed inside a 'billy', which contained a piece of bear meat. There it capsized, so we shall have sweet soup when we cook the meat. The butter, being hard and brittle, we ate like cheese. We had not gone on very far before we saw a ptarmigan sitting on the snow 80 yards away. Aikie [Añutisiak] shot it with his rifle. Fox tracks were numerous, but we saw no foxes. The dogs pulled well the early part of the afternoon, but were visibly tiring. By 4 p.m. it was becoming hard to follow the track of the front sled; at 4:30 p.m. the man ahead carried a lantern. We had not been able to sight Aksiatak's house before dark, and knew only the general direction in which it and the land lay. Yet 10 minutes after we lit the lantern we stumbled right upon the house — Aksiatak himself is away from home, but his wife, who remained with the two children, made us very welcome. For supper we had frozen fish and a few *mukpaurat*, and tea. The Eskimos drink a good deal of ice-cold water, both between and immediately after meals. Here for the first time I saw the native lamp *naneq* or *kulliq* burning — a platter of metal containing seal or whale oil, with a wick of fungus (*munik*) trained along one side. It hardly smoked at all, and gave a light equivalent to about two ordinary candles. Instead of lines of string along the ceiling and walls to dry clothes on, there are iron hooks.

The house[28] is of the usual type, except that it is built of smaller lumber than I have seen used elsewhere. The larger logs have been split in two, but the smaller ones — and some are not more than 2 inches in diameter — are set up entire. Unlike our log cabins where the timbers are laid horizontally, in these Eskimo houses they are arranged vertically. The corner-posts are notched to receive the two long beams, which act as friezes.

Figure 28. Notched corner-post.

Parallel to these, in the centre of the ceiling, is the long rafter, which forms the ridge-pole, likewise resting in the notch of a log at each end, and logs, laid side by side, run from the side-beams or friezes to this ridge pole. A rectangular opening is left or cut for a skylight, facing the south — the direction of the sun. Another small round hole is cut for the stove-pipe. Rough-hewn boards are laid down for a floor. In this house the side walls are not upright, but slope slightly inwards. Consequently the door, which swings on hinges, closes automatically. Set up in one corner is a not unhandsome wooden clock, and hanging side by side on the wall are two caps like the French or German school-boy's casquette, or the black cap of a ship's officer.

At Cape Smythe we heard a story of a very large animal that had been seen near Cape Halkett, which had three blow-holes in the ice. No one knew what it was. Our hostess here says that it is thought to be an immense polar bear, which lives all the time in the water and does not wander over the ice like its fellows. Asecaq says that an old man is said to have killed a bear with similar habits long ago, but he forgets the story. On the ice this afternoon we crossed the track of a sled with broad runners coming first from the northeast, then turning south and later west, apparently going to the fishing lake. It seemed to have been no earlier than yesterday. We noticed today, as often before, the wonderful effects of the refraction of light. Land which is really below the horizon is brought into view. A cutbank 15 feet high at a distance of 2 or 3 miles looks like a mountain. Sometimes the shore seems raised up into the sky. The Eskimos have a word for this, according to Asecaq — *kesuk*.[29] At any time in travelling over the ice, small hummocks or isolated blocks of ice assume gigantic proportions a short distance away.

Our hostess has a fine pipe. The stem is of wood split down the middle, hollowed, and lashed together again with rawhide. The actual mouthpiece is round, but the rest of the stem is four-sided. The bowl is made up of three parts. The top is a steel disk hammered over the cylindrical upright portion, which is made from the metal casing of a cartridge. This in turn fits through an iron plate into the stem. A cleaning pick of steel hung by a steel link-chain, and then by a rawhide strap from the stem of the pipe.

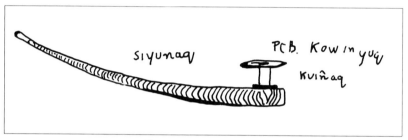

Figure 29. Mrs. Aksiatak's pipe.[30]

Her work-basket is a sealskin, complete, with a large hole cut longitudinally in the back. Here she keeps her needle-case, a metal cylinder about 8 inches long and 1/2 inch in diameter, through which, drawn by a rawhide lashing, passes a folded piece of skin in which the needles are kept. A nacre (mother-of-pearl) button prevents it from being drawn right through. I noticed the little girl give her year-old brother a good slap for something or other. We had supper (tea and hard-bread) about 9 p.m., then turned in. The weather today was mild, with a light southerly breeze.

Saturday, November 8th

We were up soon after 6 a.m. I was interrupted in a sound sleep about 3 a.m. by a cupful of water falling from the ceiling onto my face. Thereafter it dripped continuously through the cracks between the logs, and I had to shift my things and dislodge our two Eskimos a little to make room to one side. For breakfast we had bacon, rice, and *mukpaurat*, both fried and baked, an unprecedented feast. *Mukpaurat* is really the name of the baked scones only, called at Point Hope *kaqaq*; the fried variety are called *slavia* (i.e. slapjacks). Our friend Niniyak [Niniyuk] got up and lit the fire, just as he did in his own home. We loaded the sleds immediately after breakfast, and left at 9:50 a.m. for the fishing lake [Teshekpuk Lake], only a short distance away, the lady of the house assured us. We found it to be about 15 miles away by the trail we followed, but that of course may be quite near for an Eskimo. The weather was much colder than yesterday, and a fresh wind was blowing about east-northeast. This was all in our favour, for the wind was at our back most of the time, and the cold made the surface of the snow hard and the trail good. The dogs in consequence made fairly rapid progress, averaging about 4 miles an hour for the first 3 hours. Then we had to travel over land where the crust of the snow was often too weak to bear the weight of the sled, and the runners sank down several inches. Here the dogs had hard work, and required constant urging. A little before 3 p.m. we came out upon the lagoon, and crossing a corner of it arrived at two houses, or rather tents — our final destination until Stefansson turns up. On the trail we met a man and his wife coming back from the lake. The wife had a little baby on her back, and a small boy was walking beside the sled. These were the people whose sled trails we had seen yesterday. From what we could gather they had been wandering about looking for a house, being strangers in this region. Further on we met Aksiatak with his little girl, returning from the fishing lake. About 1/2 mile further back Niniyak had cached some things for him, a gun, a bag, and something else, at a post where Aksiatak had already deposited some of his own things. This was all we saw on the trail in the way of living creatures. Our course part of the time seemed to be in and out of sandspits in the delta of a river. A curious thing, noted both by Wilkins and myself independently, was the difference in colour of patches of snow-covered ice. For the most part it had the usual dazzling whiteness, but in some places it was tinged with blue, whether due to the different age of the ice or to the effect of the light on the uneven surface we could not decide. The sun at noon seemed to be only an inch or two above the horizon. The middle-aged woman (Kunaloak's wife and the mother of Ned Erie's [Arey's] wife), whom we met at Aksiatak's place before, welcomed us here, and hurried us into her warm domed tent, where she regaled us on cold ptarmigan, frozen caribou, *mukpaurat* (begged from the other tent), and tea. Asecaq and Añutisiak were entertained in the other house [tent]. We then turned out, and in the light of the half moon set up the large rectangular tent Mr. Brower made for us — large enough for 16 men to sleep in, cooking-stove and all. Presently our old lady friend came over with some frozen fish, followed almost immediately by the lady of the other tent, who dragged a bowl of frozen fish. We cooked supper on the primus and alcohol stoves, for there is no wood here, being inland[31] — rice and tea — and sent over a pot of rice to one of the tents. Asecaq and Añutisiak spent the evening with our new friends, and Wilkins and I proceeded to turn in at 7 p.m.

Sunday, November 9th

Wilkins and I turned out at 7 a.m., both feeling cold in our sleeping bags. We lit the primus and alcohol stoves, and boiled some oatmeal and made tea. Añutisiak and Asecaq came in for breakfast, then unloaded one of the sleds, put the dogs in [harness, to pull the sled], and went back to the coast for a load of firewood. Our old lady friend came in with two children and had some bear meat we had just cooked. Then she went away, and another child came in and we filled the three of them with *slavias* [slapjacks] and tea. Various things around the tent occupied our time until our two Eskimos returned about 1 p.m., when we set the wood stove going and cooked a sumptuous dinner, bear soup, boiled fish, dumplings and treacle, *mukpaurat*, and of course tea. It was then time to begin cooking again. We boiled a pot of rice and took it over to the lady of the other house, and set about baking more *mukpaurat* and rice. There are only two 10-lb boxes of biscuits left, so we are keeping them for the journey to the ships, and baking flour.

There was a band of light running through the axis of the moon (last night) as on October 22nd; tonight it was encircled with various colours, orange and green being predominant. Perhaps the colours around the moon are as bright in other parts of the world, but one seems to notice them more here. The weather today has been cold, the strong wind from the east-northeast continuing. Towards evening, however, it died away. Our neighbours obtain their water by digging a hole through the ice with an iron spike fixed on a wooden handle. A ladle of horn is used to dip out the water. The daughter of our old lady friend, a girl about 13, was digging for water this morning, while the little children were sliding on a small patch of glare ice. The old lady brought in four unfrozen fish that had been caught today.

Monday, November 10th

We rose at 7 a.m., or rather Wilkins did, for I lingered in my sleeping bag a little longer. He had considerable trouble in getting the fire to light, for our new stove is not a striking success. Boiled beans, bacon, porridge, *mukpaurat*, and tea were furnished, for now that we are settled in a semi-permanent camp we are living on the fat of the land. Kunaluak and his family left [for Cape Halkett] while we were still at breakfast. Their tent is much more comfortable than ours. It is oval in outline, or a kind of semi-ellipse, the ordinary tent of the Eskimos of Northern Alaska. The snow has drifted all round it, making it beautifully warm, and it has a passage of snow-blocks supported against a frame of sticks. Consequently as soon as Kunaluak left we moved across,[32] lit their stove, and hung up our sleeping bags and skins to dry. I then turned cook, while the other three, with the two fishing-nets, went off to the lake with Alak, the head of the other tent. He took up his three nets, securing 93 fish (one day's catch), and let our people put their nets in their place, thus saving them the trouble of making holes in the ice and of running lines along for stretching out the nets. Our nets, he said, are too deep, the lake being

Figure 30. Wood fish-net float.

very shallow; also the mesh is rather fine. The floats were made last night by our Eskimos, assisted by Kunaluak and Alak. They are of the same shape as Akuwa was making when we stayed with him [on October 31st], only his were attached by a hole at each end, whereas these had the two holes in the middle. Meantime I received a visit from Kuraluk's daughter,[33] who is living with Alak. She is about 8 years old and very deaf. I fed her with *mukpaurat*, then gave her a string to play with while I worked at cat's cradles. The others returned at 2 p.m., just as the sun was disappearing. Alak and his little girl came into dinner and we feasted on boiled fish, beans, *mukpaurat*, and tea. For the rest of the day we were occupied in making our new quarters comfortable. It has boards in the front half, and a bed of willow branches at the back, a great improvement on the snow. Our two Eskimos spend most of their time at Alak's house, but come in here for meals. We had tea at 6:30 p.m., beans and bacon, rice, *mukpaurat*, and tea. The tent was so hot that we were all bathed in perspiration. Tomorrow Asecaq is to be cook and get breakfast. He is a lazy fellow, and what work fell to the share of him and Añutisiak has been done chiefly by Añutisiak. As a matter of fact the lion's share has always been [done by] Wilkins, ever since we left the ship. The weather today has been fine, with a moderate breeze from the southwest, and the temperature fairly mild. Alak's wife brought us in a bowl full of fish while we were having dinner. He [Alak] intended to leave for Cape Halkett tomorrow, whither Kunaluak has gone, but Asecaq told us tonight that he thinks of waiting till Stefansson comes. The fish they are catching in the lake here are commonly known among the European's here as 'white fish'. They average from 12 to 18 inches, have two pectoral, two ventral, and an anal fin, a dorsal and a small second dorsal. On the back they are dark, almost black, but at the side this yields to a pale mauve tinged with pink, and underneath they are a creamy green. The back forms an arch ending in front at the pointed nose and behind in the bifid tail. The iris of the eyes is yellow.

Tuesday, November 11th

Asecaq turned out this morning and got breakfast — porridge, bacon, *mukpaurat*, and tea. He was not at all pleased at being made to do this, and has been sulky all day, infecting Añutisiak. After breakfast the two of them went out after ptarmigan, returning at 1 p.m. with three. Wilkins and I stayed in — he cooking, I working at cat's cradles. For lunch we had fried fish, slapjacks, *nerukaq*, and tea, then I and the two Eskimos went down to the lake to haul in the fish-nets. We dragged a small sled with us on which to carry the fish. The Eskimos who have been fishing here dug a number of holes in the ice about 25 yards apart, marking them with small sticks. They joined up the holes by a cord running underneath the ice, using for the purpose a pole about 24 feet long with a piece of wood 3 inches long lashed at an angle of about 40° at one end. The end of the net is let down through one hole, and dragged by means of the cord to the next. The cords at each end are then made fast, either to the original 'ground' cord, or to the ice outside the hole. This lake connects with the sea through a shallow stream, which freezes to the bottom. Consequently the fish have no outlet, and as they swim to and fro under the surface of the ice they run into the nets, their gills become entangled, and they cannot escape. We found 12 in one net, 3 in the other. The holes freeze over very quickly and the ice has to be broken afresh each time the nets are examined. For this purpose Alak has lent us two of his implements, an iron spike set in a wood handle for breaking the ice, and a sieve shovel for taking out the broken pieces of ice. The latter is rather

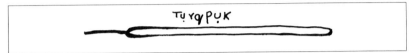

Figure 31. Alak's ice-breaker.

curious; the handle is of wood, the frame of the shovel of bone and the sieve of whale bone. Any old fragments of ice that may be left in the hole are embedded in the new ice that forms, and the hole is harder to clear out next time. Consequently the fisherman is careful to leave his holes as clear as possible. Many of the Eskimos now make their nets of

Figure 32. Alak's ice sieve.

twine obtained at Cape Smythe, but some still use sinew. Alak's are of twine; he has three in all, with bone sinkers, and wood floats.

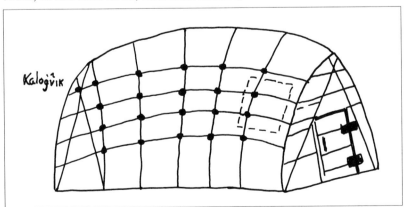

Figure 33. An Eskimo tent, with the framework of willow branches, the door of boards with leather hinges. Our tent has a window where the dotted lines come, only on the other side (the southeast). It is made from seal intestine. [D.J.]

Wilkins excelled himself as chef tonight — ptarmigan soup, baked fish, boiled beans, and dumplings. Then our Eskimos went over to the other house and we tried to draw some of the more difficult cat's-cradle figures — with rather ludicrous results. (The measurements of our tent, by the way, are roughly 14 feet long, 10 feet 6 inches wide, and 4 feet 6 inches high. We have no tape measure, hence the figures are approximate only.) We indulged in a supper tonight — tea and *mukpaurat.*

Wednesday, November 12th

A fine morning, mild, with a light southerly breeze. Añutisiak got breakfast, and the two Eskimos [Asecaq and Añutisiak] then set out [for the coast] with a sled and dog team for wood. I went out on skis with the shotgun to look for ptarmigan, and Wilkins remained to cook. About 1/2 mile from our tents is an upturned *umiak*,[34] with a spear-thrower and a pick-axe (minus the handle) on the bottom. The spear-thrower is of the old type, with a wooden handle (grooved on each face) and an ivory peg. Fox tracks were numerous, and I came across a flock of ptarmigan, but they were too shy to allow me to approach within range. I had not long returned to the tent when the Eskimos of the other tent saw a fox coming towards the settlement. I seized my rifle and tried to shoot it but the pin was frozen and the hammer consequently could not drive it home. Wilkins got his rifle and shot it just below the ear, about the best possible place if the skin is wanted — as of course it always is, for a fox such as this one, a white fox in good condition, carries about $15-$20 worth of fur on its back. The [two] Eskimos returned [with a load of wood] about 1:30 p.m., and we had lunch about 2:30. Wilkins and the two Eskimos then went down to the lake to examine the nets — there were 25 fish in all, an improvement on yesterday. I stayed to cook, and received a state visit from two of our neighbours, the two children, a boy and a girl, who ate *mukpaurat* and drank tea and gossiped as though to the occupation born. We sent a pot of boiled beans over to the next tent in the evening — a dish they would not often obtain. The moon is almost full tonight, and its beams shining on the blue-tinged snow make an almost perfect landscape. It was curious this morning to notice the distortion of the moon near the horizon — it seemed broader than it should.

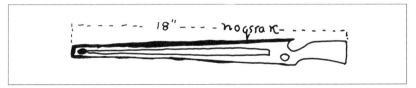

Figure 34. *Noqsrak.*

At 8 p.m. Wilkins and I went over to our neighbour's [Alak's] to spend the evening. His tent is smaller than ours, but better constructed, and with better material. His seal-intestine window, instead of facing southeast like ours, is on the opposite side of the door, and faces south-west. Ours is a fixture — sewn into the drilling of the tent.[35] His window was the same, but was broken; so he built a dome-shaped frame outside of it with small pieces of wood and snow, and framed in it a round slab of ice, slightly convex exteriorly. Being almost as clear as a poor quality window glass, it allows a great deal of light to enter. In diameter it is about 18 inches. Inside the tent a few treasures were attached to the sticks of the frame-work or stowed away at the side — an alarm clock; a rolled? gold hunting watch; a fine sewing-machine, etc. Everything was good — there were no cast-away articles. Alak and his wife were teaching our two Eskimos cat's cradles. They appeared to know a great number, with the old songs that accompanied them. Competitions in speed in producing a named figure caused great amusement. Añutisiak knows nothing of cat's cradles, while Asecaq, who is fairly proficient, was hopelessly eclipsed. Our light came from a lantern hanging from the roof — filled with some of our coal oil — and from a rude lamp modelled on the old Eskimo lamp. A pan was filled with seal oil (or whale oil) and the lid of a baking-powder tin set to float on the surface. Through a slot in the lid a broad cotton wick was drawn and set alight. By careful adjustment of this wick a moderately good light was obtained — equivalent to a candle at least — with practically no smoke. Wilkins asked Alak to skin the fox he shot today. The operation took 2 1/2 hours. Animals in the Arctic naturally carry a great quantity of fat. If any grease gets on the fur, it leaves a stain. Consequently Alak skinned the fox through the mouth, turning back the skin. It was thus removed inside out and had to be turned back. The head and neck were stained with blood. Before commencing to skin he had washed as much blood off as possible, and now after the fur was removed he went outside and stamped the stained portion in dry snow. Fat and grease adhering to the skin were carefully scraped off; this aided materially in the drying. At the end he slit down the legs and tail, and stretched the fox on a wooden stretcher Wilkins made from his ski poles. Small holes in the skin, as well as the great

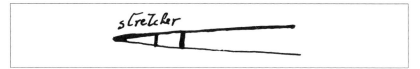

Figure 35. Stretcher for foxskin.

gaping wound in the head were skillfully stitched up by Alak's wife. Her needle case resembled that of Aksiatak's wife, the metal cylinder in this instance being taken from a brass 'tin' whistle. She had a pipe too, exactly resembling that of the wife of Aksiatak, while Alak himself had a European pipe. The tattooing on her chin was limited to one broad band in the mid-line.

Thursday, November 13th

We were so late in turning in last night that we all overslept. It was after 8 a.m. when Asecaq rolled out of his sleeping bag to get breakfast. Alak and his family left this morning for Cape Halkett or its neighbourhood.[36] Wilkins gave him a letter to give to Stefansson if they met. The weather was a little colder than yesterday, the south wind a little fresher, and the atmosphere rather foggy. Our [two] Eskimos went down to examine the nets in the afternoon; the haul was 21. I went out with my rifle on skis, and saw plenty of fox and ptarmigan tracks, but nothing living. Owing to the late breakfast we had a late dinner — a real 'spoon' dinner, of ptarmigan soup, beans, and rice, with *mukpaurat* and tea to conclude. Then a supper about 8 p.m. finished off an uneventful day. Alak has blocked up the entrance to his tent. Yesterday he cleared away the old snow and turf and returfed it, ending with a fresh covering of snow on top. It is his *umiak*, with the skin left on the framework, which lies 1/2 mile from here. Beside his tent is the rudder, shaped rather like a whaleboat rudder, but with the 'pins' on the curved [edge and] not on the straight edge. His fishing-nets and one or two other things are tied to the mast of the *umiak*, just outside the door of the tent, out of the reach of dogs. Apparently he intends to return again this winter to fish.

Friday, November 14th

A foggy day, with a cold north wind blowing. Wilkins remained at camp all day, I went out for an hour on the skis, and the [two] Eskimos went to haul in the nets. There were only 19 fish caught today. The dogs have eaten most of the rawhide lashings of one of the sleds, and last night they tore the flap of our large square tent. For dinner today we ate Wilkins' fox; it tasted very good. Our sugar is now exhausted; we are using saccharin with the tea — it seems to sweeten it all right. We have used up 40 lbs of flour in 8 days and 20 lbs of sugar in less than 3 weeks. Of course rice and oatmeal have used up much of the sugar; of the latter we have used rather less than 20 lbs in 8 days. Stefansson, in the written instructions he gave Wilkins when we left, said that he would be here about the 7th; it is now the 14th and he has not yet arrived. After dinner the two Eskimos went outside and played for an hour or so — running, jumping, football, etc. Wilkins was very seedy all day, but improved a little in the evening.

Saturday, November 15th

We had breakfast at 8 a.m., though sunrise now is not until 9:45 a.m. As it rose this morning it sent up vertically a broad streamer, like the streamers the moon emitted the other night. Asecaq got breakfast this morning, but went off without washing up the dishes; he did the same two mornings ago. He and Añutisiak had to fix up about setting one of Alak's nets, as with our own we are not catching enough fish to feed the dogs. They spent some time in digging holes through the ice, then examined our two nets — the catch was 13. Wilkins took a gun and went off on his skis after breakfast, returning about 2 p.m. He had seen only a snowy owl, which flew away at his approach. I stayed to cook — fox soup, beans, rice, *mukpaurat*, and slapjacks. We had an early dinner — about 2:30 p.m., and tea or supper at 7 p.m. The days are growing very short, and the sun's rays have hardly strength enough to cast a shadow. A camera is quite useless. Just now with the full moon the night is almost as bright as the day. At 9 o'clock this morning a beautiful band of red and orange in the southern sky marked the rising, while to the northwest but still high overhead, the moon was shining in scarce-diminished splendour. Looking out over the blue snow, not a tree, not a house was visible — only here and there a small dark spot where the snow had been blown off [the lake] and the glare ice left exposed. These brilliant sunrises and sunsets, with their rich glow of red and orange, recall the sunsets and sunrises in the Egyptian desert.[37] Wilkins was digging at the ice-hole for water when he heard a loud report as though from a gun; it was the lagoon ice cracking with the cold. Today, indeed, the air has been colder than it has been for some time; the breeze, what little there is, is from the north.

Sunday, November 16th

The night was very cold — I was cold even in my sleeping bag. Thick ice covered the water in the water can, and the *mukpaurat* in the food box were frozen hard. The hole from which we were obtaining water froze to the bottom yesterday, so Wilkins made a new one today. The dogs have made a huge rent in one corner of our square tent. The Eskimos who were living here made an ice box to keep fish in. It is a cube, with a face of about 5 feet (high enough to keep the dogs out) made from four blocks of ice about 2 inches thick, without top or bottom. The two Eskimos went off with their rifles after breakfast to look for foxes — Wilkins' success supplied the stimulus, and they set about making a wooden trap. Before returning to camp they examined the fish-nets — the catch was 21. Wilkins and I made snow shelters for some of the dogs, and a snow wall to protect others, sawing out blocks of snow with an ordinary saw that Alak left behind, and cementing them with water from the lagoon. I then turned cook while Wilkins repaired the square tent. We gave the dogs porridge today, not having enough fish. However, the Eskimos set one of Alak's nets today, so we may have better luck tomorrow. It has not been so cold today as yesterday, but is probably below zero notwithstanding. There was a light breeze from the east. I do not know whether the fact possesses any significance, but Asecaq was very unwilling to take Alak's net for our temporary use, although we told him that Stefansson would compensate Alak for it; on the other hand he was eager enough to move into Kunaluak's tent as soon as the latter left. Everywhere along the trail one uses the uninhabited houses, whoever the owner may be. Asecaq's reluctance to use Alak's fishing-net may have been due to laziness only.

Monday, November 17th

The air has been very calm and clear all day, though the temperature is fairly low. The moon has not set at all the last few days; it performs a kind of elongated ellipse, with its major axis from east to west. After breakfast I went out on the skis taking my rifle. I saw two foxes, one out of range, the other 300-400 yards off apparently; I fired at the latter but missed — badly misjudging the range. In a dull light it is impossible to distinguish mounds and hollows; sometimes one seems to be entering a broad depression, and only the difficulty in walking corrects the error of the sight. Everything is glaringly white, there are no shadows, and consequently nothing for the eye to rest upon. Not infrequently one stumbles into a large snowdrift 2 or 3 feet high without the eye being able to discern it. I got back to camp at 12:30 p.m. and Wilkins and I had tea and *mukpaurat*. The Eskimos [Asecaq and Añutisiak] returning from the lake, where they had been playing about all the morning, we boiled some rice and had tea and rice. Then Wilkins returned with the Eskimos to the lake, to bring in the rest of the fish — they had brought back half of them only — and I stayed to cook. The dogs are becoming woefully thin, for we have insufficient food to give them. Two fish a day is their allowance, and yesterday and today we gave them some porridge as well. We had dinner — beans, rice, *mukpaurat*, and tea — about 7 p.m. Another day has passed and still Stefansson cometh not. Only 27 fish were caught in the three nets — seven in the Eskimo one [Alak's]. Asecaq and Añutisiak were playing 'stick and hole' (*nipaicuq*) this evening, throwing in turns. They made the toys out of a stick. No count was kept of successful throws. Wilkins has been rather unwell the last 2 or 3 days, bad headache, and aching limbs and body.

Tuesday, November 18th

The morning was foggy, and a little snow fell. The atmosphere was a little clearer about noon, but was still very hazy. Wilkins repaired one of the harness before breakfast, and I another afterwards. As soon as breakfast was over he went off on snowshoes with his gun, hoping to come across some ptarmigan. The [two] Eskimos likewise went off to the lake and I stayed to cook and mind camp. They returned about 2 p.m., bringing 33 fish with them, the day's catch. Wilkins turned up half-an-hour later with five ptarmigan. He could not approach the flock near enough to use the fowling-piece [shot gun], so shot them with his rifle. We had dinner shortly afterwards, and for the rest of the day (it was already dark) remained in the tent. I made straps out of canvas to hang my mittens round my head. Another day without any sign of Stefansson. How often our plans (if one may call them plans) have been changed. When the *Karluk* disappeared he determined to go to Herschel Island. Suddenly he chose Point Barrow instead, intending to go to Herschel [Island] subsequently.[38] We must be at Herschel, he said, by November 20th, the time the sun disappears. A north wind sprang up this afternoon, moderately strong. The temperature, however, has not been very low.

Wednesday, November 19th

Another foggy morning. I went out shooting after breakfast and came upon a flock of ptarmigan. I fired seven times at them with my rifle — distance about 100 yards — and missed every shot. Returning in disgust I tested the rifle in camp and found I was shooting low every time — using a fine sight instead of the full bead.[39] The Eskimos returned about 2 p.m. with 25 fish. Wilkins made ptarmigan soup for dinner, beans, rice, and *mukpaurat*, then we had a late tea with the remnants. Singing and playing cat's cradles occupied us the rest of the day. I wrote down an Eskimo song and Wilkins put the music to it.[40] This kept us so interested that it was 10 p.m. before we thought of turning in. The temperature was fairly low.

Thursday, November 20th

An unpleasant day, a strong east wind blowing the snow about like sleet. Wilkins went out in the morning, met some ptarmigan about a mile away, and secured two. The Eskimos went off to the lake after breakfast and brought back 29 fish. I was cook. We had lunch at 2 p.m. and dinner about 6:30 p.m. The temperature was low; an hour after the fire went out this morning water inside the tent was freezing. At dinner tonight Asecaq held up the breastbone of a ptarmigan. It was almost transparent, but had a few minute dark spots. "This ptarmigan," he said, "was born on a cloudless day, but a little rain was falling." Later he held up another breastbone, which had a dark patch on it, and said "When this ptarmigan was born there was a black cloud in the sky." The drifting snow lashing against the intestine window of the tent today sounded exactly like heavy rain beating against a glass window-pane. The wood was wet and disinclined to burn, so, the tent being not overwarm, we turned into our sleeping bags soon after dinner.

Friday, November 21st

Stefansson, McConnell, and Alfred Hopson arrived about 11:30 p.m. [last night] while we were asleep. They left Cape Smythe November 7th and went to Point Barrow. The next day they went to *Iglorak*. From there McConnell and A. Hopson went back to Cape Smythe for a box of things. After that they stayed at the same places as we did, except that yesterday they came direct from Ikpik's house [near Cape Halkett]. They had considerable difficulty in keeping to the trail,[41] and for some time followed a wrong trail. In all they were travelling about 18 hours. We prepared a good meal for them and turned in again just after 3 a.m., the two Eskimos in Alak's tent, which they opened up. We had breakfast about 8:30 – 10:30 a.m., then the Eskimos and A. Hopson (Brick) went off to take up the nets. The weather outside was much better than yesterday, the wind having changed to the northeast and moderated considerably. We loaded up one of the sleds, placing on it most of the things that are to be left behind with me. About 200 lbs of food were left on Añop-kana's platform for me beside Ikpik's house, consisting of 60 lbs rice,

75 lbs sugar, 18 or 24 lbs dried vegetables, 25 lbs prunes, 20 lbs macaroni, one cheese (10 lbs), and one tin of coal oil. The Eskimos brought in about 300 fish, taking them from Alak's cache.[42] In our own nets there were only 10 or 11. Wilkins acted as chef today, with Stefansson superintending the primus stove.[43]

Saturday, November 22nd

We had an earlier breakfast than we have been having latterly. Then Stefansson and Asecaq went off with a sled to bring in more fish; the rest of us loaded the sleds. It was nevertheless 10:30 a.m. before we got away — four sleds and seven men. The first sled, with Wilkins, McConnell, and Añutisiak, went faster than the others, and reached Aksiatak's place at 2:10 p.m. The rest of us arrived a quarter of an hour later. The large square tent was erected at once and Wilkins set about kindling a fire in the new wood stove. It was a hopeless failure, and about 5:30 p.m. we put in the old wood stove. Stefansson, the two Eskimos, and Brick [Alfred Hopson] were having tea, meanwhile, in the Eskimo house. The old stove was better, but the wood was wet, the draught bad, and the tent covered with hoar frost, and for a long time, filled with smoke. We could not get it warm the whole evening. Aksiatak's wife came over to get our boots and dry them in her house; she stayed to drink tea and eat some rice and hard-bread, taking some over to her children. Alak and his family are living in the same house as Aksiatak. Stefansson was able to obtain only about 100 fish this morning, so that he has some 400 only for going east, not including a little whale meat (and blubber) — about 200 lbs — brought from Ikpik's. There was a fairly strong easterly wind today, blowing in our faces. It was cold too, and I had to thaw out my nose more than once. There was a brilliant meteor this evening falling from east to west.

Sunday, November 23rd

A Sunday in camp.[44] Outside a strong east wind blew the snow about in drifts. McConnell officiated as cook and we spent most of the day sitting around the fire and cooking. Stefansson and our two Eskimos remained over at the house and only appeared at rare intervals until the evening, when they all came together with Alak and Aksiatak and the latter's wife, and had dinner.

Monday, November 24th

I turned out at 7 a.m., lit the fire, and prepared breakfast. At 8:30 a.m. Stefansson sent across to the house for Asecaq, Alak, and Aksiatak, and I had to cook more. He then announced that he would leave today, and that it was time to pack up, also that Asecaq was leaving our service to do trapping here, and consequently would stay behind.[45] A sled and six dogs (the worst) were left for me, together with a quantity of food, etc.[46] The small round tent we brought from the ship and the large square one we used here were both left behind.[47] The party was reduced to four, Stefansson, Wilkins, McConnell, and Añutisiak. It was about noon when they got away. We who were left behind, Asecaq, Brick,[48] and myself, immediately cleared away the debris. We emptied the sled, placing some on the two racks belonging to the house, and others in the passage, which had a door on the outside and so was not accessible to the dogs. Then we took down the tent and cached it likewise on a rack. There was no room for our skins and sleeping bags in the house, so we left them in the passage. This occupied us until dark, when we went inside and had a meal of frozen fish, *mukpaurat*, and tea about 4 p.m. Then we sat around until 7 p.m. when we had dinner — rice, tea, and *mukpaurat*. The latter, Aksiataq's[49] wife cooked on a primus stove in the passage while her husband and Asecaq cooked the rice on a primus inside. Then we all amused ourselves playing cat's cradles, the children for part of the time playing in the passage. About 9:30 p.m. supper was served — frozen fish again — and about an hour later we turned in. We are rather crowded in this house, so they are talking of building another in a day or two for Alak and his family. The passage here is very convenient. It is formed of blocks of snow held in place by a framework of stout sticks and beams. It has a door at each end, one communicating with the outside, the other with the house.

Chapter 5. With the Eskimos in Harrison Bay (I)

Daily activities — Observations on child treatment — Cat's-cradle figures — Cleanliness — To Cape Halkett for stored provisions — Buying Eskimo drawings — Return to Aksiatak's — Sunday inactivity — An addition to the Eskimo house — Ptarmigan soup — Life on the Colville River — Daily routine of hunting and writing — Drawing maps

Tuesday, November 25th, 1913

A cold southwest wind was blowing all day with moderate strength. We had breakfast — the men at least, for the others did not get up — about 8 a.m. — frozen fish and oatmeal. Asecaq and Brick then went to look for a place to set their traps, and Alak and Aksiatak to see if any foxes were caught in theirs. I did one or two odd jobs, then set out on my skis to look for foxes or ptarmigan. The lashings of one ski were out of order, and as it was too cold to fix them up in the open I returned and fixed them up in the passage. Then, after digging small holes in the snow to shelter some of the dogs, I returned indoors and wrote and played with the children until the others returned in the afternoon. About 4 p.m. we had dinner — frozen fish, macaroni and cheese, and *mukpaurat*. The frozen fish always has rancid seal or whale oil served in a bowl alongside. Brick laid down three traps and Asecaq four. Asecaq obtained his from Alak and proposes to spend the winter here. For bait Brick brought a bottle of patent liquid manufactured in [the] U.S.A.; a few drops are smeared on the trap. Alak returned with a fine white fox, which he skinned in the evening. Aksiatak's two little girls sewed some deerskin boots under the supervision of the two women. They are very quiet children, more shy than Kuraluk's little girl, who hovered around me half the day. This last was scraping a deerskin, but did not stick to her task for 2 minutes at a time. Aksiatak's little girls do a lot of work — bring in snow and wood — look after the younger children, etc. The men cut up the wood and bring it into the passage and often into the house. They seem always to work the primus stoves when they are present. I noticed the children were scolded several times, and twice slaps were administered severe enough to make them cry — which contradicts what Stefansson told me.[1] Alak's little boy — about 4 years — was playing with his father's rifle part of the day, then with a small trap. He played with his father's watch, too, for some minutes. Brick told me today that an extra room is to be built on to this house, not a new house made. He and Asecaq go to the fish-lake tomorrow to get fish, using my sled; they will return on Thursday. We indulged in cat's cradles again this evening; the children play with the strings all day, and the elder children can make some of the figures. Growing tired of cat's cradles Aksiatak and his wife lay back and sang; Alak's wife sang half the day. No one seems to mind how loudly they sing. Alak's wife mended a deerskin boot of mine today. Our dogs are fed by the women when they feed their own dogs. The sun has left us now for a couple of months; it has been invisible for some days — since the 17th [November] I think. Alak has caught seven foxes since putting down his traps on the 15th [of November, when the trapping season opened]. At $15 a skin they will bring in quite a tidy sum. He and Aksiatak showed me their tool bags. They consisted each of an entire common hair-seal skin with a slit in the middle, like the women's sewing kit. Each had, besides European tools such as chisels, brace, and bits, etc., fish-net tools, and a lump of lead for writing. They were used for marking arrows to indicate ownership, and for various other purposes. Stefansson found numbers of them when he dug at Point Barrow, Brick says. Alak's mesh measure was a piece of wood such as Asecaq's grandfather used, about 3 inches long by 1 3/4 inches. His net-

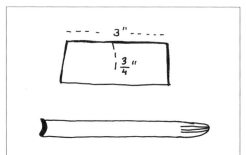

Figure 36. Alak's mesh measure and bone netting needle.

ting needle of bone was of European type. Aksiatak's mesh measure, which was made to fit the left hand, was of an altogether different shape.

For supper we had rice and tea, then followed frozen fish and whale oil. The proper way to take the oil, which is set in a pot or bowl in the midst, is to dip your fingers in from time to time and lick them. It is quite common to see a piece of chewing gum handed from one person's mouth to another. Asecaq and Brick eat from the same plate and wash in the same water. Yesterday we had grace before dinner; Aksiatak's wife said it. Today there was no grace. I noticed, however, that Aksiatak has a notebook with what appeared to be hymns written down in it.

Wednesday, November 26th

The east wind continued, of moderate strength in the morning, but increasing during the day. The men prepared breakfast as usual — oatmeal, biscuits, and tea, and frozen fish made their appearance afterwards. Alak's wife cooked some *mukpaurat* for Asecaq and Brick, and they set off as soon as it was light enough to see the trail, i.e., about 9:30 a.m., as far as we know the time here. Aksiatak went out to examine his traps, and I took my rifle and wandered along the edge of the cutbank to look for ptarmigan. Two suddenly emerged from behind a snowdrift, but immediately took flight, nor could I see where they alighted. This was all the game I saw. About 1/2 mile from the house, however, was a fox-trap made from logs — a deadfall. The bait was a large piece of whale blubber. The log was held up by a small peg, which in turn rested on a thin lath, so arranged that interference with the bait, which was accessible

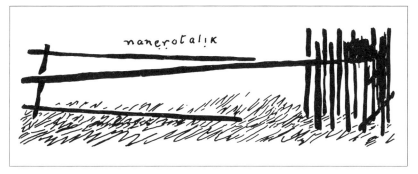

Figure 37. Eskimo fox-trap.

from below only, dislodged the peg and brought down the log upon the body of the fox. I was away nearly 4 hours and the others (except Aksiatak, who had not returned) had already lunched. However, they made the tea hot for me, boiled some fish (one whole one and the head of another) and added three or four *mukpaurat*, which were left over. Aksiatak arrived 1/2 hour later and was given frozen fish, *mukpaurat*, and tea. He was so content that he lay back and sang, whilst Alak, sleeping a few feet away, snored the accompaniment. Aksiatak's elder girl, Kukpuk (Big River), was very industrious, scraping a piece of deerskin. The second younger girl, Siniuna, was showing me some cat's-cradle figures when an interesting ceremony took place. Alak, who was suffering from constipation, had remained at home all day. Now he was to undergo first aid. His wife said a prayer of considerable length, whilst we all bowed our heads. Then he washed his chest and shoulders with soap and warm water. Aksiatak's wife rubbed him down with a towel and then said another prayer. Aksiatak himself was doing something outside during the first part of the proceedings, but entered in time to bow his head in the last prayer. The girl who was playing with me stopped as soon as she heard the prayer. Alak's wife has a curious thimble holder (*tikivik*) made of ivory by Alak himself. The thimble is inserted by pushing the edge through the slit in the side. Alak had a sweat bath this evening. He sat over the fire, stripped to the waist, and drank hot tea until he had raised a perspiration, then I rubbed him down with a towel. For dinner we had rice with cheese in place of sugar, and for supper boiled fox. Fox has a peculiar and rather strong taste, but is not altogether unpleasant. Alak taught me some more cat's-cradle figures this evening.

Thursday, November 27th

We had breakfast about 9:30 a.m., just as it was growing light. The moon is out [in the daytime] now, so it is dark at night. The wind died away before morning, and the temperature, though probably as low, seemed more bearable. Alak, who has been suffering from a pain in his chest, was still unwell, so remained indoors nearly all day. Aksiatak set about erecting a larger platform, and I helped him as far as I was able to.

We dragged on a small sled some of the larger driftwood which litters the shore. He split it and in the tops of the four corner posts cut a V-shaped notch. I dug the holes in the snow with a long knife, using for

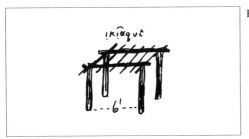

Figure 38. Eskimo platform.

a shovel a ladle of horn. Two stout beams were set in the notches, and across these were laid other beams, the end ones being rather stouter than those in the middle. This completed the platform or rack; no lashings of any kind were required. We transferred some of the things from the other

Figure 39. Notched post.

two racks to the new one; then Aksiatak set about cutting firewood. The children were playing about with the small sled, toboganning with it down a low mound of snow. There being nothing left to do I went in-doors and shaved, using a safety razor McConnell left me. The others then had afternoon tea — a frozen fish each; for me 1 1/2 fish were fried in their skins. For the slapjacks they use whale oil as well as water. It affects the eyes rather as smoke does while the slapjacks are cooking, and seems to make the cakes more sodden. One of the dogs last night was walking over the house. Aksiatak shouted at it and it went off. I was noticing today how they dispense with handkerchiefs; they blow their noses into their hand and wipe the hands on a rag or some feathers, whichever comes first to their notice. The table cloth seems to have been adopted without any notion of its real purpose; it is about 3 feet square, and is laid on the floor for each meal. Apparently it is never washed, and as no one hesitates to tread on it, its colour would puzzle an artist. Alak this morning, whilst waiting for breakfast, carved a small ptarmigan out of a stick with his pocket knife to amuse his little boy; it was very skill-fully done. Aksiatak's wife said a long prayer before breakfast, but the others took little notice of it. Here is a sketch of the thimble holder of Alak's wife. It too was interesting to watch her comb her hair with her fingers this morning. It took some time but the result appeared very satisfactory. Kuraluk's little girl, Piñasuk, is a merry little maiden, always in smiles or in tears; Aksiatak's two girls are much more staid.

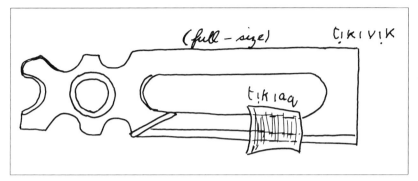

Figure 40. Mrs. Alak's thimble holder.

The evening passed quietly — I was teaching the girls to write their names. Aksiatak's little boy, who can as yet say only one or two words like *agañ* and *apañ*, took the floor for a little while and began to caper round as though dancing. The others encouraged him, while Alak's wife sang a dance song and clapped her hands in lieu of a drum. For our supper we had frozen fish and turned in immediately afterwards.

Friday, November 28th

Aksiatak was astir very early — about 6 a.m. He lit the fire, and then ate some frozen fish. Alak rose shortly afterwards, then myself, for my bed is on the boards just inside the door, and consequently in the way of anyone going out or coming in. Aksiatak went off before 8 a.m. to examine his traps. I waited for daylight and breakfast, then went off to look for ptarmigan. I saw two flocks, but it was too dark to see where they settled and I could not find them. Aksiatak's wife and Siliuna wandered along the shore, apparently collecting something. About 2 p.m. I returned and the rest shortly afterwards. Aksiatak brought back two foxes, one of which was caught in Siliuna's trap. The children have been assigned traps by both Alak and Aksiatak, but the foxes caught in them, though called their foxes, go to swell the common stock; they reap no individual benefit from them. Asecaq and Brick arrived about 4:30 p.m. with a sled-load of fish. Aksiatak has quite a Roman nose, his face is long and flat, the chin almost pointed, but there is no doubt that he is of pure Eskimo descent. I have been watching their treatment of the children rather closely, in view of what Stefansson told us on September 27th. It is true that they are allowed to play with many things — scissors, watches, etc., which a European child would never be allowed; it is true too that their whims and caprices are often humoured and given way to; but it is not true — with these two families at least — that they are never scolded or slapped, nor that they are invariably allowed to have their own way. Aluk's wife (the word is Aluk not Alak) found two holes in my sheepskin mits this morning where a dog had bitten me; she mended them as a matter of course. The weather today was mild and calm, but it was somewhat foggy. In the evening there was a fine aurora.

Saturday, November 29th

A moderate wind was blowing from the east and the atmosphere felt cold. I froze my nose slightly a day or two ago, and it was sensitive to the wind. The men were up early and went off to their traps, except Aluk. I stayed and wrote up some cat's cradles, then went out on skis to look for ptarmigan as usual. It was somewhat foggy, and in the kind of semi-twilight it was rather difficult to distinguish small objects at a distance. I saw a small dark spot which seemed to move, about 70 yards away, and taking it for a fox, I fired. The bullet went straight enough, but the object was not a fox, only a bunch of grass among the snow. Continuing I met Brick, who was returning home with his dog after setting three fox-traps. We saw one of Aluk's traps on the river bank. All that was visible was a small black sod about 6 inches high, with a short stick resting on it at one end, the other end being buried in the snow. Around were chips of frozen whale blubber. We had gone some distance past it when we saw Brick's dog approach and smell it, then become caught by the leg. Brick went back to release it while I returned to the house, which was not far off. Aksiatak arrived about the same time, Asecaq an hour later with a fox from one of Aluk's traps — the eighth [fox] for Aluk. It was not until after supper, however, that he [Aluk] skinned it, through the mouth as usual. He was busy making a short stove-pipe when we arrived, out of a tobacco tin, and removed the old stove and set in another one with an oven. The next thing was to make bread pans, and these were soon cut out of a square vegetable tin. The women at once proceeded to bake some bread using magic yeast. The bread was soon ready and tasted fine. Then he turned his energies to making a drying rack to hang above the stove. He split a stick in two, and drilled holes

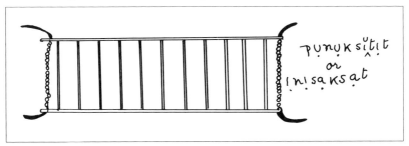

Figure 41. Aluk's drying rack.

with a brace and bit. Then with his knife he whittled away some sticks and rounded them, then made the ends fit the holes, so that the side pieces jammed against ledges on the cross-sticks. A string passed around the two corners of each end and was twisted so that it held them taut and prevented them from springing apart. This completed the work. It was then hung up over the stove. Cat's cradles again amused us, competing with one another who should make the figure *itikoraq* first. Aksiatak's little girls are very clever and quick in this amusement. Aluk seems to know an almost infinite number of figures. He has shown me about thirty already, and they say that these are only a few of those he knows.[2] The evening was cold and foggy, the stars invisible.

Sunday, November 30th

An idle day for everyone. Consequently we all rose late, and it was nearly noon before we breakfasted. The elder lady said a prayer after we rose, then after breakfast we had service. Each said a prayer, some a short one, some a long one. This terminated the proceedings. For the rest of the day we lounged about, conversed, played cat's cradles, etc. At 4 p.m. we had dinner — frozen fish as usual forming the first course. Aluk told us how they used to catch ptarmigan and foxes with a noose, à propos of a cat's-cradle figure representing a ptarmigan's nest and the noose over it. Near the fishing lake he set a noose for foxes over a hole in the ground. The string passed through a hole in a post and was tied to a stone, which fell and drew the noose tight when the bait in the hole was interfered with. He and Aksiatak are both inland Eskimos and have travelled extensively. Aksiatak said that if you go up the Colville [River], 4 days' journey in the spring time when the days are long will take you to a district where the miners are digging for gold, and 4 days' journey through their country will bring you to the forests where he has seen moose. Aluk too has seen many moose — in the same region apparently. Aksiatak and Aluk's wife are brother and sister, and Aluk's son is named after their father, hence they call him *apañ*. Kukpuk, the eldest child of Aksiatak, was born on the Colville River, and hence is called Kukpuk (great river). She has another name, Arigaicuak, but is seldom if ever called by it. Siliuna was learning to bake *mukpaurat* under the guidance of Aluk's wife. These people appreciate a joke. Aluk's wife held her finger close to the cheek of one of the children, then spoke to her. The child in turning knocked against the finger. This trick, so common with English children, seemed to afford both of them great amusement. A supper about 9 p.m. of frozen fish ended the day. The weather outside was not very attractive, for the moderate northeast wind which was blowing was rather chilling. Evening brought a fine star-lit sky, with a narrow auroral band of white light across its northern hemisphere.

Monday, December 1st

The northeast wind of yesterday increased almost to a blizzard today, consequently though we men were up early — Aksiatak at 5:30 a.m. — we spent the day indoors. The dogs for their part howled outside, causing Aksiatak's wife to yell at them several times through the skylight. Aluk fixed up his saw, sharpeninig it, and altering the position of the handle. He had to soften the steel in the fire in order to bore fresh holes. Then he sharpened his plane and one or two other tools. Asecaq and Brick cut up firewood in the passage, then played cat's cradles and lay about. Brick translated a song or two for me, which occurred in cat's-cradle figures. The women sewed, Aluk's wife using her sewing machine. The two elder girls also did a little sewing. There are about 2 hours of daylight when one can see to read, but indoors in this weather a lamp is necessary all the time. It is amusing to watch the uses to which feathers are put. There is a pillow stuffed with them; Kukpuk took some out through a small hole to wipe her fingers after using frozen fish. Generally the bunch of wing feathers from a snowy owl are used for this purpose and for sweeping the floor as well. Then feathers serve sometimes to wipe out a pot or a cup or a knife, to blow a child's nose (or one's own), to clean the lantern glass — for the hundred and one things in fact for which we use rags. Blubber again is served at table, sometimes entirely melted, sometimes in long white strips to be cut up and eaten. A tin of it is usually kept behind the stove to assist in lighting the fire, and where there is no driftwood (as is the case around Point Barrow, where the supply has been exhausted) it serves as a fuel, though turf is used perhaps more frequently. Reindeer sinew is very valuable to these people. They never use thread for sewing skin clothing when they can obtain sinew. The supply seems to be limited too, for caribou are scarce here and further west there are none, although domesticated reindeer to some extent fill their place. I had a little sinew with my sewing kit, which came from the *Karluk*, and my hostesses here were very glad to get it, as they had but little of their own. The women here are not crushed or downtrodden in any way; they seem to stand almost if not quite on the same level as the men — not quite, perhaps, because where there are a number of men the women and children eat apart or afterwards. This may be for convenience only though, for in other respects, as far as I have noticed, there is no indication of their being regarded as inferiors. Their lives seem to be spent in the alternative tasks of sewing and cooking. Aluk asked if I wanted to wash this morning, as they do just before breakfast — generally here the only time. Each had a cupful of clean water, but used the same towel, and since my towel was outside in my rucksack I declined. I have not yet discovered whether they wash for the sake of cleanliness, or as a kind of ritual, as Stefansson says; something of the former notion does seem to enter into it with some of them. I have not washed since leaving Point Barrow, and yet I do not feel unclean. Perhaps it is because we wear fur clothing instead of wool or linen. The Eskimos often wear woollen singlets night and day, and they are seldom if ever washed. There is no dust or mud here, except the earth which creeps through the crevices in the walls and roof, and one's hands at least have little opportunity of becoming very dirty from the constant handling of snow and frozen fish. Aksiatak has been busy making a snow shovel. Siliuna, his daughter, was baking bread, guided by her mother. Stefansson's theory about the little children never being hit received its death blow today as far as these families are concerned. Aksiatak's baby boy (about 15 months old) was tugging at Pungashuk's hair (or Punganahoq as they call her here). Aksiatak hit him lightly two or three times with the stem of his long pipe, then as he [the child] did not let go, he struck him a sharp knock, which made him run screaming to his mother. Aluk's wife Qapqana also gave her son a slap, which made him cry.

Tuesday, December 2nd

The bad weather of yesterday continued, so we spent the day indoors. Aksiatak continued his snow shovel. He took a rough-hewn plank and planed it down, making one side straight and the other curved. Then he planed down a smaller piece of board and fitted it on the straight side, dowelling it in. To prevent it from slipping off he drilled six holes, in pairs, and lashed the two parts together. Then he set about shoeing it with a piece of bone from the lower rib of a whale. The bone had to be shaped and grooved to fit on to the end. Aluk did most of this while Aksiatak trimmed up the wooden shovel. By 7 p.m. it was lashed on to

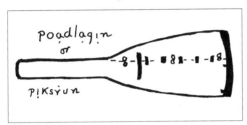

Figure 42. Aksiatak's shovel.

the shovel and he [Aksiatak] proceeded to bore holes to bind it tight. For the lashings here he used fine copper wire. The edge was scraped to make it sharp, and through two holes bored just below the handle a rope loop was made to serve as a grip for one hand. This really finished the shovel, but he rubbed the greater portion of one side with some red material, apparently red ochre (to serve as a property mark?). It had occupied him the greater portion of one day and part of another. Siliuna baked again, the women sewed, [and] I wrote and played cat's cradles with the rest. The dogs had been very noisy in the night, howling and barking; one of them persisted in running over the house. Sometimes one of the men, sometimes one of the women would shout at them. It was very cold — probably the coldest night we have had, and no one was anxious to turn out in the morning. Consequently it was nearly noon before we had breakfast.

Wednesday, December 3rd

The weather was fine this morning, the sky clear and a light breeze from the east. It was growing light when we finished breakfast, and the men went off at once to examine their traps. I stayed behind to finish off some writing, and also because as yet it was useless to go out with a rifle. About 11 p.m. I too sallied forth and wandered round for a couple of hours in search of ptarmigan but saw none. It was colder than I had thought, and I was quite glad to get back again to the house. All the glow of sunrise was visible along the southern sky, but no sun made his appearance. I shaved on my return, then had tea and fish with Aksiatak and Brick, who were also back. Two of Brick's traps had been visited, but they were badly set and the foxes escaped unhurt. Aksiatak, Asecaq, and Aluk returned with a fox each. I did some writing and some work with Brick till dinner-time. Qapqana (Aluk's wife) had a sudden seizure of what was apparently palpitation of the heart; it passed off after two or three minutes. Tomorrow Asecaq, Brick, and I go to [Cape] Halkett to obtain mine [my stores] and some of Aluk's. Asecaq says he is going to Point Barrow at Xmas with a sled, and we have been discussing what we want. It is amusing to watch the housewifely care of Aksiatak's wife in apportioning out the *mukpaurat*. She counts the number of us and passes over either the exact number of *mukpaurat* or one less. If we finish them quickly she may send across one or two more, when some of us have retired from the circle. Similarly she carefully cuts up the bread (made of magic yeast) and doles it out. She sent across a *mukpaurat* to me this afternoon because I do not eat so much fish as the rest, she said. This evening again she passed over to me two thick slices of bread because they were warm.

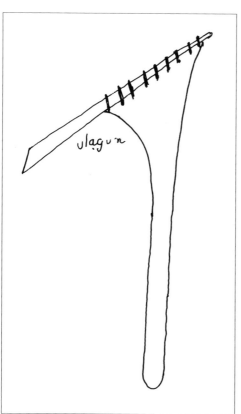

Figure 43. Adze in Aksiatak's house.

Here [Fig. 43] is a sketch of an adze lying in the passage. It is of iron, naturally, with a wooden handle, the lashings of rawhide. The whole blade of iron is some 2 feet long, the handle about 3 feet. Brick tells me that Aluk's *umiak* near the fishing lake will have the *ugruk* (bearded seal) skins kept on it all through the winter because they are new. Only old skins are removed, and in the summer when the ice opens up they are repatched and steeped in salt water to make the seams water-tight before they are replaced on the frame. The throwing-stick is used with the many-pronged spear for killing birds, especially ducks, from the kayak. It is still used at Point Barrow. Also he has used (and seen used) a bolas (*qilamitaun*), which consisted of several pieces of bone or ivory or other heavy material, each on the end of a piece of string, which was joined to all the others at the other end. It was thrown by holding the knotted ends in the hand, allowing all the weights to hang down. Aluk and Qapqana made up a harness for one of the dogs this evening, for Asecaq, Brick, and I go to [Cape] Halkett tomorrow if the weather is favourable.

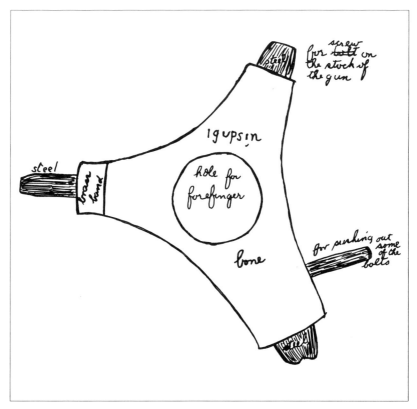

Figure 44. Aluk's screwdrivers and handle for taking his gun to pieces (full size).

Thursday, December 4th

There was a brilliant aurora last night, stretching in a broad band from northwest to southeast. It was still visible in the early morning when we rose, in the form of fainter bands of light all over the sky. The day was clear and calm, so we got away about 9:30 a.m. We took it in turns to run ahead, and steered almost due north. When close to the other side of the bay we met a man and a boy — the latter clad in a mountain-sheep coat — who had been out hunting and were now returning to their home at the point. He told us we had come somewhat out of our course, so we skirted the edge of the cutbank, which ran east and west, and after travelling about a mile we reached the post which marks the trail. A fox-trap had been set at the foot of it. Here we stopped for lunch, tea (thermos bottle), hard-bread, and baked bread, then pushed rapidly on and arrived at Añopkana's house shortly before 4 p.m. Asecaq stayed with Kunaluak and his people in the other house, Brick and I with Añopkana. In the house were the very old lady ['Lady Maguire'] we had met two or three times before, the blind lady, wife of our host, the paralysed lady, and the lady who keeps house. Aiva and her husband Samuel were away, but were expected tomorrow. Then there were Añopkana himself, and three other men, one the husband apparently of the paralysed lady. They made us very welcome, and immediately set some cold brant[3] before us, then shortly afterwards *mukpaurat* and coffee. The good lady was very lavish of her food, and we all ate together. For light they had a good stand lamp as well as an Eskimo lamp proper — the platter with seal or whale blubber and a grass wick. Over it was hanging a piece of blubber transfixed by a stick which projected from the wall. The platter was full of melted blubber, and lying on it were two sticks, which were dipped in the blub-

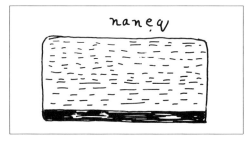

Figure 45. Blubber on wall.

ber, lit, and used as tapers. In the ceiling just above the end of the sleeping platform were three or four pegs loosely inserted in holes. At night when we went to bed these were taken out and inserted in other holes in the long beam which forms the outer edge of the platform. Here they sloped upwards at a gentle angle, and a board was laid across them and clothes bags, etc., again on that, forming a comfortable pillow. It was amusing to notice the scrupulous 'cleanliness' of our hostess. For washing up the dishes she used about a cupful of water and the same cloth with which she washes the floor. The outside and inner edges of the cups she licks clean.

They have been catching a large number of foxes here. Aksiatak's son [Itarklik], who is living in the other house, heads the list with twenty-six. Samuel shot a polar bear a little while back; a large bearskin is worth about $60. In the central rafter of the house, just above the end of the sleeping platform I noticed three pencil drawings of caribou — the form, not outlined simply but pencilled in. The artist had evidently been lying on his back when he drew them, in the same position as that in which one sleeps in such a place. The weather was very cold, if fine, and running made my boots damp with perspiration, so that I caught a severe cold. From 8 till 10 p.m. we all sat and listened to one of the men — a native from further down the coast — narrate one of the old stories of these people.[4] Long as the narrative was, the interest of the listeners seemed never to flag. Every now and then one would interrupt with a question or comment. There was a fine aurora in the evening, something like the arc with projecting streamers that one so commonly sees in books.

Friday, December 5th

Another fine day, with all the tints of a sunrise without the sun itself. The housewife was first up, and lit the fire and cooked *mukpaurat* and rice. At 7:30 a.m. we breakfasted, then one by one they went to visit their

Figure 46. The stretcher used by [?][5] at Cape Halkett for his foxskin. The cross-pieces are morticed and the whole is of wood [D.J.].

traps, the housewife to visit hers also. Brick and I loaded our stores on the sled, giving a tin of onions to our hosts, besides the tobacco (three tins) and the box of chewing gum, which Stefansson had asked me to do. About 11 a.m. I went over to Kunaluak's house and stayed for tea and *mukpaurat*. Here too I left a tin of tobacco for his wife according to Stefansson's wishes. Brick narrated the story of the evening before (in English), and I made a precis of it. The narrator of last evening showed me some of his drawings. I asked him for them (they were on a sheet of paper) but he wanted to keep it. He offered to do more for me, but wanted something in return. Finally I arranged to pay him $1 for two writing-pad sheets covered with drawings on one side, and ordered a score or so — the scenes to be typical of Eskimo life or strange animals in their beliefs. He started work at once. In skinning the foxes here they began with the mouth also, but cut off the claws, and instead of pulling the brush off the tail with the rest of the skin, cut the tail off close to the root, and split the tail down afterwards. I tried to trace, more or less successfully, one of the drawings on the ceiling — the largest, of a caribou. The paper was not sufficiently transparent and it was awkward to reach up. A second Eskimo lamp was lit, the sticks serving both as tapers and to trim and arrange the mesh. Añopkana busied himself in making a fish-net. Here is the needle and mesh used. My artist filled two sheets

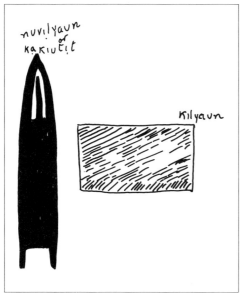

nuvilyaun
or
kakiutit

Kilyaun

Figure 47. Añopkana's needle and mesh for making his fish-net.

from my writing pad (one side only) with fairly good drawings.[6] Then it turned out that he had misunderstood the terms. He thought he was to get $1 for each drawing instead of for two sheets. I made a compromise therefore and wrote him an order on Mr. Brower's store for $2 for what he had done instead of $1. His name was Ugiagonak[7] and he is Mrs. Brower's brother; his home is somewhere near Cape Prince of Wales. It is interesting to note that the blind lady, Añopkana's wife, is the ruler of the household.

Saturday, December 6th

We were astir early, but did not breakfast (*mukpaurat* and tea) until 8 a.m., consequently it was 9 a.m. before we were away. The housewife again lit the fire and did all the work, the men watching — contrary to what usually happens in Aksiatak's house. She gave us some *mukpaurat* for lunch and filled the thermos bottle. Aksiatak's son [Itarklik] came home with us. His sled (Asecaq's) was heavily laden, as was ours also, and we made very slow progress for the first 1 1/2 miles. Then we took out the heavier things and cached them on a sled beside the trail. Nevertheless we still travelled slowly, though our sled — with five dogs — weighed about 200 lbs only. The dogs were very poor[8] — the worst

Stefansson had. At 1 p.m. we reached the post on the side of the bay opposite Aksiatak's house. The others with Brick waited to boil the kettle on the primus and make tea, although we had drunk what was in the thermos flask. I went on ahead with my sled, as it was slower than the other. It was not until 3 p.m. that they overtook me. We plodded on and reached Aksiatak's at 6 p.m., having taken 9 hours to make the journey. Here we received a warm welcome and dined on frozen fish and a huge potful of rice, with tea and *mukpaurat* following. Then we sat and talked until after midnight, with a brief interlude for supper when we had blubber (straight) and cold rice — myself the latter only. The weather was fine, with a moderate breeze from the north and consequently at our backs. It was nevertheless foggy, especially in the early part of the evening. By midnight it had partially cleared and some of the stars were visible. Asecaq's nose has a propensity to bleed without provocation, as is often the case with white people. Aluk and Aksiatak had commenced building a new room to the house for us. The frame was complete, but it has still to be turfed over and a door cut through.

Sunday, December 7th

A quiet day indoors. Everyone was up late — it appears to be the usual thing on Sunday. After breakfast Brick and Asecaq went out to examine some of their traps. The rest stayed at home, the only work they did being to cut up some firewood. We had no service of any kind this Sunday, and though grace is still sometimes said, it is less frequent than it was. Most of the day was spent in lounging about and playing cat's cradles. The women cooked, but did no sewing. Outside the weather was fine and clear, with a slight breeze from the north. The temperature seems to be fairly uniform, probably below zero at about -8°[F]. We have been using the prunes (dried) that Stefansson left me, to put in the *mukpaurat* instead of currents; they taste very well and are a great improvement on the plain cakes. I notice that [the word] *mukpaurat* here is applied to every variety of johnny cake, whether baked in the oven, fried, or boiled in lard. We went to bed early, another feature that seems to characterize Sunday here.

Monday, December 8th

We rose early, for the men wanted to go off to their traps. For breakfast, besides the frozen fish which habitually appears, we had a pot of rice. It was all eaten by the men, so the women and children who breakfasted later had to be content with fish and *mukpaurat*. I stayed in after the others went out to write up some cat's cradles, then later took my rifle and strolled out to look for ptarmigan — unsuccessfully. When I returned Aksiatak's son was already back, 'playing' on an accordion. Soon the kettle was boiling, and we had *mukpaurat* and tea and coffee. Aluk returned with two foxes, the others with none. He skinned his before dinner. Cat's cradles as usual filled in the evening. The weather today was much the same as yesterday, fine and clear, with practically no wind; the temperature, however, seemed milder. It was very late when we turned in — between 11 and 12 p.m.

Tuesday, December 9th

Whether in consequence of our tardiness in going to bed, or because there was nothing to do until daylight, we all rose very late, and it was 10 a.m. before breakfast was ready. After breakfast all we men turned out to complete the new room and attach it to the house. Aksiatak and Aluk had constructed the framework, leaving a square hole for a skylight and a small round hole for the stove pipe. The house wall, with its covering of turf and snow about 2 feet thick, separated the two. First the new room and a space of a foot or more round the sides was cleared of snow, while Aluk and Aksiatak with their small adzes dug up turf near by. A sled was used for conveying the turf to its destination. Aluk's wife was out by this time, and assisted in cleaning the walls and roof beams of snow, and in placing a layer of turf round the sides. A single layer was laid to the height of a foot or 1 1/2 feet, about 2 inches in thickness, then a bank of snow made round it and stamped down. In this way the whole room was covered in, roof and all, leaving only the holes for the chimney and skylight. Aluk and Aksiatak had uncovered the edge of the house and continued the roof of the new room to join the house roof by a row of beams laid horizontally, but at right angles to the other roof beams. Aluk now descended through the skylight and with his adze cleared away the snow and turf from the house wall, shovelling it through the skylight. He pulled away a portion of the house wall, leaving a space about 2 feet 6 inches wide for a door. It was 4 p.m. by this time, and we adjourned for dinner. Aksiatak's wife had lit a big fire outside, making a small pit in the snow to reach mother earth. Here she boiled two foxes Aluk caught yesterday, Kukpuk tending to them after the cauldron had been suspended from a stick over the fire. So for dinner we had ptarmigan and rice and *mukpaurat*. The next step was to lay the floor. Rough boards were stored on one of the platforms. These were let down through the skylight and arranged as best they could be, forming a tolerably good floor, with one bare place for the stove. Aksiatak was repairing a stove pipe, and as soon as it was ready we set up the stove on top of a 'billy' and a square alcohol can we brought from the *Karluk*, lit the fire, and dried the room. Aluk removed his things into it and his wife stitched on her sewing machine a window of seal intestine. When we turned in for the night, Aluk, his wife, Pungasuk, and Aluk's little boy, with Asecaq and Aksiatak's son occupied the new room while Aksiatak and his wife, Kukpuk, Siliuna, and the baby boy, Brick (his Eskimo name is Kaiyutak), and myself occupied the other. The weather was foggy all through the day, but not very cold. A light air came from the west.

Wednesday, December 10th

We were all up betimes, for Asecaq and Aksiatak's son were going to [Cape] Halkett to bring the stores we cached there [on December 6th]. They took my sled, it being stronger than theirs and larger, with some of our dogs in addition to their own. Brick and I went off to inspect his traps, and did not return till almost dark. We saw some ptarmigan and he shot one. One of his traps had been visited, but the fox had not stepped on the trap itself. On our return we found that Aksiatak had shot five ptarmigan with my shotgun. He and Aluk had arrived home shortly before us. We went in and changed, then they settled round a pot of blubber. Myself not being able to participate, Aksiatak's wife gave me a thin hard *mukpaurat* with a lump of cold rice on it; then she sampled a cup of tea, which was warming on the stove, and handed it on to me. This was a concession, I being a *tanik* (white man). Soon afterwards, however, dinner was ready — porridge, *mukpaurat*, and tea. Aluk's plate — a tin lid — was tainted with coal oil, which spoilt all his porridge. He took my plate and had a second helping. The girls plucked the ptarmigan, and about 6 p.m. we had ptarmigan soup with onions. Brick thinks Aksiatak's wife very stingy because she counts out the number of *mukpaurat* she gives us each meal. It is the custom, he says, of the inland people. Often he is still hungry when the meal is over. Asecaq thinks the same. I could often eat more than is available, but had considered her mathematical housewifery due rather to the fact that she is an inland woman and has probably known hard times. Aluk set up his window today. The only frame it required was four pieces of wood for the four sides of the hole, forming a square to which the intestine was attached and stretched taut by a semicircular hoop of [willow?].[9] He made two excellent stove pipes from two kerosene tins, but abandoned his own stove, where the oven was on the wrong side, in favour of mine. To connect his stove pipes with the one that attached to my stove, he cut the bottom out of an old tobacco tin.

I forgot to mention that in eating the ptarmigan soup, Aluk, Aksiatak, Brick, and I all dipped from the pot in the middle with our spoons. I made a dive and took up a leg, covered at one end, it seemed, with onions. The onions turned to feathers and claws in my mouth — the bird had been plucked to the knee, and the rest of the leg, untouched, had been left to swell the soup. The others dipped almost alternately from the soup and from the blubber pot — the manner of eating (or drinking) the blubber being to dip the three middle fingers (or two) into the pot, then suck them with great gusto. Occasionally a solid strip is taken up and eaten. I can endure one or two dips with a piece of frozen fish, but have not succeeded in acquiring a liking for it. The children — all, in fact — are expert in eating porridge, rice, etc., with their fingers — it is an excellent way to clean the pot.

The weather has been fine, though cloudy, the atmosphere moderately clear, with a light air from the east, which changed in the afternoon to the west and freshened slightly. We opened the tin of matches today that

Figure 48. Aksiatak's bone mesh-gauge,[10] *kilyaun* (slightly reduced). *Kuvrin* is another name for it; *iraok*, yet another name for it, is said to be used by both the *Nunatagmiut* and the *Kovagmiut*. [D.J.]

Stefansson left me, put away one doz[en] packages for ourselves, and gave the other four doz[en] to our hosts. In the evening Aluk and Aksiatak told of their experiences with the spirit of cat's cradles when they were young,[11] also of a mountain between the Colville and Noatak[12] rivers where it is fatal to sleep.

Thursday, December 11th

We lit the fires at 8 a.m., but did not breakfast until 11. A cold southwest wind blew all day so that it was not very pleasant out-of-doors. Nevertheless we turned out and brought in driftwood. Some was cut up for firewood, some sawn down to make a sleeping platform for Aluk's family. This occupied us until dark. Brick thought he would like to try the tin of dried beans Stefansson left us, so we opened it and used some of the packages. They turned out very stringy and rather tasteless, whether through prolonged boiling (2 hours) or because they were not much good anyhow, I do not know. However, we had a good stock of *mukpaurat*. For the rest of the day we sat and talked, played with the children, sang, and (Brick and I) wrote. The time does not seem to drag at all — at least not yet. Pungasuk received rather deserved punishment this evening — three slaps as hard as Aluk's wife could inflict. Aksiatak's little boy was worrying him [Aksiatak] so he gave him a slap which made him cry. Stefansson's dictum about little children not being punished does not apply here in the least. This evening Aksiatak drew a sketch of part of the Colville River, and he and Aluk showed me where they fished and hunted. Afterwards he gave me the map. Caribou, he says, are more numerous than they used to be in some parts of the Colville [River valley]. There are plenty of red and blue foxes, and some black ones are met with further up. Ptarmigan are numerous, also squirrels, but there are no muskrats. Moose are seen further to the south, but black bears are occasionally found in the portion of the river he sketched. The river and all the lakes are full of fish, chiefly *anakliq*,[13] which in one lake grow to a great size and are very fat. One lake, however, contains five or six different kinds of fish, though the land around seems no different save that willows are especially thick there. Some Eskimos remain on the river all the winter, obtaining their flour from the traders in summer. They do not use much flour, however, but live almost exclusively on fish.

Friday, December 12th

The southwest wind of yesterday had increased and was blowing the snow about today so that one could not see more than 100 yards away. We were late up, and so had late breakfast. Then Aksiatak's wife, dissatisfied with her husband's sketch of last evening, made one herself in my diary — the first she ever tried to make. Neither of them can read or write; they have in fact come very little into contact with the whites. Aluk and I then sawed down some large logs to make planks for his sleeping platform, a task which occupied us until 3 p.m. The others then

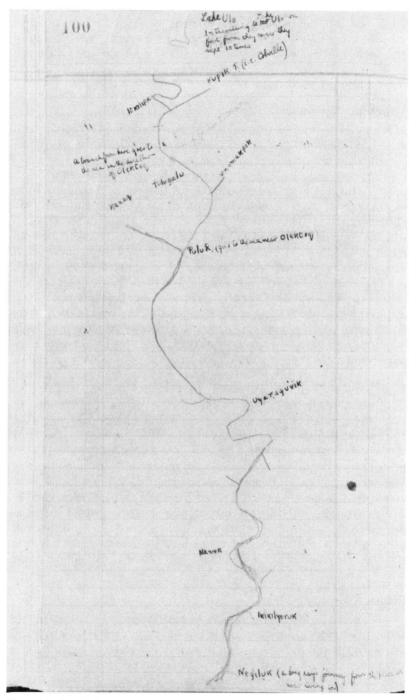

Figure 49. Mrs. Aksiatak's map of part of the Colville River. The mouth of the river is at the bottom of the page. The writing is the author's. (From page 100 in Volume 1 of the diary. See also Fig. 208.) (NAC Photo No. C136456)

had a light lunch of blubber, I a couple of *mukpaurat* boiled in blubber. Asecaq and Aksiatak's son [Itarklik] came home soon after with the stores we cached at [Cape] Halkett. At 5 p.m. we had our dinner — rice and *mukpaurat*. Mrs. Aksiatak taught me two new cat's-cradle figures while her husband continued the sketch map of the Colville [River]. Brick called me out to see the moon, which was encircled by a brilliant rainbow. When I went out only a semicircle was left, lying very close to the moon. The wind had decreased in violence and the atmosphere was very clear. The moon is almost if not quite at its full, and the night is [now] almost as light, and much more brilliant than the day. We turned in for the night at 11 p.m. I forgot to note that for supper we had boiled squirrel (squirrel, and its soup and oatmeal all mixed). We dipped from a common bowl.

Saturday, December 13th

The wind of yesterday died quite away; today the air was calm and clear. The full moon in the west sought to help the absent sun to lighten up the landscape. We breakfasted as usual about 9 a.m.; then the other men, except Aksiatak's son, went out to examine their traps. He remained to skin a fox he brought back with him from [Cape] Halkett yesterday; all his traps are set over there. I wrote for a time, then went out to look for ptarmigan as usual, and this time shot one. On returning I put it in the passage while I helped Aksiatak Junior [Itarklik] cut up wood for the two fires. Someone left the passage door open, [and] the dogs got in and ate the ptarmigan. Aluk and Aksiatak returned about 2:30 p.m. and we had tea and *mukpaurat*. Aksiatak brought a fox, but Aluk returned empty-handed. So too did Brick an hour or so later, and Asecaq. A fox had been caught in one of Brick's traps, but had managed to free itself. We dined a little late, about 8 p.m., on rice and *mukpaurat*. My [fountain] pens have been troublesome the last 2 or 4 days, perhaps the result of the continuous freezing and thawing they used to receive, or perhaps merely that I mixed this ink too thick. One of them is bent considerably. Now that there is more room I keep them inside all the time. For the rest of the day we sat about. The women sewed, I wrote, and the other men did various odd little things. Tomorrow Asecaq, Aksiatak's son, and Brick go to the fish lake with two sleds to bring back some fish. The weather this evening is fine and clear, but the southwest wind has returned, though as yet it is not very strong. Apparently it is full moon tonight.

Chapter 6. With the Eskimos in Harrison Bay (II)

Hunting caribou — Baby carrying — Eskimo language sounds — Asecaq departs for Barrow — House repairs — Accordion selections — Blizzard — Brick makes a whizzer — Aksiatak makes a foxskin stretcher — Arrival of visitors — Christmas Day — Eskimo children's wooden toys — Journey to west side of Harrison Bay — Building a house

Sunday, December 14th, 1913

The southwest wind was blowing strong this morning, so the party did not go to the lake for fish. There was no service of any kind — the only thing the men did was to cut up firewood, and the women cooked. Otherwise we lay about, wrote, and played cat's cradles. Aluk made a map for Asecaq of a portion of the Upper Colville [River], showing where they hunted caribou. One hunt, he said, they killed 140 fawns; the full-grown caribou they began to count, but became confused. The caribou were enveigled into taking a certain direction by sticks set in the ground, which frightened them off other trails. Thus they were headed towards small lakes where men waited in kayaks to spear them in the water. Aluk said that often as he lay in his kayak hidden under the willows on the bank, the deer [i.e., caribou] had jumped right over the bow of his canoe. Mt. Isuk appeared on his map — the highest mountain, he says, in this region; beside it is another high mountain, though it is but a dwarf beside [Mt]. Isuk. It is called *Sagliaq* (something lying on the lap of a person) because it 'lies in the lap' of [Mt]. Isuk.[1] Not far away is a place called *naniksraq* (a thing to make a *nanik* or Eskimo stone lamp) because here stone was obtained for making lamps. A river is named *umiaktorvik* because 'you can use your canoe on it'. Aluk's wife told a long story this evening, but asked Brick not to write it down. Aluk, Aksiatak, and Aluk's wife spent all the latter part of the evening drawing a map of the mouth of the Colville River. They had not finished by 12:30 a.m., at which hour it was adjourned, and we all retired to bed. Sunday being a day of rest the women dressed the children's hair, adorning it with red ribbon, which was plaited in. This one dressing lasts for a week it seems, and is repeated each Sunday. Aluk has a calendar written out for him on which he strikes off the days as they pass.

It is wonderful how easily the little girls carry the baby boy on their backs. They have a special coat they wear for the purpose. The boy is tucked under it from behind, the girl bends down, and the next moment the child's head appears in the hood looking over the girl's shoulder. A cord is passed round the middle of the back so that the child cannot slip down, and [is] brought round the front high up on the chest — with a woman it comes above the breasts — and is generally tied close to the armpit in front. I have seen Siliuna sometimes kneel down, get the child up on her back, and try to rise, but fall over with the weight. Then she would try again, succeed, and trot about the house or outside quite at her ease apparently. The weight falls evenly on the head (through the hood) and shoulders, it would seem, as well as on the back, so that through being distributed it is more bearable. Mrs. Brower at Barrow was very business-like in carrying her little boy. She dropped her coat over its head in front, gave it a swing round, then a slight swing to her body, and hey presto, the child was up before you knew she intended to carry it.

I am not sure if I have mentioned that the women's skin trousers and boots are all in one piece. Sometimes they cover them all over with calico trousers and boots of exactly the same shape. For outdoors they put on a pair of short boots over them. Wolverine fur is highly valued as a fringe to the hoods and at the wrists. At Barrow it is imported and sold at a high price. In the Colville district there are still wolverines existing, up on the mountain slopes. Brick told me that what Stefansson said about the *atka* protecting the child is true, and that in consequence parents are loth to punish their children, though they do punish them at times. He said that it is the relative's name the child takes, not the last dead person's in the place, irrespective of relationship. Sometimes though, a child will be named after a very close friend lately deceased. He [Brick] himself was named after the husband of a woman who was a close friend of his mother, at the request of the woman herself. (His Eskimo name is Kaiyutak.) For a time the woman used to come constantly to see him, then after a time she never even visited the house. His mother was much annoyed, and other Eskimos were displeased also, and for a time there was some talk of changing his name, but for some reason or other it was retained. The woman, it was felt, should take an interest in, and to some extent watch over the child who was named after her dead husband.

We unearthed a new sound yesterday, for which we invented a new symbol. It is half *n*, half *y*, we write it *ñ*, and [it] seems to be very common. It appears in the word for men, which is generally written *innuk*, but which we write *iñuk*. To pronounce it hold the tip of the tongue motionless against the lower teeth, and bring the back of the tongue against the palate. Sometimes I pronounce it right, sometimes wrong.

Monday, December 15th

The southwest wind is still blowing, but with less violence. Outdoors it is very cold. We were all up late. One of the dogs kept running over the house, despite the shouts of Aksiatak and Aluk. The skylights were covered with hoar-frost inside, and it [the dog] shook a lot of it down on the stove, the floor, and the clothing. For breakfast Aksiatak devised a queer mixture: rice, dessicated onions, and crushed hard-bread, all boiled together. The onions were too much for Brick. He tried to drown their taste in cheese, but even that was unsuccessful. Asecaq and the others did not feel inclined to go to the lake today, so they remained at home. Aksiatak and Brick went out to look for ptarmigan. Brick got three and Aksiatak four. We had them boiled for dinner, and for supper [we had] boiled beans. Aksiatak and Aluk finished their map of the Colville River; they did not sketch its whole course, only a portion of the lower half. Aksiatak then made a stick for tying up the dogs, in the ordinary Eskimo

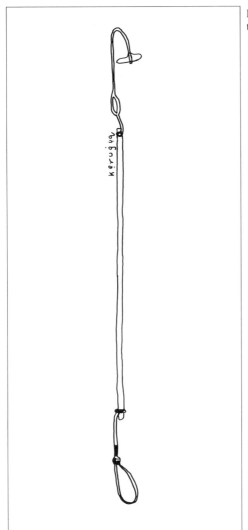

Figure 50. Aksiatak's stick for tying a dog.

fashion, i.e., a stout stick about 3 feet 6 inches or 4 feet in length, with leashes at each end. One is tied to form a loop which goes over a stake in the ground; the other has a loop in the middle and a peg at the end which goes round the dog's neck and fastens in the loop. The leashes are made so short that the dog is unable to reach and bite them — a very practical method. Brick, Asecaq, and Aksiatak Jun[ior] [Itarklik] went outside to play. They were tripping each other up, Eskimo fashion. The hands are kept tightly against the sides and the two combatants, facing each other, move round and round, watching for an opportunity of suddenly swinging out a foot behind the adversary's, jerk him off his balance, and throw him to the ground.

Tuesday, December 16th

We rose a little earlier this morning, for Asecaq and Brick were to go to the lake for fish. They took my sled and dogs, with some extra dogs of Aluk's, and got away about 11 a.m. Aluk went a little way with them, I imagine to examine his traps, for he has some along the route. He did not get back till 4 p.m., after the rest of us had dined. Aksiatak too went off, and returned about 2 p.m. with three ptarmigan; he uses my shotgun regularly and is very successful. I cut up firewood for the two stoves, a task which occupied about 2 hours. I think the Eskimos must be husbanding their supply a little, they use the hand saw a great deal in cutting up the firewood, and when they do chop through a log, they make the scarves very narrow. It may be, however, that this is their usual custom even when wood is plentiful. Aksiatak Jun[ior] manipulated the sewing machine for a time for his mother (the men often seem to do this; Asecaq was doing it yesterday for Aluk's wife, sewing on a band round the bottom of a shirt). Then he made a frame for stretching a foxskin. It differed from others I have seen in being solid, cut out of a single board, with an

Figure 51. Itarklik's frame for a foxskin.

'appendix' for the tail. Then he skinned a fox in the usual way, fastened it on the stretcher, and laid it on the rack to dry near the stove. Aksiatak set about making a stove from a kerosene tin. He fixed a door on one end, the hinge being a thin iron rod fixed perpendicularly, and the end of the door bent round it. Below was a hole for the draught. For fixing on a chimney he took a point near the end on what was to be the top, and cut out with his knife radii of a circle the size of the stove-pipe, and then lifted up the segments so that the apices stood vertical. Then from another kerosene tin he made stove-pipes — two from one tin. Flanges along the two end sides fitted into each other, when carved, to form a cylinder, and were prevented from springing out by dents at intervals along their course. For the rest of the evening Aluk, Aksiatak Jun[ior], and myself played cat's cradles, while Aluk's wife sewed. Brick and Asecaq returned about 11 p.m. They passed the house and had to return. We saw a light coming from the east and wondered what it was. They brought two large blocks of fish frozen together. Everyone turned out for a meal of frozen fish, although Aksiatak and his family had gone to bed; evidently they had felt the want of it the last few days. It was after midnight when we turned in. The weather was fine all day, but rather hazy. There was a very light breeze from the southwest and the temperature seemed much as usual. The little girls today, Kukpuk and Siliuna, made a house for a sick dog; in the snow that was piled up against the east side of the house they dug a cave and made a floor of shavings. To prevent the mouth giving way they lined the top with a piece of wood — the 'entablature of the grotto'.

Wednesday, December 17th

An unusually late rising lost us the earlier hour of daylight for we did not finish breakfast till about noon. Aksiatak's wife complained of severe pain in one eye, and spent much of the day lying down. Brick's boots have been unsatisfactory — the deerskin soles got wet the day he and McConnell farewelled Wilkins and myself from Barrow, and so have rotted and worn out. My deerskin trousers are abridged and require lengthening; also the sheepskin mits are not warm enough. Consequently today I exchanged the smaller of our reindeer skins, which we use for a bed (the other is large enough for us both), for a thick caribou skin of Mrs. Aksiatak's more suitable for boot soles. Aksiatak and his family to-morrow are going over to their son's traps (near [Cape] Halkett) for a time, so Mrs. Aluk will put new soles on Brick's boots. My trousers and mits can wait until Mrs. Aksiatak returns. Mrs. Aksiatak says Stefansson promised to send her (and I imagine Mrs. Aluk is included) two caribou skins from the ships. We spent a quiet day at home. Aluk overhauled his sled for the journey to Barrow; Aksiatak was making a new one. Aluk's sled I notice is shod with bone (the jawbone of a whale). I cut down a biscuit box and packed Wilkins' fox for transmission by post, then made up a list of things Asecaq is to bring me from Barrow. Here is the list:

1	set deer legs (for new boots for Brick)
1	pair dungaree trousers (for Brick)
10	yards brown denham [denim] (snow-shirt for myself, [the] rest for Mrs. Aluk
40	yards small lance warp (for new traces for dogs)
6	writing tablets
3	letter pads
1	dozen lead pencils
3	erasers
	Swan Ink bottle (left behind by Stefansson)
2	pair dark spectacles (for Aluk and Aksiatak)
1	dozen 3-cornered files (for Aluk, Aksiatak, and self)
2	pair small pliers for wire etc. (for Aluk, Aksiatak, and self)
1	pair scissors (for Mrs. Aksiatak)
4	large enamel plates
2	packets chocolate (for children)
1	5-gallon keg syrup
2	10-lb tins lard
3	10-lb boxes hard-bread
2	hunting knives (one for Brick's trapping and one for Aluk)
2	slabs back sinew (for the women's sewing)

Mrs. Aksiatak set to work at once to scrape our skin ready for Mrs. Aluk to make boot soles. She moistened it occasionally with a little water. Her scraper was an iron cylinder with a wooden handle, like Mrs. Hopson's [October 22nd]. Brick says the skin is scraped, then moistened and rolled up for a time to soften, then scraped again. Asecaq was preparing for his trip all the evening. Everyone retired early. The weather was fine all day, with almost no wind, the little there was coming from the west.

Thursday, December 18th

All were up early for breakfast. Outside a cold northeast wind was blowing strong, so Aksiatak decided not to go. Asecaq, however, got away about 9 a.m. or a little after; Brick went out after ptarmigan, and so did Aksiatak Jun[ior (Itarklik)]. The latter brought one back, the former none. We others stayed indoors, except that Aksiatak and Aluk cut up firewood. The rest of the day passed rather drearily, for the house was stuffy and warm. Aluk reloaded some shotgun cartridges, using refilling tools bought at Barrow. His wife sewed new soles on Brick's deerskin boots. Brick baked *mukpaurat*, I wrote, Mrs. Aksiatak scraped skins, Aksiatak smoked and talked, his son slept. Puñasuk (or Puganahoq or Puganasuk as she is variously called by Mrs. Aluk) was set to sew two narrow scraps of calico together and made to sit at the back of the room (*pavunni*) until she had finished. Mrs. Aluk started each row (there were two she had to do) and kept an eye on the child's method. I noticed this morning that Aluk spat on his hand and rubbed it over the shoeing of the sled Asecaq was taking; this was to make a film of ice on the bone shoe. He told me that they never played cat's cradles while two stars called *agruk* were visible, just before the long days of summer — why he did not know. They played other games then, like whizzer.[2] I drew a sketch of my home in the evening, which greatly interested them. There was a fine aurora about 8 p.m. — a white band of light stretching between the east and the north like a white rainbow. We retired very early, about 8 p.m., for no reason apparently except that there was nothing to do.

Friday, December 19th

We breakfasted about 10 a.m., then turned out, Aluk and Aksiatak to commence a second porch or passage to the house, for the snow beat in through the outside door, and often in the morning there has been a pile of snow both inside and outside. Aksiatak Jun[ior] and myself brought in some logs and cut up firewood, while Brick went off to bring in one of his traps. The new porch was made circular, the walls being of snow blocks cut out of a drift at the side. Across the top of these were laid rough beams split out of logs, and on these other blocks of snow forming the roof. A narrow space was left for the entrance. Soft drifted snow was now thrown over the top and into the interstices at the sides, while at the same time the inside was cleared and steps cut in the snow from the entrance to the level of the floor — a depth of about 4 feet. Aluk now took the saw and went off a short distance, where there was a low mound of hard packed snow. Out of this he sawed four blocks, two long and rectangular, two almost square. The first two he set up on end, one on each side of the entrance. On top was set one of the square blocks, forming the lintel, while the other was laid at the bottom as a kind of door step, to be stepped over, not on. It prevents the snow from being trodden back down the steps, or from drifting in. Daylight was rapidly fading by this time. At noon a brilliant yellow glow stretched along the southern sky, bounded above by the dull leaden hue of the twilight, and below along the horizon by a black band of drifting snow impenetrable to daylight. Towards the southeast it changed to a pale green tinged very slightly with red, then faded away altogether. Southwest the bright yellow darkened to orange, then to a dull red, which stretched for some distance along the sky, growing fainter and fainter, and finally vanishing altogether. The scene was wonderfully beautiful and impressive, viewed across a barren waste where the snow was driving along in clouds like dust. The northeast wind blew strong and threatened each moment to freeze the face. Indoors it was warm and comfortable. Mrs. Aksiatak wished to lengthen my deerskin trousers, so I retired to my sleeping bag and changed them there — a method of dressing and undressing decidedly awkward at first, but made easy by constant practice. A couple of hours later my trousers were finished. Aksiatak and Aluk made a rough shelf in the side of the outer porch, laying two beams side by side, with the ends set in the snow about 3 feet from the floor. On the shelf they placed blocks of snow to be used for obtaining water (our water supply in fact), underneath two or three boxes and tins. During the evening Aksiatak Jun[ior] brought in his accordion, and he and Brick gave us selections. The most interesting was an attempt to play one of the Eskimo songs while Qapqana sang it, an attempt not altogether unsuccessful. An aurora similar to last night's was visible about 10 p.m., but rather less brilliant; it stretched from northeast to northwest also.

Saturday, December 20th

A blizzard was raging outside when we got up this morning. The strong northeast wind was blowing before it clouds of dust so thick that one could see but a few yards away. We stayed indoors, Aluk spending the time profitably in making a sleeping platform. Brick continued the story we heard at [Cape] Halkett; Qapqana promised to tell him another later on, which he might write down. The women sewed, Aksiatak and his son sat about, played cat's cradles, and sought in various odd ways to pass the time. For dinner in the evening we had boiled rice saturated with whale oil. Brick is fond of the hard blubber, but could not stand this; after two or three attempts at eating he passed it over to Qapqana. I managed to swallow mine with some difficulty. Aluk's sleeping platform extends along only half the breadth of his room — it occupies, that is to say, one quarter of it. At 10 p.m. there was no aurora visible but at 1 a.m. a broad band from the northeast separated into two narrower bands, which extended to the northwest. The blizzard was raging as strongly as ever. It is strange that Aksiatak Jun[ior] should be almost as dark as a Polynesian, whereas Aksiatak himself is very fair, more so than most of the Eskimos I have seen; his body is no darker than many an Englishman's. Possibly Aksiatak Jun[ior] is an adopted son only; his mother calls him *apan* (father). I have an impression that the Eskimos in general throughout this region have lips somewhat thick and slightly everted; also that they have the habit of leaving the mouth agape.

Sunday, December 21st

Today and yesterday, the two shortest days in the year, were appropriately marked by a blizzard. As yet it shows no sign of abating. We were all up late and did not finish breakfast until about 11 a.m. Aluk and Aksiatak turned out to chop firewood, and I to help. I took the axe and went down to the beach where the driftwood lay, cut up a fine log, and carried it back to the house. Then it turned out that it was a red spruce (*ikiq*) log that Aluk was saving. The rest of the day we all remained indoors, writing, talking, and playing cat's cradles. Qapqana said that inland on the Colville River there are a great number of whalebones in one place; she herself had set some on end. There had formerly been a great flood covering all the land except this place, and the people had stayed here and killed the whales. More than this of the flood she did not know. Mountain sheep are found scattered among the mountains in every part, but they are harder to hunt than caribou. Their parents killed immense numbers of caribou, wasting a great deal of the meat. In consequence caribou became scarce, and the inland people, being short of food, have migrated to the coast. Now that they are hunted less the caribou are increasing. The red paint with which Aksiatak decorated his snow shovel — it was for decoration only, he said — came from the mountains where it is found in patches among the rocks. It is very light; perhaps it is a kind of ochre. Aksiatak had drawn a map of a portion of the headwaters of the *Kiliq* [Killik] and *Savaneqtoq* [Sagavanirktok] rivers. He explained it in the evening, then presented it to me. I asked him to draw me a sketch showing how they hunted deer. He asked for some paper as he wished to practice there and then. The ladies wished to see again the sketch of my home. I promised to make them a better one, and have already started. These two families are very fond of macaroni — they like it, Brick says, more than rice. The children had their hair dressed, it being Sunday, and the women dressed their hair also. Brick lay on Aluk's platform while Qapqana searched his head, apparently a very usual proceeding. There was a slight aurora about 10:30 p.m.

Monday, December 22nd

The blizzard raged as strongly as ever all day, so we did not venture out more than was absolutely necessary. Aluk and Aksiatak spent most of the time drawing sketch-maps of rivers they knew. Aksiatak drew the [?³] River; it took 14 sheets of a letter pad. One sheet he adorned with drawings of caribou being driven into nets and pursued in kayaks as they crossed a lake. Aluk's map is not yet finished. The children were sewing together the skins of loons and swans to make a 'mattress' on which to sleep. Brick says that sometimes a shirt is made of bird skins and used in wet weather; it does not rot if it becomes wet like deerskin. Brick partially conjugated a verb for me, and continued writing the story we heard at [Cape] Halkett. Siliuna and Kukpuk baked *mukpaurat* on top of the stove without supervision of any kind. Aksiatak Jun[ior] (his name is Itaqluq) is always playing with his watch; so too is Brick. They open the back, stop it, set it going again, alter the regulator. Then if it goes wrong they shake it violently and take out part of the works. A silver watch would not go; they poked a match down beside the hair-spring to try and set the wheels moving. A watchmaker would be horrified.[4] Itaqluq has a gold watch with 17 jewels; he plays with that in just the same way. I do not know if I have mentioned that the windows (skylights) of the two rooms here both look southward, in accordance with what seems to be the general rule.

Tuesday, December 23rd

The blizzard is over, although the northeast wind is still of moderate strength. The men, except Itaqliq, went to their traps, but returned empty-handed. Brick had not time to reach his traps; the nearer ones he has taken up, and the others are a long way off. Itaqliq and I gathered some of the driftwood and cut it up for firewood. He also partially loaded a sled, apparently with the idea of leaving tomorrow. He and his mother and Siliuna are going to stay for a time near his traps, on the other side of this bay, but south of the trail [across the Cape Halkett peninsula] to Ikpik's and Añopkana's houses. If they do not get many foxes they will come back here. Aksiatak will stay here, for all his traps are here. Aksiatak added a little to his map and presented it to me.[5] It has interesting sketches on it. I finished the sketch of my home, and put in the gardens, fountain, and greenhouse, then presented it to Qapqana. They were much interested. Qapqana has promised to tell Brick some stories as soon as he finishes the one on which he is engaged; he is very slow in writing. He made today a whizzer.[6] It differed considerably from the ordinary English form.[7] A piece of wood about 1 1/4 inches long had a deep notch cut in the middle. Round this was tied a short line of rawhide; the two ends, at equal distances from the notch, attached to short sticks, which formed the handles. The whizzer was wound round a number of times, then the strings strained and relaxed continuously. Aksiatak said that he used to have a circular disk of willow with two holes, through which passed two strings[8] — the ordinary English form, that is to say, only he did not serrate the circumference. The Eskimo name for the toy is *imigiluktaq*. Aluk partially took to pieces a dollar watch he had which would not go — a pivot broken, I think, in the balance; his only tool was a pocket knife. Last night there was a brilliant aurora, several parallel bands stretching from east to northwest, the usual direction

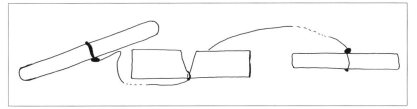

Figure 52. Brick's *imigiluktaq* or whizzer (2/3 natural size).

lately. This evening I noticed only faint signs of an aurora when I went out, but it may have developed later. The northeast wind seemed then to be increasing a little. The dogs find the outer passage a very cosy kennel; they are rather a nuisance there in fact. The door leading to it from the inner passage is held close at night by a stick passing through the handle and across the frame — on the bar principle; in the morning it is thrown on one side.

Wednesday, December 24th

Christmas Eve. Outside the north wind is blowing strongly. In the night the drifting snow rattled on the skylight like rain on a glass window. It is very cold also out-of-doors; inside the house the cauldron of water freezes each night. Aksiatak went off after breakfast, taking his snowshoes; I think he went to his traps. Brick went out to look for ptarmigan and shot one. Aluk and Itaqluq stayed indoors, Aluk trying to repair his watch. Aksiatak, when he returned, repaired one of his wife's snowshoes, the heel of which was broken. He riveted a piece of tin over the break. Then he planed down two willow sticks to make a new skin-stretcher. The two front ends were thinned down with plane and knife, and lashed together. Small holes were drilled through the joint with the bow drill and pegs of wood inserted. Five cross-pieces were fitted into the sides, and across the two last [he fitted] a piece of wood lashed round which the brush could be tied. The frame was kept rigid and the cross-pieces prevented from falling out by a twisted rawhide lashing at each end. It is the most neatly constructed stretcher I have seen. I noticed Aksiatak poured whale oil over his rice at dinner. For supper we had the ptarmigan Brick shot and the half of a codfish left by Stefansson, boiled together. The codfish had not been allowed to soak and was extremely salty in consequence. Aksiatak and Aluk each ate a small piece, made a grimace, and tried to get rid of the saline taste with mouthfuls of blubber. Qapqana, like myself on a previous occasion, put an unplucked foot of the ptarmigan in her mouth, feathers, talons, and all; we all laughed at her. The great intestine was eaten by the women and children as a delicacy. Indeed the only parts of the ptarmigan that are removed before boiling are the feathers and the contents of the crop. Some parts, e.g., the heart and the liver, are sometimes eaten raw; I saw Mrs. Aksiatak give them to the children, who relished them immensely. Brick made a gallant effort today and finished the story; I have it all re-copied in a journal similar to this one.[9] He slept last night in Aluk's room, which has more space on the floor now that he and his wife sleep on the platform. Kukpuk and Siliuna do a good deal of sewing, especially Kukpuk; both are very good children and help their parents a great deal. These people all seem to drink a lot of ice-cold water. The children often take in preference a lump of snow that has been brought in to melt, and walk about eating that as if it were candy. When first we came here I handed over to Mrs. Aksiatak my housewife[10] with a new pair of scissors for the two women to use. Brick tells me that she keeps it strictly to herself, so that Qapqana has to use a pair of scissors that are spoilt by cutting tin. The late blizzard raised a ridge of hard packed snow about 4 feet high stretching right across the entrance to the house. One can tell the points of the compass in this way, for the long high ridges are always produced by easterly or northeasterly gales along this coast. The wind tonight is as strong as ever. The only sign of an aurora that I saw was a small white patch almost directly overhead, like a faint white cloud. The nights are dark and moonless just now. It is cheering to know that the insects are not all dormant. The other day I removed a tiny caterpillar from Puganahoq's face as she lay asleep, and since then I have noticed a small black beetle, and a tiny spider. Brick says that the people are rather afraid of these small beetles, because in summer when they are numerous they may enter the ears and cause death. A few years ago when the Barrow natives went east to trade, a girl named Rosie (whom I met at Cape Smythe) went with them. She was very much afraid of these beetles, and it was noticed that some were always crawling over her as she lay asleep, although the others were immune. Qapqana told me that the curved pipe with the lashed stem that she and other women use was formerly smoked by the men also, but the latter have now discarded it in favour of the other type, which has the stem unsplit and unlashed, and the bowl generally of bone or ivory (like Diomed's pipe at Barrow).[11] Aluk and Aksiatak have fixed a number of wooden pegs in the walls on which to hang up things. Aksiatak and his family have fine coats of mountain sheepskin.

Thursday, December 25th.   Christmas Day

Aluk was astir about 5:30 a.m. and lit the fire in his room. Not long afterwards Mrs. Aksiatak emerged from her skin bedclothes and lit her fire. Then Aksiatak and I rose, while the rest slept peacefully on, except the baby boy, Katairoaq, who hovered round his mother, crying, until she was compelled to lie down and soothe him off to sleep again, while her husband fried the slapjacks. Aluk went out about 6:30 a.m., not waiting for breakfast, and did not return until 3 p.m. Like Aksiatak and Kaiyutaq,[12] who followed later, he went to examine his fox-traps. Aksiatak's are all to the south and southeast, Aluk's to the southwest and west, while Kaiyutaq's [Brick's] are now about 5 miles away to the southwest, on the other side of the river. I had an early breakfast with Aksiatak of slapjacks and tea, and later (8:30 a.m.) a plate of rice when the rest had their breakfast. I am very partial to rice, but this was boiled with whale oil, enough to make it (to my taste) rather nauseous, but not uneatable. Mrs. Aksiatak at least prefers cheese as well as sugar with her rice; the rest add it sometimes, and sometimes not. Just after breakfast Siliuna, Aksiatak's daughter, sat beside the blubber pot and the tail of her deer-skin coat was steeped in the whale oil. The other children were late in getting up and had breakfast by themselves. One of their great delights is to drain the tea-kettle through the spout with their mouths. About 9:30 a.m. it was light enough to look for ptarmigan, so I took my skis and sallied forth. A moderately strong and cold northeast wind was blowing, and the only result of 1 1/2 hours promenade on the skis was two frost-bitten patches on my face. On returning just before noon (or probably a little after, as our time, to judge by the light, seems to be behind) I found some visitors had arrived — a man, his wife, and son — the same man and boy whom we met on the other side of the bay when we went to [Cape] Halkett three weeks ago [December 4th]. I found too something less agreeable — the canvas cover to my rifle half eaten by the dogs; apparently it had blown or fallen off the rack. None of the others had returned, but a few minutes later Itaqliq arrived and we all had frozen fish, *mukpaurat*, and tea together. Qapqana had put on her best dress and boots for the occasion, but Mrs. Aksiatak had made no change except in her manner, which was more genial than I have ever seen it. Two pups belonging to the visitors were inside the house; the children were continually treading on them and making them howl. Our visitor — a middle-aged man — tried to open up a conversation with me, but I could understand almost nothing. His wife, also middle aged, was tattooed on the chin — one broad band made up of several lines; the years had not been kind to her appearance. The boy — about 12 apparently — shot his brother last year and killed him instantaneously. They were playing with a gun in the house, not knowing that it was loaded. Nothing was done to him, Kaiyutaq says, and he seems no different to any other Eskimo boy; I could observe no difference in the way he was treated. Aksiatak, coming home about 2 p.m. greeted his visitor with a hearty "Ha," which expressively signified how welcome they were. Aluk, [returning] half an hour later, simply smiled, as is his wont. He brought a fox back with him, Kaiyutaq, who returned at the same time, nothing. While these late arrivals lunched in Aluk's room, preparations for the Xmas dinner were going on apace. A large can of rice was boiling on the stove, and Qapqana and Siliuna were superintending the baking of scones. Itaqluq lit the primus stove and boiled one kettle on it, while the second boiled on one of the [other] stoves. We all gathered in a ring round the food and the kettle, save that the children dined in the other room. The 'plate' was interesting. There were three aluminum plates and an aluminum frying-pan, my own utensils, together with three aluminum spoons. Then there was an old frying pan minus the handle, two lard tin lids, and two rectangular plates cut out of tins, another dessert spoon, two teaspoons, two

ladles, and the bowl of a dessert spoon. The pot of rice was set on one
side after each person was served, then handed over to the children for
them to clean out with their fingers. In the middle was the larger kettle,
beside it the smaller one, and a frying pan with the scones. This was the
Xmas dinner. Aluk had a pain in the middle of the back, and I spent the
evening from 6 to 9 p.m. in applying fomentations — a woollen sock
heated in water as hot as I could bear, held in place by a strip of brown
denham [denim] cloth destined to repair Qapqana's trousers. The sock
was changed for another about every 5 minutes. By 9 o'clock he said it
was a little better and the treatment lapsed. Kaiyutaq skinned his
[Aluk's] fox for him, then played with his whizzer and the children,
while the others chatted in Aksiatak's room. Supper was served about
8:30 p.m., tea and scones (*mukpaurat*); of the latter there were hardly
enough to go round. Outside a brilliant aurora, southeast-northwest, lit
up the sky in honour of Xmas. It seemed scarce to touch the horizon on
either side, but to form one broad band of white light. Overhead this was
divided into several bands side by side, the more brilliant in the middle.
Along the horizon to the southwest there were dim signs of it. The stars
were visible even through the brightest portions, but were perceptibly
dimmed. I forgot to mention that our visitor wore a tonsure[13] — the first
I think I have seen here. The sun did not honour us with his presence, but
allowed a band of red light to shine along the southern horizon.

Friday, December 26th.   Boxing Day[14]

A moderately strong north wind blew all through the night, making
the snow rattle against the intestine skylight. Mrs. Aksiatak and Aluk
were astir early, lighting their respective fires. Then our lady visitor and
her son got up and turned the two pups into the passage; they had slept
close to my head all night. Then I emerged from my sleeping bag, and
set the primus stove going for Mrs. Aksiatak to boil rice, for on her stove
she had a large cauldron of melting snow. Presently the rest rose one by
one, and Aksiatak went out to cut up some firewood. Then Mrs. Aksiatak
asked me to get some snow, so I took an axe and cut out some blocks of
hard drift snow and brought [them] in, leaving some in the outer passage
for a future occasion. Breakfast was served about 9:30 a.m. and was
rather curious. Macaroni had been boiled with the rice and the whole
very badly burnt — it was a curious mixture. Scones and tea followed.
Then Kaiyutaq and Itaqliq took my sled and dogs, with some of their
own dogs as well, and went off to the fishing lake to bring back some
fish for dog meat. One of Aksiatak's dogs died in the night and was
frozen stiff. Aksiatak dragged it about 25 yards away on the snow and
left it — a simple burial. I went down to the beach and brought in a few
logs, and cut them up for the stoves. This is becoming one of my regular
occupations. It is astonishing how much wood two stoves can burn in a
day. The rest of the day we spent indoors. Aksiatak made two more skin-
stretchers, on the same pattern as the one at [Cape] Halkett (see December 4th). He brought three foxes in to thaw, which he caught yesterday,

but had left outside on the rack. Aluk also made one [a skin-stretcher], but his back began to trouble him again and he retired to his platform. The visitors slept, except the boy who played with the children. For lunch there was blubber, half a scone each, and tea, for dinner, rice boiled with prunes, and for supper slapjacks and tea. Mrs. Aksiatak certainly cannot boil rice; she either burns it or does not cook it fully. This morning it was burnt, this evening not cooked; however, it is eaten just the same. On the whole it was one of the dullest days I have had here. Outside it was cold, although as long as daylight lasted not altogether unpleasant. At noon the horizon in the south was radiant with a yellow glow deepening to orange at its lower border. On either side it darkened to a dull full red, tinged with purple or mauve. Seldom if ever have I seen richer colouring. The smoke of the house was distinctly mauve against the yellow sky. In the evening the aurora was visible again; in the early part as a fine bow stretching in what seems to be the usual direction just now, southeast to north or northwest. It changed, however, every minute. Later it showed as a series of faint arcs all over the sky, stretching parallel in the same direction.

Saturday, December 27th

Another quiet day indoors. We rose earlier than usual, as our visitor and his son were going off somewhere for the day — I could not understand where.[15] So we had an early breakfast about 7 o'clock (probably 8 a.m., for I think our time must be an hour behind at least) of scones and tea. Aksiatak, Aluk, and I turned out to cut up firewood. It was very cold and I was not sorry to retire indoors as soon as it was over. There I cleaned my binoculars, the case of which was covered with snow and ice, and the glasses frosted over. Aksiatak skinned his foxes, assisted by Aluk, stretched them on the frames he had made for them, and lay them along the ceiling. Mrs. Aksiatak made me a pair of deerskin mits fringed with red foxskin; the deerskin is not very good, for the hairs come out like they do from my sleeping bag, but they will be very much warmer than the sheepskin mits, where my hands are alternately cold and warm. They were remarking on the bad winter footgear Stefansson had made expressly for me at Barrow; it is phenomenal in size and consequently very clumsy, and ill-fitting as well. They were laughing yesterday morning about Stefansson, Kaiyutaq said. He had been telling them one of their magic songs for hunting caribou, and it was only a popular song of the day — a common phenomenon among ethnologists I imagine. The visitor and his son returned early in the afternoon. The rest of the day we lay about on the skins; some slept, some played, Aluk taught me two new cat's-cradle figures. Qapqana has a very large hump on her back; I think she is rather sensitive about it for she does not take off her coat nearly as often as Mrs. Aksiatak, and when she does she sits with her back to the wall all the time. Kukpuk too never uncovers, though the other two girls wear trousers only nearly all the time; both she and Siliuna are very good children, much better than Puganahoq, who is something of a madcap, always getting into trouble. The little boy of Aluk's seems more like a spoilt child than the rest. The two pups last night created a disturbance; their mistress turned them out for a time, then let them in again. Both today and yesterday one of them caused some excitement by repeatedly walking near and, on two occasions, right on the skylight, despite the rather frantic shouts of their mistress who was holding up the intestine window with her hands while her son rushed out to bring the dog in. The daylight certainly seems to last longer than it did a few days ago. Again there were the brilliant hues of a sunrise in the south, giving a blue tinge to the snow that covers sea and land alike. It is amusing to watch the children blow with their mouths; the tongue slightly projects and is curled into a half cylinder. Our lady visitor cooked bread today and we had it dry for supper. I think it was made with 'Magic Yeast'.[16] Aksiatak made two pump-drills for the children to

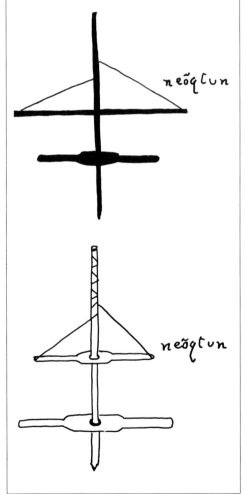

Figure 53. Aksiatak's pump-drills.

play with. Both were very well made, and would be very efficient tools if fitted with steel points; being playthings he merely pointed the wood. One drill had the pump stick lying against the perpendicular stick; in the other the pump stick had a hole in the middle through which the other stick passed.

Sunday, December 28th

A dull day indoors. Outside the air was clear and a moderate northeast breeze blowing. We were up early and had a breakfast of tea and slap-jacks. For the rest of the day we sat or lay indoors, talking and sleeping. The children as usual had their hair dressed. Soon after midday the others had a lunch of blubber straight, following it up a few minutes later with rice and tea in which I joined. About 5 p.m. Kaiyutaq and Itaqliq returned with a sled-load of fish. About a couple of dozen were rushed inside, and we were soon dining on these and a pot of rice. The wind increased slightly during the day and it was very cold out of doors. There was the usual aurora last night. Tonight it appeared in the same form — a broad arc — early in the evening, but later when we went out it had developed into a series of magnificent fans spread over all the sky except

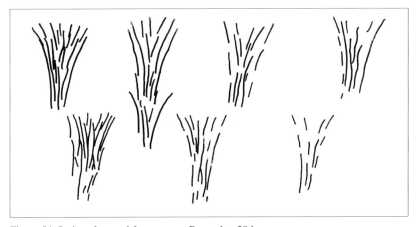

Figure 54. Series of auroral fans seen on December 28th.

the western quarter. Our visitors, I find, are come to stay. They cached their *umiak* on a platform about 100 yards from the house. The woman is left-handed, the first I have noticed among the Eskimos.[17] Itaqlik and his mother [Mrs. Aksiatak] want Brick and me to go over to the other side and live with them for a time — Brick also wants to go and trap there; so I have decided in favour of staying a fortnight or so with them. If foxes are plentiful there they will stay; if not Itaqliq and Asecaq are going east to trap.

Monday, December 29th

We were up fairly early again and had breakfast about the time it grew light. Brick went to take up his traps to set on the other side of the

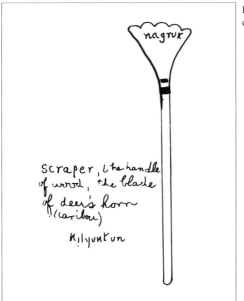

nagruk

Scraper, & the handle of wood, the blade of deer's horn (caribou)

Kılyukun

Figure 55. Scraper of wood and caribou horn.

bay when we go. Aluk and I gathered some logs and cut up firewood. Aksiatak, Itaqluq, and the other man busied themselves with odd things for a time, but remained indoors most of the day. Mrs. Aksiatak (Otoyuk) and Qapqana were dressing skins as usual. We go tomorrow across the bay, so got some of the things ready, more especially the harness. The dogs had eaten two of our harnesses, for the blizzard a few days ago heaped the snow round the posts so high that the dogs could climb on top of the rack. However, Brick sewed one up, and Mrs. Aksiatak made a new one, so we are now fixed up in that respect. Only my sled will be taken, for it is larger and stronger than theirs; also our small round tent, which will be used as a round tent, i.e., instead of the centre pole it will have the arching sticks like the proper Eskimo tent. We are not rich in varieties of food — our flour is almost finished, but we have more at [Cape] Halkett — there is a fair quantity of rice, sugar, tea, and frozen fish. Besides this there are the tins of dessicated vegetables Stefansson left, haricot beans (which were hard and stringy), spinach, cabbage, and onions, all of which are practically worthless without meat to eat them with. However, Asecaq should be back in a few days with four bags of flour, and 100 lbs sugar, a keg of molasses, two tins of lard, and three small boxes of hard-bread. I hope the sled from the ship comes soon, but hardly expect it before the 10th of January. Brick continued the conjugation of the verb 'he goes' *aulaksiroq*; it has some remarkable inflections, e.g., he said I went, I said he went, etc., which differ from each

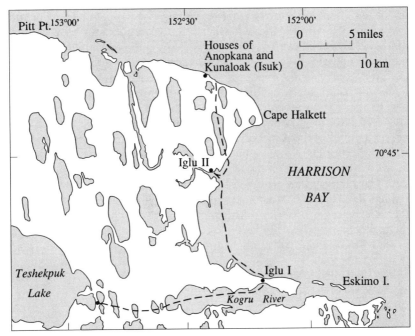

Figure 56. Map showing approximate locations of Aksiatak's house (Iglu I), the house the author helped to build Dec. 31 (Iglu II), the camp at the fishing lake, and the houses of Añopkana and Kunaloak near Cape Halkett. Approximate routes taken by the author between these settlements between November 7, 1913, and February 5, 1914, are also shown.

other (in answer to a question) from 'He told them I went'. These inflections too are extremely common. I have heard them continually, and could never understand them. There were no signs of an aurora in the early part of the evening, nor again later when we went out. A light wind blew from the northeast all day.

Tuesday, December 30th

We rose early, Mrs. Aksiatak turning out at 4:30 a.m. The visitors too rose at the same time, for they intended to return to their home at Cape Halkett. Brick misunderstood my question the other day when I asked if they were going to reside with us. Really they came over to bring their *umiak*, which had been left further along the coast, to the rack near our house. They left about 7:30 a.m., carrying a lighted lantern — we a little before 9 a.m. It was about 1 p.m. when we reached a place on the opposite shore where there was driftwood. Siliuna and her mother, the latter carrying the baby on her back, rode on the sled part of the time, and walked the other part. I felt very sorry for both of them. Siliuna became so tired that at the last she went to sleep sitting on top of my wood stove. The endurance of these Eskimo women is wonderful. After we arrived at the camping ground she [Mrs. Aksiatak] did most of the work of setting up the tent. Itaqluq seemed to find something else to do, though he cut up two long sticks for it, and neither Brick nor I knew exactly how to set it up. My tent was drawn over the sticks, snow piled round the sides, and their old tent laid on top. I put the stove in, cut up some wood, and set the fire going, while Brick lit the primus to boil tea and Otoyuk [Mrs. Aksiatak] laid sticks down for a floor and the skins on top. Brick and Itaqluq cut up more wood and brought [it] in with snow for water. Otoyuk fed the dogs with blubber; I froze the tips of two fingers trying to get it [the blubber] out of her bag. Meantime I had made tea and boiled rice on the primus — we were all desperately hungry. The weather was very cold out of doors, a moderately strong northeast wind blowing all day. The blizzard had made the snow hard, so the dogs found their task lightened. There were numerous small cracks in the ice, especially near this side. These people [the Aksiatak's] must be glad we are staying with them. We have provided nearly half the food; they have used our sled several times, and now on this trip they have our tent, sled, dogs (plus two of their own), cooking utensils (plus some of their own), stove, shovel, and sundry small things — not a bad contribution. We sat about in the tent for a while after dinner, then went to bed early. I saw no aurora when we turned in, but there was a new moon.

Wednesday, December 31st

The night was very cold. Consequently I slept little, though I lay with all my clothes on, except the snowshirt and outer boots, inside the sleeping bag. I had two pairs of woollen socks and a pair of sheepskin socks on my feet, yet they were cold all night. The tent too was very small, and my head was on the stove continually. The mouth of the sleeping bag was encrusted with ice where my breath had frozen. The others fared less badly because they had better places — I lay near the stove so that I might light the fire in the morning without disturbing the rest, especially the lady, who had undergone a pretty hard day. Nevertheless she was up as soon as I, for with a tiny residue of flour she wished to bake *mukpaurat*. The fire lit without any difficulty, but there was little wood. I lit the primus as well, but it was choked and there was no pricker, nor time at the moment to try a wooden one. So I turned out and chopped up some wood, then returned and presently woke Brick to chop more. The stove heats little on top, and it takes a long while to boil a pot. Although I was up about 7 a.m., it was after 9 when the kettle boiled. We had half a frozen fish each, three small *mukpaurat* each, and tea; our flour is finished now. Then we set to work to build a house. For tools we had a small axe, an adze, and a shovel. With these we split up driftwood logs, and constructed a house about 11 by 8 feet at the bottom, with the sides sloping inwards a little so that the turf might not fall down. Its height is about 5 feet, and the roof is practically flat. A small opening was left for the door; the bottom about a foot from the ground was formed of a piece of wood laid on the snow. Part of their old tent covers the opening, forming the door. It took us all day until 5 p.m. to erect, lay the turf, and pile snow on top, so that it was after 7 p.m. when we had dinner. We were all famished and tired out. However, we had our dinner in the new house, for we moved into it without delay. Otoyuk [Mrs. Aksiatak] assisted in all but the cutting up of the wood; I think she knows more about camping, sledging, and building houses than her son. Dinner consisted of frozen fish, rice, and tea. The house dripped a good deal, the heat of the fire melting the snow and ice in the wood and turf. This usually happens with a new house for the first day, but ours is badly constructed as well — there is too little support for the turf, suitable wood being scarce. It was 11 p.m. when we turned in for the night. I noticed that the young moon had the same band of light running like an extended chord through it, as I mentioned two or three months ago. The sky was rather cloudy, and the same strong northeast wind blew as yesterday; I saw no aurora.

Chapter 7. Facing Starvation

Brick and Itaqluq leave for Cape Halkett — New Year's Day reflections — Eskimo lamp — Story telling — Finding Aksiatak sick — Sunday activities — Eskimo game — Visitors — Reappearance of the sun — To Cape Halkett again — Warm hospitality at Añopkana's — Story of abuse of Kukpuk — Return to Aksiatak's — Eskimo joke on Stefansson — Eskimo wood carving — Asecaq returns from Barrow with letters — Eskimo card game — Eskimo songs — Eskimo eating manners — Only four dogs left — Decision to leave for Barrow

Thursday, January 1st, 1914

I lit the fire just after 7 a.m. Otoyuk [Mrs. Aksiatak] got up soon after and we cooked rice and a squirrel. (The squirrel was caught some months ago and kept frozen. It does not taste at all bad — better than fox.) The rest rose about 9 a.m. or a little after. I notice that Itaqluq is always the last up; also that he prefers to let others do things, generally speaking, than to do them himself. When we left he did very little towards loading the sled or putting the dogs in [their harnesses]. He would have left the tent sticks behind had he not been reminded, and it was not until the sled was loaded that he discovered we would want my stove. Then when we got half way across he stopped the sled for 5 minutes to think where he would camp. Yet he acquitted himself fairly well yesterday in the building of the house. After breakfast Brick and he loaded the sleds and went to Añopkana's place [near Cape Halkett] to bring flour and blubber and one or two other things, for all we have to eat now is frozen fish and a little rice, with one or two biscuits (hardbread), while the dogs have nothing. I cut up wood all day, save that I helped Otoyuk returf two places in the roof where it dripped. The weather was practically the same as yesterday. Siliuna came out to help carry the wood into the house. She found great delight in turning somersaults over a low ridge of snow and lying down behind it till I came near and pretended to throw snow at her. Thoroughly tired I re-entered the house at 3 p.m. and stoked the fire and boiled rice. Soon we had dinner — half a frozen fish each, a biscuit each, and rice and tea. Otoyuk was very tired also; she has worked wonderfully hard the last three days. The boy today was a little troublesome; he makes it much harder for her. Siliuna is very useful in carrying wood, bringing in snow, minding the boy, and in many other ways. Brick and Itaqluq may be back tomorrow night or the following.

Meanwhile here am I, the ethnologist on the Canadian Arctic Expedition, living in a tiny one-roomed house of driftwood, turf, and snow (that I myself helped to construct), with an elderly lady of perhaps 35 to 40 years and her two children, a girl of about 8 and a boy of 2 years. For food we have a little rice, which we boil, frozen fish, which we eat raw, skinning and slicing them, I with my sheath-knife, the other two with their curious-shaped *ulos*. Tea and sugar supplement this diet, while the two or three biscuits are reserved for the children. We have a stove to burn wood, a primus stove, and a very little coal oil (or kerosene), skins and sleeping clothes, three or four pots, a kettle and frying pan, with a couple of plates, three spoons, and four cups. A string across the ceiling near the stove enables us to hang up our boots and mits etc. to dry. For light we have four candles besides the one which is now burning. Itaqluq and Brick have taken the lantern. For clothes I have an inner and an outer deerskin shirt (the latter I seldom need) with a snow shirt of blue denham [denim] to wear on top, a pair of deerskin mits made for me by Otoyuk (they are bad, for the fur is coming out; the skin from which they were made was very poor), a pair of deerskin trousers with Burberry knee-breeks over them, an inner and an outer pair of deerskin boots. The boots are badly made and very cumbersome, so when the weather is not very cold and I am not likely to be standing about in the snow I wear two pairs of woollen socks, a pair of sheepskin socks, and light deerskin boots over them. Then there is my sleeping bag, also of deerskin; its fur too comes out much more than it should. My home is for the time being on the west side of a large bay which forms the western portion of Harri-son Bay — about 80-100 miles east of Point Barrow. The temperature is apparently the ordinary mid-winter temperature here; what it is in degrees I do not know, having no thermometer, but it must be uniformly considerably below zero [degrees Fahrenheit]. The sun has been invis-ible for 6 weeks, and the twilight lasts about 5 hours. Today the weather was much the same as yesterday. No aurora in early part of evening but brilliant one after moon had set.

Friday, January 2nd

Otoyuk was up first — at 7 a.m. and lit the fire. I turned out a few minutes later, and kept it stoked, and boiled the rice. There was a little flour left that I did not know of, enough to make five small *mukpaurat*, which we had for breakfast. I then set about erecting the tent to form a passage, thus keeping out a lot of the draught that came in through the cloth door. The material was eight willow sticks, a large rectangular piece of drilling [cloth], and my own bell tent. With this, and one or two stout sticks chopped from a driftwood log, I succeeded in making an apology for a passage, which Otoyuk was polite enough to call 'good'. At all events it makes the house warmer. Soft snow stamped down round the edges of the cloth and two or three large snowblocks on the east (the windy side) will keep it tight. Otoyuk took the [her small] boy Katairoaq on her back, and set out with Siliuna to lay some traps on her own ac-count. She came back just as it was getting dark, and by that time I had a good fire going and tea made. Soon we were all having lunch — the remnants of this morning's rice warmed up again, tea, then frozen fish. I turned out again to shovel soft drift snow on the roof. We put very little on the other day, because there was no soft snow handy. After this we lay about in the house, played cat's cradles a little, then I cut up some firewood. For supper I had three boiled fish-heads (scales and all), then half a frozen fish, and two fragments of hard-bread. We have been living on half rations for some days, though the others supply the deficiency with blubber. Hard-bread never tasted so good as this did. We turned in to bed soon after 8 o'clock. I saw no aurora outside. The same wind blew as yesterday and the day before.

Saturday, January 3rd

I slept very little through the night, being both hungry and cold. We had breakfast about 9 a.m., a little rice (our last) and half a frozen fish. All that we have left now is half a dozen fish, some sugar, and tea, but Brick and Itaqluq should be back this afternoon.

(later) I was chopping wood most of the day save when I helped Otoyuk make a snow wall half way round the house. She also put fresh turf on the roof around the skylight and stove-pipe. We were inside, eating half a frozen fish each, when Brick and Itaqliq came, about 2 p.m. They brought four bags of flour and about two cupfuls of rice, the latter a present to us from Kunaloak's wife. Some of the rice was boiled at once and Otoyuk made *mukpaurat*, so that about 4 o'clock I was having the best meal I have had for several days. I was ravenously hungry and could have eaten twice as much, but it was a good meal all the same. I suppose it is the lack of sufficient food, combined with sleeplessness and rather hard work the last 3 days, which has made me feel weak. I had neuralgia in one eye part of last night and my back has ached both today and yesterday. The children have not suffered, that is one comfort, but Otoyuk said yesterday we were starving, and I am afraid she too has not been getting enough to eat. However, the pinch is over, I think. I half expect the sled from the *Alaska*[1] to come about the 10th of this month. The little boy Katairoaq has very cleverly contrived mittens. They are permanently attached to the sleeves of his fur coat. At the wrist the coat has also an open wrist-mit or sleevelet, so that the boy can put his hand through like the ordinary terminus of a sleeve, allowing the mit to depend [hang down] from the wrist. We sat about the rest of the evening, Brick and I writing, and turned in before 8 o'clock; there was no aurora then. The weather was as yesterday.

Sunday, January 4th

Otoyuk baked *mukpaurat* for breakfast, and we ate besides some frozen whale skin (*muktuq*) with the blubber attached to it. The skin is black, and something like rubber, except that you can bite through it like rather hard butter; it is not brittle though like the latter. The taste reminded me of liquorice. I did not like it very much, but was hungry. After breakfast Brick and Itaqluq went off, Brick to set some traps and Itaqluq to examine his. Otoyuk followed them some time afterwards, with the boy [Katairoaq] on her back; I stayed to chop up firewood. This occupation keeps one man busy 3 or 4 hours each day, for the axe is small and the logs big, and this stove burns a lot of wood. Brick is lending six of his traps to a man at [Cape] Halkett, obtaining [in exchange] one half of the foxes caught in them. I have lent Itaqluq a box of car-tridges. The days are distinctly longer than they were; it almost seemed as if the sun were trying to rise above the horizon today. The northeast wind, which has been blowing for several days, had almost died away, although the temperature seemed if anything a little colder. Brick re-turned about 2 p.m. after setting eight traps. Otoyuk had been back a good while before and had the kettle boiling by that time, so we had a lunch of *mukpaurat* and *muktuq* and tea. Otoyuk then proceeded to bake more *mukpaurat*. It was not until 4 p.m. that Itaqluq returned with two foxes. Both were dead and frozen stiff when he found them in his traps, so he hung them up in the house to thaw. We had dinner soon afterwards — the same as for lunch and breakfast — it is indeed all we have, save a couple of fish. Otoyuk told us a short story, which Brick afterwards wrote down at her dictation.[2] We sat about until 8 p.m., then had supper. Itaqluq sold his lantern at [Cape] Halkett, and the candles I brought gave out, so we have an Eskimo lamp, or rather one of the same type. The bot-tom of an inverted rectangular tobacco tin was pressed down a little to hold more oil; then Otoyuk took some lamp grass out of her bag, and whale oil from another bag. The lamp grass she arranged on one side of the tin in a row about 1 1/2 inches long and 1/3 inch high, then put some oil on the tin so that the edge just reached the wick. Later she added a lump of blubber to the oil. The whale blubber Brick and Itaqluq brought from [Cape] Halkett the other day has too much water in it to be used for a lamp. Under the jet-black skin is a layer of blubber, then a faintly pinkish layer of something which is perhaps sinew. This, Brick says, they used to boil, then when it got cool chew up and roll in the hands till it got a little firm, after which it was left for a time and became a solid ball, which would bounce to a great height. They did not use it in playing football [i.e. soccer], for it would break, but threw it on the ground to find out who could make it bounce highest. After skinning a fox, the cer-vical vertebra used to be cut through at the joint nearest the head. Some still do this, Brick says. The idea is that the spirit of the fox will go out and become another fox, thus multiplying their number. We turned in about 10 o'clock. The moon was about at the half, and there was no aurora, neither then nor at 5 a.m. after the moon had set.

Monday, January 5th

A beautifully fine day, a very light air coming from the northeast. in the south was the usual glow. As it began to fade a distinctly green hue spread over the southwest horizon. We were all up late and it was not until 10:30 a.m. that we finished breakfast — half a frozen fish each, *mukpaurat*, and tea. The others then went to their traps, leaving me to cut firewood, and Siliuna to look after the boy [Katairoaq]. Otoyuk as usual was back first. The other two, returning about 4 p.m., each brought a fox, Itaqluq's partly eaten by one of the dogs. This is the first Brick has caught, and he is naturally feeling very pleased. I baked *mukpaurat* for about 4 hours, for lunch and dinner, while Otoyuk remade my deerskin underboots. Brick began the conjugation of a transitive verb for me, and wrote a story he heard at [Cape] Halkett — a rather strange one to European ears but typical of many which circulate among these people. Both Brick and Itaqluq skinned their foxes. For lunch and dinner we had *muktuq* and *mukpaurat*. Our Eskimo lamp met with a disaster. Otoyuk shook the cord on which my deerskin socks, with other clothing, was suspended, and a sock fell into the lamp. There was a fine mess — blubber everywhere. The scene last night when Otoyuk was telling her story was worthy of a painting. We had just dined. The others were reclining in the skins and sleeping bags, and the boy was playing with Siliuna behind them. I sat on the primus stove box (an old ammunition box cut down) and stoked the fire, trying to get warm. Two foxes, frozen stiff, were hanging by the stove to thaw. Otoyuk began to speak, then stopped. "Jennie," she said (this is the nearest these people can get to my name), "listen." Slowly and impressively she uttered each word, interrupted now and then by an eager question from Brick. From time to time a smile lit up her careworn face, and at the end she gave a half apologetic laugh. "My father told me that story," she said, "when I was a little girl," then murmured over again the chant that formed a part of the story. We sat about for some time after dinner this evening, writing and talking. On the stove the two foxes were cooking. I told one of the old Greek stories, about Atalanta and her suitors,[3] which Brick translated. At 9:30 p.m. I noticed an aurora stretching something like a rainbow in the northeast. Soon after this we turned in for the night.

Tuesday, January 6th

The northeast wind had freshened in the night and was blowing quite strong all day. We breakfasted early on *mukpaurat* and fox, then Brick and Itaqluq went off to look for fox dens. I began as usual to cut firewood, but Otoyuk came out and together we put the dogs in the sled and set out for some wood that she had seen not very far away. We brought this in, then pulled down the old passage I erected and built a new and larger one without a door. Save that it was larger and used two or three more pieces of wood, it was made exactly as I had made the other one, viz. an X in front, with a pole running from it to the top of the doorway, then the willow sticks running up to it. The tin lining of the stove-pipe hole on my tent we took off and put on the roof of the house over the stove-pipe, then [added] turf and snow above. This occupied us nearly all the daylight hours, after which I cut up more wood. Brick and Itaqluq returned about 4 p.m. empty-handed and we had tea and *mukpaurat*. I officiated as cook again today, baked the *mukpaurat* and boiled the remnant of the rice which we had for dinner about 6 p.m. Brick and I wrote for a time, but the light of our single Eskimo lamp was very poor — we have almost no blubber — so we had to give up. The rice we had was very little, only a spoonful or two each, and Otoyuk did not dole out very much flour for *mukpaurat*, so that each meal left me still hungry. This has become so chronic now that I am beginning to wonder what it is like not to be hungry. I tried blubber and *muktuq* the day before yesterday to get rid of the hunger, and the blubber and *muktuq* threatened to get rid of me — it made me feel sick a short time afterwards and produced diarrhoea. It was most exasperating, therefore, to see the boy Katairoaq playing with the *mukpaurat* as fast as I baked them, taking a bite out of this one and crumbling up that, without let or hindrance on the part of his mother. Tomorrow Brick and I are going across to Aluk's and Aksiatak's to take them flour and to bring back blubber for the lamp. We turned in about 10 p.m., at which time a strong east-northeast wind was blowing and the atmosphere was very cold. An auroral band stretched across the sky in the north; the moon was about half full.

Wednesday, January 7th

We breakfasted about 9 a.m. on *mukpaurat* and tea and got away at 9:40 with five dogs. At 11:45 a.m. we stopped for about 5 minutes to rest the dogs, and reached Aluk's at 12:45 p.m. We were travelling at about 4 miles an hour, a little east of south, so the distance across the bay here must be about 12 miles. The east-northeast wind (I have called it northeast earlier in the diary but it is more east than north) was blowing as strongly as ever, but we had it fortunately at the side; the snow was fine and hard. We found Aksiatak ill. On Saturday evening he suddenly began to cough and to spit up pus; he complained also of a pain about the lower sternum and right lung. Possibly it is a small tumor inside that has burst. They asked me about it — whether it would kill him and if fish was good for him. They have been living on fish and blubber only, having no flour and not knowing that rice was on the rack outside. We lunched soon after our arrival on fish and tea, and Brick was appointed to cook *mukpaurat*. About 5 p.m. we had a hearty meal of rice and *mukpaurat*; fish both baked and frozen was offered me afterwards, but for the first time for many days my hunger was really satisfied. Just at this time the dogs began to fight in the outer passage, [and] we found that one of Asecaq's dogs had turned up, whence we concluded that Asecaq himself was not far off. He did not make his appearance, however, in the course of the evening; perhaps he is at [Cape] Halkett. His dog started several more fights and was plainly mad, so that it had to be shot. Aksiatak developed red spots, lumps in some places over his arms and body; to relieve the irritation he leaned his bare body over the stove or sat with his back to it. For supper we had frozen fish and *mukpaurat* and turned in about 11 p.m. I had a sharp attack of diarrhoea after lunch, which lasted all the rest of the day. Qapqana [Mrs. Aluk] enlarged my smaller deerskin outer boots so that I could wear the deerskin socks inside. One of the boots, she said, was badly made; it had a twist in it, caused by the insertion of a patch. Kukpuk stitched up one or two places in my sleeping bag where the seams had burst. Aluk was making a pair of snowshoes. Having almost no coal oil they were using blubber for light, and had two ingenious lamps, made from the bottom half of a baking-powder tin with a copper tray beneath. A slot was cut at one side of the bottom of the tin for the wick — the sides of the slot being raised; on the other side was a hole through which oil could be poured if necessary, and which also admitted air. The tin was almost full of melted blubber, and the copper tray also contained a considerable quantity. The light was almost but not quite equal to that of a candle (the wick, I forgot to mention, was a cotton cloth); it was less, that is to say, than that of the ordinary blubber lamp, with its grass wick. They had tried blubber in the hurricane lantern, but it gave very little light.

Thursday, January 8th

Aksiatak relit the fire at 4 a.m. to warm his back and allay the irritation. He spent the night in a half-sitting position. We breakfasted about 9 a.m. — frozen fish, then a glorious quantity of rice and *mukpaurat*. Qapqana certainly is not stingy with her food. Otoyuk is an inland woman and has probably hardly ever known what it is to have an abundance; hence the doling out of a limited ration comes natural to her. We left at 10:10 a.m., with a side wind from the east-northeast less strong than yesterday. We missed the trail at first, but struck it after about half an hour and reached Iglu II[4] about 1 p.m. Itaqluq was away, but returned a little later, and he and Brick cut up wood; I, inside, changed my clothes, which were wet with perspiration, and baked *mukpaurat* till Brick came in and took on the job. Soon we were lunching on a frozen fish each and *mukpaurat*. Itaqluq found a fox in his trap yesterday; this he skinned in the evening while Brick and I were writing — Brick a story he heard last night from Qapqana.[5] Siliuna came in about 4:30 p.m. and said that some of my dogs were going off to the traps; one of them had previously been caught in a trap. Brick and Itaqluq brought them back, and while Siliuna watched over them made two halters of the usual Eskimo type for them, i.e., a stick with cord fastenings at each end; these with a heavy iron chain we [had] brought [along with us] sufficed for the offenders. For the rest of the evening we sat in the house talking; the light of the Eskimo lamp was too poor to write or read by for any time. About 8 p.m. we had supper. We had lunched about 2:30, so were hungry, but there was only one small *mukpaurat* between the three of us, and that was in fragments. The children were not hungry — they help themselves to anything whenever they like. Nothing remained but to turn in. Brick was already in his sleeping bag when Itaqluq brought out a lump of blubber about half the size of a cheese; between them they had a glorious feast, consuming the whole. Blubber disagreed with me the other day, and as I don't like the taste of it anyhow I preferred to remain hungry. They are all returning to Iglu I[6] the day after tomorrow, now that Aksiatak is ill, and I [will go] with them. Certainly I am not going to continue fasting as I have all the time we have been here. At 8:30 p.m. a brilliant moon — past the half — was shining outside. The wind had changed early in the afternoon, and a light breeze was now blowing from the west. There was no trace of any aurora.

Friday, January 9th

Breakfast — frozen fish, biscuits (*mukpaurat*), and tea — was over about 9 o'clock. Brick and Itaqluq went off to their traps, and Otoyuk to hers, while I stayed to pack up and load the sled, for Otoyuk wished to cross over [the bay] to Iglu I as soon as she returned. I saw her returning and had the tea ready so that we had a little *mukpaurat* and tea before we started — rather against her wish I fancy, but I was hungry. Brick and Itaqluq were going to follow either in the night — it is nearly full moon and the moon does not set — or tomorrow. We left the stove, flour, sugar, tea, a fish, and blubber for them and I left the sheepskin in case they should stay the night. We [Otoyuk, Siliuna, Katairoaq, and I] left about noon and took exactly 3 hours to cross [to Iglu I]. Otoyuk and Siliuna rode [on the sled] most of the way, while I ran ahead of the dogs. One of their dogs is lame — the leg is broken — I think in a fight with ours. I did not see it [the dog] for some days after the fight occurred, otherwise I might have set its leg. One of our dogs is lame also — it was caught in a trap — but the leg is not broken. The west wind of yesterday did not last long — it was blowing from the east again today, though very mildly. I noticed that Otoyuk did not go in at once to see her sick husband, but assisted in unloading the sled and enquired about his illness from the others. I was tying up the dogs when she went in, so did not see the meeting, but a few minutes later when I entered she was sitting beside him, displaying all the anxiety we expect from a wife. We had a good meal of fish and biscuits (*mukpaurat*) as soon as we arrived. I had four biscuits given me — each the size and shape of a sausage — about double the size Otoyuk usually makes her biscuits; I have never had more than five of hers at a meal. Aluk took my rifle (a Winchester) to pieces for me, then helped me to put it together again. It is the usual weapon among the Eskimos here and they are continually taking the breach to pieces. Aluk has made a tool [see December 3rd] for this very purpose. Qapqana was making a pair of boots for Puganahoq. The soles are measured by a span plus the fingers, the latter naturally varying with the person. It is said that a woman will make a pair of boots for her husband while he is away, which will be found to fit like a glove when he returns. The *ulo* is an excellent tool for cutting skins — far better than scissors because it can cut slanting, and thereby enable two pieces to join together better. Of course the *ulo* is used for other purposes — it is the woman's sheath-knife in fact. Aluk made for his boy an excellent wooden model of a gun, about 2 feet long. The house has been 'done up' while we were away — the roof improved, and pegs inserted in suitable places. On the ceiling are two or three ingenious wooden pegs about 5 inches long, thus:

Figure 57. Eskimo peg.

(The peg being slightly bent, while one end lies flat on the ceiling and is fastened by two nails, the other is about 1/2 inch away. On this end is a knob to prevent whatever is hung upon the peg from slipping off.) The inner passage has been practically rebuilt — it is now high enough for me to stand straight up without touching the roof with my head.[7] We are all wondering where Asecaq is, since one of his dogs turned up 2 days ago. The dogs have eaten the lashings on the rings of my ski-poles. Aluk's little boy wears trousers and boots in one [piece] — like the women's apparel. The colours along the horizon from southeast to southwest during the day are so wonderfully pure and beautiful that one hardly regrets the absence of the sun. It may be that they are no more beautiful than elsewhere at sunrise and sunset, but one certainly takes far more note of them because the landscape is limited to the bluish white snow and the black patches of soil or ice upon it. The moon and stars seem as near and friendly as when I used to sleep under them in New Guinea [in 1912], and watch them rise and set during the hours of the night. Tonight I saw no aurora; the wind was still easterly and the air seemed about as cold as usual.

Saturday, January 10th

We were up about the usual time, but breakfast was late for some reason or other. Aluk did not wait for it but had a fish, then went off to visit his traps. It was good, however, when it did come — fox, then rice (I had a second helping) and *mukpaurat*. Aksiatak seems to be improving a little; his appetite all along has been unaffected. His voice is weak, which makes me think the trouble is between the vocal chords and the left lung. I turned out to cut wood, gathering it first on the beach and then with the help of the children dragging it on the sled to the house. Brick and Itaqluq turned up early in the afternoon. Aksiatak made a wooden gun for Katairoaq today, rather larger than the one Aluk made yesterday. Qapqana could not find her *ulo* this afternoon, so she borrowed a small sheath-knife of Aluk's and cut a deerskin boot-sole with it, holding it like an *ulo*, i.e., with the handle pointing away from her, the point towards her; the edge of the palm was on the back of the blade, the thumb on one side of the handle and the fingers on the other. Aluk returned from his traps empty-handed. Both he and Aksiatak are busy making snowshoes; Aksiatak has painted a portion of his red, as he did the shovel. The children — Kukpuk and Siliuna — asked me to make them *igaluqisaq*, i.e., two small pieces of wood to throw up one after the other and catch as they come down and throw again — the same amusement as our schoolboys enjoy, only they often have three and the usual thing here seems to be two. There is a song accompanying it which Qapqana dictated to Brick. The game is to keep the 'balls' in motion till the end of the song; it requires some practice, as the song is moderately long. I took up the role of story-teller again in the evening, with Brick interpreting. I gave them the theme of the Arabian Nights — the *mise en scene*. The wind today was east-northeast and rather fresh. I saw no aurora in the evening.

Sunday, January 11th

All rose late, and it was nearly noon when breakfast was over. I borrowed Itaqluq's ramrod to clean my rifle — it is of red spruce, the tough springy wood from which bows were made. Then I shaved, to keep company with the children, who had their hair dressed. Otoyuk had the lamp especially lit for Siliuna to search her (Otoyuk's) hair. Aksiatak seems to cough less than he did; he is certainly no worse. Itaqluq brought out his accordion and gave us selections, mostly hymns. I resumed the role of story-teller and gave them some of Tom Sawyer. We cooked some tinned beans (dessicated French haricot) that Stefansson left me. They were a little softer than on the last occasion, but are wretched imitations of the true article, hardly edible; probably they are too old. Brick wrote a little of the story Qapqana told him; he is a terribly slow writer. The dogs got on to the rack, through a sled being left up against it, and ate the head of a large white bird, apparently a gull. There was a curious light in the east about 5 p.m., which lasted for some hours. It resembled a much diffused moon on the horizon, about ten times the diameter the real moon would be; the light was pure white, but not dazzling as the sun's is. Perhaps it is a kind of paraselene.[8] Later in the evening, after I had written this, it developed into what was plainly an aurora — a broad mass of white light extending to a considerable altitude. It was brightest at the top, and one could almost imagine it was a strange stormcloud rising up — white instead of black. I promised Brick today a fine bandolier I have at home[9] if we fill with stories a book similar to this one; the text has already reached p. 37 (one side is reserved for the text, the other for the translation and about one third of each page for notes).[10] The weather today was fine and clear. In the morning a light breeze blew from the east, but this died away during the day and there was a dead calm in the evening.

Monday, January 12th

The dogs raced over the house so persistently during the night that I turned out about 3 a.m. and tied up the two worst offenders. Breakfast was a little too long in making its appearance for Aluk, and he went off to his traps without any. Brick and Itaqluq preferred to wait and go off later. I cut up a little wood, then went inside to gather up stray notes etc., so as to be ready to continue work with Brick. The women were sewing as usual, and Kukpuk also for some time. Aksiatak from time to time worked a little on his snowshoes. Qapqana's trouble, Brick now says, is not in the heart but in the back — she has stabbing pains occasionally. Brick and Itaqluq returned about 2:30 p.m., Brick with a fox he found frozen in one of his traps. Aluk did not arrive until 4 o'clock, feeling desperately hungry, I imagine; he brought no fox. Qapqana told Brick a story in the evening, while I loaded some shotgun shells. Aksiatak complained that his chest was a little more painful than it had been, so we all turned in early. The moon was shining then in a sky dotted with cirri, and a very light air came from the east.

Tuesday, January 13th

We were all up late. Aksiatak had three violent attacks of coughing in the night. After a breakfast of rice and *mukpaurat* we loaded the sled and set out for Iglu II, Brick, Itaqluq, and I. There was not a breath of wind and the sky was clouded over, while the old trails had disappeared — at any rate for the first mile — through the cracking up of the old ice a few days ago, the effect I suppose of some swell outside [the bay]. In consequence we had nothing to guide us except the lines of the snow ridges, which are created by the prevailing east winds and so run practically east and west. We struck the other side of the bay too far north and thus missed Asecaq, who slept in the house last night and has crossed over today to Iglu I. He left us a little oatmeal and butter. We boiled all the oatmeal at once and made biscuits, from which we had a splendid meal.

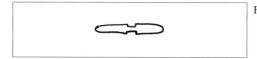

Figure 58. Peg for dog-harness.

This was about 4 p.m. Brick and Itaqluq made a few pegs for passing through loops, to take the place of swivels on [our] dog-harness, while I wrote and kept the fire stoked. Aluk has shown Brick how to whittle wood with the thumb nail against the edge of the blade, on the wood, and the blade of the knife aslant. Our oatmeal with half a dozen biscuits provided us with a good supper about 8 o'clock, as much as we could eat. Itaqluq's mother [Mrs. Aksiatak] would have been horrified. Brick began to write the story Qapqana told him last night, and I too wrote. The house is much warmer since Itaqluq put some soft snow over and round it; if it only had a board floor it would be fairly comfortable, although it gets

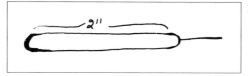

Figure 59. Itaqluq's *nepaicuq.*

cold enough during the night. I forgot to mention that Itaqluq with one of my needles made a *nepaicuq* for the game *nipaicuq*. The needle is inserted in a piece of wood about 2 inches long. Holding the stick flat in the palm of the hand you throw it into the air so that when it falls the needle sticks into a board or block of wood below; rest the stick on the back of the hand between the first and second fingers and repeat it; then with the point of the needle on the left thumb and the stick held vertically by resting the right forefingers on the end of it, jerk the right hand down so that the needle again sticks in the board. Repeat this with the point of the needle on each of the fingers in turn, then on the left side of the left wrist, then on the left elbow. One boy starts; when he misses another boy takes his place and thus the game continues. Asecaq and Añutisiak and Pauyuraq — all Point Hope boys — called *nipaicuq* the game of hole and pin [see November 17th]. A hole was made in a piece of wood and another stick pointed just enough to go into the hole. The pointed stick was held in the palm of the hand, the other, with the hole in [it] just below; then the upper stick was thrown up so that when it fell the point stuck in the hole. Brick told me tonight that the Eskimos at Barrow carry a poke made from the inflated bladder of the bearded seal when they go out seal hunting. A rope is tied to the poke, with a weight on the end, just enough to keep the poke above water, anchored like a buoy. When a seal is shot and sinks, the poke is anchored above the spot where it sank, and afterwards they drag with big hooks for the body. This of course is only practicable in comparatively shallow water. Itaqluq baked some more biscuits in the evening while we were writing and talking, to save baking in the morning, he said, but we ate them up before we went to bed. At that time the atmosphere was cloudy — neither moon nor stars were visible, and the air was calm.

Wednesday, January 14th

Brick got up at 5:15 a.m., boiled rice and baked *mukpaurat*, so we had breakfast soon after 7. It was still dark, so he and Itaqluq waited an hour or so, then set out to their traps. I fed the dogs, but Itaqluq's (or Aksiatak's) two dogs disappeared shortly afterwards, probably [having] returned home to Iglu I. I chopped up a stump and cooked some dessicated spinach Stefansson left me, then worked on the Eskimo language inside the house by the light of the lantern. Brick and Itaqluq came back at 4 p.m.; they had found no foxes in their traps. Some distance south of here they met Samuel (Aiva's husband and Añopkana's son). He told them that Kunaloak with some of his people and two sleds, and Asecaq and his sled came across to this place (Iglu II) the day before yesterday, and slept the night, then went on the next day. Kunaloak was going to the fishing lake. Asecaq, he [Samuel] said, had lost two dogs — one besides the dog which returned home [to Iglu I] and was shot just a week ago today. We found the spinach uneatable and threw it out, then made rice and more biscuits. Owing to the loss of [our] two dogs we decided to return to Iglu I tonight, for the sky was clear and the stars all visible, while the moon, which set about 1 p.m., rose again about 7:30 p.m. Consequently about 8:30 p.m. we packed up, loaded the sleds, and started out; before 11:30 we had reached our destination. A black and white dog Stefansson left me as being no good is proving an excellent leader. Qapqana lit the fire and made tea for us. We found Aksiatak a little better. Asecaq had not arrived — apparently he went to the fishing lake with Kunaloak. There was an auroral arch in the north during the early part of the evening, and a light breeze blew from the west.

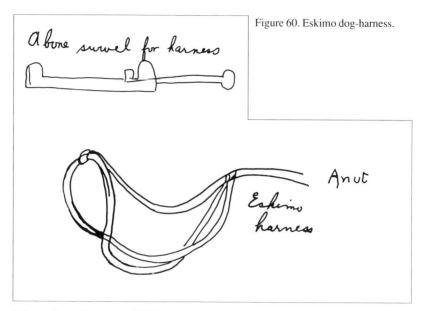

Figure 60. Eskimo dog-harness.

Thursday, January 15th

The sun almost rose today at noon. The sky in the south was so radi-
antly beautiful that one can almost believe it true that the happy land is in
the realm of sunrise or of sunset. We spent the day indoors, although the
weather was fine and clear, with only a gentle east wind blowing. Alak[11]
skinned a fox he caught yesterday, and Itaqluq rubbed flour over one of
his skins to whiten [it]. The Eskimos around here wonder why I do not
trap also.[12] It is certainly a rather cruel sport for the foxes. One that is
now hanging up was caught by the leg as usual; it had struggled in the
trap so hard that the skin has been torn away all down the leg. The other
leg is drawn up close to the body, and the lips are drawn apart showing
the fangs. It was found frozen in this state, revealing all the signs of
death-agony. About 3 p.m. Kunaloak's son, with his mother and little
boy (about 10) arrived from the fishing lake. Itaqluq had sighted them
some time before, so that we were all prepared. Yet it was curious to notice how they were received. They drove right up to the door, and only
the children took any notice. Itaqluq was cleaning a fox in the snow
some yards away, apparently insensible to their presence. They were un-
harnessing the dogs and unloading the sled when Alak and the two
women came out of the house and shook hands. Then Brick came, shook
hands, and was very energetic for 3 or 4 minutes, cutting up two or three
small pieces of wood I had brought in some time before. No one helped
with the sled or dogs, and presently all went inside, leaving Kunaloak's
son to fix up his sled alone; he was the last to enter the house. [Once] inside, the visitors made themselves at home, took off their boots and mits
and coats, and hung them up. Mrs. Kunaloak took off her shirt and
opened up a bag containing hard-bread, a tin partly filled with butter and

a little macaroni. She gave each of the children a piece of hard-bread, and Qapqana also, then to me one covered with butter. Next she set to work to boil the macaroni. She is a great chatterer, very warm hearted — she is constantly making people presents. Her husband had mits of fox-skin — the white fur outside — while the little boy had strips of wolverine fur on his coat. Katairoaq [Aksiatak's baby son] has a belt of wolverine fur, the claws hanging down. We get bigger meals here when there are visitors — they are like white people in making a show. Mrs. Kunaloak, in bustling to and fro, kicked over a can that was on the floor; "*ara*" she cried. Kukpuk tumbled some feathers out of a bag and wiped up the mess. Kunaloak's son gave Mrs. Aksiatak a tin of [condensed] milk for Katairoaq, and Mrs. Kunaloak wanted to suckle him. Before 5 p.m. we were having a good meal — first a little macaroni with which a tin of canned meat had been mixed, then rice with dried apples in it, hard-bread and butter, and tea. In the evening there was an aurora, which for a short time resembled that of December 28th, but later changed to the more usual bow. Asecaq, we learned, is not at the fishing lake — Brick and Itaqluq had been misinformed. When the Halkett sled[13] left Barrow, Asecaq stayed behind — and no one knows when he is coming. The air today was calm — there was hardly a breath of wind.

Friday, January 16th

The sun came back and was visible — or a portion of him, at least, for about an hour. We were late having breakfast. Several ptarmigan settled near the house, and the dogs chased them. Kunaloak's son took his gun and tried to get one, but it flew away. Brick and I loaded up the sled and started for [Cape] Halkett at 11:30 a.m. Mrs. Kunaloak and her people were then preparing to go back to the fishing lake and Itaqluq was going with them, taking a small sled and his two dogs, to bring back some fish. Consequently we had only four dogs to go to [Cape] Halkett, for one of mine is still lame through being caught in a fox-trap. The black and white dog — I call him 'Leader' — proved excellent; it followed the trail at a fair pace without anyone in front. It might have gone a little faster perhaps, and it had a tendency to stop and examine anything black that lay near the trail, but no dog is perfect, and this one we have only used as leader a few times. It took us 3 hours and 20 minutes to cross the bay, and it was then rapidly becoming dark. We steered a little to the left (i.e., south) of the ordinary trail across the land, and had to travel over deep snow for a considerable distance. Brick became very frightened; he thought we might tumble over the cliff or miss the house, and was very much relieved when we reached the sea [on] the other side of the peninsula near a tall sign-post. From here on there was a well-marked trail, which the [lead] dog followed of its own accord, and about three-quarters of an hour later we reached the house [Añopkana's]. After putting the sled on the rack we went into Añopkana's house. He himself was away, but we were made welcome [by his wife], and our things [were] hung up to dry. However, we had not been sitting long when a woman came over from the other house (Kunaloak's) and asked us across to dine. Kunaloak and all his people are at the fishing lake, but Mrs. Brower's brother [Asuaq] and his wife live in it. It was she [Asuaq's wife] who went to Barrow when Asecaq went [there], and who now asked us over to dine. We found there also their little girl, Amakuq, Mrs. Añopqana,[14] and Mrs. Brower's other brother [Amakuk] — the man who is always telling stories. They gave us an excellent dinner — first a tin of salmon, then hard-bread soaked in boiling water with salt and pepper, plenty of *mukpaurat* with a little butter, cocoa, and tea. Afterwards we played cat's cradles for a time. Mrs. Añopqana, though blind, was very expert in making the different figures, and taught me one I did not know before. She sewed sheepskin soles on to deerskin legs to make a pair of boots for the little girl [Amakuq], and the sewing was perfect. In her hair at the end of each of the two plaits she wears an ivory bead in place of a ribbon - I have noticed others with the same, and imagine it is the old custom. Mrs. Brower's brother [Asuaq] promised to let me have a few stores; he has not much, he said, but will give me what he can spare. I told him that for each thing he gave me I would write him an order for double the amount of it on Mr. Brower's store [at Barrow].[15] It is well worth it getting the things already up here. We sat for some time, then had supper — hard-bread and tea, and turned in after midnight. They gave me two cushions to make me more comfortable, and kept two lamps (one an Eskimo lamp) burning all night. The room was very warm, and I passed a very comfortable night. During the day there was no wind, but a light easterly arose in the evening. Up to 5:45 p.m. (the time we reached the houses) there was no aurora. In the bay there were three or four new cracks — one about a foot wide.

Saturday, January 17th

Our hostess gave us a good breakfast of cornmeal and *mukpaurat*. Brick wandered about between the two houses most of the day while I stayed in the one nearly all the time. Asuaq (Mrs. Brower's brother) gave me as many stores as he could spare, and I doubled the quantity of each and wrote him an order for the amount on Mr. Brower's store. Here is the list:

10 lbs hard-bread	10-lb bag cornmeal
4 tins salmon	1 can dried potatoes
2 tins milk	10 lbs rice
1 can butter	5 lbs lard
2 tins roast mutton	2 tins cocoa

I added one deerskin as a present, for they are short of skins. He and his wife are very well pleased — he said he was robbing me. But we are very short of food, and this may save us a journey to Barrow. Mrs. Añopqana made me a present of a bag of flour, almost full. I promised to make her a return present when the sled from the ship arrives. Yesterday I made her a present of a tin of tobacco, and Asuaq and his wife a box of chewing gum. Mrs. Añopqana said that when we run out of food Brick and I are to come and stay with them. I told her that when the ship's sled comes and I have abundance I should like to stay with her, and she replied that she would be very glad to have us. Asuaq had four balls of wool, and he wanted to make straps for his mittens. So he made skeins of the proper length of each of the four colours, using the thumb and little finger of the left hand for the two ends. He wound round the little finger, using the right hand as a carrier, then round his foot to the thumb and back again. Each skein was then cut in two. This gave him four long untwisted cords. He worked these into a sort of plait for about an inch, then Brick took two opposite cords and Asuaq the other two, and they interchanged them, Brick changing his from one hand to the other, then Asuaq his. So they worked down to the ends of the cords. I did not see how he fastens them to his mits, for that was not done today. In the plaiting care was taken not to pull the cords too tight. Brick helped him with one set, I with another. I left my denham [denim] snowshirt in the inner passage of Añopqana's house last night as it was covered with snow, which was difficult to shake off. Brick brought it in this morning; the dogs had got in and eaten up part of the hood and sleeves. Mrs. Asuaq sewed new pieces on for me, and also put two or three stitches in one of my boots. Mrs. Añopqana told about Otoyuk [Mrs. Aksiatak] a rather unpleasant story. When Kukpuk was a very little girl Otoyuk disliked her, and gave her very little to eat. Consequently Kukpuk used to take food, as the little boy and Siliuna do now, so Otoyuk shut her up in a tent apart. The smell was so bad that the other children would not go near the tent. Mrs. Añopqana said she wanted to take the child over, but Otoyuk would not let her go; however, she no longer kept Kukpuk in the tent apart. Even now she does not take Kukpuk about with her as she does Siliuna. Kukpuk certainly receives scant notice from her, and sleeps with Alak's children, not with Siliuna, though the two children are very friendly. She [Kukpuk] is very elderly in her ways [though only 12 years old], much graver than most Eskimo women even. Brick says Otoyuk is disliked by other women. Kunaloak's people made a small ante-chamber at the side of the outside entrance — a guardroom as it were. Just now it has a pile of firewood in it. Opposite it the wall is excavated a little to form another wood-bin. For dinner tonight our hostess [Mrs. Asuaq] gave us a pot of boiled beans (broad or lima beans) with a little pork in it, and plenty of *mukpaurat* with some butter. She has had more than enough food for us at each meal, which is more than I can say of any other Eskimo house I have been in. She and her husband have been extremely kind to us, although hospitality seems to be a universal trait here. Among the articles lying about the house I noticed a fine horn spoon, and a well-made ivory comb. Mrs. Brower's story-telling brother [Amakuk] is making *umiak* paddles — the handles seem very thick, but perhaps they are not finished. The handles were flattened a little so that in section they would appear oval. Mrs. Añopqana spent the day in the house with us, and about 10 p.m. Asuaq's wife escorted her across to her own home. Four of them there were playing cards — the Lapland game.

Figure 61. Mrs. Asuaq's ivory comb (left) and Amakuk's *umiak* paddle.

I watched for a time, then returned to my own quarters, where we had supper. Brick and our hostess played cards till nearly 2 a.m., when we all turned in. Outside the air was very mild, and a magnificent auroral bow stretched northwest to northeast, passing almost through the zenith. It was broadest and brightest in the middle, but at the two ends, neither of which touched the horizon, it resembled the rays of the rising sun reflected in a gently stirring sea.

Sunday, January 18th

Everyone was sleeping at 7:30 a.m. when I turned out and lit the fire. At 8:30 my hostess appeared and took charge, so that before 10 we were breakfasting on dried potatoes (boiled) with a tin of salmon mixed with them, and *mukpaurat* and coffee. Asuaq had filled our lantern for us the night before, and he now brought it out and helped to load the sled. Having only four dogs and a journey over soft snow in prospect, we were unable to take Itaqluq's seal-poke and flour bag. Just as we were starting off [for Aksiatak's] Mrs. Añopqana sent us out about 10 lbs of beans — a very welcome present. We steered almost due south for some time over very soft snow, but later over a large lagoon, between which and Harrison Bay there is only a narrow neck of land. We came out about 1/2 mile north of Iglu II, and reached the latter just as the last faint flush of sunset vanished from the southwest horizon. It took us nearly 4 hours, for we had to travel very slowly. Brick fed the dogs while I unloaded the sled, then he lit the fire and made some water while I chopped firewood. There were some *mukpaurat* left by us here last time, frozen now, but quickly thawing beside the stove and tasting as if they were only 3 or 4 hours old. With these and cornmeal we had a fine lunch, with a cup of cocoa each to wind up. For supper (or dinner, we don't trouble much about names, but this meal came on about 10 p.m.) we had the beans and *mukpaurat* and coffee. The weather during the day was very different to what it has been for several weeks. The temperature was comparatively mild, so that I tramped along without the snow-shirt and with my hands bare, and yet felt quite warm. A little snow fell continually. Wind there was none, and the atmosphere was foggy, so that all we saw of the sun was a red glow. Kunaloak's house, where Asuaq is living, was exceedingly warm; even in the morning when the fire had been extinguished for hours it was still warm. Brick told me today that one of the Eskimos told him he used to be scolded when he was young if he did not smack his lips while eating, for the Eskimos say that a silent eater eats like a thief. He [Brick] also told me that at an eclipse of the moon the women all remained indoors, otherwise the man in the moon would carry them off. I saw no aurora in the evening.

Monday, January 19th

I turned out about 9 a.m. and lit the fire. We had a few beans left over from last night, and these with cornmeal, *mukpaurat*, and coffee constituted our breakfast. It was noon when we left for Iglu I [Aksiatak's house]. A little snow was falling and the atmosphere was very foggy, but it was not cold and there was no wind. For some distance we let the dogs make their own trail; all the old trails were pretty well obliterated by the snow which had fallen since [Friday]. We drifted too far to the west and struck land more than a mile south of the house. However, we were inside the house before 4 p.m., lunching on frozen fish and biscuits. Brick was very tired and slept till 8 p.m., when we had a rice supper. Alak was making — or mending — some snowshoes, Itaqluq idling away the hours, Qapqana twisting sinew for Alak, Otoyuk dressing skins, and Aksiatak sitting in his corner, feeling a good deal better than when we left. I might have mentioned that Amakuk, the middle-aged man who was staying with Otoyuk, is something of a vagrant. He has no wife, no children, but drifts from one house to another. At Asuaq's he seemed to be a sort of servant; he attended to the fire, brought in wood, and did odd jobs of various kinds.[16] I should have entered also that both Asuaq and his wife made one or two woollen balls to wear at the shoulders in the same way as little children just beginning school are often taught, i.e., on a disc of cardboard the centre of which has been cut out. A moderately strong west wind sprang up in the evening, the temperature still remaining mild. There was no aurora visible during the first part of the night, but about midnight when I turned out to attend to the dogs there was the usual bow.

Tuesday, January 20th

The west wind of yesterday developed into a southwest blizzard today, consequently everyone stayed indoors nearly all the time. Otoyuk, assisted by Kukpuk and Siliuna, made me a pair of deerskin shoes with sheepskin upper borders; then she resoled my travelling deerskin boots. Alak had to clear away the snow from the side of the rack, for the blizzard was rapidly raising a drift which threatened to cover it entirely. Then he brought in some firewood which he sawed into suitable lengths with a small frame-saw made by himself from a clock-spring. Qapqana is making a snow shirt for Asecaq. Brick's snowshoes, made for him by Mr. Brower, were too heavy, so Alak is going to make him a pair using willow for the frame, because it is very light. The pair he has just made are for Asecaq. Qapqana asked that she might have the bag of flour I brought yesterday from [Cape] Halkett in her room, as she wished to bake some *mukpaurat* herself. Otoyuk's are very bad — like stones usually, for she puts very little baking powder in them; also she never makes enough. The first batch Qapqana made today she set in front of us and we ate them all without waiting for the tea which was being prepared; she had more ready by that time. Otoyuk too had a large number over in her corner but she only produced half a dozen for us, reserving the rest for a later meal. Brick wrote an interesting story of Jack the Giant-Killer type[17] at Qapqana's dictation, then began another — also dictated by Qapqana — which he said Stefansson had obtained as a caribou charm. The [Cape] Halkett people were laughing about it while Brick was present — it was a popular story which Stefansson had recited to them as an example of one of their charms. He had asked them to tell him any more they knew, for he would write them down and they would always be remembered — otherwise they would soon be forgotten. At the time they sat quiet and said nothing, but laughed heartily when Stef[ansson] had gone. Such is the fate I fancy of many an ethnologist — more often than is supposed. Alak taught me a rather good cat's-cradle figure in the evening — the butterfly.[18] There was the usual auroral bow and the wind moderated a little towards night.

Wednesday, January 21st

The southwest wind blew all day, gradually diminishing in strength. The atmosphere was very cold so that I got my nose and chin slightly frozen. My dog, which was caught in the trap and had its foot frozen, seems to be losing some if not all of its toes. We had breakfast about 11 a.m. Alak and Brick had theirs early — about 9 — and went to their traps, returning about 4 p.m. — Brick with a fox, his third. I cut up firewood and brought snow for water into the passage, then retired indoors where the women were sewing and Aksiatak as usual was sitting in his corner. He is rapidly getting all right again and hardly coughs at all. The sun was visible again today — or a part of him with a tiny cap on his head, brighter than the rest of him that was visible. Being on the horizon

Figure 62. The sun re-appears.

he naturally appeared very broad. Itaqluq left after breakfast for Iglu II to examine his traps over there. The dogs began to fight in the passage this evening. Brick and Alak had no boots on so I ran out, carrying my deerskin shirt, for indoors it was so hot with the two stoves that I was sitting stripped to the waist. The dogs soon separated and the chief result I obtained was a shower of snow over my naked back. The outer passage is not high enough to allow a man to stand upright, and I had knocked my head on the snow roof. This evening the sky was clear, and there was the auroral bow again. The stars shone brightly but it was very dark, for the moon is now invisible. We have no coal oil so are using blubber lamps. Alak's is the half of a large cylindrical tobacco tin closed top and bottom and set in a tin tray. The calico wick comes up through a long narrow slot lined with a piece of tin which projects on each side. On its upper side it has four holes through which a pin on the end of a stick can be in-

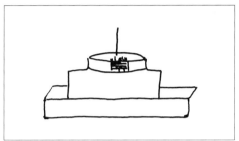

Figure 63. Alak's blubber lamp.

serted to raise or lower the wick. A hole in the middle of the lid forms a very convenient resting place for the pin. Late in the evening fan or wheat-eared aurora appeared directly overhead while in the north was the bow.

Thursday, January 22nd

We had breakfast moderately early for Brick and Otoyuk were going across to Iglu II. They set off before 11 a.m. with four of my dogs and two of Aksiatak's. The wind at this time was easterly, moderately strong. I cut up some firewood then went indoors. At 2 p.m. a howling blizzard was raging from the southwest. Aksiatak was outdoors for some time trying to cut wood; in consequence his cough reappeared. We played cat's cradles in the evening. Aksiatak made an excellent knife from a file, with a handle of willow. When we turned in about 10 p.m. the wind had greatly abated; overhead the stars were visible but there was no aurora.

Friday, January 23rd

The storm was over when we rose and the air was calm but foggy, while the temperature seemed not so low as during the last 2 or 3 days. Alak and I cut up a great pile of firewood — pine and willow — a task which occupied us till darkness set in. Aksiatak fixed a bow on to the

Figure 64. Trigger for Aksiatak's toy wooden gun.

model gun he made a week or two ago and a short barrel of wood which Itaqluq bored for him the other night. He added an arrow, a thin shaft with a broken needle in the end, while the trigger was of this shape. Smoothed with sandpaper and painted or varnished it might have come from a European shop. He found great amusement in shooting at a small wooden figure of a ptarmigan with it. At 5 p.m. a light was seen in the north and half an hour later Asecaq arrived. He had left almost all my things at [Cape] Halkett, but brought a budget of letters — mostly home letters written in June, and sent by the Geological Survey to Nome, where they arrived too late to catch us before we left. I had letters from home, Leeper, Castlehow, MacDougall, Miss Nash, and Miss de Chaumont, and a note from Mr. Cram, the postmaster, missionary government official, and schoolmistress's husband at Barrow. The last named stated that there were numerous letters at Barrow for other members of the Expedition and wanted to know what he had better do with them. There came also a pamphlet from the editor of *Globus* and *Petermann's Mitteilungen* containing the monthly notice of our Expedition. I spent the whole of the evening reading these. Outdoors there was a moderate breeze from the east, and the atmosphere was still foggy and fairly cold, while there was no aurora. I had two packets of unsweetened chocolate from Barrow and made a pot of chocolate about 11 p.m. We did not turn in till 1:30.

Saturday, January 24th

Breakfast at 10 a.m. — cornmeal with prunes in it, but the prunes were not sweet, *mukpaurat*, coffee, and tea, milk and sugar. Asecaq's dog in the night got on to the rack and ate most of the hard-bread I brought from [Cape] Halkett. Alak and I removed the things off the rack and made a new one on top of a drift, safe from the dogs for the time being. The wind at this time was northeast, i.e., rather more northerly than usual, of moderate strength, while the temperature was fairly low. About 2:30 p.m. we had lunch and a tin of apricots was produced, bought by Asecaq at Barrow. Soon afterwards when I went out the wind had shifted to the northwest, a very unusual direction. Qapqana washed some clothes in the afternoon; I gave her two handkerchiefs to wash and she asked for my Burberry trousers also, but I told her they did not matter. For dinner, about 8 p.m., we had rice with bacon in it, a queer combination.

Aksiatak received from Asecaq a pack of cards and taught me a new way of playing 'patience'. You shuffle, lay 13 cards on one side, face downwards, then place 4 cards in a row, face upwards, and a 5th above them. Whatever the 5th is you count it as if it were an ace and build on it; also whenever the same number card is turned up it counts the same and goes on top. Whenever one of the four rows is exhausted its place is taken by the top one of the (originally) 13 cards. Three cards are turned up at once, the succeeding number of an opposite coloured card takes its place in each of the four rows; the King is followed by the ace, that by 2, and so on.

Alak made an excellent box for his primus lamp, with a spare apartment for matches, alcohol etc. He made two brass hinges, using two thin nails and a small piece of brass from some tin. His lock was interesting — a hook and a nail, but the hook had a spring, being shaped thus:

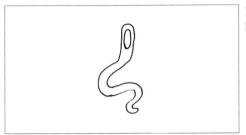

Figure 65. Lock hook on Alak's primus lamp.

Then there was a sliding door in the side; when open the stove could be pumped through a circular hole. Asecaq too made a box for his papers of very ordinary construction. Alak's son, Suivaliaq, complained of a pain in his stomach towards evening; Qapqana says he had the same 2 or 3 days ago. He got warm, then rather cold, and I had him wrapped up; his pulse was beating very fast and strong. For a while he slept, then when he woke up I gave him a little warm milk (sweetened tin milk, two-thirds water). About half an hour later he wanted water so I gave him a little water, cold, but not at zero as they usually drink it. He drank a little and 2 or 3 minutes later was sick and threw up both the milk and the water. He fretted for some time, the pain apparently not being continuous but rather spasmodic; then he went to sleep in Alak's arms. The other patient, Aksiatak, stays in the house most of the time but is really convalescent. Qapqana early in the evening dictated to me the words of a song she is always singing, and I tried to set the notes to it, with what success I cannot tell until I try it on some instrument. I wish I had my flute or piccolo here; it would be invaluable for songs. Late in the evening there was an auroral bow, with wheat-ears on each side; the temperature was comparatively mild.

Sunday, January 25th

We had a scratch breakfast about 10, some dry *mukpaurat*, and a little cold rice which lay in the bottom of the pot, and tea. An hour or two later, however, when Qapqana was baking, she gave me a hot *mukpaurat*. I spent nearly the whole day working at the music to the song Qapqana taught me. It turns out that it is one of Asecaq's composing[19] — at least the words — I think the tune is well known everywhere with slight variations.[20] He sang it for me and his rendering differed a little from Qapqana's. He also gave the meaning as far as his knowledge of English enabled him to. For some time in the evening he was lying on his back singing and beating time with a stick on the skins. For the most part the songs were wordless, i.e., consisted of meaningless syllables like '*ai yana ye*' and '*ye ye ye*', but from time to time, he put in impromptu words. I could distinguish once 'Father, Son, and Holy Ghost' and it sounded very strange. Alak's boy Suivaliaq has been all right today — he slept most of the night. Asecaq brought him a pair of trousers with a red stripe and a jacket to match, while Qapqana received a couple of shirts. He brought back also a tin of beef and a piece of ham, whether at his own cost or Alak's I don't know. Towards dusk I went outside and played chasing with the children — then made them a swing with a rope suspended from the rack.[21] I gave Aksiatak a writing pad (Asecaq brought me three that I had ordered) and he spent some time drawing a map of a portion of the Colville River with its tributaries. I wrote in the names as he pointed out the places. The wind this morning was east-northeast, a moderate breeze; it died away and a light air came out of the west with a milder temperature. Clouds on the horizon obscured the sun, but the daylight seemed to last much longer than at any time since the sun disappeared. Late in the evening there was a fine aurora; when I noticed it it consisted of 'wheat-ears' and small clouds of white light, but it was constantly changing. Kukpuk is a constant model of patience. In the house she is very quiet, and spends a good deal of time in the corner under Alak's sleeping platform, or else sitting in the back of Aksiatak's room where she is out of the way and unnoticed. Thence she observes all that happens; if a story is being told she is all ears to listen; if we are playing cat's cradles she watches and learns, although she knows already as many figures as any save Alak and myself. Otoyuk not infrequently scolds her, Qapqana less often, yet I have never been able to detect the least sign of vexation or sulkiness. Her obedience is exemplary — she might be called an Eskimo Griselda.[22] Quiet as she is, and graver than many an adult woman, she plays with the other children, though still looking after them like a governess. Siliuna is much more childish — she is the giggler of the house; nevertheless she is a very good child, very rarely cries and never sulks.

Monday, January 26th

Alak and Asecaq went off about 9 a.m. to their traps, leaving me to cut up firewood. I had just finished about 2 p.m. when the children came out for snow, so I sawed out several blocks and we carried them into the passage. Aksiatak pottered about outside for a little while then retired indoors. He finds the pack of cards that Asecaq brought very useful in helping to make the hours run quickly, and plays patience a great part of the afternoon and evening. The sun was visible for nearly 4 hours today. In the morning there was a light but very cold breeze from the southwest. Slowly it swung round to north, then back to west, then late in the afternoon to southeast. The atmosphere was splendidly clear and transparent all day. Alak and Asecaq returned about 4 p.m., empty-handed both. Alak was very tired, so slept after we had lunched (or dined?). Qapqana, growing tired of sewing, played 'patience' for a while, then lay on her back and sang in a loud voice rather nasal, to the words '*ai yana ye*', ending up with a loud emission of the breath rather like a sigh — a common ending. Though wordless the tune was well known, for Alak joined in once or twice keeping perfect time, although it changed often. As usual Qapqana beat time with her hand on some skins. Songs seem to have a 'rage' rather like our music hall ditties. Asecaq's former song, composed when we left the ship, I have heard sung almost everywhere from here to Barrow. Qapqana has had two songs going since I came, before this second one of Asecaq's I have been writing the last 2 or 3 days. This is how Aksiatak, who has never been west of [Cape] Halkett and never heard or seen a missionary, knows many hymns. The auroras seem not to appear, as a rule, until several hours after sunset, and to vanish again long before sunrise.

Tuesday, January 27th

Alak and Asecaq went off trapping after breakfast, while I cut up a log and attended to one or two things outdoors. Asecaq brought a dog from Brick's mother and it has been eating some of the lashings from the *umiak* cached on a rack by our recent visitor from [Cape] Halkett. The rack is low and by jumping up it can reach some of the sealskin lashings, so I chained it up. The sun reappeared again for the sky was very clear, and a mild east breeze blowing. Brick and Otoyuk, the latter with Katairoaq on her back, came with the sled about 2:30 p.m. [from Cape Halkett], bringing a box of things that I had ordered from Mr. Brower [which Asecaq had left at Cape Halkett the week before] and Aksiatak's seal-poke full of blubber; the latter weighed about 200 lbs. Asecaq and Alak came in about 4 p.m., Itaqluq about 5 p.m. with a fox. Brick had no foxes in his traps but found, he says, seven fox dens. I gave him some easy sentences to translate for me, in order to obtain some verb forms; also he said he would be able to write a story or two. He tells me tonight that he has not done much; he has translated the sentences and written some words on his own, but no story. I have not yet examined what he has done, but his work lately has been very unsatisfactory both in quality and quantity. I am wondering whether it is worth my while to keep him, or to go to Barrow and engage another interpreter to work out the grammar and translate the stories already written, and if possible obtain new stories. Late this evening I opened the case from Mr. Brower. There was a pleasant letter from him inside. He expected me for Christmas, he said. Almost everything I ordered he supplied except the food; for these he sent my order over by Asecaq to the other store kept by Mr. Hansen. The biscuits, Asecaq said, they would not supply, and the lard and molasses he left at [Cape] Halkett. At least he left two tins of lard there, brought one with him, and used up one on the way. He gave some molasses and lard to Asuaq, and Brick did the same later. Today as I was writing a tiny spider (*nigiroaruq*) ran over the leaf [i.e., page]. Cards was in fashion tonight, Asecaq, Brick, Qapqana, and Itaqluq playing. The wind today was easterly, very mild. There was no aurora in the early part of the evening, but at midnight there was a faint streak.

Wednesday, January 28th

Brick went away to his traps fairly early and returned about 2 p.m. with a fox — his fourth. The rest stayed about the house. I've investigated our sled and harnesses, for Aksiatak's and mine had been used indiscriminately by us both. I found that I have five harnesses besides the one to Brick's dog, but no trace. One of Aksiatak's harnesses was eaten by the dogs, so I gave him one of mine. He said that the paw of my dog which was caught in the trap was not injured, but he does not think the dog will be of any use before the summer when it can thaw out. Aksiatak and Qapqana seem very pleased with the presents from Barrow which I sent for [see January 17th]. Alak and Otoyuk are less demonstrative, the latter in fact receives everything no matter from whom in rather an offhand way — just her manner I suppose. We have no coal oil, so I tried whale oil (liquid blubber) in a small lamp I have but it was too thick to be drawn up through the wick. I spent the evening working at Eskimo language. In Alak's room, Brick, ItaXluq, Asecaq, Alak, and Qapqana constituted themselves into a choir and made the halls ring with their melodies. Asecaq improvised new words to a popular tune and taught them. Qapqana drowned all the other voices whenever there seemed to be any tendency towards a lull. There was a strong east-northeast wind all day and the air was cold. Up to 11 p.m. I saw no aurora.

Thursday, January 29th

Aksiatak set out to his traps with the others, the first time since his illness. He found that a fox had carried off one of his traps, and the rest were empty. The others also obtained nothing. I fulfilled my usual task, the chopping of firewood, then went inside to resume work on the Eskimo language. Brick had a sore throat so went to sleep soon after he came in. He showed a little feverishness in the evening, but after a perspiration issued his pulse became normal and he felt better. I made him some hot cocoa before he turned in for the night. Aksiatak taught me one of his songs, and I partly wrote the music.[23] The words are nothing, *'ai yaña ye'*, but the tune is not at all bad; it was the rage here a month or so ago. A moderate breeze from the east-northeast all day increased in strength during the evening; the atmosphere was not remarkably cold. Up to 11 p.m. I saw no aurora. Qapqana has a flour bag three-quarters full of squirrel skins. She is using them to put together again Asecaq's *atigi* (shirt) that was eaten by the dogs at the fishing lake a couple of months ago. Brick's snowshoes, made by Mr. Brower, are too heavy for him; yesterday, being tired, he left them at his traps. Alak is making him a new pair of willow. The children here go to bed about the same time as we do. Siliuna usually retires with her mother. Suivaliaq and Katairoaq as soon as they feel sleepy, but Kukpuk and Puganahoq must wait till we others are all settled in our places before turning in themselves. Tonight Puganahoq went to sleep an hour before we turned in, [and] lay stretched on the floor between the two rooms, half in one, half in the other. When we moved over to our places Qapqana dragged her across the floor to her place. Aksiatak has a very fine coat of mountain-sheep skin, and so has Siliuna.

Friday, January 30th

A day at home for everyone. Outside a moderately strong breeze from the east drove the snow along and obscured the sun, except for a few minutes at noon; the atmosphere was very cold, at least when one faced the wind. Asecaq and Itaqluq set out with a sled for the fishing lake but returned an hour later with Niniyuk, an old [Cape] Halkett acquaintance, and son-in-law of Kunaloak. They had met him coming here so turned back with him. One of my dogs is on the sick list; Qapqana thinks its tongue is frozen. At all events it will not eat. She says that one of her dogs had similar symptoms and died. That leaves me only two dogs — luckily the two best, with Brick's two dogs. Brick is all right today except for a slightly sore throat. He skinned his fox this morning and did a little work with me in the evening. Alak made a new home for one of his dogs which has two pups; he cut another hole in the snow of the outer passage. I put my sick dog in the old hole. Aksiatak did the wood chopping today, [and] he appears to be quite all right again. It was interesting to note what a brave show we presented to our visitor Niniyuk. Otoyuk cooked twice as many *mukpaurat* as usual and put them in front of us, but Qapqana surpassed her by producing a great bowl full. Aksiatak always takes from Qapqana's pile, I notice.

Eskimo manners at 'table' seem rather strange to a European. Everyone eats as fast as he can generally, and takes the best of what he sees in front of him. Often a man fingers three or four *mukpaurat* before he arrives at the one he takes. A slow eater is sure to go hungry, 19 times out of 20, or more probably 99 times out of 100. At each meal a man drinks two or three cups of tea. It must be admitted that they [these Eskimos] are very good humoured. You know that if you don't hurry up, your neighbour — [your] father perhaps — will empty the teapot and eat most of the *mukpaurat*, so you do your best to get there before him — a "survival of the fittest" method.

Niniyuk stayed with Aksiatak and his wife all the afternoon and evening — unlike all our other visitors; he was playing cards with Otoyuk for a long time. I told Brick today to take up his traps as soon as he could for we would go west. If the sled from the ship comes before we get away and Brick shows any signs of working a little better we shall stay at [Cape] Halkett at Añopqana's house and perhaps at one or two places further along the coast, returning here later. If the ship's sled does not come we shall go to Barrow. At [Cape] Halkett I have molasses and lard, left there by Asecaq. My kerosene feedcan he left on a rack further down the coast, at the large house where Wilkins and I stayed on November 3rd. My axe he left, he said, in the whale-boat house at Barrow and some one took it — he thinks Mr. Brower's workman Rexford. This evening at 9 p.m. there was a faint auroral bow east-north. At midnight this had become a magnificent arch southeast-northwest. Its form was changing momentarily, but in general it was composed of an infinite number of fine streaks set at an angle of about 30° to the direction of the arch.

Saturday, January 31st

After breakfast (*mukpaurat* and tea), Niniyuk, Asecaq, and Itaqluq set out for the fishing lake. I had to shoot my dog which was bad [sick] yesterday. Apparently the lower maxillary bone on the right side had been dislocated, and the dog was unable to keep its mouth closed. In this state its tongue froze; it could eat nothing, but howled if another dog came near it. Then I helped Alak unearth (or unsnow) a large log. He reserved the trunk for making a sled, or at least parts of one, and we cut up the knotty root for firewood. This task occupied us nearly 4 hours, after which we retired indoors to lunch on *mukpaurat* and tea, and about an hour later *mukpaurat* and cocoa. I wished to do a little grammar then with Brick, but he said he was writing a story which he began 2 days ago, one of Qapqana's. We supped about 7:30 p.m. (warm prunes, a little bacon and *mukpaurat*) after which he gave me what he had done — two small sheets, just half a page of my 'story-book'; he said he thought he would finish it this evening as it was a short story — I said nothing, but it confirms me in the belief that it is not worth while keeping him on. Kukpuk and Puganahoq were both on the sick list today. Puganahoq was sick last night and had [an] ear-ache; she woke up several times in the night and cried. This afternoon she was all right. Kukpuk had a headache this morning and was sick several times during the day. She slept part of the afternoon and evening. Brick was as well as ever. He was cleaning a foxskin part of the time, and for the rest cooking *mukpaurat* and chatting with Qapqana and Alak. Asecaq is taking up the two traps Brick has near the fishing lake. I have now but four dogs to go to Barrow — two of the Expedition's and two of Brick's or his mother's. I must leave here the dog with the frozen foot, as well as most of my things. There was a light southerly breeze all day, and the atmosphere was very cold. At 10 p.m. there was a slight auroral bow. Aksiatak and Alak both set rectangular slabs of snow behind (on the north side of) their skylights, to reflect the sunlight down through them. Brick finished the story about 10 p.m., and gave me the two fresh sheets.[24]

Sunday, February 1st

Aksiatak left early to go to his traps. Brick waited for breakfast then departed to his. Alak spliced some loops on the trace of my sled while I made a few preparations for leaving. The children had their hair dressed as usual on Sundays. It makes a wonderful difference in their appearance. All of them were well again. Aksiatak found no foxes in his traps, nor did Brick, who took his up. However, he has caught four foxes, and says he will be quite satisfied even if he catches no more. Being Sunday I did no work with him, but wrote out the music to another popular song — the one Asecaq composed on the *Karluk* and has taught all along the coast [see footnote 19, this chapter]. Cat's cradles and cards filled up the rest of the day. Aksiatak has plaited a sled-lashing for me; the old one has disappeared somehow. The atmosphere was very clear today but very cold, the wind easterly. The moon is nearly half-full and is waxing, so we shall have a good moon for our journey. Early in the evening there was a faint aurora bow east-north; at 10 p.m. none was visible.

Monday, February 2nd

Otoyuk went off early to set some traps; the rest of us waited for a late breakfast. Brick and Alak stayed indoors all day trying to finish the snowshoes Alak is making for Brick. I got things ready to leave tomorrow, then helped Aksiatak chop out a large log, which we cut up for firewood. Asecaq and Itaqluq returned [from the fishing lake] about 4 p.m. with a sled-load of fish. We all sat down at once and had a hearty meal. I managed two tail halves, Aksiatak two whole ones, and the rest I don't know how much, but a huge bowl full well-nigh disappeared. I lost my sheath-knife some time ago and was dragging off the skin with my pocket-knife when it slipped and cut deep into my thumb. Alak gave me a large pen-knife afterwards, reciprocating the present (a Wilson knife) I made him a few days ago. I wished to leave our lame dog here, but Aksiatak said he had not much dog-feed, so I shall take it along with me. I have given Aksiatak a letter for whoever comes from the ships.[25] These two families are almost out of sugar and Aksiatak of tea also, while Alak has only two bags of flour.[26] The wind was westerly all day, a light breeze, very cold; the atmosphere was as clear as yesterday.

Chapter 8. Return to Barrow

To Iglu II with Brick — Welcome at Añopqana's — Comments on Eskimo pronunciation and crafts — Overnight near Pitt Point and Cape Simpson — Iglura — Ague attack — Hearty welcome at Barrow

Tuesday, February 3rd, 1914

Two of my dogs had disappeared when we got up this morning. As soon as breakfast was over I sent Brick off in one direction and I went in the other to look for them. He found one dog — the leader — in a trap; one of its toes was frozen, but I don't know that it will disable it much. It was noon when I returned, and Brick appeared a few minutes later. We had some tea and half a biscuit each then set out for Iglu II on the other side of the bay. The dog with the frozen foot[1] followed up but tired after about a mile. I tried to carry it on the sled and lashed it on, but it struggled to get away as soon as the sled moved. It was impossible to take the dog without causing it much pain, so I was compelled, very reluctantly, to shoot it. We continued along, crossing a large crack in the ice (*qopuk*) about 1 1/2 feet wide. The leader shirked it and ran back. The next dog — Victor — jumped it without a tremor. The fourth [dog], however, was checked when half-way over, for the sled was stopped by the leader running back; the poor beast lay stretched out with its two front legs just reaching the other side; of course it was soon released from this awkward position. At 4 p.m. it grew dark and the trail was lost. We wandered far to the left without knowing it and when we finally struck the land did not know where we were. The house, we thought, was south of us — [we thought] we had drifted to the right — so we went south for some time along the edge of the land. It was all perfectly flat and we frequently had to dig through the snow to find out whether we were on the sea or the land. At last we felt sure that we were going the wrong way, so turned back. The moon was half full, but the atmosphere was foggy, so its light was dimmed. We wormed our way along slowly, sometimes drifting out on to the sea, then turning to find the land; sometimes floundering over the land in an endeavour to find the sea-edge. Occasional driftwood and kegs of ice helped us greatly, but they were not numerous and our course must have been very serpentine. At 6:40 p.m. Brick wanted to camp, or rather to pack the things so that we could sleep in the sled. We have no sled-cover — nothing to put over us and the light southwesterly breeze was intensely cold, so we struggled on. About 8 p.m. we reached a cutbank we knew and by 8:30 had gained the house. The journey had taken us 7 hours instead of 3. We could not see the house until we were about 50 yards away, when we noticed some faint dark object on our right. It did not take long to unharness the dogs, tie up the two which wandered off early this morning, hustle the things inside, and get the fire going. Brick could hardly keep his eyes open, so turned in while I kept the fire stoked with chips and odd scraps of wood about the house. There was flour in the house but no baking powder, so it was not possible to make biscuits (*mukpaurat*). At 11:30 p.m. I woke Brick up — he had been sleeping soundly for the last 2 1/2 hours — and we had supper — a frozen fish each, a little boiled rice, and chocolate. Alak and Aksiatak were practically out of sugar so we brought none with us. A pinch of salt gave the rice a little taste — the chocolate, being of the unsweetened kind, tasted rather like a dose of medicine. I made some shavings [and] filled the thermos flask with hot water for the morning, for it takes an hour to melt sufficient snow. When finally I turned in, just after 12, Brick was again sound asleep. The weather was fine and clear in the morning but gradually became foggy as darkness drew on. I saw no aurora, neither early nor late, but the foggy atmosphere might have obscured it.

Wednesday, February 4th

Brick turned out at 8 a.m. and lit the fire. I got up a few minutes later, went out and cut up firewood. We breakfasted about 9:30 — frozen fish, and dried potatoes boiled, and last night's chocolate rewarmed. Brick then went away to his traps and I searched around for a good log and cut it up for firewood. About 2 p.m. I set the fire going again and made some water. The barking of the dogs announced the arrival of Niniyuk from the [fishing] lake, on his way, like us, to [Cape] Halkett (*Isuk*). By the time he had eaten three fish and drank a little chocolate, the tea was ready. Brick appeared about 4 p.m. with his traps and a fox — half an hour later Asecaq and Itaqluq [arrived from the fishing lake]. We all had some frozen fish, tea, and a little later chocolate. Asecaq turned cook and fireman, while Brick skinned his fox. Later in the evening we had about a spoonful of rice each and half a spoonful of boiled dried potatoes. The weather was rather foggy all day, the sun invisible; a light air changed from southwest to west, then swung back again; the temperature seemed a little milder than yesterday. I found my nose was frozen a little yesterday and is preparing to peel; it is then rather painful in the cold air. Itaqluq discovered that his mother [Mrs. Aksiatak] had put baking powder in the flour so proceeded to make biscuits in boiling blubber. Niniyuk had a bottle of saccharin, so really we had a fine supper. We all squeezed into bed about 11 p.m., lying in a row, Itaqluq with his head at our feet. No aurora was visible during the evening.

Thursday, February 5th

Brick lit the fire at 9 a.m., and we all turned out a minute or two later. He went off to take up two traps that he had not been able to reach yesterday and returned before we had begun breakfast. The cooking of the biscuits this morning gave us quite a lot of amusement. First Niniyuk's primus refused to burn, being dirty. Itaqluq shaved a piece off the edge of an old baking powder tin, scraped it down on a piece of wood, bent it, and finally inserted the blunt end in a wooden handle. Thus he made a very efficient pricker with which he cleaned out the hole and set about relighting the lamp. Meanwhile Asecaq had a pan of boil-

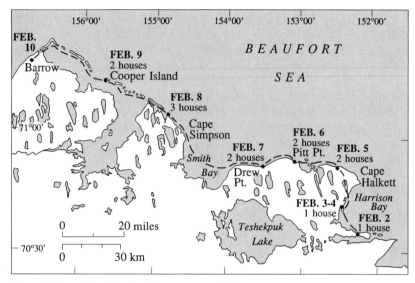

Figure 66. Route from Harrison Bay to Barrow, February 2-10, 1914.

ing blubber on the stove in which he was cooking biscuits. Suddenly there was an explosion and a biscuit shot out of the pan into the floor, splashing some blubber on the stove. Immediately a thick vapour arose, making our eyes smart and half choking us. Niniyuk and Asecaq rushed out of the house into the fresh air, I huddled into a corner and Itaqluq covered up his face. A few minutes later the primus responded to Itaqluq's efforts and he took over the boiling of the biscuits. Hardly was the pan on the primus when there was a second explosion. Itaqluq and I were both in the line of fire and received a few drops of boiling blubber. The pan was displaced slightly and in trying to readjust it we upset it. This put an end to the boiling of the biscuits. The dough that remained was baked in the oven, our baking pan being an old butter tin. We sat and ate frozen fish and biscuits until 1 p.m., when we began to pack up; 1/2 hour later we left for [Cape] Halkett. After skirting the shore for a short distance we crossed a narrow neck of land, traversed a lake about 4 or 5 miles wide, then came to land again. On the ice the trail was fairly good, but on the land the snow was soft and we sank deep into it at every step. Four or five miles of this second stretch of land brought us to Añopqana's about 5 p.m. Kunaloak's house, where Asuaq and his family were staying the last time I was here [January 16-18], is now empty, Asuaq having migrated to a house 10 or 12 miles further west. We found Añopqana at home again with Aiva and Samuel and their little girl Josephine, all of whom were away when I was here before. Besides these there were in the house Añopqana's wife, the ancient dame who saw Maguire's ship in 184[?],[2] the housewife, the paralysed woman and her son — a boy of about 13; finally there was my old acquaintance Amakuk, the vagrant, who had apparently transferred his affections to this house on Asuaq's departure. We were heartily welcomed and a great pile of excellent biscuits set before us with its indispensable accompaniment, tea. Brick brought in my molasses and lard (or the remnants of them), which Asecaq had left on a rack [a few weeks earlier]. Biscuits and molasses were a pleasant change from the almost unbroken spell of dry biscuits, which have been half my diet for the last 2 1/2 months. An hour later the whole family dined on more biscuits, and we again with them. Añopqana asked if I wanted any stores to take with me on the journey to Barrow and has promised to give me half a bag of flour and a few hard-bread (he has not many left) in the morning, and coal oil to fill my lantern. A little later one of my harnesses was brought in. It was partly eaten by a dog, as it was carelessly allowed to hang down from the rack on which the sled was placed. Aiva at once took charge of it and sewed a new piece on. This family has been exceptionally kind to me. Añopqana, Stefansson told me some time ago, is noted for his generous hospitality. He seemed pleased when I told him that I had left word for any stores that might be brought for me from the ships to be left in his rack as I intended to return there. I have promised to bring him some files when I come, the women some sinew, and Josephine a new dress. His house is much more comfortable than Alak's and Aksiatak's. It is more roomy than Kunaloak's, though the latter's [house] has two apartments; however, it hardly seems to be as warm. There have always been two blubber lamps and a large glass stand lamp filled with coal oil burning all together whenever I have been here. There were half a dozen brant hanging up on this occasion to thaw out — they were shot in the autumn and allowed to freeze. Near the stove was a large block of whale hide (*muktuk*) from which we supped about 9 p.m. The ancient dame is always very cheerful; she invariably asks me if I can talk Eskimo yet. This time she corrected my pronunciation of the word *mikiruramik*. The long syllable is - *rur* - but the tone of the voice is raised on the next syllable *'ra'*. The accentuation of Eskimo words requires as much learning as the words themselves. Mrs. Añopqana speaks in a slow rather melancholy voice — I wonder if this is not characteristic of blind people.

Three days ago I saw but failed to record a primitive fiddle, which Itaqluq, I think, made for Katairoaq. A tin was flattened, a stick inserted with a strand of sinew fixed at the inner end and passing through a hole in the pin at the other, by which it could be tightened. Near the inner end it passed over a small wooden 'bridge'. This one-stringed fiddle was struck with a stick instead of being scraped with a bow. I have met two European mechanical puzzles [toys] — no doubt they are fairly common. The Eskimos are very good at whittling wood and at executing small mechanical jobs, although there are great individual differences. Alak is notably expert, much more than is Aksiatak. The younger Eskimos do not generally display the skill of their elders. Many for example cannot make fishing-nets or snowshoes. The women have the same suppleness in the wrist that white women display (compared that is to the stiffness of a man's wrist) — also the same tendency to hold the little finger somewhat

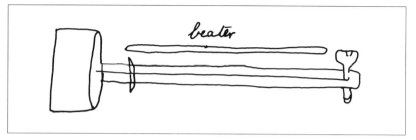

Figure 67. Itaqluq's fiddle.

apart. I have noticed this latter in New Guinea also. A light air breathed from the west all day and the temperature was fairly cold and the atmosphere inclined to fogginess. Auroral streamers were visible at 7 p.m. overhead stretching southeast to west.

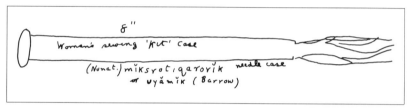

Figure 68. Eskimo woman's sewing kit case.

Friday, February 6th

At 7:30 a.m. we all turned out. Itaqluq, who had slept alone in Kunaloak's house, came in later. At 9 we had a *praegustum* [foretaste] of *muktuk*; at 10, boiled brant and its soup, at 10:30 biscuits and chocolate — a splendid breakfast. I have noticed that if I have a big meal before setting out on a journey I can go for 5 or 6 hours without feeling tired, whereas with a moderately light meal I start fresh but after about 3 hours become tired and weak, and my legs begin to ache and my hands and face become cold. A couple of hard-bread then freshen me up for another 2 or 3 hours. Today Brick and I set out at 11 a.m. We had gone a mile when we saw Aiva running after us. She brought a kerosene feed can I had left intentionally, but as she thought, through forgetfulness. Amakuk was dragging his "swag"[3] (it really resembled one) and his rifle on a tiny sled. We put the whole thing on our sled and he tramped with us for 4 hours till he branched off to the left to reach Asuaq's home. Another 2 hours saw us at the large double house Wilkins and I stayed at on November 3rd.[4] A cross-eyed man sitting in a corner greeted me (when I entered) with the word "Jennie," and I replied "*una*" (Yes, that's who it is). Asecaq told me that I was known all along the coast as Jennie. They gave us biscuits and tea, and we brought in our flour, molasses, and lard. There is one thing about an Eskimo house — you have to make yourself at home, then you find it pretty comfortable. They don't put themselves out for you either. When you arrive at a place someone always turns out to see who it is. He may stay and help you or may say "*alapa*" (it is cold) and go inside again at once. No one moves when you go in, although you generally have something to eat as soon as it can be made ready. At night everyone turns in as usual and you sit on one side waiting to see where you will find room. Once in bed they suggest perhaps how you may lie best and you make yourself as comfortable as you can.[5] We played cat's cradles for a while this evening and I learned a new figure — one that Alak had vainly tried to recall. There were a score or more foxskins hanging on a line outside the house and another row outside the other house that lies alongside. The weather today was fine with a light air from the west; not exceptionally cold. I did not notice whether there was an aurora or not.

Saturday, February 7th

Our hostess turned out at 4:40 a.m., and I, who lay near the door got up at the same time. Gradually most of the others in the house turned out of their beds, Brick at 7 a.m., just in time for a breakfast of rice, *mukpaurat*, and tea. We left at 8 a.m. and travelling slowly reached Akuwak's house at noon. Our route lay along the edge of the land, which is here very low and flat. About 5 miles from Akuwak's we met and exchanged greetings with Kaglililuña, who was going to visit his traps. We passed his house about 2 miles further on. The entrance and passage were made of fairly symmetrical rectangular blocks of snow. Akuwak[6] seemed very pleased to see us. We took our flour inside and they at once used it to make some *mukpaurat*. Just as we were beginning our lunch the lady from the second house here brought in another batch of *mukpaurat* and lunched with us. Mrs. Akuwak then put two or three stitches in the seam of one of my boots. Her husband showed me the words I had written for him when [I was] here last (Nov. 1st) and received another lesson. He is a fine old man, quite 55 years of age I should imagine, but hale and hearty, with a cheery word for everyone, and his hospitality and liberality are almost a byword. We left again about 1:45 p.m. and arrived at our destination — a house a little way beyond Pitt Point inside Smith Bay — at 5:15 p.m. There are cutbanks between Akuwak's house and Kaglililuña's, but at Pitt Point they are much more striking. The house we found was very small, and inhabited by a middle-aged man and his wife, with a young married couple (an adopted son, I think, and his wife), a girl of about 6 and another (a boy?) about 2. The man greeted us very heartily and went to more trouble to see that I was perfectly comfortable than is usual with guests. We were given tea and *mukpaurat* immediately; he noticed that I took only a small sip of mine (it was hot), so he took up my cup and tasted it to see that it was alright. In the evening a set of four was made for cards, while I lay on the platform above and watched. There is a lake near here[7] where they have nets down, so we had frozen fish for supper — the same kind *anaqliq* as at Alak's. We turned in about 10 p.m., and had hardly got into bed when another sled arrived. Fortunately there was only one man with it bringing a load of stores from Barrow. I turned out and helped him unload. He had come too late for supper he was told; we had finished ours and gone to bed (yet there was a pile of *mukpaurat* beside the door ready for the morning). However, he would find some water in the tin on the stove. He took out his cup (it is usual to bring your own cup) and helped himself, then prepared to turn in. I had already done so, as also had Brick, who came outside when I announced what the noise outside was, shook hands, said "*alapa*" (it's cold), and went in to bed again straightaway; no one else had stirred. A running conversation was kept up with the new comer, enquiries about the latest news along the coast and at Barrow, how many foxes had been caught by different people, who was at *Iglora* [on Cooper's Island; see October 28th] etc., etc. The new man squeezed in somehow between me and the stove, I don't quite know how; it was a tight squeeze for the three of us, Brick, myself, and the man. He had a most distressing cough — tuberculosis, I fancy; the young wife had three or four scars on her back, which looked like partly healed syphilitic sores. The weather was practically the same as yesterday — a little colder perhaps, for I could not prevent my nose from freezing a little more. It is rather painful just at present for it is peeling. There was an interesting aurora this evening, a perfect bow, save that the arch was truncated at the two ends. The houses between the large double house in which we slept last night and here have all lines of foxskins hung up out-

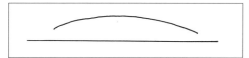

Figure 69. Bow-shaped aurora.

doors. All of them too have underground passages with well protected entrances and steps leading down. Our home tonight, however, has a small antechamber leading into a second, on the level of the ground outside, the second ends with a square hole in the floor, the outer edge protected by a substantial ledge. Three steps, each of about a foot, lead down to the true passage and this opens on to the house.

Sunday, February 8th

We turned out at 5 a.m. and with the help of two primus stoves (one the new man's) soon had breakfast. The young married couple with the two children were going to Barrow also, so we started together at 6:30. Brick forgot ten of his fox traps and a bag of frozen fish; his knife I picked up on the snow just as we were leaving, the second time I had thus rescued it, the other being yesterday at Akuwak's. Our companions had nine dogs, mostly young ones, we four, but all of ours in good training. Their sled was much heavier than ours, and I think does not run so easily. Our four dogs did better than their nine, so that for a considerable part of the way the wife, who carried her baby (of 2 years) on her back, rode on our sled. The little girl ran alongside the sled at intervals during the first part of the journey, but for most of it was tucked in their sled. We had numerous short stops to rest the dogs, and at 10:30 a.m. halted for over an hour to boil the kettle and make both coffee and tea. We had hard-bread with it, a little butter, and a little caribou fat. The trail was on the whole very good until we passed Cape Simpson, when the snow was rather soft. We gathered some wood before reaching the houses, for we had learned from our visitor of last night that one house only is inhabited and that is quite full, while the other two houses (one is Añopqana's) are empty.[8] As soon as we got there we turned in to one of the empty houses, and the woman lit a fire in the stove we brought and proceeded to make *mukpaurat*. Brick cut up firewood while I unloaded the sled and tied up the dogs. I was soon afterwards invited over to the inhabited house for tea by a young man named Neguvunna. I had nothing to take over so must remember to make him a small present as soon as possible. One of the women in the house was unwell — tuberculosis again, I think, and a little child had a very bad cold. There were four men, two women, and one child in this one small house, which seemed not otherwise notice-able. On returning I found that Brick and the others had already had some hard-bread and were preparing for a meal of tea and *mukpaurat*. My late host (Neguvunna) followed me over and had tea with us. We sat around until 9:30 p.m., when we had two frozen fish between us and then turned in. As usual I slept on the outside. The weather was much the same as it has been for several days, almost windless, the little there was being easterly. The temperature was not exceedingly cold, but the sky was a little cloudy. There was no aurora the three or four times I went outside during the evening, but the moon is nearly full — a great help to us when travelling a little late.

Monday, February 9th

I turned out at 6 a.m. and lit the fire. Our lady companion rose imme-diately and superintended the heating of rice boiled the night before last and the making of coffee. She also fried a little bacon — *mukpaurats* were baked last night. We had a good breakfast then packed up to go on to Igluraq. At 8:30 a.m. we got away and travelling slowly stopped at 11 at an empty house for lunch. Tala — the Eskimo — set the primus going and made coffee; then he warmed up a mixture of ham and biscuits with water in a frying pan — it made an excellent stew. This delayed us for an hour and a half that it was 6 p.m. before we reached *Igluraq*. My dogs travelled slowly, they did not show half the energy they displayed yester-day; nevertheless we made rather better progress than Tala's sled. The trail was good all the way; it runs along the edge of several sandspits, and passes near [several] racks. At *Iglura* there are two houses,[9] one of which was inhabited by an Eskimo, his wife, and two children, both boys, with a lad of about 14. The other house was empty but in such a state of disrepair that it would have proved a sorry resting place for the night; accordingly the family in the first house hospitably gave us shel-ter. We had two or three biscuits and a few *mukpaurat* at once, then Tala brought in his primus and set about preparing supper. The first course was frozen seal meat (raw), followed by cold boiled seal flipper, then came *mukpaurat* and tea. We were all ready for bed by this time. The house was very small, so the lad and I went out while the others made arrangements for sleeping. Outside a moderate breeze was blowing from the east, as during the day, and there was no aurora visible at this time; the moon was about full.

Tuesday, February 10th[10]

We all rose at 6 a.m., breakfasted early on *mukpaurat* and coffee, then loaded up. The man who is living in the house skinned a fox after we all turned in last night, then went outside to try Brick's snowshoes, made for him by Alak. The side of one was weak, and in running cracked right through. Its repair rests with Brick, not with the man, for of course it was an accident. This seems to be usual among the Eskimos. Alak's children broke the lashings of one of my skis while I was at [Cape] Halkett, and I had to repair it; at least I began to repair [it, but] when I was away again the dogs ate a lot of it, though how they reached it I don't know. My dogs travelled worse even than yesterday; the leader appeared to be sick. Tala very kindly gave me some of his whale meat, for most of what we brought the dogs had refused to eat. It seems that the blubber had become yellow and hard so that they could not chew it — they smelt it and turned away. The air was no colder than usual (-32° [Fahrenheit] Mr. Hopson told me in the evening), but I got cold and had my nose frozen stiff. It required first one hand then the other to unfreeze it, and in so doing my hands became very cold and I was afraid they too would freeze. Five minutes later we stopped at an empty house for lunch, just as my nose was freezing again and my hands too cold to thaw it out. However, Brick rendered me this service. It is interesting to watch how the dogs every time they lie down begin to lick the snow and ice from their paws; otherwise the feet would freeze. I had a slight attack of ague at this time and it required two hot cups of coffee and an extra *atigi* (deerskin shirt) to warm me up — after about an hour. Two other sleds turned up just after us and proceeded to lunch in the house. There was not room for all of us so the men of the second party stayed outside in the passage until we left. Slowly we travelled along and finally struck the land 2 or 3 miles north of Mr. Brower's shooting station. The dogs were very tired although well fed, and we left some of our things on the rack there. Close to Barrow, Tala had a cellar containing blubber and meat, and we stopped there to feed the dogs. About 9 p.m. — 13 hours after we left *Iglura* we reached Mr. Brower's house, where we received a hearty welcome. A huge ridge of snow had piled up between the store and the other houses, so that steps had to be cut up the sides. Mr. Brower said no news of any kind had been received from the east, either from our vessels or from the others near Herschel [Island]. He could not understand what had happened, for Mr. Stefansson had told him positively that he would be here either at Christmas or shortly afterwards. He thought it possible that the *Alaska* and *Mary Sachs* may have gone further east, the ice opening up during the gale which kept us on the island while the *Karluk* disappeared. After a good supper of goose and scones and coffee we turned in, I on my old bunk — a folding camp bed — in a corner of the store. There was a moderate breeze from the east all day and an auroral arch about 8 p.m.

Chapter 9. Archaeological Activities at Barrow

Dispatching Wilkins' movie film to New York — Writing families of Karluk personnel — Brick terminates service — Commencing study and sketching of Eskimo artifacts at Barrow — Arrival of McConnell from Camden Bay — Ordering supplies for trip to Camden Bay — Arrival of mail from Nome

Wednesday, February 11th, 1914

Breakfast at 8 a.m. following the usual routine. I sent Brick back for the things we left on the rack at the shooting station and stayed to write. Mr. Brower was polishing a mastodon or mammoth tusk. These he says have no commercial value, for the ivory splits and breaks. So many are being found that it is difficult to find a museum which will buy them. Tala, I found, is Mr. Brower's brother-in-law. I was proposing to give him a bag of flour, for we have been practically living on him for the last day or two. He came in during the morning and Mr. Brower told him. He said "What does the young man want to pay me for?" Mr. Brower scolded me for paying the Eskimos for their hospitality, following Mr. Stefansson's custom. Years ago, he said, they were offended if you did not stay with them and all that they asked in return was that you should do the like to them. Anything you got straight out from them you paid for, otherwise you took it as a matter of course that they should feed you and your dogs. Often the sled was never unloaded but just set up on a rack. When you did unload it they were very inquisitive and wished to handle and see everything, but they never asked for anything. I am afraid I have been erring greatly in this respect, following Mr. Stefansson's custom. Mrs. Brower took my big deerskin boots in hand and is having a pair of mits made from them; these are the boots that Stefansson had made here and that are so huge as to be unwearable. I went to Mr. Cram's in the afternoon to arrange about the dispatching of a parcel of cinematographic films Wilkins had sent away, but which had been returned for declaration.[1] While there I tried over the music of one or two of the Eskimo songs I had written and found one just a tone too high, the other a great deal out. Part of the evening I spent in writing, part in reading some *Daily Mirrors*[2] of Mr. Hopson's to gain a little news. Outside a cold easterly wind was blowing, but not very strong, and the atmosphere was rather foggy.

Thursday, February 12th

I have decided to remain here till after the mail goes out on March 1st, but to return for Brick's traps at once so that he can put them out here. He will do better work I think here, and I have only two dogs of my own so cannot return myself without buying more. Today we have been preparing for the trip back, for they [Brick's traps] are lying on the rack at the house on the other side of Smith Bay. I obtained some stores from Mr. Brower and others from Hansen's store, then spent some of the morning and all the afternoon at Cram's going through the Expedition's mail to try and gain the addresses of the men on the *Karluk* so as to write to their people and tell them exactly what has happened. Brick went to look for my black and white dog — the leader — which had disappeared. He tied both it and my white dog Victor together when we arrived, but they got loose somehow the next day. He did not find the leader, but in the evening learned from its original owner, a widow Tabluca, that it had been at her house in the morning but had disappeared, having followed, Kablucia[3] thought, Igawa's wife Anarogelo, who had gone to her husband to the reindeer herd. I had the sled partly loaded with our things and with a few things of Lester's, an Eskimo boy who is travelling up with us and has two dogs but no sled. However, in view of the disappearance of 'leader' and the uncertainty as to where he is, and the not altogether favourable condition of the weather, a moderate easterly wind drifting the snow a little, I decided not to leave tomorrow as I had intended. There was bright sunshine today casting quite a heavy shadow; the temperature was -28°. Mrs. Brower finished my mits this morning; the soles of the boots, which were excellent I gave to Brick's mother to resole his boots. Mr. Stefansson, so Mr. Hopson says, told him emphatically that the lad [Brick] should be outfitted at the expense of the Expedition, so I have agreed that whatever clothing he requires shall be paid for by the Expedition. He needs a new deerskin shirt, his father said, so if it is possible to obtain skins he is to have one.

Friday, February 13th

Brick enquired about 'leader' today but could learn nothing further. I spent the day indoors working at the Eskimo grammar. Outside the weather was fairly good, a light breeze blowing from the east. The atmosphere was clear and the temperature much as usual. Mr. Brower bought 23 foxskins today, making 73 for the week up to the present, an unusually high number. Mr. Cram came over to have a death-form filled in. A child died last night, Mr. Brower thinks of pneumonia, for which he gave some medicine. According to the new U.S. regulations, death certificates must contain the cause of death, names of the people who attended and prescribed medicine for the deceased; Mr. Brower had therefore to sign it.

Saturday, February 14th

Brick and I had breakfast before 7 a.m. and waited for the Eskimo Lester to turn up. He did not appear so Brick went over for him, returning about 8:30. We got away just after 9 a.m., but two village dogs persisted in accompanying us, so we had to return with them. A moderate easterly breeze was blowing and neither Brick nor Lester cared about travelling fearing it would grow stronger. The temperature was not very low, -28° F, I think. The rest of the day I was indoors working at Eskimo. There was an aurora in the evening — an arch overhead stretching north-south.

Sunday, February 15th

Brick decided to leave my service today. He says he does not like the work, it is too hard for him. Tomorrow I shall try and obtain another. I spent most of the day reading in the *Encyclopaedia Britannica* — except the afternoon when Mr. Brower showed me half a collection of old Eskimo implements and charms he sold for $500 to Mr. Stefansson to be sent to the Victoria Memorial Museum at Ottawa.[4] He sold the other half 2 years or so ago to Stefansson for the New York Museum.[5] The weather was clear all day, a light breeze blowing from the east. Brick made preparations in the evening to leave tomorrow morning, obtaining some things from Mr. Brower.

Monday, February 16th

Brick had an early breakfast and got away with Lester about 8:30 a.m.[6] I worked nearly all day at the curios Mr. Brower sold to Stefansson, making drawings of many of them, as also of a few which he retained. I am trying to draw all the different types that are represented — it will take a long time but is, I think, worth the labour. Mr. Brower told me this evening some of his experiences among the Eskimos — some of the shamanism he has seen, and his first experience of whaling. He certainly knows a very great deal about them. I went to Mr. Cram's in the afternoon and paid him $2 1/2 (obtained from Mr. Brower and entered up against the C.A.E.), the postage on Wilkins' cinematograph films that were sent back from New York for declaration and perhaps postage as well. I wished also to engage Roi and his wife Alice — Roi is the Eskimo teacher in the school — as interpreters. Roi said he would speak to his wife and let me know tomorrow afternoon when I go over. I am offering $15 a month (the pay Brick received) for 1 hour a day. Mr. Brower this evening bought his 1000th foxskin for this season. He has only seven bearskins — all poor — a very bad year. They are now hanging up in the store here and four or five women were scraping the fat off with their knives today while the men washed one or two skins in hot water. The wind increased a little during the day and made the snow drift somewhat, clouding the atmosphere. The temperature was not very low. The winter, both Mr. Brower and Mr. Cram say, has been very mild; only once or twice, the latter told me, has the thermometer registered below -40°.[7]

Tuesday, February 17th

A moderate northeast breeze made the snow drift a little and obscured the atmosphere. I spent the day sketching Eskimo implements except for a couple of hours in the afternoon when I went across to Cram's to see if Roi and Alice (the schoolteacher and his wife) would interpret for me. They preferred not to, Roi said, because he was kept too busy by Mr. Cram. The mail from [the] south is expected in Saturday or Sunday, though it does not go out again until March 1st. Mr. Brower had some *ugruk* (bearded seal — *phoca barbata*) skins in to be soaked then the fur scraped off; he is re-covering some of his *umiaks*, probably next month. The temperature was up to -7° F, the mildest it has been, I think, for months. Rheumatism, Mr. Cram says, is very prevalent this winter. The trapping around Barrow has been much more fruitful than elsewhere; the reverse has been the case for some years past. There is quite a broad expanse of open water a little way out to sea. Some of the Eskimos are sealing — taking their kayaks on small sleds out over the ice. Their weapons now are rather uninteresting — Winchester rifles and a pole with an iron hook to bring the seal in to the edge of the ice. The wooden houses here are 'lined' outside with fairly symmetrical rectangular blocks of snow resembling masonry; the roofs are covered with soft drift-snow. In some of the houses at least the passage is made of large rectangular blocks of ice — a great improvement on snow blocks being both more translucent and more permanent, for the snow always brushes off on to one's clothes and crumbles into powder with a small knock. There was an auroral arch this evening at 10 p.m. — north-south approximately.

Wednesday, February 18th

The wind increased somewhat and blew with moderate strength all day, blowing the snow about a great deal. I spent the day again in sketching implements, chiefly harpoon and arrow heads, and their stone points. In the afternoon I went over to Kablucia's house to enquire about my missing dog. The entrance to the house resembled a trap door and underground passage — but there was no door, only the square opening lined with ice blocks. This led down by two or three steps into a snow vestibule and this through a wooden door into an ice antechamber, from which a second door opened upon the house itself. A number of the school children guided me to the place — they took great delight in escorting me. The temperature was up to zero this afternoon — higher than yesterday.

Thursday, February 19th

McConnell with an Eskimo [Fred] turned up just after lunch.[8] He spent the night at Point Barrow[9] and came on this morning. He brought me a letter from Dr. Anderson saying that Stefansson had gone up the Mackenzie River and intended to make a trip out on the ice on his return (à la Mikkelsen apparently[10]) and subsequently — in the spring — to come west to Barrow. He further stated that as this would be the only chance for me to go east until late in the spring, I had better return now,[11] and that Brick should go with me according to Stefansson's suggestion, returning either with Stefansson later or by ship from Herschel [Island]. I went over to Mr. Cram's in the afternoon to get McConnell's letters and subsequently he, his Eskimo Fred, and I made a house of snow blocks (with half a dozen beams supporting the roof) in which to shelter the dogs. He had been very unfortunate on his journey, for four of his dogs are lame, their feet being worn and cut with the ice he encountered. All except one are in poor condition, though excellent dogs — Jumbo, Dub, Jimmy Britt, Denby, Charlie, and the sound dog Pickles. Jumbo is lame in three feet. McConnell brought the news that the *Elvira* (Pedersen's ship) had sunk and her crew had gone overland to the Yukon. The *Mary Sachs* is hauled up on the beach at Collinson Point [in Camden Bay] — the *Alaska* is about 1/4 mile out from shore and has a very small hole in her side. The Expedition people are living in a good hut on shore. Dr. Anderson stated in his letter that he expected to leave some time in February with Cox, O'Neill, and Chipman[12] for the International Boundary, apparently to survey along the coast to the east of that place. The weather outside today was not very pleasant, a moderately strong east-northeast wind driving clouds of snow along; the temperature was -16°.

Friday, February 20th

The weather today was no better than yesterday — worse if anything. I spent the whole of the time indoors sketching Eskimo implements, assisted in the evening by Mr. Brower. Only for some 2 hours in the afternoon McConnell and I examined the stores we possess at present and made out a list of things we shall require for the journey east. The temperature was -20° early this afternoon.

Saturday, February 21st

Similar weather again. The snow bank outside the store here must be 20 feet high and at the bottom probably 20 feet thick. Steps have to be cut up each side every day, and sometimes twice a day. Mr. Brower found some of his sleds covered up. An Eskimo brought my missing dog back,[13] but it got loose again, biting its rope. McConnell went over to Mr. Cram's in the morning and stayed all day. I worked all day at the collection of implements, for I am trying to make sketches of them all — or almost all[14] — before I leave. Mr. Brower and the boy Johnson (one of the crew of the *Transit* who is living with Mr. Brower) drew a number for me. The temperature was the same as yesterday — -20° F. At midnight there was a fine aurora.

Sunday, February 22nd

The weather outside improved a little, but the wind was still strong and the temperature the same as yesterday. I wrote two letters in the morning, one to Beuchat's mother and the other to McKinlay's people.[15] I have not the addresses of the rest of the scientific staff on the *Karluk*. For the rest of the day I was drawing sketches, assisted by Johnson and Mr. Brower again. I am hoping to finish them by Wednesday. There was no aurora visible up to 11:30 p.m.

Monday, February 23rd

McConnell busied himself in ordering stores for our trip back and in enquiring for deer legs and deerskins for sale. He gave 13 skins away on the journey down [from Camden Bay] — four each to Alak's and Aksiatak's wives, four to the aged dame who lives with Añopqana, and one to Añopqana. He had none left on which to sleep and I have only two, a sheepskin (sewn together) and a deerskin. I want a new pair of deerskin boots and so does he. I spent the day on the Eskimo implements, assisted again by Johnson. In the morning, however, I went over to the village to bring back my dog 'leader', who broke his chain on Saturday and made off home. The weather was colder — the temperature -25°, but the wind was not so strong. The Eskimos have some nets out on the ice for seals.

Tuesday, February 24th

Another day similar to yesterday but with the temperature down to -30°; a mild breeze blew from the northeast. I spliced a couple of eye-loops on to the trace of my sled and spent the day otherwise in continuing the drawing of the implements. McConnell's dogs, which were in a very bad state when he arrived, have greatly improved, but Jumbo is still very bad[16] and [Jimmy] Britt is thin. My two dogs seem to be in good condition.[17] There was a very fine aurora about midnight.

Wednesday, February 25th

The weather was much the same as yesterday. It began with a temperature of about -30° at 8 a.m., rose to -22° by 2 p.m., and was down to -28° by 7 p.m. A light easterly breeze lasted through the day. Mrs. Brower made me a pair of deerskin boots (*tutalik*) today, and Mrs. Hobson [Hopson] is making a pair for McConnell. Some of the Eskimos are securing quite a number of seals; one man today got nine I think it was. I finished sketching the implements in the collection Mr. Brower sold to Stefansson for the Museum at Ottawa.[18] Brick arrived about 9:30 p.m., having taken 2 days from Pitt Point, coming today from Añopqana's house about 8 miles this side of Cape Simpson — a distance of about 40 miles; his sled, of course, was very light and he had seven dogs, but it was a good day's journey for a boy nevertheless, even riding on the sled most of the way.

Thursday, February 26th

A fine clear day out of doors with but a very light breeze from the east and a temperature which started at -25° at 8 a.m., rose to -16° at 1 p.m., and dropped again to -28° at 8 p.m. The day was chiefly noticeable for the arrival of the mail. There were no letters for the Expedition (but telegraphic news from Canille[19] for V. S. [Vilhjalmur Stefansson]). It [the mail] caused a considerable stir in the community for there is quite a considerable correspondence between the Eskimos here (the young men and schoolboys) and the Eskimos to the south, especially at Point Hope. A Nome newspaper dated December 7th said that a boat with the name *Karluk* on it had been washed up on the beach the day before at a place a little south of Point Hope after a heavy gale. Whether the news is authentic or not no one knows for certain, but if it is, the prospect of the *Karluk* being safe seems very remote.[20] There was a fine auroral arch at midnight. The atmosphere was beautifully clear all day.

Friday, February 27th

The wind was the same as yesterday, a light breeze from the east, but the temperature was much colder — it was down to -38° at 5 p.m. We are now ready to leave in the morning for the ships.[21] The dogs are not too good — Jumbo especially is very bad still — his belly was all frozen and the hair dropped off. The atmosphere became a little foggy in the afternoon and but few stars were visible in the evening.

Chapter 10. Sled-journey to Camden Bay

Stop-off at Point Barrow — Stops at Iglora *and* Itkiaq — *Across Smith Bay — At Añopqana's — Stop at Aksiatak's — Shooting one of the dogs — Reaching Thetis Island — Meeting Billy Natkusiak — Leffingwell's survey posts — Natkusiak describes Stefansson's encounter with the* Kagmalit — *Howe Island — Blizzard at Tigvariaq Island — Reaching Leffingwell's house on Flaxman Island — Arrival at Camden Bay*

Saturday, February 28th, 1914

I posted some letters[1] at Mr. Cram's in the morning and signed the bills we had run up at the two stores. After lunch we harnessed up the dogs and set out. We are taking six of Mrs. Brower's dogs to her brother Asuaq, so that I had eight dogs (two of my own) to draw my sled — McConnell had his six dogs, Jumbo and Jimmy Britt with covers on their backs to keep them warm; his other dogs seemed in good shape. We are heavily loaded,[2] for we have about 300 lbs of seal meat. The dogs pulled well, however, so that we covered the distance to Point Barrow — 9 miles ? — in about 2 1/2 hours — from 1:30 to 4 p.m. The weather was splendid, a very light breeze coming from the east which almost died away at sunset — a clear sky and bright sunshine. The sun rises before 8 o'clock now so that we have long days to look forward to. At Point Barrow we stayed at Añukapsaña's house, which formerly belonged to Mr. Brower and so is fine and large.[3] He and his people gave us a hearty welcome, and helped us to unload our sleds and put some of the things on the rack. Soon we were dining on boiled seal meat, and shortly afterwards oatmeal, biscuits, and tea. Añukapsaña has caught 17 foxes, his son 19, and a boy of about 11 (his son?) 5. McConnell had a slight headache so lay down all the evening while I played cat's cradles and learned two new figures. These are real Barrow people — *Utkeavigmiut* — and have different names and songs for many figures to what the *Nunatagmiut*, e.g. Alak etc., have. Brilliant aurora — several concentric arches crossing the sky, the brightest in the middle — at 10 p.m.

Sunday, March 1st

We got away about 9:30 a.m. The weather was dull, a little snow falling, with a very light breeze from the northeast and a mild temperature. I had Mrs. Brower's six dogs and my own two, and for the first mile I could not keep them in check behind the other team. Consequently I gave McConnell my two dogs to add to his team.[4] In this way we kept fairly well together until 12:30, when we reached the house on the sandspit at which Tala etc., Brick, and I had lunch on the way down [February 10th].[5] We stayed here 10 minutes to rest the dogs then set out again. From the very beginning of this second start my team lagged behind. The best dog, Jack, was bleeding in the near hind foot, and a bitch, Foxy, became totally lame, and I had to unhitch it and let it run alongside. The trail was not very good, being full of small ridges, so that from 2 p.m. till

5:30 p.m., when I reached *Iglora*, I had to push on the sled the whole time. McConnell, who ran ahead the whole way, had arrived with his team about 1 1/2 hours earlier[6] and had rice boiled and tea made. Akuvak and his family were staying in one house on their way to Barrow, and they invited us over to dine. So we had a good meal of rice and figs mixed, biscuit and bacon hash, *mukpaurat* and tea. I played cat's cradles with Akuvak and his son and learned a new trick and a song to an old one. Then we retired to the other house and soon turned in. There was a fine auroral arch at 9 p.m. in the north, stretching at right angles to the north line. The wind — a mild breeze — became almost true north during the day and seemed to increase a little, but it decreased again in the evening. Our lunch ration today was figs and peanuts. McConnell seems to fancy it, but it makes me very thirsty.

Monday, March 2nd

The Eskimo Fred turned out and got breakfast — porridge, tea, and *mukpaurat* and some unfrozen bread baked for us by Mr. Hopson. Akuvak and his people were leaving early, and the son poked his head in the door about 6:30 a.m. and handed Fred a plate of *mukpaurat*. We left at 9 a.m. The trail was not good, but a little better than yesterday. My sled was about 100 lbs lighter, through the dogs eating 50 lbs for their day's ration, and McConnell taking another 50 lbs on his sled. The lame dog started out on three legs, running loose beside the sleds, but it got in the way and began to run on all fours so I harnessed it up. It pulled fairly well all day, though it limped a little. About 12:45 p.m. we reached the empty house[7] where I lunched when travelling with Tala, and finally arrived at Añutaksana's place,[8] at Itkiaq,[9] at 3:30 p.m. I blistered one of my feet rather badly — a new boot I had made by Mrs. Brower turning over on its side. A light east-northeast breeze in the morning had increased a little by noon, but seemed to abate again in the evening. There were two auroral arches in the north at 9 p.m., not very brilliant. Neguvunna invited us over to tea, and Fred and I went. Three of them came and dined with us on rice mixed with chicken soup — bread and coffee. After dinner Fred and I fed the dogs while McConnell, who cooked the rice, washed up the dishes. We turned in about 9:30 p.m. The temperature seemed not to be very low, though our noses persisted in trying to freeze, probably because we were travelling against the wind. There was brilliant sunshine all day.

Tuesday, March 3rd

A light east-northeast breeze blew all day, but the temperature did not seem very low. The atmosphere was somewhat foggy, though the sun shone out for a couple of hours about noon. About 9:30 p.m. there was an auroral arch in the north. Fred lit the primus about 6 a.m. and boiled some mush and fried a little bacon. A man and his wife invited themselves over and breakfasted with us. They came yesterday and are leaving tomorrow on their way to Barrow. We got away at 8:30 a.m., skirted

Figure 70. Maps showing route from Barrow to Thetis Island (a), and from Thetis Island to Camden Bay (b), February 28 - March 12, 1914.

the shore for 4 hours, then fell in with two sleds of Eskimos (Lester and his people) also on their way to Barrow.[10] They had a mast erected on one sled and a number of foxskins strung on to it. They had stopped to light the primus and make tea, as seems to be the usual Eskimo fashion. The trail now struck across the bay [Smith Bay]. Travelling all the way from Barrow has not been good for the snow has drifted across the track, leaving small ridges — also the surface is hard and crystalline and wears the feet of the dogs. It took us 5 hours to cross the bay, so that we did not reach the house of Lester's father[11] until 5:30 p.m. We had expected to find it empty but were agreeably surprised to see dogs outside. Four people had just arrived — the very ancient dame who was living with Añopqana, and the other three from the small house beside the large house half way between Akuwak's and [Cape] Halkett. Both the small and the large house are said to be empty now. Like others we had met they were on their way to Barrow. The house in consequence was warm and comfortable, for they had brought a stove and wood, besides having a primus. The old lady made a great fuss over McConnell, who had presented her with four deerskins (from Stefansson) on his way down [to Barrow]. The young woman (with a little girl), wife of the young man who seemed to run things, was the fair half-caste (?) girl I have noticed two or three times before. Then there was a bald-headed, middle-aged man, who was also an old acquaintance.[12] At dinner the young woman when pressed to eat said that she must not eat much because she had a little child; at least that is Fred's interpretation of a remark she made. We turned in about 10 p.m.

Wednesday, March 4th

The people were astir before 5 a.m., and we had mush (oatmeal) and biscuits and bacon. They were away by 7, and we at 7:30. The dogs travelled slowly, so that we did not reach Akuwak's (Aquvaq) house until 11 a.m. Here Asuaq and his wife, his brother, and Amakuk are staying, and here I handed over to him his dogs and cached my sled on the rack.[13] We stayed for lunch, and the lady and her husband from next door came in also — Amakuk was away looking after his traps. An hour's travelling from there brought us to Kaglililuña's (*Nunatagmiut*) house[14] — a large double house with a smaller one alongside. In the smaller one lives the pleasant young married woman we met November 3rd, when I particularly noticed her bright and cheerful disposition. We put up at the larger one (Kaglililuña's), where we received the usual hearty welcome. The weather was beautifully fine and clear all day, with brilliant sunshine. Travelling against the wind it was cold, and we had constantly to thaw out our noses, but really the temperature could not have been very low. There was only the faintest breath of air from the east. I spent most of the evening playing cat's cradles. At 10 p.m. there was an auroral arch, as usual in the north. Kaglililuña had a deerskin mask to protect his face from the cold. There were two slots for the eyes, none for the nose, and one for the mouth. He said it was very effective. The lady of the house did some sewing for McConnell — removed the fringe from the bottom of his fur coat and put it round the hood.

Thursday, March 5th

Kaglililuña and another man staying in the house were up before 4 o'clock, had a light breakfast, and went away, to their traps probably. We rose between 6 and 7 a.m., had a good breakfast, and got away shortly before 9 a.m.[15] The sled was very heavy, the trail much as it has been all along, and two at least of the dogs, Jumbo and Jimmy Britt, have bleeding feet. Shortly before noon we reached the two houses, one the very large one in which I have stayed two or three times.[16] Now both are empty, though a number of foxes are suspended from a prolonged upright of a rack, and on the rack itself are several cases. The trail then leaves the edge of the land and runs further out in the ice. We passed about 1:30 p.m. the house where Asuaq stayed for a time, and about 4 p.m. Kanak's house, now empty also, from which it was only about an hour's travel to Añopqana's. We found him and his wife at home, with the paralysed woman and her husband, Samuel and Aiva (whose Eskimo name is Iviqunna) and their child Josephine, another young man, Ikpik, the housewife and two young lads. Shortly after we arrived came a young woman and a boy, who were living when last I saw them at the large house (now empty) before mentioned. Aiva is noticeably recovering her voice, which was reduced to a whisper through a cold last winter. Kunaloak's house here is empty — he and his people being still at the lake. The weather was fine all day, the atmosphere extremely clear, and but a faint breath of air from the west — not enough to constitute a breeze. The old lady (Tupingaluk) whom we met on her way to Barrow [March 3rd] turns out to be Aiva's grandmother (*anaña*), and the housewife, Aiva's mother and Tupingaluk's daughter; the young woman who arrived after us is Aiva's sister, and the boy her son — at least he called her mother.

Friday, March 6th

No one stirred until 7 a.m. when nearly everyone turned out. We loaded the sled before breakfast and got away about 9 a.m.[17] McConnell preferred to try the trail across the land to the house Itaqluq, Otoaiyuk, Brick, and I built [Iglu II]. We followed a fresh trail, Ikpik's I think, which brought us out a long way to the right (west) of the house. It then turned sharply to the left, apparently towards the house, but we kept on steering roughly southeast, which we thought would bring us to Alak's [Iglu I]. It was about 3 p.m. when we came to the sea, for the dogs travelled very slowly and we had to rest them repeatedly. Moreover we had been delayed half an hour soon after starting through the two covers for Jumbo and Jimmy Britt being left on the rack. Fred ran back for them. At 5 p.m. the sun set, but it was moderately light for an hour afterwards. McConnell walked ahead with the lantern, Fred and I pushed on the sled. We were making only about 2 miles an hour. Twice the sled upset, once in a big crack about 3 feet wide; fortunately it was not deep, and the ice in it was solid. We had seen no trails since about 4 p.m. and were not sure of striking near the house. The dogs were about played out — we had fed them twice with blubber; we ourselves had eaten only figs and peanuts since morning. Just before 9 p.m. we decided to camp for the night. Having no tent we laid three skins on the ice on the lee side of the sled, and our sleeping bags above, and one skin on top. Our bags made pillows, and one side of the sled cover was turned over to make a wind-break. The two leading dogs, Pickles and Leader, we released from their harness and chained to two axe handles driven into the snow which covered the ice, for both these dogs bite rope and harness. Then we crawled into our sleeping bags, with our clothes on, huddled together, and drew the mouths over our heads. I was cold all night and slept very little; the other two fared better. The weather had been very clear all day, with a light air from the west; the temperature seemed fairly low. My clothes were wet with perspiration; probably the others were also, for it was hard work pushing on the sled. There was a brilliant aurora from about 6 p.m. — first the usual arches then whorls which slowly developed again into arches.

Saturday, March 7th

We turned out about 8:15 a.m., reloaded the sled and set out again. Jumbo and Jimmy Britt, especially the latter, are in very bad shape. A cutbank was visible through the glasses and we directed the sled thither. As we drew near we recognized the point [Saktuina Point] as being to the east of Alak's house, consequently we had crossed all the trails thither without observing them in the dark. Two hours brought us to Alak's and Aksiatak's, for the dogs made about 2 1/2 miles per hour. Here we received a hearty welcome and soon had a good meal of *mukpaurat*, tea and rice, the only things we had eaten since yesterday morning. Aksiatak was in, the women and the children, and one after another came Itaqluq, Jimmy Asecaq, and Alak. I was very tired and slept most of the afternoon. Dinner — potatoes and *mukpaurat* and bread and tea — was served about 7 p.m. Itaqluq promised to bring my round tent and the stove, which are in the house on the other side [of Harrison Bay, at Iglu II], over here and cache them on the rack. The weather was much the same as yesterday only colder. My nose froze every few yards and is now rather painful; once or twice I had to thaw out my cheeks, forehead, and chin. McConnell froze his nose a little, and Jimmy said he had frozen his cheek a little today. There was a faint auroral arch about 10 p.m.

Sunday, March 8th

I slept under Alak's platform, McConnell, who is better acquainted with Aksiatak and his family, slept in my old place in Aksiatak's room. I put my things together in the morning [and] divided up the powder and shot between Alak and Aksiatak. Being Sunday the ladies and children made their toilets — dressed their hair etc. Otoaiyuk fixed up a pair of deerskin slippers for me while Qapqana made my outside deerskin boots a little smaller. McConnell wrote all the morning and repaired his stove in the afternoon and the dog chains. I wrote out two cat's-cradle figures and fixed up my things — boots etc. — ready to leave tomorrow. Otoiaiyuk said that when Stefansson comes east [*sic*] she will be very glad to do all his sewing for him, because she is very grateful for the skins he sent. Of the four skins Qapqana received, one was a bad one and apparently Otoiayuk has been crowing over her. Otoiaiyuk is the one discordant element in this house; she seems to be liked by no one. The weather today appeared to resemble that of yesterday; a clear sky, bright sunshine, light air from the west. In the evening, I did not see any auroral

arch. My tent and stove, which are still on the other side [at Iglu II], Itaqluq has promised to cache on the rack here. On one rack then there is the
big rectangular tent with two of its poles and the two fish nets; on the
other — the one which is in constant use — are the long pole to the big
rectangular tent, the pole to the round tent, a pair of snowshoes, a pair of
skis, the grub-box, containing a pair of (worn) sealskin boots, deerskin
mits (one pair, not much good), large cod-line for the round tent, about
30 yards of lance warp, an aluminum teapot, and a pint bottle of alcohol
(3/4 full).[18]

Monday, March 9th

Alak, Aksiatak, and Asecaq went off to their traps early in the morning before the rest of us were up. Itaqluq followed about 9 a.m. Alak has
now 22 foxes, Asecaq 5, Aksiatak 9, and Itaqluq 37. We packed the sled
after breakfast, adding to our original load a rectangular tent, a stove,
sled-cover, snow-shovel, and two or three small things.[19] We left Qapqana and Otoiyuk about 10 lbs rice, 6 lbs or so of sugar, and a considerable quantity of tea. They are short of food now too, though Alak has a
little flour at Añopqana's. At 10:25 a.m. we got away, after saying
goodbye to the women and children. We had teased Kukpuk the day
before, saying that we would take her with us. She was half afraid when
we said goodbye that we might do so, and fled into the corner of Alak's
(the inner room). The dogs made slow progress — hardly 2 1/2 miles an
hour. Jimmy Britt and Jumbo both had *mukluk's* (sealskin) boots on their
feet (each dog one), for they were worn and bleeding through the hard
crystalline snow. Fred lost his watch on the ice the other day, after we
slept on the ice and were making for Alak's, but as our trail today coincided for a long distance with our trail then we kept a lookout and
McConnell found it.[20] Jimmy Britt was played out by the time we
reached Atigeruq,[21] the point of the peninsula on which Alak's and Aksiatak's house lies, about 12 miles away. Here there is a pole erected and
plenty of driftwood on the beach. So we erected the tent, put Jumbo and
Jimmy Britt inside and made everything as comfortable as possible for
the night. I cooked rice (mixed two tins of soup with it) while McConnell fixed up the dogs and piled snow round the tent, and Fred cut up
firewood. Behind the stove we thawed out the seal meat for the dogs.
Jimmy Britt may last another day, but it is doubtful; his tail and side
have rotted where he was frozen. It is a shame that he was brought up
here at all, for he has never carried much fur — not nearly enough for a
climate like this. The weather today began by being foggy, with a light
southwesterly breeze. The fog cleared off about 10 a.m., but the breeze
remained until we were camping, when it suddenly swung round to the
east and steadily increased in strength; by 9 p.m. a stiff breeze was blowing and we anticipate a blizzard. The temperature has felt low all day.
Qapqana made me a deerskin mask to protect my face, with two slots for
the eyes and another for the mouth. It worked fairly well today.[22] I did
not notice any aurora.

Tuesday, March 10th

A quiet day in camp.[23] Jimmy Britt was evidently on his last legs and during the night McConnell had to take him out and shoot him. A strong east wind blew all day and we wonder if it is the beginning of a blizzard. I slept badly, being cold — in the feet especially, so lay down in the afternoon and had a 3-hour nap. It was McConnell's turn to cook; after breakfast — prepared by Fred — (mush and bread and tea) he boiled beans and mince and made slapjacks. We thus had an admirable dinner at noon and a supper of boiled rice and slapjacks about 7 p.m. During the day we kept Jumbo and Denby in the tent, for outside the temperature seemed rather low. In the evening the sky was clear and a full moon shining, but we saw no aurora. On the whole the day passed quickly enough, for numerous small duties — drying clothes etc. — helped to occupy our time. I found a little interesting reading in Ker's *Mediaeval English Literature* (Home Universal Library), a book McConnell brought along.[24]

Wednesday, March 11th

A strong breeze southwest was blowing, when Fred turned out at 5 a.m., and lasted all day. We got away at 8:25 a.m. and travelled until 4:50 p.m., with several short halts to rest the dogs. Jumbo is now wearing two *mukluks* and two covers; Dub seems a little seedy also. There were no soft snow-drifts, but the surface was very hard; we crossed numerous patches of glare ice strewn with nodules and spicules of compact crystalline snow. About 4 p.m. we came to a line of stakes with several sled trails following them. Fred says that there is a whale out under the ice and three polar bears come to feed on it — the trail leads out to it. We carried a little wood on the sled and as soon as the tent was erected I turned in and heated beans and rice and made coffee — the beans were cooked yesterday and allowed to freeze, while the rice was left over from this morning. The sky was clear and the sun seemed to be trying to recover a little of its heat, but the temperature was moderately low nevertheless. We turned in as soon as dinner was over and the dogs fed, so that I had no opportunity of observing whether there was an aurora. We have gone perhaps 20 miles today, for the dogs are pulling a load of about 700 lbs.

Thursday, March 12th

The strong breeze of yesterday died away in the night and we had almost perfect calm all today, for only the faintest breath of air came from the west. I called Fred at 5:30 a.m.,[25] and he lit the primus and put the pot on, then went to sleep again. A little while afterwards when I put my head outside of my sleeping bag, the tent was full of steam. I called Fred again and he started up, took the pot off, and proceeded to light the fire, but the steam condensed as hoar-frost over everything. Half an hour later when McConnell stirred out he was astonished at the hoar-frost over his sleeping bag; he had never seen such a deposit, he said. We did not tell him the cause, and he still imagines it was a more or less natural phenomenon. We set out at 8:43 a.m., and travelled with several short stops until about 5:20 p.m., when we reached the island on which we first set foot last September after leaving the *Karluk*. Its name is *Amalektoq* [= *Amauliktok* or Thetis Island]. On a high crag of ice McConnell and Fred set up a stick, when they came west for me — about a mile to the west of the island. Our course today lay over a considerable number of patches of glare ice, some smooth and free from snow, others covered with streaks and blotches of hard snow. We crossed too several mud flats, where the sled could hardly be moved when an inch or two of soil was left exposed. The sun was really a little warm, its light clear and bright casting a moderately dark shadow; I felt quite grateful to it, although my eyes in the afternoon became a trifle painful, warning me that it will be necessary to take to glasses during the spring and that I had better start tomorrow. At the island we found a snowhouse and several sled tracks leading to it. We wonder if Billy Nekusiak,[26] an Eskimo who lives a little further east, comes here to trap. Three nuts from the sled-runner are broken off, and we had to remove their bolts this morning, as they were projecting below the steel shoe and dragging. McConnell officiated as cook tonight and shaved as soon as dinner was over. The temperature could not have been very low today.

Friday, March 13th

A moderately strong west wind blew all day, and the temperature seemed very low. I called Fred at 5:45 a.m., and we had our usual breakfast of mush (oatmeal) and bread and tea. Then the sled was loaded up and we finally got away at a quarter to nine.[27] We followed the trail that led from the house eastward, and it brought us to *Oliktoq* [Oliktok Point] at noon. So far I had travelled with but one skin shirt, but I became so cold that I had to get McConnell and Fred to partially unload the sled and enable me to get my second skin shirt out of my sleeping bag[28] — about the third time this winter that I have worn both. *Oliktoq* has a tall post with a small cross-piece on top like a vane; it was near here that we camped when we came ashore from the *Karluk* [September 28 to October 2]. An hour later saw us at Beechey Point,[29] where we found Billy Nekusiak's tent-hut. A little while afterwards Billy himself turned up; he had been about 6 miles inland trapping. He is a youngish man, formerly Stefansson's servant during his 3 years sojourn along the coast with Dr. Anderson, 1908-1912. Apparently he gave great satisfaction, for he showed us a copy of a payment receipt to him made out by V. Stefansson. In addition to $100 a year, which was his proper salary, and three-quarters [of the] skins of all animals killed except caribou and seals, he was given a skin boat (if he cared to get it from Langton Bay[30]), a team of five dogs, a .30-30 Winchester [rifle], a silk tent, and various miscellanies. Both McConnell and I noticed that it was signed V. Stefansson, Stefansson Arctic Expedition.[31] Nekusiak comes originally from Teller (Port Clarence) and is trapping up here; he has already over 40 foxes.

When McConnell came west Nekusiak was living to the east of here, but he moved westward about 4 days later. Consequently he could give us no news. His 'tent-house' here consists of walls of rectangular snow-slabs with his tent or sled-cover over the top, resting on some cross-pieces of wood. The tent-house on the island where we slept last night was made by him also, but lacks now its tent roof. I boiled rice and made tea, while Fred and McConnell put up the tent, turning out to shovel snow round the sides. Fred kept a big fire in the tent for some time to try to dry it, then I made slapjacks and boiled a packet of mince meat for supper. One of Nekusiak's dogs, I failed to remark, his leader, is of a size altogether unusual up here. There was a fine double auroral arch directly overhead at 10 p.m., the two lying so close together that their united breadth was little greater than that of a rainbow. Both were dazzling white, and a faint milky layer united them.

Saturday, March 14th

Fred turned out exceptionally early — before 5 o'clock — and lit the fire. I was very glad for I had been lying awake since 3 a.m., being cold. A moderately strong breeze was blowing from the north, a *Kannannaq* or sea breeze; but it shifted round more to the west during the day. The sun was a trifle dimmed and the temperature was low, and I was glad to wear two fur shirts and my 'mask'. The bottom of the latter froze to the top of a shirt, and I had considerable difficulty in removing it. We set out at 8:15 a.m. and travelled east-by-south over a good trail on the lee side of a chain of islands. First we left Beechey Point[32] on our right — a low bluff; from this point the shore recedes and a chain of islands 'Return Reef'[33] begins. Most — if not all of the islands — have sign posts erected upon them by Leffingwell, who has been surveying the coast. At 12:40 p.m. we overtook Nekusiak,[34] who travelled much faster than we did, boiling a teapot over a log fire amidst the snow. We 'stood by' for half an hour or so and had lunch, then set off again, Nekusiak again soon vanishing ahead with his sled. About 3:20 p.m. we passed the remains of an Eskimo hut and rack, and near by a sign post with a black-rimmed cross board on the top — a sort of 'mourning visiting card'. Half an hour later on a low sandspit we came upon Nekusiak, who had set up his tent and was warming it up with a great fire in his wood stove.[35] We set up our tent alongside and McConnell, whose day it was to cook, turned in to boil rice and make tea. Nekusiak was with Stefansson on the journey to Victoria Land. He described their meeting with one of the 'new' Eskimos — a *Kagmalit* — on the ice. He watched through a glass while Stefansson and another Eskimo approached the stranger. The latter stood up — he was a big man — carrying a seal spear and a long snow knife made of 'pieces of a rifle'. As Stef[ansson] and his companion approached the *Kagmalit* held the knife pointed outwards ready to make a lunge, but after a few words had been spoken he turned the point inwards. Stef[ansson]'s companion held both arms up to show he carried no weapon. The *Kagmalit*, Nekusiak says, spend the winter sealing on the ice and the summer, when the snow is off the ground, caribou hunting inland. In winter their homes are right out on the ice, in spring and autumn when the ice is unsafe, they live on the shore. Nekusiak is left-handed, the first Eskimo I remember to have noticed with this peculiarity.[36] In voice and manner he recalls Stefansson, especially when speaking English, which he does very well compared with other Eskimos up here. Another 5 or 6 days should see us at the ships. Poor Jumbo wears his two covers and two *mukluks* all the time, and still one of his other feet leaves a blood stain with every impress. We keep him in the tent at night — tonight in Nekusiak's, who is sleeping himself in ours. Jumbo's frozen belly must be very painful when partly thawing out beside the stove and later freezing again. Denby too seems unwell — he has hardly worked at all since we left Barrow. None of our dogs seem to fancy the whale meat Nekusiak has, so tonight we made them mush.

Sunday, March 15th

Fred got breakfast as usual and we set out at 9 a.m. Nekusiak took the tent and poles on his sled — a good 100 lbs. A strong southwest wind was blowing and driving the snow before it. The dogs travelled well, helped by the wind, for our course was east-by-south roughly. We were making for a rack on the mainland, where Stef[ansson], Dr. Anderson, and Nekusiak camped 3 years ago. McConnell had cached some stores on it.[37] The drifting snow prevented us from seeing far, but Nekusiak knew the course well. We passed the mouth of the *Kopauruq* [Kuparuk] River and a little after struck the land — an island. Skirting this we continued on and should have seen the rack in a clear atmosphere but as it was we passed it and did not discover our mistake until we reached a sign-post 2 1/2 miles away — a sign-post with three cross boards on a sandspit off Heald Point.[38] This was at noon, so we camped, had a light

Figure 71. Sign-post on sandspit near Heald Point.

lunch of biscuits and chocolate and a little ham and tea, then Nekusiak and Fred (Ailuat[39] — a *Kiñmiuñ*) (*Kiñmiutaq* is something from the *Kiñmiut* — a skin or something; *utkeavigmiutaq* similarly — a Barrow man is *Utkeavigmiuñ*) went across for the stores — chiefly hard-bread and sugar. We dined early at 5 p.m., rice and cocoa and hard-bread, with nine 'jumbo' biscuits made by the cook at the ships [in Camden Bay] and cached by McConnell. McConnell stitched up his boots in the evening; he found it less easy to imitate Eskimo sewing than he had imagined. Nekusiak said the *Kagmalit* use copper needles (he did not see any bone ones) and thimbles of bone, or thick sealskin, or the skin from the forehead of the musk-ox. They use musk-ox skins on beds, obtaining them from the mainland east of the Coppermine River. Nekusiak saw musk-ox tracks the first time he visited Langton Bay, but they are rare, he says, west of the Coppermine [River]. He told us that the *Kagmalit* would not drink tea and did not like *mukpaurat*, and gave an amusing account of how he posed as a magician, producing *mukpaurat* by boiling dough in seal-oil. A crowd gathered round, and some tasted a tiny fragment a little larger than a pin head, and took some out to other houses to show. They asked him what skin his woollen shirt was, and he said raven's skin. Stefansson said "What lie is this you are telling them?" and Nekusiak said "That all right!" Nekusiak said "I laugh all the time I there." They do not hesitate to wear deerskin clothes and use deerskin things in the winter while occupied in sealing, and sealskin things in summer when caribou hunting. He saw them playing cat's cradles as an evening game, making figures similar to what the Barrow and other people make. He told us how he and Stefansson after spending two months in Victoria Land [now Victoria Island] returned to the mainland near Cape Lyon in May. They came to a narrow lead of open water. Stefansson put coal-oil can, teapot, and various miscellanies under the sled and paddled it across with the tent pole; the water came up to his waist. Nekusiak pulled [the] sled back with [a] line, put some of [the remaining] load on, and Stefansson pulled it over. The dogs swam, with a line on their collar. Lastly Nekusiak sat on the sled and was drawn across; [he] being heavier than Stef[ansson], the water came up to his shoulders. On the other side they set up tent, lit primus, and sat over it to dry their clothes — these being deerskin, the hair came out. That night they could not sleep on account of the cold, but drank tea and ate boiled bear and seal meat (Nekusiak had shot a polar bear). When the sun rose they hung up their clothes outside and slept soundly. Nekusiak saw no fish-nets, labrets (or holes for labrets), or pipes among the *Kagmalit* or the people of Victoria Land. A *Kagmalit* boy about Kaiyutaq's [Brick's] age [15 or 16] saw him smoking, talk, then exhale the smoke and wanted to try. He was very sick afterwards and thought he was going to die. Nekusiak told him to try again; apparently he posed as a great magician there. The southwest wind abated in the afternoon, and but a light breeze blew in the evening. The temperature also became milder — it was cold in the morning. Nekusiak said that the *Kagmalit* and Vict[oria] Is[land] Esk[imos] use lake-ice windows, though there are plenty of *ugruk* [bearded seals] there. They carry the ice about with them as part of the house furniture. The *igalaq* [window] of Alaska and [the] Mackenzie River is made by scraping [the] little intestine (*iñallu*) of bearded seal or sometimes polar bear. South of Barrow sometimes walrus intestine was used. Occasionally the big intestine was employed, but it is not good, being too thick. The hair seal's intestine is too thin and frail — only good to eat.

Monday, March 16th

I called Fred at a quarter to five by misreading my luminous watch as a quarter to six. However he turned out and soon had a good fire burning. A moderately strong east wind was blowing, but it rapidly died down. We started out at 8 a.m. and reached our destination 2 miles east of Howe Island at 3:15 p.m. The atmosphere was foggy, so that the sun was hardly once visible after 9 a.m. Under these conditions it was difficult to distinguish differences of level[40] and it was impossible to pick out a good trail. This may explain why we found the going much harder today than it has been for several days, though perhaps it was really so. McConnell's extraordinary positions as he stumbled about in the snow ahead of the sled were very amusing, but I suppose we were all alike. Nekusiak forged ahead almost as soon as we left, and after midday vanished from sight altogether. He went inside Howe Island, we outside. The north side of Howe Island consists of a bluff about 15 feet high and 200 yards long. Leffingwell has set up a sign-post on it with four cross-pieces, evidently No. 4. He named it Howe Island after Dr. Howe of Mikkelsen's Expedition.[41] The island we are camped on now is very small and so nameless.[42] Nekusiak has a snow-house here, but it has partly fallen in so he is sleeping with us again. Dub has developed a sore foot and Jumbo is worse than ever — he seems to be rotting. About 1 p.m. snow began to fall and the temperature seemed to rise — though it was not very cold before. Snow fell steadily until 4 p.m., slanting with a light northeast breeze. Then suddenly a strong breeze sprang up from the south, swelling to a blizzard. This lasted about an hour, then it seemed to abate a little, but at 9 p.m. it was as bad as ever. Shall we be detained here by a blizzard — only 80 miles or so from the ships? There is a whale carcase about 6 miles west of our camp, on a mud flat. Nekusiak has three traps set round it. He has seen several unusually large foxes this winter around here — one he caught at *Amaliktoq*[43] — but he is puzzled to account for them. He is a cheerful fellow — are his boots too small, his clothes wet, his shirt covered with blubber — never mind — they can all be set to rights by and by. He told me that Stefansson took a long time to learn Eskimo — not till the second winter did he begin to understand. Sometimes Nekusiak sat and talked to him till daylight, teaching him. He did much the same with me for a couple of hours this evening.

Another method of fishing is to tie meat or other bait round a piece of bone attached to a sinew line and made fast on shore. It is left — swallowed by fish (not an eel), which is later pulled ashore.

All the above were seen by Nekusiak among the *Kagmalit*. He approves of these drawings [Fig. 72] as being correct. At [Great] Bear Lake he said the Indians catch a fish which is as heavy as a bag of flour (50 lbs) by means of an iron hook.

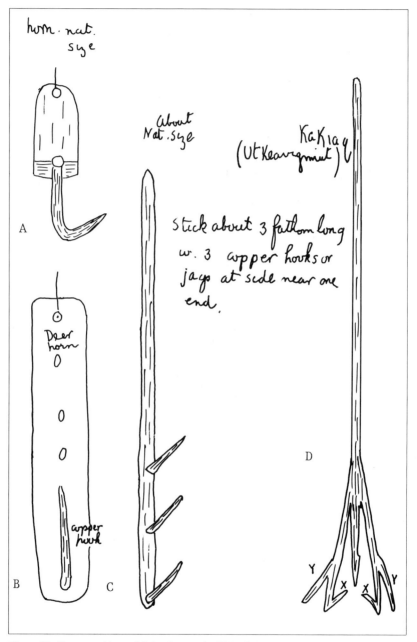

horn. nat.
sye

About
Nat. Sye

KaKiaq
(UtKeavgmiut)

A

Stick about 3 fathom long
w. 3 copper hooks or
jags at side near one
end.

Deer
horn
0

0

0

copper
hook

B

C

D

Y

X   X

Y

Figure 72. Copper and bone fish-hooks seen by Nekusiak.

(A). Ordinary form horn. Natural size. Tied pieces of fish or sinew round horn. Dangled through hole in ice and titillated. No barb. [D.J.]

(B). Deer horn with copper hook. About natural size. Saw three like this. Tie red skin through holes on one side, the other side being left blank. Nekusiak does not know what fish they were used for. [D.J.]

Tuesday, March 17th

The air was calm and the temperature very mild and a little snow falling when we set out at 9:30 a.m., but the sun was obscured by fog.
Nekusiak as usual gained a good lead — the course was almost due east,
with a slight tendency southward. At 11 a.m. a strong west wind suddenly rose — a squall in fact. It fluctuated between west and southwest,
and pushed us and the sled along at a good pace for an hour when it
abated as suddenly as it arose. The sun now shone for a time, but was
soon befogged again. About sunset it [the wind] reappeared, with rather
less violence and had abated considerably by 8 p.m. The Endicott Mountains were in plain view both today and yesterday.[44] The trail seemed
rather better than yesterday and the dogs made better progress. Jumbo
has three *mukluks* now, Charlie one, and Dub one; Denby too is unwell.
We overtook Nekusiak at his rack on Tigvariaq [now Tigvariak] Island
(*tigvaqtoq* = he crosses, e.g., from one isle to another etc.) at 3:05 p.m.
and set up the tent there. Both Fred and Nekusiaq, I notice, continually
use a double grunt to express 'yes' or to indicate that they are listening
just as we interrupt with 'yes'. I have not remarked this among other
Eskimos up here and think it may be peculiar to those further south.
Nekusiaq helped me to translate some songs I had collected. I noticed
that he softens many sounds, e.g., what I had written as '*c*' he pro-
nounces as I write '*s*'. He and Fred both say *nagovaluktoq*, whereas at
Barrow it is rather *nakopaluktoq*. At 10 p.m. when we turned in, a strong
west wind was blowing and there was a faint auroral arch.

Wednesday, March 18th

We all had to turn out about 11 p.m. last night, for the west wind suddenly swelled tremendously, creating a howling blizzard. The tent
rocked to and fro, the stove-pipe was banged out of place, and a total collapse seemed imminent. Fred rushed outside, as soon as he could get
some clothes on, followed shortly afterwards by Nekusiak and later by
McConnell. I stayed inside with my back against the wall of the tent to
hold it up — like Atlas holding up the world. The three outside fixed up
more guy-ropes then came in on the lee side of the tent, pulling up the
edge. The temperature was fairly high, but the snow was driving in
clouds. We were all tired and soon went off to sleep, again, although the
tent still swayed and creaked and the stove-pipe rattled — the end of the

---

(C). Stick about 3 fathom[s] long, with 3 copper hooks or jags at side near one end. Used
at Bloody Fall on Coppermine River. Pool below the fall is full of swirling water. The
pole is thrown in, handle being kept in hand, and pulled out. Sometimes two fish are thus
jagged; sometimes, one, sometimes none. The fish are not visible in the water. [D.J.]

(D). Kakiaq (*Utkeavigmiut*). Make hole in ice of lake - dangle white or brown bear's
tooth on string and spear fish when it comes to bait. Sometimes musk-ox tooth used and
probably other things also. There are small copper barbs set in the side of the outer prong,
used in deep water. In spearing fish in shallow water they are removed. Sometimes the
spear is used without the outside prongs (Y-Y). [D.J.]

latter we set on the floor to help to steady the tent. In the morning we had to dig a way out through the back of the tent, for the snow had banked up high on every side. The tent was torn in several places and the snow had permeated the space between the inner and outer walls, producing a compact bank. It made the tent warm, but also delayed us an hour in getting away. Nekusiak's sled was buried, ours half buried; the dogs had been set free and were all right. How long the blizzard lasted none of us knew, but the sky was clear and the air calm when we turned out at 6 a.m. Before this blizzard, and also before the big blizzard in January, the temperature was unusually high. This morning it was a little colder than yesterday and this afternoon when a light east breeze sprang up it grew still colder. The horizon was rather hazy all day. We started out at 10:30 a.m. and reached an Eskimo house at 2:15 p.m.; the trail was on the whole fairly good, but the dogs travelled slowly, Denby had to be shod with a *mukluk*, so that now all McConnell's dogs except Pickles (his sole Eskimo dog) have sore feet and wear *mukluks*. All of Jumbo's feet are bad, so he was allowed to run loose in front of the sled. Nekusiak reached the Eskimo house half an hour before us and had lit the fire to make tea. A man named Papiroq with his wife and son have been living in it, engaged in trapping. Just now they appear to be absent somewhere. Nekusiak stayed behind here; he says he is coming to the ships after the trapping season closes (i.e., after March 30th). We had tea, reloaded the sled — for he had been carrying our tent and one or two other things, and set out for Qopuk's house[45] — about 7 miles further east. Papiroq's house, by the way, is situated on a point on the mainland named *Savaqvik*,[46] i.e., a place where people have worked (so Nekusiak told me). We drifted a little south and after crossing a bay penetrated some distance into the mainland instead of crossing a narrow sandspit[47] and coming out again on to the sea ice. We had to turn northeast and before we reached the sea again the sun had set. We made for the sea at the nearest point and hastily pitched camp. During the evening a hot fire was maintained to dry the tent — it weighs about 100 lbs when dry and a great deal more when wet. This is the advantage of camping on the shore, for from a little east of Barrow it is strewn with driftwood all the way, much of it red spruce, which burns admirably. I noticed that at each tent-house Natkusiak[48] has constructed along here (I saw three) he had made a circular enclosure for his dogs with rectangular blocks of snow — a kind of cromlech.[49] About 3/4 mile west of Papiroq's house is one of Leffingwell's sign-posts or beacons with a cross-piece whose upper and lower borders are white and the middle black, thus:

Figure 73. Leffingwell's sign-post near Bullen Point.

Figure 74. E. de K. Leffingwell's house on Flaxman Island, October 1913. (Photo by K.G. Chipman, CMC Photo No. 43178).

(or so it appeared from a distance). Papiroq had caught five foxes about Xmas time — one of them a red fox, so Nekusiak told us. His house was built after the usual style but had a small intestine window in the front side near the door, which consisted merely of two curtains, the inner one of brown bear's (*ukluk*) skin. There was a large piece of rock inside. Nekusiak did not know what it was for unless perhaps as an anvil of some kind. It was about as large as a small pumpkin. McConnell showed Nekusiak the belt button which the ancient dame gave him to take to Stefansson. The ring and dot patterns with which it is covered have been made with a drill. There were two auroral arches close together about 10:30 p.m.

Thursday, March 19th

Fred turned out at 4:30 a.m. so that we had finished breakfast and were away by 8 o'clock. The atmosphere was hazy, but calm, and the temperature comparatively mild. The dogs travelled slowly — perhaps 2 1/2 miles an hour — and as we went a little astray in our course, it was 1 p.m. before we reached Leffingwell's house. We passed first a rack on which was cached an *umiak* frame, the *ugruk* skins with which it was covered having been removed. A short distance further on was a house — apparently uninhabited just now — Qopuk's house[50] (Qopuk = crack in ice). This was on the mainland. Leffingwell's house is on the southeastern extremity of Flaxman Island — 2 miles or so from shore. It is a one-story wooden building very long compared with its breadth.[51] Apparently the eastern portion is the real dwelling-house, the other half being used for storing things. About 75 yards to the northeast of the house is an Eskimo dome tent, half underground and enclosed with snow so supported that a space is left vacant between it and the canvas — on top only a few inches in breadth, at the sides 2 or 3 feet. The door as in Papiroq's house was a curtain — brown-bear's skin inside covered with canvas on the outside. An Eskimo and his wife — the man's name is Igluñasuk (i.e., Laugher)[52] — were living in it and turned out to welcome us and invite us over to tea. Leffingwell, they said, with their son (a lad) went over to the *Kopauraq* [Kuparuk] River some time ago and they did not know when he would return.[53] We found a note to this effect in the back half of Leffingwell's house — the front (east) portion where we intended to spend the night, was locked. The Eskimos told us that a week ago they learned (per an Eskimo Aiakuk) that Stefansson was not back from the Mackenzie River and that Dr. Anderson was still at the house beside the ships. At 2:35 p.m. we set out again and stopped about 5:30 p.m. on a sandspit[54] to pitch camp. The dogs, which had been fed on a little blubber at Leffingwell's, travelled slightly better afterwards. The trail was good all day — hard fairly level snow over which the sled glided easily. Throughout the day, but more especially in the morning,

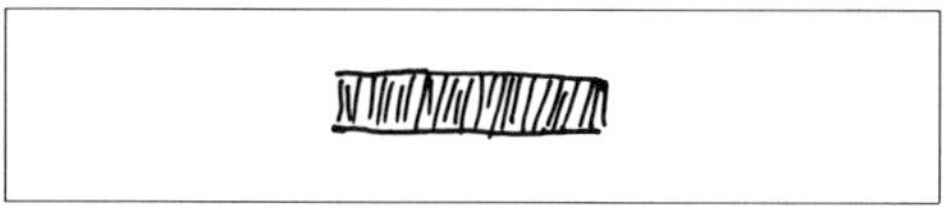

Figure 75. Basalt-like 'mirage' near Flaxman Island.

there was a wonderful 'mirage' all along the horizon from west through north to east. It seemed as though a solid grey wall encircled us, of a formation like basalt — i.e., striated or pillared. About 11 a.m. there were two bright spots in the sky rather like parhelions — one on each side of the sun at equal distances of about 15°. In the evening a strong west wind sprang up, but the temperature remained fairly mild.

Friday, March 20th

We started out at 8:40 a.m. The air was calm, the atmosphere comparatively clear. The dogs travelled fairly well, but we lost time through going out of our way round a sandspit and then having to return. About 3 p.m. we sighted Thompson's [Thomsen's] house, with three sticks set up near it, about 10 miles west of the ships. The trail was good; the dogs going well, we pressed on and reached the *Mary Sachs* and the house[55] where our party is living [in Camden Bay] about 8 p.m. The journey from Barrow is over, and I am heartily glad, for McConnell and I have not got on well together at all.[56] We found only Dr. Anderson 'at home'. Stefansson had returned from the Mackenzie River 12 days before (March 8th ?) and left on Monday, March 16th for his ice trip. He hired two white men from the *Belvedere*, [Daniel] Sweeney and Arnot Castell[57] to go out with him, taking two sleds. Wilkins, Johansen[58] and Capt. Pete Bernard (captain of the *Mary Sachs*), with two sleds were journeying 2 or 3 days, according to circumstances, out on the ice with him, as a supporting party. They were to start north on March 21st from Martin Point at the eastern extremity of Camden Bay, the most northerly point between the Mackenzie River and Flaxman Island. He [Stefansson] proposed to travel out north 15 days, taking soundings, and return rapidly in 5 days. He carried with him a Lucas[59] sounding machine previously used by Leffingwell and Mikkelsen. Wilkins obtained a cinematograph apparatus from the *Elvira* and was taking pictures. Johansen hoped to dredge for zoological marine specimens on the way back. Later

Wilkins is going west to Barrow to take pictures of the spring whaling on the ice. Cox and Chipman have gone east, Cox to work with O'Neill in the mountains, Cox at topography and O'Neill at geology. Chipman is mapping the coast between Demarcation Point and the Mackenzie [River]. Chipman and Cox were staying for a few days at Demarcation Point — whose position was accurately determined by the Survey Departments in 1912 — to rate their chronometers. Stefansson bought a motor launch for Cox and O'Neill to use on the Mackenzie. Also he bought a vessel which is up here, a little this side of Demarcation Point[60] — the *North Star* — 13 tons, and in a few days, when Capt. Bernard returns,[61] I am to go eastward with him and look after the things on board.[62] There is one white man living on the vessel — a man named Anderson.[63] O'Neill has been geologizing in the mountains about 140 miles east for some time. At the house here daily readings are taken of the barometers, thermometers, tide gauge, and anemometer (there are no anemographs and the man[ometer] and therm[ograph] are broken). At present in the absence of Chipman etc., Capt. Nahmens[64] of the *Alaska* is doing this work. [J.R.] Crawford is about 22 miles to the east trapping — he is engineer of the *Mary Sachs*. Dr. Anderson and McConnell think of trying to catch up with Stefansson before he gets too far out on the ice, leaving tomorrow. The temperature today was extraordinarily high — 27° F, only 5° below freezing. Parhelions were seen at the house — I did not notice any on the trail. There is a popular belief that they are indicative of bad weather. About midnight there was a brilliant aurora, sweeping bands of white light overhead. There was a mail for me here via [the] Mackenzie River.[65]

Chapter 11. Respite and Tragedy at Camden Bay

McConnell heads east to intercept Stefansson — Trader Duffy O'Connor leaves for Barrow — Dr. Anderson leaves for the mountains — The damaged state of the Alaska *— Writing Eskimo stories — Problems with the scientific gauges — Polar bear incident — Developing photographs — Two unwanted Eskimo children — Wilkins and others return from ice trip with Stefansson — Examining Eskimo grave — Suicide and burial of Andre Norem — Wilkins and Natkusiak depart for Barrow — Trip east to Crawford's house and back*

Saturday, March 21st, 1914

Dr. Anderson decided not to go [to catch up with Stefansson], but McConnell left about noon with an Eskimo named Aiakuk. Dr. Anderson put a typewriter at my disposal, and I spent the morning and part of the [afternoon] typing out cat's-cradle figures. Then he and I opened up two cases of books in the store — one being Beuchat's. These latter I am making a list of, and what are not useful shall repack. We could not find my own books transhipped at Port Clarence from the *Karluk* to the *Mary Sachs*. In the evening I learned two new cat's-cradle figures from Jennie,[1] the *Kiñmiuñ* (Nome) wife of [Charles] Thomsen — a sailor from the *Mary Sachs*. Strong east wind all day with a fine aurora at night.

Sunday, March 22nd

The strong east wind of yesterday continued with a velocity at 8 a.m. of 32 miles [per hour]. Aiakuk returned with a letter from McConnell, who was continuing with Crawford[2] — the engineer of the *Mary Sachs* who has been living a few miles to the eastward. If Stefansson has started out on the ice he is having very bad weather. We spent a quiet day indoors engaged in miscellaneous occupations. I have not had time yet to size up the place and the men here, being engaged in searching out books and other things I need. I am making a copy of the more important of the meteorological observations that are being made here.[3] There was an auroral band of streamers this evening about 9 o'clock, when the wind was as boisterous as ever. I am enjoying the abundance of food. We breakfast at 7:30 a.m., help ourselves to lunch (bread, butter, cheese, and coffee and generally canned fruit), dine at 5 p.m., and help ourselves to supper, which resembles lunch. The food is excellent in its variety, its abundance, and its preparation. There is no possibility of being ever hungry. Aurora at 12:30 a.m.

Monday, March 23rd

The chief event of the day was the departure of 'Duffy' O'Connor with the Eskimo Aiakuk. 'Duffy' has been up here, trading and trapping for about 3 years, having his headquarters in a house near Demarcation Point. He sold his outfit recently to Stefansson, and McConnell, after overtaking (or missing) Stefansson, is going on to take an inventory of it.

'Duffy' is now going to Nome via Barrow, for which purpose he has bought some dogs, amongst them my old dog Victor.[4] Dr. Anderson and [Daniel] Blue, the engineer of the *Alaska*, were occupied in making the final preparations for a trip into the mountains after caribou, ptarmigan, etc., leaving tomorrow if the weather clears. They expect to be away 10 days or a fortnight. Dr. Anderson suggested I should accompany them if I were not too busy, but I have a great deal on hand just now. After dinner I went with Fred to the 'dog-house', a fine building constructed exactly like an Eskimo hut, with passage etc., but larger than the ordinary house. The floor is of frozen earth, the snow having been cleared away, and a furnace in one corner keeps the room comparatively warm. The dogs are chained to the walls, each having a little stall of its own. At present there are only eight dogs in it, but there are stalls for [more].[5] Fred was feeding them on boiled rice with a little meat, salmon, and other things. He takes good care of the dogs and seems to be a good worker altogether. The easterly gale continued all day. Fred told me tonight that the spots on the moon were produced by the sun drawing very near when the moon was sleepy and scorching his face.

Tuesday, March 24th

The stormy weather continued, so Dr. Anderson did not leave. Towards noon it abated, and in the afternoon a little snow fell, and it became practically calm. The day passed quietly — everyone finding enough to keep him occupied. Dr. Anderson allowed me to copy the Eskimo names of a number of birds with the genus and species of bird. In the afternoon I continued to search for my books, which were transferred from the *Karluk* to the *Mary Sachs* at Port Clarence — but without success. There was a brilliant aurora about 11 p.m. — a curtain over the eastern hemisphere and stretching to the northwest as well. It was changing momentarily, sweeping across the sky like 'shadows' of light. As I watched, a great semicircle of brilliant white developed and faded away all within the space of about 2 minutes.

Wednesday, March 25th

The day was fine, with a light southwesterly breeze in the morning. Dr. Anderson and Blue left shortly before noon.[6] They go to Crawford's house today, and tomorrow ascend the Hulahula River to the mountains. They will return via the *Belvedere*.[7] The caribou have recently made their appearance a little to the westward, and about sixty of them have been killed already. Dr. Anderson's sled was heavily laden. He had six dogs — Blue's old team. That leaves only two at the camp here. I took a photograph of the start with Johansen's camera[8] — Dr. Anderson has not been able to find another 3A camera for me yet. After they left, Capt. Nahmens and I went over to the *Alaska* — 1 1/4 miles from the house, 1 1/4 miles from the entrance to the bay, and about 1/4 mile from the beach. The ice under the propeller had been dug away to the depth of 5 feet, leaving only a thin crust over the water. This laid the propeller open to the air. We found that a little water had penetrated through, and that the hole was filled with snow, but it would not take long to clear. The *Alaska* had a hole in the starboard side of the bow, about a foot wide, the captain said, where she bumped against a sharp piece of ice. It only penetrated the outer skin and was quickly patched. The fore half of the hull is sheathed with galvanised iron. The captain intends to transfer this to the after half, and to cover the fore half with iron-wood. At present the vessel has been stripped of almost everything. The sails are covering the store, the booms have been taken off, and the deck is bare except for a thick coating of snow. We went down into the cabin, which is aft over the propeller. It has bunks — three tiers — for about eighteen people, but some of these are to be taken out. A door communicates with the engine room [containing] a Western Standard Engine, which was in a terrible condition when the vessel left Nome. It took them 3 weeks at Teller to overhaul and refit it. The propeller too was found to be broken, and they had to send to Nome for two new ones — a two-blade for use in the ice and a four-blade one. Blue, the engineer, is said to be fairly capable. He was running his own gold mine near Nome for 2 or 3 years, but had bad luck — the mine flooded and he lost pretty well everything, so he was glad to take this job. Professionally he is a steam engineer.[9] His cabin is beside the engine room, but will be knocked out to make the latter larger, and he will sleep in the large cabin with the rest of us. The galley and the saloon are forward. When the vessel left Nome the amidships was piled so high with stores that from the wheel-house the captain was unable to see the bow.

On the beach south of the *Alaska* is the dory that belongs to it. The *Mary Sachs* lies on the beach beside the house. She entered the bay before the *Alaska* and was thus able to secure a better berth. The wind swung round to the southeast as we were returning and freshened a little. I opened one of Beuchat's cases in the afternoon — and another in the evening. The latter took a very long time as it was a very big case, and in the limited space it was impossible to turn it over, so that I had to break open the side. Fred told me two stories in the evening[10] — in English — which I hastily scribbled down. At midnight snow was falling thickly and there was a moderate west wind blowing.

Thursday, March 26th

Between 1 and 2 a.m. a howling westerly sprang up. At 8 a.m. it was blowing 45 miles an hour, and the snow was drifting in thick clouds so that it was impossible to see more than half a dozen paces. This meant a day indoors for us. Thomsen came over from the *Mary Sachs* in the morning and stayed all day. He has caught 23 foxes this season. Capt. Nahmens passed the time in making a tool box — I in typing notes and in taking an inventory and repacking Beuchat's box. The wind abated in the afternoon, and by 5 p.m. had died right away, but about midnight a gentle breeze was blowing from the southeast. Jennie and her two little girls — one, Annie, 16 months old, her own child, the other about 4 years of age, a neglected child that she is looking after — came over in the evening with her husband Thomsen. Fred told me a short story and Jennie told me another, rather longer, so that I spent a very profitable evening. Capt. Nahmens found that the tide gauge had gone wrong and was not recording; we shall examine it tomorrow. He has been searching out the amount of canvas required to make a lug-sail for a whale boat. At 11:30 this evening there was another fine aurora — two arches north-west-southeast, brightest at the extremities, but neither very markedly bright; in the east a large 'wheat-ear', a bright semi-circle; the whole was changing momentarily.

Friday, March 27th

Capt. Nahmens began to dig out the pipe that protects the tide-gauge wire, for the water at the bottom seemed to be frozen. The tide gauge is set out on the sea-ice (not in the bay) on the other side of the sandspit — about 200 yards from the house. A snow house is built over it, and a rude table has been constructed on which the clock with its graduated paper is set. A thin wire runs round the large driving wheel of the clock and connects at one end with the tide-gauge wire, while from the other a weight hangs down to keep the wire taut. The gauge itself consists of a thin wire running down through a pipe, with a heavy weight on the bottom. The pipe is filled with coal oil to prevent the water from freezing. As the tide rises it lifts the ice and the clock indicator with it, while the weighted end of the wire remains on the bottom. For two days the pencil made a perfectly straight line round the paper, so that we are afraid that there is a vacuum between the ice and the water. Not only so, but the water at the bottom of the pipe seems to be frozen. A lantern is kept burning day and night in the tide-gauge house so that the temperature is never so low as out of doors. The captain dug down about 2 1/2 feet and still had not reached water, so he postponed the task until tomorrow. A westerly blizzard suddenly sprang up early in the afternoon and raged furiously all the afternoon and evening. I spent most of the day indoors, writing and reading. Fred told me part of a long story[11] in the evening of which I took notes, but at 11 p.m. the room became so cold that we had to give up and turn in. The temperature was not really very low, however — only 2 or 3 points below zero.

Saturday, March 28th

The blizzard lasted all through the night and raged unabated this morning, but lulled in the afternoon, and at 6 p.m. there was a dead calm. A few minutes later a light breeze sprang up from the east. The wind gauge is out of order now — it has registered the most remarkable speeds — once something like 150 miles an hour. Stefansson and the others who have gone out on the ice must be having a very bad time. We are afraid they may meet with a wide patch of open water, as we have seen a water-sky several times. This afternoon, Fred, Andre Norem (the cook of the *Mary Sachs*[12]) and I cleared out the passage, which was so blocked up with snow that an outlet had to be cut through the roof. We made a fine arch doorway with some front pieces of sleds. Capt. Nahmens has been making a tool box — Fred, gun covers of green canvas. We had a phonograph concert this evening. Thomsen and Jennie and the two children came across [from the *Mary Sachs*] just after dinner — about 6:30 p.m. I notice the cook of the *Alaska* lights a fire in the same way as Eskimos, i.e., he takes a piece of wood and cuts down a series of

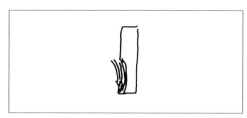

Figure 76. Stick cut for shavings by C. Brook.

shavings one after the other without detaching them from the stick until they form a bunch, when the whole bunch is split off at once. Only the cook pushes the knife away from him, European fashion, and the Eskimos draw it towards them, holding the knife with the back of the hand downwards.

Sunday, March 29th

Every event of note that has happened here this winter has occurred on a Sunday, the cook said this morning. His prophecy came true. Capt. Nahmens and I were fixing up the tide gauge at 1 p.m. when the cook called through the opening [of the snow house] "Do you want to shoot a polar bear?" We thought it was a joke at first, until assured that Thomsen had seen one beside a fox-trap this morning and had returned for his rifle. We left the tide gauge, hurriedly seized our rifles, and ran to catch up with Thomsen and Fred, who were nearly 1/2 mile ahead. We had only gone a short distance when a large black bird (a *tulugaq* or raven) flew over our heads. I fired a shot at it but missed.[13] It is the first bird we have seen (save ptarmigan) since the beginning of winter. We hurried on after this and caught up with the other two. Thomsen told us that he went out this morning to visit his traps and was approaching one set about 4 miles from the house here when a great bear rose up from beside it and faced him — not 20 yards off. He had only a single-barrelled shotgun, so beat a hasty retreat, but not before he had distinguished something white in the trap — either a fox or a bear cub. He looked behind a good many times to see if the bear was following him, but after he had gone a few yards it lay down again. The four of us hurried on afraid that we should find it gone, but when we were still a mile away we could see it moving about on the top of the mound where the trap was set. Keeping close together so as not to alarm it by an appearance of numbers we drew close up, then spread out to shoot. The bear was very uneasy, for she apparently discovered us when we were at least 1/2 mile away and walked round and round the top of the mound, but did not leave it. The reason was plain enough — her cub — about the size of a fox, only much heavier, was caught in the trap, and she could not release it without a wrench which she seemed unwilling to do or else was unable to evolve such a method of encountering the unusual situation. We approached within 20 yards of her — or at least the captain and I did, for Fred and Thomsen were some 10 or 15 yards behind us on our right. The bear stood in front of its cub, facing us and growled two or three times. We agreed not to kill the cub, then fired a volley at the mother. She pitched on her head, and slowly fell over on to one shoulder, then began to roll down the side of the mound. By this time she had received another volley, but one bullet unfortunately went astray and killed the cub — piercing the lower jaw and penetrating the neck. Still the mother was not dead and several more shots were fired — about 18 altogether before we were absolutely sure there was no sign of life. Fred was very excited and blazed away at a great rate without taking much aim, so that I, who was on his left and in front, was in far more danger from him that from the bear. There is little doubt but that it was a bullet from his rifle that killed the cub. It appears to be rather typical of Eskimo hunting — Capt. Nahmens and I both thought — to stand off some distance and empty the magazine into the object on the chance that one bullet at least will get home. It was a rather pathetic sight to watch the mother guarding her young one so anxiously. She had stayed by it for hours, and would not leave it even when attacked by four men. I greatly regretted that in the hurry of getting away I had forgotten the camera. One could have approached to within 10 yards without much risk and secured a splendid picture. It was sheer butchery on our part, but necessary, for here at the ships they have had almost no fresh meat, but only salt beef all the winter. Dr. Anderson and Blue have gone to the mountains expressly to obtain some fresh meat if possible. Thomsen and Fred began skinning the bears while the captain and I returned to the house for a sled. The captain decided to stay and finish the tide gauge and if possible fix up the wind gauge, but Andre Norem — ex-cook of the *Mary Sachs* and now general handy man about the house — returned with me. We took the only two dogs here, Jumbo and Dub, and a light sled and made good time over the bay ice. I took the camera too, although it was now late — about 5:30 p.m. when we reached the bears; however, I took four photos, but very much doubt whether they will turn out to be any good.[14] Thomsen used the intestines as fox-bait; the skins and the bodies we placed on the sled and brought back home. Fred thought he saw Natkusiak (Billy) a long way off and went to meet him and borrow one of his dogs; he was mistaken but did not return empty-handed for he found a fox in another of Thomsen's traps. Both [of] the bear[skins] and the foxskin were in very good condition and will be a good haul for Thomsen, who was engaged for 6 months only on the *Mary Sachs* and is now receiving no pay, though he keeps all the skins he can obtain whether fox, bear, or anything else (he now has 24 foxes). We had a very late dinner — about 8:30 p.m. — but we had a stew of the bear's heart, which everyone enjoyed — including Jennie, who honoured us with her company. She repaired my skin shirt today and in the evening gave me material for a few notes. In replacing the pipe for the tide gauge this morning we tied on the bottom with two thicknesses of very close-textured cloth, one smeared with gun grease, the second (which was put on double after the first had proved unsatisfactory) of the same kind of cloth with paraffin boiled in. The wire was passed through it, and the pipe filled with coal oil and lowered into the water, leaving only about 9 inches projecting above (we believe it is high water now). (The trouble with the wind gauge seems to be that it can run backward, the captain told me; he can find nothing else the matter.) The tide gauge we found had a 20-lb weight of lead attached to the bottom of the wire, and this seemed to be insufficient, so the captain attached another 20-lb weight to it as well. The water at the bottom of the pipe was frozen and the wire broken, as we had anticipated. However, it is now in running order again. The weather today was remarkably temperate, the thermometer registering 34° at 4 p.m. The atmosphere was fairly clear this morning, but became hazy in the afternoon and a little snow began to fall about 6 p.m. There was no wind until evening, when a strong breeze sprang up from the west — I estimated it at 10:30 p.m. to be about 25 miles an hour and it was increasing. Snow seemed to be falling also, but it was dark and it may possibly have been merely drift. There was a dark water-sky to the north, and it is certain that there is a large expanse of open water not many miles away. The Endicott Mountains[15] stood out wonderfully sharp and clear. The snow in the valleys showed up like the ribs of a leaf.

Monday, March 30th

The weather was beautiful and clear until towards evening when a strong westerly wind sprang up and snow began to fall. Thomsen and his wife Jennie were busy all day with the bear- and foxskins. I took some photos with a 3A camera — one of Capt. Nahmens and the tide gauge, one of the *Mary Sachs*, one of the captain again reading the thermometers and wind gauge, and one of an *umiak* with superimposed kayak cached on a rack[16] (one of three) by an inland native last fall. For the first of these photos we had to cut two apertures in the side of the tide-gauge house. Both wind and tide gauge seem to be working perfectly now. There was a water-sky again to the north today. In the evening Fred told me two stories. At 11:30 p.m. there was an auroral arch northeast-southwest, brightest in the middle, and not reaching quite to the northeast horizon.

Tuesday, March 31st

An 8-mile an hour wind was blowing from the west at 7:30 this morning, but it changed its direction continually and sometimes sank to a calm. The air was clear and the temperature before noon +34° F. The wind changed to southeast about 2 p.m. and the temperature dropped about 20°. A strong west wind again sprang up in the evening — about

Figure 77. Jennie and Charles Thomsen and daughter Annie at Collinson Point, September 1913. (Photo by J.R. Cox, CMC Photo No. 39582.)

20 miles an hour. Thomsen and Jennie finished the bearskin today — they washed it in cold water to remove the blood. The cook roasted the cub for dinner — it was fine, as good as veal, every whit. I developed some photos this evening in daylight developing tank — one or two will be passable, I think, but most of them are very poor, and three or four no

good. Jennie told me two fine stories tonight.[17] I have never remarked that the Eskimos as a rule put on their skin shirts differently to what the ordinary white man does. They throw it over their heads and shoulders, turn it round to front, and pull it down from the inside with their arms, then — the last step of all — put their arms down the sleeves. They laugh whenever as not infrequently happens a white man puts his shirt on back to front. The little girl Mrs. Thomsen (Jennie) is looking after (she is called various names, but her real name is [?][18]) is, Jennie thinks, a *Kanaka* — Eskimo half-caste. She certainly looks it. She is a very merry child — always laughing and cheerful — about 5 years old. Her father's name, she says, is Teriglu (Leffingwell's man), and she does not know who her mother is. Fred told me tonight that when he was a baby his mother wanted to get rid of him — she had too many sons, she said (he has three older brothers and two older sisters). She tied him up in a bag, laid him on his side, and pressed down on his ribs with her arm, till she thought he was dead, then she took him out. He was not dead, however, and she was going to repeat the operation when his father intervened and said "That will do, let him live." Now Fred says he is much narrower in the lower part of the chest than he should be — something he thinks was broken. Actually, however, there seems to be nothing much wrong with him — he is as strong as a bull. The tide gauge is working admirably now, and we are feeling very pleased about it. I had another unsuccessful hunt for my books in the store today.

Measurements of the Bear Cub

Total length (from tip of nose to base of tail)	2' 7"
" " of tail	3 1/2"
" " from neck to anus	1' 9 1/2"
Length of head (callipers) to alveolar point	6 1/4"
Breadth of top of head	3 7/8"
Length of ear	2 1/4"
Girth behind fore legs	1' 5 1/2"
" half-way between fore and hind legs	1' 6 1/2"
" behind hind legs	1' 7 1/2"
Length of fore leg (top of hip bone to end of toe)	1' 0"
Length of fore leg from knee to top of hip	6 1/2"
Circumference of fore leg (a) above knee	9 1/2"
" " " " (b) below "	8 1/2"
Length of fore paw	4 1/2"
Breadth " " "	4"
Length of hind leg (top of hip to end of toe)	1' 1"
" " " " (knee to top of hip)	7 3/4"
Circumference of hind leg (a) above knee	11 1/2"
" " " " (b) below "	8 1/2"
Length of hind paw	5 1/2"
Breadth " " "	4 1/4"

Teeth (on each side, 2 incisors, 1 canine, 3 molars
(and premolars)
Weight[19]   24   lbs

Wednesday, April 1st

A strong west 32-mile wind blew this morning when we got up. It diminished gradually and died right away in the afternoon but sprang up again from the east in the evening. The temperature fluctuated, but during most of the day was a little below zero. There was nothing to take us out of doors so we stayed inside all day, except Fred and Andre Norem, who went out for a short time in the afternoon for wood. We had a phonograph concert in the evening, and Jennie showed me how to sew.

Thursday, April 2nd

A 20-mile easterly was blowing this morning but died away during the day. The temperature rose from -3° at 8 a.m. to 24° at 8 p.m. At 1:30 p.m. Wilkins, Capt. Pete Bernard (captain of the *Mary Sachs*), a sailor from the *Belvedere* named Aarnout [Castel], and Añutisiak arrived. They had started out with Stefansson on the ice on March 22nd. The first day they travelled about 7 miles, but were only 3 from shore. The following morning McConnell caught up to them[20] and delayed their start until 11 a.m. At 1:30 p.m. Capt. Bernard met with an accident, pitching forward and knocking his head against the curved part of the sled between the handles in crossing a pressure ridge.[21] Three stitches were put in on the spot by McConnell and eleven more when he got back to Martin Point the same day.[22] It is healing very rapidly now. That day they got about 1 1/2 miles further from shore and the following another mile or two when arrested by open water. Their tent was pitched about 300 yards from an open lane of water, full of young and slush ice and heavy floe ice, where crossing was impossible. During the night about 200 yards of this was ground away; they had to keep a watch all night. The open lead detained them in camp the next day; the following — the 27th [March] — Stefansson sent two sleds back to Martin Point with Wilkins' cinematograph apparatus, two crippled dogs, and sundry other things to lighten the loads. They expected to rejoin Stefansson again in 5 or 6 hours, but a blizzard overtook them on the way to the Point, and they had to stay there the night. When it cleared a little about noon the next day and they started off back, they were arrested by a lane of water about 2 miles wide and extending to right and left further than they could see. They skirted it for some distance, then made for the *Belvedere*, [about 25][23] miles away, hoping to see from her masthead some place where they could cross. But opposite the *Belvedere* it was still 2 miles wide, and beyond was another lead of water. Stefansson and his party (McConnell, Johansen, Ole Andreasen, Storkerson, and Crawford) might have drifted 100 miles away by this time, so there was nothing for Wilkins to do but return to Collinson Point. He had exposed about 700 feet of cinematograph film on the trip and is anxious to get to Barrow as soon as possible to photograph the spring whaling. Stefansson and his party had provisions for themselves and dogs for about 2 1/2 months, but they were rather short of coal oil, which Wilkins was to take back. During the fourth day, when all were detained in camp they had shot eleven seals.

Friday, April 3rd

A strong westerly — somewhere about 30 miles an hour — blew all the morning but died away in the afternoon. Wilkins developed some pictures he took of the ice party. I typed notes and the others found various tasks to fill in the time. The temperature was high — somewhere about +24° in the afternoon. Añutisiak told me a short story in the evening (in Eskimo), which I roughly wrote and got translated.[24] There seems to be more and more to do every day. At 11:30 p.m. the sky was clear — the moon about half full — shining with a halo round it and a faint aurora band stretched southeast-northwest; the wind was blowing from the east at about 8 miles an hour.

Saturday, April 4th

A strong west wind was blowing this morning, but died away about 10 p.m. Later it swung round to the east. The temperature was high, for a great part of the day 28° F. Capt. Bernard and Fred went along the coast to find Billy Natkusiak, whom Dr. Anderson wishes to join the Expedition. Wilkins is going to Barrow in a few days to photograph the spring whaling on the ice and wishes Natkusiak and his dog team to go with him.[25] He continued developing his pictures today — he has a splendid set of the ice trip and others. Aarnout Castel and Añutisiak and Andre [Norem] began building a snowhouse for Capt. Bernard, who intends making a boat or something shortly. I spent nearly the whole day working at Eskimo, and in the evening Jennie told me some stories. The days pass very quietly here — there is always plenty to do — at least most of us find it so. For the last two days we have been enjoying fresh caribou meat from the *Belvedere*. A party from that vessel shot sixty odd [caribou] about a month ago, besides some mountain sheep. Nome and Teller Eskimos, when a person sneezes, say "*qaqatqain (quvuña qatqain)*" and I fancy the same custom prevails further north. Wilkins told me tonight the weight of the four sleds which accompanied Stefansson out on the ice: Storkerson's sled, 920 lbs; Capt. Bernard's, 1020 lbs; Aarnout Castel's, 640 lbs; Wilkins', 786 lbs; there were twenty-seven dogs and seven men. A fairly strong west wind was blowing at 11 p.m. when the others turned in. We noticed this afternoon remarkable clouds to the west. Overhead were alto cumuli, but in the west cumulo-nimbus, with a touch of stratus on the horizon; it is the first approach to a nimbus since last autumn.

Sunday, April 5th

After breakfast this morning Capt. Nahmens and I harnessed up three dogs and with the light racing sled set out for the former's cabin, about 7 miles to the east. He built [it] in Eskimo style some months ago and stayed there for the greater part of 2 months trapping but never caught a single fox all the winter. Now he wished to bring back some of his things. I went with him to examine a grave about 3 miles further along the coast at a point at [the] mouth of Sadlerochit River. It turned out to be the grave of a child — the captain was told it was a boy who was buried there 2 years ago. The coffin was constructed like a European coffin with sawn timber and nails and laid on the ground with some sticks driven in round the sides, to keep it in place.[26] Underneath the head of the coffin, which was oriented roughly east and west, the head east, was a European dessert-spoon laid on the surface. The body, which was not fully decayed, was fully clothed and lying on its back at full length. A mountain-sheep skin was wrapped over the feet. There seemed to be nothing else in the coffin, save snow; all the skins etc. were frozen stiff. We left it where it lay and returned to the captain's hut where we loaded up the sled and set up a square sail near the front end, for a moderately strong southeast breeze was blowing, which we would have nearly astern on our homeward journey. The sail proved a great success;[27] it lifted up the front of the sled and once capsized it. Often the wind was strong enough to start it and keep it going for a little while without any pulling on the part of the dogs, and that despite the fact that the load, including the captain and myself, weighed about 500 lbs. We sat on the sled for the greater part of 4 miles, then the wind lulled and we walked ahead. We found that Capt. Bernard and Fred had returned with Billy Natkusiak, whom they found at Leffingwell's. There was no water-sky in the north this morning, but this afternoon it was very prounouced. The temperature was fairly high — somewhere about 24° in the early part of the afternoon. The strong breeze, which helped us homeward, sprang up about 11 a.m. and lasted 3 or 4 hours, then lulled; it sprang up again for a few minutes about 4 p.m. then died away altogether.

Monday, April 6th

The day was chiefly remarkable for the constant high temperature — averaging between 25 and 30 [degrees] all day. The house began to leak, or rather the snow on top to melt and drip through the rough beams. Outdoors the surface of the snow was very soft and damp, and in the tide-gauge house the ice on the surface was melting. Capt. Bernard has his workshop finished. It is made of snow blocks, laid on four sides to form a wall about 18 ft x 12 ft x 6 ft. A tarpaulin forms the roof. If this weather continues it will cave in in 2 or 3 days. A great water-sky was visible all along the northern horizon and it seemed that open water could not be far away. So about noon Capt. Nahmens and the three Eskimos (Fred, Añutisiak, and Natkusiak) dug out a skin boat and with a sled and team of dogs went out seal hunting. They went about 4 miles and then stopped and climbed a high keg. The open water was nowhere in sight, though the water-sky was still there; it was brought near by mirage. Wilkins printed some photos in the evening, mostly for me, some from his own negatives, which were interesting from an ethnological point of view. His photos have turned out splendidly; he seems to be one of those rare individuals who do well everything they put their hands to. Jennie told me another short story in the evening. The air was fairly calm all day, but in the evening a strong westerly sprang up.

Tuesday, April 7th

The westerly of last night had died away this morning. The three Eskimos took a sled and dog team and went out over the ice to look for seals. The rest of us spent most of the day indoors writing, typing etc., except Capt. Bernard, who was in his new workshop for several hours, and Andre [Norem], who was bringing in ice and firewood on a sled. The Eskimos returned at 5 p.m.; they had gone some 4 hours northward and had then seen the open lead a considerable distance ahead of them so they turned back. A strong east wind sprang up in the afternoon, the speed being 20 miles an hour at 3 p.m. and 14 miles at 8 p.m. The temperature was a little lower than yesterday — it stayed about 20° F all day. At 8 p.m. it was 14° F. Jennie made me today a pair of spring boots, *ugruk* soles, and deerskin legs, fur inside. If the deerskin is steeped in oil for sometime, it becomes waterproof like sealskin and has the advantage of being a great deal warmer than the latter.

Wednesday, April 8th

Another quiet day indoors. I worked at Eskimo grammar most of the day, and in the evening Jennie told me four short stories. Wilkins typed letters all the time,[28] and the others found various employments. Andre Norem caused us a little anxiety this evening. He started out with a gun; he was going to examine his traps, he said. It was then about 7 p.m. Capt. Bernard met him outside — we others did not know he had gone — and induced him to return. He has been a victim of hallucinations since before Xmas, and on Xmas Eve wandered off, was lost, and though search parties were out all Xmas day, he was not found until Boxing Day; he had been wandering about 72 hours in a very low temperature. For a man of 56[29] it was a wonder he survived. He had taken his hands out of the sleeves of his coat and put them in his trousers, thus saving them from being frozen. His cheeks and chin were frozen and took a fortnight or so to heal, but otherwise he was unharmed. He had walked about the whole time, he said; when discovered he was slowly making his way to camp (Collinson Point) about 3 miles off. Since then a quiet watch has been kept on him, but he is aware of it and has been greatly depressed. The sky has been overcast all day, and the moderate breeze of the morning strengthened in the afternoon and was blowing strongly at 11 p.m. The temperature fluctuated — early this afternoon it was about 14°.

Figure 78. The author and *umiaks* cached the previous autumn by the inland Eskimos; April 1914. (Photo by G.H. Wilkins, CMC Photo No. 37120.)

Thursday, April 9th

Another quiet day indoors for most of us. The temperature was extraordinarily high early in the afternoon — it reached 45°. But a westerly blizzard sprang up in the evening and at 8 p.m. it was blowing about 45 miles an hour. The tide rose extraordinarily high today.

Friday, April 10th   Good Friday

The blizzard of last evening had hardly abated at all when we got up this morning, but it slackened during the day, until late in the afternoon the air was practically calm. The temperature fell during the night. At 8 a.m. it was -5°, at 8 p.m. -15°, a drop of 60° in about 26 hours. Wilkins took some photos today, partly for me, of the *umiaks* on the rack and two of me.[30] He developed them later, and at the same time developed the three I took the other day when I went with the captain to his cabin along the coast; all turned out fairly well.

Saturday, April 11th

The sun set at 7:45 p.m. this evening. The temperature fell to -20° last night and remained between -10° and -20° all day, and dropped to about -20° in the evening again. There was hardly any wind at all — a light breath from the west. We expected Dr. Anderson, but he did not turn up. Andre Norem seems to be rather worse than usual — he sits with a vacant stare for long periods, takes up a thing and lays it down again several times before he adopts any decisive course, and in many ways acts like a little child. He has to be under supervision all the time.[31] Natkusiak and Fred went out after ptarmigan and secured one. Capt. Nahmens was making a sail for a boat. There was a very slight aurora at 10:30 p.m., a faint bow running north-southeast in the southeast quadrant, not quite stretching to the horizon. At 11 p.m. there were three parallel bows stretching northwest-southeast.

Sunday, April 12th. Easter Sunday

An ideal Easter Sunday for this climate. The temperature was down to -18° during the night, -8° at 2 p.m., and -30° at 8 p.m. There was almost a dead calm all night and all day. The sun shone brightly and a light haze obscured the horizon. Capt. Nahmens and Castel went to the former's cabin and brought back the remainder of his goods.[32] Capt. Bernard with the Eskimos pulled down the dog-house; the dogs are all tied up outside now. Wilkins went over to a small river behind the *Alaska* this morning to take some photos of its frozen condition, but it was covered over with snow and no glare ice was visible. Aiyakuk and his wife turned up at 2 p.m. He is a youngish man who has married an elderly woman. Two lads of about 12 years came with them — their relationship I don't know. The woman's name (the boys call her mother) is Toglumunna. We had a gramaphone concert in the evening under the baton of Capt. Nahmens while the Eskimos played cards on the floor. There were at 10:30 p.m. two faint auroral arches perceptible overhead stretching northwest-southeast, but not approaching close to the horizon in either direction. Sledging has been very bad since the very warm day (Thursday) when all the surface snow began to melt. Now there is a hard crust not firm enough to bear a man or a dog, and below is soft snow often for a depth of 2 feet, and almost everywhere for 6 to 8 inches. We are wondering what is delaying Dr. Anderson and Blue.

Monday, April 13th

Another glorious day, calm and clear save for a slight haze on the horizon. The temperature was well below zero, -6° in the early afternoon. Andre [Norem] had a recurrence of his hallucinations today. He was crying while sawing wood and seeing Capt. Nahmens he went up to him and said "Have I done anything to you?" Capt. Nahmens and Castel are going east tomorrow to try and discover Dr. Anderson.[33] Capt. Bernard was in bed all day — suffering from intense pain in the side of the neck (whenever he moved his head). Añutisiak and Aiyakuk went out to look for ptarmigan but returned empty-handed. Añutisiak had the misfortune to fall and break the stock of his fowling piece — a 12-gauge [shotgun] belonging to Capt. Nahmens. Wilkins went off also to look for ptarmigan but was equally unsuccessful. Fred and Natkusiak cleared away the snow from both the outside and the inside of Johansen's tent. This morning Wilkins and I catalogued all the Expedition's books here, and I typed the list this afternoon.[34] Thus the day passes in various occupations. I have more than I can do — trying to read up Eskimo and other literature, to translate the Eskimo stories I have, revise and correct the vocabulary etc. I had a bath just before turning in.

Tuesday, April 14th

A repetition of yesterday as far as the weather was concerned. The light westerly breeze of the morning died away before noon. The temperature was comparatively mild (between -20° and zero) and the atmosphere brilliantly clear. Capt. Nahmens[35] and Castel left about 10 a.m. to go to Crawford's (25 miles east) and if Dr. Anderson were not there to continue on to the *Belvedere* (another 50 miles). The Eskimos and Thomsen were digging out the snow from the stern of the *Mary Sachs* today. Wilkins took both still and moving pictures of it. I am the meteorologist now that Capt. Nahmens[35] has gone. Capt. Bernard was all right today — he was up and working outside. Natkusiak called out in his sleep last night "What's the matter with you?" followed by some Eskimo word I could not catch. There were auroral arches last night about 10:30 stretching in the usual direction northwest to southeast.

Wednesday, April 15th

A blizzard sprang up about midnight and raged all day today. The temperature was about zero [Fahrenheit] most of the time, and the wind varied in its velocity. Some of the gusts must have been nearly travelling at about 50 miles an hour. I found it very disagreeable reading the thermometers and wind gauge this morning, as they were all snowed up, and my hands had to be warmed up several times by running inside. The tide gauge too was working badly — ice had settled on the arm along which the indicator slides, and prevented the latter from moving up and down, so that it registered a straight line only. At 11 p.m. the wind was still fairly strong and the snow still drifting in clouds, but it was much less violent than during the day.

Thursday, April 16th

The day was marked by a terrible tragedy. Andre Norem, ex-cook [steward] of the *Mary Sachs*, blew out his brains a few minutes before breakfast in the passage-way just outside the door. Wilkins was taking the meteorological observations outside and Andre spoke to him, remarking that "it was pretty raw this morning" or words to that effect. I went outside just as Andre was coming in. A few moments later as I was going inside again and, half-blinded by the sunlight outside, was feeling my way along the passage, I nearly knocked against him, and he said "I nearly bumped into you then." I could just make out a blurred form, and replied "It's dark inside here," then went on in, pausing for a moment before closing the door in case he was following. Hardly had I taken off my skin shirt when a report of a gun was heard and going out we found him lying dead, with a rifle still in his hand — he had blown his brains out. We laid him out at the end of the passage. Thomsen, the sailor on

Figure 79. Wording on monument for Andre Norem.

the *Mary Sachs*, had worked with an undertaker in earlier days, and he washed and dressed the body.[36] Then a coffin was made[37] and a wooden monument engraved.

He will not be buried until Dr. Anderson returns. His clothes and other possessions were gathered together; Dr. Anderson will decide what is to be done with them. The deceased has a sister in the States, it is said, and property in Nome.[38] Two or three times before he has been prevented from shooting himself, and once he threatened to shoot Capt. Nahmens. Yet last evening he seemed more cheerful than he has been for some time. Only yesterday afternoon he washed some clothes for me.

The blizzard lasted all night and up to about 9 o'clock then gradually died away. The temperature ranged betwen -8° and -20°. This evening the sun set at 8 p.m., but it was still faintly light at 10:30. At 11 p.m. there were a number of stars visible but no aurora.

Friday, April 17th

Andre's body was placed on the cache outside last evening, inside the coffin; the wooden memorial was set up beside the stove indoors to dry, after receiving a coat of paint. Capt. Bernard[39] and Aarnout Castel returned at a quarter to 9 [p.m.], having travelled all the way from Martin Point today — a distance of 50 or more miles. They had nine dogs and a light sled, and the weather favoured them. Nothing had been learnt about Dr. Anderson or about Stefansson and the others out on the ice. A great lead of open water lies within 1/2 mile of the *Polar Bear*, and between her and the shore is a crack about 25 feet wide. The engineer and others are working hard to fix the propeller on, in case she goes off in the next blow, as is thought very probable. The *Belvedere* suddenly sprang up 5 feet through the pressure of the water below; the jump shook things a good deal but did no damage. The weather was calm and fine all day.

Saturday, April 18th

Wilkins has decided to leave for Barrow on Monday with Natkusiak and his dog team. He has been waiting for Dr. Anderson to return but is afraid to wait longer lest he should be too late for the floe whaling. On Tuesday Aarnout Castel and the cook Charlie Brook [who had been steward on the *Alaska*] are going east with two sleds and fifteen dogs to take gasoline down to the mouth of the Mackenzie[40] ready for the launch in the spring when the ice breaks up. I am going east with them as far as the *North Star*[41] and shall examine what there is there and perhaps at Crawford's also and probably make an inventory of it, returning as I find occasion. Consequently much of the day has been spent in making pre- parations for our respective journeys. Tomorrow Norem is to be buried[42] — a grave has been made some distance to the eastward on a small emi- nence. The weather has been fine and calm all day, the temperature a little above zero.

Sunday, April 19th

Today was perhaps the pleasantest, as far as the weather was con- cerned, that we have had this year. The temperature was a little above zero, but the sun shone brilliantly and was quite hot. Andre Norem was buried about 2 p.m.; we all attended the funeral. His grave is on a slightly elevated point about 1/2 mile east of the camp.[43] Wilkins developed some photos and made a few prints, and I also made some prints in the evening. He starts away tomorrow morning and we on Tuesday probably. There is still no sign of Dr. Anderson or of the ice party. The dogs killed a fox last night but did not eat it, so that the skin was not in bad condition. I gave Wilkins a set of deer legs to give to Mrs. Añopqana and another for Qapqana.

Monday, April 20th

Wilkins and Natkusiak left this morning for Barrow where he will take cinematographic pictures of the spring whaling from the ice.[44] As soon as possible he will return and go down to the Mackenzie to join Chipman and Cox. The weather could hardly have been more favourable. The temperature was just below zero, and a light easterly wind was blowing. Tomorrow Aarnout Castel and the cook [Charlie Brook] are leaving for the mouth of the Mackenzie, freighting gasoline for the launch. I am going with them as far as the *North Star*, and Capt. Bernard as far as Crawford's. There are two sleds, but both will be heavily laden. Fred cut my beard and moustache this evening with a pair of clippers — it afforded the rest great amusement. The days are very long now — even at 11 p.m. it is not really dark.

Tuesday, April 21st

Capt. Bernard decided not to come with us — there was really no need. He has to stay and superintend the work around and on the *Mary Sachs*. Aarnout [Castel], [Charlie] Brook the cook, and myself left about 9:30 a.m. Aarnout's sled had a load of about 1100 lbs and weighed 200; Brook's, sled and all, had about 750 lbs.[45] Aarnout had eight dogs, Brook six. The first 9 miles or so to the point [Anderson Point], where Capt. Nahmens' cache is, was very heavy travelling and took us about 3 1/2 to 4 hours. After that the trail was good. About 2 p.m. we met Dr.

Anderson and Blue returning and stopped to talk and have lunch. A stump was split and lit, and the Dr. fried some ptarmigan meat on it and boiled tea; we had brought some bread. He had been unsuccessful in a search for mountain sheep, and of caribou had seen no trace, but he brought about 150 ptarmigan. The two ascended the Hulahula River to the mountains and went about 25 miles up into the range [Romanzof Mountains] but did not cross the divide. It was much warmer there, he said, than on the coast. They were caught in a blizzard the first day they started up the river and were stuck for 2 or 3 days; then they lost a dog which fell sick and died. The Dr. is coming down to the *North Star* in a few days to arrange things at various places along the line. Brook exchanged sleds with them[46] and we started out again just after 4 p.m. The dogs were very tired before we reached Crawford's [house] and Jumbo had to be released — he was dead beat. However, we made the house just before sunset. It is an ordinary Eskimo log cabin. The Dr. had given us about a score of ptarmigan, so Brook (or Charlie as he is usually called) baked three for dinner. The weather was glorious all day — a very light air coming from the west. At 10 p.m., however, it was -20° according to the thermometer outside.

Wednesday, April 22nd

Charlie baked three more ptarmigan for breakfast, which delayed us in getting away. It was 10 a.m. when we moved off, in fine clear weather, bright sunshine and a light southwesterly air. We travelled along slowly for 10 miles or so and were just reaching the eastern end of Barter Island where there is a native house when we met two sleds, Johansen, Crawford, and Dan Sweeney. Sweeney had been left in charge of the camp at Martin Point, the other two, with McConnell, were sent back from the ice on April 7th and landed about 30 miles this side of Herschel Island. They travelled along the coast, McConnell staying at Martin Point to gather up some papers etc., he had left there. He has instructions from Stefansson to take an inventory of the Expedition's things at Duffy O'Connor's and at the *North Star*. He [McConnell] is going out[47] in the summer, probably on the *Annie Olga*,[48] a small schooner lying about a mile from the *North Star* at present. He will thus sever his connection with the Expedition. He and Stefansson have not got on too well together, he told me. Crawford brought me a letter from Stefansson cancelling his earlier instructions to take charge of the *North Star*, and instructing me from June 1st to start archaeological work at Barter Island if possible, or at some other place if Barter Island is not convenient. Dr. Anderson is to hire one or two men for me — white men if possible. Johansen proposes to go up into the Endicott Mountains[49] again as soon as Leffingwell returns, the two going up together to a hot stream that was discovered up near the head of the Sadlerochit River by a winter hunting party of which Johansen was one.

I turned back with Crawford's party. We passed some ruined houses on the north side of Barter Island — which I shall probably dig out later, and in 2 hours reached Crawford's house — with the freighting teams this morning we had taken 4 hours to cover the same distance. About 1/2 mile northeast of Crawford's, Aiyakuk (or Aiyaka) lives with his wife and one son in a tent surrounded with a snowhouse. About 2 1/2 miles north of it on a sandspit, Sweeney says, are some very old ruins — older, he thinks, than those on Barter Island. I went over with Johansen to Aiyakuk's cabin — and got four ptarmigan and a little salt, while Crawford baked some bread and made coffee. Aiyakuk came in later with ten ptarmigan he shot today. There are ptarmigan tracks all round the cabin. They are changing to their summer brown now; Aiyakuk has noticed brown feathers on the throat and breast. Fox tracks seem to be fairly numerous too.

Thursday, April 23rd

We left about 10 a.m.; my watch stopped last evening so I do not know the exact time. Crawford gathered up his things and loaded them on the sleds. About 3 p.m. we reached Collinson Point. When Johansen and the others left Stefansson, they were on the edge of the continental shelf, the depth being 175 fathoms, with a bottom of mud and small pebbles. This was some 65 miles from shore, April 7th.[50] Sweeney is going back to the Mackenzie River the day after tomorrow,[51] and I shall go with him for the first day or two to look at the ruins along the coast. Probably I shall go to Icy Reef, between the *Belvedere* and Duffy O'Connor's,[52] where there are both ruins and a number of Eskimos now engaged in sealing.[53] Dr. Anderson is coming down a few days later to fix things up along the line. Capt. Bernard is camp chef now — an old occupation of his.

Friday, April 24th

Another glorious day although it was somewhat overcast this morning. I walked round the coast examining the three ruined houses in the bay. One — behind the *Alaska* — seems to be comparatively new — it has iron nails in the window frame. The other two are probably fairly recent also — Teriglu says they are and gave the names of the men who built them. Sweeney also says they were not here when he first came 28 years ago. I took a photo of one near the camp.[54] Teriglu is living in a cabin a few yards from the camp. I visited him this afternoon, and his wife put a patch on my boot. Johansen gave me this morning a skull and a few stray things he gathered last summer for me — nothing of much value except the skull. Johansen also is going down with Sweeney to Duffy O'Connor's[55] and will return with Dr. Anderson. Teriglu taught me a new cat's-cradle figure this evening. Sweeney was fixing up the sled he is to take tomorrow. The light has been very trying the last few days — we have all been wearing snow-glasses. Capt. Nahmens had a touch of snow-blindness one day. We have been getting sun-burnt too.

Teriglu told me the names of three of his children and their ages — he had a stroke to represent a year. Igiaqpuk is 6 and was born on the Igiaq-puk River;[56] Okpiluk is 4 and was born on the Okpilak River; Savagvik is 1 and was born at a point a little west of Flaxman [Island] with the same name.[57]

Saturday, April 25th

There was a strong wind blowing from the east this morning causing a considerable drift, so we decided not to leave until it cleared. Johansen spent most of the day working up his notes and I typing cat's-cradle figures, the rest in various occupations about the house. Blue, Capt. Nah-mens, and Crawford found heated arguments where facts were neglected an interesting way to pass the time. The Eskimos Fred and Añutisiak and Aiyakuk's step-son are sleeping on the *Mary Sachs* now, and Thomsen and Jennie have a corner in the house. In the evening we had a phono-graphic concert and a number of records were picked out to be lent to the *Belvedere* people.

Chapter 12. Journey to Demarcation Point

Departure eastward — Martin Point — Welcomed aboard the Belvedere *— Along Icy Reef — Arrival at Duffy O'Connor's house — Examining house ruins on Demarcation Reef — Overnight with Eskimos at west end of Icy Reef — Return to the* Belvedere *— Story of slaughter of Prince of Wales Eskimos in Kotzebue Sound — Mixed crew of* Belvedere *— Meeting Dr. Anderson — Visit with Eskimos at Martin Point — Story of seal and sea-otter hunting — Overnight solo walk from Martin Point back to Camden Bay camp*

Sunday, April 26th, 1914

A light breeze was blowing from the west when we turned out. We got away at 9 a.m., and soon after we started the wind freshened until it became almost a blizzard. We took a wrong trail to start with, and on leaving it, still held too far inside Camden Bay. We had to skirt along the eastern shore past Capt. Nahmens' cabin until we reached the point where his cache is. Here, beside the grave I photographed a few weeks ago, Sweeney pointed out an old ruined house, which Aiyaka (who has been in this part of the country since his boyhood) said was once inhabited by a *Nunatagmiuñ* family. It was deserted when Sweeney came here in 1897. From the point we kept on to Crawford's, wandering a little as the trail was obliterated by the drift, and we could not see very far. However, we reached the house about 4 p.m. and had a good meal of coffee, tinned meat, hard-bread, a pie, and *mukpaurat* made by Capt. Bernard for us. Aiyakuk and his wife came in a little later. He said that the ruined houses on Barter Island and on the sandspit about 3 miles northeast of this house were formerly inhabited by *Kagmalit* Eskimos (Mackenzie River). So too were some old ruins on the sandspit about 1/2 miles west of our camp at Collinson Point, ruins of which I was ignorant for they are now covered up completely with snow. Sweeney tells me that he has often seen a Point Hope woman doctor named Uvugra 'driving out the devil' of sickness by laying the patient on the floor, with a rope or cord passed round the neck and a stick attached to it, and held in her hand. After a long 'conjuration' she lifted the head; if it was light to lift the devil was driven out — if heavy it was still there and the process had to be repeated (see picture in Boas, *The Eskimo of Baffin Land* [*and Hudson Bay*, Fig. 2, p. 511, 1907]). Sweeney says he has seen this practised all along the coast from Point Hope and Barrow eastward.

Monday, April 27th

We made an early start at 10 minutes to 8 a.m. A strong breeze was blowing from the west, causing the snow to drift a little, but it was clearer than yesterday. Steering a little north of east we reached the eastern extremity of a sandspit after going about 3 miles. This is the sandspit, Sweeney says, that bears the three old houses in which the Mackenzie Eskimos used to live. We did not see the ruins, however, for they lay a

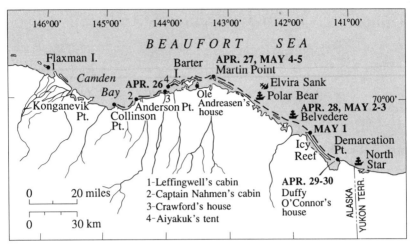

Figure 80. Route to and from Demarcation Point, April 26 - May 6, 1914. Dates indicate probable locations of overnight stops.

little west of the point where we struck the spit. Continuing we passed the ruins on the west end of Barter Island, then Iñukuk's house on the eastern end [and] at about 1 p.m. reached O. Andreasen's house, which lies on a sandspit. Here we gathered up his goods,[1] and packed them on a small sled — some 300 lbs all told. We had lunch here too, kindling a fire outside and boiling coffee. The sled with Andreasen's goods we trailed behind the other sled, and Johansen and I pulled on each side of it — he with a dog chain, I with my belt — for the dogs were very tired. It is about 20 miles from Crawford's to Andreasen's, another 10 to Martin Point. There is an old ruin near the camp at Martin Point; the house was built by an Inland Eskimo, Iñukuk says. We found Iñukuk and his mother (commonly known as Shotgun) living in a tent snowhouse beside Sweeney's tent snowhouse. Pannigavlu[2] and her son went to the *Polar Bear* to obtain a tent and are expected back tomorrow. The wind moderated considerably during the afternoon, and the atmosphere became very clear. The *Polar Bear* is about 10 miles from here and the *Belvedere* another 12 miles.

Tuesday, April 28th

We breakfasted at 6 a.m., for Sweeney had to gather up some of his stuff off a rack and out of the house. I found time to visit the old *Nunatagmiut* house about 1/3 mile to the south. Very little is left of the house, but two racks are still standing beside it. Under one — a very large one apparently intended for an *umiak* — I picked up a bone piece of a sled runner about 1 foot long. There were fragments of old tins scattered round, showing that the place had been inhabited recently. It was 8 a.m. when we left. About 2 miles east of the camp lie the ruins of two houses and a mile or so further on [lie ruins] of another two. These are

Figure 81. Oyaraq and his wife sledding with sail, en route to Barter Island, April or May 1914. (Photo by D. Jenness, CMC Photo No. 37110.)

on the left of the trail. About another 2 miles brings you to a high cutbank. Just before reaching this on a high knoll lies an old grave, for it seems to have been the custom here to bury on the ground and cover the grave with logs, not to erect a platform such as we saw in Port Clarence. At noon we came to the *Polar Bear* camp and had tea with an Eskimo woman in one of the three huts, then later dinner at 3 p.m. with Capt. Mogg and the *Polar Bear* party. Johansen visited the ship to secure a tide staff; it lies about 1/2 mile north of the camp in the ice. The *Polar Bear* is a schooner which had rather an odd crew and passenger list. Some rich people's sons in Boston half chartered her to take them big-game hunting, up in Banks Land and its vicinity. There were added two scientists — the two men now at Duffy's, who are collecting for some museum, I think. Then there is [Capt.] Mogg himself, who wished to trade on the Siberian coast. The rich men's sons — of whom I saw three — appeared to be heartily sick of the Arctic. One came in with two ptarmigan; the other two appeared to have hardly enough energy to go a dozen paces out of doors. We left there at 4 p.m. and reached the *Belvedere*[3] about 8 p.m. The last mile was rather heavy travelling, for the ice round the ship is rather heavy. The crew and officers of the ship are living on board, together with the crew of the *Elvira*,[4] which was crushed near here. Capt. Cottle[5] and his wife made us heartily welcome; in fact Johansen and I sat up until 2 a.m. talking to them.

Wednesday, April 29th

Sweeney proposed to travel in the evening because the dogs were fatigued by the heat of the day. So Johansen and I accompanied a sled which left the *Belvedere* about 10 a.m. to take a bag of flour to some natives on Icy Reef, returning with a load of wood. One of the natives who ran the sled was from Siberia; I noticed that though he conversed freely with the others he not infrequently failed to understand what was said to him. We found two or three Eskimo families encamped in tents on the west end of Icy Reef;[6] with one of them we had biscuits and tea, and left our things there, mine to remain inside the tent until I return, Johansen's to be brought on by Sweeney. After lunch we two set out to walk down Icy Reef to Duffy O'Connor's house about 18 miles away (the Eskimo settlement is about 8 miles from the *Belvedere*). We walked along leisurely examining the ruined houses scattered along the reef. It was easier to coast the reef than to keep out on the lagoon ice between the reef and the shore, for the snow had melted or been blown away in many places leaving only the slippery glare ice. The Endicott Mountains[7] only a few miles back stood out very clearly; they impressed us as being extremely steep. Naturally no vegetation of any kind was visible. We met two parties of Eskimos on their way west, the second consisting of a man named Eglun with his wife and son; this Eglun has the reputation of being one of the most progressive natives in the Mackenzie region. He has a tent house on Icy Reef and opposite it on the mainland about 1/2 mile away is his cache and a high look-out platform used when sealing. We reached O'Connor's house about 9 p.m. and found there McConnell,[8] [Joseph] Dixon, and [Winthrop S.] Brooks, the two latter being scientists from the *Polar Bear*. Dixon said he had been very disappointed at this locality and had only secured, besides ptarmigan, a single lemming. The lemming, like the ptarmigan, is changing its colour from the white coat of winter to the brown one of summer, the change here occurring first on the back. Dixon has cleverly constructed a canoe rather like a Canadian canvas canoe, cutting the ribs out of curved roots. I was disappointed to find no sealing in progress, but there is no open water visible — fortunately for Stefansson and his party. A light east wind sprang up in the afternoon but died away again soon afterwards. The days are so long now that there is really no time when it is dark. It is rather disconcerting, for it is difficult to accommodate oneself to the new conditions.

Thursday, April 30th

Sweeney arrived at 2 a.m.[9] He left again with McConnell about 10 a.m. for Matt Andreasen's place — the schooner *North Star* — some 10 miles further on. McConnell is to take an inventory of the things there.[10] I wandered among the old ruins on Demarcation Reef [Point], where there are about 30 houses and racks. A sled with four Eskimo men and one woman passed by on their way to the *Belvedere*; they were of the party which conveyed the launch Stefansson bought from that vessel to the Mackenzie. A moderately strong west wind sprang up before noon, so we spent the rest of the day indoors. Two sleds with sails set passed by the house about 6 p.m., but the travellers (Eskimos) did not stop.

Figure 82. Eskimo tent and sled, with snow blocks for wind break, Icy Reef, April 1914. (Photo by D. Jenness, CMC Photo No. 37135.)

Friday, May 1st

Dixon and I left on the return journey at 7 a.m.;[11] he is going back to the *Polar Bear* camp to prosecute scientific work there until the vessel breaks out. The walk up took 6 hours. We stayed to lunch with the Eskimo family where I had left my sleeping bag, and he [Dixon] went on an hour later. I stayed in the tent and talked with them, joining the men about 7 o'clock in another tent for dinner (ptarmigan and *mukpaurat*). The woman in the tent where I stayed is the wife of a man named Kiniq(?)[12] and is busy making spring boots for the *Belvedere* [crew]. I turned in about 10 p.m., but the others not until some hours later. The difficulty with the long days now is to know when to eat and when [to] sleep. The weather was fine all day. For a time a moderate breeze blew from the west making the air feel rather cold, but this died away in the evening. The Eskimos here on the reef seem to be hunting ptarmigan and preparing for the sealing. An old man returned with two snowy owls and two ptarmigan. They seem to be living mainly on *mukpaurat* and such birds as they shoot.

Saturday, May 2nd

We all rose late — about 9 a.m. At breakfast when I joined the Eskimo men in a neighbouring tent for breakfast, I found Eglun there. He said he had brought Heard[13] down from the *Polar Bear* camp the night before and that he was then in a neighbouring tent. I called on him a few minutes later. He said that he had made two or three plans during the winter to go hunting in the mountains, but they had all miscarried. When Stefansson went up the Mackenzie he and [Winthrop S.] Brooks had accompanied him as far as Herschel [Island]. Now he was going to Duffy O'Connor's camp to try to find a dog team to take him up into the mountains behind for a fortnight's hunting. He thought McConnell might

Figure 83. Duffy O'Connor's house and storage racks, east end of Demarcation Point, Alaska, May 6, 1914. (Photo by R.M. Anderson, CMC Photo No. 38699.)

possibly go up with him. A sled from the *Polar Bear*, which had come down with him the night before, was returning immediately, so I packed my sleeping bag on it and left. A sharp run of 7 or 8 miles brought us to the *Belvedere*. Here I found Dixon waiting for this same sled to take him back to the *Polar Bear*. Capt. and Mrs. Cottle made me kindly welcome, and I spent nearly all the rest of the day talking to them. In the evening a visit to the west-shore (Siberians from Indian Point) natives resulted in a number of interesting new cat's-cradle figures and songs, so I determined to stay another day and gather more.[14] The weather was very mild all day and the atmosphere calm. A man from the *Belvedere* brought in a seal, which he had shot about 2 miles from the ship, where it had come up out of its hole.

Sunday, May 3rd

Another day on board more or less idle until the evening, when I obtained some more cat's-cradle figures. During the day an Eskimo attached one end of a sealskin line to the crow's nest and the other to a rope down near the hatch amidship — he was hanging up to dry a rawhide line cut from a single skin. I took a photo of part of the bow of the *Belvedere*, where it was sheathed with Australian iron bark more than 20 years ago.[15] After all this buffetting in the ice it is hardly marked and as sound now as when it was put on; and yet the *Belvedere* last autumn had her stern partly broken through crashing into a heavy floe. I am thinking of sending a print to the Commonwealth office in London as an advertisement of Australian timber. Capt. Cottle has been whaling up here for some 25 or 26 years. He says that the Siberian natives used to cross over to Kotzebue Sound, the American Eskimos to Collusion Bay, about 50 miles northwest of Cape Serge[16] in order to trade. During trading there was an armistice — the trading ground was neutral territory. In [?][17] a gang of [Cape] Prince of Wales Eskimo who had turned buccaneering and sorely molested their neighbours of Kotzebue Sound tried to capture a whaling vessel, the [?][18] of which Capt. M. Kenny (?)[19] was in command. They came out under the pretext of wishing to trade, left their

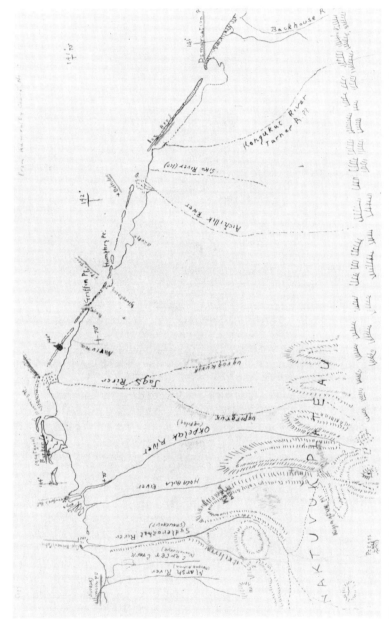

Figure 84. Author's sketch-map of the region between Collinson and Demarcation Points. The original map is at the back of Volume 1 of the diary (Jenness papers, MG30.B89 NAC) (NAC Photo No. C136457).

Figure 85. The 420-ton bark *Belvedere* in the ice northwest of Icy Reef, October 1913. (Photo by K.G. Chipman, CMC No. 43199.)

women below in the boats and swarmed on board. Suddenly one of them, knife in hand, stole up behind the captain to stab him, but was seen by one of the crew and knocked down with a hand bar. A general fight ensued, [and] the Eskimos [were] defeated. Some jumped overboard and tried to make for shore in their canoes; the boats were fired on and every one sunk. The rest hid in the forecastle but were dragged out with a great hook, knocked on the head, and thrown over the side. There was great rejoicing in Kotzebue [Sound] when it became known that the pirates had been exterminated. The *Belvedere* had so much cargo taken out of her during the winter[20] that recently she suddenly sprang up 3 feet in the night. Mrs. Cottle was greatly alarmed, as indeed everyone was. The crew is very mixed. There are seven Eskimos from Indian Point [Siberia], who in the matter of work are far superior to the American Eskimo, Capt. Cottle says. Then there are Portuguese and Negroes from [the] Cape Verde Islands[21] for the captain made three voyages between there and the West Indies in search of sperm whales. Latitude 12° North and longitude 140° East was one of his favorite hunting grounds. There is another Negro from the southern States, two Russians, one only a half breed, one half being Eskimo. Then there is a cockney from London, a 'blue-nose'[22] from Nova Scotia, Americans, and I do not remember what else. A snow bunting was flying round the ship most of the day. The temperature was a little below freezing most of the day.

Monday, May 4th

A very warm day — the thermometer must have approached 50°. Everywhere the snow was melting. I left after breakfast for the the *Polar Bear* camp with Clark and Ellis,[23] the former photographer and assistant

Figure 86. Three Siberian sailors from the *Belvedere* making an *umiak*. Foxskins drying on a line in distance. (Photo by D. Jenness, CMC Photo No. 37141.)

engineer, the latter engineer and part owner of the *Elvira*. They told me that on the 22nd September (or possibly the 23rd) the *Elvira* was abandoned at the instance of Capt. Pedersen. She was then about 7 1/2 miles out from the shore and leaking a little. In the night she disappeared — whether she sank or was carried away by the ice they do not know.[24] Capt. Louis Lane [owner of the] (*Polar Bear*) and a party of men crossed the mountains to the Yukon River during the winter, following hard upon the tracks of Capt. Pedersen (*Elvira's* captain) and Swenson[25] (trader and part owner of the *Belvedere*). They crossed the Endicott Mountains,[26] ascending the Kongakut River opposite Icy Reef. We met Dr. Anderson about 5 miles from the *Belvedere* with the Eskimos Fred and Añutisiak, Pannigavlu and her son. He had left the *Polar Bear* camp that morning, having reached it in 2 days from Collinson Point.[27] Añutisiak returns tomorrow to Collinson Point with sugar, so he will pick up my things at the *Polar Bear* camp. We reached this latter place in time for dinner at 3 p.m. I stayed 2 or 3 hours only, then left with a Russian boy, who had been interpreter up the Siberian coast on the *Polar Bear*. He wished to remove the remnants of his trapping camp, which lies about 4 miles east of Martin Point. He had caught only four foxes during the winter, but had built a very comfortable hut for himself. We made tea there with the primus stove, ate some bread and butter we brought with us, then, finding a lard can containing some frozen mush (porridge) we heated and ate this. He then packed his things on a light hand-sled he had brought and set off for the *Polar Bear* camp, while I continued on to Martin Point. It was after 10 p.m. when I reached the place, but at this time of the year it is light even at midnight. Between the *Belvedere* and Martin Point I saw a raven, some ptarmigan, snow buntings, and the tracks of a fox. Clark, the photographer, spent 4 years in the Pribilof [Islands] sealing somewhere between 1880 and 1890. He said that they killed as many as 15,000 seals a year. The young males which could find no mates went up some distance on the land to sleep during the warm days of summer. By night men stole in between them and the rookeries on the shore and drove the whole herd to the slaughtering station — it might number 15,000 as said above. There they are driven into a pen — two men can drive them once they are set going, for they huddle together like sheep. Those fit for killing are cut out like cattle a score or so at a time, and killed by a sharp knock on the top of the head with a kind of club; the rest are driven back to the sea. In 1911 the sealing grounds were closed by an international agreement between [the] United States, Russia, and Japan and England (?). Previous to that the grounds on the American side were leased for a term of 5 years.

The other man Ellis had spent some years hunting the sea otter in somewhere about the same region. The Aleuts[28] with the two- or three-holed kayaks (*bidake*) searched for them and shot them. A sea otter skin is worth from $500-$3000 according to the size and quality. Sometimes, like the hair seal, the sea otter sinks, but generally it floats after being shot. Now the industry is stopped in Alaska at least, and sea otters are very rare there.

Tuesday, May 5th

Another very warm day. I went back east 4 miles with shovel and axe to examine what seemed an old grave [Fig. 87], but found that the logs concealed a box nailed together — a recent burial — so returned. The tundra is full of small brown patches where the snow has melted away. As far as the temperature goes this is the pleasantest time of the year to travel, but sledging is extremely heavy and will soon be impossible, while one's boots are soaking wet through walking in the soft melting snow. The snowhouses are everywhere thawing and will presently be abandoned. Ptarmigan and snow bunting seem abundant and ravens not at all scarce. Squirrels are coming out, it is said, though I have not observed any. I spent the rest of the day with Iñukuk and his mother at Martin Point.[29] About 2 p.m. an elderly man and his wife turned up, travelling from the Mackenzie [River] to Flaxman Island. Johansen and I met this pair at Icy Reef [April 29th] travelling up towards the ships. They were carrying on their sled a great seal poke full of seal blubber. About 9:30 p.m. came Añutisiak, accompanied by 'Levi' (W.J. Baur) our new cook, Addison, and Sullivan. The two latter are engaged to dig out the *Alaska*; all three may possibly be retained permanently;[30] Levi and Addison were on the *Elvira*, Sullivan on the *Belvedere*. The first is a Jew, the second American, and the last an American Negro. Pannigavlu and her boy returned to Martin Point with the party. I made them a pot of tea and some boiled rice, and we turned in soon afterwards.

Figure 87. An Eskimo grave near Martin Point, May 5, 1914. (Photo by D. Jenness, CMC Photo No. 37161.)

Wednesday, May 6th

A glorious day, though not quite so warm as the two preceding, fortunately for dog-mushers. Sullivan, who has been a cook as well as an A.B.,[31] got breakfast, after which we packed 80-100 lbs of beans on the sled and set up a square-sail in the front end. The old Eskimo pair who came yesterday also loaded up, and we all set out together. The trail was much better than it had been from the *Belvedere* to the cutbank 5 miles east of Martin Point; it seemed as though that portion of the coast were especially favoured with an early spring. A light puffy east breeze gradually died away during the day leaving the sails flapping. We stopped at Inyukuk's tent-house near the east end of Barter Island and made tea. The place was constructed 2 or 3 years ago by a white man from one of the whaling ships who lost his way at the mouth of the Hulahula [River] and was never found. We reached Aiyaka's tent[32] at 8:30 p.m., having left Martin Point at 10 a.m. Aiyaka has pitched his tent on the tundra close to Crawford's old house, which is now full of water, and Teriglu has his tent beside Aiyaka's. They fed us with boiled ptarmigan and biscuits and tea, after which I lay down in Teriglu's tent till 11 p.m., then set out alone for Collinson Point.[33] There was a half daylight, but it was foggy and nothing to guide me for most of the way across the Hulahula delta (14 miles) except a very light easterly air, and a faint glow which moved round from northeast to northwest following the sun's track. At times this was scarcely perceptible by reason of the fog, and the drifts of snow (which run east-west along the north coast of Alaska and so serve as a kind of compass), have been obliterated by the wind and the warm weather. However, all went well for 4 1/2 hours, when I stumbled upon the tundra. I turned to the north-northwest, still tundra; then north, and in a few minutes was in rough ice and therefore north of the trail. I turned west, but the rough ice continued, then southwest, still rough ice, finally south. The big kegs seemed to be rather less numerous, but the snow was very soft. Suddenly the fog lifted a little, the sun half pierced through, and there 50 yards on my left was the cache at the eastern point [Anderson Point] of Camden Bay. A few yards further brought me on to a well-marked trail, and by 6:30 a.m. I had reached Collinson Point, having made the longest tramp in a day of any member of the Expedition so far — about 53 miles in 20 1/2 hours, with two breaks — one from 4 - 5:30 p.m. for lunch and the other from 8:30 to 11 p.m.

Chapter 13. Temporarily in Charge of the Arctic Expedition

Camp activities — Repair work on the two schooners — Trading with inland Eskimos — Flu-like illness among personnel — Funeral service for Eskimo woman — Having to take charge of camp — Leffingwell arrives — Doctoring sick Eskimo girl — Discussion with Leffingwell — Signs of spring — Return of Dr. Anderson with mail

Thursday, May 7th, 1914

At Collinson Point there had been changes owing to the warm weather. The snow had been cleared away from the house and from the store and a new entrance constructed for the former. Qopuk and his family had come in from the west [from near Flaxman Island], and some inland natives from beyond the mountains had been down, sold some ptarmigan and a haunch of a mountain sheep and returned to their camp about a day's journey up one of the rivers. Capt. Nahmens and Blue are busy on the *Alaska*; Capt. Bernard gives such time as he can spare from the kitchen to the *Mary Sachs*. A strong easterly blew all day and the temperature was below freezing, quite a change. Añutisiak and the others turned up about 5 p.m., the sail had driven the sled along at a great rate. Tomorrow Levi takes over the kitchen. I spent the evening developing photos of which I have a fairly successful batch.[1] I am worried though at not being able to find my book of cat's-cradle figures and songs and the grammar notes; two hours and more were wasted in a vain search. The ptarmigan have at last made their appearance at Collinson Point and yesterday some of the folks here secured about a score. At Aiyaka's, Teriglu said, they [the ptarmigan] had left that locality, but he had caught a number of squirrels in his traps; Aiyaka, however, had several ptarmigan.

Friday, May 8th

A quiet day indoors; outside an unpleasant east wind was blowing and the temperature did not rise above 32° — freezing. Capt. Nahmens with Addison and Sullivan went off to dig out the *Alaska* and Blue to fix up his engines. Capt. Bernard and Crawford were busy on the *Mary Sachs*. I was typing cat's cradles on a Hammond typewriter, but it went out of order in the afternoon and it took Blue and me some time to fix it up. Towards evening two sleds came from the mountains bringing some *Nunatagmiut* [inland Eskimos]. They pitched their tents close to our camp.

Saturday, May 9th

The east wind gave place to a west wind with driving snow. The temperature was still below freezing most of the time. Work was resumed on the *Alaska* and the *Mary Sachs*, Levi running the kitchen. I had a very slight attack of malaria in the afternoon, but it was over in a few

Figure 88. A family of inland Eskimos, *Nunatagmiut,* arriving at Collinson Point, May 1914. (Photo by D. Jenness, CMC Photo No. 37134.)

hours. My missing papers were discovered behind the chronometers. About 6 p.m. a caravan of inland Eskimos made their appearance — thirteen sleds all told.[2] They made camp also beside us and we brought one family over to dine — a man, his wife, and five children. When the *Mary Sachs* put in here last autumn it was out of sugar, for the *Alaska* had not yet arrived, and this Eskimo gave them half a bag. Their sleds were loaded high with deerskins[3] — one sled alone seemed to contain about 100. It was interesting to watch them set the willow sticks around in a circle and draw the tent over it.[4] Many of them carried brush-wood for a flooring. The sleds seemed mostly of the old type with high runners.[5] There is an elderly woman among them who is dangerously ill with some stomach trouble. We have been trying to doctor her a little and gave her some hot broth as well. Several Eskimos came over to the house in the evening and we gave them a gramaphone concert. Capt. Bernard is still troubled with his head — a peculiar kind of headache which constantly overtakes him.

Sunday, May 10th

The air was comparatively warm but very foggy right up to the evening, probably due to the evaporation from the surface of the snow. One of Blue's dogs — a blind one — wandered straight out on the ice this morning, north-northeast. Blue followed its trail for about 2 miles but saw no sign of it, and it has not come back. The Eskimos in the camp beside us are up most of the night playing, for at midnight it is light enough to see outside.[6] Levi is proving an excellent cook. Blue went off for ptarmigan in the afternoon and brought back fourteen. The three Eskimos we have, Fred, Añutisiak, and Aiyaka's son Kaiyutaq are sleeping in a tent outside now. They seem rather glad now that the *Nunatagmiut* have come. I developed some photos this morning and took a short stroll in the afternoon.

Monday, May 11th

A glorious day, warm, sunshiny, and clear. We had numerous Eskimo visitors at the house. It seems to be characteristic of the people as a whole that they keep their mouths somewhat agape. An unmarried girl was wearing four rings (silver or nickel) on one hand. One of the *Nunatagmiut* men has a black fox and a silver-grey fox besides one or two red foxes. Last night before and after midnight the Eskimos, married men, single men, and girls were playing two or three European games — a kind of prisoner's base. I felt rather seedy this afternoon and went out for a stroll to the end of the sandspit about 1 1/2 miles, searching at the same time for remains of old houses. The snow, however, is still thick upon the ground and has hardly even begun to thaw. It is hopeless to try digging here for a while. The two captains bought four quarters of mountain sheep for a gunny [sack] of flour, a baking-powder tin, and a box of chewing gum. Capt. Bernard gave an Eskimo Kunuññaña a shot gun and a box of cartridges and told him to go and shoot some ptarmigan. He was away only 3 or 4 hours and brought back thirty. I noticed that two or three of the men have worn the tonsure.[7]

Tuesday, May 12th

Outdoors a mild sunny day, with the temperature well above freezing and the snow thawing. Snow buntings made their appearance and in the evening three geese flew over. Work is prosecuted daily on the two schooners. Qopuk's wife — Onin — is making me a hat. I cut the brim and band out of bearded-seal skin and she is sewing brown denham [denim] cloth over the outside and a pink calico inside — brim and all. Thus the crown will consist only of two thicknesses of cloth. I have now decided to discard my deerskin sleeping bag until next winter and have taken a woollen bag covered with Burberry cloth which belonged to Andre Norem, but which he did not use.

Wednesday, May 13th

Another gloriously warm day — at 8 p.m. the temperature was 36° F. I visited the *Alaska* in the afternoon. Capt. Nahmens has enlarged the engine room — it was a regular Black Hole [of Calcutta] before. He is patching the hole in the bow of the *Alaska* made by a piece of ice last summer — not a very serious matter. Then he intends to sheath the bow with Australian iron bark and the stern with iron sheets. Addison, Sullivan, and Qopuk were clearing the ice from under the propeller — the engineer Blue wants to see that it [the engine] will start all right before he takes it to pieces. I had another touch of fever today; it came on while I was visiting the *Alaska*. Levi had exactly the same and in the evening Blue developed similar symptoms. Thomsen had it for 2 days recently.

Apparently it is a mild fever produced by the change of weather. Levi's symptoms and mine coincided exactly. First we felt cold and shivered all over; then we began to feel sick and the head to ache rather badly. Soon we were feverishly hot and perspiring from every pore. It lasted with Levi about 2 hours and left him rather weakened. With me it continued longer, about 4 hours, and afterwards my head and eyes ached badly and I felt rather slack. In many ways it resembled a form of malaria, but the pulse quickened very little. The two captains bought for me a quarter of mountain sheep from the Eskimos, for a gunny [sack] of flour and a tin of baking powder; I hope to take it to Barter Island with me. Capt. Nahmens bought two cross foxes — black-red — for a rifle (my Winchester), several boxes of cartridges, and two boxes of chewing gum. His own rifle was a slightly different type of Winchester — but I fancy equally good. The Eskimo from whom he bought the foxes preferred the kind I had, so we exchanged. This morning the snow bunting were chirruping outside so gaily that one could almost close one's eyes and imagine oneself back in civilization.

Thursday, May 14th

Another fine day, though it rained a little in the early part of the evening and later snowed. Jennie made me a butterfly net today, stitching it on the machine.[8] Crawford is now feeling a little seedy — everyone of the whites appears to be having a turn. The melting snow is flooding the holes in which the two schooners lie, and the men have to work in a foot and more of water. Capt. Bernard has Eskimos bailing out round the *Mary Sachs* all day and most of the evening. The sick woman — Pannigavlu,[9] seems to be sinking fast. Her pulse almost stops beating at times and she has sunk into a state of semi-consciousness. For some days no food has passed her lips. A snowy owl was killed by a native and brought for Dr. Anderson.

Friday, May 15th

Pannigavlu died at 4 a.m. The natives made a coffin for her and wrapped it in sail-cloth. About 4:30 p.m. they held a service. The coffin containing the body was already nailed down. It was set on the ground in front of the tent, and the Eskimos all gathered around. After singing various hymns, one of them, a young man, read out of a well-worn notebook some verses of the Bible translated into the Mackenzie Eskimo dialect. The men stood with heads bare, but the women covered. At the conclusion some slices of caribou fat were brought out on two plates and each person partook, as far as I could see, without exception. Then they stood around and talked. Later the coffin was laid on top of a cached *umiak*, and covered with a couple of deerskins. The husband removed the tent a little to one side, apparently in deference to an ancient custom. During the ceremony the attitude of the audience was fairly respectful, but there was no pretence of sorrow on the part of some at least; they turned carelessly away as soon as it was over and had to be called back for the 'sacrement'. The deceased leaves two daughters — one married with a little girl Sañiaq, the other still awaiting a husband. Pannigavlu is to be buried at Flaxman Island, where a great number of Eskimos have already preceded her. The weather today was colder — at 4:30 p.m. it was 32.5°, and a mild east wind is blowing. The passage to the house is flooded with water. One of the Eskimos here, Pikalo, is of a rather unusual complexion, almost a copper-bronze. Aiyaka and his family with Teriglu and his wife, and two old acquaintances from down the line (eastward) Oyaraq and his wife arrived the night before last. Crawford softened and bent over three files for me to use as scrapers in digging out the old houses. Snow fell thick during the evening, and the temperature was below freezing.

Saturday, May 16th

Snow was still falling early this morning and the temperature was below freezing all day. Two sleds left for Flaxman Island in the evening, otherwise there were no accessions or losses to our numbers. Tomorrow Pannigavlu is to be taken to Flaxman Island [for burial]. Jennie had [a] toothache rather badly today — the first molar had a large cavity in the side. I stopped it with dental cement. There was some friction tonight at dinner over who was in charge of supplying the camp — or really of the camp. Apparently Capt. Nahmens was left in charge by Dr. Anderson and the other captain [Bernard] has assumed the reins himself. We have not only discord between the leaders of the Expedition[10] but among the rank and file. I believe that as the only scientist in camp I should be in authority, though there is no direct ruling on the subject. I was not expected to be here, however, and do not know how we are outfitted as well as the two captains, because I was absent all the winter. However, now that an open quarrel has broken out I have to step in. It is very unfortunate that Dr. Anderson has not returned. He expected to arrive this very day. I had a conference with the two captains late this evening, and took over charge of the camp, investing myself with the same authority as Dr. Anderson would have if he were here. Capt. Nahmens resigned to me the keys and papers. I don't know that either party is satisfied; they waxed rather hot at times during the discussion, but I hope things go on smoothly till Dr. Anderson comes anyhow.

Sunday, May 17th

A day of rest for everyone. Outside a moderate east wind was blowing and the temperature never rose above 25° F. The gramaphone was in requisition part of the day, but for the rest most of us read or wrote or talked.

Monday, May 18th

Dr. Anderson went to Shingle Point[11] about 60 miles beyond Herschel Island, so a native boy told us today. This boy was the cook's assistant on the *Belvedere* and has been down to Herschel [Island], where he saw

Dr. Anderson. Consequently we can hardly expect the latter for another 2 days at least. In camp everything is quiet, though I have plainly incurred the enmity of one person through assuming charge. Qopuk's wife, Onin, washed the floor of the house today and afterwards washed some clothes for Capt. Nahmens, Blue, and myself. Kunuññuña, one of the Eskimos camped here, shot 27 ptarmigan today with a shotgun and cartridges we lent him. He took 13 home and we had the other 14 — a distribution which pleased him much. Some of these Eskimos are shortly going west to hunt seal. I have not mentioned that Blue's [blind] dog reappeared the other day [see May 10th]. It wandered over towards Flaxman Island, and was found and kept by some natives there, who recognised it as belonging to the Expedition. Today a fairly strong east wind has prevailed and the temperature has not risen, I think, above 15°. The snow, lately soggy and melting fast, is now almost as hard as ever. An elderly Eskimo woman took her double-barrelled shotgun today and went out after ptarmigan. She returned with two. The others told me that she goes sealing too and in other ways follows the pursuits of the men. Another woman about here, Kaiyana's wife, is said to have the same nature. Aiyaka's son, Kovun, or rather his step-son, was unwell today — a sore throat and a headache, probably the result of the weather. The *Alaska* now has one side of the bow sheathed with hardwood, and a start has been made on the other bow. The *Mary Sachs* also is undergoing steady repairs. Levi has been busy repairing our watches lately — he is by trade a watchmaker.

Tuesday, May 19th

A blizzard today from the east albeit not a very violent one. Still the wind must have been travelling about 30 miles an hour. Capt. Bernard was over at his schooner most of the day, the rest of us stayed indoors. The passage to the house, from which the snow roof had been removed, was blocked completely when we turned out this morning. A tarpaulin was stretched over it after a passage had been cut through. Kovun is almost all right today, but Crawford seems to have succumbed to the same malady. Duffy O'Connor lent his dog team to Louis Lane [owner of the *Polar Bear*] to cross the mountains, under an agreement that they should be returned. Lane apparently omitted to return them by the first opportunity, so O'Connor had to buy dogs where he could to go out [to civilization] himself via Barrow. When he left us [March 23rd] he was full of threats of how he would bring an action against Lane for damages. Amongst the *Nunatagmiut* who came here the other day was a man with O'Connor's dogs. Capt. Bernard took them in charge and we have them now in camp. The temperature this morning was 14° at 7 a.m. One of the ptarmigan shot the other day was a beautiful chocolate colour throughout the length of the neck, but the body had not changed from its winter white. Our wind gauge is in bad shape; the pivot on which it turns is badly worn, and it requires a 12-mile breeze to make it revolve at all; it ought of course to run on ball bearings.

Wednesday, May 20th

The east wind still blew, but with greatly diminished violence. Work was resumed on both schooners. The boy, Kaiyutaq,[12] who has been acting as house boy hitherto in conjunction with another Eskimo named Alfred, was working on the *Mary Sachs*. Alfred left too for Herschel Island with an Eskimo family, so that there was no one to get wood and ice. I hunted up Kaiyutaq's elder brother [Ipanna] in the afternoon for that work. Aiyaka returned in the evening from the other side of Flaxman Island, bringing word that Leffingwell was at the point this side of Flaxman and wished to come on here. Capt. Bernard proposes to go on Friday, first to Flaxman to erect a pole for Leffingwell, then returning to bring him here. Jennie is going with him for a trip. The temperature today was just below freezing for the greater portion of the day, but in the early afternoon it was slightly above.

Thursday, May 21st

The snow thawed out somewhat and had to be cleared off the roof, the little, that is to say, which had accumulated there on the lee side during the late blow. The Eskimos who have been encamped beside us are gradually dispersing along the coast to hunt seal. A sled came from the west in the late afternoon, Teriglu bringing Leffingwell. He is sleeping for quietness and rest on the *Mary Sachs*. Aiyaka has decided to return to his old home east of here tomorrow.[13] He is willing to work for me if the pay is satisfactory, so I have written to Dr. Anderson, who will pass his place, asking him to arrange for his engagement. I can live in his tent and use his boat, so that whenever necessary I can communicate with Collinson Point, and shall not be imprisoned on Barter Island until the *Alaska* comes to pick me up. Capt. Bernard goes to Flaxman Island tomorrow to get some things from Leffingwell's place. Jennie is going to stay for a few days with some of the Eskimos who left here yesterday to camp on a point[14] between here and Flaxman.

Friday, May 22nd

Capt. Bernard and Jennie got away about 10 a.m. Ipanna (Aiyaka's eldest step-son) and I cleared out one side of the store [house] where snow had drifted in during the late blow and was beginning to melt. Aiyaka left in the afternoon. I gave him a shovel to take with him. A flat piece of iron from the bow of the *Mary Sachs* is furnishing me with two narrow spades for digging out the frozen ground. Crawford has already made me three scrapers out of old files. In the afternoon a sled came from the east, Keasik bringing some bear meat. He shot a polar bear (a female) out on the ice the other day. He came into the house in the evening and said that his little girl was sick, having sores in her mouth which prevented her from eating. I went back with him, riding most of the way on the sled, to the sandspit *Qonanevik*,[15] about 9 miles west of here, where four families had pitched their tents. The girl proved to be a baby of probably 12-15 months, hardly beginning to talk; she was suffer-

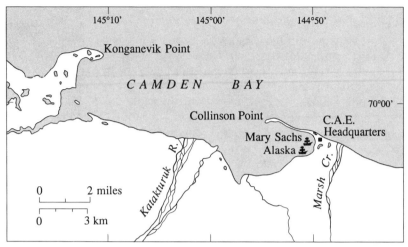

Figure 89. Map of Collinson Point area, Camden Bay.

ing from ulcers on her lips and mouth. We washed round the mouth as best we could with a solution of permanganate, but there was nothing much that could be done at the time. After a cup of tea and piece of bread I started back on foot and reached camp at 2:45 a.m. The midnight sun was well above the horizon. The snow was rather soft and sodden, though it seemed to be freezing a little on the way back. There was a light breeze from the east and the temperature during the day was well above freezing.

Saturday, May 23rd

Leffingwell spent much of the day with me discussing some questions of Eskimo grammar and examining the drawings of the Colville River and its tributaries made for me by Aksiatak during the winter. Outside the atmosphere was calm, and a fog enshrouded land and sea so that the *Mary Sachs* was hardly visible from the house. The temperature remained at 3 or 4 degrees above freezing all day, but at 8 p.m. it was 32° F.

Sunday, May 24th

I left after breakfast for the Eskimo settlement at *Qonanevik* to see how the baby girl was progressing. On the trail I saw a snowy owl which had turned partially black, losing its winter plumage; then seven birds which I took for a species of gull. On the way back another bird flew overhead, of the same species apparently as the flock of seven. Half way between Collinson Point and the camp I met Capt. Bernard returning from Flaxman Island. He had found a great deal of water between *Qonanevik* and Flaxman Island. The Eskimos were holding a service when I arrived, but it was soon over. The little girl's mouth was better, and she was eating freely, although one or two small ulcers had developed on the side of the tongue. Jennie made me some cocoa before I started back. The Eskimo tents were of deerskin, one of six, the other of five skins — they are called *itsalik*. The front portion in both was of mixed drilling and calico, with seal-intestine windows. The doors were of brown-bear skin and the wooden frame of willow. One of the Eskimos shot a seal the day before yesterday. I reached Collinson Point again at dinner time. Sullivan had been out for ptarmigan but had seen none. Blue came back soon after I did. He also had been out for ptarmigan and shot twenty, but lost his way and had to cross the *Nuvoak* River[16] a mile east of here. The water had broken out since the morning, and his dogs had to swim while he himself stood on the rails. In crossing he had the misfortune to lose a box of cartridges and his twenty ptarmigan. In the evening three seagulls flew overhead towards the east, and a flock of snipe was visible over on the tundra. The snow was thawing all day and a thick fog settled over everything and did not rise until evening.

Monday, May 25th

The temperature was at 42° for a considerable portion of the day, but in the evening it sank to freezing and snow fell. The rivers have broken out on all sides. Water was pouring round on either side of the *Alaska*, flooding the ice, until it found an inlet through the stern-hole through which it rushed like a great whirlpool. The roar of the *Nuvoak* River could be heard all night, and further east the Sadlerochit and the Hulahula [rivers] have broken out and the reflection of their dark waters cloud the sky. The melting snow threatens to flood everything. I set Ipanna to dig a trench from the storehouse towards the sea, and another will have to be dug from the corner of the house. Leffingwell is leaving for the mountains tomorrow. If he waits any longer for Johansen the snow will have disappeared altogether and he will not be able to sled up. His [Eskimo] boy Igluñasuk [Teriglu's son] killed three squirrels today and a skua gull. A great flock of brant flew over towards the Nuvoak River, and some geese made westward over the *Alaska*. The twittering of the snow buntings in the morning was very reminiscent of the south. An owl flew steadily over the tundra and a seagull was visible almost every hour of the day. The spring is certainly here. Towards midnight Dr. Anderson arrived with Johansen, Sweeney, Olsen, and a man from the *Belvedere* named Bezette (?).[17] He brought a mail from Herschel [Island], but the only news from the Canadian Government was a telegram approving of Stefansson's 'original' plans, whatever that may mean.[18] The government had received both Stefansson's telegrams from Barrow and Dr. Anderson's dispatch. I had a small budget[19] from various people, including three from home [New Zealand]. Ayakuk came[20] at the same time. They [Dr. Anderson's party] had a very unpleasant trip from Hulahula Paña, for all the rivers had broken out and they had to go through a great deal of water. Dr. Anderson had been down to the Mackenzie

[Delta] and had stayed with Cox for 2 or 3 days. Cox, Chipman, and O'Neill were all well. Castel and Brook were left at the *North Star*. There was no news of Stefansson.

Chapter 14. Archaeological Investigations on Barter Island (I)

Heading for Barter Island — Establishment of main camp — Initial recon-
noitering — Freezing weather continues — Reconnoitering east end of
Barter Island — Archaeological digging commences — Cold weather
impedes progress — Collecting a few zoological specimens — Sunday ac-
tivities — Drawing a plan of ruins on western end of Barter Island —
Wilkins arrives, heading east to North Star *— Wilkins' plans — More zoo-*
logical specimens — Eskimo's fear of skulls — Excavation on five house
sites completed — Remains of 40 old houses on sandspit west of Barter Is-
land — Another Sunday in camp

Tuesday, May 26th, 1914

I was preparing during a great portion of the day to go down the coast
with Aiyakuk. Dr. Anderson took over the charge of the camp, thus re-
lieving me of all responsibility. Johansen showed me a few ethnological
specimens he had picked up down the coast — fragments of snowshoes
etc. — of little value, though I have asked him to pack them for me. Aiyakuk was engaged to help me on Barter Island for $100 for the
2 months and his step-son Ipanna for $50.[1] The food, etc. at Martin
Point, Aiyakuk will bring down to Barter Island immediately, where it
will be at my disposal until the *Alaska* comes to pick me up. Leffingwell
made a start for the mountains, minus Johansen. He was held up by the
river, which he could not cross without getting all his things wet, so he
returned. He hopes to try again in another two days. Sweeney was dispatched to the *Belvedere* to obtain 200 lbs sugar and a large sail; Kaiyutaq[2] was sent with him in case he [Sweeney] cannot obtain permission
from Capt. Cottle to leave the *Belvedere* and join the Expedition.[3] The
two left just before 9 p.m. and Aiyaka, Tuglumunna (his wife), Ipanna,
and myself left at the same time.[4] We had to make wide detours to avoid
some of the overflow of the *Nuwak* [*Nuvoak*], Sadlerochit, and Hulahula
rivers. In some places the ice had cracked open and the water was rushing through. This bay ice is about 5 feet thick. Fortunately we met very
few places where the water was more than a foot deep. In a week or 10
days travel along the mouths of these rivers will be impossible. We saw
a *nepailuktaq* (hawk) on the way down. It was about 3 a.m. when we
reached the sandspit where Aiyakuk had left his tent. Oyaraq and his
wife and Pannigavlu[5] and her boy were there with Qovun, Tuglumunna's
youngest son.[6] A few yards away was Teriglu and his family. We
flocked into Aiyaka's tent, had a good meal of bread, *mukpaurat*, and
mountain-sheep meat, with coffee and cocoa. Then another tent was set
up alongside and Aiyaka and part of his family migrated to that, and I
with them. About 5 a.m. we turned in for the 'night'.

Wednesday, May 27th

We turned out about noon and had 'breakfast'. Soon afterwards Sweeney and Kaiyutaq left, followed later by Teriglu and family and Pannigavlu and her son. Aiyaka was gathering up his things, caching some here and taking the rest to Barter Island tomorrow. Some white geese flew over, and later some eider ducks. Qovun went off after some but returned empty-handed. Aiyaka erected a large pole anchored by guy-ropes and hoisted a polar-bear skin on it to ensure it from the dogs of any passing travellers. The other things which he was not taking were laid in a heap on a few logs that rested flat on the ground, and the whole covered over with three or four large cloths. This is the summer cache, lying directly on the ground; the winter [cache] is raised on a staging *iki-agut* so that it will not be covered by a snow-drift.[7] Late in the evening a sled came from the east, driven by a single man. The temperature about 6 p.m. was 32°, and there was a light air from the east.

Thursday, May 28th

We loaded up the sleds after breakfast and set out, Oyaraq with his sled ahead. Aiyaka went off towards the southeast to examine some traps he had set. The sleds were fairly heavy and the trail soft and slushy, with quite a number of pools to go through. Two or three flocks of grey geese flew by us, once within range, but we had no luck. We found Teriglu camped at the ruins on the west end of the [Barter] island and set up our two tents close by. Teriglu's wife gave us a good lunch of *mukpaurat* and tea, Aiyaka arrived about 6 p.m., and about the same time Qovun, who had been out with the gun, appeared with four ptarmigan. Qovun has a fair-sized bow, unbacked, with which he amuses himself. One arrow (they are unfeathered) has a cartridge shell for the head, another a lone point. After a dinner of *mukpaurat* and tea, everyone turned out and for a longer or shorter time scratched away some of the surface soil from two or three of the old ruins. A few odds and ends were found which had been shaped for some purpose, and a great number of bones, whale, caribou, fox, and bird. The temperature fell to 30°, and a moderately strong east wind sprang up towards evening. Aiyaka saw a white goose (*kañut*) today. Teriglu wants to dig out a certain ruin, Aiyaka tells me, on his own. I replied that he could dig it out if he liked and we would not interfere, but neither he nor his children should dig at those we were engaged on. The atmosphere was foggy all day, especially towards evening; a little rain fell in the afternoon. Billy Natkusiak has a cache about a mile southwest of here.

Friday, May 29th

We rose about 10 a.m. After breakfast Ipanna and Kovun set out for Martin Point to bring back the stores etc. from there.[8] Teriglu, Panni-gavlu, and two children left about the same time to go to the *Polar Bear*. I did not go to Martin Point myself, for Sweeney should be there when the two lads arrive and he knows better than anyone else what is Expedition property. There was a cold east wind blowing and the temperature at 11 a.m. was 33°. Aiyaka went out after a seal which was lying on the ice. He made a wide circuit and was within range, but trying to crawl up closer, lying flat on his stomach, when the seal heard him and dived. An attempt in the afternoon to steal up to another seal was equally unsuccessful. However, in the course of the day, he and Oyaraq and Teriglu's boys between them shot a few ptarmigan and oldsquaw ducks. Oyaraq's wife killed a lemming, which I skinned for Dr. Anderson, and Aiyaka shot an owl, which I also skinned, though I made rather a bad job of it.[9] A couple of parasites on the latter were bottled for Johansen.[10] We had the ptarmigan and ducks for supper and I had the pleasure of eating some unlaid ptarmigan eggs. They tasted very good. The lemming is a curious creature with two pairs of toes on each front foot overlapping and joined together. These people call it *kilugmiutaq* (something from the sky) and believe it grows into a fox (at least some do). Other birds have come: eider ducks, sparrows etc. I strolled up into the centre of the island with a butterfly net and some pill-boxes but found no specimens. A good deal of snow is still lying about; as it melts the water drains off in innumerable streams to the sea, cutting quite deep channels in many places. There were curious formations in the ground resembling the English neolithic camps on the hill-tops, only in miniature. Here is a rude sketch of one I measured. The centre was a slightly elevated oval sur-

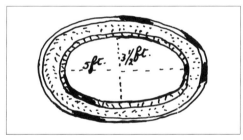

Figure 90. Elliptical ground formations, west end of Barter Island.

rounded by a miniature ditch, that again by a low rampart, and outside all ran another ditch. Some formations had only the central 'camp' surrounded by a ditch and were either oval or circular. Then there were depressions like small dewponds. We noticed something similar, I remember, on the tundra at Port Clarence.[11] The atmosphere grew colder during the day, and at 10 p.m. it had fallen to 26° F. As long as this weather continues digging is impracticable. There are twelve old houses here, one perhaps a dance house, it is so large. Another has a kitchen attached, a wigwam-shaped structure of logs in which the housewife

Figure 91. Wigwam-shaped house of logs on west end of Barter Island.

cooked over a blubber lamp. A hole at the point of the cone allowed the smoke to escape. A depression marks the site of an ice-house for storing food. We turned in after 'midnight' with the east wind still blowing.

Saturday, May 30th

We rose at noon when the temperature was 24 degrees and a strong east wind blowing. It remained well below freezing all day, and the wind if anything increased. We all stayed indoors — Aiyaka took his Remington rifle to pieces; I wrote letters[12] and sundry notes; Tuglumunna cooked and sewed. 'Stone'[13] and his wife dropped in to talk and eat from time to time. So passed an uneventful day.

Sunday, May 31st

We rose at 11 a.m. After breakfast the Eskimos held a service in 'Stone's' tent, while I wandered along the spit. About 3 p.m. Sweeney and Kaiyutaq, Ipanna, and Qovunna arrived with Teriglu, bringing nearly everything there was at Martin Point, including two tents and a stove. The tents we set up forthwith, one for a store, the other for Sweeney and Kaiyutaq to sleep in. The rest of the day we sat and talked and (I) read, turning in about 11 o'clock. The temperature remained just below freezing all day, and there was a light air from the east. Sweeney had been as far as the *Belvedere*, but there was no news of Stefansson.

Monday, June 1st

Sweeney and Kaiyutaq got away [for Collinson Point][14] before 8 a.m., just as the rest of us were beginning breakfast. The weather was calm and moderately clear, though the sky was clouded. The temperature at 7:30 a.m. was 31° but by 1 o'clock it had risen to 35°, though at 11 p.m. it was 26°. Aiyaka stalked another seal on the ice and got in a shot, but it dived, not being fatally injured. He and Qovunna then went down to Iñukuk's rack — about 3 miles east to bring in some stores — beans, sugar, etc., which had been left there. During the day numbers of oldsquaw ducks and pomerine Jaeger[15] (*isuñgaq*) flew over. One flock of oldsquaws was in regimental order — six squadrons, each of about a dozen birds, flying swift and high in a line towards the east. Tuglumunna greased my sealskin boots with seal blubber to make them soft and waterproof. When the ducks flew over she amused herself and me by imitating the notes of different birds. The oldsquaw duck says *a'haliaq*, the yellow-billed loon [says] *tu'lik*, the semipalmated sandpiper [says] *liwaliwa*, and these are their Eskimo names. Aiyaka had better luck with a seal in the afternoon — a large male. We saw him dragging it home and the dogs were hitched to the sled and sent out for it. Ipanna also went seal-hunting and saw three, but they all dived. Qovunna shot two king eiders [ducks], and four or five oldsquaw ducks at the expense of some 40 rifle cartridges. Aiyaka and I then strolled over to the east end of the island and examined the ruins of a large settlement there. It seems to be much older and more interesting than the ruins here, also the ground is less frozen, so we shall begin there tomorrow. We noticed portions of three skeletons, and near one grave I picked up a white stone labret. But the remarkable thing about the settlement was the enormous number of whale bones present. They were grouped at the houses; thus, at the end of one house were the skulls of four whales, [at the end] of another [house], three. Aiyaka had his shotgun with him and secured six or seven ptarmigan. We disturbed a snowy owl which was feasting on an oldsquaw duck, and robbed it of the latter. It is strange to observe the effect of the freezing and thawing. The ground is full of small cracks as if it had been through fire, and the running water has cut deep ditches into it. In some places these have developed into small ravines in which the snow lingers, though the stream runs underneath it. Thus it resembles a 'glacier' of snow. We had several of these to cross where we should have sunk over our head tops if the top crust after the little stamping we gave it had not borne our weight.

Tuesday, June 2nd

We breakfasted about 11:30 a.m. Ipanna and Qovunna went over to the ruins at the east end of the island about midnight and after some fossicking found two or three small curios. Aiyaka and I loaded the sled with some food and a tent, and went along the sea ice to the site, while Ipanna and Oyaraq walked across the island. We found a good deal of water on the ice and sank in several places up to our knees; the temperature at noon was 36° but it grew colder as an east wind sprang up, and we found our wet feet anything but comfortable. However, we set up the tent and began to search in earnest. The soil, however, was frozen 1 1/2 inches below the surface, so we could not do very much. The weather growing still colder, we returned home, Ipanna and I with the sled, the other two by land, hunting for ptarmigan. Ipanna and I arrived home about 8 p.m. and found the temperature 26°. Light snow fell soon afterwards and continued for some hours. I am kept very busy just now with excavation work and collecting for Dr. Anderson and Johansen. The continuance of this cold weather is rather annoying. It is not severe enough to prevent digging altogether, yet just enough to keep the ground hard and make our progress insignificant. I skinned a small bird for Dr. Anderson in the evening, and we retired about 2 a.m.

Wednesday, June 3rd

The temperature remained consistently a little below freezing all day, so we did no work outside. Aiyakuk shot a seal out on the ice, but it got into its hole. He told me that Teriglu yesterday found a seal wandering on the ice — its hole apparently having frozen or closed over; he dispatched it with a knife. A loon was shot today, two eider ducks, and a number of oldsquaws. I spent most of the time writing notes. A sled arrived from the west, Mapteraq and his family, who had been living at *Qonañevik*[16] with the other inland Eskimos. He is going to stay here for a time, hunting seals and birds. An unpleasant east wind blew all day. This

Figure 92. Tents of Teriglu (left) and Aiyaka (right), on western sandspit of Barter Island, June 1914. (Photo by D. Jenness, CMC Photo No. 37117.)

thin cloth tent grows cold at night, so we are going to sleep in a green bell tent that used to be at Martin Point. It is of thicker canvas, more spacious, and has a good stove inside. Its defect is that it is much darker. I skinned a small bird tonight for Dr. Anderson and found that one which I skinned 2 days ago and placed in the store tent had been destroyed by the pups.

Thursday, June 4th

A continuance of the cold windy weather which has prevailed the last few days. The temperature did not rise above freezing once. Snow fell for a while in the evening. Those in camp went out from time to time to shoot the ducks that settled on the ponds along the inner edge of the sandspit. I wrote out some notes on Eskimo music and skinned a small bird for Dr. Anderson in the evening. Aiyakuk, Tuglumunna, and I slept in the green tent last night. I found it rather cold, but Aiyakuk thought it was a little warmer than the other tent in which we live, where the two boys [Qovunna and Ipanna] slept. At 3 o'clock we had a great dinner party. Everyone in the camp was present except Qovunna, who was away chasing ducks. First we had the loon, boiled, then ptarmigan and stew with rice mixed with it, and tea and cocoa; next came boiled ducks; a few *mukpaurat* accompanied each course. I cried off the last one. The oldsquaws are continually flying over the tent, crying *ahalik ahalik*; the men and boys immediately rush out for their guns, if they have not already observed their approach, and fire about 10 rounds for every bird they kill. However, they have plenty of powder and shot and brass shells, so I suppose it matters little; but it is a trait of their character. Similarly they burn a lot of coal oil in primus stoves when it is altogether superfluous, then live in darkness part of the winter for lack of lighting.[17]

Friday, June 5th

The wind increased somewhat during the night and we found the green tent cold again. I am boxing my sleeping bag in with a big log on either side, so that there will hardly be room to turn; I look forward to a comfortable night. After breakfast Aiyakuk, Ipanna, and I went over to the ruins on the east end. Although the temperature of the air as registered by the thermometer has not been above 32° and only once I think as high as 32° during the last 3 days, we found the ground had thawed very slightly and were able to dig a little on four or five sites. Then we made huge fires of driftwood on top of the ruins of two houses[18] and returned home. Ipanna shot a snowy owl on the edge of the tundra, and not far from it we found a human skull which had been buried under the grass and snow. This and half a dozen small specimens from the ruins made up the day's takings, besides two or three zoological specimens — some parasites from the snowy owl for Johansen and a small bird[19] for Dr. Anderson. The latter had a thick layer of fat which clung to the skin and was extremely difficult to remove. It kept me up until 2 a.m.

Saturday, June 6th

A day very similar to yesterday, the same wind, same clouded sky, same temperature from 26° to freezing. Iñukuk came from Martin Point last night and all the men from the other tents, Teriglu, Oyaraq, Mapteraq, and Iñukuk breakfasted with us and two or three women as well. Aiyakuk and I set out soon afterwards for the eastern ruins, shortly followed by Ipanna and Qovunna with two of Teriglu's children. We found that the fires had thawed out the ground all right, but had cracked at least one flint, so the experiment is not a success; we must wait for the warm weather. The snow is fast disappearing from the tundra, and the birds are building their nests — *vere concordant amores vere nubunt alites.*[20] Yesterday we found a *kupahloaluk's* (sparrow?)[21] nest with three eggs in it; today it had four and another had three. A Baird's sandpiper's nest had four eggs too. On the tundra we found the fragments of a sled — perhaps marking a grave — and some sticks which had been used for ptarmigan snares. A small red flower is common everywhere. Our party had three bows, and Aiyakuk was contesting with Qovunna and Teriglu's oldest son who could shoot straightest and farthest. These bows have a simple notch at each end, and a grip-shape in the middle, but are not backed like the old Eskimo bows; perhaps they never were in this region. Aiyakuk fired about fifteen times at some ducks, from 200-300 yards away without success. The whole camp assembled at our tent for dinner. Oyaraq's wife brought tea, Teriglu's tea and some bread, Mapteraq's a small bowl of boiled duck. We furnished rice and *mukpaurat* and tea. Several times lately the Eskimos here have marked a spot on

Figure 93. Ptarmigan snares on Barter Island.

the tundra by two or three lumps of black sod; they can pick up such a mark 200 yards away. Iñukuk seems a quiet shy man; you would think butter would melt in his mouth. Actually he is a lazy good-for-nothing fellow, or at least has that reputation.

Sunday, June 7th

The temperature remains still the same, but the wind has almost completely died away. There were two or three sharp showers of half snow, half rain. The Eskimos assembled in Oyaraq's tent and sang hymns, ate, and talked all day. I wrote letters and worked up a few notes, had a primitive kind of bath with a wash-basin, and felt bored — a proper Sunday feeling. So passed an uneventful day.

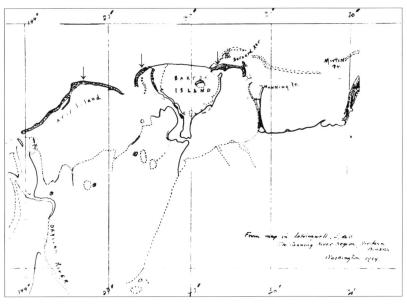

Figure 94. Author's map of Barter Island and surroundings, on which are shown (three arrows, added in 1987) the approximate locations of the Eskimo ruins.[22] (Photo by S. Presley, CMC Photo 87-3031.)

Monday, June 8th

The wind drifted round through south and west to north, [and] the temperature rose at noon to 38°F and remained above freezing all day. Aiyakuk, Ipanna, and some others stayed up all night playing cards. Teriglu and Mapteraq went seal-hunting; early this morning Mapteraq shot a seal. Iñukuk returned to the *Polar Bear* camp whither he and his mother Arluk (Shotgun) have removed since the camp at Martin Point was broken up.[23] We made a bundle of pegs and numbered them, then I made a plan of the ruins on this western sandspit of Barter Island. Digging was prosecuted more or less sporadically during the afternoon, the only finds being a bone arrowhead, the blade of a woman's knife, and a portion of a bow. Aiyakuk and Ipanna slept part of the evening while I was writing up notes. A flock of Pacific Eider ducks flew inside the sandspit, crossed its neck, and continued their course eastwards. Their appearance augurs a southwest wind according to Aiyakuk. Teriglu returned about 10 p.m. bringing a small seal home with him; another that he had shot he left out on the ice. The temperature at this time had fallen to 26° F, and a light northwest wind was blowing.

Tuesday, June 9th

Oyaraq's wife left for the *Polar Bear* camp during the day. Aiyakuk, Ipanna, and myself went over to the eastern ruins and dug about for 4 or 5 hours, when the weather grew cold and snow fell, so we returned. It cleared while we were returning, but grew much colder a little later; from 38° at 10:30 a.m. it dropped to 29° at 8 p.m. The ground is beginning to thaw a little, and we removed the top crust from four or five houses, making a few small finds. Johansen's [insect] collection will be swelled by a couple of specimens of today's taking. We found another *kupahloaluk's* [Lapland Longspur] nest this morning — the third; it contained three eggs.

Wednesday, June 10th

The weather was not very agreeable — a moderately strong east wind was blowing, and the temperature was hardly above freezing. Nevertheless after breakfast, Ipanna and I, followed later by Aiyakuk, went over to the east side and continued excavations. Oyaraq came 3 or 4 hours later, and finally Tuglumunna, who was searching for the two pups which Aiyakuk had brought along with him. Oyaraq fossicked in two or three places where he thought from the look of the ground there might have been houses, and he was right. A jade knife-sharpener was found in a grave, a fine whale-harpoon head (minus the point) on the site of one of the old houses, and sundry other things interesting though less perfect and valuable. On returning to camp about 6 p.m. we found Wilkins and Crawford and the two Eskimos Fred and Natkusiak. Wilkins was on his way to the *North Star* to take charge. According to Stefansson's instructions[24] from the ice in case of his non-appearance, Wilkins is to take the *North Star* to North Banks Land, wintering if possible at Norfolk Island, unless he can cross to Prince Patrick Land, and during the winter establish beacons along the coast.[25] He hopes to take [Aarnout] Castel as engineer, and hire a man named Seymour, once mate of the *Belvedere* and married to an Eskimo woman along the coast here, to be navigating officer. He himself will be in command and have Billy Natkusiak the Eskimo with him.[26] Crawford is going down to look at the engine, and take back sugar and salt from the *Belvedere*. Fred is to stay here with me till Crawford comes back and secure as many ducks and seals as possible for the camp at Collinson Point. The mail at Barrow was very disappointing — very few letters and no government ones;[27] I had no letters at all save one from Dr. Anderson. I am to go on the *Mary Sachs* as far as

Herschel Island at least and take an inventory of the things shipped from Duffy's.[28] Wilkins had a very hard trip to Barrow and back. He was snow blind nearly all the way there and had to hang on to the back of the sled. Three days before he reached Barrow a whale was caught, then the ice closed up and never opened again the whole 3 weeks he was there — consequently he secured no pictures of the whaling.[29] He told me Capt. Nahmens is leaving the Expedition[30] and that the command of the *Alaska* has been given to Sweeney.

Thursday, June 11th

I got up at 6 a.m. and cooked breakfast, frying some seal liver from a seal Wilkins' party shot yesterday. They got away before 9 a.m. It is very lucky for them the weather is remaining so cold, though for the Expedition it may be disastrous; there is speculation as to whether we shall get through this summer, for the ice is late in opening. A strong east wind was blowing all day, and as Aiyakuk caught a slight cold yesterday we did not go over to the east side but dug at the ruins here more or less sporadically. Oyaraq helped quite a lot; he is extremely careful and knows more than the others. A few articles were found to swell the list and two houses are almost finished. The high wind kept the ducks away, so though a party was out for 3 or 4 hours it had very little success.

Friday, June 12th

A busy day over at the eastern ruins for Ipanna and myself. I sent Aiyakuk with Fred seal-hunting,[31] but though they saw several and shot one they had no success; the seal they shot sank. Qovunna shot four ducks today and I one on the way to the ruins. Five small birds were shot for skinning and two nests full of eggs (*liwaliwak's* — Baird's sandpiper) taken and blown. I skinned one bird in the evening[32] and wrote a few notes. Tuglumunna complained of the propinquity of a skull I brought from the other side of the island; it is in the next tent. She said she heard the tent shake and rattle today for no visible cause, then the neighbouring tent in which she was sitting at the time shook as though it would fall. Aiyakuk came and asked me tonight to shut it up in a box and put the lid on; it would be all right then. The amusing thing is that I brought two more skulls over today, not knowing of Tuglumunna's fears. However, I boxed one up tonight and tied the mouth of the bag containing the other two. The weather was clear with a light west wind, except for three or four westerly squalls of wind and rain lasting from 20 minutes to an hour. The temperature was up to 40° and has been above freezing all day.

Saturday, June 13th

A fine warm day, with the sun shining part of the time and for the rest concealed behind clouds. Ipanna went seal-hunting for Collinson Point folk and brought back one seal. Fred and Qovunna went duck-shooting and returned with about fifteen, while Aiyakuk in the evening shot ten in

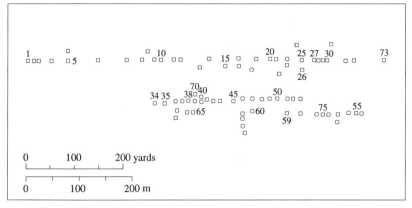

Figure 95. Sketch plan of the 76 sites (mainly remains of houses) on the eastern sandspit, Barter Island (after a plan in Jenness, 1914j).[33]

about 3 hours. I shot an eider duck, *kiñalik*, on the way to the east side, but it was in the middle of a deep pool and we had to leave it. When we returned at night a seagull was feasting on it. On the way back I shot an oldsquaw [duck]. At the time of writing (1 a.m.) shots are resounding continually from the end of the sandspit. Fred brought back two geese eggs, which we boiled and ate, the first eggs (save unlaid ptarmigan eggs) this season. Aiyakuk and I dug over in the eastern ruins, finding a few objects, and Oyaraq found four or five in one of the western ruins. The ground is slowly thawing now, and we have five or six houses nearly finished. The chief treasure today was an ivory needle-case from a grave. A little yellow flower like a buttercup has appeared — I noticed it today for the first time. There are a few flies about too, and mosquitoes will soon be here if the warm weather continues. Rapid streams of water are flowing down from the middle of the island. In some places they run over the snow of the little ravines, in others under, but by now they have cut a channel through the middle of it almost everywhere. It makes them a little awkward to negotiate. Yesterday I broke through the upper crust twice; the first time a great circular hole was made about 10 feet in diameter. There was a fine waterfall in one place; the stream ran over the top of the snow in a channel about 3 feet deep, then fell over to the bottom of the 'ravine' in a drop of about 6 feet. At the bottom was a large pool surrounded on all sides with walls of snow.

Sunday, June 14th

Service was held in Oyaraq's tent after I breakfast[ed]. I listed some of my specimens then took the shotgun and went over to the east end to pace out the distances between the ruins and so make a plan of them. The only measuring instrument I possess is a 5-foot tape (cloth), which is useless for the purpose. The day was warm with a light west breeze, but there were very few ducks around. On returning I found another service

Figure 96. Whale head bones marking site of former Eskimo house, with lagoon in distance, south side of eastern sandspit on Barter Island, July 1914. (Photo by D. Jenness, CMC Photo No. 37149)

about to start, so I was left in state in my tent, undisturbed to write notes and a letter. The sun came out towards evening, though the day had been cloudy and rain fell in the morning.

Monday, June 15th

Fred and Ipanna and Aiyakuk and others played jumping etc. half the night, so we were late in having breakfast. I sent Aiyakuk and Fred to get loons' eggs from somewhere on the other side of the island, while Ipanna and I worked on the eastern ruins. Tuglumunna washed some clothes for me, while Oyaraq cut out a long line from a sealskin and hung it up to dry. Ipanna and I found a miscellaneous lot of objects, and Oyaraq a few good pieces in the western ruins. He is invaluable both for his knowledge and the willingness with which he imparts some of it, and from his careful scratchings among the ruins at odd moments. I shot an oldsquaw duck on the way home and wasted half an hour following up another from one large pond to another and back again until I lost sight of it and gave it up. After writing up some of the day's notes, I skinned a bird for Dr. Anderson, while Ipanna went off with my shotgun after ducks etc. At the time of writing — 1:30 a.m. — neither he nor Aiyakuk nor Fred nor Qovunna are back. The temperature was about 38° most of the day but down to 34° at midnight. A rather cold breeze blew from the west, but it died away in the evening.

Tuesday, June 16th

Aiyakuk and the others returned at 4 a.m. with some 35 ducks and brant. I turned in then and did not get up till 11 a.m., when I skinned a small bird before breakfast. Aiyakuk and I went over to the east ruins afterwards, while Ipanna went shooting. The last returned with a white goose, which had a bare spot on its breast — due, Aiyakuk says, to its picking out the feathers to line its nest. He himself shot a species of hawk, which I skinned in the evening,[34] while he skinned a duck (*igniqauqtoq*).[35] Fred and Qovunna returned from shooting without success but brought a *liwaliwak* (Baird's sandpiper)[36] and its eggs. Aiyakuk and I worked for about 2 hours only, then returned, as there was a cold east wind blowing and the temperature had dropped to freezing. We had no mits, either of us, and were compelled to put our hands in our trousers from time to time to warm them. The weather was foggy and dank and unpleasant altogether. Oyaraq found a few more relics on the west end — what with birds and insects and my own work I have more than I can manage. However, Aiyakuk will have to do some of the skinning. There was an interesting example of the way ravines are formed here that we came across this evening. The melting snow and water had cracked the ground in a hollow, then worked holes down through it, whereby the water ran underground for some distance, then emerged into the open in a place where the tunnel had grown so large and the crust so cracked up that it had collapsed.

Wednesday, June 17th

Crawford turned up about 7 a.m. I had gone to bed about 2 a.m., the others later, so no one expected to be up for some hours. However, I turned out and got him some breakfast. He had come from the *Polar Bear* camp, the journey occupying 12 hours. The ice was covered with water, so that his clothes were very wet. Under the water the surface of the ice is like a series of needle points, and the dog's feet get terribly cut up. He says he has used 200 *mukluks* (boots) on his team of nine [dogs]

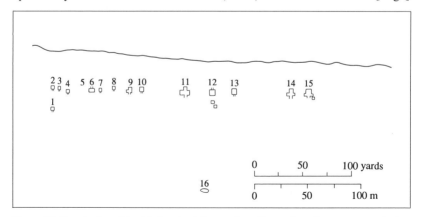

Figure 97. Sketch plan of the 16 sites (mainly remains of houses) on the western sandspit, Barter Island (after plan in Jenness, 1914j).[37]

since leaving Collinson Point. Aiyakuk made him an extra twenty this evening. He went as far as Duffy O'Connor's then returned, taking up a load at the *Belvedere*. The lagoon behind Icy Reef, he said, is open water, and the Eskimos go across in a boat. He turned in to sleep after

Figure 98. Aiyakuk digging into ruin No. 11, western end of Barter Island, June 1914. (Photo by D. Jenness, CMC Photo No. 37146.)

breakfast, while I typed a letter and some notes for Dr. Anderson,[38] then went to sleep again myself for an hour or two. Shortly after 2 p.m., the weather being cold and a moderately strong east wind blowing, Ipanna and I and Oyaraq began digging out a large house on the western end of the island beside our tents. Aiyakuk I sent off after a loon, and he returned an hour later without the loon but with two ducks. We finished the house all but two small patches where it was still frozen; the result was a disappointment, it contained almost nothing — three or four fragments of drumsticks, of lamp wicks, and half a dozen other objects. Apparently it was a dance-house.[39] We next attacked a house a few yards away, but this proved to be comparatively modern, for some of the beams had been adzed with a metal adze. We could not finish it for it was still frozen, but the finds we made were few and of little value. Altogether it was rather a disappointing day, archaeologically. Zoologically it was more fertile. Ipanna skinned a gull that Qovun shot. It had a bare patch on the breast about the size of a dollar, where the bird had plucked out the feathers to line its nest, the Eskimos say. Qovun brought in its egg also, which I blew, with four eggs of a sandpiper. Then I skinned two sandpipers[40] and Teriglu brought in a pintail duck skinned, with a parasite from it.[41] Finally Qovun brought in a Lapland Longspur and its eggs, but as it was 4 a.m. I left it over [until later]. Crawford and Fred left about midnight,[42] and Aiyakuk and Tuglumunna went with them as far as their cache on the sandspit 4 miles west. They have not yet returned.

Thursday, June 18th

Aiakuk and ToXlumana (that seems to be the correct spelling, not Tuglu[munna]) returned about 8 a.m. and turned in. I was sound asleep but got up about 11 or 11:30 a.m. to do a little work before breakfast. This [breakfast] came on about 2 p.m. A little while afterwards Teriglu came over and said that his wife had run a needle into the palm of her hand. It transpired that 2 days ago she placed her hand on a post in which a needle had been stuck. The eye of the needle penetrated deeply into her palm, then snapped off, leaving about 1/4 inch in the wound. Now she complained of pain in the last three fingers. I opened it up a little where the needle was said to have gone in but found nothing. There seemed nothing more that I could do except rub a little hazeline[43] on it and leave them some to do the same later, hoping that the needle will work out soon. The only instruments I had were those for skinning birds and cleaning eggs, and no antiseptics; it was better to leave it alone. We then continued on the second house that we attacked yesterday,[44] not very hopefully, for it seemed too recent. To our surprise we unearthed a number of valuable specimens in good condition, the chief being an etched needle case, a fine stone *uluraq* (woman's knife) with its handle, and a spear thrower. We could not finish it as it was still frozen. I was feeling wretchedly tired and aching all over too, so we gave up after some 3 hours and came back. Oyaraq, however, had been poking about the corners of two houses practically finished and discovered beside two or three other things a splendid bone arrowhead with three barbs. He is a perfect genius for discovering good things, it was he who unearthed the fine woman's knife today, just a few minutes after we started work and so lent enthusiasm to the party. Aiyakuk last night scratched about among three of the ruins on the sandspit near his cache[45] and brought back a dozen or so knife blades, three or four rather good ones, and some sticks which were used for various purposes, e.g., a drum-stick. Altogether from the number and quality of the specimens the day was a fairly successful one. Aiyakuk reported that there are at least a score of ruins there much easier to dig just now than those on Barter Island because less frozen, so we are going to work over there for as long as we can conveniently cross on foot. Today the temperature was a little above freezing, but a cold east wind was blowing. Tonight the thermometer registered 28° at 10 p.m. Qovunna shot a mallere or black-throated [Arctic] loon last night and Ipanna skinned it this evening.[46] The former also brought in a *puveoktoak*[47] shot by Ipanna yesterday but forgotten.

Friday, June 19th

After breakfast Aiyakuk and I with the dog team went over to the sandspit west of here to excavate. We found something like forty old houses, some of which he dug out more or less imperfectly a few years back. Ipanna had preceded us — he is always keen on anything new but seems unable to stick at anything. I put numbered sticks against almost all the ruins, and we worked steadily from about 4 to 9 p.m. Two graves

Figure 99. Ruin No. 16, western end of Barter Island, June 1914. (Photo by D. Jenness. CMC Photo No. 37148.)

a little way off had been dug out previously, probably by Stefansson and Leffingwell. The bones were scattered about but the skull taken — rather an unscientific proceeding. Ipanna saw five seal on the ice, and Aiyakuk stalked and fired at one but missed. There was a good deal of water, and we got wet feet — we were in up to our knees almost. Oyaraq produced a splendid harpoon head he had unearthed while we were away, and a fine board used for trimming arrow feathers. Qovunna shot five Sabine gulls and an Arctic tern. Aiyakuk skinned one of the former for me. The weather was dull all day and a few drops of rain fell; the temperature was up to 36°, but about midnight it had dropped to 30°

Saturday, June 20th

Rather a wretched day, though it ended better than it began. In the first place everyone overslept — at least Aiyakuk and his wife and I did, the three who counted. I had turned in at 2:30 a.m., slept at intervals till about 7 a.m., then dropped off into a sound sleep and did not wake till noon. I roused up the other two and we 'breakfasted' about 2 p.m. The pups had broken loose in the night, entered the tent and devoured four birds which were waiting to be skinned for Dr. Anderson, besides destroying a nest and its eggs. Aiyakuk, Ipanna, and I went over to the sandspit west of the camp and began work. I felt a bit seedy when I got up and had no sooner started work than I had to quit and lie down on an improvised bed of logs, with a fire alongside, partly sheltered from the cold east breeze by one of the ruins. It seemed to be the same kind of 'spring' fever that I had a month or so ago and lasted, like it, about 4 hours, leaving a slight headache and a feeling of lassitude. Aiyakuk and Ipanna dug and unearthed a miscellaneous number of objects. The

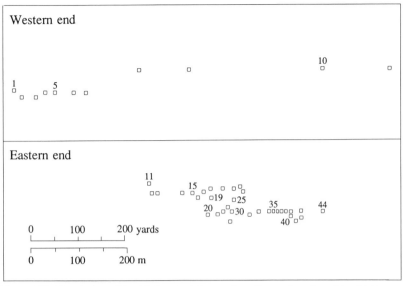

Figure 100. Sketch plan of the 44 sites (mainly remains of houses) on Arey Island (after plan in Jenness, 1914j). The former settlements were located just east of the major bend near the centre of the island.

ground seems to be frozen about as much there as on Barter Island, but Aiyakuk wanted to go over as there is always a fair chance for seals. I told him today he could continue alone there for a time, and Ipanna and I will go on with those on the east [end] of Barter Island, an arrangement which suits him perfectly, as it gives him a sealing excursion everyday. He is a very reliable Eskimo, and I can trust him to do a good deal of conscientious excavation without my being present, a thing Ipanna would never do. We returned to camp about 10 p.m. Aiyakuk made a circuit on the return journey and brought in two ducks and an Arctic tern[48] (one specimen of which the pups ate last night). Qovun shot a *kirigugiuk*, another bird devoured by the pups. The two were skinned tonight, one by Aiyakuk, one by Ipanna, while I wrote notes. Thermometer dropped from 36° at 2 p.m. to 30° at 10 p.m.

Sunday, June 21st

Outside the thermometer fluctuated between 33° and 34°, and a cold strong east wind was blowing, with a mist obscuring everything. Everyone stayed in camp, I typing notes and a letter, the rest singing hymns, eating, and talking.

Chapter 15. Archaeological Investigations on Barter Island (II)

More excavating on east side of island — Comments on Eskimo gratitude — Late ice break-up — A profitable excavation — Capturing butterflies for Johansen — Ducks, loons, seals, and birds' eggs for food — Learning to smoke an Eskimo pipe — Floors of 15 houses exposed at eastern excavation site — Writing notes and packing specimens — Low food supply — To Camden Bay in a whale boat — Return to Barter Island with more food — Teriglu sails west to meet Leffingwell — By whale boat to east end of Barter Island — Problem obtaining fresh water — Termination of work at east end of island — Packing up — Eskimo family departs for mountains — Some reflections on Eskimo behaviour — Beans — Departure for Collinson Point — Arrival at ships just on time — Specimens loaded on Mary Sachs *— Departure of* Alaska *and* Mary Sachs *from Collinson Point — Ice bound just west of Martin Point — Preparation to go by whale boat to Duffy O'Connor's place*

Monday, June 22nd, 1914

A fine sunny day, temperature up to 38° and in the evening down to 31°. A moderately strong east wind blew part of the time. Ipanna, Qovun, and one of Teriglu's boys went over with me to the eastern ruins. I made a pretence at working for a couple of hours then had to lie down, having a rather sharp attack of what certainly seemed to be malaria. When a couple of hours lying down saw no improvement we left off and came home, Ipanna going seawards and seeing two seals, one of which he shot at but missed, Qovun with my shotgun and Teriglu's boy looking for ducks, while I made the best way I could straight across the tundra to camp. Aiyakuk and his wife had left for the sandspit taking the tent and dog team with them, so that I am setting Ipanna to cook in my big sleeping tent. On reaching camp I turned in at once and dozing a little lay there till 9:30 p.m. when we had dinner or supper, after which we straightened things up and Ipanna made some doughnuts.

Tuesday, June 23rd

A day similar to yesterday with the east wind a little stronger. Qovun was out after ducks all night and brought back three, two of which were *igniqauqtoq* or Steller's Eider,[1] so Ipanna skinned one and I the other in the evening. Ipanna got breakfast, then we went over to the ruins on the east side and worked for 4 hours or more, after which he returned as yesterday via the ice, on the chance of getting a seal, and I over the tundra. Oyaraq is sick, pain in his back and stomach. This evening a service was held in his tent for his recovery; hymns were sung and prayers said. I found a Baird's sandpiper's nest today where the eggs were already hatched. Mapteraq killed six seals yesterday and one today, and he says Aiyakuk has killed one too.

Wednesday, June 24th

A fine warm sunny day with the thermometer above 40° for at least part of the time. Ipanna, Qovun, and I went over east and dug. The great find today was a jade dagger, but there were one or two other interesting objects also. Some ducks settled near us, and Ipanna with my shotgun went after them. He had no luck but found a duck I fired at yesterday (and which then flew away) lying dead on the ice. When we left work (about 8:30 p.m.) Ipanna went hunting ducks and brought in two. Qovun and I returned, but he soon went off for ducks also. There is a fine big lake of open water, behind the sandspit, about a mile in diameter. Yesterday for the first time we saw mosquitoes here. The snow has disappeared entirely from the island except at the bottom of a few deep ravines. Some of the flowers are now fading — their day is very short. One kind exactly resembles the buttercup of home [i.e., New Zealand], and there is another which reminds one of the 'bunny' or dragon flower. Flies are plentiful; great bumble-bees[2] buzz around the flowers, especially a red flower like a scotch thistle from which the Eskimos also suck the honey.

Thursday, June 25th

Qovun was out all night after ducks, except that he came in for a while to have a meal. The temperature fell to 34° at 2 a.m. but was up to 46° by noon, and the day was even warmer than yesterday. Ipanna and I went over and dug at the eastern ruins. On the way back I shot two ducks in a large pond. The wind blew them among the weeds and I had to wade in, minus trousers, boots, and socks to get them. It was nearly waist-deep and at a temperature of about freezing. Oyaraq is better tonight. I dosed him yesterday morning with Epsom salts, for he had been suffering from diarrhoea for 2 days, then in the evening gave him flour and water — rather crude doctoring. Qovun and Teriglu's boy last night made a raft and went out on the lake behind us here. The lashings gave way and they fell into the water. With the glasses we can see Aiyakuk's tent on the sandspit, and a seal hung up on a line beside it. The Eskimos, adult men and boys alike, delight in throwing stones at small birds, especially driving them from their nests. Then they set snares (nooses) over the nests to catch them. Ipanna set one tonight over an *augruaq*[3] (literally, blood-birds) nest, which had four eggs in it.

Friday, June 26th

Today was warmer than yesterday, the thermometer being above 50° at noon. At midnight it was 31°. Digging over at the eastern ruins filled in the day. At supper (or dinner) Ipanna came in for a good deal of chaff because he is not married for one reason. Teriglu told him Leffingwell would have used him for one of his beacons. Mapteraq chaffed him too, and Ipanna retorted by remarks on Mapteraq's nose, which is rather longer than the average coast Eskimos. Qovun went after some gulls with my shotgun and bagged two. He had to cross a pool of water. In going he took off boots and socks and waded but found it bitterly cold.

Returning he tried to ferry himself over by alternate weighting forward of his body on a loose cake of ice. It refused to budge, so Ipanna threw him a pole and he punted over on his ice-raft. Late this evening Teriglu brought to me two teal,[4] (*savavum tiñmiaña* he called them), a pair, which he had just shot. They are scarce around here, he said. A few minutes later he told me that his wife's hand was all right again (see June 18th). He had rubbed hazeline cream twice a day as I showed him, and the pain grew less, until today the needle (it must have been quite 1/2 inch long according to his account) emerged, and he drew it out with thumb and finger. I fancy he meant the ducks as a payment. Leffingwell and Stefansson both say the Eskimos are never grateful for anything.[5] They certainly would be considered an ungrateful people if judged by our standards, but I think it is the point of view that differs, not the level of attainment of a common standard. Teriglu's payment of the ducks was perfectly voluntary; it was a true expression of gratitude. Yet Teriglu was one of Leffingwell's standing examples of ingratitude!! Mapteraq shot four seals today. There is a fine view when the atmosphere is clear (just now a fog has crept up) from our tents over the big lagoon of water behind the sandspit to the snow-clad Endicott [Romanzof] Mountains in the distance. The sandspit curves round the lagoon on one side and the island on the other, almost enclosing it altogether, and the peaceful sheen of the tranquil water, with here and there a duck or a seagull flying over it, reminds one of a more southern clime. There are small flowers too in abundance on the tundra and especially among the ruins of the eastern sandspit, some bluish red and some quite blue, but clustered in bunches that strangely resemble the wild hyacinths of the English woods.

Saturday, June 27th

Another fine day, with the temperature about 50° at noon and down to 31° at midnight. Ipanna and I dug over at the eastern ruins, and I spent the evening writing up notes. On the way back we caught a small moth, the first seen in flight this year. Also we found the nest of a Lapland Larkspur (*kupahluk*),[6] where one egg was much larger than the other three. Ipanna skinned one of the teal in the evening and Qovun the other, while I put on the final dressings. Mapteraq was rubbing the seams of his kayak with caribou fat this evening to make them waterproof. He had a seal harpoon inside a stout stick, not very smooth, about 6 feet long with a piece of bone lashed on the end. Into the bone was hammered an iron spike on which fitted a brass head with a point shaped thus:

Figure 101. Pointed brass head on Mapteraq's seal harpoon.

A line ran from this brass head and was made tight by two half hitches to the middle of the shaft. He reported that he had seen today some fish through a crack in the ice, and SuXrana, Oyaraq's wife, went along to fish. Oyaraq showed me two hooks he made, and I sketched one. It had an ivory back shaped like a fish, with iron pins for the fins and brass ones for the eyes. The hook was an iron nail riveted through the ivory, bent and pointed. For bait he had a small piece of red flannel on the bottom of the hook, and inside that a similar piece of white skin as a backing for the flannel. The whole thing was about 3 inches long, a very small hook, he said; it was very well made nevertheless.

Sunday, June 28th

Another day similar to yesterday but a little colder, for an east wind sprang up. At midnight the temperature was 31°. Qovun and I went over to the sandspit where Aiyakuk and ToXlumana are living,[7] and I inspected what he [Aiyakuk] had done — not a very great amount, but not bad, considering that ToXlumana had been sick the last three days and kept him in most of the time. Apparently it was some stomach trouble she was affected with, but she was better today. I told him he could continue until the ice breaks up, then he is to bring his two boats — a whaleboat and a skin boat — along to my camp and we will all go over to the east end of Barter Island. We found a duck's nest (*amauligeroq*) with five eggs, but had no gun to shoot with. On returning we saw about 100 oldsquaw ducks on the lagoon behind the camp, and not 50 yards from my tent, in a small pool, were three others. The Eskimos were holding service in an adjoining tent at the time, but I shot the three nevertheless; they would not shoot, themselves, for it was Sunday. The evening was spent in writing up notes, except for a half-hour profitably devoted to duck and *mukpaurat* and cocoa. The ice is very slow in breaking up. I wonder if the ships will get free this summer and make Coronation Gulf.

Monday, June 29th[8]

A moderately strong east wind blew all day, making the air colder than yesterday. Ipanna and I dug out two houses, as far as the frozen ground would allow us to, on the west end of the island near our tents, then in the evening he and Qovun went over to see their mother and Aiyakuk. Qovun shot two spectacled eiders and skinned one [of these] for Dr. Anderson.[9] Teriglu showed me a woman's knife he found in one of the ruins. The blade was copper, and it had a curious bone handle — flat and disc-shaped, prevented from falling off by a peg above. Ipanna having leave of absence, I turned cook and made *mukpaurat* and cornmeal. The temperature fell to 31° during the evening. Teriglu came into the tent during the evening and stayed for a couple of hours, talking.

Tuesday, June 30th

Ipanna had not turned up by noon, so after breakfast I went over to Aiyakuk's sandspit and sent him across[10] while I remained to pace out the distances between the houses in order later to make a plan of them. The water is gradually extending, and Aiyakuk should be able to bring his boat over in 2 or 3 days. Teriglu had most annoyingly good luck in the sites I let him dig. There were five in all, and four proved more or less ordinary, but the last one, the nearest to his tent (No. 2),[11] was a perfect mine of treasures. Inside were two skeletons, apparently a man and his wife, and all their property was there pretty well intact — a large labret, arrow-heads, fish-hook, needle case and thimble holder, knives etc. I am arranging now to buy them from Teriglu and have further engaged him to work for me for 15 days for which he is to receive $20. Qovun shot an *amaulegeroq* (an eider duck), and we brought it across with the five eggs on which it was sitting. A moderate east wind blew all day, and the temperature was not very high. At night it fell to 31° F.

Wednesday, July 1st

Teriglu, Ipanna, and I worked on the eastern ruins from 1 p.m. till 8 p.m., making good progress. Qovun was cook and scratched a little in between times. He shot a loon in the morning as it flew overhead. When we returned we found Aiyakuk and ToXlumana had come in their boat, following the land round to the lagoon at the back of us. They returned later with the dogs, but have to break up camp and come over here tomorrow, for we are going to settle on the east end of the island until these ruins are finished. The weather was overcast all day, and it rained in the evening. The temperature never reached 40° all day, I think, for a cold east breeze was blowing, not very strong luckily. Ipanna caught a butterfly for me — the first I have seen this year[12] — the other was a moth [caught on June 27]. Qovun went out after ducks and spent several hours beside the lagoon, securing two.

Thursday, July 2nd

I sent Ipanna and Teriglu across to dig on the eastern ruins while I stayed to pack up some of the specimens here and to sketch some before packing. This kept me busy all day. Aiyakuk and ToXlumana came across towards evening. They had to go through a good deal of water. The weather was cold all day, and in the evening it snowed a little, though the wind had changed to southwest. One of the dogs got loose last night and entered our store tent and ate up some bird specimens, though they were in a tin case, and he had to push up one end with his nose. I am wondering now whether the arsenic[13] will disagree with him, or whether there is not enough to hurt.

Friday, July 3rd

A foggy day, and cold with a little rain. After breakfast, Teriglu and Aiyakuk went to bring over their whaleboats from the sandspit;[14] Aiyakuk too to break up his camp. He misunderstood me and left his tent and things there, bringing Ipanna's 20-foot whaleboat only. Ipanna and I and Mapteraq took this and some of our things, and went across the lagoon and round the back of the island. After going a short distance the water became very shallow and we had to get out and drag it along. The bottom was thick black ooze, and at one place I noticed a kind of blue clay, noticed it especially for I nearly lost my boots there — long thigh boots though they were. About 3 miles down where the water was a little deeper we came to a whaleboat, Mapteraq's. It had been Billy Natkusiak's, but he sold it[15] the other day to Mapteraq for six foxskins — three red, two white, and one black or partly black. We helped him launch it, then continued, Ipanna and I, round the back of the island, occasionally having to get out and push. But the bottom had now changed from ooze to gravel, and the channel was narrow and impeded by ice. A west wind was blowing, helping us part of the way and hindering us later. In one place we had to push off a great ice cake to make a channel; in another to drag the boat over a narrow cake. It was cold wet work, for the water came in over the top of our boots. Finally we were held up altogether — on the east side of the island, where the low flat coast rises to a cliff. Here there was a broad expanse of ice clinging to the shore, with here and there a narrow crack but no continuous lane. We left the boat and walked along the edge of the cliff, which is about 24 feet high and intersected by three or four narrow ravines where the melting snow of the winter drains off into the sea. The cliff extended for about a mile until it faces the sandspit on which the ruins are situated, where it turns westward to enclose a small bay, and becoming lower and lower, finally curves round into the sandspit. All round the shore of this bay was an open channel, but for the mile where the cliff faced eastward the ice was still solid, and likely to be so for some days. We returned to the boat, dragged her up high and dry, covered our things with the sail, and set off home — about 3 miles across the tundra. On the way we found a loon (*qaqsrauk*) on its nest and shot it, taking the eggs — two — never more than two, Ipanna says.[16] Further on we found another loon's nest with but one egg and the bird some distance away swimming in a pool. We left them, hoping to return later when it has laid another. About 9:30 p.m. we reached camp, and I boiled the loon's eggs for 10 minutes — a little too long, I think, for mine did not taste as well as it should have, or at least as I expected. Aiyakuk and Teriglu had not returned by 2 a.m. The temperature at 11 p.m. was 31° F., at 2 a.m. 28°. It is interesting to notice the lemmings' nests on the land now that the snow has all melted — an uninitiated person would mistake them, as I did at first, for old birds' nests. Ipanna, by the way, calls them *oviñaq*,[17] or *uviñaq*, but I have noticed that he has a rather marked pronunciation.

Saturday, July 4th

A fine sunny day with a temperature of 49° at noon, and a very light northwest breeze. Aiyakuk and Teriglu before breakfast hoisted the sails of their whaleboats to dry them. Later we went over to the eastern sandspit to work, though Teriglu did not turn up for some reason or other. Butterflies were numerous, for the first time, and we lingered long enough to capture a dozen or so.[18] Ipanna also shot a ptarmigan with his rifle. About 6:30 p.m. the others returned home, while I stayed behind to write up some of the remains (I had taken the typewriter across) and pack them up. When I returned about 9 p.m. they [Aiyakuk and Ipanna] had gone off after ducks, for we have just about run out of them. It is now 2 a.m. and they have not returned. I have been writing up notes ever since I came back. ToXlumana made a huge *mukpaurat* sandwich for me. She mixed chocolate and cocoa and a little water into a thick paste and laid it about 1/2 inch thick between the two halves of a large *mukpaurat* baked in a frying pan. This, (or part of it), a leg of a duck, and some beans (for the third time today), with a cup of cocoa was my dinner. The temperature has fallen to freezing, but the sky and atmosphere are clear. It is amusing to note how the Eskimos avoid a slightly overbaked *mukpaurat*; they throw away the black as much as any schoolboy.

Sunday, July 5th

Aiyakuk and the others returned about 3 a.m. They secured only about five ducks, but Aiyakuk shot a seal. We did not turn out till about noon. The weather was a little colder — the thermometer did not rise above 40°, I think, all day. I loaded some shells after breakfast and went off shooting over the tundra. After tramping about 6 hours I finally got home again with a loon and an *'isungaq'*.[19] Another loon I shot was caught under the ice, and the water was too deep to look for it. It was a relief to get away from the murdered hymns they keep up all Sunday. It is interesting that the 'sacredness', i.e., the 'idleness', of the Sunday only lasts from the time the sun is east to the time it is west, i.e. about 12 hours. After that they can shoot, etc. as usual.

Monday, July 6th

A cold dank misty day with a moderately strong east wind blowing and the temperature uniformly about freezing. I set Aiyakuk to work on the western ruins near our tents while Ipanna and I, followed later by Teriglu, worked on the eastern [ruins]. After a couple of hours or so digging I sent these two to take the small whaleboat from where we left it the other day back to the sandspit, as the ice seemed to be opening faster round the north edge of the island. I stayed and worked on for a couple of hours then returned to camp, and when the whaleboat arrived — they lingered to shoot ducks etc. and killed one brant — Aiyakuk, Ipanna, and Qovunna went over to the sandspit 3 miles west to bring in Aiyakuk's tent, fish-net, etc.; he had been unable to reach them in his full-sized whaleboat on account of the ice and the shallow water. Teriglu and Mapteraq and their families moved westward today about 1/2 mile along the sandspit nearing to the fishing place.[20] Mapteraq secured a good haul in his net this morning, though Teriglu has been less successful. Aiyakuk shot a couple of brant this morning — they are large birds and the two alone made a great potful of meat and soup.

Tuesday, July 7th

A miserable day — a cold strong east wind and a temperature of about freezing. I knocked over the typewriter[21] last night just before going to bed and broke something. Today I spent all the time in pulling it apart and trying to discover what was wrong. Now I have put it nearly all together again and it is the same as before. Ipanna dug a little on two of the houses here and Aiyakuk did miscellaneous jobs. Oyaraq made me an Eskimo pipe and I have had a smoke out of it. The stem is of willow, so it smokes very strong at present and tastes strong too. The bowl and mouthpiece are of fossil ivory. Mapteraq caught nine fish in his net last night, Aiyakuk one. It snowed for a time this evening. Three birds were skinned today for Dr. Anderson — two loons (mallere) and an *isungaq* (jaeger?).[22]

Wednesday, July 8th

Another miserably cold and windy day similar to yesterday. However, Aiyakuk, Ipanna, and I went over and worked on the eastern ruins. Ipanna had been out a great portion of the night sealing and brought in a seal this morning. He went to sleep where he was supposed to be digging, so I sent him over to the tent to sleep there. Aiyakuk shot two ptarmigan beside the tent with a .22 rifle, and we ate them for lunch. He shot at the same time a weasel (*itigiaq*), black on the back and white beneath. I am having it skinned for Dr. Anderson. He discovered in a little nook on the edge of the sandspit numbers of whale, deer and mountain-sheep bones, but especially the former. They lay in black ooze covered by an inch or two of water, though it deepened at the entrance to the nook. A significant fact was that it was on the south margin of the sandspit, which borders on a half-enclosed lagoon, and it is along that margin that lie what I suspect to be the more ancient of the ruins. We picked out of the ooze two or three bone adze's or picks, a bone knife, and a bone knife handle. Apparently the whale or whales had been dragged in and cut up on this spit. After working 4 hours or so we returned to camp. When we went across at noon there was a clear lane of water practically the whole way between the two sandspits and we anticipated getting the whaleboat across tomorrow. When we returned, however, it had closed up in one place so the project seems doubtful. Oyaraq and his wife scratched at one of the houses beside their tent and unearthed a few specimens. Aiyakuk fixed up his fish-net this evening after dinner, then took it down to the end of the sandspit to set it. A little rain began to fall, but presently turned to snow, for the temperature has been in the neighbourhood of freezing all day, and this evening the thermometer stood at 31° F.

Thursday, July 9th

A repetition of yesterday as far as the weather was concerned and the temperature, which at 11 p.m. stood at 28°. The ice is moving westward, but the inshore channel to the eastern ruins is still closed. We worked,

Aiyakuk, Ipanna, Qovun, and I, on the eastern ruins, Teriglu being occupied in painting his boat. Aiyakuk with his .22 shot a second weasel, the mate of the one he shot yesterday, and Qovunna skinned both tonight[23] — through the mouth, like a fox. Oyaraq's wife fossicked about one of the ruins at midnight last night and unearthed a fine flint arrowhead, a well marked whetstone, a wooden ladle, and the two halves of a horn ladle used for removing ice from a fishing hole. Aiyakuk set about painting his boat this evening; he used seal oil (obtained by boiling seal blubber) to mix with his paint, and it worked up fine. He says that in fairly warm weather it takes 2 to 3 days to dry. It snowed a little towards midnight.

Friday, July 10th

The wind was much the same as yesterday but the sky was clear, the sun shining brightly and the temperature about 38° F. I sent Ipanna over to the sandspit[24] to bring across a shovel which had been accidentally forgotten, also to give him a day off to hunt seal. Aiyakuk, Teriglu, and I excavated over on the eastern ruins. During the last 4 days the ground has thawed very little. Oyaraq's wife [SuXrana] again fossicked and found this time a fine blade of a woman's knife. I am smoking the pipe Oyaraq made for me. The stem being of willow and partly green, the first smoke, short though it was, made me feel as if I had drunk a very sufficient quantity of liquor; the feeling passed off, however, after about 10 minutes. Now the stem is dry and it smokes pretty well, though half a dozen whiffs empties it, the bowl being extremely small. Teriglu's boy [Igluñasuk] (about 10) and Aiyakuk were racing each other down and up the little ravines cut near the edge of the cliff by the drainage from the land. We were approaching one rather deeper than usual, Teriglu's boy well in front. "*Aiyakuk añayuqaqsruq*" (Aiyakuk's an old man), he called out and ran down the slope. Off darted Aiyakuk, overtook him just as he was beginning the ascent of the other side, seized his hand and dragged him up till the panting boy cried "*tavrani tavra*" (stop stop). A few minutes before this I had sneezed. "*Tavrani tavrani*," Teriglu said "that's what you must say — or '*qatqain*'" (i.e. *qain* = come). "It's your self stopping inside you," Aiyakuk says, "*atkin* your spirit, and you know he is there because he makes you sneeze." It was just then that Teriglu's boy called out "*Aiyakuk añayuqaqsruq.*" The sun is almost due north at this moment and the colours of different parts of the tent viewed from where I write are rather striking. The tent is a large round one of green canvas, somewhat faded of course, with a perpendicular wall all round, about 2 feet high. The northern slope [of the tent] is a brownish green, the brown predominating; in the wall directly below a yellow predominates. These two tents merge into the dull green of all the southern half of the tent, but the bag door is a bright grass green.

Saturday, July 11th

Teriglu, Ipanna, and myself worked on the eastern ruins while Aiyakuk continued on the western. ToXlumana and Oyaraq's wife found a new site, or rather a place where there were numerous remains below the surface, though no trace of a house. Oyaraq's wife in giving me their trophies in the evening told me their theory about it, viz. that a white man had been digging for gold and had thrown out these specimens along with the gravel. There were some good implements among them. We have about 15 houses on the eastern side exposed down to the floor, and we are just waiting for them to thaw out before finishing them. I finished two yesterday and stayed after the others left to write them up, sketch some of the specimens,[25] and pack them away. The wind was not so strong and the sun much warmer — I think the thermometer touched 46°. The ice has cleared out on either side of the eastern sandspit, leaving large lagoons of open water. If only it would clear off the edge of the cliff we could go along to the other side and proceed to a sandspit at the mouth of Jag's [Jago] River and get some duck eggs. A few more days and it will be too late — they will be hatching. Many of the flowers — most in fact — that bloomed first have faded and new ones taken their place. I come upon fresh species every few days. Yesterday there was a cluster of 'forget-me-nots' or flowers suggesting them. The warm sun, the sight and sound of the waves of the sea, the bumble bees and flies and butterflies and birds, and these flowers, so reminiscent of other days, are very comforting when tired out or vexed at the slow progress we are making. We will yet finish all the ruins on Barter Island, I hope, though we shall probably have to go down to Collinson Point in a few days, if possible, and get some flour. Aiyakuk has three bags, but the flour, he says, is not much good — apart from this we have barely one-quarter sack. We are having fish though, and occasional duck and seal, so that we are not badly off even though I dine twice a day on beans, and sugar is on the missing list. We have about one-half cupful of molasses — doctored with much water.

Sunday, July 12th

I took the shotgun and butterfly net after breakfast and wandered over the tundra for a few hours. There were no ducks or loons, but I captured a number of butterflies. When I returned Aiyakuk was down at the end of the sandspit — at Mapteraq's tent, so I wrote up some notes and gathered together the specimens for Dr. Anderson and Johansen preparatory to leaving for Collinson Point. The weather was glorious; around noon the thermometer registered 56°, and there was a very gentle north breeze. It grew much cooler, however, towards evening and had fallen to freezing by 11 p.m.

Monday, July 13th

We started in the small 20-foot whaleboat of Ipanna but exchanged it for Aiyakuk's large 30-foot whaleboat at the end of the sandspit. It carries a very much larger sail and is therefore faster. The wind was almost dead ahead for some distance and not very strong. It took us 3 1/2 hours to beat up to the west end of the sandspit where Aiyakuk's tent used to be.[26] After this we had to row a little, but this occupation was varied by 'potting' at ducks and loons with Aiyakuk's .22. After a time the wind, which had been shifting about a good deal, what little there was, turned definitely northeast, and later strengthened, so that we reached the captain's cache[27] about 11 p.m.[28] Outside there was a great expanse of deep water, which may extend for 50 miles, but close to shore it is shallower, and there was too much ice for us to get through. We had to turn in behind the sandspit near the cache and anchor the boat there. We had already indulged twice in tea and hard-bread, having a primus stove, and now on the sandspit we had a good meal — three oldsquaw ducks (boiled in the teapot, and half of one roasted on a stick), some chocolate, and hard-bread crumbs and tea. Mapteraq had come with us (there were Aiyakuk, Qovun, and I), bringing a large seal to sell to Dr. Anderson. We had to leave this but took the specimens and set out to walk round the bay a distance of perhaps 12 miles. The tramp was rather interesting. Near Capt. Nahmens' old cabin some large streams flowing down from the hills broaden into two lagoons, which communicate by narrow but rather deep (about 3 to 4 feet) channels with the sea. At the first we laid logs out on to ground ice kegs and jumping from one to the other crossed without difficulty but not altogether dry. At the second we made a raft, and Qovun and I crossed over on it, I squatting in front. There was a long thick log in the middle and two small side logs, with three or four sticks laid across. To land, you walked gingerly out a few feet along the middle log. Qovun rushed it and went in. A few streams and two small rivers — the *Kuvraliruk* and the *Nuvoak*[29] — that we had to cross later, were shallow, not above the knees. Squirrels were very numerous about the middle of the bay, where the knolls on top of the bank were riddled with their holes. We shot two, and I killed one with a stone. About 5 p.m. we reached Collinson Point and found that the harbour was clear of ice and that one vessel — the *Alaska* — was at anchor near the camp and had that day commenced loading. Johansen was busy packing all his specimens, and Dr. Anderson superintending the loading. Both seemed pleased with the specimens I brought along for them.[30] Johansen has now four skulls, which he found close to the camp and will pack for me.

Tuesday, July 14th

Dr. Anderson said he hoped to get away inside of 10 days, as it required only a southwest breeze to clear out the ice at the mouth of the bay. [Capt.] Nahmens has left the Expedition, and Sweeney is now in command of the *Alaska*. Johansen and Dr. Anderson went across to *Qonanevik* [Konganevik Point], and Johansen stayed there a week while the Dr. took Nahmens on to Flaxman Island, where he joined Leffing-well and goes outside with him.[31] After obtaining the stores etc. I needed, we prepared to set off back, hoping by skirting the shore and tracking to be able to take the things in a small skin boat. Aiyakuk received or arrangements were made whereby he should receive $50 worth of stuff from the Expedition (a rifle[32] and 1000 rounds) and Kaiyutaq, who had been working at Collinson Point for nearly 3 months, was paid off at his own request[33] — $20 a month — the same as Fred and Añutisiak receive. He took $49 in goods[34] and $11 in money. Mapteraq received a flour bag of hard-bread for his seal, because there are only four sacks of flour left at Collinson Point. For the same reason I too got hard-bread instead of flour. The Dr. had two fish-nets set at the mouth of the *Nuvoak* River [Marsh Creek], so they were getting a few fish. He had bought several seals from the Eskimos at *Qonanevik* [Konganevik Point] with flour. We set out after lunch and with great difficulty reached about 1/2 mile beyond the *Nuvoak* River. The ice had closed in during the night, and the channel which was there the day before no longer existed. We had to push ice kegs aside and where they could not be moved lift the canoe[35] bodily over. Finally it became altogether impenetrable, and I sent Añutisiak back with the canoe; he had been sent to take the canoe back and the seal with it. We divided the baggage into five loads and shouldered it down to the whaleboat — a long weary tramp for us all. On the way I shot a pintail duck and caught a young one, and Kaiyutaq shot two golden plovers and an oldsquaw [duck]. We stopped at Capt. Nah-mens' old cabin and had coffee (we found a little there) and the two ducks and hard-bread. Again on reaching the whaleboat (11:45 p.m.) we had a loon and more hard-bread and tea. Then we embarked with a very light north wind. The ice had opened up greatly in our absence and the schooners, could they get clear of Camden Bay, might reach nearly to Aiyakuk's sandspit.[36] The night was cold and foggy, and the wind almost died away. I for one slept little — about an hour.

Wednesday, July 15th

We travelled very slowly all night — I rowing every now and then to keep a little warm if possible. About 10 a.m. the wind freshened — from the east now, so that we were tacking all the way. About noon we reached Aiyakuk's sandspit, and after a meal I walked along to the ruins to gather some of the specimens and make notes while the others continued in the whaleboat — the distance being about 2 miles. Aiyakuk went to sleep, and the others put in about 3/4 mile beyond the ruins and stayed there — it took them 2 hours to make that distance. I joined them there, and we stood across for Barter Island, which we reached in the late afternoon. Teriglu was about to leave for *Olektoq*[37] to pick up Leffing-well, as instructed a month ago. After eating I examined the specimens he had gathered and bought most of them, giving him a letter to Dr. Anderson asking him to pay. He had worked 6 days for me and for the whole we agreed upon this price:

1 20-gauge shotgun, with 1 box brass shells and reloading tools
$9 cash or trade
Also, if easily accessible,
    1 tin lard
    1 lb tobacco
    1 tin baking powder.
I wrote letters to Dr. Anderson and to Leffingwell for him [Teriglu] to
take, and he sailed away about 11 p.m. with a fine east breeze in his
favour.[38] Shortly afterwards I turned in, being very sleepy after the hard
tramp of the day before and the sleeplessness of the night. Aiyakuk had
gone to sleep about 8 p.m.

Thursday, July 16th

A fine sunny day — temperature at 9 a.m. 36° with a moderate breeze
from the east. After breakfast Aiyakuk went along to bring the whaleboat, and I wrote some notes until he came. All along the north of Barter
Island there is now a fine wide stretch of open water with but a few floating kegs of ice. Kaiyutaq and Aiyakuk shot three or four oldsquaw ducks
as we sailed along [heading for the ruins at the east end of the island].
We had to keep tacking so the run took some time. It was not until 2 p.m.
that we really settled down to work, Aiyakuk, Ipanna, and I, while Oyaraq's wife, who had come with us, fished on the sea shore, and Kaiyutaq and Simigaq (Qovun) hunted ducks. While working we came upon
three young [Baird's] sandpipers and took two,[39] letting the third run
free; Dr. Anderson was very anxious to get some specimens because this
bird breeds exclusively in the Arctic, though it migrates south in the
autumn. I sent the others home by boat about 7 p.m. and stayed on myself digging until 8, then wrote up some notes and packed a few specimens, setting out for camp at 9 p.m. across the tundra and arriving at 10
p.m. A moderate easterly breeze prevailed all day, but just after I returned a thick fog set in, the temperature being 36° F.

Friday, July 17th

Mapteraq and his people were leaving today for Flaxman Island, but a
strong east wind was blowing most of the day so they stayed. Oyaraq
and his wife are going up into the mountains next week, Ipanna tells me.
They have been preparing for this for some weeks, intending to carry
their tent etc. on their backs, or rather on the backs of their dogs. They
have three fine big dogs and one small one — a pup still, but a good
worker. Oyaraq wishes to try for mountain sheep, whose wool is best at
this time of year according to Aiyakuk. Mrs. Oyaraq has two enormous
'sausages' made from the gullet? (*igiaña*) of the white whale; soon they
will be filled with seal oil. I brought them some presents from Collinson
Point — in return for the help they have given me here — 20 lbs or so of
hard-bread, a pipe, 2 fathoms [about 12 feet of] white drill, and a tin of
tabloid tea. They were very pleased. Aiyakuk, Ipanna, and I worked
solidly on the eastern ruins from 1 p.m. till 7:30, save for two intervals

for tea and hard-bread. We made considerable headway, for the ground had thawed somewhat. If the schooners do not appear till the end of next week I hope that everything on Barter Island will be finished and shall feel fairly well satisfied. It has meant a great deal of hard work — 4 to 5 hours a day on the average with shovel and scraper, then for me, in addition, 5 hours or so, packing, writing notes, labelling specimens etc. Then there have been specimens for Dr. Anderson and Johansen. Today I caught six butterflies,[40] and Aiyakuk, from a pool, culled half a dozen fish for Johansen, while Kaiyutaq cleaned a loon skin which I have to dress. Ipanna found a snow bunting's nest in the hollow of a whale's head and took great delight in frightening the young ones (there were four) by shouting through the hole. I saw Aiyakuk and Simigaq chasing the old birds later with stones, and Simigaq (Qovun) shooting at them with his bow and arrow. It is a great pastime apparently with both boys and grown-up men — throwing stones at birds. If ducks or loons fly near and they have no gun the first thought is to throw a stone. Aiyakuk shot a *tulik* and a mallere (two kinds of loons)[41] from the cliff this morning, and they drifted in to shore about a mile to the west, where we picked them up on the way home. He is a good rifle-shot — indeed, he has plenty of practice — I suppose in a year he uses easily 1000 rounds — mostly in spring and summer — probably more — besides shotgun ammunition. ToXlumana told me this morning — now that Teriglu and his people are gone — that they are a bad lot — not above stealing from their neighbours. Certainly they were less welcome than Mapteraq and his people. The temperature at 11 a.m. was 44° — at 10 p.m. 36° F. The sky was clear and the east wind slightly moderated towards evening but was still fresh.

Saturday, July 18th

We made an attempt to finish the ruins on the western side of Barter Island today. There were three houses and one grave, all partly excavated. Two we finished altogether, the other two — one the grave — nearly, but could not complete because the ground was frozen. The unfinished house was deep in ice and water. We dug the floor boards out with a pick, but underneath was solid ice and we had to leave it. Mapteraq and his people have not left, for a strong east wind blew all day, though it moderated slightly at night and shifted a little round to the north. This change brought some ice kegs in shore, and ToXlumana and Oyaraq's wife hastened to secure some ice for water. Normally on a sandspit when neither ice nor snow is available a hole is dug and fresh water obtained in that way, but just about here the water is salt. ToXlumana went along to a ravine on the island about 1/2 mile away for water today. I spent most of the evening packing and filled two cases, one a small sugar box and the other about twice the size. A much larger box is almost full also, and on the east end of the island one small box is packed and nailed down and another larger box is half full.

Sunday, July 19th

A day of mingled work and idleness but mostly the former. The east wind still blew strong, increasing a little in the afternoon but diminishing again later. I wrote one or two notes after breakfast, then went over to the eastern ruins and packed and labelled and wrote notes for a couple of hours or so. The weather was dull and overcast up to this time, but now the sun came up and the temperature rose well above 40°. About 4 p.m. I reached camp again and lunched, then slept an hour, after which Aiyakuk, Kaiyutaq, Qovun, and I went over to the sandspit[42] 3 miles west where I had to gather up the specimens Aiyakuk dug during his stay there. This took some time — 2 hours or so. Aiyakuk meanwhile caught me a young sandpiper[43] to bottle for Dr. Anderson. The return run took us a long time, for we had to tack continually. The cold wind scorched our faces and we had to row occasionally to keep the circulation going. However, a good supper of beans and *mukpaurat* awaited us, and this with a smoke afterwards made us feel content again. The temperature was 34° at 11 p.m.

Monday, July 20th

A moderate north breeze was blowing when we turned out this morning; the sky was clouded, the temperature below 40°. After breakfast Aiyakuk went off for his whaleboat, as he much prefers sailing over to the eastern ruins to walking. I packed specimens and wrote notes until he came along with it, then with the three boys, Ipanna, Kaiyutaq, and Qovun, embarked. We had a good quick run along the coast, Kaiyutaq expending a good deal of ammunition and bagging one oldsquaw duck. The geese and the oldsquaws are beginning to lose their wing feathers now, and depend upon their speed on and below the surface of the water to escape danger. We worked on the ruins till after 5 p.m., though they had thawed but little in the last few days. Aiyakuk helped me to pack some specimens, but I sent him and the others home after a little and continued alone. Ipanna went on foot, the others in the whaleboat, but after a couple of hours had to put back and anchor the boat in the lagoon behind the sandspit, for the wind shifting a little round to the northeast had driven a great quantity of ice inshore, and they could not work through it. I was just starting off home when I saw them coming behind; it had taken 3 hours to pack the specimens from four ruins and make a rough list of their contents. Brisk walking kept us warm going across the tundra; Kaiyutaq shot at but missed a snowy owl. Notes and specimens filled in the remainder of the evening — what little was left after dinner, for it was 9:30 p.m. when we reached camp. The temperature at 11 p.m. was 33° F., just one degree above freezing.

Tuesday, July 21st

The wind was still northwest or perhaps west-northwest. I am not sure of the exact orientation here. After breakfast we went over as usual to the eastern ruins and Ipanna dug — more or less — while Aiyakuk and I packed. With two interruptions for refreshments we kept busy from 12 noon to 8 p.m., when the other two went away in the whaleboat. The ice still packs the shore on the other side, but they went round it well out to sea and so reached camp about midnight. I took stock of the condition of the ruins after they left — a task which took me more than an hour, then walked home, dropping Aiyakuk's hammer somewhere over the first mile. Kaiyutaq was away after ducks and secured two oldsquaws and some eggs. Ipanna made a find today; in what appears to have been a dance-house he unearthed five fine whale-harpoon blades of stone, cached one on top of the other between two floor beams. It infused a tremendous amount of energy into him — for a time — though really he seems to have worked fairly well today on the whole. The temperature was below freezing when I reached camp about 10:30 p.m. It is very pleasant to lie in my sleeping bag at rest and listen to the waves once more lapping on the shore. The earth is very musical just now — the birds and the sea and the flowers and the bright warm sun (when the day is fine) make one long to be idle and lie down on the grass and sleep beside the murmuring water. Yet I have never been busier than I am now — and shall be very glad in a way when this digging is over. Qovun shot two small birds beside the camp today — Oyaraq calls them *kilatallik*[44] — I do not yet know their scientific name, but am keeping them for Dr. Anderson.

Wednesday, July 22nd

Another day of packing for myself and Aiyakuk. I did a little before breakfast, then walked over to the eastern ruins and packed alone from 1 to 4 p.m. At 4 Aiyakuk, Ipanna, and Qovun arrived — bringing the whaleboat to carry the boxes away. We then packed steadily — with two intervals for tea and hard-bread, until 11 p.m. The others then left in the whaleboat — with a good east wind behind them — while I had a final look round the ruins to see that nothing had been forgotten. I am very disappointed that they are not finished, but the cold weather has been against us. On the east sandspit 38 sites have been fully excavated (five were graves, the rest dwellings), 10 or 11 (all houses) cleared down to the floor, where the beams are still frozen, and 10 others (probably all houses) marked out for excavation are untouched. On the west sandspit beside our camp there were 16 sites, five of which were dug out by Teriglu, the rest by me. One was a grave, the others all dwellings. All have been completely excavated except one house where the floor has been removed, but the earth beneath is covered with about 2 inches of water. It would have been 1/2 day's work to make a trench for it to drain off, and I left it, hoping always that with warmer weather it would soon disappear; the luck has been against me. On the sandspit 3 miles west about 15 sites have been excavated, one or two wholly, the others either in part, or in completion of former excavations by Aiyakuk and others. Sufficient remains have been recovered from it to enable a judgement to be formed as to its antiquity,[45] which was the important consideration. I have — or will have, if my scattered notes prove as full as I think they are — rough plans of all three villages and notes of each place in each village, with a fairly complete list of everything found in it.[46] There are many sketches of the interesting objects, but latterly I have had no time to carry this on and many of the most important finds are unsketched. There is nothing to do now but to clear up the debris and get rid of all the boxes. Kaiyutaq and Oyaraq went sealing in Ipanna's small whaleboat and got two seals. There are plenty now in the open water close to shore. It was about 12:30 a.m. when I reached camp, just after Aiyakuk and the others. The temperature was 31° with a moderate cold east wind blowing. It had not reached 40° all day. I saw some plovers at the end of the sandspit on which the camp is situated and sent Ipanna after them with my shotgun. He secured one, which will be skinned later, I hope, for Dr. Anderson.

Thursday, July 23rd

Another day similar as far as the weather was concerned to yesterday. I was packing all day. We have practically no good boxes, and to go down to Martin Point where there are two good large ones might take us 2 or 3 days and even more. We have made two or three boxes with scraps of boards and used all kinds of odd little boxes. Some of our lids are quaint — cut out of sled or canoe 'boards' with a tiny saw of Oyaraq's and a knife. I shall have to repack some later in better boxes. The total number at present is seventeen, that is, those that contain specimens from the ruins. These are nearly all small, though three or four are of an average size. I sent Ipanna off to shoot some small birds that may be about, and he brought back ten or eleven; three being sandpipers — of which I have already given Dr. Anderson four or five specimens, and he has himself several more — I gave to the pups. Kaiyutaq skinned one bird, a plover, and there are half a dozen left to be skinned when there is opportunity. Ipanna and Kaiyutaq towards evening took Oyaraq and his wife with all their belongings over to the mainland to the mouth of the Hulahula [River]. He [Oyaraq] is going up into the mountains for the summer, as he wishes to get some mountain sheep; how I don't know, for he is too old to clamber about the summits where the sheep mostly dwell.

Eskimos are kind to each other in some ways. Aiyakuk, for example, says he has given Oyaraq about two bags of flour this year, and he probably spoke the truth. Yet if Oyaraq's dog were tangled up and likely to strangle itself it is quite likely that he would let it do so unhindered — "I don't care, it's not mine," he would say. If he saw Oyaraq he would tell him, but would not stir a finger himself or go a step out of his way. I have noticed this repeatedly among all the Eskimos I have been with — it seems to be typical of the people as a whole. They are unable, I suppose, to project themselves out of themselves — to love their neighbours as themselves. This perhaps explains their cruelty — or so it seems to us — to birds and animals — a child-like thoughtlessness which permits

Figure 102. The Canadian Arctic Expedition headquarters at Collinson Point, July 24, 1914. (Photo by R.M. Anderson, CMC Photo No. 38703.)

them to torment an injured bird or thrash unmercifully a dog which has provoked them — although in the latter case the dog's great value makes them refrain from doing it lasting injury.

Aiyakuk after lunch went to fix up his whaleboat and brought me back a dead jellyfish (?) he found on the beach. I put it in alcohol for Johansen. Now that my sojourn on Barter Island is about over — we leave tomorrow for Collinson Point if the schooners do not show up before — I shall have a change of diet from the everlasting beans here. True we have had duck fairly often and seal sometimes, and fish occasionally — but beans have generally turned up once and sometimes even three times a day. I asked ToXlumana today if she wanted some beans and she said "not just now" and laughed. I brought about 100 lbs here and we have used three-quarters of them in less than 2 months. Aiyakuk is going to Barrow to buy stores, taking Kaiyutaq with him. ToXlumana and Qovun will remain near Flaxman Island, Ipanna wherever he chooses to go, though first he is coming on the *Mary Sachs* as far as Duffy O'Connor's to obtain some flour.

Friday, July 24th

We left Barter Island about 2 a.m. and with a light east breeze behind us sailed down to the sandspit,[47] where Aiyakuk removed all the contents of his cache (*unisat*). This occupied an hour, and before he had finished I rejoined him, having disembarked at the other end of the sandspit to take a final look at the ruins. We then had tea and *mukpaurat* and set sail once more for Collinson Point, Ipanna and Simigaq (Qovun) following in the former's whaleboat. About 9 a.m. we reached the point in which the cache used to be[48] and found Mapteraq and his people there, unable to pass the ice which had closed into Camden Bay. We ran down to Capt.

Nahmens' old hut and found the canvas which lined its walls had been removed already, so sailed back and passing along a broad lead outside the bay we came opposite the schooners about 5 p.m. Here we tried to thread our way in, but the ice was too thick. The wind had shifted earlier in the day to northwest, which brought [the ice] in on our starboard bow. Occasionally a seal popped up in the water among the ice-cakes, and there were quite a number of loons, but our rifles were unsuccessful. Our only chance of reaching the schooners lay in running west to *Qonañevik* [Konganevik Point] looking for an opening. At last we found one, about a mile east of the latter place, and running in and turning, sailed at about 6 knots along the coast straight to the schooners, which we reached at 11 p.m. Everyone was on board the vessels except Johansen, the Dr., and Olsen, who was looking after the dogs. The vessels had practically finished loading and were hoping to get away tomorrow. We had come in the nick of time. Aiyakuk and his people slept in our deserted house, where Olsen also had made his bunk; Johansen took me into his tent. At 12:30 a.m. all had turned in save Johansen and I. Teriglu had camped inside the bay at the mouth of the Kuvialiruq [Katakturuk] River for some days, but now had his tent about 1/2 mile west of our camp. The Dr. had paid him for the specimens I bought and for the time he worked with me, so that is settled satisfactorily.

Saturday, July 25th

We turned out at 6:30 a.m. and the Dr., Johansen, Olsen, and myself went over to the *Alaska* to breakfast. As soon as we had finished she got under way, and sailed outside of the bay, touching bottom once in 6 feet of water. The engine was running well, though lubricating rather freely, and a stiff westerly breeze was blowing. This had cleared the ice out of Camden Bay, but made loading in the lagoon where the vessels lay rather difficult, hence the *Alaska* sailed round and anchored outside, opposite the camp. There she set about loading, the dogs being the last to be taken aboard. The *Mary Sachs* followed later, waiting till the tide rose; she had less to take on board also. Johansen had unearthed three crania and one complete skeleton for me from beside the camp and packed them snug in two solid boxes. All my things were put aboard the [*Mary*] *Sachs*, Ipanna's whaleboat fastened behind, and about 4:30 p.m. we were ready to leave. Aiyakuk received $50 from the Dr. in payment of his work with me (he had already received $50 in trade) and was well pleased.[49] He says that he will excavate for me again if I come along here next summer, which of course I hope not to do.[50] Ipanna sold a seal to the Dr. for dog-feed, for which he received two 1/2 lb packages [of] tea, and I am to give him another at Duffy's. I am to settle with him at Duffy's for the 2 months he worked with me, to the amount of $50; he is now on the [*Mary*] *Sachs* with me. The Dr. gave me an inventory made during the winter of the goods at Duffy's. Much of it has been consumed since. I am to check all that goes aboard the [*Mary*] *Sachs*, and if the keys are available go through the cases and separate what is useless, to leave at Herschel [Island]. My position on the [*Mary*] *Sachs* is a little awkward; plainly I am a *persona non grata*, my duty being to guard the Expedition's property as far as possible, and where that is not possible to know exactly what goes astray, so that the proper persons will be made responsible. The Dr. told me this, and other things as well, of both past and present history. The *Mary Sachs*, he said, will be given as good an outfit as can be spared and will then be left to carry out its duties in absolute and entire independence of the *Alaska* and the southern party. What we are concerned with is to see that the southern party is not robbed in any way. Now all this is known on the [*Mary*] *Sachs*, hence the delicacy of the ground on which I tread. Moreover, the stand I took when there was the quarrel between the late [i.e. former] captain of the *Alaska* [Capt. Nahmens] and the captain of the [*Mary*] *Sachs* [Capt. Bernard] last May has made me unpopular with the latter and his people. It is decidedly unpleasant, but I believe my action was right; the Dr. approved of it and so does Johansen, and after all, one does not aim at pleasing everyone. 'Levi' (Baur) is cook on the *Mary Sachs*, as far as Herschel [Island] at any rate, and the Negro 'Bob' Sullivan on the *Alaska*. Johansen tells me that both may leave at Herschel, and Sweeney, present captain of the *Alaska*, also, but the Dr., who decides on the Expedition side, has said nothing definite about it. The stiff west wind of the morning shifted round to the northwest, but changed in the evening to south. The [*Mary*] *Sachs*, following the *Alaska*, left Collinson Point at 5:10 p.m. and without any trouble from the ice reached Barter Island about 9 p.m., 28 miles in 4 [hours]. At the east end of Barter Island we nearly ran into the sandspit on which Iñukuk's old house lies, the atmosphere being rather foggy. Turning out, however, we rounded it safely, though narrowly missing some heavy ice through Eikie [Ikey Bolt] misinterpreting the captain's signals. The temperature at 11 p.m. was at freezing and the wind back in the north.

Sunday, July 26th

A day of rest in a manner. I turned in at midnight, the temperature being 30° F. At 1 p.m. we encountered heavy ice off the sandspit some 4 or 5 miles west of Martin Point. Here too was the *Alaska*, which had arrived about an hour before us. We anchored beside [it], close in to the land, and leaving a watch, turned in. The ice closed round us today. We may be stuck a week, a day, or even a month. I repacked my things all day. The dogs on the [*Mary*] *Sachs* were put ashore, but those on the *Alaska* remained on board — an interesting case of a difference in judgement concerning the ice and its probable effects. I prepared in the afternoon to leave with Ipanna for Duffy's,[51] travelling in his whaleboat inside the lagoon and dragging it across the sandspit here and on the other side of Martin Point. Capt. Bernard went away hunting in the afternoon; Crawford tinkered with his engine. A rifle .30-30 seems to have been left behind at Collinson Point. The Dr. thought it was mine and wrote my name on the cover.

Part 2

Start of the Coronation Gulf Studies

July 27, 1914 – April 12, 1915

Chapter 16. Through Rough Ice to Herschel Island

In ice near Martin Point — Feuding among ship personnel — Watching an Eskimo camp — Reaching Icy Reef — By whaleboat to Duffy's — Loading supplies on the Mary Sachs *— Passing the International Boundary — Arrival at Herschel Island — Official instructions from Ottawa — Wilkins given command of* Mary Sachs *— News of the* Karluk *and its people —* Mary Sachs *departs in search of Stefansson — Eskimo dance — Aground in a gale*

Monday, July 27th, 1914

Ipanna and I left the schooners after dinner last night about 8 p.m., to attempt to reach Duffy's house near Demarcation Point.[1] We had to pull all the way up the lagoon[2] and drag the boat over a sandbar in one place. This was hard work for the two of us, as the boat is heavy; at times we could drag it only about a foot with one effort. Here I got rather wet too, being in the water up to my knees. However we did not stop, so that though the sea water was freezing in places, we yet managed to keep warm. At Martin Point we attempted to skirt the shore on the outside instead of within the lagoon but were blocked almost immediately by solid ice. Returning to the lagoon we travelled up it for about 2 miles beyond Iñukuk's winter house and the Expedition's camp, then landed and proceeded on foot along the coast and the edge of the cliff for perhaps 3 more miles. Then, having reached a place from which I could sweep round the horizon on three sides,[3] I examined the ice. Around Martin Point it was composed of comparatively solid floes tightly wedged together with few interstices of open pools, but from about a mile to 2 miles east of the point it had opened out a little and there were scattered pools and short open leads. Nevertheless it was still dense so that it was impossible to work through it with a small skin boat, even if the floes were motionless. The cliffs rise about 4 miles east of Martin Point, and from this part on the ice seemed to be less compact, while some miles to the east was a fairly broad lane of open water stretching apparently north and south for some distance with a terminus at or close to the shore. From my viewpoint the *Alaska* and the *Mary Sachs* were visible to the naked eye, their distance off being about 9 miles in a direct line. Seawards a fog was beginning to creep up, but eastward the atmosphere was still clear. Of the *Belvedere* and *Polar Bear* there was no sign, though both vessels should have been visible through the binoculars if still in their old winter positions. Apparently the ice opened recently and allowed them to escape east. Then it had closed in again, creating the high pressure ridge visible about a mile northeast of where I stood. Ipanna and I turned back, progress further by boat being impossible. We stopped at Martin Point to boil the pot and make tea. Fossicking round the deserted camp I found about 1/2 cup of oatmeal and a couple of spoonfuls of rice. These we boiled together; added to the two loaves of bread taken from the schooner they made a hearty meal. Then we set off back, with five oldsquaw ducks we had shot, and with a fair east wind reached the schooners at 7 a.m. Only Olsen was astir on the *Alaska*, no one on the [*Mary*] *Sachs*. The *Alaska*'s cook, the Negro Sullivan, has strained his arm badly, so Olsen is doing the cooking. The *Alaska*'s people were just rising for breakfast so I stayed and reported to the Dr. [Anderson] what I had seen. All the rest of the morning I assisted Mr. Blue, the *Alaska*'s engineer, in repairing the Bijou typewriter I kicked over on Barter Island[4] and knocked out of gear. Finally we discovered that six steel balls were missing and that this was the only damage it had sustained save that the 'back' lever was bent and has yet to be straightened. We had no steel balls to replace the six lost but put in No. 2 shot, which are a trifle small but answer the same purpose. In the afternoon Ipanna, who had slept during the morning, and I went in his whaleboat to Martin Point again to clear everything of the cache.[5] We tacked part of the way and I slept during this time, but for half the distance we had to pull and paddle. Coming back Ipanna slept while I steered. The wind, which had before come from the northeast, now changed to north but was at no time strong. Dr. Anderson and two or three others from the *Alaska* turned out to drag the whaleboat over the sandspit and transfer what we brought to the *Alaska*. The Dr. gave me the whole of the meteorological reports[6] made at Collinson Point to duplicate and send out from Herschel Island, but being rather tired, having travelled all last night and slept since yesterday morning for about an hour only in the whaleboat, I am postponing them until tomorrow. The night is cold; indeed the day altogether has been chilly but little above freezing in the shade. The ice is moving slowly westward. The *Mary Sachs* was anchored so close to the *Alaska* that she crowded that vessel in to the beach and she grounded. A slight opening in the ice in front allowed of her being dragged along a little and getting clear.

Tuesday, July 28th

The [*Mary*] *Sachs* drifted a little during the night, and the ice had visibly opened considerably to the east. I did not turn out of my bunk until nearly lunch time. In the afternoon we sailed off and made perhaps 2 miles towards Martin Point before we were again blocked by ice. The *Alaska*, following behind us, was held up 1/2 mile further west, the ice closing in again. Capt. Bernard and others went ashore to set the fish-net and look for ducks, but before they had the net down the ice opened in front again, so they returned and having supper immediately set the schooner in motion once again. This time we made only about 1/4 mile. Again the captain went ashore to set the net. Eikie [Añutisiak] shot a seal and four eider ducks today, and there were four fish in the net this morning, so we are in luxury. I spent the day, after I got up, in copying out the meteorological data and after about 7 hours work am about one half way through. My relation with the captain [Bernard] is one of uncomfortable civility; he is sore because he could not have some of the Martin Point things and will not get all he wants at Duffy's. The Dr. is checking everything as far as possible and, though many things are 'missing', he is keeping a strict eye on everything and knows where it goes to. I have to do the same at Duffy's, and that annoys the captain very much. Dr. Anderson told me that as far as he could see the [*Mary*] *Sachs* would get away with all it could and find a suitable place in the neighbourhood of Banks Land — not too far away — to spend a profitable winter trapping; this and this alone is their object.[7] In accordance with Stefansson's instructions he [Dr. Anderson] is giving the vessel an outfit and hopes to be rid of her altogether as soon as she lands our stores somewhere to the eastward. Crawford, the engineer, is a very decent man, the only man on board with whom it is any pleasure to converse. 'Levi' blackguards the *Alaska* and its people when on the [*Mary*] *Sachs* and the *Sachs* when on the *Alaska*, a perfect lickspittle. Chipman may travel on the *Sachs* from Herschel [Island] and that will make things more comfortable. The *Alaska* people were swearing at the *Sachs* and the *Sachs* at the *Alaska* all the time they lay beside each other yesterday and the day before; there was a hostile civility between the two vessels, which both found intolerable. The temperature was down to freezing again this evening.

Wednesday, July 29th

A dull day, foggy, with a light north breeze as yesterday. Both we and the *Alaska* are short of flour and sugar, until we reach Duffy's; both are on their last bag of flour and using saxin.[8] During the night the ice closed in round the *Mary Sachs* and hemmed in the propeller. Crawford turned out and with the two Eskimos moved the vessel a little. She is in rather a bad position for she is twin-screwed, with three blades to each. In ice navigation two are far preferable, it is said, for when at rest they are little likely to be broken by an ice pack. Just now she is unprotected by any keg of ground ice and when the pack moves, as it is this evening with the high tide, it seethes all round the stern. The dogs were put ashore this morning and the net set at the mouth of the lagoon near Martin Point — about a mile away. The captain [Bernard] shot an *amaulik* (Pacific Eider duck) today, and a loon, but the latter sank. Eikie shot a seal, but it also sank. I copied out the meteorological notes, finishing just after supper, when most of us went ashore, and Crawford and I went up to the *Alaska*, about a mile and a quarter west. She lies in a fine position with open water all round her, dogs and fish-net on board, and everything ready to take advantage of the first opening in the ice. Yet both vessels are in a precarious position if a northerly gale springs up, for the ice will drive them straight on to the sandspit. This evening there is a light breath of air from the south. Capt. Bernard received today from Dr. Anderson Stefansson's letter of instructions and a typewritten copy of the same.[9] We are afraid Wilkins will have left Herschel Island before we are able to reach it. He is to wait until 6th Aug[ust], not later.[10]

Thursday, July 30th

The temperature in the shade on deck never rose above 40° all day and was down to freezing in the evening. I wrote an official report for Dr. Anderson to send to Ottawa;[11] we all have to send a yearly report in. This filled in the morning. In the afternoon I wrote some notes, then visited the *Alaska*, which after cruising about a little in the night looking for a lead outside, anchored within 200 or 300 yards of us. Part of the evening I spent in the engine-room with Crawford; he is the only one on board[12] with whom it is a pleasure to converse. His engine-room is large and comfortable, with linoleum on the floor and a small stove, which he sets between the two 2-cylinder engines when they are not running and warms the room. The rest of the evening passed in writing a letter[13] and in listening to the phonograph. Ipanna shot 5-6 Pacific eiders and a king eider today and brought two fish back from the net, so we are faring well. The wind was north most of the day, but there was little change in the ice.

Friday, July 31st

Still no change in our position, though the *Alaska* drew a little closer. A schooner is visible on the other side of Martin Point — we think the *Anna Olga*, though she is too far away to be sure. If it is, McConnell will probably be aboard and [also] Brook our late cook. Several from the [*Mary*] *Sachs* visited the *Alaska* whose cook, the Negro Sullivan, is having very hard luck. He strained his arm badly hauling the vessel out of the ice, and now that it is getting a little better he dropped a heavy weight (the anchor I think) on his foot and it is troubling him considerably. Capt. Bernard is troubled with one of his eyes; he thinks it is a result of the accident on the ice trip when he laid his head open against the sled [March 23rd]. A seal appeared near the vessel this evening, but our marksmen were unsuccessful. The temperature was very little above freezing all day, according to the thermometer on deck, and at 5 p.m. it was exactly at 32°. The wind was east-northeast most of the day but shifted to east towards evening.

Saturday, August 1st

I strolled along the beach this morning for a mile or so and partially dug out an old house, finding only two bone wedges and a bone pick. The ice jammed round the propeller in the night and tore out a large staple that fixed the chain. A strong east-northeast wind blew all the morning and afternoon. The vessel we saw yesterday came down a long open lead outside till she was about a mile north of us, then after anchoring for a short time went back. About the middle of the afternoon the inshore ice suddenly began to move rapidly, and both the *Alaska* and the [*Mary*] *Sachs* [began] to drift in to the beach. The *Alaska* was aground before she could extricate herself, but after supper, about 6:30 p.m. when the wind had abated a little, she was got off without difficulty. The *Sachs* had her engines working just in time to work through the slush ice and anchor to a large grounded keg. At this time we noticed a flag and some people at Martin Point, and after supper Ipanna and I in the small dingy went along inside the lagoon to ferry them across its mouth. By this time, however, they had made a raft and crossed over. There were two, McConnell and the engineer of the vessel — the *Anna Olga* — named Sunblad.[14] The *Belvedere* they told us reached Herschel about July 23, and the *Polar Bear* had passed on its way thither last Sunday. Louis Lane had come down the Mackenzie [River] in a scow ahead of the Hudson Bay steamers, to take charge of the *Polar Bear* again. Wilkins had caught 1000 fish in one draught down near the [Alaska-Canada] Boundary, and Natkusiak had shot six caribou. On the [*Anna*] *Olga*, which is on her way to Nome, were [Charles] Brook, late cook of the *Alaska*, and [Winthrop] Brooks[15] of the *Polar Bear* party, beside McConnell and one or two others. East of Martin Point there is, or was, open water as far as Herschel [Island] at least. The mail had not reached Herschel when Louis Lane passed through but should be there by now. McConnell and Sunblad left about 10 p.m. to return to the *Anna Olga*. About 9:30 p.m. the *Alaska* got under way and tried to force her way through the floe ice to the big lead a mile out.[16] They were still working, trying to push the ice kegs aside a little at 11 p.m. If they get through it will make an opening for the *Sachs*. The *Sachs'* fish-net captured seven fish, one a fine salmon trout 3 lbs in weight. The sun now no longer remains above the horizon at midnight. August should be the warmest and pleasantest month in the year, but the temperature this evening is 33°.

Sunday, August 2nd

The *Mary Sachs* got under way at 5 minutes to 1 a.m., attempting to follow in the channel made by the *Alaska*. The ice, however, had closed in again, and the *Sachs* following a different route encoutered heavy ice floes, which made her progress very slow. She 'bucked' into the ice, backed and bucked again repeatedly. I stayed in my bunk, judging that if I were needed someone would call me. When I turned out at 6:30 a.m. the *Alaska* was out of sight, but the *Sachs* was scarcely one half way through the ice to the open lead. After much 'bucking' of the ice, pushing with long poles or with our backs against the side of the vessel, we succeeded in gaining an easier route where the floes were smaller and more mobile. Breakfast was late, 10 a.m. The engines were stopped and the schooner moored to a keg. At 1 p.m. we gained the lead and made our way down the coast. While we were working out, the *Anna Olga* was trying to work in by another route, but she seemed to have struck rather bad ice. Running down the coast we encountered numerous floes and once ran hard and fast on to the shelving ledge of one. It took us nearly 1/2 hour to release the vessel. About 4 p.m. we arrived opposite the *Polar Bear's* late camp [at Humphrey Point] and moored to a keg for dinner. An *umiak* with a half dozen Eskimos on board met us just before we moored, and they came on board, amongst them Iñukuk and Kaiyana. We secured a number of fish from them, and I heard Capt. Bernard arrange to take Iñukuk and another man up to Duffy's to pay them there. Pannigavlu had carried off a number of things from Martin Point, a trunk of Stefansson's amongst them. These were at this camp, and after dinner a boat brought them ashore.[17] An Eskimo lad who was in the *umiak* gave me a loon (*tullik*) rather nicely skinned, and an old rusty iron knife with horn handle etched with ring and dot pattern. He asked for nothing in return, but I gave him about one-third tin tabloid tea. They told us that the *Alaska* was held up by ice this side of the Aichilik River, about 6 miles away. Her masts are visible from the camp ashore. Crawford had a bad time in the engine room today. He had to stand at the clutch almost the whole time, exposed to the smell and fumes of the gas. He was pretty well knocked out and refused to do any more ice 'bucking' today — he had no sleep last night, was on duty since 1 p.m., and had almost no sleep the night before last. The weather was fine all day, bright sunshine, temperature between 40° and 50° and only a very light north wind. Everyone turned in before 7 o'clock, leaving me on watch until 12. The night is calm and beautiful. The colouring in the Arctic is wonderfully chaste and delicate. Tonight the sky, flecked with cirri and strato-cumuli, is mirrored in the calm water of the sea, with strange effects of depth and distance; it requires no effort to imagine no sea at all, only twin skies with oneself between. Crawford came on deck about 9 p.m. after sleeping 2 or 3 hours. He was feeling very wretched, horribly sick and with a frightful headache, the effect of some 15 hours at the clutch exposed to the smell and fumes of gas. About 11:30 p.m. after pacing the deck for a couple of hours he was better and turned in again. I watched the Eskimo camp ashore through the binoculars. There are 15 people living there, five tents, all of calico, three rectangular gable tents and two oval, like the old Eskimo skin tents, stretched over curving willow sticks. On the beach a man was sitting watching a fish-net stretched in the water on the edge. Presently a boy went down to him and they gathered the fish —

salmon trout they looked like — eight in all I think, and flung them up on the beach; then they sat down side by side to chat for a time. Higher up on the bank in front of one of the tents four girls or women were sitting. A young fellow approached, apparently said something to them, then began to run. One of the girls or women sprang up and chased him for a short distance then picked up a clod of earth and threw it after him. Some distance away a man was approaching with a gun — clearly he had been out hunting — probably for ducks. A little while afterwards a little girl in bright red calico dress wandered down to the beach. The same girl ran after her and picked her up and threw her up the bank then scrambled up herself and stretched out on the grass beside the others. Outside another tent a man was gazing placidly out to sea, very likely watching our schooner. The sky was mirrored in the placid water and a little way out from the beach a line of small grounded ice floes stretched along for miles in each direction. Now and again an eider duck or a regiment of oldsquaws flew by. Faint and blurred in the far distance, hardly perceptible to the naked eye, were the Endicott Mountains.[18] Blue smoke curled up from one of the tents and made a dark line across the sky. The whole scene was pervaded with the peace and charm of home, with the melancholy comfort of a sunset.[19]

Monday, August 3rd

Iñukuk and two other Eskimos[20] came aboard about 1 p.m. when I called up Añutisiak to stand watch and turned in. We started out after breakfast and bumped our way along, running on one engine. The bow of the [*Mary*] *Sachs* is not shaped for working among ice, and she slides up upon the shelving ice kegs and sticks there. Then everyone has to turn to and try to push her off. Sometimes reversing the engine frees her, often it has no effect whatever. She is very slow in answering the helm too, and that makes it impossible to avoid the ice kegs. Early in the afternoon we arrived off the west end of Icy Reef where we found the *Alaska* held up by the ice. We too tied to a keg beside her and waited for the ice to open. I left after supper (about 8 p.m.) with Ipanna and another Eskimo [Frank] to sail down in the small whaleboat behind Icy Reef and reach Duffy's by that route — one easy for a small boat but impossible for a schooner by reason of the shallow water. A west wind sprang up, light but favourable, and we made fair progress. The temperature was mild — compared that is to preceding nights — probably it was about 37°.

Tuesday, August 4th

We put in at an Eskimo camp, which I mistook for Duffy's house until we drew near. It was just after 2 a.m., but we landed and roused the inmates of the two tents — an old man and his daughter — inland Eskimos. The woman made tea for us, and we had a light meal, chatting the while and discussing the news along the coast. Both these inland folk had long faces narrowing towards the chin, a characteristic, apparently,

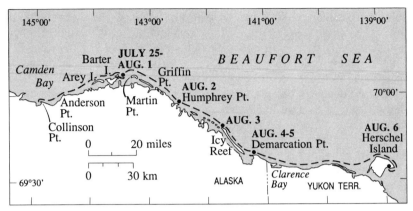

Figure 103. Map showing the route taken by the author on the schooner *Mary Sachs* from Camden Bay to Herschel Island, July 27 - Aug. 6. Dates indicate approximate locations of schooner at end of each day. The author went inside Icy Reef in a whaleboat while the *Mary Sachs* remained outside that barrier.

of this branch of the Eskimo race. The woman swayed her body forward and back whenever she spoke. We stayed only 1/2 hour then continued to Duffy's, some 2 miles further on. We passed a man and his wife, the son of the old man we had just visited (his name is Tulugaqpuk = big raven) tracking his skin boat along the shore while his wife steered. They have seen caribou about here within the last few days. About 3:30 a.m. we reached Duffy's.[21] There was a note from Brooks of the *Polar Bear* saying that he had left in a hurry to go out on the *Anna Olga*, as the arrangements of the *Polar Bear* party seemed anything but satisfactory.[22] The house showed his haste — there was a plate of fish set out on the table, a baking-powder biscuit on one side, a kettle of water on the stove, dirty dishes and pots scattered around, and everything in confusion. I started work straight away[23] while Ipanna slept and the other Eskimo [Frank] walked along the sandspit to revisit the Eskimos we had just left. Feeling rather sleepy after a time I lay down and slept an hour, then began work again. The *Alaska* turned up about 11 a.m., and both Ipanna and I went off to her immediately for lunch. Their dogs were put ashore and in the afternoon they loaded flour and sugar and other stores[24] while I continued packing and listing the things. Ipanna was paid off, so that is one trouble off my shoulders. The [*Mary*] *Sachs* arrived about 4 p.m.; she had left about 8 a.m., but was stuck on an ice keg for about 2 hours. Both schooners have experienced considerable bumping against the ice and leak a little. The *Alaska* got under way again about 8 p.m., for the Dr. [Anderson] is anxious to see Wilkins before he leaves Herschel Island and he [Wilkins] leaves not later than the 6th Aug[ust]. I have to pack all the things, make complete lists of them, check off what went to the *North Star*, to the *Polar Bear*, to various Eskimos, to the *Alaska*, and after the *Mary Sachs* takes what she needs (or wants) pack the rest to leave at Herschel Island.[25] I left off about 8 p.m. and returned to the ship, very tired and sleepy, with several days heavy work in prospect. The wind was westerly all day, not strong. The sky was clouded most of the day, but the temperature did not seem very low.

Wednesday, August 5th

Añutisiak called me at 3 a.m. and took me ashore to Duffy's house to complete listing and packing. About 6 a.m. Capt. Bernard came ashore to feed the dogs and we returned together for breakfast. Loading was resumed immediately afterwards and by 11:30 a.m. all was on board. We sailed after dinner and quickly passed the boundary post between Canada and Alaska,[26] then Matt Andreason's cache, but were held up by ice a mile or two beyond. I was opening the 10 trunks of clothes, cloth, thread etc. that were shipped at Duffy's, packing a few things that Dr. Anderson wanted, making an outfit for the [*Mary*] *Sachs* from them, and listing all the stuff. Everything has been so hurried that it is difficult to make out my lists. I spent all the evening on them, then turned in about 11 p.m. for it was too dark in the saloon to read. A fog had crept up and enveloped everything. A party from the ship went ashore and looked around and cut up firewood. The [*Mary*] *Sachs* is badly off for mittens (woollen), overshirts, socks, and baking powder and perhaps two or three other things. It has no yeast, but plenty of flour, sugar, and tea. The temperature was very mild all the morning, about 50°, I think, at noon; a light east wind was blowing, and it grew colder in the afternoon.

Thursday, August 6th

We got under way after breakfast — about 9 a.m., when the fog rolled away. After the first mile there was plenty of open water, and we kept on uninterruptedly with both engines until [?[27]]. I was working over the lists all the morning and completed the packing. About mid-afternoon we reached the western end of Herschel Island. The air had been almost calm hitherto, but now a head wind sprang up, milder than any we have felt this year, for it blows from the land across water free from ice. We skirted round the north shore, then southward, close to the mud cliffs that rise from 100 to 200 feet sheer out of the water. A strong tide was flowing eastward, about 2 miles broad, and travelling perhaps 3 miles an hour. Here and there were scattered kegs of ice, some of great size and height — the tallest probably more than 20 feet — rather surprising so late in the season and close in shore. Some were wonderfully beautiful, with deep horizontal flutings where the ice had washed or melted out when the keg floated at different levels. The delicate pale green tinge beneath a crest of overhanging white attested its purity from salt. Other kegs were dark, and one or two in the distance appeared quite black, changing to brown as we approached. 'Dirty' ice, it is called, and so it should be called in winter. But in summer, as it floats on the dark rippling water, with the bright light of the sun radiating over everything, it loses its sinister aspect and gathers something of the soft sad charm of the sunset. They range from the palest sienna to a full brown and float

conspicuously among the white or bluish brethren. The cliffs of the islands were built by a different architect. Here the draining water from the
land had channelled in divided streams from the summit and produced a
series of arches, true gothic perpendiculars extending in places for a mile
almost unbroken. Above them, resting on their apices, was the tundra
clothed with a well-trimmed lawn of brown-green grass. Beneath them in
the shade of the cliff was the dark sea, looking black and still like a deep
cavern until it emerged into the light. In one place there was a tiny bay,
with a great pile of driftwood in one corner. The settlement is far away,
so the search for fuel has not led its inhabitants here. A loon floated
peacefully on the water; it dived sharply as the captain's bullet whistled
over its head. So did two King eiders when Añutisiak fired at them.
Jennie [Thomsen] was whistling to a seal, and it did follow us for a little
way, but at a safe distance. About 8 p.m. we reached the settlement [Her-
schel Island], which lies on a broad sandspit with a deep sheltered haven
behind. Here were a number of yawls belonging to local Eskimos, and
towering above them the *Alaska* and the *North Star*. The former had
reached Herschel [Island] the night before, just in time to catch Wilkins,
who intended to leave early the next morning. Chipman, Cox, and
O'Neill had also arrived from Fort McPherson about the same time,
bringing the Mackenzie River mail.[28] Cox had been mapping in a small
motor launch the western mouth of the Mackenzie, Chipman and O'Neill
the eastern and part of the middle. On the whole they seem to have been
fairly successful, though none of them was very well pleased. The arrangements which Stefansson said he had made for them when he went
down last winter[29] were incorrect or imperfect, and they had found themselves consequently in difficulties with their equipment at the very start.
One launch, which Chipman was to use, would not run, and he worked
with a whaleboat. The government sent down two Peterborough canoes
and a number of cases of instruments and books. I received my letters
and some books from home and a set of anthropometrical instruments
from the government.[30] The food supplies are being sent by way of Barrow on a steamer, which the Hudson['s] Bay Company is sending in the
Ruby.[31] The settlement [Herschel Island] consists of the barracks of the
Royal Northwest Mounted Police, three or four large sheds, a number of
huts from which the snow has disappeared leaving the dark sod naked,
and the tents, which cover the Eskimos now that they have sloughed
their winter houses. I was introduced to the police — there are three,[32]
and they seem rather fine men. About 11 p.m. everyone began to disappear from the beach, so I went on board the [*Mary*] *Sachs* and turned in.

Friday, August 7th

A busy day packing some specimens the Dr. [Anderson] gave me. He
had received them from an Eskimo who once worked for Stefansson
around Coronation Gulf.[33] Then many things were landed from the
[*Mary*] *Sachs* and had to be sorted, listed, and packed. During the night a
southeast gale sprang up, and the *Alaska* had to be moved out, but she

Figure 104. The author packing archaeological specimens at Herschel Island for shipment to Ottawa, August 7, 1914. Photo by G.H. Wilkins, CMC Photo No. 51436.)

came in alongside the beach again next morning. The *North Star* is ready to leave tomorrow morning. The police gave me two skulls Stefansson had left there, and Chipman brought down the [Mackenzie] river a large stone lamp which Stefansson had bought. During the evening Chipman, Cox, and O'Neill were in their tent and Wilkins and I with them when Dr. Anderson came in. Chipman showed me the clippings of the questions asked in parliament (Canadian) about the Expedition on two occasions, and expressed the opinion that the Opposition was lying low. Dr. Anderson read the government dispatches. Their substance was that the southern party had already suffered through the loss of the *Karluk* and that it was not to be crippled any further by the formation of a new northern party.[34] The coast of Banks Land was rugged and dangerous for large vessels and he [Stefansson] could, with the two members of the northern party still left — McConnell and presumably Wilkins — explore its shores with one of the launches bought in the Mackenzie. Neither of the two schooners, *Alaska* or *Mary Sachs*, should be detached for that work — the southern party was to proceed unhampered to its scientific work in Coronation Gulf. (Evidently the government knew nothing of the purchase of the *North Star*.) The ice trip[35] was sanctioned (*ex post facto*), but the government said that it must be carried out without interfering in any way with the southern party. It was arranged that either Chipman or

Cox, probably Chipman, should travel on the [*Mary*] *Sachs*, and I could please myself whether I went on the *Alaska* or remained on the *Sachs* with Chipman.

Saturday, August 8th

Another change in the program. Crawford, engineer of the [*Mary*] *Sachs*, wished to leave — apparently he had no confidence in Capt. Bernard's navigation and was also dissatisfied with the quantity of supplies — the *Sachs* is very insufficiently equipped. The Dr. [Anderson] went on board the *North Star* about 7 a.m. and had a long conversation with Wilkins. As a result Wilkins takes command of the *Mary Sachs*, forming a new northern party — the *North Star* goes to Coronation Gulf with Cox as engineer and in command. Wilkins insists that he have full authority over the *Sachs* such as Stefansson would have — and will have if he is found, when Wilkins can either join the southern party or go out — (his firm wrote instructing him to do the latter).[36] He also insisted that he should have — in writing — a statement of the reasons why he was taking over the *Sachs* instead of the *North Star*,[37] viz. that Dr. Anderson and the members of the scientific staff had no confidence that the *Sachs* would — if left to its own devices — make a whole-hearted quest for Stefansson in the region — south Banks Land — where it was to go.[38] Dr. Anderson agreed to this. I told Wilkins that I would be quite prepared to attach my signature to such a document. Dr. Anderson made an extract from the new instructions of the government and from the original ones regarding trading, viz. that no private trading of any kind be allowed — all skins, curios, etc. should be turned in to the government, also a clause putting Wilkins in supreme command of the [*Mary*] *Sachs* and its outfit — not merely superintendent (watchdog as it were) of the Expedition's stores, with Capt. Bernard in real command as the latter thought (Wilkins told Dr. Anderson this in so many words and it was true). I understand at least from Wilkins that this was the tenor of the document;[39] we discussed it together before and after. He read it over to the assembled crew — Capt. Bernard, Crawford, Levi, and Thomsen, and they agree to go. It is a distinct blow to Capt. Bernard, for Stefansson's letter from the ice gave him — as he interpreted it — independent authority.[40] He was subject to Dr. Anderson only in the matter of equipment and supplies. Now he has to succumb. Wilkins is certainly the most capable all-round man on the Expedition — a splendid photographer, first-class mechanic, with a considerable knowledge of boats and motor engines, at heart a scientist though his training is imperfect, a professional electrical engineer, and something of a musician and singer. He was brought up on a sheep station in South Australia and is a splendid horseman and a good shot. Without doubt he will be able to maintain his authority without any great difficulty. Cox has some acquaintance with motor engines and has been running a small launch himself this spring on the Mackenzie [River]. The *North Star* should be safe in his hands. She is to be used by Chipman, Cox, and O'Neill in their geological and topographical work. Wilkins and I spent the whole day making complete lists of what was already on the [*Mary*] *Sachs*, what should be put on board from the *North Star*, what additional supplies were needed. The weather was fine all day, with a light northeast breeze, and the temperature comparatively low. It sank to 36° in the evening and the wind freshened considerably.

Sunday, August 9th

Great news. The steam whaler *Herman* arrived early this morning from outside, Capt. Pedersen in command, formerly of the *Karluk*, then when Capt. Bartlett took over the command, skipper of the *Elvira*.[41] Allan, originally 1st officer of the *Karluk*,[42] is her 2nd officer. He [Capt. Pedersen] picked up Capt. Bartlett in Plover Bay.[43] The *Karluk* drifted about 60 miles off the coast of Herald Island, about 65 miles from Wrangel[44] Island in January. Here she was crushed by the ice, and the water flooded her engine room. However, she did not sink immediately, for the ice held her up. Everything was put out on the ice and an ice house built. Capt. Bartlett stayed on board alone one night. Two days after she was crushed the ice opened and made a hole. She sank with the [Canadian] flag flying, and the ice closed over her again. The men made Wrangel Island with provisions for 80 days and plenty of guns and ammunition. But before the vessel was crushed three scientists (one Dr. Mackay, the other two Capt. Pedersen had forgotten; he thought they were Murray and Mamen, but probably I think Mamen was not one) and one seaman, a big man, left for the shore[45] — it is said because they did not see why they should be carried to the northwest. Capt. Bartlett searched for them on Wrangel Island but did not find them; however, the weather was good and he had no doubt that they also were safe. He himself with a Point Hope Eskimo — Claude Kataktovik — crossed over to the mainland and reached Plover Bay 'all in'[46] — he could hardly stand his feet were so broken up. (Why he went to Plover Bay and did not cross from East Cape via the Diomede Islands to Nome does not appear.)[47] The *Herman* butted through the ice at Plover Bay, picked up Capt. Bartlett, and took him to Nome, whence he was telegraphing out.[48] The Revenue Cutter *Bear* was taking him up to Barrow, thence to Wrangel Island to pick up the remainder. Wrangel Island is said to contain plenty of drift wood. Polar bears are especially numerous and about April walrus [also], so they should have plenty of food. The *Herman* found the sea free from ice as far as Point Barrow, but east of this there was ice practically the whole way. The *Anna Olga* was sighted near Return Reef — about 50 miles west of Flaxman Island. A number of us breakfasted aboard the *Herman* and the Expedition obtained five cases of fresh potatoes from her. Being Sunday no Eskimos could be procured to work on the schooners, and the departure of the *Mary Sachs* is delayed a day in consequence. In the afternoon Wilkins initiated Cox into the mysteries of the engine on the *North Star*, and we went for a short run in her. Chipman spent the day making up the list of stores on the *Alaska*, but he and I wandered over the tundra in the evening picking up Johansen, who was collecting plants. I noticed a kayak in which the stem was prolonged upward at each end to afford a grip for dragging on a sled. The Barrow people adopt a different device; they make an eye in the end. Chipman received bad news by the mail, and so did O'Neill; the former's mother is dead, the latter's very ill and her end only a matter of a few months at the most. The instructions of O'Neill's chief were practically that if the Expedition does not make the Coppermine country this year he should go out.[49] I believe the other two men, Chipman and Cox have somewhat similar instructions. Wilkins took the small launch, the *Edna*, belonging to the Expedition, and went with Blue this evening down to a point whose name I forget — but it is several miles away, 15 or more, to obtain spare parts for one of the motor engines.[50] The *Herman* made up a baseball team, and Sweeney captained another consisting chiefly of Eskimos, and they had a game this evening in which Sweeney's team won. Several of the men were drunk or half drunk during the day, and one or two at least will not be very fit for duty tomorrow. There is trouble on the *Alaska* over the crew. One man, the Negro cook Sullivan, is certainly leaving, and another, Addison, will be dismissed if he does not leave voluntarily, for he is intolerably lazy and useless.[51]

Monday, August 10th

The cook [William] Sullivan left and a new cook[52] was obtained this evening from the *Herman*. Addison also has left. Añutisiak left the *Mary Sachs*, telling Capt. Bernard he wanted to go home [to Cape Smythe], then joined the *Alaska*; he did not like the *Sachs*. Wilkins returned about noon; the *Edna's* engine had run perfectly at about 12 knots; her horsepower, I think, is 20 and her length 28 feet or thereabouts. Several of our men procured liquor from the *Herman* and were drunk. A Siberian Eskimo named Mike has been engaged for the *Alaska*. He is said to be a good boy.[53] He is married to a *Kittigariut* woman and has two children; but he is leaving these to the care of the police at Herschel Island. I issued her a number of clothes on the Dr.'s instructions, and the police are supplying her with food until we return. Chipman is making out the list of stores on the *Alaska*.[54] I had to watch on the *Alaska* for a time last night lest anything should be stolen. The weather was foggy all day. A scow-schooner came in from Baillie Island, worked by one white man Slate[55] all the way — her name is *Alice Stofen*. He had seen the *Polar Bear* off Baillie Island.[56] [Bill] Seymour and his boat's crew on that vessel had killed two whales.[57] The *Belvedere* was away off shore skirting the ice, and he had not heard whether she was successful or not. The coast was practically free from ice except just around Herschel Island. I shifted over to the *North Star* this afternoon when she was brought alongside the *Mary Sachs* to discharge.[58] For the night I made my bunk in the engine-room, but Cox will sleep there, and I shall sleep forward in the galley-cabin where there are three bunks, one for Aarnout Castel, one for me, and another for an Eskimo if we can get a man. If we take any more people they will have to sleep on deck or in the hold.

Tuesday, August 11th

A fine day. Aarnout Castel and I went over to the [*Mary*] *Sachs* for breakfast, but Levi was stretched out in drunken sleep, so we had to forage for ourselves. I found some cold rice, which had lain in the cupboard for a week or so, and breakfasted contentedly on that and coffee. Aarnout, like most of the men on our vessels, does not care for rice, so when I was through we both returned to the *North Star* and he fried some stale bread and some bacon. The chief event of the day was the departure of the [*Mary*] *Sachs* in the afternoon.[59] The vessels gave her three hoots of their whistles and dipped their flags, and she hooted and dipped her flag in return. The *Herman* left about 2 hours before.[60] A schooner — *Rosie H.* — with Fritz Wolki and another white man aboard, lay about a mile away this morning with flapping sails, for the air was perfectly calm. The *Herman* had some cargo for her, so she steamed out in the morning and towed her in. Like the scow-schooner [the *Alice Stofen*] that arrived yesterday this one also came from Baillie Island. These white men have been trading and trapping there — with indifferent success.

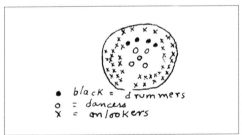

Figure 105. Arrangement of dancers, Herschel Island.

In the evening there was a great dance — *hula-hula* as the jargon calls it — in the settlement here, attended by most of the Eskimos and whites. A tent was devised of four boat sails set round in such a way that they made a kind of large wigwam. Inside, in a circle all round, sat the spectators. The drums were of different sizes and numbered four altogether. At times both men and women danced together; sometimes a single man or woman. Anyone stepped out and danced as the spirit moved him, or he was urged by others round him. Even little children danced. There is a marked difference between the women's dancing and the men's. With the men the object seems to be to strain as many muscles of the body and limbs as possible, and so some of them perform many strange contortions. Stepping out in front of the drummers he picks up from the ground the gloves which the last dancer has thrown down and draws them over his fingers or holds them one in each clenched hand. During the first part of the song, which is accompanied by light taps of the drums without the sticks bending and striking the membrane, the dancer beats time with

one foot, sways his body a little and rhythmically waves his arms keeping them still close to his sides. Sometimes he sings too, as well as the
drummers and spectators. Presently the drums strike up hard and the
song swells in volume. Every muscle of the dancer becomes rigid, each
clenched hand is stretched out in turn to one side, while the other is held
against the chest. He stamps with one foot, keeping both knees bent, con-
torts his body, shrugs the shoulders, now stoops, now throws back his
head uttering inarticulate cries. Occasionally he may jump around in a
manner resembling a hornpipe. Every individual dances in his own
peculiar way. An elderly Eskimo — the *Kugmulit* chief as he is called,
because he is more influential than any others — save one — and still re-
tains two wives — danced alone, once holding the largest of the drums
upright in his hand and rapping out quick successive strokes with constant turning of the wrist. He capered round the ring with bent knee,
singing a song which the onlookers accompanied, the three other drummers laying their drums down. With the women the dance is less violent.
They begin in much the same way, but have no gloves. Then when the
drums strike up they bend and straighten their knees a little in time with
the music and rhythmically wave their arms with the hands open and the
palms generally facing outwards until the music ceases. The dance lasts
about 2 minutes, but some at least seem to have two parts, with an interval of a minute or two between them. The dancer retires as soon as he is
exhausted or feels he has had enough. There was a big feast at the end of
the dance, given it is said by a white man, Pederson,[61] who was working
for Cox in the [Mackenzie] delta this spring. A rumour is current that he
was married today on board the *Herman* to an Eskimo woman with
whom he lived some 10 years ago. When nearly all the white spectators
had gone he rose and danced too in company with three or four others.
Dance-music seemed to me to have a different scale, different intervals,
to modern European music, and hence . . . .[62] There was an interesting
gathering of types. Besides whites and Eskimos there were Indians from
Fort MacPherson,[63] a girl half Portuguese half Eskimo, another half
Negro half Eskimo, and several half Eskimos half whites. The half-
Negro girl is about 9 years of age; she danced once or twice.

Wednesday, August 12th

A quiet morning. After breakfasting on the *Alaska*, which has a new
cook from the *Herman*,[64] we returned (Aarnout and I and Cox) to the
North Star. Aarnout turned barber and cut my hair, but we had no clippers so left the beard as it was — about 1 1/2 inches long. In the afternoon we brought the vessel alongside the beach, but as it was an
exceptionally high tide we could not anchor close enough to be of much
use without the certainty of being aground as soon as the tide fell; so we
went out again and anchored in our old position. It was a useful experience for both Cox and myself. It took him nearly an hour to start the
engine the first time, and I received a practical lesson in anchoring and
steering. It proved useful, for shortly before midnight a gale suddenly

sprang up from the south. I was alone on board, but Cox soon appeared, then Aarnout. About 12:30 a.m. we found ourselves drifting. We let go a second anchor and still we drifted. Cox started the engines, Aarnout steered then [Cox] steadied the engine while he [Aarnout] helped me haul up one anchor. Going ahead again I hauled up the other anchor as far as I could then made fast and at the signal let go. The second anchor was let out a moment later, but we found ourselves too close to an ice keg, so the manoeuvre was repeated, I steering and Aarnout at the anchors. This time we paid out a great length of cable, for the schooner was bobbing up and down like a cork and swinging through nearly 90°. This time the anchors held, though the wind increased if anything during the night. The centre board was let down to check the swinging. It was not until about 2 a.m. that all was snug; then we turned down below for coffee and hard-bread. Rain had fallen steadily for hours, and the tide rose higher and higher until it threatened to drown the dogs on the beach, and Añutisiak went over from the *Alaska* to move them. Aarnout stayed on watch; Cox and I turned in, fully dressed, ready for a call if needed. The *Belvedere* came in this evening from the east. She had been cruising round Cape Parry and stood once within some 4 miles of Nelson Head on Banks Land. Everywhere to the [solid] ice there was open water with no ice in sight. She had captured five whales and a polar bear; the latter is hanging astern. There was no word of Stefansson. Yesterday she passed the *Mary Sachs* about 20 miles off shore. The *Sachs* hoisted her flag, probably for a salute. The *Belvedere* understood it as a signal and stood over towards her, but the *Sachs* lowered the flag and kept her course, so the *Belvedere* turned and came straight on. Addison appears to have quitted the *Alaska* then joined again. Blue requires an assistant in the engine room and apparently can obtain no one else.

Thursday, August 13th

I turned out between 7:30 and 8 a.m. and relieved Aarnout. He had mixed some sourdough, and while watching the vessel I fried slapjacks. Cox turned out about 11, and Aarnout turned out again, and we breakfasted, then turned in again. The wind was still very strong when I went on watch and a high sea running, but it was visibly abating. We all rolled out in time for supper at 5 p.m. on the *Alaska*, when Mike the Eskimo officiated as cook. Cox went ashore, I returned to the *North Star*, and Aarnout went off to the *Belvedere*. The police at the station here made a very kind offer yesterday. They would give us all the butter, rice, etc. they had and take the same from our stores on the *Ruby* when she arrived. It is possible the *Ruby* may not be able to get in at all,[65] and the police are not too well supplied, so that their offer was really very generous, though the Inspector [Phillips] passed it off by saying that they were only following out the instructions of the government in helping us all they could. They seem a fine set of men (there are three of them, an Inspector for the whole district, a sergeant in command of this station, and a corporal),[66] though they could not get on with Stefansson. They have been very kind and obliging to all the other members of the Expedition.

Friday, August 14th

We loaded up the *North Star* during the day. I clipped my beard and prepared to call on Mrs. Cottle on the *Belvedere*, but Dr. Anderson came across to the *North Star* and asked me to type out the list of stores and equipment aboard.[67] The *Alaska* has a cook from the *Belvedere*,[68] but he has been on the sick list for the last 2 days, so we had our meals, Cox, Aarnout, and I, on our own vessel. Cox cooked an excellent dinner, fried potatoes, beans, and stewed apples. A strong southwest wind sprang up during the afternoon and continued all the evening. It brought a number of ice kegs into the beach, and one fouled one of our anchors. It was fully an hour before we could clear it, then the keg drifted down and fouled an anchor of the *Alaska*. The *Belvedere* intended to leave this evening for another whaling cruise, but the captain feared foggy weather so did not raise anchor. The sky was clouded nearly all day and the wind distinctly cold.

Saturday, August 15th

The wind increased to a violent gale soon after midnight. Aarnout turned out to keep watch, and I dressed to meet emergencies and lay down ready for a call. About 4:30 a.m. the vessel began to drift, dragging her two anchors. I was asleep at the time, but awoke a moment later for she turned broadside on to the gale and rolled heavily. A nasty sea was running and the spray swept the deck. Cox had been trying to start the engine, but one of the cylinders had been flooded through the exhaust pipe and was full of water. He rushed on deck to help Aarnout with the anchors, almost at the same moment that I turned out, but nothing could be done. The schooner drifted rapidly down on to the beach as if she were under steam, and soon she was pounding the bottom broadside on to the wind and [was] swept by the seas. I pumped her out while Aarnout and Cox, with the aid of Chipman, O'Neill, and another man,[69] who had turned out to watch the fate of the vessels, made a dead-man, i.e., ran a line from near the top of the mast to an anchor made fast ashore and hauled it taut to check the pounding. Nothing more could be done. The temperature was 33°, and we were soaking wet with the waves that had broken over us and numbed by the furious gale. We made for the police barracks, which opened its doors hospitably and made us welcome. Dry clothes were brought out, and soon we were comfortable, though my legs were so numbed that they only ceased to feel cold after I had been sitting for an hour over the stove. Slates' schooner, the *Alice Stofen*, was on the beach too, and said to be broken up;[70] the *Rosie H.* was aground undamaged. From the barracks we watched the fight of the *Alaska*. Her anchor was dragging too, but she had the engines working and so [was] able to make a stand. Once she was almost if not quite aground, but after several hours battling she succeeded in crossing to the other side of the bay where it seemed more sheltered and anchored there. The *Belvedere's* anchor held. The wind drove the sea high up on the beach and threatened to flood many of the Eskimo tents. After lunch Aarnout, Cox, and I returned to the *North Star*, for the gale had moderated a little, and the water receded a few feet. Cox went below to fix up the engine, for luckily everything below hatches was dry. Aarnout and I and two Eskimos set to work to clear the deck a little so as to lessen the strain on the vessel. I pumped out again, but she seemed not to be making any more water than usual. The gale freshened again and the spray swept the deck so we had to leave off. Aarnout and I again returned to the barracks, but Cox stayed below in the engine room. A couple of hours later the gale diminished in violence, and Aarnout returned to work on her, while I remained at the barracks. At 9 p.m., when I went back, the gale was over, though the wind was still fairly strong. This is another misfortune with which the Expedition has to contend; truly it has had fearfully bad luck.

Sunday, August 16th

The *Alaska* steamed back again this morning, and Dr. Anderson and the others came aboard the *North Star*. There was a light southwest wind, but the sea was comparatively calm, and the water had receded, leaving the vessel in about 1 foot of water. A line was passed from the *Alaska* to the *North Star* and made fast to the Samson post and the mainmast on the latter; then the former vessel went full steam ahead. The second jar dragged the *North Star* about 2 feet, but after that she would not budge. Nothing remained but to have the *Belvedere* pull her off.[71] We had four natives working on the vessel and everything on deck and almost all that was in the hold amidships had been landed immediately after breakfast. I acted as cook, Aarnout and Cox being busy on the vessel; it enabled me to dry some of my clothes, though my sleeping bag and sleeping skin and some other things are still very wet. However I had enough dry clothes left to be able to dispense with the outfit borrowed from the police, which I returned to them this afternoon. About 7:30 p.m. Aarnout and the Eskimos put a bridle round the *North Star*, and the *Belvedere* dragged her off without difficulty, though the rope was cut through at the first attempt by the wire bridle to which it was attached. We anchored out in the stream, near our old position. The *Rosie H.* was dragged off the mud with the winch alone. I had a long tramp in search of fresh water this morning, about 1 1/2 miles up into a small valley where there were a few very shallow pools of water from which I could dip up 3 or 4 gallons with a cup. Addison finally left the *Alaska* and is on the *Belvedere*. Olsen also is leaving today.[72] The wind in the evening moved round to the northeast and the temperature fell.

Chapter 17. On to Coronation Gulf

Departure of Alaska — Loading of North Star *— North Star sails for Coronation Gulf — Catching up to the Alaska near Clay Point — Bartering at Shingle Point — Picking up equipment at Point Atkinson — Aground at Baillie Island — Meeting Capt. Joseph Bernard — Palaiyak joins the* North Star *— Cape Parry — Meeting Klengenberg's children at Cape Lyon — Strange rock structure at Pierce Point — Fog hampers progress across Stapylton Bay — Taste of seal meat — Liston Islands — Sheltering in unknown bay — Dr. Anderson and Chipman arrive — Waiting to enter Bernard Harbour*

Monday, August 17th, 1914

The *Alaska's* people were up all night making the final preparations for leaving. Dr. Anderson came over to the *North Star* about 8:30 a.m. to give us one or two final instructions, and the *Alaska* pulled out an hour later. The *Belvedere* had already left for the west to meet Swenson, Capt. Cottle's partner, who is coming in with another vessel.[1] The *Belvedere* had only about 70 tons of coal left, too little to allow of her making another whaling cruise to the eastward and then going outside. A fresh northeast wind was blowing; it froze last night — there was about 1/3 inch [of ice] in the water can. Cox spent the whole day fixing up his engine;[2] it was not till late in the afternoon that he got it to run. Aarnout [Castel] with four Eskimos was reloading the vessel, using not the dory, for it leaks like a sieve and is useless, but the *Biffin*, a yawl dingy about 16 feet long, which had a motor engine during the spring to propel it. Cox took out the engine 2 or 3 days ago. I turned to as cook again, and between times measured the heads and faces of three of the Eskimos[3] and learned a cat's-cradle figure. The northeast wind continued to blow fresh all day. The Dr. [Anderson] tried to arrange with Slate[4] to join the Expedition, but the pay ($65 a month) was too small. The police have taken charge of what we are leaving. The nights are growing very dark now, which will make our sailing difficult, especially if we strike ice. Cox is trying to procure an Eskimo to work for us, but is experiencing great difficulty; it will mean very hard work and long hours for us all if he does not succeed.

Tuesday, August 18th

A beautiful fine warm day with a light easterly breeze. I resumed cooking duties while loading was finished. By 4 p.m. everything was on board. The police came over to see the vessel and say goodbye, after which we pulled out. Cox had some difficulty in starting the engine, and this delayed us a little so that it was 5 p.m. before we really got under way. Passing the barracks Cox was at the engine, Aarnout at the wheel, and I dipped the flag three times in salute. Then Aarnout went aloft, and I took the wheel, for the ice had come close in during the day. However, we worked our way through it and came to open water comparatively free of ice. Aarnout went below and cooked dinner, then when all was ready Cox and I dined while he took the wheel. He then dined in his turn and fed the dogs, by which time we were close to Kay Point, 25 miles from Herschel Island. A whaleboat rounded it, coming from the east, but turned down into the bay for the night before we came up. The ice hung thick around the point and beyond, so that Aarnout had to go aloft again and shout down the course. It was very difficult to hear him at times on account of the rattle of the engine, and once I ran the boat right on to an ice keg, not hearing the signal "one bell," although I was listening for it. We scraped several others, mostly unavoidably I think, for the ice was packed so close, though in at least two cases a more skillful helmsman would have worked through without touching. The vessel swings very freely, and there was a current with us, which, Aarnout said, made steering a little more difficult. About 5 miles beyond Clay Point we found the *Alaska* anchored and hove to alongside of her at 10:30 p.m., after a run of 5 1/2 hours. About an hour previously the wind shifted to southwest and freshened considerably. The Canadian (Peterborough) canoe was lowered, and I paddled over to a keg to obtain some ice for cooking and drinking purposes, not without some trouble, for the wind nearly blew me away. The other two then turned in, and I am keeping watch till 2 a.m. when I call Aarnout. We have nine dogs aboard, three of which, Jumbo, Dub, and Snap came from the *Karluk*. Jumbo and Snap are both fine leaders. The vessel, which is about 45 feet long and has a beam of 14 feet and a gross tonnage of 11, is loaded down now with something like 17 tons of freight, which includes a Peterborough canoe, a kayak, and a heavy ship's dingy. The motor engine, which belongs to the last, is stored in the hold, and the dingy is now the home of three of the dogs. The evening was not remarkably cold, probably about 40°. The southwest wind has freshened considerably and has moved the ice a little, but whether there is a lead ahead now it is still a little too dark to see.

Wednesday, August 19th

Last night's wind opened up the ice considerably, and the *Alaska* got underway about 4:30 a.m., followed immediately by us on the *North Star*, Aarnout aloft and I at the helm. However, once we got well under way, Cox and I went below for prunes and coffee, then, when Aarnout had eaten, I prepared to turn in. Hardly had I lain down, however, when the *Alaska* stopped, something having gone wrong with her engine. I had to turn out again to the helm, while Aarnout directed from aloft. So we continued till 6:30 a.m., when the ice was no longer dense enough to obstruct a direct course; then I turned in and slept, just as we were approaching King Point, where Amundsen wintered in a lagoon when he made the northwest passage.[5] About 9:30 a.m. we reached Shingle Point, a long sandspit running roughly northwest by southeast, with a lagoon behind, where vessels drawing 5 and 6 feet of water can moor with safety. Cox and I went ashore in the Canadian canoe to buy fish, but their prices in hard-bread etc. were rather high. We returned on board to take

Figure 106. Dr. Anderson and John Cox bartering for dried fish (on the racks) with natives at Shingle Point near Herschel Island, August 19, 1914. (Photo by D. Jenness, CMC Photo No. 37140.)

some of the trade things ashore, but saw the *Alaska* coming so had lunch and waited for Dr. Anderson to arrive. Then he, Cox, and I all went ashore, I with the camera to snap some pictures of men in kayaks and of the netting and drying of fish.[6] The hills behind the lagoon were of a more vivid green than any I have yet seen in the Arctic. The settlement contained about 12 tents, with three or four abandoned winter houses.[7] About 2 miles away, on the opposite side of the lagoon was another settlement. Several whaleboats lined the outer edge of the lagoon near the tents and high up on the sandspit is the remains of a schooner, the *Penelope*, wrecked here in 1906(?).[8] Dr. Anderson was well known to the natives[9] and secured the fish at a much cheaper rate than we were able to obtain.[10] The Eskimos here are greatly mixed with foreign blood and foreign customs. One girl was half French and had lived for some years with the French missionaries (?) up the Mackenzie [River]. I said to her in French "You understand French, don't you?" and she replied in English "No," then in Eskimo "I have forgotten," which was rather 'naive'. Two other girls were certainly mingled with European blood, and one or two others seemed to be Indian half-breeds. There was one old woman who must have been 80 years of age, to judge by her appearance. Several of the natives were *Nunatagmiut*.[11] After spending a considerable time in purchasing fish, both dried and fresh, we moved out about 5 p.m., the *Alaska* a mile ahead.

Thursday, August 20th

We ran all night. I was at the wheel from 8 to 11 p.m., from 3:15 to 6 a.m., then continuously from 8 a.m. till 3:30 p.m., save for 1/2 hour when Cox left his engine and took it over. In the night the sea was a little lumpy — nothing at all for a larger boat, but it made the *North Star* roll and pitch as if bewitched. Twice the engine broke down, once at midnight when Aarnout turned me out to help in hoisting the staysail and mainsail. At 3:30 p.m. the crank shaft became overheated and stopped the engine, and again we hoisted the sails. Up to about 10 a.m. the sea was clear of ice, but as soon as we entered the ice floes the swell subsided. They were not very dense; only once did we have to stop the engine to squeeze between two small [ice] pans. The *Alaska* was 2 to 3 miles ahead at 3:30 p.m., and we did not see her afterwards. At 11 p.m. when Aarnout awakened me to take the wheel again we were close to a point of land, and working carefully in we found it was Point Atkinson, the western extremity of Russell Bay. Matt Andreasen, brother of Ole Andreasen (who accompanied Stefansson on his ice trip), has a house here. He had a cache laden with stores close to Duffy's, and Stefansson last winter bought his entire outfit.[12] We had instructions from Dr. Anderson to pick up anything useful that we might find at Point Atkinson[13] and take it along if conditions favoured our putting in there. We therefore anchored close in shore — opposite the house and rack. Cox and Aarnout went over in the canoe, I stayed aboard on watch, and took the opportunity to write up the day's journal. We sighted the *Herman*[14] this afternoon steering west, apparently on her way out. The weather was calm and clear all day, with fine mirages above the ice kegs; the evening still and mild, lovely tints in the north marking the sunset and sunrise.

Friday, August 21st

Cox and Aarnout returned with a great number of steel traps (fox-traps), and towing a sled behind them. We had one sled on board, but this one was better, so we are effecting an exchange. Cox was fearfully sleepy; he has hardly closed his eyes since Herschel [Island], but watched over his engine in a room full of fumes as though the life of the whole Expedition depended on it. Aarnout and I, therefore, towed our former sled ashore[15] — rather an energetic task, for the iron fixings made it just too heavy to float. [Matt] Andreasen had a comfortable shack here, on a sandspit beside a small hillock. Beside his house were a number of Eskimo ruins, two apparently graves which had been ransacked; one of the houses likewise appeared to have undergone some excavation. On the surface were a number of large whale bones, and I picked up a section of a whale's rib. Two Eskimo families are living there temporarily in tents of white drilling, but only the two wives were at home, their husbands being away sealing. Behind the point is a lagoon and here one of their whale boats was moored. We met the men (three of them) in a second whaleboat as we steamed out. It was about 3 a.m. when we got under way again. Cox went to sleep soon after we started, and I kept the wheel, occasionally sounding with the lead for the first few miles because a long sandspit runs out towards the northeast. About 6 a.m. Aarnout took over the wheel while I cooked breakfast, then after breakfast Cox and I kept the wheel while Aarnout slept. We had to wake him up about 1 p.m. to go aloft and pilot through the ice, which was rather thick for a short distance inside Liverpool Bay. Then it thinned out and for the last 10 miles west of Baillie Island there was hardly any ice at all. A number of seals poked their heads up in the water and gazed at us at different times, and we startled an immense flock of ducks (oldsquaws, I think), which were settled on the sea in a dense long black line exactly resembling a sandspit. Once Cox and I saw a whale spout — three times — then discovered it was not a whale at all but two or three Arctic tern falling and rising above the surface of the sea in their own peculiar manner. A moderate east wind blew all day, and we had the staysail and mainsail set most of the time, thereby averaging a speed of 6 knots. Twice the sky was ominously brooding, but the threatened storm passed off; only in the afternoon the sky clouded over and a little rain fell.

Saturday, August 22nd

We made Baillie Island yesterday evening but did not reach where we wanted to. There are two entrances to the lagoon between the island and Cape Bathurst, one via the west, possible only for vessels of shallow draught, the other deeper entrance on the east. We took the western, for two reasons — it cuts off, if one's course is perfectly straight, something like 15 miles, and we understood that the whale carcase towed in here by Louis Lane of the *Polar Bear* this summer, from which we are to obtain a supply of dog meat, was on the southwest sandspit.[16] The channel is deep enough for the *North Star*, for Matt Andreasen, her former owner, always entered by this route. But we did not know the channel and were misled by the ground ice — we steered between it and the bluff instead of (probably) outside, because with the current along the bluff we expected deeper water. Aarnout was using the lead continually, and we were running very slow, but we grounded nevertheless in 4 feet. With pushing and striving we worked her out a few yards then stuck fast and could not budge her with engines or poles both. We lowered the dingy, put 22 cases of distillate in it, and then put out a kedge anchor to one side, after Cox and Aarnout had sounded a channel with a pole from the canoe. This swung her about a point, then we were simply dragging the anchor. The tide appeared to have sunk a little, leaving the bow aground in less than 4 feet and the whole vessel in less than 5 [feet], save that the stern had worked a hole 6 feet deep under the propellor. Nothing remained but to unload some of the cargo — the distillate, dingy, and kedge [anchor] had already lightened her about a ton. Cox attached an Evinrude engine to the dingy, and he and Aarnout, after supper, took a load of distillate ashore; they set out at least with that intention but found that the dingy could not get within 100 feet of the shore. Glancing back at the vessel what was their amazement to find that though she had dragged a heavy anchor without swinging a foot, she had now of her own accord swung completely round and was heading towards the beach. It was soon accounted for. The tide had risen, and a strong current was setting east, and this with a light breeze on the foresail, which we had set to help our efforts, had accomplished in 5 minutes what we had vainly striven to do for hours. We had thought of the tide rising of course — but tides here are very irregular, depending largely on the wind, and at Herschel [Island] the average tide is only 8 inches, and in Coronation Gulf 1 foot. The kedge was still out. Hurriedly we put things straight, easily hauled up the anchor and steamed back into 8 feet of water, then lowered an anchor again while we took the dingy, distillate, and canoe aboard. Thus we were saved from a very unpleasant situation — by the sheerest good luck. We were taking no chances now but sailed right round the north end of the island till we reached the *Alaska* and *Teddy Bear*[17] at 8 a.m., which we had sighted from the place at which we grounded about 5 miles away. They were anchored close in to the long sandspit at Cape Bathurst where there are now two Eskimo tents — a man named Nauyakvuk[18] and his people — and the fresh whale carcase towed in by Louis Lane this summer in return for distillate (or gasoline, I forget which) given him by Wilkins. The *Teddy Bear* is run by Joe Bernard, nephew of Capt. [Peter] Bernard, outfitted by a man in Nome. He has spent three winters in and around Coronation Gulf, one at the mouth of the Kugaryuak River, another near Cape Pullen on Victoria Land, another in an excellent harbour between Stapylton Inlet and Cape Krusenstern. The latter he describes as the best harbour he has seen in the Arctic[19] — there is wood, it is well sheltered and deep, contains plenty of salmon and trout, and is directly on the route of the caribou migration in November. Dr. Anderson has decided to make it our base if we can reach it. He [Joe Bernard] spent this last winter in Victoria Land close to some Eskimos and has a considerable collection of ethnological specimens, which he will probably sell to curio dealers in Nome.[20] He reported loose ice all the way to the [Coronation] Gulf, enough to keep the sea down but not enough to impede navigation. He had met the *Mary Sachs* near the mouth of the Horton River.[21] She has met serious trouble. The first day out they stopped for water and could not proceed because both the cook [Levi] and the engineer [Crawford] were drunk. Then they encountered rather heavy ice and had to lie off Pullen Island. After that they were struck by a southwest gale and forced right down into Liverpool Bay (the same gale drove the *North Star* on the beach) [at Herschel Island]. The launch filled with water but was bailed out safely. But a propeller blade struck a keg of ice and broke off one of the shafts, so that they could run on one engine only. Crawford wanted 3 weeks to put in a new one; also he and Levi (the cook) refused to go further than Cape Bathurst. However, Wilkins got them to go along to Cape Parry, running on one engine, from which place it is only a short run across to Banks Land. He wrote a note to Dr. Anderson from Horton River that he would go on if he could.[22] The *Alaska* pulled out just after noon. Chipman took observations for both longitude and latitude. They had secured as much whale meat as they could take and the Dr. wished to hurry on and overtake the *Mary Sachs* if she has not crossed to Banks Land. The *Teddy Bear* left before noon — for Nome if possible. We secured a native named Palaiak[23] from the *Alaska* and returned to the *North Star* for lunch. Aarnout was asleep, so Cox cooked while I bargained with Nauyakvuk and his family for a few curios. After lunch Aarnout and Palaiak cut some whale meat[24] while Cox and I slept. They finished soon after 7 p.m., and we started out again at 8:15 [p.m.]. About noon three of the Eskimos living ashore came on board and sold me three or four old ethnological specimens for calico. In the afternoon while I slept one of them, an old woman, came aboard again with her granddaughter — a half-white girl of about 12 years.[25] She brought three or four more specimens, all save one new and more or less faked. A strong tide runs through the channel here and down the coast. It helped us along though against the comparatively strong east wind, which sprang up in the afternoon. About a mile east of the new whale carcase is an old one, round which a great number of seagulls had gathered at the time we passed. There was not much ice, just enough to keep the sea calm without hindering a direct course. I was at the wheel till 10:30 p.m. when Aarnout relieved me and I had supper and turned in. The wind had moderated greatly at this time, and the air was calm and clear.

Sunday, August 23rd

The morning saw us speeding across Franklin Bay to Cape Parry, where [the] whaleship *Alexander*[26] was wrecked in 1906. The current still favoured us, the sea comparatively free of ice — indeed for about 6 miles in the middle of the bay entirely free. Stefansson and Dr. Anderson wintered in Langton Bay at the bottom of Franklin Bay,[27] and Palaiyak, the young *Kittigariut* native we have on board was with him [Stefansson]. The engine ran well and by noon we were abreast of the cape, which appears to be a tall cliff 50 feet high with a great number of high rocky islets along its face and channels in behind. Two Eskimo men belonging to the Mackenzie River branch of the race came out in a Canadian canoe and informed us that the [*Mary*] *Sachs* had passed there going eastward.[28] We imagined she may have continued to the east to escape heavy ice, though the strait across to Nelson Head, about 50 miles wide,[29] seemed to us to be fairly clear. From the masthead Cox imagined he saw the high cliffs at Nelson Head but was not sure. We stopped to speak to these Eskimos for a few minutes, then continued on our way, turning a little to the south to strike Cape Lyon. Here we were to make a small cache of flour etc. for Cox and O'Neill when they run a traverse from the Coppermine here — the country through which it is believed the copper-bearing rocks extend. We hoped to reach Cape Lyon about 6 p.m., for the chart makes it only about 30 miles, and the sea was clear of ice. But 6 o'clock saw us only half way across. The reason we discovered later; whereas from Cape Bathurst to Cape Parry the current had helped us along, so that we reached the latter long before we expected and the log registered considerably less than it should have according to the chart (our course took us nearly down to the mouth of the Horton River, then straight across), from Cape Parry to Cape Lyon the tide was against us and in the evening the wind as well. For this afternoon exactly the same kind of wind sprang up as we faced yesterday, a fairly strong easterly, which died away during the evening. The sky also resembled yesterday's — black and threatening clouds to the south, which came to nothing. In the middle of Darnley Bay the engine suddenly stopped — the distillate in the tank was exhausted. In consequence we wallowed in the trough of the sea — fortunately comparatively calm — for nearly three-quarters of an hour. Stefansson, when he issued instructions last March that a cache should be established at Cape Lyon, sketched from memory a good harbour (as he thought) between this cape and Pierce Point,[30] of which Pierce Point closed the eastern end. Dr. Anderson showed Cox another sketch, altogether different, of the same place, with three or four soundings made, Cox has the impression, by Joe Bernard. The two were so different that we did not know which to follow, if either, though we inclined, rightly as it turned out, to the latter, because it contained the soundings and Stefansson's was based on a winter inspection. About midnight, guided by a lantern light on shore — the first shore light I have seen in the Arctic save for the one that was raised each night during the winter at Collinson Point — we worked between a broad field of ice and some perpendicular cliffs of sedimentary(?) origin, probably about 30 feet high, into a roughly cup-shaped bay 2 to 3 miles wide where the bed of the sea came up at a sharp angle to form a gravel beach strewn with driftwood, so that 15 yards off shore the depth was about 4 or 5 fathoms. The two or three rocks about a mile from shore were insufficient to protect the beach from heavy ice, but the eastern cliffs, which we skirted, are indented with two or three small coves, one of which curves right round horse-shoe fashion, so that if the water is deep enough a schooner would be protected from any wind. In any case a small schooner could easily be drawn up on the beach out of the reach of the heavy ice if it was desired to winter here. Cape Lyon shelters it from the west wind and Pierce Point from the east, and the tundra gently rising behind to a plateau from the south and southwest, but it [the bay] has no protection apart from these possible coves from the north and northeast; at least this is so for the eastern part of the bay where we anchored. Yet the gravel bed would probably give excellent holding ground against any wind that is likely to come from this direction. The gorgeous glow of the sunset and sunrise behind the cliffs of Pierce Point, the gleaming white and bluish ice kegs, the dark blue sea stirred by light ripples, and the brown tundra behind made a wonderfully striking picture, the beauty of which equalled anything that I have seen — so far as it is possible to compare different scenes in this regard. We dropped anchor about 40 yards from the beach where we could see a sod house and near it the tent, which takes its place in summer. Presently a small skin boat pushed off and as it drew alongside imagine our astonishment to find its occupants a handsome lad of about 13 years and a pretty maid of perhaps 15. We knew that a man named Klengenberg with his Eskimo wife and family were in this neighbourhood, and these were two of his children.[31] At the moment they seemed like fairy inhabitants of a fairy lagoon. Their father, they said, had gone down inside the bay, and they were not sure when he would return; meanwhile they two were left alone. The evening before they had seen a schooner pass on its way east, which from the description must have been the [*Mary*] *Sachs* (though why it should be going east is rather hard to understand). Possibly there was some mistake and it was the *Alaska* they saw. (Yes.) We took them below and gave them something to eat then went ashore leaving them aboard, chatting with Palaiyak, an old acquaintance. Cox and Aarnout made the cache while I gathered firewood, then Palaiyak coming ashore, we took the firewood on board, and he procured some ice for water from a keg, then returned to shore to bring Cox and Aarnout aboard. By 3 a.m. we were steaming out and Cox and I turned in to sleep, leaving Aarnout to steer.

Monday, August 24th

Palaiyak took the wheel, while Aarnout cooked breakfast and at 9 a.m. roused Cox and me. The weather was a repetition of that on the two preceding days, a light east wind with clear blue sky flecked with white clouds round the horizon and a calm sea. We passed Cape Dease Thompson at [...],[32] noticing the strange hole in the rock, which is pictured in Stefansson's book.[33] Near the mouth of Roscoe River the tundra appeared to be channelled by mathematically parallel lines, resembling a field under cultivation.[34] Cox says he noticed the same behind Pierce Point. Here an ignition spring broke [on the engine of the *North Star*] and a new one had to be substituted. While this was being done we drifted in shore, so that when we started out again we ran into shoal water less than 2 fathoms deep, though we were about 1/2 mile from shore. However, we soon ran out of this again into deep water by turning northward. The sea here is brilliantly clear; often a deep blue, reminding one of the tropics a little. We noticed the same at Pierce Point. Further west where the turgid Mackenzie River brings in its waters it is so muddy that at 3 feet the bottom is invisible. This is the case even as far east as Baillie Island, as we found to our cost. In the afternoon again the magneto went wrong and we had to stop for that. While Cox was fixing it up two seals came close up to the vessel, no doubt wondering what the strange monster could be. I shot one but missed the other. We had fried seal shoulder for supper dressed by the masterly hand of Cox. Palaiyak skinned the seal and hung the meat in the rigging, then about 6 o'clock relieved me at the wheel. We dined (or supped) about 7 p.m., and Aarnout and Palaiyak took turns in steering throughout the evening and night. The sun in the early afternoon was delightfully warm — warmer I think than I have ever felt it this summer[35] though Cox, Chipman, and O'Neill experienced very hot weather in the Mackenzie delta — the thermometer

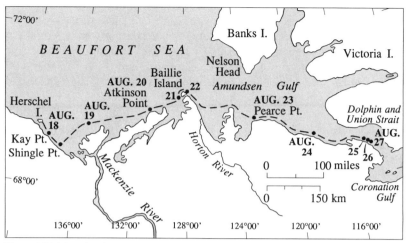

Figure 107. Map showing route taken by author on the schooner *North Star* from Herschel Island to Coronation Gulf, Aug. 18-27, 1914. Dates indicate approximate locations of schooner at end of each day.

registered 100° F once, I think Cox told me. Towards evening the temperature fell, and it grew chilly again. We have certainly been favoured with wonderfully fine weather hitherto.

Tuesday, August 25th

Aarnout roused Cox and me at 5 a.m. and I took the wheel. The sky was somewhat clouded, and a northwest wind had been blowing but had now died away. It was difficult today, as it was yesterday also, to identify the conspicuous places on the coast with the bays and promontories of the chart. The atmosphere was slightly foggy, so [we] veered to the south half a point in order that we might not lose touch of land. At 7:20 a.m. a north wind sprang up and cleared the atmosphere, when we found ourselves about 1/2 mile south of a cape, which after much consultation of chart and log we decided must be Young Point. Here the engine had to be stopped for the magneto went wrong again, and Aarnout was roused to hoist the foresail and staysail. It was an hour before the engine could be restarted, some bearings of the magneto being so worn that it could not be fixed without a new set, of which there are none on board. Consequently we ran on the battery. Following the chart, and allowing six points for the magnetic variation, I steered north-northeast across Stapylton Bay, but after we had run about 2 hours in thick fog without reaching land, we decided that we must have gone out too far, so steered east by north. This brought us up against the coast, but only after we had gone 10 miles, and the fog lifting we found ourselves off Cape Bexley. Evidently the chart here, as in so many places along the coast, is not quite accurate. In rounding the cape close in to shore we had to go through a loose pack [of ice] and ran into shoal water where the bottom was plainly visible 5 fathoms and more below the surface. It was gravel, with here a bed of large boulders, there a dark patch of sea vegetation. We were running at half speed when the engine stopped, and while we lay still a seal rose near by and was promptly shot by Palaiyak. There is shoal water off the point, which does not appear on the chart, and the bay is certainly wider and different in shape from what it is marked. The fog settled down again soon after the point was rounded, but we steamed along through open water, here and there interspersed with floe ice. Aarnout was at the wheel, so I took advantage of the opportunity and measured Palaiyak[36] with the anthropometric instruments sent down the Mackenzie [River] this summer, then cooked dinner. It was just ready at 7 p.m. when the bell rang and the engines stopped. Running on deck I found we had struck another shoal and were in 2 fathoms of water only. It took some time to work out. Once we had only a fathom of water between us and the gravel bed. The compass is extremely sluggish and refused to move once when the vessel was swinging round at a great rate.[37] Given plenty of time, however, it seems to move regularly. We ran north into deep water, then as the fog showed no signs of lifting and we must be close to the harbour where we expect to winter, we decided to run south till we struck 2 fathoms or so again and anchor till the fog lifted. Ten minutes later we had a glimpse of the coast 200 or 300 yards away as we dropped anchor in 2 fathoms, then the fog closed in again.[38] We went below for dinner, smoked, and talked till 10 p.m., when the rest of us turned in, leaving Aarnout on watch. He woke me at 11 p.m., turned in himself, and I shall call Palaiyak at 12. As soon as it is light we shall start out again if so be that the fog lifts; just now it is as thick as ever. There is a slow current setting west at the rate of perhaps 1/2 mile an hour, and a faint breeze from the east; otherwise all is still. The light and dark patches at the bottom of the sea are plainly visible, and the ship's name inverted can be clearly read in the water. One feature is lacking — there are no fish visible swimming at the bottom in and out of the vegetation. Seals appear to be fairly numerous; Palaiyak had two more shots this evening — unsuccessful ones.

Wednesday, August 26th

I kept watch again from 2 to 3 a.m. then called Palaiyak again. The weather was still foggy with a very light east wind blowing. We turned out late for breakfast since the weather did not appear propitious and enjoyed a luxurious meal of porridge, fried potatoes, bacon, and seal liver. The last is excellent — I could not have distinguished it from calves' liver. Some seal meat, especially the fresh meat of a young seal, is as good as beef or mutton, in my opinion; when boiled for 20 minutes or 1/2 hour it is as tender as either. But seal meat can be tough and 'sealy' in taste. It is naturally very dark, so that the colour is no guide in cooking. The atmosphere cleared about 11 a.m., and we prepared to move, for we found ourselves some 200 yards off a flat beach with an inlet a mile west of us and a point about a mile east. To the east were visible also two or three islands, which we identified as the Liston Islands, and north the hills of Victoria Land were faintly visible for a time. The point east of us was, therefore, probably Cape Cockburn [Cockburn Point], and our harbour for the winter some 10 miles east. The mainland near us seemed very flat and marshy; there was a large pool — not big enough to constitute a lake — a little way behind where we lay. The bottom of the sea was rocky without any cracks or crevices of any size and consequently very poor holding ground; a good breeze in the night would have put us on the beach if we had not set the engine going in time. Cox had considerable difficulty in making it start, and this delayed our departure for an hour or more. When we did run out into deep water and down through fairly thick floes of ice between the Liston Islands and the mainland, Aarnout aloft and I steering, the fog settled over us again and we could see nothing for more than 100 yards round us. However, steering east by south we struck land after about 2 hours, and working slowly along it dodging in and out of the heavy grounded floes we finally ran into a cul de sac. The fog was too thick for us to see where we were, though we thought at first that we were among the islands just outside the desired harbour, of which Joe Bernard had supplied a sketch. We moored to an ice cake and after a light lunch Aarnout and Palaiyak went off in the canoe to look for a passage. An hour or two later the fog lifted somewhat, and we saw that we were in a small semi-circular bay, not 100 yards from shore; a barren stony land with low ridges and depressions. It seemed too large to be any island here, and we were not sure where we were. The chart is not accurate enough to be a certain guide. Aarnout returned about 7 p.m. He had gone about 3 miles along the coast and saw what seemed to be a large lake or bay, but the fog had hardly lifted at all in the direction (west) that he took, and he too could not say whether we were up against the mainland or an island. For a time we heard distinct barking southeast of us, and fired several shots to attract attention and an answer, if the *Alaska* is in the neighbourhood; but no reply came. The fog settled down again, and we could not move. But the ice was closing in on us. Already once Cox and I had shifted the vessel a little, now we had to start the engine, and pushing aside some floes squeeze our way out for 150 yards to a large keg grounded in 3 fathoms and run a line out on to it. The water is so clear that we could see the bottom when the lead gave 6 fathoms.[39] Seals appear to be plentiful, and we had several shots, Aarnout securing a small one, which means another liver for breakfast. We boiled the legs and flippers of Palaiyak's seal for supper then turned in, Palaiyak keeping the first watch from 11 to 1 [a.m.]. I am now on watch from 3 to 5 [a.m.], the time at this moment being just 4 a.m. Aarnout, who was on watch from 1 to 3 [a.m.], said that he too heard distinct barking to the southeast — on the other side of the ridges. The atmosphere is still foggy, with light rain falling as it was yesterday afternoon, but it is perfectly calm and still. We were able to collect some fresh water off a large floe this afternoon. It seems strange that 'fresh' water can be obtained on sea-ice, but so it is. The surface of the ice melts, the water collects in a small depression, and there you have a fresh-water pool. It saves much time and fuel used in melting a block of ice.

Thursday, August 27th

Cox had the morning watch 5 to 7 a.m. and prepared breakfast. Indeed, he made so hot a fire that he roasted me out of my bunk. Aarnout said that he distinctly heard barking during his watch. The atmosphere was as foggy as ever, so we did not move. Several seals showed themselves, and I shot one. We had three or four shots at a large bearded seal (*ugruk*) but failed to kill it. They average about 600 lbs weight as against l00 to 120 [lbs] of the common hair seal. Suddenly we heard two answering shots to the southeast, and when we fired again other shots in answer. So we weighed anchor and steamed out hugging the shore, watching the depth all the time. Rounding a point we sighted a canoe coming towards us. It was Dr. Anderson and Chipman, who had set out to meet us as soon as they heard our shots. The channel by which they came out, and up which we were heading, is very shallow they told us, hardly deep enough for a canoe. The tents and caches of the *Alaska* were visible at its head about 1/4 mile away. We had to turn and go back round an island[40] and up another channel. Palaiyak shot a bearded seal as we were running along, but it sank just as we came abreast of it. Suddenly we found our way barred by heavy floes jammed between two islands.[41] They had been recently carried in by the northeast wind and a strong tide setting through the channel. We tried to force our way through but failed and had some difficulty in turning round again on account of the shelves of ice projecting below the water. The Dr. and Chipman returned to the *Alaska* and we ran for shelter under a small island about 1/2 mile away,[42] hoping to be able to make the harbour when the tide sets the other way. There is a rise and fall of the tide inside the harbour, Chipman says, of 5 or 6 feet. It is admirably sheltered from the winds of every quarter, but there is almost no wood. The *Alaska* got in Monday evening, when the weather was clear and calm, making a straight run from Baillie Island. She was leaking very badly, however, and required pumping for about 10 minutes every half-hour. But since some of the cargo has been unloaded she has not leaked half so much. They are hurrying on with the unloading so that she can return to Baillie Island and pick up coal and whale meat,[43] and the Dr. is thinking seriously of sending her right to Herschel [Island] to pick up the mail and stores coming by the *Ruby*. The Dr. shot a large bearded seal after they came in here, and they have also secured a large fish, though I do not know what kind it was. Añutisiak saw a caribou track, which he thought was only 2 or 3 days old, but Chipman saw what may have been the same track and he thought it dated from the spring. A cold northeast wind prevailed more or less all day, varying in strength though never very violent. Rain fell a great part of the time. The tide seemed to be ebbing in the evening, though it is really too dark to see. I hope we can get in tomorrow. It will be pleasant to have no watch at night — I am on duty now from 11 to 1 [a.m.], having changed my breakfast watch with Cox because he was too sleepy to keep awake. None of us has undressed — save our boots and possibly socks — since we left Herschel [Island], and I only once since leaving Barter Island to go down to join the ships at Collinson Point more than a month ago.

Chapter 18. First Encounters with the Copper Eskimos

Unloading in Bernard Harbour — Replacing propellor on Alaska *— Finding recent Eskimo camp — Catching salmon in Eskimo fish dam — Scarcity of driftwood — First encounter with Copper Eskimos — Tattoos and attire — Initial attempts at trade — Diseases amongst Eskimos — Departure of Eskimos to east — Departure of* Alaska *for Baillie Island — Arrival of new group of Eskimos*

Friday, August 28th, 1914

We are safe in our winter harbour, Bernard Harbour as it will probably be called, after its discoverer.[1] The fog was as thick as ever when we turned out this morning, but the sea was unruffled by any breeze, so after breakfast we raised anchor, ran down to the barrier of ice floes, which closed the narrow entrance, and strove to force our way through. It took about an hour, perhaps more, for we were all working too hard to notice the passage of time. Sometimes we were going full steam ahead for a yard or two, then astern, then ahead again, twisting this way and that wherever a thin dark streak of water marked the end of one floe and the beginning of another. Frequently we had to jump off on to the floes and push the vessel off or forward. At the narrowest point the passage cannot be more than 50 yards wide, and it is only about 200 yards long. The *Alaska* lay about 150 yards inside, and we anchored beside her, with a stern line ashore and one anchor out; then we set about unloading. The *Alaska* finished her unloading about 2 p.m., all the cargo being stacked in separate piles on the rocky shore.[2] We managed to clear the decks almost entirely before dinner, which we had on the *Alaska*. Both vessels show the effects of butting through ice; they are more or less stripped of paint in the bows from the waterline down. The *Alaska* broke a propeller blade at Herschel [Island] during the gale that left the *North Star* stranded on the beach, for she touched the bottom just once.[3] It was not known at the time, though Blue, the engineer, knew it had been damaged somehow. As a result she came all the way here with only one propeller blade, averaging about 5 knots. Tomorrow a new propeller is to be fixed on, one with four blades, for she is going straight back to Baillie Island to pick up coal, whale meat, and wood,[4] and may even return to Herschel [Island] to bring back the stores and the mail that the *Ruby* is bringing in. A strange dog has been seen around here, with a ribbon of deerskin round its neck. Pudding, by the way, one of the dogs we brought off the *Karluk* last September, was killed in a fight here 2 days ago, and another dog was injured but will probably recover. I went for a stroll after dinner and walked some 5 or 6 miles, hoping to see signs of caribou or Eskimos. But the only living creature I saw was a small bird, a sandpiper I think, besides one that I did not see but heard twitter. The weather was rather disagreeable, for a moderately strong southwest wind had sprung up, driving showers of rain before it for a time. However, it accomplished one good thing — it drove away the fog that has vexed us during the last 3 days.

Saturday, August 29th

A dismal day, with a strong wind blowing and rain falling almost all day. We landed everything off the decks and washed them down, but did not touch the flour and other stores in the hold lest they should get wet. The *Alaska* was drawn in close to the beach, the stern raised a little, and an unsuccessful attempt made to remove the propeller. The ice lies thick outside both in and off shore, so that for the present, while this wind lasts, there seems little prospect of the *Alaska* making her way out.

Sunday, August 30th

We emptied the hold of the *North Star*, which now draws only 18 inches forward and 3 feet 6 inches aft, a good 2 feet less than she did when loaded. Johansen and O'Neill went for a stroll inland in the afternoon, and after we had finished unloading I wandered west looking for driftwood[5] along the coast, then striking inland[6] met Johansen and O'Neill and returned with them. One small salmon was caught in the net this morning. After supper about 6 p.m., when the water was low, Blue removed the propeller and put on the new one, screwing the nuts on by hand. He was compelled to stand in the water; it was more than flesh and blood could endure for more than a few minutes, and he had to come out and change before tightening the nuts with a monkey-wrench — consequently the work is not finished yet. A strange dog was hanging about the shore this evening — it was noticed 2 or 3 days ago also. The weather was dull in the morning, but the sun shone out in the afternoon. The temperature, however, was low and the sea was freezing in the evening. There was a most brilliant aurora about 9:30 p.m. It began as a bow of bright prismatic colours, with two 'sheaves' or curtains close by. But

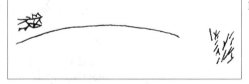

Figure 108. Auroral bow.

it changed momentarily and even as we watched became a whirling eddy of dazzling light emitting flashing streamers of red and orange to white, which faded as quickly as they appeared. The spectacle lasted perhaps 3 minutes then suddenly vanished, leaving in its place only two or three pale white bands.

Monday, August 31st

After breakfast, the weather being fine though the sky was overcast and a light east wind was blowing, the Dr. went east to inspect a fish-net he had set there the day before at the mouth of a small creek. Sweeney went that way also to look for driftwood, while Blue went inland for caribou. O'Neill and I decided to go east also and look for driftwood but to make a day trip of it so that we might go beyond where the others went. We passed Sweeney as he was returning, then the Dr. carrying the fish-net with no fish, and a bunch of dandelions, the first he has seen in this region. Pushing on we sighted two bright green patches that stood out prominently from the pervading brown, and suspecting that they marked old inhabited sites, we directed our steps towards them. They were old sites, yet not so old as we had imagined, for the inhabitants could not have deserted the place more than 2 months ago. There were rings of stones, which seemed to have held down the tent walls, and other rings much smaller inside, [on] which the stone lamp was probably set when in use. Fragments of implements, some shavings, and a few charred sticks were strewn everywhere. I picked up a fine pair of bone goggles. There were two small pits apparently made by dogs scratching down to avoid the summer heat. The settlement was divided into two parts by a large creek. In the middle of the western half were four sticks about 6 feet long 'cached' by placing three or four large stones on top and near by another stick 'cached' in a similar manner. The creek at this point is tidal, for the settlement lay at the head of a fine large harbour, well sheltered, and apparently accessible to vessels drawing at least 10 feet and perhaps more.[7] Fish dams of stones had been set in the creek, three rows one above the other.[8] The lowest (A) had several gaps in it,

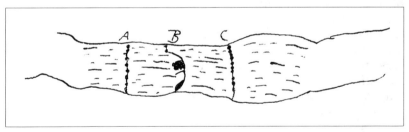

Figure 109. Eskimo fish dam on fishing creek near C.A.E. station. Stream flows from right to left.

the middle one was shaped rather like the Eskimo bow and was entirely closed save for a V-shaped opening, which guided the fish upstream. One side of this V was also the side of another closed V, which had its point downstream and was roofed with large stones so as to make a dark recess. The uppermost dam (C) was entirely closed. We were sitting on

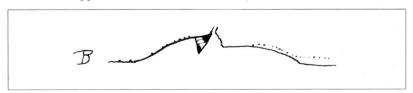

Figure 110. Detail of middle trap of fish dam in Fig. 109.[9]

the bank eating our lunch when we had an admirable illustration of the effectiveness of such a trap. A large 7 lb salmon lay in the shallow water between B and C, left half stranded by the receding tide. O'Neill pursued it with his knife, and it rushed downstream and hid in the dark cavity, the mouth of the one and only exit being narrow and difficult to find. By simply removing one or two bowlders from the roof we were able to draw the fish out with thumb and finger inserted in the gills. Near the right half of the settlement were some caches, three made by piles of stones covering in one case a seal poke full of blubber; in another four seal spears were inserted — two made of long brass tubing with iron tips at each end; the third covered two or three pieces of driftwood. A little to one side was a cache of four trimmed boards with two large soapstone lamps and a wooden bowl resting on top. The bowl was weighted down with four stones to prevent it from blowing away. Finally there were three coal-oil cans cached together with a stick or two of wood.[10] O'Neill picked up the lid of a coffee-mill; plainly Joe Bernard had not failed to leave behind traces of his visit to this region. We found afterwards, beside a small creek 3/4 mile west, three similar stone circles and a cache of dried fish. Pushing on for another 4 miles we came down to the shore. Along the whole coast there was scarcely a sign of driftwood, a small stick perhaps every 2 miles. It was nearly 7 p.m. when we made the ships again. The land is broken up into ridges and valleys at right angles to the coast, the ridges being from 100 to 200 feet high and covered with boulders and stones, limestone, diabase, and shale.[11] The few exposures are all of limestone about here, many with deep parallel scratches indicating glacial action. The valleys have in most cases small lakes at their heads, which collect the drainage from what seems to be plateau land behind, and send it forth in small streams now mostly dry. Near the coast they broaden out into mud flats. Cox was fixing up the Evinrude engine when we left, and Chipman setting up his tent and collecting his things ashore. No plans for one or two houses have crystallized yet.[12]

Tuesday, September 1st

The morning was rather cloudy but still. A strong east wind sprang up last evening and continued into the night. It loosened the ice at the entrance and blew it out of the strait so that hardly a keg was visible. Johansen enlisted Cox as engineer and boat captain and myself as A.B.[13] to tow his trawling nets down the bay with the *North Star's* dingy. We dragged the smaller net first, then the larger, but the results were rather disappointing. There were two species of kelp, *laminaria* and *alaria*, both dead, washed in apparently from the straits, one fish — a sculpin — and a number of amphipods, cetapods, and ascidia. After lunch Cox and I walked over to the old settlement 5 miles east.[14] The weather was gloriously fine and the sun quite hot in the still air, but just as we reached the place dark clouds gathered in the south and soon it was raining fast. We found four large salmon in the trap, one in shallow water, the other three in a pool about 15 feet wide and in the middle 4 feet deep. So we took the brass spears from the cache and quickly secured the first. The other three gave more trouble, the pool was just too wide for us to reach the middle, and the salmon knew it. Cox tried to shoot them, but the water was too deep. One by one we stabbed them and after 1 1/2 hours exciting quest secured all three. I took four photos,[15] then we set out homeward.

We were crossing the last ridge when down below in the valley beside a creek we sighted an Eskimo tent which was not there when we passed by in the morning. Two women, one elderly the other young, came out as we approached and after a few words invited us in. A little child of about 5 years was sitting there — a boy, I think. They put some cold boiled caribou meat before us then held an animated conversation between themselves, with occasional queries at us. Their men, they said, had gone to the ships,[16] whither we [all] soon followed, leaving behind the largest of our four fish. Sure enough we found them on the *Alaska*, three men and a boy, chattering and laughing and curious towards all they saw. They had been given a good dinner half an hour before, nevertheless they followed Cox down and helped themselves to all they saw.[17] Some of the food they did not like, and it had to be thrown into the slop-bucket. Sweeney dosed one [man] with pepper. It created much amusement; even the man himself did not appear to mind. Both the men and the women told their names then paused for you to give your name — a custom wholly foreign to the Northern Alaska Eskimo, who much prefer others to tell you their names than to tell them themselves. Both men and women have rank black hair, curling at the ends. One woman and the boy have the Mongol almond eyes more markedly than the rest. The men wear the hair close clipped on the crown,[18] but long at the sides; the women long all over, but braided into two pendant plaits in front, one falling in front of each ear. Both women were tattooed in the

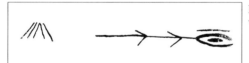

Figure 111. Tattoos on Eskimo women near Bernard Harbour.

same way — five rays from the lower lip to the chin, two parallel lines along each cheekbone, and another parallel to the lower two running from each eye to the hair. This last had short branch lines so that they resembled two Y's placed one on top of the other, or joined arrows. The costume was peculiar; I have not fathomed it yet, but both men and women wear long swallow-tailed coats with rather low necks [and] hoods at the back; knee breeks; the men seem to have long underboots with short overboots, the women a kind of legging and short boots. They are all very brown and dirty-looking now, tanned with hot summer sun on the tundra. The younger woman had a pleasant voice with greater variety of intonation than I have remarked elsewhere. All are infested with *komait*.[19] One woman rather upset the Dr. [Anderson] by transferring the entrails of a freshly killed ptarmigan to her mouth.[20] The Dr. took the three Eskimos[21] some distance east and showed them where to cut sods for the houses. He was returning when he saw the strange Eskimos and went over to their tent,[22] afterwards conducting the men to the ship.

Wednesday, September 2nd

The *Alaska's* propeller was fixed yesterday, and this morning after breakfast the *North Star* attempted to pull her off, but she was aground too firm. The Eskimos came down en masse, all seven, and stayed about the beach all day.[23] Some food was sent ashore to them at lunchtime, and just after eating one of the old men gave a short dance trying to induce the child to dance also. Chipman thought that he was possibly expressing their thanks, for they repeatedly exclaimed *inuit nakorut* (the strangers are good people). In coming the women were a little behind and one of the old men approached first as though they were uncertain whether the welcome they received yesterday would be repeated today. Aksiatak brought his bow and arrows and hunting outfit. [24] There were several copper-tipped arrows, the copper being obtained he said from an Eskimo in Victoria Land, two iron-tipped, and three (for ptarmigan) of horn with blunt points. There were only two feathers on each, curled slightly at the tip; they were attached by cutting a narrow groove into which the rib was pressed by means of a bone *kiputaq* and then made fast with a lashing of caribou sinew. The bow was backed with sealskin lashings laid longi-

Figure 112. Aksiatak's bow, Bernard Harbour.

tudinally and lashed at intervals with deer sinew, and the string also was of deer sinew. The main arch of the bow was made from a single piece of wood, but the two ends were of separate pieces. The 'string' was attached to projecting pegs at the ends. A simple notch U-shaped cut in the end of the arrow fitted firmly against the string. On his wrist tied by a sealskin lashing Aksiatak wore a hollow oval wristguard about 2 inches long by 1 1/4 inches wide. The bow and the arrows had separate sealskin cases; the arrow quiver having a detachable cap. Another small bag contained bone pins for pinning back the skin of a deer when skinning, a sinew twister for twisting on the back lashings, three or four 'prickers' or 'marlin spikes', a wedge, and a flat spoon for picking out the marrow from the split leg bones — all of bone. The heads of the arrows were beautifully fitted on and held in place by copper rivets; the bow too was well made. In the afternoon he offered four arrows in exchange for a rifle, but no one seemed inclined to accept the offer. Just before dinner the *North Star* succeeded in towing the *Alaska* off, after several ineffec-

Figure 113. Copper Eskimos watching activities of the Expedition members on the *Alaska*, Bernard Harbour, September 2, 1914. Person near boxes above the Expedition's canoe may be Chipman. (Photo by Dr. R.M. Anderson, CMC Photo No. 38733.)

tual attempts. I had my little finger jammed between the tow-rope and the woodwork of the ship in the operation, and it is rather painful in consequence. She will probably sail out tonight or tomorrow, though it is now too late in the season to return to Herschel [Island]. The weather was gloriously fine all day, with hardly a breath of wind to disturb the serenity of the sea. A light east wind sprang up in the late afternoon, and the ice seems to be returning a little; but the wind died away again in the evening, and we had a most beautiful sunset of purple and gold, with the full moon rising over a low ridge in the east. The sun sets early now — about 7 o'clock — and the nights are dark.

Dr. Anderson told me that tuberculosis had been very common around the Mackenzie and along the coast to the east and west and that its action seemed to be very rapid. A large proportion of the population in the same region had suffered from syphilis and many from gonorrhea, but in many cases they appeared to have recovered even without treatment from the whaling captains. Now there appear to be very few cases of the primary stage. He knew of several instances of insanity where the victims had formerly been syphilitic. The gonorrhea frequently resulted in stricture, but the patients had recovered without aid. Palaiyak has a bald patch on his scalp. When he was a small boy, he told me, there had been a large swelling there, and his father had opened it with a knife. The Dr. said that the Mackenzie and Baillie Island natives frequently resorted to bleeding to cure headache and backache, hence the scars on the scalps and backs of many of them.

Thursday, September 3rd

The Eskimos left this morning to go east [about 4 miles] to the fishing creek on the site of the old settlement.[25] They brought four small slices of caribou meat to sell and received in return a little bearded seal and three or four dried fish. The weather was gloriously fine, but a moderate east wind was blowing and blocked the entrance with ice so that the *Alaska* could not go out. We busied ourselves a little fixing up various tents[26] and storing inside whatever would be damaged by rain.[27] The Eskimo boys cut sods for the houses to be built later. The evening was very beautiful — a calm sea with the rich sunset glow in the west and the full moon in the east.

Friday, September 4th

A repetition of yesterday as far as the weather and our occupations[28] were concerned. The Dr. shot a seal from the *Alaska's* deck.[29] The shallow channel to the north was sounded and found to carry only 3 feet of water at high tide with a rocky bottom. The *North Star* unloaded draws 3 feet 6 inches to 4 feet aft, so it is impossible to take her out [by that channel].[30] Again a glorious evening.[31]

Saturday, September 5th

Another repetition of the two preceding days. Palaiyak went hunting and brought in a portion of a caribou — our first.[32] There is a great migration of them past here in November, Joe Bernard says, but just now they are very few and far between. Chipman, Cox, O'Neill, and I played bridge in the evening.

Sunday, September 6th

The *Alaska* left about 6 a.m.,[33] for the wind veering to the southeast opened up the ice in the passage. In consequence we had to cook for ourselves ashore,[34] and Cox took on the job for the day. While he was preparing breakfast Palaiyak and I went out in the canoe to try for a seal. We saw several, and Palaiyak fired twice, but both shots went over the top. It is difficult to aim from a canoe as the slightest movement in the water causes the vessel to rock, and the muzzle of the rifle wobbles up and down.

Just as we came to the beach we saw a party of Eskimo on the crest of the ridge about 200 yards from the tent. They were standing in line, five of them, alternately raising their open hands above their heads and then stooping, lowering them towards the ground, to signify that they had come in peace, that they had laid their weapons on the ground, and they they held nothing in their hands. We approached them first laying down our own guns and repeating their signs. Twice they repeated the gestures and we replied, then coming up we all sat down and began to talk. There were four men and a lad of about 14 years. The eldest man, father of the lad and of two of the other men, had his right hand wrapped in deerskin. A brown bear had bitten the thumb off this summer, though it was

Figure 114. The author chatting with Ayalit (with bound hand on left) and other Copper Eskimos a week after his arrival at Bernard Harbour, September 6, 1914. (Photo by F. Johansen, CMC Photo No. 42232.)

wounded through the chest with an arrow and died a few minutes afterwards. We took them down to the tents and gave them something to eat, then Chipman, O'Neill, and I went off to examine one of the fish-nets. There were two fine large salmon trout caught in it, swarming with small crustaceans, which feed on it when it rots but do not harm it while fresh. I took them back to camp while the other two brought the shovels and axes from the opposite side of the bay where our Eskimos had been digging sods, so that we might dig more nearer home; then returning we three dug steadily till nearly 1 o'clock, when we left off for lunch. The strangers were still at the camp. Johansen had dressed the old man's thumb, an operation which afforded him great pleasure and satisfaction, since it enlarged his importance in the eyes of all. We gave them tea and hard-bread and dried fish, and scraps of rice and corn meal, but the only thing they liked was the dried fish. Chipman, O'Neill, and I dug [sod] all the afternoon,[35] returning in the evening for supper. Our visitors left about 5 p.m., after examining everything around the camp. A light southeast breeze blew all day, favouring the *Alaska*, and clearing the ice out of the straits.

Monday, September 7th

Our visitors of yesterday came again this morning. Johansen and I met them as we drew near the turf-plot. As before they held up their hands and made the peace signs. I tried to photograph them doing it but was both too far away and had to lay the camera down to return their signs. They brought a number of things to barter — two pairs of boot soles made differently to those over west, some implements, and a few

Figure 115. Copper Eskimo visitors in summer attire at Bernard Harbour: Algiaq, Ayalit (with bandaged hand), Taptuna, Qamingoq, and Kallun, September 7, 1914. (Photo by D. Jenness, CMC Photo No. 36932.)

pieces of copper. We traded two empty coal-oil cans and a very small worn frying pan, an old pot, a few matches, and a half dozen needles for them, and they went away well satisfied after lunch. The women and children were 1/2 mile away on top of a ridge when we met the rest, but I told them to call them down, so the old man beckoned to them. One woman and child were left in camp, but two women and two children came, a little boy and a little girl. Both women were tattooed on the faces thus:

Figure 116. Tattoos on face of Eskimo woman, Bernard Harbour.

and from the wrists up to the elbows at least and perhaps higher. Here are the names of some of the party. The old man who had lost his thumb was Ayalit, a woman Imilguna; another man bore the name of Kaiyutaq (i.e., ladle). O'Neill and I dressed the old man's hand again. They left immediately after lunch, wishing to go out and hunt caribou [inland]. When the ice comes in (i.e., in the fall) they will come again they said. Johansen and I continued turf digging in the afternoon. We had a little amusement this morning. While we were standing with the Eskimos

Figure 117. The author applying first aid to Ayalit's injured right hand, Bernard Harbour, September 7, 1914. (Photo by J.J. O'Neill. GSC Photo No. 38682.)

waiting for the women and children to come up Johansen and I tried to shoot with their bows and arrows. Johansen set up his cap on top of his insect net and shot a hole right through the net. Many of the arrows have the shafts spliced,[36] the cement used being blood. Apparently the inten-

Figure 118. Spliced arrow.

Figure 119. The author cutting turf for the house at Bernard Harbour, September 7, 1914. (Photo by F. Johansen, CMC Photo No. 42234.)

tion is that they should break off in the wound. In the evening Chipman and I went out in the canoe after a flock of oldsquaw ducks, but I shot a seal on the way so we returned towing it back to camp. The light southeast wind of yesterday continued all day, though it fell almost to a dead calm in the evening. Chipman was cook today.

Chapter 19. Building the Base-camp Station

House construction commences — Taking depth soundings — Successful seal hunting — A gale damages the canoe — Sodding the house — Palaiyak shoots three caribou — Concern about the Alaska *— Another raging gale*

Tuesday, September 8th, 1914

Johansen [was] cook. Two of the dogs got loose in the night and ate up the caribou liver Palaiyak brought in the day before yesterday. Consequently we had no fried liver for breakfast. We made a start on the house today — the staff's house, for there are to be two, one for the four white men, Aarnout, Sweeney, Blue, and the cook to sleep and cook in, the other for the scientific staff. The three Eskimos will build a house for themselves as well, probably a snow-hut. Nearly all if not all the lumber (about 1000 feet) goes to make the staff's house, which must have a warm, dry, well-lighted structure to house its instruments and papers and to prosecute its work in undisturbed. It is to be 12 x 18 feet, with a large three-pane window in the south side and a small two-pane window in the north, the house being oriented north and south.[1] The lumber is poor, of various sizes, the heaviest being 2 x 4 inches, which we have to use for corner posts, joists, studs, and roof. Palaiyak took Denby, our largest dog, and went back this afternoon to bring in the last of the caribou meat, packing it on the dog's back in two bags hanging down on each side. The other day Denby carried about 70 lbs in this way. The caribou was a large buck with a splendid skin. In the evening Cox and I went out to look for seals and saw one which we failed to secure. The weather resembled yesterday, being beautifully fine and warm, with a light southeast breeze stirring the air. It veered to the north for about an hour, then shifted back again. There was a brilliant aurora in the evening, coloured at intervals and assuming every variety of shape. Caruso, a black dog, bit his rope and was wandering round this evening near Johansen's (the Professor's) tent. I went after him, and he deliberately walked out into the sea till the water was about 1 foot deep, then stood and looked at me. I waited for about 10 minutes expecting him to come out every moment finding the water cold, but he stayed there, so at last I sent Palaiyak to round him up with the canoe.

Wednesday, September 9th

Another beautifully fine day with the same southeast breeze. The warm weather has so dissipated and melted the ice that there is hardly any to obtain for water. Johansen did duty on the sod patch again, piling up the sods in a heap ready for transportation. I was cook, so was more or less occupied all day about the tent. Here is the day's menu. Breakfast, 7:30 a.m., cornmeal (cooked overnight in a fireless cooker), fried fish and corn bread (the last left over from yesterday), coffee. Lunch 1 p.m., six boiled ptarmigan and their soup, boiled potatoes, boiled rice, and a little cold apricots (dried apricots, boiled yesterday), baking-powder biscuits (rather hard), tea, and coffee. Dinner, fried caribou meat, fried onions, fried potatoes, a ptarmigan, and a quantity of soup left over from lunch, some cold rice (also a remainder), boiled dried prunes, baking-powder biscuits, and tea. The wind shifted to the west in the afternoon and freshened, the temperature falling at the same time. Palaiyak shot four seals in the afternoon, a hawk in the morning.

Thursday, September 10th

A fine day similar to yesterday, though it clouded over in the after-noon. O'Neill was cook; the rest of us worked on the house. We finished the framework today.[2] The sides are fully boarded and the floor, but the scantlings on the roof are about 4 inches apart; we had to leave some timber for bunks and table, and for the second house where the four white crew[3] are to live; the three Eskimos[4] will have to build a hut for themselves, probably a snow-hut, which can be erected in 2 hours by one man. Afterwards we started to pile sods round the walls, but were soon called away to supper.

Friday, September 11th

Cox [was] cook. Another all day's work on the house, piling sods. Chipman's part of the wall collapsed when it was two-thirds of the way up,[5] and the rest of us took warning and immediately began to increase the width. Palaiyak went out in the canoe for ice and shot three seals. One sank, but the other two he brought back. The wind shifted round to the north for a short time, then back to southeast. There was a fine aurora in the evening, with colours at intervals — green and red and white.

Saturday, September 12th

A moderate east breeze sprang up in the morning. In the afternoon rain fell for a short time, and the wind veered almost all round the com-pass. Chipman was cook; the rest of us continued piling sods round the walls and have now almost reached the top. We expect the *Alaska* back any day now. A bearded seal, *ugyuk*,[6] came into the harbour, and Palaiyak fired at it but missed. I felt rather seedy all day and thought an attack of malaria was impending, but it failed to develop luckily. Nevertheless we all retired early, about 8 p.m., vowing to keep tomorrow (Sunday) a holiday, after 6 days of hard work.

Sunday, September 13th

A strong westerly wind blew for some hours during the night but died away in the morning, and a moderate east breeze took its place. Johansen was cook and turned out at 7 a.m., but breakfast was not ready till 12. We ragged him very badly over it,[7] but he took it well. Cox and Palaiyak went out in a launch to get ice.[8] Seals were very numerous, they said, but they had no luck with their guns. About 2 p.m. the same two and myself went round in the launch to the deserted Eskimo settlement and sounded the two entrances on either side of an island.[9] One was very shallow, the

Figure 120. Partly constructed house at Bernard Harbour, September 11, 1914. Two layers of sod supply insulation and support. (Photo by K.G. Chipman, CMC Photo No. 43261.)

other deep, with a small low bight behind a rocky point where even a large vessel like the *Alaska* could shelter. We shot three seals (Palaiyak two and Cox one) and four oldsquaw ducks at the cost of some 20 cartridges. The sun was warm enough, but the air on the water was rather cold. The launch resembled a slaughter house on the way back. We have shot 10 seals since the *Alaska* left (Palaiyak eight, Cox and I each one). Palaiyak promises to be a valuable adjunct to the Expedition. He is a nice lad and a good hunter, though not so good as the other two Eskimos (Añutisiak (Eikie) and Mike) on a boat. Johansen gave us a combined dinner and supper at 7 p.m. Chipman worked out a longitude calculation during the day and put us in almost 142° W,[10] about 1 1/2° E of where we should be according to Rae's[11] map of this region. However, Chipman's calculation was based on one observation from one chronometer only, and the latter may very likely have suffered in the rating during the voyage from Herschel Island. We had a gramophone concert after supper and retired early.

Monday, September 14th

I was cook, so turned out before 6 a.m. and cooked cornmeal and fried a seal liver. There was a light northerly breeze, but it changed to the west during the morning. The change cleared the atmosphere, which had been very foggy, but the sky was overcast all day, and the wind increased in strength. The others continued work on the house.[12] The temperature was fairly low — about 33° F.

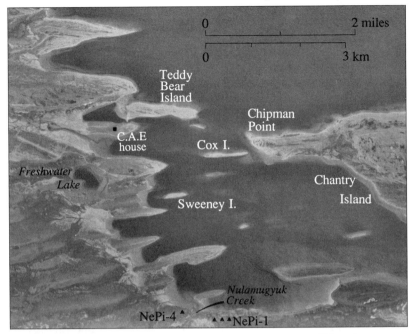

Figure 121. Aerial view of Bernard Harbour showing site of C.A.E. building, the narrow entrance to the harbour, the small lake from which fresh water was obtained, and the fishing creek (Nulahugyuk Creek) (RCAF Airphoto No. A19211-42). The DEW-line runway, roads, and huts, built in the 1950s and now abandoned, are located on the peninsula and ridge between the small lake and the C.A.E. headquarters. The location of Dorset culture tent-ring sites Bernard Harbour No. 1 (NePi-1) and No.2 (NePi-4) near the mouth of Nulahugyuk Creek is from Taylor (1972).

Tuesday, September 15th

The wind increased during the night, and the sea was a little lumpy when we went ashore in the canoe for breakfast. It became much worse in the afternoon. The canoe was lying on the beach, and the wind picked it up and carried it helter skelter over the rocks and boulders, with O'Neill chasing after it at full speed. It was badly damaged, but Cox and Chipman patched it a little. O'Neill was cook, and the rest of us as usual worked on the house. It was too stormy to venture out to the *North Star* to sleep, though we were very anxious about her, for she was tossing a good deal. I turned in to Johansen's tent, Cox and Palaiyak into one the Dr. [Anderson] set up for himself. We had to go round the tents and caches and tighten ropes and heap up boulders to protect things from the fury of the gale. The *Alaska*, if she is not in shelter, must be having a very bad time.[13]

Wednesday, September 16th

The gale raged all night,[14] but diminished a great deal during the day. Cox, Chipman, and O'Neill (the last steering) went out in the canoe to the *North Star* about 2 p.m. and bailed out the launch, which was trailing astern, half full of water. Cox set the engine going and, steaming up on the anchor which was down (a patent anchor, not very secure), they dropped a second and heavier anchor of the common type. We finished sodding the roof and three of the walls today of the house, while Cox was cooking. The front of the house we closed with a large tarpaulin. Despite the two windows, one on each side, it is very dark within, though it promises to be warm. There are several faults in construction. One wall has sagged in a great deal, and the whole building has a twist forward. We all slept ashore again, for the weather was still very stormy.

Thursday, September 17th

Still another stormy day, though the fury of the gale was over. The wind shifted a little to the south. While Chipman cooked, Cox and Palaiyak went about a mile inland to a stream to obtain some water, for there is not a keg of ice in sight save two or three some distance out by an island, which the storm washed in.[15] O'Neill and I covered the walls with white canvas and added three or four struts where the frame seemed weakest. Cox fitted in the door and the stove-pipe so that Chipman was able to transfer the stove and cooking material to the new home in the afternoon and give us our first meal there in the evening. We celebrated the occasion with a cigar all round. Cox discovered a fine comet[16] in the evening a little below B[eta] Ursa Major thus:

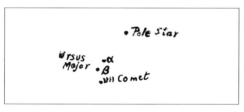

Figure 122. Appearance of the comet Delavan on September 17, 1914.

from the direction of the tail, which was plainly visible to the naked eye for some distance (10°?) it is travelling southwest. The northern lights were very brilliant, especially in the south. The wind was still fairly strong when we turned in for the night, but the sky was clear and the stars bright. We all slept on shore again,[17] and probably shall always do so henceforth. Snow fell more or less during most of the day.

Friday, September 18th

Johansen [was] cook — breakfast 9 o'clock, dinner 2:30 p.m., supper 7 p.m. The caribou meat is becoming 'high', the livers of those seals that have not been cut up are no longer fit to eat, and possibly the flesh itself is in the same condition, so our stock of meat is running low. The nets too are disinclined to furnish any fish at present. O'Neill and I set up all the bunks today. I chose one, which could conveniently be used by the others as a seat or lounge when I am away, as I hope to be most of the winter; Dr. Anderson's was arranged for in the plan, and the others drew lots for theirs. We moved our sleeping skins and bags over [from the

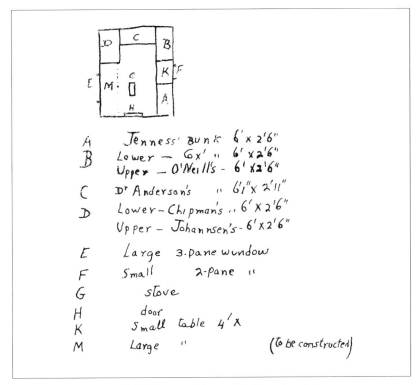

A   Jenness' Bunk   6' x 2'6"

B   Lower — 6x' "   6' x 2'6"
       Upper — O'Neill's - 6' x 2'6"

C   Dr Anderson's   " 6'1"x 2'11"

D   Lower - Chipman's " 6' x 2'6"
       Upper — Johannsen's - 6'x2'6"

E   Large   3-pane window

F   Small   2-pane   "

G   stove

H   door
K   Small table 4' x

M   Large   "   (to be constructed)

Figure 123. Floor plan, 12' X 16' house at Bernard Harbour, door facing east.

tents], all save Johansen, glad to settle down in our permanent quarters at last. Palaiyak for the time being occupies Dr. Anderson's bunk, in front of which an impromptu table is used for meals. The door is in place, but the front is covered with a tarpaulin only, though all the rest of the building is boarded and surrounded with sods. We have used nearly all the available timber and have to leave most of the rest for the other house. One of the rafters was found to be badly cracked, and the wall where the large window fits in was caving in owing to faulty construction and weak timber; we have been obliged to patch it up and support it with a strut. The wind was still strong all day, blowing from the south. The temperature too was low, rising from 31° at 8 a.m. to 32° at 9 a.m. and later 33°; it never rose above this last but dropped again in the afternoon. There is still no sign of the *Alaska*. The stars were shining and the comet plainly visible at 9:30 p.m., but an hour later the sky had clouded over.

Saturday, September 19th

A wretched day, for a moderately strong west wind brought snow and drift. It sprang up in the night and by morning the hillsides were white. The temperature remained in the neighbourhood of the freezing point all day, consequently little work was done outside. I was cook so naturally stayed indoors all the time. Incidentally, however, I set up a shelf for my books and drove in one or two nails for pegs. The outside board, which bounds my bunk, I have fitted so that it simply slides in and out of place and can, therefore, be readily removed when I leave and the bunk becomes a settee. Cox and O'Neill tacked a strip of calico along the edge of the roof on one side, and Cox and Chipman made the large table, which is set under the window (M [on Fig. 123]). In the evening we made a party at bridge.[18]

Sunday, September 20th

Another day of falling snow, though it left off for a time in the afternoon. O'Neill was cook; the rest of us lounged about most of the morning fixing shelves, reading, and doing odd jobs. Palaiyak saw a bearded seal about 10:30 a.m., and he and I went off in the canoe in pursuit while Chipman and Johansen in different directions went after ptarmigan. Palaiyak shot a hair seal but had no luck with the bearded one, though he put in six shots at it and hit it the last time. It kept jumping up out of the water like a porpoise near the boat, so that one had to be very quick to get in a shot at all. We saw some eider ducks and oldsquaws and a loon; three or four flocks of ptarmigan flew over the water southeast across the bay. Their colour is changing again to white to match the snow. Our seal was a very large one — too heavy to pull into the canoe, which was besides very leaky owing to its recent mishap in the gale [Sept. 15]. It was very slow laborious work paddling along with the seal dragging astern and a slight head wind, so that finally we had to put in to the nearest point of the shore, empty the water out of the canoe, which was becoming extremely uncomfortable, put the seal inside, and start out afresh, this time with more success. Chipman returned for dinner with one ptarmigan, Johansen with none. In the afternoon I cleaned my two guns, then Cox and I brought our things ashore from the *North Star*. The temperature did not rise above 33° all day.

Monday, September 21st

The dogs were rather troublesome in the night, for four of them broke loose. We have only three or four chains, and they are very weak (save one); the other dogs are tied with rope, which some of them succeed in breaking or else bite it through. They ate Chipman's ptarmigan and some seal meat, which was exposed. Cox was cook for the day. Palaiyak and I dug a trench on each side of the house to carry away the drainage next spring; it is easier to make now than when the ground is covered with a couple of feet of snow. O'Neill, Chipman, and Johansen made a small store or cache of the distillate and gasoline cases arranged in a hollow square, inside which they put some barrels of vinegar, the dead seals, and a few miscellaneous things, covering the whole with a tarpaulin. The wind was west all the morning but changed to east shortly after noon and freshened, making the temperature drop from 34° to 33° and bringing a slight fall of snow. About the middle of the afternoon it changed again to the west. One of the dogs gave birth to eight pups today, but three died. We put them with the mother in a tent for shelter. The comet was visible this evening at odd moments, for the sky was flecked with clouds.

Tuesday, September 22nd

A moderate east wind blew all day. Chipman was cook. Palaiyak and I visited the two fish-nets in the morning, then went out in the canoe to look for seals. One large bearded seal came within range, but Palaiyak's shot just missed. In the afternoon I strolled out to look for ptarmigan but saw nothing. Palaiyak was sealing, with equal ill-success. The others remained indoors fixing shelves, instruments, etc. The temperature was about the freezing point all day, and a little snow fell. From the hills behind no ice is visible out to sea; it is extraordinary where all the ice has gone that was here when we came.

Wednesday, September 23rd

Another day with a moderate east wind. Johansen was cook, but wanted to go ptarmigan hunting so Chipman took his place after breakfast.[19] Cox was fixing the wind gauge, O'Neill working at his geology. I did a little sewing in the morning then in the afternoon went [4 miles] east to the fishing settlement to see if there were any fish in the trap. The creek, however, was entirely frozen over, save for a narrow channel in the middle where the current keeps the water from freezing. Returning I shot a ptarmigan, the only one I saw. Johansen saw none, but discovered an old settlement to the west and a little driftwood on the beach. Palaiyak, however, had gone caribou hunting and shot three, a female and two fawns. We were just out of meat,[20] for our 20 dogs eat about a small seal a day. The evening was cold and cloudy.

Thursday, September 24th

Chipman, Cox, O'Neill, and Palaiyak with two dogs went off after breakfast to bring in the caribou Palaiyak shot. A moderate east wind was blowing, but no snow fell. They shot five ptarmigan, and Johansen, who went out hunting in the morning, got one; Chipman shot also an eider duck, and another was caught in the fish-net; further, the fish-net contained two fish, so the day was fruitful in game. Foxes had been eating the deer, though, and the ground was strewn with their tracks. They are poor eating now — no good at all, Palaiyak says. I was cook and tried to make bread, with magic yeast, and a fruit pie. The bread would not rise, but is edible; the pie cooked beautifully on top, but the paste below was a little thick and was a little doughy. No sign of the *Alaska*. We are wondering if she suffered some damage in the recent gale, or if she has gone to Herschel Island, though even in the latter case she should have returned long since unless she is blocked by ice.[21] Yet the straits here are entirely free of ice.[22] The wind freshened in the evening, and the weather outside was raw and unpleasant.

Friday, September 25th

The morning broke calm and still, with a bright warm sun thawing the snow on the ground. After breakfast (O'Neill cook), Cox, Palaiyak, and I pulled up the larger anchor [and] hoisted the sails on the *North Star* to dry them. Then while Cox was fixing up the engine on the small launch, which had been swamped in the recent storm, and Johansen and Chipman were piling up the sods we cut some time back, Palaiyak and I went sealing in the canoe. Palaiyak shot two seals and I an oldsquaw duck. An easterly breeze sprang up soon afterwards, and the sails on the *North Star* had to be lowered. The battery of the launch's engine was unsatisfactory, so we had to abandon the idea of running round the coast a little way to the west where Johansen had piled up a few sticks of driftwood. I walked round, however, for there are remains of an old settlement there, stone circles for tents,[23] and stone fireplaces. The east wind grew stronger and stronger until by evening it was blowing a violent gale. The barometer had gone down steadily, and the weather was altogether ominous.

Saturday, September 26th

The gale raged furiously all night but sensibly diminished from daylight on until for a brief interval at noon it was dead calm. Then a south breeze sprang up, which later in the afternoon veered to the west. The driving rain showers of the night and early morning gave place to bright sunshine, a brilliant sunset, and a bright starlit night with the comet in full view. It had travelled a considerable distance and its tail streamed

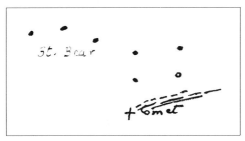

Figure 124. New location of the comet Delavan. Compare also diary entries for Sept. 17, Oct. 15, and Nov. 13.

behind much further than we had ever seen it before — right to the other side of the pointers,[24] visible to the naked eye. Cox was cook. Johansen and O'Neill went biologizing, ptarmigan hunting, and fossil collecting. Johansen found two fossils early in the morning, not in place, unfortunately, yet of great importance, for O'Neill, who was working at them all the morning, came to the conclusion that they belong to the Ordovician Period, and hitherto this region had been doubtfully assigned to either [the] Ordovician or Silurian [Period]. In the afternoon O'Neill found another fossil, which he has not yet examined. Johansen discovered two or three spiders, weavils, a butterfly grub, and one or two other things. Chipman was ransacking boxes in the morning;[25] in the afternoon he and Palaiyak went sealing without success. I spent the day developing photographs, four rolls of 10 films each; about 50% turned out well, about 60 or 65 [% are] printable. We made up a bridge party in the evening, as usual on Saturday's. Cox is our best cook. He made a meat pie and fish rolls for dinner, two fruit pies, and one or two turnovers for supper today, besides biscuits etc.

Chapter 20. Serious Trading Commences

Another Eskimo visit — Visit to the Eskimo camp — Tattoos and hair style — Trading for Copper Eskimo implements — More Eskimo visits — Serving as camp spokesman — Efforts to curb the Eskimo visits — Thoughts of forming search party to seek Alaska *personnel — Construction of food cache — The Abercrombie tent*

Sunday, September 27th, 1914

A moderately strong southwest wind was blowing this morning, which changed in the afternoon to west and increased somewhat in the evening. O'Neill and Johansen went geologizing and 'bug'- hunting in the morning. I was attending to my photographs, then searched out the sewing-machine and with Palaiyak's aid repaired my snowshirt, which was rent in several places. Johansen returned for dinner with a squirrel, which Snap, one of our dogs which is Johansen's special companion, had caught and killed. Cox was busy at odd jobs all the morning while Chipman cooked. I was putting the finishing touches on my snowshirt in the afternoon when our Eskimo friends turned up, Ayalit, Kamiñuaruk, Aksiatak, Anauyuk, the boy Taptuna, and a woman who had not visited us before, Kamiñuaruk's wife Kalyutarun, carrying her baby girl Oqomik on her back. Aksiatak and Anauyuk belonged to the first party of Eskimos who had visited us.[1] On this occasion they came about 3/4 hour after the rest. None of them showed any hesitation in approaching, though they were surprised at the sight of the house, which was not begun when they were last here. We took them inside and they were still more surprised. Chipman boiled some seal meat for them. Eskimos put their seal meat either in cold water and bring it to a boil or into hot or boiling water directly. Nor are they particular about its being fully cooked; often they take it out when the water has just reached a boil. The woman asked for a knife and cut up the meat for them and laid it on a plate, then they all set to. Soon after they had finished Aksiatak and Anauyuk appeared, peering in through the window, for they could not find the entrance. Kamiñuaruk, a youngish man, who seemed to be something of a humorist, shouted to them to climb on to the roof and come down the stove-pipe, then turned round to us and laughed heartily. I measured all the adults — full head and face measurements and stature.[2] They said Stefansson had measured them previously, though not so fully. Body measurements are impracticable at this time. They were anxious to return home before dark, as they had been on the previous occasion. We gave the woman Chipman's boots and a pair of soles we had already bought from them for her to sew on, together with a needle and some sinew. Ayalit's hand appears to be healing — he has not removed the dressing O'Neill and I put on it, but can now move his last three fingers with ease. He was much amused with one of the gramophone records in which the time was particularly prominent and gave us an impromptu sort of dance to accompany it. Kamiñuaruk brought a foxskin to sell and Taptuna an ermine skin; they were much surprised when we told them we did not desire any skins, for Joe Bernard had traded in them very largely. When they returned Palaiyak and I went with them. They are living in two skin tents up the valley just beyond our sod pile, about 1/2 mile from our house. Some of them were already in bed, sleeping naked, as far as I could see, under deerskins; at least one person had no upper garment, and the boy Taptuna (he is about 12) stripped stark [naked] as soon as we reached their camp and turned in. Palaiyak and I sat and talked to them for some time, and our visitors told those who had not come [to our camp] what had happened. Amongst other things they told about the window, which they thought was ice until we told them otherwise. They gave us raw fish soaked in seal oil to eat, and some dried fish; the first I did not care for, but the second was good. By the way, Anauyuk had helped himself to some of our biscuits and enjoyed them immensely. They told us they were all *Noahogmirmiut*,[3] which is apparently Stefansson's *Noahominmiut*.[4] I am not sure, however, whether it should not be spelt *Noahogmiñmiut*, which would be nearer Stefansson's term. Their sleds they had cached at a lake not far away. Kalyutarun was tattooed like the other two women who had visited us last time, though the cheek lines and the lines from the eyes were not quite so long; I am not certain either whether she had any marks on her forehead.[5] Her wrists were encircled (?) with lines which extended only

Figure 125. Face tattoo of Kalyutarun.

half way up the forearm, whereas in at least one of the other women they extended to the elbow. Apparently it is the fashion here for the men to wear the hair on the crown close-cut and to eradicate the beard from the sides of the face, if not altogether, while the women part their hair in the middle. Their tent was oval in shape, supported by side sticks running up to a ridge pole to which they were tied with seal or deerskin — usually the former. One of the skins of the tent I was in was a bearded sealskin, the rest deerskin. The woman lit the lamp for us — a piece of blubber set in the small frying pan that we had traded with them. Kalyutarun carried her baby[6] naked on her back, in the same manner as the western Eskimo; she had peaks on the shoulders of her *atigi*, which we had not noticed on the other woman. Ayalit wore his sealskin coat above his deerskin one, and none of them objected to eating seal meat; in fact they especially commented on it when they returned. These people wear very short mittens of deerskin with the fur outside, fitting fairly tightly round the wrist.

The women too have very short sleeves on their coats. Both on this occasion and previously the women carried everything back to their camp — foxskin, pots, etc., while the men had only their weapons.

Monday, September 28th

A light west wind was blowing all day, and the weather was fine, albeit overcast and cold. The temperature last night was down to 28° and 28° again this afternoon. A little progress was made in arranging the shelves, and the camp generally. A staging was erected on which the electric wind gauge was set and connected by a long wire to the house where the record in miles is given on a revolving drum. The Eskimos came down again this morning to trade, and I bought a considerable number of specimens from them, besides measuring three women who had not come down yesterday. The youngest woman Niaq was tattooed from the elbows to the first joint of the fingers, as illustrated:

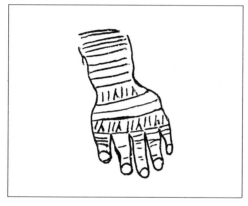

Figure 126. Niaq's hand.[7]

it did not extend, however, to the inside of the wrists and arms. The other women were similarly tattooed, but only halfway to the elbow — at least in one case and I think in the other two also. All had the same tattooing on the face,[8] only in the case of one of the elder women the lines on the cheeks and from the eyes were shorter. Consequently she had only two 'arrows' or 'Y's' beside each eye. The tattooing is done with a needle, they said, but I omitted to ask what the dye came from; the Mackenzie natives use lamp black (*utkusium pauñanik* (from *paumik*)).[9]

Trading was a very confusing and tedious task. Here are the prices as far as I recall them:

1 large enamel pot	- 1 large stone pot
1 small enamel dish	- 1 very small stone pot, 1 bone needle case
about 15 matches	- 5 skewers of bone
1 thimble	- a woman's knife and its sharpener
1 small worn frying pan	- 1 large musk-ox ladle, 1 woman's knife

For two other ladles and sundry skewers, [and] two ermine skins and a foxskin, I paid a thimble, some needles, and a few matches;

1 fox-trap (in two cases)	- 1 dressed sealskin
1 lard can	- 1 pair sealskin soles and
	1 pair sealskin overshoes
20 .303 W[inchester] cartridges[10]	- 6 copper-headed arrows
	and 2 sealing'indicators'
	on bobs.[11]

We treated them to some gramophone music. They were greatly taken with a recitation — Hamlet's soliloquy. Johansen cooked them a pot of seal meat, which they ate in one of the tents while we had our dinner, not by their choice, for they wanted to eat in the house. One of the women — rather elderly — seemed a motherly little person, and a little boy, Naqitoq, about 6 years old, was quite a charming child. They returned to their tents after dinner and I visited them later. They were eating dried fish and rank seal blubber and invited me to share — I partook of the former but not of the latter. O'Neill, who appeared a little later, declined altogether. The fish had been caught in a lake this spring (or summer?) with hooks and dried. O'Neill showed them his Brunton compass, and they were immensely amused at the sight of their reflections in the mirror. One man, Qamiñgoq [Kamiñuaruk], the humourist of yesterday, sustained his character today by grinning into the mirror exclaiming "Who is this?" "What is his name" etc., keeping the others in a perpetual state of laughter. O'Neill then made the needle revolve following his pocketknife. Aksiatak then tried to do the same using his finger, making everyone laugh when he failed. It was most amusing in the house to see Kamiñuaruk [Qamiñgoq] and Anauyuk sitting facing Chipman and jabbering away at him both at the same time —"You are good people — thank you — the seal meat was good" etc. etc. — while Chipman, who did not understand a word (save perhaps the first two) would reply "You bet your life" and one or two similar phrases, then all would join in roars of laughter. There was a fine auroral arch this evening at 10:30, with streamers stretching upwards from it. It lay in the southern hemisphere and ran from west to east.

Tuesday, September 29th

I was cook and had a busy time, for almost the whole body of the Eskimos came down from the camp — a good round dozen of them. My attentions were divided between trading and cooking, somewhat to the detriment of both. However, the Eskimos received a large pot-full of seal meat and two batches of *mukpaurat*, and we fared not unsatisfactory, so all went well. The old man Ayallik [Ayalit] had a little skin bag suspended on his chest by a cord round the neck. I asked him what was inside and he said 'his thumb' — the one the brown bear tore off. I wonder if there is some magical reason for his wearing it. His wife Kaumaq is a motherly little woman, whom we all liked. Niaq and her husband AXiatak are never backward in coming forward. He seems to be the most intelligent of the men and alone possesses a .30-30 Winchester, obtained from Joe Bernard [in 1912 or 1913]. He has kept it in admirable condition. I traded one box of .30-30 ammunition (20 rounds) for six copper-pointed arrows and two seal 'indicators' yesterday. Niaq (the nickname that we have given her is a paraphrase of 'birdseed') took it into her head to help me make *mukpaurat* and showed no little ability in the art. Palaiyak gave the boy Taptuna a cigarette to smoke, and his choking caused us much amusement. The Eskimos helped themselves to sugar etc., which they appreciate very much. I gave Niaq a small lump of salt, which she took for sugar and popped into her mouth at once. However, she swallowed it — though very slowly — she was quite a 'sport' over it. She enjoyed lard though and said a small piece of bacon fat was 'good', though I doubt her liking it. Palaiyak said they ate the liver and kidneys of a seal raw — it was not frozen or even dried. She drew several figures for me — a man, a woman, myself, foxes, etc.; generally she began at the shoulder or the foot and moved the pencil indifferently towards and away from her. The drawing of the woman was quite well executed.[12] Kalyutaryuk's baby Oqomiq was stark naked — she is only a few months old[13] and was carried on her mother's back in the same way as among the western Eskimo — but she wore deerskin socks with an outside pair of squirrel skin — the fur of the squirrel being outside and long. The Eskimos brought two pups with them which they wished to sell. Not content with one refusal they persisted again and again all day long. As far as I can remember I made the following trades:

1 small enamel bowl	- 1 fire-making apparatus complete, 1 needle case, a copper needle and a marrow spoon
1 tiny frying pan	- 1 fire-making apparatus
1 small file (2 cases)	- a horn quiver handle (etched) and a sinew-twister
1 small file	- a sinew fishing line, rod and sundry fishhooks, hook matches etc. — for other fishing outfits, a ladle and miscellaneous small implements (4 copper needles, 2 bone thimbles etc.)
1 coffee tin (empty)	- 1 fishing outfit

Snow fell most of the day and the temperature reached a minimum of 26°. There was a peculiar aurora for a few minutes in the evening — a perfectly straight narrow 'beam' of white light running from near the northwest horizon beyond the zenith.

Wednesday, September 30th

The Eskimos came again today when O'Neill was cook. They are be-coming a nuisance, and threaten to eat us out of house and home. We gave them some dry deer meat, distinctly smelly,[14] and some hard-bread. Palaiyak even refused the former, yet they seemed to like it. Johansen went ptarmigan hunting and specimen collecting this morning. He bought a rock ptarmigan from one of the Eskimos — price a safety pin. The rock ptarmigan can be readily distinguished from the willow ptarmi-gan — which is commoner along the coast — by the black streak which runs from the eye to the bill. Palaiyak and I went out sealing in the canoe, but the weather was not propitious — an easterly wind mod-erately strong and a choppy sea — so we did not go far. However, we visited one of the fish-nets and obtained a salmon trout weighing about 6 lbs. An ice keg was caught in the net and we had some trouble in free-ing it. Niaq stitched up my sheepskin mittens this morning. I opened my sewing kit and she craned her head over my shoulder to look. Taking a needle from the case I asked her "Is it a good 'one'?" "Yes, it is," she said. Then I took a piece of sinew and repeated the question, receiving the same answer. Then I told her to go ahead and patch my mittens. The change on her face was most amusing — I think she was expecting me to give them to her. However, she set to and mended them all right, for which I gave her the needle. In the afternoon Kalyutaryuk brought a pair of *ugyuk* boot soles to sell. I told her I would buy them if she sewed them on to my boots, which she did, both quickly and neatly. The payment — soles and sewing — was a large worn file — with which she was more than content. At the same time Niaq was set to put a large patch in my deerskin trousers, and later a much larger patch in O'Neill's. This oc-cupied her all the afternoon, and she received in return a tiny frying pan and one-third of a packet of matches (about 20) — a very high payment, they seemed to think, though she begged for the remainder of the fawn-skin that had been used to repair the trousers — unsuccessfully.[15] Both women were very keen to be given more work, but they are a great nuisance just now. I told them that in the winter "when the ice comes" we shall have more work for them to do, and they went away very con-tent. Their sewing was well done, in about half [the] time an ordinary western [Eskimo] woman takes. The method was exactly the same, though costume and footgear here are quite different. The others have left me to do all the trading because most of the things brought in are ethnological specimens; so when the Eskimos offer them anything they refer them to me — which is very decent on their part; the same applies too with the feeding and treatment of the Eskimos, Chipman asks what I think best to be done. Things could be made very awkward for me by a less decent lot of men; as it is they go out of their way to help me and put up with a great deal of annoyance and inconvenience. Niaq was having her head cleaned by Anauyuk this morning — the trophies furnishing him an ample repast. We gave the Eskimos a good hint that we were tired of them — told them we were out of seal meat — were going to

work all day tomorrow etc.[16] They have made free use of our bunks —
mine especially, and we all expect a host of parasitic guests as a result.
The weather was fine nearly all day though cloudy, and the wind cold.
Towards evening it snowed for a short time, and the wind changed to
southeast. The maximum temperature was 36°.

Thursday, October 1st

A dull cloudy day, with snow falling much of the time. The temperature was above freezing in the morning and the air calm, so that the
weather seemed quite mild, but a light west wind sprang up towards
noon, and the temperature fell to freezing. The Eskimos again came
down in force — 12 of them — and pottered about continually in our
way. I refused to buy any more specimens, and only took a pair of boot
soles for which I paid a fathom of white drilling. They are becoming perfect parasites, and we concluded that we should have to check them, so
Cox, who was cook, gave them rather little to eat, and from dinner time
on we kept them out of the house. This last course seemed less harsh because O'Neill and I were boarding up the front and lining it with heavy
drilling in preparation for the winter. It was far less pleasant pottering
around outside than sitting on our bunks and lounging round the fire, so
our visitors soon departed. Some ptarmigan appeared near the house, and
Chipman and Johansen secured ten. We have little hope of the *Alaska*
appearing now, and think of sending a search party along the coast as far
as C[ape] Lyon or C[ape] Parry as soon as the weather is cold enough for
sledding. Probably Chipman and Cox will go, for they can do a little
topographical work on the way. We have arranged to take week and
week in the cooking, Cox beginning. Johansen was strongly opposed to
it,[17] but the rest of us overruled him. Chipman, Palaiyak, and Johansen
set about constructing the food-cache against the front of the house.[18] It
will be 12 feet square, covered with a tarpaulin, so that if Dr. Anderson
and two or three others come along in the winter a small tent can be
erected inside.[19] Meteorological observations began today. The wind
gauge can be read in the house. Connected with a small lamp, it gives a
light; if the wind is travelling at 15 miles per hour the spark appears in
4 minutes, if 8 miles in 7 1/2 minutes. By testing each of four wires for a
spark (the wires are marked N, S, E, and W) the direction of the wind
can be ascertained. Cox is our engineer, mechanic, and head cook. He
gave us a fine pudding tonight, with white sauce.

Friday, October 2nd

Niaq and Anauyuk appeared before 7 a.m. when Cox alone was
dressed and lighting the fire. They said the rest had gone away to a lake[20]
and that they would follow as soon as they had eaten (with us). She
brought a pair of boot soles, for which I paid her a plate. Cox gave them
something to eat, then when we had all finished breakfast, a slapjack
each and a portion that was remaining of a salmon trout to take back with
them. I noticed then and on two earlier occasions as well that they put

some aside for the child or wife or husband of the family, if that person is not present. These Eskimos have a fine taste for *mukpaurat*, which name they learnt from Natkusiak.[21] These two left then; they will not return until the ice comes, when they will bring their sleds. Palaiyak went sealing in the kayak, and secured a seal and a ptarmigan. The rest of us (save Cox the cook) set to work to build the food-cache against the front of the house in the form of a hollow square, the house front forming one side. This took us all day, and even now we have not quite finished. I found time to get out an Abercrombie tent and set it up. It is peculiar in shape — requiring four sticks arranged in pairs, 'A'-shape on the out-

Figure 127. Abercrombie tent.

side, the apices being separated by an interval of about 2 feet, while the tent bellies out behind. It has an oval door (a 'mouth') with mosquito netting attached, two windows (also with mosquito netting) in the back, and the floor sewn on. It is really a summer tent, weighing 13 1/2 lbs without the four bamboo poles. This one needs some adjustments, which I shall try and make tomorrow. Also Palaiyak and I tested four primus stoves — two seem fairly good, one poor, and one useless. A light east wind blew all day. The temp[erature] at 8 a.m. was 28°, at 5 p.m. 33° F. Snow fell during most of the day. The evening was marked by a misty rain.

Chapter 21. Preparations for Winter

Favourite dog killed — Getting firewood and seals — Sled repairs — Snow arrival — Cigars for all — Lighting system fails to work — Comet farther southwest — Tent unsatisfactory — Freezing of the straits — Search for phonographs and records — Testing dog team — Waiting for freeze-up — Preparations for caching trip to west

Saturday, October 3rd, 1914

Chipman, O'Neill, and Johansen (the 'Professor' or Frits) continued to build up the grub store in the morning while I fixed guy ropes etc. on my tent. Palaiyak went out in the canoe sealing and secured six, one a small bearded seal. The weather was calm and mild all the morning, but a fresh east wind sprang up in the afternoon, so that I had to pile snow round the flaps of my tent. The store was covered with tarpaulins in the afternoon, so that it now forms a covered-in passage to the house, with an entrance at the north side. With Palaiyak's assistance I made three dog chains in the afternoon, using the chains from fox-traps. Leader, my dog, was running loose, so I chained him up at once. We played bridge in the evening, as usual on Saturdays. A strong east wind was blowing when we turned in.

Sunday, October 4th

There was a dog-fight in the night — about 3 a.m., and when I turned out to stop it there were six dogs piled on top of Leader — I roused Cox and we tied them all up again — save Leader, who was in a bad way. His belly had been torn open and the intestines were all hanging out. We carried him inside and woke Chipman, who stitched up the wound, but the poor dog died before day-break. This is the second dog lost here — Pudding was killed in a fight 2 days after the *Alaska* arrived. Both Leader and Pudding were excellent dogs; Leader was the dog I had all last winter. He was much attached to me, and used to go half mad with delight whenever I approached him. I was counting on him for my leader this winter also. Being Sunday we spent a quiet morning indoors; I made two more dog chains. In the afternoon Palaiyak and Chipman went sealing, and I strolled inland to look for ptarmigan; none of us had any success. The east wind almost died away by noon, and the temperature was above freezing. The snow has melted from the land altogether in many places. My tent withstood last night's blow satisfactorily. It is very light — a fine summer tent — but will be rather cold in winter.

Monday, October 5th

Chipman and Palaiyak went off in the canoe after seals and to gather up some wood on an island a mile or two out. They returned about 5 p.m. with four hair seals and a hare (a Keewatin hare). There was about a month's supply of wood on the island, which they stacked up.[1] O'Neill went fossilizing with considerable success; Johansen went west to look for wood and found a little, which he stacked up; also he shot two ptarmigan. I spent the day fixing up the 'racing' sled, which I expect to use this winter, then began on one of the other sleds, one which Aarnout was repairing but did not finish.[2] All the sleds require overhauling, and one or two considerable repairs. Cox is still cook; his week finishes on Thursday when I take his place. A west wind sprang up during the day and was blowing quite fresh in the evening. The temperature at noon was 37° F. Really the weather is wonderful for so late in the year. I expect the break will be sudden and sharp.

Tuesday, October 6th

A fine day, not at all cold. With Palaiyak's assistance I fixed up another sled today, then turned cook while Cox and Chipman in the launch went over to one of the islands for wood. O'Neill was fossilizing again and Johansen biologizing, but in the afternoon they put more sods round the house where it had subsided a little. Chipman and Cox brought back a good load with them, and there is still more to come — enough for about 2 months, they said, with a single stove such as we are using. Following a recipe of Cox's I made a pudding, which turned out a success. We shall all be cooks before the winter is out. Palaiyak took the canoe in the afternoon and secured two seals — both hair seals, though one was very large.[3]

Wednesday, October 7th

Palaiyak and I fixed up another sled today — the heavy Nome sled, which had been rather badly damaged. Johansen went out for ptarmigan unsuccessfully. A west wind sprang up and the atmosphere was chilly. Chipman and O'Neill went off in the launch for another load of firewood, while Cox remained to cook. This is his last day — tomorrow my week begins; instead of turning out 7:30 - 8 a.m. I must get up at 6. We are working through Duffy's and Matt Andreasen's gramophone records — a miserable lot. Snow fell in the evening.

Thursday, October 8th

The ground was white everywhere this morning with snow. A west wind was blowing, but it ceased to snow, so Johansen went west again to look for biological specimens and for wood. He returned quickly, however, with the news that he had seen a fresh caribou track nearby only about 1/4 hour old. Palaiyak immediately set out in pursuit, and returned about 5 p.m. empty-handed. He had followed the tracks for some miles, then it began to snow and drift so he returned. The caribou swam two bays, he said, then struck inland to a large lake (where Palaiyak had previously shot his caribou); he believes it is browsing somewhere in the neighbourhood. He noticed a wolf's track also; we hope it does not discover the caribou and run it down or drive it away. All the lakes inland in the neighbourhood are frozen. Cox made a switch-board for the wind gauge so that we can more readily tell the direction, then he made some

Figure 128. Completed house and storage area, Bernard Harbour, with schooner *North Star* in the harbour beyond. Viewed from the south, Oct. 5, 1914. (Photograph by F. Johansen, CMC Photo No. 42235.)

dog chains. It snowed all the evening and a moderately strong west wind blew, while the temperature about 6 p.m. was 27° F. We have given up all hope of seeing the *Alaska* this fall, and speculate as to what has befallen her.[4] We are comfortable enough — with a good house and plenty of provisions,[5] and enough fuel for a year; the only difficulty is the dog-feed, and we have about 3 weeks supply of that.[6]

Friday, October 9th

A moderate west wind blew all day. Johansen went out to look for ptarmigan — unsuccessfully. O'Neill fossilized with better fortune. Chipman, Cox, and Palaiyak went out in the launch to the island to bring in more wood, but the sea was too rough to allow them to land. Snow fell for a time, the temperature was the lowest we have yet experienced, the minimum being 22°.

Saturday, October 10th

It was snowing and blowing from the west this morning at the rate of 20 miles an hour, consequently we all remained indoors for the greater part of the day. Progress was made in the repair of the dog-harnesses, and Cox and Johansen finished the lining of the [house] walls inside with white drill. The temperature in the night fell to 20° [F]. Cox became sleepy after supper so we did not make up the usual Saturday-night bridge party, but spent the evening quietly reading. The wind decreased in the afternoon, and there was hardly a breeze at all by 10 p.m.

Sunday, October 11th

A strong southeast wind sprang up during the day. At 6 p.m. it was blowing 24 miles an hour. Nellie, one of our dogs, took shelter in the grub-cache just outside our door this morning; she is in the last stages of parturition. Everyone remained indoors. Cox developed some photos, and O'Neill made a beginning of developing his. Looking through the window Palaiyak discovered Nellie, another of the dogs with the same name, running off with a ptarmigan, which Johansen was keeping in his tent as a specimen for the doctor [Anderson]. All the ptarmigan we have yet seen are rock ptarmigan; no willow ptarmigan. I forgot to mention that we all won a cigar yesterday at dinner — Chipman vowed 4 days ago that each man should receive a cigar on the first occasion when Johansen sat down to a meal at the same time as the rest of us; he is always behindhand in everything. Our stove is a miserable affair now; one side has partly worn out and it is impossible to heat the oven. Cox tried to make a fruit pie the other day and the pastry would not cook. I tried again today with appalling results. It was *4 hours* in the oven and then only just cooked; a hammer was put on the table to break the crust. The temperature was 17° last night. Chipman traced some arms for me so that I can mark in the tattooing.

Monday, October 12th

A blizzard today, the first real blizzard of the season. The temperature was down to 27° F at 5:20 p.m., and the wind averaged about 30 m.p.h. Nellie produced a litter of pups, seven in all. They seem fine little creatures, all different colours. Chipman, O'Neill, and Cox all continued developing, drying, and packing their photos. Johansen skinned some ptarmigan (five rock [ptarmigan]) for the Dr., and I was cook. The day passed quietly and uneventfully.

Tuesday, October 13th

The wind was blowing 18 miles an hour on the average, and the temperature [was] about 20° F. In the afternoon slush ice was rapidly forming in the bay. Sundry occupations kept us busy during the morning indoors. In the afternoon the launch was pulled up on to the beach in anticipation of the winter. Steam condenses on the ceiling of the house, so on the first fine day we propose to put in a ventilator. Cox and O'Neill unpacked the distillate lighting plant this afternoon and are going to try and install it. It was shipped on the *Belvedere* so was not available last winter. Tomorrow is my last day as cook, then Chipman comes on. Cox complains that I always forget to use salt. So far no one has fallen sick, so I am hoping for a successful issue to my week. Palaiyak is constantly drawing various objects. I have kept three or four that he has made and given him a book[7] to draw others for me; he is something of an artist.

Wednesday, October 14th

A beautiful fine, sunshiny day, though the temperature was down to 20° F most of the time. The bay was frozen over when we rose in the morning, and in going out to the *North Star* to bring the launch ashore, it was necessary to break through the ice in front of the bow of the skin boat with a club. The launch was dragged up on to the beach and covered with a tarpaulin for the winter. Cox and O'Neill continued working at the lighting plant, installing pipes and burners etc., in the house, while the plant was set up in the grub cache just outside. Chipman and Palaiyak carried the kayak out to the open water at the entrance to the harbour, and the latter went sealing. He shot a bearded seal, but it sank; however, he secured a foetid seal (*natsiq — Phoca foetida*).[8] This is probably the last chance this year of sealing on the open water. Johansen began developing his photos and completed three rolls of films,[9] while I put in my last day as cook. Chipman relieves me.

Thursday, October 15th

This seems to have been the time Collinson was frozen in at Cambridge Bay (South Victoria Land) in 185?[10] The thermometer was down to 18° at 8 a.m. and 16° at 5 p.m. Last night it touched 6° F. A light east wind blew at the rate of about 9 miles per hour. There was an aurora last night and again tonight. The comet has travelled still further southwest; its position now is:

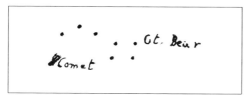

Figure 129. Comet Delavan on October 15.

Cox and O'Neill gave up their efforts with the lighting plant.[11] The engine will not run in the cold cache and there is — at present at least — no room in the house for it. There were other difficulties, but this was the chief. I made two single trees for two sleds — or rather made one and repaired another, and Palaiyak joined up the drilling for a sled-cover on the sewing-machine. Travelling will not be so pleasant here with only a primus stove. A large white dog was prowling round the camp this morning. The ice in the harbour was 3 inches thick today, and the sea has frozen for a short distance outside. Four of Nellie's pups are males and four female. We have decided to kill the four female ones for they would be a nuisance later, and if the mother has only four to rear they will grow faster and stronger with less risk.

Friday, October 16th

A little snow fell in the morning, but the weather cleared later. The temperature at 8 a.m. was 15° F, at 5 p.m. 14° F. Palaiyak went caribou-hunting. About 3 miles away he saw two, but at the same time he started the large dog or, as he rather thinks, the wolf which was prowling round the camp yesterday. It fled towards the caribou and started them. He fired four times at the 'wolf', unsuccessfully, then returned, as the caribou had gone beyond recovery. Cox and O'Neill fixed the ventilator in the roof, a contrivance made the other day by Chipman. I made a few arrangements for leaving shortly,[12] then spent the day writing up notes. Johansen measured the ice in the bay this afternoon — it was 4 inches thick in the spot he measured but is not uniform all over. The sea outside appears to be freezing today. Sledding over land is impracticable here on account of the boulders which everywhere strew the ground — it is all boulders in fact, and they project above the thin carpet of snow. Johansen also swept through the hole in the ice with a hand net and obtained a small jelly fish, one or two amphipods, and a *Clio borealis*. A light northeast breeze was blowing at 8 p.m.; there were auroral streamers.

Saturday, October 17th

I slept in my tent last night to test it. The atmosphere remained calm until about 4 a.m., when an easterly breeze sprang up, increasing in strength during the day, until it veered to the southeast towards evening and blew 25 miles per hour. The temperature fell to 10° F during the night, but had risen to 17° by 8 a.m.; at 5 p.m. it was 20°. Cox, O'Neill, and Johansen pulled up the anchor on the *North Star* through a hole in the ice.[13] I took down my tent, which was covered with a thick coating of ice all round the bottom and over the whole front, the snow which settled on it during a snowstorm melted, then froze solid. Instead of weighing only 13 lbs (minus poles — four [of] light bamboo) the tent weighed about 40 [lbs]. I took it into the house in the afternoon to dry, after first scraping off most of the ice with a spoon. The day was spent in various occupations indoors, for the wind made it unpleasant to linger outside. A considerable number of sculpins, averaging perhaps 5 to 6 inches in length, had been accumulated by Johansen as specimens after being captured in the fish-nets; there were perhaps 12 all told. Now that he has examined them and no longer required them he cleaned them all for Chipman to cook. They were served for supper, and we each received, as Cox said, their 'flavour', for after they were cleaned and washed there was really little left save bones; all this after he had worked at them for 2 hours and dirtied half a dozen dishes. However, Chipman came to the rescue with a fine pudding.

Sunday, October 18th

As with the cooking so with the meteorological observations we are taking it week about, and my week begins today. However, as it was Sunday and breakfast to be at 9 a.m. instead of 8 a.m., at which latter hour (plus at 5:20 in the evening) the observations are taken, Chipman took the morning ones for me, his duties as cook constraining him to rise earlier than the rest of us. We passed the day quietly indoors, reading most of the time. Johansen went for a stroll in the afternoon while

Palaiyak had a joyous skate on the bay ice, using a pair of skates belonging, I think, to no one in particular. A fairly strong wind was blowing, 28 miles [per hour] southeast in the morning, 23 east-southeast in the evening, but the temparature was comparatively mild — averaging about 20° F.

Monday, October 19th

Dull weather with a southeast breeze increasing from 9 miles [per hour] this morning to 15 1/2 this evening. However, the thermometer rose at the same time from 16° to 24°. Palaiyak went east after breakfast, and only 2 or 3 miles away saw 16 seals lying beside their holes on the ice. He wounded one, but it dived into its hole, the bullet striking it not in the head but in the shoulder. Chipman, Cox, and Palaiyak took the stove out of the *North Star* this afternoon. It is to be substituted for the one we are using in the house. Johansen measured the thickness of the ice in the harbour — 5 1/2 inches. I worked at Eskimo grammar all the morning — at the notes of Barter Island excavations in the afternoon.[14] We no longer think it possible for the *Alaska* to make its appearance.[15] The wind died away in the evening and at 7:30 p.m. snow was falling.

Tuesday, October 20th

A quiet day indoors for most of us, reading and writing and various miscellaneous employments. Palaiyak saw 13 seals out on the ice, but could not approach them because it was too thin. The maximum temperature was 26.3° F and the minimum 18.5° F, and though the weather was dull part of the day there was hardly a breath of wind, and the air seemed quite mild. Johansen went out for a while looking for ptarmigan and anything else he could find but saw nothing. Cox and Chipman removed the stove from the fo'castle of the *North Star* and brought it in. It was substituted today for the old one and proved a great success. Chipman is burning wood, of which we have enough stacked up around the coast to last till Xmas. It gave three times as much heat as the old stove, so that now we can bake in the oven.

Wednesday, October 21st

Maximum temperature 23°, minimum 14.7° — an overcast sky but very little wind. Palaiyak went out to look for caribou but saw nothing. The rest of us stayed in camp. The temperature of the room reached 70°, the highest it has yet been.

Thursday, October 22nd

Colder weather. Maximum 20.5°, minimum 8.2°, and a west wind which increased from 14 to 19 miles per hour between morning and evening. Johansen again went to look for ptarmigan but saw nothing. I took a stroll over the island at the mouth of the harbour to look at the Eskimo tent-rings there and to see the ice conditions. The straits are rapidly freezing. There is very little open water around here and in a few days I shall be able to travel. Snow fell intermittently all day. Chipman and I searched the store tent for the phonographs, records, and blanks. We found all except the phonographs — the blanks and records in broken cases. Cox was washing clothes this evening.

Friday, October 23rd

Minimum temperature today 7°, maximum 14°, the sky overcast and a moderate northwest wind in the morning decreasing continuously through the day. Snow fell intermittently. Cox, Johansen, and Palaiyak harnessed up a dog team and went off to gather wood. They brought one load in the morning and another in the afternoon. The ice was still thin, and the sled broke through in one place, and they were in the water up to their knees. Chipman and I found the two phonographs[16] and set them up. There are about 200 blanks, besides a large number of records.[17] Unfortunately all the latter are 4-minute records, and the spindle on the machine is made for 2 minutes. To play them at all we have to take off the connection and move the needle along with the finger — a simple and effective method but rather tedious. Some of the records are good, the majority are very poor.

Saturday, October 24th

Temperature at 8 a.m. [was] -3.5°, the first time this year it has been below zero [Fahrenheit]. The minimum for the 24 hours was -7°. A west breeze of 16 miles an hour entirely died away during the day. Chipman and I set out to harness Blue's dogs but found the collars all too small. It occupied us almost the whole morning to set them right. In the afternoon, however, we harnessed them up and brought two loads of sods to the house. This is the team I am to use this winter. They have never been used as a team by any one save Blue himself, so I was anxious to see how they would shape.[18] They proved fairly satisfactory, and as they are a homogeneous set, which keep together and do not fight with each other, they should give little trouble. The weather was brilliantly fine — the sea freezing hard. Johansen took a long stroll out on the ice. Palaiyak went to look for seals — the snow was too crunchy to make caribou-hunting of any use, for they would hear a man's footsteps a long way off. He saw no seals but shot an arctic hare, which we ate for supper. We played bridge this evening, [it] being Saturday. About 8 p.m. there was a brilliant aurora, but not coloured.

Sunday, October 25th

Outdoors a foggy day, with the temperature well above zero; in fact most of the day above 20° F (?). Johansen takes the meteorological observations this week. We idled away the day in reading[19] and writing, talking, and listening to the gramophone. I compared the two phonographs and packed the one which seemed the less satisfactory.

Monday, October 26th

Another foggy day. Johansen took a line of soundings across the mouth of the harbour; the ice was 7 feet? (inches ?) thick, the greatest depth [to the channel bottom] at the entrance, 11 feet. The temperature was very mild, and a little snow fell. I ransacked the store tent for some trade articles to use this winter, and the others filled in the time at various occupations. Blue's dog Nellie has one pup living, a brown one. I shall not be able to use her for a time. The winter is unusually late in closing in; it is useless for me to set out along the coast as long as there is a possibility of finding the ice too thin at the mouth of Stapylton Bay or the Eskimos not yet returned to the coast.

Tuesday, October 27th

Again the temperature was above 20° all day. Snow fell continuously, making the atmosphere very thick. There was another dog-fight last night, two or three dogs breaking their chains. Johansen was sounding in the harbour again. Cox wandered out for an hour or two with his gun to get some exercise, the rest of us spent most of the time indoors.

Wednesday, October 28th

Cox and Chipman harnessed a dog team and brought in three or four loads of firewood.[20] I gathered together food, etc., for my prospective trip. The weather was mild, the thermometer being in the neighbourhood of 15-20°. Palaiyak saw a seal, but did not secure it. The ice outside was very soft, Chipman said, about 3 inches slush, and 2 inches solid. There was open water not far out.[21] Snow fell part of the day.

Thursday, October 29th

The wind was blowing 18 miles an hour this morning — from the west, and the thermometer had fallen. Jumbo and Dub between them tore the roof off the seal cache.[22] Cox spent most of the day repairing dog chains.[23] Johansen's week as cook began today.

Friday, October 30th

The west wind was blowing 22 miles an hour this morning and snow was drifting. It abated in the evening. We all stayed indoors, Chipman developing photos,[24] the rest of us reading and writing. Palaiyak saw two ptarmigan near the house, but they flew immediately.

Saturday, October 31st

It was blowing 11 miles an hour at 8 a.m., so I did not start out, but partly loaded the sled in readiness for the first bright day. The temperature was 9° F this morning, 4° F this evening. The weather was dull all day, but very little wind. Chipman went to look for caribou but saw nothing save three foxes, not even a caribou track. However, near the big lake some 6 miles away he met Akhiatak, who had gone there for a bundle of dried fish he had cached. They had a meal of dried fish and a chat, neither understanding the other.[25] He [Akhiatak] sent me, *pro* his wife, Niq, a dried fish. Palaiyak went seal-hunting, out at the open water about 3(?) miles away. He shot two seals, but could not secure them, the wind blowing them out of reach of his line. The rest of us stayed in camp, though Cox and O'Neill examined the fish-net, which Johansen and Palaiyak had set under the ice outside the harbour. There is open water-sky all along to the west, north, and east. I shall leave tomorrow morning, if the weather be favourable, for the west, make a small cache at Clifton Point for Chipman and the other person who goes to Cape Lyon in a week or two to enquire about the *Alaska*, then I shall return to look for the Eskimos round Cape Bexley.

Sunday, November 1st

After breakfast — at 9 a.m. — Johansen[26] and I, with a scratch team of four dogs (Jumbo, Dub, Dock, and Bob) left with the racing sled and travelled 12 or 13 miles along the coast to the west to examine the condition of the ice. Everywhere it was several inches thick and beautifully smooth, with but a thin covering of hard-packed snow. Jumbo excelled himself on the return journey, following the outward trail at a steady trot in the darkness without erring once. We had a long discussion in the evening about my travelling alone, a thing which is neither desirable nor expedient when it can be avoided. The others were strongly opposed to it,[27] and it was arranged that Cox and I should leave on Tuesday for Stapylton Bay to find out whether the Eskimos have returned to the coast yet. We shall, if possible, arrive back at the camp on Sunday Nov. 8th after caching 100 lbs of dog-feed at Hope Point[28] — the eastern extremity of Stapylton Bay. Monday week (Nov. 9th) Chipman and O'Neill set out for Cape Lyon, and Johansen and I will accompany them to put in a cache at Wise Point, about 75 miles from here. If, however, Cox and I find Eskimos in Stapylton Bay, Johansen will not leave [Bernard Harbour], but after putting in the cache at Wise Point I shall return alone the 30 or so miles [from Wise Point] to the Eskimo camp. There is a little open water all along the middle of the straits, but it seems to be closing up. The caribou should be migrating over from Victoria Land very shortly.[29] The weather was fine all day, almost windless. For a while a few flakes of snow fell, and the sun shone out during a brief interval. The temperature was 0° F at 8 a.m., 9° at 5:20 p.m. The moon is nearly full, the sun at noon very near the horizon. We light the lamps about 3:30 p.m. Palaiyak shot a large hare.

Monday, November 2nd

In the morning O'Neill and Palaiyak brought in a load of ice then went off to the open water. They watched for about 20 minutes but saw no signs of seal so returned. The water was covered with a film as though it were freezing over. Chipman and Cox were occupied with various minor matters about the camp, and I was rearranging the things Cox and I leave with tomorrow. The afternoon passed quietly in much the same way, and the evening in reading, writing, and talking. The weather was calm and mild, the sun shining out for part of the day. The temperature was 4° F at 5:20 p.m.

Chapter 22. First Foray by Dogsled

Heading west — Limestone circle — Open water near Stapylton Bay — Caching pemmican — Return to headquarters — Lessons learned

Tuesday, November 3rd, 1914

Johansen was a little late in getting breakfast. He said he had wakened several times in the night for he was afraid that the alarm might not go off. When it did sound he promptly turned it off and went to sleep again. (The other day, not being sure where to set the hammer, he placed it mid way between 'alarm' and 'silence'!) We were delayed another half hour after breakfast in digging a seal out of the cache; it was frozen both to the ground and to its fellow. However, we [Cox and I] set out at 10 a.m. with five dogs, Blue's team Bruce, Donald, Scotty, Sam Jones, and another small woolly dog named Telluraq. The snow was soft and sticky, Bruce (the leader)[1] and Scotty would not pull, and we made poor progress. We had travelled perhaps 12 to 13 miles when we camped — at 4:15 p.m. (it was just dark) and were hardly beyond the place Johansen and I reached last Sunday. Cox fed the dogs, I cooked on the primus stove. We had a pot of beans already cooked and frozen and some of these we warmed in a frying pan, then we had cold pemmican (Hudson's Bay Co. brand 40% fat and 60% meat), hard-bread, boiled rice, and cocoa. We turned in about 8 p.m. The temperature was above zero, but I do not know how much. The sky was overcast all day, but there was very little wind.

Wednesday, November 4th

We set out at 8:10 a.m. I had to turn out three times during the night on account of the dogs — two of which broke loose. It was much foggier today than yesterday, and almost immediately after starting we ran into rough ice and had to worm in and out of it for some miles, here and there chopping away excrescences and reducing the inequalities to make a negotiable passage. The dogs pulled fairly well, on the whole. We stopped at noon in the shelter of a big ice keg and had a lunch of doughnuts and raisins (the doughnuts presented to us by Johansen on leaving). The dogs were now very tired and could hardly be made to move at a snail's pace, so we camped about 2 p.m. on a point which may be Cape Bexley. There is considerable driftwood all along the shore here for many miles. Outside — about 2 miles from the beach — is a great lane of open water extending east and west, with two small breaks apparently. On a ridge just behind our camp is a stone circle about 6 feet in diameter. The ground is strewn with limestone boulders, with a few of granite and diabase interspersed. Cox was cook tonight. A moderate west wind blew all day and felt very cold because we were travelling so slowly.

Thursday, November 5th

Cox was up and prepared breakfast. We were away again this morning at 8:10 a.m. Rounding a point close to our camping place we noticed that it more resembled Cape Bexley than what we had considered such the night before. Beyond was a shallow saucer-shaped bay about 5 miles broad with a small island in the middle — South Bay — though its shape is rather different to what it appears on the chart. At the western end of it we suddenly came to a great lead of open water with an extremely narrow band of heavy ice kegs between it and the shore. Cox went ahead and cut a way through with the axe. Once or twice we had to pass over thin slush ice and the dogs did not appreciate this at all. Finally about noon we reached a point[2] beyond which was more heavy ice fringing the shore and the lead of water extending to the horizon and round to the south deep into Stapylton Bay. Another point was visible to the southwest, and beyond that apparently was Stapylton Bay with its open water. To try to go further meant risking a breakdown with the sled, traversing much heavy ice through which we should need to cut a passage, with the practical certainty of finding no Eskimos at all in Stapylton Bay owing to the open water preventing their building snow-huts on the ice and pursuing their usual winter occupation of sealing. This had been the main purpose of the journey. We cached seven tins of pemmican (112 lbs) on the ridge just above the shore, erecting a log of driftwood over the site, and after a lunch of pemmican, raisins, and hard-bread, set out back, reaching our camping ground of the night before about 3:15 p.m. The dogs were tired so we pitched the tent on the same spot, but directed towards the west instead of the east, owing to the wind having changed from west to east. The weather was comparatively mild, the snow and ice sodden and mushy, making the sled heavy to drag. From 8:20 a.m. till 10:30 a.m. there was a fine display of parhelia thus:

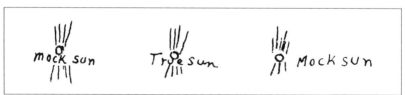

Figure 130. Parhelia near Cape Bexley.

Part of the time only the parhelion on the right was visible, and even when both were plain the rays streamed north of them and only once or twice south to the horizon as well (e.g., as shown in sketch). At sunrise the horizon opposite the sun had a markedly green tinge. We did not tie any of the dogs up, for they did not seem inclined to fight or create a disturbance. I took turn again as cook.

Friday, November 6th

A strong west wind sprang up in the night but had abated a little when we turned out in the morning. The ice cracked close in shore just below where we were camped among the grounded floes, and the water flooded it for some distance along to the depth of about a foot. In trying to find a shallow passage out with the sled to the unflooded ice I stepped in over my boot tops and had to change my socks. The dogs made rather better time with the lightened sled, about 3 miles an hour, though the ice was very mushy. We made our first camp about noon — after 4 hours travel — we set out at exactly 8:10 a.m. again by a curious coincidence — thereby making in 4 hours what took us 6 [hours] in coming west. There we lunched in the shelter of an ice keg, and pushed on again for the home camp. By mistake we ran inside the deep bay behind Cockburn Point, which we had failed to notice before. The dogs began to flag though it was only about 8 or 9 miles to camp, but we spurred them on, and at last sighted the light from the small north window. We made home before 6 p.m., the dogs being absolutely played out, though they had travelled only about 25 miles. We were both almost as tired as they were. The first trip of this winter is over, and we have gained a little experience.[3] First, a single tent is very bad. The one we had — 'my' tent that I tried a few weeks back — is made of good material and very light, while its shape, though not beyond improvement, is fairly good. But it is single [layered], and with a stove in it, especially a primus stove, a thick layer of condensed steam forms like frost all over the inside; everywhere you touch against the side or roof you are plastered with white, and during the night it dropped continuously on top of you like steady rain. When rice was being boiled the air was so thick that we could hardly see one another, even though we had the door open a little and an icy draught blowing in. Being single again it was much colder than a double tent would be. Another thing we learned was that we could have used a wood stove equally well at the two spots on which we camped, and presumably at most places between Cockburn and Hope points there is plenty of driftwood to be picked up within 200-300 yards of any spot on which the tent might be erected. A wood stove is warmer, can be maintained continuously — a primus burning for an hour or more begins to 'taste' — and enables wet mittens, socks, etc., to be dried; all our clothing was wet when we returned and it is extremely unpleasant to put on frozen shirts and trousers or boots in the morning. Of the dogs on the team, Telluraq and blind old Sam Jones were splendid workers, the rest miserable. The high temperature — hardly once even during the night was it below zero [Fahrenheit] — made the ice soft and sticky, and the sled dragged heavily in consequence. I developed a sore foot just on the outside of the bottom between heel and toes — in the identical place where it troubled me last year when we left the *Karluk*; apparently it is a strained muscle.

Chapter 23. Brief Respite at Bernard Harbour

Weatherbound — Foot injury and ailing dogs — Reappearance of Eskimos — Cook week commences — Chipman and O'Neill head west — Trading — Shortage of dog-food — Eskimo personalities — Poor condition of dogs

Saturday, November 7th, 1914

A strong northwest wind blew all day, snow fell and drifted, and the weather generally was 'blizzardy'. Johansen and Palaiyak brought in a load of ice and another of wood, the rest of us stayed indoors. Palaiyak shot three seals out at the open water during the week.[1] Cox examined a rock exposure near Cape Bexley and found it to be dolomite or a limestone that was almost a marble. I have been working recently at a Barrow grammar and continued today. The temperature was 15° this morning and 6° tonight.

Sunday, November 8th

Another day with a strong wind blowing, the temperature somewhat cold — -14° in the morning and -11° at night. We all lingered in camp, as there is nothing to occupy us out of doors.

Monday, November 9th

The temperature was about the same as yesterday, with a moderate west wind. Johansen went out to look for ptarmigan, saw two, and shot one. Palaiyak also wandered off but saw nothing. Two of the dogs I used on the trail, Bruce the leader and Donald, are half crippled. They were chained up like all the other dogs, but the foolish creatures lay buried in the snow, lying in pools of their own urine, which froze, and froze them to the ground. They had to be cut out and are now loose, limping on three legs whenever they move about. Bruce is a miserable sight, thin and brown and limping, despite plenty of food and care. My foot was troublesome during the night and again today; I cannot set it square on the ground. It feels much like a sprain and is caused, I think, by walking with heelless boots on soft snow, so that the weight of the body, instead of being distributed between the ball and the heel of the foot, is distributed evenly all over and the middle feels the unusual strain. However, as it is only the left foot that is affected, it would seem that it has been strained a little at some time and is weaker than it should be.

Tuesday, November 10th

Another cold day like yesterday, with a fresh westerly breeze blowing. Johansen again went out to look for ptarmigan, and so did Palaiyak, but [they] secured none. The rest of us remained in camp all day. My foot was very painful and kept me awake much of the night. One of the dogs broke his chain, entered the food cache, and ripped open a bag of rice and one or two other things, besides insolently chewing up the dog-whip. With this cold weather Chipman and O'Neill expect to be able to leave for Cape Lyon next Monday.[2]

Wednesday, November 11th

Weather like yesterday. O'Neill and Chipman busy preparing for their trip. Palaiyak visited his fox-trap — a deadfall he has set up about a mile away. The day was uneventful. A bright aurora in the evening; the two preceding nights also there were auroral streamers.

Thursday, November 12th

Weather the same as yesterday. The most eventful feature of the day was the appearance of Akhiatak just before noon. He, his wife Niq, and his daughter Naqitoq[3] with Hitqoq and a boy Hogaluk, came down by sled from inland and camped not far to the eastward of here. He himself came along the coast by sled, I imagine to cache some things, and took the opportunity to visit us. We entertained him to dinner and his manners, for an Eskimo, were exemplary. He was well clad — the costume being altogether different to his summer dress. instead of baggy trousers open just below [the] knees and coat cut short at the waist in front, he wore two long deerskin coats, [a] new one inside (fur in) and [an] old one outside (fur out). Likewise he had on two pairs of trousers — the inner tucking into the shoes apparently,[4] the outer ending in a fringe of deerskin fur just below the knees. The coats were trimmed with similar fur, and the inner one had for extra trimming a narrow white sealskin band all round the bottom. He carried a snow-knife of steel, for now they will be living in snowhouses instead of a tent. Johansen took some soundings in the outer harbour — he has been taking them at intervals of 7 feet, which on a map of 1 inch to the mile will represent about 1/500 inch!!! Scotty, the third of Blue's dogs, was frozen to the ground this morning (like Donald and Bruce [on Nov. 9]), and I had to dig him out, then thaw out the ice on the foot with a primus stove in the cache. One toe seemed to be frozen, but he is not limping. Bright aurora this evening. O'Neill's birthday; he is 28.[5]

Friday, November 13th

Temperature between -10° and -20° (-19° at 8 a.m., -14.5° at 5:20 p.m.) as it has been the last 4 days; but today there was no wind at all and it was very pleasant out of doors. O'Neill and Johansen with a dog team brought in a load of wood. Palaiyak found a fox in his deadfall. He is making me a stove out of two kerosene tins and stove pipes of [the] same material. We are going to cut down meals to two — breakfast 8 a.m., dinner 2 p.m., with a light supper about 8 p.m.[6] My foot is better today, though I can't walk with it flat on the ground. Aurora this evening, and comet still visible, though very low in the west.[7]

Saturday, November 14th

The morning dawned calm but a trifle foggy. Before noon a blizzard was beginning. Johansen had gone off somewhere, but soon returned. The wind increased to nearly 30 miles an hour. We were congratulating ourselves that we had a secure house and need not turn out to fasten down a tent. But in the middle of a bridge game — about 10 p.m. — Palaiyak reported that the tarpaulin roof of the cache was in danger. We turned out and had a lively time weighting it down with logs, sacks of coal, ice blocks, anything and everything. Cox and Chipman froze their toes — they just turned white — but thawed them out inside before any damage was done. The drifting snow felt very like hail, and the temperature was about -15° or perhaps even lower.

Sunday, November 15th

I began my week as cook. Breakfast 9 a.m. The velocity of the wind at 8 a.m. was 43 miles per hour, the temperature -15°, with the minimum at -23° during the night, the lowest we have recorded this winter. It was an indoors day and there we all remained.[8] The tent in which Blue's dogs had been placed was blown down, and two of the dogs half-buried in snow; they were dug out in the morning. Unlike the other dogs they won't stir now and then to shake the snow off. The four pups of Nellie were brought indoors for warmth; they howled fearfully during the night. All four try to suck at once, and as only two can do so at one time the other two scratch their mother, who punishes them; the result is a long growl, a sharp snap, and prolonged howling. The sky was clear this evening and the wind had abated somewhat. There was a bright coloured aurora.

Monday, November 16th

The temperature was -14° and the wind blowing 25 miles [per hour] at 8 a.m., but there were signs that the worst was over. By evening the wind had dropped to 13 miles [per hour], the sky was clear, and the aurora visible. The pups of Nellie were again brought into the house to warm up. Before dark the others were able to turn out for a few minutes while it was yet light and straighten things up. The pup of Blue's Nellie is dead; it was prematurely born and undersized. Cox cooked some rice for the dogs to warm them up. I was ragged at breakfast for bad stoking [of the fire], and Johansen and O'Neill took it over. They raised the temperature of the house up to 36° F. I retaliated by giving them only fried potatoes and boiled rice for lunch. (Bad temper![9])

Tuesday, November 17th

A busy day for Chipman and O'Neill, who were preparing to leave in the morrow.[10] The weather was fine, temperature fairly low (about -20° F) and only a light northwest breeze. O'Neill and Johansen exercised the team by bringing in a load of ice.[11] I made a batch of doughnuts for the two who were leaving, a batch of 'magic' yeast bread, and a batch of baking-powder biscuits, fearing that the yeast bread might not turn out good. Luckily my fears were abortive. The *Noahognirmiut* turned up about 9 a.m. — Aksiatak, his wife Niq, and their little daughter Naqitoq, the elderly woman Iguaq,[12] another man Hitqoq, and a boy (the last-named's nephew) Hogaluk. We set the women to work. Niq quickly made a pair of deerskin socks for O'Neill, while Iguaq put a large patch in his trousers and a small patch in Chipman's coat. This occupied all the morning. We gave them a good dinner, then paid them for their work and traded for some goods they brought for sale. There was a fine pair of sealskin overshoes, which came up front and back to the ancles, where they could be secured if desired with a piece of string. They fitted neatly over Chipman's mocassins, so he is taking them with him. The most noteworthy specimen they brought was a fish-spear with a horn point, and two copper points on each side of it at right angles, set in heads of horn also, thus:

Figure 131. Horn point on fish-spear, Bernard Harbour.[13]

The whole was lashed securely with rawhide. Other things comprised copper needles, and a musk-ox horn ladle. We gave them two skins to scrape and sew into a sleeping bag for me, and another skin to convert into socks. Brilliant aurora in [the] evening.

Wednesday, November 18th

Breakfast was over before 8 a.m., but Chipman and O'Neill did not leave before 10:30. They had about 700 lbs weight on their sled[14] and at Point Hope would pick up the 112 lbs [of] pemmican Cox and I cached there for them. The weather was not promising, for the temperature was -21° F, and a moderately strong east wind was blowing, which though fair, was extremely cold. The barometer was also steadily going down, and during the afternoon a blizzard developed, the wind attaining the speed of 29 miles per hour. About 8 p.m. it had increased to 40 miles [per hour]. The snow was hard and in fine shape for travelling, which was one consolation. Their dogs pulled well and were making about 3 miles an hour when Cox and Johansen turned back. Palaiyak has two or three fox-traps set, which he visited today, and reported that the Eskimos had stolen one. Their honesty is not above question. We lent them needles and thimbles for sewing yesterday and they failed to return them; when we asked for them they handed them over with a bad grace. I made two pies in the afternoon but did not put enough lard into the pastry so it is hard.

Thursday, November 19th

The wind had diminished a little this morning — 29 miles [per hour] — and the temperature [was] 1/2° F. It was snowing thickly, so that travel would be difficult along this unknown coast where there is no beaten trail. Probably Chipman and O'Neill stayed in camp — in their sleeping bags.[15] Three Eskimos appeared shortly before noon — Aksiatak, Niq, and Iguaq. They brought my sleeping bag and two pairs of deerskin socks which they had sewn. I paid them each two fathoms calico for their work. At the same time I bought also a small stone lamp, a pair of good deerskin mittens (for Palaiyak), and an iron harpoon head.[16] This last, they said, was made by a Victoria Islander from a piece of iron obtained from [Capt.] Joe Bernard. In shape it closely resembles (if it is not identical with) some bone and horn harpoon heads of Barrow in Stefansson's collection,[17] and with others figured in Swenander's monograph on *Harpun Kastril . . . . spetsar von Väst Grönland.*[18] Another interesting specimen I bought was a blubber-pounder of musk-ox horn with the handle cut out to fit the fingers.[19] Eskimos have smaller hands and feet than Europeans, as most Arctic travellers have remarked; hence boots bought from them are almost invariably too small. So with this blubber pounder; the handle was too small for even my fingers;[20] strangely too, Aksiatak's mittens which I bought for Palaiyak were also too small for any of us save Palaiyak, and rather small for him, though he is a smaller man. We enquired then about the fox-trap of Palaiyak's which had been taken. Hitqoq removed it, they said, because he thought Palaiyak had thrown it away. It was in his house and he was going to return it. This was plainly a lie, but it was diplomatic to accept it as true. We told them that this winter we should have plenty of sewing for them to do, but that if they removed any trap or any other object belonging to us we should neither give them any work to do nor trade with them nor have anything at all to do with them. They protested then that they had not stolen the trap, and the matter was dropped. It was then arranged that I should go over to their camping ground in 2 or 3 days,[21] and they would make me a snowhouse alongside of theirs. Later on they will guide me to the Eskimos on the Victoria Land side, for which I shall pay them. They seemed very pleased at this. They are waiting at the fishing creek for Ayallik and the rest, and when they arrive the whole party will cross over to Liston Island and seal around there. The caribou, they said, when migrating north in the spring, pass here, but in the fall return through the country of the *Nagyuktogmiut*, whom Stefansson places between the Coppermine and Kent Peninsula, only off the coast of Victoria Land.[22] This is a serious problem for us, because we have dog-food enough to last until Xmas only, and shall now be compelled to try and secure seals from the Eskimos. From Stefansson's book[23] and Anderson's Appendix [therein] one gathers that the autumn migration passes by here also, but this appears to be a mistake.[24] The Eskimos ate with us, quickly adapting themselves to our manners, a trait common, I fancy, to most primitive peoples.

Another point common to them I imagine to be an undeveloped personality or rather individuality. Hence the individualist is the man of note and influence. The easy merging of one man's will into another's makes for the 'tolerance' of Eskimo society, where each person does what he likes without interference. It would account in part for the ease with which they are dominated by Europeans, their pliant wills yielding submissively to the aggressiveness of the outsider. Perhaps too it accounts in part for the hold that missionary teaching has upon the Mackenzie and Barrow natives, the driving power of the missionary forcing his convictions — in so far as they are understood — upon his auditors. Even with us it is always easier to acquiesce than to oppose.

The rest of the day passed quietly. The wind was blowing 19 miles [per hour] at 5:20 p.m., but only about 7 [miles per hour] at 7 p.m. There were bright auroral streamers at 7 p.m. running northwest by southeast; the temperature at 5:20 p.m. was -2.4° F. It may be worth noting that the skins for my sleeping bag were scraped by Aksiatak, though his wife did the sewing. Oyaraq used to scrape skins for Leffingwell.[25]

Friday, November 20th

There was very little wind when I turned out this morning, and the sky was clear though a little foggy. Cox, Johansen, and Palaiyak spent the day in lining the store outside with snow-blocks so that we shall have no repetition of the scene of the other night when the roof was nearly blown away. I cooked and prepared for my prospective departure. Two days ago Cox and Palaiyak made a snowhouse for the dogs, and Blue's team was put in there yesterday with Telluraq. They were all right last night, but this morning Nellie was dead — nor could we discover the cause unless it be old age. Donald was frozen in as before and Scotty lying in a pool of his own urine — though neither was tied. The stitches in the former's legs had broken out — I believe what we thought were cuts are corrupt sores. We took him inside the house and washed and bandaged them. Bruce seems to be on his last legs. He is thin and tottering and will probably not last many days more — senile decay I fancy. This breaks up my team altogether and we are in somewhat of a strait, for besides the two bitches with pups there are only Jumbo, Denby, Ukumala, and Panaski. Jumbo and Ukumala are both on the sick list — the latter quite lame — and Denby requires housing in the winter; Panaski is old though frisky just now, and I shall have to take him. Palaiyak tells me tonight that Ilavinuk[26] made him no return for all the foxes and caribou he procured for him — of foxes nearly 100. By the way, his [Palaiyak's] mother had an exceptionally large family — four boys and two girls still living, and four children who died — ten in all. Mauss in *L'Annee Sociologique*[27] doubts the existence of an Eskimo family of eight (vol. IX, 1904-5, p. 61, n. 2) — he says "il y a probablement une erreur d'observation." Teriglu had two boys and three girls, and his wife was again pregnant — the eldest (a boy) was only about 12 years. In both these cases none of the children were adopted. No doubt these are exceptional cases, but Mauss goes too far when he says "le maximum semble être 4 à 5 enfants!" The maximum temperature today was zero; the weather was fine, with only a light east wind.

Chapter 24. First Encounter with Victoria Island Eskimos

Living in an iglu — Aksiatak sleeps at the station — To Victoria Island — Iglu construction — First contact with the Puivlirmiut *— Welcome dance — Taking physical measurements — Sleeping with an Eskimo family — Return to Bernard Harbour — Planning a longer visit — Snowhouses at Putulik — Living and trading with the* Puivlirmiut *— Learning new cat's cradles — Wife exchanging — Observations on customs and activities — Return alone to headquarters*

Saturday, November 21st, 1914

A beautiful fine day with a very light east breeze. I got breakfast then turned over the cooking to Johansen; it was the last day of my week and I wanted to get away among the Eskimos. The sled was half loaded when Hitqoq and Hogaluk[1] appeared, the former bringing Palaiyak's fox-trap which he had stolen. Hogaluk brought an interesting harpoon, which he wished to trade for a fox-trap — Johansen is going to sketch it for me. I left about 11 a.m., Cox and Palaiyak accompanying me to take the sled back.[2] Hitqoq had brought word that Aksiatak had built a house for me.[3] On the way I photographed Palaiyak's fox-trap[4] — of stone — a simple contrivance — a short stick set upright on another cross-piece of wood

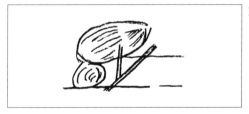

Figure 132. Palaiyak's fox-trap.

laid on the ground in a small 'box' made of stone. Two heavy stones were placed on a stick resting on the upright and pointing outwards. Bait (blubber) was placed underneath on the ground, and the fox had to move the upright to secure it, when the stones fell on its head. This trap had already killed two foxes.

I found my house built as Hitqoq said,[5] and turned my things into it at once, then Cox, Palaiyak, and I visited the Eskimo iglus. These consist of two round snowhouses, which touch on one side.[6] The walls are broken through where they touch, making a common passage from one house to the other. At this place a 'bay' or cupola is constructed, in the bottom of which a small hole was cut through for a door. In this bay is an ice window, and another in one of the houses, giving more light than would penetrate through the snow alone. The door (which is closed from the inside by a snow-block) leads to a passage which is enlarged in the middle of its course to serve as a store for guns, snow-shovel, etc. Then it curves to the north so that drifting snow will not pile down it and block it up. Outside various sticks, seal spears etc. are planted in the snow around the houses. The Eskimos gave us dried (raw) salmon trout to eat, and about 2 p.m. Cox [and Palaiyak] left. I cooked some rice on the primus in my house and entertained most of the Eskimos to supper, later visiting their house again. It was only 5 p.m., yet Hitqoq and Iguaq[7] were in bed. I sat and tried to talk to them for an hour or so,[8] then returned to my own house, turned into my sleeping bag and wrote up the day's notes, stopping every few minutes to warm my hands in the bag. There was an aurora in the evening about 4 p.m.

Sunday, November 22nd

It was rather cold in my hut last night. I turned out about 8 a.m., cooked some oatmeal on the primus, had a meal, and took the rest over to the Eskimos' hut. Hitqoq and Hogaluk had already gone to the lake to fish by jigging with a hook and line and did not return till 2 p.m.; they secured no fish, but found two foxes in their traps. I spent the day alternately in my own hut and in the Eskimos'. A strong east wind sprang up, and Aksiatak turned out to make a proper passage for my hut. I gave him and his wife [Niq][9] hard-bread and cocoa afterwards, and later in the afternoon cooked a pot of rice in their hut, and we all had a meal. Aksiatak with a bow drill was fashioning a harpoon head of soft iron, holding the head in a socket at the end of a piece of antler. Iguaq was fixing a water dish made by dividing a coal-oil can in two lengthways. She was turning over the rim, placing under it short thin rods, some of iron, some of copper (beaten out with two stones), and biting the rim down over them. Niq repaired Cox' boots and lengthened my sleeping bag, first scraping the skin for this latter. I paid her a bowl and a fathom of calico. I wrote notes, measured the house,[10] gave Aksiatak a lesson in the use of the rifle, and generally made myself at home. In the evening one of the dogs broke into my hut and chewed up Cox' boots. Niq will repair them tomorrow. The lamp in one house was burning low along half its length. I took the temperature — 3 feet from the lamp it was 35° F, at the back of the room 30° F, outside -2° F.

Monday, November 23rd

A strong west wind was blowing this morning — the temperature was -2° F. The temperature in my hut last night when I turned in (the lantern was burning) was 8° F; this morning — lantern burning again — it was 6° F. Aksiatak and the two children [Naqitoq and Hogaluk] appeared while I was cooking oatmeal, and I gave them a light meal, sent the rest over to their hut and went over and had a dried fish. My handkerchief amuses the Eskimos greatly. I wrote down their names for [the] different parts of the body, and measured the passage, then about 11:30 a.m. set off for Bernard Harbour, reaching there at 12:30 p.m. Johansen (cook) gave me a good meal — Cox was riveting the broken tops of the stove and making an excellent job of them. Palaiyak had written me out a short story (in Mackenzie dialect).[11] I left again at 1:45 p.m.; it was growing dark and I could not see the [Eskimo] houses, but struck their store caches, so soon found the place. Hogaluk had securely blocked up the entrance to my house while I was away to keep the dogs out. I cooked some rice in their house and we all had a meal. I limit them very severely on the sugar. Aksiatak was finishing his harpoon head, Hitqoq cutting up horn with a curious hooked knife by scratching grooves and deepening

Figure 133. Hitqoq's hooked knife.

them, then breaking out the [triangular] sections with a small iron-headed adze. Niq repaired Cox' mits and shoes, Iguaq was making a shirt from the calico they received from me.

Tuesday, November 24th

A fine clear day, with the sun visible above the horizon. I took a photo of the Eskimos double hut.[12] The floor was just thawing enough to wet through my deerskin boots and deerskin socks, and as they were unpacking their sealskin pokes full of winter clothes and I had to stay and see them, I nearly froze my feet. Aksiatak finished his harpoon head, and Niq made herself a pair of overshoes then myself a pair. Hitqoq skinned his fox, using for part his curved whittling knife, for part Iguaq's *ulo*. Unlike the western Eskimos who skin from the mouth like a seal, he began with the legs and skinned it like a caribou.

Wednesday, November 25th

Aksiatak had the sled outside my hut at 8 a.m. I cooked some porridge, then a hole was made in the side of my hut and all my things loaded on to their sled. Thus we returned to Bernard Harbour.[13] Aksiatak courageously sleeps in our house tonight, then tomorrow he and I go to one of the Liston Islands, and the next day to the *Purplermiut*[14] Eskimo. I shall make a cache of food with them, stay 2 or 3 days, then return and cross over later. The day was taken up with preparations for the journey. I tried to fix up the double tent but it was dark outside and there was no room either inside or in the store to set it up, so I had to [leave][15] it. I showed Aksiatak some pictures of Eskimos etc.[16] In one picture, which represented some Eskimo implements and toys, he tried to take up the picture of a toy dog with his fingers. None of them have the least understanding of a map. They are all extremely curious and have no hesitation in asking for anything and everything that takes their fancy, but do not mind being refused. Aksiatak had a bed made for him on the floor beside Palaiyak, but sat on it for a long time, too much afraid to lie down. We all turned in — save Johansen, who was washing up — and that gave him a little courage so that at last, overcome by sleep, he stretched himself out and in a moment was unconscious of everything. He will be a hero forever hereafter in his own eyes and in those of his countrymen.

Thursday, November 26th

Cox and I set up the tent after breakfast, but it evidently required at least 2 to 3 hours work repairing it, so I decided to leave it behind. We got away at 10 a.m., but four of the home dogs followed us, and later when we were 3 miles off, Jumbo [came after us], both of which incidents delayed us. We passed through a lot of tolerably rough ice and did not reach *Ukullik*[17] (one or all three of the Liston Islands) till after 3 p.m. Akhiatak built a snowhouse, while I unhitched and fed the dogs and later filled in the interstices with soft snow. My ignorance of a snow iglu and its ways amuses him greatly. We ate dried fish, pemmican, hard-bread, and rice, and turned in at 6:45 p.m.

Friday, November 27th

The iglu was fine and warm last night — at least, I was in my double sleeping bag, jammed between Akhiatak on one side and two boxes on the other. I lit the primus before 7 a.m., and by 8:30 we had started. The first 6 or 7 miles were through broken ice — rather rough. I ran across once to examine a big rock exposure — there are many — on one of the Liston Islands.[18] It appeared to be limestone or dolomite with outcrops of marble. I could see no fossils, but the light was bad, and I did not stop to search. Akhiatak took us too far to the east-northeast instead of steering northeast, so that about 1 p.m. when we came to good ice with very little snow on it (not enough for an iglu) the land was hardly in sight. We circled to the east and the dogs, beginning to travel a little better, reached Victoria Land at 4:30 p.m. Akhiatak again built a snowhouse, while I filled the lantern — unharnessed and fed the dogs, and unloaded the sled, then filled in the chinks in the wall. I cooked rice and made cocoa, and we had some dried fish also. Akhiatak then turned in while I refilled the primus and blocked the doorway. Again he laughed heartily over my unskilful handling of snow. There was no wind practically till about 4 p.m., when a light cold breeze sprang up from the east. The sun acc[ording] to the declension should have appeared yesterday for the last time, but it was visible again today well above the horizon — probably refraction. It was splendid travelling weather. His [Akhiatak's] dog Itaiyuk is leader — not much good, though it is improving. Then comes Panaski, an old dog, but a good worker, Telluraq, the gamest dog in the outfit, small as he is, [then] Sam Jones and Scotty, the former old but hard working, the latter young and lazy and slightly footsore besides. Akhiatak builds a snowhouse about 9 feet x 6 feet x 4 feet high in about an hour easily. He cuts out the opening for the door last, cutting out blocks for about 3 feet inside to make a floor and leaving the 6 feet or so behind it for the sleeping platform. I look forward to a comfortable night — a great boon in the Arctic after a hard day's travel. Tomorrow we search the coast to the south for the *Purpliurmiut* as far as the point.[19] There was an aurora about 3 p.m. [with] streamers and wheat ears.

Saturday, November 28th

Nearly a disastrous morning. I closed the doorway very airtight and this morning the primus refused to burn and the lamp to go on. Not till I had wasted half a hundred matches did the truth dawn on me that the air was foul. We were thus delayed an hour in getting away. When we did I left a cache in the hut of rice, pemmican, hard-bread, and a few odds and ends. We travelled northwest, running inside of the bays. In one large bay we circled round two small islands. A few miles along the coast we fell in with an old sled trail leading northwest and followed that for a short distance then lost it. It was very cold and I had continually to thaw out my nose. At last we reached a fox-trap on a point of land — made of snow — a small rectangular doorway with lintel and side (jambs?) posts of single snow-blocks led into a small square chamber where a perpen-

Figure 134. Snow fox-trap on south side of Victoria Island.

dicular stick supporting the roof was pivoted on another stick, the end of which, pointing inwards and raised an inch or two above the ground, bore a piece of blubber. The fox had to enter the chamber to seize the blubber, and in so doing displaced the upright stick and brought the roof down — a snow-block weighted with a stone. Footsteps from this guided us across a bay, on the far side of which we fell in with four Eskimos all coming from different directions. Akhiatak ran ahead at the top of his speed, flinging up his arms with [the] peace sign, and they ran to a common centre in the direction of their settlement. I saw Akhiatak throw up his arms, making the signals of peace, then he was hid from view behind the land. About a mile further on I found him with four young men, who returned my peace signals, and stood up in a row when I approached — the tallest man on the right. He told me his name, I told him mine, then, standing in front of the second I repeated mine. He gave me his name — or as it proved afterwards his two names. They were so long that I failed altogether to grasp them, and stood for a moment hesitating, then said "Phew, what a long name." They seemed amazed for a moment, then seeing me laugh, they roared with laughter also. The other two presented themselves in turn likewise, then we all set out towards their settlement. One or more went ahead with me, the others rode on the sled, this apparently being the proper etiquette. They were immensely pleased, and one of them — a merry-faced handsome youth — wanted to hug and rub noses with me all the time. Then they wished to race with me — and I was glad to find I could outstrip them all. The huts[20] were situated at the head of a large practically land-locked bay[21] — it seemed quite land-locked with a creek flowing out of it, but they said the water was salt. As we neared the settlement Akhiatak went ahead with a youth on either side and began to run, then the other two youths arranged themselves on either side of me and told me to run too. They began to shout *kovluna*,[22] and men, women, and children poured forth to meet us. Several of the children had small hoops in their hands and sticks — the former about 1 foot in diameter and the sticks 2 to 3 feet long —as far as I could see in the hustle and stir. The men and women had learned the custom of shaking hands from Joe Bernard, but they told me their names and I told them mine. One of the old men immediately led me into his hut and stood me on his platform, then brushing my boots and clothes, seated me and sat down beside me. Everyone crowded in and a perfect babel arose — constantly they repeated *nagojugut* (we are friendly), *inuit nagojut* (the people are friendly), *inuit ileanaitut* (the people are glad). After a while I went out and unharnessed the dogs while the Eskimos built me a snow-hut into which my things were hustled.[23] Then I was conducted to another man's house. At length I returned to my hut, where I found Akhiatak playing the big man. He had already set the primus going — to everyone's admiration. I had to squash him and take charge of the primus, which he did not know how to manage.

After the meal (I cooked enough for about three people and had a good plateful myself) we all adjourned to one of the larger huts for a dance. They were glad, they said, and so wanted to dance. The huts (there are 6(?)) are all double — like Akhiatak's — save that from the one entrance the passages separate for each of the two iglus in some cases, whereas in others (like Akhiatak's) there is only one passage leading into the forecourt. It was in this forecourt that the dance took place. A man held the drum in his left hand about the level of his head and beat it with a short stick held in the right hand — alternately turning his wrists. The drum was about 20 inches in diameter, of skin laid on one side only of a frame (of wood?) and fastened by a lashing of rawhide round the rim — probably put on green and tightening as it dried. The drummer did not move his feet, but bent his knees up and down to the accompaniment of a song, in which the circle of spectators joined. This lasted for a couple of hours or more, while I sat on the platform and watched them. At last, about 10 p.m., I announced that I would retire to bed in my hut and was conducted thither and the door closed behind me.

Sunday, November 29th

I slept badly, for the hut was small, my sleeping bag wet, and the air very cold. I heard footsteps outside about 5 a.m. and later about 7 — someone listening to see if I was astir. I now lit the lantern, and immediately some one outside called my name. I lit the primus, then told them to come in, and immediately a crowd flocked in and filled the place. I cooked oatmeal, then told Akhiatak I was going to one of their huts to measure them and would give each man I measured a fishhook and each woman some matches. They were pleased with this and flocked in after me to the hut of Akhiatak's cousin, where I was so crowded that it was almost impossible to work. However, I scattered them a little and kept steadily measuring till about 1 p.m., when most if not all of the men were finished.[24] I was hungry and said I would eat before proceeding to the women, and was presented with some deer fat liver (dry), for which, of course, I paid. I now measured most of the women, but two or three said they did not wish to be measured so trading began.[25] Two or three times when they clamoured too much I stopped trading and leisurely lit my pipe until they calmed down a little — it seemed fairly effective. During an interval I said my hut the night before was very cold and asked at whose house I should sleep the coming night. Immediately a young man near me named Haviuyaq[26] said "mine," so I said "all right." Later in the evening my things were transferred to his hut,[27] where I found his wife Itoqanna — a pleasant woman who had badgered me less than the others — when I was naturally glad that I was to sleep in their hut. Her husband, however, I found almost as bad as the rest, who clamoured around and pestered me so much at times as almost to upset my temper. One man in particular was such a nuisance that at last I refused to have anything to do with him. I cooked some rice in Haviuyaq's hut on the primus and made cocoa, so that I had a good meal myself and something for the Eskimo spectators as well. Finally about 10 p.m. they left and we all turned in for the night — myself in my sleeping bag on one side of the platform, and Haviuyaq and his wife under a common sleeping skin on the other. The wife always sleeps apparently at the far end of the platform nearest the lamp and furthest from the entrance. Like the western Eskimos their feet are against the back wall and their heads towards the door. Haviuyaq has a .45-70 rifle for which he wanted cartridges.[28] I arranged that he should take me to the *Haneragmiut*,[29] and told him that if he came to our base I thought we had cartridges there that would fit his gun. He agreed to return with me [to the station] the next day.[30] There was an amusing episode in the morning. Some Eskimos rushed up to me and said that there were three ptarmigan nearby. I seized my rifle and set out towards them, followed by the whole tribe and their dogs. I waved them back, but my own dog Telluraq had sighted a ptarmigan and chased it, though I called to him to come back. The ptarmigan flew on to the top of the rise. I drove Telluraq back then shot the bird — there was only one in sight. It was still fluttering and I was pressing on it with my foot when Telluraq suddenly pulled it out from under me and ran off with it, chased by myself and the Eskimos, like the proverbial dog with the cricket ball. The chase was so hot that at length he was obliged to drop it. An Eskimo grabbed it up and I saw it no more, nor ever learned where it disappeared to.

Monday, November 30th

Aksiatak was astir at 4:30 a.m. in the neighbouring hut, so I and my host and hostess turned out also. I lit the primus and cooked some oatmeal. Itoqanna gave me also some raw deer meat, which was quite good. She was very anxious for a bowl and offered me a pair of women's deerskin *kamik's* for them (her own). Curiously enough they are separate and reach barely up to the thighs — boot and leg being in one. How they are held up I do not know, but it must be by a strap in some way. I gave her a coffee tin and one or two small things, which pleased her very much. Practically every man and boy in the village put his hand to loading the sled — a great nuisance. Haviuyaq's cousin [Huputaun] was travelling with us also,[31] and brought two dogs, which we hitched on to one side of the sled and Haviuyaq's two dogs to the other. I left with Itoqanna one-half can [of] coal oil, a bowl, and a coffee tin full of lard to be kept for my return. We set out at a great speed and continued so over the smooth bay ice mile after mile — one at a time riding in turn on the runners at the back of the sled. The dogs pulled well, but we had 30 miles or so to travel before reaching *Ukullik* (the Liston and Sutton Islands) where our iglu was (direction Magnetic South or true southwest), and the dogs were well tired when we reached our destination. The three men set about knocking out the front of the iglu to build it larger, while I unhitched and fed the dogs and unlashed the sled. The house was ready by the time I had done this latter and our things hustled inside. It was fairly comfortable when the primus was set going. I thawed out a big fish and some caribou meat for them and boiled some rice. They thought it was the proper thing to eat up anything I had — self invited though one of them was (Huputaun) — in fact he was the one most vociferous in voicing his demands. He had three very large bull caribou skins as a bedding and another large thick skin to cover him. These were so warm that they all lay naked beneath the skin covering while I tumbled in a similar condition into my sleeping bag. I had trouble with my nose all day — which persisted in its efforts to freeze. The sky was beautifully clear — almost calm — and the sun was visible for some time — the result of refraction.

Tuesday, December 1st

The primus was lit at 7 a.m. We got away about 9 a.m. and made Bernard Harbour about 1 p.m. Ayallik and his people had been down and paid them [the Expedition members] a visit, while Aksiatak's folk were there when we arrived. Cox had bought a number of specimens for me — two bows, a small stone pot, a copper *ulo* etc., besides a number of fine salmon trout. Ayallik's wife (Cox thought) had stolen a small frying pan, and Aksiatak's people when they left made off with a large cup. The women seem to do the stealing, concealing the things in the large trouser's legs. I told Aksiatak about the former, but the latter theft was not discovered till after he left. I paid him a bowl and some calico, and gave him a large knife in return for which he was to bring tomorrow a big stone lamp. I bought from Huputaun another big stone lamp for the same price, and brought back from the *Puivlirmiut* — besides other specimens — a large stone pot, while another large pot I bought was left over there. Haviuyaq and Huputaun made themselves at home. They did not hesitate to say what kind of food they wanted — dried fish, seal meat, caribou meat — and refused white man's food save hard-bread. All the Eskimo I have met here, with the possible exception of Itoqanna, will beg and clamour for anything they fancy, like children without the least shame or hesitation. If you give them a needle they will say "thanks, give me some matches too." Itoqanna seemed different. I offered her a safety pin and she offered in return a bone fastening to a bag or something, and another bone fastening in exchange for a skin needle she saw I had. We made special effort to treat our two guests well, but they seemed not to appreciate it in the least. The sun was visible again today.

Wednesday, December 2nd

The sun has disappeared for 6 weeks or so, though fine clear weather marked his departure. The temperature yesterday was down to about -27°, but today it was around zero. I was busy preparing for a prolonged stay among the *Puivlirmiut* with Haviuyaq and his wife. All the tribes about here, he said, the *Noahognirmiut, Puivlirmiut, Akulliakuttogmiut* and the *Haneragmiut* will gather shortly around the Liston and Sutton Islands sealing. He knows the *Kanghiryuajiagmiut*[32] — the blond people Stefansson speaks of — and will take me to them in [the] spring over the mountains when the caribou come, about April. It is too cold, he said, to cross the mountains in winter, and round the coast it is a very long way. Hitqoq and Hogaluk turned up in the morning — the latter bringing the big stone lamp Akhiatak sold me — a fine specimen. We told him about the cup and he brought it back in the afternoon. Iguaq — the thief — is forbidden the house for a month. Cox found a saucer has disappeared also, but does not know whether it was Akhiatak's or Ayallik's people who stole it. The latter are camped over on an island about 3 miles from here.[33] Akhiatak's and probably Ayallik's [people] also are moving over to the Liston and Sutton Islands tomorrow. Our two guests Haviuyaq and Huputaun were a great nuisance. I bought a good dog from the latter with a saw, and a pair of deerskin boots with a fox-trap. Both of them pestered me time after time wishing me to buy this and that. I told them I was busy preparing to leave tomorrow[34] and put them off for a while till I had a spare moment; Palaiyak too told them the same for me. They became excited, declared they were going off to Akhiatak's at once, put on their boots etc. I told them it was all right — they could leave when they liked, but incidentally showed Palaiyak the rifle I was going to give to the man who should take me to the *Kanghiryuajiagmiut* in the spring. They calmed down then, and Hitqoq appearing at the same time, they waited till we others had dinner then had their own. As they were leaving just afterwards to go to Akhiatak's house Palaiyak, following some instructions I had given him quietly before, told Haviuyaq that if I liked living in his house they would get plenty of presents and he could take me to the *Kanghiryuajiagmiut*, but if I didn't I should go and live with some other native and bestow all the rewards on him. Haviuyaq, Palaiyak told me afterwards, is anxious to have me. We spent a quiet evening, in various occupations, Cox making me an ice spear out of an old chisel, and Palaiyak lashing it on to a handle. Haviuyaq remarkably resembles the picture of Ahngoodloo in Peary's *Snowland Folk* ([1904], p. 48).[35] Palaiyak, who was missionary trained, told them the missionaries were coming in here next year and would teach them so that they might go to heaven. They said they did not want to go to heaven; this place was a good place — there were plenty of caribou. Haviuyaq asked him why he clipped his (Palaiyak's) hair short, [since] he had a rifle; Haviuyaq wore his hair long because he had a rifle.

Thursday, December 3rd

We were having breakfast at 7:30 a.m. when Ayallik and most of his people came in. As usual they were much in the way, but I got the sled loaded despite them and set out towards *Ukullik* to meet Haviuyaq and Huputaun on the ice. Johansen went with me, for the sled was moderately heavy. We reached the rough ice — about 5 miles out — without seeing any signs of them. Alone with a heavy sled and only five dogs I could not attempt to negotiate the broken ice, so we turned aside to the island[36] where Ayallik's people are camped. On the way we saw a hut just vacated and the sled trail with the tracks of four men leading from it towards *Ukullik*. Evidently they were the tracks of Hitqoq, Hogaluk, Haviuyaq, and Huputaun — they must have left before daylight. From Ayallik's people later we found that this was so. We met a few minutes later Kaumaq (Ayallik's wife)[37] who, Cox said, had stolen a small frying pan. She guided us to their huts — three single snowhouses, well built — in a drift of deep snow beside an island. On the way I arranged to sleep with them the night. She was carrying a large pot, which I doubt her ever receiving in legitimate trade. I asked her if it were not ours but could not understand her reply, so I put it on my sled and it now rests on top of her house. I shall try to judge from their attitude towards it whether it is theirs or ours. I saw two frying pans in her hut — one received for a pair of boots, she said, the other for a ladle. In face of this I could say nothing, though I doubt it. She gave us cold, boiled seal meat — Anauyuk speared a seal the other day. Later Johansen returned to the station, while I stayed with sled and dogs, and arranged with Kamiñgoq to accompany me across to the *Puivlirmiut* in return for a pan, an empty lard tin, and a fox-trap. Ayallik's people made me very comfortable, fed me (though I cooked rice as well), gave me a little meat for my dogs, and did not pester me to give them matches etc., or to buy things from them. The weather was calm and clear, moderately cold, but with no appearance of the sun. We turned in about 6:30 p.m. Kaumaq, I noticed, instead of sleeping innermost as is usual, slept one in as it were — her husband was innermost.

Friday, December 4th

Ayallik had to take some [meat] to the station [at Bernard Harbour] so I went with him. All were astir about 4:30 a.m., and we had dried fish and blubber for breakfast. We did not leave, however, till about 8 a.m. and then caught up with Kamiñgoq and others also on their way thither.

They are a plague at the station, but the three families leave tomorrow for *Ukullik* to seal over there and I with them, so they should be less trouble in the future. I traded with them for various things, notably a fine harpoon and a woman's outer coat, then tried to induce them all to return with me,[38] but only Ayallik came. The rest said they would follow soon, but were plainly expecting a meal. Johansen and Palaiyak were taking soundings of the outer harbour, and returned just as I was leaving. Donald[39] was frozen in this morning as before. I doubt his living very long. We saw a fresh trail leading to *Ukullik* — Akhiatak's people. All the four neighbouring tribes gather there — the *Haneragmiut, Noahognirmiut, Puivlirmiut*, and the *Ahuttokullugmiut*.[40] Kaumaq gave me some seal meat almost as soon as I entered, and I cooked rice again. As we were turning in each received a dried fish. Tonight there are sleeping in the hut Ayallik, then his wife, next the little boy Ivagluk, then Anauyuk (brother of Ayallik — his wife is dead), then myself. Taptuna, the boy who slept last night between Anauyuk and me, has gone to sleep in Kallun's hut, as we were rather crowded last night. The weather was again beautifully calm and clear, though tonight there is a ring round the moon. Anauyuk is snoring gloriously. I have noticed several Eskimos doing this, and two (one [of them] Palaiyak) talking in their sleep. On these snow platforms, if you want to pass water during the night you get out from under your sleeping skin and do so against the snow at the bottom or side of the bed or (if you have one) use a *qorviq*. There is a cavity under the middle of the platform covered, I think, with boards. It serves to pack bags etc. underneath. Near my head is a stone with a small hollow set on sticks in the wall — it is a lamp. I saw one burning in Kamiñgoq's house, tended by Aqara, his daughter(?). The lamp expired during the night — so did the one in Haviuyaq's house. I sketched Kaumaq's arm this morning[41] — she is tattooed (by means of a copper needle, sinew, and lamp black) on both forearm and upper arm. Imilguna says she herself has none on the upper arm.

Saturday, December 5th

We were all up before 6 a.m., and after a breakfast of dried fish and blubber loaded the sleds. A hole was broken in the wall for the purpose, as it was much simpler than through the long passage. Ayallik was given a pot of sealskin (*kataq*) full of water with which he coated the mud runners of the sled. Nevertheless the resultant ice coating had worn off before we reached the islands[42] and the tracks of all three Eskimo sleds were brown with earth. We left at 8 a.m. while it was still dark and stumbled for an hour over broken ice. Taptuna accompanied me with my sled — twice it upset with him and once with me at the handles. Eskimo sleds, having all the weight close to the ground and many sticks and other things placed crosswise above, cannot easily upset. The wife of each family hauled on the sled ahead of the dogs, the men close to the sled but in front, a little behind them so that they could prod them [the dogs] with their sticks. Kalyutarun carried her baby [Okomiq] on her

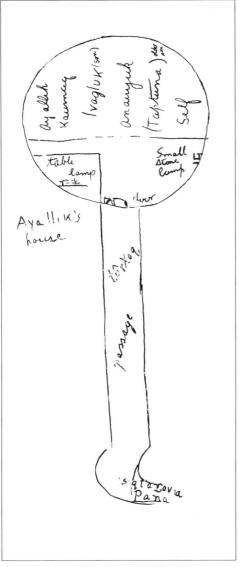

Figure 135. Plan of Ayallik's snowhouse at the Liston and Sutton Islands, December 5, 1914.[43]

back. All carried walking sticks to help them along — in the case of the men to beat the dogs also. About 9:30 a.m. we came to smoother ice, but snow had been falling in the night and was still falling so that the sledding was not very good. My seal was on Kamiñgoq's sled, and my dogs were doing fairly well, so I took Ivagluk on mine practically the whole way. We reached the middle (southeast) of the Ukullik Islands (*Putulik*[44]) about 2 p.m. Taptuna went ahead at the last to prod the snow with a horn snow-sounder, but Ayallik condemned the place he suggested and found another where it was deeper. Kaumaq immediately took their unhitched dogs back to help on Kallun's sled, which was far behind, and after fixing up my own dogs I went back to drag on Qamiñ-goq's. All the men began to build snowhouses at once. I tried to light the primus, but there was a moderate west wind and the attempt was unsuccessful, so I helped Kaumaq shovel snow round the bottom of the hut, then when it was nearly built lit the primus inside. Soon there was water for all to drink — which is saying something, for they had about 3 pints each; then I cooked rice and melted more snow for water. Taptuna laid a layer of blocks round the outside of the house, and Kaumaq and I filled in the interspace with soft snow; the bottom was thus made more secure and air tight. A hole was left in the side through which everything was passed in. Then the hole was closed while they made a passage of snow-blocks and roofed it over. Kallun and Qamiñgoq made similar houses, but only one common passage with separate openings into it and no common forecourt or open space between their two houses. All the snow-blocks above the first layer rest on one block and overlap on the next. One or two small blocks only violate this rule. The roof or dome blocks rest on three or even four, set on a bevel. The last key-stone is pushed up from below through the roof, then gently lowered, and it and neighbouring blocks trimmed until it exactly fits.[45] An oval of snow-blocks was then set round inside and the space between them and the walls filled with snow from the floor so as to make a platform. The hollow centre of the oval was then covered with pieces of wood laid across so that there was a storage for bags etc. underneath. The table was then set up; resting on the snow wall at one end and on a curious board with a long elbow at the other set thus:

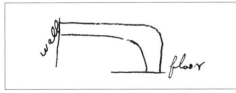

Figure 136. Ayallik's table.

Behind the table the two stone lamps were set on two sticks laid in the same way as the table. A stick set perpendicularly on the elbow board and another resting on this running horizontally, parallel to the elbow board, supported the drying rack (*iñitat*) at one end, and two sticks running lengthwise to the wall parallel to the table took the weight of the frame at the other.[46] The bed platform was covered with several small mats of bound willow twigs; above these were laid musk-ox skins, fur downwards, and above these again deerskins fur upwards — then the sleeping skins, and my [sleeping] bag. We each had some dry and mouldy fish to eat first, then rice; later Kalyutarun brought in two large pieces of frozen salmon (two had already gone to the third house). She gave one to Anauyuk and the other to me. Anauyuk's was divided evenly amongst the rest, but all save Ivahluk refused to share mine, just why I do not know. Later when all had turned in save Anauyuk, and I was writing my diary in my sleeping bag, we all had some boiled seal meat. The

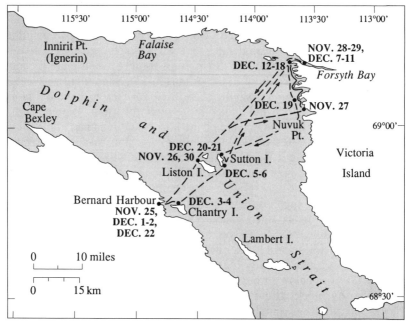

Figure 137. Map showing routes taken by author on trips to visit the *Puivlirmiut*, between November 26 and December 22, 1914.

ice window was carried on the sled and will be set up tomorrow. Taptuna sleeps with us tonight — Ayallik, Kaumaq, Ivahluk, Anauyuk, Taptuna, and I, in that order. Lamp and table as before are on the left of the door — so too in Qamiñgoq's hut, but on the right in Kallun's.

Sunday, December 6th

Qamiñgoq and I were to cross over to the *Puivlirmiut* today, but we were delayed by one thing and another till 8:30 a.m., and just as we started the harness of one of his dogs broke. He had no spare harness — this had to be repaired — so we postponed the trip till tomorrow. All the men, after the few minutes occupied in putting the ice windows in the houses, went sealing, but Qamiñgoq alone was successful. He brought back a large foetid seal, speared at its hole, drawn by his two dogs. His wife when she saw him coming merely said "*Qowana nakemmun*" (hooray for the seal) then went inside. A small piece of the blubber, cut from the breast, was given to each of us, and Kalyutarun (Qamiñgoq's wife) skinned and cut up the seal in her house. Portions were sent to the other two houses, and I received special parts — part of the great intestine, part of the heart, and later some boiled meat. I bought part of the liver with some blubber for a needle and fried the former with salt and pepper as a special dainty for myself. The Eskimos loathe salt and pepper. Part of the day I spent in Qamiñgoq's house then went out to look for ptarmigan (and later learned there are none here). Talking, jotting down words, measuring Ayallik's hut filled up the rest of the day. Ayallik is very anxious for me to stay the winter in his hut, as he finds it means good trade and many presents. Kaumaq must have an instinct that it is Sunday, for she combed her hair with a small bone comb and cleaned the heads of the rest. She wanted to clean mine (eating the contents), but I assured her it was clean.

Monday, December 7th

I had a very comfortable night, being snug and warm in my new sleeping bag. On the whole the night is the most comfortable time in these Eskimo houses. I turned out at 5 a.m. and cooked some cornmeal, then loaded the sled. We started out at 7 a.m., Qamiñgoq and I;[47] Taptuna[48] wished very much to come and was rather persistent, but I sent him back. We travelled by moonlight for a couple of hours, then day dawned sunless but fine, though a little foggy. The dogs made fair time on the whole, and we had two trails to follow, mine when I returned, and Akhiatak's when he crossed over 2 or 3 days ago.[49] Twice squalls of westerly wind struck us — helping us on though they lasted but a short time. Near land — about 2:30 p.m. — we came on a deserted hut, where Akhiatak and his people spent the night. From there we lost the trail in the dark, and when we found the land did not know which way to go. However, we floundered along, occasionally spotting a trail for a moment, until about 4:30 p.m. we struck the Eskimo camp.[50] I fed the dogs about 200 yards away, then went right into their camp without their noticing. The first house I poked my head into was Akhiatak's new one, and they were all surprised. My things were bundled into Haviuyaq's[51] house, and his wife gave me a four-course meal: caribou fat, frozen caribou meat, a dried fish (very mouldy), and finally a portion of boiled caribou leg. There was no water at hand so I boiled the kettle on the primus and made cocoa for myself. This family luckily dislikes English food, one reason for trying to settle with it this winter. The man, however, is an unconscionable beggar, constantly asking for presents. If he gives me a piece of meat to eat, he wants payment enough for a whole caribou, despite his being my guest for 3 days[52] without a request of any kind — like a European guest in fact. His wife, too, I am afraid, hardly upholds the first opinion I had of her, though so far (I have given her several presents) she has asked me to pay her for the meal only that she gave me tonight. Still, she ate a good portion of the coffee tin of lard that I cached with her, and from the experience I have had of all these people I should be thankful she did not eat all. I set them playing cat's cradles and found they know several I have learned to the west, besides several new ones.[53] They must not play save when the sun is away[54] — and it made its appearance for the last time yesterday, a fraction of a rim. I learned tonight the reason of their prolonged stay on the coast before sealing. The women are making their winter clothes of deerskin and they must be finished before sealing is commenced.[55] Eskimo children are old fashioned little things in many ways — hence their charm. Many of them have a habit when they enter a house of executing a kind of Pyrrhonic[56] dance first on one foot then on the other.

Tuesday, December 8th

We turned out soon after 6 a.m. Haviuyaq had some caribou cooked and asked me if I should like some, but wanted to know at the same time what I would give him in return. So I cooked some cornmeal instead and ate that. There was the usual bother over trade afterwards. One man, Quputim by name, nearly caused serious trouble by seizing a big knife which I had great difficulty in making him hand over.[57] Ikpuquaq was very serviceable in supporting me, but everyone else kept out of it. Things looked very awkward at one moment. The man and his wife left during the morning to go along to the *Nagyuktomiut*,[58] I think. I bought a considerable quantity of caribou meat from Ikpuquaq with two boxes of .30-30 ammunition, some frozen fish (*tacim ekalloa*), and some dried fish, the latter for the dogs. Then with the large knife [Quputim had seized earlier] I bought a lot of caribou meat from Haviuyaq, with some good deerskins from which Itoqunna is making me a coat of the fashionable shape and a pair of deerskin mits. She has been working on the *atigi* all day. With a bowl and a lard can I bought an outer and an inner woman's coat, with another lard can a pair of women's trousers. Two fox-traps were stolen from my sled — I cannot find out by whom. A number of us played cat's cradles in the evening. Many are the same or little different from those known to the west, but their songs here seem very crude. These people are not going to *Ukullik* till the sun reappears. They are now making deerskin clothes, for these must not be made on the ice, while sealskin clothes must not be made on land. I fried some caribou this afternoon and made rice and cocoa, so had a good meal. Two bolts on my sled have broken, the two on the left runner at the back end. I knocked one out and put in a fresh one, but it is too long, and I do not know whether it may not be necessary to extract it later. By an oversight I have no small sled bolts with me. The weather was fine all day, but a fresh west wind sprang up towards evening. The pipe which I lost on the trail was found by Akhiatak and returned to me this morning. Of course he wanted payment, but I had made him a present of a fox-trap the other day so he did not get one.

Wednesday, December 9th

A strong west wind blew all day causing a little drift and apparently a rise of the tide, for water flooded the ice in the bay. I arranged with Qamiñgoq that he should return alone to *Ukullik* while I stay here. One of the stolen fox-traps was found on the sled this morning, but the other is still missing, so I have refused to do any trading. In one of the snow-houses a line was passed down through two holes in the roof and small loops made at each end. Some of the young men amused themselves by performing a simple gymnastic feat thereon, hanging by the arms, then half circling and placing the feet in the loops and releasing the hands, hanging full length head downwards. Then they had to half circle up and catch hold again with the hands and drop. One or two women tried to perform the same trick. Itoqunna finished my *atigi* today — the second day's work — and started on trousers for her husband. The tattooing on the faces of the women — or at least of two of them — was done by their mothers, that on the arms by themselves. I had an excellent supper tonight — fried fish, boiled caribou meat, rice, and cocoa. Afterwards I learned a new cat's-cradle figure and found amusement in inducing some of the Eskimos to draw. None showed Palaiyak's talent. Itoqunna told me that her father, a *Puivlirmiutaq*, was stabbed and killed not many years ago by a *Noahognirmiutaq* named Hitqoq apparently[59] — not the man I know by that name; I could find or understand no reason for it. I asked Itoqunna to make me a good pair of sealskin overshoes, but she said not now, but when they were on the ice — in her case, at least, the taboo carries weight. The names of these Eskimos sound fearfully long when they tell you both [names] at once, for they add to each the termination -*viunilu* (i.e. either). An elderly woman, Taqtuq, told me this morning that she had seen in her sleep a hand and forearm abstracting the traps from my sled, but did not know whose hand it was. However, she thought even this much information a great achievement.

Thursday, December 10th

Last night's wind had abated and half the settlement left this morning for the sea.[60] However, Haviuyaq and his people did not go, so I also stayed. A snow-shovel was put up during the morning about 120 yards away and several of us tried our marksmanship. Haviuyaq, with my rifle, put five successive shots — some distance apart — through it, while after about twelve shots I only succeeded in putting one through. It was very humiliating, and I could not find out where my shots went. Two shots, later at 200 yards, seemed to prove that I was either canting very badly or the rifle carries far to the left. I must test it thoroughly in a good light when I can see where the shots go. The rest of the day was spent in visiting the different houses. Haviuyaq is a conceited fellow and has been rather a bother the last few days, but his wife Itoqunna seems the quietest and perhaps the most intelligent woman in the settlement. It was all the more vexing that Haviuyaq should have succeeded so well at shooting, though he failed at 200 yards. The dog that I bought from Huputaun broke loose this morning and followed him,[61] but a boy brought it back. I bought from Ikpukkuaq a bow and quiver with arrows, feathers etc., complete for a saw, and a small stone pot for a coal-oil can. Several articles of clothing and other things I have arranged to buy at *Ukullik*. The women sew in exactly the same way as the women [to the] west, the thimble on the forefinger, and the needle pushed through with the side, not the top of the thimble. It is then seized on the other side with thumb and middle finger, drawn right through and turned on its side, then the thimble is set behind it and the thread drawn right through, and the needle inserted for the next stitch. Generally it is not drawn taut till the second stitch. The sewing is always, I think, carried from right to left, the left hand bringing the two parts together that are to be stitched.

Friday, December 11th

There was an interesting insight into the customs of these Eskimos last night. After 'supper' Itoqunna disappeared, and Niq entered the house. I was playing cat's cradles with three of the children. She took Itoqunna's place and a little later turned in to bed. Itoqunna, I believe, slept with Niq's husband Akhiatak — an exchange of wives for the night — very likely in connection with the change from the summer hunting of caribou on land to the winter's sealing on the ice. In the morning Niq turned out, mended the trousers of Haviuyaq's father, who sleeps in the other part of the house, and generally took the place of Itoqunna. A little later Itoqunna came in, said not a word, but went into the other part of the house, trimmed the lamp, and appeared to wait for Niq to depart, which she did quietly a few minutes later. No words passed between the two women, but when Itoqunna entered, Haviuyaq laughingly asked me "Where is Itoqunna?" — alluding to my question of the night before, whereupon everyone laughed. I do not know if everyone exchanged wives last night, though Haviuyaq asked me if I still wanted to sleep alone. The custom is, of course, well known among savages from books, but strangely enough it shook my nerves more than anything else I have seen in the Arctic — even more, I think, than Andre Norem's suicide.[62] Itoqunna resumed her usual place in the house today and is sleeping with her husband tonight. I have not dared to enquire yet whether it was in connection with the sealing — though I feel rather ashamed of my weakness in this respect as an ethnologist.

Two or three told me today that on the ice caribou and fish may be eaten raw, but must not be cooked, and I promised not to cook any. Ikpukkuaq said that long ago some people cooked caribou on the ice and the ice cracked up and they perished. Others agreed that a similar result would happen if they infringed the rule. More people — Wikiaq's and Iguaq's[63] — left today and tomorrow the rest of us — Haviuyaq's, Akhiatak's, and Ikpukkuaq's — leave. Ikpukkuaq is not coming to *Ukullik* till the sun reappears — nor possibly the others either, when a great number of people — *Haneragmiut* and *Ukulliakutogmiut* included — gather also; the *Nagyuktomiut* do not come. I strolled with two of the children up the river[64] — which appears to be a tidal estuary here — in places 1/2 mile or so wide, to see their traps. We passed and demolished a rabbit or a fox carved from a snow-block by these children and set up on the ground. Two of their traps were home-made to this extent — the springs and chains were obtained from Joe Bernard;[65] the rest they had made themselves. One had copper jaws, the other iron. The latter I obtained from Ikpukkuaq in exchange for a good trap. The children had made a little box of snow-blocks — the bait (seal blubber) set inside and the trap laid on the surface at the mouth fully exposed. Haviuyaq was fixing up the runners of his sled — chipping off excrescences of frozen earth and generally smoothing it. I bought a stone lamp (comparatively small) and a large wooden bowl from Ikpukkuaq for a machete — a big price — but he was a good ally when Quputim tried to make off with the big knife, and I wished to reward him. He was very anxious for me to stop with him when we leave tomorrow and to accompany me in the spring to the *Kanghiryuarmiut,* but I am pledged to Haviuyaq as long as I have no cause for complaint. I told Haviuyaq, however, about it, thinking that it will make him more solicitous about my comfort. It was very cold today — even in the house I had to wear mits, though outside it was fine — with a very faint easterly breeze. There was a fine aurora in the evening. Ikpukkuaq, I forgot to mention, is to bring lamp and bowl to *Ukullik* when the sun returns, though I gave him the machete now to show my confidence in him. Fish are speared, I learned today, both in winter and in summer with the *qaqiviuk*(?) or three-pronged trident — in winter, I imagine, through a hole in the ice when they are attracted by lowering a bait on a line. I have been much confused by the use of the word *iglopuk* for double(?) or large(?) snowhouses and also for our station in Bernard Harbour. These people are a great nuisance when I am writing or thinking — they have no conception apparently of a man's wishing to be silent. There are two uses of signs for speech — screwing up the nose for "no" and lifting the eyebrows for "yes." Some use these signs much more than others — Itoqunna I have noticed particularly. She told me tonight that if we want any sewing of deerskins this winter it could be done on land at the station but not on the ice.[66]

Saturday, December 12th

We were to travel some 4 miles today to the new settlement,[67] so we had to turn out perforce before 4 o'clock because they could not tell how long it would be before daylight. It was foggy and a strong east wind causing some drift, but it abated somewhat later and snow fell. We sat about for an hour and a half or more, then Haviuyaq, with water made by Itoqunna over the stone lamp, iced the runners of his sled. I loaded my sled and hitched up the dogs, then waited for the others to finish. The ice window was taken out, and the things passed through the opening thus made.[68] We did not leave till 9:45 a.m., when Akhiatak and Ikpukkuaq — the only other two families remaining — also left. *Qimirjuak*[69] seems to be the name of a portion of the coast or possibly an island near here (a little west) — it is not the name of the river, which is *Ugjuq.* Haviuyaq's father [Haviraun] is sick, so he stood on the runners of my sled as it was fairly light and the travelling was good. Haviuyaq built a large single iglu for himself, Itoqunna, his father and younger brother [Utuallu], and myself.[70] I attempted great execution with a snow shovel, filling in the gap between the outer and inner wall; the outer wall was carried up two blocks in both Akhiatak's and Haviuyaq's houses, whereas in Ayallik's and Qamingoq's it was carried up only one block. I fed the dogs, then while Itoqunna and another woman (her cousin?) were fixing up the inside arrangements and the men (save Haviuyaq's father) were making the passage — Akhiatak's branches off from ours[71] — I lit the primus and made some water. Then when the passage was finished and the house reopened (to put the things in, a hole is left in the side nearest the sled, which is closed up before the passage is begun) I brought in some things from my sled and boiled rice. When I was heating the water Itoqunna told me that we could not cook either fish or caribou now. Akhiatak, I find, is Haviuyaq's cousin,[72] his father [Taptuna] being an elder brother of Haviuyaq's. Several people spent the evening in the hut and we played cat's cradles, whereby I learned two new figures. Tomorrow Akhiatak and I go along the coast [southward] towards *Nuvok*[73] and bring in the food I cached there. I have dog-food for one day only, but there is a tin of pemmican there.

Sunday, December 13th

Akhiatak and I left with an empty sled for *Nuvok* where I had cached my things — before 9 a.m. It was barely twilight. We caught up to two young fellows with a small sled who were going the same way for a bag of blubber. Three lads who had lost their way about a mile out were directed to their settlement — even Eskimos near home seem to lose their way. Travelling at a fair pace we reached the house at noon, put the things on the sled and returned. The whole journey was about 24 miles, and we did not regain the settlement until dark. I was anxious to get in before dark if possible, for it is easier to feed the dogs in the daylight, so the last part of the way I neither rode on the sled myself nor would allow the other three. Hitherto we had taken turns. But the ungrateful fellows, whenever my back was turned, would stand on the back and check the pace until I became angry and turned them away. These Eskimos seem not to have developed a sentiment of gratitude. Favours showered on them only make them worry you for more. It was interesting to notice the apparent affection shown by Itoqunna and Haviuyaq for each other, despite the temporary change in the marital relations the other night. Akhiatak said today that they changed wives because they were relatives (Akhiatak and Haviuyaq are first cousins); apparently it has no connection with the change from land-hunting to sealing. If I give Itoqunna a hard-bread or similar thing she always keeps half for her husband — and others do the same. The products of the chase seemed to be shared among the different families more or less equally. Anyone in the house when a meal is in progress receives (or is at least offered) something. One of the women was mending an old pair of deerskin trousers. When I asked her about it she said they were very old and worthless, otherwise she could not sew them on the ice. Akhiatak asked me today if I were going with Ikpukkuaq's people to the *Kanghiryuagmiut*. Apparently there is no love lost between Haviuyaq's kinsmen and Ikpukkuaq's. I told him I did not know — that I would like to go with Haviuyaq and his wife, but that while Itoqunna was satisfactory Haviuyaq was a bother through his constant begging. Apparently he told Haviuyaq, for this evening the latter, who had experienced an unsuccessful day's sealing, left me strictly in peace. Others too who entered seemed to realise that I did not want to be bothered, so I had a quiet pleasant evening — the pleasantest I have yet had. Matches are in great demand for lighting the lamp in the morning. Huputaun sent in a little caribou meat for matches, and another family brought a couple of dried fish for the same purpose. Itoqunna has just prosecuted a search of Haviuyaq's head — in bed.

Monday, December 14th

After breakfast this morning I visited Wikkiaq's house. He has a charming little daughter named Alunaq — the same name as my dog — and I called her the other day, half in jest, my daughter — she is about 11 years of age. It caused much amusement and the title has stuck to her. Her mother stitched some rents in my mits, for which she received a present of matches. Thence I visited Qiñaloqunna's iglu — the roof of which is very flat and has to be supported with a small board resting on a perpendicular pole set in the floor. Qinaloqunna is Ikpukkuaq's elder brother[74] and father-in-law of Huputaun, Haviuyaq's first cousin (son of his father's elder brother). Hence the two families are connected by marriage (both are *Puivlirmiut*, Haviuyaq says), though there seems to be some jealousy between the two, and each is seeking to replace the other in my favour and go with me to the *Kanghiryuagmiut*. Haviuyaq's is the last house at one end of the settlement, and Ikpukkuaq's the last at the other [end]. Thence I went on to Ikpukkuaq's iglu, led by his little daughter Qanajuq — as charming if not more so than Alunaq. Ikpukkuaq with all the other men had gone sealing, so I did not stay. Only Haviuyaq and Qiñaloqunna were left in the village, besides women and children — the former because of a ripening boil on his stomach, the latter because he is old and crippled with a bad knee; in addition he is blind in one eye — the right. I forgot also Haviraun — Haviuyaq's father — who is sick — stomach trouble of some kind.

Three or four of the children amused themselves and me by dancing in Qiñaloqunna's iglu to the beating of a small child's drum. Apparently there are at least three kinds of dances; the first where one stands in the middle beating the drum while the others stand in a circle round the drummer, all singing in concert, the only movement of the feet being that of the drummer as he faces one or other of the circle; this was the kind of dance which celebrated my first arrival.[75] In the second kind one beats the drum and sings while another jumps from one foot to the other, shaking the head from side to side and keeping the knees bent. The third resembles more a western dance, one drumming while another prances about in time, gesticulating and waving the arms. (As I write this in bed, next to Haviuyaq, Itoqunna has just finished what she said was a very productive search of his head.) The children, boys and girls, were playing at building snowhouses, using proper snow-knives made by hammering out a file, with the usual horn handle and its oval tip, bound round with willow. Knives over west also used to be made (and probably some are still) by hammering out files. A ptarmigan was seen near the village but was frightened away. I searched round for it but could not find it. Haviuyaq's boil having come to a head he pricked it with a needle and squeezed it on to a piece of caribou meat. He asked to be allowed to give this to my dog Scotty, because it is the biggest dog in my team. If I understood him aright, when I go away the dog will carry away the 'contagion' with it. I told him he might, and he proceeded to take it out but dropped it on the floor. One of his dogs attempted to seize it, and he hastily and, as it seemed, anxiously drove it off.[76] It can't hurt Scotty, and it was an interesting insight into one of their superstitions.

One of the women made me a pair of sealskin overshoes — too large — to wear outside my deerskin boots. I got her to make them smaller before paying her, but they are still badly fitting. However, my need is pressing, for my deerskin boots are already spoilt with the thawing snow floors. Itoqunna will make me a decent pair soon. There was a light west wind blowing all day, with one or two brief squalls, which started the snow drifting. I presented Haviuyaq with a file and Itoqunna with another (a small one). Some of the natives here like sugar and chocolate, some do not — they call it 'salty' (*mamaitoq*). Children generally like it. These people have a curious custom when they are a short distance away e.g., as in standing on the edge of a crowd or when running ahead of the sled, of nodding the head to you or raising the hand to the shoulder and shaking it; you are supposed to respond. The men all returned in a body, all alike unsuccessful. There is no taboo on the names of dead, for Itoqunna told me the name of Haviuyaq's mother without any hesitation, though she added immediately that she is dead. Generally though they tell you at once that the person is dead and seem to expect the matter to be left at that without further enquiry as to the name. I enquired of Itoqunna why some have one, some two, and some even three names, and she said they were named according to the number of people who had recently died — receiving their names. It is an interesting fact that the children seem to grasp what I am trying to say quicker than the older people — I have noticed this on several occasions. A patch was sewn on my deerskin boots today and Itoqunna repaired her deerskin *kummuk's* [*kamik's*] — it is only new deerskin that must not be sewn on the ice, she said. Wikkiaq's people wanted me to sleep in their house last night, and Ikpukkuaq repeated today his proposal of yesterday to the same effect, and also asked whether I was not going to use him and his people to take me to the *Kanghiryuagmiut* in the spring. This is making Haviuyaq very uneasy; he is beginning to realise that my choice of him and his wife depends on how I like them this winter.

Tuesday, December 15th

A fine day, fairly clear and almost calm. The men went sealing again while I visited various houses and learned three or four cat's cradles.[77] Then I went for a short stroll and returning, visited more houses.[78] Haviuyaq became rather a nuisance tonight again. I shall not have him to go to the *Kanghiryuagmiut.* Qiqpuk's wife is tattooed, like Ayallik's, on the upper arm as well as on the lower, in the same way. I bought a caribou shoulder from Ikpukkuaq this evening. The men were again unsuccessful at sealing. Anauyak and Taptuna turned up in the evening. Anauyuk said he had killed two seals and Ayallik two, while Qamiñgoq had been successful also. A crowd poured in as usual when I began to cook rice, but I refused to feed any save Haviuyaq's own household and a man who brought me a little deer meat as payment. The sleds here are placed upside down on two blocks of snow, apparently to protect the runners or to keep them from drifting over, for they are certainly not out of reach of the dogs.

Wednesday, December 16th

A dull day, the temperature fairly high. A little snow fell at intervals. I have been noticing the boulders along the coast. Here dolomite or limestone predominates, with a little granite and diabase. Twelve miles southeast at *Nuvuk,* limestone seems to be almost absent, and the bowlders seem to me to be mostly granite. Haviuyaq at the last settlement[79] had a large anvil of granite (?) in which there was a thin vein of copper on the surface about 1 1/2 inches long. A crowd poured in to share my rice this morning, but I fooled them by having a cold breakfast of frozen caribou meat and hard-bread. A little later I melted some water for Haviraun and made myself some cocoa at the same time. Then I repacked two or three boxes and put some of my things on the sled ready to start any day. Afterwards I visited one house after another, eating a little caribou fat or dried fish in each and paying for it with matches. We played cat's cradles a little, but I learned only one trick — from Akhiatak, who seems very expert in the game. Haviuyaq and his folk appeared much sobered today at the signs of my approaching departure. His father tonight, who has been suffering with his stomach for some time and has hardly left the house, stitched a small strip of caribou fur on the right shoulder of my *atigi* (the outside calico one) and said something about my 'reaching the station soon', but exactly what it was I could not understand. Following his and Haviuyaq's instructions, I then moistened my hand (in reality I spat) with my tongue and rubbed his stomach all over. He seems to be a little congested also, and I promised to give him something in the morning (Epsom salts), which will cleanse him out. Haviuyaq said that the 'disease' would be expelled (let 'fall' *kataktoq*) in the process. One of the men told me that the only other tribes they meet when they go inland in summer are the *Nagyuktomiut* and the *Umingmuktomiut.*[80] From the latter they obtain their musk-ox skins and stone lamps and pots — trading copper-pointed arrows and knives. Haviuyaq said today his boil was all right, thanks to my dog. The wood for the large dishes is said to come from trees (*nepaatomiñ*) inland.

Thursday, December 17th

A blizzard followed yesterday's mild temperature, and the men all remained in camp save one or two who went to their fox-traps. Several houses developed cracks during the night. They lie on the edge of the reef, and the west wind caused the tide to rise and crack the ice. Haviuyaq's house is nearest the end of the reef and consequently his house suffered most.[81] Apparently there is not enough deep snow to build a new one, so the cracks were stuffed with snow at intervals during the day. I spent nearly all the time in other houses and found out one interesting fact. Quputim, who tried to take the big knife a few days ago [Dec. 8], has not left to join the *Nagyuktomiut* — a story I always doubted, for the two tribes seem to have no intercourse in winter and little in summer. He had been keeping out of my sight all the time. Today I happened to enter his house and saw him. I asked another man his name and he naively replied that it was not the man who had tried to take the knife, for he had gone to the *Nagyuktomiut*. When I pressed for the name they were unwilling to tell me, till finally the man himself gave me another — possibly his second name. I pretended to believe. My dog Alunaq, I learned today, went with the two men who left yesterday to bring back blubber from the other side of *Nuvok*. They said he was unharnessed and followed of his own accord, but I suspect otherwise. Haviuyaq and his people are afraid the water will flood the hut during the night and drown them in their sleep. I sounded all round with my ice-pick and fell through in one place, making one foot wet. The water is flooding in from one side only — all the rest seems firm. What I fear most is the collapse of the hut. They appealed to me about it, and I calmly told them that they might sleep securely — the water would probably rise a little but not enough to hurt. I hope I don't prove a false prophet. I gave Haviraun a dose of salts this morning, and he said this evening his stomach was a little better. Another old man Qiñaloqunna, who has a bad knee, asked me to do something for it. I told him I would fetch him something from the station. I am buying dried fish for dog-food daily with matches. Itoqunna made me a pair of sealskin overshoes. They are not very good but better than any I have had yet. I made her a present of a large aluminum pot I promised her some time ago. The men spent much time in polishing their iron harpoon-heads and knives with pieces of fur. I am pretty sure they will leave here as soon as the men return with the blubber for the lamps. Haviuyaq did nothing to patch up his house. Itoqunna strewed snow on the floor, and Akhiatak and Haviuyaq's younger brother [Utualu] did it all. He did not even help his wife remove the big lamp and other things from the weak side of the house. He talks of going to the station, but he shan't as far as I am concerned. These Eskimos do not whistle and are much interested whenever I happen to.

Friday, December 18th

A moderate southwest wind all day. My prophecy of last night was luckily fulfilled. We were not drowned in our sleep! The water rose a little, and the house cracked but did not fall. Another house also cracked and is supported by a stick set upright on the floor. Both Akhiatak and Haviuyaq built new houses, and I assisted in shovelling snow, then visited Ikpukkuaq's house, learned a cat's-cradle figure, and wrote two dance songs and bought a dressed doll made by Qanayuq. At Akhiatak's house I learned two more figures. The men who went for blubber returned today bringing back my dog Alunaq. Tomorrow all leave for *Nuvok*, for seals seem to be absent about here. The next day Akhiatak's family and I go on to *Ukullik*. I want to spend Xmas at the station. Akhiatak is waiting to turn in with Itoqunna alongside me, he and Haviuyaq having exchanged wives again for the night. But this time the men visit the wives, not the wives the men. Itoqunna is apparently asleep.

Saturday, December 19th

Akhiatak left as soon as he was dressed, and a few minutes later Haviuyaq entered and took his usual place. Apparently such incidents are so usual as to pass unnoticed. I did not hurry over turning out but lit the primus and had a good meal while the others were loading their sleds. Consequently I was not ready when they left — about 7 a.m., but caught up to them about a mile off. It was still dark and the two sleds of Haviuyaq's people were trailing along in the rear. I took his father Haviraun on my sled, and as he must weigh nearly 200 lbs it greatly increased the load, so now my sled was last. However, all halted for a rest a few miles on, and I caught up then. Haviraun was seated on another sled and my dogs could now travel faster than any. My two 'daughters', Alunaq and Holoaq,[82] were hauling on a small sled bearing blubber, with two dogs in front of them, so I let one of them watch my sled — which now had a child on it — and took her place. It greatly amused the Eskimos. A grown-up man of another family would quite naturally allow a child to tire itself out while he walked idly along; it is no concern of his. We stopped for another rest a couple or more miles further on, and most of the people gathered in a circle round Anauyuk while he delivered a long oration — with constant interruptions from the bystanders, especially from Taqtuk (Ikpukkuaq's wife), who seems to like to hear the sound of her own voice. Another woman then gave a long excited speech, apparently about Haviraun and his sickness;[83] I could understand only a word here and there, not enough to catch the drift, but heard the word *tornraq* (spirit) mentioned. Anauyuk's speech seemed to be about the hunting conditions and the sealing, with some reference to us thrown in. I stood and listened until I could no longer keep my nose from freezing so started my sled moving, and everyone set out for their sleds at the same time. We had gone only about 200 yards, however, when we stopped to camp. As usual I shovelled snow in between the inner and outer wall, then went inside and set the primus burning while the men made the passage. Huputaun is now our neighbour instead of Akhiatak. All the houses seem to be arranged differently — for no apparent reason except the whim of the moment. There is some reason for the change with us. Akhiatak and his people leave for *Ukullik* tomorrow (and I also if all is well) so that the second house off the passage would then be vacant. Haviuyaq and his wife seemed much sobered by my prospective departure and were unusually considerate in their attitude. Two or three families wanted me to stay in their houses tonight. A fairly strong west wind sprang up this evening. Auroras have been frequent lately, but somehow I have forgotten to record them.

Sunday, December 20th

At 6 a.m. Itoqunna, who had been up for some time, told me it was very cold outside and Akhiatak and his family were not going to *Ukullik* today. At 7 a.m., just when I had lit the primus, Anauyuk and Taptuna entered and said they were going as soon as it was light, i.e. about 8:30 a.m. I said I could go with them. I divided up the remainder of the hard-bread — a considerable number — among the crowd that always gathered when I cooked, sent two to different old men. Then I cooked a considerable quantity of rice, had a good meal myself, and gave the rest to the Eskimos — seeing that Anauyuk and Taptuna had a good share. Haviuyaq and Itoqunna both rather annoyed me as I was packing by begging for various things — an axe, a knife etc., though both had received large presents and an inordinate quantity of food. Of six hard-bread — the last six — which I had put in a box for the three of us on the trail today and told the Eskimos were for that purpose — three were stolen while I was loading the sled, a particularly mean trick. The sled was moderately heavy and the snow soft, so our pace was rather slow, and we did not reach Ayallik's house[84] till 5:30 p.m. Twice after dark the sled upset in broken ice. My reception at Ayallik's contrasted favourably with that among the *Puivlirmiut*. He was of great assistance in unloading the sled, promised seal meat for my dogs, though it was not till later that I told him I would give him caribou meat in return. No sooner had I entered than the two girls from Qamiñgoq's and Kallun's houses[85] came in with seal meat especially for me and did not ask for payment as the *Puivlirmiut* invariably did. I sent some food over to their houses later, when I made cocoa and rice. Space being limited Anauyuk is sleeping with his feet towards the door, contrary to the usual custom. The things I had left inside the house were all safe — those on the roof I have not yet seen. I should not mind staying with this family in the least during the winter if owing to their number they did not consume so much of my food — not more than the *Puivlirmiut* [do] — and these people make a return with their own food and do not worry me for payment. The *Puivlirmiut*, on the other hand, if they picked up a piece of paper which dropped from my packet, or gave me an inch of meat when I visited their houses, wanted matches or something for payment and often begged without even that excuse, and this though a crowd always received a share of my food when I cooked quite freely. They were rather getting on my nerves — my only rest was in bed, and even then early in the morning someone would bring in a little caribou meat or dried fish for the dogs and want to rouse me to pay them — though they knew I should refuse till I got up. They handled everything — pried into every box when I was not looking, and I never knew from one day to another whether I should not wake to find half my things stolen. I believe only the fear that I should refuse to buy anything at *Ukullik* later — I refused to buy over there because one or two things were stolen — prevented any extensive stealing. At Ayallik's I feel a little more secure, though these people too stole from the station. I stayed with the *Puivlirmiut* as long as I did only because I was securing ethnological material, but I could not stand it much longer.

Monday, December 21st

Outside it seemed to be very cold. I went for a short stroll to get warm and almost succeeded in freezing my nose. Inside even the Eskimo women found it cold, for I saw them breathing on their hands to keep them warm. It must have been below freezing in the houses, even though the lamps were burning. Shortly after we went to bed last night one of Ayallik's dogs began to howl in the passage. Ayallik told his wife [Kaumaq] to stop it or something to that effect, and she slapped on a pair of shoes and tumbled out of bed — stark naked save for the shoes — quietly removed the door (a snow-block), and hit it (the dog) a crack with the snow-beater (*anauytuk*). I slept pretty well, but woke once to find my sleeping bag frozen to the wall in one place. The men went sealing during the day but were all alike unsuccessful. I spent most of the day indoors, where Kaumaq was making me a pair of sealskin shoes to fit over my deerskin boots, the third attempt. She is just finishing now, but though like the others [who had made such boots for me] she had my boots to copy, she seems to have been little more successful. The shape is a little different to what the women are used to, and they seem unable to adapt themselves to it. From one and another during the day I learned half a dozen or so cat's cradles, but on the whole it was miserable with the cold. The most comfortable time — the only comfortable time generally — is in one's sleeping bag. I bought one or two articles with fox-traps — dried fish for dogs (five large ones [for] one trap), a seal-harpoon [and] bow and drill (but not mouthpiece) with another trap, and bow and drill and mouthpiece with a third [trap]. The last were from Ayallik and were interesting because the bow was of musk-ox bone and must have come from the *Umiñmuktomiut*,[86] the drill of whale bone from a whale, which they said was stranded on the coast of West Victoria (?) Land, the mouthpiece of caribou ancle.

Tuesday, December 22nd

Back again at the station. Chipman and O'Neill have not returned, though they hoped to be here for Xmas. I left a good many things at Ay-allik's house, then set out alone at 10:15 a.m. (by my watch, which I found to be more than an hour fast). The ice was a little broken in places, and Telluraq tried to make short-cuts instead of following in my trail, with the result that the sled upset several times. It was not until I was within about 4 miles of the mainland that any difficulty arose. Here there had been a crack, which in closing had piled up blocks of ice 15 - 20 feet high. I skirted along it for some distance until I found one place more penetrable, then cut some sort of passage with the axe, and with numerous upsets we forced a way through. An hour later — it was just growing dark[87] — I was at the station, warm and comfortable. I brought them as a Xmas present about 50 lbs caribou meat.[88] Everything had gone on smoothly. All three — Cox, Johansen, and Palaiyak — were trapping foxes; Palaiyak had about twenty to his credit, Frits [Johansen] ten, and Cox four.[89] They had seen no Eskimos since we left and were feeding the dogs on boiled fox and rice combined. A strong west wind sprang up in the evening, and the thermometer was down to -26° F, making travelling rather unpleasant. Aurora in the evening.

Chapter 25. Christmas, Trading, and Trip to Victoria Island

Return of Dr. Anderson, Chipman, and O'Neill — Christmas Day activities — Snow-hut for the Eskimos — Trading restrictions at the station — Trading at Putulik — Primitive Eskimo drawings — Puivlirmiut *dance — Shaman's performance — Return to station with goods and meat — Construction of kitchen — Return to the islands — West to visit the* Haneragmiut *— Measurements and dances — Reappearance of sun terminates cat's-cradle studies — Return to base — Recording Eskimo songs — More Eskimo studies — Writing up notes — Preparation for trip up Coppermine River*

Wednesday, December 23rd, 1914

I searched round during the daylight for hardwood to repair my sled; then proceeded to type out my notes of cat's cradles — incidentally learning one or two more from Palaiyak. Cox was working up his survey notes of the Mackenzie delta — or rather of one part — the west and part of the middle branch, the rest of the middle and the eastern branch having been surveyed by Chipman. Frits [Johansen] was cook. Palaiyak visited his traps and returned with two foxes. I found that the fox-trap — Eskimo-made save for the spring — which I secured in exchange for a good trap, had been stolen, whether by the *Puivlirmiut* or by the *Noahognirmiut* I do not know. The temperature was between -15° and -20° F all day, and a moderately strong west wind blowing, though it died away in the afternoon but sprang up afresh in the evening.

Thursday, December 24th

Xmas Eve. Frits had great difficulty in lighting the fire as there was a strong west wind, which created a big draught in the stove and blew out his matches. We breakfasted about 10 a.m., dined about 4 p.m., and supped about 10 p.m. I was busy on the repairs to the sled during the daylight hours — a chilly occupation in the store, for there is not room to bring the sled indoors. Inside the house was cleaned out by Frits and Cox, while I cleaned up my corner and labelled and stowed away in a big canvas bag all the Eskimo clothing that has been bought here for specimens — quite a considerable number. Then we had a musical concert on the phonograph. While I was away Frits sang into the phon[ograph] a Danish song, and Palaiyak sang twice — two dance songs (*ai yaña* etc.),[1] forming one record, and the song for the game of 'juggling' — both turned out pretty well. Cox is making some candy — recipe: sugar, water, milk, salt, butter, and cocoa. A strong west wind blew all day, and the weather was not at all pleasant. Chipman and O'Neill are not here to spend Xmas with us. Cox has been reading the article on Painting in the *Encyclopedia Britannica*[2] and found that Frits' father is spoken of very nicely there as the leading Danish landscape painter and portrayer of quiet home scenes.

Friday, December 25th.   Christmas Day

A red letter day. Chipman, O'Neill, Dr. Anderson, Aarnout Castel, the cook Sullivan (Cockney), and Eikie [Añutisiak] turned up about 10 a.m.[3] They tried to reach the station last night but had to camp at Cockburn Point. The *Alaska* went to Herschel [Island] but found that neither the *Ruby* with our supplies nor any other ships had come in — only the *Herman* had rounded Barrow and reached Herschel Island this year.[4] The *Belvedere* (5 whales), *Herman* (5 whales), and *Polar Bear* (9 whales) had all left for the outside, but no one knew whether they had got out safely. A Hudson's Bay [Co.] schooner with a large quantity of supplies obtained from the *Herman* was wintering at Horton River, in charge of a *Kittigariut* Eskimo named Jimmy. So the *Alaska* set off back without either mail or supplies but with distillate and coal. She reached Baillie Island safely, but there encountered a furious gale with a 4-foot rise of tide, which left her aground. They had to unload her to get her off, and by the time she was afloat again it was too late in the season to make it worth while reloading her and risking the chances of reaching us. Dr. Anderson and Aarnout attempted to reach Point Atkinson to obtain a sled we left there [on Aug. 2], but the trail was too bad and the attempt had to be abandoned. So they left Sweeney, Blue, and Mike living on the *Alaska* (with two Eskimo families ashore) and set out to join us — Dr. Anderson, Aarnout, Sullivan, and Eikie, with one sled. They met Chipman and O'Neill at Keats Point, where the latter had been detained 6 days by blizzards. At Baillie Island there are two whale carcasses, and innumerable foxes and polar bears have gathered there. The *Alaska's* people had shot 16 bears (Mike four in one day), and the two Eskimo families 24 when the Dr. left, besides catching a great number of foxes. The *Alaska* had a rack almost overwhelmed with bear meat.[5] Cox met the sleds when he was out visiting his [fox]-traps.[6] We spent the rest of the day rejoicing indoors — Johansen [was] cook. In the evening the Dr. gave each of us a present of some letter paper stamped "Canadian Arctic Expedition" on the top.[7] The weather was very mild and calm in the morning, but it breezed up towards evening. We had a good dinner,[8] with a Xmas cake to end up with — one of Mrs. Scholefield's,[9] I think — and some crackers and chocolates. Everyone enjoyed the day immensely.

Saturday, December 26th

A strong west wind caused a good deal of drift all day. Aarnout and the two Eskimos[10] set about building a large rectangular snow-hut to be covered with a tarpaulin. It is to have a stove inside for warmth and for cooking dog-food, and the two Eskimos will sleep there, for now there are four men sleeping on the floor. I was busy repairing my sled part of the day and learning and typing cat's cradles the rest. Cox prepared breakfast, then Cockney [Sullivan] took charge of the cooking.

Sunday, December 27th

A quiet home day. The others wrote and read in the house, while I, forgetting it was Sunday, set about finishing my sled. Aarnout helped me in lashing and drawing the pieces tightly together. Only when I asked Palaiyak to fix a lashing and he asked whether I wanted it done today did I learn that it was the day of rest, when one ought not to work. The weather was comparatively mild, with only a mild breeze, the air a trifle foggy.

Monday, December 28th

My sled was finished today and I was busy writing up some notes, the rest occupied in various ways round the house. Aarnout and the two Eskimos finished their hut — a tent inside four snow walls covered with a heavy tarpaulin. The wood stove inside keeps it as warm or even warmer than our house.

Tuesday, December 29th

The cook was sick today — I was sick yesterday, indigestion and nausea. Cox turned out and prepared breakfast and acted as cook for the day. O'Neill made some preparations for building a room in the store where cooking can be done and the others sleep,[11] leaving the house for the scientists — it could be warmed with the small heater. I spent most of the day writing notes and in the afternoon set up the outer cover of my double tent and marked it where straps had to be sewn on. The evening passed in playing cat's cradles and talking with Palaiyak.

Wednesday, December 30th

Ayallik and [his brother] Anauyuk turned up suddenly about 8 a.m., having walked over from *Ukullik*. They brought word that the *Puivlirmiut* had all migrated over to *Putulik*,[12] one of the Ukullik Islands. A little later some of the *Puivlirmiut* appeared and others still later — both men and women.[13] They were a great nuisance hanging round inside the house, but the Dr. followed exactly the same policy that we had done, allowing them in the house and giving them the remnants of the meals. I bought a few things from them, including a large stone pot and some caribou meat, but refused to buy the majority of what they brought so that they would have no inducement to come to the station — a course Dr. Anderson approved. Palaiyak and I managed to fix up the inside lining to the tent, sewing on a number of straps — an unpleasantly cold outdoor task. It is now all ready for the trail. Owing to the Eskimos, however, I was unable to get the other things ready and could not break into the ammunition pile as I had intended. Two or three of the Eskimos went home — the rest stayed until late in the evening, the men building a snowhouse shortly after dark (it was moonlight). I lent them a stone lamp, a blubber-pounder, and some wick to warm their hut, and they had brought a small lamp of their own. The weather was beautifully clear all day with hardly a breath of wind; the temperature was moderate. Tomorrow Palaiyak and I hope to cross over to the [Liston and Sutton] islands to buy some deer [i.e., caribou] meat and specimens. Cox found a fox in his trap today.

Thursday, December 31st

We kept the Eskimos out of the house during breakfast, though they vainly tried to open the door. The dogs broke into the seal cache in the early morning, so Chipman and others set to work to repair it. I was greatly delayed by buying caribou meat from the Eskimos.[14] The Dr. had some experience of trading with them when he proceeded to buy a bag of fish. The operation took him (and I was incidentally mixed up in it part of the time) a good half hour. It was not till 11:40 a.m. that Palaiyak and I got away[15] preceded by some of the Eskimos, and followed by Ikpuk- kuaq and his sled. The ice was fair except in one place, but we did not reach the islands till dark and the settlement not until 4:30 or there- abouts. The *Puivlirmiut* are camped on the island called Putulik [Sutton Is.], about 3 miles from Ayallik's old home, for he and his people have joined them, taking my things with them.[16] Palaiyak was rather disgusted with the way they crowded into the hut when I cooked rice. He seems rather to despise these people and regard his own as vastly superior. We are both sleeping in Ayallik's house tonight — it would have caused us a good deal of trouble to set up the tent with the crowd about. The dogs had eaten something before leaving, so I gave them some sealskin with a good deal of blubber on [it] at night — bought with a block of matches from Ayallik. Snow fell during the day, and the air was very mild, only -2° F at 8 a.m. I have arranged with Akhiatak that he help Palaiyak build a snowhouse over my tent tomorrow — it will have to be a big one. I am rather afraid of a blizzard though tomorrow after the mild weather today. The Dr. is going to Fort Norman when the sun returns, taking Palaiyak with him for the caribou hunting up the Coppermine [River].[17] A sled goes with him to put a cache in somewhere there, and it is possible he may want me to go with it.

Friday, January 1st, 1915

Palaiyak and I had a comfortable night but were inundated with visi- tors in the morning when the primus was lit. When breakfast was over Akhiatak and Qamingoq and Utualu, with Palaiyak, built a large snow- hut in which we set up my tent. Then the lamp I bought from Ikpukkuaq some days ago was set up inside, with blubber and wick, and lit by one of the women, Kaullu, and when all was comfortably arranged inside I proceeded to buy from the Eskimos, keeping them outside the tent. In this way matters went pretty well till about 3 p.m., when several began to crowd round, and I stopped buying altogether and turned them all out. Then we cooked some rice and allowed Akhiatak and Niq and Naqitoq and Haquna to share the meal. Several tried to get in, but I turned them out immediately and only let them in when we had finished. Palaiyak learned one or two cat's cradles, which he will teach me later. Akhiatak

told me (through Palaiyak) that many years ago they had regular intercourse with the western natives (before he was born). Both groups visited the other, and three women from here married over there and
remained. Possibly an old woman who lived until very recently at Baillie
Island was one, for Dr. Anderson said they told him she came from here.
Haviuyaq and Quvyiktoq say they are going to the *Pallirmiut*[18] and want
to go with me, but I don't relish their company. Haviuyaq is going to
bring his sister [back], Palaiyak says. Uglu killed two seals today, and I
bought one with a box of .30-30 cartridges. While the house was being
built I strolled along the beach, gathering two or three rock specimens.
There is very little wood on the west end of this island — enough for 3
or 4 days only. On the northwest end are some fine rock exposures. They
appear to be limestone or dolomite. There is a story about the island
south of this — *Ahuñahuña*.[19] The big rock on the west end was once a
giant man who crossed over from the mainland when the ice was thin —
unseen by the sun — though it was summer. His nose is still visible. The
weather was mild today, but a west wind seems to be springing up this
evening. Our tent is very warm — so warm that at supper tonight I sat
stripped to the waist, though both the door of the tent and the door of the
snow-hut were open.

Saturday, January 2nd

Several people wanted to come in when Palaiyak lit the primus at
7 a.m., but we kept them strictly outside until I got up half an hour later.
We entertained four people to breakfast, turning the others out. Then
when everything was in order I began to trade and bought some caribou
meat, clothes, and a few specimens until I became rather tired, so
finished trading and turned them out, leaving three women to look after
the tent. Palaiyak went visiting and so did I — I to Haquña's house to
see the drawings she is making for me. Everything was in order when I
returned to the tent, so I gave the women a light meal of seal and caribou
meat, and a little later Niq, Palaiyak, and I had one ourselves. Niq said
she had no food, which means that she and Akhiatak are living on the
food given them by the other Eskimos in accordance with their com-
munistic habits. I told her that it was all right for her to come and eat
with me and make no return of food, under the circumstances, also that
Akhiatak should dine with me tonight, and further gave her a little fish
and caribou meat to take to her house, but I said that when they have
plenty of food I should expect her to give me a little without payment, as
is the proper custom. It so happened that Akhiatak secured a seal today,
and after he dined with me he invited me along to his house and gave me
some boiled seal meat, with some raw meat to take away. I bought the
seal's liver from him to fry with salt and pepper for Palaiyak and myself.
Wikkiaq brought me a little caribou meat and asked for matches, but I
said that his daughter Alunaq was dining with me and that I would also
send some rice to him when it was cooked. Itoqunna this morning
brought a little boiled seal meat, so she had breakfast with us. They are

apparently beginning to understand that I am not going to buy food from them and then let them eat it, or give them my food freely while paying for every scrap I receive from them. Two or three other men were successful in sealing today.

Towards evening they built a dance-house. Huputaun and Ikpukkuaq with their families are living in a double house.[20] The front of this was torn out and made into a large dome-shaped forecourt, into which both rooms looked. This forecourt is the dance-house (*qalligi*). They danced in the evening — both the songs and the dances similar to the old Mackenzie [delta] ones, Palaiyak said. Three of the dances we timed — they lasted just 10 minutes. They had no drum, but Haquña, who was the first to dance, used a pot and a snow-beater. Most of them, however, used nothing. All seemed to wear short mits when they danced. The people stood all around in a circle and sang, while the dancer performed in the middle. He began the song himself, and the rest joined in as soon as they picked up which one it was. Whenever the chorus threatened to die down he picked it up and sang loud to make it recover. Ikpukkuaq's dance song was not well known, and two or three times when the chorus stopped and someone said it was finished he had to start them off afresh. The movements in some of the dances were more violent and spasmodic than in others — shaking the head, flinging the arms about and leaping about now on one foot now on both.

After the dance there was an *añatkok* performance — the *añatkok* being no other than my old acquaintance Qamiñgoq. In the Mackenzie [delta region] when a man plays the *añatkok* he is *añatqaqtoq* — here he *onipqaqtoq*, which in the Mackenzie [delta region] means 'tells a story'. Qamiñgoq announced that he was going to perform, and the people gathered round. He began by talking as usual, then suddenly uttered cries of pain and put his hand to forehead and eyes as though in agony. This was followed by a period of dumbness, during which the bystanders suggested what he wished to say and he nodded eagerly to the person who was correct. In this way he told about two men to the eastward who had just died — one through the cat's-cradle spirit. (In the Mack[enzie region] and apparently here also the figure *tutañokin* (Barrow name) has the magic power of driving away the spirit. The man who had just died had not been able to excel the spirit in his speed in making the movements[21]). Again he suddenly uttered cries of pain and slapped his hand to his forehead, then began to speak in a half ventriloquistic tone — something like falsetto — this time about the lack of success of two men (one [of whom was] Huputaun) at sealing. They had done something with an axe, he said, which frightened the seals. He removed the axe and they would presently be successful. A third time he cried with pain, then spoke in his natural tones, but low and husky, and said that he saw the dogs stealing some fish. Someone said my dogs, and he said no, not mine. I heard the words 'my dogs' and turned out with others. It was Raullus' fish which were stolen by some of their own dogs. How Qamiñgoq knew I have no idea. When I came back the performance was almost over. He suddenly began to stagger — his soul *nappan* was returning. Akhiatak put his hand on the back of his neck, Qaiyorunna his on the side of the neck. Huputaun asked me to lend him some matches and tapped Qamiñgoq on the head with them, and presently, as this seemed to have no effect, gave him a sharper rap. They told me then to put my hand on him, so I placed my hand on the side of his head, when he immediately opened his eyes and looked at me (during the performance they were open and a little wild — a very little — but when he began to stagger he closed them). For a moment he gazed at me, then smiled, picked himself together, and began to converse with the rest in a natural manner. This ended the performance, and soon afterwards I returned to my tent. There was nothing so strange in his actions as to lead one to believe he was in an abnormal state of mind — it was more like a fairly clever imposter's trick. Palaiyak believes in him and says he has plenty of *tupilek* or familiar spirits — one to make a sick man well, one to create plenty of seals etc. Palaiyak is looked upon as an *anatkok* too because of a trick of apparently joining together a string which has been cut in two — a trick taught him the other day by Chipman. A man Quñahoq, who has a bad knee, gave him some seal meat and a pair of mittens to make his knee better and said that if he were married he would have given him his son. They wanted him to marry the widow Kaullu, who was offered to me the day of my arrival with Akhiatak.[22]

Sunday, January 3rd

More guests to breakfast, after which I bought a few things till all my stock was exhausted. Some women then stayed inside and I tried to learn some songs from them — or rather Palaiyak tried without success to write some down. I had more luck and learned one, after which I fried a seal liver bought from Akhiatak last night. I used about half a candle for fat, then added a little caribou fat on the sly, for caribou meat must not be cooked on the ice. It was a great success. Itoqunna mended one of my boots. Haviuyaq, Quvyektoq, and Utualu have gone to the *Pallirmiut* and are bringing back Kaullu's little boy. Palaiyak was offered Kaullu for a wife — like myself at different times. Kaullu was anxious to give him her son — why, I don't quite know, unless it be to make him rich and powerful as an *añatkok*. Qiqpuk's grandfather (Qiqpuk is Ikpukkuaq's adopted son (*tiguaña*)) came from the west and belonged to the Mack[enzie] people. At that time there was regular intercourse, the western people bringing knives, both men's and women's, in exchange for copper and stone lamps and arrows. At the present time these [*Puivlik*] people trade with the *Itkillik* Indians near Great Bear Lake,[23] giving dogs for knives and guns (?). Haquña, who is only about 16 or 17 [years old], has seen them. Possibly this explains the '*a ha*' which I have heard used for 'yes', and which Palaiyak remarked as *Itkillik*. Ayallik made his table strut himself, journeying far to the south.[24] Qiqpuk appears to have seen the *Ekalluktogmiut* people,[25] but of this I am not sure. My dogs stole some of Kaullu's sinew, and I have promised to pay her for it when I come back from the station. I am going back tomorrow,[26] if the weather is good, and shall leave my tent and the smaller of the two stone lamps here to use when I return, for the sled will be fairly heavy with caribou meat, a seal, and specimens. Three men killed seals today. The weather was dull and fairly calm, and the temperature moderate.

Monday, January 4th

Palaiyak and I left before 10 a.m., but travelled slow, with a heavy load. About 3 p.m. we struck broken ice and drifted rather far south towards Chantry Island. However, we were able to get our bearings before dark and made the station by 4 o'clock. We brought about 100 lbs deer meat, a seal, a large stone lamp, and a quantity of Eskimo clothing[27] and ethnological specimens. I left the tent, a little food and coal oil, the primus, and a stone lamp at the Eskimo settlement. A tabloid-tea tin with matches had disappeared, and I left word for Qamiñgoq to discover it by his magic. The weather was dull and foggy, with a moderate easterly breeze and a little snow. The temperature was comparatively mild. All was well at the station. They had started on the construction of a galley or kitchen, which will occupy half of the store. Aarnout [Castel] and the cook are to sleep there.

Tuesday, January 5th

Similar weather to yesterday, though the wind was a little stronger. Johansen went over to Chantry Island for wood. I was busy writing notes, packing specimens, and preparing to leave again. Cox, Chipman, O'Neill, and Aarnout worked on the kitchen, which is nearly ready. Bridge in the evening.

Wednesday, January 6th

The kitchen is finished and Aarnout and the cook are sleeping there. The cooking stove has been removed to it, and we have a small stove burning coal in the house. The Dr. was sewing most of the day, the others busy on the kitchen or other odd tasks, myself in preparations for leaving tomorrow and in writing. The weather was fairly clear, the thermometer only -10° F and a light easterly breeze.

Thursday, January 7th

Palaiyak and I left about 10 a.m. Alunaq[28] had disappeared, so I took Sam Jones as before, with Jumbo leader. About 2 miles out Denby chased us, and I sent Palaiyak back with him. By the time he overtook me I was half way across to *Ukullik*. The most westerly of the Ukullik Islands is called *Ilavillik*[29] (the burying ground), because years ago a number of *Pallirmiut* died there. They had caught plenty of seals in the spring so stayed there during the summer and died of starvation. The most northerly island is *Putulik*[30] (the place with a hole), for a man once harpooned a seal on the south side and it dived and was killed by another man on the north side, so they know there is a hole underneath it. We reached the settlement about 3:30 p.m., just as it grew dark. Everything was in order save that my lamp was replaced by a smaller one belonging to Kaullu. Her house was cold, she said, and she was using my lamp because it was larger. The usual crowd turned up for supper. I was invited almost immediately into Haviuyaq's house (by Itoqunna) to feast on caribou and seal meat. Haviuyaq was becoming much afraid because I did not care for him and we had no cartridges to fit his gun — a .55-70.[31] In the evening there was a dance, this time with a large drum — a deer-skin stretched over one side of a wooden hoop. It was beaten on either side, but generally on the under side, with a short undecorated stick — not across the rim as over west, but directly on the membrane. We turned in about 10 p.m., being rather tired.

Friday, January 8th

Palaiyak lit the primus about 7 a.m. and fried a seal liver and boiled mush. After breakfast Akhiatak and Palaiyak went off to set the seal-net, while I spent the day in trading.[32] I bought about 200 lbs caribou meat, over 100 dried fish, a seal, a large quantity of clothing, and some miscel-lanies. Qamiñgoq, the *añatkok*, discovered my tabloid-tea tin of matches in his sleep; Kaullu had taken it. She returned it to me yesterday, but says Uñahaq took it and gave it to her — a lie. I gave Qamiñgoq the tin and two blocks of matches. The Eskimos are catching a good number of seals now. There was dancing in the evening, which I attended, and then two seances[33] — by Anauyuk and Qamiñgoq. Anauyuk's was very matter-of-fact — he spoke in his natural tones, once or twice a little abruptly. Qamiñgoq, who enquired about our journey (Akhiatak, he and I) to the *Haneragmiut* tomorrow, acted as before — a rapid speech, cries of pain, wild eyes, dumbness, nodding his head at accepted suggestions of the meaning of his gestures — a moment's gasping, excited talk in falsetto voice, then a gasp, a glance to the roof and a sharp cry — his spirit (*nap-pan*) had returned and all was over.[34] Unlike the previous occasion his *nappan* had no difficulty in re-entering. Anauyuk said that Wikkiaq's *nappan* had been stolen by a dead man, but that my dog Jumbo had brought it back. The natives are in great glee over the trading, as well they might be.

Saturday, January 9th

We had a rather peaceful breakfast, then loaded the sled. I had to wait a little while for Qamiñgoq, then we set out[35] — Akhiatak to catch up to us. We had gone about a quarter mile when who should overtake us but Itoqunna, who said she wanted to see her younger sister, who lives among the *Haneragmiut*, so she was going with us. We travelled at nearly 4 miles an hour on the average until about 3 o'clock (6 hours) without reaching land — going in a northerly direction but veering to the west. Then Akhiatak and Qamiñgoq built a snowhouse, while Itoqunna filled in the cracks and I unharnessed and fed the dogs — my own six and their three. For supper we had hard-bread, dried fish, rice, and two of them a little caribou meat.

Sunday, January 10th

I lit the primus at 6:45 a.m., but it went out and I found it was empty. Qamiñgoq had slept in his clothes with an *atigi* thrown over him, so he brought in the coal-oil can. We used up all the mush practically for breakfast, and my rice was almost used up for supper. My mittens were wet through, and the weather very cold though clear and calm. My nose is a little frozen, and I had great difficulty in keeping my hands warm. We reached the combined settlement of *Haneragmiut* and *Akulliakut-tugmiut*[36] about 1 p.m., the sun having just set — it reappeared (by re-fraction) for the first time today. There was a bad stretch of rough ice just in front of the settlement, but Jumbo proved an excellent leader. The men were away sealing, and the women and children only left. They did not introduce themselves at once as before, but separately on their own initiative in the houses. Akhiatak and Itoqunna (she is virtually his wife for the trip)[37] made their home in one of the houses occupied, I think, re-ally by a single man, but empty during the day, and I am staying with them, while Qamiñgoq stays in another house. The men returned after dark, then flocked into the house to introduce themselves and see me. Itoqunna's *nukka* (younger sister) is a child of about 13 or 14, who has no tattooing on the face, but is tattooed on the backs of the hands — I have not seen her arms. One of the women offered to sleep with me tonight, but I declined. Like the others these people cannot understand a man not wishing that sort of thing. Two men killed seals and brought me small pieces of fresh blubber for presents. Itoqunna seemed sleepy so I postponed attending the dance, which was postponed till tomorrow, and turned in, but the crowd became such a nuisance as I was writing my diary that I turned them all out and was left alone in peace. They wanted to handle and look at everything like all the natives here [in the region].

Monday, January 11th

Itoqunna brought another woman in as I lay alone in my sleeping bag and offered her for the night; her husband, she said, wanted three car-tridges in payment. I told her as best I could that a white man should sleep with his wife only,[38] but they cannot understand all the same. I was rather cold during the night; the house snowed on everything. When I did turn out about 8 a.m. I boiled the handful of oatmeal that was left, then crumbled hard-bread with it to make it go further. This with some frozen caribou meat gave a tolerable meal. The people danced in the dancing hall — which was similar to that among the *Piuvlirmiut.* I measured eight people, mostly *Akulliakuttugmiut*,[39] then watched the dancing and finally returned to our hut, where I bought a little meat and one or two other things. Apparently they have not much food on hand, and as I don't fancy buying food for Itoqunna, Akhiatak, and myself, I am leaving to-

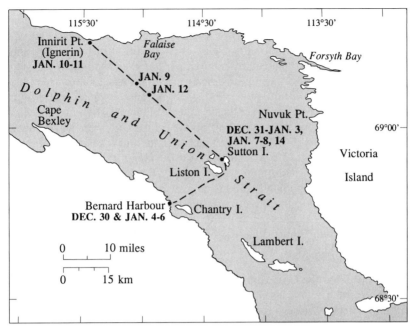

Figure 138. Map showing the routes taken by the author to Sutton Island (Dec. 31 to Jan. 8) and to Victoria Island to visit the *Haneragmiut*, Jan. 9 to 13, 1915.

morrow, before the dog-food is quite exhausted.[40] The weather is very cold, but fine. Cat's cradles are tabooed since yesterday when the sun appeared. I did not mention that yesterday when we arrived, Itoqunna's elder sister had a cry in her hut, with Itoqunna sitting quietly beside her — weeping for joy. The three sisters form an interesting trio — the woman just past her prime — the woman in her prime [Itoqunna] — and the girl just preparing for marriage. It would be still more interesting if one could only discover their different outlooks upon life. The settlement resembles in every way the *Puivlirmiut* — they are kindred people; some *Puivlirmiut* or [people] who call themselves thus are living here. The tattooing of the women is the same. It was uncomfortably cold in the snow-hut today; I should not like one for a permanent dwelling.

Tuesday, January 12th

Akhiatak dressed and went out about 5 a.m., leaving Itoqunna and me alone in the hut. We did not turn out till 7:45, for I was warm and comfortable in my sleeping bag. Then I made tea on the primus and we had a little dried fish, frozen fish, seal meat, and hard-bread. The sled was then loaded, Itoqunna taking back with her the younger sister Uñelaq and a young girl Arnauyak,[41] who is to marry Utualu (Itoqunna's brother-in-law). Their things were loaded on my sled. Another young fellow, a relative of Taptuna named Kehullik, wanted to come. I told him I couldn't take him, but he planted some things on the sled and Qamiñgoq said twice they were his. About 1 mile from the settlement I saw he was coming and found they were his things so pitched them off the sled. Qamiñgoq showed up less favorably today than he has hitherto done, and Akhiatak was more than usually bumptious, so I shall read them a lesson at *Ukullik*.[42] I allowed only the women to ride on the sled and turned the two men off. We did not leave till 10 a.m., because I wanted good light to work through the heavy ice beside the settlement. The *Haneragmiut* and *Akulliakuttugmiut* came with us about 1/2 mile on their way to seal. We travelled about 3 1/2 miles an hour or more and reached our former hut on the ice about 2 p.m., but kept on till about 3:30 p.m. when we camped, the two men building a snow-hut.[43] I froze my nose rather badly while camping — my hands tried to freeze so I had to let my nose go too long. My dogs had rather less than full rations, so I gave nothing to their dogs — they are all feeding at my expense, dogs and all, and using my sled to carry their things. Palaiyak says I am far too good to them, and I believe him. The weather was cold but fine and clear, with a very light west breeze. We could see *Ukullik* part of the day; it lies east-northeast (compass) from the *Haneragmiut* settlement.[44] I had no chance to see the formation of the land along the coast, for we kept well out. It looked from the distance to be about 20 to 50 feet high, rising in terraces. One of the capes is named *Iñnerin*. Beyond (*avatiñnuani*) the *Haneragmiut* settlement is *Tulukkaq*. Near (east of) *Ignerin* is *Tifittoq*, another cape;[45] *Ignerin*[46] is the place where the *Haneragmiut* settlement is.

Wednesday, January 13th

The alcohol tin was in place this morning beside the primus, but it was empty; it was too cold for it to evaporate, even if the lid had not been tight. It must either have escaped through a small hole in the bottom or been emptied by someone in the night. Anyhow, it put the primus out of action, for it was too cold to fiddle about for kerosene and a wick. We had a scanty meal, our food being exhausted. The weather was fine but foggy, with a very faint west breeze. We got away about 9 a.m. and reached the island[47] about 3 p.m. Qamiñgoq annoyed me a good deal by trying to sneak rides on the sled when I was in front, so I read him a lesson tonight by not allowing him in the tent. I told the people who were gathered for a dance in the dance house some plain truths about them — with the names of the thieves. The other day I learned by listening to the conversation going on round me that the man who had stolen my fox-trap a month or more ago was Qunaluk. I told them tonight and gave instructions for him to bring it back tomorrow. Two men and a woman (Kaullu) stole and ate some caribou meat the other day. The children told me their names tonight. I told the people I was going west and maybe should not come back to them. They are rather scared about the whole matter, especially at the loss of trade — of course, I knew all this because I am an *añatkok*. Jumbo is a great *añotkok* — he brought back Wikkiaq's *nappan* (soul) and cured his sickness, so Taqtuk tied a string of deerskin round his neck when I went to the *Haneragmiut* to keep him warm, and so in gratitude he would bring back the soul of her little son who is ailing. These people expose their babies so that they die of cold, not infrequently. While I was away Huputaun and Qiqpuk took my note to Dr. Anderson,[48] who sent Aikie over with the big sled. Aikie left this morning with two (three?) seals (one caught by Palaiyak in his net), all the caribou meat and dried fish, and one or two other things — a heavy load even for seven dogs. He brought over the powder primer and lead [in exchange] for Ikpukkuaq's caribou meat, which I paid him tonight, and will take the meat when we cross over the day after tomorrow. I bought some dried fish for dog-food from Haviuyaq (twenty-one for half a bar of lead), and three seal livers for ourselves, for both Palaiyak's food and mine are exhausted, and we have only seal and caribou meat and a few hard-bread. Seal meat is good with salt and pepper, but very insipid otherwise, especially cold boiled seal meat. The caribou meat we must not cook, being on the ice. Palaiyak is 21 years old. I saw a raven today — some evidently remain here all the year. Palaiyak caught no foxes — they are apparently scarce on the island.

Thursday, January 14th

We had a good breakfast of seal liver and tea. On a diet of straight meat I find I drink at least five times as much as on a diet of partridge [ptarmigan] and rice. Dried fish and seal meat unsalted seem to make me particularly thirsty. After breakfast Palaiyak and I took up the seal-net.[49] There was one small seal caught in it — the second. The net was set at right angles across a narrow crack through two holes, one on each side, each upper end being attached to a stout piece of wood laid across the hole. One hole only was opened when examining the net — since yesterday this one had frozen over to a depth of about 3 inches. The other hole was frozen to a depth of about 20 inches — the result of a week's freezing. The bottom of the net is weighted with stones to keep it stretched. The seal apparently follows along the crack to its hole (*uglu*), pushes the net in front of it, and gets its fore feet hopelessly entangled. Its struggles only increase its helplessness. The Eskimos did not seal tonight; they said they wanted to dance, but the real reason, I think, was because it was very cold, with a cutting west wind. Quniluk appeared at the door of the tent and swore black and blue he had not stolen the trap and knew nothing about it, until I began to think I was mistaken, especially when others backed up his statement. The whole settlement was in a state bordering on panic lest I should 'magicise' them and lest all trading and intercourse should end, greatly to their loss (and mine, if they only knew it). However, I arranged to buy from certain ones different things and to take four of them to the station tomorrow — Wikkiaq and Qaiyorunna, each of whom wants to sell a seal, the latter's daughter Haquñaq (Qiqpuk's wife), and the little girl Qanaiyuq, Ikpukkuaq's daughter. The two latter I want to sing into the phonograph, and Quñaiyoq is bringing a number of clothes to sell. Also I arranged to leave in Kaullu's care (Kiligavik's house) the stone lamp I bought some time ago, so that they can use it to keep the house warm. Haviuyaq's big stone lamp (it is 39 1/2 inches long in front) I am buying in the spring too, when it is no longer needed. Haquñaq brought the book of drawings she made for me; they are very crude, and mostly of people, but some of the faces are fairly good.[50] Though they lie and steal most execrably, even among themselves apparently, they seem to have implicit faith in me. I can take things to the station under agreement to pay later (which I have avoided in almost every case — not the paying, I mean, but the taking away without paying); they leave their things in my tent and sometimes do not recover them for days. Kaullu gave me a knife to give to a lad among the *Haneragmiut* and wants me to bring her little son back from the *Pallirmiut*[51] when I go there. Qiñaloqunna wants me to bring his daughter — a young widow — from the same place (I hope not to, though).[52] In many ways they show their confidence and I try to take every care never to abuse it. Yet Haviuyaq was unwilling that I should pay Wikkiaq and Qaiyorunna for his bow at the station tomorrow, for he says the people here are always stealing and he was afraid he should not receive it; he said I could take it with me and pay later, but I arranged for himself to bring it in 4 days time. In the evening Utualu brought the stolen fox-trap — late when all were supposed to be asleep. He said Qunaluk had stolen it, and Qiñaloqunna was implicated. I told him I should forget about the whole matter henceforward, and if they stole no more, matters should stand on the same footing as before. Everyone in the settlement knew all about it. The day has been rather tiresome, but fairly profitable. It is only during the dark days when the sun is away that they must not sew new deerskin clothing on the ice. Now they are making boots and mittens, and other clothing as required. Yet caribou meat must not be boiled. Tomorrow if the weather is good we return to the station. Palaiyak hungers for white men's food — we have tea only — and says that both himself and his underclothes are very dirty. He wears European underclothing, which I avoid for that very reason.

Friday, 15th January

We packed the sled after breakfast, putting the tent on Wikkiaq's sled. Kaiyorunna, Wikkiaq, Haquñaq, and Qanayuq all came. The two former were rather afraid, especially Kaiyorunna. The weather was cold, especially in the afternoon when we had a light head wind. The temperature at 5 p.m. was -27° F. The lowest recorded yet was on the night of the 11th, when it reached -43.5° and -40° at 8 a.m. However, the atmosphere today was clear and the sun visible for the second time this year — the first time, it was seen at the station. About 3 miles from the station we saw Johansen returning from Chantry Island (*Qigiaqtarjuak*)[53] with a load of wood on his sled. It was about 3:30 p.m. when we made the house and settled the Eskimos in Eikie's tent. Later in the evening we brought them into the house and entertained them. They were very quiet, did not handle things, and kept out of the way. My little 'daughter' Qanayuq was greatly admired. Her mother Taqtuk was seen by Dr.

Anderson near Gray's Bay (east of the Coppermine River). She had gone with her husband to obtain a stone lamp from there and her husband died in the region.[54]

Saturday, January 16th

The Eskimos appeared outside the house just after we finished breakfast — or rather Haquñaq did. She said they were cold down in the tent, for the fire was out. So they all came into the house, and Haquñaq was set to work mending clothes. She had suffered with a headache the evening before, and I gave her a phenacetin tablet. It was all right this morning. Then I traded with the two men in Eikie's tent and gave them seal meat to cook and some dried fish. Cox and Chipman called in and stayed for some time. I found I had made a mistake in trading with primers for cartridges, selling the wrong ones to some people, so now I shall have to run over to *Ukullik* to rectify the mistake as well as possible. Haquñaq contrasted strongly with the other women who had sewed for us here. She brought back needle, thimble, and sinew unasked, put them away neatly in my housewife,[55] and handed it over to me. The sewing she did was carefully done, and she looked the things over to see if they needed mending in other places. In the evening I got the phonograph[56] to work, and obtained four records, two from Haquñaq, one from Qanayuq, and one from Qaijorunna;[57] all were fairly good, but unfortunately one of Haquñaq's was broken in packing it away. Kaijorunna sang first, and when he heard his own voice again issuing from the machine he did not recognise it but asked if there was an Eskimo inside. Later when he heard the break's and exclamations in the other's songs he did not know what to make of it, but became rather scared. Haquñaq thoroughly enjoyed singing the last time, and finally broke down with laughter, some of which was recorded. Her father Kaiyorunna was rather worried about it afterwards, though I assured him that I had Palaiyak and Johansen boxed up as well as them. This party has been very little trouble to us (save myself); there would be little objection to their presence at the station if the others behaved in the same way. I tried to get Haquñaq to count. She wanted to tell me six cartridges, so she held up three fingers and said *piñahut* (three), then another three, and said *piñahut* again. I started her on her fingers *attauhiq* (one), *mallrok* (two), then she said *attauhiq* again, and on being corrected, said *piñahut*. For the fourth finger she was at a loss, but Wikkiaq said *sitamat*. Beyond four neither of them could count, nor have I met any Eskimo here who could; for anything above three they say *amihunik* (a lot). They returned to Eikie's tent about 11 p.m., well content with their reception by the powerful *añatkut*, the *qovlunat*.

Sunday, January 17th

Our Eskimo visitors left about 10:30 a.m. I bought one or two more things from them, and gave them some trail food and warm water to put on the sled runners. Kaiyorunna took a deerskin mitten — poured a little water on his hand, rubbed it lightly on the runner, then put his hand in a deerskin mitten and rubbed to and fro. A piece of red ribbon Dr. Anderson gave me and which I bound round Qanajuq's forehead excited great admiration. I spent the day in preparations for leaving tomorrow, and the evening in playing bridge. The temperature averaged about -25°, and there was a light northwest breeze. A fine aurora in the evening.

Monday, January 18th

It was -20° and blowing 15 miles an hour — head wind. There was a little work I wanted to do as soon as possible, so Palaiyak and I stayed over today. I found there are about 16 *Puivlirmiut* whom I have not yet measured. With the help of Palaiyak and Aikie I translated two or three dance songs, then worked on cat's cradles so as to leave my notes on that subject in a satisfactory condition for working through later. Johansen was out for a short time and reported the weather very unpleasant — the breeze freshened a little during the day.

Tuesday, January 19th

Palaiyak and I left about 10 a.m.[58] A light northeast [breeze] was blowing at 8 a.m., 4 miles per hour, and the temperature was -21°. It had increased to about 12 miles when we left; it increased still more on the way across, and as it was dead in our faces we felt it keenly. Both my ears are slightly frozen, and I think Palaiyak's are also. We made good time, having a light sled and clear trail, and reached the settlement [*Putulik*] by 3 p.m. I am sleeping in Ikpukkuaq's house, Palaiyak is in the other half, which is Huputaun's; the big forecourt is the *qalligi* (dancing house).[59] I fixed up about the primers and bought a liver, which we fried for supper. The men seem to be averaging still about three seals a day; today it was either four or five.

Wednesday, January 20th

I lit the primus about 8 a.m., as soon as Taqtuk turned out of bed; then leaving Palaiyak to cook I did a little trading.[60] As soon as it was full day I began measuring some [of the *Puivlirmiut*] whom I had not measured before. Altogether I measured seven, and there are eight or nine more to be done some time. Visits to one or two houses — taking four photos (two of camp and two of Haquñaq to try and show tattooing) — and more trading, ate up the day. Ikpukkuaq had a bullet stuck in his .303 Savage. He lashed another rifle to it muzzle to muzzle and tried to blow it out, with the natural result that he burst the barrel. He tried to repair the split by hammering, then wanted me to repair it at the station — an impossible task. They were playing the same old game in the dance-house of hanging by the toes from two loops in a cord passing through the roof by two holes. A dance was held in the evening. I bought Qanayuq's belt with some beads.[61] All the women wear the same kind of belt — a sealskin cord with a bone toggle on one end and a loop on the other. I measured the upper arms of two women, Taqtuk and Kaullu; one was 14 inches, the other 14 1/4 inches.

Thursday, January 21st

Palaiyak and I left for the station after breakfast. Ikpukkuaq complained of a pain in his stomach; he wanted me to give him my belt to wear to cure it. Yesterday Kaiyorunna brought me two caribou pins stuck in the side of a small bag made from the belly skin of a caribou. He would not let me look inside the bag, but directed my attention to the good workmanship in the pins. Later I found the bag contained four scraps of skin only. Probably I was to carry away some disease or ill-luck in the bag, and the pins were only a sop to make me accept it. The weather was cold, and we had to face a moderate head wind (westerly), but made good time and managed, with difficulty, to keep our noses and ears from freezing. At 5 p.m. it was -27° and blowing 12 miles an hour. There was a magnificent coloured aurora about midnight. We brought a seal across and some caribou meat, with one or two articles of clothing. Everything at the station was as usual. The cook ['Cockney' Sullivan] is not very satisfactory — he does not 'cook' the things, just heats them; we eat unswollen rice, fruit etc., unboiled porridge. A hare was caught at the islands yesterday, and I bought it for the doctor [Anderson].

Friday, January 22nd

Temperature was -27° F all day, and the wind increased from 15 miles per hour at 8 a.m. to 18 at 8 p.m. A little later, at 11 p.m., it was -21° and drifting quite a little. No one stirred much out of doors. The Dr. was typing all day, I writing up notes, Cox, Chipman, O'Neill, and Johansen similarly engaged, and also writing letters. I developed a roll of photos taken just before the sun left and just after it reappeared. One was good, two are possibly printable, the rest were spoilt.

Saturday, January 23rd

A blizzard raged all day today, with a low temperature, -27° F. Everyone stayed indoors, writing notes, reading etc. Aarnout [Castel] has been sewing two toboggan covers, some woollen mittens etc. in preparation for the journey to Fort Norman.[62] We played our Saturday evening game of bridge — Chipman and I vs. Cox and O'Neill.

Sunday, January 24th

The blizzard continued unabated, and the day was a repetition of yesterday, save that less work was done, being Sunday. There was a brilliant aurora visible in the evening.

Monday, January 25th

The morning was calm and clear, with the Liston and Sutton Islands visible. O'Neill and Johansen visited their traps. Johansen obtained only a frozen cheek, for he returned about 3:30 p.m. when a breeze had sprung up. O'Neill secured a fox foot — the fox had bitten it off when caught in the trap. I have now my notes pretty well in hand — typed from the pencilled notebook to my tin of papers. One of the toboggans has to be repaired. A moderate breeze sprang up towards evening, and it was cold out of doors. There was a fine aurora in the evening. Chipman and Cox are plotting the delta of the Mackenzie from their summer observations. O'Neill has just typed his geological report on the delta.[63]

Tuesday, January 26th

There was a moderate breeze in the morning, which increased to nearly 20 miles an hour by evening. The day was very foggy to begin with, then with the increasing wind the snow began to drift and everything promises another blizzard. The barometer is steadily going down. The temperature at 5:20 p.m. was -25° F. I have practically finished copying out my notes and am ready to take the trail again as soon as the Doctor decides to leave [for Fort Norman].[64] Aarnout was overhauling some of the harnesses. This evening Palaiyak wrote down the words of two of the phonograph records — short portions being reproduced at a time on the machine and constantly repeated until he wrote it correctly. O'Neill obtained a very large fox in his trap today — it weighed 12 lbs and was pure white. The Dr. took measurements of it — tip of nose to tip of tail, length of tail, and length from heel to tip of longest toe on one of the hind feet. This last, he says, is fairly constant for all foxes. We were all weighed yesterday. I am the lightest — 140 lbs (minus 6 lbs or thereabouts for clothes), though this is at least 10 lbs heavier than I have ever been before.

Wednesday, January 27th

A westerly blizzard with a cold temperature; thermometer -36° and wind at times 30 miles an hour. Naturally everyone stayed indoors, writing and reading and talking. Eikie and Palaiyak spoke into the phonograph in the evening, and Eikie sang three short songs; the latter were successful, but the former not, for they stood rather far away and their voices lack resonance. All three of Eikie's songs[65] were composed by Jimmie Asecaq, the Point Hope Eskimo who left the *Karluk* with us in Harrison Bay. The last song treats of this drifting of the *Karluk* in the ice; it was composed at the fishing lake[66] on the way to Barrow. The Point Hope natives have a story to the effect that long ago a number of them travelled round the coast day after day till they came to a great extent of land on either hand, with but a narrow isthmus linking them together. Eikie accordingly says that they travelled all round North

America, east and south, till they reached the Isthmus of Darien,[67] where passing over, they travelled north up the west coast till they reached their own land again.

Thursday, January 28th

Another day of wind and drifting snow but not nearly so bad as yesterday. One or two of the men went out for a short time. I was fixing up my harnesses, for the Dr. is taking the double trace harness (which I have been using) right through to Fort Norman, believing that they are more satisfactory in timbered country than single trace, with the dogs arranged in pairs on either side of a towline. Johansen told the Dr. this morning that he would like to go too, on the chance of securing some biological specimens on the Coppermine [River]. So he and Palaiyak will have one toboggan, the Dr. and Aarnout another, and I my sled. Johansen will return with Palaiyak and me. The atmosphere was very clear today, and the Liston [and Sutton] Islands clearly visible.[68] The days are lengthening too — the sun did not set till 3:10 p.m. The temperature, however, was -36°; it is always colder after the sun returns.

Friday, January 29th

The coldest day we have yet experienced, the minimum registering -44.7° F. There was a slight westerly breeze too, which made it feel all the colder. The air was very clear, like yesterday. Johansen and Chipman, with two sleds, went off for wood. My dog Alunaq, which I bought from Huputaun, was killed in a dog-fight last night. We knew nothing of it until this morning. He was tied up in Eikie's tent with another dog, to prevent his running away to his former master, as he has done twice. Some — perhaps all — of the dogs that are running loose broke into the tent during the night and concentrated on him. It is rather a serious loss for me, for he was a good worker. Cox visited his traps today, but found nothing. Like me he has trouble with his nose in cold weather — it persists in trying to freeze. The night is beautifully clear, with the moon at the full.

Saturday, January 30th

The coldest day of the year hitherto — the minimum being -46°, and the wind at the time over 14 miles an hour. At 11:30 p.m.[69] it had risen to -40°, the wind remaining about the same. We were busy preparing to leave on Monday Feb. 1st. The Dr. tested my rifle, two shots at 50 yards at a pemmican can (one miss, one bull's eye), and one at 100 yards (one bull's eye). I had the last shot at 100 yards and scored a bull's eye also. Evidently I was canting the other day[70] among the *Puivlirmiut*, though the foresight does look to be on one side. We had the usual Saturday evening game of bridge.

Sunday, January 31st

Minimum -45°, but there was only a very light breeze and the temperature felt less severe in consequence. We were very busy preparing to leave tomorrow. It will be late in the morning even now before we get away. Cox and Cockney [Sullivan] are playing chess, Aarnout making a box for the two thermos bottles, Chipman writing, O'Neill reading, Johansen sewing, the Dr. gathering things together, and the two Eskimos looking at whatever is doing. I have just packed my box and have to sort out my footgear. It is 10:40 p.m.

Chapter 26. Journey up the Coppermine

Off with two toboggans and a sled — Past Cape Lambert and Cape Krusenstern — Sighting Cape Kendall — Killing three caribou — Leaving food cache at mouth of Coppermine River — Wolf attack near Bloody Fall — Camping at site of Stefansson's old camp — Reaching tree line — Johansen finds beetles destroying trees — Dr. Anderson and Castel head for Fort Norman — Temperature goes below -50°F — Sighting caribou — Return to mouth of Coppermine River — Encountering Eskimos on the ice — Measurements, singing, and dancing — Heading for the station — Eskimo treatment of old and young — Freezing temperatures — Arrival on schedule

Monday, February 1st, 1915

We expected to leave today but were not ready. However, we got the two toboggans and my sled partly loaded. In the evening I started to put a new sole on one of my Coronation Gulf deerskin shoes, which had no hair on the inside. The fitting got me into some difficulty, and Aarnout [Castel] took it over and finished it about midnight. The temperature was -25°, and a light easterly breeze was blowing.

Tuesday, February 2nd

We breakfasted at 7 a.m. and got away before 10 a.m. The temperature was -12°, and the barometer going down rapidly, so we expected a blizzard. I had my sled with five dogs, Pannechuak taking the place of Alunaq. Johansen and Palaiyak took one toboggan with seven dogs, Aarnout the other with six dogs, and the Dr. [Anderson] went ahead. The weight of the things on my sled came to 497 lbs, but some extras were added, so it was over 500 lbs, a heavy load.[1] The others were less heavily loaded in comparison.[2] However, travelling was good, and we made about 15 miles southeast before camping at 4 p.m. We are all sleeping in the Dr.'s tent — which is built after the western Eskimo fashion — dome-shaped.[3] The Dr. cooked (beans and doughnuts already cooked at the station), while the rest of us fixed up the sleds and dogs. There was just enough driftwood about to cook the meal tonight and possibly tomorrow morning's.

Wednesday, February 3rd

Aarnout got breakfast and we were away by 9 a.m. The weather was calm and clear and we made fairly good progress. The Dr. lost his tobacco pouch and pipe just after we started. We passed Cape Lambert, whose cliffs — dolomite underlain with red sandstone! — rise to a height of about 40 feet[4] and extend southeast to northeast for about a mile. Johansen gathered a few lichens from them. Pushing on we made camp on the shore of a bay at 3:10 p.m.[5] There was no wood so we had to use the primus and the Khotal stove, which sadly frost-up the tent inside. The Dr. has been looking for a place to cross the land, but the

Figure 139. Dr. Anderson and his party pause while passing Cape Krusenstern en route to the Coppermine River, February 4, 1915. From left to right, Aarnout Castel, D. Jenness (leaning on his sled), Silas Palaiyak, and Dr. R.M. Anderson. (Photo by F. Johansen, CMC Photo No. 42241.)

beaches are all rocks and boulders, which would rip the runners off my sled. My dogs pulled splendidly again today — I am quite proud of them. Snow fell intermittently.

Thursday, February 4

I was cold last night sleeping against a badly frosted wall. We started out 9:15 a.m. in calm dull weather, with the thermometer at -8°. Snow fell, but at noon it cleared up beautifully. The thermometer then was at -4°. At 4 p.m. it was -10°, the barometer being fairly steady. We passed Cape Krusenstern, whose northern face is a dolomite cliff about 25 feet high, the eastern [face], about 2 miles further on, similar cliffs about 50 feet high. The travelling was good for the sled, and my team pulled excellently; we led easily all the time. The toboggans seemed to drag, and Johansen's team especially lagged behind. Probably we made 15 miles before camping. We could see three islands of the Duke of York's Archipelago, where Palaiyak thinks the *Pallirmiut* are living. Seal holes are numerous in every crack. Wood we missed last night but picked some up 1/2 hour after we started, at a place where we saw ptarmigan tracks. Further along, about 2 miles west of [Cape] Krusenstern, we saw a very large stick of wood and a low cache of stones, which was probably set up by Richardson.[6] Stone rings (old blubber caches etc.) are fairly common all along the coast. We have a very comfortable camp with plenty of wood.

Friday, February 5th

Johansen prepared breakfast, consequently we were a trifle late in starting out. The loads were rearranged; I took five boxes of pemmican on my sled — 70 lbs — which, with a quantity of wood, brought the load nearly up to its first weight — 500 lbs. The temperature was -10°, the weather foggy. We passed Point Lockyer[7] about 10.15 a.m., 3/4 hour after starting, and steered west-southwest for a time, then west stopping 23 minutes for lunch, and finally for camp at 3:15 p.m. — after making 15 or 16 miles — on a low gravel spit with a limestone cliff a little behind it. It must be about 8 miles north of Cape Hearne. The dogs were very tired, for a little snow had fallen in the night, and with their heavy loads it was not the easiest travelling. The temperature when we camped was -5°. It was almost calm all day, with but a faint west breeze; a little snow fell. The barometer has risen and is now 30 [inches] and the wind is increasing; everything promises a blizzard.

Saturday, February 6th

I took my turn at cooking breakfast. We were away at 8:55 a.m. Our camp seems to have been 4 or 5 miles northeast of Cape Hearne, which must be the high limestone cliff we saw with lowland running out into the sea. We made good time, with a faint northeast breeze, and the thermometer -10° and barometer 30.05 inches. At noon the thermometer was -8°, at 5 p.m. -7°. There was a seal on the ice today. We passed its hole where we could see the ice melted around it where it had been lying, and claw marks. Palaiyak wandered off[8] with the rifle, followed two rabbits' tracks, and shot one, which he skinned this evening. At 4:15 p.m. we were still 3 miles or so from Cape Kendall, and as it was growing dark we camped beside an old crack, where there was ice to weigh down the tent and snow for water. The wind is increasing considerably. Cape Kendall is a very high bluff. There is an island,[9] not very high, about 2 miles apparently east-southeast of us. A raven flew overhead today. The barometer is rising, tonight it is 30.1 [inches].

Sunday, February 7th

Aarnout made breakfast and we started out at 8:40 a.m., temperature -12°, and a moderate northeast breeze, which made the air feel rather cold. We passed Cape Kendall an hour later. It has two islands a little east of it and is itself a sheer cliff of cubical blocks of diabase — the whole about 150 feet high. Numerous wolverine tracks were visible on the snow on the land behind the cliff. Rounding the point there were two or three more similar escarpments, then a little southwest a basalt cliff with limestone below. We steered southwest for what we thought was an opening in the land, judging the outer portions to be the islands off Mackenzie Point. The charts differ in their configuration of the coast. We ran into low land and began to ascend it to cross over to the ice we expected to find on the other side. It was killing work for the dogs, especially my team, for the sled crushed through much more than the toboggans. We were almost on top of the ridge when we found a broad stretch of tundra on the other side with a stream running (in summer) down the middle and beyond that another ridge before reaching the sea again. There was nothing to do but to go back and round the true point of Mackenzie. Just then nine caribou (two fawns) were sighted feeding on

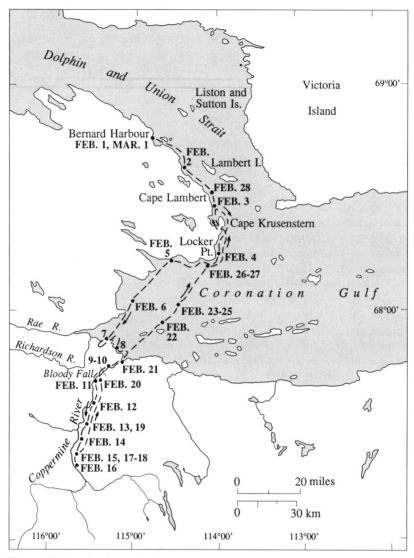

Figure 140. Map showing author's routes on the Coppermine River journey, February 1 - March 1, 1915.

the tundra about a mile to the east. Palaiyak went after them, while we plodded slowly back to the coast and made camp there, at dusk. Palaiyak returned presently — he had approached the caribou, which ran away — later he drew near them again, but darkness came on and he had to return. Probably they are sleeping a mile or two away and he may secure one or two in the morning. We found enough driftwood — mostly willow — for one day, and the Dr. has boiled the rabbit for the morning. We turned in about 9 p.m., the weather about the same, the barometer at 30 inches.

Monday, February 8th

Thermometer -16° at 9 a.m. and light northeast breeze; -12° at 3 p.m., and light southeast breeze. The Dr. made breakfast and we set out about 8:30 a.m. About 4 miles in an east direction took us to the point of Mackenzie Point, about 1/4 mile off which lies a fair-sized island with cliffs about 40 feet high facing west. We steered southwest from there and met Palaiyak, who had followed up the caribou immediately after breakfast. He had seen about 100, he said, and killed one. We continued on and after travelling about 3 miles came to low land on the south side of a small bay, into the head of which flows a small river (Richardson's Bay).[10] In crossing we had sighted caribou and the Dr. and Palaiyak, immediately we struck land, took my emptied sled and went after them. Each secured one and wounded three or four more — making three killed. One whole caribou and portions of another were brought back and both we and the dogs had a good meal from it.[11] Meanwhile Aarnout, Johansen, and I made camp and fixed up the sleds and dogs. Ptarmigan are numerous about here, and both wolf and fox tracks were in evidence. Driftwood is scattered here and there — largely spruce.

Tuesday, February 9th

We left at 9:10 a.m. and travelled along the coast eastward for about 2 miles when we picked up the caribou killed by the Dr. yesterday. Another 2 miles or so brought us to the western mouth of the Coppermine River, which is really for about 3 miles from the sea a wide estuary fringed with diabase cliffs some 40 feet high. Its width here varies from perhaps 1 to 3 miles, and it flows out between various small diabase (Richardson says basalt)[12] islands, forming its three mouths. We made a small cache of caribou meat on the western ridge,[13] using the stones off an old Eskimo cache. Continuing up the river, it narrowed to a few hundred yards with curious mud banks, which in various places on either side formed series of pyramids sloping back and up from their peaks to the flat plateau behind thus:

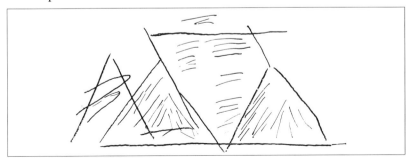

Figure 141. Pyramid-shaped mud banks near mouth of Coppermine River.[14]

On top of the banks were willows, which about 5 miles from the mouth attained in one or two places the height of a man. Johansen found marine fossils in the mud banks. It began to grow dark when we were some 3 miles north of Bloody Fall, so we camped — about a mile above two old Eskimo snow-huts — just under the left bank.[15] River snow is apt to be full of sand, so it is always better to find a crack and knock off a block of ice which is clean. River or small lake ice is much more level than sea ice, and the snow does not form such heavy drifts; hence it is often very slippery, the feet sinking through the 1 or 2 inch crust of snow to the black smooth ice below. The temperature was -9° when we started and a faint east breeze blowing. The atmosphere was clear, and altogether it was a splendid day for sledding. None of us have seen trees since we reached the Arctic, and I have not even seen willows more than a foot high [until today].

Wednesday [February 10th] — [no entry]

Thursday [February 11th] — [no entry]

Friday, February 12th

We stayed in camp Wednesday. A wolf bit my right arm and the Dr. shot it.[16] I have been unable to use the arm since, but it is rapidly healing. The temperature has been mild the last 3 days, up to +10° yesterday. Today it was -8° at 8 a.m., -6° at 5 p.m., with a fairly strong gusty southwest wind. Yesterday the wind was about the same. A cache of food was made at Wednesday's camping place just below Bloody Fall. On Thursday we passed through Bloody Fall, where there was open water in places, and passed through very bad ice for about 5 miles, when we camped on the site of one of Stefansson's old camps.[17] Palaiyak shot three caribou,[18] and they were brought into camp this morning by him and the Dr., and some of the meat cached there. We left at 12.15 p.m. and went up on top of the ridges on the right (east)[19] bank because the bed was full of rough ice quite impassable for a sled, with here and there open water. We sighted the first trees (spruce) — the northern tree-line here — on the left bank about 3:30 p.m., but none on the right bank till 5 p.m., just as it was growing dark, when we reached a grove of small trees with dry stumps of larger trees among them. Travelling was slow and difficult by reason of slopes and very soft snow.

Saturday, February 13th

Strong southwest breeze this morning, though it diminished during the day. We started out about 9:45 a.m. and continued south along the plateau above the river, up and down inclines — mostly up, over willow brush and deep soft snow — all of us wearing snowshoes. About 12:15 we stopped for lunch, and Palaiyak, who had just sighted five caribou, was sent off after them. A run across a small lake, a short further climb, then a fairly continuous descent for about 3 miles brought us, after a 10 mile tramp, to a grove of fairly large spruce trees in a little valley,

Figure 142. Arctic wolf lies dead after attack on the author, Coppermine River about 3 miles below Bloody Fall. (Photo by R.M. Anderson, CMC Photo No. 39130.)

through which a stream flows in summer. We made camp here.[20] At dark Palaiyak appeared; he had shot and skinned two caribou. It was fine and clear tonight — we are well sheltered here.

Sunday, February 14th

After breakfast Palaiyak and I went off to bring in the two caribou he shot yesterday. A cross fox was eating one of the carcasses. Palaiyak shot it in the leg, but it escaped. He followed it while I brought the meat to camp in the sled, but he did not overtake it. I fell on my right arm and damaged it a little — the arm has swollen again and its recovery will be delayed 2 or 3 days. Aarnout and the Dr. were busy, the latter in repairing the [Alpine] tent they are taking away (it was badly torn by the dogs), the former in fixing up the toboggans, stove etc. In the evening a little food was taken out for the three of us who return to the station and the departing toboggan partially loaded. Johansen was chopping at the spruce trees all day — bug hunting. He found a number of dead beetles and larvae and one live larva, which he is keeping to rear. Altogether he is very pleased with his success.

The wolf which bit my arm [Feb. 10] came into the camp just as we were finishing breakfast. It was a female, white in colour, and was snapping at the dogs, who came near. We all ran out half naked. Johansen went out first and discovered its presence — it was biting Snap. He tried to shoo it off with the flapping front of his woollen shirt. The Dr. and Aarnout ran for the rifles, Palaiyak was looking round to see where the wolf was. I saw it running behind the sled, and picking up a big bowlder, heaved it at its head. It dodged then ran at me and tried to seize my bare leg (I had on only a pair of trousers and a pair of sealskin slippers). I gripped it by the back of the neck, and it screwed its head round and fastened its teeth in my arm. I tried to choke it with the left hand — unsuccessfully — but after a moment it let go and moved away a little, when the Dr. immediately shot it.

The weather was mild today — rather foggy. Snow fell.

Monday, February 15th

The Dr. and Aarnout with a toboggan, and I with a sled, left camp before 10 a.m. on the second stage of the formers' journey. I go on 1 day with them to carry part of the load. The weather was beautifully clear, a light easterly air, and the thermometer [reading] -22°. In the evening it was -28°. We had fairly good travelling along or just above a series of small lakes, the Coppermine [River] being a mile or so on our right. We sighted five caribou, then a black or silver-grey fox at which the Dr. fired twice — unsuccessfully. It came quite close, but Aarnout's team broke loose and chased it so that the Dr. could not get a decent shot. There was a fine spruce grove about 3 miles south of our last camp, and a very fine one about 12 miles south at the head of a lake about 1 mile long. Near this we made a small cache, then tried to cross the divide which separates the lake from the Coppermine. There were some nasty ridges, however, and we [got] stuck before we were half way across — the toboggan was too heavy for a steep slope. So we camped beside a miniature lake of about 1 acre in area. The Dr. made a fire outdoors and soon had rice cooked and water boiling for tea. There was an unusual parhelia today, thus:

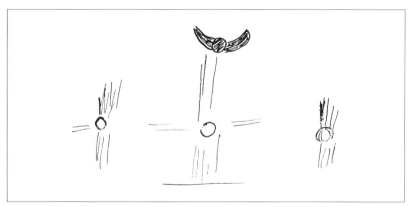

Figure 143. Parhelia observed from the Coppermine River.

The lower sun was not visible. The upper sun had horns like a Goth's helmet. It was visible for about an hour in the early afternoon. Near the cache the Dr. saw a black or silver-grey fox, which he thinks was the same he fired at some miles back — it had made a circuit and shadowed us all the time.

Figure 144. Campsite for the author, Johansen, and Palaiyak on the east side of the Coppermine River, below Sandstone Rapids, February 15, 1915. The low temperature (about -40° F) helps accent the smoke from their portable stove. This was the northern limit of the tree-line on the east bank of the river. The Copper Eskimos obtained the timber for their sleds from a nearby grove of trees. (Photo by F. Johansen, CMC Photo No. 42249.)

Tuesday, February 16th

It was -39° F at 8 a.m. when Aarnout was loading the toboggan and I my sled. I left about 9:30 a.m. for our last camp where Johansen and Palaiyak were, before the Dr. and Aarnout started on their long journey to Fort Norman. They were making two trips, each with half their load (about 700 lbs altogether) over the rest of the divide to the Coppermine — about 1/2 mile. He [Dr. Anderson] has a heavy toboggan and a team of seven dogs. The Dr. estimated he was about 40 - 45 miles from Dismal Lake. The weather was calm and clear, with a fine parhelia similar to yesterday. About half way (6 miles) to camp I ran into a herd of some 20 caribou. The dogs bolted in pursuit, and before I could capsize the sled and so stop them the herd was already disappearing over a ridge some 300 yards away. I fired at the last of them but apparently missed. Palaiyak is an infinitely better hunter than I — he secured a caribou and two rabbits yesterday and another caribou today. He saw today, he said, about 200, besides one wolverine, and 11 wolf tracks and a red fox. Game is therefore very plentiful in winter in the lower half of the Coppermine valley. Frits (Johansen) this evening shot three ptarmigan close to the camp. He is very successful with his bug-hunting here. The numerous dead spruce trees which are found everywhere in the spruce groves, and the spruce trees still standing but with some of their branches withered and dead, almost all, he says, have been destroyed by these boring longicorn and bark beetles (Cerambycidae, Scolytidae).[21] The temperature this evening was -45°, but the weather calm and clear, with bright starlight and a faint aurora. My arm was much better today — I can use it almost as freely as ever. The valley of the Coppermine from here to where I left the Dr. and Aarnout is properly speaking about a mile wide. The river bed itself seems to be sunk in a gorge, low or deep in different localities, and is full of limestone boulders. The valley on the left [west] side is bounded by a range of hills almost high enough to be designated mountains, on the right by low ridges separating a chain of small lakes from the river (in one the largest about 1 mile long, Stefansson's party caught a pike in summer). These give place to the east to a series of ridges and plateaus culminating a few miles (3 or 4 apparently) in another range of high hills. Here and there in little pocket valleys beside the lakes, around creeks flowing down from the hills, and along the banks of the Coppermine itself, are groves of spruce trees, becoming thicker and larger as the river is ascended. The Dr. says there is a little cottonwood about also. Low willows are thick everywhere in the valleys and on the ridges. The grove in which Frits and I are camped is said by the Dr. to furnish the Eskimos with timber for their sleds. Stefansson found the trunks of spruce trees cut down, trimmed, and set upright in the ground for sled runners. Probably they take their wood from any of these groves, for it is but a short distance from one to the next, generally little more than 2 - 3 miles, and the timber is larger a little farther up. Our camp here is on the banks of a picturesque creek issuing after 300 - 400 yards in the valley of the river. Trees make a wonderful difference to the landscape — it is a touch of home.

Wednesday, February 17th

Temperature -48° F in the morning — a record. Palaiyak hitched up a dog team and went to bring in the caribou he shot yesterday. Frits left shortly before noon to bug hunt in the grove about a mile south. There is open water beside this grove and clouds of mist rise from it. I stayed in camp to watch the tent and dogs and did a little sewing, amongst other things making a deerskin cover for Caruso, whose side has two great bare patches from mange. Frits returned just before dark — he had broken the axe handle very badly. This was serious for we have no spare axe or handle, and this spruce is useless for the purpose. Palaiyak and I turned out to rustle wood — tearing down small trees and branches with our hands and breaking them up. After supper I lashed the axe handle together, but it is not very good, for the crack extended nearly to the bottom, and at the top it comes apart entirely. The foxes had eaten half the caribou Palaiyak went for — there were fox tracks everywhere, he said. The weather was calm and clear all day.

Thursday, February 18th

Temperature at 8 a.m. -51°(?). The thermometer was registered to -50° only, and the column sank below that, then the mercury began to freeze. Palaiyak went caribou hunting[22] but saw none till about 2 p.m., when he observed a herd a long way off so returned to camp. Near camp he saw a black wolf and fired at it but missed. Frits continued his bug-hunting.[23] When he came in tonight he expressed himself well pleased with the results he had obtained. The axe-handle was unable to withstand the strain of another day's chopping and snapped completely. I kept camp again, repaired a large rent in the inner tent canvas, cooked, and read. There was no wind at all in this glade, but on top of the plateau, Palaiyak says, the snow was drifting before a southwest breeze.

Friday, February 19th

We omitted to take the temperature today, our thermometer being a clinical [one], packed in Frits' box. It was about 10:30 a.m. before we got away. The temperature seemed much the same as yesterday. On the top of the plateau outside the sheltered valley a moderate southwest breeze was blowing — behind us luckily or we should have suffered some freezing. As it was we nearly froze during lunch. We travelled northeast for about 4 miles to pick up a caribou carcase left by Palaiyak 2 or 3 days ago, where he had shot the animal. He had set two traps beside it, and each contained a white fox, still living. Then we travelled due north for a couple of hours or so over fairly level tundra interspersed with small lakes. In front of us lay a line of ridges running apparently northeast, so I changed the course to northwest to run inside of them close to the river. In this way we luckily struck the identical valley that led to our old camp and picking up the trail pitched tent about 4 p.m. on its old site. Palaiyak turned cook while Frits and I arranged everything outside. Frits put the cocoa tin containing my full supply of saxin[24] (one bottle of 500 tablets, and two [bottles] of 100 each) in the stove when we packed this morning. Neither Palaiyak nor I knew of it so now it has disappeared — for good. The sun shone brightly all day, and in the sheltered valleys it was quite pleasant. This is the limit of the tree-line on the east bank of the river.

Saturday, February 20th

We did not get away till 10:20 a.m., but made good time. I steered a little too far inland, but we did not lose more than 1/2 mile on the curve. We encountered nearly 200 caribou, some of which approached within 200 yards of the sleds. Frits' dogs gave chase, and he, encumbered with his snowshoes, could not stop the dogs or overturn the toboggan or even sit on top (he waddles in his snowshoes like a great duck). They chased the deer about a mile circuitously, then the deer disappeared over a ridge and the dogs stopped. Frits gave them individually a sound thrashing, but they tried to stampede again at the next herd — only this time Palaiyak was on hand to stop them. We coasted the western edge of the ridges and came down from the plateau near the mouth of the large creek that runs into the broad valley of the Coppermine [River] on the east side just above Bloody Fall. Here there is a considerable amount of driftwood, and while Frits and I made camp Palaiyak went back up along the left [east] bank a couple of miles to the caribou cache we made on the point where we camped [Feb. 12]. Wolverines had got into it last night — despite the stones — and eaten some of the meat but not much. We have now rather a heavy load of caribou meat to cross the rough ice in the valley here. The creek has cut steep banks in the mud — about 100 feet high, I should judge. Directly south of them are perpendicular faces of basalt or diabase. A good deal of slate is scattered among the boulders in this valley. The weather seemed a little milder today, though we did not take the temperature. There was no wind, and the steam was rising up from dogs and caribou like smoke. The sun was quite warm, comparatively speaking. Palaiyak had a fit of temper this evening because I told him not to follow any wolverine tracks he might see at the cache — the wolverine might be miles away and it was already late in the afternoon. He hardly spoke a word the whole evening, but seemed to be recovering a little towards bedtime. The dogs were the natural objects on which he vented his resentment. Caruso's mange is worse — one side of his body is almost bare.

Sunday, February 21st

Palaiyak took the toboggan today instead of Frits. In consequence we got away nearly an hour earlier, at 9:30 a.m. Following down the right bank of the Coppermine we escaped the rough ice and crossed over to the left bank just above Bloody Fall without difficulty. A strong head wind blew out of the gorge here and nearly froze us, but it disappeared as soon as we entered the gorge. The cache 3 miles south at our old camp — the wolf camp — was intact. We took from it what had been cached for us, had lunch, hard-bread and chocolate, and continued down to the first cache at the mouth of the river. Frits deserted us almost immediately to collect fossils from the bank, leaving Palaiyak with both sled and toboggan — I going ahead to make the trail. Both were heavily laden, so our progress was slow. I took a photo of the two deserted Eskimo [snow-huts] 1/25 second, stop [f] 8 (No. 2, Frits' roll).[25] We reached the cache at dark just in time to see a wolverine steal away. Both wolves and wolverines had been busy at it, but the extent of the damage we have not yet ascertained. A little driftwood was dug up out of the snow, very wet, and as soon as the tent was up I turned in to cook. Frits appeared while we were gathering wood. He had collected a number of shells from the mud bank.[26] The Khotal stove was set going, as the wood was scanty and poor. It was 10 p.m. before we had supper. The weather was glorious all day — just now a westerly wind is blowing, about 6 miles an hour. The temperature this morning was -26° F.

Monday, February 22nd

The wolverines and wolves seemed to have eaten nearly all the meat in the cache, though we did not pull it all down to examine, but covered it up again as securely as possible. Palaiyak stayed behind to set another trap, for the one set by the doctor [Anderson] had been carried off. I steered by compass north-northwest for about 8 miles, then north-north-east[27] along the edge of a large island[28] with basaltic cliffs on its southern face descending in a long series of terraces to the north, then due north again for about 5 miles, altogether about 15 or 16 miles. We came to a place where a seal had been caught — perhaps two months ago, as was evidenced by a block of ice smeared with blood and blood tracks around. Half a mile north (compass) of this, where we camped at 4 p.m., were tracks of dogs. Rae's chart seems to be more accurate here again than the admiralty chart, though the latter marks more islands. Neither marks as many islands as there really are. The temperature was -12° F this morning, -13° F this evening. A fresh east-northeast breeze sprang up during the day and made the air feel very cold, as we were travelling against it. It seems to be freshening up tonight. The weather was foggy all day, which was rather annoying both for picking a trail and for setting the course.

Tuesday, February 23rd

After travelling about 4 miles north magnetic we saw three people and some dogs on the ice. Approaching them we discovered them to be two men and a boy. They were rather afraid at first, but came up quickly when we made the peace sign and led us to their settlement, which was about 5 miles away northeast magnetic, about 4 miles north of the island they call *Kulliksak*.[29] Here was a large settlement,[30] and all the people who were not sealing turned out to welcome us. We set up the tent, and as the settlement was on the ice and we had practically no wood, we borrowed three small stone lamps, which soon made the tent comfortably warm. Each of us in turn had seal meat in one or other of the houses and set out our footgear to dry. I had a little sewing done to two pairs of slippers. We turned them out when we cooked rice and let them in again after we had finished, to regale themselves with the scraps. Palaiyak wandered about the houses enjoying himself, while Frits and I were entertained by a large crowd in the tent. They behaved very well, for they are growing used to white men. Many have guns, there are some spy glasses, Palaiyak says, and pots and kettles etc. abound.

Wednesday, February 24th

Having no wood the Khotal stove was used for breakfast. It bucked on making tea, so we let that go. As usual a crowd waited outside till we had finished in order to gather the scraps. I then exchanged some of our deer meat for seal meat and sent Palaiyak away to the island [*Kulliksak*] with another man for driftwood. Frits and I then went to the dance-house, which is a large dome erected over the forecourt of a single (not a double) house.[31] The house is inhabited by the 'rich' man with two wives,[32] who met white people (Melvill and Hornby[33] and a party of Indians and a French priest) on [Great] Bear Lake last summer and obtained many things in trade — cartridges, a dozen packages needles etc.

besides what he obtained from Joe Bernard. Each wife has one side of the hut, with table and lamp of her own. Some of the people went sealing, others made caches of blubber and meat, in preparation for journeying west to the *North Star* or its neighbourhood, others danced in the dance-house, while I measured the heads and stature of some of the men, and Frits wrote down the figures. This occupied us all the forenoon, when we turned out to take some photos.[34] Returning later to the dance-house I found the rich man in the middle of afternoon tea. He had two small cups and two saucers, and tea, obtained at [Great] Bear Lake and was regaling himself, his two wives, and the assembled company. He offered me tea, but I declined. The whole proceeding was intended to impress me with his wealth and importance. He has a Roman breviary (in Latin), a French Illustrated Scripture lesson book, and part of an American magazine — pipe, some plug tobacco, a .22 rifle (Winchester 1904), a double-barrelled Hollis Fowling piece, and I think a larger rifle.[35] A little boy came riding into the settlement on a sealskin in lieu of a sled, drawn by two dogs. The sleds are placed inverted on snow-blocks, a foot or so from the ground. Against many of them here lean long poles large enough for whaleboat masts — they are their tent poles, they said. All the houses open south. Most are single, but there are two[36] double houses. They are scattered over a large area, probably 300 yards long south to north, while the greatest breadth between two houses east-west is about 125 yards; the reason of their dispersion is the shallow snow surface of the ice, which only allows of the construction of a snowhouse here and there. Two blind puppies in a house wore miniature harness, deerskin collars — the rest sealskin — train the youth while he is young! Several of these Eskimos — among them the 'rich' man[37] and an elderly man — have markedly Indian features — there must be mixture. Another middle-aged man has a pug-nose and features screwed up so as to make him uglier than Socrates. One man is extremely short, only about 5 feet 1 inch. Palaiyak discovered an interesting superstition. Cottonwood (*niññoq*) must not be cut or burnt in winter, otherwise very cold weather will ensue. While I traded and cooked in the tent, Johansen taught the crowd of Eskimos a number of European games, fox and mouse etc.; they had a merry time, everyone enjoying it immensely. The Eskimos said they do not hunt the caribou which remain all winter in the Coppermine basin because their cartridges are few and their bows would snap in the intense cold. They have the same taboo against cooking caribou meat on the ice. The weather was beautifully fine and not very cold.

Thursday, February 25th

Another fine day, but with a little west wind which made it cold. I measured thirteen people in the dance-house, and Frits again wrote the figures for me. The rich man scraped the hair off a deerskin, stretched it over the large drum, and three of them together lashed it round with stout cod line. The edge of the skin protruding below the lashing was wound round a big stick, and the membrane levered tight. The people danced and sang and performed a gynmastic feat on a thick tight rope of twisted seal lines stretched across the dance-house just under the dome. The feat consisted in almost touching the rope with the toes, then with a half circle coming to an upright position balanced on the arms, swing back and half round and out, straightening the legs and half circle back to the same upright position. In the afternoon I played 'wolf'[38] with some of the people, then had some seal meat in the house of the man we met on the ice — his name is Kigodlik (Fishhead) and he seems a fine old man (he is about 40). Palaiyak took a census of the people for me. The evening was taken up with supper and with talking to the crowd that afterwards thronged the tent. The people were preparing to mush tomorrow towards the station. One of the persons I measured — an old woman with white hair — said she had seen many white men when she was a girl. I had to make it rather a leading question, so the fact is somewhat doubtful, though it is quite possible she saw Richardson's or Ray's [Rae's] party[39] — she being a *Walliarimiutaq* from the neighbourhood of Ray [Rae] River. This people is a very mixed crowd — there is a *Nagyuktomiut* man, a *Kanghiryuarmiut* woman, *Noahognirmiut*, *Haneragmiut*, *Piuvlirmiut*, *Akulliakuttugmiut*, *Pallirmiut*, and *Kogluktomiut*.[40] A young fellow here, having no lead for making a bullet when recharging a .38-55 rifle made one of copper. These Eskimos do not whistle and are greatly interested to hear us.

Friday, February 26th

We left at 8:30 a.m., having been preceded by all the Eskimos — 22 sleds.[41] However, we soon overtook them, or rather most of them, for they straggled one behind the other.[42] Some of them travelled fairly fast, for Eskimos. Altogether we travelled about 18 miles, with two rests, and practically reached the mainland southwest of Point Lockyer,[43] about 2 miles from the point. However, coming to snow banks 1/2 mile from the land they decided to camp. The rich man set up a large skin tent — conical shape — the others built snowhouses. We set up our tent, Frits turned in to cook, and I sent Palaiyak over to the coast to look for wood. He did not find very much, but did not travel far along the shore. The rich man sent over a pot of seal meat to be boiled on our stove. There were some interesting features in the migration.[44] The rich man had his two wives hauling on the front of his sled, then six dogs, then he himself pulling behind the dogs.[45] A little baby was carried on top of the sled part of the way, with a deerskin round and over it like the hood of a perambulator; part of the way it was tucked in a little nook in the deerskin at

Figure 145. Uloqsaq and his dogs pull his heavy sled, east of Cape Krusenstern, February 26, 1915, en route to Bernard Harbour. (Photo by D. Jenness, CMC Photo No. 37028.)

the side of the sled. The mother took it in her lap once to feed it and in so doing exposed it quite naked for a considerable time to the cold air. She put on it fresh loin cloths — a square of deerskin with an outer one of sealskin — (another baby had both of deerskin with a hole in the inner one through which the penis passed). They were tucked up under the fork and tied by a string round the waist. It had a small piece of deerskin on the back also but none on the breast, for when the mother carries it on her back the breast rests against her own body. At one of the rests some of the people played skipping with a rawhide line, round the middle of which they had lashed a piece of polar-bear skin. A man held each end, swung it under the feet of the skipper and over his head, then back again under his feet in the opposite direction.

Saturday, February 27th

The Eskimos had decided to wait over a day and seal. It is one of the features of their winter travelling that they cannot carry much food with them, but gather it on the journey. One man had camped several miles back yesterday near a seal hole he discovered. They are very skilful in discovering seal holes themselves — a little ridge of snow which seems to the uninitiated person no different from the thousands of others round it catches their eyes and they detect its peculiar features and immediately probe it with a knife or snow-sounder. The dogs scent out many holes, especially along cracks in the ice. Even an untrained dog can do this — Sam Jones does. Frits went off with the sled for wood; Palaiyak and I remained in camp to gather such ethnological information as we could. A light westerly wind was blowing and the thermometer was -29°, so that it was cold out of doors. Unmarried girls wear long trousers more or less close fitting, like the western Eskimo women. Tupik's trousers fit very tight; Aqulluk's are rather loose. Sometimes they tattoo before marriage (Aqulluk is fully tattooed), sometimes after — Tupik has no tattooing, though she must be about 15 years of age, and the rich man's younger wife is tattooed on face and hands but not as yet on the arms. The Eskimos of Coronation Gulf, if they have little children whom they do not want to keep, give them to others or expose them, when they soon die. However, they do not desert their old people when they become feeble — nor, Palaiyak says, did the Mackenzie Eskimos, though Pannigavlu's people in Kotzebue Sound [Alaska] did so. In fact she herself was with a party who left a feeble old man to die on the trail. Some women here have several children, often as many as five they say, but the mortality is very high. Within recent years there has been a great decrease in the numbers of Eskimos here — two (or three — see notebook[46]) summer's ago as many as fifteen died in one summer (from sickness they said) — of the Coppermine Eskimos only; last summer only one died.

Sunday, February 28th

We left about an hour after the other Eskimos — at 9 a.m. A strong northwest wind was blowing, which threatened during the day to develop into a blizzard, but it abated somewhat towards evening. We travelled fast and quickly overhauled two sleds — the rich man's, which was heavily laden (hence an excellent reason for having two wives) and another, which had stopped to melt a little snow over a wood and blubber fire and re-ice the runners, from which the ice had been scraped off by the stones.[47] The men had caught a number of seals yesterday and one bearded seal — I saw one seal being carried on a sled. Towards noon we overhauled other sleds and at 2 p.m. reached the foremost, which had stopped to camp — the man had already constructed a snow-hut. We did not go round Cape Krusenstern but cut across the isthmus behind — in which are several small lagoons. The snow was a little soft on the land, but there were not many stones. We passed close to a high cliff (40 feet?) on our left and emerged on to the sea ice — after what seemed about 12 miles — about 1/2 mile east of another cliff at the bottom of Lambert (?) Bay,[48] behind Cape Krusenstern. A small sled which the rich man was hauling behind his large sled we took in tow, but left it where the Eskimos were camping and pushed on, partly to obtain wood along the coast for our stove, but mainly because it was still early and we wanted to make the station tomorrow.[49] The abating of the wind about this time cleared the atmosphere of drifting snow, so that we could see our route. We made another 8 miles or so and camped at Cape Lambert about 5 p.m. — after sundown. Palaiyak searched the beach for a couple of miles or more back but found only a few sticks, so that we have to supplement the wood stove with the Khotal lamp tonight and tomorrow morning. Altogether we made about 20 miles today — the dogs pulling well — apparently realising that they were homeward bound. I froze my nose a little in the latter half of the day and so did Frits, though we both wore masks of blanket wool, with slits for eyes and mouth. I had to remove mine after about 4 hours as it iced up over the nose — my nose is a perpetual fountain here. Some of the Eskimos intend quickly to return to their last camping place, for in two houses the entrances were blocked with snow, while in others the long tent poles, the ice windows, and other gear were left outside, and in one [house] two or three large bags, filled with blubber and other things [were outside]. On the sleds the ice windows are packed among the skins or bags; so, too, the stone lamps wrapped in a sealskin; in both cases near the bottom on account of their weight.

Monday, March 1st

Palaiyak was up early and we broke camp at 8:30 a.m. It is about 25 miles from the east end of Cape Lambert, where we were camped, to the station, and round the cape there is a little broken ice. The weather was very cold, -34° F at 8 a.m. (though it rose to -31° during the day) and a moderate northwest wind was blowing directly in our faces. We passed our first camp on leaving the station about noon, and Palaiyak went along and picked up the Dr.'s tobacco pouch, which he lost there [on Feb. 3]. By 5 p.m. we were at the station — they had expected us for more than a week — though we had carried out our program without a hitch and returned on the exact day the Dr. had appointed for us. Everything was well at the station. The *Ukullik* natives had been over several times and brought 17 seals, with one or two specimens. The widow Kaullua had been across with a little girl — prospecting for a husband but unsuccessfully — no one took pity on her. Cox had taken three phonograph records — moderately good — for me. The natives have now shifted from the islands towards the west and are only about 3 hours journey away.[50]

Chapter 27. Trading Farther Afield

Arrival of Coppermine River Eskimos — Seance for a murder charge — Trading — More observations of Eskimo behaviour — Medical treatment for Ikpukkuaq — Arranging for visit to Kanghirjuarmiut *— Dog losses — Eskimo reactions to their voices on records — Visiting Ikpukkuaq — Brief surveying trip east with Cox — Meeting Dr. Anderson and Castel — Return to the station — Preparation for prolonged trip to Victoria Island*

Tuesday, March 2nd, 1915

Temperature -24°. The wind was north in the morning but shifted to the west and increased in strength. At 5 p.m. it was blowing 16 miles an hour, and it seemed to be stronger later — at 10 p.m. there was almost a blizzard. Six sleds arrived about noon — bringing a band of Coppermine River Eskimos. They flooded the house but soon left to build snow-huts in the long snow drift that had formed at right angles to the *North Star* on its eastern side. Cox, O'Neill, and I took each 10 photos of the different stages,[1] and Chipman vigorously shovelled snow round the walls. Two more sleds turned up just before dark. The Eskimos filled the house all the rest of the day and evening. I took two phonograph records from them, but it was impossible for anyone to work.[2]

Wednesday, March 3rd

A busy day, fixing up things about the house by daylight and purchasing articles later from the Eskimos. It was cold and rather stormy out of doors. The rich man Uloqsaq and his two wives turned up and built a snowhouse beside the others, joining passages with another man's house.[3] We kept them out during the day and let them flood the house in the evening.

Thursday, March 4th

A fine day albeit cold. Haviuyaq and Quvjextoq appeared from the *Puivlirmiut*,[4] bringing the news that a young man named Arnaqtaq had suddenly fallen sick and died there, and the people thought I had bewitched him because my fox-trap was stolen.[5] I bought a number of things from the Eskimos, spending practically the whole day in their huts purchasing — wolverine skins, clothing of all kinds,[6] bows and arrows, stone pots and lamps etc. In the evening Palaiyak said the Eskimos were going to have a dance and their doctor, Uloqsaq, would find out who had caused Arnaqtaq's death.[7] So I went down after supper and found them just beginning, with Cockney [Sullivan], our cook, there. There was an interesting seance, Uloqsaq being possessed by a dog. He attributed the death to a white man a long way off, not to us — being too shrewd not to know where their interests lay and perhaps a little intimidated by my presence and partial (to him uncertain how great) understanding of what was said. He jabbered at a tremendous rate in what his father said was white man's talk and looked to Cockney and me to bear him out. Cock-

Figure 146. Coppermine River Eskimos building snowhouses beside the schooner *North Star*, Bernard Harbour, March 2, 1915. (Photo by D. Jenness, CMC Photo No. 37020.)

ney did not drop to the trick, but I pretended to understand and nodded my head and replied in French,[8] which the [Eskimo] doctor fully 'understood' of course. His gestures were sufficiently explanatory of what he wanted us to do, and I directed Cockney. The two danced a kind of Scotch dance — an Indian dance, really, with Scotch elements in it[9] — to the great delight of the audience, the doctor all the while 'conversing' with me in his wild gibberish. The deceit was rather a strain on us both, and he was evidently relieved when I said I was sleepy and would return to the station. He led the way out and waited to speak to me outside, but as two women followed us closely I addressed him in French and 'accidentally' dropped the word *aqago* (tomorrow) in the midst of it, pointing at the same time to his house. He jumped to it at once, motioned for us to go on to the station, and retired himself to his own house. Cockney gave a most amusing account of the whole performance to the other men. He was badly scared, he said, at one time thinking the doctor was telling them to kill us. When the doctor talked gibberish and I 'understood' he thought I was hypnotized by him!! The weather was fine and clear all day.

Friday, March 5th

Another day spent in buying,[10] the weather again fine, though a moderate breeze sprang up and increased towards night. O'Neill's pictures of the snowhouse building turned out but medium, mine were all light-struck and overexposed[11] — the shutter of the camera is defective; Cox has not developed his yet. The Eskimos held a short dance in the morning, and I decorated the [Eskimo] doctor with a snow-shirt. It was amusing to see the conscious grin on his face every time he looked at me during the dance. It reminded one of the Roman augurs, who could not pass each other in the street without smiling. O'Neill is having a sleeping bag made. Most of the sewing that the women do in this region is rough, with stitches far apart, but one woman here sews very fine and neat. Cox and Eikie went with two sleds to Cockburn Point for wood. The Eskimos had the run of the house in the evening. I took six phonograph records from them, five of which turned out well. My little 'daughter' Qanayuq walked over with another child from the *Puivlirmiut* settlement[12] with the message that Ikpukkuaq was sick and wanted to see me. Haviuyaq said his wife Itoqunna wanted to see me also and wanted me to bring over some of our food; it's a case of cupboard love with her. I told them I was coming over in a few day's time when I had mended my sled, in which seven bolts along one runner and two along the other are broken or missing, and one of the side slats forming the bedding is broken.

Saturday, March 6th

Nearly all the [Coppermine River] Eskimos went over to the *Puivlirmiut* settlement, though the wind was 20 miles an hour and the temperature -24° — a blizzard. True they had it behind them. They proposed to return tomorrow, but the temperature was -26°, and the wind 23 miles an hour this evening, from the northwest. I was labelling and packing clothes most of the day and did a little buying from the Eskimos who remained. Palaiyak and I tried to worm out a little information from two or three of them, unsuccessfully, though we located the place from which they obtain their copper as 5 or 6 miles above Bloody Fall on the west side. The old Saturday evening bridge game made the evening pass quickly, the Eskimos sitting quietly watching. One man caused great amusement by asking if Chipman and O'Neill were my sons. We told him we were all Johansen's sons, for a joke, though I enlightened him afterwards. The Eskimos judge of age by the development of the beard and moustache,[13] which are always somewhat scanty with them and late in appearing. The others keep more or less well trimmed, but I allow mine to grow a week or two before clipping it, hence I am regarded as an old man.[14]

Sunday, March 7th

Rather bad weather all day. I spent some time in labelling specimens, mending my sled, and purchasing more things from the Eskimos. The latter came up in the evening. Cox had the electric cells set up and we had much amusement. First several joined hands and received shocks, then small trinkets were placed in a bowl of salt water, the wires connected, and they had to extract them. Cockney gave three a small dose of horse-radish. One man was plucky enough to swallow it, the other two spat it out immediately. All appreciated the joke.

Monday, March 8th

Another bad day, barometer falling rapidly, temperature mild, thick snow falling; natural result [was] a blizzard towards evening. Trading again occupied much of the day. Four or five families returned from the *Puivlirmiut* camp and raided the house in the evening. They told us the names for a few prominent points along the coast.[15] The four Eskimo men who have stayed here all the time did not seal yesterday — they said they could catch nothing here. Consequently they were short of food. We gave a little to the women and children, but nothing to the men lest they should be tempted to depend on us. Today they went sealing, but had no success. However, the returning natives brought a little food over with them; otherwise they had only sealskin to eat. One man told Eikie yesterday that they had eaten two old boots yesterday.

Wednesday, March 10[16]

None of the men went sealing; there are no seals about, they say. I spent the whole day trading and superintending the sewing of three or four women in the house. We gave them all a seal in the evening and a few of the women and children some hard-bread, for they said they were leaving tomorrow. They promised to give us seal meat for our days if we travel east and they have plenty. While I was away 19 seals were bought at the station from the *Ukullik* group. One day the fat widow Kaullu and the little girl Holoaq strolled over and stayed the night. Both slept on the floor. It is a curious commentary on Eskimo morality that the former asked Eikie with which white man she was to sleep. She is with child and told Eikie that plenty of men had contributed to cause that, widow as she is. There is one thing to be said for them, however; girls are pure until they marry. Ayallik's wife [Kaumaq] has been taken over by Qamiñgoq, the latter told us — a case of borrowing, apparently; I don't know whether Ayallik has Kalyutarun in exchange. The Eskimos came up[17] in the evening and I obtained five good phonograph records from them — one a magic song to procure success in hunting.[18] Cox and Johansen made an ethnological discovery today. They saw a child lift its face up towards its mother, who forthwith bent down towards it. A 'smack' was heard, and Johansen remarked that it was the first time he had known of an Eskimo kissing. Cox was more observant — the child's nose was clean after the operation. The result was Cox's retirement to the purity of the air outside. The weather was clear and bright all day, with only a light westerly breeze. It was amusing to watch one of the women tonight when the phonograph recorded a song. The eyes were almost bursting their sockets — she had never seen or heard anything like it. Kaullu sent over two pairs of sealskin slippers and a pair of mittens for which she wanted me to take her a knife for her little boy Utuaiyoq, another instance of her implicit faith in us.

Thursday, March 11th

Many of the Eskimos of the Coppermine [River] district returned today from the *Puivlirmiut* camp. Our people shot five ptarmigan, which are growing numerous round the station. I myself spent the whole day buying clothes and specimens. The Eskimos came inside in the evening and we treated them to electric shocks, which amused some and frightened others. Then at their own request the phonograph was brought out and half a dozen records taken.[19] They played the fool a little, shouting into the machine, following the initiative of the rich man Uloqsaq.[20] However, the records turned out fairly well. The weather was fine all day, though a little cold, and a moderate breeze blowing.

Friday, March 12th

I was pretty well ready to leave this morning,[21] but we were much worried by persistent intrusions of Eskimos. More of them returned, some of the *Puivlirmiut* as well, who are going east with them to visit the Coppermine River Eskimo who stayed behind. We arranged with Uloqsaq to provide him with a rifle and cartridges, and he is to hunt seal, and when they come, caribou. We buy his surplus seals and take part of the caribou meat. When the Dr. [Anderson] returns he will decide whether he wants to keep him [Uloqsaq] permanently or not. He is the only Eskimo here I have yet met who has any idea of service; he has hunted for white men at [Great] Bear Lake. Of his two wives, the elder is a good seal and caribou hunter, and both are good seamstresses. Palaiyak and I got away after lunch, accompanied by Kalyutarun, Qamiñgoq's wife, who had brought back a dog Chipman bought from them a while ago, but which had strayed back to them. This dog and the dog I bought from Qiñorlik were incorporated in my team, replacing Pannichuk and Scotty; of the latter there is no trace. The weather was beautifully fine and mild in the morning, but became foggy at noon and snow fell later. We found the combined *Haneragmiut, Aqulliakattañmiut, Puivlirmiut,* and *Noahognirmiut* camped about 5 miles east of the former settlement on *Putulik.* Two of the *Aqulliakattañmiut* had died and one *Puivlirmiut,* Arnaqtaq, during the winter — *iñminnih,* they said (of their own doing). We turned into Ikpukkuaq's house, a large single house with two other single houses opening on the same passage. Ikpukkuaq seems to have some kidney trouble, to judge by the place in which he locates the pain. I gave him vegetable laxative in the evening and shall give him iron and arsenic tomorrow.

Saturday, March 13th

A quiet day spent in the Eskimo settlement. The men went sealing about 10 a.m., and returned for the most part about 5 p.m. The weather was fine and clear, with a light breeze blowing and a moderate temperature. I gave Ikpukkuaq a little iron and arsenic, then visited Akhiatak, who dislocated his ancle playing with another man.[22] He has it in splinters and seems to be resting it well. His wife Niq has a little baby about 2

Figure 147. Interior of Copper Eskimo snowhouse, in temporary settlement on the ice 5 miles east of Sutton Island, Dolphin and Union Strait, March 13, 1915. (Photo by D. Jenness, CMC Photo No. 37019.)

weeks old, who is named Itaiyuk after his grandfather — and so bears the same name as Akhiatak's dog. Visiting two or three other houses and the taking of four photos[23] filled in the day. I asked Kalyutarun to make a pair of long deerskin socks for Palaiyak, and she made a very bad pair out of an old *atigi*. I took them but paid her very little for them. Her husband, Qamiñgoq, who is an *añatkok*, forbad Ikpukkuaq to eat the stomach of caribou, as long as he was suffering from stomach trouble, and his wife Taqtuk from making him new clothes. Consequently when I arranged with Ikpukkuaq to visit his copper deposit on Victoria Land in a few days, if he is well, he asked me to bring him a pair of inner trousers to wear on the journey. I arranged with him further to go with me to the *Kanghirjuarmiut* people, following the caribou next month. If some of them are crossing over to the *Ekalluktomiut* we will go with them, otherwise we shall continue on to Lake Tahiryuak, about a day's journey on from [north of] the head of Prince Albert Sound, where caribou and fish abound all the summer and some of the *Kanghirjuarmiut* resort. I am to supply Ikpukkuaq with a rifle and ammunition and have promised to take sled and dog-team, fish-net, tent, and other equipment.[24]

Sunday, March 14th

Palaiyak and I left for the station after breakfast. A moderate east wind blew at our backs and snow began to fall about noon. The temperature was only -11° F. We met Qiqpuk[25] and his wife Haquñgaq returning to the settlement. Only Kuniluk and his family and Qanayuq, they said, were left at the station. Everything was well. The Saturday evening bridge game had been postponed from the night before, and we played it tonight.

Monday, March 15th

I had intended to return to the Eskimo settlement today, but a boy who returned from the east reported that Qinollik and many of the Copper-mine River Eskimos are living just the other side of Chantry Island, so I sent Palaiyak over with the sled to see if my dog Mafa were there. This dog I bought from Qinollik and took over to the settlement near *Ukullik* 3 days ago. There it was tied up by its own harness, but chewed its rope in the evening and made off. Palaiyak returned about 7 p.m. Nothing had been seen of the dog. This is the second I have lost lately, for Scotty dis-appeared altogether about a week ago. The Eskimos thought he was going crazy in the evening, and certainly he had a little foam round his mouth. At all events, he disappeared the same night and has left no trace. Numerous wolf tracks have been seen to the east of the station, and it is thought the wolves have killed them. Qanayuq makes herself quite at home at the station. She knows she is a privileged person, keeps out of everyone's way, does a little odd sewing for us, and generally distracts us all and keeps us amused. This winter she harpooned a seal, but could not pull it out, so Quvyektoq, an Eskimo man, came to her aid, killed the seal, and pulled it out. Her father [Ikpukkuaq] wants me to teach her to shoot caribou next summer. I let her fire three shots from my .22 auto-matic rifle, and certainly she has a fair idea of how to hold a gun. Quniluk and his family were in the house most of the afternoon and eve-ning, and I obtained three fairly good phonograph records. Quniluk cau-tiously gazed down the horn and saw a tiny man there — a *tornraq* — the being who reproduced his songs.[26] When a man's voice was repro-duced it was the figure of a man he saw, about 1 1/2 inches high, when a woman's a diminutive woman. When his little boy Taipana sang into the machine and his song was reproduced,[27] he saw the figure of a little boy about 1/2 inch high. Quniluk's wife Qormiaq was more critical — she saw nothing after two inspections. Qanayuq could see the figure every time. The temperature dropped a little this evening — it was -19°, but the winter seems to be broken.

Tuesday, March 16th

A strong southeast breeze blew all day and the temperature at 8 a.m. was -20°. I wrote up some notes in the morning and left with Qanayuq and Kuniluk's family (save himself) immediately after lunch for the Eskimo settlement. Chipman and O'Neill expect to leave tomorrow for the west to begin their scientific work this spring.[28] Johansen went out in the morning to search the coast for wood[29] and was not returning till the afternoon. The wind was sideways to us, for our course was almost due

north, and we reached the settlement at sunset. Ikpukkuaq says he is
pretty well alright again; Akhiatak I have not seen yet. I cooked rice and
cocoa in the Khotal stove — the first time I have used it; it worked well.

Wednesday, March 17th

Fully half of the settlement had already migrated west,[30] and we followed them today. A strong east wind blew at our backs, but the weather
though dull was not very cold. Snow fell in the afternoon. We travelled
about 10 miles slightly north of west. Akhiatak was carried on his sled,
with Niq pulling in front. Instead of constructing a snow-hut, Ikpukkuaq
put up his spring tent, a great oval of deerskins sewn together stretched
over a frame of poles in the same way as Uloqsaq's. It took about
4 hours to set it up, build the two low outer snow walls and the short passage, by which time the sun was close to its setting. There are about 18
houses in this settlement now that we have arrived. Ikpukkuaq adopted
Arnauyuk[31] in the winter, so last night there slept in his house Qanayuq,
Taqtuk, Ikpukkuaq, [my]self, Higilaq, the little boy,[32] and Arnauyuk, in
that order. In this settlement, as in the last, there are three houses all
opening on to one passage.[33] The sleeping skins (*kipiq*), which many of
the people use, are sewn together at the bottom like a bag.

Thursday, March 18th

The weather was very mild today, though the sky was clouded. Ikpukkuaq went sealing with the other men. I stayed in camp [and] helped
Taqtu to extend the tent so that there might be room for Arnauyuk to
sleep inside. Visits to other houses filled in the rest of the day. Two ptarmigan appeared in the centre of the settlement. Two Eskimos fired three
or four shots at them at close range but missed them. The children played
chasing, skipping, and one or two other games, in which I joined for a
while. The men were very successful in their sealing. Both Qiqpuk and
Ikpukkuaq killed two, and one man three. Arnauyuk and Qanayuq gave
me a lesson in cutting up a seal this evening, and I mended the lid of a tin
for Haquñgaq. So passed the day.

Friday, March 19th

I returned to the station, taking with me a new dog I bought this morning named Alunaq. The weather was a trifle foggy, with a light east
breeze but very mild. Once during the day the thermometer was up to
+28° F. The settlement lies a little west of north from the station, distance about 20 miles. For most of the distance the ice is broken and
awkward to travel through. I reached the station about 4 p.m. and found
all well. In the evening I developed a roll of films I had exposed; about
half turned out to be printable — one luckily being the interior of a
snowhouse.[34]

Saturday, March 20th

Palaiyak went away to the Eskimo Coppermine River settlement just east of Chantry Island today to see if my dog Mafa was there. It broke loose at the other settlement the night I arrived [Mar. 12] and ran away. Palaiyak found no trace of it; the Eskimos think the wolves have killed it and Scotty also. Quniluk lost one of his dogs today. He [Quniluk] is still hanging round the station for no apparent reason. He said today he has no gun and had sold his bow to a Coppermine River Eskimo. Uloqhaq is with the Eskimos east of Chantry Island.

Sunday, March 21st

Palaiyak left this morning with Quniluk and his boy Taipana. A moderate west wind was blowing, but the temperature was not very low. Cox gathered a few things for our trip east in a few day's time, and Frits and I wrote up notes.

Monday, March 22nd

Palaiyak returned this afternoon with three new dogs, besides one which broke loose from the sled and ran back — four altogether that he had bought. Ikpukkuaq came with him, bringing the .303 Savage and .30-30 cartridges, which he wished to change for .44.[35] I spent most of the day revising the phonograph songs, which Palaiyak is writing down from the records. He uses Mackenzie equivalents very often or writes what the words should be in ordinary speech, besides which he employs the 'missionary' script, which with Eskimo more than with most languages is altogether inadequate. Ikpukkuaq sang a dance song in the evening; it extended through five blanks and was not finished then (three turned out good, two no good); I had no more blanks out; the rest are all on the *North Star*. This vessel seems to be leaking badly the last few days. Cox, Johansen, and Cockney took 82 buckets of water out of her hold today.

Tuesday, March 23

Ikpukkuaq left this morning with the .44 cartridges he received in exchange, the case of ammunition I am taking over to Victoria Land, and a few things I am caching on the shore on the Victoria Land side[36] before crossing over to Prince Albert Sound. Qanajuq, he said, had gone to *Ukullik* to bring back some blubber they had cached there. Cox and I were busy preparing to leave tomorrow for a trip of about 10 days along the coast, enabling Cox to do a little mapping[37] and take a few observations before the Dr. returns, when he proposes to go east again with Aarnout, at least as far as Rae River, up the Rae River, and overland to Stapylton Bay, making a kind of square route. Palaiyak wrote down three more songs recorded in the phonograph today. The weather was fine but a little colder — about -15° F part of the time.

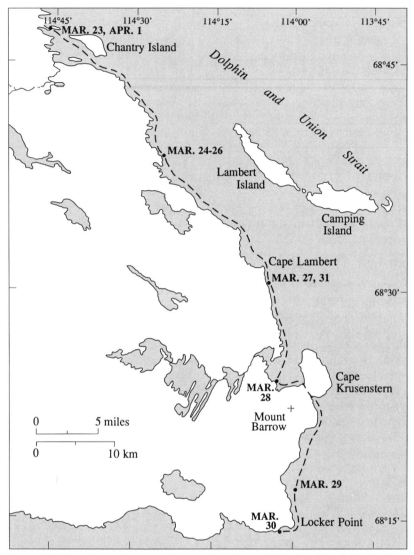

Figure 148. Map showing the route taken by the author and John Cox, March 24 - April 1, 1915. Their return trip took 2 days to cover what the outward trip had taken 5 working days to traverse.

Wednesday, March 24th

Temperature -24°, with a light west wind at 8 a.m. It died away later and the temperature rose. Cox and I got away just before 10 a.m., the team consisting of Jumbo, Telluraq, and three new Eskimo dogs. One of these is only a pup a year old. The load was about 400 lbs,[38] which proved rather too heavy for the dogs. Our progress was slow — about 2 miles an hour, though John (Cox) said this evening it was about as fast as he could travel and take bearings at the same time along this coast with its many islets, indentations, and promontories. Jumbo froze himself 2 days ago and seemed to get worse today, so tomorrow I am going back with him and [will] bring two dogs instead, making Telluraq leader. We camped in about the same place as when the Dr. and I came east — some 12 miles only, it now appears, from the station. Our tent is single, which is rather a nuisance, for it frosts up very badly. We were lucky though to find two spruce logs so had a comfortable fire this evening.

Thursday, March 25th

Temperature at 8 a.m. zero, weather partially foggy but calm. We had just finished breakfast when we heard a shout and found Haviuyaq and Itoqunna just appearing with a sled. They were going to the station, they said, to trade two bearded-seal skins for a rifle!! We decided to return also and reorganize our dog team, so we all went together, reaching the station at 1 p.m. We bought a dog — Niq — from Haviuyaq, and a large stone lamp,[39] and left Frits to purchase one or two other small things while we returned to our camp. Jumbo and two of the Eskimo dogs we had used before were left behind. Snow fell in the afternoon and the barometer fell heavily, while the temperature was fairly high. Haviuyaq and Itoqunna are sleeping in a snow-hut beside the station. There were three caribou tracks on the ice yesterday, and less than half way between our camp and the station are the deserted houses of the Coppermine River Eskimos.

Friday, March 26th

A gale sprang up in the night. We had just finished breakfast again this morning when Haviuyaq and Itoqunna appeared on their way home. It was still blowing strongly so we decided to stay here the day unless the weather cleared. About 10 a.m. John [Cox] rustled a little wood from the beach while I entertained the two Eskimos in the tent. They left 1/2 hour later, and John went off to take some bearings along the coast, but returned a couple of hours later as the weather grew worse again. We had two ptarmigan for supper tonight, brought from the station. The wind had moderated a good deal and the barometer is rising very rapidly, while the thermometer is going down — it is -14° F now at 7 p.m. John saw a rabbit today. A small creek runs into the bottom of this bay at its eastern end.

Saturday, March 27th

Temperature -12° at 9 a.m. and a moderately strong west wind blowing, luckily behind us. We left at 9:50, the weather being a little hazy. The dogs pulled fairly well, and we jogged along slowly, going a little inside two or three of the bays to enable Cox to see the bottoms of them. It is very hard to distinguish low land from the ice, and one bay Cox examined several times through the glasses but could not determine certainly whether it was land or not. About 3 p.m. we reached an Eskimo settlement, 2 miles west of Cape Lambert. Here with others Haviuyaq is staying, and Uloqhaq, the latter in his skin tent. He had shot a caribou a day or so ago and gave us two fine shoulders of meat, to prove apparently that he was carrying out his contract. All the others were Coppermine River Eskimo, and all save Uloqhaq were living in snowhuts — about three altogether, mostly single. We stayed but 5 minutes, then pressed on, passing Cape Lambert and camping on the beach just beyond. We obtained three logs of wood from the Eskimos and picked up a little on the beach — enough for tonight and the morning. This was unexpected luck, for we had feared we should have to employ the primus. Cox went on top of Cape Lambert at its eastern end and found by aneroid that its height was 80 feet. It slopes backwards and upwards, so that 100 yards or so behind it is probably about 100 feet high. Cox thought the strata underlying the limestone of the cliff was not sandstone, as Frits judged, but a shaly limestone. He entered Uloqhaq's tent and saw there a large naturally hollow slab of limestone being used for a lamp besides the ordinary soapstone lamp. Small limestone lamps are fairly common, being used mostly by little girls in their corner of the hut. The wind abated in the afternoon, and began to veer round different points of the compass, now west, now north, now east. The temperature at 6:30 p.m. was -18° F.

Sunday, March 28th

We waited till noon to enable Cox to obtain a latitude. He took a longitude also in the morning.[40] The weather was fairly clear and we continued along the coast until we sighted some Eskimo houses and tents at the bottom of the deep bay west of [Cape] Krusenstern. I then continued straight there while Cox worked along the shore. Hardly had I reached the camp when two herds of caribou were sighted. Two Eskimos (Huputaun and Aneraq[41]) and myself, with our rifles, tried to head them off, but they had too big a start. They had apparently crossed [Cape] Krusenstern by the long portage and were crossing over to Victoria Land. We put up at Huputaun's tent, which was exactly like Ikpukkuaq's. There are four tents in this settlement, and about five snowhouses.

Monday, March 29th

The whole settlement migrated to the other side of [Cape] Krusenstern today by a short portage running practically due east from near the bottom of the bay past Mt. Barrow on its northern side and out onto the sea below the first promontory south of [Cape] Krusenstern. The distance across is only about 1 1/2 miles, with one or two small detours to avoid stones, and is fairly level, dropping down a bank 10 or 12 feet high on to the sea ice on the eastern side. Cox and I began to follow the bay round, then he continued round the coast while I followed the Eskimo trail. I overtook them at the end of the portage and migrated with them till they made camp about 3 p.m. Cox turned up an hour later — the distance round was only about 12 miles, our new camp being some 3 miles north of Point Lockyer[42] and 1 1/2 miles out to sea. Again we put up at Hupu-taun's tent. The weather was fine and clear, temperature mild, and no wind to speak of.

Tuesday, March 30th

We stayed in camp till noon for longitude and latitude observations,[43] then travelled down the coast till we struck a large log of cottonwood set on end on the beach about 5:30 p.m. We were then a little south of Point Lockyer, off which lies a flat coast of shingle, invisible till one is almost upon it. The weather was fine and fairly clear, the temperature at 10 a.m. -25°, at noon -12° F, later probably still higher. The barometer was very high — 30.75° — at noon. Just as we reached the log we turned our glasses on to a sled a mile southeast[44] of us and saw it was the Dr. [Anderson] and Aarnout [Castel] returning. We all camped on the same spot, beside the log. They had a very hard trip after we left them — floundering in deep snow. The load they started out with was too heavy so they cached half of it. Finally they reached Dease River (it took 4 days to Kendall River from Melville Creek) only to flounder in more deep snow. There was no sign of Indians, whence the Dr. thought there could be no white men on [Great] Bear Lake.[45] Supplies were running low — they had not sufficient to make Fort Norman — so they turned back, killing some caribou on the way. The Eskimos were a great trouble to Cox when he was taking his observations — he does not appreciate them a bit.

Wednesday, March 31st

We cached about 60 lbs of both Hudson['s] Bay [Co.] and Under-wood (dog and man) pemmican on the beach[46] and left about 10:30 a.m. for the Eskimo camp to pick up the dog which we lost yesterday.[47] We reached there just after noon, stayed a few moments, then continued on across the same portage the Eskimos and I made 2 days ago. It is about 1 1/2 miles long and easy travelling. Reaching the old settlement in the bay [Pasley Cove] we found Haviuyaq and his people had just arrived from the west and were unloading their two sleds. They wanted us to camp there, but we pressed on and made the east end of Cape Lamburne [Lambert] at 6:50 p.m., where we knew there was wood. We all turned into one tent — John's and mine — and had a hearty supper. The weather was cold, -18° at 10:30 p.m. and a strong northeast wind blow-ing, luckily almost behind us for half the way.

Thursday, April 1st

We broke camp and started out for the station at 11 a.m., having about 25 or 26 miles to make. It was -6° F and blowing strong from the north-east. The snow was drifting so that at times we could not see more than 100 yards ahead, but the wind was behind us all the way. We passed numerous caribou tracks and finally made the station about 8:30 — just after dark. Uloqhaq, his two wives, and a boy whom he has adopted, had reached the station today, and some of them spent the evening.

Friday, April 2nd

Good Friday. Unpleasant weather out of doors, with a fairly strong breeze and drifting snow, and a temperature a few degrees below zero. We spent the day indoors engaged in miscellaneous occupations. The doctor [Anderson] ratified the contract made with Uloqhaq, and issued him, besides the .30-30 rifle, a .44, with cartridges and reloading tools, himself to use the .44, his wife the .30-30.

Saturday, April 3rd

Palaiyak went hunting and came upon a herd of caribou. He shot one and wounded three, then returned home, but went out again in the afternoon and despatched the whole herd, eight in all. I spent the day fixing up a small tent I am taking away for the summer, Aarnout in fixing up a sled for Cox and himself when they go east to survey the country between Rae River and Stapylton Bay, the rest in miscellaneous occupations. A moderately strong breeze was blowing, with a little drift, but the temperature was not very cold. I finished cutting out the old folding door of the tent, replacing it by one of the 'bag' type.

Sunday, April 4th.   Easter Sunday

Palaiyak, Aarnout, and Uloqhaq's adopted son brought in the caribou Palaiyak shot yesterday. The foxes were already beginning to make inroads on them, for they were unfrozen, being piled together and covered with snow. I put in an extra width of cloth all round the bottom of my tent to make a partial floor, hoping thereby to keep out mosquitoes. The temperature was about zero, with a moderate breeze all day.

Monday, April 5th

Preparations for our forthcoming journeys occupied most of us all day. Palaiyak and Uloqhaq went hunting but saw nothing. Frits went out for ptarmigan but saw nothing likewise. The weather was fine and clear, the temperature -7° at 8 a.m., zero at 5:30 p.m., and -14° at 10:30 p.m. A light westerly breeze lasted out the day. The phonograph was brought out in the evening, and Palaiyak wrote out the words of two songs.

Tuesday, April 6th — Sunday, April 11th

The Dr., Cox, and I have all been busy this week preparing for our journeys,[48] Palaiyak and Aarnout assisting. There were tents to alter and repair, sleds to be fixed up, and various other matters to attend to. The weather the first 2 or 3 days was blizzardy, but yesterday and today it was beautifully fine and, in the sun, quite warm, so that one could work with bare hands. Ikpukkuaq and two or three other families turned up on Thursday with Uloqhaq, who had been over to their settlement. They left next day to hunt bearded seal to the eastward, leaving only Akhiatak and family, Qanajuq (Jennie), and Uloqhaq's adopted boy. On Saturday four Eskimo men arrived to sell seals (three) and one or two other things and returned again this morning. Ptarmigan have been seen close to the house three or four times today but are easily alarmed, so that we have had no success with the .22 rifle. No more deer have made their appearance. The *North Star* was found to be leaking very badly yesterday, so Aarnout has to remain here and attend to her, Cockney taking his place as Cox's dog-driver.

Monday, April 12th

Another fine day, the sun warm, a fresh east breeze blowing, and the temperature at 5:30 p.m. -6° F. Uloqhaq, Qamiñgoq, and Ikpukkuaq with their families returned today. They had killed two *ugyuk* [bearded seals], and six caribou. Ikpukkuaq returns to the settlement near *Ukullik* tomorrow, and I go with him. Probably I shall not return to the station again before November. The Dr. and Cox are preparing to leave, the latter the day after tomorrow. We were all very busy making final preparations. Wikkiaq and his wife Uñahaq, with their newborn baby turned up today. There is no seclusion of the women at and after childbirth here as among the Point Barrow natives in former times.

Part 3

Leading a Nomadic Life on Victoria Island

April 13, 1915 – November 8, 1915

Chapter 28. To Victoria Island

First settlement on the ice — Brief trip to Cape Pullen — Tent dwellings — Hunting at seal holes — Taqtu's shamanistic performance — Rabbit hunting on Read Island — Return of the caribou — A blizzard strikes — Reading The Odyssey *— Establishing a base on Victoria Island — Two rifles among fifteen people — Caching supplies*

Tuesday, April 13th, 1915

I loaded the sled after breakfast, but Ikpukkuaq and his people were in no hurry to leave, so it was after 11 a.m. when we set out. The trail was fair though obstructed with a little broken ice in places. The temperature at 8 a.m. was a few degrees below zero and a light easterly breeze brought a little snow, which somewhat obscured the atmosphere. We travelled rather slowly and did not reach the settlement till 6 p.m. — the distance being about 20 miles.[1] Everything I had left or sent over seemed to be all right save the primus, of which the needles had been lost and coal oil mixed with the alcohol. There should have been more wire for needles, but that is missing too, so I shall have to try and file down a small needle. Spare alcohol I have with me. Most of the people have left this settlement. Arnauyuk [Kila] is married to Ayalligaq. Avrunna, Taqtuk's son, who with his wife is living now with Ikpukkuaq, gave me seal meat for my dogs. Frits had left with a dog team to obtain ice[2] from the east and Aarnout with another team for wood from the west, before I left. I have three Eskimo dogs that have been bought recently in my team, one of them very wild though a good worker. The other two, Niq and Maffa, are friendly enough. I pick up another dog here, which was bought some time back but ran away.

Wednesday, April 14th

A quiet day in the Eskimo camp, lying or sitting on the sleeping platform most of the time, for there are no caribou about here and the seals have not yet emerged on top of the ice. They were bearing young about a week ago. Bearded seals are absent here, the natives say. I fixed up a couple of harnesses, incidentally, and pottered round the camp. The weather was mild though not very clear. Several men went sealing and obtained two or three, I am not sure which.

Thursday, April 15th

A foggy day but the weather [was] very mild. In the morning I melted lead in the frying pan over the primus and cast 44 bullets for Ikpukkuaq. Kehullik and Qanajuq were conveying blubber and some of my things towards the land[3] to lighten the sleds when we go, and I accompanied them. I had 10 tins of pemmican and a case of hard-bread on the sled — they, four blubber pokes. These blubber pokes have a loop of rawhide generally at one end or both to facilitate handling them, as they frequently weigh 100 - 150 lbs. The temperature at 9 p.m., when it was still light, was zero out of doors but 43° F in the tent, with about 18 inches of the lamps burning — a tribute to the warmness of the spring tent of deerskins, for the door was open and only six of us inside. They are treating me very well — as suits their own interests of course — but I really am much more comfortable among these Eskimos than I have ever been before. I showed Ikpukkuaq how to complete loading his cartridges, and he finished quite a number — 8 oz. of lead makes apparently about 200 bullets for a .44 rifle. Tonight I learned that Qiqpuk and his people are not going with us to Victoria Land as they have said all along, but leave tomorrow to join Uloqhaq at the station — he is a kinsman. The change in their plans took place today and was announced to Ikpukkuaq's people this evening — these Eskimos, like the western [ones], can never stick to any fixed plan but change their purposes from day to day.

Friday, April 16th

A fine day though foggy. The whole settlement migrated today, most of them to a site about 10 miles north,[4] and I accompanied the train. Instead of putting up his big spring tent, which he intends sending away tomorrow to be cached on the shore, Ikpukkuaq built the walls of a regular snow-hut, laid some poles across the top, and covered it over with one of my tents then two musk-ox skins. A half circle of snow was built round it on its unprotected side, the interspace filled up with soft snow, and the bags of clothing etc., laid on top, thus protecting the edges of the roof, which was further pegged down into the snow wall. The other side of the house was protected by a regular snow-hut, the two having a common passage. It made a rather low dwelling but comfortable nevertheless.

Saturday, April 17th

The Eskimos asked me this morning to go with Ikpukkuaq and bring back some deer fat cached last fall, and I rashly consented, only half understanding the project. While preparing to leave I found it was some distance away[5] — would take 2 days, one man said. This was rather a surprise, nevertheless I took coal oil for 2 days, rice, and sugar, thinking Ikpukkuaq would take a little food as well. We set out at 10 a.m. due west in foggy weather with a strong east wind behind us. After travelling about 20 miles we came to a deserted settlement[6] with one hut inhabited by a *Haneragmiut* man. Here we stopped for a few minutes to eat some seal meat then pressed on, stopping at 7:30 p.m. to camp. Ikpukkuaq built a snow-hut[7] and I tried to set the primus going, but it proved obstinate. The needles to clean out the hole were lost — by Ikpukkuaq's people while the primus was left with them — and two new needles I made of tin proved unsatisfactory. However, I finally managed to make a new needle and set it going. It was 11:30 p.m., however, before we were able to turn in.

Sunday, April 18th

We had a comfortable night, with a mess of rice in the morning. We should reach the cache today, Ikpukkuaq said, and we travelled from 8 a.m. to 7:15 p.m. without making it, about 30 miles, besides yesterday's 30 miles. We made the unpleasant discovery that the coal-oil tin leaked and was quite empty, so now we have no fuel to cook the rice. We came about 4 p.m. to a high limestone cliff — Cape Hamilton — 200 ft ?[8] high and about 1/4 mile long, which the natives call *Mikumauq*. It is the most conspicuous feature along this coast. About 6-7 miles more took us across [Lady] Richardson Bay, and we camped behind Cape Pullen[9] (*Hinieluk*). The snow drifts were very soft and deep just here. I searched the coast for wood, while Ikpukkuaq built a snow-hut, and gathered an armful of tiny sticks in about 1/2 mile of coast — enough to light a small fire on a flat stone inside the snow-hut and boil rice. Ikpukkuaq made a sort of chimney, but the smoke nevertheless was fearful. We turned in again at 11:30 p.m. The shore here is strewn with limestone, with here and there a block of red granite full of quartz crystals or a black rock like diabase. The wind was westerly today and the weather clear and bright most of the time. We saw a seal on the ice and I took a shot at it, but hit it low in the shoulder so that it dived into its hole. This is the first seal we have seen this season on the ice. Behind [Lady] Richardson Bay there are several lakes, which teem with fish, Ikpukkuaq says. The land all around here he calls the land of the *Haneragmiut*. It would have been amusing, were it not a serious matter for us, to watch his efforts to kindle a fire with some coal-oily paper I gave him; he put it on top of the wood like blubber, set it alight, and proceeded leisurely to lay sticks around and over it. He seemed to have no idea of making shavings, so that the western Eskimos have probably derived the practice from the whites.

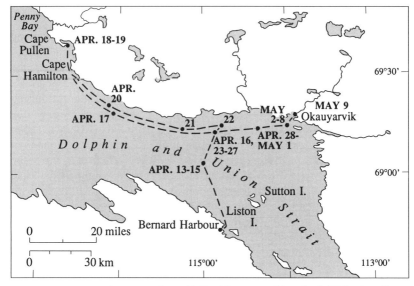

Figure 149. Map showing route taken with Ikpukkuaq to and from Lady Richardson Bay, Victoria Island, late April, 1915.

Monday, April 19th

Ikpukkuaq turned out about 4 a.m. to go off and bring the deer fat. It is close to here, he said, and he would be back before dark. My eyes are very painful — a combination of irritations produced by a cold, smoke, and snow-blindness, I think — so I stayed in camp. This is the most unpleasant trip I have had this year, for my stomach is constipated, and we travel all day without eating a bite — yesterday more than 11 hours on the morning rice. I am nearly exhausted by camp time and am troubled with a pain in the stomach while travelling. I lay in my sleeping bag for 3 hours after Ikpukkuaq left, then lit a fire and boiled rice and tea, eating besides a little frozen seal meat he left me. Then I went out to explore the coast a little, but my eyes were too painful, so I returned and lay down, and finally stripped and tumbled into my sleeping bag again for warmth. The weather is clear and foggy by turns, with a moderate west wind. Ikpukkuaq turned up at 8:30 [p.m]. just after I had lit the fire and put rice on to boil. He had a very heavy load of deer fat and deer meat so had been long in returning from the cache. Behind Cape Pullen there is a deep bay not marked on the chart[10] — at least it seemed to be closed at the bottom and I understood from Ikpukkuaq that it was, though it was full of ice kegs as though it were a strait. It ran in thus from [Lady] Richardson Bay:

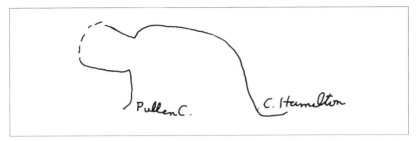

Figure 150. Sketch of bay behind Cape Pullen.

Tuesday, April 20th

We left before 8 a.m. after a light breakfast of frozen deer meat and deer fat. Both were decidedly 'tippy', some would say 'rotten', so that I could not manage to swallow very much. The weather was clear and bright, with a fresh westerly breeze at our backs. We travelled slow, the sled being very heavy, but kept on with one or two short halts till after 6 p.m. after making about 25 miles. I picked a small piece of limestone out of its bedding at Cape Hamilton about 80 feet from the ground. The cleavage of the limestone is horizontal and perpendicular, but mainly horizontal. Beside the cape we saw two ptarmigan, but they flew before we could shoot. The next cape to the eastward is *Niahognayuk*, and the coast for a few miles east of that again is *Qinaruk*. Beyond that, about 25 miles from Cape Hamilton, is *Tuluqaq*, the 'home of the ravens', because these birds are especially numerous there. We are camped about 4 miles west of it now.

Wednesday, April 21st

We left at 9 a.m. after eating a little deer meat in our sleeping bags.[11] The weather was perfect, with a light westerly breeze. About an hour later we passed *Tuluqaqaq* (little raven), a limestone cliff apparently some 50 feet high, running almost north and south. A mile or so further on is *Tuluqaq* itself, whose cliffs are a little higher and run east and west. A shallow bay about 12 miles broad succeeds and projects to a promontory at its eastern extremity, called *Iñnerin* (or *Iñnerit*) because pyrites (*iñnerin* or *iñnerit*)[12] is found here. The settlement of the *Aqulliakattuñmiut* that we were making for was about 5 miles southeast of *Innerin*, for though *Aqulliakattuk* is the country round Cape Bexley and Stapylton Bay, its people share with the *Haneragmiut* the district around *Innerin* on Victoria Land. We made the settlement just before 5 p.m. Five families are living there, and we turned into the *iglu* of a young married woman named Añopqunna. All are living in snow-huts, not in tents, for this is one of their settlements early in the winter, which they have reoccupied. This house has a deep recess near the door for a dog, and a pup is tied to a stake at the back of the sleeping platform by its harness. The woman has a copper pot obtained she thinks from the Indians, though she does not know for sure. We had a substantial meal of our own 'rotten' deer meat and some seal meat cooked by our hostess, while more was brought in later from other houses. As soon as we arrived Ikpukkuaq had picked out a little deer meat and deer fat from our load for each of the houses — enough for about a meal for one person. The coast from *Iñnerin* to Cape Pullen is formed by a series of shallow indentations backed by low ridges apparently about 50 feet high, but rising a little higher at the capes, where there are generally exposures of limestone — the prevalent formation. Both Ikpukkuaq and I were tired out when we made the settlement tonight. He drank about a quart of water, then two cups of tea, then a large musk-ox ladle full of seal broth. Last night[13] he drank my teapot-full of water — 2 quarts, and more in the night, besides which he is eating ice all day. We travelled about 20 miles today.

Thursday, April 22nd

We left about 9 a.m., expecting to reach our camp about 3 p.m. A strong east wind blew directly in our faces, causing a low drift. In the afternoon this diminished, but snow fell. The atmosphere accordingly was obscured all day, and we could rarely see more than 100 yards away. There was no trail, and we wandered about till 5 p.m. looking in vain for the settlement, then decided to camp. We had no matches, for I gave away my last block yesterday to our hostess as payment for dog-food, so I ate some frozen deer meat and turned into my sleeping bag.[14] Ikpukkuaq thought he might still find the settlement so wandered about for an hour then returned and turned in also. Altogether it was a rather miserable day.

Friday, April 23rd

It was still foggy at 6 a.m. but less than yesterday. After a light breakfast of deer fat in our sleeping bags we dressed, loaded the sled, hitched up the dogs, and set out south. The atmosphere grew clearer and after we had travelled about 2 miles we sighted the settlement about 1 1/2 miles west of us. Both of us were dead tired when we reached it, I being more exhausted than Ikpukkuaq, for I am unable to eat the quantity of rotten deer meat and fat that he finds palatable — even good. The men were away sealing; they returned in the evening with five seals. The weather became beautifully fine about noon — clothes of all descriptions were hung out to dry — suspended on sticks, laid on bags etc. Caribou passed here yesterday — the first seen this season on this side of the straits.[15]

Saturday, April 24th

I sent Avrunna to the station for a number of things, principally rice and sugar. Jennie (Qanajuq) accompanied him. They took my sled and three of my dogs, with two of their own, and left about 7:30 a.m. The weather was fine and warm, but rather foggy; probably the temperature was above freezing in the sun. I spent a quiet day in the Eskimo camp watching the women hanging out their clothes etc. to dry, and reading some of *The Odyssey* and a little German. Ikpukkuaq also stayed in camp making a box in which to carry cartridges during the summer's packing. He showed considerable mechanical skill in a small way in using his simple tools, dressing the wood, hammering out pieces of copper and soft iron for nails and fitting the pieces together. He even grooved it for a sliding lid. The men returned successful from their sealing again. Two families moved away to live about 10 miles west, and Haviuyaq and his people are living about 6 miles southeast of us.

Sunday, April 25th

Kehullik and I went to bring in the blubber and pemmican we cached a week or so ago.[16] Ikpukkuaq went sealing with the men, and Avrunna's wife Miluqattaq accompanied them also, first borrowing a knife from me to enlarge the seal hole in case she harpooned a seal. The women were busy about the camp setting things out to dry again, for the weather was fine and warm again, though still somewhat hazy. I took several photos, one being of the dogs dragging home seals in front of the hunters.[17] Ikpukkuaq obtained a seal, but Miluqattaq had no luck. Avrunna turned up about 8 p.m. with a pleasant note from Johansen and the things I had sent for, with a few additions he had kindly added. Frits [Johansen] also sent four marrow bones and a ptarmigan, but Avrunna and Jennie in typical Eskimo style levied toll on them and ate two marrow bones on the way.

Monday, April 26th

Kehullik, another man, and myself left about 7 a.m. to cache blubber and some of my things one stage further on. The weather was stormy, a strong east wind driving the snow into our faces, but the temperature was fairly mild. We went about 6 miles, placed everything in a pile and laid snow-blocks round them. The rest of the day I spent pretty well in feasting, reading, and talking. About noon I cooked rice with raisins, and we had malted milk and sugar with it as well, followed by cocoa. Later I had a marrow bone and a hard-bread, a little pemmican, a little seal meat and deer fat, and as a grand finale, cooked the ptarmigan and the meat from the marrow bone and mingled rice with the soup. Ikpukkuaq and his people would not touch the meat, though the caribou was killed this spring, and he told me the other day that fresh meat can be cooked on the ice (Uloqhaq and others had no scruples over [on] the other side[18]). Apparently he is chary of cooking or eating any caribou meat at all on the ice. The weather continued stormy all day. Avrunna and Milukattuk are the most affectionate couple I have seen among these people. They are constantly fondling each other and disconsolate at the other's absence.

Tuesday, April 27th

A stormy day similar to yesterday spent by everyone indoors. The snow had drifted greatly in the night and covered up most of the things round the house. My sled and two coal-oil tins were completely hidden, but we dug them out. The smaller coal-oil can — a 2-gallon can — I found had developed a bad leak in the bottom and fully half of the oil

Figure 151. Copper Eskimos rest briefly during migration northward to Victoria Island, about 20 miles west of Read Island, April 28, 1915. (Photo by D. Jenness, CMC Photo No. 37094.)

had been lost. I emptied what was left into the other can, which is a 5-gallon can now practically full. Luckily Frits had sent me a 2-gallon can of his own full of oil. He says it does not leak, so I shall cache it on the shore with some food for the autumn. Reading *The Odyssey* and a little German, talking, and eating filled up the rest of the day. A sled turned up with three men who had been away a few days on some business or other.[19] Avrunna is becoming a little independent and inquisitive, so I made a beginning of reducing him a little to a more respectable level. So far I have every reason to be satisfied with Ikpukkuaq and his family, despite many 'peculiarities' rather repugnant to a European but natural to them.

Wednesday, April 28th

We turned out at 5 a.m., some before, to pack up and load the sleds. The weather was beautifully fine, but a rather cold east wind blew all day in our faces. There were seven sleds in the migration train, exclusive of my own. We travelled very slowly, for the sleds were heavily laden and the snow soft and deep. The late 2-day's gale had not hardened the surface, for fresh snow fell at the same time. During one of the stops to rest the Eskimos lit a fire of shavings in a pot sheltered from the wind by snow-blocks and hung another pot containing snow over it — to re-ice the sled-runners I thought; but no, they were thirsty and wanted to drink. One wonders how much alcohol they would consume if it were procurable and how long the race would last in consequence. The sun is now so warm that it is necessary to kick snow up against the sides of the sled-runners whenever they stop to rest. About 3:30 p.m. all were too tired to proceed further, so camp was made. At the last settlement the snow-huts dripped a good deal, so now everyone set up his tent above a ring of snow-blocks. These tents are the same as the summer tents — made of deerskins supported on a frame consisting of a ridge pole supported by a half cone of poles at each end. I took three or four photos during the day, one of the Eskimos setting up their tents.[20] Our tent is similar to what we had before — snow-blocked walls with my tent and musk-ox skins laid over the top. We stay here over tomorrow, then move on again east.[21] Ikpukkuaq and his wife were telling me about childbirth, but I could understand very little. Apparently one woman acts as midwife and thereafter regards the child as in part her own.[22] I wish I could talk freely to them, for they are very communicative and would teach me many of their customs. This evening I upset a cup of tea on one of the skins, to Taqtu's great annoyance; but what vexed her most was the perfect indifference Ikpukkuaq displayed. She was laughing over it 5 minutes later.

Thursday, April 29th

A strong east wind was blowing again today. All the men went sealing save one, who returned with me to the cache we made 2 days ago and brought in the things. Ikpukkuaq returned successful, and I saw what I have not noticed before — Qanajuq poured water into the seal's mouth, because seals have an intense desire for water. This was the custom at Barrow also. He [Ikpukkuaq] generously presented me with the liver and heart to fry. It was cold in the tent today, for the breeze developed into a semi-blizzard and whistled through every chink and crevice. In the evening Taqtu and I turned out to pile snow-blocks on different things so that they might not be blown away. Taqtu was telling me how they fish through the ice in the fall. They jiggle with a baitless hook attached to line and short rod through a hole in the ice and build a wall of snow-blocks round them to shelter them from the wind. It is a cold occupation nevertheless, she says. She asked me too if we weep when anyone dies, as is their custom.

Friday, April 30th

A strong east wind blew early in the morning. Before noon it died away, the sun came out, and all the women hurriedly cleared their clothes and other possessions, which were outside, of the snow that had accumulated, and set them out to dry.[23] The men went sealing, and Ikpukkuaq secured two seals. I watched them standing over the seal holes through the binoculars. Some stood upright over the holes, some stooped till the upper half of the body was horizontal. I saw one man poise his harpoon, another pull his harpoon out of the hole, but did not see one actually strike. Incidentally, I cleared the roof of our tent of snow and my own belongings and kept a look out for caribou, but none appeared. Ikpukkuaq presented me with the liver of one of the seals, which I fried in a little lard I brought. The wind changed towards evening and blew fairly strong from the west, so Taqtu and I built a curved extension to the passage. She was almost as awkward as I in fitting the blocks together; very few women, I fancy, could make a snow-hut.

Figure 152. Spring tent of Copper Eskimos with clothes set out to dry, near the southwest shore of Victoria Island, April 30, 1915. (Photo by D. Jenness, CMC Photo No. 37006.)

Saturday, May 1st

A beautifully fine day. Most of the men went sealing, but two men with a sled went east to cache some blubber pokes,[24] and Qanajuq and I accompanied them with my sled and half of my things. We saw four seals on the ice. I stalked three, but two dived before I was near enough to shoot, and the other I either missed or did not kill outright. We did not reach the land but cached the things about 6 miles off after travelling about 10 miles. The sealers were more successful than I. Ikpukkuaq secured two and another Eskimo three. I had livers in plenty for supper. Returning to camp I repaired my sled, many of its lashings being broken. A very light air breathed from the west, and the sun shone out warm while the sky was a bright blue, a good beginning for the month of May. On our trip an old seal hole was discovered. It was covered with a little snow, which the Eskimos quickly scraped away. Beneath was a small hole about a foot in diameter, full of salt water — the real seal hole. Between it and the surface, beside the seal hole, was a small cavity in which the young seal is nourished. The salt water was full of melting ice, which was quite fresh as soon as the water was allowed to drain out of it — a matter of 2 or 3 seconds. Such a pool is a great find when one is thirsty.

Sunday, May 2nd

Another fine day with a light easterly breeze. We migrated again — east and travelled perhaps 15 miles before camping, about 4 miles west of a small island. Two sleds left us at the start to strike the land due north, but two others joined us from two houses about an hour after we started, keeping our total up to eight sleds. We sighted one seal on the ice, and Ikpukkuaq stalked it, but it dived too soon. Everyone has a tent erected now on snow-blocks with an ordinary snow-block passage. I forgot to mention an interesting performance which took place the night before last. I had turned into my sleeping bag, but several people were in the house and we were talking. They asked me something and I assented, not knowing exactly what was meant, whereupon Taqtu took a strap, passed it round my head at the nape of the neck and asked me a series of questions, I having my eyes shut and being presumably asleep. At each question she lifted my head by the strap and judged whether the answer were affirmative or negative by the weight on the strap, my head being apparently 'light' for yes and 'heavy' for no. Most of the questions I could not understand, so my answers were not very satisfactory it seemed. Another interesting performance took place last night after I had written up the day's log. Taqtu gave a shamanistic performance by request, apparently for the benefit chiefly of the two families who were quitting our train. It took place in our tent and followed the usual course. First she gave an oration, then suddenly put her hand to her forehead and uttered several cries of apparent pain; the *tornraq* was passing into her. Then at the constant solicitation of the audience she murmured some words in a thin hollow voice, hardly audible, repeated them several times, her eyes staring wildly at the same time. Again she was silent for a moment or two, then gave a long sigh, rubbed her eyes, and the performance was over. Throughout there were constant comments and requests to speak on the part of the audience.

Monday, May 3rd

The weather was so fine and warm this morning that I left for the day with only a light *atigi* and a thin Burberry snow-shirt. The snow was melting on the ice, and our footgear suffered in consequence, for we have no real spring boots. Ikpukkuaq, Avrunna, Kehullik, Haugaq, and I went over to Read Island. We secured nine rabbits and three ptarmigan. I was particularly fortunate, securing three of the rabbits out of the nine, with only seven cartridges, whereas the others, Ikpukkuaq and Avrunna, after following the rabbits all about among the rocks for several hours and expending about three dozen rounds each, secured only three each. We had an excellent supper in consequence. The other men went sealing, and Tuhajoq ("he hears or understands") secured a bearded seal. The two families who quitted us yesterday rejoined us today. There were a few caribou tracks on the island, but we saw none of the animals themselves. A strong west wind sprang up towards evening, but the sky is still clear. The sun is so warm that we are all sunburnt, and my nose is peeling a little. Its warmth seems to be doubled by reflection from the snow as it is on the water. A slight breeze still chills one so that one may feel warm on one side and freezing on the other. Read Island consists of low gravel terraces of limestone or dolomite, with here and there bowlders of diabase and red granite, the latter containing hornblende, mica, and quartz, the latter in large quantities. The rabbits were not without a few parasites, but my collecting box was cached the other day; I put two or three specimens in an empty cartridge shell. Read Island is called *Qigiaqtanneuq* by the natives, and the shore of Victoria Land just opposite is named *Iglulik*. Three of my dogs, of whom Telluraq is the ring leader, are distinguishing themselves by their talents for thieving. They devoured some of Taqtu's caribou fat today. When the seal was sighted yesterday and the rabbits today, a signal was made to the more distant Eskimos to keep quiet and on the lookout by lowering the outstretched hands to the ground several times. Ikpukkuaq tried to quiet the startled rabbits by emitting a smacking sound with his lips in imitation of the sound they make themselves (when feeding?). Ptarmigan seem to be attracted by camps. One shot today was close to the settlement, and during the winter several settled in the midst of Eskimo villages. Probably the dark objects in the midst of the white snow bear some resemblance to bare ground and so draw their attention.

Tuesday, May 4th

Another fine day of mild weather though dull most of the time. It brought much hard work but was on the whole satisfactory. I had lit the primus before 7 a.m. and was meditating dressing when caribou were sighted. The primus of course had to go by the board. Ikpukkuaq, another Eskimo Pihhuaq, and I rushed off to the land to intercept them there — a distance of some 3 miles. There Pihhuaq shot a rabbit. The caribou — five in number — stopped to browse on the first sandspit, and we had to wait over an hour before they came within range — about 150-200 yards. I killed my beast but missed twice as they fled. The other two both missed. Ikpukkuaq followed them up while Pihhuaq and I returned to camp from which a sled had come to carry back the trophy. I had been in camp about an hour and had just finished my first meal of the day when another herd was sighted; Avrunna and I set out this time and were again successful. I shot three — a buck and two does, and severely wounded a fourth. He killed a fawn and finished off the doe I wounded as it staggered away. I thus luckily maintained the reputation I gained yesterday. There is no difficulty in detecting my victims. The Ross bullet, which has a copper tip, makes a small perforation where it enters but bursts and produces a terrible gash where it goes out — about 3 inches in diameter. It has great force behind it, for the bullet which struck the buck passed through its body the same as the rest, though this caribou was shot at a range of about 400 yards. We reached camp again about 7 p.m. and sent a sled back for the dead. About 8 p.m. four more caribou were seen coming across [the strait] to the land, and Avrunna alone went off to intercept them on the ice. He fired two or three shots but missed. Naturally there is great rejoicing in camp. The temperature this evening was +19°, but the air was perfectly calm. When the Eskimos skin and cut up a caribou, they cut a tiny portion off the liver and the kidney and sometimes of other parts off the intestines and throw them away with the word *tamaijja* (there you are).

Wednesday, May 5th

A blizzard from the west. Luckily we are well supplied with food. Avrunna went off to the land to look for a caribou that was wounded yesterday but escaped by itself. He saw nothing; the drift had obliterated all tracks. The rest of us stayed in camp; indeed Ikpukkuaq and I did not dress till well on in the afternoon. We feasted at intervals and I read some Homer.[25] In the evening Taqtu imitated the peculiar intonation of the *Kanghirjuarmiut* Eskimos; both men and women there are said to pronounce their words in a strange and ludicrous tone, the women differently to the men. Long ago too, when pressed by famine one winter and unable to procure seals, they ate their dead, chopping them up with axes like caribou. The Eskimos here are horrified at the thought. They had heard too that white men ate Eskimos long ago far away to the south, but I assured them that this was not true. Taqtu then began to sing dance songs and imitated a woman who thrust her head alternately back and forth, preening her throat like a goose or turkey.

Thursday, May 6th

The blizzard continued. I turned out about 10 a.m. and a few minutes later a herd of caribou rushed by the camp pursued by the dogs. They were visible but a few moments, then were swallowed up by the mist of drifting snow before ever we could fire a shot. Avrunna again followed them to the land and spent the day there with the same ill-success as yesterday. Towards evening the blizzard abated and everything points to a fine day tomorrow. A flock of ptarmigan sped past the camp flying before the wind. The day passed in sleeping and eating and on my part in reading. I have now finished four books (13-16) of *The Odyssey* and am half way through the fifth (17th).[26] This weather is trying to one's clothes. They become coated with snow, which melts in the sun's warmth and become soaking wet.

Friday, May 7th

The blizzard had ended, but the weather was colder and a strong west wind still blowing. Ikpukkuaq turned out at 5 a.m. to intercept some caribou while I was still asleep. He took my binoculars and did not return to camp till nearly noon. Before that time I had left with the sled to bring in the things I cached on the ice a few days ago. I had gone about 4 miles and was walking some distance ahead of the sled, which was empty, when the dogs struck caribou tracks. Telluraq led, and away the dogs went full speed to land, dragging the sled behind them. There they altered their course and ran along the coast. When they had gone about 3 miles and were only a mile or two from camp, Avrunna met them and seeing me following brought them back. They all had their tails hanging down now between their legs and seemed to feel very foolish. Avrunna and I then went to the cache together and brought in the things. Ikpukkuaq was now in camp — he had killed one caribou. Without saying anything I took my binoculars and locked them away in my box, a crowd of them looking on. Ikpukkuaq later asked me about it and confessed he ought not to have taken them without permission; I thought it timely to administer a rebuke if our good relations are to continue through the summer. Avrunna and Milukattaq went over to Read Island after rabbits, the latter with my .22 automatic rifle. They obtained three, one with the automatic. Ikpukkuaq presented me with the tongue of the caribou he killed, and I boiled it with rice, as the tongue is very rich in fat and makes an excellent soup. Before we could partake of it, however, a herd of caribou showed up, and I hastened off to the land to intercept them there. The tramp was futile for the herd passed away far to the west. I noticed the other day when Ikpukkuaq shot a ptarmigan that he kneeled on the snow over its dead body and muttered a spell or incantation. I asked him about it today and he says it was the ptarmigan song (*aton*). If I understood him aright the same '*aton*' is sung over caribou and even men, but perhaps he meant that each of these has its *aton*. I hope to obtain the words later. A caribou fell through a crack into the water today and fell an easy victim to the harpoon and knife of one of the men who was out sealing.

Saturday, May 8th

The westerly wind continued all day today, though it diminished towards evening. Avrunna went off early after caribou and wounded one, which later in the day he killed. Ikpukkuaq with two or three others went off to cache some blubber pokes on Read Island.[27] They searched for rabbits, but they had all left the island.[28] Late in the afternoon Oqalluk left to bring back some caribou meat from the Kimiryuak River (where I first met the *Haneragmiut* last fall).[29] It was deposited there last fall by Qiqpuk and Ikpukkuaq. No caribou appeared near camp, so I did not leave, seeing no reason why I should hunt for a whole community and make them more or less dependant on me instead of hunting themselves. I hope to do my share to support myself and Ikpukkuaq's family this summer, and in fact of the game shot here I have four out of the eight caribou to my credit and the fifth crippled by me before it was killed, and three out of the twelve rabbits, but none of the three ptarmigan. At present I should be glad to see some of these people go away, but one family at least besides Ikpukkuaq's and his step-son Avrunna's intend going to Prince Albert Sound. The weather outdoors was rather unpleasantly cold, with the wind blowing, and my eyes are somewhat painful with a touch of snow-blindness.

Sunday, May 9th

We migrated to the land this morning,[30] a distance of some 4 miles. On the way two caribou were sighted, and Avrunna and I pursued them. I fired three shots at long range but missed; we could not approach close to them for they had seen us almost as soon as we saw them. Avrunna went after some others seen a little later but met with equal unsuccess. At the land was a joint cache of Ikpukkuaq's and Qiqpuk's containing amongst other things the summer tent of the former.[31] This he brought out, and I cut the snow-blocks to set it on, while Taqtu patched it; a very cold work in the slight westerly breeze. Milukattuk donning an old *atigi* and the long working mits of her husband, Avrunna, built a circle three tiers high of snow-blocks on which to set their tent, and I filled up the cracks and made a roofless passage for it two blocks high. I had just finished this when two caribou were sighted and I had to go in pursuit, but they saw the camp and fled far inland. Returning I fell in with Avrunna, and we returned together, only to leave immediately in pursuit of some caribou sighted to the east. This led us about 2 miles, but we secured a caribou each; a third was lamed but got away, though we followed it for a mile or so. I received my first initiation into skinning caribou and made rather a poor show of it; it was very cold work. The caribou I shot was not killed outright, so I put another bullet through its head; the proper way, the Eskimos said, is to hammer its forehead with the muzzle of the rifle or stick a knife into the nape of the neck. In the evening — we reached camp again about 8 p.m. — Taqtu gave another seance,[32] this time summoning her *tornraq*? into her *atigi* rolled up into a bundle and bound with her belt. Her *tornraq*, she said, was a dead relative of hers (*ataciara*?).[33] Both she and the spectators addressed questions to it, and a positive or negative answer was given according as Taqtu found it heavy or light to lift. The performance was a very shallow one. She had the four fingers of her right hand under the string and the thumb above, and quite plainly regulated the answers herself. Once a young man Kehullik wanted to test it when she said it was very heavy, but she would not let him. Several times she yawned during the performance, and once or twice the conversation drifted on to other topics, but no one seemed to doubt the genuineness of Taqtu. They asked me if I had left my *tornraq* in my own land and I told them yes. As far as I could gather she was enquiring about the prospects of food — caribou and fish. Some of the dogs were muzzled today by a cord fastened round the nose to prevent them howling or barking and startling any caribou that might come near. The Eskimos told me tonight that many years ago when Taqtu was a baby (i.e. about 1875) a number of Eskimos were out on the ice in Prince Albert Sound one spring when a storm arose, broke up the ice, and they were drowned. I find there are three families going to Prince Albert Sound[34] besides Ikpukkuaq's and Avrunna's — 15 people all told, of which number four are children and one a decrepid old woman.[35] There are only two rifles — mine and the one I have lent Ikpukkuaq and which Avrunna, his stepson, also uses. Consequently the hunting will fall mainly on us, for I allow no one else to use my Ross,[36] having but 400 rounds of ammunition. I have a .22 automatic and Ikpukkuaq a wretched .22 single shot; the rest have bows and arrows. I don't like the prospect of their depending on me for hunting, but can't very well avoid it. However, I am obtaining some good enthnological notes, and the more there are to travel with the better opportunity there is of seeing native life. Kehullik seems to be rather given to weeping. Twice on the trail he has leaned against his sled and wept unrestrainedly. In about 4 minutes it is all over and he chatters again as usual. One or two of the women also weep frequently, often in the middle of a conversation. Ikpukkuaq's tent is larger than the others. It is made entirely of deerskins, with a ridge pole supported by four or five poles at each end so as to make it pyramidal there, and by poles at intervals along the sides. Its general shape is then rectangular but with rounded ends, and it is raised about 2 feet above the floor on snow-blocks. Such a tent takes about an hour to set up — a great disadvantage, besides which it must weigh with all appurtenances about 60 lbs.

Monday, May 10th

Rather foggy weather with a light east breeze. A little snow fell towards evening. Ikpukkuaq wandered out with his rifle but saw nothing. Avrunna did the same with my .22 automatic and shot a fawn with it by a lucky shot. I wandered out with Ikpukkuaq a little later to the top of a ridge overlooking the sea to watch for caribou. Here around a large bowlder he made a low snow wall, semicircular, sufficient to shelter us from the breeze without obstructing the outlook. We saw nothing, after remaining there about an hour. Just before evening three caribou showed up and we went forth again to intercept them, but they winded the camp or heard the dogs and fled far away. Ikpukkuaq was busy part of the day emptying his cache. The dogs are becoming a nuisance through constant fighting. Two of Ikpukkuaq's dogs are lame, and my dog Qaqiaq has just had its ear split. Telluraq is becoming a regular warrior, though I never knew him to fight before, and Pamaski, who was a regular coward at the station, has been ringleading so many fights that I have tied him up; he half killed Niq and I believe lamed Ikpukkuaq's dogs.

Tuesday, May 11th

A fine day with a moderate east breeze and bright sunshine, but the temperature in the shade well below freezing. Ikpukkuaq was feathering arrows for Haugaq. One side of the feather is trimmed by cutting away the '*pinnae*'(?) on a piece of wood (*qeorvik*), then holding one end in the mouth, scraping the rough pen with a knife. Avrunna filed and cut away with an *ulo* the edges of some primers that were too large for a .44 rifle cartridge to make them fit. Milukattuk went off to a couple of fox-traps she set yesterday, and the children with their bows and arrows to look for small game, principally ptarmigan. The women set out their things to dry in the sun. Later Ikpukkuaq gathered things together for caching here, while the women packed their store of blubber to leave here also.[37] Avrunna went to a fox-trap he had set and found a fox in it. At the same time he took his rifle to look for caribou, and was later joined by Tutik and myself, who had gone out with the same object, the former with his bow, I with the Ross rifle. Two caribou were sighted and I shot one, while the other we badly missed, though Avrunna wounded it in the leg. The Ross has a single sight supposed to be accurate up to 500 yards. At any range up to 200 yards it seems to carry very high, and I find nearly all my bullets going above the mark. Tutik skinned and cut up the caribou, and the children turning up,[38] I took all the fore part on my back (about 70 lbs?), a boy shouldered the hind quarters, Qanajuq the head, and the skin was left for Tutik later. So we trudged back to camp. My bullet had pierced the food sac, which is always filled with the blood and tied up for conveyance to camp. The blood in this case dripped through the bullet hole and out of the carcass and down my back and legs — a full pint. The rest of the day I spent in camp reading, taking two photos,[39] cooking, and talking. One ptarmigan was shot with bow and arrow during the day.

Wednesday, May 12th

A foggy day with a little wet snow falling. I packed up what I am caching here — cartridges, food etc.,[40] surrounded by a crowd who begged or fingered half they saw. The curiosity of these Eskimos is unbounded. Later I went to the top of a ridge and took the compass bearing of two of the Ukullik Islands (the most easterly, 150°30'E, the middle island, 152°30'E). I have not had an opportunity to take a latitude and azimuth, so do not know the variation of the compass here, but it cannot be so very much different from that at the station.[41] We are camped at the spot marked on Ray's [Rae's] map 'May 18th', apparently, at the head of a small bay. Read Island must be further west.[42] The Eskimos say Stefansson started to cross the land to Prince Albert Sound from here.[43] It appears to be a regular route.[44] We leave tomorrow for a lake, which we shall reach, they say, after one sleep. There they intend to fish through the ice. The women were busy all day packing up what is to be left behind here. All the families made their caches close together on the side of a low ridge,[45] piling the things on the ground in a heap, covering them with skins and a few stones round the sides. Ikpukkuaq cached his sled and piled his things on top of it, while my tins[46] were placed underneath. In the evening caribou were sighted and we tried to intercept them, but they saw us and fled. On the way back I shot a rock ptarmigan (*nighaqtoq*).

Chapter 29. Encounter with the 'Blond' Eskimos

Migrating inland 20 miles — Unsuccessful caribou stalking — Ice-fishing for lake trout — First caribou kill — On the move again — Native fishing gear — To Lake Numichoin — Midnight seance — Absence of natural fuel — East to Lake Tahirjuaq — Interrupted sleep — First signs of Kanghirjuarmiut *— Another seance — A serious discussion — The* Kanghirjuarmiut *arrive — Welcoming dance — Exchange of gifts — Announced departure*

Thursday, May 13th, 1915

Warmest day this spring. We broke camp and travelled slowly practically due north for about 12 miles over an undulating plain interspersed with small lagoons. A little vegetation was visible here and there, but I had little opportunity to examine it. On the top of a ridge were two large bowlders of pink granite full of beautiful quartz crystals, lying amidst loose gravel consisting almost entirely of limestone. We saw a few caribou tracks but no caribou. Some ptarmigan showed up and the Eskimos fired at them several times but missed. About 8 p.m. we stopped to camp. Our tent is pitched on the ground,[1] the others are raised on snowblocks as before. Ikpukkuaq has left his kayak on the coast at the cache. Avrunna made a semicircular wall of snow and inside this Milukattuk cooked some deer meat over a small wood fire, while I made rice and cocoa on the primus inside the tent. To protect their sleds from the sun's heat the Eskimos had skins hanging down over the side.[2]

Friday, May 14th

We had just turned out to load the sleds this morning when caribou were sighted near some low hills to the northeast. Ikpukkuaq and I went in pursuit, leaving the others to break camp and trek to the lake. We spent a weary day from 8 a.m. to 9 p.m. chasing the caribou up hill and down vale, with the very worst luck. It was a good illustration of Eskimo patience in hunting. The first two caribou were in an open plain, and it was impossible to approach them without being seen. So we turned aside to stalk a herd on the top of a ridge. For 2 hours we circled round them trying to find a way to steal up close without being detected. At last we managed to crawl up almost within range, when suddenly they moved, saw us, and fled. We followed and stalked three others. They were grazing on the side of a slope, and we crept up to the top and waited for them to draw near. It was bitterly cold, though the sun was warm and temperature but little below zero, for a strong icy east wind blew over us. Two came close, and I wanted to shoot, but Ikpukkuaq signed to me to wait, as he thought they would approach still nearer. Instead of that they passed out of sight round the side of the slope. The third came within range but also passed out of sight. We stole down the slope till within 150 yards or so of them and fired but missed. Still we followed after them, for caribou were numerous everywhere, though difficult to approach from the nature of the country. Ikpukkuaq drew near to three and

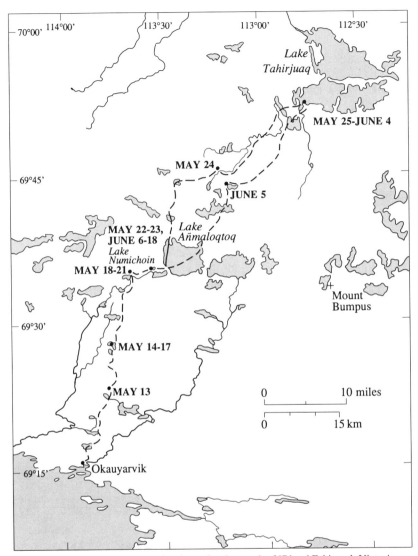

70°00' 114°00'   113°30'   113°00'   112°30'

Lake
Tahirjuaq

MAY 25-JUNE 4

MAY 24

69°45'

JUNE 5

MAY 22-23,   Lake
JUNE 6-18   Añmaloqtoq
Lake
Numichoin
MAY 18-21

Mount
Bumpus

69°30'

MAY 14-17

MAY 13

0   10 miles

0   15 km

69°15'   Okauyarvik

Figure 153. Map showing route taken by author in search of 'Blond Eskimos', Victoria
Island, May and June 1915.

signalled for me to lie down, as they were approaching. I mistook the
signal and thought he wanted me to join him, so hurried towards him.
The caribou saw me and fled. We wandered on and sighted two others,
but there was no way of approaching them. They seemed to be slowly
making their way towards the ridge we were on, so we lay down behind
it, building a wind-break of snow-blocks for shelter. There we lay quiet
for nearly an hour till we were both nearly frozen. They had moved a
little, and there seemed to be a chance of stealing round behind them. So

we circled round for half a mile or so when we discovered that they had made a sudden move forwards and were within 100 yards of the wind-break we had made. Back we rushed, but one of the caribou suddenly came into sight over the ridge. I was in front and had to drop flat and re-main perfectly still, but Ikpukkuaq, who was further behind, stole up round close to it, fired, and wounded it in the leg. Both fled into the open where we could not get within range. A little later we sighted two others about a mile away. These two we tried to stalk, but had to cross a small lake where we should be in sight. We crept along side by side, bent double and stopping whenever the caribou looked up. Once they saw us move and watched us. We dropped on our knees and remained as mo-tionless as possible for nearly 5 minutes. Then, their suspicions being lulled, they went on grazing and we stole along on hands and knees till out of sight. But just as we were going up the back of the ridge behind them two dogs that had strayed from camp suddenly appeared on a ridge about half a mile away and alarmed the caribou which fled. It was now 8:30 p.m. and we had been more than 12 hours unsuccessfully chasing caribou, with nothing to eat or drink since a light breakfast at 7 a.m. Nevertheless, Ikpukkuaq wanted to go after some caribou about a mile away, tired and hungry though we both were. I had hunted enough, how-ever, to satisfy myself so said I was going back to camp, and he reluc-tantly returned also. We sighted three snow-blocks set up in line, at a distance of about 20 yards from each other. This was to guide us to camp, which we reached at 9 p.m. The country here, 16 miles or so north by east of our cache on the coast, consists of a succession of small hills and valleys, with lakes in the valleys.[3] The tops of the ridges are now al-most bare of snow and are covered with stones, principally limestone or dolomite, with here and there bowlders of pink granite, diabase, and some red clay. The lakes are full of fish — lake trout (*tacim ekalloa*) — and the camp is situated at the side of one.[4] The Eskimos set to work im-mediately to dig a hole through the ice with an ice pick or chisel and jiggled for the trout. By 11 p.m. they had caught nearly a dozen, besides having fresh water for cooking and drinking instead of being compelled to melt snow. On a ridge we saw stones which marked the former site of a tent, and two stones set up and pointing to a lake to indicate it con-tained fish in plenty.

Saturday, May 15th

It was a fine calm day when we turned out this morning, the atmo-sphere very mild. All the men went hunting, and Milukattuk accom-panied Avrunna, Ikpukkuaq, and me. We began to stalk some caribou, which became alarmed and moved. Milukattuk and I then stalked one lot while Ikpukkuaq and Avrunna went after another. I luckily dropped two caribou with two shots, and Milukattuk and I skinned both and cut one up, then started after other caribou. These latter, however, were in a posi-tion unapproachable without being detected, so we returned to camp. A strong west wind (*uñaliaq*) suddenly sprang up, but the temperature re-

Figure 154. Ikpukkuaq jiggling for trout in Lake Ekallugak, south entrance to the Colville Hills, southwestern Victoria Island, May 16, 1915. (Photo by D. Jenness, CMC Photo No. 36971.)

mained mild. Qanajuq, Haugaq, and I with my sled went off to pick up the caribou. On the way the wind changed to north and the snow began to drift quite a little. Ikpukkuaq and Avrunna secured one ptarmigan, the others nothing. Many fish were caught today by jiggling; Qanajuq in the space of 1 1/2 hours secured five. They are almost all small — about 1 foot long — and all of the same species — lake trout. It is light now at midnight. So hot is the sun as reflected by the snow that I am badly sunburnt, and the skin of my nose is peeling — rather distressing in a cold wind — it feels as if it is freezing all the time.

Sunday, May 16th

Temperature at noon 10° F with bright sunshine, but the north wind almost as strong as yesterday. Taqtu and Kehullik went off with my sled to bring in a caribou which Ikpukkuaq wounded yesterday and which they expected to find dead. Avrunna left earlier to track it down. Ikpukkuaq, whose calves are out of order, went over to another lake to fish, and most of the men went hunting. I walked up to the top of a ridge and took a compass bearing on Ukullik Island, then spent the rest of the day in camp, making a set of canvass footgear for Telluraq, my dog; his feet gather snow between the toes, it turns to ice, and soon wears the skin off, and he is lame. Taqtu returned about 7 p.m. with two caribou on the sled, one shot by Kehullik with his bow and arrow, the other wounded by Ikpukkuaq yesterday. The latter was partly eaten by foxes. Avrunna returned an hour later — he shot one caribou. Ikpukkuaq brought back half a dozen fish.[5] A mistake — Kehullik did not kill the caribou, Ikpukkuaq [did] with his rifle.

Monday, May 17th

The north wind had moderated greatly this morning and before noon changed to south. We turned out about 8:30 a.m., and I cooked cornmeal while Avrunna jiggled for fish at a fish-hole and the others lay in their sleeping bags. Afterwards I took a second compass bearing on Ukullik [Island], as the atmosphere was clearer than yesterday and the islands a trifle less faint. An attempt to obtain a latitude with the repeating circle resulted in very cold hands and feet only, so after helping to build a wind-break to shelter Milukattuk (who was stitching deerskins for a tent out of doors) and taking the temperature in the shade — 10° F and in the sun 30° F — I took the .22 automatic and wandered over the hills. East by north there is a range of hills running apparently northwest by southeast, with one prominent peak[6] — about 25 miles from here apparently. This must be Stefansson's Museum Range.[7] The Colville Hills here are a succession of ridges and valleys stretching east and west, most of the larger valleys containing small lakes, which in some cases communicate visibly above ground, in others would seem to drain through underground channels.[8] The hills are strewn with limestone or dolomite, mixed with pink granite and diabase bowlders, and a little flint and shale. Nowhere have I seen an exposure of rock. There is little vegetation, though the ground in places is covered with a reddish clay. I met Kehullik out hunting with another boy, carrying bows and arrows. We fell in with ptarmigan in two or three places, and I shot two and Kehullik one with my automatic, and the boys killed two (one was already wounded) with their bows and arrows. Their marksmanship with bows and arrows is very poor, even the men's. Avrunna went hunting and secured one caribou. Ikpukkuaq and two other men, Oqalluk and Tuhajoy, fished in a neighbouring lake, but obtained about five each only for several hours fishing. All the fish are lake trout (*ihun* or *tacim ekalloa*).

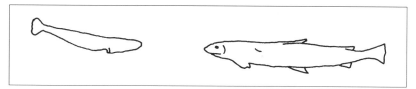

Figure 155. Author's sketch of lake trout.

Tuesday, May 18th

We broke camp again this morning about 10 a.m. and travelled till about 6 p.m., with numerous stops so that we made only about 10 miles. Even this was not 10 miles north, for we wound in and out following the line of the lakes, crossing from one to another at the gaps between the ridges where the divides were low. Probably we are only some 6 miles north of our last camp and about 22 miles from the coast. Three caribou were sighted, and Avrunna and I went in pursuit. I did not shoot, but he fired twice without success, and they fled far away. Ptarmigan were frequent. Time and again the Eskimos shot their arrows at them and missed; I had no better luck with two shots from my .22. At the divides and in many places on the lakes the snow was soft and deep, and Ikpuk-kuaq's sled[9] capsized three or four times. On the lakes the Eskimos avoid glare ice, for their sleds slide every way then stick on the barest patch of snow where dogs and Eskimos alike are standing on the ice and unable to gain a foothold. As soon as the tents were erected the men left the women to fix up the sleds and the interiors and went off to the lake be-side which we are camped to dig holes through the ice and fish. Several lake trout were caught before supper. The fishing outfit consists of 'rod' and line, with an iron hook, barbless, and a bait of whitefish flesh and skin, a copper or iron pick *turq*,[10] chisel shaped, at the end of a long pole, and a small wooden scoop[11] with bone 'freeboard' to make it larger, also at the end of a long pole; a sealskin bucket (*qataq*[12]) to hold the water scooped out, and a sealskin bag or haversack to hold the fish.[13]

Wednesday, May 19th

Ikpukkuaq sighted caribou before breakfast, but they seemed to be coming in our direction so the dogs were tied up, and we waited for some time, then climbed the hills in pursuit of them. We intercepted them some distance up, and Ikpukkuaq and I both fired and missed, then he fired again and dropped one. A little later Avrunna went off with Ik-pukkuaq's gun in pursuit of some and killed one. We crossed the ridges eastward, crossing two or three lakes, beside one of which — Numichoin — were the remains of a former camp of Ikpukkuaq and his people where they met the *Kanghirjuarmiut*. About 4 miles east of our camp is a large lake, some 4 miles by 3 miles (Lake Añmaloqtoq)[14] and on the edge of this I counted fifteen caribou. Others were on the hill-side and Ikpukkuaq, Avrunna, and Oqalluk went in pursuit of them, but without success. A weasel (*tiriaq*)[15] was chased but disappeared in a hole under a rock. However, Milukattuk shot a rabbit with my rifle. They said there were no rabbits inland — or rather hares, for all are Arctic hares here. Taqtu boiled a pot of deer meat outdoors today with heather.[16] Weather fine and clear, bright sunshine, but chilly west breeze.

Thursday, May 20th

Another day similar to yesterday. After eating a plate of corn-meal at 9 a.m. I left to follow our old sled track to search for the cleaning rod of the automatic .22, which was missing. Milukattuk followed me to look for a boot of Avrunna's, which had likewise dropped off the sled. On the way I shot three ptarmigan. We found what was missing then climbed a high knoll to look for caribou. A herd of five was sighted and we lay in wait for them. Milukattuk took first shot with my rifle and waiting till a fine bull was within 20 yards brought it down with a shot through the shoulder.[17] She handed me the gun, and I dropped another bull as they fled. The rest of the day we spent stalking caribou. About 5 p.m. we lay in wait for another herd, but as it did not approach we carefully stalked them [the caribou] to windward till within 30 yards or so. Milukattuk again took first shot but missed. However, I dropped a cow a few minutes later as they fled — with a lucky shot when they were 300 yards or more away. We skinned all three, cut two up, and carried the skins back to camp — some 6 miles away, which we reached about 10 p.m., tired and very hungry. Ikpukkuaq went away for caribou after we left and had not turned up at midnight. The sun sets now about 11:30 p.m. Two families which left us on the ice turned up today — rather an unwelcome sight to me. Avrunna killed a Lapland longspur, the first seen this season. A woman brought some fish to sell me, but I told her I would buy no food as I could get more than I wanted with my rifle and was indeed sharing the caribou I shoot with them. I put my case pretty plainly before them, as I was rather annoyed at the lack of decency she showed and was rather gratified to find the other Eskimos approved of me. I have shot more caribou than any of them, besides lending Ikpukkuaq (and Avrunna) the rifle with which all the other caribou save one have been obtained. For a fortnight we have been living almost entirely on caribou, save during the last 3 days when fish have partly superseded it.

Friday, May 21st

A day similar to yesterday but with a light easterly breeze. Avrunna left early and returned about 11 p.m., having killed three caribou. Pihhuaq, one of the Eskimos who turned up yesterday, secured one with a rifle of his own. I turned out about 9 a.m., and after breakfast was occupied with sundry odd jobs round the camp. About noon Qanajuq and I left with my sled to bring in the three caribou shot by Milukattuk and myself yesterday. We sighted two caribou, but they heard the dogs and fled; later we saw three more, but these winded the dogs and fled while I was stalking them. The three caribou proved too much for my sled, and three crossbars were pushed out of their stanchions on one side. A number of ptarmigan were seen and I shot five and Qanajuq two with my automatic. Ikpukkuaq remained in camp all day. The weather is so warm that when moving about one needs no mits, and the women do much of their work out of doors. The blubber lamps are needed hardly at all save for cooking, and even that is now done out of doors, sometimes with *oqauyaq* roots.

Saturday, May 22nd

The whole settlement suddenly decided to move to Lake Numichoin,[18] a small lake about 2 miles northeast as the crow flies, but 4 miles by the circuitous route it is necessary to follow with sleds. The weather was fine and clear again with a light south breeze. Our new camp is on the point of a ridge where it projects into the lake. Last summer Ikpukkuaq and his people were camped here. It was on this spot they met the *Kanghirjuarmiut* Eskimos[19] and completed the change from the winter to summer life by caching their sleds here. They propose doing the same this year, for they have dragged their sleds up on the bare ground and the mud shoeing, being exposed to the sun, is fast cracking and breaking off. As soon as the tents were set up Ikpukkuaq and some others went off to bring in the four caribou he shot the other day. Sleds were impracticable in the hills, so the dogs dragged the meat home wrapped in polar-bear skins (Fig. 156). They saw no caribou, but Ikpukkuaq shot two ptarmigan. I strolled some distance back into the hills and saw three caribou far away and travelling fast north, so did not pursue them. Close to camp, however, were some ptarmigan, and I shot two of these. Tuhajoq made a hole in the ice of a neighbouring lake and caught a magnificent lake trout 99 cm long. It is pleasant to have one's camp on (comparatively) dry ground instead of wet slushy snow. The uplands are fast losing their snow mantle but are sadly barren and brown.

Sunday, May 23rd

We turned out about 10 a.m., having turned in about 1:30 a.m. Ikpukkuaq remained in camp to fish, Avrunna and another man went off for caribou in one direction and Kehullik and I in another. The former returned about 9 p.m. unsuccessful. Kehullik and I saw one herd only, of four, which were approaching from the south. We followed their course along the top of a ridge and intercepted them as they passed grazing along the foot. I shot three out of the four, the fourth I missed as it fled. Ikpukkuaq was unsuccessful in his fishing, but two other men obtained about five each in a lake near by. About 7 p.m. I set a line through a hole in the ice, but up to 10 p.m. had caught nothing. Incidental to hunting, cooking etc., are other small duties, e.g. today I mended a woman's tobacco tin, treated another's eyes with boric acid. The women were busy setting out their caribou meat to dry in the sun, scraping skins, and feasting. Milukattuk made a tent just before the last migration, from skins obtained this spring (two are from caribou I killed), and she and Avrunna, with Pihuaq and his wife Itkelleroq and child Hanna, are living in it. Ikpukkuaq shot two ptarmigan today. All that I have seen on Victoria Land hitherto have been rock ptarmigan. Today for the first time I noticed flies — the small black 'blow-fly'. The temperature about 4 p.m. was 44° F in the shade, the warmest it has yet been, but about 7 p.m. ice was forming in the fishing holes. All the sleds were stripped of their mud runners today. Meat is lying everywhere about the camp — on sleds, stones, sealskins, boards. Where meat is absent there are dogs tied to large stones by their harness. Two of my dogs broke their harnesses last night and perpetrated some stealing. These Eskimos put a 'brake' on quarrelsome or mischievous dogs by tying a cord round the neck and passing a foreleg through it so that the poor beast has to hobble round on three legs.

Figure 156. Copper Eskimos dragging caribou meat to camp on polar-bear skins, Lake Añmaloqtoq area, southwest Victoria Island, May 22, 1915. (Photo by D. Jenness, CMC Photo No. 37093.)

Monday, May 24th

About midnight [last night] we had an interesting seance in our tent, Taqtu (Higilaq) performing. She was inspired by a wolf or a dog, I don't know which, and hiding her face behind Ikpukkuaq inserted two large canine teeth (dog's?) in her mouth, which she protruded one from each corner and mumbled her oracles as best she could with these impediments. When this was over she cunningly slipped them in one of her big boot legs unseen by everyone save myself, who was lying in the back of the tent.[20] The object of the performance was to discover whether we could make the journey to Lake Tahirjuaq[21] and back successfully, as I was urging Ikpukkuaq to do, in fulfilment of his engagement during the winter. At Lake Tahirjuaq we expected to find the *Kanghirjuarmiut* or Prince Albert Sound Eskimos. The answer was of course satisfactory, for Ikpukkuaq knew I should be vexed if we did not try to find them, as this was one of the objects of my visiting Victoria Land. We set out about noon — the whole settlement save Tuhajoq, his wife, and the little boy

Haugaq, who were all rather bad travellers.[22] There were two sleds besides mine, with the mud runners removed, leaving only the wood protected by whale-bone shoeing.[23] But one family — Oqalluk's — dragged its outfit wrapped in a polar-bear skin, drawn by three or four dogs. The women and children rode a good deal on the sleds and bearskin, and occasionally the men. We travelled about 10 miles north through valley and pass, over lakes and ridges, till we emerged from the Colville Hills near a high conical hill, where we changed our course to east. Much of the snow had melted from this hill and there was a large pool of cold sparkling water on a small flat beneath it, beside which we found a mouse?[24] drowned. Apparently it had nested below the hill and was caught in the thaw. We travelled about 6 miles east, then sighted three caribou, which approached to within about 200 yards of the sled. I shot one, a fine bull, so we camped on a small bare ridge near by. During the day I shot four ptarmigan and Ikpukkuaq two. Three or four of the men went after caribou, but had no luck. Our camp tonight is rather peculiar. There is a lean-to of skins with four people sleeping under it, a small [inverted V] tent closed at the back but open in front, and my own [triangular] tent 4' high X 6'6" long X 5' wide, in which Ikpukkuaq, Taqtu, and I are to sleep.[25] The dogs are tied to stones, and the sun at midnight is just above the northern horizon. The weather was beautifully warm and bright, though the temperature fell below freezing at night. I cooked a big pot of deer meat[26] because no one else has fuel — there is no 'heather' here and their oil and lamps they left behind. They are filling their stomachs with raw meat quite unconcernedly.

Tuesday, May 25th

Another fine bright day, but instead of yesterday's light n[ortherly] breeze a strong east wind blew all day. We set out about 9:30 a.m. and travelled about 14 miles east before reaching Lake Tahirjuaq [Lake Quunnguq]. Caribou were sighted several times, and we stopped to let the men hunt them. Pihuaq bagged three and Avrunna wounded one. I did not leave my sled except at the last to shoot a couple of ptarmigan. Ikpukkuaq wandered about all day looking for ptarmigan but secured three only. Lake Tahirjuaq is long and broad — its greatest length apparently being from east to west — roughly as far as I can see 10-15 miles, while north-south it must have a breadth of some 8 miles. It is hard to form an estimate because it is studded with islands of every shape and size. We are camped on the south shore, on the point of a ridge where the numerous large stones mark an old camping site. It is here, my Eskimos say, that the *Kanghirjuarmiut* habitually camp, though for some reason or other they have not appeared this spring. The men have dug holes through the ice and are fishing. A river runs out of the north side of Lake Tahirjuaq to the sea. I acquired by accident this evening the reputation of possessing second sight. I had just cooked some ptarmigan on the primus and wanted Ikpukkuaq to come and partake. So I asked Qanajuq, or meant to ask her "Is Ikpukkuaq fishing," but through using a wrong word I said "Has Ikpukkuaq caught a fish." It so happened that he was jiggling for lake trout through a hole in the ice about 1/2 mile away and about that very time caught a big trout. Some of the Eskimos thought I must have seen it occur, though [I was] in the tent at the time far away. So they wanted to know if the *Kanghirjuarmiut* were near or whether we should find them tomorrow. Even Ikpukkuaq, who was rather skeptical of my ability to answer this latter question, asked if I would let Taqtu tie a cord round my foot or head and receive answers by lifting. I told them I did not know where the *Kanghirjuarmiut* are, but of course a plain statement of that kind did not carry conviction.

Wednesday, May 26th

A dull cloudy day with fairly strong east breeze. There was a seance[27] last night after I turned in (about 1 a.m.), to discover whether the *Kanghirjuarmiut* would come today or not. Taqtu rolled her *atigi* into a bundle and addressing questions to it judged by its weight whether the answer was yes or no. Last night the answer was yes. She performed in the open air, the weather being mild and our tents too small to admit an audience. However, she was not quite satisfied with her own powers of divination, for she asked me quietly this morning — as I lay in the tent in my sleeping bag and she sat beside me mending my boots, everyone else being out of hearing — whether they would come today. I told her she knew for she learned that last night. Ikpukkuaq went off after caribou and secured [?].[28] A large number of fine lake trout were caught, and I cooked a pot-full for the Eskimos, as they have no fuel, and much prefer cooked fish to cold raw fish, the weather being so mild that they will not freeze quickly. I was rather amused latterly by their manner of addressing dogs. The night before last they were howling a great deal, and Taqtu shrieked to them "And yet you have reached camping place." Last night a man told a woman to tie his grandfather up — the dog having the same name as his grandfather. Apparently though they do not consider the grandfather's spirit to have entered the dog, for there is generally a child or adult with the same name at the same time; besides, the dog is sold or beaten like other dogs and generally belongs to another family. They are not cruel to their dogs, though when they do strike them they strike hard. In winter they feed them in the houses out of their musk-ox ladles, calling them in one by one and driving each out when it has finished, either with the cry "*hoq hoq*" or with the addition of a blow with the snow-duster. Yet they consider themselves first. After a day's travel the dogs are not fed, for they are tired and do not want to eat, the Eskimos say. They feed them the next morning. This practice has one advantage — it saves dog-food for the day — but most dog-drivers would not recommend it. Occasionally dogs are muzzled to prevent them barking or howling and frightening away caribou, or if quarrelsome one foreleg is looped through a cord tied round the neck so that it hobbles on three legs. Pups are reared in the houses, either at the back of the sleeping platform or in a little alcove made in the snow wall at one side of the door

Figure 157. Copper Eskimo camp at Lake Tahirjuaq (Quunnguq), awaiting arrival of 'blond' Eskimos from Prince Albert Sound. Southwest Victoria Island, May 26, 1915. Author's tent is on right. (Photo by D. Jenness, CMC Photo No. 36992.)

but still within the house. Here a bed is made for them of willow-matting and generally sealskins as well. To prevent them from wandering all over the sleeping platform they are tied by a harness made especially for them to a stick driven into the snow. Neither to his dogs nor to anything else is the Eskimo cruel. He does not inflict pain needlessly for the pleasure of it, though he will allow a wounded caribou to be in agony for hours without troubling to dispatch it. The link that binds dog and men is naturally closer than that which binds him to seal or caribou, and so he uses the word *kia* (who) for dogs as well as persons, but *huna* for other animals which have no individual names. Occasionally, however, *huna* is used for dogs, but I think very rarely. There was a consultation this evening as to whether the *Kanghirjuarmiut* would come here or not. The Eskimos say they have never been beyond this place, but always met their northern neighbours here. But they know that from the north side of this lake a river flows to the sea[29] — which they call *Nalluarjuk*. I am wondering whether Stefansson did not make a mistake when he placed Lake Tahiryuak north of the Kaglorjuak River instead of south of it and the source of the Nalluarjuk River, whose position he apparently marks fairly accurately.[30] Ivjarotailaq, who had been absent all day hunting caribou, returned after midnight. He had shot a bull and a doe. Away to the northeast out on the ice he saw three objects, he was uncertain whether they were men or stones.

Thursday, May 27th

Another cloudy day with a strong west wind. A little snow fell in the night, and the weather generally was colder. The dogs were a great nuisance in the night, but I found them less annoying than the Eskimos, Taqtu especially. She constantly yelled at the dogs in a strident voice that pierced my ears, and as she lay next to me in the tent there was very little sleep possible for some time. When she was not yelling at the dogs, she was yelling to the other Eskimos, or telling Ikpukkuaq on her other side how the dogs were preventing the *qovluna* from sleeping; at the rare intervals when she was silent the other Eskimos were yelling at them. Altogether with dogs howling and Eskimos yelling, half the night was passed restlessly.[31] Kullaq turned out to tie up one of her dogs which was loose; instead of turning in at once she went down to the lake and caught a trout, then returned, undressed, and went to sleep. I turned out about 8:30 a.m. before anyone else was up, went to the top of the ridge behind the camp and sighted a caribou about a mile away through the binoculars, so stalked it and brought it down at the second shot — my fifteenth caribou this month at the expense of about 40 cartridges. Taqtu with a couple of dogs brought it in on a bear's skin later. Avrunna and Pihhuaq went away with their rifles to the northeast to look for the *Kanghir-juarmiut*, Ikpukkuaq, Oqalluk, and Tucik to a part of the lake a little more distant to fish. Ikpukkuaq is suffering from what I fancy is rheumatism in the calves of his legs. He has spoken of it frequently to me, so this morning I prescribed massage with warm water night and morning. The women crowded into my tent today to sew, as it was cold outdoors. They were a great nuisance, but I couldn't very well turn them out. Little things of this kind an ethnologist has to put up with in this country. In the afternoon Milukattuk and I went out with my Ross and .22 automatic. We sighted two caribou lying down on the ice between two ridges. In circling round them we stumbled on to another herd of seven and found ourselves between two fires, unable to approach one lot unseen by the other. Finally we stalked the first two. My first shot wounded one in the leg, the second brought down its mate, the range being just over 200 yards. The first caribou escaped. Meanwhile the larger herd, startled, fled into the wind but stopped to graze about a mile away. We hurried after them and just overtook the last three as they were leaving the last ridge that offered cover to us. In our haste I carelessly allowed my head to be seen and the caribou fled. I fired four shots at them when about 400 yards away and lamed one, but it escaped — bad hunting on my part. We reached camp again about midnight. Avrunna and Pihhuaq had returned; the former shot a caribou. They had seen no traces of the *Kanghir-juarmiut*. Ikpukkuaq, Tucik, and Oqalluk had spent the day fishing; the first obtained one, the others none.

Friday, May 28th

Colder weather. The dogs again proved a great nuisance by their howling, and Taqtu a worse [nuisance]; I told her so this morning. A caribou was sighted near camp about 6 a.m., and Ikpukkuaq pursuing it brought it down. Towards noon a herd of seven was seen approaching, five being bulls. Avrunna went off to intercept them, and Ikpukkuaq, Pihhuaq, and I tried to intercept them near the camp, but the wind was blowing directly towards them and they fled. Avrunna followed after them, and later in the day when they stopped to feed he shot two. Pihhuaq went in another direction and shot a bull through the stomach; he expects to find it dead tomorrow. Ivyarotailaq went off to the north and saw two stones freshly set up (*iñuhuit*) as signposts — by *Kanghir-juarmiut*, so the whole camp is in a high state of excitement over our chances of meeting them. I went with Kullaq to show her where the caribou was I shot yesterday. A seagull and a fox were busy on it, but fled at our approach. She took it back to camp wrapped in a polar-bear skin drawn by Telluraq and Panaski — my two dogs — while I wandered to the top of a high 'sugar-loaf' hill to look for caribou. I sighted six far off, but they were travelling towards Museum Range away from me (to the east). A little later I saw four more far off approaching up the wind towards me and went off to one side to lie in wait for them, but they disappeared. However, two others showed off to one side not far from camp, and I stalked those, but could not approach near. At the expense of four cartridges I brought one down at a range of more than 300 yards, skinned and cut it up, and carried skin and one leg back to camp. Taqtu asked for my two *atigis* tonight to discover by questioning and weighing them whether we should find the *Kanghirjuarmiut*. She is about to do this now that I am writing.[32] The weather was a little colder today with a strong west wind. I have not been able to take a sight of the sun since we have been here owing to cloudy weather. The seance was rather entertaining. Taqtu rolled my two *atigis* into a bundle and tied her belt round it so that a part of the cord hung loose. She told me to say to the bundle that it was to be heavy for an affirmative answer, [I] being a *qovluna*. Then she asked it question after question, or others at the door of the tent asked and she tried the weight of the bundle. When she wanted it to be light she drew it straight up, when heavy she gave a slight twist to her hand so that the back of the hand pressed the bundle down while the fingers and wrist were ostensibly trying to lift it. It was the most palpable fraud imaginable, on a par with the protrusion of large canine teeth. The answers were supposed to emanate from me, or rather from the spirit that dwells in me. The answer in the case was that the *Tormiat* or *Kanghir-juarmiut* are coming tomorrow. If this proves untrue it is my spirit that lied, not the medium Taqtu. Avrunna asked me whether it were not lying, and I being in rather a quandary told him Taqtu knew. It is very convenient for the medium to be able to refer failures to the spirit. Ikpuk-kuaq tells me that from the north end of this Lake Tahirjuak[33] [Quunn-guq] flows the river Kaglorjuak, which Stefansson places further north and gives a very different source; from the northwestern end flows the Nalluarjuk and both [rivers] enter Prince Albert Sound. In summer, if we do not find the *Kanghirjuarmiut* now, and Ikpukkuaq's calves are better, we shall make the circuit of the lake, he says, and perhaps reach the sea, following the caribou. I sincerely hope we do. I wanted to cross the lake and go down the Nalluarjuk River with Avrunna and Milukattuk now to look for the *Kanghirjuarmiut*, but the proposal was negatived.

Saturday, May 29th

It was rather warmer than yesterday this morning, but grew cold towards night. Taqtu was busy scraping sealskins for water boots, Oqalluk and Pihhuaq went after caribou that were shot yesterday to bring them in. Ikpukkuaq and Tucik fished all day, the former obtaining two trout, the latter none. Milukattuk with my .22 went after ptarmigan and shot four, while Kehullik shot one with his bow and arrow. I went out to look for caribou and was stalking a herd of five when they sighted or winded the children and fled far to the northwest. A light north wind this morning swung round to west, then in the afternoon changed to east. At night it was breezing up. The *Kanghirjuarmiut* did not show up today.

Sunday, May 30th

A strong east wind blew all day and at night was accompanied by a heavy fall of snow. Avrunna and Oqalluk went off to look for the *Kanghirjuarmiut* but returned about 2 a.m. unsuccessful. Ikpukkuaq sighted a herd of caribou from the knoll behind the camp, and Pihhuaq, Ikpuk, Tucik, and I went after them, Tucik with his bow and arrows. It was my day out for I bagged five, while Ikpukkuaq wounded one which escaped, and Pihhuaq and Tucik none. It was a herd of twelve, consisting mostly of young bulls. Tucik and Pihhuaq were given one each as their share, the rest fell to Ikpuk and me. Itkelleroq and Kehullik brought four in on a sled, but Tucik carried the whole of his (save the head) on his back for the 2 miles or so to camp. The women each day collect fuel (*oqauyaq*) for cooking one meal, as it is not very plentiful about here, at least until the land has cleared a little of snow and it is visible.

Monday, May 31st

Last night's gale changed to a blizzard from the northwest during the night, accompanied by a heavy snowfall and a sudden drop in the temperature, which yesterday was so mild that there was even a large pool of water near the camp for the first time. No one stirred till long after noon, then some of the women rose to sew and to bring in frozen caribou meat to eat. I rose at 6 p.m. to cook a pot of caribou meat for all on the primus, and a little rice for Ikpuk, Taqtu, and myself. We had a serious consultation about finding the *Kanghirj[uarmiut]*. Ikpuk's calves are painful, otherwise he says he would gladly go down to Prince Albert Sound and look for them with me; as it is he will go if I insist, but does not relish the journey.[34] The difficulty is that the season is so late now that we cannot afford to spend any time hunting for them round the sound, as the snow will melt before we can get back and we shall be stuck, with hardly any cartridges left, for we brought but few with us. These Eskimos do not know where they [the *Kanghirjuarmiut*] are; sometimes they suggest that they are all dead, sometimes that they have gone elsewhere. It is clear that this is their usual rendezvous, but for some unknown reason (perhaps the presence of the [*Mary*] *Sachs*[35] to the north) they have not come this spring. In summer if Ikpuk's legs are all

Figure 158. Copper Eskimos help newly arrived Prince Albert Sound Eskimos to unload their sled, Lake Tahirjuaq (now Quunnguaq), southwestern Victoria Island, June 1, 1915. (Photo by D. Jenness, CMC Photo No. 36986.)

right we propose when packing to go round this lake to the north in the hope of meeting them somewhere; otherwise Ikpuk says he will go with me overland to them next winter. It is better ethnologically to spend a summer with the band I am with and watch their summer life than to run around the country, now meeting them, now alone. No one yet has spent a summer living the life of the Eskimos in their midst, so I have a unique opportunity, and still have a chance of seeing the 'blonds'. A herd of caribou was seen near camp, and Avrunna and Pihhuaq stalked them without success. The blizzard moderated towards evening.

Tuesday, June 1st

A cold day, cloudy, with a light west wind. A family of *Kanghirjuarmiut* appeared about noon,[36] with a sled, a man Kunana, his wife Nateksina, their adopted baby Allikumik,[37] and a young man Imeraq. All have dark black hair, with a brown tinge towards the light, but the man has a tawny moustache and beard, both rather sparse. Their eyes are brown, of different depths, their features Eskimo, the cheekbones being high but not exceptionally prominent. The woman's face tattooing is the same as that in Dolphin and Union Strait. Their foreheads are rather receding. As soon as they had set up their tent and we had all partaken of their food inside it, two of the men set to work to make a dance house of snow-blocks and roofed it with skins and my sled-cover. Then came the dance of welcome, interrupted about midnight by the arrival of a second sled with three more *Kanghirjuarmiut* natives.[38] Again we partook of their food, but it was too late to resume the dance, so one by one we turned in at 3 a.m.[39]

Figure 159. Double tent of two Prince Albert Sound families, Lake Tahirjuaq (or Quunnguq), southwestern Victoria Island, June 2, 1915. (Photo by D. Jenness, CMC Photo No. 36985.)

Wednesday, June 2nd

Another cloudy day, though it brightened in the afternoon. The first part of the day was spent in trading.[40] I bought two hair-seal and one bearded-seal line for harness traces, pack-straps etc. The rest of the day was spent in dancing.[41] While in the dance house I said suddenly to Milukattuk, by way of a joke, ''tukturaluk''(caribou). She immediately rushed out, for some of them at least believe I have second sight. Sure enough she saw caribou to the southeast, though a long way off and moving away. Entering again she asked me where and I pointed to the southeast luckily, the direction from which most of them have come. This has established my reputation for second sight, which is not a bad thing, as it may check any tendency to make free with my things. The two *Kanghir[juarmiut]* women sat in my tent tonight with one or two *Puivl[irmiut]* Eskimos, and I tried to find out something about their land, but they pretended ignorance. Luckily Stefansson had given the names for certain places, and I had the chart, so that I managed to elicit some information.[42] They are all amazed that I should know anything at all about their land and movements.[43] It appears that there is another lake named *Tahirjuaq* somewhere near where Stefansson places it, and the main body of the *Kanghir[juarmiut]* has gone thither. It is close to the copper deposits, which they say are in a cliff (*imnek*). One of these women lost her son, who was drowned in a river when journeying to (or from) the country of the *Ekalluktogmiut*.[44]

Thursday, June 3rd

Oqalluk went after two caribou shot by Avrunna yesterday to drag them in. I went hunting and shot three after some bad shooting. I told Taqtu when I returned and she said Qanajuq and Kehullik would bring them in as usual. Later Kehullik appeared with two skins (I had brought

Figure 160. Copper Eskimos dressing for a dance, Lake Tahirjuaq (Quunnguq), southwestern Victoria Island, June 2, 1915. (Photo by D. Jenness, CMC Photo No. 36997.)

back one), the leg bones, and heads. I asked why the whole lot had not been brought and they said they were going back to Lake NumiXoni [Numichoin] tomorrow, and the sled would be too heavy with all the meat. So they would feed the dogs as they passed, and the rest of the meat the two *Kanghirjuarmiut* families here would pick up, as they remain here. Ikpukkuaq and his people will not go to the other Lake Tahirjuaq where all the rest of the *Kanghirjuarmiut* are. Some said yesterday they were going, now they all refuse and say they are returning [to Lake Numichoin] tomorrow. It is very aggravating, but I half-expected something of the kind. I presented two of the caribou skins, heads, leg bones, and carcases to the two *Kanghirjuarmiut*. I told them it was a free gift, but they each made me a present, one of deerskin socks, the other of winter boots. They offered more but I declined. Then I bought a muskox toggle for the sled and fitted it so that it will be drawn Eskimo fashion, which is more convenient for the mode of life I am living, tying dogs to stones by their traces, hitching other dogs to the sled etc. The weather was typically spring today, warm and bright, though freezing at night. Yesterday I measured the five *Kanghir*[*juarmiut*] adults.[45] They show no signs of 'blondness' that do not appear in the more southern Eskimos. Incidentally Qanajuq meddled with my steel tape while I was not watching and broke it. I spent 2 or 3 hours today mending it so as to be usable, though a decimetre shorter.

Friday, June 4th

I told Ikpukkuaq last night that I should not leave today but intended to stay over another day. However, if he and his people wished to leave it would be all right, as I would follow them later. He said "no," if I wished to stay he would also, and Taqtu added "How should Ikpukkuaq separate from you; all together we will travel this summer." I tried to take a latitude, but the day was too cloudy. The only day on which it was possible to take a sight of the sun since we have been here was yesterday and then I was away hunting. Every other day the sun has been obscured. The Eskimos brought in the three caribou I shot yesterday and for the rest of the day sat around in their tents or danced in the dance-house. It is interesting to notice how skilfully an Eskimo woman uses her fingers for a dish rag, to drain a pot, clean a plate etc. The weather was cold and raw today, the temperature all the time being well below freezing. In the tent today one of the *Kanghirjuarmiut* women, Nateksina,[46] who was sitting beside Taqtu, suddenly leaned forward and pressed her face against Ikpukkuaq's. He never stirred but went on 'writing' in my notebook.[47] Taqtu, however, smiled as did Nateksina. Just now Ikpukkuaq asked me if I noticed the incident. He seems rather to be offended than flattered, though I imagine Nateksina, acting on the impulse of the moment, wished to show her esteem for Ikpukkuaq.[48]

Chapter 30. Lake Numichoin

Farewell dance — Southwesterly journey — Taqtu 'divines' meaning of barking dog — Ikpuk weeps for dead brother — Southerly to Lake Numichoin — Trouble with Tucik — Scarcity of caribou — Shortage of dog-food — Fishing for food needs — Much snow still in places — Ptarmigan numerous and changing colour — Repairing a bow—Preparing to move northeast

Saturday, June 5th, 1915

I cooked the last of the rice I had with me this morning then tried to take a latitude but could not work the vertical circle and bring the two suns together for a long time, and then it was past noon and useless. The Eskimos held a farewell dance, while one of the women cooked caribou meat over a heather fire. Then we loaded the sleds and set out, but Qanajuq and another child were still asleep and did not overtake us till some time after we had made camp. We travelled slowly southwest by west for about 15 miles and stopped to camp just before midnight (the sun is above the horizon the 24 hours now), on a ridge beside the hill at whose base we found plenty of water before. I gave Telluraq a holiday today, allowing him to run free, despite the remonstrances of the Eskimos. He has worked very hard all the winter and enjoyed his day off exceedingly, racing about like a young pup. The weather was gloriously fine and warm, comparatively speaking, despite a somewhat chilly west wind. Two of my dogs, Niq and Alokpik, are on the sick list, through fighting, or rather being jumped on by Ikpukkuaq's dogs. Ikpukkuaq went off almost as soon as camp was made to dig a hole through the ice and fish, though the other Eskimos tried to dissuade him on the ground that everyone was tired after the day's journey. Taqtu asked to be allowed to 'divine' with my *atigi* again and I assented.[1] They were anxious to find out what was foreboded by Telluraq yesterday suddenly barking; normally they said it forebodes death to someone. This seance was rather interesting, as Taqtu sought to make me her accomplice.[2] I put the *qovluna* (white man) into the bundle — I alone saw him enter. I put him back again when he went out — I told her when she might take her belt off and end the seance. I answered all her questions in an evasive manner, letting her interpret as she wanted to. The final answer was that it boded ill to someone — *ihuilleramuniñunnun*. At the beginning I told her the *kila* (divination by a bundle) lied, but she said it was true regarding the *Kanghirjuarmiut's* coming. She said she is constantly divining in this manner. The women gathered some *oqauyaq* off the bare tops of the ridges towards the end of the day's journey, to serve as fuel to cook the evening meal. Some of us went along like bees sipping at every little thimbleful of water we could find in the cracked soil on the ridges. I am growing Eskimo in my ways — careless about dirty pots or dirty person — drink more cold water — tend to have my mouth agape when travelling. It requires an effort to keep 'white'.

Sunday, June 6th

The warmest day this year. We set out about noon, but had not gone far when Ikpukkuaq began to weep loudly, and others joined in from sympathy. What he was weeping over I don't know.[3] At any rate he was as cheerful as ever 10 minutes later. Our course all day was compass south,[4] and the distance to Lake Numichoin about 14 miles. Consequently it must be about 25-28 miles from Lake Numichoin to Lake Tahirjuaq in a due north compass course.[5] Shortly before we reached the big Lake Añmaloqtoq (whose southwest extremity is only about 1 mile from Lake Numichoin), I shot a *qealiauq* (a plover),[6] the first seen this year. At Lake Añmaloqtoq,[7] in a little bay on the north side, we stopped for a couple of hours[8] for the men to dig holes through the ice and fish. Ikpukkuaq caught one weighing perhaps 10 lbs, and we cooked it and deer meat over heather and willow fires. Avrunna and Pihhuaq went caribou hunting. Avrunna shot one, and later at Lake Numichoin Pihhuaq another. On restarting from Lake Añmaloqtoq I experienced the first serious trouble I have had with these Eskimos. Tucik[9] hitched my dog Alokpik to his bearskin, without saying anything, though it was lame and in consequence running free. I quietly unhitched him. Two minutes later I found him [Tucik] hanging on to its trace, making the dog drag him along. He would not let go the trace, so I cut it. An hour later, perhaps, he hitched the dog on to his bearskin again. I took my rifle off the sled and field glasses, told Ikpukkuaq I was going caribou hunting, and waited for Tucik and his load to catch up. The Eskimos ahead, seeing there was trouble, stopped and shouted to Tucik's wife, who was riding on the bearskin, to let the dog loose. This she did before she caught up to me. I intended to cut the traces of his team if Alokpik were not loosed when they came up. The rifle was for effect partly, partly in case Tucik tried to use the bow and arrows he carried. These Eskimos avoid an open fight or quarrel, though they will stab a man when off his guard without scruple. I calculated on this fact to pull me through. The Eskimos were much concerned[10] and asked me this evening if I intended to shoot a dog or Tucik. I left the question unanswered, but I think there will be no further trouble. Tucik once or twice before has shown signs of being a nuisance, though he and his family are practically supported by the other Eskimos, and this spring largely by the deer I myself have shot. I told the Eskimos that henceforth I should give him no food or deerskins as before. The birds (Lapland longspurs) were singing merrily this morning; it was pleasant to lie in one's sleeping bag and listen. In crossing a marsh we had to go over some rather thin ice covering a few inches of water, for the snow is fast melting from the slopes. Higilaq (Taqtu) broke through in one place and floundered about in 2 or 3 inches of water like a hippopotamus, screaming that she had wet her feet. We laughed heartily at the comical sight. I was annoyed this evening on reaching our destination by the action of Tuhajoq. For a month past he has lived mostly on caribou meat, largely provided by myself, besides which I have given him two or three skins. While we were absent he dried a number of lake trout, some of which he brought to me as soon as we arrived. I thought it was a return present; nothing of the kind, he wanted to sell them for a knife. Naturally I refused.

Monday, June 7th

It was very foggy last night, and today the sky was clouded and [there was] mist on the tops of the hills. We did not turn out till nearly noon. I tried to cook some ptarmigan in the primus, but it would not work, partly because it leaks, I think, and partly because (as I found on examination) there was practically no oil in it. I have no alcohol so am compelled to light it with kerosene and a piece of rag. Then I spent several hours wandering along the ridge tops searching for caribou without success. Ikpukkuaq says there will be few now till the hot days of summer, when they are driven over the land by the mosquitoes. Ikpukkuaq fished, but had no success likewise; one that he hooked dropped off. We are eating the caribou meat dried a week or two ago, dried fish, and one meal a day of boiled caribou meat. The flowers are beginning to bloom — today I saw several pink *saxifraga* opening out their blossoms. The children spend most of the night wandering about after ptarmigan with their bows and arrows or jiggling for trout in the lakes, then come back in the morning and sleep during the day. Taqtu and Ikpuk are very fond of taking other people's little children into their sleeping bag; several times they have nestled Itkelleroq's little girl Hanna for an hour or more, till the child began to cry for its mother. It is strange to see a girl approaching puberty sleeping in the same bag as an adult man. Yet Qanajuq sleeps with Ikpukkuaq and Taqtu, or Avrunna and Milukattuk, or even with Kehullik in a tent alone, though he is well past puberty. Last winter too when I was returning from my visit to the *Haneragmiut*, Itoqunna's sister Unelaq, who is at about the age of puberty, slept in the same bag one night as her sister and Akhiatak. The birds are becoming very numerous. Today a seagull was caught in a fox-trap Ikpukkuaq set for it and killed; its mate, when the trap was reset, was caught also by the foot, but flew away with the trap.

Tuesday, June 8th

A damp foggy day, with the temperature at noon at freezing. Ikpukkuaq, Oqalluk, and I went off after breakfast to a small lake (Lake Periñeoq)[11] about 3 miles west of the camp to fish. The atmosphere cleared somewhat when we reached the fishing ground, so I went up on the ridges and searched the slopes and valleys for caribou but saw nothing save two fresh tracks. Oqalluk had no luck at his jiggling, but after I returned to the lake Ikpuk caught three small trout. Their lack of success made it not worth while to dig another hole and fish, so I waited till they were ready to return, and we all made our way back together. Avrunna and Tucik had fished close to camp with a little better success, and in the evening Haugaq and Qanajuq each caught one fish. Tucik brought me a fish this evening as a sort of atonement, but I refused to accept it. However, when his wife Mikineroq was sitting in our tent while we sipped cocoa and some was left in the pot, I poured out a cup and with a show of hesitation gave it to her, thereby signifying that I was prepared to forget if they behaved decently in the future. This course seemed the most prudent since they form part of the group with which I seem destined to spend the next few months. My dogs, I fear, must suffer from the scarcity of caribou; they will get one fish, broth to drink, and bones to gnaw, bones already gnawed clean by us.[12] This puts them on the same footing as the dogs of the Eskimos, but Telluraq and Panaski are used to a square meal every evening and will feel the change. I try to save my bones for them, because they have more meat on them. I noticed three different flowers today and picked one specimen for Johansen; the others were too poor to be worth collecting. A *taligruk* (small bird)[13] was caught in a trap; I intend to skin it for the Dr. [Anderson] presently, though it is now midnight. We go to bed at midnight or later and turn out shortly before noon. This evening Taqtu wanted to pour the fish broth into my aluminum frying pan, which I use as a plate, and let my dogs lick out of it. I stopped her and told her how a girl in my country allowed a pup to lick her, got worms in her stomach, and died. She dropped to it at once, so poured the soup into a tin saucepan which is used at night as a urine pot — poor dogs, but they don't seem to mind. The weather is foggy and clammy this evening again.

Wednesday, June 9th

A beautifully fine day till late afternoon when the sky clouded over, the west wind increased, and a snowstorm arose, followed later by drift after the sky cleared. The men went fishing at a lake about 3 miles east-southeast, and I went to look for caribou again till the snowstorm rendered further search useless. Amid the drifting snow I passed within 200 yards of camp without seeing it, but the sky cleared a few minutes later and enabled me to recognize the country before the drift recommenced. The fishermen had good luck and returned each with a number of fish, mostly about 3 lbs in weight. Ikpukkuaq, Avrunna, and Milukattuk did not return with them, but went to an adjacent lake to weep over the grave of Ikpuk[kuaq]'s elder brother, who died there some years ago.[14] No caribou have been seen for 3 days now, and they seem to have all gone north.[15] The dogs were fed on bones and blubber this evening. The wind makes the air feel very cold, and I can hardly write, though the temperature is but little below freezing. Taqtu was greatly concerned about me when the snowstorm arose lest I should not be able to find the camp.[16]

Thursday, June 10th

A cold clammy day, temperature at 8 p.m. 26° F, a strong north wind blowing, and snow falling at intervals. No one fished because it was too cold, and Ikpuk and I did not turn out of bed till 5 p.m. The children wandered about near the camp shooting at longspurs, sandpipers etc. with their bows and arrows. I picked two or three flowering plants near camp and pressed them for Johansen, but spent several hours reading Homer; I have now finished *The Odyssey* up to and including Book 20.[17] I wanted to write over some pencil notes in ink, but found my ink frozen.

Friday, June 11th

A day similar to yesterday, the temperature being continuously below freezing. Nevertheless there are many small pools of water, and ducks and geese are showing up. The night before last Avrunna shot a goose, and today I saw a flock of eider ducks (Pacific Eider) and another flock of geese swimming in the water. Despite the strong west wind and occasional snowstorms most of us went fishing. I caught one and nearly froze my feet in the process, as they were wet through walking over marshy tundra. The others caught some one, some two or three, and Ikpukkuaq eleven. He did not return to camp till 3 a.m. As we sat jiggling in the middle of a lake four caribou suddenly topped the ridge near by, one a fine bull. None of us had rifles, but Ikpukkuaq tried to intercept them with my .22. However, they saw us and fled. I shot eight ptarmigan and Ikpukkuaq one. They are rapidly changing colour, the females sooner than the males. Last night after turning into my sleeping bag I skinned a small bird (*qopanoaqparjuk*)[18] for the doctor [Anderson]. Avrunna is suffering from headache, so last night they asked me to bind my belt round his forehead. The pain shifted in consequence to the back of his head this morning, so neither he nor his wife Milukattuk went fishing. I am giving him a laxative tonight; it should do him more good than my belt, which makes rather a hard pillow. Taqtu has just asked to be allowed to use my *atigis* for divining again.[19] She wants to find out if any of us are going to die, and if so from what cause. I told her the *qila* (divination by bundle) lies, but she asserted that it proved true regarding the *Kanghirjuarmiut*.

Saturday, June 12th

Snow fell at intervals about noon and after, though the temperature at 11 a.m. was 38°. Later the sun came out. The men had caught enough fish to last a day or two so stayed in camp. I went out for 4 or 5 hours to look for game and secured five ptarmigan, but dropped one on the way back. I set up my second tent today — the one I intend for Ikpukkuaq and his family this summer. It is of white Burberry, — A-shape in front — with a bag door and mosquito netting. It is much bigger than the other tent and higher, besides admitting much more light. Ikpuk melted some old bullets in a frying pan over a heather fire — with some difficulty — and moulded fresh bullets with which he reloaded some cartridges. Avrunna is better today and went out after ptarmigan, securing four. Towards evening the sky clouded and it became very cold — considerably below freezing. I skinned a longspur[20] (*nahaulik*) for the Dr. before a critical audience and clipped my beard (2 months growth) with a pair of clippers I brought. Tucik is still out of favour and still trying to make amends through his wife by sending more cooked fish to me than usual.

Taqtu boiled fish this evening over the stone lamp, with seal blubber for fuel, as in winter. It is rather difficult in their skin tents because of the draught through the rents, the half gaping roof, and the open entrance.

Sunday, June 13th

A cold windy day, temperature at 2 p.m. 28° with occasional snow flurries. I remained in camp all day, but some of the men went fishing. Tuhajoq caught two very large fat trout, and Kehullik another. I was interested to see Taqtu use lye for tanning scraped sealskin with which she was going to patch water boots. Avrunna and Milukattuk went out for ptarmigan with my .22 automatic and secured five.

Monday, June 14th

The northwest wind which has been blowing for 4 days now continued unabated, but the sky was clear, though the air very keen. Ikpukkuaq, after a breakfast of dried deer meat, went off to look for caribou, Milukattuk accompanying him with my .22 automatic to shoot ptarmigan. I boiled some ptarmigan and had a hot breakfast, then likewise went out to look for caribou, in the opposite direction to Ikpuk. About 3 miles northwest I passed a lake where Tucik and his wife were fishing and continued on for 2 or 3 more miles to the northwest end of Lake Añmaloqtoq without seeing any sign of caribou. Finally I returned to camp, which I reached about 8 p.m. Ikpukkuaq, Avrunna, and Milukattuk turned up about 3 a.m. They had secured one caribou (a bull), the only one they saw. After I had disappeared from view to the north, Tucik saw three caribou travelling north. The sky clouded over in the afternoon, but the wind dropped a little. Taqtu finished her water boots today; they are of tanned sealskin throughout and shaped like the baggy, winter, deerskin boot, strapping into the belt. The season here is late, but apparently not more so than usual, I gather from Taqtu. It is now the middle of June, and the snow is still thick in most places, with but few pools of water, and those small.

Tuesday, June 15th

A fine day, but cloudy. The north wind had moderated considerably but was still chilly. I turned out just after 8 a.m., boiled a little rice and set out west to look for caribou while the camp still slept. I travelled about 10 miles without seeing a trace of caribou, then returned a little to the north of my outward trail, reaching camp about 9 p.m. Small birds were numerous, and I saw some ducks, ptarmigan, a seagull, and a raven. The last flew from the west (my left) to just above my head, croaked twice, then flew away to the west again — a very bad omen, so no wonder I saw no game. A white fox peered over the top of a ridge at me but disappeared before I could fire. Ptarmigan are very numerous here; almost every little patch of wet tundra between the foot of a ridge and the lake below it shelters a pair - *nighaqtoq* and *agnadluk* — male and female rock [ptarmigan]. The female[s] are dark now on the back, but

Figure 161. Ikpukkuaq in summer costume, Lake Numichoin area, southwestern Victoria Island, mid-June 1915. (Photo by D. Jenness, CMC Photo No. 36965.)

the males have hardly begun to turn. It is the male one sees first, the glossy sheen of its plumes, though white as the snow itself, contrasting with the latter's dazzling brightness. Higilaq[21] foolishly thought me lost or said so. Really she does not want me to go out hunting for there is food enough in camp and she has to mend my boots. One day's tramp on

Figure 162. Higilaq, wife of Ikpukkuaq, in summer costume, Lake Numichoin area, southwestern Victoria Island, mid-June 1915. (Photo by D. Jenness, CMC Photo No. 36966.)

the stony ridges wears off a patch or makes a hole in it.[22] Their spring footgear in this respect is much inferior to the western. Higilaq is lazy too — she much prefers talking to working; cooking she doesn't mind so much, as she can sit down idle most of the time and gossip. Caribou are

Figure 163. Skin tent and two summer caches at Lake Numichoin, southwestern Victoria Island, June 17, 1915. Dogs chained to stones and widely separated to prevent fighting. (Photo by D. Jenness, CMC Photo No. 36983.)

certainly few and far between, but there are some in the neighbourhood, or at least pass by us, for all the tracks point north as though these are late stragglers who stayed near the south coast to graze long after the rest had migrated to the interior. I should like to shoot two or three for the dogs, as they are very poorly fed just now.

Wednesday, June 16th

A fine day, but cloudy; temperature above freezing all the time but still a cold north breeze. The women told me today that they did not like my constant excursions because my boots required constant mending, while caribou were so scarce that it was not worth while to hunt. The men, save Tucik and Avrunna, remained in camp. The former went fishing, the latter after caribou in the same direction (east) as Ikpuk and he the other day. I backed the larger fishing-net, but it was rather chilly to continue and put on the floats and sinkers. Higilaq and Ikpuk told me last night that there is a *tornraq* (devil) on the hills a little west of here, which seizes men by the ear and kills them. Yesterday she feared it had killed me. I set Milukattuk to work sewing a mosquito net door to the small green tent. She is very willing to sew anything for me, often offering to mend things unasked. Today I found out the reason; she has had more use out of my .22 automatic than anyone else and though on the whole she has been fairly successful, yet she is conscious of having expended a good deal of ammunition to no effect; so she sews for me to make amends. I gave her a file to sharpen her *ulo*, a valuable present in the eyes of these people, and one which pleased her very much. The weather changed in the evening and a heavy snowshower fell, while the temperature dropped considerably.

Thursday, June 17th

Avrunna and Tucik (who had accompanied the former, not fished as I thought) turned up some time in the morning. The former had shot two caribou a long way off to thc northcast. So now we are all preparing to pack over in that direction, where alone caribou seem to exist to any extent — here occasional stragglers pass by, generally unseen. Milukattuk and I finished the mosquito-net door today — it seems satisfactory. I am giving Ikpukkuaq the large tent for himself and family while myself with Avrunna and Milukattuk will live in the small tent. Avrunna I don't relish much — he has the impudence of a beggar, and I gave him a dressing down today; but his wife — hitherto at least — has been more solicitous for my comfort than anyone save Ikpukkuaq — she is worth six Higilaq's. I can endure the man if the woman is useful sewing and mending. Everyday there are patches to put on boots, harnesses to repair or something. But if the arrangement proves unsatisfactory I shall change over to the larger tent to Ikpukkuaq again. The weather was fine today, but still the chilly north breeze continues. I turned out to take a sight of the sun about noon, but it clouded over just at that time. There has not been one day when it was possible to obtain a meridian sight. Ikpukkuaq mended Qanajuq's bow today — making two new horns. The whole bow had to be taken to pieces, the new parts fitting and the whole rebacked and lashed. It occupied him about half the day — the rest being spent in eating and talking. It is interesting to watch them string a bow. One horn is pressed against the outstretched foot (the man sitting down) so that it is bent in, while the other foot in the middle of the curved portion pushed out the centre, and the left hand on the other horn draws in the top. He used a curious tool for bending the ends of the horns — a piece of wood with a square hole near one end — practically the same as the smaller arrow-straightener. Their dog-packs are simply sealskins with holes round the edges for lashing it up like a poke. In winter they can be laid flat and used on the floor — or for any of the many purposes for which a sealskin is of service. There was great excitement in the camp tonight through the appearance of a weasel (*tiriaq*).[23] Everyone scampered out of the tents and chased it with sticks and stones. Our tent was nearly knocked down, but no one minded. The weasel escaped after all.

Friday, June 18th

Ikpukkuaq is no fool. He announced this morning that he was going after caribou over on the east side of [Lake] Añmaloqtoq where Avrunna secured his caribou. Being a long way off, he would not return till tomorrow morning. Meanwhile the women should prepare to pack over there, caching most of the things here. Just before leaving he came to me and suggested that we all leave as soon as Higilaq had made me some dog packs (I said I wanted two) i.e., leave tomorrow morning. He would join us when we made camp over there. I agreed and let him take my binoculars. He thus escapes packing a load on his back across country as the rest of us will have to do. Everyone was busy today packing up and caching what is to be left on the sleds.[24] We are leaving a considerable quantity of dried deer meat and a tin and a half of dog pemmican. Taqtu held a seance about midnight with my *atigi*. It differed in one detail from the ordinary run of seances; another man's spirit entered the *atigi* and made it extremely 'heavy'. I had to thump the ground at the head and sides of the *atigi* to drive it out.[25] The weather was fine till evening, when it clouded and a little snow fell. The same north wind prevailed.

Chapter 31. A Nomadic Fishing Life

Back packing to Lake Añmaloqtoq — Description of Eskimo backpacks — Marriage plans for Qanajuq — Ikpuk dismantles his .44 rifle — Native method of cooking eider ducks — Footwear problem — Cold north wind delays summer — Food supply dwindles — Departure of small Eskimo groups — Aversion to eating raw fish — Fog deters hunting — Seance to dispel fog — Weakening through hunger — Another seance to dispel the fog — Return of Ikpuk and companions with meat and fish — Eastward in search of caribou — Long days of hunting — Ikpuk's two stories — Small red flowers — Shooting a young bull — Chasing loons — Fetching the caribou meat

Saturday, June 19th, 1915

We cleared up the camp this morning, and packing some things on the dogs and the rest on our own backs we crossed Lake Añmaloqtoq and camped on the edge of a small arm of the same lake at its northwest extremity, which goes by the name of *Kauwaktoq* and is a well-known fishing place. It was here that Avrunna shot his caribou. Here too we found Ikpukkuaq and Kehullik, who had accompanied him. They carried the skins and heads of two bull caribou he had shot some distance to the north. They hunted yesterday and through the night, then slept all day today till we appeared. I was surprised at the weight of the loads these Eskimos carry; Oqalluk's pack must have reached 150 lbs, but his I think was unusually heavy. They have a broad deerskin strap across the forehead and a narrow sealskin strap (or two straps) or line crossing the chest and passing round the arms just below the shoulders. Dog packs are sealskins, oval in shape — the long sides lacing across. Each end is filled like a bag, the middle is left empty so that it lies flat on the dog's back. The harness trace is then lashed over one side, under the belly, and over the other side when it is drawn taut, made fast to the end of the harness. Of my dogs, Qaqiaq and Mafa alone are good packers. Qaqiaq carried about 30-40 lbs. The north wind seems to have taken possession of the country; it blew strong and cold all day, and a few spots of rain fell, and the sky was clouded over continuously. Many of the men and women fished after camp was made and several lake trout were caught. Ikpukkuaq and Kehullik returned to bring in the caribou shot. Qanajuq is a very good packer, Higilaq a very bad one — she is growing old, is very fat, and in consequence lazy. She wanted me yesterday to solder on a large chip of stone which had broken off the corner of her stone lamp, using bullet lead and the primus, but I assured her it was useless for the purpose. Tuhajoq the other day made a very decent pair of spring water boots — the women seemed rather surprised that a man could sew so well. It is the fashion just now in camp to sing the dance songs taught by the *Kanghirjuarmiut* recently[1] — they are all the 'rage'. Taqtu (Higilaq) yesterday had another 'confidential' chat with Qanajuq about her approaching maturity and her possible marriage next winter; the child can't

Figure 164. Higilaq, heavily burdened, and Ikpukkuaq, unleashing the dogs, prepare to pack overland near Lake Añmaloqtoq, southwestern Victoria Island, late June 1915. (Photo by D. Jenness, CMC Photo No. 36989.)

be more than 12 years old, hardly that I think. There is no pre contract. I asked Higilaq afterwards whom she was to marry, and she mentioned a youth among the *Walliarmiut* (Coppermine River Eskimos).[2] I said "Perhaps Qanajuq won't have him," and she replied, "Perhaps not." Kullaq is Higilaq's adopted daughter (like Arnauyuk and Haugaq), and Tuhajoq is her elder brother, while Tucik is a close relative, but exactly how close I have not learned; she told me but I did not understand. Our whole group are *noakatvait* — kinsfolk — for I am the 'adopted' son of Higilaq and Ikpukkuaq. In my case the adoption is very special — more in the nature of a business proposition if they understood what that meant.

Sunday, June 20th

I turned out about 10 a.m., and after eating some dried caribou meat Avrunna, Milukattuk, and I set out after caribou. We left before noon and did not reach camp again till 1 a.m. The country to the north here is an exact replica of that on the south side of Lake Añmaloqtoq — a series of ridges and lakes. We had gone perhaps 5 miles when snow began to fall heavily, driven before a strong north wind. It was useless looking for caribou through the clouds of snow, so we decided to wait where we were till the atmosphere cleared. Avrunna and I sat with our backs to the wind, leaving an acute angle between us where Milukattuk lay in shelter. So we remained for half an hour or so. I found it very cold, but Avrunna dropped his head on his chest and went to sleep. The sky did not clear, so we decided to go no further north but make a wide circuit home. On a ridge top we saw a rabbit[3] and following it up overtook it where it lay hidden as it thought behind a large stone. There Milukattuk shot it with my .22. I have noticed that rabbits can almost invariably be brought to

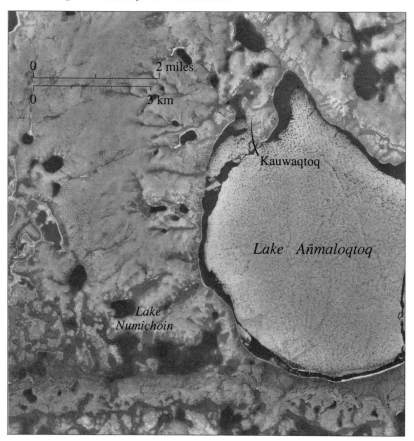

Figure 165. Vertical aerial photograph of the west half of Lake Añmaloqtoq, southwestern Victoria Island, still largely ice-covered; smaller lakes are ice-free. Lake Numichoin and Kauwaktoq are shown. (RCAF Photo No. A15776-78.)

bay as it were on a bare patch of ground; they will run to its farthest corner and crouch behind a stone, allowing the pursuer to approach within a few yards rather than run across the snow to another bare patch. Continuing amidst clearer weather, we came upon some ptarmigan; Avrunna shot one with his bow and arrows, Milukattuk one with the .22. We were some 3 miles from camp when rounding a ridge we suddenly came upon two fawns, which after a little wild shooting I managed to drop. They were so small that we decided to carry them home, all except the heads, entrails of one, and some leg bones.[4] I shouldered one, Avrunna the other, Milukattuk the guns, skins, rabbit, and ptarmigan. After about 1 1/2 miles Avrunna turned his pack over to Milukattuk, so a little later I turned mine over to him and took Milukattuk's original pack. We were all three very tired and hungry when we reached camp, glad to turn in at once and eat some cold, boiled fish in our sleeping bags.

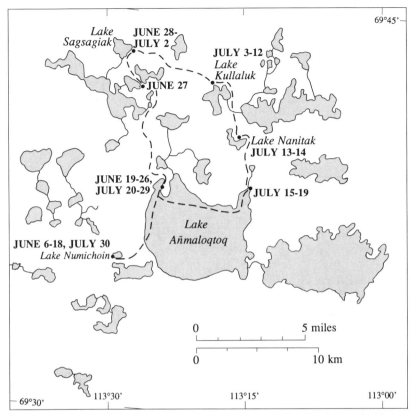

Figure 166. Map showing route taken by the author among the fishing lakes north of Lake Añmaloqtoq, June and July, 1915.

Monday, June 21st

Dull in the morning, brighter in the afternoon, and beautifully fine in the evening. I was first out in the morning about 10 a.m., having slept not too well through aching pains in the head and nape of the neck caused by the heavy load (about 70 lbs) of deer meat yesterday. Ikpukkuaq saw a bull caribou yesterday and wounded it with an arrow,[5] but it fled far away. Some of the men fished though not with much success. Ikpukkuaq obtained three small ones, which he fried in deer fat for me — over a heather fire in an aluminum plate. Taqtu cooked rice and a pot of chocolate for me this morning, and Milukattuk boiled the 'billy' for tea tonight. Ikpuk this morning took a freak into his head to take to pieces the .44 rifle he is using. He removed every screw he could see, and thus took out some of the parts, then was stuck over the rest, nor could he put it together again. I took it from him and finding the crowd of them a nuisance with their suggestions of how to go about it, went off to my tent and puzzled over it there. In the end it all went satisfactorily together except the small spring at the side of the bolt, which makes it open and close with a spring. This I was unable to replace right, but it really makes no difference to the action. Ikpuk was much upset — indeed all the Eskimos were — at the prospect of the rifle proving unserviceable during the summer and autumn, hence they were much relieved when I set it right. I think it has taught him a good lesson. Some eider and oldsquaw ducks appeared in a pond 1/4 mile away, and a crowd of us went after them. I shot an oldsquaw, the rest took flight. Higilaq brought me a small plant for Johansen (*igutaq*).

Tuesday, June 22nd

The wind changed at last. About midnight the sky cleared, and the weather became beautifully mild and calm; it was perhaps the most cheerful time this spring. Then a strong south wind arose but it too died away towards evening, and tonight it is calm and clear, though the temperature is below freezing. The men went fishing; Milukattuk and I, after setting two fox-traps for sea gulls, wandered east to look for caribou and to fish in one of the lakes. In both alike we were equally unsuccessful, but we came upon three ptarmigan — a male and two females. Milukattuk failed with the .22, but when her four cartridges were expended we chased them with stones and killed one — a female — inside which was an egg almost ready to lay. Miluk devoured it [the egg] (and the kidney) with great relish. Returning to camp about 6 p.m. I went over to the pond where we saw ducks yesterday and where during the night Ikpuk shot three king eiders. There I had better luck and secured two king eiders and two oldsquaws. Ikpuk had no luck fishing, but the others fared better; Avrunna secured ten. The snow is beginning to melt a little more rapidly. Birds are plentiful — ducks, loons, geese, terns, plovers, and ravens, and seagulls, besides the smaller ones.

Wednesday, June 23rd

Another beautifully fine day with a light south breeze, which is not so cold as the north wind. Avrunna went fishing, the rest remained in camp. Oqalluk was attempting to repair a pot [made] of [a] kerosene tin — but it was too far gone. Tuhajoq was hammering out copper arrowheads with two stones for anvil and hammer [Fig. 167]. Taqtu is making a tent for the winter from the caribou skins obtained this spring. At the neighbouring pond I shot a king eider and four or five oldsquaws. Some geese lit there in the evening, and I fired at them but missed or at least failed to kill and they flew away. The Eskimos have a curious method of cooking eider ducks. They pluck the feathers off the body, leaving them on wings and feet, then skin it, and boil the meat as usual. After the meat is cooked they place the skin with all its fat in the pot, turned inside out, and let it boil. The fat melts and forms a thick scum on the surface of the water. This is carefully dipped up with a musk-ox ladle and allowed to cool, when it congeals like lard. In this state it is eaten with great relish, small lumps being broken off and sent to each family. Sometimes instead of making tallow, the amount of fat being small (*purnaq* is its name), it is

Figure 167. Oqalluk trying to repair a cooking pot made from a kerosene tin (left), Tuhajoq making arrow heads from a caribou antler, Lake Numichoin, southwestern Victoria Island, June 23, 1915. (Photo by D. Jenness, CMC Photo No. 37052.)

drunk at once, the bottom of the ladle being dipped into the surface of the broth and the fat licked off it. Today Tuhayok's wife mixed up the undigested herbs in a caribou's stomach with water till it looked rather like spinach set to soak; this too they eat. Taqtu for some time saved the marrow bones of caribou after we had eaten the marrow. About a week ago she boiled them and made a plate of tallow similar to that obtained from ducks. Avrunna secured but one fish and two ptarmigan with his bow and arrows. There has been no sign of caribou. I spent most of the day putting floats and sinkers on a fish-net. It is very long — about 35 yards, with 2-inch mesh, and I have only about 12 floats of cork. Wood is altogether lacking; I have been searching about the tents for scraps thrown away and raised about six tiny pieces. I have another net — about 12 yards long, with 1-inch mesh — which I thought to stretch across the pond for ducks, but am afraid I shall not be able to raise floats for it.

Thursday, June 24th

A cold cloudy day, with the eternal north wind again. Rain fell in the night and caused much melting of the snow. The lake is now almost bare, and the ice on the surface is soft. At the edges pools of shallow water are forming in which loons and ducks settle from time to time. Ikpuk shot two loons — a *kaksauk* and a *mallere*[6] — Milukattuk, a female king eider and a hawk. I spent the day backing and fixing floats and sinkers on the small net — floats of wood and sinkers of horn and stone. About 11 p.m. Ikpuk, Milukattuk, and I set it in the pond where ducks are constantly settling, in the hope that some will get caught by the head or feet, though the mesh is only 1 inch. Tucik and Kehullik fished — the former caught several, the latter one. They saw two caribou, which they reported on their return. Avrunna followed after them, but they had gone far to the east across Lake Añmaloqtoq. Avrunna and Tuhayok were making copper-pointed arrow-heads part of the day. Ikpuk is showing much kindness now that I am living on straight meat like them. He lit a fire yesterday and today and made the last pot of chocolate for us to drink. I have tea left, that is all. He and Oqalluk and Avrunna have all pressed me to help myself to any dried caribou meat or fish they have whenever I feel hungry — their staple foods. Avrunna and his wife rather disturbed me two nights back with their marital attentions, so I told them today to keep over to their side of the tent at night. There was a comical sight today. Ikpuk broke through the ice into shallow water when chasing after a loon. He began to change as soon as he returned, but before he had completed his toilet another loon settled in the same pool. Off he rushed after it over the ice, clad in nothing but his *atigi* — the front reaching only to his waist while the long tail behind dangled between his legs. Avrunna during the night shot three eider ducks, and these with the loons and some ptarmigan we ate today. Taqtu has at last made me a pair of water boots. I put them on today to set the net, and they let in the water like a sieve, are in fact useless as far as water is concerned. She hasn't taken much trouble with my footgear all along — my boots have been unsatisfactory most of the time — though she makes a great fuss about every patch she puts on. I am fair game apparently in her eyes. Milukattuk promises well so far. It is strangely hard to find a satisfactory couple — either the man is a nuisance and his wife good, like Avrunna and Milukattuk, or the man is good and the wife unsatisfactory, like Ikpuk and Taqtu. Oqalluk is a very decent fellow — he is quiet and unassuming, never begs, and is always ready to help in any way; his wife Kullaq talks a lot and begs somewhat, but is no worse, possibly a little better than the average. Tucik and Mikinnerok are a poor lot — I wouldn't trust them with a cent. Tuhayok is elderly but is rather a decent fellow in his way, though always on the look-out for a trade, naturally enough perhaps; his wife Hattak is elderly too — declining in years and, therefore, is never prominent.

Friday, June 25th

Rather a cold day, with the north wind, though the sun shone out at times. A little rain fell towards evening, which soon turned to snow. The men and Milukattuk went fishing. Tuhayok had good luck and caught eight or nine, others less. I stayed in camp, having no boots to wear now that there are pools of water everywhere. For some reason or other no oldsquaws appeared at all today and hardly any eiders. I shot an eider and a loon after wasting a lot of valuable ammunition. Higilaq has at last finished my water boots, and they are fairly satisfactory, that is to say they seemed to keep the water out though they are some inches too big. The children and some of the women went out to gather *oqauyaq* for cooking. It was interesting to watch the children making houses of pebbles[7] — the outlines or ground plan, as it were. In winter they do this with snow-blocks. No caribou were seen today, though Ikpuk searched for them. The fish-net we set last night secured nothing; I do not think any oldsquaws have settled in the pond since, and eiders and loons are too big to be entangled. Fox-traps were responsible for the capture of a seagull and a hawk. One fox-trap was lost, being insecurely anchored, a gull or hawk carried it off.

Saturday, June 26th

Still the infernal north wind, blowing about 30 miles an hour and bitingly cold. Avrunna and Milukattuk turned up about 7 a.m. They had fished unsuccessfully, had seen two caribou, a doe and a tiny fawn, but had no guns and could not draw near enough to shoot with bow and arrow. I turned out just before noon while the others were still in bed and looked about for ducks, but there were none. One by one the others turned out and we breakfasted on boiled fish, after which I went off to look for caribou, carrying both .22 and Ross rifles. Of caribou there was not a sign, but I shot two ptarmigan and a king eider, for dog-food. Most of the Eskimos fished but with little success. Three small salmon (*eqal-lukpiajuk*) were caught and a few lake trout, all rather small. I was much comforted today by the sight of several brooklets running down the slopes, chattering and laughing in the glimpses of sunshine. There was a snow-shower this evening. We are running short of food. The daily catch does not provide enough and our reserves of dried fish and dried caribou meat are nearly exhausted. The dogs are the first to suffer — they are all hungry. Tucik and his wife and boy left this morning for the lakes further north. A *tullik*[8] — the largest of all the loons — settled on the water near camp this evening, but flew again almost immediately. Ducks are scarcer than they were. The outlook is not very promising. Summer, when caribou may be expected to come about again, seems as if it will never arrive. The constant theme of the Eskimos is the scarcity of fish.

Sunday, June 27th

The north wind still blows but less violently. The sky was at times cloudy, at times clear. The scarcity of food (fish and caribou) led to another separation. Oqalluk and his family (Kullaq and Ukpik) went northeast to other lakes, Tuhayok and Kehullik and Hattaq southeast to others, while Ikpuk's family and Avrunna's with myself came north by west about 5 miles as the crow flies.[9] We stopped at two lakes to fish, and I took a couple of photos.[10] At the first lake nothing was caught but two small salmon trout, at the second nothing at all. Finally we camped beside a third lake, and while Taqtu cooked some dried deer meat, Ikpuk, Avrunna, Milukattuk, and I all fished. Avrunna caught two lake trout, the rest of us nothing. Later I went up onto the neighbouring heights to look for caribou but saw only three tracks of yesterday.

Monday, June 28th

Rain fell in the night. The north wind still blows, and this evening it is very foggy. We breakfasted on dried caribou meat and some scraps of cold, boiled meat left over from yesterday, then packed up and moved camp to a place about 2 miles further north.[11] My sleeping bag got pretty wet yesterday on a dog's back, today the tent got wet. We all began to fish in a neighbouring lake, as soon as we had deposited our packs and tied up the dogs, and spent several hours in this occupation. Ikpuk caught one and I one, Milukattuk three fat ones, and Avrunna several. Taqtu boiled some for supper, the rest were cut open and hung up to dry. We saw fresh caribou tracks but no caribou. The dogs dined on a few fish bones and fish soup. The amount of fish boiled was limited, so I was still hungry when we turned in; the others ate raw fish and blubber.

Tuesday, June 29th

It blew hard in the night, but a little less hard this morning. It was very foggy, however, or rather a thick, wet mist enveloped everything. Leaving Taqtu and Qanajuq to mind camp, the rest of us went fishing, this time with considerable success — about two dozen all told, of which I caught only three; I am but a novice at jiggling and dropped three when hauling them up. Several were eaten there and then, but I find raw fish very indigestible so prefer to go hungry. After fishing about 7 hours, we set out back for camp but sighted caribou, so Ikpuk and I rushing close to the tents signalled to Qanajuq to bring our rifles. Luck has been all against me latterly and was no different today. The caribou saw us, and though we both fired, I four times, we killed none. I rushed after them and followed for nearly a mile in the fog without seeing any further trace of them, so set out back. I was steering for camp and as it proved, fairly correctly, when I heard the Eskimos shouting to me. For a long time I could not ascertain their direction, the fog causing the shouts to sound first from one then from another direction. They consider I was lost, though I think myself that the chances of my finding the tents were fairly good. Our bad luck at hunting compels the dogs to go without food today. Personally I feel little better, for the mist made the heather [*Dryas*] all wet and Taqtu was unable to light a fire; in consequence whereof we have eaten today only raw fish, a little blubber, and some dried caribou meat, myself only the last, which leaves one still desperately hungry and with an unquenchable thirst. Still better days are in store, I hope, both for my own sake and especially on account of the dogs. The temperature could hardly have been more than 2° or 3° degrees above freezing all day, and the north wind is very keen and icy — this too in the last days of June. I ought to be in first-rate condition from the outdoor tramping, but short rations have reduced my strength. It's a pity I can't adopt an Eskimo's digestion as well as his clothes; the others are all fat and content.

Wednesday, June 30th

When we turned out about 10 a.m.[12] the weather was a little clearer, so everyone went off for the day in quest of food. I went north by east[13] for caribou, Ikpuk, Avrunna, Milukattuk, and Qanajuq north, for caribou and fish both, Taqtu and Haugaq east to fish. I went about 3 miles, then a thick mist, driven by the north wind, concealed everything so I turned back. At intervals the mist cleared, and in one of these I sighted the camp to the east of me, for I had gone a little astray. Four dogs were loose, and one had dragged the stone to which it was attached; all five apparently had demolished the fish Taqtu hung up to dry, and a few of Milukattuk's. I tied them up then stayed in camp (it was 5:30 p.m. when I arrived) until Taqtu and Haugaq appeared, shivering in my sleeping bag, being both cold and desperately hungry; a scrap of dried caribou meat was all I had eaten all day. Taqtu and Haugaq had caught a few fish, which she boiled in her tent.[14] Thus I had at last a meal, hot too, though only about half enough. Afterwards she used my *atigi* at her old game of *'qila'*, removing or rather discovering and appeasing the spirits of the offended dead who were creating the fog and the scarcity of fish.[15] Some were the spirits of white men, and I named them for her — William, Mary, etc. — and at her direction told them we were friendly people, not evil minded. Some refused to go out of the *atigi* but rendered it very 'heavy'. My thumping at the side and head were of no avail, so she jammed the edge of her *ulo* or knife on the head of the *atigi* and turned them out by that means. Some were Eskimo dead — one her first husband Nerialaq, one Arnaqtaq; all she appeased with fair words and protestations of good-will, till at last the *atigi* announced that the weather would clear tomorrow and enable Ikpuk and his party to find their way back, as they had apparently been unable to return on account of the mist, which was now thicker than ever.

Thursday, July 1st

The weather was again a very little clearer about 10 a.m., and we could see ridges 300 yards away. We breakfasted on fish hung up to dry but still quite fresh and raw, and a little dried caribou lung — the only food we had. Then, leaving Haugaq to mind camp, Taqtu and I went east to fish. She caught six — four small salmon trout and two medium-sized lake trout — I one, a fair-sized lake trout. Then for a long time no fish bit at the hook and we decided to return lest Haugaq, who is only about 6 or 7 years of age, should grow lonely and cry. On the way back we gathered *okauyuk (Dryas integrifolia)*[16] for fuel. The *Dryas* is very stunted and spreads over the ground in little tufts, like *laikapodium*, only very small — a large tuft is about the size of a laurel leaf. Consequently it takes a considerable time to gather enough to make a fire and boil a pot of water. Much of it again grows on damp ground and is useless. The camp was all safe, so Taqtu and I fished again at the lake alongside, and here I caught two and she one. Some of the fish she cooked for supper, and for the first time for about a week I had as much as I could eat. Even a short tramp like today's tired me out, so weak have I become for want of food. There was an amusing spectacle in the camp this evening if there had been any spectators to see. Taqtu tied a cord round her face so as to distort her nose and show up the white eyeballs, then with a set fox-trap in one hand and my pocket knife (I have lost my sheath knife) in the other, confronted the mist and defied it. "We are angry" (*ilanaqotin* = we are vexed with you), she cried, and Haugaq and I, holding back on her arms one on each side as if to restrain her, echoed her cry, laughing aloud, laughter also being a part of the program. "You are a nuisance," she cried and finally flung the trap down on to the ground and made it spring, intimidating the fog as it were. Now it was my turn, and with my face distorted by the cord, I too defied the fog, with Higilaq and Haugaq laughing and holding on to my arms. Later the mist cleared a little — we frightened it away (*kanivjaqtugut taktugmun*). Ikpuk and his party have not turned up; it was apparently too foggy all day to find the way. Perhaps they will turn up tonight, as the fog seems to be clearing, and the north wind has almost died away. They must have found it very cold last night, being without shelter, but with their fishing gear with them, will probably have had plenty of raw fish to eat, even if they secured no caribou. It is the irony of fate that it should be they and not I who got lost, after all their forebodings about me and my ignorance of the country.

Friday, July 2nd

The wind changed to east in the night and cleared away the mist, at last. The dogs were a great nuisance. Telluraq ate his own and part of Panaski's trace, Mafa a part of his, and all three roamed about the camp. Ikpuk and his party turned up about 8 a.m. and gave a good account of themselves. Knowing they could not find their way back as long as everything was wrapped in mist they had fished with great success. Ikpuk had shot a fawn, Avrunna a bull caribou, while a doe they had missed. All were sleepy, but we boiled a pot of tea first, after which they went to sleep, whilst I wandered a short distance east to look for caribou. Taqtu boiled some caribou meat and we all had a good meal. Yesterday for the first time this year I saw a bumble bee, and today with bright warm sunshine flies settled in swarms on the drying meat. The dogs at last had a good feed. The land is now mostly bare of snow, and water is forming rapidly round the edges of the lakes. A roaring torrent was rushing down from one lake to another. The drainage here is to the south, so the divide must be further north. No rock exposures are to be looked for in the neighbourhood, as the bedding is all red clay.

Saturday, July 3rd

Today witnessed a further splitting up of our band, due to two causes, both alimentary: first, the probability of meeting caribou further east, for which reason Ikpuk, Taqtu, Haugaq, and I migrated thither; second, the fishing success of Ikpuk, Avrunna etc. at a lake to the north the other day, where they cached some of the fish. Avrunna, Milukattuk, and

Figure 168. Copper Eskimos sleeping in open-air bivouac, Lake Kullaluk, about 4 miles north of Lake Añmaloqtoq, southwestern Victoria Island, July 3, 1915. (Photo by D. Jenness, CMC Photo No. 36980.)

Qanajuq therefore went north, and I lent him my .22 automatic in case he met caribou. Ikpuk and I left Higilaq and Haugaq to pack across with the dogs to our new camping-site[17] and went hunting, doing a little fishing at such lakes as we crossed. Two of my dogs, Mafa and Niq, insisted on following us. We caught two fish, but they dropped out of the dog-pack, and [we] shot a female eider and a ptarmigan. From the top of a ridge we saw Lake Tahirjuaq,[18] in the neighbourhood of which we are to hunt this summer. Far off Ikpuk, whose sight is far better than mine, sighted a caribou with the binoculars, and we set off after it. As we drew near we saw another. Both proved to be females, each accompanied by a young fawn, all of which we secured. One we skinned, cut up, and packed on the back of the dogs and of our own; but as we were returning to skin the other we saw Higilaq and Haugaq fishing in a lake not far off, accompanied by the dogs. We signalled to her, and all together returned to the caribou which still remained to be skinned, and packed it also on the backs of the dogs. I was very tired and hungry when we reached camp, about 1 a.m., having eaten nothing since the morning, and told Higilaq she wasn't cooking enough and I was starving. She said that during the recent bad weather the heather was wet and would not burn. The weather was beautifully fine and sunny all day with a moderate south breeze. We left the two tents behind, so have an open-air bivouac tonight [Fig. 168].

Sunday, July 4th

Higilaq cooked a good lot of deer meat last night. Ikpuk and I ate some (cold) for breakfast and packed some on Mafa's back, and with Mafa and Panaski went east to hunt, leaving about noon. For some hours we saw nothing but some eiders and ptarmigan, of which Ikpuk shot one eider and three ptarmigan with his .44. Fishing gave us four lake trout, which we cached in the snow, as camp was near. At length we saw three caribou and stalked them. I shot one, and Ikpuk wounded another, which Mafa, breaking loose from the stone to which he was tied, ran down on the edge of a lake about a mile off. They proved to be fine bulls, too heavy to carry home, so we took the legs and heads only and a little of the meat.[19] A weary tramp of some 6 miles, with heavy packs, brought us to camp at 8 a.m., after a hunt lasting 20 hours. We met Tucik early in the day. He and his family had experienced little success in fishing. We sent him to our camp to have a feed of deer meat, and tomorrow he and his family will join us, as the lake beside which we are camped yielded a good number of fish to Higilaq yesterday. Ikpuk told me two stories today.[20] The snow bunting, he says, chirps "*pisiksiitutin, pisiksiitutin*" (you have no bow). Long ago a man named Pisiksi (bow) married a strange woman who talked like the snow bunting. She went off with another man named Ahina, and her husband, transforming himself into a brown bear, followed her and bit her to death. The other story I could not properly understand. Either the wolf ate a fox and became sick and his tail dropped off, or the fox bit it off. In any case it once had a long tail which made it slow in chasing caribou. Now it is light and quick.[21] I told him the story of the fox and the crow.[22] The day was warm and sunny with a moderate south breeze. The snow has vanished from the hills save in some sheltered slopes, and large lanes of water are forming round the edges of the lakes, by the streams pouring down the hillsides. Here and there the water has found a hole right through the ice, thence escapes below. From some of the small lakes the ice has all melted, save on the bottom. The sight of blue water reflecting the warm sunlight is very pleasant after months of snow and ice.

Monday, July 5th

We did not turn out till about 5 p.m. Higilaq was fishing in a pool near by with great success, and after a light breakfast of cold, boiled deer meat we joined her. The streams from the hills had bored several holes near the edge of the lake, close together. In the largest of these — lit up by the sunlight — she was fishing and caught about twenty in the space of an hour. We, fishing all around her, could hardly raise a nibble. About 11 p.m. we all quitted, Higilaq with thirty-one fish (two salmon trout, twenty nine lake trout), Ikpuk seven (lake trout), I three (lake trout), Haugaq none. Tucik's family turned up about midnight and according to custom produced some food as soon as they arrived for us to partake of, themselves eating of it later. There was great excitement today over a fish Higilaq hooked but when she pulled it out of the hole, [it] dropped off into the lane of water flowing on top of the ice. Ikpuk chased it about with the ice-pick, while the rest of us mounted guard over the holes through which it might find an entrance back into the lake. At last with a good thrust he speared it. The weather was fine and sunny, but the wind had changed to east and was rather chilly. The ground is covered with small red flowers like primroses.[23]

Tuesday, July 6th

Warm bright sunshine again when we turned out, but chilly east wind. I overheard Mikinneroq and Higilaq talking this morning, and the latter say "The Eskimos are glad when the white men reach them" (*inuit qovlonat tikitpata qowanaq pukput*). She patched my boots while Mikinneroq cooked. Then she went east to bring in the caribou meat we left behind 2 days ago, while Ikpuk, Tucik, and I went west, Ikpuk packing a load of caribou meat to deposit at our last camp.[24] Fishing gave Tucik three lake trout, Ikpuk one, and I never had a bite. Tucik speared his with the *qaqivuk* as they came to nibble round the hook.[25] We had some

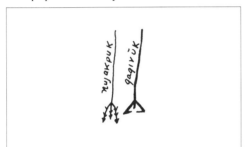

Figure 169. Ikpukkuaq's *nujakpuk* and Tucik's *qaqivuk*.[26]

trouble crossing the lanes of water on to the broad ice of the lakes, as they are growing both wide and deep. Leaving the deer meat at the old camp we went further east to fish but saw a caribou and shot it — a yearling. Returning we found Avrunna and folk had just reached the old camp. After eating some of their fish, of which they had a good store, we packed my small tent and a few miscellanies and all made our way to the camp we left this morning. The sky had clouded in the afternoon, and now rain fell steadily. Higilaq, Ikpuk, and I are sleeping in my tent. Avrunna and Tucik have each converted two or three skins into a conical tent supported by walking sticks, handles of ice-picks, fish-spears etc. The rain made cooking impossible.

Wednesday, July 7th

It rained all night and today till nearly noon when the sky cleared. Mikinneroq cooked a little food. During the meal Ikpuk announced his intention of going north after caribou, and Avrunna, Milukattuk, and Tucik said they would accompany him. He asked me if I was going, and I said "No, since my clothes were all wet and the weather was cold" — a strong north wind blowing. I refused to lend Avrunna the .22 automatic because it was in filthy condition when he returned it last time. They left immediately with their sleeping bags. Mikinneroq went off fishing, Taqtu and Qanajuq went to bring in the caribou Ikpuk and I shot 3 or 4 days ago and which yesterday she could not find. I too went fishing and during the day caught three lake trout. A thick mist sprang up similar to the mist of the other day, and I hurried back to camp and tumbled all the sleeping-gear skins and clothing that had been set out to dry into the two tents, then returned to fish. Mikinneroq turned up about 11 p.m.; she had caught nothing. Taqtu and Qanajuq did not appear till 1 a.m., but this time they brought the caribou meat. Mikinneroq had turned in, and Taqtu was very tired, so we ate semi-raw fish. Fish seem to require from a week to 10 days fine weather to dry properly, the time naturally increasing with the size and fattiness of the fish. Taqtu said she had some difficulty in finding her way back owing to the thick mist; Qanajuq was inclined to go astray all the time.

Thursday, July 8th

The sky cleared before noon and our footgear was set out to dry in the sunshine. Mikinneroq cooked some deer meat, after which we went fishing, I carrying my rifle. Higilaq and Mikinneroq fished alongside the camp with great success. Qanajuq and I wandered south to other lakes, but soon from the top of a knoll I sighted a caribou far off and leaving Qanajuq went off in pursuit. For an hour I searched around the hills where it had disappeared, then suddenly it appeared running towards me on top of a low ridge, pursued apparently by mosquitoes. A lucky shot standing pierced its heart. It was a young bull with horns about 9 inches long. I skinned it and cut it up, then with skin and leg bones set out for camp, some 7 miles away. Near camp, however, on a lake, I saw Qanajuq and Qimuktun (Mikinneroq's son) chasing two loons up and down the lane of water round the edge of the lake, giving them no time to recover their breath and fly, but frightening them under the water again as soon as they appeared. Tucik appeared with bow and arrows, but his shafts were futile, so I sent Qanajuq off for my .22. Meanwhile Qimuktun and I kept the loons under while Tucik strode an ice-raft and recovered his shafts, poling with his fish-trident. When the .22 was brought I shot both loons and we all returned to camp, where a meal of cold, boiled fish awaited us. It was pretty to see the feathered tips of the arrows dancing up and down in the water, the metal heads keeping the shafts in a vertical position. Mosquitoes made their appearance for the first time today.

Friday, July 9th

The day opened with a clear sky, but a north wind in place of yesterday's east. Towards evening rain fell and the weather became cold. Tucik brought word yesterday that Ikpuk had shot a bull caribou. We all fished today with medium success — about fifteen all told. The women and children gathered fuel just as the rain came on. I fell asleep while fishing today, not having turned in till 4 a.m. and being awakened at 9.30 by the loud conversation of Mikinneroq and Higilaq. Mikinneroq has just announced that tomorrow she and Tucik are leaving, to return to their tent some 5 miles south. Here they have only a rude shelter formed by two skins. The family has behaved fairly well since the trouble over Alokpik, my dog, a month back, but I can't trust them. Ikpuk and his family treat me very decently as far as they know how — they can't, of course, understand many of my ways. This evening I learned two short chants from Higilaq and Qanajuq. Higilaq shouted to the weather to clear up "We are miserable when it rains — it is not warm — they have no tent (Ikpuk and party) — clear up!" She did the same before [July 1] when Ikpuk and party were away caribou hunting. The bad weather apparently is 'alive' — at least is influenced by threats and entreaties.

Saturday, July 10th

The two loons when cooked made a meal for all of us this morning. I then with three dogs went off to bring in the caribou I shot 2 days ago. Two *kilguviuk* (duck hawks) had made some depredations on it, but most of the carcase was intact. Returning I had a little trouble with the dogs. Panaski and Mafa, instead of following exactly in my footsteps when passing from the land on to a lake, went off a little to one side and broke through the ice. There they were floundering in the water, with heavy packs of meat on their backs, their forefeet on top of the thin ice but unable to draw themselves up. Mafa did the same thing leaving the lake. When we drew near the camp again the three dogs made a bee-line for it on to the lake. Panaski struggled up safely on to the ice, but Qaqiaq and Mafa couldn't draw themselves up. One of my feet broke through the ice in pulling Mafa up, but by good luck I escaped a ducking. Tucik and his people left for their tent today. The weather was beautifully fine and warm with a south breeze. In the evening, however, the breeze increased and the air was sharp and keen. Higilaq and Qanajuq caught a few fish.

Chapter 32. Malnutrition

Insatiable thirst and stomach disorder — Ikpuk returns with caribou meat — Insects and blooming plants abound — Killing of unwanted puppies — Moving southeast with heavy packs — Successful fishing — Return to Lake Añmaloqtoq — Treating stomach disorder — Advising Eskimos to beware of unscrupulous 'white men' — Seance to discover reason for illness — Mosquitoes plentiful — Migration plans changed — Drying fish — Severe stomach pains — Collecting botanical specimens — Aversion to dried food diet — Shooting a troublesome dog — Catching butterfly specimens — Growing weaker because of chronic dysentery — Contemplating writing articles — Violent gale strikes — Avrunna fetches cached pemmican and malted milk — Caching equipment at Lake Numichoin

Sunday, July 11th, 1915

The strong south wind blew all night and this morning, but abated in the afternoon. I went fishing in the lakes a little to the north and caught five lake trout and another on returning to camp. Higilaq caught two in a lake to the south. Ikpukkuaq arrived alone about 10:30 p.m. with a load of deer meat. During the 5 days he has been absent he shot a bull caribou, a doe, and a little fawn, while Avrunna shot a doe and a fawn. They saw others but did not secure them. My stomach is badly out of order these last few days. An insatiable thirst possesses me and parches my mouth and throat; I think drinking too much water is reducing my strength and giving me stomach pains and diarrhoea. Probably the thirst is created by the exclusive meat diet and the want of vegetable food. I try to limit the quantity of water I drink, but it is very hard with beautiful, clear, cold streams at one's feet every few yards. The water is wonderfully transparent and blue — sometimes it almost fascinates me till I feel half constrained to dive under — I hope to bathe in the summer, but now its temperature is 'freezing'.

Monday, July 12th

Another day past. I count the days till l can eat some European food — it will be 2 months yet at least. My thirst continues, unappeasable, my mouth and throat so dry that to eat some boiled loon this morning I had to drink a little water with each mouthful. Avrunna and Milukattuk turned up towards noon with heavy packs. I went fishing to the same lake as yesterday but today caught only one trout. I hooked another and was pulling it out when my pipe dropped into the water — I rescued the pipe but lost the fish. Ikpuk at another lake speared several. We return tomorrow to our last camp at [Lake] Sagsagiaq. This lake at which we have camped for several days is named *Kullaluk* — it is about 4 miles east of *Sagsagiaq*. Taqtu cooked a large quantity of deer meat for today and tomorrow, this evening. A strong south wind blew all day. I think it will clear the straits of ice and allow the *North Star* to go east to Kent Peninsula[1] — possibly too the *Alaska* to Herschel [Island], if the same wind is blowing at Cape Bathurst. A few butterflies and mosquitoes have appeared, and flies are innumerable. Flowers too are blooming and the sky is often very lovely, especially in the evening when the sun is low in the north. Were it not for these, life would be almost unendurable. I was more than usually disgusted yesterday at the sight of the Eskimos eating fish. They never clean them but eat the black ordure with great relish. The hands and faces of both Taqtu and Qanajuq were smeared all over with it, and Taqtu drew my attention to it expressly. Last night one of her dogs bore a litter of pups — six. Taqtu killed four today — she called to me to look while she struck their heads with a stone. She seemed to take great pleasure in it. "Will you never die," she cried, as they lay quivering on the ground. It is to Qanajuq's credit that she ran away to avoid witnessing the sight. Still more disgusting is the use to which a tin saucepan is put — a *qorvik*[2] at night and by day a dog pot and a serving-up bowl for the Eskimos. I take care as far as possible my food is served up on an aluminum plate.

Tuesday, July 13th

A dull cloudy day but comparatively warm. Mosquitoes numerous — my head and face are somewhat swelled with their bites.[3] We broke camp. Ikpuk, Avrunna, Milukattuk, and Qanajuq went to [Lake] Sagsagiaq to pick up the food cached there, then went on to *Kauwaqtoq*, our old camp[4] — save Ikpuk, who picked up my tent and other things at *Sagsagiaq* and took them to Tucik's camp on Lake Nanitaq, 3 or 4 miles north by east of *Kauwaqtoq*,[5] where Higilaq, Haugaq, and I joined him in the evening. We three, with eight dogs, packed the meat and camp gear from [Lake] Kullaluk — a heavy load. My pack must have weighed something like 100 lbs, and Higilaq's was similar. Consequently we had to rest every 200-300 yards. Little Haugaq packed 40-50 lbs, and all the dogs were well laden. It was a very fatiguing day, and we are all very tired. Being unused to packing I am stiff and sore — in head, neck, back, and legs especially.

Wednesday, July 14th

I was very stiff and sore this morning, especially in the back. We ate some dried fish, then Ikpuk and Tucik went fishing. I waited till Mikinneroq boiled some deer meat, and we had a good meal, then went fishing also, followed by Taqtu and Mikinneroq. I found a good lake, still almost completely frozen over, and caught nine. The others had fair success, but Tucik and Ikpuk with their spears killed a great number in shallow water. My tent last night proved mosquito-proof, though they crawled all over the roof and sides and net door. The wind changed to north in the morning, and the tent heated up a great deal — the door facing south, so that with the change of wind no steady breeze entered. The north wind this time was quite warm, though cooler than the south wind. It drove away most of the mosquitoes. In the afternoon the sky [turned] cloudy and the weather became cooler though still warm enough to sit outside bare-headed in comfort. Tomorrow we migrate to Lake Añmaloqtoq,[6] but to the east of *Kauwaqtoq.* We had tea tonight for a change — it is seldom there is fuel enough or the weather permits it. It is just 3 months yesterday since I left the station. The children snared a longspur; like the Alaskan Eskimos they set a noose of string over the nest and catch the parent birds. The deer meat Mikinneroq cooked today was full of maggots, which (cooked) Ikpuk and the others ate with great gusto.

Thursday, July 15th

A weary day. After a meal of boiled fish we started to break camp when suddenly two caribou were sighted. Ikpuk and I went in pursuit, but by incautious stalking in a variable wind we were scented, and they fled far away. We followed a couple of miles or so, then lost track of them altogether. Returning we broke camp, Ikpuk leaving first, and set out for Lake Añmaloqtoq, to about the middle of its northern side where there is a fairly large bay. My pack was not so heavy as the other day, yet it weighed about 70 lbs. Packing is heart-breaking work when you are not used to it. I don't look forward with much pleasure to the next 2 months. Yesterday I took some iron and arsenic, and my stomach today feels much eased in consequence. Many fresh flowers are blooming — forget-me-nots, buttercups (or rather a cross between a buttercup and a primrose),[7] and many others. A few butterflies are noticeable and mosquitoes numerous, though as the wind was northerly, they kept in the hollow valleys and were not very troublesome. One of the greatest pleasures I have is to wash in the rushing streams, icy cold though they are. Higilaq rather annoyed me this morning. The packs for two of my dogs were cached near Lake Añmaloqtoq with other things by Ikpuk 2 days ago. We shall recover them tomorrow, but she wanted me to buy dog-packs (sealskins) from Tucik. She is constantly trying to play such tricks on me — says she has lost her needles, or Haugaq has lost them, where is my sewing-kit, she hasn't a file, won't I give her one (she carefully left the one I gave her at Lake Numichoin), and so on. I am rather disgusted with her, though since I jumped on her a week or so ago she sees that I have cooked food fairly regularly, not merely dried fish or caribou. In this though she has an eye to herself, for she much prefers cooked food but dislikes the bother of cooking. Tucik and his wife have done most of the cooking lately in their tent, as it is easier than outdoors in the wind. My tents having doorways do not let the smoke out like their skin tent in which the front is open. Ikpuk is very solicitous about my comfort however. He met us a little way from camp tonight and took my pack, while I took Haugaq's. The sun is very low in the north now at midnight, but still visible. The sky was beautifully clear and the sun quite hot today, while the wind was cool and refreshing — altogether a very pleasant day for tramping if one were light and in fit condition. This fish and caribou diet seems to maintain only half my strength and I soon tire. Last summer I could race about and go 30 miles without fatigue — now I crawl along like a man of 60. Still, the days are creeping by and winter will soon be at hand when I can return to the station and enjoy good well-cooked food cleanly served, and the pleasant company of the other members of the Expedition. Last night Ikpuk and Tucik were talking about the strangeness of the members of the Expedition not wishing to "marry" any of their women, and I tried to explain to them that we considered it wrong and to warn them of the fate which probably awaits them when other white men, less scrupulous, enter their land — a fate which has overtaken the Eskimos to the west and carried many of them off. It is sad to see the ravages our diseases make among the natives in all parts of the world, but it seems inevitable. Tonight I slept alone in my small green tent — a welcome change — having relegated Ikpuk and his family back to the larger white tent, while Avrunna and his wife are still at Kauwaqtoq. A *tulik*, largest of all the loons, flew overhead while we were pitching camp, and the Eskimos vainly tried to attract it and induce it to settle by imitating its cry.

Friday, July 16th

A bad day. I was awakened about 6 a.m. by a sharp pain in the stomach — liver gone wrong, I fancy, with the indigestible food. Consequently I lay in till 1 p.m., then as the pain eased off, dressed, ate a little cold, boiled deer meat, and set out to fish. My bad luck followed me even here, for I broke through into the icy water well above my knees and had to return to camp. The children — Haugaq and Kimuktun — were minding camp; I sent them to gather *oqauyaq* and boiled a billy of tea while my boots and trousers dried. Again I sallied forth to fish and spent a couple of hours or so at that occupation without receiving a bite. My stomach was uneasy all the time; I have taken vegetable laxative to clear it out but fear it won't remedy the evil — only good food can do that, and that is unprocurable. It is not as if wood were available — I could cook for myself. But it takes an hour to gather *oqauyaq* for two meals, and if there is much wind you cannot cook out of doors even with a wind-break. Tonight there is a cold, strong, gusty east wind, and cooking even inside a tent is impossible. The Eskimos have brought me dried deer meat and dried fish — medical diet for bad stomach. I shall leave it strictly alone, even though I must turn in desperately hungry. Higilaq and Mikinneroq had no success in fishing, but Ikpuk and Tucik caught a good number in another lake. While writing this last, Taqtu appeared and asked me to go over to their tent as she wanted to hold a 'consultation' over me, divining with my *atigi*.[8] She took off the footgear from one of her legs and made a cushion of it for the *atigi*, then carefully rolled up the *atigi* — the sleeves tucked one on each side of the cape, and looped her belt round both neck and sleeves — resting the head of the *attigi* on the 'cushion'. Then she orated "It's mighty unpleasant to be sick — what's the cause of it?" "*Uggroqtun* (are spirits oppressing you)?" she asked me. I raised my eyebrows — "yes." "Who are you?" she asked, and by a series of questions discovered it was a *Wallinirmiut* (Eskimo to the west). I was told then to enquire its name and suggested "Ayakuk."

The bundle answered "yes." "What are you doing here?" said Taqtu, "Jenness isn't here — he's far away. What do you want here?" and at her signal Ikpuk banged the hood and sleeves with the edge of the *ulo*. That disposed of one spirit, but the *qila* became heavy again almost immediately — another had entered and was *uggroqto*-ing. "Alak," I suggested this time. The same driving of it away followed, but it refused to go (and the *qila* grow light). So at Tucik's suggestion she blew on the cape — this was effectual. "It's heavy again," said Taqtu. Ikpuk caught hold of the cord. "No," he said, "it's light." "Heavy, surely!" said Taqtu, not too well pleased, I fancy, at her husband's interference. "Go ahead," said Mikinneroq. She didn't tell me to ask its name this time, but said "Go away — we don't want you here" and banged it with the *ulo* and blew on it. This disposed of all the malignant spirits — the bundle was light — there is nothing to prevent my becoming well.[9] I forgot to mention that at the beginning she enquired of it whether my stomach was out of order of its own accord (*iñmiñnik*), and it replied "No." "Who was it then — a white man (*qovluna*)?" "No." "Someone from Bear Lake?" "No." "A *Wallirnirmiut*?" "Yes." Personally I place more faith in the laxative I took this morning and the two pills of iron and arsenic tonight. I told her when she cooked to cook my food thoroughly, that should help also. Both she and Ikpuk were very anxious for me to have Haugaq sleep in my tent — "We don't like sleeping alone," they said. I consented to please them, though I should myself prefer to be alone. It is very chilly tonight with the strong wind. My stomach is very uneasy, but not as painful as it was this morning. I hope it will be all right tomorrow, but doubt it as the trouble has been coming on for the last fortnight. I console myself by thinking of the dainties I shall have when I reach the station — and back in Canada next year — oatmeal, eggs, butter, bread, chocolate, sausages, vegetables, fruit etc. It is strange how one's mind dwells on these things when one is hungry or badly fed.

Saturday, July 17th

My stomach was better today, but I am very 'washed out', and it requires an effort to move about. Ikpuk and I went to *Kauwaqtoq* and brought everything that was there to a place on the ice about 1 1/2 miles south of here. The dogs dragged them on a bearskin over the ice. Avrunna, his wife, and Qanajuq are still at *Kauwaqtoq*. They gave us a mess[10] — some boiled fish heads. The Eskimos are drying the fish and cooking only the heads. Generally, however, they cook the body for me, as they know I don't care for the heads. We fished through a hole in the lake Ikpuk made the day before yesterday. The water was deep — deeper than the length of the line. In such cases, when a fish is hooked, instead of pulling it up hand over hand when it would probably drop before it reached the surface, then run back from the hole with the line, I hooked a fish and ran back,[11] but my line snapped and I lost both fish and hook. Ikpuk caught three and I one in about 3/4 hour, then we made for the camp, the hour being about 10 p.m. Mikinneroq cooked a great number of fish heads — I ate a little of some and satisfied my appetite with cold boiled deer meat. Higilaq and Tucik arrived an hour later with a number of fresh fish. Telluraq is proving an excellent pack dog, though he never had a pack on his back before this summer. The weather was fine and warm, with a light mild east breeze; mosquitoes were abundant and I was bitten a good deal — they find me more tasty than the Eskimos — but I have now my hat and veil. Ikpuk used a loon's (*qaqsauk*)[12] skin to brush them away. He told me some good news. To the north, he said, fuel is scarce, so we shall soon return round the east end of Lake Añmaloqtoq to [Lake] Numichoin (where the sleds etc. are cached and I have 1 1/2 tins of dog pemmican). Caribou abound there and near the coast in summer, he said, when mosquitoes are rife. This change in our plans is to accommodate me and enable me to have cooked food — otherwise we should live largely on dried meat and dried fish. Higilaq remarked about the colour of my eyes [blue] differing from theirs. In reply to my question, she said the *Kanghirjuarmiut* had eyes like them, not like me. "How could they, being Eskimos?" Certainly the two families I saw were typical Eskimos. Ikpuk (and many other Eskimos) use barbless fish-hooks — it is easier to adjust the bait, but with an unskilful fisher more fish are dropped.

Sunday, July 18th

There was a light south wind when we rose this morning, but towards noon it changed to west and increased in strength till at night it was blowing a gale. Taqtu went off early to look at a fox-trap set for sea gulls, saw fish at the mouth of a creek alongside, and hailed the others, who rushed off with their spears. I went out on the lake fishing at the same time, as there was evidently going to be no breakfast cooked. I did not care to risk dried fish or caribou. The others followed me a little later — their spearing resulting in only some half dozen fish. A heavy squall of rain came on about noon. The others donned sealskin coats or put sealskins over their backs, converting the fish bag into a cape. Having neither I got pretty wet and found the fishing for the rest of the day bitterly cold in consequence. The Eskimos brought out a little dried fish to eat, and I tried some but the pain in my stomach showed signs of recommencing, so I told Higilaq I wanted some fish cooked for supper. We returned to camp about 8 p.m. with a fairly good bag of fish — Ikpuk's family with about twenty. Avrunna's family had turned up and tumbled into my tent, but Milukattuk was soon turned out again to cook in Mikinneroq's tent. They gave me a good plateful of fish, nearly twice as much as I could eat, but as there will probably be no cooking tomorrow morning I am keeping it on one side. There is quite a large quantity of fish drying now — their food in the beginning of winter before sealing commences. One of my eyes is almost closed with mosquito bites received yesterday. The tent is proving mosquito-proof, but very warm, too warm sometimes.

Monday, July 19th

A dull cloudy day, but comparatively warm, with a light west wind. We fixed up the large fish-net I brought, and Ikpuk, Avrunna, Tucik, and I went east to a lake about 2 miles off while the women went out on Lake Añmaloqtoq to fish. The three Eskimos took off their trousers, tied their boots as tight as they could round the leg just below the knee, and set the net at one end of a large pool of water in a corner of the lake. Then armed with their long three-pronged fish-spears and the fishing line, they searched the pond all over, stabbing at every fish they saw. Tucik secured five, Avrunna five, Ikpuk three, and the net two. One of Ikpuk's was very large, weighing, I should think, 20 lbs. This occupation must have taken them quite 1/2 hour, and they were immersed up to their hips at times in the icy water. One could not but admire their endurance. I wandered along the shore in the meantime, intending to jiggle through the ice, but saw two fish in the lane of water along the shore and cast the line for them, drawing it immediately back to shore, as the Eskimos do. The hook finally caught in a bowlder on the bottom, and in trying to tug it loose the line snapped. The water was so beautifully transparent that I thought it could be no deeper than my knees at the most and started to wade in. It was considerably deeper, and I was soaked well above the knees before reaching the place where the hook should be. So I returned to shore, stripped, and walked in, but when the water reached almost to the waist I found it too cold to endure and hurried out. Water at the freezing point may be endurable to Eskimos, but not to me. Hooks don't matter anyhow — I have plenty. We then went on to another lake, where Avrunna and Tucik waded again after fish but found none. They then on the way back jiggled in various places, and each caught two or three small ones. Milukattuk and Higilaq each caught a number of fish, but Mikinneroq[13] had no luck. I had a severe pain in the stomach part of the day, but it went away again. We saw the fresh tracks of a large bull caribou, but not the animal. Fresh flowers were noticeable again today.

Tuesday, July 20th

It was very warm during the early part of the day but grew cool towards evening. Today was one of the worst days I have had. From early in the morning I was kept awake by the pain in my stomach, which did not leave me till well on in the afternoon, and then only partially. We moved camp to the northwest end of Lake Añmaloqtoq, setting out with packs and dogs across the ice and stopping there to fish. When we moved on again and made camp[14] it was still fairly early — about 7 p.m., so the Eskimos went off again to fish close by, the women and children (save Milukattuk) to gather *oqauyaq*. I stayed in camp, using the opportunity to gather some flowering plants for Johansen. Everyone returned save Higilaq, of whom there was no sign up to midnight — she had lingered fishing as usual. Ikpuk and Avrunna turned in, as did Tucik and his wife. Milukattuk told Qanayuq to cook, Avrunna told Milukattuk, and neither did, so I turned out to cook for myself one of the fish I caught today. This set Milukattuk astir, but just then Higilaq appeared and took over the cooking. I told her that if she did not cook for me she wouldn't receive much from me when we returned to the station in the winter. In less than 1/2 hour I had boiled fish showered on me by Higilaq, boiled caribou meat by Mikinneroq, and soup (the water in which they were boiled) by both. The fact is they don't cook fish at this time of the year save the heads, but dry it for the winter. Consequently their diet consists two-thirds of dried caribou meat and dried (or raw intestines of) fish, one-third of boiled fish heads and boiled (fresh or dried) caribou meat. I, however, can't stand the dried food diet and don't want dried fish in the fall, as I have food in plenty cached on the coast (eight cans dog pemmican, 40 lbs rice, 40 lbs sugar, and 56 lbs hard-bread); and since I catch far more fish than I eat and the dogs are fed on scraps only, besides the caribou I kill, I consider I have a fair claim to boiled fish.[15] It is simply a matter of making them understand, if I can, my point of view as well as their's. They fancy my sickness is due to magic and that diet has nothing whatever to do with it. I was surprised at the number of different species of plants in flower — about a dozen. I found real buttercups just coming out — the half buttercups, half primroses with which the ground is clothed are the flowers of the *oqauyaq* that we burn for fuel.

Wednesday, July 21st

The warmest day this year, as far as I could tell without a thermometer.[16] Higilaq turned out early and boiled some fish. We had hardly finished breakfast when my dog Alokpik slipped his harness and started off back to our last camp[17] where we left a lot of fish to dry. We called him but he would not return. I followed and shot him[18] just as he reached the old camp. He has been a great nuisance all along — though he pulled and packed fairly well, but was very wild and constantly broke loose and committed depredations in the camp. But his worst fault was that he was an insufferable howler and set the other dogs in a turmoil, thereby destroying all chance of caribou approaching the camp. Ikpuk, Avrunna, and Tucik went off to spear fish, the rest of us, save Qanajuq and Haugaq, who minded camp, jiggled in Lake Añmaloqtoq.[19] Of the jigglers I had the best luck, seven. Tucik speared a great number, while Ikpuk and Avrunna have not as yet appeared (11 p.m.). Qanajuq cooked some fish for me — as I returned 1/2 hour before the rest — in an empty man-pemmican tin, which makes a tolerable pot. Mosquitoes were very thick on the land, but only stragglers on the ice. I took some lead and opium today, and my stomach is a little more settled, not so painful as yesterday, while the violent diarrhoea has almost ceased. My scolding of Higilaq yesterday has caused everyone to be very solicitous for my comfort.

Thursday, July 22nd

Ikpuk and Avrunna turned up a little after midnight. They had not visited the fish-net[20] but speared a great number of fish in another lake. Telluraq again ate part of his trace in the night. Morning was bright and sunny with hardly a breath of wind; later a moderate south breeze arose, but it was hot all day. Mosquitoes were more numerous than ever; had I no veil they would have eaten me alive. Avrunna went to examine the fish-net, and Qanajuq accompanied him; it contained three trout and a loon. The loon had rent it somewhat, so they brought it back. Higilaq alone went fishing, the rest of us stayed in camp all day, Ikpuk sleeping most of the time, Milukattuk making a tent for the fall. I caught a few butterflies etc.[21] for Johansen, but slept part of the day inside my tent and part of the time went over some of my notes. My sickness seems to have issued in a chronic dysentery, which is both aggravating and weakening. Oqalluk's and Tuhajoq's families join us here, and when the fish is dried we move to [Lake] Numichoin again and hunt caribou through the summer to the west and south of that place. Ikpuk and Avrunna shot five brant (geese) yesterday at a lake to the east. Geese and fish might be made very palatable under other conditions, but here they are insipid and indigestible. I am heartily sick of Eskimo life with its filth and squalor, and long for decent food and rest and quiet. Eskimos have a curious custom with young pups; they pull out their legs to make them grow big and blow into their noses to sharpen their scent for seals. Little children too are 'enlarged' by pulling at their arms and legs. One of Higilaq's pups has been christened with the name of Ikpuk's elder brother, who died 2 or 3 years ago near here; had it been a child it would have received the same name (or names, for it takes all the names of the person). Ikpuk asked me today if I liked longspur eggs — they are about the size of a sparrow's. I told him no, but duck's and geese eggs I should enjoy if ever they secured any.

Friday, July 23rd

We all went fishing on Lake Añmaloqtoq today save Qanajuq and Haugaq. I had good fortune in the jiggling and secured twelve. Ikpuk caught about the same number, the others less. A cold west wind sprang up in the afternoon, and the atmosphere became foggy. My stomach would not stand the diet today, so save for a little boiled fish for breakfast I am fasting.

Saturday, July 24th

Being weak and tired I stayed in my sleeping bag pretty well all day, while the others went fishing. The Eskimos are growing somewhat concerned — it burdens them for the time, though food is plentiful now, and they know that the welcome and presents they receive from us at the station this winter depend largely on my safe return. Qanajuq cooked me two ptarmigan that she killed yesterday — they were more palatable than the fish. The west wind of yesterday developed into a cold gale from the west during the night. It is still blowing but not so hard. The women returned fairly early from their fishing. Tucik's stepson Qimuktun, however, turned up first and cooked some fish for himself and me. Later Milukattuk boiled a pot of tea. Feeling too weak to move about I sought distraction in pondering over the effect civilization has had on the Northern Alaskan Eskimos and its probable effects here, with a view to writing a short essay on the subject and publish perhaps in the *Hibbert Journal*.[22] This sickness has been useful to me in one way at least; it has given me leisure for thought, which I have not known for a long time. I must confess, however, that a considerable portion of the time my thoughts run to the glorious feasts I shall have at the station and back in Canada — things which never occur to me when in health.

Sunday, July 25th

Rain fell during the night, and the west wind sprang up strong again this morning. My dysentery is less violent, and I am hoping for a speedy recovery. It is about time — I am so weak I can hardly crawl about. The Eskimos are speculating as to whether I am going to die and ask me if the folks at the station will be angry and hostile to them if I do. Ikpuk offered this morning to have some of my 'white man's' food brought up from the coast, or for us to go down to get it, but I told him it was too far — we might perhaps in summer. He and Avrunna and Tucik returned about midnight with a good number of fish and three or four geese. The latter were cooked for breakfast about 2 p.m., and I managed to make a moderate meal. Avrunna and his wife had a quarrel. I don't know what over. She wept loud and long and did not go fishing with the others — nor did I. The strong wind and cloudy sky made the air feel very cold, and I was shivering all day, though I put on extra clothes. Even at night in my sleeping bag I have been cold lately, through weakness I suppose. I began to make notes on the N. Alaskan Eskimos today and started the essay at the back of this diary,[23] for want of paper. The fishers returned about midnight, having met with fair success. Avrunna tried to make peace with Milukattuk, who has fasted all day through ill temper, but she declined to listen to his overtures and they are still at loggerheads.

Monday, July 26th

Heavy rain fell in the early morning, and the strong west wind continued. It moderated a little just after noon, and the Eskimos went off, some to fish, some to bring in food and clothes cached at earlier camps because [they were] too heavy to pack. But a violent gale broke out 2 or 3 hours later. Qanajuq was cooking me some brant in Ikpuk's new skin tent, which he set up here in place of the Alpine tent I supplied him with because it does not flap in the wind. His fish-spear, which formed one of the supports, snapped, and down flopped the tent. The children, who alone beside myself remained in camp, displayed great capacity in coping with the situation in the gale. I dressed and turned out to help, but they had already extricated the cooking gear and poles. The tent was left as it lay — to protect the sleeping skins, and Qanajuq set out to cook again, in Tucik's tent. So strong was the wind and so feeble the *oqauyaq* fire that it was 4 hours later before she succeeded in cooking a small scrap of meat in a cupful of water, and then it was so smoked as to be almost inedible. Ikpuk and Tucik re-erected the former's tent, and Taqtu, when she arrived, cooked me a little fish — rather cleanly for Eskimos — because I gave her a good rating about the little concern she took of me. Everyone was glad to turn in after a cold and miserable day. Miluk and Avrunna have made up their quarrel, and all is right again.

Tuesday, July 27th

Still the western gale — with rain squalls. No one stirred till after noon, then Taqtu cooked some fish. Avrunna went to Lake Numichoin to bring me my pemmican and a scrap of malted milk. He is showing up better now that I am half helpless — of course he knows it pays him. The dysentery seems to have stopped, though my stomach is very uneasy and at times troublesome. I wish I were not so appallingly weak. The weather outdoors — and in too — was bitterly cold, and the Eskimos did not go fishing as usual. They have a good store of dried fish now and are only waiting for fine weather and the other two families to rejoin us to start caribou hunting.[24] Probably the weather will be more settled after this gale. I spent the day in my sleeping bag — writing at intervals till I tired. Avrunna reappeared about 7 p.m. He had crossed the lake[25] and gained the shore on the other side without difficulty — this on the 27th July. He brought a bag of dog pemmican and a tin containing a mixture of malted milk and sugar.[26] Taqtu warmed the pemmican for me with water — I made a drink of 1 1/2 spoonfuls of the milk and sugar with cold water — and had a better meal than I have had for many a day. Snow fell this evening.

Wednesday, July 28th

The west wind changed to north in the night, but otherwise there was little difference. Snow showers fell at intervals all the morning. Then the weather moderated. Mikinneroq went fishing but had little success — the rest remained in camp. I continued yesterday's diet, with the addition of tea, and feel much better today, though the dysentery has not quite ended. The Eskimos remarked how thin I had become. My essay on the Alaskan Eskimos has come to a standstill till I can think it over more. Meanwhile I am jotting down some of my experiences in Papua;[27] they should make interesting magazine articles with photos to accompany them, but I don't know whether I shall ever have time to write them up or if it would be fair to Oxford to publish them if I do.[28] The sun sets at night now below the horizon. This gale has withered almost all the flowers — truly their day is short. Not a fly of any description has appeared for 3 or 4 days, but the mosquitoes I am afraid are not far distant. A flock of eight or nine Arctic tern flew screaming overhead a few minutes ago.

Figure 170. Avrunna, Higilaq's son, mending his bow, Lake Añmaloqtoq, southwestern Victoria Island, July 29, 1915. (Photo by D. Jenness, CMC Photo No. 37058.)

Thursday, July 29th

A change at last in the weather — clear sky and light north breeze. The three Eskimo men packed most of the dried fish some distance towards Lake Numichoin and cached it. When they returned Ikpuk wanted to set out at once for Lake Numichoin with all the camp gear, but as he had said nothing about it before, we were not ready. Fuel was plentiful for once and we had tea twice. Mikinneroq and Taqtu fished but caught nothing. Ikpuk moulded some bullets and loaded some cartridges. I wrote some notes, measured Milukattuk's head,[29] took a sample of her hair, and three or four photos.[30] Taqtu held a seance in evening[31] — *tornraq* not *qila* this time.

Friday, July 30th

We packed to Lake Numichoin. My pack was light — 30 lbs or so — but it tired me out. However, my stomach has ceased to pain me, and the dysentery seems to be going away, though I have still a parched mouth and unslakable thirst and dare not drink as I list. We are going down to the coast to hunt caribou there and will visit *Oqauyarvik*, where I hope to get some rice and hard-bread. Two slabs of chocolate I had left at Numi-

choin proved very welcome. We made a pot of chocolate with one —
everyone enjoyed it. I am leaving my camera here with most of my
things, to lighten my pack during the summer — I don't expect any
special feature of Eskimo life to turn up to photo. Mosquitoes plagued us
all day, for it was warm sunny weather with light south breeze. Lake
Numichoin and all the small lakes here are free of ice and shine blue like
the tropic sea.[32] The evening glow was particularly lovely. I find the
pemmican diet nourishes me, but is very dreary. The poor dogs suffer,
but the first caribou I kill they shall have a square meal. I am leaving
here, too, the flowers and grasses I have gathered for Johansen. We do
not return to Lake Numichoin till the fall — 2 months hence. I had a
good swill in the lake — my feet and the upper half of my body — it was
too cold to bathe. The children, however, stripped and played about in
the water and on the shore (at 10 p.m.) as our children do at the seaside[33]
— how they can stand water about 32° F I don't know.

Chapter 33. Packing West in Search of Caribou

Eskimo method of boiling meat — Onto the tundra plain — Temple-like dolomite outcrop — Gathering plants for Johansen — Bathing in a creek — Food cache at Oqauyarvik *— An unsuccessful caribou drive — Abundance of cockle shells — Seance — Cooking meat on a hot stone — Communal bathing — A successful caribou drive — Stalking a caribou — Discussion about lightning — Stomach ailment returns — Pyrite locality — Crossing the Kugaluk River — Camping among diabase blocks — Gale winds and snow — Another successful caribou drive — False alarm about bears — Two polar bears — Waiting for skins to dry — Caching unneeded meat — View of mainland to south*

Saturday, July 31st, 1915

We left Lake Numichoin with lighter packs than ever before — our summer packs in fact. Our route carried us south over 'squaw-head' tundra and stony soil. A caribou was sighted when we had proceeded only about 3 miles.[1] Ikpuk and I stalked it, and getting within close range I brought it down. Immediately Ikpuk signalled our success by running from side to side three or four times, and the others immediately set about making camp. Qanajuq and Haugaq brought pack straps and the meat was packed to camp. The dogs at last have had a good feed. So have we all for that matter, though I found the meat not very tasty. Eskimos don't know how to cook. They put about two cups of water in the pot and boil four or five times its volume of meat in it. Only a small portion of the meat is immersed at one time — the rest projects and frequently is well smoked before it in turn is immersed. The amount of meat that has to be cooked and the scarcity of fuel — together with the size and shape of their pots — is responsible for this. The heather [*Dryas*] has sprung up so we are burning that and willow (willow twigs principally), 'oqauyaq' chiefly to start the fire. Showers of rain fell in the evening. The caribou had a good layer of fat along its back. I boiled down a little in my frying pan to make some dripping and fry a steak later. The Eskimos tell me I should have pounded it first on a stone. Before supper I had a bath in a lake — it was very cold and I just soaped all over, dunked under once, and shot out onto the bank. How fresh one feels afterwards! My stomach gave me some trouble last night but seems better today. Ikpuk is making a hat after the model of one I made last spring — the rim of *ugyuk* skin. I have given them enough mosquito netting to go all round. In the marsh where the caribou was killed mosquitoes were very thick. The rain drove them away. The temperature is mild, for the wind is south.

Sunday, August 1st

A bright sunny day, but the wind was very changeable. In the morning it was north then it shifted to west, then south; in the evening it was north again. We broke camp fairly early in order to travel before the mosquitoes appeared, but the change of wind brought them out as numerous as ever. We trekked south, out of the Colville Hills on to the tundra plain between them and the sea. The plain is more stony than turfy. About 5 miles from the sea is the first outcrop of rock I have seen since leaving the coast — it is dolomite. In one place it resembles the floor of a stone temple — the dolomite being in blocks and here almost level, while two pillars of stone blocks, some 5 feet high, made the portals.[2] The pillars, Tucik said, were set up as rests for a *kayak*, which was cached here. About a mile further south from the top of a knoll a bull caribou was sighted. Ikpuk, Tucik, Avrunna, Miluk, and I went after it but found it impossible to stalk up close, there being no concealment. Ikpuk went round it to try and drive it towards us, but it fled far off. We followed a mile or more, then all but Ikpuk gave up the chase. He is still absent. Returning we pitched the tents, and Miluk pounded some back fat, fried it for lard, and then fried me some meat. Taqtu and Mikinneroq both boiled some deer meat, so we had plenty of cooked food. I lost a box of cartridges today. They were in a bag in a dog pack. The pack was too long for the dog and trailed on the ground. The end of the sealskin pack was ripped open on the bowlders, then the bag and the cartridge box, the cartridges dropping out one by one. I am getting stronger now with the better food. Last night for the first time for weeks I enjoyed a sound rest — sleeping 6 hours without waking. The pain in my stomach and the dysentery have both disappeared, and the intolerable thirst seems to be slackening a little. I hope this is a good augury for the month. The day's tramp and subsequent hunt has made me very tired, but that is only to be expected. The Eskimos are showing the greatest consideration for me just now — I imagine they want me to be in form for caribou hunting. Also they talk much about the things I am to give them when we return to the station.

Monday, August 2nd

A fine sunny day with fresh east breeze. Ikpuk turned up at 3 a.m. He had shot two bull caribou.[3] We broke camp about 9 a.m. and set off southwest, camping not far from where the caribou lay.[4] Avrunna, Tucik, and Milukattuk went caribou hunting and secured a bull. Taqtu and Mikinneroq brought in the caribou shot by Ikpuk. Ikpuk and I stayed in camp. He cleaned the caribou skins and set them out to dry — then boiled a pot of tea while I gathered *oqauyaq*. Taking refuge in my tent from the mosquitoes, he sewed my cloth mits on to the sleeves of my *atigi*. In the right mit he 'adjusted' the thumb and put in a fore-finger — it is now too small and out of shape altogether, but it pleased him to do it, and it really doesn't matter. I gathered three or four flowers for Johansen — among them a wild rose[5] — and had a glorious bathe in a deep pool near by where a stream cut through a small dolomite cliff. My legs gave out on me today — I don't know why. While Ikpuk sewed my mits I wrote some notes — Papuan experiences that may some day appear in print.[6] Ikpuk couldn't be bothered setting up his tent, so he and Higilaq

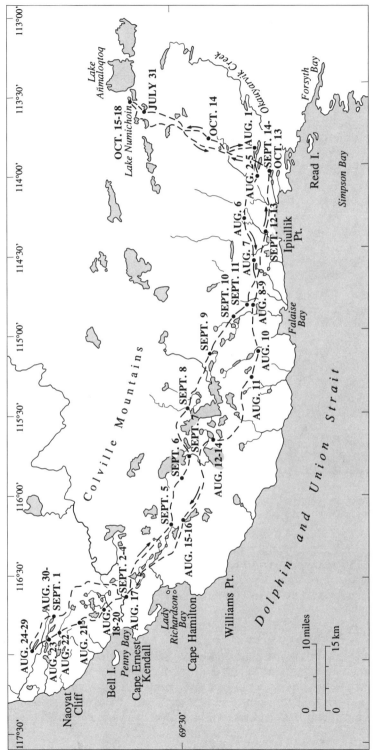

Figure 171. Sketch map of route taken by author back-packing west from Lake Numichoin, southwestern Victoria Island, July 31 - October 15, 1915.

Figure 172. Aerial view westward along the southwest shore of Victoria Island, with Okauyarvik Creek entering Dolphin and Union Strait after winding diagonally across the glacial drumlin field. (RCAF Photo T330L-87.)

are sleeping in the open. Avrunna's dog bore two pups yesterday. The poor creatures are pulled this way and that to make them grow. The other day Higilaq carried her pups in the hood of her *atigi*. Latterly they have been tied in a poke and carried on the back. Willow is very plentiful on the plain here.

Tuesday, August 3rd[7]

A little rain fell in the night and heavier [rain] in the morning. Ikpuk and Taqtu had to turn out and erect their tent. Everyone stayed in bed in consequence till about noon, when the rain practically ceased. Mikin-neroq and Taqtu both cooked deer meat during the day. Yesterday Milukattuk found five duck eggs. She boiled them but the Eskimos —

save Mikinneroq — found them distasteful (really they were quite fresh), so I came in for three. Towards evening I went down to the creek to bathe. The Eskimos followed me — both men and women — and discovered me in the water. They were much interested in my swimming but more especially when I put up my arms and sank then reappeared. When I came out (very soon, for the water was cold) Avrunna, Milukattuk, and Ikpuk all bathed — they 'dog paddle' but cannot swim. There is no false modesty or real modesty either among these people — it is perhaps impossible with their mode of life.[8] Yesterday the Eskimos momentarily sighted the *North Star*,[9] at a minute when the sun shone out clear. The sea is still covered with ice apparently. It is strange to watch the Eskimos file past with heavy packs on their backs, a walking-stick in one hand with a cup on the end, or if a woman, a pot with cup inside, while the other [hand] carries a loon's skin to flap the mosquitoes away from the face. Instead of stooping down to take a drink they dip up the water in the cup on the end of the stick. The wind changed to west this evening, but the air is mild.

Wednesday, August 4th

Ikpuk, Avrunna, Tucik and his boy, Qanajuq, and I all went down to *Oqauyarvik*. They had some dried fish and caribou meat to cache, which was packed by the dogs. In a straight line the distance should not have been more than 5 miles, but owing to the necessity of zigzagging round the many lakes and ponds we must have doubled the distance. I took about half the rice[10] and sugar cached there and a tin of pemmican — or rather emptied a tin of pemmican into a bag, as a tin was impossible to pack. Ikpuk and Avrunna then separated from us. They said they would go along the coast and look for caribou and bird's eggs. Tomorrow we are to shift camp to the west and they will join us. So we had a weary tramp home. We raised two ptarmigan among the willows, which left their young and flew. The Eskimos caught the young and made them cry to draw the parents near. By this means Tucik shot one with his bow and arrows. We deviated slightly from the track to visit a caribou cache made by Ikpuk last summer — a bull caribou. The meat had been cut up and covered with stones as usual. It was full of worms, but the dogs had a big feed, and the Eskimos cracked the marrow bones and ate the contents. It was after midnight when we reached camp. The weather had been fine and bright in the morning. Later it clouded and became very close and warm; then rain fell, but the air was still close. I perspired freely — for the first time for many weeks — a sign, I take it, of returning health. Feeling clammy I took a bathe as soon as we reached camp — then supped on cold, boiled deer meat and turned in. The tundra here is half lakes, half a grassy plain, with here and there dark patches of olive-green — willows — which are both larger and thicker here than in the Colville Hills.

Thursday, August 5th

A cloudy morning, but a cold strong west wind replaced the light south wind of yesterday. I boiled some rice and thoroughly enjoyed it after the straight meat and fish diet of the last 6 weeks. Then we broke camp.[11] Rain came on — a heavy shower — which wet our clothes and sleeping gear somewhat, despite our efforts to keep them covered. A caribou was sighted, and Tucik and I set off after it. It sighted us and fled. I sent two shots after it but missed — both were at long range. The rain cleared off shortly after, but the wind kept up, and the weather remained cold.

Friday, August 6th

Rain fell till about 9 a.m., then the sky cleared a little. A fairly strong and rather cold west wind blew all day. We migrated west and met Oqalluk's and Tuhajoq's families.[12] Uniting we continued west, searching for caribou. At last about 5 p.m. two were sighted, and nearly all of us went in pursuit of them. A caribou 'drive' was organised. Milukattuk and Qanajuq were sent off behind them, while the men set up a row of stones with a lump of black turf on top — it looked like a row of men sitting down, with black heads. Then they arranged themselves at intervals along the line, and Ikpuk and I took up positions one at each end. We alone had [high-powered] rifles, though Avrunna had my .22 automatic.[13] Miluk and Qanajuq rounded the caribou and hoo-hoo'ed,[14] but the caribou, after running first this way and that, finally fled in the direction exactly opposite to that in which we lay in wait. The Eskimos, one must admit, were cheerful despite the disappointment. Food is running low — there is nothing for the poor dogs. (Ikpuk and Avrunna turned up about 7 p.m. last night, Ikpuk about an hour before Avrunna. They had stalked a bull caribou, but Ikpuk had missed it. Avrunna followed it and fired several times, but he too was equally unsuccessful).

Saturday, August 7th

Beautifully fine summer weather with a light west breeze, which changed in the evening to east. The Eskimos had no breakfast, having nothing to eat. I had soaked a little pemmican in water last night and shared it with Ikpuk, Avrunna, and Miluk. Ikpuk boiled some tea, then we broke camp. Soon we came to a fair-sized stream running very swiftly.[15] Everyone took off their footgear and trousers (save Tucik, who tied his boots tight below the knees and removed his trousers only). The packs were taken off the dogs and carried across. It was a weird sight — young and old wading half naked, steadying themselves with walking-sticks. Some brant were seen, and the men chased them about in the water (like the loons last month), shooting with their arrows. They killed six — the rest escaped. We pressed on till we came to a high ridge. We searched the horizon for caribou but found none. The Eskimos here ate raw brant and some of my pemmican, then decided to camp, it being about 4 p.m. Avrunna and I went off to look for caribou, I north and east,

Avrunna north and west. Ikpuk and Oqaq [Oqalluk] saw me on top of a ridge,[16] mistook me for a caribou, and came chasing after me. They returned as soon as they found out their mistake, and I went on but saw no caribou though I scoured the land everywhere with the glasses. Cockle shells were numerous in patches up to the foot of the Colville Hills,[17] but I never saw any in the hills themselves. Here and there, almost reaching the Colvilles, were dolomite exposures, sometimes low cliffs, sometimes an area of slabs, flat and level like the floor of an ancient temple. I reached camp again about 10 p.m. Avrunna returned an hour later. He had shot a bull and brought back the skin, legs, and back fat. The Eskimos had a good meal of boiled brant and raw back fat. After this Taqtu enquired of the *qila* (my *atigi*) about the absence of caribou. First a white man *ugioqtoq*-ed. I found out it was Peter, told him there was no food for him, and ordered him back to his land, whereupon Taqtu banged his 'head' with the saw and sent him packing. After that I couldn't follow the drift of the conversation for some time. Other people *ugioqtoq*-ed some unknown people and were driven out. Then Ivjarotailaq (a dead relative of Ikpuk's) *ugioqtoq*-ed, and Ikpuk was roused from sleep to appease him.[18] Apparently I appease white men, and the Eskimos individually other kinsfolk. The Eskimos are very happy-go-lucky over the question of food — if they are short today, tomorrow they say there will be plenty. They offered me liberally of their food this evening though they knew there would be none for the morning, and I insisted I had my own food, which of course I share with them, though all — save Avrunna and Milukattuk perhaps — carefully abstain from taking much, asserting that it is mine, and I should be ill or at least not happy if I had it not. Avrunna and Milukattuk, especially the former, help themselves freely — indeed, the former makes too free use of my things, takes possession of my hat, binoculars etc. whenever he can. He is the fly in the ointment at present, though a good hunter and very energetic.

Sunday, August 8th

We broke camp, the Eskimos eating backfat and a little raw brant. Avrunna, Miluk, and Qanajuq went to pick up the caribou he [Avrunna] shot yesterday. They had not reached camp this evening, which was rather annoying as they had not only my tent and cooking gear but my sleeping bag as well. I have turned into Ikpuk's tent for the night and sleep in my clothes — no great hardship save that they are rather damp. We made about 15 miles, passing *Fiffitoq*,[19] which is a high knoll or hillock on the coast some 20 miles west of *Oqauyarvik*. Ikpuk and I were a good way ahead of the rest and reached a commanding hill on which he decided to camp. He searched the land for about 20 minutes with the binoculars without seeing any sign of caribou, when suddenly three emerged from behind a low ridge not 500 yards away, saw us and fled north. As soon as they were out of sight we rushed after them, but when we had gone a mile or so from the top of a ridge we saw them a couple of miles off making fast for the coast — they had doubled on us. We watched them till they were out of sight then returned to camp. There some of the others had arrived, and Oqalluk reported seeing a young caribou about 2 miles southeast. Off we went again, accompanied this time by Tucik. We travelled about 3 miles, searching everywhere, but saw no signs of caribou, so returned to camp. Tucik shot an oldsquaw [duck], which was swimming about in a lagoon with its young. He took off his trousers and waded about, shooting arrow after arrow till at last he transfixed it. The young he did not trouble about. It was 1 a.m. when we reached camp. The Eskimos had cooked a little dried fish and offered me some, but I declined. I cooked double quantity of rice in the morning and shared with them, and shared again my pemmican during the day. The weather was fine with a fresh east breeze, which kept away the mosquitoes. The temperature was mild.

Monday, August 9th

Weather similar to yesterday, though the breeze died away this evening and the mosquitoes turned out at once. Avrunna and his people turned up about 9 a.m. They brought some cooked deer meat — he had shot another caribou.[20] We breakfasted on that, after which Ikpuk and I went hunting. Ill luck still dogged us. We had gone about 1 1/2 miles when two caribou, doe and fawn, started up and fled north. They had been invisible, though only a few hundred yards off, the fawn being a dirty white and the doe the same colour on belly and rump, so that they merged into the colour of the land. Only when a caribou turns sideways on is it visible any distance at all. Then it shows black, and as the land is dotted with black rocks of diabase the caribou is only distinguishable by its movement. However, from the top of the ridge we saw a caribou 2 or 3 miles off, and by making a long circuit closed on it, and I had the luck to drop it. We looked about for other caribou but saw none, so skinned and cut up our victim and proceeded to cook a meal.

Ikpuk initiated me into cooking on a hot stone. We gathered dry sticks of willow and found some flat slabs of dolomite. Then on the shelter of a turfy bank about 2 feet high he constructed a fireplace. Three slabs on end set on top of the bank made a wind-break. Two side slabs on end and a large flat slab for the meat resting on top of them, with another underneath for the fireplace, gave us a very respectable approximation to a Dutch oven. He covered the top slab with a layer of moss, poured water over it, then laid slices of meat and back fat on the moss, covering both with a large inverted grassy turf. To light the fire he gathered a little dry grass, put a match to it, and held it up in the wind till it was kindled to a blaze. Then he laid it on the bottom slab and piled tiny sticks of willow on top. The meat soon cooked on the under side, when he turned the turf back, poured more water on, and turned the meat over. We had a fine meal, for the meat was excellent. He roasted two lumps of the liver in the fire turf; when the black was scraped off they too tasted delicious. Next he cooked a second batch of meat and roasted two marrow bones. The latter cooked in about 3 minutes, and when the bone was broken, slided right out — there was no need of a *haudlun* or marrow scraper. Marrow thus cooked is more tasty than raw, though both are fine eating, even if Huxley does declare only a savage eats marrow.

We packed the meat and skin about 1/2 mile, then cached it on a small knoll to pick up tomorrow and returned to camp, which we reached about 9 p.m. The country here is the same as further east, turf-heads and bowlders and lagoons, with here and there an exposure of dolomite. The same white shells (*olivae?*)[21] strew the ground in patches, especially where it is clayey. The dogs have had a solid meal at last and the Eskimos too, and all are sleeping contentedly. I am very tired with the strenuous exertions of the last 2 days, but more content. My stomach is not half so troublesome, though not in very good order, and the insatiable thirst still possesses me. Still one more day has passed. The sea appears to be fairly clear of ice, so I expect the *North Star* has sailed to *Uminguk*[22] as intended, with O'Neill, Johansen, Cox, and perhaps the Dr. aboard.

Tuesday, August 10th

A dull day with first a south breeze, then west, then north, and now in the evening east. People were sighted west of us when we turned out this morning, and when we packed thither after breakfast we discovered it was Pihhuaq, his wife Itkelleroq and child Hanna, and kinsman Ivyarotailak.[23] They had been fairly successful in their hunting and fishing and had made a cache of food on the coast. At the moment they came from further west and had reached the caribou cached by Ikpuk and me yesterday. We sat and talked and ate for some time, while Higilaq cut up the meat and fed men and dogs. The Eskimos partook liberally of both back fat, intestine, and ribs — raw — while I, after cracking a marrow bone, betook myself to the pemmican. We then continued on, till about 4.30 p.m. we came to a large lagoon where the Eskimos decided to bathe.[24] A dozen of us plunged in, including Higilaq and Milukattuk; it was a case of *honi soit qui mal y pense*. Finally we stopped and made camp on a small knoll about 7:30 p.m. The women cooked a considerable quantity of deer meat, and Milukattuk pounded much of the blubber on a stone, using another stone as a hammer, then boiled it in my big pot. We ate the fat, and the pure lard was partly drunk while hot, but most of it allowed to freeze. No caribou were sighted all day, though we made perhaps 10 miles.

Wednesday, August 11th

A cold boisterous east wind blew all day, and the sky was clouded. We turned out early, for a young caribou suddenly showed up near camp, sighted it, and fled. Before 9 a.m. we were away and travelled about 5 miles. Then Avrunna and Oqalluk made a detour to look for caribou, while the rest of us continued on. We saw a bull lying down in the line of Avrunna's route, so pitched camp at a lake near by, and all the men save Tuhajoq went caribou hunting to the northwest. Three young caribou were sighted about 6 miles from camp, and Pihhuaq, Ikpuk, and

I each secured one. We cached the meat on top of a hill near by to pick up tomorrow. About 1 mile west of our present camp is a deep gorge made by a medium-sized stream. With the brown stony hills on each side it reminded me of the Gorge du Tarn[25] in France. North of the gorge is a broad sandy plain — perhaps 3 miles in diameter, on which I noticed two or three species of plants (one a dandelion) not before seen.[26] On this plain were old footprints of Eskimos, "their own," Ikpuk said, "of the previous year." The temperature this evening must be close to freezing. It is interesting to see what heavy packs Eskimo women can carry. Yesterday and today, in addition to the usual bundle of skins etc. Itkellerok carried her little child Hanna on top, sometimes lying across her neck on the bundle, sometimes astride.

Thursday, August 12th

A gale from the east. Nevertheless we broke camp, after I had cooked some rice, and set out for *Kiahiqtorvik*,[27] the place where we cached the caribou meat yesterday. We all crossed safely the stream in the gorge except Kanayuk, who had not reached it. I went back to look for her — she was delayed by the dogs, whose packs required constant adjusting. She had just seen a doe and fawn, which fled east. Meantime the rest went on and we found ourselves alone. A sandstorm was raging on the plain — like drifting snow, and it was impossible to see any distance. However, guided by the wind we crossed right and were close to *Kiahiqtorvik* when we saw Haugaq. He signalled to us and told me they had seen deer and were organising a drive and wanted me to join them. However, I could not leave the dogs then, as they would follow me and frighten the deer, so we went on to *Kiahiqtorvik*, where the camp was to be. There we found Mikinneroq and Hukka (Tuhajoq's wife) and could see the deer on the plain on the other side of the lake. The Eskimos had just taken up their positions and were signalling to Mikinneroq to go round to windward of the deer and set them in motion. Kannayuk and I went with her. The deer scented us when about 1/2 mile off and fled towards the west where the hunters were. Ikpuk shot a doe and fawn, Avrunna two does and two fawns, Pihhuaq missed. Some of the deer fled back and were running to and fro on top of the ridge about 500 yards from me. I opened fire and shot a yearling in the leg. Tuhayok and Milukattuk followed it, and it took to the lake. Miluk stripped and followed it till she was waist deep, firing twice with Ikpuk's .22, but it swam to the opposite bank. However, Tuhayok went round and as it fell exhausted shot it with his bow. A doe galloped back towards me, and I fired a shot at it but missed. Then at the last a fawn approached and I shot it, making a total of eight deer for the drive, out of fifteen or sixteen.[28] My rifle missed fire once, owing to sand in the breach.[29] We returned to camp, everyone in great glee (save Pihhuaq, who seemed much disappointed and wanted to go off hunting after other caribou but was dissuaded by his wife and the others). Tucik, Oqalluk, and Pihhuaq's wife Itkelleroq appropriated some of the meat, and Tuhayok took the yearling. I let him keep the skin to make him a pair of trousers and gave him the fawn skin as well. The Eskimos who have no guns certainly benefit by attaching themselves to those that have. It says much for the Eskimo good temper and social nature that there is no quarreling. Heavy rain fell in the evening and the wind abated a little, but it is still cold.

Friday, August 13th

It rained most of the night and was still 'spitting' in the morning. Consequently we kept to our sleeping bags till late. Miluk taught me a new cat's cradle figure, then said they would teach me in the winter, as it wasn't right to make them at other times. She and Avrunna were rejoicing greatly over his success and maintained a constant chorus, broken only by remarks to each other and to me. I do not understand the geology of this plain, unless it was a lake once. The sand bed extends into the hills south, and overlies the dolomite, and onto the plain north where it overlies the yellow clay.[30] Lake Kiahiktorvik, at the foot of the isolated hill of the same name, has banks of clay in places 7 to 8 feet high, but I have noticed no fossils in it. We picked up a musk-ox bone (lower part of thigh) on the sandy plain. The rain stopped and the fog cleared way about 4 p.m. so the Eskimos went hunting. I stayed behind to gather some flowers for Johansen[31] and to search the banks of the lake for fossils — but of the latter I found none. The women cooked, sewed, and talked. Kullaq boiled my billy in her tent, and we had tea. Avrunna and Pihhuaq each secured a caribou.

Saturday, August 14th

The morning was foggy, so most of the Eskimos stayed in camp.[32] Avrunna and Oqalluk went to bring in the caribou shot by the former yesterday. The air cleared about 4 p.m. A fresh east breeze blew all day, but this evening seems to be dying away, and a few mosquitoes have turned out. Like the heroes of Homer we spent the day in eating. My stomach is troublesome again and the diarrhoea is returning, why I don't know, unless this constant meat diet does not suit my constitution. This evening I cooked a little rice. The Eskimos [are] now indulging in raw back fat. They are always saying of a dog — *aqeatulaitpoq* (there's no bottom to his stomach), but I think it applies more truly to themselves. The men were shooting with their bows and arrows at two marks alternately — clods of earth about 1 foot square set up at a distance of 40 yards from each other. About one shot in twenty hit — certainly not more — so that their marksmanship is not very accurate.[33] They say that the bow is only good up to about 30 yards when caribou hunting. Ikpuk drew me a sketch of a caribou drive and men lying in artificial pits ready to shoot when the caribou approached.[34] Higilaq amused me. She asked me, when only she and Itkellerok were in the tent, whether I saw Allikumik the *Kanghiryuarmiut* woman 'kiss' Ikpuk.[35] I said "Yes." Then she asked if I saw Kullaq do the same in [the] spring. I said "No, did she?" She answered that she herself had not seen it, but others had (I guess Itkellerok) and told her. I would tell her, wouldn't I, if I saw any woman 'kiss' him. I laughed and said "What did it matter anyhow?" She said "He's such a fine looking man." Apparently even an Eskimo woman can be jealous. Some of the children bathed this evening. They have been amusing themselves making *tallus* (artificial pits for shooting from) and setting up *inyukhiut* or rows of earth clods as for a caribou drive. The country all along here is full of such contrivances made in former years.

Sunday, August 15th

We broke camp this morning. Pihhuaq, Oqalluk, and Tucik with their families went northeast, the rest of us north.[36] Our packs were fairly heavy on account of the deer meat. We travelled rather slowly but after going some 4 miles sighted a caribou. Ikpuk, Avrunna, and I went after it. There was no ridge to hide behind, close to [it], but we crawled on hands and knees through the willow brush for a couple of hundred yards. Then Avrunna tried to attract it by walking away in a stooping position, with his gun held upright to look like an antler. Formerly it was the walking-stick that was so held. The caribou saw him but took no notice, so he walked in the same manner towards it, with Ikpuk and I concealed behind. Thus we approached within 250 yards or so, when we lay down and I shot it. It was a bull with a lot of back fat. Continuing on, after giving the dogs a feed, we suddenly spied two caribou approaching close to. Ikpuk and I ran towards them, but there was no cover. However, at about 350 yards I dropped one and wounded the other, which was already limping, having been shot apparently earlier in the day by Pihhuaq. It walked slowly away and Ikpuk fired at it and wounded it again. However, it continued to walk on. While we were occupied with the first caribou a fog suddenly came on and concealed the wounded one from sight. We then camped beside a large lake named *Tahialuk*[37] a few yards further on, and if the weather clears will pick up the wounded caribou tomorrow; it cannot be far off. The weather was alternately clear and foggy, and a moderate, rather cold north breeze blew all day.

Monday, August 16th

Rain fell at intervals during the night, but the atmosphere was clear this morning, though the sky was cloudy. Ikpuk and Tuhayok left early to look for the caribou wounded yesterday. They found it not far away, lying beside a rock, but not dead. It had broken a foot, and Pihhuaq or someone had previously wounded it in the thigh, while Ikpuk had missed. They killed and skinned it, cached most of the meat, and brought the fat and sinew to camp. All the Eskimos save Higilaq, and Tuhayok's wife and Haugaq went off to look for caribou. I too stayed in camp feeling pretty seedy. No caribou were seen but Avrunna shot a golden (brown) crane (*tattilgat*).[38] Rain fell from time to time and the sky was dark and leaden. The wind, which had been east in the morning, changed to west this evening. Lake Tahialuk is about 3 miles long by a mile broad. It runs along the foot of the Colville Hills and has at its back a peak called *Anoridlik*[39] (the windy place). We move on west tomorrow, to fish at a place called *Kugaluk*, where a rock overhangs deep water. Kannayuk and Kehullik taught me one or two songs and played cat's cradles. Kannayuk carefully closed the door of the tent so that no sunlight, she said, should enter, for one should play cat's cradles only in the dark days of winter.

Tuesday, August 17th

I had a restless night, with severe pain in the stomach and frequent diarrhoea. It eased a little in the course of the day. We packed west for some 8 miles to *Kugaluk*,[40] where there is a lot of pyrites. Formerly, Ikpuk says, this was the place where the Eskimos obtained all their pyrites for making fire. We had just commenced to pitch camp when Ikpuk sighted a caribou. The hunt was successful. Ikpuk wounded it, and I finished it off as it fled. Three small fish from 4 to 6 inches long were caught in a stream here — they have come up from the sea. Ikpuk calls them *tareomiutat* (sea fish).[41] Miluk caught a small lake trout as well. A flash of lightning was seen yesterday — a rare phenomenon here I fancy. Higilaq was going to hold a seance over it, with the *qila*, but for some reason or other it did not come off. Miluk asked me whether I saw it and if it was caused by the sky (*okilaq*)[42] or by spirits (*ugioqtun*).[43] She said they are afraid when they see it. I assured her lightning (fire, as she called it) was common in our country, and we took no notice of it. From the top of a ridge we could see *Hinieluk* (Cape Pullen)[44] quite plainly. Probably it is 10 miles away or more.

Wednesday, August 18th

I was mistaken in my bearings yesterday. We were camped[45] behind [Lady] Richardson Bay, and Cape Pullen was about 6 miles south by west of us. We left a lot of caribou meat to dry, and Hakka, Tuhayok's wife,[46] with their tent, to look after it, and about 10 a.m. packed west by north, crossing first a very large stream named *Kugaluk*, then later another *Ataucikkiaq*.[47] The former flows from the northeast out of the lakes, and its banks are wide apart and moderately high. The latter flows between very narrow high steep banks of clay superimposed on dolomite. I saw an exposure of the latter and examined it for fossils, but there were none. *Ataucikkiaq* flows direct from Mt. Qiñmiktorvik, which is directly behind Cape Pullen and one of the most prominent peaks in the Colvilles. In consequence the stream is now much diminished in volume, a mere tricklet, though it evidently pours down a great volume of water in spring. Both streams enter the sea, northwest of Cape Pullen — through a mud flat about 1 1/2 [miles] wide. Their mouths are about a mile apart — Kugaluk [River] being the most easterly.

We could see *Nauyat*[48] in the distance. The bay behind the island *Kigiaktaryuk*[49] seems to be very shallow, for there are large rocks or little islets in several places. I caught a few butterflies and insects for Johansen,[50] our packs being reduced to a minimum, and Ikpuk carrying my

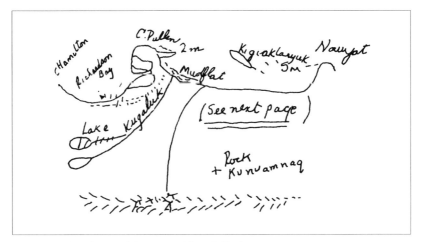

Figure 173. Sketch map of the coast at 'Cape Pullen'.

books[51] and sleeping bag. A yearling caribou was sighted to the east about noon, and Avrunna shot it, caching the meat. About 8 p.m., from the rock *Kunuamnaq*[52] where we are camped, we sighted another, a young bull, which I secured. The weather was fine till towards evening, when the wind, which had swung from east through south to west, brought rain and fog. The little heather near camp was wet, so we could have no fire. The Eskimos ate raw back fat, I a little of my remaining stock of pemmican. There is some story I think connected with this rock. At or near *Qiñmiktorvik*, Higilaq's great grandfather killed a polar bear. Joe Bernard wintered in the deep bay behind Cape Pullen[53] that forms an arm of [Lady] Richardson Bay.

Thursday, August 19th

Three caribou were sighted this morning from the camp and all the Eskimos save Haugaq went off to organise a drive. I too stayed in camp. The caribou were too clever, however, and fled in the wrong direction. They passed not far from the camp, and four dogs broke loose and pursued them. I fired at a distance of from 400-500 yards and wounded one, which the dogs followed till it dropped exhausted about half a mile away. The Eskimos were very disappointed after all the trouble they had taken setting up *inuhuit* (stones or turf to look like men). They had spent 3 hours at the task to no effect. Avrunna went up to the top of Mt. Qiñmiqtorvik to look for the other two, but saw no trace of them. Ikpuk went down to the shore to look for wood and returned in the evening with a large board full of nails and several smaller pieces, apparently thrown or dropped overboard from a whaler. I went to the top of the ridge just behind Cape Pullen, some 5 miles off, to examine the geography of the country. A long mud or sand reef runs out from Cape Pullen towards *Kigiaktaryuk*, and a little way off its point is a small sandy islet. *Kigiak-*

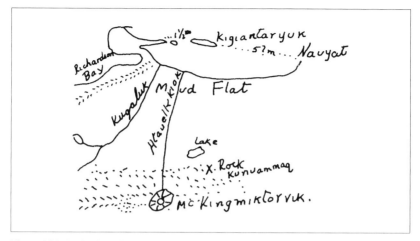

Figure 174. Author's revised sketch map of the coast at 'Cape Pullen'.

taryuk itself is perhaps 50 feet high and apparently rocky. I could not see the sea beyond (south of) Cape Pullen on account of falling snow, but saw the bay where J. Bernard wintered, and that it was separated from the sea on the north side by a mud flat about 1 mile wide. There could be no doubt of this being the bay, not a lake, for there were two ice-kegs in it. Returning I recrossed the two streams Kugaluk and Ataucikkiaq. The former, about 3 miles from the sea, was 20 yards or more wide and over knee deep. Its banks were in places 1/4 mile apart. Willows of consider- able size — the largest I have seen since the Coppermine [River] — were noticeable in one or two places along the bottom of the east bank. Ataucikkiaq on the other hand was a mere tricklet in one place, dry in another. Snow began to fall about 4 p.m., half snow, half rain, then in the evening pure snow. The wind was westerly all day. Miluk was very sick last night and today has a headache. My diarrhoea is distressing, but the pain in the stomach is easier. I passed a good night last night. The child- ren collected green willow, and I gathered two large, dry willow bushes from Kugaluk [River] with which Higilaq cooked.

The land rises in a series of gravel terraces from the clay flat to the ridges of the Colville Hills. The rock *Kunuamnaq* is really a number of huge rocks formed by the shattering of one giant crag of diabase, I think. The largest is about 12 feet high; all lie together in a cluster, forming a conspicuous landmark on the slope below Mt. Kingmiktorvik.[54] Kugaluk [River] is a comparatively long stream, probably 10-15 miles.[55] It is still quite large 5 or 6 miles from the mouth.

Friday, August 20th

Snow fell in the night and changed to rain during the morning. It ceased about 4 p.m., but the atmosphere remained very foggy for an hour later. We stayed in our sleeping bags till it ceased, the Eskimos alter- nately singing,[56] playing, talking, and sleeping. They are just like children — one mocks the others words till both laugh or they pinch and slap each other's bare limbs. Miluk boiled some rice for me after the rain ceased, then she and Avrunna roasted a little meat over the fire. Later Kehullik cooked. Ikpuk and Tuhayok were busy with the long plank found by the former yesterday on the shore. They split it down and are now trimming the long poles thus obtained for fish-spear handles. All are rejoicing in the discovery. Tuhayok this morning was singing a song to dispel the spirits that were causing the bad weather, and Kehullik tied a string round his nose and head and took a knife in his hand to frighten them away, though half in jest. The wind, which was southeast this morning, has changed to west, and the weather is cloudy and cold. The tents — which are both single — dripped and wet our sleeping gear and clothes a little, adding to the discomfort. Kannayuk slept in my tent last night. She entered when I was asleep, and when I woke I didn't care to disturb her and turn her out, though four in a tent 5 feet wide is rather too much of a squeeze. She tucked into the joint sleeping bag of Avrunna and Milukattuk. I told them this morning that it was not to occur again. They said she was afraid of Ikpuk and Higilaq, who slap her, so she does not care to sleep in their tent. I must speak to Ikpuk about it. Avrunna went off about 7:30 [p.m.] to look for caribou from the top of Mt. King-miktorvik.

Saturday, August 21st

Snow fell in the night and the wind increased to a gale. However, being short of food we set out about 9 a.m. It was bitterly cold struggling against the wind — or rather when we stopped to rest. Snow fell at intervals and about 1 p.m. a heavy snowstorm assailed us, and as it was impossible to see any distance we camped beside a small lake — having travelled about 5 miles northwest.[57] The ground everywhere is white as though it were winter. The snow ceased falling about 5 p.m. We had all turned into our sleeping bags to get warm, but Avrunna now turned out to look for caribou. I have a stiff neck where the wind last night blew on me through a rent in the tent. The gale still continues almost as strong as ever. I wonder how it will affect the schooners. The Eskimos feasted on raw meat and raw back fat — raw meat is about equivalent to a bread and butter diet with us, while back fat raw or cooked is a luxury like jam or cheese. I ate some of my dog pemmican — it is now almost exhausted. Miluk is whiling away the hours in song — her voice dins in my ear like a barrel-organ. I lie and dream on the future — friends in England — home, and form plans which may or may not be realised. Strange how one visions every stage of the journey — the boat voyage — the meeting etc. Is it mere home-sickness, or a weakening of the intellect? I have been wondering if the Canadian Government will give me 3 months leave of absence when we return. I shall go straight home and try and spend Christmas there once more.[58]

Sunday, August 22nd

The ground was covered with a thick mantle of snow this morning. The west wind still raged, and a little more snow fell, but during the day it abated considerably and the sky cleared. This evening it is clouding again. We packed about 2 miles, then sighted eight caribou. A drive was organised. Tuhayok shot a fawn with bow and arrow,[59] Ikpuk wounded a doe and a yearling, which I finished off. The other caribou did not approach either Avrunna or me. Another caribou was sighted, another drive organised, and Avrunna shot it with bow and arrow. We camped on the spot. Higilaq has presented a weird sight the last 2 days. She had only one *atigi*, and when the cold snap came she improvised one out of Kannayuk's sleeping bag.[60] I spoke to Ikpuk today about Kannayuk's fearing to sleep in their tent because they beat her. He told the others, and they thought it rather a joke, saying it was their custom; however, I assured him I should be very angry if it continued and believe it will cease. They dare not offend me because I control the supply of ammunition and other desirable things, and can refuse to allow them any this winter. The cold has killed off all the flowers, though the land is nearly bare again with the rapid melting of the snow.

Monday, August 23rd

Still the cold wind from the west and a cloudy sky, though this evening there are signs of it veering. We broke camp and travelled west[61] about 2 miles. Higilaq and Kannayuk were delayed by the packing, and I stayed behind to help them; the rest were some distance ahead. We set out to follow them, but had gone only half a mile when Higilaq sighted three caribou. Kannayuk and Higilaq both went on to signal to the others by waving their *atigis*, while I ran back to intercept the deer. They sighted the women and fled but approached within about 400 yards of me, and I shot one and lamed another. The latter with the uninjured caribou fled, and though I followed a little later, leaving Higilaq to skin the one killed, they had both disappeared. Three more caribou were sighted by us all further on. A drive was organised, but they fled in the wrong direction. Ikpuk and Avrunna followed, while I went back to search for two of my dogs, Panaski and Mafa, which had refused to follow Higilaq. Ikpuk and Avrunna each secured a caribou, and the former very considerately brought me a liver to fry for myself, though they love to eat it raw. The meat of their caribou they cached, bringing in only the skins and the fat and the leg bones. The skins are very beautiful now, the hair short and a mingled black and white. They make admirable bed skins or light clothing. Higilaq has rather an arduous task cooking for us all[62] though she uses my big aluminum pot — it has to be filled four to six times to provide two meals, one for the night and one for the morning, then usually there is blood broth to make afterwards. The children gather the willow twigs and roots. Besides this she has to mend Ikpuk's, Haugaq's, my own, and her own boots. Milukattuk does nothing but mend her own and Avrunna's and lends no hand with the cooking. I gave her somewhat of a reprimand tonight. Ikpuk offered to cook the liver for me, but I declined as he has had a fairly strenuous day. They told Miluk to, but she refused, so I cooked myself; then she had the face to cry out for some of it as she lay snug in her sleeping bag. Both men and women scrape the fat off the skins and lay them out to dry. There is still a little snow on the hills and a small patch here and there on the low ground.

Tuesday, August 24th

Fine weather at last. The wind west in the morning changed to south, and the sun shone warm. The night was cold, however. We packed northwest[63] just beyond *Nauyat* and saw the holes scratched by two polar bears about 3 days ago while it [the snow] was drifting. Immediately a hunt was organised for them, but they had disappeared. However, we came upon a herd of seven caribou. A drive was fixed, and Ikpuk himself, stalking close behind them, proposed to set them in motion by shooting. The deer fled the wrong way, but he managed to secure one — a doe. The Eskimos followed after them, save Kehullik and I, who returned to camp where we had left Higilaq and Haugaq. While we were fixing up camp and gathering fuel, Higilaq sighted 'three bears'. I examined [them] through the binoculars — certainly there was something moving — possibly two animals — which were white and so not caribou. I finished boiling the pot of rice I had set on a fire, though the Eskimos were nearly frantic with excitement, then we went after them, leaving Haugaq in camp. Higilaq and Kehullik carried bows and arrows. We went about 3 miles, then discovered two white swans in a lake — the 'three bears'.[64] I fired four shots at them but missed, then we returned to camp, close to midnight. The others turned up 1/2 hour later — the caribou had vanished, but they brought a little wood and a quantity of old whale bone from the beach.

Wednesday, August 25th

A sharp frost in the night, and the water in the pots was frozen. The wind was east and very keen, but the sun warm. I was much amused yesterday by another instance of one of the Eskimo superstitions. During the excitement attending the discussion over the traces of polar bears, I lay quietly resting against a pack, with my eyes closed. Presently I opened them and said for a joke — "*nannuraluk*" (bears). Immediately they turned and said "Where?" I said "In the country behind the *Kanghirjuarmiut* — they are coming" (*qailektoraluk*). Miluk at once announced that I had seen them as I lay sleeping, and Avrunna asked me if that were so. I left the question unanswered. The sea yesterday was a lovely deep blue — only to the southeast were there traces of ice. A pot of meat was cooked for breakfast, after which we set out northwest[65] again. Three miles or so brought us to the top of a high ridge, from which we sighted two caribou. A drive was organised, and we lay in the 'trenches' half an hour to an hour. One came up close to Tuhayok. He shot it in the leg with his arrow — a flesh wound, which sent it galloping past and away over the plain out of sight. The other broke through the line of *inuhuit* and fled pursued by several dogs, which saw it and broke loose. We were returning to our packs when two polar bears were sighted. *Nannuraluk* (bears)! Ikpuk waved his *atigi* over his head and capered from one foot to another to signal to the others. A mad rush to our packs followed to bring up three or four dogs. We raced towards the lake for which the bears were making and sat down on the opposite side, watching them swim across and ready to shoot and loose the dogs on them as soon as they landed. Unluckily they smelt or saw us — they could not help seeing us, indeed, as there was absolutely no cover — and fled back and over the hills. Ikpuk, Avrunna, Tuhayok, Kehullik, Miluk, and I followed with the dogs as fast as ever we could — through boggy tundra, up and down ridges, and across streams — Ikpuk and Avrunna with one dog soon led and disappeared from sight. About 4 miles away they caught up with the bears, and Ikpuk shot the cub, which was but a few months old. The mother fled, and they pursued her in turn. Avrunna, being younger and more active than Ikpuk, took the rifle. The dog rounded up the bear about 2 miles further on, and he [Avrunna] shot it. Meanwhile, the rest of us following after, sighted the cub lying on the ground, and ignorant that it was dead, proceeded to stalk up behind it. I led, naturally, having the only rifle, and approached within 20 yards before we saw the blood on it — a second 'April Fool' for us. We waited there till Ikpuk and Avrunna returned, when the cub was skinned and cut up. Ikpuk carried the skin — a heavy load with all the fat on it — the dogs the hind legs and some of the fat, and we returned to camp at midnight, very tired and hungry. Higilaq, Kannayuk, and Haugak had pitched our tents, and Higilaq had cooked a little meat, which we ate and gladly turned in. The aftermath of the slaughter of the bears reminded me of the wild pig hunt at Bwaidoga and the natives there.[66] Kehullik shot his arrow into the cub just as the Bwaidogans drove their spears into the dead boar. Pandemonium broke loose — everyone had his own story to tell about it, and everyone spoke at once. Every detail was repeated over and over again. The day was memorable for me in another respect. For the first time for weeks I was free from repeated diarrhoea and my thirst less virulent. I hope it is a happy augury for the future. We wonder now whether Higilaq did not actually see the bears yesterday, though we missed them when we went to look.[67]

Thursday, August 26th

Cloudy weather with a light west wind. A little snow fell but melted almost immediately. Some bear meat was cooked for breakfast and was very palatable, though three-quarters fat. Ikpuk made a tiny bow and arrow to leave beside the bear's head. This is done with bears, both polar and brown, and wolves, which are all fierce animals, in order to appease their spirits. We packed northeast[68] to the place where Avrunna shot the mother. Two caribou were seen close to, and Ikpuk and Avrunna went after them. There was no sheltering ridge close to, so Avrunna held his gun vertically above his head and stooping walked to and fro, then away from them so as to attract their attention and induce them to follow. They did follow a little way and approached Ikpuk, who was lying in cover, but were very suspicious. Ikpuk fired several shots but missed. The two men then followed them over the plain and saw other caribou, but darkness came on and they had to return empty-handed. We are to stay at this place till the skins are dry,[69] then return along the foot of the Colvilles to [Lake] Numichoin. Winter is approaching — the nights are cold, and a little ice formed on small pools by night does not melt by day.

Friday, August 27th

A fine day with a rather chilly east wind. We waited for Kannayuk to cook a pot of bear meat. As she had *oqauyaq* only for fuel it took about 3 hours; willow brush gives twice as much heat. Some caribou were in sight, about 3 miles away, and we all (save Higilaq) went out after them. The drive this time was successful. The four Eskimo men took their places in pits at a little distance from each other, and with rows of *inuhuit* extending a little further along, then up each side. I took up a position some distance along one side to intercept any caribou that escaped them and broke back. Ikpuk shot two, one of which he had to follow a couple of miles afterwards. Avrunna wounded one but not severely, and I shot it for him and killed a fourth; one escaped. The carcases of three of the caribou were to be thrown away, but I propose returning tomorrow to secure one at least. The Eskimos said they had plenty of meat and wanted only the skins. With the skins they take the sinew and back fat and leg bones. The meat they said is too heavy to pack back to [Lake] Numichoin. It is a shame to shoot caribou and then let them lie for the ravens and foxes, and I am sorry I killed my victims. Until meat is required I shall shoot no more. We returned to camp with fair back-loads. Higilaq was cooking bear meat, and I wanted to fry some caribou liver alongside. She was not sure whether it was right to do so, the bear being a sea animal and the caribou a land. She asked Tuhayok, but he didn't know, so I said it would be all right as the bear was a land animal in summer. This satisfied her, and gave me a good meal of fried liver.

Saturday, August 28th

A fine day with a southeast breeze — cold when not moving, but pleasant tramping. We stayed in camp till afternoon cooking and feasting, then I took four of my dogs and brought in the caribou I killed yesterday. Ikpuk, Avrunna, and Miluk went caribou hunting to the north. I let Avrunna take my .22 on condition that he did not throw away the meat. The camp is full of meat and skins. Tomorrow they propose to return to *Kugaluk*. I found three ravens had eaten all the back fat of my caribou and had left the meat untouched. I fried some liver and steak this evening in pounded back fat — it was as good as lard. The dogs are so satiated they can hardly move. I had a recrudescence of violent diarrhoea today, but it seems to have gone off this evening. What provoked it I haven't the least idea.

Sunday, August 29th

Another fine day with east breeze. I could see the mainland quite distinctly through the binoculars, the long coast of low hills extending from the east till it reached a sharp promontory marked by a high rock, then a blank (a dip south?), and again very high land for some distance — southwest of our position here — the [ ][70] Mts., I imagine. There was no sign of Clerk Island.[71] Tuhayok and Kehullik left this morning to return to *Kugaluk* — we leave tomorrow. Avrunna went caribou hunting and secured one. He cached the meat under stones, as I told them if they threw it away I should give them no ammunition. This perturbed them very much. They said they wanted the skins for clothing, but the meat was too heavy to pack. As a matter of fact, I am certain they have enough summer skins for clothing,[72] but probably they intend to trade with others less fortunate. They said they would cache the meat under stones and it would do for dog-food next summer, if not for themselves, at least for other Eskimos. I doubt whether any Eskimos will find it before it is consumed by worms and foxes, but let it pass at that. Our packs tomorrow will be heavy. The rest of us remained in camp, distracting ourselves in various ways — Ikpuk making arrows for Haugaq, the women cooking, sewing, and cleaning skins, and I sewing and writing. My threat re ammunition produced a rather unexpected effect, quite unintended. Marrow bones were showered on me, Ikpuk boiled tea and rice, Miluk looked over my clothes to see if there was any sewing she could do and fried some caribou liver for me. My rice has suffered badly in transport — it was soaked in water in a dog pack[73] and has clotted and lost half its nourishment and flavour. Still it is a great luxury, and a variety from perpetual meat. Fried deer liver is good too, though I have neither salt nor pepper.

Chapter 34. Packing East

Starting east with heavy packs — Comments on shell occurrences — Number of skins to clothe a native — Kugaluk River gorge — Alternating feast and famine — Tanning sealskin for boots — Lakes frozen over — A vessel sighted — Obtaining cached rice, sugar, and pemmican — Caribou pits and old tent rings — Setting fox-traps — Successful caribou hunt — Intestinal ailment again — Some seasonal superstitions — Work prejudices — Caching caribou meat — Caribou drive — A domestic quarrel — Eskimo names for some stars — Storing meat in icy lake water — Skinning a caribou — Eating fox meat — Seal hunting — Caching caribou to take to headquarters — Caching skins at coast

Monday, August 30th, 1915

East wind, bright sunshine, atmosphere rather hazy. Night was cold — nearly 1/4 inch ice on surface of water in pot. We packed south by east for some 5 miles and camped on a hill overlooking a medium-sized lagoon,[1] which is almost divided into two by a long spit from one side and a short one running to meet it from the other; between them is a shallow bar. Our packs were heavy — mine about 60 lbs, the others (except the childrens') heavier still. Some of the dog packs must have weighed 60 lbs. We are crossing a large valley between a north branch of the Colville Hills which comes out on the coast about 10 miles north of *Nauyat* [Naoyat Cliff] and a south branch which follows the coastline at an interval of 2-3 miles roughly speaking. The rock is still dolomite — I saw an exposure today. A medium-sized stream runs out into the sea apparently some 6 or 7 miles north of *Nauyat*. It is very shallow now but must be considerable in spring. Butterflies and mosquitoes and other flying insects have all disappeared since the snowstorm of a week ago. I saw a small brown moth one day that was the only exception. The dogs have grown fat and contented with the abundance of fatty food. We are packing a large quantity of bear fat for fuel and light at [Lake] Numichoin; it is as good as seal blubber. We can see *Qiñmiktorvik* peak south of us, apparently some 8-10 miles away. This is *Hanerak* — the country of the *Haneragmiut*, who have ceased to form a separate entity. Ikpuk and Avrunna saw no deer but went down to the shore and recovered a plank already trimmed by the latter for a sled-runner. It was hewn out of a log which drifted up on the beach at *Nuvuk* in the country of the *Kanghirjuarmiut*, whence Avrunna obtained it in trade. They decided, however, to cut it up for tent poles, as their sleds are in good shape.

Tuesday, August 31st

A cloudy day with a cold fairly strong south wind. Ikpuk, Avrunna, Miluk, and Kannayuk went caribou hunting. I returned to a creek we crossed yesterday and found a few live shell fish in the water — strombi, I think, or possibly volutes.[2] I put four in formaline for Johansen. Yesterday I saw a fish about 1 1/2 inches long in the same creek. Whether it remains in a state of suspended animation frozen in the ice during the winter I don't know, for the creek is so shallow that it must freeze to the bottom. The deepest pool for a mile or so hereabouts in the creek is not more than 4 feet. This was the only fish I saw, though I searched about today. The surface of still water is freezing everywhere. Higilaq cooked deer meat and I boiled a pot of tea. I find that cold water excites my diarrhoea, but tea does not, even when I drink four times as much as I would of cold water. A little rain fell in the afternoon. Nowhere on the land here have I seen the white cockle-like shells — *pinnae olivae?* — which are so common east of the place about 15 miles west of *Tiffiktok*,[3] where the Colvilles send a spur down towards the sea (*Iñnerin*, I think).[4] In the lagoon at that place (camp Aug. 11th), I saw some shell fish but had no opportunity to collect any. I forget what species they were, but fancy they were the same as in the creek here. The exact meaning of this change in the distribution of the shells I don't quite understand, but imagine the country east of *Iñnerin* must have been submerged in more recent times.[5] Higilaq told me today that she gave Wikkiaq and his wife a pot and an *ulo* as the price for adopting their baby child — just before Uñahaq gave birth to another. This Wikkiaq held on to the things but refused to hand over the baby. Kehullik likewise was a victim last winter. The knife I took to him from Kaullu when I visited the *Aqulliakattuñmiut* camp was seized by Tucik, why Kehullik did not know (or would not say) except that Tucik wanted it. Ikpuk was up early this morning and split Avrunna's sled-runner into three or four long poles, using a horn[6] for a wedge and a stone for a mallet.[7] The chips came in useful for fuel, as both willow and heather are scarce here. While Higilaq was cooking she heard a slight noise behind her as of something scratching on a skin. Her first thought was *ugioqtun?* Are there spirits beleaguering us?

Wednesday, September 1st

A little rain fell in the night and during the day, but in the afternoon the wind changed to north and the sky cleared. Ikpuk and party turned up about midnight; they had killed two yearlings, which they carried back to camp. Incidentally they had fished for lake-salmon fry about 1 [to] 1 1/2 inches long, catching them with their hands as they hid under the stones; they ate them raw. We stayed in camp all day, feasting. Miluk, Kannayuk, and Haugaq went off to the lake in the afternoon to catch more fry. Ikpuk tells me that Eskimos from *Umingmuk* (Kent Peninsula) will visit the station this winter. They previously travelled to *Mikumeoq* (Cape Hamilton) when Joe Bernard wintered near there. He believes too that some of the *Kanghirjuarmiut* will come after the sun reappears. I enquired how many skins are required to clothe a man (or woman). It appears two are necessary for the *kulitak* or heavy sealing coat, two for the outer light *atigi* (because it is decorated), one for the inner, two for the trousers and footgear — seven all told. All of these are of summer skins save the *kulitak*, which is of heavy winter skin.

Thursday, September 2nd

We broke camp and travelled south to *Kugaluk*, where we left Hakka [on August 18], a distance of 14 or 15 miles. A strong cold east wind blew all day, and a few drops of rain fell. Ikpuk made a detour to our camp of Aug. 19th *et circa* to bring in the long poles he made from the plank he picked up on the shore. The rest of us made as straight a line as we could for the intervening lakes and reached camp about 8 p.m. very tired and hungry. Kehullik had caught a few *ihun*[8] by jiggling in Kugaluk [River], and Hakka boiled them for our supper — a very scanty meal. No caribou were sighted all day. A few toadstools were noticeable on the surface of the ground. Avrunna complained of sore sinews in the calves of his legs, Ikpuk's old complaint.

Friday, September 3rd

Steady rain in the night and early morning, which cleared away about 10 a.m. This has been a common feature in the weather this summer — it reminds me of the wet monsoon season in Papua in this respect. Avrunna and Kehullik fished and caught several lake trout; so also did Tuhayok. The rest of us stayed in camp. Ikpuk split a heavy iron hoop to make a seal-spear.[9] The women propose to boil down the great quantity of back fat we have and make lard (*puiniq*), which is more portable. I am fairly hardened to unclean cooking now, but received something of a shock the other day when I allowed Higilaq to fry some liver for me in back fat and found her chewing the back fat thoroughly to make it melt better in the pan. I thought of the Samoan girls chewing the *kava*,[10] but they were select maidens, not ugly old hags.

Saturday, September 4th

Rain fell in the night and throughout most of the morning. The wind was west and very strong and cold. Avrunna and Kehullik and Kannayuk went fishing and caught several lake trout. There is a small gorge[11] in the Kugaluk River about 3/4 mile north of our camp, where the stream cuts through a bed of dolomite that runs southeast by northwest. The gorge is about 300 yards long and varies from 50 to 100 yards wide, while the cliffs are some 40 feet high. It is here that the Eskimos fish,[12] jiggling from a ledge half way down the face of the cliff in the deep pool below. Pebbles of pyrites are found in the bed of the river nearby.[13] I found no fossils either in the dolomite itself or in the clay overlying it, but on the steep sloping face of a hill 1/4 mile south that fringes the east bank were a few fragments of the white *pinna*? shell so frequent on the plain further east. We spent half the day in our sleeping bags, for the wind was too cold to do anything outside. Last evening the women pounded a lot of back fat and boiled it down for lard.[14]

Sunday, September 5th

Cloudy day but clear in the evening. Calm but fresh east breeze towards dark. We packed east about 8 miles and camped beside a lake on the north side of Mt. Anovidli,[15] and so about 2 miles north of our old camp at Lake Tahieluk.[16] No caribou sighted and we are running out of food — save back fat, with which we are loaded, and a little dried meat. The Eskimos fished. They worked a bowlder on top of another large bowlder that was submerged on the edge of the lake and speared the young trout as they darted out from under. Kehullik used a small *qaqivuk*, the others lashed a piece of antler on their walking-sticks — the antlers having broad flat heads. The fish varied from 3 inches to 1 foot and were immediately eaten raw.

Monday, September 6th

Blue sky, bright sunshine, bitterly cold boisterous east wind. We packed east over more hilly country for about 7 miles, stopping at one lake to allow the Eskimos to fish. They caught only two lake trout, about 1 foot long. We camped near a rather large lake named *Pisiksitorvik*, where formerly many *Haneragmiut* fell sick and died, Ikpuk says. Actually our camp is on the edge of a smaller lake named *Teriglu*, the name of an Eskimo over east, they say, and the name also of a Port Clarence native.[17] One of the dogs smelt fresh caribou tracks, and Ikpuk, Avrunna, and I went off after them. We travelled some 4 miles, then struck a herd of three does and two fawns. I shot a doe, Ikpuk a fawn, and two we believe are wounded; Ikpuk saw them lying down afterwards, but it was then almost dark, the sun having already set. We took the hind quarters of the fawn back to camp for food, as the Eskimos had only dried meat to eat and I a very little rice, while the dogs have nothing. We shall pick up the rest tomorrow. It was nearly midnight when we reached camp again. I was very hungry and tired, having eaten only a scrap of cold, boiled caribou meat in the morning before starting and about 1 inch of dried meat while packing. Miluk had boiled me some rice (and burnt it); I had taken care to put some in a pot with water and instruct her to boil it for me before we went caribou hunting.

Tuesday, September 7th

Snow fell in the night and the wind turned to west. This morning it was blowing very fresh. We stayed in bed till late, and Higilaq cooked the fawn meat for breakfast. Then we packed some 3 miles southeast towards where we shot the caribou yesterday. Tuhayok and Higilaq went to bring them in, Ikpuk to look for the others, and Avrunna to hunt for more. Tuhayuk returned first, bringing in a doe wounded by Ikpuk yesterday and found dead. A seagull had been busy pecking at the skin. Higilaq brought in the doe and fawn killed yesterday. Ikpuk later brought in most of a fawn wounded yesterday and dispatched by him today. Avrunna saw no caribou. I fried the liver of the doe I shot and put it in a bag for my lunch when we pack.

Wednesday, September 8th

Hard freeze in the night; bright warm sunshine the first part of the morning, then cloudy sky and cold. Wind a light south. Higilaq cooked breakfast while I boiled a few ribs to put in my lunch bag, and Avrunna and some others fished in an adjacent lake. They had half a meal of raw fish. We packed east some 7 miles, with very heavy loads — mine was about 80 lbs, as besides my normal pack of the last few days I carried two green skins.[18] No caribou were sighted and we finally camped about 5 p.m. at the side of the bed of an almost dried-up stream on an old campsite. Here there was a lot of willow, both dry and green, and we had better fires than I have seen since I joined the Eskimos. En route some of the Eskimos fished in a lake without much success.

Thursday, September 9th

A strong cold west wind with occasional snow flurries. Hard freeze in the night. The smaller pools and lagoons are freezing over. We packed east. I boiled a pot of tea before leaving, as wood was plentiful and good. We travelled 8-10 miles, then camped under the lee of a hill. The women are gathering *kanoyak* seeds (like cotton [-grass] seeds) for their lamps at every opportunity. No caribou seen all day, consequently no dog food. Heather [*Dryas*] for fuel tonight. We passed an old camp. A little to one side of it was a tent-site where there were broken tent poles. I picked up too in this place an *ulo*, a caribou 'blood' pin, a needle-case, and the wooden toggle of a woman's belt. Evidently it was a grave, though no bones were visible. I took two of the tent sticks along for fuel, but at the expostulation of the Eskimos[19] dropped them. They were intended to make the dead person a fire to keep her warm, they said. I did not tell them of the other finds, which I have concealed in a tin. Three days, I think, should take us to [Lake] Numichoin.

Friday, September 10th

Pearl's birthday[20] — 25 years old. I wonder how she is celebrating it. We had a heavy fall of snow in the night and snowstorms at intervals during the day. This with the high east wind causing drift made a regular blizzard. Still we packed and travelled 6-7 miles east, having no fresh food. No caribou were sighted through the clouds of snow, and the weather being cold and our packs heavy we camped early — about 4 p.m. As I write I witness a curious Eskimo custom that occurs almost daily. Miluk has to put a patch of sealskin on Avrunna's boots, and the patch must be tanned first. She made water[21] into a little tin pot just outside the tent door, put the patch in it, and set the pot ready for the morning just inside the tent above where her head will be tonight. Out of doors it would freeze. We are not bound for [Lake] Numichoin. I misunderstood Ikpuk the other day. Instead we go to a place near *Oqauyarvik*, where my food cache is. There we stop and hunt caribou, which should be returning in numbers to the coast now that the land is becoming covered with snow, preparatory to crossing the strait. When they have crossed we go to *Numichoin*. Three days fine weather should take us to our destination, Ikpuk says, and that should end our packing, thank heaven. My ink is frozen, and we cannot light a fire for the heather is damp. Neither can we cook, even if there were anything to cook save dried meat or tea. Luckily my stock of fried liver is not quite exhausted.

Saturday, September 11th

A continuation of yesterday's cold stormy weather, but with a north-west wind instead of an east. The temperature is uniformly below freezing, and nearly all the smaller lakes are frozen. We packed east again but had gone little more than 2 miles when Avrunna, who was a good way ahead, saw two caribou rapidly crossing our line of route from the north. He ran forward, intercepted them, and shot both with my .22 — a yearling and a fawn. We camped on the spot, and I went a mile south to *Tiphiktoq* (not *Fiffitoq*, as I wrote it before [Aug. 8] — a hill some 20 miles west of *Oqauyarvik*).[22] There is nothing striking about it — some dolomite exposures, that is all. A good-sized lake separates it from the sea. The sea, as far as I could discern, was mostly open water, with a little ice here and there.

Sunday, September 12th

The wind shifted to west again, and the weather was a repetition of the last 2 or 3 days. Almost all the lakes here are now entirely frozen over. We packed about 9 miles east and camped in an old site on the bank of a large stream, flowing east out of a fair-sized lake called *Tunuñeoq*.[23] On the opposite bank is the cache of Pihhuaq, and his people made in the spring. When we reached Lake Tunuñeoq the Eskimos laid poles and walking sticks under their packs and dragged them over the smooth ice. This place is called *Ipiyudlik*,[24] and is a well known spot. No caribou were sighted all day. The ptarmigan (two were seen) are turning white again, and the only other birds seen latterly are snow buntings[25] and ravens. Higilaq is talking of questioning the *qila* tonight about the scarcity of caribou. She was going to question it the other day about Avrunna's sore calves — she wanted me to spit on my hand and rub them — but the operation never came off, as they were better next day. The lakes in the plain here close to the sea contain a few fish which come up the streams from the sea, the Eskimos say. They are probably salmon then that spawn in the creeks. I saw a young fry about 1 inch long under the ice today. On the edge of Lake Tunuñeoq are piles of dead volute (?) shells. Probably there are live ones in the lake itself, but as it is frozen I cannot ascertain. We stay at this place to intercept the caribou, which should now be commencing their annual migration[26] back along the south coast of Victoria Land eastwards to *Nagjuktok*, whence they cross Coronation Gulf to *Ninitak* and the Coppermine [River].[27] Apparently the sea freezes over in that region earlier than in Dolphin and Union Strait, where many of the caribou cross in spring, probably because the current is less rapid.

Monday, September 13th

A good deal of snow fell in the night, but the wind shifted to south and was much less violent, while today there has been bright sunshine. All stayed in camp save the children and Avrunna; the last mentioned went caribou hunting but had no success. Pihhuaq and his people turned up. They had been north to Lake Añmaloqtoq while we went west. Yesterday he shot a fawn and today a bull caribou. A vessel was seem far out in the offing — it created great excitement. Almost certainly it is the *Alaska*, but it was too far off to see. Possibly though it is the *North Star* returning from Kent Peninsula.[28] How I wished I could signal to it and be taken on board.

Tuesday, September 14th

Higilaq had a seance last night — *qila* with my *atigi* — about the scarcity of caribou. A lot of white people *ugroktun*-ed but not my countrymen. Finally she discovered that the caribou would come presently, but whether few or many she could not learn. I told her yesterday that I was going to *Oqauyarvik*[29] in a day or two to get some of the food I have there. This led to an abrupt development. Ikpuk announced this morning that he, Higilaq, and Haugaq were going to camp just behind *Oqauyarvik* and hunt there. I agreed to go with them and sleep in their tent (an Abercrombie white Burberry single), leaving my small green tent[30] and .22 automatic for Avrunna to use, on condition that whatever caribou I cache he is to help the Eskimos at the station to freight over. Also he is to give Tuhayok two skins to make a heavy coat *kulitak* for the winter. Ikpuk and family and I then packed east. We camped about 5 p.m. beside a fair-sized lake some 3 miles from the cache on the coast.[31] I left them to fix up camp and, taking Telluraq, went off to bring in a little rice, sugar, and pemmican. Two bearded seals kept bobbing their heads up out of the water amidst the ice at the mouth of the large creek that flows into the sea at *Oqauyarvik*. I fired at them — one re-emerged, the other didn't, and I believe I shot it. There was no boat to go out in and see, but it ought to wash ashore. Telluraq was an abominable nuisance. The food I made him pack was very light, but he crawled along at a snails pace and kept sitting down. Darkness came on, and I lost sight of him altogether, and when I returned some distance and called him he did not come. I struck out for where I thought the camp should be, but made another lake about 1/2 mile east. However, I heard Ikpuk shouting to me and found the camp at last — thanks to that. Telluraq turned up a few minutes later — the scoundrel — about 11 p.m. They had boiled a little dried meat and back fat for me and made tea, for which I was very grateful. The weather was mild all day — with a light south breeze that changed in the afternoon to west.

Wednesday, September 15th

Two caribou, doe and fawn, suddenly topped the ridge beside the camp early this morning, saw the tent, and fled. This was extremely annoying. Ikpuk and I tramped north for several hours afterwards and returned without sighting any caribou. The dogs have had nothing to eat almost for 4 days now. Higilaq and Haugaq went down to the cache at *Oqauyarvik* and brought back a few dried fish, a sealskin tent to cook in, and a few other things.[32] They saw no sign of the bearded seal. Willow is very plentiful here; we intend to gather a lot for fuel before the land is covered with snow. A strong west wind blew all day and the temperature was just below freezing. I wore Ikpuk's sealskin *atigi* (*nauk*) and found it very warm. Ikpuk amused himself by setting up near every caribou pit (*tallu*) that we came across a mark — one stone on top of another to indicate supposedly the spot where the archer in the pit shot the caribou. I expect later wanderers here will believe that caribou were actually shot in these spots. *Kayaks* are few in this region. They are used for hunting deer, both in the lakes, and less often in the sea — the kayaker stabbing the deer with a small knife lashed to the end of a pole. They use a double-bladed paddle. I asked Ikpuk today about the old stone house which Stefansson locates about here.[33] He knows of no stone house with a doorway, but says there are here and there stones piled on top of each other (dolomite blocks?), which are the homes of spirits *tornkin*. I think it must have been one of these Stefansson saw, possibly the pillars I noticed on Aug. 1st, which should be close to his line of route. All over the land there are caribou pits (*tallu*)[34] and oval rings of stones or turf about a foot high on which a tent has formerly been set. Then there are piles of stones where meat or skins were once cached, single large bowlders set on end on hill tops to indicate the direction in which dead game lay or something, lines of stones set up for caribou drives, and two stones on end at some interval pointing to a lake where there are fish — all these are familiar signs everywhere. Higilaq last night was burning a small lamp in the tent — a hollow stone about 4 inches [in] diameter, with bear fat (crushed to oil) for fuel and *kanoyak* seeds for wick. Today I had a feast of *kovlut* berries[35] — they are very like our small red currants to look at. The leaves are red too, bright red when not faded, and look lovely where they strew the ground in patches. Many of the berries never reach maturity, many are eaten by the birds — longspurs and ptarmigan. We have seen no ptarmigan latterly, a bad sign to the Eskimos, who say the caribou return in numbers when the ptarmigan come back to the coast. All the lakes are now frozen over and even the rushing streams are frozen in many places. The dried fish Higilaq brought back is full of worms. Sea salmon are found in a few lakes here — they ascend the streams. At this time (or a few weeks later) they are bright red in colour. It is much pleasanter with Ikpuk's family alone than with the crowd; they really are very decent to me as far as they know how and try to make me comfortable, though Higilaq is always asking if I am not going to give her this or that when I return to the station. All our thoughts are now centred on the caribou. Sometimes they return here in great numbers in the fall, but occasionally only a few appear.

Thursday, September 16th

Ikpuk turned out early and went to the look-out knoll to search the landscape for caribou. He sighted one coming eastward and ran back for his rifle and to raise me. I tumbled out of my sleeping bag and we both raced after it. It had gone some distance, however, and we travelled about 2 miles before sighting it again — about 1/2 mile northeast of us. Then when we thought we had overtaken it, it had vanished. The wind was shifting, and apparently it scented us. We thought at first it was lying down and searched all round but could not see it. Then Ikpuk said "I'll go over on to the hill yonder (east) and have a look. You wait here." After a time I saw him waving his *atigi* and interpreted it to mean 'come'. He was about 1/4 mile away, and I could not be sure how he waved it, for waving upwards over the head means 'come' and waving down towards the ground means 'return'. I followed after him, but he travelled fast from one hill top to another, and after going some 3 miles in this way I lost sight of him altogether. He had the binoculars, without which at this time of the year I find it hard to sight caribou unless they are close. Accordingly I returned to camp (actually this was the signal he gave), which I reached about 3 p.m., very tired and hungry, having eaten nothing since the night before. Higilaq boiled the billy and we had cocoa and cold dog pemmican. Ikpuk turned up about 7 p.m. He had overtaken the caribou and shot it (it was a young bull *aññohadluk*),[36] but so far from camp that he brought in only the skin, leg bones, sinew, and (for me) the liver, with enough meat for supper and breakfast. So for supper we had tea and boiled caribou and retired about 9 p.m. very satisfied. In the hurry of tumbling out this morning I could not find one sealskin slipper, so seized one of Ikpuk's. That foot felt very uncomfortable all day, and at night when Higilaq was turning the boot inside out to dry she found the missing slipper in the bottom. It caused great amusement. Ikpuk noted sea salmon under the ice of a lake from which a large stream flows to the sea — it was red, this being spawning time. The Eskimos know of this; they [the salmon] chase each other in pairs round bowlders — mating, Ikpuk told me, and the Eskimos spear them with the *qaqivuk* as they do not bite at the hook. Ikpuk has no *qaqivuk* here. I learned last night the true meaning of the songs called *aqeutaq* (pl[ural - *aqeu*]*tain*).

Figure 175. Head of a fish-spear (*qaqivuk*).

They are incantations, to drive away the malignant spirits that brood around, and have been handed down from one generation to another; they are songs of *inuit pivuliñni* (men of the first times). Ikpuk was singing in bed a song which referred to a story about a woman, a wolf, and a man; he told it to me but I could not follow it. The weather was calm and mild all day, with a light breeze that shifted from south to east and back to south. The temperature was below freezing all the time. I cut a quantity of willow in the evening for fuel later.

Friday, September 17th

The wind changed to west in the night, and the temperature was lower. Ikpuk went to the lookout place — a ridge nearby on the top of which he has made a semicircular stone wall for shelter — but saw no caribou. Higilaq took his place, later I, then Haugaq. I boiled a pot of tea, and we had frozen meat and a little pemmican for breakfast. At intervals during the day one or other of us went to the lookout station to search for caribou, but none showed up. Ikpuk went off for a short time to set four fox-traps for foxes, for Higilaq saw a fox today. He was cleaning his .22 and the cord broke, leaving the cloth wad in the barrel. At present we have no means of extracting it. He was busy part of the day scraping deer skins. A medium strong south wind sprung up in the afternoon. The sea as far as I can discern is free of ice.

Saturday, September 18th

Ikpuk went off to look for caribou, Higilaq and I to *Oqauyarvik* to bring in some clothes, fish spear and pole, hard-bread, and a few other things. Ikpuk saw no traces of caribou and speaks of going east to the coast[37] opposite Cape Krusenstern to intercept them there. I am not keen on going, as we have but a single wall tent and no means of drying our footgear, so it would be very cold and unpleasant. As it is, it is cold enough, and there is still a chance of caribou turning up in numbers. Ikpuk proposes to go fishing (spearing) tomorrow for sea salmon. We saw no *ugyuk*[38] at the coast. In crossing the stream I went first and broke through the ice into the water with one foot — it wet me half way up the thigh. Luckily we were returning and had change of footgear, for the temperature was well below freezing and a strong cold west wind blowing. I fed my dogs on pemmican today and yesterday. How I long to be back in civilization! We saw the skeleton of what I believe to be a white 'whale' (*kilaluvak*) on the coast and a quantity of driftwood — all very small pieces. Incidentally we set three traps for foxes, making stone 'boxes' with the bait at the far end and the set trap at the opening.

Sunday, September 19th

Comparatively calm in the morning, strong west wind at noon, which greatly abated towards night. Ikpuk left early to spear salmon. He took his rifle and my binoculars in case he saw any caribou. The rest of us stayed in camp keeping a lookout for caribou, also Higilaq and Haugaq gathered a little dry willow and *kannoyak* seeds for the lamp. The other day they gathered *munnik*, the tufty-rooted moss, which serves as torch. I scraped half a skin for Higilaq, and she scraped the other half — it is to make her a pair of trousers. The weather was very cold with the high wind. Owing to the absence of caribou Higilaq wants to pack to [Lake] Numichoin and fish; Ikpuk would like to go east to intercept them. I favour Higilaq's plan, as there is a lamp and a skin tent at [Lake] Numichoin. This time of the year is bound to be uncomfortable, living with the Eskimos, worse luck. Ikpuk returned after sunset with seven or eight salmon and four ptarmigan. All the salmon were males, so had no ova. We had a good supper, in consequence, of boiled fish. The wind died away entirely at night.

Monday, September 20th

A north wind stronger around noon than in the morning or evening. Our bad luck followed us again today. Four caribou suddenly showed up and Ikpuk and I, rushing off, took up our positions to intercept them. They were quite close when suddenly Haugaq topped a ridge near by returning from the fox-traps. The caribou fled. I fired a number of shots after them at about 500 yards and wounded one, which later I followed. It caught sight of me and fled north, but slowly. I pursued for some 3 miles, then lost sight of it. I think it must be lying down somewhere and propose to follow with a dog tomorrow. Ikpuk chased after the other three and at close range shot one through the nose and missed another; all alike escaped. The pup, in the meantime, entered the tent and ate almost all the cooked fish. In the hurry Ikpuk and I did not wait to put on our boots but raced off in sealskin slippers — which made our progress over the stones and turfy ground rather painful. One of my slippers is worn right through and my ancle is somewhat sore. Ikpuk fell on his back on the ice and hurt himself a little but not seriously. I had rather a perilous passage across one lake which was only partly frozen. The ice cracked under my feet, developing quite an attack of nerves in me. There were no snowstorms today for a change, but a clear sky. Ikpuk scraped a skin today for a pair of trousers for me.

Tuesday, September 21st

Beautiful sunset last night with brilliant moonlight slightly coloured in the east. The north wind continued today but brought mixed luck. Tucik, Oqalluk, and Tuhayok, with their families, turned up[39] — to eat the caribou we shoot. Nungutok, they reported, had shot five and had cached some of the meat for the station. Pihhuaq shot a bearded seal. Haugaq and I with one dog went north to look for the caribou I wounded yesterday. We sighted three on the way, and I made a wide circuit round a big lake to intercept them. When I reached where they ought to be they had disappeared, nor could I discover any trace of them. However, a little further on I intercepted a doe and fawn and secured both. Returning with heavy loads I saw two caribou to the east but did not stalk them — luckily, for I found on reaching the camp that Ikpuk had gone after them.

A little ice is visible in the strait. The absence of big ice kegs in any numbers should make for an early opening up next summer. Ikpuk returned at dark. He had wounded a doe and expects to secure it tomorrow.

Wednesday, September 22nd

Ikpuk left early to look for the doe. He found it near where he had shot it, with its leg broken, and dispatched it. Also the fawn which accompanied it he shot. I cooked breakfast for myself first, then went with two dogs to bring in the caribou I shot yesterday. My route crossed Ikpuk's and we went together in search of other caribou but saw none. Three foxes had made havoc with my caribou. What was left made just a back-load for me, so the dogs packed Ikpuk's victims. I had fried liver and cocoa for supper, but feel very sick, why I don't know. I was troubled today again with diarrhoea. The weather was fine and clear with a moderate west breeze.

Thursday, September 23rd

I was very sick during the night and troubled also with diarrhoea. All day I have been very seedy and feel even more so this evening, despite a meal of rice and cocoa. Diarrhoea is still troublesome. Kehullik and I went off caribou hunting but saw no game, so returned early, I being very fatigued and hungry, having gone without breakfasting. Ikpuk and the other Eskimos went down to the coast, the former to shoot bearded seals, the latter following in his train. Yesterday when some of the Eskimos went to inspect their caches on the coast they saw about ten bearded seals, some in the water, some on top of the ice. The weather was bright and clear, with warm sunlight but cold west breeze. Our single tent is beginning to frost up badly at night. Ikpuk returned about 8 p.m. having shot two caribou and a small bearded seal.[40] He stalked many other seals, but they either dived before he fired or he missed; three caribou escaped.

Friday, September 24th

Fine day with south breeze. Ikpuk and the others went down to the coast again, while Tucik and I went north for caribou. We again saw none. Ikpuk secured another bearded seal but saw no caribou. Still troubled with diarrhoea both by night and by day. I have discovered another superstition. The marrow bones (after marrow is extracted) must not be thrown to the dogs at this season when the caribou are returning (nor I think in the spring either); it would annoy the dead Eskimos. For the same reason Higilaq would not make a dog harness of deer legs now, but will after the return migration is over. They will not boil seal meat and caribou meat together, but cooked seal meat this morning and caribou meat this evening. At the coast they speared a few bull-heads (*kannayun*[41] — sculpins), which they eat raw. Another delicacy is the frozen meat round leg sinew of caribou. The back fat they like to keep for the winter — when they nibble a little every now and then, especially in the mornings. I rallied Higilaq this evening because she could not make the caribou come despite her being a shaman. She thought it a great joke. There is a little discrimination in the work of the women and men. As a rule the men will not gather fuel, and only cook when the women are busy at something else and they themselves have nothing else to do. Also they consider it beneath their dignity to carry the pots and utensils. Yet they don't mind scraping skins and occasionally do a little sewing.

Saturday, September 25th

A gale from the east. Higilaq turned out at 2 a.m. and by the light of a small blubber lamp made me a pair of trousers, as my old ones were full of holes. The skin was scraped by Ikpuk 2 days ago and the cutting out and sewing took her about 3-4 hours. They are very thick and warm, but want fixing up a little round the knees. After a mixed breakfast of frozen raw, frozen boiled, and hot boiled caribou meat, Ikpuk, Higilaq, and others went down to the coast, partly after other seals, partly to bring in some things there. I stayed in camp to watch for caribou, as Ikpuk thinks there is more chance of their passing here than further north. It was a cold unpleasant day altogether. Snow fell thick towards evening. The Eskimos returned with a few sculpins. Higilaq had tied my fork on the end of her walking stick to stab them, and broke one of the prongs in consequence. No caribou sighted all day.

Sunday, September 26th

The snow changed to rain in the early morning and the white coat with which the land was covered vanished in many places. The wind dropped, then changed to west during the day, and in the evening died away. The weather altogether was cold and clammy. Two flocks of ptarmigan flew past the camp. A sharp lookout was kept for caribou, but none showed up. Ikpuk and I made a small cache of meat for the station, partly from one of my caribou, partly from one of his own. He drew a sketch of salmon pursuing each other round the stones at the edge of a lake where the Eskimos spear them.

Monday, September 27th

Fortune smiled at last. Ikpuk announced that he was going fishing and sealing, and I said I was going north for caribou. However, while breakfast was being cooked a man showed up in the west, and we waited to hear the news. It was Ivyarotailaq, come for cartridges for Avrunna. He said he had seen a large herd coming our way, but having no gun himself had not stalked them. Ikpuk rushed to the lookout place but could see no sign of them. It was then noon, and I went north as proposed, followed by Tucik, while Ikpuk, considering the caribou had passed and were lost, went down to the sea. From the top of a knoll not very far from camp I sighted the caribou just a little east of us, but the west wind was blowing direct from us to them. They winded us and fled. We followed and after a long chase headed them, and I shot seven out of the eight that formed the herd. Three were does and five fawns; a fawn escaped. A doe and fawn I gave Tucik. We skinned them and cached all the meat save two forelegs from one of my caribou and some legs and back fat from Tucik's, and with the skins returned to camp. We did not reach the tents till 11 p.m. Ikpuk had boiled (and boiled very successfully) a pot of rice for me. At the coast he had shot one seal — a foeted seal, not an *ugyuk*, and several ptarmigan. In caching the caribou we had great difficulty in obtaining stones, for though the ground was littered with bowlders they were all frozen in. The weather was fine and clear and the temperature but little below freezing, so that it was not at all cold skinning the caribou, luckily.

Tuesday, September 28th

Again fortune smiled on me. It was a beautifully fine day, mild, with a light east breeze. Ikpuk said he was going sealing again but suggested I should watch in camp for caribou. Being tired from yesterday I had no objection, though it was evident that Ikpuk had little hope of any turning up. About noon while I was cleaning my rifle, a herd of about twenty was sighted close by, and I went after them. I found it impossible to stalk close as there was no cover, but dropped three (a bull, a yearling, and a fawn) at long range and wounded two others. These last, however, escaped, and I only found out they were wounded through Tucik who, having returned to where we shot the deer yesterday to recover a forgotten skin, came upon the fleeing herd on his way back. I waved to Higilaq and Kullaq, who were watching, to come over, and we set to work to skin the beasts. Two were not dead, only unable to rise. I was going to dispatch them with the rifle, but Higilaq remonstrated, on the ground that it would damage the skins and waste ammunition. With the corner of a large flat stone she knocked in their foreheads, killing them almost instantly. While we were skinning, a caribou showed up to the east — one which had separated from the rest of the herd and was straying back. I went after it and shot it. It proved to be a doe. Thus my total today was four out of a herd of perhaps twenty. Ikpuk shot a bearded seal — one of two that he saw on the ice, but it sank, and he returned empty-handed. I am caching the bull and the doe. The yearling I gave to Oqalluk, who has been very decent all along. He has never begged for even a match (though his wife has a little) and has often been helpful. Tucik, on the other hand, both begs constantly, takes all he can, and is ungrateful. Yesterday I found he had cut off the leg bones of one of my caribou and left them out of the cache. He tried to evade my question about it, and I believe intended to appropriate them himself; however, I made him put them back in the cache. Today he wanted me to give him the skin that he brought in, though it was he who forgot it yesterday, and the reward (two caribou, skins and all) that he received yesterday was twice as much as any Eskimo would have given him. To Ukpiq, Oqalluk's son, I gave a fawn skin today, but the majority either I or Ikpuk will keep — I want a sleeping bag and heavy coat, and Higilaq has to make another deerskin tent — the one she made in the spring she said is tearing badly. I gave her a skin today for a sleeping bag for Kannayuk. This caribou hunting is weary work. Yesterday it was 11 p.m. when we returned to camp, today I did not make it till just before 10 p.m.; on both occasions we left about noon. Ikpuk gave some leg bones to the dogs today, and when I told him Higilaq had prevented me from so doing a few days ago on superstitious (*qaligimun*) grounds, he said these leg bones were from caribou shot far off (by myself yesterday, some 5 miles away). Caribou shot close to camp alone were under the ban. So in skinning the caribou today, Higilaq would not cut the ears off at the roots, as usual, but pulled them right out; nor would she allow any of the *nerukkaq* to escape, both for the reason that the dead Eskimos would take offence (*qaligimun*). I cut off the ears of the doe and threw away the stomach, for it was growing dark. I told Higilaq that being a white man it did not matter — there could be no offence.

Wednesday, September 29th

Another fine day. Ikpuk said he was going north to look for caribou and asked if he might take my binoculars. I said "yes," as I did not intend to go off myself, and he was evidently very disappointed at missing the caribou the last two days. At camp no caribou were seen. I brought in the doe I shot last evening — it was only about 1/2 mile away — and spent the rest of the time writing, making a pull-through for my rifle, and sewing a little. There is evidently a little jealousy and ill feeling amongst the Eskimos against Tucik, though not expressed openly to the persons most concerned. Higilaq and Kullaq were talking a great deal between themselves — about my giving him two needles the other day because (as he said) his wife had none to sew with (he lied, they said), about his receiving two whole caribou and then wanting the skin that was forgotten and brought in by him. Higilaq roundly declared he had purposely left it behind in cache (it was certainly he who omitted to bring it, though the skin was mine). Ikpuk and Oqalluk, who accompanied him, did not return till after dark. He had shot three caribou — a doe and two yearlings — but was very dispirited because he had repeatedly missed though the caribou were very close. He saw five separate herds. The deer after being skinned were sunk in the water of a lake under the ice, where they will keep fresh without freezing. Later the ice will be dug out (*turk*-ed),[42] and the deer taken out.

Thursday, September 30th

Higilaq told me last night that of old, people wore foxskin mits (*poallu*), foxskin *kulitak* (outer *atigi*), and foxskin slippers (*ilupekuk*). She remembered seeing three men thus clothed when she was a girl. Early this morning she rose and taking my woollen shirt and flannel (not the deerskin *atigi*), made a *qila* of it, and enquired why Ikpuk had failed yesterday. I was thought to be asleep till the later stage of the performance, and there were Ikpuk and Taqtu [Higilaq] alone (besides me) in the tent. She discovered that it was because she had sewn a lot of deerskin clothing here (*iqaligimi*) and Ikpuk had hammered on a lot of stones (to loosen them for caches, tent ties, etc.) whereat the dead *inuit* were offended. Strange I have never been to blame, and she never questions whether I am, probably because she uses my *atigi's* and 'I' interpret out of them. After breakfast Ikpuk, Oqalluk, Tucik, and I went north caribou hunting. We reached the caches Tucik and I made the other day without seeing any game. The foxes had dislodged the stones of two caches and eaten the hind quarters of three deer — two mine and one Tucik's. I found too — to my great vexation — that Tucik had not removed the intestines of four of my deer, though I told him to do so while I gathered stones for the caches. Consequently they smelt somewhat rank and probably the meat is tainted a little too. I was greatly annoyed with him and told him so. His own two deer likewise contained the bowels, so there could be no question of exchange. However, I arranged that Ikpuk should take my four deer and give me four others when he shot them, as the three he shot and sank in the lake the other day were the same as the rest — contained the entrails. My fifth deer was all right — I had disembowelled it myself. Returning we made a wide circuit to the west and chanced upon a fawn, which I shot. While the Eskimos skinned it I went up on to a neighbouring hill and sighted a herd of eleven caribou to the northwest. We cached the fawn and went after the herd. There was no cover near it, and it was rapidly growing dark. Tucik was sent round behind them to set them in motion by his shouts, and Oqalluk stationed at one side to frighten them off from that direction. Ikpuk and I dodged about behind a low ridge as they appeared to come now here, now there, and finally came within range. In the stampede and fusilade that followed Ikpuk's first shot, he dropped a doe, I two does and a young bull. Oqalluk was presented with a doe entire, Tucik the hindquarters of another. The meat was cached on the spot, save Tucik's portion, and with skins, leg bones, and sinew we set out for camp, stumbling in the dark over the broken tundra and sliding on the ice of the lakes. It was about 11:30 [p.m.] when we made camp, tired and hungry. Higilaq had [a] stomach ache or something equivalent, and everyone was snug in bed.

Friday, October 1st

Yesterday's west wind freshened during today, and the weather was colder. Tucik and Oqalluk went off in the morning and speared a few sculpins. Oqalluk saw a few caribou, but they disappeared. The rest of us stayed in camp. Higilaq scraped the skins of the deer killed yesterday, Ikpuk made a sculpin spear-head, double-pointed, out of a leg bone of a caribou. Towards evening he and I cached the bull and the quarters of the doe I shot 2 days ago. It was unpleasantly cold in the tent, and we were too tired from yesterday to go hunting.

Saturday, October 2nd

A domestic quarrel last night. It originated with Higilaq, who rated Kullaq over some blubber, which she had given to the dogs or something. Kullaq retorted, and the two women exchanged real Billingsgate,[43] ending up with Kullaq subsiding into tears. Ikpuk scolded Higilaq, then retired to the tent, where both he and I turned into our sleeping bags. A little later Higilaq entered, undressed, and snuggled down beside Ikpuk. He let her lie for 2 or 3 minutes then told her to go sleep in the empty tent alongside, which we use for cooking. She rose and took hold of her *atigis* to dress, but Ikpuk pulled them away from her. She was now frightened and dived out through the tent door stark naked, while Ikpuk quietly settled down alone in his bag. It was a bitter cold night, freezing hard, with a strong west wind. I judged it wise to interfere and assert my authority in my own tent to prevent further quarrels in the future, so after about 5 minutes I told Ikpuk to tell her to come in again. He tumbled outside and returned a moment later to say she was not in the tent, but had gone he knew not where. It was certain, however, that she must be in one of the tents, as no person of flesh and blood could stand the temperature out of doors stark naked, so a few minutes later I slipped on some clothes and enquired at the other tents. She was in Tucik's tent. I told her to come back. She said Ikpuk was angry. I told her 'it was all over; let her come back' and re-entering the tent told Ikpuk to let the matter drop — we wanted to sleep. She followed me and we all settled down quietly.[44] She was rather sulky this morning, but everything seems all right tonight. Ikpuk and I went north hunting but saw no caribou. We carried back a doe he shot the other day and sank in the shallow water of a lake under the ice. Tucik and Oqalluk are busy caching things under a pile of stones preparatory to leaving for Lake Numichoin.

Sunday, October 3rd

Yesterday's north breeze continued and the temperature was well below freezing. Oqalluk and Tucik and their families left for Lake Numichoin. Ikpuk and Higilaq carried two bags of deer fat down to *Oqauyarvik* to cache. Ikpuk was going to look for seals while Higilaq speared sculpins. I went north again after caribou but saw none. We are wondering whether any more will pass or whether they have not all migrated east, though the ground is almost free of snow. The Colville Hills show white, and everything is settling down for the winter. Four or five foxes have been caught, but their fur is still a dirty brownish white. Ptarmigan are fairly common now; they have almost completed their change to white. Oqalluk poked his head inside our tent yesterday morning and reported five (undried) slabs of sinew missing that belonged to Higilaq; Mikinneroq, it was said, had stolen them. Nothing was done about it. Ikpuk shot two *ugyuk* on the ice today.

Monday, October 4th

Much colder weather — east breeze. Ikpuk and I went north caribou hunting, saw a herd of thirteen and killed three. Three others were severely wounded, but we could not follow them because it was dark. We sank the three in water and carried the skins back to camp, which we reached about 11 p.m. Ikpuk told me the names of two or three stars on the way back. The Pleiades are *nannorjuit* polar bears, Aldebaran below them is *ugleorjuit* because it follows them; two stars in the Wain (beta ? and a faint star near it) are *tuktujuin* = caribou, Jupiter is *uvloreaq ugjuk* the bearded seal, and Arcturus is *Hivulik* = the leader. Of the caribou shot today the three killed were my victims and go to the station. One of the three wounded also is mine. Falling stars are the stars *'ana'* ( )[45], but bright meteors are 'fire' *igniq*.

Tuesday, October 5th

The tent latterly has been covered with frost on the inside. The east wind blew fairly strong and the weather was very cold. Ikpuk and I went after the caribou wounded yesterday. I froze the tip of my index finger on the trigger yesterday, and the tips of my ears are slightly frostbitten. We found two dead — they had expired close to where they were shot, but in the dark we could not follow them. Both smelt rank, as the stomachs had not been removed and their contents had fermented and tainted all the meat. The Eskimos don't mind that, however, and Ikpuk carried the smaller of the two back to camp. The doe whose leg was broken yesterday we found beside a lake, with its fawn grazing peacefully near. I shot the fawn, and we skinned it and sank it in a lake. The doe I wounded, but it hobbled away and we drove it before us towards camp. About 3/4 mile from camp it tried to break back, and we killed it and sank it also in a lake. A fox had committed some depredation on one of the dead caribou. Higilaq had taken down the cloth tent and laid it round the small sealskin tent, then she put deerskins outside that again. The combination makes a more comfortable tent than the cloth tent, as it is, if anything warmer and does not frost up so badly. Moreover, Higilaq can cook in the open doorway, which at night will be closed with a skin. Ikpuk talks of going east alone to hunt caribou round the Kimilyuak River, while the rest of us return to fish at [Lake] Numichoin. Light east breeze but very chilly. The aurora has been brilliant latterly — wheat ears being prominent in the early evening. The legs of the two caribou which we found dead were frozen. Consequently we were unable to remove the skin and had to carry the legs in the skin to thaw out later. In skinning the bull, Ikpuk slightly modified the usual method. He cut from nose down to midway between the horns, whereas usually two cuts are made down each side of the face to the eyes then to the horns. Consequently he had two holes in the skin to represent the eyes. He said this was regularly done with bulls where the horns are large and meeting almost on the forehead. Ikpuk's axe comes, he says, from Hudson Bay. It was obtained in barter from the *Arkiliniñmiut* Eskimos by a *Neni-*

tagmiut[46] native, from whom again Ikpuk obtained it. Ikpuk has frozen both his wrist knuckles (outer) by crawling on the ice when shooting seals; they are perfectly black.[47] It speaks highly for his endurance.

Wednesday, October 6th

A beautifully calm fine day — the temperature hardly below freezing. Ikpuk went down to *Oqauyarvik* to shoot seals and spear sculpins, and Haugaq accompanied him. Higilaq brought in the doe we sank in a lake near by yesterday, while I stayed in camp and wrote out the headlines of my report on these Eskimos. Ikpuk had no success in the sealing. Higilaq brought in a quantity of *kanoyak* seeds for the lamp.

Thursday, October 7th

Another mild day, almost calm though cloudy. We did not turn out till about 11 a.m. Then we had a breakfast of cold, boiled meat and frozen meat in our sleeping bags, and Ikpuk and I left to take up the three deer we sank in water 2 or 3 days ago and cache them under stones. One we had some difficulty in removing, as its head had frozen to the ice. Ikpuk was troubled with diarrhoea today — my complaint extended to him. Higilaq is busy each day setting out the deerskins to dry (scraping the fat off them first). No caribou seen today. The birds and the flowers have gone (save ravens and ptarmigan) and now the caribou seem to have all gone.

Friday, October 8th

Wind changed to east and blew strong. Snow fell in [the] night, and today it drifted a good deal. The weather was very cold and unpleasant. The dogs have been a nuisance lately, biting or breaking their ropes.[48] Last night Niq broke loose and chewed up three skins. Ikpuk went down to *Oqauyarvik* to get a little wood to make a hot fire in which to soften a bar of iron, I think. Haugaq went to look at the fox-traps. Higilaq and I stayed in camp keeping a watch for caribou, but none appeared. Ikpuk returned early. The day altogether was tedious and uncomfortable, and I was glad when night came and it was time to turn in. A few more days and we should be able to build a snow-hut.

Saturday, October 9th

Ikpuk and I went north to look for caribou but saw none. From behind a low knoll we sighted a fox just below. Ikpuk, lying hidden, made a squeaking noise with his lips like a young bird. The fox came right up to within a half dozen yards then saw Ikpuk and fled. His [Ikpuk's] shots were futile. Two caribou Ikpuk had sunk in a lake were dug out and cached under stones, after which we returned to camp. Higilaq boiled some foxes for supper. They are good eating when fat, but very rank when lean. A light north breeze blew all day, and the temperature was wintry.

Sunday, October 10th

Higilaq turned out about 10 a.m. and saw Avrunna and his people approaching. Towards noon Ikpuk, Avrunna, and their wives went off with packs of skins to cache near the coast. Avrunna had great success in his caribou hunting and has about fifteen cached. They saw great numbers near their camp but they [the caribou] seem to have passed to the north of ours. I am a little vexed with Milukattuk. When we separated a month ago I gave her four blocks of matches to keep her and Itkilleroq supplied until we joined again. She kept the matches herself and refused to give Itkilleroq any. I asked Taqtu [Higilaq] about it and she said "Oh Miluk is an Eskimo and we don't make presents like the whites." It shows that their 'communism' doesn't extend nearly as far as many writers claim. Haugaq is greatly delighted at Kanayuq's arrival; he has been longing for her for some time. I too have missed her, for she is a bright cheerful child, with very winning ways. She is gifted too with more shrewdness than most Eskimos and does not bother one or get in the way. The weather was chilly and clouded, with a few flakes of snow falling all the time. Pihhuaq has shot three bearded seals (Ikpuk has four to his credit). They have been very numerous, poking their heads in great numbers out of the water. I was told today that in the domestic quarrel the other day [October 2] Oqalluk slapped his wife Kullaq and tore her *atigi*. I heard her crying in her tent in the evening.

Monday, October 11th

Ikpuk found three foxes in the traps down at *Oqauyarvik*, which he skinned last night. Two were very fat and were cooked today. A fat fox is good eating but a lean one is very rank. Avrunna and I went north to look for caribou but saw none. We had just returned about 6 p.m. when the children came into camp. They had seen a bull down near the sea, but it had sighted them and fled. Avrunna took Ikpuk's rifle and followed in the direction Qanayuk pointed out it had gone. Ikpuk took up the fawn I shot from the lake in which it was sank and cached it under stones. I have approximately eleven cached now for the station — out of twenty-two I have shot here. There is a little snow on the ground now but not much. The weather was cloudy and cold all day, with a light north wind. The sea is freezing over. The Ukullik Islands seemed today as if they had been lifted up into the sky. Avrunna turned up just after dark; he had not seen the caribou.

Tuesday, October 12th

Ikpuk told me last night that before they had rifles they killed comparatively few caribou in spring, but lived almost entirely on fish. He told me two cures for snow-blindness, one to smoke the eyes over an *oqauyaq* fire, the other, which is mentioned by Hanbury,[49] to tie a louse to a thread and let it scratch the sclerotis.[50] Near the Kimilyuak River, he said, a white fish (white whale) stranded once. They ate it and found it delicious. Near the same place an *ugyuk* once dragged a man under the water; he had speared the animal and had the harpoon line attached to his wrist.[51] He wants to teach me to seal this winter. Snow fell in the night, and the land is white now. A light air breathed from the west all day. Ikpuk and Avrunna went west along the coast to look for caribou. I north. I saw no trace of any and returned to camp about 3 p.m. Further north the land is still free of snow; the fall was only local apparently. The weather was foggy, so it was impossible to see far. Ikpuk likewise saw no trace of caribou. He returned about dark.

Wednesday, October 13th

Ikpuk, Kannayuk, Haugaq, and I packed skins and other things down to the coast to cache. I cached my Ross rifle, having no more use for it now that the caribou season is over. From the coast I took the remnant of the rice and sugar, a can of dog-pemmican, and half the remaining hard-bread. Five cans of pemmican still remain. Ikpuk brought back his sled, dragged by the dogs here over the snow. Probably he will have to carry it further back. We leave tomorrow for Lake Numichoin.[52] The weather was fine and calm, with bright sunshine.

Chapter 35. Return to Bernard Harbour

Heading north to Lake Numichoin — Damaged caches at Lake Numichoin — Eastward to Lake Kigiaktaktok — Starting south to the coast — Down the Oqauyarvik Creek — Camp at foot of Colville Hills — Waterfall — Some superstitions — Winter sewing commences — Gathering cached supplies — Snowhouse cracks — Preparations for crossing to mainland — Reaching Liston Island — Arrival at headquarters — News, strangers, and mail

Thursday, October 14th, 1915

We left for [Lake] Numichoin this morning. Ikpuk's sled has no bone or mud along the bottom, just the bare wood. My dogs and his were harnessed to the sled and he pulled. Higilaq and I also pulled at times. For some distance there was a fairly thick coat of snow, but near the Colville Hills it grew less and the sled had to be dragged over the stony ground. We saw fresh tracks of caribou and a large flock of ptarmigan. At sunset we reached a snow drift which would serve for the walls of a house but was not hard enough for the roof. Ikpuk and Avrunna each made a hut, covering them with the tents. Ikpuk's is so low that the space between my face and the roof is only about 6 inches.[1] Dressing will be a problem in the morning. He made a sort of passage with the sealskin tent for Higilaq to cook, and she has heated pemmican and hard-bread for me and is now boiling caribou meat. The weather was very unpleasant, cold and snowing, and a fairly strong north breeze.

Friday, October 15th

We have made [Lake] Numichoin and sleep in one of three empty [snow-]huts recently vacated by Oqalluk, Tuhayok, Tucik, and their families. Avrunna, his wife, and the children occupy the other. Avrunna and Miluk left before us. He had my .22 but saw only a couple of ptarmigan, one of which he shot. Ikpuk, Kannayuk, and I carried packs to lighten the sled, which dragged very heavily. When we reached the first lake in the Colville Hills, which contains fish, we stopped to lunch on a scrap of frozen deer meat and a hard-bread each (we left after a breakfast consisting of a cup of tea and a hard-bread). Here Ikpuk remained behind to fish. The rest of us went on, but Higilaq, who was supposed to know the way, lost her bearings. Luckily we struck the track of Avrunna and his wife, which set us right. Soon after Ikpuk overtook us; he had speared two fish, one only about 4 inches long. Hurrying on, suddenly we sighted two caribou — a bull and a doe. I had left my rifle at the coast, but Ikpuk had his. He rushed off after them, but they had seen us and in the growing dark he could not follow them. The rest of us made Lake Numichoin at dark, and Ikpuk turned up 2 or 3 minutes later. The stone lamp left here was soon set going, Miluk boiled me a little tea, some pemmican and hard-bread were fried, and we have turned in, feel-

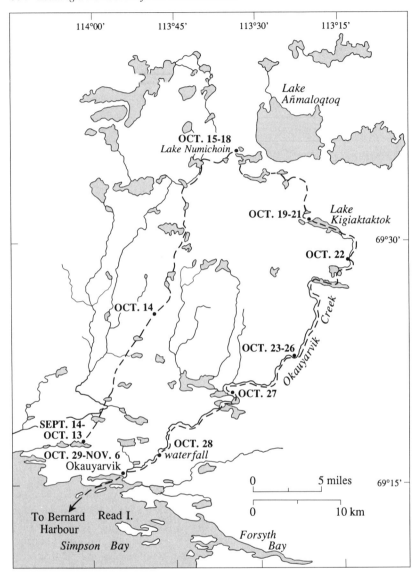

Figure 176. Map showing author's route from the southwest coast of Victoria Island to Lake Numichoin and back, October 14-29, 1915.

ing more comfortable in this snow-hut than for many a day. The weather was the same as yesterday, save that no snow fell and the drift was less. We passed many fresh caribou tracks.

Saturday, October 16th

Our caches were dismantled.[2] The foxes have eaten all the white skins from the bellies of the caribou killed to the north of Lake Añmaloqtoq.[3] Further, they have chewed up some of the lashings of my sled, the toggle to which the traces are attached is missing, the lashings being chewed away, and I cannot find my polar-bear mits and one or two other articles. The weather was milder, only a light breeze blowing. I repaired the lashings and fixed up the harnesses of four dogs. Ikpuk dug up some mould,[4] shredded it in the hut, and mixed it with water into large soft balls. With these he overlaid his sled-runner.[5] Higilaq and Kannayuk went fishing and caught four or five fish, three very large. Avrunna fixed up his sled likewise then went fishing, but secured only one small one. The breeze is freshening this evening. We leave tomorrow for another lake to fish.

Sunday, October 17th

A blizzard from the north. Ikpuk went off fishing without breakfast, to Taqtu's [Higilaq's] great annoyance, and returned about 4 p.m. with half a dozen small lake trout. The rest of us stayed in camp. It was very cold in the hut — water froze in the pot — and most unpleasant. Higilaq asked me suddenly whether Ukpik and Nerialaq (the latter her first husband), both dead, were not living among the *Wallirnirmiut*, i.e., Eskimos to the west.[6] Ekallukpuk, the Pallik[7] River Eskimo, who according to Stefansson had seen Richardson and Rae in 1852,[8] was living there, she said. I read [*The*] *Odyssey* 23[9] — it is a pleasure to have a little literature again.

Monday, October 18th

Temperture -4° F at 4 p.m. and a moderate north breeze, making the weather feel very cold. Avrunna took my sled and went to *Kauwaktok*[10] to bring back some dried fish cached there in the summer. The children and Miluk went fishing but had little success. The rest of us stayed in camp. Ikpuk attached a horn end-piece to the handle of my snow-knife to lengthen it so as to allow of its being gripped by both hands. Our hut is cold, he says, because it is built on a sloping bank, and the passage opening is lower than the house itself. He told me that long ago they had only horn knives to build their houses, knives like the *haviuyak* of the present day, which is only used for *anyu* (i.e., the snow for cooking).[11] Then they made knives of copper, such as the one he now uses on land, where the blade may encounter stones. Last of all they obtained knives from the whites.

Tuesday, October 19th

We were up at the first streak of dawn to load the sleds. I warmed a little pemmican for breakfast and then had two cups of soup. Our course was approximately east[12] over lake after lake. At one we stopped to fish, and Ikpuk caught one and Higilaq one. Avrunna and his wife went over to another lake to fish, so when Ikpuk's family started off again, Kannayuk and I took over Avrunna's sled and Haugaq superintended mine. We came to a large lake, *Kigiaktaktok*,[13] after going about 5 miles, and here found the three families which were with us in the summer.[14] Ikpuk built a snowhouse and I put a wall round the outside. Meanwhile Higilaq and Kannayuk fished, and Higilaq caught two. I fished afterwards and caught one. In the evening Tucik made me a present of three fish — one a fine specimen weighing a good 10 lbs. Kehullik promised a basket (*uñedlaq*) of dried fish if I gave him a knife, as he has none to build a snowhouse. The foxes ate the sinew lines of several fish lines that were cached at [Lake] Numichoin. Luckily for the Eskimos I was able to supply fishhooks and three lines.[15] Many caribou tracks have been visible about here, the Eskimos say, so tomorrow Avrunna is going hunting with my .22. It appears that he understood when I lent him the .22 and ammunition at *Epiudlik* [*Epiullik*] in the fall that some of the caribou he killed were to go to the station, and Ikpuk understood the same. As he killed and cached more than he needs I am accepting their interpretation, which was after all only a fair arrangement, and shall take a few from him — one quarter or one third. The settlement here is exactly similar to those made on sea-ice.[16] The weather was foggy all day — a little snow fell, at 6 p.m. the temperature was +4° F. Latterly there have been brilliant auroras.

Wednesday, October 20th

Foggy in the morning, clearing later to bright sunshine. The Eskimos went fishing, I stayed in camp. Higilaq caught four, Ikpuk, Kehullik, Kannayuk each one, Miluk none, Oqaq three, Tucik four — the others I don't know about, but their success was not very great. Tuhayok went to bring back the dried fish he cached near here in the summer and found the foxes had eaten them. Consequently Kehullik paid for his knife with frozen instead of dried fish. Tomorrow Ikpuk with my sled proposes to bring in his dried fish.

Thursday, October 21st

Ikpuk went to bring back his dried fish.[17] He and Higilaq had a discussion about it last night. At first she said she and Kehullik would go, then she wanted Ikpuk and I. I declined, and Ikpuk said he would go and she too. This vexed her, and she was peevish during the evening — sat down and began to pick *kannoyak* seeds, saying nothing but looking as though she might burst into tears at any moment. This morning both got ready to leave, but at the last moment Ikpuk exempted Higilaq, so she and Kannayuk have gone fishing. This Lake Kigiaktaktok has proven a disappointment, so all the Eskimos have gone further afield today [to fish]. The weather was foggy and a little snow fell. Haugak and Ukpik amused themselves by building a small snow-hut — early training for future work. Everyone had good luck fishing today — Ikpuk, who returned at dusk caught most — about a dozen.

Figure 177. Tucik re-icing his sled runner while travelling down Okauyarvik Creek, southwestern Victoria Island, October 22, 1915. (Photo by D. Jenness, CMC Photo No. 36987.)

Friday, October 22nd

We left for *Oqauyarvik* and the coast this morning in foggy weather and a mild east breeze. Travelling southeast to the end of Lake Kigiak-taktok, we entered the stream which flows into the sea at *Oqauyarvik*, this lake being its source. Consequently the stream must be (including its windings ?) about 25 miles long. The trail was good — slightly downhill and often almost glare ice. At one place we rested, and Ikpuk and Higilaq crossed a ridge to fish in an adjacent lake. Tucik and Oqaq re-iced their sled runners, tipping the sleds and resting each runner in turn on a couple of stones.[18] After a time we went on and had proceeded about a mile when Ikpuk appeared behind us running. He had seen four caribou — he said there were a great many (*amisuralgaluit*). He and Avrunna went after them while the rest of us made camp. Kehullik built a snowhouse for Ikpuk (and me), with the assistance and advice of some of the others, while I cut snow-blocks and shoved them inside for him. Ikpuk and Avrunna turned up just after dark — two caribou, doe and fawn, fell to Ikpuk, one (a young bull) to Avrunna, and one (also a young bull) escaped. In the fishing Ikpuk caught five, Higilaq one, Avrunna five, and Kehullik three or four, I don't quite know which.

Saturday, October 23rd

Weather similar to yesterday — foggy with light east breeze, rather cold. We migrated some 8 or 9 miles down the Oqauyarvik River. In one place it tumbles (in summer) down a rocky cascade where a low cliff of broken dolomite blocks lines the north edge of a lake. Here we had some trouble in finding a passage. My sled worked through the bowlders fairly easily — Telluraq for once proving an excellent leader.[19] The other sleds stuck occasionally despite 1/4 hour spent in breaking away some of the rocks. We camped on the south edge of a small lake just beyond. There was not snow enough for houses, so all erected tents and made snow passages. A caribou (young bull) was sighted en route, and Avrunna and Ikpuk went after it, but it saw the latter and fled east, passing so close to the sleds as to set the dogs in a turmoil. We are out of the Colville [Hills] now and not far from *Oqauyarvik*. Tomorrow the Eskimos are going to fish in an adjacent lake. Ikpuk emptied the stomach of only one of his caribou yesterday, though he knows the meat becomes tainted and I do not care for it. He did it purposely for tonight he emptied it and threw the contents away. I am wondering if he feared I might claim the animal in exchange for one of mine on the coast from which the intestines were not removed, according to the arrangement he made with me. However, as he has not exchanged any (save one) I shall retain those on the coast, not hand them over to him as proposed. One or two rabbits were seen among the dolomite bowlders, and Avrunna shot one. In working through the cascade a few willow twigs were placed over two or three sharp-edged stones which could not be dislodged to prevent them scraping the ice off the sled runners.

Sunday, October 24th

A fine, bright, sunny day, cold, with hardly a breath of air. The Eskimos went fishing, and Avrunna and Ikpuk hunting as well. I stayed in camp, fixing up my sled and writing up some notes on 'skins and their treatment' among these Eskimos.[20] Avrunna shot two caribou, a yearling and a doe, Ikpuk none. The fishers had fairly good luck everyone, so are in the best of spirits save Ikpuk. We are just at the foot of the Colvilles, as I found by going up on top of a knoll. Ikpuk shot a ptarmigan close to camp.

Monday, October 25th

Another fine day, foggy in the morning, but the fog was raised by a light north breeze. The other families left for further down the creek, but as Ikpuk wished to hunt we stayed behind and Higilaq and I fished — I caught six, Higilaq four. I put four aside for the station, letting Higilaq take out the stomachs which the Eskimos like to eat. There were two sun dogs (parhelia) on either side of the sun today; the other day three. I have never seen the one below the sun — perhaps because when the other three have been visible the sun has been too low for the fourth to show up. Ikpuk's dogs are becoming a nuisance. They are constantly jumping on one or other of mine, two or three of them at a time. My dogs foolishly fight each other and don't defend themselves as a pack, though Panaski, the warrior amongst them, sometimes goes to the help of Niq or Mafa. Telluraq curiously enough the other dogs do not attempt to attack, though he is no fighter.[21] Ikpuk turned up after dark. He shot a bull caribou, one out of a large herd that he saw.

Tuesday, October 26th

Another fine calm day, cold. We did not migrate as Ikpuk had to bring in the caribou he shot yesterday — it was too heavy to pack in one load by himself. He returned early and reported that he had seen four caribou, but they had been alarmed by the dogs before he could stalk close. Haugaq and I stayed in camp while Higilaq and Kannayuk fished. There was a big dog-fight at dawn this morning. I rushed out with a stick, stark naked, kicking down the snow door, and stopped it before any dog was seriously hurt. Ikpuk told me this evening that one of his bags of dried fish is for me to take to the station and offered me the bull caribou he shot yesterday. The latter I declined, telling him that I had enough caribou cached. He wants ammunition in the winter, enough for two or more summers in case no other white men come. I have promised him that he shall have it, and other things as well. Higilaq and Kannayuk did not return till long after dark. They had caught only five fish, Kannayuk three and Higilaq two.

Wednesday, October 27th

We set out at daylight and camped at dark but only travelled about 12 miles. The lashing of Ikpuk's sled toggle broke twice and had to be repaired, and we stopped several times to try for water. We were lucky to strike water at camp-time — for the creek is frozen to the bottom in all but a few places. No game of any description was seen. The weather was foggy and occasionally there were flickers of snow. Stones in the bed of the creek were troublesome — they broke away a little mud from Ikpuk's sled — a rather serious affair. My sled capsized once while the children were steering it, I meantime hauling on Ikpuk's sled. Luckily the only damage was a broken bolt, which I have repaired.

Thursday, October 28th

Again we moved on. Mafa in the night chewed up his harness and line. Higilaq made three slits in a broad strip of sealskin thus:

Figure 178. Higilaq's sealskin 'cape'.

the middle one for the head, a most ingenious contrivance. About 8 miles from camp we reached a lake where Avrunna and Oqalluk and their families were camped[22]. The men were caribou-hunting — Avrunna had shot five since leaving us. We had a meal of frozen deer meat then continued for 4 miles or so, when we reached a waterfall about 10 feet high. At the foot of this we camped. We had partly unloaded the sleds when

Figure 179. Copper Eskimos migrating southward to the sea along Okauyarvik Creek, southwestern Victoria Island, October 29, 1915. Author's sled on extreme right. (Photo by D. Jenness, CMC Photo No. 37057.)

Tucik and Tuhayok appeared. The former's sled was cached just below the falls, and their camp but a short distance below. The waterfall is very picturesque, though the leap is but slight and the volume of water small. It is crescent shaped, the main flow of the stream falling on the western side, but about one-third falls on the east. I intend to photograph it in the morning if the conditions are favourable — it was dusk when we reached here today — too late to attempt a photo. The weather was beautifully fine and bright with but the faintest breath of north wind.

Friday, October 29th

We were astir before light, but early as we were Avrunna and Oqalluk and their families reached us before we had started to load up. It was too dark to photo the falls, so I shall return one day and do that. We overtook Tuhayok and Tucik just finishing loading up — about a mile downstream. Here there was a water hole, and Ikpuk, Avrunna, and Oqalluk took advantage of it to re-ice their sleds. A couple of buckets of water were poured out on the ice and the sleds run through it. Further on Avrunna's sled capsized and everyone helped to lift it again. We reached the mouth of the creek about noon. The others set up their tents — Ikpuk made a snowhouse, I cutting blocks outside and passing them in to him. The weather was foggy, and the light west wind of the morning had freshened considerably by night — I fancy a blizzard is impending. When we overtook Tuhayok and Tucik today, Kannayuk took advantage of the halt to remove her footgear. Her sealskin shoes, *mutkolik* and *il-ipikuk*, were all frozen solid, and the *alektik* — the innermost — were frozen at the toes. Higilaq told me last night that the dead sometimes go to the moon. The mountains of the moon are a man Ikpuk had heard — according to Higilaq they are the moon's dogs. She told me that the *ni-glivik* (brant?)[23] was bathing once and a man stole her clothes, wishing to marry her. Cat's cradles must not be played when the sun is above the

Figure 180. Copper Eskimos righting Avrunna's overturned sled, just south of a 10-foot waterfall about 4 miles above the mouth of Okauyarvik Creek, southwestern Victoria Island, October 29, 1915. Author's sled is on the left. (Photo by D. Jenness, CMC Photo No. 37053.)

horizon during the day, because long ago it pinched (?) a man all over who was making them.[24] In Ikpuk's house I have a medium-sized lamp on my side — to dry my clothes — we have blubber too in abundance, and now I have kerosene for the primus.

Saturday, October 30th

A fine day, with only a few flakes of falling snow. Ikpuk and others went over to the island, *Kigiaktanneuk*,[25] to examine their blubber pokes. A fox had eaten some of Ikpuk's, and Tucik's had leaked. He shot a rabbit and a fox there. Avrunna went to look for caribou and to set fox-traps — he saw no caribou. I recovered my [Ross] rifle, which was cached about a mile away — the barrel I found was beginning to rust — I am out of 3-in-1 oil, so use caribou marrow. I found three knives still left in my trunk, so traded two for fish and gave Kannayuk the other — a present which set her aglow with pleasure. During the night a dog — or several — chewed one of my pemmican cans and ate some of the contents. The women have started their winter sewing — preparatory to going out on the ice to seal.[26] Taqtu chipped out a rectangular block of ice with the *turq* for a window[27] — so that she might have light to sew by.

Sunday, October 31st

The light east wind of the morning freshened during the day till it caused a considerable drift. This with a little falling snow obscured the atmosphere considerably. Ikpuk and I brought in three of the caribou we had cached to the eastward for the station. We saw no game of any description. The caribou were frozen together and we had some difficulty in separating them by means of stone wedges and mallets. Nuñutoq reported two small lanes of water in the ice out to sea — it is a little too early to attempt to cross yet, for these will be lanes of water round the Ukullik Islands. Ikpuk tells me that the bay here at *Oqauyarvik* and the western entrance are both deep so it should make a good anchorage. Roughly its shape is thus:

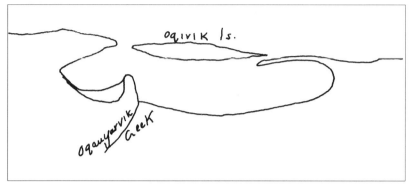

Figure 181. Author's sketch map of the bay at *Oqauyarvik*.

A mile or two south of Oqivik Island is Kigiaktanneuk [Read] Island. There was a domestic quarrel this morning.[28] Kannayuk was vexed at something Higilaq told her to do and sulked in a corner. Kehullik jeered at her behind her back and she hit back and caught him in the eye. Then he had a cry, and Higilaq poked Kannayuk two or three times with the *anautuk* or snow-beater, and she had a cry too. They soon made it up and tonight Kannayuk is going to sleep with Kehullik instead of with us as usual.

Monday, November 1st

A dog — we think Mafa — chewed open a pemmican can and ate more than half the contents. I cached the remaining four under heavy stones and intend to leave them here for my projected spring journey to Prince Albert Sound.[29] Ikpuk and I then brought in a bearded seal he cached near here in the fall, and he cut up the meat, reserving some for dog-feed, and the rest for our own eating; a portion was sent to each house. Kannayuk saw two caribou on the ice not far from camp, but they were alarmed by the dogs and fled far away. Higilaq made me a pair of sealskin shoes the day before yesterday and is beginning my heavy winter coat. Ikpuk is busy making a seal harpoon shank out of a broad piece of iron obtained from [Capt.] Joe Bernard. He is splitting it in two with stone anvil and hammer and cold chisel. Our house from the first day it was set up has cracked repeatedly each night — with explosions like a gun fired near by. The ice along the edge of the creek is cracked and the snow covering and our snowhouse crack with it. Every morning the cracks have to be filled up and again at night. It proves clearly the strength and cohesion of the house that, though cracked from one side to the other, it does not collapse.

Figure 182. Ice-covered 10-foot waterfall about 4 miles above mouth of Oqauyarvik Creek, southwestern Victoria Island, November 3, 1915. (Photo by D. Jenness, CMC Photo No. 38528.)

Tuesday, November 2nd

Foggy in the morning, but bright warm sunshine in the afternoon — practically no breeze. Tuhayok and I with my sled brought in four caribou cached by me in the fall some 6 or 7 miles back. We saw no caribou, but fresh tracks of two. Ikpuk brought in the caribou I had cached at our fall hunting camp near by. Two that I brought in go to Ikpuk in exchange for one of his not yet brought in — mine containing the intestines. I have now seven caribou here for the station and five still to come in. Ikpuk saw three caribou, but his dogs barked and startled them when close to. Of the other Eskimos, Avrunna and Oqalluk have now built snowhouses to live in instead of their tents.

Wednesday, November 3rd

Ikpuk re-mudded his sled and with my sled brought in a load of cached deerskins. I went up to Oqauyarvik Falls (about 4 miles) to photo it[30] and look round for caribou. Of the latter I saw none. Ikpuk employs his spare moments in scraping deerskins — I do the same at times. Tuhayok built a snowhouse today. The weather was at times foggy, at times clear, with a very light north air.

Thursday, November 4th

Our house cracked more than ever in the night, not only right across the roof but round the side. Consequently we made a new one, the passage joining on to that of Tuhayok's. Building and moving occupied us the whole day. Tuhayok helped in the building. Tucik at the same time built a house for himself alongside. Avrunna and Kannayuk have gone to *Epiudlik* [*Epiullik*] to bring in the caribou he cached there. I told him yesterday I would take four of them. He has fourteen cached, all told. The children latterly have been spearing sculpins through the ice. Kannayuk yesterday speared one. It was a fine day with bright sunshine, save when a bank of fog concealed the sun — it is now very low at noon and the daylight hours are growing few. Yesterday I took a sample of Avrunna's hair for microscopic examination,[31] and the temperatures of both him and his wife.

Friday, November 5th

Ikpuk and I went to bring in four of my caribou cached some 7 miles back. From a knoll beside the cache he saw some caribou far off through my binoculars, so he went after them, leaving me to return alone. I had a little trouble in one or two places, for the sled was heavy and there were several inclines; once I had to drop two caribou, run the sled up a bank, and reload again. Incidentally I lost a mitten — it dropped from the sled. Higilaq has nearly finished my heavy *atigi* — she began the sewing today. The weather was fine with a light north breeze. Ikpuk turned up about 6 p.m. There was but one caribou — a small fawn — which he shot and carried back entire.

Saturday, November 6th

A semi-blizzard from the north — it was not cold enough and the wind hardly strong enough to call it a blizzard. I prepared to leave for the station tomorrow if it is fine. From Ikpuk I obtained three fine bed-skins and five slabs of sinew — all that I am demanding of the caribou I have secured, save the meat cached for the station. Higilaq, however, is to make me a set of new clothes this winter. I gave Ikpuk the remainder of the .44 ammunition — several boxes — and a set of reloading tools, with a full bar of lead — also a large file and a pair of large scissors. Avrunna returned today with his caribou, and Pihhuaq and his family accompanied him — so that our little settlement of six families is now complete.[32] As our white belly skins were eaten by foxes in the summer and our summer fawn skins are few, some also being devoured, I have arranged with Pihhuaq's people to have two yearling (*inirnerin*)[33] skins and two white bellies for my trousers and to send him by Ikpuk a box of primers.

Sunday, November 7th

Ikpuk and I got away before daylight.[34] The ice was very smooth, but the snow soft, as no wind had blown to harden it. The sled in consequence dragged heavily, and we cached two boxes on an island about 3 miles out.[35] Just beyond was a crack not completely frozen over, but we managed to cross without difficulty. Thence on we made good progress and after travelling some 25 miles reached the west side of *Iluvik*[36] and built a snow-hut just at sunset. There was quite a little driftwood on this end of the island. The primus for once worked well, and we had a snug camp for the night.

Monday, November 8th

We left soon after 8 a.m. in perfect weather. The ice was rather broken all the way across, in contrast to its smoothness on the north side of the islands. We reached the station just after noon. There were tracks of several caribou on the ice only 2 or 3 days old. At the station the only member of the staff was Johansen, who told me the news — Stefansson landed at Norway Island from his ice trip; Wilkins came to Bernard Harbour in the spring; the *Ruby* reached Herschel Island with stores for us, which were freighted in here by the *El Sueno*; the *Polar Bear* and *El Sueno* going north to join V. Stefansson's base at Cape Kellett; Stefansson discovered new land north of Prince Patrick Island, to be explored this winter; the survivors of the *Karluk*; the European war. I had a big mail — letter from McKinlay amongst others, and one from V. Stefansson saying that if I liked I could join their base at Cape Kellett and work among the Eskimos from there. The Dr. [Anderson] and the [Geological] Survey men had gone east to Cape Bathurst in the summer and had failed to return. Sweeney, his Eskimo wife, and Mike left 4 days ago to look for them, going via the south coast of Victoria Land. At the station were a number of Mackenzie River Eskimos, including Palaiyak's sister[37] (Palaiyak has joined Stefansson, as has Wilkins also in the *North Star*), Klengenberg's half-caste boy Patsy,[38] a new white engineer for the *Alaska* (Blue having died in the winter of scurvy), a white missionary named Girling (whose schooner was blown ashore at Clifton Point in the summer), and a RNWMP Corporal Bruce (come to enquire into the alleged disappearance of two French missionaries from Great Bear Lake). There are now two large rooms at the station — the old kitchen being entirely rebuilt and the place seems very comfortable. I spent most of the time hearing the news and reading my mail.

Part 4

Completing the Odyssey

November 9, 1915 – August 15, 1916

Chapter 36. Quiet Time Around Bernard Harbour

Arrival of Dr. Anderson, Chipman, Cox, and O'Neill — Departure of Girling — Gathering of Eskimos — Trading for skins and ethnological specimens — Starting work on Eskimo religion and folk-lore — Time for cat's cradles — To the Ukullik Islands — Eskimo marital problems — Return to the station — Sharing Christmas with the Eskimos — Preparation of report for government — Translating songs on phonograph records

Tuesday, November 9th, 1915

The Dr. [Anderson] and the [Geological] Survey men [Chipman, Cox, and O'Neill] turned up this afternoon. They had been frozen in at Epworth Bay but had plenty of food — white [man's] food — deer meat and fish. The launch and canoe, which they had there, they left and sledded west to the station as soon as the ice was solid enough. The day passed quietly, everyone looking at their mail or papers.[1] There is a big crowd here, and some of the local Eskimos are camped near by. The weather was again beautifully fine and bright, with only a light breeze.

Wednesday, November 10th

A quiet day in camp, reading letters and papers. O'Neill received word that his mother had died, also of his promotion in the [Geological] Survey. A great deal of food was brought in by the *Alaska* and *El Sueno*. Stefansson bought the *Polar Bear* and bought or chartered the *El Sueno*, giving the *North Star* as part payment. In a letter to me he stated that at their camp at Cape Kellett they have . . . Eskimo . . . dogs.[2] Fine weather. Deer seen close to camp but none killed.

Thursday, November 11th

Ikpuk with my sled and dogs returned to *Oqauyarvik* today. Eikie and a new Eskimo named Ambrose[3] started out with him but struck deer, and Ambrose shot three, so they returned. We were busy reading papers and letters. Girling, who seemed a very decent broad-minded young fellow, intends to set out tomorrow for his camp at Clifton Point.

Friday, November 12th

Eikie and Ambrose left for *Oqauyarvik* and Girling for Clifton Point. The latter has 3 years to put in among these Eskimos. He proposes to return here in January and visit the Eskimos at the Ukullik Islands with me. Caribou were again sighted today, but were scared away by the Eskimos encamped at the fishing lake to the south.

Saturday, November 13th

Quiet day in camp. More caribou sighted but none secured. The neighbouring Eskimos secured two, we hear.

Sunday, November 14th

Cox secured three caribou, others who were out none. Fine weather but cold east wind. Our papers and letters still fill up our time.

Monday, November 15th

A large number of Eskimos turned up today, and more are coming. They hunted round the Pallik [Rae] River in summer. Uloksak is amongst them. In the spring he took Qiqpuk's wife Hakungak, so now he has three.[4] We are keeping them out of the inner room — our room — but let them enter the kitchen except at mealtimes. The doctor has four brown-bear skins and skulls, bought from the Eskimos to the eastward. Cockney went out this morning and shot seven caribou out of a herd of eight. Cox in the opposite direction secured three, and Chipman, Corporal Bruce, and the Eskimo Maffa, all shooting at once, secured one. The weather was fine, temperature about -17°, with a rather chilly northwest breeze.

Tuesday, November 16th – Thursday, November 25th

Quiet days in camp. Sweeney and his Eskimo wife Añayu Annarihopopiak, and Mike turned up on the 21st. They had been as far as Tree River, where they met some Eskimos who told them that the Dr. and his party had returned to the station.[5] The Eskimos have been coming in two's and three's and four's till now there must be between 100 and 150 people here, camped on the edge of the water below the station. I have traded a good deal with them for skins and ethnological specimens. The rest of the time has been spent in writing up notes, taking phonographic records, measuring natives, and taking fingerprints (or rather Corporal Bruce took them for me), developing photos etc. The topographers let loose two small balloons today, sent up by the Meteorological Office for testing the currents in the upper air. They tried to follow them through the telescope but failed, and the balloons soon disappeared from sight in the fog. Today for the first time for weeks the weather was very foggy; hitherto we had bright and generally calm weather. The Eskimos have stolen a few things around the camp, but not so much as they might have.

Thursday, November 25th – Tuesday, December 14th

Quiet days in camp. The crowd of Eskimos in small parties crossed over to the Ukullik Islands to seal. The topographers sent up two or three balloons successfully. The Dr. is preparing for his trip to [Great] Bear Lake after the sun comes back, with Corporal Bruce. For a week we took tidal measurements in a snow-hut beside the island at the entrance of the harbour.[6] Continuous readings were taken every half hour and even of-tener, the men taking watches. Being very busy with my own work I was left out of the schedule and had only one watch — 12 p.m. - 9 a.m. It afforded some amusement, as both the Dr. and O'Neill on two separate occasions failed to find the hut in the darkness. A search party found the Dr. and guided him; O'Neill returned to the station and was guided across by Cox and myself. A small polar bear was shot by Adam — one of our Eskimos — off Chantry Island. [On] December 13th Paucina, Mr. Girling's Eskimo, turned up with a letter from the latter asking us to purchase him three dogs, as three of his had died. I started work on religion and folklore, with Higilaq, Milukattuk, and Avrunna, but they were very loth to impart anything with other people around. Cat's cradles are now in season, and I am giving much time to them.

Wednesday, December 15th

Corporal Bruce, Paucina, Patsy, and I crossed over to the Ukullik Islands today and turned in to Ikpuk's hut, as it was too dark to set up the tent and rustle wood. The primus refused to burn, so we ate cold pemmican, raisins, and hard-bread, and boiled tea and pemmican over the blubber lamp. The weather was cold, -24° F, with an 18-mile wind from the west when we left, though it decreased during the day. Paucina brought his own sled and team of three dogs, and so was able to take part of our load, which was very heavy. Owing to the weight indeed I was unable to bring the phonograph. Jennie (Kannayuk) has a bad cold. A dance was held in the evening, and Utugaum[7] gave a shamanistic performance. People entering the dance-house or leaving it at such a time do so very quietly.

Thursday, December 16th

A fine day most of which we spent in setting up a snow-hut with the tent erected inside. Then the corporal cooked. We had a good quiet meal and sent over a good meal to Ikpuk's. There was a dance in the dance-house in the evening for a short time, after which the young folks played 'wolf'. I am sleeping with Ikpuk tonight, the other three in the tent. Avrunna opened a cache of meat, which he had made in the ice.

Friday, December 17th

I bought the third of the dogs for Mr. Girling this morning, and Paucina got away about 11 a.m. One of his dogs — bought from Ayalligaq — had followed its master sealing. Paucina reckoned on returning from the station for it. I did a little trading in the houses and made presents of calico to Jennie and Haugaq. Patsy brought in a load of wood; the Corporal cooked in the tent, where it was warm and comfortable. A dance and seance was held in the evening. I missed the seance, being occupied with Patsy's lesson,[8] but the Corporal was present. Maffa and the other *Kogluktualuk* natives arrived from the station today. The weather was fine but cold.

Saturday, December 18th

I am continuing to sleep with Ikpuk, though there is room in the tent now that Paucina has gone; it pleases the old man. Patsy wandered round the islands, prospecting for future sources of wood. The Corporal remained most of the day in the tent cooking and reclining on the warm bedding. Uloksak exchanged his two elder wives Koptana and Kukilukkak for Milukattuk the night before last.[9] The old man Ikpuk has made a very fine pipe stem of musk-ox horn for Johansen, decorated with etched lines. I visited different houses trading a little, then tried with Patsy's help to extract a little information out of Niq, Milukattuk, and Jennie.[10] A dance was held in the evening, followed by wrestling bouts. The ill-success of the sealers — they had obtained not even one seal — was forgotten in the excitement. We are cooking caribou meat — that is not tabooed because we are on the land — yet Taktu told me last night that when we cooked fish — I bought two yesterday — we should turn everyone out of the tent, as it is taboo. We sent a pot of rice over to Ikpuk's last night. He and Taktu were in the dance-house, so it was suspended over the blubber lamp to keep warm. Various people entered the hut and helped themselves to it till finally, when I discovered it and took it back to our tent, it was nearly empty.

Sunday, December 19th

Very few men went sealing, and they had no success. The majority danced and swung on a horizontal rope set through the walls of the dance-house some 7 feet from the floor. The weather was fine but cold. I traded a little and visited one or two houses, but the day was rather monotonous.

Monday, December 20th

A semi-blizzard prevailed. Ikpuk turned out to put a new roof on his hut, as the old one was unshapely and draughty, and I assisted. The Corporal cooked. Most of the Eskimos stayed in camp and held a dance. In the morning a sled arrived with frozen fish, dried fish, and caribou meat, and towards evening another sled turned up with Uloksak's food.

Tuesday, December 21st

Fine weather again. Patsy brought in a load of firewood. I visited two or three houses while the Corporal stayed in the tent and cooked. He is absolutely sick of the Eskimos. I had some in the tent in the evening, amongst them Aneraq, Uloqsaq's father, a fine old man; from him I obtained a little information. Kukilukak, Uloksak's eldest wife, cut her hand very badly while attempting to cut meat; I have bandaged it up as well as possible, but am rather afraid of it. About 11 p.m. Arnauyuk, Qiqpuk's young wife, came running to my tent to hide from Añivrunna, who had tried to drag her to his hut and make her spend the night with him, though he is married himself. Kanneyuk and Añopkunna ran to Arnauyuk's help, and tipped Añivrunna over into the snow, whereupon all fled to their houses. I thought it was all a game at first, till I found Arnauyuk some time after asking Higilaq if she thought it would be safe to try and get home. I saw her safe as far as her passage and heard her laughing inside the house, so knew all was well. No one seemed to regard the matter very seriously.

Wednesday, December 22nd

Another fine day. Higilaq discovered that one of the skins in the tent, which was resting directly on the snow, was soaking wet and spoilt. She gave me a good rating for it, as indeed I deserved; she is very amusing, however, on such occasions. I was invited over to Milukattuk's hut for a meal of deer meat, and while there she sewed the skin of a northern squirrel on to the hood of my calico snow shirt. Along the back it had black and white strips of deerskin, which made its appearance very remarkable. There was dancing as usual in the evening.

Thursday, December 23rd

We left after breakfast for the station, taking Alunaq and Jennie along with us for Christmas. We had two tide cracks to cross, each about 3-4 feet wide. I was testing the first with my foot when it broke through and I got my footgear a little wet — not enough, however, to necessitate changing as long as we kept moving. The snow was soft and deep, which made the pulling very heavy; however, we reached the station before dark. Shortly after our arrival two sleds appeared, coming from the east. There were six natives — three men and three women. One, a middle-aged man, came from the district of *Pallik* — which seems to be a little inland from Hudson Bay, north of the Aqillinniq River.[11] He left his country 3 years ago and has been hunting at *Suniñaiyoq*,[12] which seems to be about 3 day's journey south or southeast of Arctic Sound. While hunting there last summer he heard of us, so came along. He has traded with Indians from *Imaryuak* (Great Slave Lake ?), and with white men on a salt-water lake (inlet?)[13] near Hudson Bay, apparently in the neighbourhood of Wager Inlet — a new Hudson['s] Bay post. The second was a young man from the *Aqillinoriq* itself. He had left a wife behind and brought one along, whereas the *Pallik* man left two behind and brought one. The third was also a young man, albeit taller than the other two, whose home is *Kilusiktok*, or the bottom of Arctic Sound. He is a fellow tribesman of Kukluka and others. They were up inside the station in the evening but kept quiet and did not obtrude themselves.

Friday, December 24th

Everyone was busy preparing for Christmas. Johansen made a Christmas tree of willow twigs with paper flowers and candles. Flags were hung up in both rooms. The engineer Hoff[14] has fixed up a carbide gasometer, with three burners, so that we have a very good light in the 'scientists' room. The weather was fine but cold, the minimum being -35°. Yesterday morning when we crossed over [from the islands] it was -31°, but the wind was behind us.

Saturday, December 25th. Christmas Day.

The weather was milder, temperature -15°, with a little snow falling. After breakfast we turned out to hold sports — racing, jumping etc. The Eskimos won nearly all the events, which perhaps was just as well. They found their stockings full of presents. Even Jennie and Alunaq had silk 'grub-bags' filled with precious gifts, calico, needles etc. Cockney gave us an elaborate lunch and a still more elaborate dinner — plum pudding, mince pies, candy, and what not.[15] The new Eskimos gave a dance in the evening in the kitchen, using a frying pan for a drum. The music is considerably different from that here, about as different as the dialect. I took four phonograph records from them.[16] The *Pallik* man is very civilized — his chief desires are tea and tobacco. He has a .303 rifle, for which we have no cartridges. His costume is a little different from that of the Eskimos here. He wears an *atigi* long, equally in front and back, but slit up the sides, and on his feet he has deerskin shoes with fur both inside and outside the soles — useful enough on land snow, but impracticable on sea ice. In his pipe, which has a soapstone bowl with metal cap and chain obtained apparently from the Indians, he smokes a mixture of willow and bearberry leaves. His sled is similar to those used here, but much narrower, with the runners smaller and lighter and the cross-bars closer together and more numerous. He carries a sail too of deerskin shaped thus:

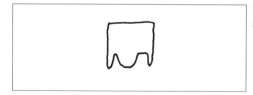

Figure 183. *Pallik* native's deerskin sail for sled.

e.g., a kind of square sail. The women are none of them tattooed. Their coats are like the men's, save for the long hood. One has large 'bags' in her long deerskin *ipijait*, just above the ancles — for no particular purpose, she says.

Sunday, December 26th

A quiet day in camp, part of which was spent in buying skins from the *Pallik* and *Aqillinniq* Eskimos, who had numbers of musk-ox, deer, wolf, brown-bear, fox, and wolverine skins. I gathered together some of the things I am taking over to *Ukullik*, and typed out a short report to the government for the Dr. to take to [Great] Bear Lake when he leaves — he says about January 20th.

Monday, December 27th

I had intended to return to *Ukullik* today, but my 'children' Jennie and Alunaq have enjoyed their stay so much that they wished to postpone our return for a day. It enabled Ciss[17] to make an *atigi* for Milukattuk and Unalina one for Alunaq. The eastern Eskimos who have spent Christmas here went across to *Ukullik*. A light east wind blew and some snow fell. Ciss made me a tobacco pouch for a present today, very unexpectedly.

Tuesday, December 28th

Again we postponed our return. I have been going to bed late the last few days and felt very sleepy this morning. Consequently when Cox — who was first up — said the wind was blowing 21 miles an hour and the snow drifting a little, I determined to stay in bed and not go. I slept till 10 then dressed. The children are in no hurry to return. The *Pallik* Eskimo and his companions went across to *Ukullik* to visit and trade with the natives there. Patsy, Jennie, and Alunaq helped me to write down and translate three phonograph records. The weather became much milder when day broke; the temperature in the early morning was -1/2° F.

Chapter 37. Folk-lore and Folk Songs

Return to Ukullik Islands — Conflict with native medicine man — Seances — Collecting native stories Dancing after sealing successes — Brief respite back at the station — Reading and writing lessons for Patsy Klengenberg — Problems collecting stories — Dealing with theft of a rifle — Blizzard — Another trip to the station — Infanticide — Dr. Anderson and Corporal Bruce leave for Great Bear Lake with mail — Visit from author's Eskimo 'children' — Back to the islands in a blizzard — Seance — Termination of studies and return to station — Writing up notes — The Eskimos on record — Writing down words of songs — Preparing to journey east

Wednesday, December 29th, 1915

We left after breakfast, though the wind was strong and snow drifting. The temperature at 8 a.m. was -9° [F]. We made the settlement just after dark. Everything was safe and in order, and Higilaq had dried our skins. Ikpuk even had the teapot boiling and made chocolate immediately for us. Then I tumbled into my tent, lit the fire, and made rice and coffee. We entertained some company in my tent, then at the solicitation of some of the Eskimos I went to see Naqitoq, Aksiatak's boy, who fell yesterday from the roof of the hut and broke his thigh. They wanted me to take the case over. I found the boy in his sleeping bag with his left thigh in splints — but the splints did not reach the knee. They were bound over a wrapping of deerskin. The parents told me that they had given the boy to Qoeha — an *añatkok* — who offered to make him well if they let him keep the boy after. He was just going to '*tornaq*' over him when I arrived. I told them that they could choose — either let Qoeha doctor him or I would take him to the station tomorrow and the Dr. and I would try and fix him up. I don't know whether it is a simple fracture or not, as I did not take off the splints, but the leg seemed to be swelling, and in any case it ought to have better splints. I left then, and have not learned what decision they have reached. Arnauyuk is again a divorcee. Qiqpuk did not like her, so they have separated, and she returned to Ikpuk's.

Thursday, December 30th

The Eskimos held another dance today — the farewell visitors' dance. The ceremonial part — one or two running round the dancer — the dancer's dancing companions — was precisely the same as occurred in the summer at Lake Tahiryuak.[1] Only a few Eskimos sealed, and only two seals were obtained. Aksiatak and Qoeha decided that they would not send Naqitoq to the station unless I was especially insistent, which of course I was not. I told them to put full-length splints on his leg, but doubt if they will do it. Ikpuk was very anxious for me to take the case in hand. Three men held seances in the evening, Qunaiyoq in the morning. The latter said some of the Eskimos were threatened with danger by spirits — Avrunna was one — so Milukattuk would not fix up Patsy's sleeping bag today. She further said some Eskimos over east would be travelling along a cliff and would fall into a hole and perish. The children brought in a load of wood for me today. Atqaq and Kaqkavina left for the east this morning.

Friday, December 31st

I did a little buying today.[2] The weather was rather cold with a fair breeze, but the Eskimos sealed with great success — nine [seals] in all. There is accordingly great rejoicing. The dogs have rambled over the top of the house the last two nights and stolen a little meat. It is amusing to hear Ikpuk or Higilaq brandishing the seal-harpoon (minus the head) inside the house, listening for the sound of the dog on the roof so as to stab it through the wall. Kanneyuk, Haugaq, and Arnauyuk are to sleep in my tent tonight. They do not like sleeping at other peoples', Kanneyuk says, and it is only natural. Ikpuk is very anxious that Patsy and I should continue to sleep with them. Ugluaq made overtures to Arnauyuk today, but she rejected him — she doesn't like him, she told us. Ikpuk spent most of the day in my tent; it is comfortable and warm. Higilaq too came over for a short time and taught me one [or] two short tales.[3]

Saturday, January 1st, 1916

An unpleasant day, with a strong west wind and a little drift. The Eskimos did not go sealing. I did a little buying, then spent a couple of hours trying to extract two or three stories out of Avrunna and Milukattuk. The Eskimos danced vigorously most of the day. Miluk lengthened Patsy's sleeping bag for him. Kukilukkaq's hand [see Dec. 21] is healing nicely.

Sunday, January 2nd

A lucky day for the Eskimos — they killed nine seals. Añivrunna got two. The weather was not very good, for a cold breeze blew. Pausanna came across from the station to secure a dog he had left behind. He brought a loaf of bread, a little cold bacon, and slapjacks as a present to us from Cockney. He is living about 14 miles west of the station with his wife — trapping. On the 9th January he returns to Mr. Girling, who starts for our station on the 15th. He spent the evening in taking a census of the village, while we had Ikpuk in our tent and obtained a good story from him.[4]

Monday, January 3rd

Pausanna returned this morning to the station. I gave him a note to give to Dr. Anderson, asking the latter to issue him a can of tobacco. Ikpuk was very anxious to buy a pair of fancy stockings from him, but had not the equivalent so I added the tobacco. Some of the Eskimos sealed and got four. Sometimes they find a great number of seal holes, sometimes hardly any. Nor does the seal always come up to the surface after the hole is found — it may be sleeping in a little 'hut' alongside. A dance was held in the evening. Uloksak was in my tent during the day, and I told him that he could not expect me to treat him very liberally if he did not tell me any stories. He said there was someone always hanging about the tent and he was afraid to tell. However, he came over late in the evening and told us a few shamanistic stories.[5] I asked him whether he would care to have Ikpuk present, and he said no, Ikpuk would be angry with him. The weather was cold with a sharp west breeze.

Tuesday, January 4th

A cold day, nevertheless the Eskimos went sealing and caught ten. Kehullik and Qiqpuk went across to *Oqauyarvik* to bring back the deer and bearded seal left there by Ikpuk and myself. They took three of my dogs with them. Uloksak came in for dinner, and afterwards when we had turned everyone else [out] he told us a few stories.[6] Milukattuk, who was in for an hour or so, told us a little about their burial customs. The last night or two we have had little supper parties in our tent — about 11 p.m. — the three children who sleep in it (Arnauyuk, Kanneyuk, and Haugak), Patsy, and I. Chocolate, hard-bread, [and] pemmican. The children enjoy it immensely.

Wednesday, January 5th

Another cold though fine day. Kehullik and Qiqpuk returned. They left the bearded seals, as they were frozen to the ground, but brought the caribou. By mistake they brought also the four cans of pemmican I left over there for my trip to Prince Albert Sound. Ikpuk went sealing but had no luck. The Eskimos got nine today, so held a dance — just as they did last night. Uloksak told us two or three more stories tonight, and Miluk two short ones this morning.[7] I took out the phono[graph] at Ikpuk's request and secured another record — not a very good one. I fancy the changes of temperature affect the cylinders. I know it has caused several to crack, but I think also it affects their hardness and makes some very 'scratchy'.

Thursday, January 6th

Cold weather but fine. Añivrunna and his wife went over to the station for something or other. The Eskimos had great luck today and secured eighteen seals. Six Eskimos sent over livers and a little meat and blubber. Ikpuk made a pipe-stem for my broken pipe. I moulded some cartridge bullets for Kinordluk and visited Niq to find out how Naqitoq was; he seems to be progressing all right. My sugar, tobacco, and other things are almost all used up so I am going back to the station tomorrow if it is fine and spend 4 or 5 quiet days there.

Friday, January 7th

Patsy and I returned to the station. The weather was a little cold but fairly clear and fine when we left. Hardly had we got really started, however, when a blizzard sprang up from the west right in our faces. At times it was impossible to see more than 20 yards ahead. However, we managed to keep the trail and reached the station before dark. Nothing had happened of note while we were away. Añivrunna and his wife returned to the islands today, but we did not see them, as they did not follow the trail.

Saturday, January 8th – Wednesday, January 12th

Quiet days at the station. On the 10th four boys came over from the islands to get some things of Uloksak's. They had no sleeping gear on their sled, but we fixed them up in the house for the night. Eskimos from the east are expected to turn up any day, according to reports brought by Naugaluaq and Kaksarina. This was one reason for Añivrunna's trip across the other day. The Dr. and the Corporal are slowly preparing for their trip to Great Bear Lake.

Thursday, January 13th

Patsy and I crossed over to *Ukullik* again today. All was well among the Eskimos. As we drew near the first island we saw an Eskimo approaching. He hailed us and stopped beside a seal hole apparently. Again we heard him hail, so I left Patsy to take the sled in to camp and went over, thinking perhaps he had speared a bearded seal and could not haul it up without aid. But as I drew near he came towards me and hailed 'The White Man'. "Yes — Hitqoq" though it turned out not to be Hitqoq but Kigiuna or 'Nuts to You' as the boys christened him. "I've no luck at all in sealing." "Oh," I replied. "Ikpuk has been very successful in his sealing," he went on. "That's good news." "I'm going to search round a while, then shall return to camp." "All right, I'm going straight to camp," and thus speaking I began to move off. "I say," he started, "have the eastern natives turned up." "No, they haven't appeared yet," I said, and again started off. "I say." "Yes?" "I'll be going home soon." "All right." "I say" — this when I was a dozen yards away — "When I get a seal you'll buy some of the meat, won't you?" "Perhaps." "Dog food, you know." "Yes," and again I went on. After I had gone some 30 yards more he suddenly hailed again. "I say." "Well?" "My name's Kigiuna." "Yes, Kigiuna, Nuts to you." "Yes" — he laughed and this time allowed me to go off without further remarks. Kigiuna is a middle-aged man, somewhat crazed. He has one distinguishing feature which marks him off from all other men about here — two small tattoo marks on the bridge of the nose — made apparently for amusement, because he says they mean nothing. Tusayok[8] has been ill — the Eskimos thought he was going to die. Taktu, his sister, would neither sew nor eat seal's liver — probably forbidden by a doctor[9] — though the prohibition against the wife's sewing is always I think in force in such cases. He is said now to be recovering. So too is Naqittoq according to his father.

Friday, January 14th

A fine day though foggy and with a little snow falling at times. The temperature was very mild. I was late up, though a little ahead of the children who sleep in my tent. We watched the men going sealing, some with one, some with two and three dogs, leading them by their traces or letting them run loose behind or ahead of them. One, Uloksak, came up to me. "Aren't you going sealing? Take my spear." "No," I said, "I went sealing yesterday and killed two so I'm going to stay in camp today and dance." This made them all laugh — the counter went home. I turned into the tent to cook breakfast. The Eskimo women crowded the door. One, Itkelleroq, brought a little frozen deer fat. She and my summer companion, Milukattuk, and Hakuñgak were allowed in and shared our breakfast, the remainder being sent over to Ikpuk's family. Patsy went out immediately he had finished breakfast. The women stayed on for some time. Milukattuk brought Avrunna's boots to dry in our tent, as it takes about one-tenth of the time it does over the blubber lamp. Niptanauaq brought a pair of fancy men's trousers to sell — she took lead for bullets in exchange. After a time I turned them out and went over to Itkelleroq's to pay a debt — some lead for a sleeping bag. Maffa's wife fed two of my dogs that had followed me — she is one of the best women amongst these Eskimos. Then I wandered up to the top of the island *Iluvik* to find the height above sea level — 150 feet.[10] Two boys were despatched for a load of wood, and I helped Higilaq and Arnauyuk clear up the sleeping platform — cut and shovel away the ice all round the bottom of the sides. By then it was time to return to my tent and melt snow for cooking water. Higilaq and some children came over and stayed to talk and eat pemmican and hard-bread. The Eskimos returned at dark, one after the other. They killed twenty-one seals — Ikpuk one. An hour later I was flooded with seal livers — brought by the hunters that they might share some of my food. As the hunters approached the camp with their seals the children ran out to meet them, and falling on the seals, pretended to stab and kill them. They told Patsy to do the same; it is supposed to give the hunter luck in his sealing. Jennie, Kesullik, and Haugak were in to dinner, and I sent some food over to Uloksak and Ikpuk. Some of these Eskimos go about in woollen or cotton shirts and *atigis*, without a deerskin shirt under or over them — an excellent way to get colds. I warn everyone I see — but some of them just put it down to a white man's foolish notions. Ikpuk came over for a short time and told us a good story, then went off to the dance which was in progress. I gave Patsy his lesson in reading and writing, then as Ikpuk and Higilaq came over boiled a pot of cocoa for supper. Visitors were numerous. I turned all out save Naneroaq and his wife, Ikpuk and Higilaq, but almost immediately Maffa, his wife, and Munnigorina appeared, three of the Dr.'s

Eskimos. I supplied cocoa and hard-bread to all but Ikpuk and Higilaq
and turned them out, then feasted the two latter. Ikpuk shortly went out
to go to bed, but a moment later shouted to Higilaq — who was lying
comfortably back on the skins — "They're playing games." Higilaq
jumped up as if she were shot and floundered out of the tent door, nearly
upsetting stove, pots, and all. The Eskimos were wrestling — both men
and women — outside the dance-house, as the weather was very mild.
Pissuaq and Puññik had a quarrel and pelted each other with dog excreta.
Jennie this evening was in Uloksak's hut, and heard a noise which she
said was caused by spirits (*ugioktun*). She rushed out and told us, though
she said she wasn't afraid. Patsy went over to look, laughing at them —
he said he wanted to see one of these spirits. However, fate was unkind
— he saw nothing. A quiet supper about midnight with my two 'children' Jennie and Kila, and Patsy finished up the day. Patsy and I turned
into Ikpuk's hut to sleep, leaving the children in tranquil possession of
the tent for the night.

Saturday, January 15th

A semi-blizzard raged from the east so no one went sealing. Instead
they spent the day in the dance-house, or in my tent as it seemed to me.
However, the result was a little more information from Milukattuk and
Uloksak. Ikpuk dressed in all his finery for the dance — he borrowed
Patsy's undershirt and put on top all the calico overshirts he possesed. At
their formal dances each man — or woman — has his dancing partners
— either one or more, man or woman — not necessarily related by blood
or marriage. It is a well-recognised relationship and endures until one
dies or they have a quarrel. Kuniluk gave a seance in the evening, which
we attended. After him Senaññuk, or Arnauyuk, entered the ring and
made a pretense at giving another — but never came to the point; she
would utter a few words then laugh, say a few more, and laugh again.[11]

Sunday, January 16th

A fine day though the wind freshened towards evening till the snow
began to drift considerably. The Eskimos caught eleven seals and sent
me three or four livers. I cooked a big pot of deer meat with some rice,
and we fed about eight people besides ourselves. Higilaq and Ikpuk told
us a few items of information, but it is extraordinarily hard to extract
anything out of them. There is much I think they could tell, but they
don't seem to understand what is wanted. They can't narrate a story
completely. Generally they begin in the middle and give the words of
one of the personages, then stop as if that explained everything.

Monday, January 17th

The westerly wind blew fairly strong all day. Kinordluk came into
Ikpuk's house early this morning to say that his rifle had disappeared. He
had wrapped it in an *atigi*, having no case for it, and laid it on the roof of
his house. *Atigi* and gun have disappeared, so there is no doubt it has

been stolen. I have put an end to all trade, both now and in the future, between us and the Eskimos, and told them that probably Mr. Girling will not trade either rifles or cartridges with them unless the gun is recovered. I have a suspicion Uloksak knows something about it.[12] He comes in usually each evening to tell me stories and is to have his .44 rifle changed to a .30-30 if I am satisfied with him. I told him tonight I wanted that rifle recovered. I think it will be recovered some time, if the embargo on trade is maintained. The rifle can always be recognised, for I removed a small spring in the side of the breach during the summer.[13] No sealing today.

Tuesday, January 18th

Maffa left this morning for the station, on his way to the Kogluktualuk [Tree] River to bring back the Dr.'s and O'Neill's specimens. Kohoktak will join him in a day or two. The weather was fine, but the barometer dropped alarmingly, and I have predicted a gale. Twelve seals were caught today, Kilugoq securing two. No news yet of the missing rifle, so no trade. Uloksak was in narrating a few stories in the evening.

Wednesday, January 19th – Friday January 21st

The blizzard came all right. It kept the Eskimos from sealing, so they spent the time in the dance-house. At first they did not hold a seance about the weather, for some said that as I had predicted it, I must know when it would cease and how. But on the 21st, when many were reduced to eating sealskin, two or three doctors gave seances and discovered that the storm was due to our cooking deer meat. Kinordluk's rifle was discovered — by Uloksak — on the snow some distance from the houses. I have secured three or four phonograph records in the last day or two.

Saturday, January 22nd

The weather showed signs of clearing this morning. Uloksak and his wife Kukilukkak started out for the station, and Patsy and I followed a little later. Qohoktak, however, had preceded us too, but as the Dr. proposed to leave on the day after tomorrow, Qohoktak returned again to *Ukullik* for his wife. The Eskimos were leaving to go sealing just as we set out too. The blizzard came on as bad as ever just after we left, but we managed to hold the trail and got across before dark.

Sunday, January 23rd

The blizzard which has raged the last few days continues unabated. Nevertheless, Qohoktak and his wife and child, Taglu and his wife Ekkiahoaq, and Kannuyauyuk and his wife Kaiyuina came over from the islands. The last woman had a baby yesterday morning, but not caring to be troubled with rearing it, and there being no one willing to adopt it, she exposed it out on the snow in the blizzard a little way from the camp. This is the first case of infanticide that has occurred, to my knowledge, since we came into this country.

Monday, January 24th

Still blowing hard. However, a sled and a toboggan were loaded up and the Dr. hopes to get away in the morning. He, the Corporal, and Adam (Uvoiyuaq, a Mackenzie native) go right through to Great Bear Lake;[14] Cockney, Ambrose, and Eikie put in a cache for them somewhere near Bloody Falls. Ambrose is to hunt caribou there too.

Tuesday, January 25th

The Dr. and his party with the train of four Eskimo families who followed him from the east in the fall (Maffa, Qohoktak, Taglu, and Kannuyauyak) set out this morning. Shortly after noon Kanneyuk, Alunak, and two boys appeared. I am giving up my bunk to my two 'daughter's' (for Jennie, by the revised version, is my younger sister), and taking the Corporal's bunk up above them.

Wednesday, January 26th – Tuesday, February 1st

The westerly gales continue incessantly. My two 'daughters' are very happy here. In true Eskimo style they wait till all the rest of us are in bed or just turning in before they follow suit. From my bunk above I hand them down some chocolate, and they fight for it between themselves. The weather clears for an hour or two, sometimes, then breezes up again till the snow drifts before a wind from 30-45 miles an hour. The two boys went back home the 26th, sleeping one night in the kitchen. Naugaluaq and his wife [and] Anivrunna and his wife turned up. They propose to go east immediately as soon as the weather clears. Kesullik and Allgiaq turned up, the former bringing word from Higilaq for Kanneyuk to return. Finally, on the 1st, Aksiatak and Ugluaq came over — to see the white men, they said. However, they received little encouragement, only Kesullik was allowed to sleep in the house (kitchen), save of course Jennie and Alunaq, and the rest received only scraps to eat.

Wednesday, February 2nd

The weather cleared somewhat for an hour or two in the morning, and Patsy and I, with Kehullik and the two little girls, left for the islands. However, we had not gone far when the blizzard came up as bad as ever. We lost the trail when half way over, but guided by wind kept a good course and reached the village safely. We heard voices when near by and made for them. In this way we were actually passing the village within 30 yards, as it was hidden by the drifting snow. The voices came from the returning sealers, who, despite the weather, had ventured out through scarcity of food. They had little success, only obtaining four. Still it will help to keep them going. We turned into Ikpuk's hut for the night; this time Haugaq slept out in another hut and the other two children, Jennie and Kila, slept in the same hut as us. With six of us sleeping there it promises to be warmer than before when there were only four of us.

Thursday, February 3rd

The blizzard continued unabated all day. Consequently the Eskimos spent the day in the dance-house, singing and dancing. In the evening Uttugaum held a seance, attempting to invoke or rather find Kannakapfaluk, the woman who lives in the depths of the sea and superintends the seals and the weather. It was the first time he said that he had tried to approach her, and it seemed like it, for the seance was altogether unsuccessful. He made a long tedious oration wherein, according to etiquette, he might not refer directly to what he meant, but let the bystanders guess and assent when they guessed right. He spoke about two ducks, a fish, a man who had knocked down two sticks, he thought (presumably the sticks that hold up the sky), someone in the moon etc., but no one could make much out of it. Then he invoked his spirit, said that he was no longer a man but some animal, and tried to find Kannakapfaluk. At this time he was stooping low and speaking in a high-pitched voice quite different to his previous loud strident voice. It soon ended, and he rose up saying that he couldn't find her. A little later he held a seance for seals, but no one could see the seal holes, as they should have done.[15]

Friday, February 4th

The weather was fine though clouded; best of all there was no wind. All the Eskimos went sealing. Patsy and I took down the tent, a rather tedious and not altogether easy task, as it was frozen in all round the sides. For a time, having nothing to do, we especial[ly], we played with the children, tumbling each other in the snow. I was much annoyed to find some Eskimos had slit open a pemmican can and stolen some of the meat. More annoying still, someone stole my snow knife. The Eskimos secured thirteen seals today.

Saturday, February 5th

Another fine day, until we left and had drawn near the station, when a stiff west breeze sprang up. Mr. Girling had arrived the day after Patsy and I left for the islands, with him a lay missionary named Merritt — a young man. They had been delayed by the weather. All was well at the station.

Sunday, February 6th

A stiff west wind towards evening, otherwise a fine day. Chipman proposes to go over to *Ukullik* to bring in some of our dogs there and to buy two fresh ones. I brought three across with me yesterday; two others that I intended bringing had gone with their masters sealing. Girling and Merritt go over also. Kesullik is to receive a .44 rifle for two dogs; he has been anxious to make the trade since last fall.

Figure 184. An Edison recording machine similar to the one used by the author to record the songs of the Copper Eskimos, 1915-16. The round cardboard carton encloses the waxed recording cylinder, which is about 4 inches high. (Photo courtesy CMC. No. LAR-Vn-90.584)

Monday, February 7th

There was a stiff westerly breeze in the morning so the party did not leave. The weather cleared up about noon. Higilaq let me have one of her dogs, Atigihyuk. Yesterday we found it had disappeared, chain and all. The day passed quietly writing up notes and working up the phonograph records.

Tuesday, February 8th

Chipman, Patsy, Girling, and Merritt left for the islands, in fine clear weather. In the afternoon Naneroak, his wife Niptanaciak, and a boy Avakunna appeared. The two former had come to trade, the boy apparently because he wanted a change of scene. They keep quiet fairly well and are little in the way. I took two phonograph records from them and had their help in writing out the words of others.[16] They are sleeping in the kitchen on the floor.

Wednesday, February 9th[17]

The weather was stormy this morning, the snow drifting hard. Nanneroak and the other two in consequence said they would stay over another day. The weather cleared, however, at noon, though towards night the wind sprang up a little. The air has been keen the last few days — the thermometer ranging from -25° to -38°. Chipman and Patsy turned up about 5 p.m., being preceded by two Eskimo boys about an hour earlier; the latter had come over to enjoy the hospitality of the white man. Chipman said the four of them slept last night in Ikpuk's house and were very comfortable. Patsy told me tonight that Niptanaciak was implicated in the stealing of the pemmican the other day. I taxed her with it and she admitted it, saying that she and the others were hungry. I tried to make her feel a little ashamed, the correction which seems to be most suitable in unimportant cases of this kind, for really some of them are like children. She and her husband helped me today to write down the words of some more records, and I took three fresh ones this evening. Some of the Eskimos at the Ukullik Islands are migrating west out on to the ice the first fine day.

Thursday, February 10th[18] – Monday, February 14th

Quiet days at the station, with comparatively good weather. Mr. Girling and Merritt returned on Saturday 12th, and with them Uloksak and two wives, Avrunna, Milukkattuk, and Kaneyuk. Uloksak and one wife, Hakungaq, go east with us, as well as Avrunna. He expected to load his things on my sled and live in our tent, but I told him he could do neither — four was as much as the tent would hold, and our sled would be heavy. However, we reached an agreement that he take a sled, build a snow-hut for himself and his wife, and carry part of our load. In return we feed him, and until he reaches Eskimos, his dogs. I have been very busy latterly writing down and translating the words of the phonograph records and have now finished about fifty. Avrunna has received his .44 rifle promised him last fall in return for the stories he was to teach me, and Uloksaq for similar services has had his .44 changed to a .30-30 rifle.

Chapter 38. Visiting the Eskimos in Coronation Gulf

Cold start to trading trip east — Encountering Ikpuk's first wife — Theft of some provisions — Meeting Eskimo with crucifix and cassock — Passing some islands — Sleeping-bag difficulties — Trouble with Uloksak — A young companion joins the party — Food shortage among Tree River Eskimos — Reaching a small settlement — Tree River cache — Intestinal problems — Hepburn Island — Dease and Simpson's cairn — Blizzard at Jameson Islands — A deserted snow-hut village — Measuring natives and trading — Another blizzard — Caribou hunt — Return to Tree River — Journey northwestward — Plagued by illness — Confined to camp with dwindling supplies — Cape Krusenstern portage — Meeting Cox and O'Neill heading east — An Eskimo crowd near the station

Friday, February 15th, 1916

-30° in morning. We got away at 9:15 [a.m.], and with an interval of about 10 minutes for lunch travelled till 4:15. The dogs were now growing tired and so were we, it being the first day out. We are camped at the point some 3 miles west of Cape Lambert, and managed to gather quite a fair quantity of driftwood for fuel. Milukkattuk (with Kanneyuk and Kukilukkaq and Holoraq) returned home at the same time as we left. Her last words to me were not to let Avrunna marry over east. She is almost due for a baby, so we lent her a sled to take her home. The weather was fine and bright, but the light west wind shifted to the southeast during the day, and I found it very hard to keep my nose from freezing. Avrunna proved himself willing and useful this first day, and I hope he continues.

Wednesday, February 16th

Uloksak and his wife came over for a meal of oatmeal, bacon, dog-biscuits, and tea, and we left at 9:20 a.m., with a moderate east wind causing a low drift. We kept a mile or more off the coast, passing within 1/4 mile of Cape Lambert, and made the short portage across the land behind Cape Krusenstern which I made last year with the Eskimos. On reaching the sea on the other side we met two sleds — Haviuyak, his wife Itoqunna and Utualu with one, and Qoehuk, Hupo, their baby, and Kanneyuk[1] with the other. The latter hearing that the white men at the station were not trading, turned back. We followed their trail to the settlement l 1/2 miles southeast of Cape Lockyer [Locker Point], meeting Qiñaloqunna dragging his own sled, and a little behind him Kitiksiq, Ikpuk's first wife, who was going to rejoin him, the Eskimos say. We reached the settlement about 6 p.m. and turned into a small empty hut. There we had some trouble with the primus, but finally managed to cook a good meal and tumbled in, Avrunna sleeping next door at Aiyallik's, and Uloksak and his wife in another house. We made about 25 miles, with the wind almost in our faces from the portage, so that all of us were

Figure 185. The author and H. Girling, the Church of England missionary, leaving Bernard Harbour for Coronation Gulf, February 15, 1916. (Photo by F. Johansen, CMC Photo No. 42352.)

sore tried at times to keep our faces from freezisng. Uloksak and Avrunna are both shaping well so far. We noticed several seal and *ugyuk* holes, and fresh rabbit tracks.

Thursday, February 17th

Cloudy day, rather foggy, with southeast breeze. Last night Añivrunna stole a little hard-bread off the sled — today when none of us were watching, a crowd of Eskimos opened up the sled and emptied a bag of rice — more than 20 lbs — into their mits. In consequence trade is tabooed. We obtained two small blubber lamps from Kaulluaq last night with blubber, and when we set up the tent this morning she shifted them over and set them burning inside while Avrunna went for wood. He brought back a good load, so we had a good warm tent and a fine supper of boiled deer meat and rice soup. I bought dog food (sealskin and blubber with some matches, and two shoulders and a hind quarter of a deer for one box .30-30 cartridges). Kaulluaq did some sewing for us and spent the day in the tent; she seemed quite pleased to see me again.[2] The settlement here comprises about 15 houses, but I have not taken a census. A man named Noqallaq has a crucifix (bone Christ on ebony cross) obtained from [Great] Bear Lake, and a cassock with hood, sewn (by his wife probably) down the front. Some of these people were down at [Great] Bear Lake last summer, but saw neither white men nor Indians. Qomiq's boy, a lad about 10, is unable to walk, his ancles and one wrist are swollen — apparently some disease of the joints. He crawls about on his knees. A girl Aqulluk — unmarried — is tattooed on cheeks and forehead, but not on the chin, from left hand to elbow, but only on left hand and wrist.[3]

Friday, February 18th

A gloriously fine day. We broke camp at 9:45 [a.m.] and set out east. The ice was a little broken in places, but on the whole the trail was good. We passed several islands, those north of us a good many miles away, three [to the] south quite close to us. Avrunna and Uloksak took their rifles and went to look for rabbits. They saw one but failed to get it. We finally stopped about 4:45 to camp 10 miles perhaps from an island east of us. Some islands southeast seem a little nearer. A little girl Nallvahhoq is travelling with us. We carried a little wood on the sled, enough to keep the tent warm while we cooked on the primus.

Saturday, February 19th

Another beautifully fine day. The wind swung to the east in the afternoon — in our faces, and as the temperature has been very low latterly we felt it keenly in our faces. All of us were very cold last night. My sleeping bag is wet and frozen at the bottom, and wet through with kerosene at the top, being accidentally placed above the kerosene tin on the sled — it is a cheerful prospect for a night's rest. We had a little scene this morning. Uloksak and his party were kept outside the tent till Girling finished cooking, as all of them in at once leaves no space to move. It annoyed him and he loaded up, sending his wife and the little girl in to eat but refusing to come himself. He started off, but the little girl was still eating in our tent. Thinking him gone, we finished off the oatmeal and bacon that was being kept for him, but suddenly he turned back ostensibly for the little girl, and put his head inside. We told him he could have a little frozen deer meat, which he did, after which he left, without waiting for our tent, which was supposed to go on his sled. We loaded up and set out, fixing a hauling strap on in front and taking turns in hauling. In this way we made some 7 miles east to an island about 1/2 mile long on which Avrunna collected a little wood. Here we lunched then set out, but soon sighted Uloksak and his party, the little girl bringing the dogs back to help us along. I told him if he gave any more trouble he would get no ammunition from us, and fancy that will keep him steady. He seemed inclined to make amends this afternoon, hauling fairly steadily on our sled. We stopped to camp at 4.30, and Girling, who is permanent cook, set to work to boil some deer meat. The wind appears to be freshening this evening.

Sunday, February 20th

A day of idleness. An easterly blizzard arose during the night, so today we did not move. Our wood lasted till well into the afternoon, when Uloksaq, Avrunna, and Patsy turned out to enlarge the snow-hut of Uloksaq's. When they had finished we shifted our things over into it, fed the dogs, cooked supper on the primus, and turned in. Uloksaq told us one or two short stories as we lay in bed. The little girl Nalvahhoq is half starved. This Coppermine lot that we just left have been hard put to it this winter. Some have stolen food from others and eaten [it] themselves. The little girl is going from her parents to her father's brother to live. The snow-hut we have tonight is long and narrow, thus:

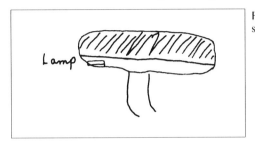

Figure 186. Top view of Uloksaq's snow-hut, Coronation Gulf.

Monday, February 21st

The weather was foggy most of the day, and snow fell at intervals, but the east breeze was very light. We broke camp at 8:40 a.m., and Patsy took his rifle to look for rabbits on some islands southeast of us, while we continued east-southeast. Avrunna and Uloksaq searched two islands for rabbits, but shot none, though they saw two. As the air was thick, and it was impossible to see far, I decided to camp on the point of an island shortly before 2 p.m. lest Patsy should lose his way. But soon after, while we were still fixing up camp, he turned up with the news that he had met Maffa, Kohoktak, and another family on their way to the station. They had made a short journey yesterday, and camped west of our present camp, so that the nearest people to us, their *Piññannoktok*[4] kinsfolk, should be only a few miles east. Uloksak and his wife immediately (about 3 p.m.) set off to reach them, but agreed to let the little girl spend the night with us. I believe they will have to camp without finding the Eskimos, as there were only about 2 hours of daylight left, and the weather was very hazy. The *Kilusiktomiut*[5] are scattered about in small parties all along the coast east of Tree River. All these Eskimos have been very short of food this winter. Kanuyauyaq shot five [deer], Kohoktak three deer near Tree River. From what they said, Patsy believes they cached the stores sent down by the doctor [Dr. Anderson] beside the whaleboat at Tree River. We made only about 14 miles today.

Tuesday, February 22nd

A beautiful day, with warm sunshine and but the lightest westerly breeze. We had a roaring fire, some of the wood being red spruce. Consequently we lingered, drying out some of our clothes, and did not start till 10 minutes to 9. Our load was heavy with the tent on top, and we made slow progress, following Uloksak's trail. Towards noon we noticed Maffa's and Kohoktaq's trail crossing Uloksak's — the latter in the dark had gone astray. We followed Maffa's and soon sighted five men sealing. They gathered together as we approached and, abandoning their sealing, returned with us to their settlement. There are five houses inhabited now, and four or five more deserted. We tumbled into a double hut, one wing of which had been inhabited by Qohoqtaq and his family, the other by Kannuyauyaq. We occupied both. Opening on the same house is Taglu's house. Uloqsaq and his wife had, as we expected, missed the way in the dark and did not reach the settlement till this morning. The people were very decent, helped us in with our things, lit lamps in our houses, and generally assisted to make us comfortable without bothering us. When we set out to cook, Eqqiahoaq (Taglu's wife) filled our pots with water, thereby saving half the kerosene we would otherwise burn. I did a little trading in the evening.

Wednesday, February 23rd

A fine day, but with a chilly east wind. Uloqsaq and Avrunna, the latter influenced by the former, are very anxious to push on to the people further east, but I am not inclined to move yet. I tried to get Avrunna to do something, seal or hunt, so that he would be more content. Patsy went out towards the land — about 8 miles off — but it started to drift a little before he reached it, and he turned back, picking up on his way a fox that was caught in a trap. The Eskimos were out sealing all day but had no success; they did not return until after dark. I measured all the adult women in the place — reserving the men till some more favourable opportunity.

Thursday, February 24th

A gloriously fine day with but a light east breeze. Uloksak and his wife left for the eastward; I am glad to see them go, as both are utterly untrustworthy, the wife [Hakungak], who was but a child last winter and apparently perfectly honest, having been corrupted by her new husband. Uloksak is a shrewd enterprising fellow, utterly unscrupulous, who has most of the natives under his thumb. With a stern master who kept him strictly to account he would make an excellent servant, but at present he sadly needs discipline. Patsy and Avrunna took the sled and tent and went off to the land to look for game, and NadrvuXoq the boy who accompanied us the other day and whom we all took for a girl, (even Patsy), went with them. I measured three of the men, took a few photos,[6] and visited next door. The sealers again had no success; one speared a seal but failed to kill it. They say the seals have many holes, and as the men are few (only six) and cannot watch all, they frequently fail to appear. Our Eskimo neighbours are real treasures compared to those we have met west — not officious or bothersome, and perfectly honest. Taglu on his own initiative put two windows in our double house to give more light this morning, and his mother-in-law Hattorina constantly superintends the lamps or sends someone to fill up the chinks[7] in the roofs.

Friday, February 25th

Another gloriously fine day. The sealers got two seals and brought us quite a quantity of the meat for a present. Patsy and Avrunna arrived after dark. They had seen no deer but shot five rabbits. I sent three to the

Figure 187. Snowhouses and sleds mounted on snow-blocks, Duke of York Archipelago, Coronation Gulf, February 24, 1915. (Photo by D. Jenness, CMC 37018.)

different houses, and we kept the other two ourselves. Maffa was supposed to have cached a 50-lb box of oatmeal at Point Epworth, with other stores, and I had told Patsy to bring back a 10-lb bag, but he reported that there was no oatmeal there. There is flour, however, and we are going across to pick up a little for soup the day after tomorrow. I measured the two remaining men this morning and took a few pictures.

Saturday, February 26th

Another glorious day. The sealers had no success. We packed up some of our things, which we are leaving here — a case of dog pemmican, my trunk (locked) with miscellanies, a bag of sugar, a half bag of hard-bread, and a can of man pemmican. Other things we prepared for the trail tomorrow. Our family next door continues splendid, but one family — Hitaq's — is accused of stealing, the man of a few matches, and the son (a small boy) of hard-bread. Taglu presented me with a stone pipe of his own manufacture. Incidentally we fixed up the sled, which had suffered somewhat in the runners from the heavy loads.

Sunday, February 27th

We left today in fine sunny weather, though the temperature was low and the east breeze chilly. First we went south 7 miles to the mouth of the Kogluktualuk [Tree] River and took about 3 lbs flour from the cache left by Maffa for the [Geological] Survey men. Patsy and Avrunna then went after rabbits, while Girling, Nalvuhhoq, and I followed the coast east. We were disappointed in wood, which we had expected to find as abundant as at the mouth of the Kogluktualuk River. Actually we found over the 10 miles or so we travelled only enough to cook the evening meal. Avrunna and Patsy secured each two rabbits, and the former a ptarmigan also. Avrunna built a snow-hut, to which we adjourned after supper. I was wearing an ordinary shortwaisted *atigi* underneath an old western *atigi* and a snowshirt. As a result I got a cold in the stomach, which has resulted in violent diarrhoea. Girling and I had considerable trouble setting up the tent and lighting the fire through the cold, the others not having yet arrived.

Figure 188. Cox, O'Neill, and Chipman at foot of Dease and Simpson's rock cairn east of Port Epworth, Coronation Gulf, September 30, 1915. It was constructed in 1839. (Photo by R.M. Anderson, CMC Photo No. 38750.)

Monday, February 28th

We had a very comfortable night in the snow-hut, though I had to turn out at 3 a.m. We continued northeast and are now camped on the northwest end of Hepburn Island (*Igluhugyuk* — big house). Avrunna and Patsy again went hunting and shot a rabbit each. We passed Uloksak's tracks following some deer, and Avrunna saw the skins of deer, which Kanuyauyaq and perhaps others had shot and thrown away the skins as useless. There is a considerable quantity of wood on the northwest end of

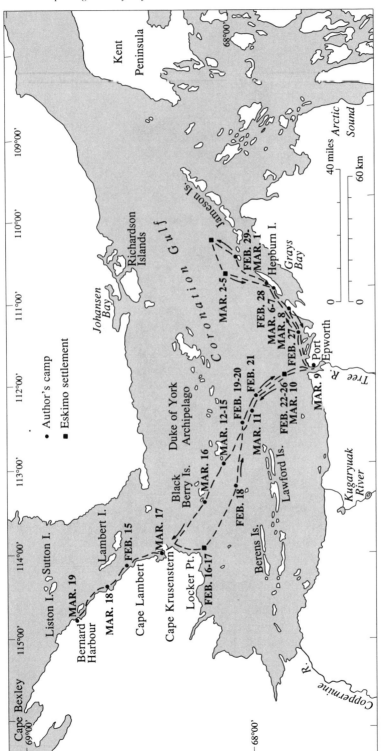

Figure 189. Map showing approximate route taken by the author in Coronation Gulf, February 15 – March 18, 1916.

Hepburn Island, and we found a little in a pocket on the coast about 5 miles west of Gray's Bay. Some 12 miles west of Gray's Bay is the high pillar and cross built of stones by some early explorers — probably Franklin's party, though no mention of it is made in his book. It is perhaps 12 feet high, and the bottom stones would require three or four men at least to move.[8] The weather was bright and sunny, with a light east breeze — less cold I think than yesterday. I found the day very tiring through the violent diarrhoea by which I am still attacked. I have taken flour and water tonight, hoping that may stop it.

Tuesday, February 29th

We set out about 9 a.m. and travelled about 10 miles due north to the north side of the nearest of the Jameson Group of islands. The chart here puts them too far off shore.[9] This island is steep and craggy, containing no wood, but a little was obtained on a lower island about 1/2 mile east. The two islands are called by one name, *Huloktok*.[10] The third island with a very high bluff on its southeast extremity, is *Imnahugyuk* (big crag). Patsy wandered off with his rifle over the north [side] of Hepburn Island and shot a rabbit. On the north end of our present island we found an empty snow-hut, and though it was only a little after 2 p.m. we decided to camp, as the wind was breezing up from the west and the snow beginning to drift. Patsy and Avrunna went off for wood to the adjacent island and brought back some that had been stacked up by some previous person. To save coal-oil we let them two turn into the tent for the night so that they could get the stove going in the morning, while Girling, Nalvahhoq, and I are to sleep in the [snow-] hut. We found our coal-oil can had leaked through a hole in the bottom and is almost empty — a rather serious event.

Wednesday, March 1st

A semi-blizzard so we stayed in camp. Avrunna and Patsy went over again to the adjacent island but found very little. I slept part of the day, for the dysentery (as I think it must be) continues unabated and is rather weakening. We are going to bed early — about 6 p.m. — as we want to save the wood to cook with in the morning.

Thursday, March 2nd

The semi-blizzard continued this morning, but we decided to make an island some 12 miles north of us, if possible, near which the Eskimos are said to be camped. A trail leads thither from last night's camp. This we followed and after travelling about 9 miles came to a deserted village of thirty-seven huts. We stopped a few minutes to lunch then followed some trails which led from the village southwest, with the blizzard almost dead ahead. Luckily it was not a severe blizzard, otherwise we could hardly have made before dark the 10 miles which brought us to the new encampment. The first house was that of Avrunna's foster brother or something, and into it we all turned. It happens also to be Nalvahhok's real brother. Here we learned that a band of perhaps sixty had gone east instead of southwest — one day's journey and therefore about 20-25 miles from here. On the other hand Uloksak, with ten families, has gone to the station — I fancy he wants to beat the big drum acting as escort, but fear they will be sadly disappointed by their welcome, and it will reduce his credit. Kannuyauyak and possibly one or two others have returned to Tree River. These people were not visited by Stefansson, and some at least have never seen a white man, not even Joe Bernard, though he wintered 18 miles east of Coppermine [River].[11]

Friday, March 3rd

The blizzard abated considerably, but the Eskimos did not go sealing though they had nothing but sealskin to cook. Instead they flooded our hut all day. I measured about a dozen of them — all men — Girling writing the figures and notes while I measured — paying two needles and a fish hook to each subject. Then I did a little trading,[12] and we settled down to cook supper. The Eskimos have behaved very decently and though curious have refrained from handling everything or stealing. Though they crowd round at mealtimes they are very restrained, contrasting greatly with the natives further west. A dance was held in the evening to welcome Avrunna, who has two dancing companions (*numikattik*) here — a man and his wife. The dance-house was very small, and they had no drum, but it did not diminish their enjoyment a whit. Our host and his wife are very quiet and decent — keeping away from everything but doing any little thing we want.

Saturday, March 4th

Blizzard from west all day. We stayed over, not caring to face it. The Eskimos too did not go out but made a drum and held a dance besides flooding our hut all day. It was very cold in the hut nevertheless. We had oatmeal and dog pemmican (Underwoods) mixed for breakfast and cooked two rabbits for dinner at night, feeding the family we are staying with. It is fortunate for them that we are here. On the whole it was rather a miserable day as we could not keep warm. There are some big lamps here. These Eskimos have no taboo against sewing on the ice in the dark days because the ice is solid and will not crack. But like the natives further west they will not cook on the ice deer meat that has been cached under stones, for then the stones would be cold and make the weather cold. The fall sewing of new clothes is done by the *Kilusiktok* natives at the island *Igloryuallik* in Bathurst Inlet, by the *Piññaññaktok* at *Igluhugjuk*, [and] by the Victoria Land (*Nagjuktok*) natives on that island.[13]

Sunday, March 5th

Still the blizzard. We remained in camp as yesterday, and everything passed in the same way, though we did not feel the cold so much. We cooked our last two rabbits.

Monday, March 6th

The weather had moderated greatly this morning so we decided to start back for Tree River. Three Eskimo families suddenly announced their intention of going to the station via Tree River also, but our own food supply being low — enough for about 3 days — we slipped them by going south. We intended to strike the mainland a little west of Hepburn Island (*Igluhugyuk*), but the blizzard sprang up shortly after we set out and we found ourselves running along the shore of the island. Patsy went over to look for rabbits, saw one, but failed to get it. We reached our old camp there, picked up some of the wood which we had left, went on for 2 or 3 miles more, and camped beside another small wood pile made by Patsy when we passed the other day. It was only 2:30 p.m., but we should not have reached more wood for 3 or 4 hours. Both Patsy and I found it extremely cold and fatiguing — in fact I had great difficulty in keeping my nose and forehead from freezing. We have a very comfortable camp tonight, with plenty of wood, though the blizzard is raging as much as ever.

Tuesday, March 7th

The weather was as bad as ever this morning, yet Patsy and Avrunna both expressed a desire to go and look for rabbits. While they were away Girling and I went back along the shore for a load of wood. Atigchyuk, Higilaq's dog, followed us, not pulling on the sled because he is lame. He lost us and did not return to camp for some hours. Patsy chased a rabbit from the mainland to Hepburn Island but lost track of it close to our tent. Avrunna had better luck and shot one. The weather shows no sign of abating yet.

Wednesday, March 8th

A gloriously fine morning though cold. We left at 8:15 [a.m.] but soon a moderately fresh west breeze set the snow drifting low. It became intensely cold travelling against it. My knees, face, and hands were all striving hard to freeze, and once I had to thaw out Girling's nose. So, soon after reaching the mainland I decided to camp, there being a little wood on the spot and more in a gulley a couple of miles further on. Avrunna had gone hunting and Patsy had just left with the same object, but we called the latter back. He has proved invaluable to us all along, infinitely superior to anyone else I have ever travelled with here, and today he almost eclipsed himself in the work of making camp. I had announced that I would go along with him to the gulley for more wood, but Girling slipped off unnoticed, and when Patsy was ready to start out I was obliged to remain and mind camp. They had barely reached the gulley when Patsy sighted caribou at the foot of the cliff. He had no rifle with him, but luckily Avrunna showed up near by, quite unexpectedly, and he wounded one. The dogs went mad with excitement, but Patsy cut the trace of the leader and let it pursue the deer. It soon overtook it, and the animal turned to gore it, but with a spring it seized its throat and brought it down. Consequently tonight we gorged the dogs and ourselves with meat and have a good quantity to carry away with us tomorrow. The wind died right away early in the evening, but soon sprang up again. The night is beautifully clear and starlit but very cold.

Thursday, March 9th

We were late in starting out, for the caribou meat took a long time to cook. However, the weather was comparatively mild, compared that is with what it has been. A little snow fell, and the atmosphere was foggy. Avrunna went hunting and shot a rabbit. He fired thrice at another but missed. The dogs pulled well, and we made the 18 miles or so to Tree River by 4:15 p.m. Avrunna went off wooding and saw a wolverine, but had no rifle with him. Our camp tonight is under the shelter of the high diabase cliffs on the east side of the harbour. Patsy and Avrunna opened up the cache left for the [Geological] Survey men by Maffa and took out one bag of hard-bread (5 lbs), two cans of dog pemmican, and about 3 lbs of flour. The wolverine had tried to get into the cache but could not dislodge the heavy stones. Tomorrow we shall take about a gallon of coal oil from another cache nearby. The monument about 9 miles east of Tree River — a pillar of stones surmounted by a stone cross — was erected, the natives say, by Hanbury's party.[14] Fresh caribou tracks were noted on the ice today, but no caribou seen. Yesterday every one of us was frozen in some part of his person — Girling and I on the noses, Patsy on one cheek, and Avrunna, who in the excitement of chasing the caribou, had raced along without mits or hood, on a part of one hand, the ears, and the forehead.

Friday, March 10th

We had a tranquil night. While Girling was cooking breakfast I went up on top of the cliff and gathered two or three plant specimens — poor and useless I fear — for Johansen. Patsy filled a 10-lb malted-milk can with a mixture of coal oil and distillate, while we loaded up the sled. We took our time in breakfasting and loading up and did not get under way till 10:30 a.m. Travelling slowly north we reached the settlement about 1:30 p.m. and soon set up our tent. The settlement has grown with the coming of three or four families from the east. All the things I had left with Taglu's people were safe. Hattorina lengthened my trousers and patched my shoes, while Eqqeahoaq repaired Girling's boots. I am buying dog-food from them with a small file and have presented Hattorina with an 8-inch knife, besides some 4 lbs of dog biscuit. Taglu and Kannuyauyak each secured a seal today — the only two hunters who were successful. Girling is a little off colour and retired to bed early. When we cooked this evening a woman was inside the tent and a crowd at the door. I told them we were going to eat so they all retired and closed the door immediately — a great contrast to the Eskimos further west who have been spoilt by the presence of J. Bernard and of us, and become intolerable thieves and beggars. The weather was bright and clear all day, with a light breeze from the southwest, fairly cold, though as it was behind us we did not notice it.

Saturday, March 11th

Fine clear day of bright sunshine, with a very light east breeze at times veering to southeast and south and southwest, and finally in the evening south. We packed up after breakfast and travelled west-northwest, passing the small island on which we camped on our way to Tree River, then camping about 3 p.m. on the island where we had lunched. We had then gone about 16 miles, and though the weather was gloriously fine I preferred to camp because no other island was within reach that day, and there were several small repairs to execute — a rent in the tent, the handle of the sled broken, etc. Naugaluaq and his wife TamoXuina, whom I have nicknamed Tamogluña (let me eat) accompanied us with their sled, carrying our tent and a large sealskin for dog-food. They contrast greatly with Uloksaq and his wife, who lived on us entirely and butted into the tent as though it were their own, whereas this couple come over one at a time, wait to be invited before entering, and have brought an outfit of their own. The [British Admiralty] chart is altogether inaccurate concerning the islands here — in fact it is useless. We are much amused at the volume of liquid Avrunna drinks. The other night he drank fourteen breakfast-cups full — three of soup, two of tea, and the rest ice-cold water — all within the space of 3 hours. Tonight I think he has exceeded this.

Sunday, March 12th

A light southwest wind was blowing when we started out at 8:40 [a.m.] in bright sunlight. We travelled northwest, the dogs making good time, and reached a cluster of islands forming a regular archipelago — *Iperviksaq* and *Nannuktun*[15] — two of them with high cliffs we left on our right. By noon we reached the n[orthern] extremity of the first of these islands and could see *Pauneraqtoq*,[16] another of them, one of the largest, some 10 miles ahead, but the wind, which had been slowly increasing, began to blow more violently, and I sent Avrunna and Patsy to see if the island we were passing sheltered any wood. They were absent but a few minutes, but in that time it had begun to drift heavily, and as they found a good quantity of wood I decided to camp. It had been cold — Girling, myself, and even Patsy had constantly to thaw out parts of our faces. I was under the further disadvantage of not being well, having been wakened in the night with a severe pain in my stomach, which effectually put an end to any idea of breakfast; the little chocolate I nibbled at lunch had a bitter taste, and when Girling made a concoction of thick rice soup and pemmican mixed for me, the three or four mouthfuls I was alone able to swallow soon resulted in violent sickness. Avrunna was very anxious to push on; he is feeling the absence of Milukattuk.

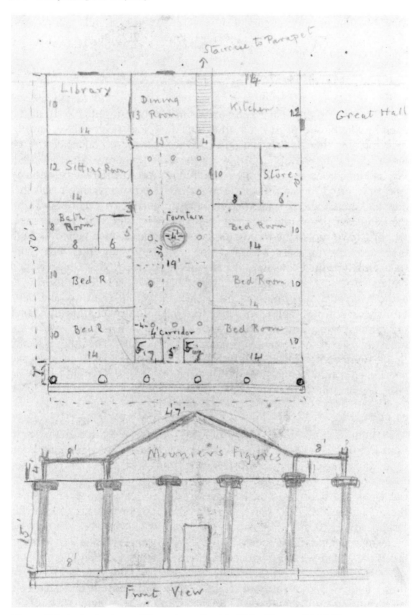

Figure 190. Author's plan and front view of an ideal island home. (NAC Photo
No. C136455)

Monday, March 13th and Tuesday, March 14th

Two days of blizzard which confined us to camp. Our food supply is running low — especially dog-food — so we are hoping it will clear tomorrow. Avrunna and Naugaluaq went over to a low island 3 miles or so away for wood this morning and brought back half a sled load. The weather at present seems more boisterous than ever.

Wednesday, March 15th

Another day of blizzard, though it abated a little about noon and a little more towards evening, coming more in gusts. It was useless to leave camp, as we could not see far ahead. In the afternoon Avrunna and Naugaluaq (the latter with Patsy's rifle) went over to Nannuktok Island to look for rabbits. We have cut down our rations, have two meals a day, with a little scrap of pemmican and some boiled cocoa (or chocolate) for lunch. The dogs broke into Naugaluaq's snow-hut in the afternoon while TamoXuina was in our tent and ate up their blubber, besides tearing to pieces a fine pair of long deerskin boots belonging to the woman. I have been amusing myself by drawing a plan of an ideal small home in some warm country on a promontary or island, overlooking the water. The idea of some such house — modelled on a Roman House[17] — has been floating in my head for many years, but the sudden impulse to crystallize it on paper was occasioned by reading Bacon's Essay yesterday on Building.

Thursday, March 16th

It was almost calm at daybreak so after breakfast we set out. Hardly had we started, however, when the wind sprang up again and it was bitterly cold. We passed by the first two of the islands which made the group *Pauneraktok* — the middle one and the largest has high perpendicular diabase cliffs running west-northwest - east-southeast — and were rounding the last of them when the wind began to blow more violently than ever and the snow to drift. I decided, therefore, to make camp. Quickly the tent was set up to accommodate all of us, as Naugaluaq and his wife have no blubber left for their lamp. Avrunna and Patsy went over to the islands to look for rabbits, and Avrunna secured one, which we are cooking for the morning. We found a quantity of wood luckily on this island and have a comfortable camp.

Friday, March 17th

The weather seemed to be a little better this morning. In any case we had not enough wood for all day and tomorrow morning, so we set out hoping to make [Cape] Krusenstern and possibly beyond. It was bitterly cold, and we all, except Naugaluaq's wife, got a little frostbitten.[18] We made good time, nevertheless, but I steered a little wrong (the chart throughout the run through the islands has been quite useless) and hit the short portage across the neck of [Cape] Krusenstern instead of the point. As we drew near we saw Eskimos engaged in sealing, and they all gathered to meet us. Their houses lay just to the south of the portage, close to the shore. They are the same lot who stole our rice, but have been supplemented by ten families of *Kilusiktok* Eskimo whom Uloqsaq set in motion. We avoided their camp, crossed the portage, and stopped at two empty snow-huts in the bay west of it to camp, as there is no wood. Naugaluaq and his wife had turned aside to get blubber in the Eskimo camp, and though he said he would follow us, I did not expect him to do so till tomorrow. However, he turned up while we were cooking and fitted out the other hut to sleep in. They had eaten, they said, in the Eskimo camp and obtained a little blubber and a small piece of bearded-seal meat — very little, because food was scarce. As we had been feeding them the last few days they brought the seal meat over and left it in our hut. However, I told them to cook it for themselves and said we would send very little food over to them in consequence. We saw on the east side of the portage many wind-breaks around holes in the ice where the Eskimos had been fishing for tomcod. The place is noted for the quantity of tomcod, but they must have been very short of food to fish at this time of the year in the intense cold.

Saturday, March 18th

A fine bright day, with only a light west breeze. We got away at 8:55 a.m. and travelling well reached a point within some 18 miles of the station about noon. Here we met Cox and O'Neill and Eikie with a heavily laden sled, accompanied by Kohoktak and his wife Munnigorina, on their way to Bathurst Inlet. They told us the doctor and the Corporal had returned without reaching [Great] Bear Lake, the Corporal with his face badly frozen. They had been 11 days in reaching the Coppermine [River], but had shot ten caribou on the way. Chipman and the Dr. have gone to Croker River, which the former wishes to map and descend a neighbouring river. Johansen has gone to Mackenzie River on South Victoria Land, as he wanted to get out after being confined to the house all winter and thought he might botanise a little. Sweeney is left in charge of the station — the only other two white men there being the Corporal and the engineer [Hoff]. It was about 3 p.m. when we stopped to camp, some 12 miles from the station. About 6 p.m. sleds appeared behind us, and a little later the first of the Coppermine crowd appeared. Others followed until soon a settlement rose all around us, some being the Coppermine Eskimo who stole our rice and five families *Kilusik-tomiut*. The latter we distinguished and when some asked for water we gave it to them. The Coppermine bunch we strictly excluded. Huputaun, the ringleader in the stealing, made several overtures — sent a pot over full of snow to be melted on our stove, then his child to come into our tent — we turned both propositions down at once.

Chapter 39. Thievery and a Search for Johansen

Arrival of eastern natives — Partial recovery of stolen ammunition — Return of Dr. Anderson and Chipman from Croker River — Search for the thieves — Ikpuk's discomfort with two wives — Confronting a thief — Off to search for Johansen — Finding a cairn with a note from Johansen — Return to Bernard Harbour

Sunday, March 19th – Tuesday, April 4th, 1916

Quiet days at the station. The Dr. and Chipman returned April 2nd. Numbers of Eskimos settled round the station; many were eastern people — *Kilusiktok*.[1] Amongst them was the celebrated shaman Ilaciaq, who has the repute of being the best shaman anywhere in the country. I photographed him[2] and retained him for some days, promising to pay him if he would tell me some of their folklore. He was very willing to tell anything except what related to religion — on this topic he was inclined to be reticent. Incidentally he 'shamanised' twice into the phonograph and the records turned out splendid.[3] It was a real performance such as they constantly have amongst themselves, with the audience interrupting, ejaculating, and interpreting. I traded a good deal with the *Kilusiktok* natives, especially for clothes and skins — their clothes on the whole were very much more elaborately adorned with insertions of red and white and black than those of the Eskimos around here. The Coppermine River crowd who stole our rice also visited us, but were strictly excluded from the house, as were also some of the *Ukullik* natives; no trading was done with them. They perpetrated some petty thefts, and when a party of them left on March 31st we discovered that they had carried off a case of pemmican. Sweeney and the Corporal, with Patsy and Ambrose, chased after them and recovered it. A little had been already divided up and eaten, and to pay for this they took away two boxes [of] .44 cartridges from the thief Nanneroak. This man, not having the courage apparently to commit the theft himself, sent his wife up in the night to take the case off the cache. Then he opened it in his hut, left one can with some natives who remained behind, and carried the rest off leaving very early in the morning. The Dr. and Chipman ascended the Croker River for some 25 miles in a straight line from the coast — ascending Mt. Davy (2000 feet), whence they could see the country for at least 15 miles south. They found an extraordinary cañon with sheer cliffs of dolomite rising up 300 feet on each side, above which again was superimposed about 50 feet of gravel. The morning they arrived Sweeney discovered that 2000 rounds of .22 automatic ammunition had been stolen out of the store tent, besides some pork out of the passage. Further a whole case of Remington .30-30 ammunition was missing from the cache. The natives have constantly asserted that Uloksaq has made away with a quantity of ammunition and other things. The presumptive evidence against him in regard to the Remington .30-30 ammunition was fairly strong, so we took possession of his .30-30 rifle until he cleared himself, or the ammunition was

recovered. He protested his innocence, asserting that Ugluaq and Aksiatak had stolen them. As a matter of fact, Ikpuk has recovered five boxes
of .30-30 ammunition from Ugluaq, and Uloksaq brought in eight boxes
of the Remington .30-30 on April 1st from Aksiatak, he says. Tomorrow
I am going over to the settlement with him to enquire into it from Ugluaq
and Aksiatak themselves, and Mr. Girling is going with me. The weather
has been much milder since we returned to the station.

Wednesday, April 5th

A beautiful fine sunny day. Girling, Uloksaq, and I left about 9:30
a.m. for the Eskimo settlement out on the ice. About 14 miles to the
north-northeast we came upon a number of empty huts from which they
had migrated but 2 days ago. There were trails leading off both east and
west; we took the west [trail]. Another 10 miles brought us to a settlement where Ikpuk is living, but not the two men we wanted; they have
gone east, the Eskimos told us.[4] I tumbled into Ikpuk's house, Girling
into Avrunna's, and Uloksaq into someone else's. In the evening the
sealers returned — Avrunna alone had been successful. Ikpuk and
Higilaq turned Kila and Kanneyuk out of the hut at bed-time, and
Higilaq did the 'head lifting' performance, using me as the subject; the
purpose was to induce my spirit to come to their help whenever they are
in distress, after I have gone away. It was rather touching to witness their
simple faith and trust in me.[5] Kitiksiq, Ikpuk's first wife, has reclaimed
him, but he clings fondly to Higilaq. So Kitiksiq has a hut next to
Ikpuk's, opening on to his passage, and is supported by him, while he
lives with Higilaq. The two women disregard each other as far as
possible and Ikpuk evidently feels the burden. Kitiksiq sometimes
entered the hut of Ikpuk and Higilaq and jabbered away to me or to
others in the house. If she addressed a remark to Ikpuk he either took no
notice or replied in the curtest manner possible.

Thursday, April 6th

A strong east wind set the snow drifting nearly all day so we stayed in
camp, neither Girling nor I having more than one skin shirt to oppose to
the cold. The day passed wearily for the time hung heavy on our hands,
though I learned one or two cat's-cradle figures.

Friday, April 7th

A glorious day. Girling, Uloksaq, and I left at 8:20 a.m. for the other
settlement, behind the more southern of the Ukullik Islands and some
22 miles away. We reached there by 2 p.m., and I ransacked the tents and
bags of Aksiatak and Ugluaq (they lived in one tent) and Sinisiaq, who
was also suspected of being implicated in the theft of the .30-30 ammunition. From the former we recovered three boxes, from the latter
eight. I also seized the latter's .22 rifle (he is suspected of stealing the .22
ammunition) till he should clear himself, and four boxes of .30-30
bought by Aksiatak in the fall as well as his bow and case. The women

Figure 191. H. Girling, Church of England missionary (far right) with a group of Copper Eskimo women and children at *Ukullik* settlement, Dolphin and Union Strait, about 24 miles north-northeast of Bernard Harbour, April 5, 1916. (Photo by D. Jenness, CMC Photo No. 36956.)

tried to oppose it, but could naturally do nothing. Then we waited till the sealers returned. One by one they came, the last being Ugluaq, to whom everybody attached the blame. As they came in an old man Iglisiaq told them to put away their harpoons and assemble; this they did but all had long knives. Girling and I had automatic pistols concealed in our pockets, ready for any emergency. Luckily they were not required. Ugluaq thought his last hour was come; especially when Aksiatak caught hold of him and urged him to own up. All the men appeared to side with Aksiatak — Ugluaq apparently not being very popular. One man, Atigihjuk, got a bad fright. Girling, who was standing on guard on the outskirts of the crowd, saw me apparently in the centre of a scrimmage (really it was Ugluaq trying to escape). He put his hands into his pocket and shoved a cartridge into the barrel of his Browning automatic ready for immediate use if required. Atigihjuk, standing beside him, heard the sound and shifted out of the way rather abruptly. But the most amusing sight was Uloksaq standing well out of the way, on top of my sled, with his snow-knife held high and orating at the top of his voice. The upshot was that we recovered three more boxes and restored to Aksiatak and Sinisiaq their property as their explanations were plausible and were supported by the others (though I misdoubt both). At 8:30 [p.m.] we left to return to the station, but in the semi-darkness steered a little too far east and struck the land west of the station. For half an hour or so we stumbled about some small bays and low spits, then, not knowing exactly how far off we were, Uloksak built us a snow-hut and we tumbled in. We had no food, since a breakfast of mixed pemmican and oatmeal, only a cake of chocolate for lunch, and the tiniest scrap of seal meat at the Eskimo settlement. We had travelled about 38 miles and were tired out and hungry. Uloksaq lay down in his clothes — Girling and I half undressed and crawled into our bags. We had but one sleeping skin and that was under Girling. Uloksaq and I lay on the sled cover. It was 2 a.m. when we turned in.

Saturday, April 8th

We turned out before 5 a.m., for the sun was already up. Portaging across two necks of land we were at the station before 6 a.m. Two or three more families of *Kilusiktok* Eskimos had arrived during our absence. Johansen, who left with Adam for Mackenzie River on Victoria Land on March 6th (the same day the Dr. and Chipman left for Croker River), has not shown up yet, though he was due on April 1st. I am going off to look for him the day after tomorrow, with Patsy. He may be all right, but he is a very poor traveller and had a poor team of dogs. Uloksaq was given his rifle back today — he has received a good lesson, if nothing else, as indeed have all the Eskimos round here.

Sunday, April 9th

A busy day getting together an outfit to leave in search of Johansen tomorrow — Patsy and I.[6] More time was taken up in trading with the *Kilusiktok* natives.[7] Nanneroak and his wife Niptaniaciak had the effrontery to return and even to enter the house in the evening; they were promptly turned out. The weather was bright and clear, with a moderate easterly breeze; the temperature at noon was about +20° F.

Monday, April 10th

Patsy and I left just after 9 a.m. and passing by the e[astern] edge of the most s[outherly] of the Ukullik Islands [Liston Island] picked up Johansen's sled trail and followed it for some 2 miles east of that island. Then as our dogs were tired out we camped — at 4:30 p.m. The weather was beautifully fine and warm, though a fresh east wind blew. This died down after we camped, and inside our tent it was delightfully warm, though we had no wood stove. We saw the Eskimo settlement some 2 miles or 1 1/2 miles w[est] of us but did not approach it. On the east end of *Ahuñahuñak* [Liston Island] we cached a tin of dog [pemmican] and a tin of man pemmican, beside a large stone on top of which we placed a smaller stone holding down a piece of red paper. If we miss Johansen he ought to see the mark and find the food; I hardly think the Eskimos will steal it after the lesson they received the other day. Travelling was heavy today, the snow being soft and 'drifty', so our progress was very slow. I was pushing or pulling on the sled the whole time.

Tuesday, April 11th

Morning dawned fine and bright, with hardly a breath of air. Later it clouded somewhat, though the atmosphere was clear most of the day. We started early — at 7:15 a.m. — and the dogs working better than yesterday reached the nearest point of Victoria Land east-by-south of the Ukullik Islands some 18 miles by 1 p.m. Here we stopped to lunch and

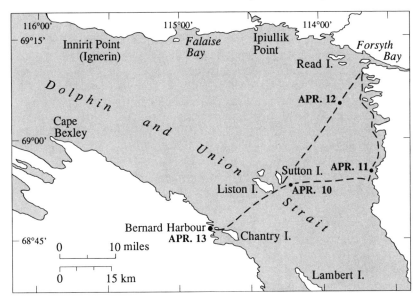

Figure 192. Map showing route followed by the author in search of F. Johansen, April 11 - 13, 1916.

to rest the dogs. Then we resumed our journey, following the coastline to the south. Hardly had we made another 1/4 mile when we encountered a sled trail leading north; we had crossed in without seeing it 1/2 hour before, in a place where the sled and footprints had left almost no trace on a patch of hard-packed snow. Evidently it was Johansen's and Adam's — and only 2 or 3 days old. Why they were following the coast north instead of crossing direct to the Ukullik Islands I don't know, unless it was to pick up a can of Hudson ['s] Bay pemmican cached a few miles north in the fall by Mr. Girling, when he accompanied Sweeney across the strait while the latter was off to look for the Dr. and the [Geological] Survey men. We followed the trail north and about 4 p.m. reached another point beyond which lay a large bay. Here we decided to camp, and almost immediately sighted a pile of snow-covered wood already cut up — evidently Girling's and Sweeney's camp in the fall. Our camp tonight is very comfortable. All day the temperature has been so mild that mittens have been almost a superfluity. The dogs' feet keep becoming clogged with ice, and we have to stop every 2 or 3 miles to remove it. We could tell Johansen's trail by the size of the footprints and also by the toes being turned out, while Adam's were almost straight. We saw, too, a raisin box thrown away.

Wednesday, April 12th

We followed Johansen's trail for some 16 miles northwest along the coast. We saw it dip deep into a shallow bay — apparently between the Clouston and Forsyth bays of Rae's map.[8] We did not follow it down but cut across the narrow mouth of the bay and picked it up on the other side. At the point just before turning in to Forsyth Bay (apparently) was a small stone cairn, and in it a note from Johansen himself[9] — the outside of the note had in pencil a request to the finder to send it to the Canadian Government. The note contained a detail[ed] account of his journey with all he noted on the way and was extremely interesting, and amusing. It finished up with the remark that he was leaving that day (April 9th) for the Ukullik Islands, with 2 days' rations left. We saw his trail — it was heading back south down the coast, but he must have curved round later towards the islands. We could faintly descry the islands southwest of us (compass south), so headed straight for them and made another 8 miles or so before camping. We left at 7:40 a.m. and stopped at 4:55 p.m. In making camp we discovered a dehydro can full of chocolate, raisins, tea etc. had dropped out of the back of the sled. I went back a mile or so to look for it but could see no trace of it, and it is not worth returning 20 odd miles to pick it up. A good day's hike tomorrow should take us to the station — it is only about 30 miles. Snow fell thick at intervals during the day, making the atmosphere hazy and the trail at times obscure and difficult to follow. Tonight the sky is clear and the wind has changed from east to west. The weather is still very mild.

Thursday, April 13th

An early start well before 7 a.m. brought us to the deserted Eskimo settlement at the Ukullik Islands soon after 1 p.m. Here we stopped and cooked some rice and coffee inside the dance-house. A raven had left its foot prints everywhere on the snow inside — they are fond of visiting empty houses. As we were setting out again we discovered that the steel runner of the sled was broken and doubled back under. We filed a portion off — the best we could do, but it still left the runner far from satisfactory and the sled heavy to pull. Then we set out for the station, which we reached about 8 p.m. Johansen himself came out to meet us. There seem to have been great doings since he returned, the day after I left. He told Chipman the geologists and topographers were not doing their duties — sitting about in the house when they should be exploring the unknown coasts. Apparently he went so far that the atmosphere began to fume with sulphur — all parties becoming inflamed.[10] Weather gloriously fine all day.

[The text of Johansen's note retrieved by the author, which was but one of several left by Johansen at assorted localities on southern Victoria Island, according to Chipman (1913-16, Apr. 12, 1916) follows:]

Main Record.
Canadian Arctic Expedition 1913-16.
Southern Party.

April 9, 1916.

This (Forsyth Bay, Wollaston Land) is the farthest N.W. reached by me (with Herschel Island - Native companion) on an exploration trip along the coast of Wollaston Ld. I left headquarters Bernard Harbour on the mainland side of Dolphin and Union Strait opposite *Liston and Sutton Isls.* March 6, crossed via these Isls. to Wollaston Land and followed this to *Lady Franklin Pt.* From the latter place I went to the islands (3) in Coronation gulf S.E. of it, returning via *Miles Isls.* to Wollaston Land and followed then this coast through the sound between *Richardson Isls.* and Wollaston Ld. to *Murray Pt.* (Welbank Bay) where I reached farthest E. and met natives March 25.

Went then W. through the sound back following the coast more closely than on the way out until I reached the so-named *Mackenzie River*, which I examined all along its mouth and for a mile inland and found to be nothing but an intricate system of drainage creeks (only the lowest part of the most E. of these resembles a river (broad, deep-lying bed W. high Willows)) and lakes in swamps in a sandstone terrain. Rechristened it *Raes Creeks.* Found a good portage from here across the base of peninsula terminating in *Pt. Ross*, and followed then the coast rather closely to *Pt. Peers*, which I found to be nothing but one of the Miles Isls. by gravellars and bays connected with Wollaston Ld. Gave therefore the name Pt. Peers to the broad sandstone point E. of Raes Pt. Peers instead. Found a good portage from a deep bay (creek from N.W.) a few miles W. of Pt. Peers and came via this portage (tundraswamp W. many lakes) down in *Austin Bay*, which is much shorter (E-W) than given on maps, the inner 2/3 of it being the named tundraswamp. Followed then the coast of Wollaston Ld. up to here (Forsyth Bay). Saw the W.S. peaks of Museum - range from Clouston Bay: 335-340 N.

On the most Eastern of Okallik Isls. (Liston Isl.) I found many fossil corals in the Silurian *limestone*-bedrock.[11]

The coast of Wollaston Land all the way from Clouston Bay N. to Lady Franklin Pt. S. is a monotonous, low *gravel and tundraland*, where no rock exposure nor rivers are seen. Inland on the peninsula terminating in Lady Franklin Pt. I found the presilurian *sandstone* in many low outcrops; from W. of Raes Pt. Peers this formation comes to the sea

(Coronation Gulf) and gets much higher both here and inland; and it composes all the country from here far inland, until the bay just E. of Raes Mackenzie River has been reached.

From this bay E. *on both sides* of the sound (and the islands in this sound) between Richardson Isls. and Wollaston Ld. is nothing but often very high cliffs of (tertiary?) *basalt* to be seen, until the peninsula terminating in Murray Pt. has been reached, where occur the presilurian *sandstone* below; above this is the Silurian *limestone* and above this again (higher parts of [the] peninsula) the tertiary basalt. The many smaller islands close to (off) Murray Pt. consist of Silurian limestone.

The (tertiary) basalt alone composes the islands visited S.E. of Lady Franklin Pt., all the Miles Isls. (also Raes Pt. Peers) and (apart from a little *sandstone-reef* (Adams reef) I found near the coast about half way between Raes Pt. Peers and Pt. Ross) all the islands in the gulf between Miles Isls. and Richardson Isls. and also these latter ones. Took many *compass-bearings* from Adams reef E. to Murray Pt. from islands and points surveying especially the sound (which runs magnetic N-S and contains more bigger and smaller islands than given on the map) between Wollaston Ld. and Richardson Isls. (there are only 2 of the latter ones) and the mouth of Raes Mackenzie River. Found plenty caribou in this sound (middle of March) also hares.

The peninsula of Pt. Ross runs much more E-W than N-S, so that it hides the mouth of Raes Mackenzie River and the bay E of this, the sound is best seen from the 2 small basalt isls. (which I named Twin Isls.) off Pt. Ross; and the best mark of the S entrance to the sound are 2 (and an intermediate very small one) basalt isls. in its mouth inside Ross Pt.

The peninsula of Murray Pt. is really 1 (2) islands by marine formations connected W. Wollaston Ld. Richardson Isls. should be given as 1 very big Southern (Western) one bordering the sound all the way and then 1 smaller (besides the ones in the sound) in the bay (many lesser isls. here) between this big island and Murray Pt. E. of Murray Pt. the coast looked very low, the Eskimos we met here told about a river (Savaktok) open all winter, short, running (going inland) first N. then W. and coming from lakes — 3 days travelling E. of us; the river may thus safely be placed in or near Byron Bay. Discovered out in the gulf a new big island between Murray Isl. (which is close to Richardson Isls.) and Miles Isls. (about half way) and a *chain of small isls.* (the latter terminating N. in Twin Isls.) N. of this new Isl. — all these islands (composed of basalt) thus connecting the Miles Isls. with Richardson Isls. Back of them could Bale Isls. be seen.

At the mouth (E-side) of Raes Mackenzie River is a *basalt outcrop* (point and small isl.) connected W. the otherwise sandstone land by tundraswamp; ca. 1 mile inland and marking about the middle of the river (mouth) here is a very conspicuous (a good landmark coming from E or S) (ca. 50 feet high) tabular cliff, composed of a *basalt dike* intersecting the sandstone and limestone; named this O'Neills cliff. Similar basalt dikes are seen in the cliffs on the N.E. side of the Murray Pt. peninsula. Biological collections made during the trip.

Left a *record* in a cairn on a smaller island about in the middle of the sound between Richardson Isls. and Wollaston Ld. March 27, and another dito [sic] in cairn on O'Neills cliff (Raes creeks) March 29; other cairns erected by me on this trip only mark places of observations (bearings).

Shot 2 caribou in the named sound and we have thus (we have 5 dogs and started with 4 weeks supplies) been able to extend the trip and investigate things, we met more closely and farther than originally planned. Had very cold weather (w. frequent W. snowstorms) until March ca. 20; since then almost continuously E. wind w. mild weather, even in snowstorms. Much loose snow feel [*sic*] at this change of temperature.

Met no *natives* apart from those in Welbank Bay, all the way, but saw signs of them (meatcaches, tentrings) everywhere. Okallit Isls. are seen from Wollaston Ld. to be 3 [islands] (230- 242W).

More or less *driftwood* found along the coast of Wollaston Ld. all the way from Simpson Bay to Miles Isls. (enough for camp purpose); but *scarcely any further* E., the named Isls. and the ones farther out in the gulf barring and receiving the driftwood coming from the W.

Found plenty *copper*[12] (small crystals) in quartz veins on Miles Isls. The country seen has everywhere been subjected to glaciation; to a tremendous extent is this the case where the sandstone and especially the basalt bedrock comes to the surface.

Today we went into this long and narrow fjord separating Clouston and Forsythe Bays and found at the head of it that a river (probably the Kimiryuok) comes out in a little defined riverbed (sandflats and dunes) on both sides up the river, so far we could see in the thick and snowing weather, were the same low gravel slopes as at the coast.

Owing to the weather we did not go up the river, which not seemed to be so big that we could afford to explore it (we could not see the Museum-range today); maybe it affords access to the interior of Wollaston Land; its direction seems to be the same as the fjords at its mouth.

The *coast W. of here* is high (rocky) as we saw it from Clouston Bay 2 days ago. Apart from Dolphin and Union Strait E. of Okallit Isls. and Coronation Gulf between Miles Isls. we saw no *sea-ice* too difficult (rough) to travel over. No open water seen.

Have only dog and man food left for a couple of days and are therefore returning today via Okallit Isls. to Bernard Harbour where I have promised to be back in the beginning of April.

(Sgd.) Frits Johansen.
Naturalist.

Chapter 40. West with Girling

Departure west with Girling — Foot trouble — Unsatisfactory rifle — Arrival at Girling's mission hut near Clifton Pt. — Revising and translating Alaskan folklore texts — Examining shore west to Croker River — Hunting caribou — Two new Eskimo stories — Setting out for the station — Night travel — Startling news

Friday April 14th – Tuesday April 18th, 1916

Quiet days at the station. When we returned yesterday we found no Copper Eskimos at all there — all had gone east. This happy condition lasted 2 days, then three sleds came over from Ikpuk's settlement and pitched their tents beside us. One was Avrunna's, who is shortly going over to *Puivlik*[1] to spend the summer. The following day Ikpuk and others appeared. They have finally abandoned sealing, though Ikpuk proposes to go a little distance east and shoot *ugyuk* and caribou. He was given the .30-30 rifle I promised him last winter — Kanneyuk to receive his .44. Avrunna received a can of powder, a box of primers, and a bag of shot, to last him, with what he already has, over the summer. On the 18th caribou were seen close to the station. Our folks and the Copper Eskimos rushed off after them but Adam alone got one. Avrunna, however, was away hunting at the time and he killed one and wounded two others, which he expects to find dead when he returns. The Dr. is preparing to go east to Bathurst Inlet again, and the engineer [Hoff] is accompanying him as far as Tree River to bring back the boat engines cached there last fall. Chipman left to map the coast from Rae River east, the day before I returned, e.g. April 12th. All expect to return to the station some time in the beginning of June.

Wednesday, April 19th

Girling, Patsy, and I left for Clifton Point[2] with a good southeast breeze behind us. We had gone some 2 miles when we saw people from the station racing over the ice — evidently in pursuit of a herd of caribou, of which our dogs too got wind. We stopped at Pausanna's old snow-hut — about 15 miles — to boil some tea, then continued another 8 or 9 miles and camped, with plenty of wood. Girling resumed his old duties of cook.

Thursday, April 20th

We started just before 9:30 a.m. with weather similar to yesterday and made Hope Point [Cape Hope] by about 4 p.m., though we set up the tent and stopped 1 1/2 hours for lunch. My waterboots have blistered my feet somewhat, and my left ancle is very painful. Tomorrow unfortunately we have to make a long hike — to Young Point [Cape Young]— but perhaps they will improve. Patsy shot a ptarmigan (willow) close to our camp. Hitherto we have seen no seals on the ice. I must be wearied with travelling, for I find it hard and fatiguing though the weather could hardly favour us more. Tonight the wind is blowing strong, but there is little drift because the surface of the snow has been partly converted into ice by the warmth of the sun.

Friday, April 21st

Crossed Stapylton Bay today, skirting the inside of the rough ice, and camped on Young Point, where Chipman and O'Neill camped last May. The weather was fine and clear, though the sky clouded. The wind swung from east to north, then to west, and finally to east again. We saw three seals on top of the ice. Patsy went after two of them. At the first he fired four shots from my Ross — all went over the top — for the Ross with its single sight (supposed to be accurate up to 500 yards) shoots high up to about 250 yards. He then wounded it with the .22 and it dived. The other he missed with the Ross — again the shot went over. We saw a polar bear's tracks on the ice. The snow here was brownish coloured from the sand blown off the sand dunes to the west.

Saturday, April 22nd

Moderate east wind and snow falling but temperature mild. We broke camp at 8:15 a.m. and travelled as far as a whale carcase a few miles southeast of Wise Point. There we camped, though it was still forenoon, so that we could cut up some of the meat and blubber and cache, both for Patsy and I when we return and for Mr. Girling later. I have the same stomach pain when travelling as I had last spring about this very time and again this winter when we went to *Kilusiktok*. Wood is plentiful all along here — mostly cottonwood.

Sunday, April 23rd

Set out 8:45 a.m. in foggy weather. Instead of following round the coast we portaged over the land, though the last part proved to be stony. Jokingly we are naming it Johansen's portage. We came out near the cliffs of the East Cape Wise and there stopped to lunch. Continuing we passed the West Cape Wise, some 14 miles further west, and camped on a point 2 miles beyond where the men put in a cache last spring. The dogs pulled rather badly today, having gorged themselves yesterday on the whale carcase. It was 6:45 p.m. before we stopped to camp. The sky cleared in the afternoon and the weather was gloriously warm. Hardly a breath of wind stirred all day, but a strong east wind seems to be springing up this evening.

Monday, April 24th

We opened the cache this morning and found it empty. We left a little food of our own in the same spot for our return. About breakfast time Patsy saw a young seal on the ice close to the camp and shot it. We put it on the sled and set out for the Mission hut of Mr. Girling just beyond Clifton Point. The weather was gloriously fine like yesterday, and I searched the land round Clifton Point and the Inman River for the old wood hut Chipman thought he saw. There was nothing but driftwood — 600 yards or more from shore, relics of a time not very remote when the sea washed the shore 30 feet or so higher than it does now.[3] We reached the auxiliary schooner *Atkun*[4] — she is rather smaller than the *North Star* (about 48 feet long) — and the mission hut (Camp Necessity it is called) about 4:30 p.m. and found that the other two white men, Merritt and Hoare (the latter the engineer) had left that same morning with Pausanna for Pierce Point where the schooner *El Sueno* is wintering. This latter vessel freighted our supplies into Bernard Harbour last summer, and its master Allen was ordered to report to Dr. Anderson there in May.[5] The Dr. left a note for him at Camp Necessity, and when Allen reached this place on April 22nd he found it unnecessary to go further. Merritt and Hoare went back with him to help him out, as he had only one dog. Pausanna, the Barrow native, and his family have their tent beside the mission cabin. Wood — heavy logs — strew the beach for miles in both directions. Patsy, who left us about 4 miles from the camp, brought three ptarmigan with him when he arrived.

Tuesday, April 25th – Sunday, April 30th

Quiet days in camp. The 26th and 27th saw a slight blizzard from the west, and the wind has fluctuated between east and west continually. The temperature, however, is very mild. With the help of Pausanna and Patsy I have revised and translated almost all the stories Brick Hopson wrote for me in Harrison Bay the first winter. April 29th a flock of ptarmigan was seen near camp. Pausanna shot fifteen and Patsy shot the five remaining — the whole flock was destroyed. Then the former went inland for caribou. Previously he had seen none, but on this day he sighted a herd of four, three of which he shot. Another herd of ten grazing near by, but unseen by him when he was stalking the first herd, scattered. April 30th he went to bring in the caribou he had shot. He saw another herd of seven but did not attempt to get any as it was Sunday;[6] probably had he been out of meat he would have gone after them. I followed the coast along for some 10 miles to the mouth of Croker River, looking for some reported wood and sod house-ruins but saw none. There are some stone circles, the remains of caches and tent-ties, but no houses. Ptarmigan are appearing more numerously — snow birds are comparatively common, squirrels and mice[7] are running about — and generally life is beginning to abound. Even the land is bare in small blotches and grass starting to sprout.

Monday, May 1st

We all went hunting today and coming across a herd of seven caribou — the same sighted by Pausanna 2 days ago — secured four of them. Instead of packing them home we piled them together, laid the skins over the top, and placed snow blocks all round, then trudged back to camp. The weather was gloriously fine, warm, and bright, with a light east breeze, which later swung round to the west.

Tuesday, May 2nd – Thursday, May 4th

Three days of easterly blizzard, which confined us to the hut. I have been working busily on the Barrow folklore texts, with the help of Patsy and Pausanna, and finished them today. There is still much work to be done revising them and labouring at the grammatical forms, but the most essential part is now finished. Patsy is feeling a little off colour these days. The wind died right down this evening and the sun shone clear, so about 11 p.m. Girling, Pausanna, and I went and brought in the deer that we shot on Monday. They were frozen hard. Patsy shot three more ptarmigan this afternoon.

Friday, May 5th

I went back to the little gorge on Atkun Creek and gathered some plants for Johansen[8] while Girling and Patsy went wooding and Pausanna sealing. Pausanna dictated two short western stories to me today, and I have them translated.[9] He has promised to write some out for me and bring them when he comes along to the station with Girling about the end of this month. The weather was typically spring. About 2 miles from the mouth of Atkun Creek, on the top of the cliff above the gorge, I noticed an old camping-site — evidently a single tent. Pausanna helped me to repair my sled, which was in a sadly battered condition.

Saturday, May 6th

Another beautiful day with a light east breeze. The snow is melting fast around here. We loaded up our sled, Patsy and I, and Girling cooked a bagful of 'bannock' bread for us. About 8:30 p.m. we set out for the station, preferring to travel by night because it is cooler and the surface of the snow harder than by day. About 1:30 a.m. we reached 'Cache Point' 18 miles away, both of us footsore, and Patsy very tired. He tumbled into the tent and cooked while I emptied our cache and did the outside work. We have nearly a sled load of luxuries — bannock, raisins, a little cheese and dried fruit, a tin of marmalade and piece of deer meat — all presents from Mr. Girling.

Sunday, May 7th

We slept from about 4:30 a.m. till nearly 2 p.m. The tent was delightfully comfortable with the warm sun. Patsy went up on top of the adjacent ridge after breakfast and sighted a seal. He went out for it while I stayed and typed notes. Just after 5 p.m. he returned without a seal — they were two bearded seal, a mother and its young. He got within 370 yards of them — the larger saw him and dived. He fired at the younger, which he struck, but it retained vitality enough to slide down its hole, which it left full of blood. We had a light supper then set out at 8:40 p.m., passed the high dolomite cliffs of the most westerly C[ape] Wise and pressed on towards the easterly. A seal was sighted on top of the ice, but it smelt us (the wind was west) and dived. We reached our old lunching ground on the west end of the E[ast] C[ape] Wise after travelling

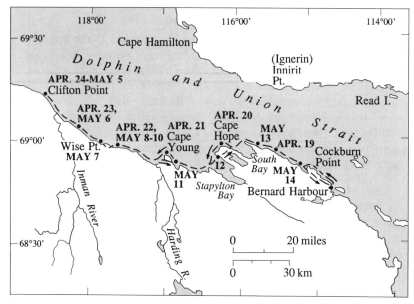

Figure 193. Map showing route taken by the author to Girling's camp, April 19 - May 15, 1916.

some 15 miles and decided to camp. Patsy had worn a great hole through the bottom of his boot and the sock inside and had but a single thickness of a thin sock to protect his foot. Both my feet were badly blistered, and one large blister had burst. We soon had the tent up, a little tea made, and turned into our sleeping bags. The weather had been fine and clear up to midnight, but the wind then swung to south, and it became foggy.

Monday, May 8th

We slept till nearly noon. After breakfast Patsy went up on top of the cliff to look for seals. He saw three or four and started off after the nearer one. It turned out to be a red fox. He sent three shots after it but it got away. The other seals he could not find in the rough ice. We had dinner about 6 p.m. and set out before 8. A little snow was falling, making the weather hazy, and there was a light west breeze. Reaching the whale carcase — some 10 miles away — we camped. I am lame in one foot, a blister that burst showing signs of festering. Near the whale carcase are many remnants of stone caches — evidently of great age. Probably they were made by Copper Eskimos.

Tuesday, May 9th

My foot has been giving me great pain so that I was unable to sleep. I have been bathing it constantly in hot water. The weather was not as pleasant as it has been — a strong east wind creating a low drift. A little snow fell at the same time. Owing to my foot I decided not to move tonight and am busily typing notes and working at Eskimo grammar with Patsy.

Wednesday, May 10th

My foot is much better but still very painful at the least touch. Patsy saw four bearded and one stinking seal lying round a single hole about a mile from camp. He stalked them but all dived save one *ugyuk*, an old bull, which he shot. Later he went back with the sled and brought all the meat and a small part of the skin in. Probably the animal entire weighed 600 lbs, but with the skin and blubber removed its weight was reduced to half that amount. We cached most of the carcase under stones for Mr. Girling to use later.

Thursday, May 11th

A hazy day. We stayed quietly in camp till evening, I writing grammatical notes. About 8 p.m. we started out, and by midnight had made a portage of some 2 miles across the neck of Young Point, thereby avoiding broken ice and an extra 3 or 4 miles. The portage is very good, low ground, marshy, and so in winter ice covered with but few stones and not much vegetation projecting through the snow. A snow storm overtook us before we reached 'Cache Point' on the west side of the portage, and the sky was obscured in consequence. Patsy was suffering from a bad headache and my foot began to give trouble again, so we camped about a mile southeast of the portage. Wood was plentiful and we soon had the fire lit and supper cooked. Before we left, Patsy caught a couple of small flies — the first seen this season.

Friday, May 12th

A quiet day in camp, breakfast about noon, light lunch (biscuits) 3:30 p.m. and dinner (seal meat and rice) about 6 p.m. The weather was dull but almost calm, the atmosphere rather hazy. Patsy had a continuance of his headache. We started out before 8 p.m. to cross Stapylton Bay. It was slightly foggy when we set off and the fog increased at intervals. There was no guide save the light breeze — at times hardly perceptible — and the direction of the snow drifts, which as the prevailing winds in winter are east and west run also in that direction. Following these indications we travelled along, but dipped a little too far south and missed Hope Point [Cape Hope]. We could not see land till within 200 yards of it, and though we knew we were somewhere down in Stapylton Bay we did not know how far. Consequently we camped — about 4 a.m. — on a bare plot of ground with drift wood in plenty.

Saturday, May 13th

Our last camp was only 2-3 miles southeast of Hope Point. A strong northwest wind rose and a little snow fell during the day. We slept till noon, spent the time till 7:30 p.m. in camp, then started off again. Instead of following the coast, however, we portaged across to South Bay and struck out for Cape Bexley. From the west end of [Cape] Bexley we travelled along another 4 miles, then camped in the identical spot where Cox and I cached some pemmican at the beginning of November 1914. Despite the strong wind the temperature was very mild.

Sunday, May 14th

Rose at noon — stayed in camp till 7:30 p.m. then started out again. We prefer travelling at night for several reasons: it is cooler for both men and dogs and the dogs pull better; it is warmer in the tent by day; the snow is harder and travelling easier. The only disadvantage is that it is a little harder to see the points ahead. Snow glasses are not needed from 10 p.m. to 2 a.m. just now. Slowly we travelled down the coast, passed Pausanna's old hut, and about 2 a.m. stopped in the bay just west of Cockburn Point to camp. A strong west wind was blowing and snow falling and drifting a little. Wood was plentiful.

Monday, May 15th

Slept till noon and left at 2 p.m. for the station, having only about 8 miles to go. We did not go round Cockburn Point, but crossed direct over the land from the bay to the station. On the way we saw two caribou and Patsy shot one. Startling news greeted us at the station — a telegraphic account of the war up to November 1915, and the crossing over of Inspector La Nauze, Constable Wight, Ilavinirk, and Arden[10] from [Great] Bear Lake. They met the Corporal [Bruce][11] with Chipman just east of the Coppermine [River], took him along, struck an Eskimo settlement near Lambert Island, and from them learned that the two French priests had been murdered near the mouth of the Coppermine [River] by Sinnisiaq and Uloqsaq — the latter is a *Kilusiktok* man I met this winter, not our old acquaintance. The Inspector pushed on to the station, then crossed to *Nuvuk* on Victoria Land, where he intends to arrest Sinnisiaq. Weather fine and clear. Engineer [Hoff] returned from Tree River with motor engines. He left the Dr. there. Chipman and O'Neill propose to go out via [Great] Bear Lake with the returning police party packing overland.

Chapter 41. Murder Charges

Committal of murder suspect — Sweeney's serious hand injury — Return of Inspector La Nauze with second prisoner — Arrival of Wilkins and Palaiyak — News of Stefansson's party — Packing of specimens completed — Cox maps Bernard Harbour — Payment to Ikpuk and family

Tuesday, May 16th, 1916

Inspector La Nauze and his party returned this morning with Sinnisiaq and his wife. He [Sinnisiaq] was very frightened, thinking he was going to be killed; so too was his wife. They recovered the .44 rifle of one of the priests, which was in Qiqpuk's possession. At *Nuvuk* they found quite a large party of Eskimos. While one of the police party watched the prisoner the others slept. Sweeney has poisoned his hand. He has tried various remedies, iodine, plasters, lysol etc., but it is getting worse and going up the arm. I have begun treating it with boracic acid; he is in great pain. Weather fine and bright. Inspector La Nauze has a touch of snow blindness and so have I. The Eskimos in the vicinity have killed many bearded seals and caribou this spring and have sold them at the station.

Wednesday, May 17th

The Inspector intended to leave tonight to arrest Uloqsaq II, who is said to be at the Kugauyaq[1] River close to the Coppermine [River]. However, so much time was taken up in a formal commitment for trial of Sinnisiaq that he is postponing his departure till tomorrow. The committal took place at the station, and he asked me to attend so that I could lend him assistance if necessary. Ilavinirk interpreted. I took little part in the proceedings, wishing to have my name kept out of the case altogether.[2] Consequently the Corporal in stating his case for the prosecution made no mention of my part in acquiring evidence and the property of the murdered men. Once I put in an objection on the prisoner's behalf — the Inspector evidently wishing me to say something. Sinnisiaq was formally committed for trial and is left in the Corporal's charge to be taken out to Herschel Island this summer. I had a long talk with the Inspector afterwards and am to make up a short document containing information concerning the Copper Eskimos for the benefit of the Police Department in their future dealings with the natives. I intend to address it to the Commissioner of the [Royal] North West Mounted Police,[3] to whom the case of the murder will be sent. He will refer the whole matter to the Premier, and my statement will almost certainly accompany it. Sinnisiaq will probably, the Inspector says, be kept at Herschel [Island] for a year or two, then brought back. At present it seems that the priests did not behave wisely and that the natives acted from motives of self-defense — but there is a slight conflict of evidence. My chief reason in sending in a statement, which will make no reference to the case at all, is to urge that precautions be taken against the indiscriminate influx of white men and western Eskimos saturated with diseases, which would sweep off half the population here within 20 years[4] and that the government may have more information to guide them in introducing regulations etc. for the police administration of the country. A patrol will almost certainly be established in here within the next year or two,[5] and it is imperative that salutary legislation should begin at once — before our diseases (venereal, tuberculosis, measles) have appeared amongst these natives. Sweeney's hand bad today.

Thursday, May 18th

A chilly east wind. The Inspector, Constable Wight, Ilavinirk, and Patsy left about 9 a.m. Patsy is to accompany the Inspector back here with the prisoner Uloqsaq II if he is found, while the others go overland to [Great] Bear Lake. Ikpuk and his family, and one or two other Eskimos who are living on him, turned up yesterday. The Corporal is left in charge of Sinnisiaq and finds the problem of watching him and preventing any attempt to escape very difficult. I am the only one left to interpret for him and am constantly called on to smooth things over. It is an extremely awkward problem for us all — police and Expedition — but for the moment the affair is going fairly smoothly. My position as ethnologist here is beginning to involve grave responsibilities which should normally be no part of the duties of an ethnologist. Sweeney's hand, under the treatment of boracic acid, shows signs of improvement. I have had to administer a sleeping draught 3 nights now. Yesterday he was nearly crazy with pain, his pulse throbbing rapidly, and signs of fever apparent. I gave him ammonium bromide, which depressed the heart action and relieved him very much. I think he has turned the corner, but for a time it looked as though he would lose his arm if not his life. Mrs. Sweeney (Añaiyu) is unwell — she is within some 2 months of delivery and probably her indisposition is in consequence of that. She has too a bad cold. I gave her quinine.

Friday, May 19th – Tuesday, June 13th

Sweeney has been laid up ever since my return. His hand improved steadily with bathing in antiseptic, a little lancing, and redressing several times a day. Finally a kind of boil emerged in the thumb from which I extracted a good deal of pus. The Dr., Cox, and O'Neill returned on the 6th, and the Dr. has now taken the case over. Today he lanced it deeply in the palm and extracted a great deal more matter. Probably it will heal now more quickly, but Sweeney has narrowly escaped losing his arm if not his life. Johansen developed similar symptoms of poisoning at the root of a finger nail. I lanced it; nothing came out at the moment, but overnight all the pus was ejected and his finger is now well. Patsy too ran a nail deep into his foot and could only hop about for 3 or 4 days. He too is all right again. Finally Corporal Bruce yesterday, through firing both barrels of a shotgun at once, got the breech-lever driven deep into his hand in the cleft between thumb and forefinger. It seems to be healing now.

Figure 194. A cheerful Higilaq in summer costume, Bernard Harbour, June 12, 1916. (Photo by R.M. Anderson, CMC Photo No. 39058.)

The Inspector (La Nauze) and Patsy returned to the station on May 26th with their prisoner Uloksak [II]. They found him on an island near the mouth of the Coppermine [River] with a few other families. He came without any trouble. Three or four days after they had gone to get him we got rid of Sinnisiaq's wife; Higlu (Higilaq's foster son) and Jennie took her over to the Eskimo settlement at *Nuvuk* on Victoria Land.

I was in charge of the station till the Dr. returned on June 6th. The engineer [Hoff] gave a little trouble once or twice and had to be told his place, as did Cockney once. The engineer has been a bigger plague to everyone than Cockney. Once he came to blows with the Corporal, and the two had to be separated. The Dr. told us he would have fired him long ago but for the necessity of packing him out with us. As it is if he gives more trouble he will fire him at Herschel Island. I am still in charge of the ordinary work about the place — stores, Eskimos etc. — while the Dr. is busy with his own specimens. All of us are busy packing our things to go out. I have eighteen cases of specimens packed and still much more to continue with.

There has been a settlement of several Eskimo families on the point about 200 yards from the house. We have had no trouble with them as all save Ikpuk's family, and latterly Kohoktok's, are strictly excluded from the house. I have taken a number of photos, which turned out pretty well,[6] and have now most of the phonograph records written down and translated. My tent is pitched in the Eskimo camp, and there Patsy and I sleep each night. Kila and Jennie too sleep in our tent, but usually turn in in the early hours of the morning and don't get up till noon, so we hardly ever notice their presence save during the afternoon and evening, whenever we happen to be down there.

Wednesday, June 14th – Sunday, June 18th

The chief event of the last four days was the unexpected appearance of Wilkins and Palaiyak from the north. His news in brief was this. The *Mary Sachs*, with Capt. Bernard, Levi, and an Eskimo family, is at Cape Kellett, as it was last year; there are fair prospects of getting her off when desired for the return to Alaska. This summer the attempt will not be made, for there are not enough men there to launch her, but it will probably be done in the summer of 1917. The *North Star* with Wilkins, Aarnout Castel, Billy Natkusiak, and another man wintered in the northwest of Bank's Land near Cape Prince Alfred. He [Wilkins] had instructions to try and make Winter Harbour in Melville Island, but could not round the cape on account of heavy ice. Stefansson on the *Polar Bear* tried to follow Wilkins up the west side of Bank's Land, and finding that impossible went round the east side through Prince of Wales Strait, but was unable to proceed beyond Mt. Adventure. Consequently that vessel wintered there, almost opposite McClure's old wintering place. During the winter there was freighting up to Melville Island for a new base in Winter Harbour in 1916. Storgersen mapped part of northeast Victoria Land — triangulating with compass from a base and taking a few sextant observations.

The New Land has been explored and mapped for about [?][7] miles and is to be further explored this spring by Stefansson and a party. An ice trip had been planned for early spring west from Cape Alfred, but Storgersen did not turn up to take part in it, believing he had not sufficient dogs, as many had died during the winter. There had been a great number of Eskimos — combined *Kanghiryuarmiut* and *Kanghiryuatjagmiut* off outside Minto Inlet, with whom they had much trouble. Two sleds from [Cape] Kellett or the Sound[8] which visited them were stripped of everything by the natives. Stefansson proposes to go out by the Northeast Passage, in the *Polar Bear*, sending the rest of the party out next summer (1917) in the *North Star* and *Mary Sachs* via Herschel Island.

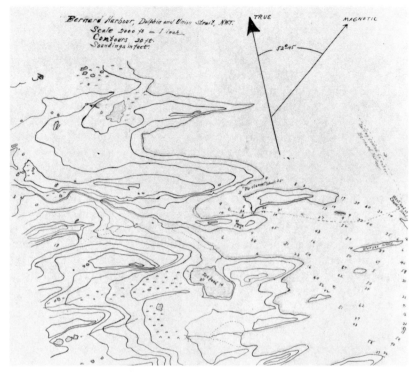

Figure 195. Topographic map of Bernard Harbour, N.W.T., prepared by John Cox, June 1916.[9] (CMC Photo No. K87-891.)

Wilkins for many reasons wanted to go out — at least as far as Herschel [Island] for his mail, and most likely right outside. Stefansson was very anxious for him to remain and take the leadership of the party that will explore the new land this spring, but he declined.

Sweeney's hand has been painful latterly but I think it is improving. The Dr. lanced it again this morning, as the old incision failed to drain any more pus. A great deal was expressed in the new incision he made. The hand must have been utterly rotten; the skin has peeled off the palm and will probably peel off all over.

I am making slow progress with my packing and have already twenty cases packed. The weather has been fine and warm the last two days, and the snow is melting fast. Ducks (oldsquaws and eiders) are plentiful, and geese occasionally fly over. The Eskimo settlement has diminished to five families, though others are fishing not far away.

Monday, June 19th – Wednesday, June 28th

Busy days at the station packing. By today all my specimens are on board, boxes and packages, forty-four in number, though I think I have omitted Nos. 34 and 35 by accident, and so the numbers run up from 1 to 46. In addition I have packed a box of anthropological books — my own,

Beuchat's, and the Expedition's, which is ready to go on board tomorrow. The bay is fast clearing of ice, the ship is free, the ice round the sides having been cracked up with powder (placed in bottles under the ice and fired with a waterproof fuse). The ship is half loaded already with food and specimens. Sweeney's hand is rapidly getting well — and all the rest of us are well and looking forward to getting out in a month or less. Cox, with Patsy to help him, has mapped the harbour on a large scale and started to map inland a little, but has postponed it temporarily to pack. All the Eskimos have left us and gone to spear the salmon as they migrate up the mouths of the streams to the east of us. Mike and Eikie went over to one of the islands off Cockburn Point one day and brought back about 180 eggs — eider ducks' and a few seagulls'. Yesterday the Inspector with his two prisoners went over and brought back about the same number. I have 'paid off' Ikpuk and his family — making provision for their future to some extent by caching about all his goods in the station house for Girling to deliver to him by instalments. Ikpuk gladly consented to the arrangement; he has taken a 10 1/2 power monocular and the .22 automatic (having already received from me a .30-30 rifle and Jennie a .44) with two cases of cartridge each for his .30-30 and the .22. In the house are stored for him 28 boxes of .30-30 ammunition, 8 cans powder, 2000 primers, 10 bags (100 lbs) shot, 4 large knives, 5 files, 2 combs, a pot and a small fish-net, needles, thimbles and fishhooks. He has taken one file, a hammer, a saw, a large fish-net, and a large single tent. Avrunna is to receive of this 4 cans powder, 5 bags shot, and 1000 primers.

Chapter 42. Journey to the Stone Hut

Photographing salmon spearing — Packing overland with Patsy and Jennie — Brief stay at second fishing creek — Camp near Cape Krusenstern — Taboo on washing iron utensils — Examining the stone hut near Locker Point — Mosquitoes abundant — Forced stopover — Travelling by night — Jennie's explanation for an echo — Influence on fish migration — Canoe trip back to station

Thursday, June 29th, 1916

Patsy and I left this morning to pack down to Cape Lockyer [Locker Point], where I wish to examine an old stone hut on top of a hill behind the cape. Wilkins came with us as far as the fishing creek[1] to get some photos of the Eskimos spearing fish. The salmon are now migrating, mainly at night up the creeks to the lakes, and the young fish are coming down at the same time from the lakes to the sea. The salmon from the sea average about 8 lbs in weight and about 2 feet long; the young fish are only about 8 inches long and weigh about 1/3 lb. The former are caught in traps of stone at the mouth of the creek, the latter at other stone traps a little higher and at others again at the outlets of the lakes. While the men race about in the water spearing with the *qaqivuk* the large salmon, the women catch them as they flee for shelter into dark box-like cavities of stones and string them on a line. We waited till the first migration of the evening took place, when about 40 salmon were caught. The Eskimos, mainly the children, ran to the upper series of traps and caught the little fish in their hands. Both Wilkins and I took photos of the performance,[2] then Patsy and I with Jennie continued on to Lockyer [Locker Point] — at about 10:15 p.m. Weary packing over very stony ground took us to the second fishing creek,[3] some 12 miles from the station, where Qamiñgoq and Qaritaq alone were camped. The camp we had just left comprised about nine families. We reached Qamiñgoq's camp about 4 a.m. on the 30th. The weather was gloriously fine — as indeed it has been for the greater part of this month, the wind shifting from east to west then back again to east. Mosquitoes were thick for a time when the wind was light, but disappeared as it freshened in the early morning.

Friday, June 30th

We slept most of the day. About 2 p.m. I turned out and boiled a pot of oatmeal and some tea. We were obliged to leave Mafa, one of my dogs, because his feet were blistered with the stones and he could barely limp. I bought five semi-dried fish from Havgun, paying a knife for them, on the understanding that she should look after Mafa till my return. Then we set out, but travelled only some 4 or 5 miles. We had then reached a large lake called *Kogluktuaryuk* — about 1 1/2 miles in diameter — a few miles west of Cape Lambert. The main body of the lake was still covered with ice, but there was a broad lane of water round the edge,

Figure 196. Copper Eskimos spearing salmon in stone weirs at the mouth of Nulahugyuk Creek, three miles south of the C.A.E. headquarters at Bernard Harbour, June 29, 1916. (Photo by D. Jenness, CMC Photo No. 37078.)[4]

and we could not get on to the ice to fish. Qaqcaq, my other dog, was growing lame — for the country is very rough, covered with broken dolomite — so I decided to camp, lest he be entirely incapacitated to-morrow. We found heather [*Dryas*] and boiled some tea, after which Patsy and Jennie went off to look for ducks and rabbits, while I stayed to mind camp. While they were absent I wandered over to look for fossils in an exposure of dolomite rock. I found no fossils, the dolomite, which shows up here in many places in low cliffs, seeming identical with that at Cape Lambert. On the surface of the ground among the dolomite debris, the only other rock is an occasional bowlder of diabase. However, on the way back to camp I nearly trod on a Pacific eider sitting on a nest of four eggs. Patsy and Jennie returned about 3 a.m. (July 1st), by which time I had a pot of rice cooked for them. They had seen no rabbits, but brought a female Pacific eider and three eggs. Mosquitoes worried us a good deal during the evening, for there was but a light east breeze. Jennie is very good company, always laughing or singing — she is enjoying the trip immensely, and both Patsy and I enjoy her company.

Saturday, July 1st

A strong east wind sprang up some time in the morning, and as there was no sheltered place in which to cook we stayed in bed till about 4 p.m. Then we rose, ate some dried fish, pemmican, bread and jam, and set out. Just before leaving, Jennie brought over three of the four eggs in the duck's nest I had found, and then within 20 yards of camp found herself another nest of five eggs, four of which she added to the list. So we started out with an eider duck and ten eggs. After packing about 2 miles we found shelter under a low dolomite cliff and cooked these over a heather fire. Slowly we pushed on over one dolomite ridge after another, passing along the edges of several lakes — varying from mere ponds to a mile or more in length, finally stopping about 2:30 a.m. to camp. The sky was cloudy all night and the wind cold, but there were at least no mosquitoes. We camped on a site where two Eskimo families had pitched their summer tents, as was evidenced by two oval rings of sod about 6 inches high and with a major axis of about 6 feet. We have passed many *inyuchiut* (stones for caribou drives) on our way hither. On the coast just north of Lake Kogluktuaryuk we could see through the field-glasses three Eskimo caches (winter clothes etc. cached near the shore). Our tramp today took us 8 or 9 miles on our way.

Sunday, July 2nd

Rain fell throughout the morning — heavy rain in big drops. It soaked through the foot of the tent and wet Patsy's sleeping bag, the sleeping skin, and my two shirts with sundry other things. The wind blew strong and cold, and we could light no fire, the heather and willow twigs we collected last night all being wet. We set out about 6:30 [p.m.], and crossing ridge after ridge of dolomite and skirting many lakes, reached at midnight a camp of six Eskimo tents beside a stream[5] flowing out of a large lake into the deep bay west of [Cape] Krusenstern. There beside them we pitched our tents and boiled oatmeal, a loon's (*mallere*) egg Patsy found on the way, and tea in the tent of Ayallik, Ikpuk's brother. Just as the tea was boiling salmon trout appeared in the stone weirs beside us, and all the Eskimos, Jennie included, rushed off to spear them. Jennie missed them all, some got one, some two, and one man three. It is just the end of the salmon migration, so the number of the catch was small, though none which entered the weir escaped. Soon the Eskimos will scatter over the land south after caribou. I took the teapot down to the creek to wash it out. One must not wash it directly in the creek or the fish will smell the contents and not come up. I took an aluminum cup to dish up the water in, and the Eskimos told me iron was taboo in the fishing creek while fish were running. However, I washed out the pot, then showed them the difference between iron and aluminum, and assured them aluminum was not taboo, a distinction they appeared to swallow all right. The east wind seemed to be abating somewhat and the sun was now shining so that we could set our things out to dry.

Monday, July 3rd

I turned out at 10:30 [a.m.] and cooked some oatmeal, after which Noqallaq, Jennie's cousin, and I left for *Qiqigarnaq*,[6] the hill behind Cape Lockyer [Locker Point]. Our course led us beside many ponds and lakes and over several stony ridges for some 9 or 10 miles, for the large creek which flows by our camp falls not into the bottom bay behind Cape Krusenstern but on the west side of it. The slopes of *Qiqigarnaq* were covered with dolomite shale, with one or two fossilless dolomite exposures on the north side. On the top we found the stone hut, erected (some of the Eskimos say) by white men long ago.[7] It is 6 feet high, with a diameter of 7 feet at the bottom and 2 feet 2 inches at the top (inter-

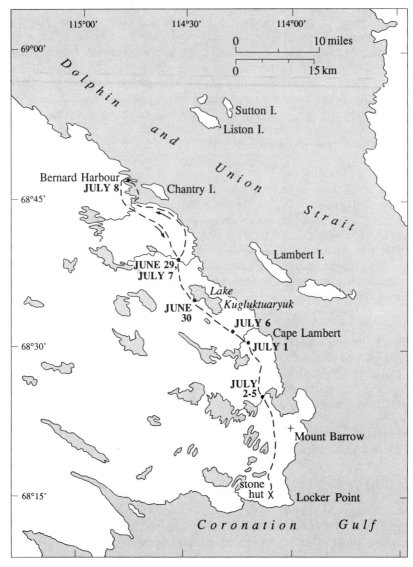

Figure 197. Map showing author's route to and from stone hut near Locker Point,
July 1916.

nally), shaped like a truncated cone, the orifice at the top being closed by
flat slabs. The doorway faces west- southwest and was 18 inches wide by
30 inches high, being raised 16 inches above the floor of the hut. There
were no signs of the hut ever having been inhabited by man — indeed it
was too small — but rabbits, lemmings, birds etc. had left their traces.
Abutting on the doorway externally were two stone tent rings and some
15 yards to the north a stone pillar made by laying six or seven flat

Figure 198. The old stone hut near Locker Point, looking east, July 3, 1916. (Photo by D. Jenness, CMC Photo No. 37070.)

dolomite slabs on top of each other — probably entirely from amusement. Nearby was a stone shelter behind which the Eskimos had crouched from the wind while scanning the landscape for caribou. We ate lunch beside the house,[8] dried fish and chocolate, then set off back to camp. We had gone almost half way when suddenly on the opposite side of a lake two caribou appeared — a *nukatukak* (2-3 years old)[9] and a doe that had never borne a fawn (*noraitok*). A stern chase delivered them into our hands, and tired and footsore we reached camp just before midnight, carrying the skins and a leg bone on our backs. Patsy meanwhile had been over to Mt. Barrow, round which he chased a rabbit till at last it dropped beneath a .22 bullet. Some of the Eskimos went down to the shore and brought back a number of eggs, of which I bought a dozen with matches. With eggs, duck, and tea, we had a good supper. A number of fish came upstream and were speared during the day. Jennie went spearing them without boots and cut her heel on a stone; consequently we shall be unable to leave tomorrow as intended on the return journey. The weather was very warm, with a very light east breeze; mosquitoes plagued us badly.

Tuesday, July 4th

Another glorious day with a light north breeze. Mosquitoes again abounded, but as we stayed in our tent much of the day they did not worry us much. Patsy had collected a few specimens, flies, bugs, [and] fish for Johansen, and skinned the rabbit for the Dr. Jennie was up all night so slept most of the day. The Eskimos held a seance last night, Toqalluaq ('Socrates', because he is the ugliest man in the country) performing.[10] I was in bed at the time, but Patsy attended. The procedure — official at least — was the same as at others. He invoked his spirit, said something, then laughed and had to cover his eyes and recall his spirit.

This happened repeatedly, as he apparently could not control his laughter when any of the audience laughed. He spoke [about] a boy whose legs were too long (Patsy), about a man with long whiskers (myself — for which reason the Eskimos commonly call me *injuqoaq* — old man). I was called Patsy's father and accused of frightening the fish by dipping up water from the creek in an iron cup. Unluckily for Toqalluaq the Eskimos had a phenomenal catch yesterday. He has tabooed all sewing today.

I saw today for the first time amongst the Eskimo the bull- roarer — it is a toy only, called *imilguptaq*, i.e., the whizzer.[11] In the evening I made a pot of chocolate and ate some deer meat the Eskimos cooked. They are having an easy time, lying about their tents all day waiting for fish to show up in the weir. From time to time someone goes down to look and gives a whoop if any appear, whereupon everyone rushes out, clothed or naked, grabs a spear, and runs down to the creek. This morning the women were inside the tents, the men outside, and the men fooled the women by hailing when there were no fish. The women had their revenge in the afternoon when all the men were inside waiting for my pot to boil. For the children this is perhaps the pleasantest period of the year. The weather is warm, there is perpetual sunshine, and almost their sole duty is to brush away the mosquitoes that swarm around them. These diminish somewhat in the 'night' hours, so the children usually roam about all night, playing on land and water, looking for eggs and mice,[12] snaring small birds, and bathing in the creek or in an adjoining lake; by day they sleep in the tents with the door blocked up with skins.

Wednesday, July 5th

A day similar to yesterday but with a west breeze instead of a north [one]. The Eskimos cooked fish heads and one fish, of which we all partook. The day passed quietly in camp, hiding from the mosquitoes in the tents. Jennie, who had been up all night, was sent to bed about 10 a.m. so that we could leave in the evening on our return journey. She brought in a large lemming (*kilañmiutaq*) with four young ones inside it.

Thursday, July 6th

Jennie was playing all night with the other children. I turned out about 10 a.m., Patsy about 4 p.m. There was nothing to do in camp save lie about, read, and write. The Eskimos cooked some fish heads and one or two fish, of which we partook. In the afternoon I cooked oatmeal and tea, then roused Jennie, and we left at 6 p.m. The day had been very warm, with a light but cool westerly breeze, and hosts of mosquitoes. Twice the Eskimos had rushed to their weir to spear fish — with considerable success, securing about twenty altogether. The evening was cooler, and we slowly retraced our way towards the station, camping after 6 or 7 miles just beyond our former camp. We might have proceeded further, but both Patsy and I were tired. Jennie was disappointed indeed at our not continuing on, but she had no pack, her foot not being fully healed, and I was carrying both hers and my own, some 70 lbs altogether. As we skirted a small lake we saw two black brant, which Patsy shot. There was a small islet in the lake; on this they had a nest. We saw too a female eider duck on it and two seagulls hovering round, all [of] which had nests in the same place. The water was rather too deep to cross over to it by wading, so we let them stay; however, on the shore of the same lake we nearly trod on another eider sitting on a nest of four eggs, two of which we took along. These and the two brant we cooked for supper, then boiled rice (brown) in the soup and also made tea, so that we had quite a feast. Jennie is a queer little thing. She was sadly out of temper at being wakened this afternoon, then had a cry on leaving her Eskimo friends. Ten minutes later she was chatting gaily with Patsy, quite forgetting all her troubles. As soon as we stopped to camp I sent her off to gather a dog-pack full of heather for fuel. This she did, first changing her foot-gear, then turned into the tent to mend her boots while I cooked. After supper Patsy took the glasses to look round on the chance of seeing a brown bear, and she followed him. He has been made a present of my Ross rifle — with the Dr.'s permission — and is very proud of it, not unnaturally, for it is in excellent condition and a fine weapon for large game — deer, bears etc. The [Geological] Survey men have divided a case of ammunition for it, which was left over, between him and Girling, so that he is well supplied for a year anyhow, unless he is extremely wasteful. We saw an interesting sight this evening — a seagull chasing a loon (mallere), which was flying too near the seagull's nest. The loon did not seem perturbed at all, but quietly settled on the water, whereupon the seagull, which had well-nigh overtaken it, flew over and back to its nest. The other day we saw an eider (female King) chasing a seagull for the same reason, and the seagull did not relish it at all. The Eskimos have a curious custom with reference to the salmon migrating up and down stream. If caught going up, their heads (if they are lain on the ground) or their backs (if hung up to dry) must face upstream, and vice versa if captured when migrating to the sea. Then the other salmon will follow in their wake, as though their companions were still continuing their journey, and be captured likewise in the same weirs. Probably a similar process of reasoning explains why lake trout caught by jiggling should be laid with heads facing the hole in the ice, though I could never obtain any other reason than that "it had always been the custom to do so." The mosquitoes were a little less numerous at midnight when we stopped to camp, as the sun was clouded and the air rather chilly, but 2 or 3 hours later they came out again as thick as ever. Everything promises another glorious day tomorrow (or today, for it is now 4 a.m. July 7th).

Friday, July 7th

A moderate east breeze was blowing during the day, not sufficient, however, to keep down the mosquitoes. I turned out about 2 p.m. and cooked with heather, then wakened Patsy and Jennie. We set out about 5 p.m. and travelled with many stops till 11:30 [p.m.], when we reached our old camping place beside Lake Kogluktuarjuk.[13] On the way we gathered seven eider duck's eggs. Jennie shot an eider, and Patsy killed a squirrel. All of these we cooked, mixing rice with the soup and making also a pot of chocolate. Five of the duck's eggs had chickens inside in a very advanced state, and Jennie was horrified by them and especially at Patsy's eating them. We continued then our journey and about 5 a.m. July 8th reached the fishing creek [*Kogluktuaryuk*] where Qamiñgoq and Qaritaq were camped. Since we passed, Mammaq and Itilorunna have joined them. Our arrival wakened them all up, a fortunate event, for the salmon were just coming into the mouth of the creek. Half an hour later every adult in the place was out spearing them. They lent Jennie and Patsy spears, and the former secured five while Patsy got six. Qamiñgoq got ten, and everyone was successful more or less, so that there is great rejoicing. It seems that the fish began to come up in numbers after we passed on our journey down the coast, as Qaritaq came and said "You bade the fish come up — they came so we have killed great numbers." We were passing between a dolomite cliff and a lake this evening when Jennie shouted. The shout was re-echoed, whereupon she stopped and re-peated it. The echo set her laughing and that too was echoed. This gave her more delight than ever, and she shrieked and shouted and called out in every fashion that she could conceive of. I said to her "What is it?" "*A tornraq*" (spirit), she replied. "But where?" I asked. "Inside the cliff." "Is it dangerous?" "No," she answered, "didn't you hear it laugh?" The mosquitoes were thicker today than I have ever seen them. They buzzed round the tent like bees and swarmed round our faces while we walked as thick as any swarm of bees. We had no veils, only Patsy had gloves, and we vainly strove to beat them off our faces with handkerchiefs. Even the dogs howled and had to be let loose. No wonder the caribou are driven maddened over the land and take shelter on wind-swept promon-tories and isthmuses. Patsy has told me a fuller account of how I made the fish swarm up this creek. As we were leaving to go east along the coast Qaritaq had asked me to "will that the fish should come up." That same evening after we had left a large shoal of them did actually migrate up and were speared. The doctrine of the 'power of the will' plays as great, perhaps a greater part in Eskimo philosophy than in our own.

Saturday, July 8th

Qaritaq and his wife left about noon to visit the settlement at the fish-ing creek near the station. We followed about 5 p.m. after a meal of boiled fish. The mosquitoes were worse than ever, for though there had been a fresh west breeze during the morning, it had died entirely away soon after noon. We took our dog Mafa, which though apparently well cared for in our absence, was still lame, and travelled along close to the beach, because it was less stony. After going about 2 miles we came to a small cave in a low dolomite cliff, beautifully cool. There we took shel-ter for an hour, driving out the mosquitoes by burning paper and *oqauyaq* at the entrance. Then we continued on our way and reached the creek about 11 p.m. All the Eskimos had gone inland to hunt caribou as

Figure 199. Tent rings and racks with drying fish, Higilaq's camp at the mouth of Nulahugyuk Creek, near the C.A.E. headquarters at Bernard Harbour, July 1916. (Photo by J.J. O'Neill, CMC Photo No. 38615.)

the salmon migration had ended, and left only Ikpuk's family and Mammaq's. Mammaq himself we saw at the more eastern creek this morning, but he had left his tent and wife here. The Eskimos had been very successful in their fishing, more so than last year. We were much delighted to find our own boys here — Eikie, Palaiyak, Mañilenna, and Adam. They had come in two kayaks and the Peterborough canoe, for there is plenty of open water in shore now, and the bays are quite clear. We boiled a pot of tea, then leaving Jennie, who badly wanted her playmate Patsy to stay, embarked, Patsy in a kayak, I in the canoe, while Mañilenna walked round the coast. It was 3 a.m. when we reached the station and everyone [was] asleep. I found my bunk and Johansen's had been taken down, evidently to put up some more bunks on the *Alaska*. The *Alaska* is now fully painted, even to her name, and looks quite respectable. The boys have found specks of copper in the diabase bowlders about here recently, exactly similar to O'Neill's discovery in Bathurst Inlet. The bowlders here, however, he says, must have come from the Coppermine [River] region, which goes to prove that the copper that the Eskimos obtain there — amygdaloidal — has a basis in solid rock just as in Bathurst Inlet. O'Neill has been trying to discover the proportion of copper in his specimens by the specific gravity, and though his methods are necessarily extremely rough, the percentage comes to well over 1%, which is the amount that is actually worked in the big Michigan mines with great profit.[14]

Chapter 43. Return to the Outside World

Final visits with Ikpuk and family — Start of voyage back to Alaska — Disorientation in fog — Ice-bound at Young Point — Aground briefly — Picking up Klengenbergs at Keats Point — Baillie Island — Farewell to Klengenbergs — A few days at Herschel Island — Paying off native help — Contracting a severe cold and fever — Barrow and purchasing archaeological materials — Visit from Jimmy Asecaq at Point Hope — Delayed by a gale — Influenza strikes the others — On to Nome

Sunday, July 9th – Tuesday, July 11th, 1916

Fine weather with light breezes, mostly east and northeast. We are ready to leave any day now. The ship is loaded, save for a few personal effects round the house; Cox has finished his mapping [of the harbour], and we are just filling in time till the ice conditions seem favourable for a move. Ikpuk and his family we took in the skin boat (Evinrude attached) to the station on July 10th. The salmon, which had ceased migrating up the streams, causing the Eskimos at the fishing creek to go inland, suddenly resumed their migration, and Ikpuk's family, being alone, have speared a great number. He has presented me with a musk-ox skin and the skin of the polar-bear cub he shot last summer on Victoria Land, when I played so inglorious a part in the hunt. If the government allows me to keep them I shall take the bear skin home. Higilaq unpacked the fine set of clothes she made especially for me this winter. I have only worn them once or twice, then let her put them away, intending to take them out with me. Patsy and I paddled the two girls[1] back to the fishing creek this evening in the Canadian canoe. We found seventeen salmon in the weir and had a lively time spearing them. Palaiyak followed us in a kayak and took back a score of fish heads which Higilaq gave us.

Wednesday, July 12th

We practically finished loading today. There seems to be a large body of open water to the west beyond Cockburn Point. Ikpuk, Higilaq, and I took his dried meat in the canoe and cached it on the island at the mouth of the harbour. The two girls walked back to the station this evening, bringing all the dogs. No more fish had entered the weirs, and the young fry had ceased migrating seawards. Weather fine and clear.

Thursday, July 13th

We packed the last things aboard and got away about 7 p.m.[2] The Canadian canoe was presented to Ikpuk, to his great delight. Outside Chantry Island we had to work through a good deal of ice and finally anchor behind the second point west from the station. The weather was fine, clear, and practically calm. We have drawn for watches — the six Eskimos take 6-hour watches, three Eskimos on each. The six scientists take 4-hour watches each in this order: Dr. Anderson, 8-12 a.m.; O'Neill, 12-4 p.m.; Cox, 4-8 p.m.; Johansen, 8-12 p.m.; Wilkins, 12-4 a.m.; my-

Figure 200. Avrunna, Ikpuk, and Higilaq beside the C.A.E. building, Bernard Harbour, July 11, 1916. (Photo by R.M. Anderson, CMC Photo No. 39415.)

Figure 201. Jennie (Kanneyuk) and Kila (Arnauyuk) at Bernard Harbour, July 11, 1916.
Partly loaded *Alaska* on left. (Photo by R.M. Anderson, CMC 38997.)

self, 4-8 a.m. Breakfast 6 a.m., lunch, 12 [noon], dinner 6 p.m. The engineer [Hoff] refused to take Mike back into the engine room — he was
taken from him a week or so ago because Hoff had struck him in a fit of
temper — so runs the engine alone. He had some trouble in starting up
this evening.[3]

Friday, July 14th

A strong west wind set the ice moving. We remained at anchor for
some hours and shifted after breakfast to the shelter of the larger island
off Cockburn Point. The Dr. landed on it to photograph the Pacific eider
ducks that were sitting on their nests all over the island. He found, too,
three terns' nests. Johansen collected a few specimens. After lunch we
moved out to an ice keg for water, then worked out through the ice into a
great stretch of open water extending to the horizon. The swell was considerable, and put the Inspector and Johansen out of action, besides disturbing the appetites of the majority of us. We are heading west this
evening, making about 3 knots.

Saturday, July 15th

The Dr. was on deck when I turned out to my watch at 4 a.m. and
asked me if I recognised the coast. I told him it looked to me more like
southwest Victoria Land than the mainland round Wise Point. There had
been a fog in the night and some doubts as to the accuracy of the compass. The sky was clouded, the sun invisible, the wind thought to have
changed to east. Just after breakfast the sun came out for a moment and

Figure 202. C.A.E. headquarters, Bernard Harbour, July 12, 1916, with supplies cached in front of house. View is north-west. (Photo by J.J. O'Neill, CMC Photo No. 38621.)

we found ourselves heading east, and we were off *Oqauyarvik*!![4] Apparently during the fog they had made a circle. We turned about and are heading southwest-by-south, which should be almost due west.

Sunday, July 16th

We passed Young Point [Cape Young] about midnight. An hour or two later we ran into heavy ice, which blocked us 2 or 3 miles east of Wise Point. For a time we remained tied up to an ice keg, then the west wind made the ice close in on us and we had to shift. We beat out to try and find an opening westward, but finding none returned and tied up again. Again the ice closed in on us and we had to return for shelter behind Young Point. There we tied up to a large ice keg. Ambrose, about 9 p.m., shot a small seal. The Eskimos were cutting it upon the ice keg when it [the ice keg] split in two. We tied up to the larger half, the other went drifting down the bay.

Monday, July 17th

At the end of my watch (8 a.m.) the ice driven by a northwest wind threatened to hem us in, so we pulled in the anchor and worked up along the shore to the tip of Young Point. The ice was thick round the point, and in working along it we passed too close to the shore and grounded. The tide fell rapidly, and the *Alaska* keeled over to an angle of about 25, so that the water nearly came over the side. A line was run from the mastheads to shore and drawn tight. This straightened her, and we are now waiting for the tide to rise again and set her afloat. Should it not rise high enough we shall have to unload the oil-tanks off the deck.

Figure 203. The author (with oars) about to return to the *Alaska* after bidding farewell to Ikpuk and Higilaq (on right), Bernard Harbour, July 13, 1916. (Photo by G.H. Wilkins, CMC Photo No. 51277.)

Tuesday, July 18th – Saturday, July 22

The *Alaska* floated off at high tide, and we moved up to the tip of Young Point. From here we made one or two unsuccessful attempts to move west; each time we were compelled to return to Young Point. The wind was westerly all the time and the ice drifted a little, so that we had to move two or three times to avoid being jammed or pushed up onto the beach. On the 21st Patsy discovered two old graves and brought me in a number of implements[5] together with one skull. Today we managed to make our way through to a big lead of open water, though half an hour before we left it had seemed impossible. We are now making good time for Baillie Island, through a sea with comparatively little ice.

Sunday, July 23rd

We made Keats Point in the evening. There we found Klengenberg, Patsy's father, and his family. We took their whaleboat in tow for Baillie Island. He has found at Cape Parry, he says, copper in quantity diffused through the rock. He had five children with him — three boys and two girls, besides Patsy and two married girls elsewhere — eight in all. Keats Point contains a magnificent harbour lined with sheer diabase cliffs. One of the islands off the point, Patsy says — the largest — contains the ruins of two or three old wood and sod houses.

Monday, July 24th

A light south wind sprang up for an hour or two in the evening and we hoisted sail. Almost no ice was encountered during our passages across Darnley and Franklin bays. We put in at Cape Parry for Cox to take an observation[6] — Chipman's survey of Langton Bay in the spring of 1915

Figure 204. The heavily loaded *Alaska* awaiting the author's return before sailing for Nome, July 13, 1916. (Photo by D. Jenness, CMC Photo No. 37182.)

put it considerably west of where it is placed on the charts, at the bottom of Franklin Bay in fact. It is thought that the whole of the Parry Peninsula has been pushed too far east on the chart, and Cox's observation was to discover whether this were true of the tip of [Cape] Parry. Since he does not possess the nautical almanac for 1916 — none having come in last summer — he is unable to work the observation out. We were delayed about an hour there,[7] then sped across Franklin Bay, tying up for a few minutes to an ice keg to take on water. We reached Baillie Island about 11 p.m. A Hudson ['s] Bay post was established here last summer and several Eskimo families are camped on the sandspit.

Tuesday, July 25th

A westerly gale. Nearly everyone stayed in his bunk in consequence. The Dr. is not very well — kidneys apparently. Muññilenna, Eikie, and Patsy leave us here and have to be paid off.

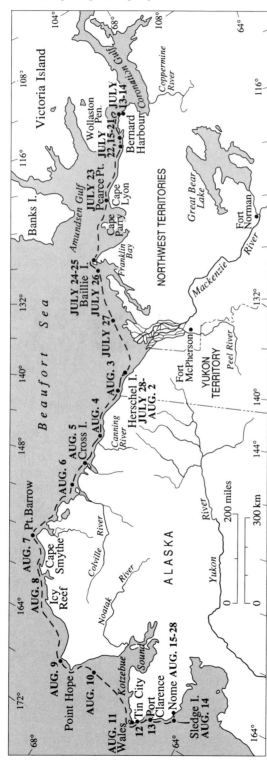

Figure 205. Map showing route taken by the members of the southern party on the *Alaska* from Bernard Harbour to Nome, Alaska, July-August, 1916.

Figure 206. The author reflects momentarily on board the heavily loaded *Alaska* en route from Bernard Harbour to Herschel Island. Near Cape Parry, July 24, 1916. (Photo by R.M. Anderson, CMC Photo No. 39209.)

Wednesday, July 26th

Patsy,[8] Eikie, and Muññilenna were paid off today. Patsy's father made me a present of two white and one blue[9] foxskin because, he said, I had devoted much time to teaching Patsy to read and write. I wished not to take them, but he seemed aggrieved so I gave in.[10] Eikie is going to marry Patsy's sister,[11] if he turns out well; the Klengenberg family,[12] including Eikie, are going to the Coppermine River this summer to trade and trap. There more than anywhere else they can procure a living for themselves. Two elderly men on the beach here are wearing white stone (dolomite?) labrets[13] — one in each corner of the mouth. I saw at least two half-caste children — besides the Klengenberg's. The storm had abated considerably this morning; by noon the weather was practically calm. We left at 7 p.m. for Herschel Island. A few miles out we saw a polar bear swimming in the water with two others about a mile away. It

Figure 207. The Klengenberg family at Baillie Island, July 26, 1916. From left to right, Etna, Jorgan, Mrs. Kenmek Klengenberg (with Bob in her arms), Patsy, Andrew, Captain Christian Klengenberg, and Lena. (Photo by D. Jenness, CMC Photo No. 36912.)

was then at least 6 miles from land. The ship was headed out and we ran right past the bear, almost grazing it, so that whoever wished could take a photo.[14]

Thursday, July 27th

Fog most of the night and day. The wind was east, and when I went on watch in the morning I hoisted the mainsail, but we were making most of the wind with the engine. Practically no ice encountered all day; a slight swell caused misery to one or two on board.

Friday, July 28th – Wednesday, August 2nd

We reached Herschel Island the evening of the 28th. That same evening the Hudson ['s] Bay [Company] gasolene schooner *Fort McPherson*, with Phillips[15] the trader on board, left for Bernard Harbour to establish a post. We spent several quiet days at the island, unloading and loading.[16] All our natives were paid off; only Sweeney's wife goes a few miles further west to join her people. The Inspector[17] found that he had to stay in the [Mackenzie] delta this winter and was very piqued over it.

Thursday, August 3rd[18]

A glorious day. We pulled out and headed down the coast westward. Añaiyu[19] was left about 25 miles west of Herschel Island with an Eskimo family; her own people were in the neighbourhood, but as there was a good deal of ice about we did not know whether we should be able to pick them up.[20]

Friday, August 4th – Monday, August 7th

Travelling along the coast.[21] The chief incident was our running aground about 1 1/2 miles off shore, some 5 miles west of Collinson Point, when a fairly fresh east breeze was blowing. It took 4 hours hard work at the winch to get us off. Incidentally most of us got wet and caught colds. I was most unfortunate, my cold being very severe and made more disagreeable by feverishness, whether malaria or not I don't know. My temperature was high, but my pulse as far as I could tell was fairly steady. Consequently I have spent all the time subsequent to the evening of the 5th in bed, unable to take my watch. While tied up at Cross Island or thereabouts last night we saw the *Herman*[22] pass by. Close to midnight on the 7th we made Barrow, having encountered comparatively open ice all the way from Herschel Island.

Tuesday, August 8th

We unloaded a few more things, nine dogs, two sleds, some empty gasolene drums.[23] I bought two boxes [of] archaeological specimens from Mr. Brower.[24] There is a new schoolmaster at Barrow in place of Cram and his wife, a man named Richardson. The Revenue Cutter had not turned up, only the *Herman*, and she had brought no mail. There was no mail for the Expedition, though our last Ottawa letters at Herschel [Island] were dated November 1915. We left again in the afternoon, put across to a big ridge of ice to take on water, then travelled full speed west-southwest (compass) in the full confidence that at last the dangers from ice — the greatest of all dangers in the Arctic — were practically over. My fever yielded at last this morning, but my cold is as bad as ever, giving me a very sore throat and chest, so that I can hardly utter a word. However, I was able to stand my watch today. We were broken in to coal-heaving on the *Karluk* coming up;[25] now it seems we are to be trained as A.B.'s.[26]

Wednesday, August 9th

We rolled in a broken sea all day, flying before a northeast breeze. About 10:30 p.m. we passed Cape Lisburne and were approaching Point Hope. The ship's pump was in poor shape, and the bilge in the ship becoming considerable. In one more violent lurch than usual a little bilge splashed on the fly-wheel of the engine and stopped it. This piqued the engineer, who immediately turned in, and when asked some minutes later if he couldn't keep the engine running to Point Hope at least — only 2 more hours — he swore he couldn't without the gravest danger of ruining them. All sails were hoisted, and everyone was resigning himself to seeing Point Hope not earlier than noon tomorrow, when the engineer turned out, rubbed his fly-wheel dry, and started the engine again. The whole trouble had simply been a display of childishness and 'cussedness'.

Thursday, August 10th

Glorious weather. We reached Point Hope safely and were inundated with Eskimo visitors, including our old *Karluk* friend Jimmy Asecaq. I spent most of the morning buying archaeological specimens from them. Incidentally I traded off my heavy *atigi*, made for me last fall by Higilaq, and obtained a mat made from skins of eider ducks and loons. We resumed our voyage about 2 p.m., bidding goodbye to Mr. Orr,[27] the English missionary. Kotzebue Sound is notorious for bad weather, so we ran down to Cape Thompson before striking south (compass).[28]

Friday, August 11th

Rain in the night, a fine morning, marred by fog towards noon. This cleared away, however, in the afternoon and showed us land on the port bow; towards evening we approached Cape Prince of Wales — we are outside the Arctic circle, 'sour-doughs' of 3 years standing. A strong north wind sprang up in the evening. We anchored under the village of Eidanoo [near Wales], and were visited by two canoe-loads of natives, but an hour later[29] found our anchor dragging and had to move further east some 2 miles. There under some high bluffs we found shelter from the seas, but not from the wind, which blew in violent gusts down the face of the cliffs. We have both anchors out,[30] and for an hour she has stood without drifting, but we do not know how long it will last, and one of us bestrides in turn the anchor chains all the time. We are getting close to Nome now.

Saturday, August 12th

The gale continued all day but our anchors hold. We could see opposite us on the shore two or three empty shacks and the ruins of an old mining plant, for the rock here is cassiterite (tin oxide) and has been worked (though through mismanagement, apparently, it did not pay) for the mineral. From 10 p.m. till 2 a.m. it is fairly dark now.

Sunday, August 13th

The wind abated considerably in the early afternoon, and we sailed along the coast to the beginning of the sandspit that runs in to the Reindeer Station at Port Clarence. The spit is about 15 miles long, and to go inside the bay would have been out of our way. The wind is still pretty strong; our anchorage is in smooth water, 2 1/2 fathoms, but the bottom is hard, and the anchor seems to be dragging a little all the time. Cox was down with influenza today — feverish and temperature 100.8° F. The Dr. has been seedy for some days with the same thing; none of us in fact feel in condition.

Sunday, August 14th

The wind had dropped a good deal, so after breakfast we hoisted sail and under combined engine and canvas set off for Nome.[31] About noon the wind died down and rain fell.[32]

Epilogue

My father's Arctic diary ended on August 14, 1916, but from the diaries and notes of Dr. Anderson and Wilkins, and from other sources it is possible to relate some of the events that happened thereafter.

Nome

The *Alaska* docked at Nome early in the morning of August 15. After arranging for the removal of its valuable cargo, Dr. Anderson and his scientific companions disembarked, sent telegrams in several directions of their safe arrival at Nome, and got rooms at the Golden Gate Hotel.

That evening several of the men visited Jafet Lindeberg, to thank him for his efforts to rescue the *Karluk* survivors on Wrangel Island in 1914 (he had at his own expense chartered a vessel, the *Corwin*, for that purpose). Then they went to a movie theatre to see *Quo Vadis*. The next day Lindeberg took them on a visit to his Pioneer gold mine.

Disposal of the *Alaska* was a major item of business before Expedition members could leave Nome, and Dr. Anderson sought guidance on this matter from the Department of the Naval Service in Ottawa. Instructions ultimately arrived, and he had the schooner hauled up on the beach, from where it was sold many months later.

Passage was then arranged for Expedition members on the S.S. *Northwestern* for Seattle on August 28. My father had an especially large load to take to Ottawa besides his bag of personal effects: 40 boxes and 9 bags of ethnological specimens, a box of books, and three kayaks and paddles (Anderson, 1913-16, Aug. 23, 1916).

During the rest of their stay in Nome, Expedition members had time to visit several local people. One of these was Dr. D.S. Neuman, the local government health officer, who had a remarkable collection of Eskimo artifacts, "probably the most complete in the world" (Wilkins, 1913-16, p. 81).

To Seattle and Ottawa

The S.S. *Northwestern* left Nome during the afternoon of August 29, with Dr. Anderson, Cox, Jenness, Johansen, O'Neill, and Wilkins on board. Johansen disembarked at Ketchikan on September 9, in order to return to Ottawa via Prince Rupert and Jasper Park. The others reached Seattle two days later and dined the same evening at the College Club, where each one was called upon to give an after-dinner speech.

From Seattle they shipped the Expedition's freight to Ottawa via Vancouver, and Cox, Jenness, O'Neill, and Wilkins followed the same route east. Dr. Anderson, however, accompanied by his wife, went first to Victoria for a few days to settle some Expedition matters with George Phillips, the Store Officer for the Department of the Naval Service there, and to ship the Expedition papers and instruments from there to Ottawa. Men and equipment arrived safely in Ottawa before the second week in October.

Chipman, who had backpacked across country on June 1 from the mouth of the Coppermine River to Great Bear Lake and journeyed from there to Fort Norman and Edmonton, arrived in Ottawa only a few weeks earlier than the others. With the safe arrival back in Ottawa of all six scientific members of the Southern Party, there remained only the arduous task of assembling and preparing for publication the extensive collections of notes they had written during the previous 40 months, a task that stretched over more than 25 years and was never fully completed.

Subsequent Activities of My Father

Settling into a small apartment on Osgoode Street in Ottawa my father spent the next several months getting his notes and reports underway and his collections straightened out. Within 6 months he completed manuscripts for C.A.E. volumes on Eskimo folk-lore and string figures, had labelled and catalogued all of his Arctic specimens, listed all of his photographs, and written several chapters for his monumental work on the life of the Copper Eskimos. In addition, he published a brief article on his ethnological results in the *American Anthropologist* before the end of the year and followed it with a longer one on the Copper Eskimos in the *Geographical Review* early in 1917. His third publication, appearing early in 1918 in the *Geographical Review* was the article on the Alaskan Eskimos he wrote in the back of his diary during the summer of 1915 on Victoria Island (Jenness, 1918). While accomplishing this he also sought clarification on his possible future with the Geological Survey in Ottawa; he was offered employment at a salary of $140 per month while he wrote up the material he had collected in the Arctic, but nothing after that. By the spring of 1917, dissatisfied with his employment situation and much disturbed over the war news from Europe, he enlisted as a private in the Canadian Army, along with his colleague John Cox, and within a few months was shipped to England, though not before becoming engaged to Dr. Sapir's secretary, Eilleen Bleakney.

After two years with the Canadian Army, much of which was spent as a gun spotter at the war front in France, my father returned to Canada, married, and following a three-month vacation to New Zealand, settled down to complete his Arctic reports. His first report, a classic account of the life of the Copper Eskimos, appeared in 1922 and was followed during the next six years by volumes on the string figures, folk lore, songs, and vocabulary of these native people. An additional volume on the material culture of the Copper Eskimos was written by 1932 but remained unpublished until 1946. My father's final volume, on the archaeology of the Eskimo ruins of Barter Island, remained unpublished, in rough manuscript form only, just as he had prepared it in 1914. His share of the reports issued by the Canadian government with the results of the

Figure 208. The author with the partly frayed first volume of his Arctic diary, after receiving a Guggenheim Fellowship in 1954. The map is the original drawing of Fig. 49. (Photo by Newton Associates, reproduced with the permission of the *Ottawa Citizen*.)

Canadian Arctic Expedition 1913-18 amounted to four volumes, totalling 1436 pages, far exceeding the contribution of any other member of the Expedition. Collectively they constitute the definitive early work on the Copper Eskimos.

From 1926 to 1942 (with a brief gap in the early 1930s) my father was Chief of the Division of Anthropology of the National Museum of Canada, and his time was divided between administrative duties and field studies of the Canadian Indians. By 1932 he had published his major work *The Indians of Canada*, which after almost 60 years is still a leading book on that subject. Early in this period he also published a popular account of his life among the Copper Eskimos, *People of the Twilight*.

During the 1939-1945 war years my father was seconded to other branches of the Canadian government, where he could best contribute to the war effort. He retired shortly after the end of the war and for the next two decades until his death in 1969 travelled widely, carried out valuable research, and wrote extensively. In 1954 he was awarded a Guggenheim Fellowship and began writing an account of his experiences during his first year in the Arctic (1913-14). Within a year he had completed his manuscript, *Dawn in Arctic Alaska*, which was published in 1957. In the early 1960s he commenced and published a monumental comparative study of the Eskimo administrations of Alaska, Canada, Labrador, and Greenland (Jenness, 1962, 1964, 1965, 1967a, 1968a), five reports which he regarded as his final tribute to his Eskimo friends.

In 1968 he was made a Companion of the Order of Canada, the country's highest honour, in recognition of his many scientific contributions on Canada's aboriginal peoples. Three years later, largely through the efforts of Dr. William E. Taylor, Jr., then Director of the National Museum of Man in Ottawa, he was further honoured posthumously with his name being given to the large peninsula immediately north of Wollaston Peninsula in southwest Victoria Island. Years earlier his name had been given to a small Arctic island off the southwest corner of Borden Island and also to a river flowing into Parry Bay on the east side of the Melville Peninsula, north of Hudson Bay.

My father died peacefully at his home near Ottawa in November 1969 and is buried in Beechwood Cemetery in Ottawa.

Subsequent Activities of the Other Scientists

Dr. R.M. Anderson, soon after his return from the Arctic, was asked to serve on an Arctic Biological Committee, which was charged with the task of seeing that all of the material collected by the Expedition members was carefully studied, written up, and published. In 1919 he became secretary of that committee and later the editor for the entire series of volumes, on which he laboured long and hard to see them into print. Only fourteen of the sixteen originally proposed volumes were eventually completed and published. Nine of the volumes were to have been biological treatises, ranging from insects to botany, fishes to crustaceans and other creatures; five were to have been ethnological, anthropological, and archaeological; and the other two were to deal with geological and geographical aspects and to narrate the stories of the Northern and Southern Parties respectively. The narrative accounts of each party, the definitive studies of mammals and birds seen and collected, and the results of the archaeological work in Northern Alaska failed to see the light of day; indeed, the first two were never written. By the late 1920s most of the C.A.E. reports had been published and in 1946, with the appearance of my father's volume on the material culture of the Copper Eskimos, Dr. Anderson's role as overseer of the publication of these reports at last ended.

From his return in 1916 until his retirement in 1945, Dr. Anderson pursued his studies and collections of mammals for the National Museum of Canada, building up an extensive collection of specimens from throughout the country. During much of that time he was Chief of the Biological Division at the Museum. He died in 1961. Two geographic features in Canada's north were later named in his honour: Anderson Headland, on the west side of Baffin Island, and Anderson Brook, on the southeastern side of Southhampton Island, in the northern part of Hudson Bay.

K.G. Chipman, the senior topographer on the Expedition, remained with the Geological Survey of Canada and its later offshoot, the Topographical Survey, for the rest of his professional career. In 1924 he and his colleague J.R. Cox published their Expedition results in a C.A.E. report on the topography of the Arctic coast west of the Kent Peninsula. Chipman died in 1974. The west end of Chantry Island, at the mouth of Bernard Harbour, was named Chipman Point in his honour.

J.R. Cox enlisted in the Canadian Army a few months after his return from the Arctic and served nearly two years at the war front in France. After returning briefly to the Geological Survey of Canada in 1919, he left in 1920 to work in India for an oil company. His career subsequently took him on an assortment of business projects to Peru, Kenya and Uganda, and the U.S.A. before he retired to Arizona. He died there in 1977. A small island off the west end of Chantry Island, in the mouth of Bernard Harbour has been named Cox Island in his honour.

F. Johansen remained with the Geological Survey of Canada for two years after his return from the Arctic, then was employed for some years by the Department of the Naval Service and its successor the Department of Marine and Fisheries. By 1925 he had published C.A.E. reports on insect life in the western Arctic, arctic vegetation, and crustaceans, and was working on a report on arctic fishes when he returned to Denmark in the late 1920s. He died in Denmark in 1957. A large bay near the Richardson Islands, on the south coast of Victoria Island, has been named in his honour.

J.J. O'Neill worked for the Geological Survey of Canada following his return from the Arctic until 1920, when he accepted a commercial job in India. Returning from there in 1921 he joined the faculty of geological sciences at McGill University in Montreal. His C.A.E. report on the geology of the Arctic coast of Canada west of the Kent Peninsula was published in 1924. In 1929 he became head of the geology department at McGill, then in 1935, Dean of Science, and from 1949 until his retirement in 1952 he was vice-principal. He died in Ottawa in 1966.

V. Stefansson, the Expedition's leader, returned from the north in the fall of 1918, after a lengthy and nearly fatal struggle with typhoid fever and pneumonia, and thereafter pursued a busy career in the United States as author and lecturer for many years. The publication in 1921 of his popular account of his part of the Expedition, *The Friendly Arctic*, created much ill feeling among the scientific members of the former Southern Party, owing largely to his accusation of their disloyalty and disobedience at Camden Bay in 1914. Their collective indignant responses in 1921 and 1922 to his published charges, together with the sharp criticism of the tragic 1921 Wrangel Island expedition he organized and dispatched, and other factors, all led to his being out of favour in many parts of Canada for many years thereafter (Diubaldo, 1978, p. 206). His failure to prepare for the C.A.E. Report Series an account of the activities and scientific findings of his Northern Party has meant that the fourteen published volumes of that series deal almost exclusively with the work of the Southern (Geological Survey) Party. Stefansson died in 1962 in New Hampshire. Eight Canadian geographic features have been named in his honour: two lakes, two creeks, a mountain, a township in Ontario, a large island on the northeast side of Victoria Island, and the northernmost point of land Stefansson discovered, on Meighen Island.

G.H. Wilkins returned from the Arctic to Seattle and thence to Ottawa with Cox, Jenness, and O'Neill in September 1916. He then headed home to Australia, where he was given a commission in the Royal Australian Air Force and was assigned the task of making a true photographic record of the war activities in northern France. Wounded nine times and cited in dispatches for his bravery, he was awarded the Military Cross with bar. Following the war he went south with the British Imperial Antarctic Expedition in 1920-21 and the Shackleton Quest Expedition in 1921-22, then led a British Museum (Natural History) Expedition conducting biological studies in eastern Australia for some three years. Returning to the United States in 1925, he headed once again into the Arctic, making sorties by airplane off northern Alaska in 1925, 1926, and 1927. In 1928 he and his pilot of previous Arctic flights pioneered polar flights by flying from Barrow to Spitzbergen, for which he was knighted by King George V of Great Britain. Within months he was off again to Antarctica, where he made the first inland flight and charted hundreds of miles of coast by aerial photography. He returned to Antarctica in 1929, soon after his marriage, and recognized that a large area formerly thought to be land was merely ice-covered sea. He followed this experience by purchasing an obsolete submarine from the U.S. navy, renaming it *Nautilus*, and being the first to take under-ice motion pictures while on a journey that took him to latitude 82° N. After four more trips to Antarctica, a journey around the world on the dirigible *Graf Zeppelin*, and the maiden voyage of the famed dirigible *Hindenberg*, he flew in a large flying boat into the Canadian Arctic in 1937, using Coppermine, Aklavik, and Barter Island from which to make long-distance sorties over large tracts of the Canadian and Alaskan Arctic in a futile search for six lost Russian aviators. He served with the U.S. armed forces during the Second World War and died, after an extraordinarily adventurous life, in 1958. His ashes were subsequently scattered by U.S. submarine over the ice at the North Pole. A strait between Borden Island and Mackenzie King Island has been named in his honour.

Subsequent Activities of Others

Very little is known about what happened to many of the people the author met during his three years in the Arctic. The following are brief notes I have assembled from various published and unpublished sources on some of them.

Ikpukkuaq and **Higilaq** remained around Bernard Harbour and southwest Victoria Island for some years after the departure of the Southern Party in 1916. Rasmussen (1927, p. 283) met and stayed with them near the Sutton and Liston Islands in February 1924 when he passed by on his epic Fifth Thule Expedition sled journey westward across the Canadian Arctic coast. Both Ikpukkuaq and Higilaq were alive at the time of the formal marriage of Higilaq's son John Avranna (Avrunna) to Lucy Milukkatuk at Bernard Harbour in September 1926, but Higilaq evidently died in late 1927, a probable victim of the influenza epidemic that struck the Bernard Harbour region that summer. Ikpukkuaq's name appears occasionally in the daily journal entries of the Hudson's Bay Co. manager at Bernard Harbour from 1928 until 1930, sometimes alone, sometimes (as in March 1, 1928) with Avrunna and his family. Ikpukkuaq married Kihak after Higilaq died, but she died at Read Island early in 1931 (Walter Vanast, verbal communication, 1990). The photographer-journalist Richard Finnie met Ikpukkuaq at Bernard Harbour in the summer of 1930 (Finnie, 1940, p. 34) and the following spring filmed him building a snowhouse near Locker Point. A copy of that brief film is housed in the National Archives of Canada. Ikpukkuaq was then living near or with his ailing daughter, Jennie Kanneyuk, and her husband Kekpuk and their little son. Sometime after Jennie's death in March 1931, he returned to the Read Island area, where he is mentioned once in August 1932 in the daily journal of the Hudson's Bay Co. post manager as a fisherman for the rival Canalaska Co. He is reported to have died in the summer of 1933 at or near Basil Bay (Death records, Coppermine Hamlet).

Jennie Kanneyuk, my father's 'little sister' during his travels on southwestern Victoria Island in 1915, was the wife of **Samuel Kekpuk** when Finnie reached the Coppermine region in August 1930. By then she was far from well, however, suffering greatly from spinal tuberculosis; she was so crippled, in fact, that in the spring of 1930 she had had to be carried on a sled to the Locker Point area where the annual caribou hunt was to take place (Bethune-Johnson, 1986, p. 50). She died in March 1931 at Coppermine and was buried by Rev. J.H. Webster in the Church of England cemetery on an island in the mouth of the Coppermine River. Samuel Kekpuk died near Bernard Harbour in April 1933, from unstipulated causes, and was buried on Read Island. Their son Aime Ahegona, his wife Betty, and several grandchildren and great-grandchildren now live in Coppermine.

Avrunna (or Avranna), Higilaq's son, and his wife **Milukkatuk** continued hunting caribou and trapping foxes on southwest Victoria Island and sealing near the Liston and Sutton Islands for many years after 1916. Avrunna's name is listed several times in the daily journals kept by the managers of the Hudson's Bay Co. posts at Bernard Harbour, when he made visits there during the winters of 1928 and 1930, and at Read Island from 1933 to 1938. They had several children. Milukkatuk died of flu in May 1949 and was buried by Rev. Webster in the Church of England cemetery on the island at the mouth of the Coppermine River. Avrunna died the following March while hunting caribou inland. Two children and several grandchildren and greatgrandchildren now live in Coppermine.

Kila Arnauyuk, Ikpukkuaq's adopted daughter, after two unsuccessful marriages in 1914 and 1915 (which are reported in my father's diary), married an Eskimo from the Mackenzie River delta and accompanied him to his home. Some of her later often tragic marital history to 1931 has been set forth by Finnie (1940, pp. 85-93). After her marriage to a prospector named Bill Storr, she lived near Coppermine for several years, where both Kila and her husband were well known to Finnie in 1930 and 1931. Some years later they moved to Stapylton Bay, where they operated a trading post from 1939 to 1943.

Charles Klengenberg (whose baptismal name was Christian Klengenberg Jorgensen) moved with his family to the west end of Coronation Gulf in the summer of 1916, establishing a trading post at Coppermine. In 1919 he established a second one at Rymer Point, near Read Island on the southwest shore of Victoria Island, which his daughter Etna (Edna) and her husband Ikey Bolt operated until 1932. Klengenberg's wife Kenmek lived there for many years with Etna and Ikey Bolt. In 1920 he set up another post, at Arctic Sound in Bathurst Inlet. A few years later Klengenberg retired to Vancouver, where two of his daughters resided, in order to write his memoirs. He died there suddenly in the spring of 1931 just before his autobiography was completed (MacInnes, 1932). A large bay at the northwest end of Coronation Gulf is named after him.

Patsy Klengenberg, having acquired a good knowledge of English from his year with the Southern Party and from my father's teaching efforts, later became a successful trader and business man. In 1917 he served as a translator during the well-publicized trials in Edmonton and Calgary of Uluksak and Sinnisiak, the two Coronation Gulf Eskimos accused of murdering two Roman Catholic priests on the Coppermine River in 1913. He later had various dealings with mining entrepreneurs in the Great Bear Lake region, sailed his own boat between Coronation Gulf and Herschel Island, and ran a trading post on Wilmot Island near the east end of Coronation Gulf for some years. Patsy married Mary Yakalun from the Rymer Point area, Victoria Island, in 1924, and had two daughters, Amy and Dora Kelly. Patsy's wife died in 1937, and he re-married soon afterwards. About that time also he adopted a young boy, Donald Ayallik, who in August 1946 vainly sought to rescue Patsy when the latter was caught in an engine-room fire on his schooner *Aklavik* at Cambridge Bay. Patsy drowned in an attempt to swim to shore from the burning boat and was buried at Cambridge Bay.

Ikey (Añutisiak) Bolt married **Etna (Edna) Klengenberg** soon after they met in 1916 (MacInnes, 1932, p. 275). For many years after 1920 they operated a trading post at Rymer Point on Victoria Island northeast of Bernard Harbour, where Etna's skill as a seamstress soon revolutionized the costume designs in the Coronation Gulf region. She also carried out a strong crusade against the practice of infanticide among the Copper Eskimos, especially with regard to girl babies, and even travelled to Ottawa to confer with government officials on the matter (MacInnes, 1932, p. 320). In the mid-1930s Ikey and Etna moved to the west side of Victoria Island near Minto Inlet. By the late 1940s they moved to Coppermine where Ikey became caretaker and interpreter for the first government school established there. In 1953 he was awarded the Coronation Medal in recognition of his services. He died at Coppermine in 1981 (Sperry, 1983, p. 218) and in 1987 his wife followed him in death. Both are buried in the Anglican cemetery at the mouth of the Coppermine River.

Rev. H. Girling, the Church of England missionary, and his assistants, **G.E. Merritt** and **W.H.B. Hoare,** established their mission in the C.A.E. house at Bernard Harbour in 1917 and carried on their work with the Copper Eskimos. Girling was especially interested in the native language, having shared many lengthy discussions with my father on the subject when they were together during the winter of 1915-16. In 1919 he returned to England on furlough. On his way back to Canada he contracted pneumonia and died in Ottawa early in 1920 at the age of 30. Girling had just completed a translation of the Gospel of St. Mark into the dialect of the Copper Eskimos and had been working on an Eskimo grammar and dictionary at the time of his death. A point a few miles west of Coppermine, misspelled Gurling Point, has been named in his honour.

Sinisiaq (or Sinnisiak) and **Uloqsaq** (Uluksak), the two Copper Eskimo men charged with the murder of the French Roman Catholic priests on the Coppermine River in 1913, were taken to Herschel Island by the RNWMP on the C.A.E. vessel *Alaska*, and disembarked there in August 1916. From there, the two prisoners were escorted by the police up the Mackenzie River the following spring for trial at Edmonton and Calgary in August 1917. Their trial being the first of any Eskimo under British law attracted widespread attention. Both prisoners were found guilty of murder and sentenced to death, but their sentences were commuted to life imprisonment at Fort Resolution on Great Slave Lake. In the spring of 1919 they were released, following review of their case, and sent back to Coronation Gulf. Uluksak died of tuberculosis at Coppermine in 1930 and is buried there. Sinisiaq died in the summer of 1931 at Stapylton Bay.

Billy Natkusiak (later known as Billy Banksland) worked for Stefansson for a year after he and Wilkins were at Bernard Harbour in 1915, then he returned to his life as a hunter and trapper. He ultimately found his way to Baillie Island, married a Mackenzie delta woman, Topsy Ikiunak, in the early 1920s, and fathered six children. In 1939 he and his family moved to Holman Island (now Holman) on the west side of Victoria Island, where two of his children are now well-known artists. Natkusiak died at Holman in 1947 and was buried in the old cemetery there. A peninsula in north-central Victoria Island carries his name, as also does a widespread Precambrian basalt formation that caps high ridges inland from Holman.

In 1958 my father received an unexpected letter from Professor Henry E. Childs, Jr., in Alaska, who supplied most of the following information on the fates of several of the Alaskan people my father knew. Professor Childs obtained the information from Pete Savolik (Suivaliaq in my father's diary, the young son of Aluk and Qapqana in Harrison Bay).

Aluk moved to Wainright in 1933 and died there two years later. His wife, **Qapqana**, died in 1915 on the Colville River. Their adopted daughter, **Pungasuk** or Imeroon, married a native of Barrow and died there in 1938.

Kukpuk or Cookpuck, eldest daughter of Aksiatak and Otoyuk, died in 1933 of the flu. Her younger sister, **Siliuna** or Seeluk, was married and living in Fairbanks in 1958.

Jimmy Asecaq still lived in Point Hope in 1958, and **Alfred Hopson** was running a combined coffee shop and dance hall at Barrow. **Charlie Brower** died in 1944, leaving a large family. His trading post by 1958 had become a restaurant and souvenir shop.

Aiyakuk moved to Aklavik on the Mackenzie delta and died many years before 1958. **Mapteraq** moved to the Colville River area in 1933 and died in 1957. His family was still living at Anaktuvuk Pass the following year.

The following information on Aksiatak, his wife Otoyuk, and son Itarklik comes from Spearman et al. (1985).

Aksiatak lived and trapped in the Colville River area for some years, but moved in 1938 to the Killiq and Ningulik valleys, then in 1940 to the Ulu valley, where he soon became leader of a small group of natives. Because of wartime shortages of ammunition and other supplies and his wife's illness, he moved his family south in 1942 to the gold-mining Wiseman area, and a year or two later to the Fairbanks area. He was no longer alive by the early 1980s when Spearman interviewed his son Itarklik.

Itarklik (more recently known as Arctic John Etalook) continued trapping in the Colville River region for some years, but by the late 1920s and early 1930s was roaming farther afield, hunting and trapping with his younger brother Katairoaq, up the Kuukpik River as far as Umiat and into adjoining river valleys. He then moved to the Wiseman area along with his parents in the early 1940s, where he and his wife remained until about 1972, before moving to Fairbanks, where he died in the spring of 1984 (Spearman et al., 1985).

End of an Odyssey

My father commenced this Arctic Odyssey with his departure from New Zealand in April 1913 and terminated it 3 1/2 years later with his arrival in Ottawa in September 1916. Half a year later, in response to his strong sense of duty to the British Empire, he enlisted for overseas duty in the Canadian Army and spent nearly two years on active duty. He returned to Ottawa in 1919 and within a few years completed his seven reports for the C.A.E. Report Series.

In a letter to Vilhjalmur Stefansson from Oxford, dated February 20, 1919, shortly before his return to Ottawa, my father wrote:

> "Now that the war is over, and I can see everything with a clearer vision, I am glad that I was able to take an active part in it . . . I felt that I . . . could not honourably stand aside, and let others fight the battle of civilization."

Of the immense effort he had put into his duties in the north and during the few months he was in Ottawa before enlisting, he had this to say, in the same letter:

> "I am conscious that there are many important data which I failed to obtain, partly through imperfections of my own, partly through the necessity of having to cover the whole field — linguistic, sociological, technological, and anatomical . . . I did my best, both for my own sake and for the cause of science, and because I would not bring discredit on an expedition which it was an honour to accompany."

During the rest of his professional career and beyond, after he had retired, my father strove quietly and diligently to render assistance whenever possible to the warm and friendly people he had known and respected in Canada's Arctic. It is unfortunate, perhaps, that he never had the opportunity to return to visit them, though both Ikpuk and Jennie urged him late in 1930 to do so. By the 1930s, however, my father's efforts had been officially channelled into studies of Canada's other native peoples, the Indians, it was still extremely difficult for a private individual to travel into the Arctic, and because of the depression there was no money for further government-sponsored ethnological work in the Coronation Gulf region. With a saddened heart he responded to his adopted kin:

"I shall never forget my father and my younger sister. Though I would like to see you, it cannot come to pass. It is too far away. I am getting old. Do not be frightened. When we die we will meet each other. We will be happy all together" (Finnie, 1940, p. 169).

Postscript

In September 1990, a short while before this book went to press, I had an unexpected telephone call from Coppermine from Allen Ahegona, one of Jennie Kanneyuk's grandsons. My wife and I had met Allen and his wife Linda during our brief stay in Coppermine in July 1989, at which time we saw their new little daughter Kanayok, namesake of her great-grandmother, my father's 'younger sister'. In the spring of 1990 Linda and Allen had a son, whom they named Ikpukkuaq. A few months later, when we were again in Coppermine, both Linda and little Ikpuk-kuaq were seriously ill in a hospital hundreds of miles to the south.

Allen's telephone call was to tell me he wished to change the name of his small son to Diamond Jenness Ahegona, following the practices of his forefathers, in the hope that the illness that had befallen his child would depart with the original name and that good health and fortune would bless the newly named child. At the urging of his father Aime, he sought my approval for the renaming, adding that they would call the child "Jennessie," for that was how my father had been called. My entire family was proud to accept their compliment to our father.

Allen then reminded me of my father's message to Jennie Kanneyuk and Ikpukkuaq, quoted above, which he had read in Finnie's book, and said "Then my son and daughter will be as your father said, for Kanneyuk and Jennessie will be happy together again."

Three generations and 75 years after my father hunted with Ikpukkuaq and Kanneyuk and their people on Victoria Island, the odyssey has come full circle.

Appendix 1.

People Encountered or Mentioned by D. Jenness, 1913-1916

Included are variations in names and spellings I have found in the accounts of other members of the Canadian Arctic Expedition. The superscript numbers cite the sources of the spelling variants; all sources are listed in the references. Names without superscript numbers are variations within Jenness' diary or from Appendices 5 and 6. This list of names may provide one of the first published records of early Copper Eskimo family names and relationships.

1. Jenness, 1922a
2. Jenness, 1923a
3. Jenness, 1924a
4. Jenness, 1928a
5. Jenness, 1957
6. Anderson, 1913-16
7. Chipman, 1913-16
8. Finnie, 1940
9. Johansen, 1913-16
10. Letter, Childs to Jenness, 1957
11. McConnell, 1913-14
12. McKinlay, 1913-14
13. McKinlay, 1976
14. Roberts and Jenness, 1925
15. Spearman et al. 1985
16. Stefansson, 1913
17. Stefansson, 1921
18. Wilkins, 1913-16

Aarnout — see Castel

Acicaq — see Asecaq

Adam — see Uvoiyuaq, Adam

Addison, Ralph — crew member of the ill-fated *Elvira*, hired by Dr. Anderson to dig out the *Alaska* at Collinson Point; left Expedition August 1914

Adluat — see Ailuat, Fred

Agara — Copper Eskimo daughter of Qamiñgoq (?), Bernard Harbour

Agluak — Copper Eskimo shaman

Agnavigak, Ambrose — young Herschel Island native man hired by Stefansson summer of 1915; husband of Unalina (Palaiyak's sister), father of small girl Annie

Ahangik — see Tucik

Ahina — native man in story told by Ikpukkuaq

Ahluk — see Arluk, Mrs.

Aiakuk — see Aiyakuk

Aikie — see Bolt, Ikey

Aikuk — see Aiyakuk

Ailuat, Fred (Adliak[6], Adluat[11]) — Cape Prince of Wales Eskimo hired for 1 year at Nome, July 1913, to work on the *Mary Sachs*. Accompanied McConnell from Camden Bay to Barrow to get Jenness and return. Left Expedition July 1914

Aitauq — Coronation Gulf Eskimo man photographed at Bernard Harbour, 1916.

Aiva (Iviqunna, Evakana[11]) — young wife of Samuel (Paninona) at Cape Halkett, northern Alaska

Aiyaka — see Aiyakuk

Aiyakuk (Aiakuk, Aiyaka, Ayakuk, Ayacook[5], Aikuk[6], Iakuk[11], Ajakok[9], Iakok[18]) — Alaskan Eskimo who helped Jenness excavate on Barter Island, June-July 1914

Aiyalligak — Copper Eskimo, Liston and Sutton Island area, husband of Arnauyuk briefly in 1915

Aiyallik — see Ayallik

Ajokok — see Aiyakuk

Akhiatak — see Aksiatak

Akseatak — see Aksiatak

Aksiatak (Aksiataq, Arksiatark[5], Akseatak[11]) — Colville River Eskimo at Harrison Bay with whom Jenness stayed Nov. 1913 - Feb. 1914; husband of Otoyuk

Aksiatak (AXiatak, Akhiatak, Aqxiataq[6,14], Axiatok[7] Copper Eskimo man encountered at Bernard Harbour shortly after the C.A.E. established its base camp there

Aksiatak Junior — see Itaqluq

Aksiatak, Mrs. — see Otoyuk

Aksiataq — see Aksiatak

Aksiatark — see Aksiatak

Aksiatark, Mrs. — see Otoyuk

Akuvak — see Akuwak

Akuvak, Mrs. — wife of Akuvak, near Okulik, northern Alaska

Akuwa — see Akuwak

Akuwak (Akuvak, Akuwa) — elderly Alaskan Eskimo man living near *Okulik*, northern Alaska

Alak — see Aluk

Alfred — young Alaskan Eskimo boy who got wood and ice for the C.A.E. camp at Collinson Point, northern Alaska

Alice — wife of Roi, schoolteacher at Barrow, northern Alaska

Allan, Alexander (Allen) — captain of the motor schooner *El Sueno*, intent on trapping east of Cape Parry, contracted by Stefansson in August 1915 to take supplies to Bernard Harbour

Allan, John F. — first officer on the *Karluk* before it left Esquimalt, B.C., June 1913, then second officer on the *Herman*, 1914

Allen — see Allan, Alexander

Allgiaq — Eskimo living at Liston and Sutton Islands, N.W.T.

Allikammik — see Allikumik

Allikumik (Allikumiq, Allikammik[1]) — adopted baby of Prince Albert Sound Eskimos Kunana and Nateksina, on Wollaston Peninsula, Victoria Island

Allikumiq — see Allikumik

Allis, Mr. (Ellis, Ellice[7]) — Engineer and part owner of the *Elvira*

Aluk (Alak, Arlook[5]) — Alaskan Eskimo living at Harrison Bay; husband of Qapqana, Aksiatak's sister

Aluk, Mrs. — see Qapqana

Alunak — see Alunaq

Alunaq (Alunak[7]) — daughter of Wikkiaq, Bernard Harbour, age about 11 in 1915, one of Jenness' 'daughters'.

Amakuk (Amatuk, Ugiagonak, Amarcook[5], Ugiarnaq[3], Two wolves[5]) — Alaskan Eskimo, widower, brother of Mrs. Brower and Assuaq, artist and story teller

Amakuq — little daughter of Assuaq, Cape Halkett, northern Alaska

Amarcook — see Amakuk

Amatuk — see Amakuk

Ambrose — see Agnavigak, Ambrose

Amundsen, Roald — first explorer to navigate Northwest Passage, east to west, 1903-1906

Añaiyu — see Añayu Annarihopopiak

Añayu Annarihopopiak (Añaiyu, Eunice) — Eskimo wife of Daniel Sweeney

Añivrana — see Añivrunna

Añivrunna (Anivrunna, Angivranna[1], Añivrana[14]) — young Copper Eskimo man in Bernard Harbour area

Añopkana (Angopkana, Anupkona, Añopqana, Angopcana[5], Angupkana[11], Anubconna[18]) — elderly northern Alaskan Eskimo with house near Cape Halkett, another house west of Cape Simpson; noted for his generous hospitality

Añopkana, Mrs. — blind wife of Añopkana, near Cape Halkett, northern Alaska

Añopkunna — see Añopqunna

Añopqana — see Añopkana

Añopqunna (Angopqana[2], Añopkunna) — young Copper Eskimo woman, age 18, near *Innerit*, southwestern Victoria Island, and later at Sutton and Liston Islands

Añukapsaña (Añutaksana) — Alaskan Eskimo living in house formerly owned by Mr. Brower at Point Barrow, northern Alaska

Añutaksana — see Añukapsaña

Añutisiak — see Bolt, Ikey

Anarak — see Aneraq

Anarogelo — wife of Igawa, a reindeer herder at Cape Smythe, northern Alaska

Anaumiq — young Coronation Gulf Eskimo, daughter of Itivilrunna photographed at Bernard Harbour, 1916

Anauyuk — Copper Eskimo shaman first encountered by the C.A.E. personnel at Bernard Harbour, 1914; brother of Ayallik

Anderson, Dr. Rudolph M. (the Dr.) — zoologist in charge of the Southern Party of the Canadian Arctic Expedition

Anderson, Martin — see Andreasen, Matt

Anderson, Oley — see Andreasen, Ole

Andreasen, Matt (Martin Anderson) — brother of Ole Andreasen; sold *North Star* and provisions to Stefansson; also owned shack and provisions at Point Atkinson, N.W.T.

Andreasen, Ole (Oley Anderson) — sailor with Stefansson on the ice trip 1914; owned house 10 miles west of Martin Point, northern Alaska

Aneraq (Anarak[6]) — 50-year old father of shaman Uloqsaq, Coronation Gulf area

Aneyaq — Coppermine River Eskimo man, recorded song No. 77, Bernard Harbour

Angatitsiak — see Bolt, Ikey

Angivranna — see Añivrunna

Angopcana — see Añopkana

Angopkana — see Añopkana

Angopqana — see Añopqunna

Angotitsiaq — see Bolt, Ikey

Angupkana — see Añopkana

Angutisiak — see Bolt, Ikey

Angutitshak — see Bolt, Ikey

Anivrunna — see Añivrunna

Annie — baby daughter of Jennie Thomsen, Camden Bay, northern Alaska

Annie — young daughter of Ambrose Agnavigak and Unalina, Bernard Harbour

Anubconna — see Añopkana

Anupkona — see Añopkana

Apattoaq — see Tigsaq

Apattoq — see Tigsaq

ApeXoaq — Coronation Gulf Eskimo woman photographed at Bernard Harbour, 1916

Aqara — daughter of Qamiñgoq

Aqulluk — young tattooed unmarried Copper Eskimo woman near Bernard Harbour

Aqxiataq — see Aksiatak

Arctic John Etalook — see Itaqluq

Arden, D'Arcy — trader and explorer, well known in the Mackenzie River region, who lived on the Dease River north of Great Bear Lake 1914-16; he met Inspector La Nauze at Fort Norman in July 1915 and guided him and his small party to Coronation Gulf

Arey, Ned (Ned Erie, Ned Eric[9]) — prospector, married to one of Kunaloak's daughters, northern Alaska

Arigaicuak — see Kukpuk

Arlook — see Aluk

Arlook, Mrs. — see Qapqana

Arluk, Mrs. (Shotgun, Ahluk) — mother of Iñukuk on Barter Island, Alaska

Arnaqtaq — young Victoria Island Copper Eskimo man whose death was blamed on Jenness

Arnaugak — see Arnauyuk

Arnaun — see Holoraq

Arnauyuk (Senañnuk, Kila, Kila Arnauguk[1], Kala[6], Kila Arnaugak[8], Lucy[8]) — orphan girl, age about 14 in 1915, adopted by Ikpukkuaq, married Aiyalligak in 1915, then Qiqpuk, then several others and finally Bill Storr

Arnold — see Castel, Aarnout

Arnot — see Castel, Aarnout

Artegi — see Atigihjuk

Asatshak — see Asecaq

Asatsiak — see Asecaq

Ascetchuk — see Asecaq

Asecaq (Jimmy Asecaq, Acicaq, Asicaq, Asetsaq[2], Jimmy [5,13], Asatshak[11], Asiatsiak[17], Ascetchuk[18]) — Point Hope Eskimo on the *Karluk*, interpreter for Jenness Sept.- Nov. 1913

Asetsaq — see Asecaq

Asicaq — see Asecaq

Assuaq — see Asuaq

Assuark — see Asuaq

Asuaq (Assuaq, Osuaq, Assuark[5]) — Cape Prince of Wales Eskimo, brother of Mrs. Brower, lived with wife in Kunaloak's house at Cape Halkett, northern Alaska

Asuaq, Mrs. — wife of Asuaq, Cape Halkett, northern Alaska

Atigihjuk (Attigiruaq, Atigihyuk[1], Attigiriak[6]) — Copper Eskimo man, husband of Hattorina, photographed near Tree River in February 1916 and seen later near Bernard Harbour

Atigihyuk — see Atigihjuk

Atorinna — see Hattorina

Atqaq — Eskimo man, age 22, from Thelon River region

Attigiriak — see Atigihjuk

Attigiruaq — see Atigihjuk

Avakana — see Avakunna

Avakunna (Avakana[14]) — young Eskimo boy wintering at Liston and Sutton Islands

Avrana — see Avrunna

Avranna — see Avrunna

Avrunna (Avranna[1], Avrana[3], the Runner[4]) — son of Higilaq, step-son of Ikpukkuaq, older brother of Qanajuq; husband of Milukkatuk, Bernard Harbour area

AXiatak — see Aksiatak

Axiatok — see Aksiatak

Axiranna — Copper Eskimo man photographed west of Read Island, Dolphin and Union Strait, 1915

Ayacook — see Aiyakuk

Ayakuk — see Aiyakuk

Ayalit — see Ayallik

Ayalligaq (Aiyalligak[1], Ayaligaq[2]) — young Copper Eskimo who married Arnauyuk (Kila) in the spring of 1915, divorced her the next winter

Ayallik (Ayalit) — Copper Eskimo man, age 55, husband of Kaumaq; had his thumb bitten off in a fight with a bear near Bernard Harbour

Ayallik (Aiyallik)— Copper Eskimo man, age 50, brother of Ikpukkuaq; seen at second fishing creek, near Cape Krusenstern, 1916

Azzun — Coronation Gulf Eskimo man photographed at Bernard Harbour, 1916

Bartlett, Bob — captain of the *Karluk* and last person on it when it sank in January 1914; walked from Wrangel Island to the Siberian coast and thence east to Emma Harbour where he was rescued by Capt. Pedersen and the *Herman* in May 1914.

Baur, W.J. (Levi) — hired as cook for the *Mary Sachs* to replace Andre Norem; had been on the *Elvira* before it sank

Bernard, Joseph — captain of the schooner *Teddy Bear*, trader, wintered in Coronation Gulf 1910-13 and southwestern Victoria Island 1913-14, advised Dr. Anderson about best harbour for C.A.E. headquarters; nephew of Peter Bernard

Bernard, Peter — captain and part owner of the *Mary Sachs*; perished on Banks Island, 1916

Beuchat, Henri — French anthropologist on the *Karluk*; perished trying to reach Wrangel Island after that vessel sank, January 1914

Bezette — see Pechette

Big River — see Kukpuk

Big-tooth — see Kiguina

Blew — see Blue

Blue, Daniel (Blew) — Engineer on the *Alaska*; died of scurvy and/or pneumonia in May 1915 at Baillie Island

Bolt, Ikey (Aikie, Eikie, Añutisiak, Angatitsiak[6], Angotitsiaq[3], Angutisiak[18], Angutitshak[11], Eigil[6], Ikey[4]) — Point Hope Eskimo hired at Barrow, northern Alaska, to replace Pauyuraq, October 1913

Brick — see Hopson, Alfred

Brook, Charles (Brooks) — steward and cook on the *Alaska*; left Expedition end of July 1914

Brooks — see Brook, Charles

Brooks, Winthrop S. — American scientist on the *Polar Bear*. Left on the *Anna Olga* for Nome at the end of July 1914

Brower, Charles — manager for H. Liebes (fur) Company and part owner of the Cape Smythe Whaling and Trading Company, Barrow, northern Alaska

Brower, David — second son of Charles Brower, Barrow, northern Alaska

Brower, Mrs. — Eskimo wife of Charles Brower, Barrow, northern Alaska

Brower, Tommy — eldest son of Charles Brower, Barrow, northern Alaska

Bruce, Corporal W.V.— R.N.W.M. Police man sent to Bernard Harbour in 1915 to investigate the murder of two Roman Catholic priests

Castel, Aarnout (Arnot Castel, Castell, Arnold[9], Castel[5]) — sailor on the *Belvedere* hired by Stefansson; in charge of the *Alaska* to Bernard Harbour summer of 1914, the *North Star* to Banks Island with Wilkins summer of 1915

Castell — see Castel, Aarnout

Castlehow — friend of author's (in New Zealand?)

Chatterbox — see Oqalluk

de Chaumont, Miss — friend of author's (in New Zealand?)

Chipman, Kenneth — chief topographer with the C.A.E. Southern Party

Ciniciaq — see Sinnisiaq

Ciss (Sis[6,7]) — Eskimo wife of Mike and mother of two small children (Mike and Ikey)

Clark — photographer and assistant engineer from the ill-fated *Elvira*; sold his photographic equipment to Stefansson for Wilkins' use

Cockney — see Sullivan, James

Collinson, Capt. Richard — wintered with his ship *Enterprise* at Walker Bay, Victoria Island in 1851-52 and the following winter at Cambridge Bay during his search for Franklin

Cookpuck — see Kukpuk

Cottle, Capt. S.F. — captain of the *Belvedere* in winter of 1913-14 and of the Hudson's Bay Co. supply ship *Ruby* in 1915

Cottle, Mrs. — wife of Capt. Cottle on the *Belvedere*

Cox, John — assistant topographer with C.A.E. Southern Party

Cram, G.W. (Cramm[18]) — missionary, postmaster, and government official at Barrow, northern Alaska

Cram, Mrs. — wife of G.W. Cram; school mistress at Barrow, northern Alaska

Cramm — see Cram

Crawford, J.R. — engineer of the *Mary Sachs*; left C.A.E. at Baillie Island, August 1915

Diomed — old Eskimo with pipe, Barrow, northern Alaska

Dixon, Joseph — American scientist on the *Polar Bear*

Dr. — see Anderson, Dr. Rudolph M.

Duffy — see O'Connor, Edward 'Duffy'

Egaryuk — Copper Eskimo wife of Oqormik, said to be mother of Haquñgaq

Eglun — one of the most progressive Eskimos in the Mackenzie River region; had tent-house on Icy Reef, near Demarcation Point, northern Alaska

Eigil — see Bolt, Ikey

Eikie — see Bolt, Ikey

Ekallukpuk (Ekalukpik[16]) — elderly Copper Eskimo man who had seen Rae and Richardson in 1848 at the west end of Coronation Gulf

Ekalukpik — see Ekallukpuk

Ekkeaheak — see Ekkiahoaq

Ekkiahoaq (Eqqeahoaq, Eqqiahoaq, Ekkeaheak[1], Ikkiahuag[6], Iquaq[7]) — wife of Taglu, near Bernard Harbour

Ellis, Mr. — see Allis

Eqaryuk — Copper Eskimo wife of Ilaciaq and mother of Paglik

Eqqeahoaq — see Ekkiahoaq

Eqqiahoaq — see Ekkiahoaq

Eric, Ned — see Arey, Ned

Erie, Ned — see Arey, Ned

Eunice — see Añayu Annarihopopiak

Evakana — see Aiva

Fishhead — see Kigodlik

Fred — see Ailuat, Fred

Frits — see Johansen, Frits

Gilley, Capt. George (Capt. M. Kenny, Capt. Gilly[5]) — captain of a whaling ship attacked by Cape Prince of Wales natives in 1877; story told to Jenness near Icy Reef, northern Alaska

Gilly, Capt. — see Gilley, Capt. George

Girling, Mr. H. — English-born Church of England missionary who attempted to sail his small vessel to Bernard Harbour in August 1915 but was forced to winter near Clifton Point, Amundsen Gulf. Moved to Bernard Harbour in 1918.

Haggilak — see Higilaq

Hakka (Hattak, Hattaq, Hukka) — elderly wife of Higilaq's older brother Tuhayoq, mother of Kehullik

Hakuñgak — see Haquñgaq

Hakungak — see Haquñgaq

Hakunggaq — see Haquñgaq

Hanna — baby daughter of Pihhuaq and Itkelleroq

Hansen — rival storekeeper to Charles Brower at Barrow, northern Alaska

Haquña — see Haquñgaq

Haquñaq — see Haquñgaq

Haquñgaq (Hakuñgak, Haquña, Haquñaq, Haquna, Hakungak[1], Haqunggaq[2]) — young (about 16) Copper Eskimo woman, wife of Qiqpuk early in 1915, but taken by Uloqsaq to be his third wife late in 1915; daughter of Kaiyorunna

Haquna — see Haquñgaq

Haqunggaq — see Haquñgaq

Hattak — see Hakka

Hattaq — see Hakka

Hattorina (Atorinna[6]) — mother-in-law of Taglu, wife of Atigihjuk, Coronation Gulf, N.W.T.

Haugak — see Haugaq

Haugaq — Copper Eskimo girl photographed near Tree River, 1916

Haugaq (Haugak[1], Knife-blade[4]) — son of Haviraun, nephew and adopted son of Ikpukkuaq, 7 or 8 years old in 1915

Havgun — Copper Eskimo woman encountered at fishing creek about 12 miles southeast of Bernard Harbour

Havgutaq — Bathurst Inlet Eskimo woman, recorded song for Jenness, 1916, but recording broken

Häviaq — Coppermine River Eskimo boy, recorded song No. 28, Bernard Harbour

Haviraun (Haviron[1]) — Copper Eskimo man, father of Haviuyaq, Utualu, and Haugaq, brother of Ikpukkuaq, Bernard Harbour area; died in 1915 and his grave near Cape Lambert was photographed by Wilkins

Haviron — see Haviraun

Haviuyaq (Haviuyak[1], Havayuyok[7], Snow-knife[4]) — Copper Eskimo man, husband of Itoqunna, brother of Utualu and Haugaq, cousin of Aksiatak, at Bernard Harbour

Heard — see Hird

Hieyaq — Copper Eskimo woman photographed at Bernard Harbour

Higeloq — see Higilaq

Higilak — see Higilaq

Higilaq (Taktu, Taqtu, Taqtuk, Taqtuq, Higilak[1], Higeloq[6], Icehouse[4], Haggilak[18]) — Copper Eskimo wife of Ikpukkuaq, Bernard Harbour area. Had 3 children (2 survived) by previous marriage to Nerialaq (who may have been Ikpukkuaq's older brother — see Jenness, 1922a, p. 167), who vanished while hunting near Lake Numichoin, Victoria Island, years before. Went by name Taqtu or Taqtuk (= liver) till about June 1915, then changed to Higilaq without explanation. One of eight shaman in Dolphin and Union Strait during winter of 1914-15

Higlu — Higilaq's foster son, near Bernard Harbour

Hikkok — young son of Coronation Gulf Eskimos Kaiyuina and his wife Igeyaq, photographed at Bernard Harbour, 1916

Hird, John (Heard) — Harvard University sportsman on the *Polar Bear*

Hitaq — Eskimo man with wife and son encountered in Coronation Gulf

Hitqoq (Hitkok[1,6]) — Copper Eskimo man encountered at Bernard Harbour, age about 40 in 1916; brother of Iguaq, uncle of Aksiatak and Hogaluk

Hoar, T.M. — see Orr

Hoare — see Orr

Hoare, W.H.B. — engineer with the Church of England missionary H. Girling, wintered near Clifton Point 1915-17, before moving to Bernard Harbour in 1918

Hobson, Alfred — see Hopson, Alfred

Hobson, Fred — see Hopson, Fred

Hoff, J.E. — hired by Stefansson from Capt. Cottle on the *Ruby*, August 1915, replacing Blue (who died May 1915) as engineer on the *Alaska*

Hogaluk — Copper Eskimo boy, nephew of Hitqoq, at Bernard Harbour

Holoaq — young Copper Eskimo daughter of Huputaun; one of Jenness' 'daughters', Bernard Harbour area

Holoraq (Huloraq[1] or Arnaun[1]) — Coronation Gulf Eskimo woman, age 40, who spent part of winter near Bernard Harbour

Hopson, Alfred (Brick, Kaiyutak, Kaiyutaq, Alfred Hobson[3]) — 15-year old son of Fred Hopson, hired Oct. 1913 at Barrow, northern Alaska, as interpre-ter-guide for Jenness; terminated services Feb. 15, 1914

Hopson, Fred (Hobson) — cook for Charles Brower at Barrow, northern Alaska, father of Alfred and other children; married to local native woman

Hopson, Mrs. — native wife of Fred Hopson, mother of several children

Hornby, John — English game-hunter and trader, who built cabin on Great Bear Lake with C.D. Melvill about 1908, and remained there for several years; met Stefansson and Dr. Anderson in 1908 and 1911

Howe, Dr. George P. — medical doctor with Mikkelsen-Leffingwell expedition of 1906-1907

Hukka — see Hakka

Huloraq — see Holoraq

Hupo — wife of Qoeha, encountered near Cape Krusenstern, Coronation Gulf

Huputaun — Coppermine River Eskimo man, Bernard Harbour

Iakok — see Aiyakuk

Iakuk — see Aiyakuk

Icehouse — see Higilaq

Igawa — Alaskan Eskimo from Barrow working with reindeer herd

Igeyaq — Coronation Gulf Eskimo woman, wife of Kaiyuina and mother of Hikkok, photographed at Bernard Harbour, 1916

Igguaq — see Iguaq

Igiaqpuk (Ikiakpuk) — adopted daughter of Teriglu, age about 6, looked after Jennie Thomsen's baby Annie at Camden Bay, northern Alaska 1914

Iglisiaq — elderly Copper Eskimo man near Bernard Harbour

Igluñasuk (Iglunasuk, Laugher) — young son of Teriglu near Flaxman Island, Alaska; worked for Leffingwell in 1914

Iglunasuk — see Igluñasuk

Iguak — see Iguaq

Iguaq (Iguak[1], Igguaq[6]) — elderly Copper Eskimo woman at Bernard Harbour, mother of Aksiatak, sister of Hitqoq

Ikey — see Bolt, Ikey

Ikiakpuk — see Igiaqpuk

Ikkiahuaq — see Ekkiahoaq

Ikpakhuak — see Ikpukkuaq

Ikpakhuaq — see Ikpukkuaq

Ikpik — Alaskan Eskimo with a cabin near Cape Halkett; said by Wilkins to be Pauyuraq's cousin

Ikpuck — see Ikpukkuaq

Ikpuckhuak — see Ikpukkuaq

Ikpuk — see Ikpukkuaq

Ikpukhruak — see Ikpukkuaq

Ikpukkuag — see Ikpukkuaq

Ikpukkuak — see Ikpukkuaq

Ikpukkuaq (Ikpuquaq, Ikpukkuak, Ikpuk, Ikpakhuak[1], Ikpuck[3], Ikpakhuaq[2,3,14], Ikpukhruak[6], Ikpukkuag[6], Ikpuckhuak[8]) — Copper Eskimo man who adopted Jenness and took him to Wollaston Peninsula, Victoria Island; second husband of Higilaq; age about 40 in 1916; younger brother of one of three men named Ayallik known to Jenness

Ikpuquaq — see Ikpukkuaq

Ilaciaq (Ilatsiak[1], Ilatsiaq[2], Iliciaq[6], Ilätciaq[14]) — 50-year old Coronation Gulf Eskimo shaman, husband of Eqaryuk and father of Paglik

Ilätciaq — see Ilaciaq

Ilatsiak — see Ilaciaq

Ilatsiaq — see Ilaciaq

Ilavinirk (Ilavinuk, Ilavinik[7]) — Alaskan Eskimo who was hired by Stefansson in 1908, and in 1909 adopted Palaiyak; was interpreter for Inspector La Nauze in the questioning of murder suspects in 1916

Ilavinuk — see Ilavinirk

Iliciaq — see Ilaciaq

Imeraq — young Prince Albert Sound Eskimo man

Imeroon — see Pungasuk

Imilguna — Copper Eskimo woman encountered soon after the arrival of the C.A.E. at Bernard Harbour in 1914

Iñukuk — Alaskan Eskimo with tent house near east end of Barter Island and at Martin Point, northern Alaska; lived with his mother, Arluk

Ipanna — oldest stepson of Aiyakuk, helped Jenness at Barter Island, northern Alaska, in June and July 1914

Iquaq — see Ekkiahoaq

Itaiyuk — baby son of Niq and Aksiatak, Bernard Harbour area

Itaqlik — see Itaqluq

Itaqliq — see Itaqluq

Itaqluq (Itaqliq, Itaqlik, ItaXluq, Aksiatak Junior, Itarklik[5], Arctic John Etalook[15]) — son of Aksiatak, at Harrison Bay, northern Alaska, age 18 in 1913

Itarklik — see Itaqluq

ItaXluq — see Itaqluq

Itigagyuana — sister of Kaullu, daughter of Kiligavik, Bernard Harbour area

Itilorunna — Copper Eskimo with Mammaq at fishing creek southeast of Bernard Harbour

Itivilrunna — Coronation Gulf Eskimo man, father of Anaumiq, photographed near Bernard Narbour, 1916

Itkellerok — see Itkelleroq

Itkelleroq (Itkilleroq, Itkellerok, Itkellrok[1]) — Copper Eskimo wife of Pihhuaq, on Victoria Island with Jenness in 1915; mother of baby girl Hanna

Itkellrok — see Itkelleroq

Itkilleroq — see Itkelleroq

Itokanna — see Itoqunna

Itoqanna — see Itoqunna

Itoqunna (Itoqanna, Itokanna[1]) — Copper Eskimo woman, wife of Haviuyaq, near Bernard Harbour

Ivagluk (Ivahluk[1]) — small Copper Eskimo boy, Bernard Harbour area

Ivahluk — see Ivagluk

Iviqunna — see Aiva

Ivjarotailaq (Ivyarotailaq, Ivyarotailak[1]) — Copper Eskimo widower, living with Pihhuaq and Itkelleroq on Victoria Island, summer of 1915

Ivjarotulaq — dead relative of Ikpukkuaq

Ivyarotailak — see Ivjarotailaq

Ivyarotailaq — see Ivjarotailaq

Jennie — see Thomsen, Jennie

Jennie — see Qanajuq

Jennie Kannayuk — see Qanajuq

Jennie Kanneyuk — see Qanajuq

Jennie Thompson — see Thomsen, Jennie

Jenny — see Thomsen, Jennie

Jerry — see Pauyuraq

Jimmy (Jimmy Memoranna[6]) — Mackenzie River (*Kittigariut*) Eskimo man in charge of Hudson's Bay Co. schooner wintering at Horton River, N.W.T. in 1915; husband of Sinnekpiak

Jimmy Asecaq — see Asecaq

Johansen, Frits (Johannsen, Fritz) — marine biologist with the C.A.E.

Johnny — see Kaiyutaq

Johnson — boy from the *Transit* living with Charlie Brower; helped Jenness drawing Eskimo implements

Josephine — little daughter of Samuel and Aiva, Cape Halkett, northern Alaska

Kablucia (Tablucia) — Eskimo widow in Barrow, Alaska

Kaglililuña (Kakarelana[11]) — Eskimo trapper with house near Pitt Point, northern Alaska

Kahina — Copper Eskimo woman photographed in Coronation Gulf, 1916

Kaijorunna — see Kaiyorunna

Kaioranna — see Kaiyorunna

Kaiyana — Eskimo on Barter Island, northern Alaska

Kaiyaryuk — Coppermine River Eskimo man, recorded songs No. 24, 42, at Bernard Harbour

Kaiyorana — see Kaiyorunna

Kaiyorunna (Qaijorunna, Qaiyorunna, Kaijorunna, Kaiyorana[1], Kaioranna[6], Qaiyorana[14]) — Copper Eskimo man in Bernard Harbour area, husband of Qiqpak; father of Haquñgaq (fem.) and Qavyektok (male) (Jenness, 1923a, but in same reference Haquñgaq's parents are stated incorrectly as Oqormiq (father) and Eqaryuk (mother))

Kaiyuina — Coronation Gulf Eskimo man, husband of Igeyaq, father of Hikkok, photographed at Bernard Harbour, 1916

Kaiyuina — wife of Kannuyauyak, near Bernard Harbour

Kaiyutak — see Hopson, Alfred

Kaiyutaq (Johnny) — second son of Tuglumunna, Camden Bay area, northern Alaska

Kaiyutaq (= ladle) — Copper Eskimo man encountered soon after arrival of the C.A.E. at Bernard Harbour

Kakarelana — see Kagliliña

Kaksarina — see Kaqkavina

Kala — see Arnauyuk

Kallin — see Kallun

Kallun — young Copper Eskimo man photographed at Bernard Harbour, 1914

Kallun (Kallin) — young Copper Eskimo woman from Coronation Gulf area

Kalyutarun (Kalyutaryuk, Kalyutaryun[2]) — Copper Eskimo wife of Qamiñqoq, mother of baby Oqomiq, near Bernard Harbour

Kalyutaryuk — see Kalyutarun

Kalyutaryun — see Kalyutarun

Kamiñuaruk — see Qamiñgoq

Kamingok — see Qamiñgoq

Kamingyok — see Qamiñgoq

Kanaiyak — see Qanajuq

Kanaiyok — see Qanajuq

Kanak — Eskimo with house east of Pitt Point, northern Alaska

Kanayuk — see Qanajuq

Kanayuq — see Qanajuq

Kaneyok — see Qanajuq

Kannakapfaluk — woman in Copper Eskimo folklore who lives in the sea and superintends the seals and the weather

Kannayuk — see Qanajuq

Kanneyuk — see Qanajuq

Kanneyuk — Coronation Gulf Eskimo man encountered near Cape Krusenstern

Kannuyauyak (Kannuyauyuk, Kannuyauyaq, Kanuyauyaq[2]) — Coronation Gulf Eskimo man from near Tree River, seen near Bernard Harbour; husband of Kaiyuina; son of Atigihjuk (male) and Hattorina (female); older brother of Ekkiahoaq (female); age about 25 in 1916

Kannuyauyaq — see Kannuyauyak

Kanuyauyaq — see Kannuyauyak

Kannuyauyuk — see Kannuyauyak

Känuva — Coppermine River Eskimo boy, recorded song No. 29 at Bernard Harbour

Kaqkavina (Kaksarina, Qaqsarvik[2], Kakshavinna[6], Kakshavik[6], Qaqsavina[14]) — Eskimo from west of Hudson Bay, age about 45 (Anderson, 1913-16)

Katairoaq (the boy, Katairuak[11]) — 2-year old son of Aksiatak at Harrison Bay, northern Alaska

Katairuak — see Katairoaq

Kataktovik, Claude — young Eskimo widower hired by Stefansson at Point Barrow, northern Alaska, August 1913; accompanied Capt. Bartlett on his trip from Wrangel Island to East Cape, 1914

Kaudluak — see Kaullu

Kaudluk – see Kaullu

Kaullu (Kaulluak[1], Kaulluaq[2], Kaudluk[6], Kaudluak[6]) — Copper Eskimo woman with young daughter, Bernard Harbour, age about 25 in 1915, daughter of Kiligavik (male), sister of Huputaun (male) and Itigagyuana (female); "the Merry Widow"; married briefly to Billy Natkusiak in June 1915

Kaulluak — see Kaullu

Kaulluaq — see Kaullu

Kaumaq — Copper Eskimo woman, age 45, at Bernard Harbour, wife of Ayallik

Keasik — Alaskan Eskimo with sick daughter, Camden Bay area, northern Alaska

Kehullik (Kesullik[1], Misty[4], Kexullik[14]) — young Copper Eskimo man (about 17 in 1915) on Victoria Island, son of Higilaq's older brother Tuhajoq and his wife Hakka

Kekpuk — see Qiqpuk

Kenny, Capt. M. — see Gilley, Capt. George

Kesullik — see Kehullik

Kexullik — see Kehullik

Kigiuna (Big-Tooth[2]) — Copper Eskimo with whom Jenness had strange conversation near Bernard Harbour

Kigodlik (Fishhead) — Copper Eskimo man near Bernard Harbour

Kikpak — see Qiqpuk

Kikpuk — see Qiqpuk

Kila — see Arnauyuk

Kila Arnaugak — see Arnauyuk

Kila Arnauguk — see Arnauyuk

Kilgavik — see Kiligavik

Kiligavik (Kilgavik[2]) — Copper Eskimo man, age 55, father of Kaullu and Huputaun, Bernard Harbour area

Kilugoq — Eskimo man near Bernard Harbour

Kimuktun — step-son of Tucik, 1915, Victoria Island

Kinordluk — Copper Eskimo man near Bernard Harbour

Kiniq — see Qaqnik

Kiirkpuk — see Qiqpuk

Kitiksiq — first wife of Ikpukkuaq, encountered by Jenness near Locker Point, Coronation Gulf

Kitriq — Copper Eskimo woman, wife of Noqattaq, photographed at Bernard Harbour, 1916

Klengenberg, Christian (Klingenberg[6], Klingenburg[9], Klengenberg[6,7], Charles Klinkenberg[17]) — Danish whaler, married to Alaskan native; was hunting and trapping in Darnley Bay region in 1914; taken with his family on the *Alaska* to Baillie Islands in 1916; later established trading posts at Coppermine (1916), Rymer Point (1919), and elsewhere in Coronation Gulf; original name Christian Klengenberg Jorgensen

Klengenberg, Patsy (Patsie[7]) — 15-year old son of Christian Klengenberg, hired in the spring of 1915 as hunter, and as interpreter for Jenness

Klinkenberg, Capt. Charles — see Klengenberg, Christian

Knife — see Uloqsaq

Knife-blade — see Haugaq

Kohoktak (Qohoktak, Kohoktaq, Kohoktok, Qohoqtuq, Qohoqtaq[2], Kokshuktok[6], Kokaktok[6], Kokoktuak[7]) — Tree River Eskimo, husband of Munnigorina, brother of Maffa; in Bernard Harbour area, 1916

Kohoktaq — see Kohoktak

Kohoktok — see Kohoktak

Kokaktok — see Kohoktak

Kokoktuak — see Kohoktak

Kokshuktok — see Kohoktak

Koñuñnuna — see Kunuññaña

Kopak — see Qopuk

Koptana (Koptanna[1], Kuppanna[6]) — second of three wives of Uloqsaq, Bernard Harbour area

Koptanna — see Koptana

Koruna — 18-month old son of young Eskimos at Okalik, northern Alaska

Kotney — see Sullivan, James

Kovanna — see Qovun
Kovun — see Qovun
Kugluglu — see Qanajuq
Kukialuk — see Kukilukkak
Kukilukak — see Kukilukkak
Kukilukaq — see Kukilukkak
Kukilukkak (Kukilukak, Kukilukkaq, Kukkilukkak[1], Kukkilukak[1], Kukilukaq[2,14], Kukialuk[6], Kukioktok[6]) — first of Uloqsaq's three wives, Bernard Harbour area; from Bathurst Inlet area; age about 25 years
Kukilukkaq — see Kukilukkak
Kukioktok — see Kukilukkak
Kukkilukak — see Kukilukkak
Kukkilukkak — see Kukilukkak
Kukluka — Eskimo from Bathurst Inlet who came to trade at Bernard Harbour
Kukpuk (Big River, Arigaicuak, Cookpuck[5]) — 12-year old eldest daughter of Aksiatak at Harrison Bay, northern Alaska
Kulahuk — Bathurst Inlet Eskimo man, recorded song No. 6 at Bernard Harbour
Kullak — see Kullaq
Kullaq (Kullak[1]) — Copper Eskimo wife of Oqalluk; adopted daughter of Higilaq
Kullaq — Coronation Gulf Eskimo woman, wife of OXomiq, photographed at Bernard Harbour, 1916
Kunaloak (Kunaluak, Kunarluark[5], Kunualak[18]) — Eskimo at Cape Halkett, northern Alaska; had one daughter married to Japanese hotel owner on Yukon River, another married to Ned Arey, prospecter; also son about 10 years old
Kunaloak, Mrs. — wife of Kunaloak, Cape Halkett, northern Alaska
Kunaluak — see Kunaloak
Kunana — Copper Eskimo man from Prince Albert Sound
Kunana — Bathurst Inlet Eskimo man who may have recorded songs No. 9, 41 at Bernard Harbour, 1916
Kunarluark — see Kunaloak
Kuniluk (Qunaluk, Quniluk) — Copper Eskimo male shaman, husband of Qormiaq and father of Taipana, Bernard Harbour area
Kunualak — see Kunaloak
Kunuññaña (Kunuññuña) — Eskimo at Camden Bay, northern Alaska
Kunuññuña — see Kunuññaña
Kuppanna — see Koptana
Kuraluk — a Barrow Eskimo man hired by Stefansson for the *Karluk*; played a major role in keeping the survivors alive on Wrangel Island after the ship sank; father of a little deaf girl, Pungasuk, living with Aluk; had house near Cape Halkett full of whale meat

La Nauze, Charles Deering — Inspector in charge of Great Bear Lake Patrol of the Royal North-West Mounted Police, stationed at Herschel Island, N.W.T. Travelled from Fort Norman to Great Bear Lake in 1915, then to Coppermine area in spring 1916, to investigate murder of two Catholic priests; arrested two suspects and arraigned them at Bernard Harbour; returned to Herschel Island on the *Alaska* with the C.A.E. in 1916
Lane, Capt. Louis (Lewie Lane) — owner of the *Polar Bear* caught in ice near Icy Reef, northern Alaska, 1913-14
Laugher — see Igluñasuk
Leaf — see Milukattuk
Leeper — friend of Jenness (in New Zealand? or Oxford?) who wrote to him

Leffingwell, Ernest de Koven — American geologist living at Flaxman Island, northern Alaska, 1913-14, mapping the coast and Canning River area

Lester — Eskimo boy at Barrow, northern Alaska, who went east to Smith Bay with Alfred Hopson, while Jenness was at Barrow

Levi — see Baur, W. J.

Listener — see Tuhajoq

Lucy — see Arnauyuk

MacDougall — friend of Jenness (in New Zealand? or Oxford?)

Mackay, Dr. Alistair Forbes — surgeon on the *Karluk*; perished attempting to reach Wrangel Island after the ship sank in Jan. 1914

Maffa (Mupfi[6], Mupfa[6,7]) — Tree River Eskimo man about 30, hired in June 1915 as assistant to Cox and O'Neill; husband of Kilauluk (age about 45), father of 4-5 year old girl, Minguyuk (or Mingoyualuk), brother of Kohoktak

Maguire, Capt. Rochefort (McGuire) — Commander of British supply ship H.M.S.*Plover*, one of many vessels searching for Sir John Franklin. His ship was prevented by severe ice conditions from getting east of Point Barrow, and he wintered there between 1852 and 1854.

Maguire, 'Lady' — octagenarian Eskimo woman living with Añopkana, northern Alaska; given this nickname because she had visited Capt. Maguire's ship at Point Barrow when it wintered there in 1852-54; mother or mother-in-law of Añopkana

Mamen, Bjarne (Mamen) — Norwegian hired by Stefansson as assistant topographer, June 1913; perished on Wrangel Island, May 1914

Mammaq — Copper Eskimo man at fishing creek about 4 miles from Bernard Harbour

Mañilenna (Muññilenna, Mungalina[6], Mongalini[7]) — young Mackenzie River Eskimo man, hired by Stefansson at Herschel Island, August 1915, to work for southern party of C.A.E.

Manigyoranna — see Munnigorina

Manigyorinna — see Munnigorina

Mannigyorina — see Munnigorina

Mapteraq (Mapterark[5]) — inland Eskimo man who lived on Barter Island, northern Alaska, with his family while Jenness was there

Mapterark — see Mapteraq

McClure, Robert — captain of the ship *Investigator* sent from England in 1850 to search for Franklin; abandoned his ship in Mercy Bay, Banks Island in 1853; it later was discovered by Copper Eskimos

McConnell, Burt — secretary to V. Stefansson and 'assistant to the C.A.E. magnetician'; had one-year contract with C.A.E., which was not renewed; left Expedition in July 1914; played active role in the rescue of the survivors of the *Karluk* on Wrangel Island

McGuire — see Maguire

McKinlay, W.L. — C.A.E. magnetician on the *Karluk*; sole scientist to survive the sinking of that vessel; rescued from Wrangel Island 1914

Melvill, C.D. (Melville) — English game-hunter and trader, acquaintance of Stefansson and Dr. Anderson, had cabin with Hornby on Great Bear Lake

Melville — see Melvill

Memoranna, Jimmy — Mackenzie River (*Kittigariut*) Eskimo man in charge of Hudson's Bay Co. schooner wintering at Horton River, N.W.T., in 1915; husband of Sinnekpiak.

Merritt, G.E. — assistant to Church of England missionary H. Girling; wintered near Clifton Point 1915-17, while seeking to establish a mission at Bernard Harbour; took charge of Bernard Harbour mission in 1920 after death of Girling

Mike — Siberian Eskimo hired by Dr. Anderson at Herschel Island, 1914; husband of "Ciss"

Mikineroq — see Mikinneroq

Mikinneroq (Mikineroq, Mikinnerok, Mikinrok[1]) — Copper Eskimo wife of Tucik, on Victoria Island, summer of 1915

Mikinnerok — see Mikinneroq

Mikinrok — see Mikineroq

Mikkelsen, Ejnar — Danish explorer, co-leader of Mikkelsen-Leffingwell expedition to northern Alaska, 1906-07; sledded back to Fairbanks

Miluk — see Milukattuk

Milukatak — see Milukattuk

Milukattak — see Milukattuk

Milukattaq — see Milukattuk

Milukattuk (Milukkattuk, Milukattaq, Miluqattaq, Miluk, Milukkattak[1], Milukattak[2], Milukatak[14], Leaf[4]) — wife of Higilaq's son Avrunna, both with Jenness on southwestern Victoria Island in summer of 1915

Milukkattak — see Milukattuk

Milukkattuk — see Milukattuk

Miluqattaq — see Milukattuk

Misty — see Kehullik

Mogg, Capt. William (Capt. Mogg) — whaler friend of Charles Brower, captain of the *Olga*, which wintered at Cape Halkett, northern Alaska 1908-9, where Stefansson first met him; captain of the *Polar Bear*, which was caught in the ice near Icy Reef, northern Alaska, 1913-14

Mongalini — see Mañilenna

Muññilenna — see Mañilenna

Mungalina — see Mañilenna

Munnigorina (Mannigyorina[1], Manigyoranna[6], Manigyorinna[6]) — wife of Kohoktak, near Bernard Harbour

Mupfa — see Maffa

Mupfi — see Maffa

Murray (James Murray) — oceanographer on *Karluk*; perished with Dr. Mackay attempting to reach Wrangel Island after that ship sank in Jan. 1914

NadrvuXoq — see Nalvahhoq

Nahmens, Capt. Otto — hired July 1913 at Nome by Stefansson to be captain of the *Alaska*; left the C.A.E.in June 1914

Nalvahhok — see Nalvahhoq

Nalvahhoq (NadrvuXoq, Nalvuhhoq, Nalvahhok) — young Eskimo boy with Jenness for part of his Coronation Gulf trip, 1916

Nalvuhhoq — see Nalvahhoq

Naneroak (Naneroaq, Nanneroak) — Eskimo man from east of Bernard Harbour; husband of Niptanaciak

Naneroaq — see Naneroak

Nanneroak — see Naneroak

Naqitoq (Naqittoq) — son of Aksiatak and Niq, Bernard Harbour, about 6 years old in 1914; given to shaman Qoeha in 1916 for healing Naqitoq's broken thigh

Naqittoq — see Naqitoq

Nash, Miss — friend of Jenness (in New Zealand? or Oxford?)

Nätein — Coppermine River Eskimo man, recorded songs No. 44, 45, 90 at Bernard Harbour

Nätein — adopted young son of Coronation Gulf shaman Ilaciaq, recorded songs No. 11, 39 at Bernard Harbour

Nateksina — Prince Albert Sound Eskimo woman, wife of Kunana; mother of Allikumik

Natkusiak, Billy (Nekusiak, Nekusiaq, Natkutsiak[11]) — Alaskan Eskimo who worked for Stefansson between 1908-1911, trapped between Camden Bay and Colville River 1913-14, and was hired to work with Wilkins for the C.A.E.'s Northern Party in 1914

Natkutsiak — see Natkusiak

Naugaluaq — Copper Eskimo man in Bernard Harbour area; husband of TamoXuina

Nauyakvuk (Nauyavuk[6]) — elderly Eskimo man at Baillie Island

Nauyavuk — see Nauyakvuk

Neguvunna — young Eskimo man living in one of three houses west of Cape Halkett, northern Alaska

Nekusiak — see Natkusiak

Nekusiaq — see Natkusiak

Nerialaq — first husband of Higilaq; older brother of Ikpukkuaq; vanished while hunting near Lake Numichoin, Victoria Island, 1912 or earlier

Niak — see Niq

Niaq — see Niq

Niaqeptoq — Copper Eskimo man, photographed near Tree River, 1916

Nigaktallik (Nigaqtälik) — Coronation Gulf Eskimo man, photographed at Bernard Harbour, 1916; recorded song No. 52, at Bernard Harbour, 1916

Nik — see Niq

Nilgak (Nilgaq[2]) — Prince Albert Sound man, about 35, crippled, husband of Utuaiyok, encountered by Jenness at Lake Quunnguq, Victoria Island

Nilgaq — see Nilgak

Niniyak — see Niniyuk

Niniyuk (Niniyak, Nunivak[18]) — Eskimo husband of attractive Eskimo woman near Cape Halkett, northern Alaska, with new double house; son-in-law of Kunaloak

Niptanaciak (Niptaniaciak; Niptanatciaq[14]) — wife of Naneroak, near Bernard Harbour; may be same person as Niptanauaq

Niptanauaq — Eskimo woman near Bernard Harbour

Niptaniaciak — see Niptanaciak

Niq (Niaq, Nik[1], Nironella[6], Niak[7]) — Copper Eskimo wife of Aksiatak at Bernard Harbour; age about 25; mother of two boys (Naqitoq and Itaiyuk)

Nironella — see Niq

Noqallaq — Coronation Gulf Eskimo with crucifix and cassock obtained from cabin of two murdered French Catholic priests near Great Bear Lake

Noqallaq — young Copper Eskimo man, cousin of Qanajuq (Jennie); accompanied Jenness from fishing creek in Pasley Cove to the stone house on the hill behind Locker Point. May be same person as had priests' items; probably the son of Ikpukkuaq's older brother Ayallik

Noqattaq — Copper Eskimo man, husband of Kitriq, photographed at Bernard Harbour, 1916

Norem, Andre (Andrew Norham) — cook on the *Mary Sachs*, 1913-14, who committed suicide at Collinson Point, northern Alaska, April 1914

Norham, Andrew — see Norem, Andre

Nuñutoq (Nungutok) — Copper Eskimo man on Victoria Island, summer of 1915

Nungutok — see Nuñutoq

Nunivak — see Niniyuk

O'Connor, Edward 'Duffy' — trader, wintered 1913-14 near Demarcation Point, northern Alaska; had earlier built then abandoned shack at Collinson Point used by C.A.E. members 1913-14; sold his supplies to Stefansson in March 1914 and went west to Barrow

Okalluk — see Oqalluk

Okomik — see Oqomiq

Okpiluk — 4-year old son of Teriglu, Camden Bay, northern Alaska

Olesen, Louis (Olsen; Olavus Olsen[6]) — sailor hired by Stefansson at Nome to work on the *Alaska*; left the C.A.E. at Herschel Island in 1914

Oloksaak — see Uloqsaq

Olsen — see Olesen, Louis

Olsen, Olavus — see Olesen

O'Neill, John J. — geologist with C.A.E. Southern Party

Onin — wife of Qopuk near Camden Bay, northern Alaska; made hat for Jenness

Oqaitok — Bathurst Inlet Eskimo woman, recorded song No. 36 at Bernard Harbour, 1916

Oqalluk (Oqaq, Okalluk[1], Chatterbox[5]) — Copper Eskimo man, age 40, with Jenness on Victoria Island summer of 1915

Oqaq — see Oqalluk

Oqomik — see Oqomiq

Oqomiq (Oqomik, Okomik[1]) — crippled baby daughter of Kalyutarun and Qamiñgoq, Bernard Harbour; killed by exposure, 1916

Oqormiq — Copper Eskimo said to be father of Haquñgaq (Jenness, 1923a), but see Kaiyorunna and Qiqpak

Orr (T.M. Hoar[6], Hoare[18]) — resident missionary at Point Hope, Alaska (see footnote 27, Chapter 43)

Osuaq — see Asuaq

Otoiaiyuk — see Otoyuk

Otoiyuk — see Otoyuk

Otoyuk (Otoiaiyuk, Otoiyuk, Mrs. Aksiatak, Mrs. Arksiatark[5] — wife of Aksiatak at Harrison Bay, northern Alaska

Ovayuak — see Uvoiyuaq, Adam

Oyaraq (Stone[5]) — Eskimo with wife who worked with Jenness on Barter Island, northern Alaska

Oyaraq, Mrs. — see SuXrana

Paglik — daughter of Coronation Gulf shaman, Ilaciaq, and his wife, Eqaryuk

Palaiak — see Palaiyak

Palaiyak (Palaiak, Silas Palaiyak[6], Pelayak[7], Poleiak[9], Palaiyak[7,9]) — young Mackenzie River Eskimo who worked with Stefansson and Dr. Anderson during their 1908-1912 expedition; adopted son of Ilavinirk; hired by Dr. Anderson at Herschel Island, 1914

Paninona — see Samuel

Pannigabluk, Fanny (Pannigavlu, Pannagabaluk[7]) — Eskimo woman with young son who had been Stefansson's seamstress during his 1908-1912 expedition; hired briefly for work at Martin Point and on the *North Star*, northern Alaska, spring of 1914, and later by Stefansson on the *Polar Bear* in August 1915

Pannigavlu — see Pannigabluk

Pannigavlu — elderly inland Eskimo woman near Camden Bay, northern Alaska, died May 1914

Pannigavlu — elderly Eskimo woman in Kotzebue Sound, northern Alaska

Paperok — see Papiroq

Papiroq (Paperok[11]) — tall Eskimo with wife and adopted son in house at or near Bullen Point, Alaska; lived previously in Mackenzie River region

Parted-Hair — see Tucik

Patsie — see Klengenberg, Patsy

Patsy — see Klengenberg, Patsy

Pauchina — see Pausanna

Paucina — see Pausanna

Pausanna (Paucina, Pautcana[3], Pauchina[6], Pouchina[6]) — Barrow, Alaska Eskimo helper with Church of England missionary H. Girling; had camp with wife and children near Bernard Harbour 1915-16

Pautcana — see Pausanna

Pauyourak — see Pauyuraq

Pauyuraq (Payuraq[2], Pauyourak[11], Jerry[13], Pyurak[18]) — Point Hope Eskimo youth on the *Karluk* who accompanied Stefansson from the ship to Barrow, northern Alaska; left the C.A.E. October 1913

Payuraq — see Pauyuraq

Pearl — Jenness' youngest sister in New Zealand

Pechette, Louis (Bezette) — man from the steamer *Belvedere* who went to Barrow with Capt. Nahmens in June 1914

Pedersen, Capt. C.T. (Pederson) — captain of the schooner *Elvira* caught and lost in ice near Icy Reef, northern Alaska, 1914; later captained the *Herman* (1914-1922)

Pedersen, Peder L. (Peter Peterson; P.L.P.[7]) — hired by Stefansson to run launch for Chipman on Mackenzie delta, spring 1914

Pederson — see Pedersen, Capt.

Pelayak — see Palaiyak

Peterson — see Pedersen, Peder L.

Phillips, G.A. — Department of the Naval Service employee at Victoria, B.C.; helped supply and coordinate the loading and departure of the Canadian Arctic Expedition in 1913

Phillips, Inspector J.W. — R.N.W.M. Police officer-in-charge at Herschel Island

Phillips, W.G. — manager of Hudson's Bay Co. post at Fort McPherson, established new post at Bernard Harbour in 1916

Pihhuaq (Pihuaq, Pissuaq, Pissuak[1], Pixuaq[14]) — Copper Eskimo man, a distant relation of Ikpukkuaq's, husband of Itkelleroq, father of baby girl Hanna. Was with Jenness on Victoria Island in 1915

Pihuaq — see Pihhuaq

Pikalo — Eskimo man, Camden Bay region, northern Alaska

Piñasuk — see Pungasuk

Pisiksi — native man in story told by Ikpukkuaq

Pissuak — see Pihhuaq

Pissuaq — see Pihhuaq

Pixuaq — see Pihhuaq

Poleiak — see Palaiyak

Pouchina — see Pausanna

Puganasuk — see Pungasuk

Puñasuk — see Pungasuk

Puññik — Eskimo man near Bernard Harbour

Punganahoq — see Pungasuk

Pungashuk — see Pungasuk

Pungasuk (Piñasuk, Punganahoq, Puñasuk, Puganasuk, Pungashuk, Imeroon[5]) — deaf Eskimo daughter of Kuraluk, age about 8 in 1913, staying with Aluk, Cape Halkett area, northern Alaska

Pyurak — see Pauyuraq

Qaijorunna — see Kaiyorunna

Qaiyorana — Coppermine River Eskimo woman, recorded songs No. 58, 63, and 74 at Bernard Harbour, 1915

Qaiyorana — see Kaiyorunna

Qaiyorunna — see Kaiyorunna

Qamiñgoq (Kamiñuaruk, Qamiñqoq, Kamingok[1], Kamingyok[6]) — Copper Eskimo shaman encountered after arrival of C.A.E. Expedition at Bernard Harbour; husband of Kalyutarun

Qamiñqoq — see Qamiñgoq

Qanajuq (Kanayuk, Kanayuq, Kannayuk, Kugluglu, Qanaiyuq, Qanayuk, Qanayuq, Jennie[4], Jennie (Kannayuk), Kaneyok[14], Kanneyuk[1], Jennie Kanneyuk[8], Sculpin[4]) — daughter of Higilaq, age about 12 in 1915, Bernard Harbour area; 'adopted sister' and 'little sister' of Jenness

Qanaiyuq — see Qanajuq

Qanayuk — see Qanajuq

Qanayuq — see Qanajuq

Qapqana (Mrs. Aluk, Mrs. Arlook[5]) — inland Eskimo wife of Aluk at Harrison Bay, northern Alaska; Aksiatak's sister

Qaqnik — Eskimo with wife west of Demarcation Point, northern Alaska

Qaqsarvik — see Kaqkavina

Qaqsavina — see Kaqkavina

Qaritaq — Copper Eskimo encountered at fishing creek about 12 miles southeast of Bernard Harbour

Qavyektok — see Quvyiktoq

Qimuktun (Kimaktun[1]) — Mikineroq's son and step-son of Tucik, age about 13

Qiñaloqunna — older brother of Ikpukkuaq, father of Huputaun's wife, Bernard Harbour area

Qiñollik — see Qiñorlik

Qiñorlik (Qiñollik) — Copper Eskimo man who sold dog to Jenness near Bernard Harbour

Qiqpak — Copper Eskimo, wife of Kaiyorunna, mother of Haquñgaq

Qiqpuk (Kikpak[1], Kiirkpuk[6], Kikpuk[7], Kekpuk[8]) — adopted son of Ikpukkuaq, age about 16-18 in 1915, husband of Haquñgaq briefly in 1915, then of Arnauyuk (Kila) for 2 weeks, and ultimately of Qanajuq

Qoeha (Qoehuk, Qoesuk[2], Qoexuk[14]) — Copper Eskimo *anatkok*, husband of Hupo, kinsman of Uloqsaq, Bernard Harbour area; was given Naqitoq, Aksiatak's son in 1916

Qoehuk — see Qoeha

Qoesuk — see Qoeha

Qoexuk — see Qoeha

Qohoktak — see Kohoktak

Qohoqtaq — see Kohoktak

Qohoqtuq — see Kohoktak

Qomiq — Coronation Gulf Eskimo with crippled child, near Locker Point

Qöpana — Coppermine River Eskimo woman, sister-in-law of Añivrunna, recorded song No. 32 at Bernard Harbour

Qopanna — Copper Eskimo woman photographed near Tree River, 1916

Qopuk (Kopak[11]) — Alaskan Eskimo with house near Flaxman Island; husband of Onin and uncle of Ikey Bolt

Qormiaq — wife of Kuniluk, near Bernard Harbour

Qormiq — Copper Eskimo woman, 15 years old, photographed near Tree River, 1916

Qovun (Kovun, Qovunna, Simigaq, Kovanna[5]) — stepson to Aiyakuk, youngest son of Tuglumunna

Qovunna — see Qovun

Quñahoq (Qunaiyoq) — Copper Eskimo man, Bernard Harbour area

Qunaiyoq — see Quñahoq
Qunaluk — see Kuniluk
Quniluk — see Kuniluk
Quputim — Copper Eskimo man, Bernard Harbour area, who struggled with Jenness for a knife
Quvjextoq — see Quvyiktoq
Quvyektoq — see Quvyiktoq
Quvyiktoq (Quvyutoq, Quvjextoq, Quvyektoq, Qavyektok[2]) — Copper Eskimo man, Bernard Harbour area; son of Kaiyorunna (m) and Qiqpak (f), brother of Haguñgaq
Quvyutoq — see Quvyiktoq

Rae, John — Scottish arctic explorer, who with Sir John Richardson in 1848-1849 searched for Franklin from the Mackenzie delta to the Coppermine River; in 1851 he explored the shore of Wollaston Peninsula and around Coronation Gulf
Rexford — man working for Charles Brower at Barrow, northern Alaska
Richardson, Mr. — school teacher at Barrow, northern Alaska
Richardson, Sir John — arctic explorer and naturalist; served as surgeon and naturalist on two Franklin expeditions (1819-22 and 1825-27) and led a search party for Franklin in 1848-49 between the Mackenzie and Coppermine rivers
Roi — Eskimo teacher at Barrow, northern Alaska
Rosie — Eskimo girl at Barrow, northern Alaska
Runner — see Avrunna

Samuel (Paninona[11]) — husband of Aiva near Cape Halkett, northern Alaska, father of Josephine; Añopkana's son; may be same person as Ikpik
Sañiaq — little granddaughter of dead Pannigavlu, northern Alaska
Savagvik — 1-year old child of Teriglu, Camden Bay, northern Alaska
Savolik, Pete — see Suivaliaq
Sculpin — see Qanajuq
Senaññuk — see Arnauyuk
Seymour, William — second mate on the *Polar Bear* in 1914; with Stefansson and his Northern Party 1915-1917
Shotgun — see Arluk, Mrs.
Siliuna (Siniuna) — 6-8-year old (second) daughter of Aksiatak at Harrison Bay, northern Alaska
Simigaq — see Qovun
Sinisiaq — see Sinnisiaq
Siniuna — see Siliuna
Sinnekpiak — Eskimo wife of Jimmy Memoranna, Horton Bay
Sinnisiak — see Sinnisiaq
Sinnisiaq (Sinisiaq, Sinnisiak[1], Ciniciaq[14], Summinak[18]) — southwest Victoria Island Eskimo, age about 35 in 1916, charged with murder of two Roman Catholic priests near Great Bear Lake
Sis — see Ciss
Slade — see Slate, Harry C.
Slate, Harry C. (Slade) — owner of the old schooner *Alice Stofen*, which was wrecked at Herschel Island, August 1914
Snow-Knife — see Haviuyaq
Socrates — see Toqalluaq
Stefansson, Vilhjalmur (Stefannson; V.S.) — leader of the Canadian Arctic Expedition, 1913-18
Stone — see Oyaraq

Storgersen — see Storkersen

Storkersen, Storker (Storgersen) — sailor and trapper hired by Stefansson in Mackenzie Valley in 1914 to go on his ice trip from northern Alaska, March 1914

Storr, Bill — Trader, Coronation Gulf region, husband of (Kila) Arnauyuk in 1930s

Suivaliaq (Pete Savolik[10]) — small son of Aluk at Harrison Bay, northern Alaska

Sullivan, Bob (Sullivan, William[6]) — crew member of the *Belvedere* hired to dig out the *Alaska* at Camden Bay and be cook on the *Alaska*; left the C.A.E. in August 1914

Sullivan, James (Cockney, Kotney[9]) — 28-year old cabin boy on the *Herman* hired as cook for the *Alaska* by Dr. Anderson, Herschel Island, August 1914

Summinak — see Sinnisiaq

Sunblad, John (Sunblade) — engineer of the *Anna Olga*, northern Alaska

Sunblade — see Sunblad

SuXrana (Mrs. Oyaraq) — Eskimo wife of Oyaraq, on Barter Island, northern Alaska

Swanson — see Swenson

Sweeney, Daniel — man hired by Stefansson from the *Belvedere*, replaced Capt. Nahmens as captain of the *Alaska*, northern Alaska; married Eskimo woman Añayu Annarihopopiak from Herschel Island area in 1915

Swenson, Olaf (Swanson) — owner of Seattle walrus and trading schooner *King and Winge*, who rescued the *Karluk* survivors from Wrangel Island in 1914; trader and part owner of the *Belvedere*

Taagluk — see Taglu

Tablucia — see Kablucia

Taglu (Tahliq, Taagluk[7], Tagluk[6,14]) — Tree River Eskimo man, husband of Ekkiahoaq, photographed in Coronation Gulf, 1916

Tagluk — see Taglu

Taipana — little son of Kuniluk, Bernard Harbour

Taipana — see Utualu

Takoheqina — Coppermine River Eskimo woman, recorded songs No. 73 at Bernard Harbour

Taktu — see Higilaq

Tala — Alaskan Eskimo, brother-in-law of Charlie Brower, Barrow, northern Alaska

TamoXuina — wife of Naugaluaq, encountered in Coronation Gulf; nicknamed Tamogluña (= let me eat) by Jenness

Taptona — see Taptuna

Taptuna (Taptona[9]) — Copper Eskimo son of Ayallik and Kaumaq, age about 13 in 1914, encountered at Bernard Harbour after arrival of C.A.E.

Taqtu — see Higilaq

Taqtuk — see Higilaq

Taqtuq — see Higilaq

Tekelroq — Copper Eskimo woman photographed with Higilaq near Read Island, 1915

Terigloo — see Teriglu

Teriglu (Terigloo[5], Tiriglok[6], Terigluk[11]) — Eskimo man, father of 4-5 year old girl with Jennie Thomsen at Camden Bay, northern Alaska; worked with Leffingwell; had wife and 3 other children; camped on Barter Island in June-July 1914, when Jenness worked there

Terigluk — see Teriglu

Thompson, Mrs. — see Thomsen, Jennie

Thomsen, Charles (Thompson) — sailor and handyman on the *Mary Sachs*, husband of Jennie Thomsen; had trapping house west of Camden Bay, northern Alaska; perished on or near Banks Island 1916

Thomsen, Jennie (Jennie, Jenny, Mrs. Thompson, Jennie Thomsen[3], Jennie Thompson[5]) — Nome (*Kinmiun*) Eskimo woman, wife of Charles Thomsen; hired by Stefansson as seamstress for Northern Party; mother of 16-month old Annie in 1914; helped Jenness with language and Eskimo stories

Thomsen, Mrs. Charles — see Thomsen, Jennie

Tigsaq (Apattoq, Apattoaq[2]) — elderly Coronation Gulf man photographed at Bernard Harbour, 1916

Tiriglok — see Teriglu

Toqalluaq (Socrates) — Copper Eskimo shaman with negroid facial type encountered at fishing creek at Pasley Cove, near Bernard Harbour

ToXlumana — see Tuglumunna

Tucik (Tutik, Tutsik[1,2], Ahangik[1], Parted-Hair[4]) — Ikpukkuaq's nephew, husband of Mikineroq; was with Jenness on Victoria Island summer of 1915

Tuglumunna (ToXlumana, Tuklumanna[6]) — elderly Eskimo wife of Aiyakuk, mother of Ipanna, Kaiyutaq, and Qovun, Barter Island, northern Alaska

Tuhajoq (Tuhajoy, Tuhayok, Tuhayoq, Tusayok[1], the Listener[4]) — elder brother of Kullaq and Higilaq, father of Kehullik, Bernard Harbour area; was with Jenness on Victoria Island in 1915

Tuhajoy — see Tuhajoq

Tuhayok — see Tuhajoq

Tuhayoq — see Tuhajoq

Tuklumanna — see Tuglumunna

Tulugaqpuk — Eskimo man encountered just west of Demarcation Point, northern Alaska

Tupik — young Copper Eskimo woman near Bernard Harbour

Tupingaluk — elderly Eskimo woman, grandmother of Aiva, encountered near Barrow, northern Alaska in March, 1914

Tusayok — see Tuhajoq

Tutik — see Tucik

Tutsik — see Tucik

Ugiagonak — see Amakuk

Ugiarnaq — see Amakuk

Uglu — Copper Eskimo man, Bernard Harbour

Ugluaq — Copper Eskimo man, Bernard Harbour area. May be same man as Uglu

Ukpik (Ukpiq) — son of Oqalluk and Kullaq, age about 8 in 1915, on Victoria Island

Ukpik — Eskimo man known to Higilaq, but deceased

Ukpiq — see Ukpik

Uloksak — see Uloqsaq

Uloksoak — see Uloqsaq

Uloqcaq — see Uloqsaq

Uloqhaq — see Uloqsaq

Uloqsaq (Uloqhaq, Uloksak, Knife[5], Uluksoak[6], Uloksoak[7], Uloqcaq[14], Oloksaak[18]) — 'rich' Copper Eskimo shaman, age 30 in 1915, in Coronation Gulf area; by 1916 had three wives: Kukilukkak, Koptana, and Haquñgaq; father of Ikotak and kinsman of Qikpuk

Uloqsaq II (Uloqcaq[14]) — Copper Eskimo man charged with the murder of two Roman Catholic priests on Coppermine River in 1913

Uluksoak — see Uloqsaq

Uñahaq (Unahak[1], Ungahaq[2]) — Copper Eskimo wife of Wikkiaq, Bernard Harbour area

Uñelaq (Unelaq) — young sister of Itoqunna, encountered in Dolphin and Union Strait

Unahak — see Uñahaq

Unalina — Herschel Island wife of Ambrose Agnavigak; sister of Palaiyak

Unelaq — see Uñelaq

Ungahaq — see Uñahaq

Utoqeq — Coronation Gulf Eskimo man photographed at Bernard Harbour, 1916

Utoqeq — Coppermine River Eskimo woman, recorded songs No. 12, 80

Uttugaum — see Utugaum

Utuaiyok — wife of Nilgak, Prince Albert Sound man, encountered at Lake Tahirjuaq (now Lake Quunnguq)

Utuaiyoq — small son of Kaullu, Bernard Harbour

Utualu (Utuallu, Utualuk[2], Taipana[2]) — Copper Eskimo man, Bernard Harbour, brother of Haviuyaq

Utuallu — see Utualu

Utualuk — see Utualu

Utugaum (Uttugaum) — Copper Eskimo shaman near Bernard Harbour

Utunin — Copper Eskimo man near Bernard Harbour

Uvilloq — Copper Eskimo woman photographed near Bernard Harbour, 1916

Uvoiyuaq, Adam (Ovayuak[6]) — young Mackenzie River Eskimo hired August 1915 by Stefansson to work for the C.A.E. at Bernard Harbour

Uvugra — Point Hope woman doctor, northern Alaska

Wight, Constable D.E.F. — member of Royal North-West Mounted Police Great Bear Lake detachment, who accompanied Inspector La Nauze to Coronation Gulf in spring 1916 and returned with Chipman in June 1916

Wikiaq — see Wikkiaq

Wikkiak — see Wikkiaq

Wikkiaq (Wikiaq, Wikkiak[6]) — Copper Eskimo man, Bernard Harbour area; husband of Uñahaq, father of Alunaq

Wilkie, Fritz — see Wolki, Fritz

Wilkins, George Hubert — official photographer of the C.A.E.; put in charge of the *Mary Sachs* August 1914 to find and supply Stefansson

Wolki, Fritz — owner and captain of the sailing ship *Rosie H*, trader and collector in Franklin Bay region, 1914; later sold the small schooner *Gladiator* to Stefansson

Appendix 2.

Eskimo Words Used in Diary

Eskimo words entered in the diary before August 1914 are N. Alaskan; native words thereafter are mainly from the western Coronation Gulf region, although some are of N. Alaskan or Mackenzie Valley derivation, reflecting the influence of the interpreters Palaiyak and Patsy Klengenberg. The first date that a word or term appears in the diary is given in the list below. Words in italics and brackets were provided in 1989 by Rosemarie Avrana Meyok, an Innuinaqtun (Copper Eskimo) language specialist at Coppermine, Northwest Territories, and reflect modern spelling and interpretation in that region. As no interpreters familiar with Coronation Gulf dialect(s) existed in 1914-16 some spellings and meanings on this list may be inaccurate. For some words Jenness supplied meanings in his diary, for others the meanings have been deduced from his diary text or have been supplied by Ms. Meyok. As might be expected, words used in Jenness' second and third year are generally more accurate than those heard and used during his first year in the north.

Word	Chapter and Date	Meaning
acan [*atchan?*]	(3) Oct. 24/13	father's older sister
aga [*aaka*]	(3) Oct. 24/13	mother
agan [*aakan*]	(4) Nov. 27/13	mother [*your mother*]
agnadluk [*arnalluk*]	(30) Jun. 15/15	female rock ptarmigan [*female for all animals*]
agruk [*arluk*]	(6) Dec. 18/13	name for two stars close to each other that appear just before spring (Barrow)
a'haliaq [*aahanngiq*]	(13) Jun. 1/14	oldsquaw duck
ahalik ahalik [*a',a',ahangik*]	(13) Jun. 4/14	sound made by oldsquaw duck
Ahuttokullugmiut	(24) Dec. 4/14	see Akulliakattangmiut
akamuktoaq [*aqamuktuq*]	(3) Oct. 22/13	Eskimo game, pulling with interlocked wrists (Barrow)
akublagaq	(4) Nov. 3/14	Eskimo game, balancing sticks on nose (Barrow)
Akulliakattangmiut	(24) Dec. 2/14	Eskimo group living near Stapylton Bay
alapa [*alappaa*]	(8) Feb. 6/14	it is cold!
alektik [*aligtok*]	(35) Oct. 29/15	inner 'shoes', caribou fur stockings
amaulegeroq [*amauligiruuq*]	(15) Jun. 30/14	eider duck [*it is said to be an eider duck*]
amauligeroq	(15) Jun. 28/14	duck's nest
amaulik	(16) Jul. 29/14	Pacific eider duck
amihunik	(25) Jan. 16/15	a lot
amisuralgaluit [*amihuraaluit*]	(35) Oct. 22/15	a great many

anakliq [*aanaakniq*]	(5) Dec. 11/13	whitefish (also ekalusaq)
anana [*anaanattiaq*]	(10) Mar. 5/14	grandmother
anatkok [*angatkuk*]	(25) Jan. 2/15	shaman
anatkut [*angatkut* pl.]	(1) Sep. 27/13	shaman or witch doctors (Barrow)
anatqaqtoq [*angatkuktuq*]	(25) Jan. 2/15	playing the shaman [*in a trance*]
anauytuk	(24) Dec. 21/14	a snow-stick [*bat*]
anayugaqsruq [*inutquaq*]	(15) Jul. 10/14	"is an old man"
angekok [*angatkuk*]	(1) Sep. 27/13	witch doctor or shaman
annokadluk [*nukatukkaaq*]	(34) Sep. 16/15	young caribou bull
anut [pl.]	(7) Jan. 4/14	harness[es] for dog (Fig. 60)
anyu [*aniu*]	(34) Oct. 18/15	snow used for some specific purpose
apan [*aappan*]	(2) Nov. 27/13	[*your*] father
aqago [*aqagu*]	(27) Mar. 4/15	tomorrow
aqeatulaitpoq [*aqiattulaitpuq*]	(33) Aug. 14/15	there's no bottom to his stomach [*he never gets full*]
aqeutaq [*aqiutaq*]	(34) Sep. 16/15	incantation to drive away evil spirit(s)
Aqulliakattak	(28) Apr. 21/15	country around Stapylton Bay and C. Bexley
Aqulliakattunmiut [*Akulliakattangmiut*]	(28) Apr. 21/15	Eskimo group living near Innirit, Victoria Island
Arkilininmiut [*Aqiliningmiut*]	(34) Oct. 5/15	people living around the Aqilinik (Thelon) River
arnakata [*arnaqataa*]	(1) Sep. 27/13	his cousin
arnaq	(1) Sep. 27/13	woman
ataciara [*attiara*]	(28) May 9/15	a familiar spirit [*dead relative a person is named after*]
atataruak [*ataatattiaq*]	(3) Oct. 24/13	grandfather
Atigeruq	(10) Mar. 9/14	name of peninsula in Harrison Bay, Northern Alaska
atigi	(7) Jan. 29/14	shirt [*parka*]
atka [*atqa*]	(1) Sep. 27/13	guardian spirit [*his name*]
atkin [*atqin*]	(15) Jul. 10/14	spirit [*your name*]
aton [*atuun*]	(28) May 7/15	a type of Eskimo dance song
attauhiq [*atauhiq*]	(25) Jan. 16/15	one (1)
augruaq [*haavraq*]	(15) Jun. 25/14	red phalarope ("blood-bird")
aulaksiroq [*aullaqtiqtuq*]	(6) Dec. 29/13	he goes [*he takes off*]
avatinnuani [*avatinnuanga*]	(25) Jan. 12/15	beyond [*just beyond*]
bidake (= bidarka)	(12) May 11/14	2- or 3-holed kayak (Alaska)
ekallukpit [*iqalukpik*]	(17) Aug. 19/14	salmon trout

Ekkalluktogmiut [*Ikaluktuuttiarmiut*]	(25) Jan. 3/15	Eskimos on southeastern Victoria Island opposite Kent Peninsula [*Cambridge Bay people*]
eqallukpiajuk [*iqalukpiayuk*]	(31) Jun. 26/15	a small salmon
eqalusaq [*iqalugaq*]	(2) Oct. 12/13	whitefish (see anakliq) [*small or young fish*]
Haneragmiut [*Hanirarmiut*]	(24) Jan. 9/15	Eskimo living around Hanerak
Hanerak [*Haniraq*]	(34) Aug. 30/15	region around C. Hamilton, S.W. Victoria Island
haudlun [*haulluun*]	(33) Aug. 9/15	marrow scraper
haviuyak [*havik*]	(35) Oct. 18/15	snow-knife, made of horn
Hinieluk [*Hinialuk*]	(28) Apr. 18/15	Cape Pullen, S.W. Victoria Island (now Singialuk Peninsula)
Hivulik [*Hivulliq*]	(34) Oct. 44/15	Arcturus, the leader (name for the star)
Huloktok [*Huluktuk*]	(38) Feb. 29/16	'wings' = two most westerly of the Jameson Islands (see fn. 10, ch. 38)
Huluktok	(38) Feb. 29/16	see Huloktok
huna	(29) May 26/15	(name used for animals without identifying names) [*this one?*]
igalaq [*igalaaq*]	(10) Mar. 15/14	window (of iglu)
igaluqisaq [*igaluqihaq*]	(7) Jan. 10/14	two pieces of wood used in children's game
igiana	(15) Jul. 17/14	gullet of whale
Iglanacuk	(10) Mar. 19/14	see Iglunasuk
iglopuk [*igluqpak*]	(24) Dec. 11/14	large (snow) house
Igloryuallik [*Igluryualik*]	(37) Mar. 4/16	'the place which has old houses' = island north of Algak I., Bathurst Inlet
Igluhugyuk	(38) Feb. 28/16	'big house' = Hepburn Island
Iglulik	(28) May 3/15	south shore Victoria Island west of Read Island
Iglunasuk [*Iglanatchuk*]	(10) Mar. 19/14	'one who is always smiling' (a child's name)
Ignerin	(25) Jan. 10/15	see Iñnerin
igniq [*ingniq*]	(34) Oct. 4/15	'fire' (name given to bright meteors)
igniqauqtoq [*igniqauqtuq*]	(14) Jun. 16/14	Steller's Eider duck
igutaq	(31) Jun. 21/15	name of a plant [*bee*]
ihuilleramuninunnun [*ihuiguhuktun*]	(30) Jun. 5/14	'it bodes ill for someone'
ihun [*ihuuq* (s.), *ihuun* (pl.)]	(29) May 17/15	lake trout
ikiagut	(14) May 29/14	elevated cache

ikiaq (ikiq)	(1) Sep. 26/13	red spruce
ikun [*ikuun*]	(3) Oct. 23/14	knife or skin-scraper of horn or stone
ilanaqotin [*ilanaqutin*]	(31) Jul. 1/15	we are angry
ilipikuk [*ilipiqquk*]	(35) Oct. 29/15	sealskin footwear [*duffle socks*]
ilupekuk [*ilupikuk*]	(34) Sep. 30/15	skin slippers
imigiluktaq	(6) Dec. 23/13	name for Eskimo toy (a whizzer)
imilguptaq	(41) Jul. 4/16	whizzer, an Eskimo toy
Imnahugyuk	(38) Feb. 29/16	'big cliff' = third Jameson Island from west
imnek [*imnaq*]	(29) Jun. 2/15	cliff
iñallu [*ingaluat* pl.]	(10) Mar. 15/14	the little intestine
Ingnerin	(25) Jan. 10/15	see Iñnerin
inirnerin [*inirnirin*]	(35) Nov. 6/15	yearling caribou [*adult caribou*; see nukatukak]
initat [*innitat*]	(24) Dec. 5/14	drying rack
injuquaq [*inutquaq*]	(41) Jul. 4/16	old man
inminnih [*inmingnik*]	(27) Mar. 12/14	of their own doing
inminnik	(32) Jul. 16/15	of its own accord
Iñnerin [*Ingnirin*]	(25) Jan. 10/15	("pyrite"), a shore prominence about 12 miles W. of Falaise Bay, S.W. Victoria Island. Now called Innirit on topographic maps
innuk	(6) Dec. 14/13	men [*two people*]
inuhuit [*inukhuit*]	(29) May 28/15	marker stones, directional indicators [*inukshuk*]
inuit ileanaitut [*inuit ilianaitut*]	(24) Nov. 28/14	the people are glad [*the people are are not happy! i. aliahuktut = the people are happy; iliranaitut = friendly people*]
inuit nagojut [*i. nakuuyut*]	(24) Nov. 28/14	the people are friendly
inuit nakorut	(18) Sep. 2/14	the strangers are good people
inuit pivulinni [*i. hivullirni*]	(33) Sep. 26/15	"men of the first time", i.e., early man
inuit qovlonat tikitpata qowanaq pukput [*i. qablunaat tikitpata quyanaqpakput*]	(31) Jul. 6/15	the Eskimos are glad when the white men reach them
inyuchiut [*iñutchiut*]	(42) Jul. 1/16	see inyukhiut
inyukhiut [*inukhiut*]	(33) Aug. 14/15	rows of earth clods or stones set up for hunting
ipijait [*ipirait*]	(36) Dec. 25/15	woman's skin trousers
iqaligimi	(34) Sep. 30/15	deerskin clothing
iraoq	(5) Dec. 9/13	see kilyaun
isungaq [*ihunngaq*]	(14) Jun. 1/14	pomerine jaeger
itigiaq [*tiriaq*]	(15) Jul. 8/14	weasel [*itigiaq = look at that weasel*]

itigoragmiksoaq [*itigurangmikhuaq*]	(3) Oct. 22/13	Eskimo game, pulling little fingers
itigoraq [*itiguraq*]	(5) Nov. 29/14	name for a cat's-cradle figure
Itkillik [*Itqillit, itqilrit*]	(25) Jan. 3/15	Indians near Great Bear Lake
itsalik [*ittalik*]	(13) May 24/14	deerskin tent
ivalugun [*ivalurun*]	(3) Oct. 22/13	cross piece of wood drill (Fig. 18)
Kagmalirmiut	(2) Oct. 6/13	Eskimo from Kagmalik River branch of the Colville River, Alaska
Kagmalit [*Karmalit* pl.]	(10) Mar. 14/14	Victoria Island Eskimo [probably = Kogmollik of Stefansson (1919, p. 151, 156)]
kaksauk [*qaqhauq*]	(31) Jun. 24/15	red-throated loon
kalnaq	(3) Oct. 22/13	long-stemmed pipe (Barrow) (Fig.20); see kuiñaq
kamik	(1) Sep. 21/13	Eskimo boot
Kañianergmiut [*Kanianirmiut*]	(2) Oct. 6/13	Eskimos from Kangianik (= upper Colville) River
kanermiksoaq [*kanirmikhuaq*]	(3) Oct. 22/13	Eskimo game, pulling elbows
kaneyoq [*kanayuk*]	(24) Sep. 24/15	sculpin (sing.) (sea fish)
Kanghirjuatyagmiut [*Kangiryuayarmiut*]	(41) Jun. 14/16	Eskimos living around Minto Inlet, Victoria Island
Kanghiryuarmiut [*Kangiryuarmiut*]	(24) Dec. 11/14	Eskimos living around Prince Albert Sound, Victoria Island
kanivjaktugut taktugman [*kangivaktugut taktungman*]	(31) Jul. 1/15	we frightened it away [*we landed on shore because of the fog*]
kannannaq [*kanannaq*]	(10) Mar. 13/14	north wind
kannayun [*kanayun* pl.]	(34) Sep. 24/15	sculpins (pl.) (sea fish)
kannoyak [*kannuuyaq*]	(34) Sep. 15/15	cotton grass (*Eriophorum*)
kanoyak	(34) Sep. 9/15	see kannoyak
kanut [*kangut* pl.]	(14) May 28/14	white geese
kaqaq	(4) Nov. 8/13	baked scones (Point Hope, Alaska)
kata [*qata*]	(1) Sep. 27/13	(from arnakata)
kataktoq [*kataktuq*]	(24) Dec. 16/14	'let fall' (eliminate)
kataq	(24) Dec. 5/14	pot, dish (see qataq)
kealiauk	(30) Jun. 6/15	see qealiauq
keruguq [*karugaq*]	(6) Dec. 15/13	stick used to tie Eskimo dog (Fig.50)
kesuk [*kisuk*]	(4) Nov. 7/13	water-sky, or black sky over open water
kia	(29) May 26/15	who?
kiglin	(3) Oct. 23/13	[edge of] scraper (Fig.21) [*edge of anything*]
Kigiaktanneuk	(35) Oct. 30/15	see Qiqiaqtanneuq

Kigiaqtanneuk	(35) Oct. 31/15	see Qiqiaqtanneuq
kila	(30) Jun. 11/15	see qila
kilalurak [*qilalugaq*]	(34) Sep. 18/15	white whale
kilanmiutaq [*qilangmiutaq*]	(42) Jul. 5/16	a large [*white*] lemming
kilatallik	(15) Jul. 21/14	long-billed dowitcher (a small water bird)
kilaun [*qilaun*]	(3) Oct. 16/13	Eskimo drum (Fig.15)
Kilermiut	(2) Oct. 6/13	an Alaskan inland Eskimo tribe
kilguviuk [*kilgavik*]	(31) Jul. 10/15	duckhawk [*falcon*]
kilugmiutaq [*qilangmiutaq*]	(14) May 29/14	[*white*] lemming
Kilusiktok [*Kiluhiktuq*]	(38) Mar. 4/16	region around small river at bottom of Arctic Sound, Bathurst Inlet
Kilusiktomiut [*Kilusikturmiut*]	(38) Feb. 21/16	all the natives who winter on the ice off Bathurst Inlet
kilyaun	(5) Dec. 9/13	bone mesh gauge for fishing (Fig.48)
Kiñmium	(10) Mar. 15/14	member of Kiñmiut group or 'tribe'
Kiñmiut	(10) Mar. 15/14	an Alaskan Eskimo group
kiñmiutaq	(10) Mar. 15/14	something from the Kiñmiut
kina atka [*kina atqa*]	(1) Sep. 27/13	what is his name?
kinalik [*qingalik*]	(14) Jun. 13/14	[*King*] eider duck
kinmiaq [*kingmiaq*]	(3) Oct. 22/13	mouthpiece of wood drill (Fig.18)
kipiq [*qipik*]	(27) Mar. 17/15	sleeping skins [*sleeping bag or blanket*]
kirigugiuk	(14) Jun. 20/14	N. Alaskan name for an unidentified bird
kitixliqmiksoaq [*qitiqhimigaq*]	(3) Oct. 22/13	Eskimo game, pulling middle fingers
Kittigariut [*Kittigaayiut*]	(16) Aug. 10/14	Mackenzie River native
Kogluktomiut [*Qurlukturmiut*]	(26) Feb. 25/15	Eskimo living in Coppermine River valley
Kogluktualuk [*Qurluktualuk*]	(36) Dec. 17/15	Tree River
komait [*kumait*]	(18) Sep. 1/14	lice (and other parasites on humans)
kovluna [*qablunaaq*]	(24) Nov. 28/14	white man
kovlut [*kablat*]	(34) Sep. 15/15	red alpine bearberry
kugmulit [*kagmalit*]	(16) Aug. 11/14	name used by Mackenzie delta natives for all Eskimos farther east
kuiñaq	(4) Nov. 7/13	long-stemmed pipe (Barrow) (Fig.29)
kulitak [*qulittaq*]	(34) Sep. 1/15	heavy skin coat (outer skin atigi)
kulliq [*qulliq*]	(4) Nov. 7/13	Eskimo lamp (see also naneq)
kummuk	(24) Dec. 14/14	deerskin boot (see kamik)

Kunuamnaq	(33) Aug. 18/15	name for blocks of rocks west of Kugaluk River, S.W. Victoria Island
kupahloaluk	(14) Jun. 6/14	see kupahluk
kupahluk [*kupaglualuk*]	(14) Jun. 27/14	Lapland longspur
kuvrin	(5) Dec. 9/13	see kilyaun
liwaliwa(k) [*livilivilaaluk*]	(14) Jun. 1/14	Baird's sandpiper (also its song)
mallere [*maliriq*]	(31) Jun. 24/15	Pacific loon
mallrok [*malruk*]	(25) Jan. 16/15	two (2)
mamaitoq [*mamaittuq*]	(24) Dec. 13/14	'salty' [*smells/tastes terrible*]
mikilyeragmiksoaq [*mikirarmikhuaq*]	(3) Oct. 22/13	Eskimo game, pulling ring fingers
mikiruramik	(8) Feb. 5/14	[*Eskimo game, pulling with ring fingers*]
Mikumauq [*Mihumeuk*]	(28) Apr. 18/15	Cape Hamilton, S.W. Victoria Island
mukluk	(10) Jun. 17/14	[*English word for*] seal-skin boot
mukpaurat [*muqpauyat*]	(4) Nov. 3/14	baked scone, flap-jack, pancake-like food [*bannock*]
muktuq [*maktaaq*]	(7) Jan. 4/14	whale blubber and skin (muktuk is English version of word)
mumik	(3) Oct. 16/13	drum-stick (N. Alaska) [*dance*]
munik [*manikhaq*]	(4) Nov. 3/13	moss used as wick in Eskimo lamp
munnik	(38) Sep. 19/15	see munik
mutkolik [*mitqulik*]	(34) Oct. 29/15	footwear [*caribou-leg skin footwear*]
naga [*naagga*]	(4) Nov. 4/13	no!
nagojugut [*nakuuyugut*]	(24) Nov. 28/14	we are friendly
nagovaluktoq [*nanguvaluktuq*]	(10) Mar. 17/14	(word used by Billy Natkusiak and Fred) [*teasing someone*]
Nagyuktok [*Nagyuktuuq*]	(37) Sep. 12/15	region near Lady Franklin Point, Victoria Island [*Richardson Islands*]
Nagyuktomiut [*Nagyuktuurmiut*]	(24) Dec. 8/14	Eskimos living around Southern Victoria Island [*Richardson Islands*]
nahaulik [*nahaullik*]	(30) Jun. 12/15	Lapland longspur (bird)
nakopaluktoq [*nakupalloktuq*]	(10) Mar. 17/14	(a Barrow, Alaska, word; variant of nagovaluktoq, q.v.) [*think he's doing fine?*]
Nalluarjuk [*Nalluaryuk*]	(29) May 26/15	a river flowing into Prince Albert Sound, Victoria Island
naneq [*naniq*]	(4) Nov. 7/13	Eskimo lamp
nanik	(6) Dec. 14/13	Eskimo stone lamp (see naneq)
naniksraq	(6) Dec. 14/13	thing to make a nanik (also a place name)

nannorjuit [*nannuryuit*]	(34) Oct. 4/15	polar bears (stars)
nannuraluk [*nanuraaluk*]	(33) Aug. 28/15	polar bear
napan [*nappan*]	(1) Sep. 27/13	soul
napata [*nappata*]	(1) Sep. 27/13	soul (see napan)
natsiq [*natriq*]	(21) Oct. 14/14	foetid seal [*seal*]
nauk	(34) Sep. 15/15	[*where is...*]
nauyat	(34) Aug. 18/15	sea gull
Nennitagmiut [*Nannitarmiut*]	(34) Oct. 5/15	people living on the west side of Bathurst Inlet
neoktun [*nauktun*]	(3) Oct. 22/13	stem of wood drill (Fig.18)
nepaatomin [*napaaqtumin*]	(24) Dec. 16/14	trees [*from the tree; trees = napaaqtuq*]
nepaicuq [*napaadjak*]	(7) Jan. 13/14	toy, to play nipaicuq
nepailuktaq [*napailuktaq*]	(14) May 26/14	hawk
nerukaq [*nirukkaq*]	(1) Sep. 27/13	half-digested moss in caribou stomach
Niahognayuk [*Niahug nayuk*]	(28) Apr. 20/15	Williams Point, 6 miles S.E. of Cape Hamilton, S.W. Victoria Island
nighaqtoq [*nikhaaktuuq*]	(28) May 12/15	male rock ptarmigan
nigiroaruq [*nigiruaruk*]	(7) Jun. 28/14	spider [*snaring; spider = aahivak*]
niglivik [*nirlivik*]	(35) Oct. 29/15	black brant
Ninitak	(34) Sep. 12/15	region west of Bathurst Inlet
ninnoq [*nin'nguq*]	(26) Feb. 24/15	cottonwood
nipaicuq [*napaadjak*]	(4) Nov. 17/13	Eskimo game, stick and hole, or hole and pin
Noahognirmiut [*Nuahungnirmiut*]	(26) Feb. 25/15	Eskimo group near Cape Krusenstern [*Nuahungniq = Eskimo from Cape Krusenstern area*]
Noahognirmiutaq	(24) Dec. 9/14	Eskimo from Cape Krusenstern area
noakatvait [*nuatqatigiit*]	(31) Jun. 20/15	kinsfolk [*neighbours; kinsfolk = katangutigiit*]
noqsrak	(4) Nov. 12/13	toy gun (Fig.34)
noraitok [*nurraittuq*]	(42) Jul. 3/16	caribou doe that has not fawned
nuitkikpaqtuk [*nuitqikpaktuk*]	(1) Sep. 27/13	"they [*both*] kept coming up again"
nujakpuk [*nuyakpak*]	(31) Jul. 6/15	barbed fish-spear (Fig.169)
nukatukak [*nukatugaq*]	(42) Jul. 3/16	2- to 3-year old caribou [*yearling; see inirnerin*]
nukka [*nukaa*]	(25) Jan. 10/15	[*his/her*] younger sister
numikattik [*numiqatigiik*]	(38) Mar. 3/16	dancing companions
Nunatagmiut [*Nunataarmiut*]	(10) Feb. 28/14	inland Eskimo, N. Alaska [*also used for people from the Aklavik area*]
okauyak [*ukauyak*]	(29) May 30/15	a shrub (*dryas integrifolia*)
okilaq	(33) Aug. 17/15	see qilaq

onipqaqtoq [*unipkaaqtuq*]	(25) Jan. 2/15	tell a story (Mackenzie region); see anatqaqtoq
oqauraq [*uqauyaq*]	(29) May 30/15	see okauyak
ovinaq [*avinaq*]	(15) Jul. 3/14	lemming nest
Pallik [*Paalliq*]	(35) Oct. 17/15	Rae River region; may also refer to a region west of Chesterfield Inlet, Hudson Bay
Pallirmiut [*Paallirmiut*]	(25) Jan. 1/15	Rae River Eskimo (obsolete term)
pavunni [*kilumi*]	(6) Dec. 18/13	back of the house
pinahut [*pingahut*]	(25) Jan. 16/15	three (3)
Pingangnaktok [*Pingangnaqtuq*]	(38) Feb. 21/16	district between Tree River and Bathurst Inlet
Pinnannoktok [*Pinnannuqtuq*]	(38) Feb. 21/16	people inland between Tree River and Bathurst Inlet
pisiksakaqtilutik [*pitikhaqqaaqtillutik*]	(1) Sep. 27/13	"after they have been shot at"
poallu [*pualuk*]	(34) Sep. 30/15	skin mitts
puiniq	(34) Sep. 3/15	lard made from caribou back fat [*hardened caribou fat when cooked*]
Puivlirmiut	(24) Dec. 1/15	Eskimo living near Forsyth Bay, Victoria Island
puluo	(3) Oct. 16/13	handle of Eskimo drum (Fig.15)
purnaq	(31) Jun. 23/15	fat (from an eider duck)
puveoktoak [*puviuktuuq*]	(14) Jun. 18/14	pectoral sandpiper
qailektoraluk [*qailiqturaaluk*]	(33) Aug. 25/15	they are coming
qaligimun	(34) Sep. 28/15	superstitious
qalligi [*qalgi*]	(25) Jan. 2/15	dance house
qaqatqain [*qaigguin*]	(11) Apr. 4/14	expression used by Nome and Teller Eskimos when someone sneezes (also quvuna qatqain)
qaqiviuk [*qaqiviuk*]	(24) Dec. 11/14	two-pronged fish spear
qaqivuk [*kakivak*]	(34) Sep. 16/15	see qaqiviuk
qaqsrauk [*qaqsrauq*]	(15) Jul. 3/14	loon
qaqtuk [*qaiqtuk*]	(17) Aug. 19/14	herring (see fn.7, ch. 17)
qataq [*qattaq*]	(29) May 18/15	bucket, dish, pail (see kataq)
qatqain [*qaigguin*]	(15) Jul. 10/14	come
qealiauq [*qealiayuq*]	(30) Jun. 6/15	black-bellied plover (bird)
qeorvik [*qiurvik*]	(28) May 11/15	a piece of wood
Qigiaqtanneuq [*Qikiqtanayuk*]	(28) May 3/15	Read Island
qila	(30) Jun.11/15	a bundle, usually a coat, used for spiritual divining

qilamitaun	(5) Dec. 3/13	Eskimo bolas (N. Alaska)
qilaq [*qilak*]	(33) Aug. 17/15	sky or heaven
Qinaruk [*Kaniqhuk*]	(28 Apr. 20/15	cape 4 miles east of Williams Point
qopanoaqparjuk [*qupanuaqpaar yuk*]	(30) Jun. 11/15	horned lark (bird)
qopuk [*quppaq*]	(8) Feb. 3/14	ice-crack
qorviq [*qurvik*]	(24) Dec. 4/14	chamber pot
qovluna [*qablunaaq*]	(25) Jan. 16/15	white man (sing.)
qowana nakemmun [*quana nikhingman*]	(24) Dec. 6/14	hooray for the seal! [*thank you for it (the seal) got hooked*]
quvana qatqain	(14) Apr. 4/14	see qaqatqain
Sagliaq	(6) Dec. 4/13	'something on lap of person' (name of a mountain in Alaska)
savavum tinmiana [*savavum tingmianga*]	(15) Jun. 26/14	teal (bird) [*bird or duck from ...area*]
sieraq [*siiraq*]	(17) Aug. 19/14	connors (small fish)
sitamat [*hitamat*]	(25) Jan. 16/15	four (4)
siyunaq	(4) Nov. 7/13	a long pipe stem of split willow (Fig.29)
slavia	(4) Nov. 9/13	fried variety of mukpaurat (Point Hope word)
tacim ekalloa [*tahim or tarium iqalua*]	(24) Dec. 8/14	frozen fish [*fish from the lake/sea*]
taligruk [*taliruq*]	(30) Jun. 9/15	ruddy turnstone (bird)
tallu [*talu*]	(34) Sep. 15/15	caribou hunting pit (sing.)
tallut [*talut*]	(33) Aug. 14/15	caribou hunting pits (pl.)
tamaijja [*tamadja*]	(28) May 4/15	"there you are" [*there they are coming in the distance*]
tanik	(5) Dec. 10/13	white man
tareomiutat [*tariurmiutat*]	(33) Aug. 17/15	a variety of small sea fish [*creature*]
tattilgat [*tatilgat*]	(33) Aug. 16/15	brown crane (bird)
tavrani tavra	(15) Jul. 10/15	stop! stop! [*there! there!*]
Tigeragmiut [*Tikirarmiut*]	(2) Oct. 5/13	Point Hope Eskimos
tiguana [*tiguanga*]	(25) Jan. 3/15	adopted son [*his adopted child; tiguaq = an adopted child*]
tigvaqtoq [*tigvaqtuq*]	(10) Mar. 17/14	he crosses over to a place [*he drifts out to sea*]
tikermiksoaq [*tikirmikhuaq*]	(3) Oct. 22/13	Eskimo game, pulling fore fingers
tikivik [*tikigarvik*]	(5) Nov. 26/13	thimble holder
tipuk	(17) Aug. 19/14	herrings
tiriaq	(29) May 19/15	tundra weasel
tonraq [*taanraq*]	(24) Dec .19/14	a tiny man, a spirit [*a ghost*]

Tormiat [*Tuurmiat*]	(29) May 28/15	Prince Albert Sound natives [*strangers*]
tornkin [*tuurniqin*]	(34) Sep. 15/15	home of the spirits
tornuaq [*turruaq*]	(4) Oct. 28/13	an (evil) spirit
tuktujuin [*tuktuit*]	(34) Oct. 4/15	caribou! (pl.)
tuktukiuk	(2) Oct .5/13	bad (rancid) caribou (Alaskan word to describe bacon)
tukturaluk [*tukturaaluk*]	(29) Jun. 2/15	caribou [*usually said with amazement*]
tullik [*tuullik*]	(14) Jun. 1/14	yellow-billed loon
tulugaq [*tulugaryuaq*]	(11) Mar. 24/14	raven
Tuluqaq [*Tulukkak*]	(28) Apr. 20/15	cliff ("home of ravens") near Tuluqaqaq
Tuluqaqaq [*Tulukkakaq*]	(28) Apr. 21/15	a limestone cliff ("little raven") 20 miles E. of C. Hamilton, Victoria Island
tupilek [*tupilak*]	(25) Jan. 2/15	a shaman's familiar spirits [*devil*]
turXoq [*tuqhuuk*]	(24) Dec. 4/14	passageway into snowhouse [*porch*] (Fig.135)
tutalik	(9) Feb. 25/14	deerskin boot
tutanokin [*tutanukin*]	(25) Jan. 2/15	a cat's-cradle figure (Barrow word)
uggroqtun [*akhuuqtun*]	(32) Jul. 16/15	are spirits oppressing you? [*trying very hard*]
ugioqtun [*ugiuqtun*]	(33) Aug. 17/15	shades of the dead, spirits
ugleorjuit [*ugliuryuit*]	(34) Oct. 4/15	Aldebaran (stars)
uglu [*aglu*]	(25) Jan. 14/15	seal hole in ice
ugroktun	(34) Sep. 14/15	see uggroqtun
ugruk	(5) Dec. 3/13	bearded seal (Alaska)
ugyuk [*ugyuk*]	(34) Sep. 18/15	bearded seal
ukluk [*akhak*]	(10) May 19/14	skin of brown bear
ulo [*ulu*]	(2) Oct. 5/13	woman's knife or skin scraper
Ulumiut	(2) Oct. 7/13	Alaskan Eskimo group (see fn.11, ch. 2)
uluraq	(4) Nov. 4/13	semi-lunar knife [*blade of woman's knife*] (Fig.25)
ulvoreaq ugjuk [*ubluriaq ugyuk*]	(34) Oct. 4/15	Jupiter, the bearded seal (planet)
umiak [*umiaq*]	(3) Oct. 17/13	[*large*] skin-covered boat
umiaktorvik [*umiaqturvik*]	(6) Oct. 14/13	river
Umingmaktomiut [*Umingmaktuurmiut*]	(24) Dec. 16/14	Eskimo living east of Bathurst Inlet
uñalaq [*ungalaq*]	(29) May 15/15	west wind
uñedlaq [*unidlaq*]	(35) Oct. 19/15	'basket'
una	(8) Feb. 6/14	this one
unisat [*piruyat*]	(15) Jul. 24/14	cache

Utkeavigmiun [*Utkiavigmiun*]	(10) Mar. 15/14	Eskimo man from Barrow
Utkeavigmiut [*Utkiavigmiut*]	(2) Oct. 6/13	Cape Smyth Eskimo man
utkusium pauñanik [*utkuhikhaq paunanik*]	(20) Sep. 28/14	lamp black
uvinaq	(15) Jul. 3/14	lemming nest (see ovinaq)
Walliarmiut [*Uallinirmiut*]	(32) Jul. 16/15	Eskimo to the west
Walliarmiutaq [*Uallinimiutaq*]	(26) Feb. 25/15	Rae River native (female)

Wallirnirmiut
    [*Uallirnirmiut*]
	(35) Oct. 17/15	general term for all Western Coronation
		    Gulf Eskimos

Appendix 3.

Lists of Items Traded by D. Jenness with the Copper Eskimos, Bernard Harbour Region, N.W.T., 1914-1916

During his two years with the Copper Eskimos in the Coronation Gulf region, Jenness obtained for the National Museum of Canada, largely by trade, more than 2500 items of clothing, cookware, hunting and fishing equipment, tents, skins, and other cultural artifacts. All told, these form probably the finest collection of Copper Eskimo material in existence. They are currently housed by the Canadian Museum of Civilization, Hull, Québec, Canada. A 34-page typed list of the items collected (*Eskimo specimens, collected by D. Jenness, Canadian Arctic Expedition, 1913-1916, received at Victoria Museum, Sept. 1916*) is on file with the Canadian Ethnology Service of that Museum.

I came upon the two lists reproduced on the following pages while conducting research on my father's diary during the past five years. Typewritten by him on 5 x 7 note paper at Bernard Harbour, they reveal both the minute details of his methodical bartering and a clear insight into the relative value of the newly encountered white man's goods to the native people at that time. That the people he traded with were satisfied with their transactions is evident from their willingness, sometimes eagerness, to return with new items to trade, as well as the good rapport my father continued to have with them for the rest of the time he remained among them.

My father mentioned his first trading activities in his diary on September 28 and 29, 1914, but was too preoccupied with helping build the Bernard Harbour headquarters and related matters for the next few weeks to have time for any further trades. The first major trading period, therefore, was between late December 1914 and March 1915. For the next seven months he was wandering about Wollaston Peninsula on Victoria Island and was more occupied with simple survival than with trading. His second major trading period commenced after his return to Bernard Harbour and covered the period from November 1915 to March 1916. Thereafter his travelling and the scattering of the native people ended all further trading.

Most of his trading, therefore, took place during the winter months while he was at Bernard Harbour or around the Liston and Sutton Islands (about 15 miles distant), for that corresponded with the times when the Copper Eskimos gathered near these islands to hunt seals. The size of one such native gathering is recorded in my father's diary entry for November 16-25, 1915 "... there must be between 100 and 150 people here, camped on the edge of the water below the station." For a brief period little Bernard Harbour was a well-populated community!

The first list (winter 1914-15) reveals numerous trades for caribou and seal meat and dried fish, items that are not found on the second list. The explanation for this is that the men at Bernard Harbour had inadequate supplies of food for their dogs during the first winter. This inadequacy was the result of two factors: (1) most of the dog pemmican originally slated to be shipped in to the Coronation Gulf area for the use of the Southern Party had been sent instead with Wilkins on the *Mary Sachs* to Banks Island for the use of Stefansson's dogs, for Stefansson and probably also Capt. Joseph Bernard had assured the men of the Southern Party that there would be plenty of caribou available during the fall migration around the west end of Coronation Gulf; and (2) all of the Southern Party's Eskimo hunters except Palaiyak had gone west on the *Alaska* with Dr. Anderson. The late freeze-up in the fall of 1914, however, resulted in the caribou crossing the strait between Victoria Island and the mainland far to the east of Bernard Harbour. The resultant scarcity of game in the fall of 1914 meant that Palaiyak's efforts were inadequate, hence my father was called upon to obtain meat and fish from the Eskimos gathered at the Liston and Sutton Islands. Adequate supplies of dogfood arrived on the *Alaska* in August 1915, however, so that my father was able to devote most of his trading during the second winter to the collection of ethnological specimens for the National Museum. The second winter also saw two Eskimo women, wives of men hired in the summer of 1915 to hunt and work for the Expedition, at Bernard Harbour to make clothing and footwear for the scientists and others. Such apparel had had to be obtained by my father by trade during the first winter along with the supplies of meat and fish, as is shown by the frequent trades for skin boots and for sewing services on the first list.

The two lists reproduced below are as my father prepared them except for minor editorial additions and modifications, and I have supplied the locale where each day's trade took place, drawing upon the diary for that information. Dashed lines mark where pages end on the original lists.

The original list for the first trading period is in the R.M. Anderson papers, Jenness file, Zoology Division, Canadian Museum of Nature, Ottawa. The original list for the second trading period is with the Canadian Arctic Expedition (1913-16) documents, under D. Jenness, Box 3, File 1, Archaeological Survey of Canada, Canadian Museum of Civilization, Hull, Québec. Some 1916 items included on the first list are shown here on the second list.

Trade List for December 1914 to March 1915

Dec. 30th, 1914 (Bernard Harbour)

1 pair deerskin boots	1 fox trap
1 large stone pot	1 box .30-30 cartridges
1 caribou thigh	1 fox trap
1 pair deerskin boots (worn)	8 .30-30 cartridges
1 pair sealskin slippers	1 tin pot
1 pair long deerskin mits	4 .30-30 cartridges

Dec. 31st, 1914 (Sutton Island)

1 large stone lamp	1 saw
1 bag [of] fish	2 boxes .30-30 cartridges

For building snow house around tent	3 fish-hooks, 3 .44 cartridges, and 5 .30-30 cartridges
1 caribou head	1 fox trap
8 arrows, 2 musk-ox ladles	12 .44 cartridges
2 arrows, 2 musk-ox ladles	4 .44 cartridges
1 pair woman's outer trousers	1 empty lard can
1 caribou thigh and leg	1 wash-bowl
1 pair deerskin boots	1 empty coal-oil can
2 pieces caribou meat	13 .30-30 cartridges

1 pair man's trousers, 1 large copper ulo, 1 copper skin scraper	20 .44 cartridges
1 deerskin poke, 1 pair long mits	1 fox trap
1 deerskin atigi, 1 pair deerskin pants	20 .44 cartridges
1 pair deerskin pants	1 box .30-30 cartridges
2 caribou quarters	1 box .30-30 cartridges
1 piece caribou meat	4 .30-30 cartridges
5 arrows	5 .30-30 cartridges
5 fish	5 .44 cartridges
2 caribou shoulders	1 box .30-30 cartridges
1 caribou saddle	6 .44 cartridges
1 caribou saddle	8 .44 cartridges
1 pair deerskin boots	1 fox trap
10 dried fish	1 fox trap
1 pair woman's pants (worn)	1 pair sealskin slippers
1 fathom calico, 1 pair deerskin boots	1 fox trap
1 piece seal meat, 20 dried fish	3 .30-30 cartridges
1 pair long deerskin mits	2 fathoms calico

1 saddle caribou meat	7 .44 cartridges
1 pair deerskin boots	1 fathom calico
1 pair sealskin slippers	1 fathom calico
1 seal	1 box .30-30 cartridges
1 pair deerskin mits	1 coal-oil can
1 pair deerskin boots	1 fox trap
5 (?) lbs caribou fat	1 bowl
4 pieces caribou meat (shoulders)	1 box .30-30 cartridges
4 pieces caribou meat (shoulders)	1 box .30-30 cartridges, 7 .30-30 cartridges
1 pair sealskin slippers and [for] tending blubber lamp	1 fox trap
1 ugyuk line	7 .44 cartridges, 4 fish-hooks
1 large wooden bowl	1 flour bowl
1 small white deerskin	2 fish-hooks and 1 empty milk can
1 needle case and attachments	3 needles
1 musk-ox fork	1 cocoa tin (empty)

1 needle case with copper needle
1 small wooden bowl
1 needle case and attachments

1 large needle
1 empty cocoa tin, 1 needle
2 needles

Jan. 5th - 15th, 1915 (Sutton Island)

3 duck's feet with lamp wick
2 caribou heart linings
1 musk-ox ladle
1 pair deerskin boots
1 copper knife
1 swan's foot with wick and a fork
1 small wooden dish
2 copper needles
  lamp-torch
1 fishing line
1 pair short mits
3 small duck's feet with wicks
1 needle case
1 fawn-skin cap
2 copper needles and a bone handle
1 bear-tooth handle

3 needles, 1 fish-hook
1 needle
2 fish-hooks, 1 needle
1 18" 3-cornered file
4 fish-hooks, empty milk can
2 fish-hooks, 1 block matches
1 needle, 1 fish-hook
2 needles
1 fish-hook
1 fish-hook, 1 block matches
2 fish-hooks
1 block matches, 1 fish-hook
3 fish-hooks
2 needles
1 block matches
2 fish-hooks

----

  drawings [by Haquñgaq, Jan. 14]
1 needle case and attachments
  attachments of needle case
1 seal's liver
1 pair sealskin slippers
1 large musk-ox ladle

1 large lamp torch
1 duck's foot bag with wick
  [for] stitching boots
2 copper knives
1 pair [snow] goggles
2 needle cases and attachments
  few scraps deer meat
1 seal's liver
1 seal's liver
12 lbs caribou meat
1 bow and equipment
41 dried fish
1 pair sealskin slippers,
1 pair deerskin boots
30 lbs (?) caribou meat
30 lbs (?) caribou meat

1 empty pemmican can
1 block matches
1 block matches
1 block matches, 1 needle
2 needles and empty cocoa tin
2 fish-hooks, 1 needle,
1 empty cocoa tin
2 needles
1/2 block matches
1 needle
5 large needles, 4 fish-hooks
2 blocks matches
3 needles, 1 block matches
1 block matches
1 needle, 1 block matches
1 needle, 1 block matches
1 lard pail
20 .44 cartridges
1 canister [gun] powder

1 pair calico trousers
1/2 box No. 2 1/2 primers
1/2 box No. 2 1/2 primers

----

1 pair sealskin slippers	1 small lard pail
30 lbs (?) caribou meat	1/2 bar lead
8 dried fish	1 fathom calico
50 lbs (?) caribou meat	1/2 box No. 1 primers
66 dried fish	1 canister powder, 1/2 box No. 1 primers
1 heavy man's atigi, 1 pair breeks [breeches]	
1 woman's atigi	30 .44 cartridges
1 large copper knife	1 flour bowl
1 pair deerskin boots, 1 pair woman's outer trousers	1 tin saucepan
2 pair sealskin slippers	20 .44 cartridges
1 caribou thigh	1 pair calico trousers
1 seal	10 .30-30 cartridges
1 pair deerskin boots	1 large pot
50 lbs (?) caribou meat	10 .30-30 cartridges
1 woman's atigi, 1 pair deerskin boots, 1 pair woman's outer trousers, 1 pair sealskin slippers	1/2 bar lead
1 pair deerskin boots, 1 wooden bowl, 1 wooden dish	1 box .44 cartridges
	1 box .30-30 cartridges

1 bow [with a] few attachments	7 .30-30 cartridges
1 caribou thigh	10 .30-30 cartridges
for helping with seal net	3 .30-30 cartridges
6 lbs (?) caribou meat, 1 wooden bowl	1 flour bowl
[for] repairing boots etc.	1 enamel saucepan
1 pair deerskin boots	1 pair calico trousers
1 pair deerskin boots, 1 pair sealskin slippers	1 pair calico trousers
1 pair deerskin boots, 1 dancing cap	1 lard pail
1 seal	1/2 box .44 cartridges
1 pair sealskin slippers	1/2 block matches, 1 empty milk can
1 fishing line	1 large fish-hook
2 caribou tongues	1 1/2 blocks matches
2 caribou tongues	1 empty tobacco tin
1 seal's liver	1 needle, 1/2 block matches
seal meat	1 needle, 2 blocks matches
seal meat	1 large fish-hook, 1 empty butter tin
1 frozen fish	2 empty milk cans

2 frozen fish	1 needle, 1 block matches, 1 large fish-hook, 1 empty cocoa tin
1 pair sealskin slippers	1 empty milk can
1 pair sealskin slippers	1 empty milk can, 1 needle, 1 fish-hook, 1/2 block matches
1 pair short mits	3 needles

1 new man's atigi	20 .44 cartridges
60 lbs caribou meat	1 box No. 1 primers,
	1 cannister [gun] powder, 1/2 bar lead
1 pair deerskin boots,	
1 pair sealskin slippers	1 fox trap
1 seal liver	1 needle
1 seal liver and meat	1 tin milk (empty)
1 pair sealskin slippers	1 tin plate
2 pairs sealskin slippers	2 needles, 2 fish-hooks,
	1 block matches
1 pair deerskin socks	1 fathom calico
[for] drying and mending boots	1 block matches
[for] watching tent and lamp	1 needle, 1 empty milk can

Jan. 15th, 1915 (Bernard Harbour)

1 atigi, 2 pairs breeks [breeches], 1 pair	2 fathoms red zephyr
inner socks, 1 pair deerskin boots	2 boxes .30-30 cartridges
1 pair sealskin slippers, 1 pair long mits	
1 bow and equipment	20 .44 cartridges
1 pair long mits, 1 pair short mits,	
1 fishing line	1/2 bar lead
1 woman's atigi	1/2 bar lead
1 pair sealskin slippers	4 .44 cartridges
1 small stone lamp, 1 harpoon with	
copper head, 4 arrows	1/2 bar lead, 6 .44 cartridges
1 pair deerskin boots, 1 pair sealskin	
slippers	1 fox trap
1 atigi	1 flour bowl
[for] singing into phonograph	1 fathom red zephyr

For anthrop. measurements etc.	3 blocks matches
2 ugyuk lines	1/2 bar lead
1 seal line	1 box No. 1 primers
1 pair long mits	1 fox trap
1 pair sealskin slippers,	
1 pair short mits	1 fathom calico

Jan. 16th, 1915 (Bernard Harbour)

1 light atigi, 1 pair breeks [breeches]	1 box No. 2 1/2 primers
1 atigi	1 canister [gun] powder
1 seal harpoon	1/2 bar lead
2 woman's atigis	1 box No. 1 primers,
	1 canister [gun] powder
1 pair deerskin boots,	
1 pair sealskin slippers	25 .44 cartridges
1 pair sealskin slippers,	
[for] sewing at station	25 .44 cartridges
1 pair woman's trousers	1 pemmican can (empty)

1 pair woman's trousers,
1 pair sealskin slippers

1 pair deerskin socks

1 pair sealskin slippers,
   [for] sewing at station

1 flour bowl

1 fathom calico

20 .44 cartridges

Jan. 20th, 1915 (Sutton Island)

1 stone pot

  [for] sewing

1 seal line, 3 caribou hearts

50 lbs caribou meat

1 3-pronged spear

1 bow complete, 1 pair deerskin socks,
1 light atigi

25 .44 cartridges

5 .44 cartridges

1 box .30-30 cartridges

1 box .30-30 cartridges

1 fathom calico

2 canisters [gun] powder,
1 box No. 2 1/2 primers

Feb. 24th, 1915 (about 20 miles north of Coppermine in Coronation Gulf)

2 atigis, 2 pair short pants,
1 pair deerskin slippers,
1 pair deerskin socks

4 pieces sinew

3 seal's livers

1 blue fox skin
   for measuring heads

1 bow and equipment

1 bow and equipment

1 bow and equipment

1 dog

2 pair deerskin boots,
1 pair deerskin socks

1 box .44 cartridges

12 needles

6 needles, 1 block matches

1 wolf trap

8 fish-hooks

1/2 machete

1 wolf trap

1 wolf trap

1/2 machete

2 fathoms calico

1 atigi, 1 pair deerskin socks

1 pair old deerskin boots

1 snow-knife

1 snow-knife
   for sewing

1 pair long mits

1 flour bowl

1 block matches

2 fathoms calico

2 fathoms calico

2 fathoms calico

2 fathoms calico

March 3rd, 1915 (Bernard Harbour)

1 wolverine skin, 1 pair deerskin socks,
1 pair sealskin slippers
1 pair deerskin slippers

2 wolverine skins

1 sleeping skin

1 sleeping skin

1 heavy deerskin

1 box .44 cartridges

1 box No. 2 1/2 primers,
1 canister [gun] powder

1/2 bar lead

1/2 bar lead

12 .44 cartridges

1 seal line and head	2 fathoms calico
1 seal line and head (small)	1 fathom calico
?	1 fox trap
1 bow and attachments	1 box No. 2 1/2 primers
1 bow and attachments	1 wolf trap

March 4th, 1915 (Bernard Harbour)

1 foetus seal	10 .44 cartridges
1 atigi	1 wolf trap
1 atigi (old), 1 pair deerskin socks, 1 pair sealskin slippers	1 flour bowl
1 ornamental dancing cap	1 5-inch knife
1 stone pot	1 8-inch knife
1 stone pot	1 canister [gun] powder
1 stone lamp	1 wolf trap
1 pair deerskin boots, 1 pair sealskin slippers	1 fox trap
1 seal harpoon	10 .44 cartridges
1 pair pants, 1 pair deerskin boots, 1 pair sealskin slippers	20 .44 cartridges
1 bow and equipment	1 canister [gun] powder
1 man's atigi, 1 pair man's pants	1 box No. 2 1/2 primers
1 pair deerskin boots, 1 pair deerskin short socks, 1 pair deerskin long socks	20 .44 cartridges
2 pair spring boots	1/2 bar lead
1 man's atigi, 1 pair pants	1/2 bar lead

1 large snow-knife, several pieces of copper	1/2 box .44 cartridges
1 pair long mits	1 fox trap
seal meat and dog food for three days	1 box No. 2 1/2 primers, 1 canister [gun] powder
2 arrows, 1 snow sounder	10 .44 cartridges
[for] sewing	1 fathom calico
1 pair man's trousers, 1 pair woman's trousers, 1 pair deerskin boots, 1 pair deerskin socks	1/2 bar lead, 1 flour pan, 2 fathoms calico
1 musk-ox skin scraper, 1 snow-knife	15 .44 cartridges
1 pair deerskin socks	1 pair old scissors
[for] sewing	2 fathoms calico
1 man's atigi	20 .44 cartridges
1 small stone lamp	5 .44 cartridges
2 seal toggles, 3 sealing pins	5 .44 cartridges
child's old atigi and pants	6 .44 cartridges
2 needle cases and thimble	1/2 block matches

1 pair seal slippers	2 blocks matches
1 pair long socks	10 .44 cartridges
1 pair seal slippers	5 .44 cartridges

1 seal harpoon head and line,	
1 skin scraper	1 fathom calico
1 stone pot	1 8-inch knife

March 5th, 1915 (Bernard Harbour)

3 wolverine skins, 1 stone pot	1/2 bar lead, 1 canister powder,
	1 box No. 2 1/2 primers,
	1 8-inch knife
1 man's atigi	1 8-inch knife
1 skin scraper	1 thimble
1 needlecase and attachments	1 block matches
1 large snow-knife	1 fox trap
1 man's atigi, 1 pair man's pants,	
1 pair pup seal's mits	1/2 bar lead
1 man's atigi	1 flour bowl
1 stone lamp	1 wolf trap
1 man's atigi, 1 pair man's pants,	
1 pair deerskin boots, 1 pair sealskin	
slippers, 1 man's atigi	1 canister [gun] powder
1 pair man's pants, 1 pair deerskin	
boots	1/2 bar lead

1 double copper hook	1 fox trap
1 woman's atigi, 1 woman's	
outer trousers	1 flour bowl
1 wolverine skin, 1 pair spring boots	1/2 bar lead
1 pair man's pants, 1 pair woman's	
trousers, 1 man's atigi	34 .44 cartridges
1 pair deerskin socks (long),	
1 pair deerskin socks (short),	
1 pair deerskin boots, 1 man's atigi	1 box .44 cartridges
1 man's atigi, 1 pair man's pants	1/2 bar lead
1 pair man's trousers with feet,	
1 man's inner atigi	1/2 bar lead
1 man's atigi, 1 pair man's pants	25 .44 cartridges
1 pair sealskin slippers, 1 musk-ox	
horn box, 1 musk-ox drinking cup,	
several pieces of copper	25 .44 cartridges
2 horn snow-bailers	5 .44 cartridges

1 small stone lamp, 1 pair deerskin long	
socks, 1 pair deerskin boots, 1 pair	
man's trousers	1/2 bar lead
1 pair man's trousers, 1 man's atigi	1/2 bar lead

1 pair deerskin socks (long), 1 pair deerskin socks (short), 1 large wooden dish	1 flour bowl
1 man's atigi, 1 pair man's trousers	1 canister [gun] powder
1 woman's atigi	1 saucepan
1 seal-line and head, 1 skin scraper, 1 small ulo	1 fathom calico
1 pair woman's trousers	15 .44 cartridges
1 pair deerskin boots, 1 pair deerskin socks, 1 pair sealskin slippers	1 wolf trap
1 man's outer trousers, 1 man's inner trousers	1 flour bowl
2 woman's atigis	1 cooking pot
1 man's atigi, 1 pair man's trousers	1 cannister [gun] powder

---

1 pair seal slippers	5 .44 cartridges
1 pair seal slippers, 1 pair long socks	15 .44 cartridges
1 pair sealskin slippers, 2 woman's atigis	1 box No. 2 1/2 primers
1 pair outer deerskin boots, 1 pair woman's trousers, 1 pair sealskin slippers	1 flour bowl
1 child's coat and trousers	15 .44 cartridges
2 pair long socks	1/2 box .44 cartridges
2 pair short socks	10 .44 cartridges
1 man's atigi, 1 pair man's pants, 1 pair deerskin boots	1 box No. 2 1/2 primers
1 fancy snow-beater	5 .44 cartridges
1 pair deerskin boots	10 .44 cartridges
1 pair spring boots, 1 pair long socks	1 box No. 2 1/2 primers
2 pairs sealskin slippers	14 .44 cartridges
2 long sets of atigi strings	16 .44 cartridges
1 pair long trousers	1 flour bowl
[for] sewing	1 flour bowl
[for] sewing	2 fathoms calico
[for] sewing	2 fathoms calico

---

1 pair small water boots, 1 pair long socks	1 flour bowl
1 pair sealskin slippers	2 blocks matches
1 dancing cap	1 1/2 fathoms zephyr
1 pair short socks	2 blocks matches
1 pair long mits	1 8-inch knife
[for] sewing	10 .44 cartridges
2 decorated bone handles	4 .44 cartridges
adze and long trousers	1 box .44 cartridges
[for] scraping skins	2 fathoms calico

March 11th, 1915 (Bernard Harbour)

[for] sewing	6 .44 cartridges
[for] sewing	2 fathoms calico
[for] sewing	2 blocks matches
[for] sewing	1 8-inch knife
[for] singing into phonograph	8 blocks matches

March 12th, 1915 (Bernard Harbour)

caribou meat	1 box .44 cartridges
1 seal	1 8-inch knife
2 pair sealskin slippers, 1 pair deerskin socks	15 .30-30 cartridges

1 pair new sealskin mits	10 .44 cartridges
1 ugyuk line	15 .44 cartridges
1 pair sealskin slippers	5 .44 cartridges
1 pair sealskin slippers, 1 small stone lamp	10 .30-30 cartridges
1 small stone lamp	8 .30-30 cartridges

March 16th, 1915 (Liston and Sutton Islands area)

2 pairs water boots	5 yds calico

March 17th, 1915 (Liston and Sutton Islands area)

1 small seal	15 .44 cartridges
1 sealing harpoon head and line	10 .44 cartridges
1 seal	1 8-inch knife
2 seals	1 box .44 cartridges
1 seal	1/2 box .44 cartridges

March 20th, 1915 (Bernard Harbour)

1 dog	1 box .44 cartridges
1 dog	2 boxes .30-30 cartridges
1 seal	1 box .30-30 cartridges
1 dog	1 box .44 cartridges
1 dog	3 boxes .30-30 cartridges

March 22nd, 1915 (Bernard Harbour)

4 boxes .303 Savage [ammunition]
10 boxes .30-30 Winchester ["] changed for 6 boxes .44 cartridges

1 dancing cap	12 .44 cartridges

March 25th, 1915 (Bernard Harbour)

1 large stone lamp	1 box No. 2 1/2 primers, 1/2 bar lead, 1 canister [gun] powder
1 dog	1 box No. 2 1/2 primers, 1/2 bar lead, 1 canister [gun] powder
1 bearded seal liver, 1 pair sealskin slippers	2 fathoms white drill

March 30th, 1915 (about 3 miles north of Locker Point, Coronation Gulf)

1 dog and harness	1 1/2 box .44 cartridges
3 caribou tongues	13 .44 cartridges

April 2, 1915 (Bernard Harbour)

Issued to Uloksak	1 .44 rifle, 2 boxes .44 cartridges, 1 set reloading tools, 1 long cooking pot

March 1915 (Bernard Harbour and Liston and Sutton Islands areas)

1 bow and equipment	1/2 box .44 cartridges
outer and inner man's atigis	28 .44 cartridges
1 pair short deerskin socks, 1 pair long mits	
1 woman's ulo	1 fox trap
musk-ox skin scraper	6 .44 cartridges
seal toggle	5 .44 cartridges
whittling knife	4 .44 cartridges
2 seal toggles	5 .44 cartridges
2 seal daggers	8 .44 cartridges
musk-ox pounder	9 .44 cartridges
bow and equipment	5 .44 cartridges
1 woman's coat, 1 woman's trousers	1/2 box .44 cartridges
1 seal dagger	1 18-inch pot
1 skin scraper, 1 seal toggle	3 .44 cartridges
1 small stone lamp, man's outer and inner atigis	5 .44 cartridges
2 woman's atigis, 1 pair man's outer boots	1/2 bar lead
1 goose foot with seal-pins, 1 skin bag with seal-pins	1 box .44 cartridges
	2 blocks matches
1 seal-line and head, 1 musk-ox skin scraper, 1 woman's belt, 1 pair long socks, 1 box for drill	1 box No. 2 1/2 primers

Trade list for November 1915 to April 1916

Nov. 10, 1915 (Bernard Harbour)

[for] services rendered (Ikpuk)	1 10-inch knife

Nov. 16, 1915 (Bernard Harbour)

1 winter skin, 1 pair woman's boots, 1 pair man's boots, 1 bow and case	4 boxes .30-30 cartridges
1 fish spear, 4 fish spear heads, 1 pair deerskin boots, 1 pair sealskin socks, 1 pair sealskin waterboots, 1 nigsik	3 boxes .30-30 cartridges
1 thimble case	1 thimble
1 pair sealskin shoes	1 thimble, 1 needle
1 loon skin	5 .30-30 cartridges
1 bundle dried fish	1 enamel pan
1 stone pot	1 10-inch snow-knife
1 pair deerskin boots (woman's)	1 fox trap
1 pair deerskin boots (woman's)	1 enamel pan
1 set fish-spear heads	1 thimble, 2 needles
1 pair sealskin boots, 1 pair sealskin socks	1 fox trap

1 pair bearskin mits	1 pair scissors
1 slab sinew	1 thimble
1 snow-knife	1 enamel pan
1 large frozen fish, 1 pair long mits	1 enamel pan
[for] freighting [from Victoria I.]	1 fox trap
1 fish spear	10 .44 cartridges
1 pair deerskin boots, 1 pair deerskin mits	30 .44 cartridges

Nov. 18, 1915 (Bernard Harbour)

1 bow and case	1 box .44 cartridges
1 bow and case (woman's)	10 .44 cartridges
2 forks	4 needles
1 arrow straightener	5 .44 cartridges
1 lump copper	5 .44 cartridges
1 pair child's mits	5 .44 cartridges
1 pair sealskin slippers, 1 fish spear	15 .44 cartridges
1 fire-making apparatus	10 .44 cartridges
1 musk-ox ladle	1 thimble
3 bone thimbles	1 thimble
1 bow and case	1 can [gun] powder

1 pair deerskin boots, 1 pair deerskin
socks (long), 1 pair deerskin socks
(short), 1 pair sealskin shoes

1 nigsik (fish gaff), 3 fish spears

1 bow and case

1 sealskin coat

1 bearded seal line

1 winter deerskin

1 blubber pounder

[for] mending [a] bow

bow and case

1 pair waterboots, 6 dried fish

large bundle dried fish

1 fish spear, 2 small stone pots

1 fish line, 1 fish spear, 1 wood bowl

1 set sealing pins, 1 seal toggle

1 stone lamp (large)

1 stone pot

1 stone pot

1 ice pick

1 bow and case

1 thimble (bone)

1 copper needle

1 stone lamp, 1 large wooden dish

1 set spear-heads (fish)

1 pair woman's waterboots

1 needle case

1 box (250) No. 2 1/2 primers

1/2 bar (8 lbs) lead

30 .44 cartridges

20 .44 cartridges

1 box .44 cartridges

10 .44 cartridges

1 thimble

1 thimble

1 can [gun] powder

1 fox trap

1 10-inch snow-knife,
10 .44 cartridges

1 can [gun] powder

1/2 bar (8 lbs) lead

2 blocks matches

1 can [gun] powder,
1 box .44 cartridges

1 box .44 cartridges

1 saw

1 box No. 2 primers

1 can [gun] powder

2 needles

1 thimble

1 tin saucepan

1 thimble

1 saw

1 thimble

Nov. 20, 1915 (Bernard Harbour)

1 bundle squirrel skins

1 stone pot

1 stone pot, 1 stone lamp, 1 dog

3 sets fish-spear heads

1 large fish gaff

1 winter deerskin

1 child's trousers

1 white belly skin

1 white belly skin, 1 pair waterboots,
1 pair sealskin socks

1 snow-knife

1 bow and case

1 pair deerskin boots, 1 pair sealskin
shoes, 1 pair mittens

2 1/2 fathoms print [cloth]

1 long iron pot

1 .44 rifle and set of loading tools

20 .44 cartridges

10 .44 cartridges

1 long iron pot

25 .44 cartridges

20 .44 cartridges

1 box .44 cartridges

1 8-inch knife

1 box .44 cartridges

1 box No. 2 primers

1	small lamp, 1 blubber pounder	20	.44 cartridges
1	pair waterboots	15	.44 cartridges
1	copper-headed skin-scraper,		
1	blubber pounder	10	.44 cartridges
1	seal scoop	15	.44 cartridges
2	bearded seal lines	2	boxes .38-55 cartridges
	fishing line	5	.44 cartridges
1	seal scoop	5	.44 cartridges
2	harness toggles	2	blocks matches
1	fishing line, 1 seal scoop	2	fathoms print [cloth]

- -

Nov. 22, 1915 (Bernard Harbour)

1	bow and case	1	10-inch knife
1	arrow straightener	1	thimble
1	pair waterboots, 1 seal scoop	25	.44 cartridges

Nov. 24, 1915 (Bernard Harbour)

1	fish gaff	1	box .38-55 cartridges
1	woman's belt	1	block matches
1	fish gaff	10	.44 cartridges
1	dog, 1 stone lamp, 4 wolverine		
	skins	1	.44 rifle and set of reloading tools
4	harness toggles	15	.44 cartridges
1	seal indicator	3	needles
3	fall deerskins	1	can [gun] powder, 200 No. 2 primers
1	bow and case	1	box .44 cartridges
2	wolverine skins	1/2	bar (8 lbs) lead
1	pair waterboots	15	.44 cartridges
1	pair deerskin boots	100	No. 1 primers
1	fish gaff, 1 fish spear	1/2	bar (8 lbs) lead

- -

Q	[1?] pair woman's waterboots	1	can [gun] powder
1	fish spear		
1	fish spear	1/2	box .44 cartridges
1	clothes bag		
1	fishing line	10	.44 cartridges
1	small stone pot	4	needles, 2 blocks matches
2	pair sealskin shoes, 1 bearded seal		
	line, 1 foetid seal line	1	long iron pot

Nov. 25, 1915 (Bernard Harbour)

3	wolverine skins	2	cans [gun] powder
1	sled toggle, 5 harness toggles		
1	seal scoop	100	No. 1 primers
1	fishing line	100	No. 1 primers

1	seal harpoon, 1 fish gaff,		
1	sled toggle	1	box .44 cartridges

Nov. 27, 1915 (Bernard Harbour)

1	deerskin	100	No. 1 primers

1	atigi, 1 pair trousers	100	No. 1 primers, 1 can [gun] powder, 3 fathoms ticking
	issued to Milukkattuk	1	long iron pot

Nov. 28, 1915 (Bernard Harbour)

1	box .44 cartridges changed for	2	1/2 boxes .30-30 cartridges
1	can [gun] powder changed for	2	boxes .30-30 cartridges
1	deerskin poke	1/2	bar (8 lbs) lead
1	pair deerskin socks, 1 pair sealskin shoes, 1 fish spear	1	box .44 cartridges
1	water bag	2	blocks matches
1	pair sealskin shoes	10	.44 cartridges
1	bow and case	1	box .44 cartridges
1	copper-headed ice pick	1	box .44 cartridges
1	fishing line	1	box .38-55 cartridges
1	pair waterboots, 1 pair sealskin socks	1	box .44 cartridges
1	small lamp	7	.44 cartridges
1	new stone lamp	1	box .44 cartridges

Nov. 29, 1915 (Bernard Harbour)

1	deerskin	1	box .30-30 cartridges
1	white deerskin belly	1	box .30-30 cartridges

Nov. 30, 1915 (Bernard Harbour)

1	knife	100	No. 1 primers
2	rosaries, 1 cross (for Corporal Bruce)	2	boxes .44 cartridges
1	large bail dried fish	1	box .44 cartridges
1	pair deerskin boots, 1 pair deerskin socks, 1 bearded seal line	1	box .44 cartridges
1	pair mittens	1	pair scissors
1	fish spear	100	No. 1 primers
	woman's waterboots	100	No. 1 primers
	man's waterboots	25	.44 cartridges
1	pair trousers, 1 seal harpoon, 1 seal scoop, 1 seal indicator, 1 seal poke	3	boxes .38-55 cartridges
1	fish gaff	20	.44 cartridges
1	bow and case	1	11-inch knife
3	seal indicators	12	.44 cartridges

1 ice pick	1 long iron pot

---

issued to Jennie [Kanneyuk]	1 long iron pot
1 pair fancy deerskin boots, 1 white [caribou] belly skin	1 10-inch knife
1 bag dried fish, 3 frozen fish	1 10-inch knife
2 horn snow-knives	15 .30-30 cartridges
big deerskin bag	1 box .44 cartridges
1 sealskin shoes	5 .44 cartridges
1 sled toggle, 1 seal scoop	20 .44 cartridges
1 big deerskin bag	1 box .44 cartridges
2 horn snow-knives	10 .30-30 cartridges
1 harness toggle	1 thimble
1 deerskin	1 box .38-55 cartridges
2 deerskins	1 box .44 cartridges
1 pair scissors	5 .44 cartridges
1 pair woman's waterboots, 1 pair man's waterboots	30 .44 cartridges
1 small stone lamp	10 .44 cartridges
1 bow and case, 1 horn snow-knife, 1 iron snow-knife, 1 seal scoop	2 boxes .44 cartridges

---

1 small lamp, 1 horn snow-knife	20 .44 cartridges
2 woman's atigis	1 box .44 cartridges
1 bow and case	1 can [gun] powder, 1/2 bar (8 lbs) lead
1 snow sounder, 1 seal probe, 1 seal indicator, 1 seal scoop	250 No. 2 1/2 primers
1 sealskin bag	30 .44 cartridges
1 deerskin	1 box .38-55 cartridges
2 deerskins	2 boxes .38-55 cartridges
1 horn turf pick	5 .44 cartridges
1 pair man's waterboots, 1 pair woman's waterboots, 2 fish gaffs, 1 fishing line, 1 horn turf pick	4 boxes .30-30 cartridges
dog	1 box primers, 1 can [gun] powder, 1/2 bar (8 lbs) lead
1 squirrel-skin atigi	1 1/2 fathoms ticking

---

1 sleeping skin	1 box .30-30 cartridges
1 pair snow goggles, 1 drill set, 1 drill, 1 drill mouthpiece	34 .44 cartridges
1 groover	1 thimble

Dec. 3, 1915 (Bernard Harbour)

3 deerskins, 1 white [caribou] belly skin	2 boxes .44 cartridges

Dec. 4, 1915

1	horn snow-knife		
2	harness toggles	2	blocks matches
1	bundle dried fish	1	10-inch knife
1	pair deerskin boots	20	.44 cartridges
1	bearded seal line	1	box .44 cartridges
1	bale dried fish	1	10-inch knife
1	deerskin	1	box .38-55 cartridges
4	shoulders caribou meat	2	boxes .38-55 cartridges
1	pair waterboots	15	.44 cartridges
1	deerskin	35	.44 cartridges
1	deerskin (large bull)	1	box .44 cartridges
1	sealskin bag	1	box .38-55 cartridges

1	horn turf pick	10	.30-30 cartridges
1	blubber pounder, 1 fishing line	20	.44 cartridges
1	big ulo	1	box .38-55 cartridges
1	bow and case	1	box .44 cartridges
1	sealskin bow case, 1 bundle arrows	1	box .44 cartridges
1	fancy cap, 1 pair deerskin shoes,		
1	pair woman's waterboots	1	box .44 cartridges
1	pair sealskin shoes	10	.44 cartridges
1	seal spear	10	.44 cartridges

Dec. 5, 1915

1	atigi	1	can [gun] powder
1	atigi	1	can [gun] powder

Dec. 6, 1915

	sleeping bag, atigi	2	boxes .44 cartridges
1	bearded seal line	200	No. 1 primers
1	scraped deerskin	1	box .44 cartridges
2	man's atigis	2	cans [gun] powder
2	pairs man's trousers	200	No. 1 primers

1	wood dish	1	can [gun] powder
1	horn snow-knife	1	thimble
1	horn arrow-straightener	10	.44 cartridges
1	pair sealskin shoes, 1 seal scoop	15	.44 cartridges
1	bow and case	1	box .44 cartridges
1	fishing line	20	.44 cartridges

Dec. 7, 1915

1	work-bag and drill set	20	.44 cartridges
1	pair deerskin boots (made)	1	can [gun] powder

1 pair waterboots — 1/2 bar (8 lbs) lead

Dec. 9, 1915

1 fish gaff, 1 man's tool kit — 1 box .44 cartridges
1 table prop (for Milukkattuk) — 1 can [gun] powder

Dec. 11, 1915

1 bearded seal line, 2 priests' books (for Corporal Bruce) — 2 boxes .44 cartridges
issued to Milukkattuk — 10 .44 cartridges; 1 long iron pot
1 bearded seal line, 1 atigi — 1 box .44 cartridges
issued to Munnigorina — 1 child's shirt

Dec. 14, 1915

1 deerskin atigi, 1 scraped deerskin — 2 boxes .44 cartridges
1 musk-ox scraper, 1 fishing line, 1 sled toggle, 1 strap for hauling on sled — 1 box .44 cartridges
1 pair long mits — 15 .44 cartridges
1 pair short mits — 10 .44 cartridges
2 white [caribou] belly skins — 1 box .44 cartridges

Dec. 16, 1915 (Liston and Sutton Islands)

1 pair deerskin boots, 1 pair sealskin shoes, dog food — 1 box .44 cartridges
building snowhouse, bringing load of wood — 1 box .44 cartridges

Dec. 17, 1915 (Liston and Sutton Islands)

1 dog (for Mr. Girling) — 1 12-inch knife
1 dog (for Mr. Girling) — 1 machete
1 unborn seal, 1 large ulo, 1 large musk-ox ladle — 1 box .44 cartridges

Dec. 18, 1915 (Liston and Sutton Islands)

1 blubber pounder — 2 fathoms print
1 pair deerskin socks — 2 fathoms print
1 pair waterboots and socks — 1 box .30-30 cartridges
2 frozen fish, 1 fishing line, 1 seal scoop — 1/2 box .30-30 cartridges
3 horn snow-knives — 1/2 box .30-30 cartridges
1 pair sealskin shoes — 2 fathoms print

Dec. 19, 1915 (Liston and Sutton Islands)

1 dog (for Mr. Girling)	3 boxes .38-55 cartridges
1 musk-ox ladle	2 fathoms print
presented to Ikpukkuaq for services rendered	1 large spoon, 1 12-inch knife
presented to Kanneyuk for services rendered	1 12-inch knife, 2 fathoms print
presented to two children	4 fathoms print
2 marlin spikes for bow	1 thimble
reward for finding watch	1 thimble
to 3 children	3 aluminum thimbles
3 dried fish	1 aluminum thimble, 3 needles
paid to Milukkattuk	2 fathoms print, 1 thimble

Dec. 22, 1915 (Liston and Sutton Islands)

dog food	1 thimble, 6 needles

Dec. 24, 1915 (Bernard Harbour)

1 pair deerskin trousers	1 8-inch triangular file
1 pair spring boots	15 .44 cartridges

Dec. 26, 1915 (Bernard Harbour)

1 pair deerskin shoes	1 thimble, 3 large fishhooks
1 musk-ox skin	1 canister [gun] powder

Dec. 27, 1915 (Bernard Harbour)

1 pair deerskin socks	10 .44 cartridges
1 deerskin	6 bars lead
[for] bringing load of wood	1 1/2 fathoms print, 10 .44 cartridges, 1 aluminum thimble

Dec. 31, 1915 (Liston and Sutton Islands)

1 wooden dish	4 bars lead
1 pair fancy deerskin trousers	1 box (250) No. 2 primers
2 pair sealskin shoes	4 bars lead
1 pair child's boots	2 blocks matches
1 pair sealskin shoes	2 blocks matches
1 large wooden bowl	1 box .44 cartridges
1 pair deerskin trousers	1 can [gun] powder
1 copper-headed fishline	16 bars lead
1 man's atigi	1 set reloading tools
1 pair deerskin trousers	1 can [gun] powder
1 pair deerskin long boots (woman's), 1 pair man's deerskin boots	1 box .44 cartridges

1 small stone lamp	9 bars lead

1 caribou	1 box (250) No. 2 primers, 8 lbs lead
1 bow and attachments	1 box .30-30 cartridges
seal meat	1/2 box .30-30 cartridges
1 child's doll	1 aluminum thimble
1 child's doll	1 aluminum thimble
[given] to child	1 aluminum thimble
seal meat	10 .30-30 cartridges, 2 needles

Jan. 5, 1916 (Liston and Sutton Islands)

1 1/2 boxes .30-30 [cartridges] changed for	1 1/2 boxes .38-55 cartridges
1 pair sealskin shoes	10 .38-55 cartridges
for bringing in deermeat	1 box .30-30 cartridges

Jan. 6, 1916 (Liston and Sutton Islands)

1 pair waterboots and socks	10 .30-30 cartridges
1 seal scoop, 1 sled toggle	12 .30-30 cartridges
for services rendered (Ikpuk)	1 can [gun] powder
1 pair trousers, 1 pair long socks	1 box (250) No. 2 1/2 primers
2 rosaries (for Corporal Bruce)	1 box .30-30 cartridges
1 sleeping bag	8 lbs lead

Jan. 14, 1916 (Liston and Sutton Islands)

1 pair fancy trousers	1 can [gun] powder

(*Note*: the following two entries are from the First Trade List)

1 pair trousers	10 bars lead (1 1/2 lbs)
1 man's atigi	100 No. 2 primers

Jan 16, 1916 (Liston and Sutton Islands)

1 cup	2 thimbles
1 cup and ball (toy)	3 needles
1 cup and ball (toy)	1 thimble
1 pair deerskin boots	5 bars lead

Jan. 17, 1916 (Liston and Sutton Islands)

1 outer atigi, 1 inner atigi	1 can [gun] powder

(*Note*: Entries for Feb. 3, 8, 16, 20 and 21, are from the First Trade List)

Feb. 3rd, 1916 (Liston and Sutton Islands)

to Ikpukkuaq (for services rendered)	18 bars lead (3 lbs)

Feb. 8th, 1916 (Bernard Harbour)

1 heavy man's atigi, 1 woman's outer atigi, 1 woman's inner atigi, 1 woman's fancy trousers, 1 dressed sealskin, 1 pair deerskin boots, 2 pair sealskin shoes, 1 doll	2 cans [gun] powder, 300 No. 2 primers, 1 box .38-55 cartridges (20), 12 bars lead (2 lbs), 10 assorted needles

---

Feb. 16, 1916 (a few miles southeast of Locker Point, Coronation Gulf)

1 seal	1 box .22 automatic [ammunition]
1 seal	20 .44 [cartridges]
1 pair mittens (for J.R. Cox), 1 pair boots for Mongolina	1 box .22 automatic [ammunition]
2 heavy deerskins	empty tins

Feb. 20, 1916 (Bernard Harbour; not transacted by D. Jenness, who was in the middle of Coronation Gulf about 35 miles northwest of Tree River on this date. Unalina was Palaiyak's sister, married to Ambrose)

issued to Unalina	1 can powder to buy two light deerskins for atigi for herself

Feb. 21, 1916 (on small island in middle of Coronation Gulf, about 25 miles north-northwest of Tree River; no record in diary of this transaction)

2 seals	1 box .44 [cartridges]

Feb. 22, 1916 (temporary Eskimo settlement in Coronation Gulf, about 13 miles north of Tree River)

1 inner atigi	100 No. 2 primers
1 outer atigi	1 canister [gun] powder
seal meat	100 No. 2 primers
dog food	8 bars lead (1 1/3 lb), 2 fathoms print
1 Eskimo tool-bag and tools	5 bars lead
1 wrist toggle for sealing	4 large needles
seal meat	100 No. 2 primers
1 Eskimo tool-bag and tools	4 blocks matches
2 1/2 boxes .30-30 given in exchange for	1 box .44 cartridges

(*Note*: the following three entries are from the First Trade List)

2 seals	1 can [gun] powder
2 seals	1 old saw
1 pair mittens	1 empty tin

Feb. 24th, 1916 (Coronation Gulf, about 13 miles north of Tree River)

for services rendered	2 fathoms print

Feb. 25th, 1916 (Coronation Gulf, about 13 miles north of Tree River)

1 pair deerskin long socks	6 bars lead

(*Note*: the following four items are from the First Trade List)

1 pair boots, 1 pair mittens, 1 pair slippers, 1 heavy deerskin	1 box primers and 1 empty tin

March 3rd, 1916 (Temporary Eskimo settlement in Coronation Gulf, about 8 miles north of Hepburn Island)

dog food, 1 inner atigi	1 box .44 cartridges
1 pair sealskin shoes, 1 pair mittens, 1 slab sinew	1 8-inch knife

2 slabs sinew	2 thimbles, 8 large needles
payment for anthrop. measurements	24 needles, 12 fish-hooks
[for] sewing and drying clothes	3 bars lead
1 dog	3 boxes .38-55 cartridges
5 slabs sinew	25 needles, 5 aluminum thimbles

March 11th, 1916 (On small island in Coronation Gulf, about 32 miles north-northwest of Tree River; a few miles north-northwest of Feb. 21 locality. This transaction actually occurred on Mar. 10, at the same Eskimo camp visited Feb.22-26)

dog food	1 flat 7-inch file
seal meat	1 8-inch knife

March 19th, 1916 (Bernard Harbour)

[to Avrunna] for service during sled journey from Feb. 15th to Mar. 19th	1 canister [gun] powder, 20 bars lead, 250 No. 2 primers, 1 box .44 cartridges, 1 set .44 reloading tools

March 20th, 1916 (Bernard Harbour)

2 fawn skins	1 canister [gun] powder
3 thin summer skins	1 canister [gun] powder
1 fawn skin	15 bars lead
1 wolverine skin with skeletal parts	1 box .44 cartridges
1 wolverine skin, 1 red fox skin	1 set .45-70 reloading tools
1 wolverine skin	5 bars lead
5 wolverine skins	1 box .44 cartridges
1 red fox skin	1 set .44 reloading tools, 1/2 bag shot
2 wolverine skins	1 canister [gun] powder

2	wolverine skins	10	bars lead
1	white fox skin	1	canister [gun] powder
4	white deer belly skins	250	No. 2 primers
4	fawn skins	1	bag shot
1	man's outer atigi, 1 man's inner atigi	1	canister [gun] powder

March 21st, 1916 (Bernard Harbour)

2	wolverine skins	1	box .44 cartridges
14	deer skins	2	canisters [gun] powder, 500 No. 2 primers, 2 bags shot, 1 set .44 re-loading tools

- -

	woman's outer atigi, woman's inner atigi, woman's outer breeks	1	canister [gun] powder
	man's outer atigi	200	No. 2 primers
	man's outer and inner breeks	1	bag shot
	man's deerskin boots, 3 deerskins, 1 man's outer atigi, 1 woman's outer atigi	2	canister's [gun] powder
1	woman's inner atigi	1	bag shot
4	white deer belly skins		
5	deerskins	1	10-inch knife, 1 can [gun] powder
2	pair deerskin boots	1	can [gun] powder
1	man's outer atigi	200	No. 21; primers
1	white [caribou] belly skin		
2	dancing caps	500	No. 2 primers
2	pair woman's long boots	1	can [gun] powder
2	woman's outer atigis	1	bag shot
1	pair man's outer breeks	1	10-inch knife
2	man's outer atigis	1	fox trap
1	pair man's outer boots	1	cooking pot
9	deerskins	1	cup (aluminum)
3	white deer belly skins	1	14-inch file (used), 1 thimble

- -

March 24th, 1916 (Bernard Harbour)

1	deerskin	1	thimble, 1 empty pemmican can
1	sealskin atigi	3	canisters powder
1	wolverine skin	2	bags shot
1	large stone lamp	500	No. 2 primers
1	large stone pot, 3 deerskins, 1 pair man's outer breeks, 1 pair woman's outer breeks, 1 pair deerskin boots (issued to engineer), Priest's vestments and books (delivered to Corporal Bruce)		
		6	boxes .30-30 cartridges
1	man's outer atigi	1	canister [gun] powder
1	man's outer breeks	1	bag shot

1	large deer-leg clothes bag [for] anthrop. measurements		
	issued to Patsy Klengenberg	30	needles, 15 fish-hooks, 2 thimbles
		1	Ingersoll watch (received in return - Ingersoll watch - broken)

March 26th, 1916 (Bernard Harbour)

1	wolvering skin and bones	1	box .30-30 cartridges
1	bow and case	1	can [gun] powder

March 31st, 1916 (Bernard Harbour)

	paid to Ilaciaq for instruction in folklore	1	can powder, 1 bag shot,
		200	No. 2 primers
1	man's atigi	1	8-inch knife
4	pair deerskin boots	2	plugs Navy 5 tobacco
1	pair sealskin shoes	2	cans [gun] powder
2	men's outer atigis	1	bag lead
2	men's inner atigis	1	can man pemmican
1	woman's outer atigi	3	lbs sugar, 200 No. 2 primers
1	seal	200	No. 2 primers
1	child's combination suit	1	can [gun] powder

April 3rd, 1916 (Bernard Harbour)

1	pair woman's boots		
1	pair man's boots	1	bag shot
1	woman's inner atigi		
1	woman's outer atigi	1	can [gun] powder

April 9th, 1916 (Bernard Harbour)

1	fawn skin	1	can [gun] powder
1	wolverine skin	200	No. 2 primers
2	short-haired deerskins	1	bag shot
1	long-haired deerskin		
2	wolverine skins	2	bags shot
9	short-haired deerskins	500	No. 2 1/2 primers, 2 cans powder
1	outer atigi	1	bag shot
1	pair man's boots, 1 pair outer trousers	1	can [gun] powder
1	man's outer atigi, 1 man's inner atigi	1	can [gun] powder

April 14th, 1916 (Bernard Harbour)

	to Kesullik for services	100	No. 2 primers

April 18th, 1916 (Bernard Harbour)

to Avrunna for services	1	can [gun] powder, 1 bag shot,
	200	No. 2 primers
to Ikpukkuaq for services	1	.30-30 rifle

Appendix 4:

The Arctic Collections of D. Jenness, 1913-16

During his three years in the Arctic Jenness made extensive ethnological and archaeological collections for the National Museum of Canada in Ottawa, the result of his continuous and tireless efforts in carrying out his official expedition duties. These contributed significantly towards his later acclaim as Canada's foremost anthropologist.

The ethnological collections consisted of more than 2500 specimens obtained by trade between 1914 and 1916 from the Copper Eskimos around the west end of Coronation Gulf and on southwestern Victoria Island. These include fur garments for both male and female, young and old, hunting and fishing equipment (bows and arrows, various types of spears, knives, fish hooks and lines, etc), women's cooking and sewing utensils, tents, and kayaks, many of which are listed in Appendix 3. It also includes 92 Edison wax-cylinder recordings of Eskimo (principally but not exclusively Copper Eskimo) songs and shamanistic performances. These specimens and recordings are housed in the Canadian Museum of Civilization (formerly the Canadian Museum of Man, and earlier yet the National Museum of Canada), in Hull, Québec. They have been catalogued in detail by that organization.

The archaeological collections brought back by Jenness from the 1913-16 Canadian Arctic Expedition came from the following localities: (1) Nome, Alaska — a small collection made on site by Jenness and his colleague Henri Beuchat while en route north on the *Karluk* in late July 1913; (2) Barrow, Alaska — material purchased from Charles Brower by Viljhalmur Stefansson, mainly in 1912, and by Jenness in 1916; (3) Barter Island, northern Alaska — a collection of some 3300 artifacts collected personally by Jenness in June and July 1914; (4) Young Point, Amundsen Gulf — a small collection made by him in July 1916 ; and (5) a small collection purchased by him at Point Hope, Alaska, in 1916, while he was en route back to Nome and Ottawa. These archaeological specimens, like the ethnological specimens, are stored in the Canadian Museum of Civilization and have been listed in full by that organization.

Jenness' Coronation Gulf (Copper Eskimo) and Barter Island materials constitute the finest and most complete collections from these two regions in existence.

Still unheralded, however, are the small but valuable contributions Jenness made during the same period to Canada's National Collections of birds, insects, plants, animals, mosses, and shells. In spite of inadequate facilities, equipment, and means of transportation for what he gathered, he nevertheless collected several dozen specimens of animal and plant life for his scientific colleagues, Dr. Anderson and F. Johansen, during his travels in places they were not likely to visit. Furthermore, he recorded in his diary meteorological data, topographic information, and geological observations for the benefit of two other scientific members of the Southern Party of the Canadian Arctic Expedition, Chipman and O'Neill. As the information on

these contributions is widely scattered and not readily found, I have prepared the following lists based upon evidence in the diaries of Jenness and
some of his colleagues, in published reports of the Expedition, and in
various Canadian government science research buildings in Ottawa.

A. Birds

1. *In the National Bird Collection*

(Ornithology Section, Canadian Museum of Nature, Ottawa, Canada)

RMA Fld No.	Mus. No.	Genus & species	Name	Date Collected	Locality
37	10322	*Calioris bairdii*	Baird's sandpiper	Jul 19/14	Barter Island
35	10323	*Calioris bairdii*	Baird's sandpiper	Jul 16/14	Barter Island
36	10324	*Calioris bairdii*	Baird's sandpiper	Jul 16/14	Barter Island
34	10325	*Anas acuta*	pintail duck	Jul 14/14	Camden Bay
561	9950	*Pluvialis squatarola*	blackbellied plover	Jun 6/15	L.Añmaloqtoq
562	9951	*Arenaria interpres*	ruddy turnstone	Jun 8/15	L.Numichoin
563	9952	*Eremophila alpestris*	horned lark	Jun 10/15	L.Numichoin
564	9953	*Eremophila alpestris*	horned lark	Jun 16/15	L.Numichoin
565	9954	*Calcarius lapponicus*	Lapland longspur	Jun 12/15	L.Numichoin

Comment: The 9950-54 specimens are males, all from Victoria Island, N.W.T.; the
10322-25 specimens were juveniles, sex indeterminate, all from north coast of
Alaska. Name given 10322-24 in field was *Pisobia bairdii*, 10325 was *Dafila acuta*,
9950 was *Squatarola squatarola*, and 9952 was *Otocoris alpestris*. Dr. Anderson recorded the receipt of Field specimen Nos. 561-565 in his field notes Nov. 18, 1915.
RMA Fld No.= R.M. Anderson Field Number. Mus. No.= Museum Number.

2. *Other birds collected by D. Jenness on Barter Island for Dr. Anderson*

(information from Jenness diary, R.M.Anderson field notes July 13/14, and
records in the Zoology Division, Canadian Museum of Nature, Ottawa,
Canada)

Mus. No.	Eskimo name	Name	Sex	Date Collected
7886	*nepailuktak*	short-eared owl		May 29/14
8791	*kirigavik*	duck hawk (perigrine falcon)	m.	June 16/14
8794	*mit-kutai-lak*	Arctic tern	m.	June 20/14
8795	*isunyuk*	parasitic jaeger	f.	July 5/14
8797	*puviaktok*	pectoral sandpiper	?	June 5/14
8799	*liwaliwak*	Baird's sandpiper	f.	June 16/14
8800	*liwaliwak*	Baird's sandpiper	f.	June 12/14
8801	*livalivaurak*	semipalmated sandpiper	f.	June 17/14
8802	*augruak or savwak*	red phalarope	f.	June 12/14
8806	*tutalik*	spectacled eider duck	m.	June 29/14

8807	*tutalik*	spectacled eider duck	f.	June 29/14
8808	*ignakauktok*	Stellar's eider duck	m.	June 23/14
8809	*ignakauktok*	Stellar's eider duck	m.	June 23/14
8810	*ignakauktok*	Stellar's eider duck	m.	June 29/14
8811	*sagavuptingmia*	Harlequin duck	m.	June 26/14
8812	*sagavuptingmia*	Harlequin duck	m.	June 26/14
8813	*kurugaq*	pintail duck	f.	June 26/14
8815	*mallere*	Pacific loon	?	June 18/14
8816	*mallere*	Pacific loon	m.	July 7/14
8817	*mallere*	Pacific loon	?	July 7/14

Comment: Jenness collected in all about 50 bird specimens in northern Alaska between late May and mid July 1914, mostly on Barter Island. These he sent to Dr. R. Anderson at Camden Bay on June 16 and July 13 (recorded in Dr. Anderson's field notes, June 18, July 13, and July 24, 1914, with Eskimo names in italics). I have found CMN (formerly National Museum of Natural Sciences NMNS) specimen numbers for the 24 listed above; the remaining specimens, listed in Dr. Anderson's field notes, may not have been retained. They were:

1. Golden plover (*tulik*), m., E. end Camden Bay, Alaska, July 14/14.
2. Ditto, f., July 14/14.
3. Black-bellied plover (*tullik*), f., Barter I., Alaska, June 22/14.
4. Yellow-bellied loon (*tulik*), m., mouth Hulahula R., Alaska, July 13/14.
5. Sabine's gull (*kirigugiuk* or *ikirigugiuk*), m., Barter I., June 30/14.
6. Ditto, m., June 30/14.
7. Red-throated loon, sex ?, Barter I., date June or July/14.
8. Sanderling (*Calidris arenaria*)(*taligvaruk*), sex ? Barter I., June 6/14.
9. Semipalmated sandpiper (*kurukkuruk*), sex ? Barter I., June 13/14.
10. Ditto, sex ? Barter I., June 3/14.
11. Pacific eider (*amauligerak*), f., Barter I., June 29/14, with 5 eggs and nest.
12. Pacific loon (*mallere*), f., Barter I., July 2/14.
13. Pacific loon, m., Barter I., July 5/14.
14. Ditto, f., Barter I., July 5/14.
15. Pintail duck, juvenile in alcohol, Barter I., July 14/14.
16. RMA Field No. 236. *Somateria v-nigra*, m., Barter I., June 15/14.
17. RMA Field No. 237. *Arctonetta fischeri*, f., Barter I., June 15/14.
18. RMA Field No. 238. *Anser albifrons gambeli*, m., Barter I., June 15/14.
19. RMA Field No. 239. *Anser albifrons gambeli*, f., Barter I., June 15/14.
20. RMA Field No. 240. *Branta canadensis hutchinsii*, m., Barter I., June 15/14.
21. RMA Field No. 241. *Eniconetta stelleri*, m., Barter I., June 15/14.
22. RMA Field No. 242. *Eniconetta stelleri*, f., Barter I., June 15/14.
23. RMA Field No. 243. *Arctonetta fischeri*, m., Barter I., June 15/14.
24. RMA Field No. 244. *Arctonetta fischeri*, m., Barter I., June 15/14.

The last nine specimens correspond to numbers 17, 18, 22, and 23 in a list in the Summary Report of the Geological Survey for the calendar year 1914 (p. 164). This report (p. 163) states that 212 bird skins had been packed for shipment to Ottawa during 1914. It would appear that nearly 25 percent of these specimens were collected by Jenness.

B. Insects

1. *Butterflies*

(National Collection of Insects, Department of Agriculture, Ottawa, Canada, Described by Arthur Gibson, 1920, pages on which the various species are described in Gibson are indicated within brackets)

1. Family Pieridae: *Eurymus hecla glacialis*, 8 males, 3 females, Barter Island, northern Alaska, July 4, 17, 19, 21, 1914. [6I]

2. Family Pieridae: *Eurymus nastes*, 1 female, Barter I., northern Alaska, July 17, 1914. [11I]

3. Family Satyridae: *Oeneis taygete*, 1 male, bay southwest of Cape Krusenstern, Coronation Gulf, N.W.T., July 3, 1916. [12I]

4. Family Satyridae: *Oeneis semidea* var. arctica, new variety, 3 females, Wollaston Peninsula, Victoria Island, N.W.T., summer 1915 (possibly near Lake Añmaloqtoq, July 22). [13I]

5. Family Satyridae: *Erebia fasciata*, 2 specimens, sex ?, bay southwest of Cape Krusenstern, Coronation Gulf, N.W.T., July 3, 1916. [16I]

6. Family Satyridae: *Erebia rossi*, 1 female, just west of Lake Añmaloqtoq, S.W. Victoria Island, July 22, 1915. [17I]

7. Family Nymphalidae: *Brenthis chariclea*, 1 male, 1 female, Wollaston Peninsula, Victoria Island, summer 1915. [20I]

8. Family Nymphalidae: *Brenthis polaris*, 6 females, July 2,4,5,11,17, 1914 and 1 male, July 5, 1914, Barter Island, northern Alaska; 2 males, bay southwest of Cape Krusenstern, Coronation Gulf, N.W.T., July 3,4, 1916; 1 male, Lake Añmaloqtoq, Victoria Island, July 29, 1915; 2 females, Lake Añmaloqtoq, Victoria Island, July 22, 1915; 1 female, Wollaston Peninsula, Victoria Island, summer 1915. [23I]

9. Family Nymphalidae: *Brenthis frigga alaskensis*, 2 males, 3 females, Barter Island, northern Alaska, July 4, 11, 1914. [24I]

10. Family Nymphalidae: *Brenthis frigga improba*, 9 males, 5 females, Barter Island, northern Alaska, July 1,2,4,5,11, 1914. [24I]

11. Family Lycaenidae: *Plebeius aquilo*, 1 male, about 6 miles north of Lake Añmaloqtoq, Victoria Island, N.W.T., July 1, 1915. [29I]

12. Family Noctuidae: *Barrovia fasciata*, 1 male, Barter Island, northern Alaska, July 11, 1914. [33I]

13. Family Noctuidae: *Anarta leucocycia*, 1 female, Cape Pullen (Lady Richardson Bay), S.W. Victoria Island, N.W.T., August 18, 1915. [35I]

14. Family Lymantriidae: *Gynaephora rossi*, 1 female, Barter Island, northern Alaska, June 24, 1914. [37I]

15. Family Geometrida: *Lygris destinata*, 4 poor specimens, Cape Pullen (Lady Richardson Bay), Victoria Island, N.W.T., August 18, 1915. [41I]

16. Family Geometrida: *Psychophora sabini*, 2 poor specimens (one Cape Pullen, Lady Richardson Bay, Victoria Island, August 18, 1915; other Wollaston Peninsula, summer 1915). [42I]

17. Family Geometrida: *Aspilates orciferaria*, 1 specimen, Kugaluk River, about 4 miles from mouth, Victoria Island, N.W.T., August 18, 1915. [44I]

18. Family Pyralidae: *Titanio* sp. 1 poor specimen, Cape Pullen (Lady Richardson Bay), Victoria Island, N.W.T., August 15, 1915. [45I]

19. Family Eucosmidae: *Eucosma* sp., 4 poor specimens, species indeterminate,
    Barter Island, northern Alaska, June 27, July 11, 1914. [46I]

Comment: These 69 specimens were collected by Jenness for Frits Johansen. Several
are pictured in the Gibson reference.

2. *Diptera (two-winged flies)*

(Described by J.R. Malloch, 1919; pages on which the various species are
described in Malloch are indicated in brackets)

1. Family Chironomidae: *Diamesa arctica* n. sp., female, one mile west of Lake
    Añmaloqtoq (type locality), S.W. Victoria Island, N.W.T., July 22,
    1915. [37C]
2. Family Chironomidae: *Chironomus* sp., male, Barter Island, northern Alaska,
    July 2, 1914. [37C]
3. Family Chironomidae: *Tanytarsus* sp., male, one mile west of Lake Añmaloqtoq,
    Victoria Island, N.W.T., July 22, 1915. [37C]
4. Family Simuliidae: *Prosimulium borealis*, n. sp. male, Wollaston Peninsula (type
    locality), Victoria Island, N.W.T., summer 1915. [41C]
5. Family Empididae: *Rhamphomyia erinacioides*, n. sp., male, Barter Island (para-
    type), northern Alaska, July 11, 1914. [46C]
6. Family Syrphidae: *Scaeva pyrastri*, 2 specimens, Barter Island, northern Alaska,
    June 10, 1914. [54C]
7. Family Oestridae: *Oedemagena tarandi*, female larva from under caribou skin,
    Read Island, off S.W. Victoria Island, N.W.T., May 4, 1915. [56C]
8. Family Callaphoridae: *Cynomyia cadaverina*, six specimens, Barter Island,
    northern Alaska, June 15, 20, 23, July 2, 1914. [58C]
9. Family Anthomyiidae: *Mydaeina obscura*, male and female, one mile west of
    Lake Añmaloqtoq, S.W. Victoria Island, N.W.T., July 22, 1915. [62C]
10. Family Scatophagide: *Scataphaga furcata*, 24 specimens, Barter Island, northern
    Alaska, June 8, July 2, 1914; 1 specimen, Cape Pullen (Lady Richard-
    son Bay), S.W. Victoria Island, N.W.T., August 18, 1915. [81C]

Comment: The new species *Diamesa arctica* was named after its collector.

3. *Mallophaga (bird and animal parasites)*

(Described by A.W. Baker, 1919; pages on which the various species are
described in Baker are indicated in brackets)

1. *Trinoton querquedulae*, female, taken from Pintail duck at Barter Island, north-
    ern Alaska, June 1914. [4D]
2. *Philopterus ceblebrachys*, numerous males and females taken from snowy owl
    at Barter Island, northern Alaska, June 5, 1914. [5D]
3. *Philopteras cursor*, male and female and immature specimens taken from short-
    eared owl at Barter Island, northern Alaska, May 1914. [5D]

Comment: These specimens are not credited to Jenness, as collector, but his diary records that he collected a parasite from a pintail duck on June 17 (specimen 1), parasites from a snowy owl (specimen 2) on June 5, and that he skinned a short-eared
owl on May 29, 1914, so there can be little doubt that he collected the three species
listed above for F. Johansen. Specimens of *Pediculus humnus capitis* (head lice)
were collected by Jenness from Copper Eskimos (Nuttall, 1919, p. 11D footnote).

4. *Coleoptera (forest insects)*

(Described by H.C. Fall, 1919 (Carabidae); J.D. Sherman, Jr., 1919 (Dytiscidae); C.W. Leng, 1919 (Rhynchophora); pages on which the various species are described in Fall are indicated in brackets)

1.   Family Carabidae: *Nebria* sp., female, Collinson Point, Camden Bay, northern Alaska, May 9, 1914. [14E]
2.   Family Carabidae: *Pterostichus agonus*, female, Demarcation Point, northern Alaska, May 20, 1914. [15E]
3.   Family Carabidae: *Amara brunnipennis*, Kugaluk River, about 4 miles from mouth, S.W. Victoria Island, N.W.T., August 18, 1915. [16E]
4.   Family Dytiscidae: *Agabus nigripalpis*, one specimen, near Lake Añmaloqtoq, S.W. Victoria Island, N.W.T., July 1915. [19E]
5.   Family Rhynchophora: *Trichalophus stefanssoni*, Spec. No. 292, Cape Krusenstern, Coronation Gulf, N.W.T., July 1916. [20E]

5. *Tenthredinoidea (saw flies)*

(Described by A.D. MacGillivray, 1919; the page on which this species is described in MacGillivray is indicated in brackets)

1.   *Amauronematus aulatus*, n. sp., female, Barter Island, northern Alaska, June 16, 1914. [17G]

6. *Apoidea (bumble-bees)*

(Described by F.W.L. Sladen, 1919; the page on which these species are described in Sladen is indicated in brackets)

1.   *Bombus arcticus*, one queen, Barter Island, northern Alaska, June 25, 1914. [29G]
2.   *Bombus sylvicola*, one queen, Barter Island, northern Alaska, July 4, 1914. [29G]

7. *Spiders*

(Described by J.H. Emerton, 1919; the page on which this species is described in Emerton is indicated in brackets)

1.   *Lycosa pictilis*, Barter Island, northern Alaska, June 1914. [5H]

Comment: This specimen is not credited to Jenness as collector, but he appears to have been the only member of the Expedition who was on Barter Island in June and collected for Johansen.

C. Mammals

(The following specimens collected by Jenness are in the National Collection of Mammals, Zoology Division, Canadian Museum of Nature)

Mus. No.	Genus and species	Name	Date Collected	Locality
2448	*Dicrostonyx sp.*	white lemming	May 29/14	Barter Island
2492	*Mustella erminea arctica*	tundra weasel	July 9/14	Barter Island
2493	*Mustella erminea arctica*	tundra weasel	July 8/14	Barter Island

Comment: As Dr. Anderson was a mammalogist, there was little need for Jenness to collect mammal specimens. CMN (formerly NMNS) records indicate he collected one other specimen, a foetus of a ringed seal in the Liston and Sutton Islands in December 1914 (NMC No. 4993), but it was discarded some years later without explanation.

D. Plants

In the National Plant Collection

(Botany Division, National Herbarium of Canada, Canadian Museum of Nature, Ottawa, Canada)

Mus. No.	Field No.	Family	Genus & Species	Date Collected	Locality
39281	406	Poaceae	*Elymus alaskanus**	July 26/15	L. Numichoin**
39282	405	Poaceae	*Elymus alaskanus**	Aug/15	S.W. Victoria I.
28015	659	Cyperaceae	*Eriophorum triste**	July/15	L. Numichoin**
46180	408a	Salicaceae	*Salix arctica**	Aug/15	S.W. Victoria I.
46155	404b	Salicaceae	*Salix arctica**	Aug/15	S.W. Victoria I.
48284	308e	Salicaceae	*Salix Richardsonii**	Aug/15	S.W. Victoria I.
43029	655	Polygonaceae	*Oxyria digyna*	July/15	L. Numichoin**
54879	658	Caryophyllaceae	*Silene involucrata**	July/15	L. Numichoin**
54880	658a	Caryophyllaceae	*Silene involucrata**	July/15	L. Numichoin**
54805	657	Caryophyllaceae	*Silene uralensis var. arcticum**	Aug/15	S.W. Victoria I.
57623	653	Ranunculaceae	*Anemone parviflora*	July/15	L. Numichoin**
56306	654	Ranunculaceae	*Ranunculus pedatifidus**	July/15	L. Numichoin**
62580	652	Cruciferae .	*Draba groenlandica**	July/15	L. Numichoin**
64122	411	Cruciferae	*Braya humilis**	July/15	L. Numichoin**
64186	413	Cruciferae	*Braya glabella Richards.**	Aug/15	S.W. Victoria I.
64233	412	Cruciferae	*Parrya nudicaulis*	July/15	L. Numihoin**
64232	650	Cruciferae	*Parrya nudicaulis*	July/15	L. Numichoin**
66628	390	Saxifragaceae	*Saxifraga oppositifolia*	Aug/15	S.W. Victoria I.
——	574	Rosaceae	*Potentilla rubricaulis*	Aug 2/15	S.W. Victoria I.
76426	388	Leguminosae	*Astragalus alpinus*	July/15	L. Numichoin**
511129	387	Leguminosae	*Oxytropis arctica**	Aug/15	S.W. Victoria I.
77198	386	Leguminosae	*Oxytropis varians**	Aug/15	S.W. Victoria I.
77507	389	Leguminosae	*Hedysarum mackenzii*	July/15	L. Numichoin**
82548	575	Onagraceae	*Epilobium latifolium*	July/15	L. Numichoin**

87897	579	Ericaceae	*Rhododendron lapponicum*	Aug/15	S.W. Victoria I.
88532	577	Ericaceae	*Cassiope tetragona*	July/15	L. Numichoin**
89244	576	Ericaceae	*Arctostaphylos rubra*	Aug/15	S.W. Victoria I.
91998	578	Plumbaginaceae	*Armeria maritima ssp labradorica*	July/15	L. Numichoin**
94313	410	Boraginaceae	*Mertensia lanceo lata var.Drummondi* *	Aug 11/15	S.W. Victoria I.
96162	324b	Scrophulariaceae	*Castilleja pallida ssp. elegans*	Aug/15	S.W. Victoria I.
97439	307b	Scrophulariaceae	*Pedicularis capitata*	Aug 15/15	S.W. Victoria I.
97852	283b	Scrophulariaceae	*Pedicularis lanata*	July/15	L. Numichoin**
102460	349	Compositae	*Aster pygmaeus* *	Aug/15	S.W. Victoria I.
103707	375a	Compositae	*Erigeron humilis* *	Aug/15	S.W. Victoria I.
107825	317b	Compositae	*Chrysanthemum grifolium*	July/15	L. Numichoin**
108258	337b	Compositae	*Artemisia hyperborea*	Jul-Aug/15	S.W. Victoria I.
109069	335b	Compositae	*Arenica alpina ssp angustifolia*	July/15	L. Numichoin**
109956	329a	Compositae	*Senecio atropurpureus*	Aug l0/15	S.W. Victoria I.
110821	401	Compositae	*Senecio congestus* *	Jul-Aug/15	S.W. Victoria I.
110823	414	Compositae	*Senecio congestus* *	Aug/15	S.W. Victoria I.
———	403	Compositae	*Crepis nana ssp Nana*	Aug/15	S.W. Victoria I.

*not the genus and species as originally identified.
**specimens shown with Lake Numichoin locality are from an area of 10 miles radius of that lake, which is 1 mile west of the southwestern part of Lake Añmaloq-toq in southwestern Victoria Island.

Comment: The 41 specimens named above are listed in Porsild (1955), who mentioned seven other plants collected by Jenness at the time, but which lacked field numbers. I did not find them in the National collection in 1988.

E. Mosses

Genus and Species	Date Collected	Locality
Ditrichum flexicaule var. densum Braithw.	July/15	Near Colville Hills, S.W. Victoria I. N.W.T.
Barbula vinealis Brid.	May 6/16	Atkoon Cr., Clifton Pt. N.W.T.
Bryum pallescens Schleich.	May 6/16	Atkoon Cr., Clifton Pt. N.W.T.

Comment: Jenness collected the above-listed three of the 68 species of true mosses brought back by the Canadian Arctic Expedition; most of the rest were collected by Frits Johansen (Williams, 1921, p. 3E).

F. Shells

Collection Station	Genus & Species	Date Collected	Locality
5285	*Mya truncata* Linn. *Macoma inconspicua* Broderip and Sowerby *Saxicava pholadis* Linn.	Aug. 9?/15	mud formation ca. 300 ft above sea level, between Colville Hills and SW coast, Victoria I., N.W.T.

Comment: The bivalve shells listed above were in marine sediments deposited following the retreat of the last continental ice sheet. Jenness observed their occurrence up to about 300 ft a.s.l. but had no means of determining their real maximum elevation (the upper limit of marine invasion, now known to rise eastward in this region), which is about 400 ft a.s.l. at Cape Baring, on the west end of Wollaston Peninsula, where deglaciation occurred about 10,710 years ago (Sharpe, 1988, p. 263). This small shell collection is recorded in O'Neill (1924, p. 33A). The exact locality from which the three species listed above were collected is unknown, but O'Neill mentioned that Jenness collected specimens from silty mud on the east bank of the Kugaluk River 1/4 mile below the gorge some 4 miles above its mouth (O'Neill, 1924, p. 52A), and this may therefore be the locality.

Jenness also collected modern fresh-water shells near Williams Point (see footnote 17, Chapter 33).

Appendix 5.

Singers of the Copper Eskimo Songs Recorded by D. Jenness, 1914-16

Jenness recorded some 137 songs by native singers during the winter months between December 24, 1914, and March 1916. All were made on a portable Edison recording phonograph, using 4-inch wax cylinders (numbering 92 in all), which permitted up to 4 minutes of recording. Recording was done mainly in the Canadian Arctic Expedition headquarters building at Bernard Harbour, Dolphin and Union Strait. My father generally played the results back to the performers after the recording sessions, and their reactions ranged from fright through amazement to amusement. Some of the singers thought a spirit was reproducing their words. The recordings were later played to one or two other natives and translated into English by Palaiyak, a native from the Mackenzie delta region, or by Patsy Klengenberg, son of the Danish whaler-trader Christian Klengenberg and his Wainwright, Alaska, native wife. The wax recordings were sent later to Miss Helen Roberts in New York City, who after many playings transcribed them into common musical notation. She and my father then co-authored their classic report *Songs of the Copper Eskimos* (Roberts and Jenness, 1925).

In 1961 the songs were transferred to metallic audiotapes for the National Museum of Canada by Eugene Arima. The original rather worn wax cylinders are now stored by the Canadian Centre for Folk Culture Studies, Canadian Museum of Civilization, Hull, Québec. A few, regrettably, were broken after Miss Roberts had transcribed them and can no longer be heard; some others are badly damaged but were taped by Mr. Arima. The whereabouts of the recording machine my father used is not known.

Of the 137 native songs recorded, more than 100 were by Copper Eskimos. The rest were mainly by natives from Hudson Bay, the Mackenzie delta region, and northern Alaska. The Copper Eskimo songs are listed below. The first two columns contain the original wax-cylinder identification numbers; the next two columns are the song number and page number of the musical transcription in Roberts and Jenness (1925); next is the name of singer, 'tribe', and sex, then the type of song (dance, magic, weather incantation), and (if known) the date of the recording. I have prepared this list from a basic list provided by the Canadian Museum of Civilization, incorporating additional or corrective information from Jenness' diary and the Roberts and Jenness (1925) reference. Spelling of the singers' names follows that in the 1925 reference except where non Roman letters have been used or inconsistencies occur.

Cat. No.	Song No.	Page No.	Singer	Type of Song
IVC20	1a 105	327	Kaneyok (Puivlik girl)	– weather incantation
	1b 103	323	Kaneyok (Puivlik girl)	– weather incantation

IVC21	2a	66	245	Kaneyok (Puivlik girl)	– dance song
	2b	68	248	Haquñgaq (Puivlik girl)	– part of dance song
IVC22	3	99	315	Qormiq (Coppermine R. man)	– magic song
IVC23	4			(*wax cylinder broken, not transcribed*)	
IVC24	5			(*wax cylinder now broken but notated by Roberts & Jenness*)	
	5a	44	185	Nätcin (Coppermine R. man)	– magic song
	5	94	309	Nätcin (Coppermine R. man)	– weather incantation
	5c	45	185	Nätcin (Coppermine R. man)	– part of dance song
IVC25	a	108	332	Ciniciaq (Puivlik man)	– weather incantation
	b	50b	208	Ciniciaq (Puivlik man)	– dance song
	c	50	206	Ciniciaq (Puivlik man)	– dance song
	d	16	88	Ciniciaq (Puivlik man)	– dance song
IVC26	8	40	170	Ikpakhuaq (Puivlik man)	– dance song, self-composed
IVC27	9	10	64	Unëhaq (Dolphin & Union St. girl)	– dance song
IVC28	10	77	274	Aneyaq (Coppermine R. man)	– dance song
IVC29	11	71	257	Taipana (Puivlik boy)	– dance song; Mar.15/15
IVC30	12	64	241	Uloqcaq (Coppermine R. shaman)	– dance song
IVC31	14	82	289	Uloqcaq (Coppermine R. shaman)	– dance song
IVC32	15	38	163	Hupo (Puivlik woman)	– dance song
IVC33	16	52	213	Nigaqtälik (Coppermine R. man)	– dance song
IVC34	17	56	223	Kuniluk (Puivlik man)	– dance song; Mar.15/15
IVC35	18	43	182	Haquñgaq (Puivlik woman)	– dance song
IVC36	19	73	264	Takoheqina (Coppermine R. woman)	– dance song
IVC37	21			(*wax cylinder broken, not transcribed*)	
IVC38	22	27	127	Haquñgaq (Puivlik woman)	– Prince Albert Sd. dance song
IVC39	23	34	149	Haviuyaq (Puivlik man)	– dance song
IVC40	26	33	146	Qoexuk (Coppermine R. man)	– dance song
IVC41	27			(*wax cylinder broken, not transcribed*)	
IVC42	28	23	114	Añivrana (Puivlik man)	– dance song
IVC43	29a	107	331	Ikpakhuaq (Puivlik man)	– weather incantation
	29b	92	307	Ikpakhuaq (Puivlik man)	– weather incantation
	29c	95	310	Ikpakhuaq (Puivlik man)	– weather incantation
IVC44	32	74	267	Qaiyorana (Coppermine R. woman)	– dance song
IVC45	33a	59	231	Avrana (Puivlik man)	– dance song
	33b	51	212	Avrana (Puivlik man)	– dance song
	33c	67	247	Avrana (Puivlik man)	– dance song
IVC46	35	12	69	Utoqeq (Coppermine R. woman)	– old dance song

IVC47	37a	63	240	Qaiyorana (Coppermine R. woman)	– part of dance song
	37b	58	229	Qaiyorana (Coppermine R. woman)	– part of dance song
IVC48	39	65	243	Haiyakuk (Coppermine R. woman)	– dance song
IVC49	40	80	282	Utoqeq (Coppermine R. woman)	– dance song
IVC50	41a	42	179	Kaiyaryuk (Coppermine R. man)	– dance song
	41b	24	116	Kaiyaryuk (Coppermine R. man)	– dance song
IVC51	42 abc	–	–	Kuniluk (Puivlik man)	– dance songs

(Kuniluk's songs are not given in Roberts and Jenness, 1925)

| IVC52 | 43 | – | – | Havgutaq (Kilusiktok woman) | – dance song |

(cylinder broken, music not transcribed)

IVC53	45a	79	280	Aqxiataq (Noahogniq man)	– dance song
	45b	84	293	Aqxiataq (Noahogniq man)	– dance song
	45c	76	272	Aqxiataq (Noahogniq man)	– dance song
IVC54	46	60	233	Iguaq (Dolphin & Union St. woman)	– dance song
IVC55	47	81	284	Milukatak (Dolphin & Union St. woman) learned from Nilgaq, Prince Albert Sd. man, summer 1915	– dance song
IVC56	48	18	94	Avrana (Puivlik man)	– dance song composed by Ikpukhuaq
IVC57	49	21	105	Añivrana (Coppermine R. man)	– dance song
IVC58	50a	62	238	Kaneyok (Puivlik girl) learned from Imeyaq, Prince Albert Sd. man, summer 1915	– dance song
	50b	53	216	Kaneyok (Puivlik girl) learned from Kunana, Prince Albert Sd. man, summer 1915	– dance song
IVC59	51a	30	139	Ivyarotailaq (Dolphin & Union St. man)	– dance song
	51b	104	325	Ivyarotailaq (Dolphin & Union St. man)	– magic weather incantation
IVC60	52	20	100	Taptuna (Coppermine R. man)	– dance song
IVC61	53	8	56	Pixuaq (Dolphin & Union St. man)	– dance song
IVC62	58a	55	221	Haquñgaq (Puivlik woman)	– dance song
	58b	2	33	Haquñgaq (Puivlik woman)	– dance song
IVC63	59a	96	311	Haquñgaq (Puivlik woman)	– magic weather incantation
	59b	97	312	Haquñgaq (Puivlik woman)	– magic weather incantation

	59c	93	308	Haquñgaq (Puivlik woman)	– magic weather incantation
	59d	88	301	Haquñgaq (Puivlik woman)	– magic sickness healing song
IVC64	60	32	142	Añivrana and Qopäna (Coppermine R. man and his sister in law)	dance song
IVC65	61	128	368	Qaqsavina (Hudson Bay man)	– dance song
IVC66	62	129	371	Qaqsavina (Hudson Bay man)	– dance song
IVC67	63	130	376	Atqaq (Thelon R. man)	– dance song
IVC68	64a	126	363	Atqaq (Thelon R. man)	– dance song
	64b	127	365	Atqaq (Thelon R. man)	– dance song
IVC69	65	70	254	Kuniluk (Puivlik man)	– dance song from Prince Albert Sound
IVC70	65a	61	236	Kukilukaq (Bathurst Inlet woman)	– dance song
	65b	31	140	Kukilukaq (Bathurst Inlet woman)	– dance song
IVC71	66	78	276	Ikpakhuaq (Puivlik man)	– dance song from Prince Albert Sound
IVC72	67	75	269	Haquñgaq (Puivlik woman)	– old dance song
IVC73	68a	54	219	Kexullik (Dolphin & Union St. youth, nephew of Higilaq)	– dance song
	68b	15	84	Kexullik (Dolphin & Union St. youth, nephew of Higilaq)	– dance song, composed by his father Tusayoq
IVC74	69	28	131	Häviaq (Dolphin & Union St. boy)	– dance song composed by Taptuna (Coppermine R. man)
IVC75	70	57	226	Haquñgaq (Puivlik woman)	– dance song
IVC76	72	22	110	Ikpakhuaq (Puivlik man)	– dance song, self-composed
IVC77	71	72	259	Haquñgaq (Puivlik woman)	– dance song learned from Kälupik (Dolphin & Union St. man), who had learned it from a white man in a dream
IVC78	73a	35	151	Uñahaq (Puivlik woman)	– dance song, self-composed
	73b	4	40	Uñahaq (Puivlik woman)	– dance song, self-composed
IVC79	74	7	50	Kaneyok (Puivlik girl)	– dance song from Prince Albert Sound
IVC80	75	1	29	Higilaq (Dolphin & Union St. woman)	– dance song, self-composed
IVC81	76a	106	329	Kaneyok (Puivlik girl)	– magic weather incantation
	76b	90	304	Kaneyok (Puivlik girl)	– weather incantation (but listed as old dance song)
	76c	91	306	Kaneyok (Puivlik girl)	– weather incantation (but listed as old dance song)

IVC82	77a	100	317	Añivrana (Coppermine R. man) – magic weather song (joins with song 101, page 319)
IVC83	78a	109	334	Añivrana (Coppermine R. man) – magic weather song
	78b	110	335	Añivrana (Coppermine R. man) – magic weather song
	78c	111	336	Añivrana (Coppermine R. man) – magic weather song
	78d	112	337	Añivrana (Coppermine R. man) – magic weather song
	78e	113	338	Añivrana (Coppermine R. man) – magic weather song
IVC84	80	48	201	Kaneyok (Puivlik girl) – old dance song
IVC85	81a	5	43	Kaneyok (Puivlik girl) – dance song composed by Tusayoq, Higilaq's older brother
	81b	83	291	Kaneyok (Puivlik girl) – old chant
	81c	85	297	Kaneyok (Puivlik girl) – old chant
IVC86	82a	131	378	Tamoxuina (Bathurst Inlet girl) – dance song from Hudson Bay
	82b	132	380	Tamoxuina (Bathurst Inlet girl) – dance song from Hudson Bay
IVC87	83	17	91	Kexullik (Cape Hope man) – dance song
IVC88	84	46	186	Niptanätciaq (Coppermine R. woman) – dance song with three versions
IVC89	85a	102	321	Näneroaq (Coppermine R. man) – Incantation to the Longspur (a bird)
	85b	89	303	Näneroaq (Coppermine R. man) – magic weather song
	85c	86	298	Näneroaq (Coppermine R. man) – magic weather song
	85d	87	300	Näneroaq (Coppermine R. man) – magic weather song
IVC90	86a	25	119	Niptanätciaq (Coppermine R. woman) – dance song
	86b	47	198	Niptanätciaq (Coppermine R. woman) – dance song
IVC91	87	13	72	Näneroaq (Coppermine R. man) – old dance song
IVC92	88a	19	97	Avakana (Dolphin & Union boy) – dance song composed by his mother Apatoq
	88b	29	135	Känuva (Coppermine R. boy) – dance song composed by Hävgaq, a man who had lately died
IVC93	89	3	36	Haquñgaq (Puivlik woman) – old dance song
IVC94	90	6	46	Kulahuk (Bathurst Inlet man) – dance song
IVC95	91a	49	205	Uloqcaq (Bathurst Inlet man) – dance song
	91b	14	78	Uloqcaq (Bathurst Inlet man) – dance song
IVC96	92a	41	173	Uloqcaq (Bathurst Inlet man) – dance song
IVC97	92b	9	60	Uloqcaq (Bathurst Inlet man) – dance song
				(92a and 92b are shown in Roberts and Jenness, 1925 as being sung by Kunana, a Kilusiktok man, from Hood R. or more generally from Bathurst Inlet)
IVC98	93	36	155	Oqaitok (Bathurst Inlet woman) – old dance song
IVC99	94	26	122	Ilätciaq (Kilusiktok shaman from Bathurst Inlet) – dance song which he also composed

IVC100	95a	11	66	Nätcin (adopted son ca. 13 of Ilätciaq)	– old dance song learned by Ilätciaq from Eqaluktok natives in southeastern Victoria Island
	95b	39	166	Nätcin (adopted son of Ilätciaq)	– old Kilusiktok or Bathurst Inlet dance song
IVC104	7	69	251	Ikpakhuaq (Puivlik man)	– dance song

Appendix 6.

Arctic Photographs Taken by Diamond Jenness, 1914-1916

Based on a list originally prepared by Jenness, which is on file with Photo-theque, Canadian Museum of Civilization, Hull, Québec; negatives are stored at the same locality, except where otherwise noted. The original negatives are stored by the National Archives of Canada. Dates not on the original list were determined from Jennesss' Arctic diary and related sources. A date followed by a question mark is probably correct but not certain. Where a month is followed by a question mark, the reliability of the month is uncertain.

Date	CMC No.	Subject
		1914
Apr. 5	37125	– Modern Eskimo grave, dogs, and Capt. Nahmens. Near mouth of Sadlerochit River, northern Alaska.
Apr. 5	37159	– Three Canadian Arctic Expedition dogs used by D.Jenness — Telluraq, Denby, and Dub — pulling lightly loaded racing sled with some assistance from a sail, Collinson Point, Camden Bay, northern Alaska.
Apr. ?	37126	– Igiaqpuk, 6-year old daughter of an Eskimo woman from Barrow and a whaling-ship sailor; the mother was dead, and the child had been borrowed from her step-father Teriglu by Jennie Thomsen to be nursemaid for her child. Collinson Point, northern Alaska. (See sketch in Jenness, 1957, p. 144.)
Apr. 22	37129	– Johansen, McConnell, and Crawford, returning from Stefansson's ice party, encountered at east end of Barter Island, northern Alaska.
Apr. 22?	37139	– Eskimo ruin No. 16 on west sandspit, Barter Island, northern Alaska. May be late May or early June 1914.
Apr. 24	37158	– Remains of old house at Collinson Point, Camden Bay, northern Alaska.
Apr. 29	37119	– Frame of winter house, lined with snow blocks and covered with canvas, Icy Reef (near the Canadian border), northern Alaska. Marine biologist Frits Johansen standing beside house.
Apr. 30	37135	– Eskimo tent with snow windbreak and sled, Icy Reef, northern Alaska.
Apr. 30	37143	– Some of Eskimo ruins, Demarcation Point, northern Alaska.
Apr. ?	37160	– Canadian Arctic Expedition headquarters after roof had been cleared of snow. Collinson Point, Camden Bay, northern Alaska.
May 1	37128	– Group of 9 Mackenzie River Eskimos at Icy Reef, northern Alaska.
May 4	37115	– Fox-skins drying, Humphrey Point, near Canadian border, northern Alaska.
May 4	37131	– Tent of *Nunatagmiut* woman at Humphrey Point, northern Alaska.
May 4	37141	– Three Siberian Eskimos making a skin boat for sealing, Humphrey Point, northern Alaska.

May 4	37164	– Two Siberian Eskimos, from whaling ships icebound nearby, at Humphrey Point, northern Alaska.
May 5	37151	– Eskimo ruin at Martin Point, east of Barter Island, northern Alaska.
May 5	37161	– Eskimo grave near Martin Point, east of Barter Island, northern Alaska.
May 9	37118	– *Nunatagmiut* (Inland Eskimo) tent, Collinson Point, Camden Bay, northern Alaska.
May 9	37123	– Arrival of *Nunatagmiut* (Inland Eskimos) at Collinson Point, Camden Bay, northern Alaska.
May 9	37134	– *Nunatagmiut* (Inland Eskimos) arriving at Collinson Point after migrating across Philip Smith Mountains (called Endicott Mountains in 1914), northern Alaska.
May 9	37156	– *Nunatagmiut* (Inland Eskimo) setting up tent, Collinson Point, Camden Bay, northern Alaska.
May 9	37157	– Arrival of *Nunatagmiut* (Inland Eskimos), Collinson Point, Camden Bay, northern Alaska. (See also 37123, 37134.)
May 11	37113	– *Nunatagmiut* (Inland Eskimos) camp, Collinson Point, Camden Bay, northern Alaska.
May 11	37116	– *Nunatagmiut* (Inland Eskimo) children playing 'tag' at midnight, Collinson Point, Camden Bay, northern Alaska.
May 11	37137	– Scene in a camp of the *Nunatagmiut* (Inland Eskimos), Collinson Point, Camden Bay, northern Alaska.
May ?	37124	– *Nunatagmiut*'s (Inland Eskimo) sled, Collinson Point, Camden Bay, northern Alaska.
June	37127	– Seal poke full of blubber, Barter Island, northern Alaska.
June ?	37122	– Aiyakuk's cache on Arey Island, just west of Barter Island, northern Alaska.
June ?	37114	– A *Nunatagmiut* (Inland Eskimo) man, Mapteraq, Barter Island, northern Alaska. (See sketch in Jenness, 1957, p. 193).
June ?	37110	– Oyaraq and his wife sledding with a sail east of Barter Island, northern Alaska.
June ?	37111	– Sealskins pegged out to dry, near Barter Island, northern Alaska.
June ?	37112	– Oyaraq's wife scraping blubber from a sealskin, near Barter Island, northern Alaska.
June ?	37117	– Tents of Aiyakuk and Teriglu on Barter Island, northern Alaska.
June ?	37142	– East sandspit, Barter Island, northern Alaska.
July ?	37144	– Lagoon with abundant whale bones, south side of east sand-spit, Barter Island, northern Alaska.
July ?	37145	– Eskimo camp, west sandspit, Barter Island, northern Alaska. D. Jenness' white tent and bell tent in distance.
July ?	37146	– Aiyakuk, D. Jenness' Eskimo helper, digging in ruin No. 11, west sandspit of Barter Island, northern Alaska.
July ?	37147	– General view of west sandspit of Barter Island, northern Alaska.
July ?	37148	– Close-up view of Eskimo ruin No. 16, west sandspit of Barter Island, northern Alaska. (See also 37139, 37150, 37152.)

July ?	37149	– Whale skulls mark site of ruins, east sandspit of Barter Island, northern Alaska.
July ?	37150	– Eskimo ruin No. 16, west sandspit of Barter Island, northern Alaska. (See also 37139, 37148, 37152.)
July ?	37152	– Eskimo ruin No. 16, west sandspit of Barter Island, northern Alaska. (See also 37139, 37148, 37150.)
July ?	37153	– Trap door in Eskimo ruin No. 12, west sandspit of Barter Island, northern Alaska.
July ?	37154	– Eskimo ruin No. 12, Aiyakuk and Oyaraq (D. Jenness' Eskimo helpers) digging, west sandspit of Barter Island, northern Alaska.
July ?	37155	– Eskimo grave on east end of Barter Island, northern Alaska.
Aug. 19	37130	– Mackenzie River Eskimo woman cutting up fish for drying, Shingle Point, west of Mackenzie delta, N.W.T.
Aug. 19	37132	– Mackenzie River Eskimo man examining fish nets in kayak, Shingle Point, west of Mackenzie delta, N.W.T.
Aug. 19	37133	– Mackenzie River Eskimo man drawing fish out of net, Shingle Point, west of Mackenzie delta, N.W.T. Canadian Arctic Expedition vessels *Alaska* and *North Star* in distance.
Aug. 19	37136	– Eskimo camp at Shingle Point, west of Mackenzie delta, N.W.T., showing winter huts deserted in summer for tents.
Aug. 19	37138	– Mackenzie River Eskimo camp at Shingle Point, west of Mackenzie delta, N.W.T., showing fish hung up to dry.
Aug. 19	37140	– Dr. Anderson and John Cox buying fish at Shingle Point, west of Mackenzie delta, N.W.T.
Aug. 19	37162	– Mackenzie River Eskimo in kayak, Shingle Point, west of Mackenzie delta, N.W.T.
Aug. 31	36994	– Cache beside fishing creek (Nulahugyuk Creek) near Bernard Harbour, left by Eskimos in summer.
Aug. 31	36995	– Same as 36994. Shows two stone lamps, dish, and table boards left by Eskimos. Part of 'Bernard Harbour' in distance.
Sep. 1	37001	– Fish traps near mouth of Nulahugyuk Creek, 4 miles south of C.A.E. headquarters in Bernard Harbour. John Cox, expedition topographer, on right. Looking northwards towards outer harbour, now called 'Bernard Harbour'. (See also 37073.)
Sep. 7	36932	– Five Dolphin and Union Strait Eskimo men: Kallun, Qamingoq, Taptuna, Ayallik, and Allgiaq. Bernard Harbour, (Fig. 4 in Jenness, 1922a, p. 35.)
Sep.	36970	– Ayallik, Dolphin and Union Strait Eskimo man, wearing his thumb (which had been bitten off by a bear) around his neck for a good-luck charm. (See also 36963.)
Sep.	36962	– Kaumaq, portrait, Dolphin and Union Strait Eskimo woman. Bernard Harbour. May be October.
Sep.	36963	– Ayallik, portrait, profile. Dolphin and Union Strait Eskimo man, with thumb (bitten off by a bear) tied around neck. Bernard Harbour. (See also 36932.)
Nov. 24	37039	– Snow-hut near Bernard Harbour, on last day before sun disappeared.

1915

Feb. 24	37016	– Eskimo camp, with dance house on right. Duke of York Archipelago, Coronation Gulf. May be February 25. (Plate IIIA in Jenness, 1922a, p. 255.)
Feb. 24	37018	– Snowhouse and sled mounted on snow blocks, in Eskimo settlement, Duke of York Archipelago. May be February 25. (Plate IIIB in Jenness, 1922a, p. 255.)
Feb. 24?	37008	– Snow-hut and sled, Duke of York Archipelago, Coronation Gulf.
Feb. 24?	37024	– Eskimo men going sealing near Tree River, Coronation Gulf. (Fig. 35 in Jenness, 1922a, p. 112.)
Feb. 26	37026	– Copper Eskimos migrating west to Bernard Harbour. East of Cape Krusenstern. (Fig. 37 in Jenness, 1922a, p. 117.)
Feb. 26	37027	– Copper Eskimos resting during migration westward. East of Cape Krusenstern.
Feb. 26	37028	– Heavily laden Copper Eskimo sled during migration westward; dogs are hitched with individual traces. East of Cape Krusenstern. (Plate XLII in Chipman and Cox, 1924, p. 49B.)
Feb. 26	37033	– Spring tent of Uloksak, 'rich' Coronation Gulf Eskimo with two wives. Near Locker Point, west end of Coronation Gulf. (See Plate I in Jenness, 1923a, p. 67B for portraits of Uloksak by G.H. Wilkins (51561, 51562); see 37028 for picture of Uloksak's sled and possessions.
Feb. 26	37034	– Uloksak making snow passage to spring tent, near Locker Point. (See also 37033.)
Feb. 26	37103	– Coppermine Eskimos migrating northwest to Bernard Harbour. South of Locker Point, Coronation Gulf.
Feb. 26	37104	– Same as 37103, but viewed from ahead of migrators.
Feb. 26	37032	– Meeting with Copper Eskimos, who are migrating westward to Bernard Harbour. Cape Krusenstern area. (See also 37026, 37027, and 37028.)
Mar. 2	37010	– Copper Eskimos building a snowhouse. House nearly completed. Bernard Harbour. (See also 37011-37013.)
Mar. 2	37011	– Same as 37010, initial stage of construction.
Mar. 2	37012	– Same as 37011, closer view of initial stage of construction.
Mar. 2	37013	– Same as 37010, Eskimo man closing gaps in roof while Eskimo woman (squatting in front of sled) passes goods into house. Child at left.
Mar. 2	37017	– Snowhouse building, same as 37010. Bernard Harbour,
Mar. 2	37020	– Scene in Eskimo camp beside schooner *North Star*. Bernard Harbour.
Mar. 2	37029	– Distant view of Eskimo settlement beside schooner *North Star*. Bernard Harbour. (See also 37020.)
Mar. 2?	37054	– Copper Eskimo sled left loaded while making camp, another sled and woman in background. Bernard Harbour.
Mar. 13?	37019	– Interior of Eskimo snowhouse, Eskimo settlement on ice 5 miles east of *Putulik* (Sutton Island), Dolphin and Union Strait.

Mar. 13?	37109	– Eskimo camp at *Ukullik* (Liston and Sutton Islands), snow-hut at right built by some boys for two little girls, the regular families having skin tents.
Mar.	36934	– Qopanna, Coronation Gulf Eskimo woman, in doorway of snow-hut, Coronation Gulf.
Apr. 13?	37100	– Snowy view of Ahunahunak Point, Sutton Island, Dolphin and Union Strait.
Apr. 14?	37062	– Higilaq packing blubber and pemmican to send ahead before the migration next day towards Victoria Island. Dolphin and Union Strait.
Apr. 25	37037	– Nine Copper Eskimo children playing 'tag'. Dolphin and Union Strait.
Apr. 25	37023	– Return of Eskimo sealing party, dogs dragging seals ahead of sealers. Same locality as 37022.
Apr. 25?	37022	– Axiranna bringing in two seals with dogs. Temporary Eskimo camp about 25 miles west of Read Island, Dolphin and Union Strait.
Apr. 25?	37025	– Flensing (cutting up) a seal, Dolphin and Union Strait. Probably same locality as 37022.
Apr. 28	37046	– Copper Eskimos making a fire on the ice to obtain drinking water. About 10 miles west of Read Island, southwestern coast of Victoria Island.
Apr. 28	37092	– Copper Eskimos preparing to migrate north from a spring camp; loading up a sled. About 25 miles west of Read Island, Dolphin and Union Strait.
Apr. 28	37094	– Brief rest during a migration northward to Victoria Island. Probably about 20 miles west of Read Island.
Apr. 28	37097	– Eskimos load up a sled before migrating north to Victoria Island. About 25 miles west of Read Island, Dolphin and Union Strait. (Sequel to 37092.)
Apr. 28	37004	– Setting up Ikpukkuaq's spring tent; passage still to be made. Dolphin and Union Strait, about 10 miles west of Read Island, southwest Victoria Island.
Apr. 28?	37021	– Eskimos unloading sleds and setting up spring tents. Temporary camp about 10 miles west of Read Island, Dolphin and Union Strait.
Apr. 28?	37060	– Copper Eskimos stop for lunch on the trail, sled runner protected from sun by tent cloth, en route to Oqauyarvik Creek, southwestern Victoria Island.
Apr. 30	37006	– Spring tent, clothes set up to dry. Dolphin and Union Strait near southwest shore of Victoria Island. (See also 37004 and 37098).
Apr. 30	37061	– Copper Eskimos spring camp, sealskins pegged to walls to dry, Dolphin and Union Strait.
Apr. 30	37098	– Drying day in spring camp on ice; 10 miles west of Read Island, Dolphin and Union Strait.
Apr. 30?	37043	– Copper Eskimo spring camp on ice, Dolphin and Union Strait. (See also 37099.)
Apr. 30?	37099	– Distant view of spring camp on ice; 10 ? miles west of Read Island, Dolphin and Union Strait.

Apr. ?	36969	– Group of *Noahognirmiut* (Cape Krusenstern area Eskimos) eating dried fish, Bernard Harbour.
Apr. ?	36925	– Haqungaq, 16-year old daughter of Oqormiq and his wife Eqaryuk (Jenness, 1923a, p. 32B) or of Qaiyorunna (Jenness, 1913-16, Jan. 14, 1915) and his wife Qiqpak. Dolphin and Union Strait Eskimo woman. Dolphin and Union Strait. She later became the third wife of the shaman Uloksak (Jenness, 1922a. p. 159).
Apr. ?	37063	– Interior of Copper Eskimo spring tent after tent had been taken down. Dolphin and Union Strait.
May 7?	37095	– Copper Eskimo women (Higilaq and Tekelroq) tying up bags of blubber to be cached for the summer on Read Island, southwest coast of Victoria Island. Locality probably about 1 mile west of Read Island.
May 12	37031	– Copper Eskimo camp, possibly at mouth of Oqauyarvik Creek, near Read Island, southwestern Victoria Island.
May 16	36971	– Ikpukkuaq jiggling for trout in Lake Ekallugak, south entrance to Colville Hills, southwestern Victoria Island. (Fig. 40 in Jenness, 1922a, p. 129.)
May 22	37093	– Copper Eskimos dragging caribou meat to camp on polar-bear skins, Lake Añmaloqtoq area, Colville Hills. (Fig. 41 in Jenness, 1922a, p. 130.)
May 22	36984	– Copper Eskimos sleeping under a lean-to (windbreak). Northeast of Lake Añmaloqtoq, Colville Hills, southwestern Victoria Island. (Plate VC in Jenness, 1923a, p. 259.)
May 22	37003	– Copper Eskimos sleeping under a windbreak, northeast of Lake Añmaloqtoq, Colville Hills, southwest Victoria Island.
May 25?	36982	– Copper Eskimos cutting up a caribou. Lake Tahirjuaq (now Lake Quunnguq), southwest Victoria Island.
May 26?	36992	– Copper Eskimo camp at Lake Tahirjuaq (now Lake Quunnguq), Jenness' tent on right. Southwest Victoria Island.
May	36991	– Copper Eskimos shooting ptarmigan with bows and arrows. Southwest Victoria Island.
May	37007	– Summer tent raised on snow blocks during a cold snap. Near Lake Añmaloqtoq, Colville Hills, southwest Victoria Island.
May ?	36927	– Milukkattuk, wife of Avrunna (36926), southwest Victoria Island. Profile portrait. See also 36928, 36951, 36964.
May ?	36928	– Same as 36927, front view, in front of skin tent.
May ?	36933	– Higilaq, profile. See 36918. Southwest Victoria Island.
May ?	36964	– Left foot of Milukkattuk, warped by boot. Southwest Victoria Island.
May ?	36966	– Higilaq, wife of Ikpukkuaq (36965), portrait, Dolphin and Union Strait Eskimo woman, in summer costume. Southwest Victoria Island.
May ?	36990	– Higilaq and Ukpik, 8-year old son of Oqalluk and Higilaq's adopted daughter Kullaq, riding on a polar-bear skin pulled by dogs. Southwest Victoria Island.
May ?	37036	– Caribou meat drying, Kanneyuk by Copper Eskimo summer tent, Milukkattuk on left cutting up more meat. Possibly Lake Tahirjuaq (now Lake Quunnguq), still frozen in background.

May ?	37044	– Higilaq cooking, open-air bivouac, near Lake Añmaloqtoq, Colville Hills, southwest Victoria Island.
May ?	37045	– Cooking inside a snow windbreak. Southwest Victoria Island.
May ?	36965	– Ikpukkuaq, portrait, Dolphin and Union Strait Eskimo man, in summer costume. Southwest Victoria Island.
June 1	36986	– *Puivlirmiut* (southwestern Victoria Island Eskimos) helping newly arrived *Kanghiryuarmiut* (Prince Albert Sound Eskimos) to unload their sled. Lake Tahirjuaq (now Lake Quunnguq), southwest Victoria Island.
June 1	36996	– Arrival of Kunana and his small party of *Kanghiryuarmiut* (Prince Albert Sound Eskimos) to visit the *Puivlirmiut* (southwest Victoria Island Eskimos) at Lake Tahirjuaq (now Lake Quunnguq), southwest Victoria Island.
June 2	36997	– Dressing for a dance. Lake Tahirjuaq (now Lake Quunnguq), southwest Victoria Island. (See also 36981.)
June 2	36985	– Double tent (two summer skin tents) of two *Kanghiryuarmiut* (Prince Albert Sound) families. Lake Tahirjuaq (now Lake Quunnguq, southwest Victoria Island. (Fig. 30 in Jenness, 1922a, p. 85.)
June 2	36981	– Copper Eskimos dressing for a dance. Lake Tahirjuaq (now Lake Quunnguq), southwest Victoria Island. (Fig. 42 in Jenness, 1922a, p. 132.)
June 2	36967	– Two *Kanghiryuarmiut* (Prince Albert Sound) Eskimo men, Kunana and Nilgak, eating boiled caribou meat, and *Puivlik* (southwest Victoria Island) Eskimo woman Kullaq (an adopted daughter of Higilaq), eating the same, in background. Lake Tahiryuaq (now Lake Quunnguq), southwest Victoria Island, (Plate IVB in Jenness, 1922a, p. 257.)
June 6	37047	– Copper Eskimos digging holes in ice at northwest corner of Lake Añmaloqtoq, Colville Hills, southwest Victoria Island.
June 6?	37048	– Halt while packing overland, in order to fish in lake. Possibly Lake Añmaloqtoq, Colville Hills, southwest Victoria Island.
June 17?	36983	– Skin tent and two summer caches at Lake Numichoin, dogs widely separated and chained to stones. Colville Hills, southwest Victoria Island.
June 18	37050	– Clearing up camp preliminary to summer packing overland, Lake Numichoin, one mile west of Lake Añmaloqtoq, Colville Hills, southwest Victoria Island.
June 23	37052	– Oqalluk making a cooking pot from a tin can, Tuhayok making arrow heads from a caribou antler. Lake Numichoin, Colville Hills. (Fig. 66 in Jenness, 1922a, p. 230.)
June 25	37038	– Two Copper Eskimo children (Kanneyuk, Ikpukkuaq's 12-year old stepdaughter, and Kehullik, 17-year old son of Higilaq's brother Tuhayok) playing, making houses of pebbles. Near Lake Añmaloqtoq, Colville Hills, southwest Victoria Island. (Fig. 63 in Jenness, 1922a, p. 220.)
June 27?	36972	– Haugaq, 8-year old nephew and adopted son of Ikpukkuaq, bringing *Dryas integrifolia* back to camp for fuel, near Lake Añmaloqtoq, Colville Hills, southwest Victoria Island. (Fig. 32 in Jenness, 1922a, p. 99.)
June ?	36989	– Ikpukkuaq releases his dogs while Higilaq sets out with her backpack, near Lake Añmaloqtoq, southwest Victoria Island.

June ?	36999	– Spring tent with entrance blocked to enable cooking within. Southwest Victoria Island.
June ?	37035	– Caribou meat hung up to dry, possibly at camp just west of Lake Añmaloqtoq, southwest Victoria Island.
June ?	37049	– Camp at Lake Numichoin, Colville Hills, southwest Victoria Island.
June ?	37056	– Copper Eskimos sleeping in open air, near Lake Añmaloqtoq, Colville Hills, southwest Victoria Island.
July 3	36980	– Copper Eskimos sleeping in open-air bivouac. Lake Kullulak, north of Lake Añmaloqtoq, Colville Hills, southwest Victoria Island.
July 29?	36926	– Avrunna, son of Higilaq by a first marriage, mending his bow, Lake Añmaloqtoq, Colville Hills, southwest Victoria Island. (Fig. 43 in Jenness, 1922a, p. 135). (See also No. 37058.)
July 29?	37058	– Avrunna, Higilaq's son, mending his bow, front view. Lake Añmaloqtoq, Colville Hills. (See also No. 36926.)
Jul. ?	37211	– Portrait of Copper Eskimo man, seated, Bernard Harbour. Photo by G.H. Wilkins for D. Jenness. May be June 1916.
Jul. ?	37212	– Koptana, Coronation Gulf Eskimo, seated and scraping a skin, Bernard Harbour. Second wife of the shaman Uloksak. Photo by G.H. Wilkins for D. Jenness. May be June 1916.
Oct. 16	37087	– Avrunna (36926) smoothing the mud runner of his sled. Lake Numichoin, Colville Hills, southwest Victoria Island.
Oct. 16	37090	– Ikpukkuaq putting mud on his sled runner, his nephew (and adopted son) Haugaq (age 8) carrying the balls of mud to him. Lake Numichoin, Colville Hills, southwest Victoria Island.
Oct. 20	37005	– Autumn camp at Lake Kigiaktallik (the source of Oqauyarvik Creek), southwest Victoria Island.
Oct. 22	36987	– Tutsik re-icing his sled runner while travelling down Oqauyarvik Creek, southwest Victoria Island.
Oct. 22	36988	– Oqalluk and Tutsik digging for water in Oqauyarvik Creek to ice their sleds. Southwest Victoria Island. (Fig. 45 in Jenness, 1922a, p. 143.)
Oct. 28	37055	– Fall tent of Copper Eskimo, Oqalluk, at Oqauyarvik Creek, on lake about 4 miles above 10-foot waterfall near its mouth, southwest Victoria Island.
Oct. 29	37053	– Righting Avrunna's overturned sled, Oqauyarvik Creek below 10-foot waterfall, near coast of southwest Victoria Island.
Oct. 29	37057	– Copper Eskimos migrating to the sea near the mouth of Oqauyarvik Creek, southwest Victoria Island.
Oct. 29?	37059	– Passing goods into a tent at camp at mouth of Oqauyarvik Creek, southwest Victoria Island.
Oct. 29?	37091	– Avrunna and his family migrating south to coast, southwest Victoria Island.
Oct. 30?	37086	– Tuhayok's cache at mouth of Oqauyarvik Creek, south coast of Victoria Island. Cache was left here in spring of 1915 and recovered in fall.
Oct.	37009	– The building of a snow-hut. Sled used to bring snow blocks. Southwest Victoria Island (Oqauyarvik Creek?).

Oct.	36993	– Two snow-huts with single passage and Avrunna putting mud on his sled runner. Near southwest coast, Victoria Island.
Oct.	36998	– *Puivlirmiut* (southwest Victoria Island Eskimos) migrating to the southwest coast, Victoria Island. Jenness' sled in rear.

1916

Feb. 16	37015	– *Inuxuit* (stones), now snow covered, set up in a row for caribou drive. Cape Krusenstern. May be March 17.
Feb. 24	37014	– Snowhouses, Tree River area, Coronation Gulf, with windbreak alongside one house and a sled on top of another.
Feb. 24	37040	– Attigiryuaq (age 50) and Tahliq (age 22), Tree River Eskimo men, the latter harnessing a dog before going sealing. Tree River area, Coronation Gulf. (Fig. 58 in Jenness, 1922a, p. 204.)
Feb. 24	37096	– Part of Copper Eskimo settlement, Tree River area. Coronation Gulf. May be February 25.
Feb. 24	37102	– Distant view of *Pingangnaktomiut* settlement, near Tree River, Coronation Gulf.
Feb. 24	37041	– TamoXuina, Coronation Gulf woman in winter travelling dress, front view. Tree River area, Coronation Gulf.
Feb. 24	37042	– Same as 37041, side view.
Feb. 24?	37030	– Windbreak for Eskimo seal hunter, Coronation Gulf.
Feb. 25?	37089	– Snowhouse with bags on the wall, Tree River area, Coronation Gulf.
Mar.	36930	– Kahina, portrait, Tree River Eskimo woman. Tree River area, Coronation Gulf.
Mar.	36931	– Qormiq, portrait, 15-year old Tree River Eskimo girl, Coronation Gulf.
Mar.	36936	– Haugaq, Tree River Eskimo girl. Tree River area, Coronation Gulf. (Fig. 61 in Jenness, 1922a, p. 215.)
Mar.	36942	– Niaqeptaq, Tree River Eskimo man wearing deerskin headband to cure headache. Tree River area, Coronation Gulf. (Fig. 53 in Jenness, 1922a, p. 172.)
Mar. ?	36948	– Uvilloq (Uritaq?), Dolphin and Union Strait Eskimo woman. Bernard Harbour.
Apr. 4	36935	– Ilatsiaq, portrait of greatest shaman among Coronation Gulf Eskimos. Bernard Harbour.
Apr. 5	36956	– Group of Eskimos at ice camp west of *Ukullik* (Liston and Sutton Islands) with H. Girling, Church of England missionary (Fig. 68 in Jenness, 1922a, p. 238.)
Apr.	36949	– Unahaq, portrait, Dolphin and Union Strait Eskimo woman. Liston and Sutton Islands.
Apr.	36957	– Alunaq, portrait, Dolphin and Union Strait Eskimo girl. At ice camp west of Liston and Sutton Islands.
Apr.	37065	– Ahunahunaq Point, Liston Island, snowbound.
Apr.	37105	– Spring camp at *Ukullik* (Liston and Sutton Islands), Dolphin and Union Strait.
Apr.	36929	– Utoqeq, Coronation Gulf Eskimo man. Bernard Harbour.
Apr.	36937	– ApeXoaq, portrait. Coronation Gulf Eskimo woman. Bernard Harbour.

Apr.	36938	– Nigaktallik, Coronation Gulf Eskimo man. Bernard Harbour.
Apr.	36940	– Azzun, Coronation Gulf Eskimo man. Bernard Harbour. (Plate VII, lower right, in Jenness, 1923a, p. 79B.)
Apr.	37051	– Kehullik, young (17 years) Copper Eskimo, shooting his bow and arrow. Bernard Harbour.
Apr.	36919	– Kanneyuq, daughter of Higilaq. Bernard Harbour.
Apr.	36920	– Kanneyuq, daughter of Higilaq. Bernard Harbour.
Apr.	36939	– Paglik, daughter of Ilatsiaq (36935) and Eqaryuk. Bernard Harbour. (See also Plate IX in Jenness, 1923a, p. 83B.)
Apr.	36973	– Kitiqsiq's snow-hut with roof of skin, Bernard Harbour.
Apr.	37181	– Canadian Arctic Expedition 'flagship' *Alaska* in ice, Bernard Harbour, Dolphin and Union Strait.
May	36958	– Aqulluk, portrait, Dolphin and Union Strait Eskimo woman. Bernard Harbour.
May	36959	– Kitriq, portrait, Dolphin and Union Strait Eskimo woman. Bernard Harbour. (See also 36946, 36961.)
May	36960	– Group of Copper Eskimos at Bernard Harbour.
May	36961	– Noqattaq and Kitriq, Dolphin and Union Strait Eskimo man and his wife. Bernard Harbour.
May ?	36941	– Aitauq, *Asiak* Eskimo man living among Coronation Gulf Eskimos. Bernard Harbour. (See also Plate VI in Jenness, 1923a, p. 77B.)
May ?	36943	– Kallun, Coronation Gulf Eskimo woman, showing face tattooing. Bernard Harbour.
May ?	36944	– Naugalluaq, portrait, Coronation Gulf Eskimo man, front view. Bernard Harbour.
May ?	36945	– Same as 36944, side view. Bernard Harbour.
May ?	36951	– Milukkattuk, wife of Avrunna (36926), Dolphin and Union Strait Eskimo woman, showing tattooed hand. Bernard Harbour. (See also 36928, 36929, 36964.)
May ?	36953	– Tokalluaq (Toqalluaq), profile. Coppermine River Eskimo man, a shaman. Bernard Harbour. (Fig. 59 in Jenness, 1922a, p. 206). (See also 36954.)
May ?	36954	– Same as 36953, portrait, front view.
May ?	36968	– Tigsaq (also known as Apattoq), elderly *Asiak* (Coronation Gulf) Eskimo man, wearing snow goggles while shaving wood outside his tent. Bernard Harbour.
May ?	36974	– Kitiqsiq clearing up interior of her spring tent after tent had been taken down. Bernard Harbour.
June 29	37076	– Mannigyorina, Copper Eskimo woman, ready to start for fishing creek near Bernard Harbour, with spear and cord for stringing the salmon. Nulahugyuk Creek.
June 29	37077	– Mannigyorina, Copper Eskimo woman, with baby on her back, watching the salmon ascending the creek. Nulahugyuk Creek, near Bernard Harbour.
June 29	37078	– Copper Eskimos race to fishing creek upon hearing the salmon are running upstream. Nulahugyuk Creek, near Bernard Harbour.

June 29	37079	– Copper Eskimos spearing salmon in stone weirs, Nulahugyuk Creek, near Bernard Harbour.
June 29	37080	– Same as 37079. Closer view. (Plate VIIA in Jenness, 1922a, p. 263.)
June 29	37081	– Same as 37079.
June 29	37082	– Copper Eskimo men spearing salmon, women catching them in the stone traps and stringing them on a line. Nulahugyuk Creek, near Bernard Harbour. (Plate VIIB in Jenness, 1922a, p. 263.)
June 29	37083	– Copper Eskimos return to camp with their salmon catch. Nulahugyuk Creek, near Bernard Harbour. (Plate VIIC in Jenness, 1922a, p. 263.)
June 29	37084	– Copper Eskimo children catch by hand young salmon fry swimming downstream to the sea from Lake Hingiktok. Fish are trapped by a set of stone weirs a few yards above the weirs that are used to spear the larger salmon migrating upstream. Nulahugyuk Creek, near Bernard Harbour.
June 29	37085	– Stone weirs in fishing (Nulahugyuk) creek near Bernard Harbour.
June	37002	– Qaritaq and his wife Havgun making a deerskin tent. Bernard Harbour.
June	37072	– Copper Eskimo Oxomiq's tent closed with a sealskin; his wife standing beside tent. Bernard Harbour.
June ?	36947	– Kila, portrait, Dolphin and Union Strait Eskimo girl. Bernard Harbour. (See also 37107, 37108.)
June ?	36977	– Toqalluaq, Coronation Gulf Eskimo man, holding up Ikpuk-kuaq's kayak frame. Bernard Harbour.
June ?	36978	– Higilaq and Kila (her adopted daughter) pegging out deer-skins to dry. Bernard Harbour.
June ?	36979	– Hieyaq, Copper Eskimo woman, cutting up deer meat for drying. Bernard Harbour.
June ?	37064	– Copper Eskimo camp (on right) at Bernard Harbour, tents and supplies of expedition on left.
June ?	37088	– Remains of stone cache of the Copper Eskimos, near Bernard Harbour.
July 2	37073	– Copper Eskimo camp at Noahognik Creek, which flows into Pasley Cove near Cape Krusenstern.
July 2	37074	– Men, women, and children returning from spearing salmon in Noahognik Creek, near Cape Krusenstern.
July 3	37066	– View north from *Qiqigarnaq*, hill behind Locker Point. West end of Coronation Gulf.
July 3	37067	– Tent stones and cooking place on top of *Qiqigarnaq*, hill behind Locker Point. West end of Coronation Gulf.
July 3	37069	– Stone windbreak used as a shelter by Copper Eskimos while awaiting caribou. Located on top of *Qiqigarnaq*, hill behind Locker Point, west end of Coronation Gulf.
July 3	37070	– Stone house on top of *Qiqigarnaq*, hill behind Locker Point. West end of Coronation Gulf. View to east.
July 3	37071	– Stone house on top of *Qiqigarnaq*, hill behind Locker Point. West end of Coronation Gulf. Young Eskimo examining

country through Jenness' binoculars is Noqallaq, cousin of Kanneyuq (36916, 36919, 36920) and nephew of Higilaq (36913, 36918).

July 3	37101	– View north from *Qiqigarnaq*, hill just west of Locker Point. West end of Coronation Gulf.
July 7	37075	Two stones for markers (*nukkutain*) pointing to a place on the lake at which to dig holes through ice for fishing. Lake Kogluktuaryuk, west of Cape Lambert.
July 13	37180	– Shore of Bernard Harbour, Dolphin and Union Strait, on departure of Canadian Arctic Expedition.
July 13	37182	– *Alaska*, flags flying, ready to leave Bernard Harbour.
July 13	37183	– Close view of C.G.S. *Alaska*, loaded and ready to leave Bernard Harbour.
July 13	37184	– Same as 37183.
July 13	37185	– Rear view of C.G.S. *Alaska*, about to depart from Bernard Harbour for Nome, Alaska.
July 26	36911	– Three Eskimo men: Manilenna (Siberian), Añutisiak (Alaskan), and Mike (Mackenzie River). Baillie Island. All worked for the Canadian Arctic Expedition 1913-18.
July 26	36912	– Klengenberg family, Baillie Island. Father was a Dane, mother was an Eskimo from Wainright Inlet, Alaska. From left to right: Etna, Jorgen, Kenmek (Mrs. Klengenberg), Bob, Patsy (in cap), Andrew, Christian (Charles) Klengenberg, Lena. Patsy served as D. Jenness' interpreter in 1916. (Fig. 69 in Jenness, 1922a, p. 241).
July	36917	– Portrait of Anaumiq, daughter of Itivilrunna, a Coronation Gulf Eskimo, Bernard Harbour. See also 36924.
July	36918	– Higilaq, wife of Ikpukkuaq, Dolphin and Union Strait Eskimo woman, side view showing tattooing on left arm. Bernard Harbour.
July	36921	– Hikkok, young son of Kaiyuina, a Coronation Gulf Eskimo, Bernard Harbour. (Plate VIIIa, in Jenness, 1922a, p. 265).
July	36922	– Coronation Gulf Eskimos: Kaiyuina and his wife Igeyaq, Bernard Harbour.
July	36923	– Kullaq, Coronation Gulf Eskimo woman, wife of OXomiq (Oxemiq). Bernard Harbour.
July	36924	– Itivilrunna, Coronation Gulf Eskimo man, father of Anaumiq (36917). Bernard Harbour.
July	36946	– Kitriq, portrait, Dolphin and Union Strait Eskimo woman. Bernard Harbour. (See also 36959.)
July	36950	– Hattorina, portrait, Coronation Gulf Eskimo girl. Bernard Harbour.
July	36975	– Kitiqsiq cooking out of doors, using *Dryas integrifolia* for fuel. Camp is littered with caribou meat drying in the sun. Bernard Harbour. (Plate IVC in Jenness, 1922a, p. 257.)
July	36976	-- Ikpukkuaq putting a steel runner on his sled. Higilaq? standing and watching him. Bernard Harbour in background.
July	37000	– Camp scene. Eskimo women pegging out deerskins to dry. Bernard Harbour.
July	37068	– Eskimo archer's pit for shooting at Caribou, Bernard Harbour.

July	37106	– Oxomiq's summer tent, Bernard Harbour.
July ?	36916	– Kanneyuq (Jennie), teen-age daughter of Higilaq by first marriage, asleep in tent at Bernard Harbour. See also 36919, 36920.
July ?	36952	– Tigsuq (Tigsaq or Apattoq), portrait, elderly Dolphin and Union Strait Eskimo man with snow goggles. Bernard Harbour.
July ?	36955	– Kitiqsiq, portrait, Dolphin and Union Strait Eskimo woman. First wife of Ikpukkuaq. Bernard Harbour.
July ?	37169	– Same as 37168. (Fig. 54 in Jenness, 1922a, p. 175.)
Aug. 10	37178	– Three Eskimo *umiaks* off Point Hope, Alaska.
Aug. 10	37179	– Same as 37178.

(Photos by D. Jenness listed among J.J. O'Neill's photos; negatives at the Geological Survey of Canada)

Nov. 3/15	38527	– Falls of dolomite on Oqauyarvik Creek, S.W. Victoria Island, 4 miles from coast. (Fig. 3 in Jenness, 1922a, p. 25.)
Nov. 3	38528	– Same as 38527, but closer view.
Nov. 3	38529	– Same as 38528, but closer view, looking north.
Nov. ?/15	38530	– Cuesta of dolomite parallel to south coast, Victoria Island, 5 or 8 miles inland from mouth of Oqauyarvik Creek, looking southeast. (Fig. 2 in Johansen, F., 1921, p. 53K.)

(Photo by D. Jenness listed among R.M. Anderson's photos; negative at CMC)

| Mar. 29/14 | 39127 | – Polar-bear cub in fox-trap, Collinson Point, northern Alaska. |

(Photo by D. Jenness listed among F. Johansen's photos; negative at CMC)

| Feb. 21/15 | 42254 | – Deserted Eskimo snowhouses on Coppermine River near its mouth. |

(Photos by G.H. Wilkins for and listed among photos by D. Jenness; negatives at CMC)

Apr. 10/14	37120	– Eskimo *umiaks* cached in the winter of 1913-1914 at Collinson Point, Camden Bay, northern Alaska. D. Jenness beside *umiak*.
Apr. 10/14	37121	– Eskimo *umiak* with kayak on top, cached at Collinson Point, Camden Bay, northern Alaska.
July 10/15	37165	– Kukilukaq, 25-year old Coronation Gulf Copper Eskimo woman. First wife of shaman Uloksak. (See Plate XI, lower right, in Jenness, 1923a, p. 87B.)
July 1915	37163	– Grave of Victoria Island Eskimo, Haviron, who died April 1915. Near Cape Lambert, Dolphin and Union Strait.
July 1915	37168	– Corpse of Haviron laid out in burial with belongings, near Cape Lambert, Dolphin and Union Strait.
July 1915?	37166	– Keyuq, a Dolphin and Union Strait Copper Eskimo woman. Bernard Harbour. (See Plate XII, lower left, in Jenness, 1923a, p. 89B.)

July 1915? 37167 – Keyuq (or Keyak), same as 37166 but showing arm tattooing, Bernard Harbour.

July 1915? 37213 – Iguaq, Dolphin and Union Strait Copper Eskimo woman, Bernard Harbour. (Plate X, upper left, in Jenness, 1923a, p. 85B.)

July 1915? 37214 – Same as 37123, Bernard Harbour. (Plate X, upper right, in Jenness, 1923a, p. 85B.)

July 1915? 37215 – Amigailaq, Dolphin and Union Strait Copper Eskimo man, Bernard Harbour. (Plate VIII, upper left, in Jenness, 1923a, p. 81B.)

July 1915? 37216 – Utugaum, Dolphin and Union Strait Copper Eskimo man, Bernard Harbour. (Plate VIII, upper right, in Jenness, 1923a, p. 81B.)

July 1915? 37217 – Keyuq (or Qeyuq), Dolphin and Union Strait Copper Eskimo woman, Bernard Harbour. (Plate XII, lower right, in Jenness, 1923a, p. 89B.) (See also 37166, 37167.)

July 11/16 37107 – Kila, young Dolphin and Union Strait woman. Head and shoulders portrait showing facial tattooing, head uncovered.

July 11/16 37108 – Kila, same as 37107 but head covered by hood of *atigi*.

July 11/16 36913 – Portrait of Ikpukkuaq and Higilaq (Dolphin and Union Strait Eskimos) in full Copper Eskimo costume, Bernard Harbour.

July 11/16 36914 – Same as 36913, showing rear of costumes, Bernard Harbour.

July 11/16 36915 – Same as 36913, closer front view, Bernard Harbour.

Appendix 7.

Arctic Expedition Letters of Diamond Jenness, 1913-1916

The following is a list of all known letters and notes and their sources.

	Date	From	To	Pages	Source
1.	May 1, 1913	Jenness	Sapir	2	2
2.	May 13, 1913	Jenness	Sapir	2	2
3.	May 16, 1913	Jenness	Sapir	1	2
4.	May 22, 1913	Jenness	Sapir	2	2
5.	June 10, 1913	Jenness	Sapir	2	2
6.	July 3, 1913	Jenness	Balfour	9	6
7.	July 7, 1913	Jenness	Barbeau	3	3
8.	July 7-11, 1913	Jenness	Marett	4	4
9.	Aug. 6, 1913	Jenness	Sapir	4	2
10.	Oct. 16, 1913	Jenness	von Zedlitz	4	5
11.	Oct. 17, 1913	Jenness	Marett	4	4
12.	Oct. 26, 1913	Jenness	Sapir	4	2
13.	Dec. 2. 1913	Jenness	Sapir	4	2
14.	Dec. 14, 1913	Jenness	Scholefield	4	8
15.	Feb. 2, 1914	Jenness	'Arctician'	2	1
16.	Feb. 27, 1914	Jenness	Sapir	4	2
17.	Apr. 19, 1914	Jenness	Anderson	3	1
18.	May 21, 1914	Jenness	Anderson	2	1
19.	undated (May 28/14)	Jenness	Anderson	1	1
20.	May 30, 1914	Jenness	Sapir	4	2
21.	May 31, 1914	Jenness	Anderson	2	9
22.	June 17, 1914	Jenness	Anderson	10	1
23.	June 29, 1914	Jenness	von Zedlitz	5	5
24.	July 30, 1914	Jenness	Sapir	2	2
25.	Aug. 2, 1914	Jenness	Marett	5	4
26.	Aug. 10, 1914	Jenness	Barbeau	1	3
27.	Jan. 5, 1915	Jenness	Sapir	5	2
28.	Jan. 8, 1915	Jenness	Anderson	2	1
29.	Dec. 26, 1915	Jenness	Sapir	2	2
30.	Jan. 11, 1916	Jenness	von Zedlitz	12	5
31.	July 18, 1916	Jenness	Commissioner, RNWMP	6	7
32.	Aug. 18, 1916	Jenness	Sapir	2	2

1. Jenness file, R.M.Anderson papers, Vertebrate Ethology Section, Zoology Division, Canadian Museum of Nature, Ottawa, Ont.

2. Jenness letters, E. Sapir correspondence, Research Reference Section, Canadian Ethnology Service, Canadian Museum of Civilization, Hull, Que.

3. Jenness file, M. Barbeau correspondence, Document Collections, Canadian Centre for Folk Culture Studies, Canadian Museum of Civilization, Hull, Que.

4. Committee for Anthropology papers, File # Ms. UDC/C/2/4, Bodleian Library, Oxford University, Oxford, England.

5. Prof. W. von Zedlitz papers, Hocken Library, University of Otago, Dunedin, New Zealand.

6. Henry Balfour papers, Pitt Rivers Museum, Oxford University, Oxford, England.

7. RG85, vol. 571, File 244, National Archives of Canada, Ottawa, Ont.

8. File ED J43, Archives of British Columbia, Victoria, B.C.

9. MG30 B40, vol. 2, File 2-2, National Archives of Canada, Ottawa, Ont.

Contract between D. Jenness and the Geological Survey of Canada
(unsigned copy enclosed with letter to H. Balfour, July 3, 1913)

I hereby agree to the following contract with the Geological Survey of Canada. I am to undertake ethnological field work among such Eskimo tribes as may be designated by Mr. Stefansson, the length of time estimated for this work being three years. In consideration of the anthropological services rendered the Geological Survey of Canada, a salary of $500 per year is to be paid for the length of time spent in services on the Stefansson expedition, the beginning of this period being dated from the day on which Wellington, New Zealand, was left. At the expiration of the expedition, the Geological Survey undertakes to put me under salary for as long a period of time as is required to work up for publication the scientific results obtained by myself, provided that all such time be actually spent in preparation of manuscript for publication for the Survey.

All manuscript notes, ethnological specimens, photographs, and such other scientific material of whatever nature as result, from the expedition are to be the exclusive property of the Geological Survey of Canada, and are to be turned in to the Survey as early as possible, and not later than the acceptance of the manuscript.

Special attention is called to the following clauses:–
1st. There shall be no trading or other commercial transactions done during the time spent under the auspices of the expedition, except for the expedition itself, or the Geological Survey of Canada.

2nd. No news is to be given out except through the official reports made to the Geological Survey of Canada, and every reasonable care shall be exercised to prevent the leakage of news.

3rd. Magazine articles, popular books, and lectures for gain are not to be written or delivered before one year after the return of the Expedition.

4th. Summary reports of the progress of investigation are to be made to the Geological Survey, yearly if possible, and the final report, or reports, on the scientific results of the expedition are to be prepared as soon after the return as practicable.

5th. All mail sent out is to be put in a bundle addressed to the Geological Survey of Canada, from which it will be forwarded to its destination.

[Signed by D. Jenness June 10, 1913; copy to be signed by R.W. Brock, Director of the Geological Survey of Canada, and transmitted to D. Jenness' father in New Zealand; an unsigned copy made by D. Jenness sent to H. Balfour and R.R. Marett at the University of Oxford (Jenness, 1913a)]

Notes

Prologue

1.
From its inception the Expedition was planned as a three-year project and was known as the "Canadian Arctic Expedition of 1913-16" (see for example Cook, 1918, p. 22), but early in 1919, shortly after Stefansson's return from the Arctic, the Deputy Minister of the Naval Service notified the Chairman of the Editorial Committee on Governmental Publications that the dates on the C.A.E. publications had to be changed to recognize the contributions made by Stefansson and members of his Northern Party in 1917 and 1918 (Desbarats, 1919). This modification, which by its timing could only have originated from Stefansson himself, was agreed to by Cook's Committee and the Deputy Minister of Mines, thereby overriding the unanimous wishes of the members of the Arctic Biological Committee, who had the responsibility for getting the C.A.E. results published (Hewitt, 1919). A few weeks later, in the spring of 1919, the Canadian Government officially changed the name to "Canadian Arctic Expedition 1913-18." Ironically, in spite of this change, no account whatsoever of the accomplishments of Stefansson's Northern Party was ever published by the Canadian Government in the C.A.E. Report Series.

2.
There is at present no single depository of correspondence written by the six scientific members of the Southern Party during the period 1913-16. Since commencing work on my father's diary in 1985, I have uncovered thirty-one letters he wrote while in the Arctic, as well as a number written by his five colleagues, some of which are housed in obscure places. Those that I have cited in my footnotes are listed (with their locations) among the references.

3.
After reaching Ottawa in September 1916, Cox worked for the Geological Survey for six or seven months then, like my father, enlisted in the Canadian Army and went overseas a few months later. Unlike my father, however, he did not remain long with the Geological Survey after the end of the war, departing within a year of his return from overseas. In the early 1970's he responded to an enquiry from the National Archives in Ottawa by saying that he had left his diary in Ottawa many years before (J. Kidd, verbal communication, 1988). It is possible, therefore, that it still exists somewhere within the Department of Energy, Mines and Resources, Ottawa.

4.
Beuchat perished after the sinking of the *Karluk* early in 1914.

5.
The C.A.E. Report Series was to have contained 16 volumes when completed, but only volumes 3 to 16 were published. Volume 1 was to have contained V. Stefansson's account of the Northern Party as Part A and Dr. Anderson's account of the Southern Party as Part B. Volume 2 was to have contained Dr. Anderson's descriptions of the mammals of the western Arctic as Part A and descriptions by Dr. Anderson and P.A. Taverner of the birds of the western Arctic as Part B. The four parts of these two volumes were never written.

6.
At that time, citizens of Canada were considered British subjects. They attained the status of Canadians only after the passage of the Canadian Citizenship Act late in 1947.

7.
Professor R.M. Marett had instructed both Barbeau and my father in anthropology at the University of Oxford. He wrote Barbeau late in January 1913 informing him that my father had completed his research project in New Guinea and asking if Barbeau could find him a job with the Geological Survey of Canada (Marett, 1913). Though primarily a student of the classics during his three years at the University of Oxford (1908-1911), my father received a diploma in Anthropology in 1911 as well as his humanities degree. Two colleges at the University of Oxford, together with several individuals (including Sir Arthur Evans, famous for his archeological finds in Crete less than a decade earlier), then provided him with funds to carry out anthropological studies for the university among the primitive Northern d'Entrecasteaux natives of the southeast coast of Papua, New Guinea (Jenness and Ballantyne 1920, pp. 5-6 1928). He worked among the

natives there for about a year, but contracted malaria and returned to his parents' home in New Zealand late in 1912 to recuperate.

8.

This is the same salary as was offered to an 18-year old Ottawa high-school graduate, Eilleen Bleakney, in 1911, for her appointment as stenographer in the same Department of Mines. It was also the minimum starting rate of pay in the federal civil service at that time (G.M. Bleakney, verbal communication, 1988). Of course, her salary did not include the benefits of food, lodging, clothing, and transportation 'enjoyed' by the author for the next 3 years (1913-16). By a curious coincidence Miss Bleakney became secretary to Dr. E. Sapir, the author's employer, in which office she met the author upon his return from the Arctic in 1916. She married him in April 1919, a week after his return from serving with the Canadian Army in France.

9.

O.E. LeRoy (1914) advised the Deputy Minister of Mines that the contract between the Geological Survey and Mr. Jenness had provided for the payment of his expenses from New Zealand to Vancouver but said nothing about paying his expenses from Ottawa back to New Zealand, adding "it is assumed that the Survey is responsible."

10.

The *Karluk Chronicle* was a daily newsletter typed and edited by B.M. McConnell between June 18, 1913, and July 7, 1913, for the entertainment of the men on board the *Karluk* (McConnell, 1913).

Chapter 1. – Stranded

1.

These two were hired at Point Hope by Stefansson to serve as hunters and dog-drivers. They were eighteen to twenty years old.

2.

Burberry is a trade name for various fabrics, often containing wool, used for outdoor wear. It was popularized through use in all-weather coats worn by British and allied soldiers in the First World War, and Burberry coats today command high prices. The name derives from the originator of the fabric, John Burberry. Drill was a strong durable cotton fabric in a twill weave made in various weights for clothing, tents, etc.

3.

The second team was hitched to a heavy freighter sled driven by Pauyuraq and accompanied by Wilkins and Jenness. The first team was driven by Acicaq (Asecaq), led by Stefansson, and accompanied by McConnell. Its dogs were Snap (leader), Joe, Buster, Charlie, Denby, and Jimmy Britt and were hitched in tandem to a lighter sled. Wilkins' moving picture of the departure from the ship was lost when the *Karluk* sank, but the departure was also photographed by McKinlay (1976, Fig. 17).

4.

The tracks were those of James "Big Jim" Allen, a well-known Alaskan whaler (Allen, 1978), and seven native companions, who were travelling with a whaleboat from the *Belvedere*, a whaling ship caught in the ice east of Flaxman Island. They were en route to Point Hope, where Allen had a whaling station and the natives had their homes. The latter had been hired to work on the whaling ship only for the summer months (Anderson, 1913-16, Sept.7, 1913).

5.

They were not Leffingwell's (see Footnote 4). Ernest de Koven Leffingwell, an American geologist, had been invited at Nome by Stefansson to sail on the *Mary Sachs* to Flaxman Island, northern Alaska, where he intended to complete geological mapping he had commenced in 1909. In exchange for his passage he served as ship's pilot. The *Mary Sachs* was separated from the *Karluk* in a dense fog on July 30, 1913, before it reached Point Barrow.

6.

Identified as Amauliktok Island by Stefansson (1921, p. 57). Named Thetis Island by E. de Koven Leffingwell (1919, p. 100), which is the name shown on modern maps of the region. It is the westernmost of a chain of sandy islands known as the Jones Islands and is about 4 miles off the mainland.

7.

Cross Island is located within a chain of offshore bars about 12 miles northeast of Prudhoe Bay. The *Karluk* anchored nearby on August 11 (Bartlett, 1915, p. 25), when its eastward progress was stopped by ice. The author went ashore at that time with his fellow anthropologist Henri Beuchat to examine some old Eskimo ruins (McConnell, 1913-14, Dec. 3, 1913). From there the *Karluk* steamed north for 10 miles to avoid the near-shore ice, only to become totally and permanently entrapped. By September 20, when this diary begins, the ship was some 20 miles north of the mouth of the Colville River, about 60 miles northwest of Cross Island.

8.
Eskimo-made boots.

9.
This was the residue of either the Jim Allen party en route to Barrow from the *Belvedere* or shore parties from the *Mary Sachs* and the *Alaska*, which visited Spy Island many weeks earlier (according to Leffingwell, as reported in Wilkins, 1913-16, Dec. 11, 1913), or of both parties. Frits Johansen, the marine biologist with Dr. Anderson's Southern Party on the *Alaska*, collected five spiders (*Typhocraestus spetsbergensis*) on Spy Island, Sept. 3, 1913 (Emerton, 1919, p. 3H).

10.
They were to bring back Mamen (assistant topographer) and Malloch (geologist), another dog team and sled, and additional supplies (McConnell, 1913-14, Sept. 22, 1913).

11.
The author is referring to British Admiralty chart #2435 (Mackenzie River to Bering Strait), which shows Beechey Pt. (not Cape Beechey) at about the locality now known as Oliktok Pt.; Oliktok is shown farther east on the old chart. The name Becher Pt. appears on the chart for the feature now known as Beechey Pt.

12.
Coming as it does after Capt. Bartlett steered the *Karluk* northward from Cross Island, evidently against Stefansson's wishes, this statement, if verifiable, is of some significance.

13.
'Tabloid' tea was a compressed tea-leaf with the mid-rib and stalk removed, the product of the firm Burroughs, Wellcome & Co. Each hinged-lid tin contained 100 or 200 small individually tin-foil wrapped packages. The word 'Tabloid' was a trade mark registered in 1884 and used on many of this company's products. Arctic and Antarctic

expeditions commonly carried such products with them (Burroughs Wellcome & Co., 1934).

14.
The author had contracted malaria in New Guinea the previous year. Recurrences of the illness plagued him frequently during his three years in the Arctic.

15.
September is an early spring month in the author's homeland, New Zealand.

16.
Herschel Island was the initial destination for the Canadian Arctic Expedition, where the supplies and men on the three ships (*Karluk*, *Alaska*, and *Mary Sachs*) were to be redistributed to meet the respective needs of Stefansson's northern exploration party and Dr. Anderson's southern scientific party.

17.
This photograph "Looking for the *Karluk* from Spy Island" is not in the collection of the Canadian Museum of Civilization.

18.
Stefansson (1921, p. 60) stated that McConnell, Wilkins, and Jenness all remarked on the great superiority in taste of the seal meat cooked in true Eskimo style (cut in pieces, dropped into cold water, boiled, and served underdone) to the seal meat the cook on the *Karluk* had served them. McConnell found that the seal meat was similar in taste to polar-bear meat (McConnell, 1913-14, Sept. 27, 1913), while Wilkins described the blubber as quite palatable also, having a taste not unlike mutton fat (Wilkins, 1913-16, Sept. 27, 1913). Jenness offered no opinion in his diary or letters.

19.
Wilkins (1913-16, Sept. 27, 1913) recorded the same message in his diary, adding "V.S. says I am duty bound to comply with the request, but I am afraid the shops that I will find around here do not sell picture postcards and I don't ever expect to go to the north pole to photograph it."

20.
Because Pauyuraq and Acicaq were from Point Hope, the author's initial contact with the Eskimo language provided him with words from that locality, which were often different from words used by Eskimos farther east. He frequently recorded these

local variations in his diary by writing (Point Hope) or (Point Barrow) after newly learned words. Ultimately he compiled the linguistic variations into a report (Jenness, 1928b).

21.
This quotation is probably referring to seals reappearing at their breathing holes.

22.
For Stefansson's discussion of this subject, see Stefansson (1913a, pp. 397-402; 1913b, pp. 873-874). Wilkins (1913-16, Sept. 27, 1913) also recorded that Stefansson had told them how the names of Eskimo children are chosen, and why the children are never forbidden anything or punished.

23.
In Amundsen Gulf, almost 400 miles east of the Alaska-Canada boundary.

24.
A shaman or medicine-man.

25.
This was the remains of a house used briefly by Leffingwell and Mikkelsen after their epic 70-day trip on the ice north of Alaska in 1907 in search of land (Wilkins, 1913-16, Sept. 29, 1913).

26.
"Jenness had another attack of the Ague today and was pretty bad for an hour or so. We repeated the treatment of wrapping him up as warm as possible and giving him hot drinks. . . . He worries so much about the trouble that he thinks he is giving us, that I think that does him as much harm as the attack of Ague" (Wilkins, 1913-16, Oct. 1, 1913).

Chapter 2. – Off to Barrow

1.
They were engulfed in fog shortly after setting out for the island, and the two Eskimos expressed concern that Wilkins was leading them out to sea. Fortunately the fog lifted briefly and they could see the island about a mile behind them and a couple of miles out to sea. They had steered too far to the west, and "It was lucky for us that the fog lifted or else I don't know where we would have brought up" (Wilkins, 1913-16, Oct. 2, 1913).

2.
"Jenness is very weak and was just about done up when we arrived at camp although he rode quite a way on the sledge" (Wilkins, 1913-16, Oct. 3, 1913).

3.
The *Alaska* and *Mary Sachs* were 65-foot schooners (the *Karluk* by comparison was 125 feet long) added to the Canadian Arctic Expedition at Nome, Alaska, to accommodate the personnel, equipment, and additional supplies needed for the division of the Expedition into Northern and Southern parties. Most of the author's scientific equipment was on the *Mary Sachs* after the Expedition left Nome, though his personal possessions were with him on the *Karluk*.

4.
They are now known as the Eskimo Islands (Orth, 1967, p. 318).

5.
The habitats of these small Eskimo groups and the rivers along which they lived are shown on a map in the back of *My Life with the Eskimo* (Stefansson, 1913a). A note on this map states that the Kangianik River is the upper Colville River. The Kagmalik River, also shown on this map, may be the Chandler River. It is not listed in Orth (1967). The author probably got his information from Stefansson at the time.

6.
"This was not a very severe attack today but every one leaves him weaker and I will be glad for his sake when we reach Point Barrow so he can get some palatable food for he eats hardly anything now" (Wilkins, 1913-16, Oct. 6, 1913).

7.
McConnell also showed concern for the author's health. "Jenness is frail and liable to sudden attacks of ague, so it really is not right to leave him alone in camp" (McConnell, 1913-14, Oct. 7, 1913).

8.
Temperature readings throughout this diary are in Fahrenheit.

9.
Pemmican was a common food concentrate used by Arctic explorers. The Canadian Arctic Expedition had one variety for the men,

another for the dogs. One pound a day was considered adequate nourishment (the 'standard ration' of Peary) for a dog (Stefansson, 1921, p. 485). The man pemmican contained some dried fruit in addition to the meat and fat of the dog pemmican. The Expedition had three different brands, one American (Underwood), one British (Hudson's Bay), and one Norwegian (Bovril). According to Chipman (1913-16, Dec. 10, 1914) the Underwood brand contained 53% meat, 35% lard and tallow, 9% dried fruit, mainly raisins, and 3% sugar. Stefansson contended that such pemmican was not bad if eaten with something else, though he later stated that the pemmican supplied the Expedition was deficient in fat and unsatisfactory (Stefansson, 1921, p. 485). In March 1913, however, when Dr. Anderson was having tests made on the purity of pemmican samples in New York (he had heard that pieces of glass and metal had been found in the pemmican supplied other exploration parties), Stefansson cabled him from London "Damn purity tests order pemmican immediately we have no alternative" (Stefansson, 1913c). These orders led to the purchase of the Underwood brand that Stefansson later called unsatisfactory. He also found the dog pemmican unsatisfactory (Stefansson, 1921, pp. 485-486).

10.
This was Teshekpuk Lake, some 15 miles to the west. In the 1890's the Cape Smythe Eskimos believed it contained large and ferocious man-eating fish (Brower, 1944? pp. 137-138).

11.
Aksiatak's son was eighteen-year old Itarklik, years later known as Arctic John Etalook, the source of much information about the ways of his people, the *Ulumiut*, in the early 1900's (Spearman et al., 1985, p. 31).

12.
This was H.T. (Ned) Arey, an American miner and prospector originally from Cape Cod, Massachusetts, and long a resident along the northern coast of Alaska. In 1888 he teamed up with Charles Brower, Patsy Grey, and several others to start a trading and whaling station near Point Barrow (Brower, 1944? p. 104 et seq.). Later he spent several years with E. de Koven Leffingwell on Flaxman Island (Stefansson, 1913a, pp. 68, 380). Leffingwell named the island west of Barter Island after him; this

island had originally been called Barter Island by Sir John Franklin (Leffingwell, 1919, p. 93).

13.
This theory was discussed on September 27th.

14.
The author wrote Dr. E. Sapir in Ottawa "We came away [from the ship] very ill-prepared for a long sled trip and of course without winter clothing of any kind" (Jenness, 1913g). According to Wilkins they were clad in summer clothing (Thomas, 1961, p. 71), and Stefansson (1921, p. 68) admitted that the men had been improperly dressed when they left the ship. The clothing they were wearing when they left the *Karluk* on September 20, 1913, can be seen in a photograph in McKinlay (1976, Fig. 17).

15.
There were actually four houses, but only two were occupied, the other two having whale meat in them. Stefansson's party was able to take whale meat for their dogs for the journey to Barrow from one of the two houses, for it belonged to Kuraluk, a Barrow Eskimo on the *Karluk* (Wilkins, 1913-16, Oct. 8, 1913). The smaller inhabited house belonged to Ikpik, Pauyuraq's cousin; the larger house belonged to Paninona (i.e., Samuel), the son of Añopkana (see Oct. 11) (McConnell, 1913-14, Oct. 8, 1913).

16.
The author, apparently unfamiliar with this popular North American card game, spelled it "polka." The Eskimo men learned to play cards from the whalers on the ships at Point Barrow (Wilkins, 1913-16, Oct. 8, 1913) and from the Lapland herdsmen who brought domesticated reindeer to Alaska in the late 1800's (Jenness, 1957, p. 103).

17.
On a similar sketch drawn in a letter to Professor R. Marett, Jenness (1913f) indicated that the two wings on the plan view were used as store rooms for pots etc., the skylight was made of seal gut, and there was a door at the left end of the passage.

18.
There were twelve people, according to McConnell (1913-14, Oct. 9, 1913), fourteen men and the young woman [Aiva] according to Wilkins (1913-16, Oct. 8, 1913).

19.
Stefansson also was unwell and had to ride on a sled, alternating with Wilkins (McConnell, 1913-14, Oct. 9, 1913).

20.
The walls of these houses were plastered with old newspapers, including the *San Francisco Examiner* (McConnell, 1913-14, Oct. 10, 1913).

21.
Wilkins took two pictures of the cutbank on this date, but only one appears to have survived (CMC Photo No. 51449).

22.
Mr. Leffingwell postulates a glacial origin for Flaxman Island only, and for such places along the coast as contain the Flaxman formation, but not for all the cutbanks that display protruding edges of ground ice. [D.J.]

23.
This was to appease the two Eskimos, who objected to going straight across Smith Bay (McConnell, 1913-14, Oct. 10, 1913). See also footnote 8, Chapter 4, regarding the Eskimo fears of crossing Smith Bay.

24.
Charles Brower and his companion Patsy Grey were probably the first white men to discover the several pitch lakes in this region (Brower, 1944? p. 70).

25.
These houses were at Ikiak, near Tangent Point (McConnell, 1913-14, Feb. 15 and 16, 1914).

26.
These fish were frozen, a little bigger than sardines, and very fat. "I ate as many as anybody else, McConnell also liked them, but Jenness did not care for them as well" (Wilkins, 1913-16, Oct. 11, 1913).

27.
Also known as hardtack, an unleavened bread or biscuit, a common item of food supplied sailors in those days.

28.
The man was Añopkana, father of Samuel near Cape Halkett; he lived here near Point Barrow until the trapping season opened (in mid November) then moved east to the settlement near Cape Halkett (McConnell, 1913-14, Oct. 11, 1913).

29.
She was an octogenarian, whom the members of the party nicknamed 'Lady McGuire' (Jenness, 1957, p. 33). She apparently took a great fancy to Wilkins, stroking his beard, patting him on the back, and repeatedly asking his name, which she pronounced "Oolikan" (Wilkins, 1913-16, Oct. 11, 1913).

30.
Rochfort Maguire (not McGuire as spelled in the diary and in Jenness, 1957) was Commander of H.M. supply ship *Plover*, a support vessel for the two British naval vessels under Capt. McClure and Capt. Collinson that were searching east of Point Barrow for survivors of the Sir John Franklin expedition of 1845. The *Plover* wintered over 1852-53 and 1853-54 in Elson Lagoon, just east of Point Barrow (Bockstoce, 1988b, p. 232; Murdoch, 1888, p. 52).

31.
She attributed her paralysis to a 'spell' cast upon her by a shaman whom she had refused to marry when she was a young girl (McConnell, 1913-14, Feb. 14, 1914).

32.
The vessel was 3 or 4 miles offshore for at least 2 days, close enough that Añopkana could see its rigging. He was certain it was the *Karluk* (Stefansson, 1921, p. 67). As shown on Fig. 2 (taken from a map in Stefansson, 1921) it was indeed the *Karluk*, for she was just offshore east of Point Barrow at that time, and no other vessel was in the ice on that part of the coast.

33.
They were heading east to their winter camps for the trapping season. There were five sleds and about 20 Eskimos (Wilkins, 1913-16, Oct. 11, 1913).

34.
A map in Stefansson's *The Friendly Arctic* shows the position of the icebound *Karluk* on October 5 as some 15 miles northeast of Point Barrow. Thus its masts might have been visible to persons in that settlement. From there it moved seawards and westwards until it sank near Wrangel Island (Ostrov Vrangalya) on January 11, 1914.

35.
A near serious accident occurred just at this time. While leading the two sled teams, Wilkins came upon a narrow patch of thin

new ice and beckoned to Stefansson and Pauyuraq to hurry the dogs and sled across, which they did successfully. Pauyuraq then tried to warn the second sled team of the danger, shouting "Don't stop on the young ice." All the second team heard was "Stop," and so they stopped the dogs just as the sled reached the thin young ice. Jenness got off the sled and immediately began to sink with the ice, but Wilkins shouted to his dogs and they managed to pull the sled safely across. "There was a little talk by V.S. (in strong language) about blockheadedness in general and we proceeded on our journey" (Wilkins, 1913-16, Oct. 11, 1913).

36.
The author both here and on Oct. 28 refers to three houses, though both Wilkins and McConnell, in their diary entries for Oct. 11, 1913, mention only two. Stefansson's diary has no entries between Oct. 1, and Dec. 17, 1913.

37.
Charles Brower was born in 1863 in New York City and went to sea at the age of thirteen. In 1886 he settled at Cape Smythe and by 1913 was owner-manager of the main trading post in that settlement, the Cape Smythe Whaling and Trading Company (Stefansson, 1913a, p. 47). For many years he was the United States' most northerly citizen and was known throughout Alaska as the "King of the Arctic" (Brower, 1944?

frontispiece). Later he became a member of the famous Explorers Club in New York City (Brower, 1944? p. v). In 1913 Barrow was the post-office name for the settlement the author called Cape Smythe. Said to be the largest Eskimo settlement in Alaska at the time (Stuck, 1918a), it lay 10 miles southwest of the smaller native settlement of Point Barrow. It was built on a bluff some 50 feet above the sea (Brower, 1944? p. 119).

38.
Collinson Point is in Camden Bay, about 290 miles east of Barrow. News of these ships had been brought by Jim Allen and his Eskimo companions from the *Belvedere.*

39.
The *Elvira* had in fact been wrecked by the ice and abandoned by this time, as Stefansson learned later. It sank on September 24 (Chipman, 1914a).

40.
It was indeed the *Karluk* (see footnote 32, this chapter). That vessel, being a brigantine rather than a schooner, carried square-rigged sails on its two masts rather than the type of sails carried by schooners. The story of what subsequently happened to it, its crew, and its scientific personnel is well documented in books by R.A. Bartlett and R.T. Hale (1916), and W.L. McKinlay (1976).

Chapter 3. – Re-equipping at Barrow

1.
The store was part of a large building erected by Brower and his partner Tom Gordon in 1893, after backing by H. Liebes and Co. of San Francisco, the largest furriers on the American west coast. The building also contained living quarters, a workshop, and a kitchen (Brower, 1944? p. 19).

2.
Fred Hopson was Charles Brower's cook and an enthusiastic amateur photographer. Both Hopson and Brower appear in an 1898 photograph in Bockstoce (1986, p. 294).

3.
This was Brower's second wife. His first wife, also an Eskimo, died during a measles epidemic in 1902 (Brower, 1944? p. 192).

4.
This was one of the first of many string figures the author learned during his Arctic

experience, which he subsequently compiled and published (Jenness, 1924b). He expected them to be ethnologically valuable in working out Eskimo affinities and contacts (Jenness, 1914e). Most Eskimos played string games only during winter months when the sun was below the horizon.

5.
An Australian bushman's teapot. Wilkins, being an Australian, would have used this term. It was used also in New Zealand (Jenness, 1968b).

6.
Alfred Hopson, aged 15, also known as Brick, was the oldest of Fred Hopson's children. He was hired by Stefansson to be the author's Eskimo interpreter for $15 per month (Jenness, 1914b). He spoke English well and could read and write (Jenness, 1913h).

7.
An uncrystallized syrup produced in the re-
fining of sugar.

8.
Their wages were $2.50 per day (Wilkins,
1913-16, Oct. 17, 1913) or about $70 per
month. The author was being paid about $42
per month and expenses, young Hopson
$15.

9.
According to Stefansson the Eskimos
believed that the animals were never caught
and killed unless they wanted to be. The
fox's "God or Ruling spirit" was a knife, and
to get a knife from a man the fox allows itself to be killed. When a man catches a fox
he cuts its throat and then buries his knife
for a day or so, during which time the fox
will return and take up the spirit of the knife.
Then the man can dig up his knife and use it
again and catch and kill more foxes. If the
man fails to cut the fox's throat and bury his
knife, the foxes will no longer let themselves be caught by him. The same principle
applies to other animals, but they require
different objects. The younger Eskimos who
had come into contact with the missionaries
took no notice of these old beliefs (Wilkins,
1913-16, Oct. 20, 1913).

10.
Stefansson (1913a, pp. 56-57) had just published this explanation.

11.
The General Orders of the Expedition, made
binding on all members of the party when
they joined it, stipulated that any private
equipment (other than purely personal effects) would be considered the property of
the Expedition and would be at the disposal
of the Expedition (Anderson, 1913-16, Aug.
8, 1914). (See also footnote 23, this chapter.)

12.
A nursery children's game in which a ditty
beginning with these words is sung, and the
players take sides according to their answer
to the question "which will you have,
oranges or lemons?"

13.
Mrs. Cram, the schoolteacher, and her
husband, G.W. Cram, the missionary, Jus-
tice of the Peace, and Commissioner, were
from Seattle, Washington, and had been at
Barrow for 14 years (McConnell, 1913-14,
Oct. 18, 22, 1913). Neither could speak the

Eskimo language, and Mrs. Cram used an
interpreter for the junior classes (Wilkins,
1913-16, Oct. 23, 1913).

14.
Brower had at least five children by his first
wife, Toctoo, whom he married in 1888:
Elizabeth, Flora, Jim, Bill (all of whom were
educated in the U.S.A.), and a baby who
died the same year as Toctoo (1902)
(Brower, 1944?). Brower's autobiography
does not mention his remarrying but does
mention David (Brower, 1944? p. 222), who
was part of his second family, as noted here.

15.
This included a lengthy report to Mr.
Desbarats, the Deputy Minister of the Naval
Service, in Ottawa (McConnell, 1913-16,
Oct. 24, 1913) in which Stefansson stated
that he planned to leave Jenness with the
Colville River Eskimos for the winter be-
cause his health was not adequate for the
journey to Camden Bay (Hunt, 1986, p. 90).

16.
The mail was leaving Cape Smythe Nov. 1
by dog team for Nome. The author wrote 10
letters (McConnell, 1913-16, Nov. 3, 1913),
three of which have been found (Jenness,
1913e,f,g).

17.
This type of whaling, known as shore whaling, declined dramatically between 1907 and
1914 after the market for 'whalebone'
(baleen) softened (Bockstoce, 1986, p. 252).
Charles Brower was probably the first white
man to participate in this dangerous but
(then) rewarding activity, soon after his arrival in the area in 1884 (Brower, 1944? p.
36 et seq.).

18.
Bone or wooden ornament worn in a hole
pierced through the lower lip (Jenness,
1957, p. 27). Twenty years earlier all men
and boys over fourteen in the Cape Smythe
region wore them (Brower, 1944? p. 146).

19.
Stefansson wanted to send a report to Ottawa when the mail left on November 1, as
well as some dispatches to various newspapers with which he had commercial contracts for articles. McConnell had been
taking dictation in shorthand from him for
several days and was typing it up on Mr.
Cram's typewriter (McConnell, 1913-14,
Oct. 26, 1913). Wilkins would have preferred being advised of the change of plans

earlier in the day, for it was then 8 p.m. and the sleds had to be unloaded and reloaded differently (Wilkins, 1913-16, Oct. 26, 1913). McConnell knew a full day before Wilkins (and Jenness) of Stefansson's change in plans (McConnell, 1913-14, Oct. 25, 1913).

20.
Asecaq, and a newly hired Añutisiak.

21.
The families of Aksiatak, Aluk, and Kunaloak.

22.
In order to catch enough fish to feed the dogs on their journey east to Collinson Point. Stefansson, McConnell, and young Hopson left Cape Smythe on November 7th, but did not reach the fishing lake until November 20th.

23.
The author's personal .303 Lee-Enfield, which Stefansson then gave to McConnell in exchange for a carbine (probably a .44 Model 92 Winchester) that McConnell brought from the *Karluk* (McConnell, 1913-14, Oct. 16, 1913). The payment was drawn on the Department of the Naval Service because that department was funding Stefansson's expenses. The author sent the $30 order to Dr. Sapir in Ottawa with the request that it be forwarded with his monthly salary to the author's father in New Zealand (Jenness, 1914c) in partial repayment for money lent him to get to Canada.

24.
After 9 p.m. Stefansson dictated instructions to Wilkins, whom he was putting in charge of the small party leaving the next day; there were no instructions for the author (McConnell, 1913-14, Oct. 16, 1913).

Chapter 4. – With Wilkins to the Fishing Lake

1.
And to help them travel more quickly so that they could reach *Iglurak* the same day (Wilkins, 1913-16, Oct. 27, 1913).

2.
At Stefansson's insistence (McConnell, 1913-14, Oct. 27, 1913).

3.
Here spelled *Iglura*, but the author also spells it *Igluraq* and *Iglora* later in this diary. Spelled *Igloorak* and *Iglurak* in Wilkins (1913-16, Oct. 11 and 28, 1913). Stefansson (1913a, p. 51) stated that *Iglorak* was the Eskimo name for a sandspit shown on the [British Admiralty] charts as Cooper's Island. Orth (1967, p. 236) lists *Iglorak* and *Iglurak* as variants for Cooper Island.

4.
Though not back to full strength yet, he had not had an ague attack since getting some quinine from Mr. Brower (Wilkins, 1913-16, Oct. 28, 1913).

5.
Probably at or close to the locality shown as "Ikiak" on modern topographic maps, on a sandspit in Mackay Inlet, near the mouth of the Simpson River. The author reported only two houses at the time of his previous visit (October 11; see also Jenness, 1957, p. 21), and again on March 2, 1914. In his diary, he wrote *Ekiuroq* (with dots beneath the E and o) for this place name on this date, but spelled it *Ikiuraq* on November 1st, *Itkiaq* on March 2, 1914.

6.
Asecaq acted as interpreter (Wilkins, 1913-16, Oct. 29, 1913).

7.
The author meant "from the west." This family moved into the third house (Wilkins, 1913-16, Oct. 29, 1913).

8.
Both Asecaq and Añutisiak were crying at this meal, and they said a prayer, the only time they ever did. [D.J.] According to Wilkins (Thomas, 1961, p. 73), when they reached the west shore of Smith Bay, the two Eskimos insisted the party travel around the bay because a storm was coming. This would have increased their journey by 40 miles, and thinking the Eskimos were trying to lengthen the journey because they were being paid by the day, Wilkins insisted they all cross the bay. The Eskimos lagged behind for some time, then caught up and tearfully begged Wilkins and the author to return to shore before the storm struck. Wilkins insisted upon following Stefansson's instructions and they continued across the bay, a distance of 16 miles. The storm forced them to camp part way across.

9.
Drew Point, on the east side of Smith Bay. The author later corrected this misidentification (Jenness, 1957, p. 30). Wilkins (1913-16, Oct. 31, 1913) also called it Pitt Point at the time.

10.
Spelled *Ukallik*, meaning 'hare', in Jenness (1957, p. 30). Probably a coastal locality just north of the lake shown as Okalik Lake on modern topographic maps. Though his diary entry for October 9 mentions only two houses at this locality, he later described them as "three empty cabins" (Jenness, 1957, p. 21).

11.
Wilkins (1913-16, Oct.31, 1913) gives a more vivid description of their struggle across Smith Bay against the strong headwinds and the resultant frost-bite suffered by all four men.

12.
On October 22nd.

13.
The story was based on fact. In 1871 thirty-three ships out of an Arctic whaling fleet of forty were trapped by pack ice and lost along the 25 miles of coast between Icy Cape and Point Franklin, southwest of Barrow (Bockstoce, 1986, p. 159). Brower (1944? p. 24) passed the battered hulks of several of the wrecked ships in 1883 and wrote of the bodies of Eskimos still in their houses who had died after drinking liquids from the ships' medicine cabinets, which they had thought to be whisky. None of the surviving Eskimos would enter the houses of the dead, so the bodies of the dead remained untouched for many years.

14.
Wilkins was able to give presents to the Eskimos (some tobacco and chewing gum given him by Stefansson) in appreciation for their kindness (Wilkins, 1913-16, Nov. 1, 1913).

15.
Hymn books written in the Eskimo language were produced from a box under the bed (Wilkins, 1913-16, Nov. 2, 1913).

16.
"One would start a hymn and another would stop them and say they were singing the wrong tune and then this one would start the tune he thought was right, and in some cases neither were right.They were pleased when Jenness and I joined in with the singing" (Wilkins, 1913-16, Nov. 2, 1913).

17.
This word is in Greek letters in the diary.

18.
"Where men and women perform the duty of nature. Yesterday when anyone suddenly passed wind while they were playing all broke their sides with laughter. Such is their custom." (Translation by Prof. R. Jeffreys, Carleton University, 1986.)

19.
A large pancake or flapjack (see author's explanation on November 8th).

20.
While the author was inside the house saying goodbye the two sleds unexpectedly departed, and he had to run quite a distance to catch up to them (Wilkins, 1913-16, Nov. 3, 1913).

21.
Kuraluk, a Cape Smythe Eskimo, was on the *Karluk* at this time; he later played a major role in helping many of the survivors stay alive until their rescue from Wrangel Island after the sinking of that ill-fated ship.

22.
There were three families in this house, the finest Eskimo house they had seen so far. It was also the first one they had seen with some decoration: several picture postcards of prize fighters hung on the walls (Wilkins, 1913-16, Nov. 3, 1913).

23.
About 800 pounds (Wilkins, 1913-16, Nov. 5, 1913).

24.
She was very concerned about his condition and asked many questions about how he had gotten so frost-bitten (Wilkins, 1913-16, Nov. 5, 1913).

25.
Purchased at Cape Smythe by Stefansson (McConnell, 1913-14, Oct. 15, 1913). They may have been Waterman's pens comparable to the ones with which the Expedition was originally equipped. The author had written his notes in pencil from September 20 to October 14, 1913.

26.
The author had stayed overnight with Ikpik on October 8th and met him again at Cape Smythe (October 15th). Ikpik had enlarged his house since then (Jenness, 1957, p. 33) and the author, Wilkins, Acecaq, and Añutisiak were invited to stay in his house on this occasion (Wilkins, 1913-16, Nov. 4, 1913).

27.
Stefansson had stated in his instructions to Wilkins that he would arrive at Aksiatak's on November 8 (Wilkins, 1913-16, Nov. 6, 1913), which meant he would have reached Cape Halkett by November 6 if on schedule.

28.
The house measured 12 x 22 feet, was divided in the middle, and was well built (McConnell, 1913-14, Feb. 11, 1914). McConnell used the name *Kipootik* for the house's locality, a name he may have heard Aksiatak or Aluk mention.

29.
The word means a 'water-sky' according to A[lfred] Hopson, the black sky over open water (or over land). [D.J.]

30.
A more finished reproduction of this pipe, drawn by an artist in Italy under the author's direction in the mid-1950's, appears in Jenness (1957, p. 34).

31.
As this region was north of the tree-line, firewood was obtained only along the seashore, washed down the rivers from the interior.

32.
Having gladly accepted Kunaluak's offer to use his tent (Wilkins, 1913-16, Nov. 10, 1913).

33.
Called "Imeroon" in Jenness (1957, p. 41).

34.
An open skin boat.

35.
The next four lines in the diary were stroked out by the author. They read "his can be drawn aside, letting in a little fresh air. A large block of thin ice set up about a foot outside of it and so joined to the tent with

snow and (on each side) by narrow laths of wood protects the window without blocking out all the air or light."

36.
To join Aksiatak and his family (Wilkins, 1913-16, Nov. 13, 1913).

37.
The author probably saw such sunrises and sunsets en route to England from New Zealand in 1908 or upon his return three years later, after his graduation from the University of Oxford.

38.
Herschel Island had been the wintering place of the American whaling fleet and was a port of entry into Canadian Arctic waters for the American trading ships. The settlement consisted of a small Eskimo community, a Church of England mission, and a Royal North-West Mounted Police post. The police had overland communication links via Fort McPherson to Edmonton and also to Fort Yukon, Alaska. There was a Hudson's Bay Company post at Fort McPherson. In 1913 Herschel Island was the only regular source of supplies east of Barrow (Cape Smythe) on the north coast of Alaska and northwestern Canada.

39.
The author was no novice with a rifle, having won several shooting prizes while a student at the University of Oxford 2 or 3 years previously, but this was not his own rifle (see October 26).

40.
"Jenness was very interested in this and although he cannot sing three notes in tune and has no ear for music at all he knows something of the theory" (Wilkins, 1913-16, Nov. 19, 1913). Wilkins was apparently unaware that the author played the flute rather well and enjoyed classical music very much. Nor could he have anticipated that the author would soon publish four of these northern Alaska songs (Jenness, 1922c) and later coauthor (with Helen Roberts, a folksong specialist from New York City) a major publication on Eskimo songs (Roberts and Jenness, 1925).

41.
They had intended to go to Aksiatak's house but had become lost in fog (Wilkins, 1913-16, Nov. 21, 1913).

42.
Alak had previously given the author's little party permission to take as many fish from his cache as they needed for dog-food (Wilkins, 1913-16, Nov. 21, 1913).

43.
"After supper we all started to get to bed early for we intended to get up early in the morning. V.S. and Jenness started an argument on some theosophical matter and sat there each half way into their sleeping bags, neither of them new [sic] anything about it according to their own evidence, yet they kept on jawing away for hours and none of we others could get to sleep for the noise they made. About ten o'clock (we had gone to bed at seven) they postponed their argument long enough to have a cup of tea. It was then resumed and would have continued for I don't know how long had it not happened that the dogs began to fight. We all lay quiet and V.S. went out to stop it; this broke the thread of their argument and as V.S. was getting into his sleeping bag he remarked with a self satisfied air 'That this showed the value of their discussion, for it kept them awake so that they could stop the dog fights, and that he guessed the others had been sleeping soundly for some time.' The 'others' had been doing their best to sleep but had spent most of their time saying things under their breath that they would not like to see in print, and they now took pains to let the two 'Philosophers' know it" (Wilkins, 1913-16, Nov. 21, 1913). This was evidently a continuation of an argument that commenced soon after Stefansson's arrival, for McConnell (1913-14, Nov. 20, 1913) wrote that after eating, "The Chief and Jenness got into an argument regarding Philosophy, but Wilkins, 'Brick' and I retired at 3 a.m."

44.
Stefansson decided the weather was too bad to start out for the ships at Collinson Point (Wilkins, 1913-16, Nov. 23, 1913).

45.
The author regretted this arrangement, for Asecaq had been troublesome (Jenness,

1913h). Asecaq retained his entire outfit, including the rifle and other supplies issued him while on the Karluk and at Barrow (McConnell, 1913-14, Nov. 24, 1913).

46.
Some 300 pounds of food, mainly rice, sugar, and oatmeal, most of which was cached 20 miles away, near Cape Halkett, where a stranded whale would also supply dog meat. Additional supplies were to be sent to him from Camden Bay, Stefansson assured him, as soon as possible. With sufficient supplies he planned to remain with these Eskimos until June or early July, then go eastward to join the others at Camden Bay (Jenness, 1913h).

47.
Wilkins reported that they left not only all provisions and dogs that could be spared for Jenness, but unlimited credit at Barrow if he did not care to remain with the Eskimos long. He also commented that he thought Jenness would gradually regain his strength now that he had a supply of quinine to prevent further ague attacks and was not required to go on the trail. "I hope Jenness has a comfortable time this winter for he is a fine fellow and a pleasant companion and we have spent a congenial time together" (Wilkins, 1913-16, Nov. 24, 1913).

48.
Stefansson told the author that since 'Brick' Hopson's salary was very small he was to be allowed time and facilities for trapping while he was in the author's service. Stefansson also told him that the agreement made with Brick's father regarding how long Brick was to be the author's interpreter was rather indefinite, but it was probable that he would remain until the end of the trapping season (Jenness, 1913h), i.e. a few months.

49.
The diary at this point has "Anutisiak's," which the author later crossed out and wrote "Aksiataq's"; this appears to be the only time he used this spelling variation of Aksiatak.

Chapter 5. – With the Eskimos in Harrison Bay (I)

1.
See author's entry of September 27.

2.
At least 13 of Aluk's string figures were subsequently published by the author (Jenness, 1924b, Figs. XIII, XVI, L, LXXIV, LXXVI, LXXIX, XCI, XCVII-D, CVIII, CXXVII, CXXIX, CXXXV, and CXLII). The source of these figures is attributed to "a Colville River Eskimo." Some other figures in this volume, whose source is attributed to the "Inland Eskimos of Northern Alaska" may also derive from Aluk (or his brother-in-law Aksiatak), but most of them were probably learned from the Eskimos who came north from the mountains to Camden Bay and eastward in 1914. Chants often accompanied the making of the string figures.

3.
A small, dark wild goose.

4.
This may be the story "The wolf's bride" (Jenness, 1924a, pp. 38A-42A). It was told by Ugiarnaq, a native from near Cape Prince of Wales, to the residents at Cape Halkett on January 1, 1914, and dictated later to the author by Itarklik and Alfred Hopson, who were at Cape Halkett on that date.

5.
He came from near C. Prince of Wales [D.J.]. Probably one of Mrs. Brower's brothers, Assuaq or Amakuk, the latter the artist.

6.
Four of these drawings are reproduced in the author's article "Eskimo art" (Jenness, 1922b, Figs. 1, 6, 11, and 14). Three others appear in his book *Dawn in Arctic Alaska* (Jenness, 1957, pp. 60 and 125). The where-abouts of the original drawings is not known.

7.
Also spelled Ugiarnaq (Jenness, 1924a, p. 38A). Also called Amakuk and "Two Wolves" (Jenness, 1957, p. 59). He was a widower.

8.
Stefansson, McConnell, and Wilkins had taken the well-trained dogs that came from the *Karluk*, which McKinlay (1976, p. 47) described as twelve of their best dogs, as they had been supplied by Scotty Allan of Nome. "Scotty" Allan was said to have been the best dog trainer in Alaska (Garst, 1948, p. 143). Left for the author were five native dogs purchased by Stefansson at Barrow in October.

9.
The author left a space in his diary at this point, so that the identity of the material forming the hoop is not known.

10.
iraoqitsoq = mesh the breadth of the 3 mid fingers taken bet[ween] 1st and 2nd joints. *iraokturoq* = mesh the breadth of the 4 fingers and the thumb taken over the knuckles [D.J.].

11.
Their three stories appear in Jenness (1924b, pp. 182B-183B).

12.
The Noatak River flows into Kotzebue Sound southwest of the headwaters of the Colville River. Aluk lived on this river during his youth (Jenness, 1924b, p. 182B).

13.
Whitefish, *Argyrosumus* sp. (Jenness, 1928b, p. 18).

Chapter 6. – With the Eskimos in Harrison Bay (II)

1.
The exact location of these two mountain peaks is not known. Neither is listed in Orth (1967).

2.
See Fig. 52.

3.
In his diary the author had written "Kiliq" but then stroked it out, so that the identity of the river remains unknown.

4.
The author's father was a watch and clock maker in Wellington, New Zealand.

5.
This map has not been found.

6.
A toy that makes a whizzing noise when whirled around. It was a common toy in Canada, the U.S.A., England and perhaps elsewhere in the early 1900's.

7.
The author must have seen comparable toys during his 4 years (1908-1911) as a graduate student at the University of Oxford, or even earlier in New Zealand.

8.
A similar homemade toy in Canada and the United States in the 1930's used a circle of string looped through two of the holes of a large coat button. Winding the string, then alternately stretching and relaxing it made the button revolve and make a whizzing sound.

9.
The whereabouts of this journal is unknown.

10.
A pocket-case for needles, pins, thread, scissors, etc.

11.
Described on October 22nd.

12.
Alfred Hopson had received two forenames when he was a baby, the English name Alfred and an Eskimo name. He was nicknamed Brick by his father and called Kaiyu-taq (or Kaiyutak) by his Eskimo mother (Jenness, 1957, p. 80). The Eskimos with whom the author was living probably used the name Kaiyutaq, which may explain its use by the author here.

13.
The top of the man's head was shaved, resembling the shorn heads of men of some religious orders. Most of the male Copper Eskimos seen by the author during the next two years also wore a tonsure (Jenness, 1923a, p. 40B).

14.
Boxing Day, the day after Christmas, is traditionally a holiday in England, New Zealand, Canada, and other British Commonwealth countries. The origin of the name is somewhat obscure.

15.
The two went off to the southern part of Harrison Bay to bring back an *umiak* [skin boat] they had cached there, in order to leave it on one of the platforms alongside Aksiatak's house, where the presence of the dogs would prevent foxes or wolves from chewing at the sealskins on the boat (Jenness, 1957, p. 80).

16.
A brand-name product at that time.

17.
The author encountered his first left-handed male Eskimo, Billy Natkusiak, on March 14, 1914.

Chapter 7. – Facing Starvation

1.
One of the two schooners transporting the Expedition's Southern Party, the *Alaska* was winterbound at Collinson Point, in Camden Bay, about 180 miles to the east. Stefansson had promised in late November to send a sled with supplies from the *Alaska* to the author as soon as possible.

2.
This story, "The mad hunter," appears in Jenness (1924a, p. 33A).

3.
Atalanta, according to Greek legend, was a beautiful, swift-footed maiden who offered to marry any man able to defeat her in a race, with death the penalty for failure. One of her suitors was Hippomenes, to whom Aphrodite, before his race, gave three golden apples that had been plucked from the garden of the Hesperides. These he dropped one by one; Atalanta stopped to pick them up and so lost the race (*Encyclopedia Britannica*, 1956, vol. 2, p. 595).

4.
This was the author's name for the house on the west side of Harrison Bay that he helped build December 31st. It was about 12 miles northwest of Aksiatak's house (Iglu I). The Eskimo word *iglu* (commonly written *igloo*) refers in Alaska to a house constructed of wood, turf, and snow. All Eskimo houses visited by the author along the north shore of Alaska were of this type. The word has been popularly misused in southern Canada and the United States for an Eskimo house

constructed solely of blocks of snow. Such snowhouses were constructed in the winter months in the central and eastern Canadian Arctic because the tree-line east of the Mackenzie River delta was much farther to the south than in Alaska, and very little wood could be found along the coast. The author first encountered the snowhouse among the Copper Eskimos in the Coronation Gulf region in 1914.

5.
Probably one of the four stories told by Qapqana (Mrs. Aluk) that appear in Jenness (1924a, pp. 33A-38A).

6.
Aksiatak's house.

7.
The author was 5 1/2 feet tall.

8.
A mock moon.

9.
In New Zealand.

10.
The whereabouts of this Eskimo story book is not known. However, four of Qapqana's stories, representing most if not all of Brick's entries, were published in Jenness (1924a, pp. 33A-38A).

11.
Although the author clearly stated on November 28 that this name was Aluk, he returned to his earlier spelling (Alak) on this date.

12.
All members of the C.A.E. were under strict orders from the Canadian government not to interfere with the fur trade nor to trap any of the fur-bearing animals unless these were needed for food, clothing, or scientific specimens. "Even without this prohibition I doubt whether I could have found the heart to set any fox traps after witnessing the torture they inflicted on the unhappy creatures" (Jenness, 1957, p. 92).

13.
The sled going to Cape Halkett.

14.
At this point the author changed the spelling from Añopkana to Añopqana.

15.
The food supply left for the author by Stefansson in November was practically exhausted and would only last another two weeks (Jenness, 1957, p. 98). Dissatisfied with the semi-starvation diet he had been forced to live on since mid-December, he decided to take advantage of his unlimited credit at Brower's store in Barrow to obtain enough supplies from Asuaq to tide him over until the supplies promised him by Stefansson arrived from Camden Bay.

16.
Amakuk's wife had died childless many months before, leaving him without a woman to cook for him and to make and mend his clothing. He drifted from house to house, hunting and trapping to pay for his board and lodging, and performing various odd jobs, such as chopping wood and carrying snow, in return for the housewife's care of his wardrobe. Being strong and active, and therefore an asset wherever he went, he was always welcomed (Jenness, 1957, p. 100). The author first met him at Kunaloak's near Cape Halkett November 4 and 5, then again on December 4 and 5, 1913.

17.
This is probably "The orphan's gratitude" (Jenness, 1924a, pp. 36A-38A).

18.
This cat's cradle is described and illustrated in Jenness (1924b, pp. 128B-129B).

19.
In this song, composed early in September 1913, Asecaq expresses his despair of seeing again his home in Point Hope. It is reproduced in Roberts and Jenness (1925, pp. 387-388; English translation on p. 505) in the original version as written by the author about a month after Asecaq composed it and also in Añutisiak's recorded and transcribed version two years later. It is also reproduced in a version harmonized by an English organist friend of the author's (Jenness, 1922c, pp. 381-382 and 1957, p. 105).

20.
Asecaq had taught the song to various Eskimo families between Harrison Bay and Barrow. Another song composed by Asecaq about October 1, 1913, at Oliktok Point was recorded by Añutisiak and is reproduced in

Roberts and Jenness (1925, p. 390; English translation on p. 505).

21.
Nearly 50 years later Professor H.E. Childs, Jr. wrote the author that his assistant in northern Alaska, Pete Savolik, who was Alak's son Suivaliaq, remembered Jenness' 1913 visit with his family vividly, "particularly your kindness in making him and the other boy a swing" (Childs, Jr., 1958).

22.
Griselda was a peasant woman in medieval legend, a model of wifely obedience and patience to the cruel tasks laid on by her nobleman husband Walter. Her story is told in the final tale of Boccaccio's *Decameron* and in the "Clerk's Tale" in Chaucer's *Canterbury Tales*.

23.
Aksiatak's song is reproduced in Jenness (1922c, p. 380).

24.
Probably one of the four stories attributed to Qapqana in Jenness (1924a, pp. 33A-38A).

25.
Aksiatak gave this letter (Jenness, 1914a) to Burt McConnell a week later, when he arrived from Camden Bay to take the author back to the Expedition headquarters (McConnell, 1913-14, Feb. 10, 1914).

26.
The author left some items with Aksiatak and Aluk to be picked up later. Some of these were missing when Wilkins arrived to collect them (Wilkins, 1913-16, May 29, 1914).

Chapter 8. – Return to Barrow

1.
This was the dog the author wanted to leave behind with Aksiatak (see entry for February 2), not the one found in the trap earlier in the day.

2.
The year was 1852. Commander Rockfort Maguire, R.N., captain of the H.M.S. *Plover*, charted part of the Alaskan coast and recorded the existence of a native village at Cape Smythe, which he called "Otki-a-wing." He spent the winters of 1852-53 and 1853-54 at Point Barrow (Murdoch, 1888, p. 52; Bockstoce, 1988a), prevented from sailing eastward by ice conditions during those years. Brower (1944?, pp. 23, 25) stated that the Eskimo settlement, which he called "Utkiavie," was on a bluff 50 feet above the ocean and in 1883 was the biggest native settlement in Alaska.

3.
An Australian and New Zealand term for a pack, such as a blanket roll, carried on the back of a foot traveller.

4.
The author mentioned the presence of two houses here on November 3rd.

5.
When you leave you do not say goodbye — there seems to be no word for goodbye in Eskimo. You take your things and go out, load up your sled, and leave with never a word. Often though they bring out some of your things, cup etc., and perhaps may help you to load up. You generally contribute something in the way of food so that your hosts lose nothing by their hospitality; for they really are glad to see you. [D.J.]

6.
Akuwak had caught 21 foxes [D.J.]. Wilkins later photographed Akuwak at Point Barrow on March 20, 1914 (CMC Photo No. 50833).

7.
Okalik Lake is 4 miles to the south, Nalvakruk Lake, which is somewhat larger, about 6 miles to the southwest. The lake referred to here may have been Teshekpuk Lake, some 14 miles to the south, the same large lake in which Alak fished.

8.
The locality was probably Ikiak, where the author stayed on October 29th.

9.
The author stated that there were three houses and a platform at *Iglura* on October 28, when he last was there.

10.
The author's 28th birthday.

Chapter 9. – Archaeological Activities at Barrow

1.
Wilkins had sent them ashore at Cape Smythe the previous August for posting to the Gaumont Company in London, England. The Customs office at New York had returned the parcel because no value had been shown on it when Mr. Hopson posted it (Wilkins, 1913-16, Apr. 2, 1914). The package apparently contained three reels, with scenes from the early part of the Expedition, including ones around the *Karluk* at Esquimalt, B.C., ethnological specimens and assorted scenes at Nome, Alaska, and Stefansson leaving the *Karluk* for Cape Smythe early in August 1913 ("A complete list of Titles and sub-titles included in the cinimatographic [*sic*] record of the CANADIAN ARCTIC EXPEDITION," L file, Anderson papers, CMN). These reels are not among the Wilkins' films held by the National Archives of Canada.

2.
A New York newspaper.

3.
Originally written "Tabluca," the author corrected it later to "Kablucia."

4.
These specimens were received by the Museum in Ottawa on November 4, 1914, and subsequently given Accession numbers IX-F-2989 to 3704 (MS 1532, vol. 30, Archaeological Survey of Canada, Canadian Museum of Civilization, Hull, Quebec). The cost of the specimens was $1000, not $500, of which $233 was still owing in July 1914 (Brower, 1914).

5.
This was the American Museum of Natural History, New York City, which had co-sponsored (with the Geological Survey of Canada) Stefansson's previous polar expedition, the Stefansson-Anderson Expedition of 1908-1912.

6.
They were accompanied by Pauyuraq. While coming west from Camden Bay to fetch the author, McConnell and Fred encountered Brick, Lester, and Pauyaraq in a house on the Tapkaluk Islands (McConnell, 1913-14, Feb. 18, 1914).

7.
The author neglected to include the minus sign in his diary entry.

8.
Dr. Anderson had received a letter dated January 4, 1914, from Stefansson, who was then at Herschel Island, asking him to send a sled to Cape Halkett to fetch Jenness. The letter reached Dr. Anderson on January 16. McConnell and Fred (also known as Ailuat, an Eskimo hired at Nome in July 1913 to work on the *Mary Sachs*) left Camden Bay January 24 with twenty days' supplies (Anderson, 1913-16, Jan. 16, 19, 24, 1914). They reached the house of Aksiatak and Alak on February 10, where they learned that the author and Brick Hopson had gone west to Barrow. McConnell gave four reindeer skins each to the wives of Aksiatak and Alak, which Stefansson had promised them the previous November (McConnell, 1913-14, Feb. 10, 1914).

9.
At Añukapsaña's (or Añutaksaña's) house, a large (about 20 X 30 foot) structure originally built by Mr. Brower as a whaling station. Within two hours of McConnell's arrival most of the forty-four inhabitants of the little community showed up to visit and exchange news. McConnell attributed their apparent friendliness to his connection with Stefansson, who was "very popular with the Eskimos along the entire coast" (McConnell, 1913-14, Feb. 18, 1914).

10.
Ejnar Mikkelsen (a Danish adventurer and explorer) and Ernest de Koven Leffingwell (the American geologist on Flaxman Island) attempted unsuccessfully to discover land north of Alaska. By dog-sled they struck out from Flaxman Island in the spring of 1907, northwards across pack-ice in search of land, returning only after 70 days. Their little ship, the *Dutchess of Bedford* was crushed by the sea ice during their absence, so its materials were used to build a house on Flaxman Island (which Jenness reached on March 19, 1914, en route to Camden Bay). From there Mikkelson returned in the fall to civilization by means of a 2500-mile sled journey around the Alaskan coast to Nome, thence inland to Fairbanks and Valdez, and from there by ship back to Seattle (Mikkelsen, 1955). Leffingwell remained at Flaxman Island.

11.
In a letter to Dr. Sapir, the author wrote "I don't know why I am wanted now, but imagine it is to assist in taking the meteoro-

logical observations" (Jenness, 1914b), since McKinlay, who was to have taken such observations, was thought to be with the *Karluk*. The author had originally expected to remain with the Eskimos at Harrison Bay until late spring (Jenness, 1913h).

12.
Kenneth Chipman was chief topographer, John Cox assistant topographer, and John O'Neill the geologist for the Southern Party of the Canadian Arctic Expedition.

13.
It had disappeared two days previously (McConnell, 1913-14, Feb. 20, 1914).

14.
He sketched and made notes on the implements in order to learn their names and uses, and also so he could compare them with the types he expected to find on Victoria Island (Jenness, 1914b). The whereabouts of both sketches and notes is unknown.

15.
The author was probably endeavouring to reassure the relatives that all was well and to give them what news he could of the Expedition. Henri Beuchat was the French ethnologist and William McKinlay the Scottish magnetician on the *Karluk*. Although the author was not aware of it at this time, Beuchat had already perished. McKinlay was among the survivors rescued in September 1914 from Wrangel Island (McKinlay, 1976).

16.
His flanks and part of his belly had been frozen and his feet were badly damaged by the sharp ice in the journey to Barrow (McConnell, 1913-14, Feb. 16, 1914).

17.
Of the six dogs Stefansson left with the author in late November, two later had to be shot because of serious injuries, one had to be returned to Mr. Brower's brother-in-law at Cape Halkett, and another belonged to Brick (Jenness, 1914b).

18.
Brower was often able to explain to the author what some of the implements were, even when the local Eskimos did not know (Jenness, 1914b).

19.
Candle, a settlement in the southeast corner of Kotzebue Sound, Alaska, which had telegraphic facilities at that time.

20.
The Nome report probably referred to the same event as that of a Washington dispatch late in 1913, which stated that a life buoy (not boat) from the *Karluk* had washed ashore at Kivalina, a small village north of Kotzebue Sound. As the life buoy was found considerably before the January 11, 1914, sinking of the *Karluk*, it was probably washed overboard in a storm the *Karluk* encountered when it crossed Kotzebue Sound on July 28, 1913 (Desbarats, 1914c).

21.
The *Alaska* and *Mary Sachs* at Camden Bay, 285 miles to the east.

Chapter 10. – Sled-journey to Camden Bay

1.
One of these letters was to Dr. E. Sapir in Ottawa, reporting the author's activities since the previous December and news of the men at Camden Bay (Jenness, 1914b).

2.
About 500 lbs on McConnell's sled, 400 lbs on the author's. Included were about 18 lbs of mail McConnell was taking for persons along the coast as far as Herschel Island, 20 lbs of butter for Leffingwell on Flaxman Island, and some seal meat for Asuaq near Pitt Point (McConnell, 1913-14, Feb. 28, 1914).

3.
About 20 X 30 feet (see footnote 9, Chapter 9).

4.
This gave McConnell eight dogs to the author's six (McConnell, 1913-14, Mar. 1, 1914).

5.
On the Tapkaluk Islands, which McConnell called "Topkarluk" (McConnell, 1913-14, Mar. 1, 1914).

6.
McConnell's dogs were trained sled dogs purchased at Nome. The author's dogs were Eskimo dogs belonging to Mrs. Brower. "Eskimo dogs are accustomed to frequent rests on the trail, while our dogs keep on going all day with only two or three rests in the whole time, or even without a single rest" (McConnell, 1913-14, Mar. 1, 1914).

7.
This was the house of Stefansson's former seamstress (McConnell, 1913-14, Mar. 2, 1914).

8.
The house was Añopqana's, not Añutaksana's (or Añukapsaña's), the latter being at Point Barrow. The author, McConnell, and Fred spent the night in Añopqana's old house, the other one being occupied when they arrived at 3:45 p.m. (McConnell, 1913-14, Mar. 2, 1914).

9.
This locality, near Tangent Point, is now called Ikiak. The author previously called it *Ikiuraq* (Nov. 1); he had stopped there also on October 11 and 29, and February 8. This was where he first encountered Añopqana (Oct. 1).

10.
To trade their furs (McConnell, 1913-14, Mar. 3, 1914).

11.
Near Drew Point. McConnell had hoped to reach Pitt Point, but the author's dogs were tiring before they even started across Smith Sound (McConnell, 1913-14, Mar. 3, 1914).

12.
Unnamed but described on December 25 as "wearing the tonsure."

13.
The author states (Feb. 28) that the six dogs were Mrs. Brower's and were to be turned over to her brother (Asuaq). After that transaction took place, he and McConnell were left with one sled, eight dogs (of which two were somewhat incapacitated) and a load of about 700 lbs (McConnell, 1913-14, Mar. 4, 1914).

14.
The author had much trouble with this man's name. He spelled it Kagliluña on his first encounter, February 7, but on March 3, 4, and 5 stroked out that spelling and in-

serted quite a different version, complete with Greek letters. For simplicity I have retained the original spelling. Kagliluña's house was a few miles west of Pitt Point. *Nunatagmiut* was a name given by Alaskan coastal natives to the native people of the interior (Stefansson, 1913a, p. 181).

15.
An hour-long argument between McConnell and the author delayed the start of the trip (McConnell, 1913-14, Mar. 5, 1914), but the subject of the argument was not disclosed.

16.
The author had stayed there November 3 and February 6. McConnell incorrectly interpreted it as Asuaq's house (McConnell, 1913-14, Mar. 5, 1914).

17.
Fred had gathered about 200 lbs of whale meat and blubber for dog-food, which McConnell and he had cached here on their way west, February 14, and this had been added to the sled load. They hoped it would last them until they reached Howe Island, where Billy Natkusiak had cached a supply (McConnell, 1913-14, Feb. 14 and Mar. 5, 1914).

18.
If they had had two dog teams they could have taken all of this equipment east to Camden Bay. However, with only one dog team the author was forced to leave these items here. Some were later picked up by Wilkins (Wilkins, 1913-16, May 29, 1914).

19.
McConnell thought their load was about 900 lbs and commented that two of the eight dogs were of no use to pull such a load (McConnell, 1913-14, Mar. 9, 1914).

20.
It was a watch McConnell had lent to Fred when they left Collinson Point (McConnell, 1913-14, Mar. 9, 1914), which probably accounts for McConnell's desire to retrieve it.

21.
Atigaru Pt. on modern maps. Alak's house was on the north side of Kogru River, on the narrow peninsula that is terminated eastward by Saktuina Pt, a few miles to the west of Atigaru Pt.

22.
McConnell was less enthusiastic about the mask. "Jenness' deerskin mask was so full

of ice that he could not see where he was going" (McConnell, 1913-14, Mar. 9, 1914).

23.
The stop-over was mainly to give Jumbo a rest, as they did not want to lose him (McConnell, 1913-14, Mar. 10, 1914).

24.
From Collinson Point for the author (McConnell, 1913-14, Mar. 10, 1914).

25.
It had been arranged that Fred would prepare breakfast each morning, while the author would alternate with McConnell in preparing the evening meal (McConnell, 1913-14, Mar. 11, 1914).

26.
Billy Nekusiak (Natkusiak) worked for Stefansson during his 1908-12 expedition. McConnell met him while journeying west late in January and seeing tracks of a large dog around the snowhouse concluded that he was probably somewhere nearby, for he knew Natkusiak had an unusually large dog (McConnell, 1913-14, Mar. 12, 1914). Natkusiak and his dog are pictured in Stefansson (1921, p. 608).

27.
"Jenness thought there might be something of ethnological interest at the snow house, so he delayed the start about 20 minutes" (McConnell, 1913-14, Mar. 13, 1914).

28.
Fred put the shirt on Jenness "who was absolutely helpless, and who probably would have frozen to death had he been alone" (McConnell, 1913-14, Mar. 13, 1914).

29.
Beechey Point is 16 miles east of Oliktok Point, too far to be reached in one hour. The author is referring to an unnamed point 3 or 4 miles east of Oliktok Point. The British Admiralty chart (2435) at that time showed Beechey Point at the locality now called Oliktok Point. (See also the author's comment on Sept. 22, 1913, on the inaccuracy of the chart they had.)

30.
Langton Bay, at the south end of Franklin Bay, between Cape Bathurst and Cape Parry, east of the mouth of the Mackenzie River, is more than 600 miles to the east.

31.
The author's comment refers to the omission of Dr. Anderson's name, for the expedition was generally known as the Stefansson-Anderson Expedition.

32.
Beechey Point appears to be correctly identified here.

33.
Franklin had applied this name in 1826. It was changed to Return Islands by Leffingwell (1919, p. 89).

34.
Nekusiak (Natkusiak) had just taken up his traps when the author's party met him and was about to head east. He and McConnell agreed on camping sites each day before they started off (McConnell, 1913-14, Mar. 13, 17, 1914).

35.
Though able to travel much more quickly Nekusiak (Natkusiak) repeatedly waited for the others to catch up, because his provisions were all gone (McConnell, 1913-14, Mar. 14, 1914).

36.
See December 28, however, for an earlier observation of a left-handed Eskimo, a woman.

37.
When he was heading west late in January. The rack was on Heald Point (McConnell, 1913-14, Mar. 25, 1914) on the east side of Prudhoe Bay, an embayment whose name (given by Franklin in 1826) has much greater importance today than it had in 1914. In 1988 it was the largest daily oil-producing field in the Western Hemisphere.

38.
McConnell had camped on this sandspit north of Heald Point six weeks before (McConnell, 1913-14, Jan. 31, 1914).

39.
McConnell (1913-14, Mar. 13, 1914) called him "Adluat."

40.
The dogs did not seem to be troubled by this effect of the light. [D.J.]

41.
Dr. George P. Howe was a medical doctor on the Anglo-American Polar Expedition 1906-1907 with Mikkelsen and Leffingwell.

42.
It was near Anxiety Point, just east of Howe Island.

43.
Thetis Island, on which the author landed on September 21, 1913. Spelled Amauliktok by Stefansson (1921, p. 57).

44.
The name "Endicott Mountains" was used in the early 1900's for all of the mountains running roughly east-west near the north coast of Alaska between the 145th and 154th meridians (Schrader, 1904, p. 40). The mountains visible from that part of the coast where the author was travelling are now called the Sadlerochit Mountains and Shublik Mountains and are about 40 miles distant.

45.
In reality Aiakuk's house, because Qopuk's house was west of Papiroq's, in Foggy Island Bay (McConnell, 1913-14, Jan. 28, 1914).

46.
Also spelled *Savagvik* (see author's entry for April 24, 1914), *Savakvik*, and *Shavugavik* (Leffingwell, 1919, p. 94). Now known as Bullen Point (Orth, 1967, p. 167), it is on the east side of Mikkelsen Bay. Qopuk's house was apparently at or near the point now known as Point Hopson.

47.
Near Point Gordon, 10 miles west of Flaxman Island.

48.
Initially spelled Nekusiak here, the author later corrected it to Natkusiak.

49.
A chromlech is a prehistoric tomb or monument consisting of a large, flat stone laid across upright stones. In pagan Ireland cromlechs were regarded as the graves of giants.

50.
Probably Aiakuk's house (see footnote 45, this chapter).

51.
Leffingwell's camp, which in 1914 consisted of a house and a nearby shack for stores, is now a U.S. National Historic Site.

52.
This was Teriglu, also spelled Terigloo (Jenness, 1957, p. 143), whom the author encountered later on Barter Island. Igluñasuk was Teriglu's son, who at the time was away with Leffingwell. The author evidently got the names confused on this occasion. Igluñasuk (*iglanacuk*) means "one who is always smiling" (Jenness, 1928b, p. 31).

53.
Leffingwell went to the Kadleroshilik River on March 5, 1914, to undertake triangulation observations, then worked westward to the Kuparuk River. He returned to Flaxman Island on April 21 (Leffingwell, 1919, p. 18).

54.
On Brownlow Spit [Point Brownlow], about 3 miles west of Leffingwell's beacon (McConnell, 1913-14, Mar. 19, 1914). However, Leffingwell stated (1919, p. 40) that the triangulation station was at Brownlow Point. If the station and beacon were one and the same, McConnell's mileage figure is incorrect. He may have meant 3 miles east of the beacon.

55.
Duffy O'Connor had built the house a few years previously. It measured about 20 x 30 feet.

56.
McConnell mentions having disagreements with the author but provides no details (McConnell, 1913-14, Mar. 5 and 20).

57.
Sweeney later became master of the *Alaska*; Aarnout Castel, a sailor, later went with Wilkins and became master of the *North Star*.

58.
Frits Johansen was the marine biologist and naturalist with Dr. Anderson's party.

59.
The Lucas was thoroughly overhauled and is in good condition. It reads up to 400 fathoms, but having only a small reeling wheel takes about an hour to wind up. It weighs about 27 lbs. [D.J.]

60.
It was actually about 10 miles east of Demarcation Point.

61.
From the trip out on the ice with Stefansson. Though Peter Bernard sold his ship, the *Mary Sachs*, to Stefansson at Nome for $5000 in July 1913, he retained one-third interest in it, remained its captain, and was to get the ownership back after three years (Chipman, 1913-16, Aug. 3, 1913). However, he perished on or near the north shore of Banks Island during the winter of 1916-17 (Stefansson, 1921, p. 653). The *Mary Sachs* was beached on the west side of Banks Island in 1914.

62.
Stefansson also left instructions for McConnell, as soon as he returned to Camden Bay with the author, to go to the *North Star* and make a complete inventory of the 20 tons of goods it held (McConnell, 1913-14, Mar. 20, 1914). This apparent confusion because of Stefansson's duplication of instructions was later corrected when Stefansson sent another letter to the author cancelling his earlier instructions (see diary entry, Apr. 22).

63.
This was Matt Andreasen, owner of the *North Star* until he sold it to Stefansson.

64.
Otto Nahmens, a young American sailor and miner around Nome, was hired by Stefansson in 1913 as captain of the *Alaska*.

65.
Forwarded from Fort McPherson (McConnell, 1913-14, Mar. 20, 1914).

Chapter 11. – Respite and Tragedy at Camden Bay

1.
Jennie Thomsen with her husband Charles and child Annie were taken on board the *Mary Sachs* at Nome in late July 1913. They were added to Stefansson's 'new' Northern Party in the summer of 1914, with Jennie as seamstress at $25 per month. She replaced the seamstress hired for the 'original' Northern Party, who was with the shipwrecked *Karluk* party on Wrangel Island on this date. Jennie's husband, Charles, a seaman, froze to death off the north coast of Banks Island during the winter of 1916-17.

2.
They were going east to 'Duffy' O'Connor's house at Demarcation Point and the *North Star* some miles farther east (Anderson, 1913-16, Mar. 22, 1914), but hoped to catch up to Stefansson and his party en route.

3.
William McKinlay was to collect meteorological and magnetic data for the Southern Party for the first year, then transfer to the Northern Party. He was on the ill-fated *Karluk*, however, and following his rescue from Wrangel Island in September 1914, returned to his home in Scotland and military service. The meteorological observations for the Southern Party were, therefore, recorded by whichever scientist was at the headquarters camp to make them.

4.
Victor was sold to O'Connor for $15 (Anderson, 1913-16, Mar. 23, 1914), although prices for dogs in the Herschel Island region had been running considerably higher (to $50) the previous fall (Chipman, 1913-16, Oct. 16, 1913; Anderson, 1913-16, Oct. 17, 1913).

5.
The author left a space at this point in his diary, presumably intending to insert a number later.

6.
Dr. Anderson had been trying to get away on this hunting trip since the first of January, but was repeatedly delayed and frustrated by Stefansson's changes in plans and instructions.

7.
A 440-ton bark (Bockstoce, 1977, p. 78) caught in the ice a mile or two off-shore near Humphrey Point, some 60 miles east of Camden Bay. It was carrying a considerable cargo of supplies originally intended for delivery to Dr. Anderson's Southern Party at Herschel Island.

8.
This picture is not on Johansen's photograph list and is assumed to have been discarded.

9.
Daniel Blue died of scurvy on May 2, 1915, after the *Alaska* was trapped by ice at Baillie Island en route eastward from Herschel Island the previous September (Anderson, 1916b, p. 7).

10.
Probably two of the six stories attributed to Fred in the author's Eskimo folklore book (Jenness, 1924a, Nos. 14, 21, 22, 23, 24, and 37).

11.
Probably story No. 23 (Jenness, 1924a, pp. 49A-52A).

12.
Andre Norem was the steward from the *Mary Sachs* and alternated as cook weekly with Charles Brook, the steward from the *Alaska* (Stefansson, 1921, p. 95).

13.
The author was trying to collect a specimen for Dr. Anderson's bird collection.

14.
Only one (CMC Photo No. 39127) appears to have survived.

15.
The mountains visible from Camden Bay are now called the Sadlerochit and Shublik Mountains and lie on the northern side of the Brooks Range. They were named by Leffingwell (1919, pp. 50-51). (See footnote 44, Chapter 10.)

16.
These photographs are not recorded on the lists of photographs taken by the author, Johansen, or Dr. Anderson and were presumably discarded. Wilkins photographed the *umiaks* for the author on April 10, 1914 (see author's entry for that date).

17.
Thirteen of Jennie's stories were published by the author (Jenness, 1924a, pp. 44A-47A, 53A-58A, 60A-64A, 68A-69A).

18.
The diary has no name at this point, only an empty space. However, a photograph (CMC Photo No. 37126) of a little girl, taken by the author in 1914, lists her name as Iqiaqpuk, daughter of Teriglu, Collinson Pt. Her mother was an Eskimo woman, now dead, but the father was from a whaling ship, and may have been Negro, judging from the child's frizzly hair and head shape (Jenness, 1957, p. 145). Wilkins also photographed the same little girl (CMC Photo No. 50722), whom he listed as Ikiakpuk. She had been left with Jennie some two months before by Teriglu, her adopted father, who was working with Leffingwell (Anderson, 1913-16, Apr. 26, 1914). She was to help look after Jennie's baby daughter Annie.

19.
The author collected these data on Thomsen's bear-cub specimen for Dr. Anderson in the latter's absence. The back of the first volume of the author's diary contains the following checklist of items to be measured: Measurements of Animals (Skins for Mounting)
1. Length of Head and Body to root of tail (set up stick at each end and measure dist[ance])
2. Height of shoulders from ground
3. Girth bet[ween] forelegs
4. Circumference of neck
5. Depth of Flank (taken w[ith] 2 sticks)
6. Circumf[erence] of foreleg (at the femur)
7. Head of Humerus to Head of Femur
8. Length of Tail.

20.
He had brought mail from Barrow for Stefansson and Wilkins (Wilkins, 1913-16, Mar. 23, 1914).

21.
The cut was about 9 inches long, across the head from temple to temple, "so that his entire forehead was hanging down over his eyes" (McConnell, 1913-14, Mar. 23, 1914).

22.
Stefansson wanted to take Capt. Bernard to the *Belvedere* for treatment by Capt. Cottle, who had some medical experience, but Capt. Bernard said he would rather have his friend Crawford sew up the wound than a stranger. Crawford was at Martin Point, so Stefansson, McConnell, and two others took Capt. Bernard there. After viewing the severity of the wound, Crawford said he could not sew it up, so McConnell performed the operation, which was done without benefit of anaesthetic. The next day, leaving Capt. Bernard with A. Castel, Stefansson, McConnell, Crawford, and Ole Andreasen returned to their camp on the ice (McConnell, 1913-14, Mar. 23, 1914).

23.
An empty space appears here in the diary, but the distance of about 25 miles has been

determined from information the author provided elsewhere in his diary.

24.
This story, entitled "The woman and her grandfather's skull," is published in Jenness (1924a, pp.64A-65A).

25.
There were not enough dogs at Collinson Point to spare Wilkins a team to go to Barrow, and Natkusiak not only had a good dog team but wanted to go to Barrow (Wilkins, 1913-16, Apr. 3, 1914).

26.
The author photographed the grave (CMC Photo No. 27125).

27.
The author photographed the sled and sail (CMC Photo No. 37159).

28.
Wilkins wrote to the *Daily Chronicle* (London) and to his firm, the Gaumont Co. He was delaying his departure for Barrow as he expected Dr. Anderson to return any day and wished to converse with him before leaving (Wilkins, 1913-16, Apr. 5 and 8, 1914).

29.
Chipman (1913-16, Oct. 31, 1913) recorded Norem's age as 58, but the grave marker (Fig. 79 and CMC Photo No. 50807) lists it as 52.

30.
CMC Photo Nos. 37120, 37121, and 50806. No. 50806 (Frontispiece) is perhaps the best picture taken of the author during his three years in the Arctic.

31.
Wilkins' diary does not mention Norem's problem prior to April 17, 1914, which suggests that the supervision was not obvious.

32.
Like Charles Thomsen, who had a trapping cabin some 9 miles west of Collinson Point, Capt. Nahmens spent some of his winter trapping around a cabin some 10 miles east of Collinson Point. Both men were now needed for Expedition activities (Wilkins, 1913-16, Apr. 12, 1914).

33.
Wilkins asked Capt. Nahmens and Castel to enquire after news of Dr. Anderson and

Blue as far east as Martin Point, as he was anxious to head for Barrow before the season progressed any further (Wilkins, 1913-16, Apr. 14-20, 1914).

34. The whereabouts of this list is unknown.

35.
Erroneously written as Capt. Bernard in the diary.

36.
Both Thomsen and Wilkins dressed the body and laid it in the coffin (Wilkins' letter to Dr. Anderson, dated Apr. 19, 1914, quoted in Anderson, 1913-16, Apr. 21, 1914).

37.
The coffin was built by Capt. Bernard (Wilkins, 1913-16, Apr. 14-20, 1914).

38.
More information about Norem, who was of Norwegian birth, is given in Anderson (1913-16, Apr. 21, 1914).

39.
Capt. Nahmens, not Bernard.

40.
Stefansson (1914d) wrote Dr. Anderson that he was sending Capt. Bernard instructions to take charge of the freighting of 300 gallons of distillate, some other oils and sundries, and about 1200 lbs of food to the Mackenzie delta, using at least two teams of dogs. These were Expedition supplies that had been shipped on the *Belvedere* from Nome, destined for Herschel Island, and were now needed for Cox and Chipman for their planned survey of the Mackenzie delta during the spring and early summer.

41.
The *North Star* was a 10-ton, gasoline-motor powered, 40-foot fishing schooner, drawing less than 5 feet of water. It had been caught by ice conditions as it sought to reach Nome from Herschel Island in August 1913, and wintered in Clarence Lagoon, some 10 miles east of 'Duffy' O'Connor's place at Demarcation Point. Stefansson had bought both the vessel and its supplies from its owner, Capt. Matt Andreasen, four months before. Stefansson planned to use these supplies and those he had also purchased from 'Duffy' O'Connor to help outfit his new Northern Party, so that he could continue with his polar exploration despite the loss of the *Karluk* and its personnel.

42.

The men had intended to await Dr. Anderson's return to bury Norem, but with the news that nothing had been heard about either Dr. Anderson or Stefansson, Wilkins decided to head west immediately, and Capt. Bernard decided to start freighting the supplies from the *Belvedere* to the Mackenzie delta the following day, leaving few dogs and spare men at Collinson Point. The burial was, therefore, undertaken while both men and dogs were available (Wilkins, 1914).

43.

"He was buried on the top of a low bluff on east bank of Marsh Creek, about two miles east of the house used by the Canadian Arctic Expedition at Collinson Point, near Mr. Chipman's survey beacon. The grave was dug through three or four feet of solid earth and then down into solid white ice (ground-ice) to about six feet in depth. The mound was rounded up with earth, and marked by a painted headboard inscribed with his name and the date of his death. The coffin was made by Captain Bernard, of pine boards, lined with cloth. Buried in the solid palae-ocrystic ice which underlies the ground here, the body should be permanently preserved." (Anderson, 1921). Wilkins photographed the headstone after the burial (CMC Photo No. 50807).

44.

Only one whale was killed by the whale-hunters near Barrow in 1914. Unfortunately, Wilkins arrived too late to film that event, and though he waited six more weeks, he did not get the films he had hoped to (Thomas, 1961, p. 80). (See also author's diary entry for June 10, 1914.) Natkusiak was offered $100 plus all expenses for taking Wilkins to Barrow and back, a trip of about 800 miles (Wilkins letter to Dr. Anderson, Apr. 19, 1914, quoted in Anderson, 1913-16, Apr. 24, 1914). In the three-quarters of a century since Wilkins sought to film the off-shore whale hunt a significant cultural change has occurred in the Barrow region, for in October 1988 thousands of dollars were spent trying to save the lives of three small California grey whales trapped by ice near Point Barrow. The valiant and successful efforts of the local people were shown nightly on North American and world television for nearly three weeks.

45.

Capt. Bernard decided to send gasoline and provisions from the Collinson Point supplies

because the drums were smaller than those farther east and the assortment of groceries was preferable (Wilkins letter to Dr. Anderson, Apr. 19, 1914, quoted in Anderson, 1913-16, Apr. 21, 1914).

46.

Dr. Anderson gave Brook a heavy new "Point Barrow sled," taking a light "Thompson sled" in exchange, it being too light for heavy freighting (Anderson, 1913-16, Apr. 21, 1914).

47.

To return to the U.S.A. As things transpired, however, he played an important role in the rescue of the survivors of the *Karluk* from Wrangel Island in September 1914 (McConnell, 1915, p. 353; see also Stefansson, 1921, pp. 726-730).

48.

The vessel's name was *Anna Olga* (Anderson, 1913-16, May 6, 1914; McConnell, 1913-14, July 17, 1914).

49.

The Sadlerochit Mountains south of Camden Bay.

50.

Lat. and Long. at the place of separation 140° 30'W. L. 70° 20'N. On the night of the 26th [March], the big blizzard which opened up the ice and prevented Wilkins from returning, they drifted about 50 miles, according to Storkerson's observations. [D.J.]

51.

Sweeney was to convey the Expedition's distillate, food, and other supplies from the *Belevedere* and *North Star* to the Mackenzie delta for Cox and Chipman. Capt. Bernard advised Dr. Anderson that Sweeney should be put in charge rather than Castel, as the former knew the country better and had more trail experience. Dr. Anderson listed in his field notes the supplies to be moved (Anderson, 1913-16, Apr. 24, 1914).

52.

E.B. O'Connor, known in Nome and elsewhere in Alaska as 'Duffy', established his trading post at Collinson Point, about 1911 (Stefansson, 1913a, p. 379). It proved to be too close to Leffingwell's trading camp on Flaxman Island, so he moved to Demarcation Point some time before the Canadian Arctic Expedition reached Collinson Point.

53.
The information available at that time suggested that the best place for the author to carry out ethnological and archaeological field work was at the Eskimo sealing camp on Icy Reef (Anderson, 1913-16, Apr. 24, 1914). This trip thus allowed him to assess where he should commence his field investigations.

54.
CMC Photo No. 37158.

55.
Johansen was to collect tidal equipment used at Martin Point and take tidal observations at Demarcation Point, as well as undertake biological collections. The tidal observations were expected to provide information to supplement that obtained at Martin Point and Collinson Point on the direction of the tides along that part of the Beaufort Sea (Anderson, 1913-16, Apr. 24, 1914).

56.
This was probably Ikiakpuk Creek, now known as Eagle Creek, a tributary of the Canning River (Orth, 1967, pp. 292, 447).

57.
Savakvik Point, now known as Bullen Point (see footnote 46, Chapter 10). Teriglu had five children: two boys, age 8 or 9 and 4 or 5, and three girls, two of them age 5 or 6 and one age 2 or 3. The oldest boy was with Leffingwell west of Flaxman Island (see footnotes 52 and 53, Chapter 10), and the 4 to 5 year old boy was up the Hulahula River with the Eskimo Pikalo. One of the older girls, Ikiakpuk, had been left with Jennie Thomsen as nursemaid for two or three months when Teriglu was on Flaxman Island (Anderson, 1913-16, Apr. 26, 1914). Wilkins photographed Ikiakpuk [Igiaqpuk] on Mar. 6, 1914 (CMC Photo No. 50722); the author photographed her a few weeks later (CMC Photo No. 37126).

Chapter 12. – Journey to Demarcation Point

1.
Ole Andreasen, a brother of Matt Andreasen (captain of the *North Star*), had gone on the ice trip with Stefansson.

2.
Fanny Pannigavlu (her name is now generally spelled Pannigabluk) was a widowed Alaskan Eskimo who served as seamstress for Stefansson during his 1908-1912 Arctic expedition. Her only son, Alik Alaluk, was born in 1910. Wilkins photographed Fanny and Alik near Martin Point on March 18, 1914 (CMC Photo Nos. 50769, 50770), and O'Neill photographed the two about the same time (GSC Photo No. 38378). In 1915 both mother and son were baptized at Aklavik by the Anglican missionary, the Rev. C.E. Whittaker, whose All Saints Church registry recorded Pannigabluk as wife of Stefansson and Alik as son of Fanny and Stefansson (Finnie, 1978, p. 3). The church and its records were destroyed by fire in the early 1980's. Some members of the C.A.E.'s Southern Party were aware of and commented on the relationship, notably Chipman (1914b), but neither the author nor Dr. Anderson mentioned it.

3.
A 140-foot bark, built in Maine in 1880, the *Belvedere* served in the western Arctic whaling trade longer than any other steamer.

Capt. Cottle bought it in 1911, sold it to a Seattle company in 1913, and promptly sailed it back into the Arctic as a trader and freighter (Bockstoce, 1977, p. 78).

4.
The *Elvira* was a small, 86-foot schooner on only her second whaling voyage into northern Alaskan waters. After bending her shaft and propellor near Herschel Island she was taken in tow by the 76-foot *Polar Bear* in an effort to get out of the Beaufort Sea before freeze-up. Trapped by ice east of Barter Island, the *Polar Bear* Bear used its engine to work shoreward behind heavily grounded ice flows before becoming ice-bound for the winter, but the *Elvira*, lacking engine power, remained seaward of the grounded ice and was lost on September 23, 1913, during a gale. A photograph of the three ships near Barter Island shortly before their separation appears in Bockstoce (1977, p. 106).

5.
Capt. Steven F. Cottle was well known to Stefansson, having taken the latter to Herschel Island from near the Colville River in 1907 and from Herschel Island to Cape Bathurst the next year, when he was captain of the whaler *Karluk*. Mrs. Cottle always accompanied her husband (Stefansson, 1913a, pp. 48, 118-119).

6.
Some of these natives are shown in a photograph taken by the author (CMC Photo No. 37128).

7.
The mountains visible from Icy Reef are the British Mountains, at the eastern end of the Brooks Range.

8.
McConnell, just back from Stefansson's ice party, met Castel and Charles Brook at Martin Point, and they sledded him and his things east to Duffy O'Connor's house at Demarcation Point (McConnell, 1913-14, Apr. 23 and 24, 1914). There he learned that W.S. Brooks had several weeks earlier made an inventory of Duffy's supplies (a copy of Brooks' list, with an added note by McConnell mentioning a few overlooked items, is in the Inventory file, Anderson papers, CMN). Reasoning that if he made another inventory it would show a lack of trust in Brooks, whom Stefansson had left in charge of the supplies, McConnell sat around, typed, and read old magazines until the author's party arrived five days later (McConnell, 1913-14, Apr. 26-30, 1914).

9.
The author told McConnell that Sweeney was in charge of freighting supplies from the *Belevedere* and *North Star* to Herschel Island and Shingle Point (McConnell, 1913-14, Apr. 29. 1914). The author was then going to study the Eskimos and old Eskimo sites while en route back to Collinson Point.

10.
Dr. Anderson had written a letter to McConnell, which Sweeney brought from Collinson Point for him, instructing him to undertake the inventory of the *North Star* supplies (Anderson, 1913-16, Apr. 24, 1914).

11.
Johansen stayed at O'Connor's house to take tidal measurements and collect biological specimens with Brooks, who was collecting for the Harvard Museum. The author obtained from McConnell the 3A Kodak camera McConnell had brought ashore from the ice trip (McConnell, 1913-14, Apr. 29, 1914).

12.
The author later corrected the name Kiniq here to Qagnik.

13.
John Heard, Jr. (spelled Hird by the author) was one of the four young Harvard sportsmen on the *Polar Bear*.

14.
Twenty-one are included in Jenness (1924b, pp. 185B-187B).

15.
This photograph is not listed in the author's collection and must have been discarded as unsatisfactory.

16.
Cape Serdze Kamen, Siberia.

17.
The diary has a blank space where the date was to be inserted. The year was 1877 (Bockstoce, 1986, p. 189).

18.
The diary has a blank space where the name of the sailing vessel was to be inserted. It was the trading brig *William H. Allen* (Bockstoce, 1986, p. 189).

19.
Capt. George Gilley. A brief description of the incident, which arose after the illegal trading of whiskey to the Cape Prince of Wales Eskimos for foxskins, appears in Brower (1944?, pp. 65-66); a fuller account of the incident appears in Bockstoce (1986, p. 189-191).

20.
To feed both her own crew and that of the sunken whaler *Elvira*, nearly one hundred men in all.

21.
These islands are in the Atlantic Ocean west of Senegal.

22.
People from Nova Scotia are often colloquially called 'bluenosers', a reference to the famous 19th century Nova Scotian sailing ship *Bluenose*.

23.
Mr. Ellis had wanted to go with Chipman up the Mackenzie River to Fort McPherson, but changed his mind and was returning to the *Polar Bear* (Anderson, 1913-16, Apr. 23, May 4, 1914).

24.
The *Elvira* sank at 5:42 p.m. on September 23, 1913, and its crew moved onto the *Belvedere* (Anderson, 1913-16, Oct. 12, 1913).

25.
Olaf Swenson was an agent for the Hibbard-Swenson Co. of Seattle, the company that bought the *Belvedere* from Capt. Cottle in 1913. During the summer of 1914 McConnell went from Barrow to Nome on Swenson's schooner *The King and Winge*. While at Nome he persuaded Swenson to attempt to reach Wrangel Island to rescue the survivors of the *Karluk*. Swenson, a born leader according to McConnell, undertook the trip, with McConnell as passenger, and succeeded in rescuing the survivors on September 7, 1914, a day before the arrival of the U.S. Coastguard cutter *Bear*, which had the *Karluk*'s Capt. Bob Bartlett on board (McConnell, 1913-14, Aug. 22, Sept. 3 and 7, 1914).

26.
The British Mountains.

27.
Dr. Anderson was heading for the Mackenzie River delta to check on the progress of the topographic work of Cox and Chipman. He was undoubtedly carrying Expedition mail to leave at Herschel Island with the Royal North-West Mounted Police, from whence it would go south via Fort McPherson.

28.
Natives of the Aleutian Islands, southwestern Alaska.

29.
Sweeney had left Iñukuk in charge of some of the Expedition's equipment (Anderson, 1913-16, May 3, 1914).

30.
Dr. Anderson hired Baur to replace Andre Norem as cook for the *Mary Sachs*, Sullivan (and presumably also Addison) at $2.50 per day for general work on the *Alaska* until they reached Herschel Island (Anderson, 1913-16, May 4, 1914).

31.
Ordinary seaman. The A.B. stood for able-bodied or ordinary.

32.
On Arey Island (see May 26, 1914).

33.
Addison, Sullivan, Levi, and Añutisiak apparently left for Collinson Point after eating.

Chapter 13. – Temporarily in Charge of the Arctic Expedition

1.
They included the following eleven photographs taken by the author prior to May 8, 1914: CMC Photo Nos. 37110, 37115, 37119, 37128, 37129, 37131, 37135, 37141, 37143, 37151, and 37164.

2.
The author's photographs of their arrival are: CMC Photo. Nos. 37123, 37134 (see Fig. 88), and 37157.

3.
The natives expected to trade with members of the Expedition.

4.
The author's photographs of the inland natives setting up their tents are: CMC Photo Nos. 37113, 37118, 37137, and 37156.

5.
The author photographed one such sled (CMC Photo No. 37124).

6.
The author's photograph of the Eskimo children playing at midnight is CMC No. 37116.

7.
See footnote 13, Chapter 6.

8.
Many Alaskan native women had small hand-operated sewing machines. The Expedition's sewing machine was probably a sturdier model.

9.
This is not the Pannigavlu (= Pannigabluk) who had travelled with Stefansson a few years earlier.

10.
The author is referring to the conflict between Stefansson and Dr. Anderson over the nature and extent of Dr. Anderson's authority, a conflict that surfaced first in Victoria

in early June 1913, then a month later at Nome, then erupted again in December 1913 and March 1914 at Collinson Point (Diubaldo, 1978, pp. 79-81, 84-86, 90-99).

11.
To see John Cox, who was fixing up a motor launch Stefansson had bought for Chipman and Cox to use when mapping the Mackenzie delta in the summer (Anderson, 1913-16, May 10, 1914).

12.
Also known as 'Johnny', he was the second of three sons of Aiyaka's wife Toglumunna. He should not be confused with the Kaiyutaq who was Brick Hopson (see footnote 12, Chapter 6).

13.
On Arey Island.

14.
Konganevik Point.

15.
Konganevik Point.

16.
Marsh Creek.

17.
This was Louis Pechette, who worked at Martin Point with Stefansson before the latter embarked on his ice trip in March 1914, then sought further work with the Southern Party (Anderson 1913-16, May 4 and 25, 1914). Late in June Pechette went west to

Point Barrow with Leffingwell and Capt. Nahmens (Anderson, 1913-16, June 24, 1914).

18.
Stefansson's original plans called for the Northern Party, under his command, to carry out geographic and oceanographic explorations north of Alaska and west of the already known Arctic Islands, while the Southern Party, under the direction of Dr. R. Anderson, was carrying out detailed scientific studies in the Coronation Gulf region. A month after he became separated from the ice-entrapped *Karluk*, its scientists, crew, and supplies off the north coast of Alaska, Stefansson sent a long report from Barrow to the Department of the Naval Service in Ottawa proposing that he pick up necessary supplies and equipment and proceed with his original exploration plans. The telegraphed reply from the Deputy Minister of the Naval Service, sent care of the RNWMP at Herschel Island via Dawson, Yukon, included the following statement "Your decision to pursue expedition as per original plans is approved" (Stefansson, 1921, p. 72). By mid-May, when Dr. Anderson learned of it upon his arrival at Herschel Island, Stefansson was somewhere northwest or north of Banks Island, and it was many months later before Stefansson received it.

19.
A supply of mail.

20.
From Arey Island.

Chapter 14. – Archaeological Investigations on Barter Island (I)

1.
These two wages were arranged by Dr. Anderson (Anderson, 1913-16, May 26, 1914). Curiously the author years later erred in stating they were $100 and $50 per month (Jenness, 1957, p. 178). Compare Aiyakuk's wage ($50 per month) with that of the author (about $42 per month). The author, of course, had food and clothing, such as they were, paid for by the government. The use of Aiyakuk's tent and *umiak* was included in the price agreed upon, as were the sewing and cooking services of his wife, Tuglumunna.

2.
Second son of Tuglumunna, also known as 'Johnny'.

3.
Dr. Anderson wrote Capt. Cottle of the *Belvedere* asking him to release Daniel Sweeney so that he could join the C.A.E. as mate and general utility man. Sweeney, an excellent sailor with 15 years experience along both the Alaskan and Canadian Arctic coastlines, and an efficient traveller and dog-driver, was willing to sign on at $65 per month (Anderson, 1913-16, May 28 and June 1, 1914).

4.
They took little with them but the author's personal outfit; food supplies, tents, and other equipment were to be collected at the cache left by Stefansson's ice party at Martin Point (Anderson, 1913-16, May 26, 1914).

5.
The author previously encountered Panni-gavlu (Pannigabluk) on April 27 and May 4 and 5 at Martin Point. Two weeks later she and her small son joined Wilkins, who was en route to Clarence Lagoon to get the *North Star* ready to sail to Banks Island as per Stefansson's instructions (Wilkins, 1913-16, June 11, 1914).

6.
A boy of about twelve years (Jenness, 1957, p. 191).

7.
The author photographed Aiyaka's summer and winter caches on the west end of Arey Island (CMC Photo No. 37122).

8.
Stefansson had left supplies at Martin Point when he headed north in late March. Dr. Anderson listed these supplies (Anderson, 1913-16, May 3, 1914) and later brought most of them back to Collinson Point, leaving but a small supply for the author (Anderson, 1913-16, May 24, 1914). This consisted of provisions (dried beans, sugar, cocoa, malted milk, and tea), as well as two tents, a stove, cooking and eating utensils, and for excavation work, a shovel, pick, and axe, all of which Ipanna and Kovun brought back from Martin Point on this occasion (Jenness, 1914i).

9.
The white lemming (Spec. No. 2448, NMNS) and the short-eared owl (Spec. No. 7886, NMNS) are two of three small mammal and more than 34 bird specimens collected by the author from Barter Island that are now in the National Collections of the CMN.

10.
See Appendix 4(B3).

11.
In July 1913, while the *Karluk* underwent repairs at Teller, near Port Clarence, for 13 days, the author and Henri Beuchat undertook local ethnological and archaeological investigations (Beuchat 1913a) on the tundra near the town. See data in Cameron and Ritchie (1923, pp. 3c, 15c-22c.)

12.
One was to Dr. Sapir in Ottawa reporting on the author's activities during the previous two months (Jenness, 1914c).

13.
'Stone' was the Eskimo Oyaraq (Jenness, 1957, p. 168).

14.
Sweeney took a letter and two skinned specimens from the author to Dr. Anderson, as well as a note dated May 29 listing birds and their Eskimo names seen by Aiyaka near the mouth of the Hulahula River (Anderson, 1913-16, June 1, 1914). The note is in the Jenness file (Anderson papers, CMN).

15.
The pomerine Jaeger (*Stercorarius pomarinus* (Temminck)) is a gull-like predatory sea bird, 20 to 23 inches long, comparable in size and somewhat in colour to the oldsquaw duck (*Clangula hyemalis*).

16.
Konganevik Pt.

17.
The author had observed the natives' improvident use of ammunition and coal oil (kerosene) along the north Alaskan coast during the previous eight months (Jenness, 1957, pp. 177, 182).

18.
In an attempt to speed up the rate of thawing and thus the excavation rate (Jenness, 1957, p. 189).

19.
A pectoral sandpiper, *Pisobia maculata*, of unstated sex, now Spec. No. 8797, CMN.

20.
"In spring loves are in harmony, in spring the birds marry." (Translation by Prof. R. Jeffreys.) The author appears to have been quoting from one of the classics he had studied at university.

21.
Dr. Anderson had earlier identified the *kupahloaluk* as *Calcarius lapponicus lapponicus*, the Lapland Longspur (Anderson, 1913-16, June 1, 1914). The author had sent him this Eskimo name for the bird on June 1 (see footnote 14, this chapter). The Lapland Longspur belongs to the sparrow family.

22.
This is part of a map drawn by the author for his archaeological notes on Barter Island.

The name Bernard Harbor was proposed by E. de K. Leffingwell (1919) in honour of Capt. Joseph Bernard, who wintered there in 1909-10; the harbour was unnamed when the author was there in 1914 so it is unlikely that the map was drawn before 1919. The original of this map is with the author's archaeological manuscript (Jenness, 1914j). The locations of the three sites shown on Figure 94 are based mainly on the locations shown on Plate 1 in Hall (1987).

23.
Iñukuk had been in charge of the Expedition's supplies left at Martin Point by Stefansson in late March (Anderson, 1913-16, May 3, 1914). His caretaking duties were no longer needed after Ipanna and Qovunna collected the residual supplies on May 31.

24.
Johansen, on his return from the ice party some weeks previous, had brought a letter for Wilkins from Stefansson with new instructions, details of which are recorded in Wilkins (1913-16, June 6, 1914). They included the statement that Stefansson would be glad to put Wilkins on the Expedition's pay roll. Wilkins was a Gaumont Co. employee at that time.

25.
The author expressed his sympathies to Wilkins over his change of plans (Wilkins, 1913-16, June 10, 1914).

26.
Natkusiak was to be paid $25 per month, and four of his five dogs (the fifth dog was too old) were to be purchased for $25 apiece for Wilkins' party (Anderson, 1913-16, June 10, 1914).

27.
There was a report of 200 to 300 lbs of mail cached somewhere south of Barrow and word of some mail lost or damaged by the sinking of a mail steamer (Anderson, 1913-16, June 6, 1914). The report was evidently false, however, for no such supply of mail ever materialized or was found to have been lost or damaged.

28.
Supplies purchased earlier by Stefansson from Duffy O'Connor at Demarcation Point were to be divided between the Southern and Northern parties at Herschel Island. (See also footnote 23, Chapter 16.)

29.
The whale had been caught by a brother-in-law of Charles Brower. Brower was probably the first white man to participate in the unusual form of whale hunting practiced by the northern Alaska Eskimos from the edge of the shore ice. He has described in detail his first such experience in 1883, south of Barrow (Brower, 1944?, pp. 39-51). Wilkins had hoped to capture the whale-hunting action on movie film.

30.
Capt. Nahmens had a special arrangement with Stefansson that he could spend six months of each year trapping foxes. He had expected to make a small fortune in this manner, but did not catch a single fox during the winter of 1913-14 and became disgusted with the country and restless and discontented. Dr. Anderson, therefore, considered it best to let him leave the Expedition (Anderson, 1913-16, June 24, 1914).

31.
A constant supply of fresh meat was required for both humans and dogs, and game was scarce around Collinson Point. Dr. Anderson had, therefore, sent Fred along with Crawford and Wilkins (when they were heading east to the *North Star*) to shoot as many seals, ducks, and geese as he could around Barter Island and to bring them back when Crawford returned from Duffy O'Connor's place at Demarcation Point (Anderson, 1913-16, June 10, 1914).

32.
Both a female Baird's sandpiper, *Pisobia bairdi*, and a red phalarope, *Phalaropus fulicarius*, of unstated sex, were collected by the author on this date. They are Spec. Nos. 8800 and 8802 respectively, in the National Collection, CMN.

33.
The exact location of this ancient settlement is not known, but it is believed to have been 1/2 to 1 mile east of the point of attachment of the sandspit. The settlement was obliterated many years ago during airport runway construction (Hall, 1987, p. 21.)

34.
A male duck hawk or peregrine falcon, *Falcoperegrinus anatum*, now Spec. No. 8791, CMN.

35.
A Stellar's eider duck (see also footnote 1, Chapter 15).

36.
A female, now Spec. No. 8799, CMN.

37.
The exact location of these sites is not known, but they are believed to have been located about 1 mile west of the point of attachment of the sandspit. The remains of the former settlement were removed for construction material during the building of a DEW-line station on Barter Island in the early 1950's (Hall, 1987, p. 1).

38.
This three-page typed letter with accompanying six pages of zoological notes is in the Jenness file (Anderson papers, CMN).

39.
This was house No. 11 on the author's sketch map and in his field notes (Jenness, 1914j) (see also Fig. 98).

40.
One of these specimens was a female semi-palmated sandpiper, *Ereunetes pusillus*, now Spec. No. 8801, CMN.

41.
The parasite species is listed in Appendix 4B3.

42.
Heading west to Collinson Point from their trip to Duffy O'Connor's place at Demarca-

tion Point for supplies. They took with them a letter dated June 17 and assorted zoological notes from the author, which are now in the Jenness file (Anderson papers, CMN). The zoological notes are also reproduced in Anderson (1913-16, June 18, 1914).

43.
'Hazeline' cream was a soothing ointment containing an alcoholic distillate from the witch hazel plant. The word 'Hazeline' was a registered Trade Mark (Burroughs Well come Co., 1934, p. 140). Some first-aid kits produced by this company contained tubes or jars of the 'Hazeline' products.

44.
From the description and artifacts listed in the author's field notes (Jenness, 1914j), this appears to be ruin No. 14.

45.
On Arey Island.

46.
Identified by Dr. Anderson as *Gavia arctica*, unstated sex, now Spec. No. 8815, CMN.

47.
A pectoral sandpiper (Anderson, 1913-16, July 13, 1914, CMN).

48.
Sterna paradisaea, now Spec. No. 8794, CMN.

Chapter 15. – Archaeological Investigations on Barter Island (II)

1.
This is about the easternmost known occurrence of this species of duck, which normally breeds in northeastern Siberia (Godfrey, 1966, p. 75). These two specimens, along with one skinned on June 16, are probably the three male specimens in the National Collection recorded as collected by the author June 29, 1914 (Spec. No. 8808, 8809, and 8810, CMN).

2.
The author collected two species for Johansen (Appendix 4B7).

3.
Red phalarope (*Phalaropus fulicarius*) (See Appendix 4A2, Spec. No. 8802, where the *augruak* is identified.)

4.
Two male harlequin ducks, *Mistrionicus histrionicus*, now Spec. No. 8811 and 8812, CMN. The author also collected a female pintail duck, *Dafila acuta*, Spec. No. 8813, CMN. The Eskimo name for the pintail duck is *kurugak* according to a handwritten note dated June 2, 1914, with Jenness (1914f).

5.
The author undoubtedly had heard Leffingwell's views from conversations with him at Collinson Point, and Stefansson's from conversations as well. See also Stefansson (1913a, pp. 97-98).

6.
Lapland Longspur (*kupahloaluk*) (see diary entry of June 6, 1914).

7.
They were on Arey Island, which the author thought was a sandspit.

8.
The author typed a letter to his classics professor (von Zedlitz) in Wellington, New Zealand, on this date (Jenness, 1914e). It and four later letters to the professor are in the Hocken Library at the University of Otago, Dunedin, New Zealand.

9.
Two spectacled eider ducks (*Arctonetta fischeri*), one male, one female, collected by the author on this date, are in the National Collection (Spec. No. 8806, 8807, CMN).

10.
The author sent Ipanna back to the main camp on Barter Island, probably to continue skinning the specimens they had collected.

11.
For the location of house ruin No. 2 see Figure 97.

12.
Brenthis frigga improba, now in the National Collection (see Appendix 4B1).

13.
An arsenic compound was used to kill parasitic insects on the specimens.

14.
Arey Island.

15.
Natkusiak had no further need of it as he was heading east with Wilkins to the *North Star* to prepare for their voyage in search of Stefansson.

16.
The Arctic loon usually has two eggs (Godfrey, 1966, p. 12).

17.
Oviñaq = brown lemming (Dr. R.M. Anderson note in Jenness, 1913-14, July 3, 1914).

18.
Four species were represented: *Eurymus hecla glacialis* McLach.; *Brenthis polaris* Bdv.; *Brenthis frigga alaskensis* Lehm; and *Brenthis frigga improba* Butler. In all, 44 specimens of butterflies and moths collected by the author on Barter Island and 24 collected around Coronation Gulf in 1915-16 were placed in the the National Collection

of Insects, Ottawa (Gibson, 1920). (See Appendix 4B1.)

19.
A jaeger or Arctic skua.

20.
Towards the southwest end of Arey Island.

21.
A Bijou typewriter, which Dr. Anderson tried to repair later (Anderson, 1913-16, July 26, 1914).

22.
Probably Arctic loons (*Gavia arctica pacifica*) one male, the other of unstated sex (now Spec. No. 8816 and 8817, CMN) and a female parasitic jaeger (*isungaq*), (*Stercorarius parasiticus*), (now Spec. No. 8795, CMN). The local Eskimos used the name *isungaq* (or *i-sung-ok*) for all species of jaeger (Anderson 1913-16, June 1, 1914).

23.
Both weasel specimens are now in the National Collection (see Appendix 4C).

24.
Arey Island.

25.
The author's sketches of some of the artifacts from the eastern ruins are in his typed manuscript (Jenness, 1914j).

26.
At the southwest end of Arey Island.

27.
Capt. Nahmens' cache was at his cabin on Anderson Point, about 10 miles east of the Expedition's camp at Collinson Point (Anderson, 1913-16, July 13, 1914).

28.
This should be 11 a.m., for they left Barter Island at midnight (Anderson, 1913-16, July 13, 1914).

29.
These were later named Carter and Marsh creeks (Leffingwell, 1919, pp. 94, 97; Orth, 1967, pp. 189, 624). The author wrote *Kuvralivruk* for Carter Creek on his sketchmap (Fig. 84).

30.
The author brought 31 bird skins, two weasel skins, and several birds' eggs from Barter Island for Dr. Anderson, and a num-

ber of butterfly, moth, and other insect specimens for Johansen. The bird and animal specimens are listed, most with their Eskimo names and collection dates, in Anderson (1913-16, July 13, 1914). See also Appendix 4.

31.
Capt. Nahmens later went from Flaxman Island to Point Barrow with Leffingwell and Louis Pechette in July in Leffingwell's dory. Dr. Anderson had found Capt. Nahmens rather "young and inexperienced for the job," though "his work has been faithful and energetic" (Anderson, 1913-16, June 23, 30, 1914). Capt. Nahmens was only 29 whereas Capt. Peter Bernard was 57 (Chipman, 1913-16, Oct. 31, 1913).

32.
A Winchester .30-30 valued at $15 (Anderson, 1913-16, July 14, 1914).

33.
To return to Barter Island with his stepfather Aiyakuk (Anderson, 1913-16, July 14, 1914).

34.
A 20-gauge shotgun, 50 shells and reloading tools (valued at $10), 1000 .30-30 shells (valued at $35), and 4 traps ($4) (Anderson, 1913-16, July 14, 1914).

35.
A small skin boat to carry their provisions back to "Ten mile Point" (Anderson Point), where they had left Aiyakuk's whaleboat. Añutisiak accompanied them to bring the small boat back to Collinson Point (Anderson, 1913-16, July 14, 1914).

36.
Arey Island.

37.
Oliktok Point, just east of the mouth of the Colville River.

38.
Teriglu reached Collinson Point on July 22 and was paid off as the author requested, the artifacts and wages being worth $50 of goods (Anderson, 1913-16, July 22, 1914).

39.
These two bird specimens are now in the National Collection in Ottawa (Spec. No. 10323 and 10324, CMN). (See also Appendix 4A).

40.
Some of these are in the National Collection in Ottawa (see Appendix 4B).

41. The *tulik* is a yellow-billed loon (*Gavia adamsi*); the *mallere* is the Pacific loon (*Gavia arctica pacifica*).

42.
Arey Island.

43.
Probably a Baird's sandpiper (*Pisobia bairdi*), now in the National Collection (Spec. No. 10322, CMN). (See Appendix 4A).

44.
They were possibly long-billed dowitchers (*Limnodromus griseus scolopaceus*), which the *Nunamiut* Eskimo called *Kilyaktalik* (Irving, 1958, p. 74).

45.
Hall (1987, p. 258), after a thorough study of the author's Barter Island artifacts and notes, concluded that "most of the features were built and utilized between 550 and 400 years ago," that is, between approximately the years 1450 and 1600.

46.
Hall (1987) reported in detail on the author's entire collection of Barter Island material.

47.
Arey Island.

48.
Anderson Point (Jenness, 1957, p. 212). This point was named after Dr. R.M. Anderson by Leffingwell (1919, p. 93).

49.
Fred Ailuat, the Eskimo hired at Nome as assistant on the *Mary Sachs*, was also paid off on this date. His year with the Expedition was up and he wanted to return to Nome, going west in Teriglu's whaleboat. He was paid $240 for his year's service (Anderson, 1913-16, July 25, 1914).

50.
The author was eager to get started on his main scientific project, the study of the Copper Eskimos. However, when the *Alaska* two years later stopped briefly at Kamarkak (probably the locality now called Komakuk Beach, near the Alaska-Canada boundary) to let off Sweeney's wife (Anderson, 1913-16, Aug. 3, 1916), he received a large box

of archaeological specimens collected by Aiyakuk at and near Barter Island in 1915. Some of the artifacts obtained on that occasion are mentioned in Jenness (1914j, pp. 54-55).

51.
The author was "…hoping to get there ahead of us and sort out some of the stuff there"

(Anderson, 1913-16, July 26, 1914), and Ipanna was to take the $50 owed him as pay in goods from Duffy O'Connor's supplies (Anderson, 1913-16, July 25, 1914).

Chapter 16. – Through Rough Ice to Herschel Island

1.
The author was to sort Duffy's supplies for division among the Expedition's three schooners, and Ipanna was to receive some supplies to complete his payment for work with the author on Barter Island (Anderson, 1913-16, July 25, 1914).

2.
This is now known as Jago Lagoon, between Manning Point and Martin Point, inside the offshore barriers east of Barter Island (Orth, 1967, p. 469).

3.
The author had trekked into the high land south of Tapkaurak Lagoon, about 7 miles west of the *Polar Bear* winter quarters near Humphrey Point (Anderson, 1913-16, July 27, 1914).

4.
On July 6, 1914 (see author's diary entry for July 7, 1914).

5.
The cache had been left by Stefansson when he started his ice trip on March 22. The author brought back two saws, some coal oil and cans, and some boxes (Anderson, 1913-16, July 27, 1914).

6.
A red notebook containing the original meteorological records of the Southern Party, August 11, 1913 - August 15, 1916, is in the Anderson papers, CMN.

7.
Such activities by the men on the *Mary Sachs* would have been totally contrary to the official government orders, which stated: "The members of the party will not engage in any private trading or make any private collections of specimens…"(Desbarats, 1913). This was later restated by Desbarats (1914a) to Stefansson: "The general rule which obtains on all Government expeditions is that the members of the party are en-

gaged solely on Government business and any objects which they obtain belong to the expedition and to the Government." Both letters are reproduced in Anderson (1913-16, Aug. 7, 1914).

8.
Bottled tablets of saccharin manufactured by Burroughs Wellcome Co. Ltd.

9.
Capt. P. Bernard was to take the *Mary Sachs* east to the Cape Krusenstern area, unload its supplies for the Southern Party, then proceed northwest to Banks Island as far as Cape Kellett. (A copy of Stefansson's general instructions to Capt. Bernard, dated April 4, 1914, is in the Bernard file, Anderson papers, CMN.)

10.
Wilkins, on Stefansson's instructions (which are quoted in Wilkins, 1913-16, June 6, 1914), had taken the 10-ton gasoline schooner *North Star* (purchased earlier by Stefansson from 'Capt.' Matt Andreasen) from Clarence Bay, just east of the Alaska-Canada boundary, to Herschel Island. He was to see that the schooner was equipped with sufficient supplies for 2 years and then proceed to the northwest coast of Banks Island, to photograph the Eskimos there and rendezvous with Stefansson's party (Stefansson, 1921, p. 125). Wilkins arrived at Herschel Island on July 24 and awaited the arrival of Dr. Anderson and the mail from Fort McPherson and Nome before heading for Banks Island (Wilkins, 1913-16, July 24, 27, 1914). With him were Aarnout Castel, Billy Natkusiak, and Pannigabluk and her young boy (Anderson, 1913-16, Aug. 1, 1914).

11.
The author's report was abridged in the Summary Report of the Geological Survey for the calendar year 1914 (1915, p. 174). This publication (p. 176) also recorded the receipt from the author of a 262-page manu-

script "Eskimo Ethnological Notes" (MS. 58), the present whereabouts of which is unknown.

12.
On board the *Mary Sachs*.

13.
A two-page handwritten letter to Dr. E. Sapir in Ottawa, telling him of his archaeological work on Barter Island (Jenness, 1914d).

14.
Spelled Sunblade in the diary, this was John Sundblad (Anderson, 1913-16, Aug. 1, 1914). Sunblad and McConnell had come ashore from the *Anna Olga* at the sand bar outside Martin Point and walked along it until they came to the entrance of Jago Lagoon. Soon afterwards they were picked up by the author (McConnell, 1913-14, Aug. 1, 1914).

15.
Withrop Brooks had been looking after the stock of goods at Duffy O'Connor's for the Expedition, while collecting specimens for the Museum of Comparative Zoology, Cambridge, Massachusetts (Anderson, 1913-16, Aug. 1, 1914).

16.
Sunblad and McConnell told Dr. Anderson that if his two ships could reach the lead they would probably have clear sailing to Herschel Island. After about 7 1/2 hours of bucking the ice the *Alaska* finally reached the open lead at 4:15 a.m. and headed east (Anderson, 1913-16, Aug. 1, 1914).

17.
The author probably meant that a boat brought the Martin Point items *from* the shore.

18.
The mountains visible from the schooner are now known as the Romanzof Mountains, at the eastern end of the Brooks Range.

19.
During his evening watch the author wrote a five-page letter to Professor R.R. Marett at Oxford, about his activities since the winter. He stated he was sending a copy of his diary to his parents in New Zealand, who would forward it through a friend in London to the professor. The author then added that although his diary was private, "I have carefully refrained from anything personal against members of the expedition or anything of that nature" (Jenness, 1914g).

20.
One named Frank, the other a boy. Both planned to return to Humphrey Point with Ipanna (Anderson, 1913-16, Aug. 3, 1914). Iñukuk had taken care of the Expedition's supplies at Martin Point for a time after Stefansson left on his ice trip.

21.
Duffy O'Connor's camp was located about 3 to 4 miles west of the Alaska-Yukon boundary, a mile from the west end of the spit (Anderson, 1913-16, Aug. 4, 1914). On a modern topographic map the west end of the spit is about 7 miles from the international boundary, so Dr. Anderson's distances may have been incorrect; or perhaps the sandspit has extended westward since 1914.

22.
The *Polar Bear* went east to hunt whales once it broke free from its winter ice-trap near Humphrey Point (Anderson, 1913-16, Aug. 6, 1914). Brooks chose to leave that vessel as well as the Arctic at this time, so took passage west on the *Anna Olga*.

23.
Dr. Anderson, in response to instructions from Stefansson (1914d), asked the author to make an inventory of O'Connor's supplies and equipment, for division between the Southern Party and the new Northern Party Stefansson had organized.

24.
Dr. Anderson listed the food and supplies taken on board the *Alaska* (Anderson 1913-16, Aug. 4, 1914).

25.
This was the only record of the supplies Stefansson bought from O'Connor. The author's 4-page list is in the Inventory File, Anderson papers, CMN.

26.
This international boundary had been established by survey just two years before, in 1912 (Leffingwell, 1919, pp. 86-87).

27.
The author's diary has a blank space here suggesting that he had intended to write in the hour they turned off the engines.

28.
Chipman was the first to reach Herschel Island by boat from the Mackenzie River in 1914. Arriving at 1 a.m. his boat was quickly followed during the night by a stream of other boats, including one containing Cox (Chipman, 1913-16, Aug. 5, 1914).

29.
Stefansson had journeyed early in January with Inspector Phillips and Constable Parsons of the Royal North-West Mounted Police from Herschel Island to Fort McPherson, a Hudson's Bay Company post on the Peel River (Stefansson, 1921, p. 104).

30.
The books included works of Goethe, Heine, and Schiller, according to a note on the inside back cover of the second volume of the author's diary. They had been mailed from New Zealand. The instruments came from Ottawa.

31.
The *Ruby* was unable to get to Herschel Island in 1914 because of adverse ice conditions.

32.
The Herschel Island detachment at that time consisted of four men: Inspector J.W. Phillips, Corporal W.A. Johnson, and Constables J. Parsons and A. Lamont. Dr. Anderson reported that only Johnson and Parsons were at Herschel Island when he arrived on August 5, Inspector Phillips and Constable Lamont having gone to Fort McPherson and not yet having returned (Anderson, 1913-16, Aug. 5, 1914), but one of them had evidently returned just before the author reached Herschel Island. The fourth arrived before August 13, for the author on that date again mentions that there were three present, and by then Corporal Johnson had left on the *Herman* to act as customs officer for any trading activities it might conduct at Baillie Island or elsewhere in Canadian waters.

33.
These were a few ethnological specimens from Darnley Bay and vicinity, given to Dr. Anderson by Ilavinirk (Anderson, 1913-16, Aug. 7, 1914).

34.
These instructions were in a letter dated April 30, 1914, from G.J. Desbarats (Deputy Minister, Department of the Naval Service) to V. Stefansson, which ended with the following statement "... the main point to be born in mind is that the work of the southern party should be carried out as originally proposed and that it should not be weakened for the purpose of organizing another northern party" (Desbarats, 1914b).

35.
Stefansson's trip north from Martin Point in search of unknown land, which he commenced on March 22, 1914.

36.
Wilkins was 'on loan' to the Expedition from the Gaumont Co., Limited, London, England, but was still on the company's payroll and thus responsible primarily to it. He had received two letters from the company asking him to return to England as soon as possible, so his decision to stay with the Canadian Arctic Expedition forced him to break his contract with that company. He stayed with the Expedition because he recognized that he was its most suitable member at Herschel Island to take charge of the relief ship searching for, and taking provisions to, Stefansson's little party on Banks Island (Wilkins, 1913-16, Aug. 6, 1914).

37.
Wilkins was not enthusiastic about taking the *Mary Sachs*, though it was larger than the *North Star* (Chipman, 1913-16, Aug. 9, 1914).

38.
For Dr. Anderson's views on the intent of Capt. Peter Bernard, see the author's comments on July 28.

39.
A copy of this document is reproduced in Anderson (1913-16, Aug. 8, 1914).

40.
The essence of Stefansson's instructions to Capt. Bernard was in a letter from Stefansson to Dr. Anderson (Anderson, 1913-16, Apr. 23, 1914). Capt. Bernard was to deliver 10 tons of supplies near Cape Krusenstern for Dr. Anderson's party then bring the *Mary Sachs* to Banks Island for a 2-year stay.

41.
Early in 1913 Stefansson asked Capt. Theodore Pedersen to find a vessel on the Pacific Coast that could be purchased for the Expedition. Pedersen selected the 125-foot brigantine *Karluk* in preference to the smaller *Elvira* (86 feet) or *Jeannette* (115

feet), even though it was the oldest of the three whaling ships (28 years old), and took it from San Francisco to Esquimalt, on Vancouver Island, where it underwent considerable refitting. Capt. Bob Bartlett shortly thereafter replaced Capt. Pedersen, who promptly sailed the *Elvira* to the Arctic for some San Francisco fur traders. That ship got caught in the Arctic ice and sank near Humphrey Point in September 1913. Capt. Pedersen then travelled by sled over the mountains to Fort Yukon and from there back to Seattle, from where he sailed in charge of the *Herman* in the spring of 1914.

42.
John F. Allan was responsible for much of the pre-sailing arrangements of the *Karluk* in Esquimalt, including its loading. He resigned (he may have been dismissed for incompetence (McKinlay, 1976, p. 12)) just before it sailed, however, in the spring of 1913, and was replaced by Alexander ('Sandy') Anderson, who perished trying to reach Wrangel Island in February 1914, soon after the vessel sank.

43.
From Emma Harbour, some 200 miles southwest of East Cape, Siberia (Bartlett and Hale, 1916, p. 280). While trading south of East Cape before going to Herschel Island, Capt. Pedersen heard that Capt. Bartlett was at Emma Harbour and sailed the *Herman* there to pick him up.

44.
Spelled Wrangell in the diaries of both the author and Dr. Anderson and in many newspaper accounts at that time.

45.
The four in the group that struck off for land on February 5, 1914, three weeks after the ship sank, were: Dr. Alistair F. Mackay (surgeon), James Murray (oceanographer), Henri Beuchat (anthropologist), and S. Stanley Morris (seaman) (McKinlay, 1976, pp. 77-79). All four perished before reaching Wrangel Island.

46.
Kataktovik accompanied Capt. Bartlett only to East Cape. Bartlett made the journey to Emma Harbour, in Plover Bay, with Baron Kleist and a Mr. Caraieff (Bartlett and Hale, 1916, p. 268).

47.
According to Capt. Bartlett, it was too late in the season to cross Bering Strait safely by

sled and too early for boats. He expected to be able to get passage on a ship from Plover Bay long before he could cross safely from East Cape (Bartlett and Hale, 1916, p. 264), and events proved him correct.

48.
As Nome was iced in when they got near it, the *Herman* took Capt. Bartlett to St. Michaels, from where he telegraphed the news of the *Karluk* disaster (Bartlett and Hale, 1916, p. 281).

49.
Revised instructions for O'Neill from Dr. R.W. Brock, Director, Geological Survey of Canada, were enclosed with a letter dated November 22, 1913, to Dr. Anderson (Brock, 1913).

50.
Wilkins and Blue went with Billy Annette to Kay Point where Annette had a camp. He was the former owner of the *Edna*, a speedy 30-foot launch Stefansson had purchased for the use of the Southern Party topographers. Dr. Anderson, however, decided that the *Edna* should go with the *Mary Sachs* to help place caches and beacons along the coast of Banks Island (Anderson, 1913-16, Aug. 9, 1914), a decision severely criticized later by Stefansson (1921, pp. 273-274).

51.
Dr. Anderson paid off three men at Herschel Island, all originally from the ill-fated *Elvira*, who had been hired in the spring at a rate of $2.50 per hour for temporary work with the Southern Party. They included the cook William Sullivan, assistant engineer Ralph Addison, and cook W.J. 'Levi' Baur. Sullivan then joined the *Herman*, Addison the *Belvedere*, and Baur went as cook for Wilkins on the *Mary Sachs* (Anderson, 1913-16, Aug. 11, 1914).

52.
James 'Cockney' Sullivan, a 28-year-old from London, England. He had been cabin boy on the *Herman*, that position now being filled by the departing cook, William Sullivan. 'Cockney's' wages as cook were to be $65 per month (Anderson, 1913-16, Aug. 11, 1914).

53.
Mike was hired at $30 per month, which was more than any other Eskimo on Dr. Anderson's Southern Party was paid, because of his greater efficiency (Anderson, 1913-16, Aug. 14, 1914).

54.
Chipman's lists would complete the inventorying of the three ships, because the author and Wilkins made lists of the supplies on the *Mary Sachs* and *North Star* on August 8. Dr. Anderson wanted complete lists of all supplies and equipment carried on all three vessels "... in order that the Government might have full knowledge of how the three ships of the Expedition were outfitted, so that there may be no apprehension or fear that any of the vessels have gone off insufficiently provisioned..." (Anderson, 1913-16, Aug. 13, 1914). Dr. Anderson mailed a copy of the completed inventories of the above stores and the reserve stores left with the RNWMP at Herschel Island to the Department of the Naval Service in Ottawa and also left a copy with the police at Herschel Island (Anderson, 1913-16, Aug. 13, 1914).

55.
Harry C. Slate (spelled Slade in the diary) had brought the schooner, said to be 50 or 60 years old, to the Arctic from San Francisco in 1912, wintered that year at Herschel Island, the next at Baillie Island. On the journey mentioned on this date, he had made the 275-mile trip from Baillie Island in 7 days, alone, with no life boat, his schooner so rotten as to be scarcely seaworthy (Anderson, 1913-16, Aug. 10, 1914).

56.
Capt. Louis Lane had headed east to catch whales once the *Polar Bear* got free of its winter entrapment near Humphrey Point, Alaska. Short on fuel, he had obtained 600 gallons of distillate from Wilkins at Herschel Island on the strength of a letter from Stefansson. This he promised to repay the next year (Wilkins, 1913-16, July 28, 1914) but failed to do so. He did, however, tow a whale carcass in to Cape Bathurst for dog-food for the Expedition as repayment (see author's entry for Aug. 22).

57.
Bill Seymour was second mate, Billy Mogg first mate to Capt. Louis Lane at the time. A detailed account of the killing of one of these two whales, together with photographs of the incident, appears in Bockstoce (1977, pp. 11-14).

58.
After Wilkins took charge of the *Mary Sachs* all supplies for the Southern Party were removed from it and exchanged for the Northern Party's supplies on the *North Star*. The author on this date wrote a short note to his former Oxford classmate Marius Barbeau in Ottawa, telling him briefly of his work on Barter Island and of the imminent departure of Wilkins (Jenness, 1914h).

59.
Wilkins had intended to leave in the morning, but his engineer (Crawford) and cook (Baur) were in no condition to work, having earlier purchased a case of whisky from the *Herman*. O'Neill photographed the departure of the *Mary Sachs* (CMC Photo No. 38433). Accompanying Wilkins were Capt. Peter Bernard (sailing master), James Crawford (engineer), Charles Thomsen (seaman), Mrs. Jennie Thomsen (seamstress) and their little daughter Annie, Billy Natkusiak (seaman and hunter), and 'Levi' Baur (cook). Also on board were Mrs. Storkersen and her child (Anderson, 1913-16, Aug. 11, 1914). Pannigabluk and her son were not on board, for she had been paid off in provisions at Herschel Island by Dr. Anderson for her work at Martin Point and on the *North Star* (Anderson, 1913-16, Aug. 8, 1914). She rejoined the Northern Party after Stefansson reached Herschel Island in August 1915 (Noice, 1924, p. 38), however, and Wilkins photographed her on May 1, 1916 near Minto Inlet, Victoria Island.

60.
The crew of the *Herman* was anxious to get east to the whaling grounds, for whalebone (more exactly, baleen) from the bowhead whales had risen temporarily to about $2.75 per pound and was more profitable than trading for furs (Chipman, 1913-16, Aug. 10-17, 1914).

61.
This was Peder L. Pedersen, whom Stefansson had engaged as engineer to put the launch *Edna* into condition and run for Chipman (not Cox) in the Mackenzie delta survey. Neither he nor the boat gave satisfactory service (Chipman, 1913-16, Aug. 22, 1914; Stefansson, 1921, pp. 109-110, 273).

62.
The author did not complete this sentence.

63.
The Hudson's Bay Company's post and associated community, about 80 miles south of the mouth of the Mackenzie River. Now spelled Fort McPherson.

64.
James 'Cockney' Sullivan.

65.
Ice conditions along the north coast of Alaska did, in fact, prevent the *Ruby* from reaching Herschel Island in 1914.

66.
The fourth member of the detachment, Corporal Johnson, who Wilkins discovered was originally from Tasmania (Wilkins, 1913-16, July 24, 1914), had gone on board the *Herman* on Aug. 11 to serve as a customs officer for any trading this U.S. vessel might carry out while in Canadian waters (Chipman, 1913-16, Aug. 10-17, 1914).

67.
Chipman was making copies of the *Mary Sachs'* inventory for Dr. Anderson and the author was to do the same for the *North Star* inventory. Dr. Anderson wanted to ensure that his Southern Party had as adequate and suitable supplies as conditions permitted before he headed east from Herschel Island. Some provisions were simply not available, but he had been hoping the *Ruby* would arrive from the west with both the mail and the provisions he had ordered and was delaying the departure for that reason. Once the inventories and copying of ships' papers for the *Mary Sachs*, *Alaska*, and *North Star* were completed, however, he delayed no further (Anderson, 1913-16, Aug. 14, 1914).

68.
The cook, James Sullivan, was acquired from the *Herman* at this time. However, he had served on the *Belvedere* before becom-

ing cabin boy on the *Herman* (Anderson, 1913-16, Aug. 11, 1914).

69.
This other man, identified simply as Phillips by Chipman (1913-16, Aug. 10-17, 1914) was W.G. Phillips, the Hudson's Bay Company employee who had brought Geological Survey supplies to the Expedition at Herschel Island on the small Hudson's Bay Company schooner from Fort McPherson (Anderson, 1913-16, Aug. 6, 1914). Phillips later (1918-1921) became manager of the company's trading post at Bernard Harbour (called Fort Bacon and then Fort Thomson when he was there) (Hudson's Bay Company Archives, Winnipeg, Manitoba, A.74/45).

70.
The waves "pounded her bottom out," but because the vessel was considered almost valueless no effort was made to save it (Anderson, 1913-16, Aug. 14, 1914).

71.
The 420-ton, steam-whaler *Belvedere* had far more power than the much smaller, 50-ton *Alaska*.

72.
Louis Olesen had been hired by Stefansson at Nome in July 1913 for the *Alaska* (Stefansson, 1921, p. 109). When Capt. Nahmens quit the Expedition in mid-July, Olesen expected to be put in charge of either the *Alaska* or the *North Star*. When that did not take place, he decided to end his employment with the Expedition (Chipman, 1913-16, Aug. 10-17, 1914).

Chapter 17. – On to Coronation Gulf

1.
Olaf Swenson (spelled Swanson in the diary), owner of the little trading schooner *The King and Winge*, had expected to reach Herschel Island with provisions and supplies from Seattle for Capt. Cottle and the *Belvedere*, but had been delayed through going to Wrangel Island to rescue the survivors of the *Karluk* (see footnote 25, Chapter 12). As a result Capt. Cottle changed his plans for further whale hunting and headed west (Chipman, 1913-16, Aug. 10-17, 1914).

2.
Cox wanted to be sure that the engine on the *North Star* was in condition for the trip to Coronation Gulf.

3.
These were Aqoyaq, Seputiatoq, and Unalina (Jenness, 1923a, pp. B33-B34, B37).

4.
The owner of the ill-fated schooner *Alice Stofen*. (See author's diary entry for Aug. 10, 1914 and footnote 55, Chapter 16.)

5.
Captain Roald Amundsen navigated the little 47-ton converted herring-boat *Gjoa* through Canada's Northwest Passage between 1903 and 1906, the first man to cross northern Canada by boat from east to west (*Encyclopedia Britannica*, 1982, vol. 13, p. 258). Stefansson met him at Herschel Is-

land during the summer of 1906 (Stefansson, 1913a, p. 3). A photograph of the ruins of the house Amundsen occupied 1905-1906 appears in Stefansson (1913a, p. 36).

6.
The author took three photographs showing an Eskimo man in his kayak at Shingle Point (CMC Photo Nos. 37132, 37133, 37162) and four other photographs of parts of the Eskimo settlement there (CMC Photo Nos. 37130, 37136, 37138, and 37140). Photo No. 37140 shows Dr. Anderson and Cox bartering with the natives for fish.

7.
Several fish nets were set along the outer edge of the spit at right angles to the beach. One contained 22 fish at the time. Great numbers were drying on poles in the settlement, and two women were busy cutting and cleaning others. Herrings *qaqtuk* or *tipuk* seemed the most numerous, but there were also connies (Fr. *inconnu*)(Esk. name *sieraq*), whitefish — *ekalusaq*, and salmon-trout *ekallukpit*. [D.J.]

8.
The 43-ton *Penelope* was one of a number of small schooners that entered the Arctic waters in 1900 or later for commercial whaling and trading. It remained in the Arctic and in 1904 was sold to a group of Eskimos at Herschel Island. It was wrecked at Shingle Point in September 1907 (Bockstoce, 1977, pp. 118-119). Bockstoce (1988b, p. 232) observed the wreckage there in 1984 and remarked that it had been the only Eskimo-owned commercial whaling vessel.

9.
Most of the dozen or so Eskimo families camped there were actually strangers to Dr. Anderson, but he knew one family well (Anderson, 1913-16, Aug. 19, 1914), having met them while he was on the 1908-1912 Stefansson-Anderson Expedition.

10.
Dr. Anderson purchased about 250 lbs dried fish, 60 lbs fresh fish, and 20 lbs of caribou meat, as well as flour, biscuits, bar soap, and cloth. The fish, almost all whitefish (Anderson, 1913-16, Aug. 19, 1914), were food for the many dogs with the Expedition.

11.
A general term for inland natives. For a discussion of these people and a map showing their general location at that time, see Stefansson (1913a, p. 282; map in back of book).

12.
For $13,000 Stefansson obtained a considerable amount of provisions and trading goods from Matt Andreasen, as well as the little gasoline-powered schooner *North Star*. The boat and most of the supplies had been located at Clarence Bay, a few miles east of the Alaska-Yukon Territory boundary. A partial listing of the supplies obtained from Andreasen is in the "Inventory" file (Anderson papers, CMN).

13.
As Stefansson had bought all of Matt Andreasen's supplies these now belonged to the Canadian Arctic Expedition.

14.
Dr. Anderson reported passing the *Polar Bear*, which was going west, about 9 a.m. on this date (Anderson, 1913-16, Aug. 20, 1914) when the *Alaska* was off Pullen Island. As the *Alaska* was some miles ahead of the *North Star*, the timing suggests that the author mistook the *Polar Bear*, which was two-masted, for the *Herman*, which was three-masted. As Dr. Anderson had sailed on the *Herman* in 1910 (Stefansson, 1913a, p. 436), he is not likely to have misidentified the ship. Alternatively, both whaling ships may have been in that region on the same day. The *Polar Bear* had been seen near Baillie Island on August 10, and the *Herman* had headed east from Herschel Island on August 11 (Chipman, 1913-16, Aug. 10-17, 1914); both were seeking pot-head whales. Photographs of both the *Herman* and the *Polar Bear* are shown in Bockstoce (1977, pp. 100 and 109).

15.
Dr. Anderson attempted to retrieve this sled a few months later, after the *Alaska* became ice-bound at Baillie Island, but was turned back by adverse snow conditions (Anderson, 1913-16, Nov. 1-8, 1914).

16.
See footnote 56, Chapter 16.

17.
The *Teddy Bear* was a 13-ton gasoline schooner from Nome, Alaska, captained by Joseph Bernard. It is pictured in Stefansson (1913a, p. 336).

18.
In addition to Nauyakvuk (or Nauyavuk) there were four other natives: Tashawanna (wife of Nauyakvuk), John Angasinauk, his wife Betty Aganvuk, and daughter (more probably granddaughter, as the author states later on this same date) Violet Mamayauk (Anderson, 1913-16, Aug. 21, 914).

19.
Capt. J. Bernard gave Dr. Anderson a sketch map of the harbour (Chipman, 1913-16, Aug. 21, 1914), which proved very helpful, for the harbour had two entrances, but only one had a channel with sufficient depth to allow passage of the Expedition's ships. This is the first mention of the geographic feature later to be named Bernard Harbour.

20.
Capt. J. Bernard sold his collection of some 3000 Eskimo artifacts from Coronation Gulf to the University of Pennsylvania (Macbeth, 1923).

21.
On the evening of August 19, 1914, Wilkins left two letters (dated August 17 and 19) for Dr. Anderson with the natives at Baillie Island. Their contents are included in Anderson (1913-16, Aug. 21, 1914).

22.
Capt. Bernard brought this letter to Baillie Island. Of it Dr. Anderson wrote, "Mr. Wilkins' letter, written from off the Smoking Mountains, Franklin Bay, stated that the *Mary Sachs* was doing much better than he had anticipated at Baillie Island, and they were running very well under sail with one propellor" (Anderson, 1913-16, Aug. 21, 1914). The letter, however, was not reproduced in Dr. Anderson's field notes, nor is it among his papers.

23.
Dr. Anderson hired Silas Palaiyak at Herschel Island shortly before leaving for Coronation Gulf, though Palaiyak's sister Unalina had tried to dissuade her brother from leaving the island (Anderson, 1913-16, Aug. 14, 1914). He was needed now to help spell the three tired members of the *North Star*. Palaiyak, then 21 years old (Jenness, 1923a, p. B33), was the adopted son of the Mackenzie River Eskimos Ilavinirk and Mamayauk; all three had worked with Dr. Anderson during his 1908-1912 expedition (Stefansson, 1913a, p. 131).

24.
The whale meat was needed for dog-food.

25.
The only young girl at Baillie Island then was Violet Mamayauk (Anderson, 1913-16, Aug. 21, 1914). Her photograph, taken by G.H. Wilkins two years later (on July 26, 1916; CMC Photo No. 51337), appears in Stefansson (1921, p. 389); a drawing based on the same photograph appears in Jenness (1957, p. 115) to portray "Aiva," an attractive Alaskan woman. Wilkins also photographed Violet Mamayauk with her mother on the same day (CMC Photo Nos. 51338, 51338, and 51340).

26.
This 158-ft. bark, probably the largest whaling ship to operate in the western Arctic, ran hard aground onto the rocky shore at Cape Parry under full sail and engine power in a dense fog (Stefansson, 1913a, p. 120; photo facing p. 150) on August 12, 1906. The ship's crew abandoned her and sailed in whaleboats 360 miles west to Herschel Island where they found another vessel, the *Charles Hanson*, and left the Arctic on it (Bockstoce, 1977, p. 90). Capt. Charles Klengenberg later pirated timber from the wrecked vessel to repair his scow in Darnley Bay and convert it to a schooner (MacInnes, 1932, p. 266). A cabin built alongside the wreck of the *Alexander* housed Dr. Anderson and a native companion Pikaluk briefly in the winter of 1909-10 (Stefansson, 1913a, pp. 144-145).

27.
A small house at the bottom of the bay, built by a whaling ship's crew about 1897 served as the headquarters and storehouse for Stefansson's and Dr. Anderson's scientific collections for three years (1909-1911), although they spent less than three months there during that period. In addition to Palaiyak, Stefansson was accompanied by Billy Natkusiak and Pannigabluk (Stefansson, 1913a, pp. 125-126).

28.
Wilkins reached Cape Parry the night of August 20. He wanted to sail for Banks Island from there, the night being clear, but Mrs. Storkerson, whose husband was with Stefansson, wanted to be taken to her father, Capt. Klengenberg, who was living near Cape Lyons, so Wilkins headed east across Darnley Bay the next day. Unsuccessful in

finding Klengenberg, he sailed from Cape Lyon to Nelson Head on Banks Island on August 22 (Wilkins, 1913-16, Aug. 20-22, 1914).

29.
Nelson Head is a prominent cliff on the south shore of Banks Island. The strait is now known to be about 70 miles wide.

30.
This inked sketch map, dated Mar. 9, 1914, and signed by V. Stefansson, is in the Stefansson Correspondence file (Anderson papers, CMN).

31.
These were Patsy and Edna Klengenberg, whom the Expedition members were to encounter again. (The author spelled the name Klinkenberg on this date.) Stefansson first met Capt. Charles Klengenberg at Herschel Island in 1906 and learned from him about a group of Eskimos to the east who used copper implements, hunted with bows and arrows, and who had had virtually no contact with white men. Stefansson thereupon resolved to organize an expedition to study them, which resulted in the Stefansson-Anderson Expedition of 1908-12, co-sponsored by the Geological Survey of Canada and the American Museum of Natural History (Stefansson, 1913a). Stefansson spelled the name Klinkenberg, Dr. Anderson spelled it Klingenberg, but the captain in his autobiography spelled it Klengenberg (MacInnes, 1932). Many Arctic residents today pronounce the name Klinkenberg, but at Coppermine in July 1989, the captain's son Bob, in response to my deliberate question, pronounced it Klengenberg (soft 'g'). Capt. Klengenberg was a Danish whaler who had married an Alaskan Eskimo woman and now hunted and trapped in the Darnley Bay region. His oldest daughter, whom he called "Weena," went with Wilkins on the *Mary Sachs* to Banks Island in search of Stefansson and her husband S. Storkerson.

32.
The author did not indicate the time in his diary.

33.
Three photographs and a copy of Richardson's sketch of what he called "Torso Rock" are in Stefansson (1913a, facing p. 316). This peculiar shoreline feature lies west of Cape Dease Thompson.

34.
Now known as tundra polygons.

35.
Dr. Anderson observed about the same time on this date that the temperature on deck of the *Alaska* was around 40° F, whereas up in the crowsnest it was 60° F (Anderson, 1913-16, Aug. 24, 1914).

36.
Palaiyak's measurements appear in Jenness (1923a, pp. 33B and 37B). The procedures the author followed when using his portable Swiss-made instrument are given in the same publication (pp. 5B-6B). A photograph of Palaiyak appears in Stefansson (1913a, facing p. 268).

37.
They were getting near the magnetic pole, although they were not fully aware of that fact at the time.

38.
About this same time Dr. Anderson, wandering on the hills west of the harbour (which he later named Bernard Harbour) caught sight of a two-masted schooner to the northwest, which he rightly assumed to be the *North Star* (Anderson, 1913-16, Aug. 25, 1914).

39.
Gazing down into it this afternoon we could see myriads of tiny black "fish" about 1/8 or 1/16 inch in length; they were so thick that it resembled soup, to use Cox's expression. [D.J.]

40.
Officially named Teddy Bear Island in 1960, after the vessel in which Capt. Joseph Bernard wintered in the small harbour immediately to its west in 1911-12.

41.
Probably between Teddy Bear Island and Cub Islet.

42.
Probably Cox Island.

43.
The whale meat was needed to ensure the Expedition had enough dog-food for the winter.

Chapter 18. – First Encounters with the Copper Eskimos

1.
Dr. R.M. Anderson introduced the name Bernard Harbour to honour Joseph F. Bernard, captain of the schooner *Teddy Bear* (and nephew of Capt. Peter Bernard on the *Mary Sachs*), who had spent the winter of 1912-13 in this little harbour. Dr. Anderson (1920) wrote "I named the harbour, after consultation with all the scientific men of the party, and it was so mentioned in our reports sent out in the fall of 1914 and published in 1915." V. Stefansson (1920) later asked the Canadian government to reject Dr. Anderson's name for the embayment, claiming prior usage of the name for a harbour on Barter Island, northeastern Alaska, but his efforts were unsuccessful. However, the name Bernard Harbor (named after the same Capt. Joseph Bernard, who wintered there in 1909-10) still appears on U.S. maps of Barter Island. Stefansson also claimed that he and Billy Natkusiak discovered the Coronation Gulf harbour in May 1910 (Stefansson, 1921, p. 740, footnote), before Joseph Bernard wintered there, a claim Dr. Anderson strongly disputed (Anderson, 1920). The name was originally given to the small harbour west of Chantry Island (Anderson, 1918, p. 35) but a few years later was applied (possibly in error) to the large embayment (including the small harbour) that is sheltered from Dolphin and Union Strait by Chantry Island (O'Neill, 1924, geologic map), and is shown thusly on modern topographic maps of the region.

2.
The unloading was done "in a systemless sort of way" (Chipman, 1913-16, Aug. 26, 1914).

3.
The propellor on the *Alaska* was a two-bladed type. Its shaft had been racked by an eccentric motion during the voyage to Coronation Gulf, which the engineer (Blue) wanted to investigate before starting back for Baillie Island. After the vessel was partly unloaded the broken condition of the propellor was discovered; one of the two blades was broken off about 3 inches from its hub. The damage was thought to have occurred when the vessel scraped bottom at Herschel Island during the storm of August 15 (Anderson, 1913-16, Aug. 29, 1914).

4.
The *Alaska* was expected to return within a week unless it went on to Herschel Island (O'Neill, 1924, p. 8A).

5.
Capt. Joseph Bernard had assured Dr. Anderson that there was a lot of driftwood around the harbour, but "if there ever was any driftwood, the *Teddy Bear* must have used it all" (Anderson, 1913-16, Aug. 29, 1914).

6.
Somewhere in the hills inland the author caught a live lemming, which he took back to Dr. Anderson (Anderson, 1913-16, Aug. 30, 1914). A young male, it was one of the first of about five dozen lemming specimens collected and brought back to the National Museum by the Canadian Arctic Expedition. It is now Spec. No. 2948 in the National collection in Ottawa (David Campbell, personal communication, Sept. 21, 1987). Although the author collected many bird specimens for Dr. Anderson, which ultimately became part of the National Collection in Ottawa, he collected only four mammal specimens that are registered in the National Collection (see Appendix 4C).

7.
This large harbour is shown on modern topographic maps as Bernard Harbour.

8.
In July 1989 three rows of stones still crossed this creek in the same general locality, though oriented somewhat differently, and a small shack lay close by.

9.
At this point in his diary, the author added "(see Boas. Esk. of Baffin Land etc. p. 475)." Boas's report must have been at Bernard Harbour. Boas (1907, p. 475) described dual fish dams on Southampton Island: "Another dam is built across the stream a little below the first dam. The lower dam has an opening in the centre, so that a pool is formed between the two dams. After the fish have accumulated in the pool, the opening in the centre of the lower dam is closed and the fish are speared in the pool."

10.
Articles of stone, wood, or metal did not need much protection from beasts of prey, such as foxes, wolves, and especially wolverines, and could be cached openly in this fashion. The natives to whom these items by the fishing creek belonged had cached their sleds and heavy spring tents at a lake a few miles inland, and their more perishable goods on Chantry Island. The spring cache-sites were often the same as the winter assembling places (Jenness, 1922a, pp. 121-122).

11.
These ridges are part of an extensive drumlin field formed during the last glaciation of the region and reshaped (rounded and winnowed of fine materials) by post-glacial marine erosion some 10,000 years ago up to about 450 feet above present sea level in that region. Similar marine-rounded drumlins occur for many miles along the south side of Victoria Island north and east of Bernard Harbour.

12.
Chipman and Cox, however, had measured the lumber brought with the Expedition from Nome, finding 1000 feet of boards. After Dr. Anderson told Chipman he wanted two houses built, Chipman quickly prepared plans based upon the lumber available and his calculated need for at least 1200 square feet of sod. He was anxious to get started with the construction (Chipman, 1913-16, Aug. 31, 1914).

13.
Able-bodied seaman.

14.
In 1963 Dr. William E. Taylor Jr. found evidence of Dorset culture, which he estimated to be nearly 1800 years old, associated with old tent rings near the mouth of the fishing creek (called Nulahugyuk creek in Jenness, 1922a, p. 16) about 3 miles south of the site of the C.A.E. headquarters in Bernard Harbour and 450 miles west of any then-known Dorset sites (Taylor, 1972, pp. 28-32). In September 1987 Dr. Taylor mused briefly to S.E. Jenness on what the effect might have been on the development of Arctic archaeology had the author investigated these sites in 1914, a full 11 years prior to his recognition of the existence of such a culture (Jenness, 1925).

15.
One of these photographs has survived (CMC Photo. No. 37001).

16.
Palaiyak encountered the Eskimos during the day while he was hunting caribou and persuaded them to set aside their fears and visit the two ships and Expedition members (Chipman, 1913-16, Sept. 1, 1914).

17.
They had become somewhat acquainted with the 'white-man's food' through contact with Capt. Joseph Bernard two years earlier (Anderson, 1913-16, Sept. 1, 1914). They seemed to like apricots, did not like salt or macaroni, and tried just a little bread, cookies, and tea. They were not offered any butter (which was in short supply) lest they would have eaten it all (Chipman, 1913-16, Sept. 1, 1914).

18.
According to Dr. Anderson, the Eskimos grabbed the hairs by the edge of the thumb and a steel or copper knife and cut (or pulled) them out. By doing this regularly they kept the hair short (Chipman, 1913-16, Sept. 1, 1914).

19.
Lice and other parasites found on human beings and lower animals, and also the grubs on the caribou were indiscriminately called *komait* (Dr. R.M. Anderson, *in* Stefansson, 1913a, p. 448).

20.
This incident took place in the woman's tent before Dr. Anderson returned to the ships (Chipman, 1913-16, Sept. 1, 1914).

21.
Mike, Palaiyak, and Eikie Añutisiak. Dr. Anderson took them about a mile east of camp to a lake for sod cutting (Chipman, 1913-16, Anderson, 1913-16, Sept. 1, 1914). Mike and Eikie accompanied Dr. Anderson when the *Alaska* departed on September 6.

22.
Palaiyak was with these Eskimos when Dr. Anderson arrived at their tent. They had traded with Capt. Bernard when he wintered in the harbour two years previously (Anderson, 1913-16, Sept. 1, 1914).

23.
Dr. Anderson had issued instructions that they were not to be invited aboard the *Alaska* again but were to remain on shore (Chipman, 1913-16, Sept. 2, 1914). There Dr. Anderson photographed them (CMC Photo Nos. 38731 and 38733).

24.
Aksiatak was one of the Copper Eskimos the author met on the previous day. His bow (or one similar to it) is well illustrated in Jenness (1946, p. 123, Fig. 151).

25.
The settlement O'Neill and the author had encountered on September 1. This was almost certainly the site that Taylor investigated in 1963 (Taylor, 1972).

26.
One was an 8' X 12' wall tent to be used as a cook tent (Chipman, 1913-16, Sept. 3, 1914). Others included a 10' green Bell tent for Johansen's boxes and laboratory equipment, two similar tents (one for Geological Survey boxes, the other for skins, clothing, bags etc.), and an 8' X 8' pyramidal tent for Dr. Anderson's equipment (Anderson, 1913-16, Sept. 3, 1914).

27.
Chipman, O'Neill, and the author then asked Dr. Anderson what plans he had for house construction. Dr. Anderson replied by instructing Chipman to go ahead with the plans he had drawn up (Chipman, 1913-16, Sept. 3, 1914).

28.
Most of the day was spent arranging the stores and equipment in the various tents (Chipman, 1913-16, Sept. 4, 1914).

29.
The *Alaska* was still in the harbour because the ice was drifting fast to westward outside the islands at the mouth of the harbour and some of it had penetrated the smaller islands near the outer entrance (Anderson, 1913-16, Sept. 4, 1914), thus blocking the *Alaska*'s departure for Baillie Island.

30.
On the north side of the island now called Teddy Bear Island.

31.
The moon was nearly full that night and the dogs howled in a most unearthly manner, greatly disturbing the sleep of the men (Anderson, 1913-16, Sept. 4, 1914).

32.
Palaiyak also reported seeing a camp of 11 Eskimos who were en route to Bernard Harbour (Anderson, 1913-16, Sept. 5, 1914).

33.
On board the *Alaska* were the Southern Party's best team of dogs and seven men: Dr. Anderson, Seamen Daniel Sweeney (acting captain) and Aarnout Castel, cook James 'Cockney' Sullivan, engineer Daniel W. Blue, and two Eskimos, Mike and Añutisiak (Anderson, 1913-16, Sept. 6, 1914). Dr. Anderson hoped to obtain fuel (both driftwood and coal at Baillie Island) because of the scarcity of fuel at Bernard Harbour, mail and provisions at Herschel Island, and return before the freeze-up. Baillie Island was a common port-of-call for whaling vessels at the time.

34.
Up until this time they had been eating food cooked by Sullivan on board the *Alaska*.

35.
Dr. Anderson thought that enough sods had been cut before he sailed west, but Chipman found they had cut only about 450 square feet, and his calculations indicated they needed to cover some 1214 square feet of space with sods to make up for the inadequate supply of lumber for the two dwellings they planned to erect. It was, therefore, necessary to cut a lot more sod (Chipman, 1913-16, Sept. 5, 1914).

36.
"Arrows are spliced neatly near middle, blood being used as glue, and are feathered. The bows were made of three spliced pieces of spruce (Chipman, 1913-16, Sept. 6, 1914). The author (Jenness, 1946, p. 126) later noted that the shapes and methods of splicing of this type of arrow were rather fully illustrated by Stefansson (1914a, Figs. 32-38).

Chapter 19. – Building the Base-camp Station

1.
The orientation was east-west, with the door facing east (Chipman, 1913-16, Sept. 20, 1914). The author later corrected his orientation (Jenness, 1928a, p. 9).

2.
Chipman photographed the house during and after construction: CMC Photo Nos. 43261 (during construction), 43262 (completed house, about Sept. 18, 1914), 43263 (house and nearby shed after snowfall).

3.
Sweeney, Blue, Castel, and Sullivan, who were with Dr. Anderson on the *Alaska*.

4.
Eikie Añutisiak (later known as Ikey Bolt), Palaiyak, and Mike.

5.
This was an incident not mentioned in Chipman's diary. He did record, however, that the sods, now obtainable near the house, were placed flat and in a double layer (Chipman, 1913-16, Sept. 11, 1914).

6.
The Copper Eskimo's word for bearded seal, *ugyuk*, differs slightly from that used by the Eskimos on the northern coast of Alaska, *ugruk* (Jenness, 1928a, p.125).

7.
The porridge was cold, the coffee was over-boiled, the liver was overcooked, and the hot cakes were "not a success" (Chipman, 1913-16, Sept. 13, 1914).

8.
Both the harbour and the nearby strait were free of ice, which forced them to go "some distance to get ice for water" (Chipman, 1913-16, Sept. 10, 1914).

9.
This small unnamed island lies just outside the mouth of the fishing creek where Taylor (1972, pp. 29-32) found Dorset Culture artifacts in 1963. Cox and the author were mainly interested in visiting the Eskimos at their fishing site on this occasion (Chipman, 1913-16, Sept. 13, 1914), but finding them gone, they examined the harbour facilities for a possible alternative shelter for the *Alaska* and *North Star*. They returned with

four ducks and three seals (Chipman, 1913-16, Sept. 13, 1914).

10.
Modern topographic maps, however, indicate their locality was at 114° 47'W.

11.
Dr. John Rae, an officer of the Hudson's Bay Company, travelled with Sir John Richardson in 1848 from the mouth of the Mackenzie River to the Coppermine River. Rae returned in 1851 to explore the south shore of Victoria Island (Rae, 1852).

12.
Tar paper was installed on the roof by Cox and O'Neill in the morning, then 3-inch thick strips of sod were added onto the tar paper, and the wall frame was further braced (Chipman, 1913-16, Sept. 14, 1914).

13.
It was. However, after 2 days of battling fog, snow squalls, rough seas, and occasional ice patches following its departure from Herschel Island early in the morning of September 13, the *Alaska* pulled safely into the shelter of Baillie Island at 9 p.m. September 15 (Anderson, 1913-16, Sept. 13-15, 1914).

14.
The wind was still from the northwest (Chipman, 1913-16, Sept. 16, 1914).

15.
The waves in the bay were too high to risk using the damaged canoe to fetch ice for fresh water even if they had seen any ice kegs (Chipman, 1913-16, Sept. 17, 1914).

16.
The comet Delavan, discovered only 9 months previously by an observer in Argentina. It disappeared past the sun on October 26, 1914 (Dr. Ian Halliday, verbal communication, 1976).

17.
In the tents, for only one bunk had been constructed in the house at this time (Chipman, 1913-16, Sept. 17, 1914).

18.
The author now made the fourth hand in this weekly Saturday night activity (Chipman, 1913-16, Sept. 19, 1914).

19.
Johansen arose at 5:40 a.m. but did not have breakfast ready until 8:40 a.m., his tardiness drawing various comments from the others. Their efforts to train him proved ineffectual (Chipman, 1913-16, Sept. 23, 1914).

20.
Both men and dogs preferred fresh meat to canned pemmican. Capt. Bernard had assured Dr. Anderson that the locality was along the fall caribou migration route, and the men had counted on laying in a winter's supply of caribou meat. The late freeze up of Dolphin and Union Straits, however, forced the caribou to migrate farther east and the men had to turn their efforts to seal hunting (Jenness, 1928a, pp. 12-13).

21.
The *Alaska*, after reaching Baillie Island on September 15, took on sacks of coal, whale meat, and newly purchased dogs, while waiting for the northwest gale to subside. In trying to get out of the harbour early on September 20 it ran aground. The tide soon dropped 3 to 4 feet and the vessel had to be unloaded before it was finally floated free on September 24. Estimating that it needed

3 days to reload, Dr. Anderson deemed the season too late to risk the trip back to Bernard Harbour, there being no safe winter harbour en route. Consequently the *Alaska* wintered where it was, and Dr. Anderson later returned to Bernard Harbour by dog sled (Anderson, 1913-16, Sept. - Dec. 1914).

22.
Chipman, from a hilltop south of their camp, was able to look across the straits to Victoria Island, and reported no cakes of ice in sight (Chipman, 1913-16, Sept. 24, 1914).

23.
Elsewhere the author (Jenness, 1922a, pp. 81-82 and Fig. 29) discusses and illustrates ground plans and dimensions of several stone rings "near Bernard Harbour."

24.
The pointers are the two stars of the Big Dipper (Ursus Major) that point to the North Star.

25.
Salvaging the contents because some of the boxes had gotten wet at Collinson Point (Chipman, 1913-16, Sept. 26, 1914).

Chapter 20. – Serious Trading Commences

1.
On September 1 and 2, 1914.

2.
These measurements helped the author conclude later that there was no valid evidence of admixture with Europeans, as Stefansson (1913a) had proposed, nor physical basis for subdividing the Eskimos in the region into local groups (Jenness, 1923a, pp. 46B-B47). Physical characteristics of Ayallik, Aksiatak, Anauyuk, and Kalyutarun are given in Jenness (1923a, pp. B8-B9, B25), their photographs on p. 73B (Aksiatak, CMC Photo Nos. 51602, 51603, p. 79B; Ayallik, CMC Photo No. 36963; Anauyuk, CMC Photo No. 42227), and p. 85B (Kalyutarun, CMC Photo No. 51043, 51044).

3.
They lived a short distance south and southeast of Bernard Harbour and, in the summer of 1914, numbered only 19 individuals (Jenness, 1922a, p. 34).

4.
These were the *Noahanirgmiut*, a small group of natives Stefansson met hunting seal

on the ice northeast of Lambert Island, Coronation Gulf, early in May 1911 (Stefansson, 1913a, p. 264).

5.
Curiously Kalyutarun has no obvious facial tattoos in the three photographs of her in Jenness (1922a, p. 166, CMC Photo No. 51040; 1923a, p. 85B, CMC Photo Nos. 51043 and 51044) and no mention of tattooing is given in the facial description of her (Jenness, 1923a, p. B25). All three photographs (by G.H. Wilkins, who listed her as Kaluta) were taken in July 1915.

6.
A girl named Oqomiq (Jenness, 1922a, p. 166, Fig. 51).

7.
Hanbury (1904, pp. 143-144) reported that all of the older Eskimo (or 'Husky') women were tattooed on the hands, wrists, and lower part of the arm. The tattoo design he illustrated is similar though not identical to Niaq's.

8.
Niaq or Niq is pictured in Jenness (1923a, p. 87B, CMC Photo Nos. 51604 and 51605), but like Kalyutarun (see footnote 5) shows no facial tattooing, nor is it mentioned in her facial description (Jenness, 1923a, p. 26B). The photographs were taken (by G.H. Wilkins) a year after this encounter (July 10, 1915).

9.
The author later discussed the tattooing of the Copper Eskimos and provided drawings of several varieties of face, hand, and arm patterns (Jenness, 1946, p. 53 and Fig. 45). Figure 45b is probably Niaq's hand and arm. Chipman also sketched what appears to be Niaq's tattooed hand and Kalyutarun's face on this same day (Chipman, 1913-16, Sept. 28, 1914).

10.
These were .30-30 cartridges (Chipman, 1913-16, Sept. 28, 1914), a correction the author made September 29. Aksiatak had a Winchester .30-30.

11.
Seal floats (Chipman, 1913-16, Sept. 28, 1914).

12.
The whereabouts of these drawings today is unknown.

13.
Early in 1916 this little girl froze to death after being exposed by her mother, who said the child was bewitched and a burden, because she was still unable to stand or walk, even though she was about 3 years old (Jenness, 1922a, p. 166; Fig. 51 on p. 166 is a photo of mother and child by G.H. Wilkins, CMC No. 51040).

14.
This caribou meat had apparently been obtained by Wilkins in July when he was at Clarence Bay, Alaska (Chipman, 1913-16, Sept. 30, 1914).

15.
In additional trading, one marrow spoon and two bone pins were obtained in exchange for two fish hooks (Chipman, 1913-16, Sept. 30, 1914).

16.
Other tactics were also used to discourage their presence and familiarity (Chipman, 1913-16, Sept. 30, 1914).

17.
He argued that he preferred to give up one day in five from his research work than one week in five (Chipman, 1913-16, Oct. 1, 1914).

18.
As this was the last day they had allowed for the return of the *Alaska* before freeze up, the men started hauling supplies from their unloading site for the combined provision cache and shed, utilizing provision containers for the walls and the lumber that had been left for a second house for the roof, then covering the whole structure with canvas (Chipman, 1913-16, Oct. 1, 1914).

19.
The tent would provide sleeping quarters for the extra men accompanying Dr. Anderson from the *Alaska*. There was insufficient coal for more than one stove for the party, but a Primus stove could heat up a sheltered tent (Chipman, 1913-16, Oct. 1, 1914). The Expedition members had not yet discovered the supply of wood around Chantry Island with which they were able to supplement their fuel supply over the winter.

20.
These natives would not be back until they could travel by sled and go out on the ice (Chipman, 1913-16, Oct. 2, 1914) to hunt seal for their food needs while travelling.

21.
Probably in the summer of 1910, when he and Stefansson were in the region (Stefansson, 1913a, pp. 203-208).

Chapter 21. – Preparations for Winter

1.
Chipman observed that half the wood on the island's gravel beach was rotten, the driftwood higher on the beach being more rotten than that lower down. His opinion of the length of time things remained unaltered in the Arctic differed considerably, therefore, from that expressed by Stefansson in his book *My Life with the Eskimo* (Chipman, 1913-16, Oct. 5, 1914).

2.
Before he went west on the *Alaska* on September 6.

3.
In the month since the departure of the *Alaska*, the six-man party at Bernard Harbour had supplemented its food supply (and that of the 20 dogs) by 18 seals, three caribou, 30 ptarmigan, 13 ducks, and one Arctic hare (Chipman, 1913-16, Oct. 5, 1914).

4.
Chipman too was concerned about the vessel and its crew, about this time noting that they had taken only 6 weeks' food supply with them (Chipman, 1913-16, Oct. 14, 1914). The *Alaska*, however, was safely anchored in the harbour at Baillie Island, its occupants hunting ducks, foxes, and polar bears (Anderson, 1913-16, Sept. 29 - Oct. 8, 1914) for fresh meat and dog-food.

5.
Chipman discusses briefly their careful rationing of luxuries, for which they could not expect replacements before the next summer. Butter and cheese would be eaten only on Sundays; they would save their one slab of bacon; they could consume about half a tin of canned milk each day; and dried fruits would be available once a day (Chipman, 1913-16, Oct. 8, 1914).

6.
This was the main reason Palaiyak went hunting almost daily.

7.
One of Palaiyak's drawings is reproduced in Jenness (1922a, Fig. 65, p. 226), but the whereabouts of the book and its original drawings is unknown.

8.
The Mackenzie River delta term *natsiq* or *nat.ciq* means 'a pup seal' (Jenness, 1928a, p. 85). Palaiyak, being a Mackenzie River native, would have used this term.

9.
Most of these pictures were of flowers and other plants, taken in Northern Alaska in July 1914, but a few were scenes about Bernard Harbour, taken in early September 1914, including two showing the author trading with some Copper Eskimos (CMC Photo Nos. 42232 and 42233).

10.
1852.

11.
Their useable lighting consisted of only three lanterns, together with a tin lamp that had been obtained from Leffingwell's cabin on Flaxman Island. Chipman commented that the bulky lighting equipment, weighing a ton or more, was not designed for Arctic use and was a costly item to ship to Nome, thence on the *Belvedere* to Herschel Island, from whence it was brought on the *Alaska* to its present site, where it was too cold to work. He was much irritated by the lack of an alternate lighting system (Chipman, 1913-16, Oct. 14-15, 1914).

12.
On a short trip to Stapylton Bay in search of another group of Eskimos and also to test his dog-team and equipment (Jenness, 1928a, p. 16).

13.
The inner harbour was entirely frozen over, with 5 inches of ice (Chipman, 1913-16, Oct. 17, 1914).

14.
These Barter Island notes, typed on 5" X 8" pages, are at the Archaeological Survey of Canada, Canadian Museum of Civilization, Hull, Quebec (unpublished MS. No. 85).

15.
There was ice most of the way out to Liston Island but to the west of that island was still open water (Chipman, 1913-16, Oct. 22, 1914).

16.
Edison recording phonographs (Jenness, 1928a, p. 57). The author uses the word "gramophone" for the two C.A.E. machines that played commercially made recordings.

17.
The blanks (cylinders about 4" long) were for recording Eskimo material, the records (about 75 in all) were for the listening pleasure of the men (Chipman, 1913-16, Oct. 23, 1914).

18.
Chipman commented that of the 20 dogs left at the station 14 "cannot be relied on for any long trips or hard work," the best team of dogs having gone west on the *Alaska*, and though Blue's long-haired dogs were slow, they should prove suitable for Jenness' needs once they got used to him (Chipman, 1913-16, Oct. 23-24, 1914).

19.
A big box of clippings addressed to V. Stefansson yielded old news items and several

reviews of his book *My Life with the Eskimo*. Chipman commented especially on the authoritative, fair, and generally favourable review of that book by the *Athenaeum* (Chipman, 1913-1916, Oct. 25. 1914), a literary weekly published in London.

20.
From Chantry Island. They also brought a load of fresh blue ice for drinking water from an ice keg in the next bay (Chipman, 1913-16, Oct. 28, 1914).

21.
West of Liston Island (Chipman, 1913-16, Oct. 28, 1914).

22.
Three other dogs were loose and two sled lashings, ski lashings, and a portion of the kayak had been eaten (Chipman, 1913-16, Oct. 29, 1914).

23.
Cox was the all-round handyman of the Southern Party (Chipman, 1913-16, Oct. 29, 1914).

24.
Four rolls of film (Chipman, 1913-16, Oct. 30, 1914) taken in the Mackenzie River delta and at Bernard Harbour. The author can be seen talking with some Copper Eskimos in two of them (CMC Photo Nos. 43253 and 43254).

25.
An amusing version of this encounter appears in Jenness (1928a, p. 22).

26.
Johansen was on duty as cook but was relieved by Chipman so he could get some fresh air (Chipman, 1913-16, Nov. 1, 1914).

27.
For some time Chipman, Johansen, and O'Neill had warned the author that it was inadvisable for him to travel alone, but on this date they collectively told him they would not let him go alone (Chipman, 1913-16, Nov. 1, 1914).

28.
Shown on modern topographic maps as Cape Hope.

29.
The southward migration of the caribou from Victoria Island to the barren grounds could only take place when the waters of Dolphin and Union Strait froze over adequately. Because freeze-up was late in 1914 the caribou migrated farther east along the south shore of Victoria Island and finally crossed Coronation Gulf well east of Bernard Harbour.

Chapter 22. – First Foray by Dogsled

1.
He was old and not expected to survive the winter (Chipman, 1913-16, Nov. 3, 1914).

2.
Cape Hope.

3.
They were also able to advise Chipman that his proposed trip to Cape Lyon was impractical at this time (Chipman, 1913-16, Nov. 6, 1914).

Chapter 23. – Brief Respite at Bernard Harbour

1.
Chipman reckoned they now had enough seals on hand to supply dog-food until Christmas (Chipman, 1913-16, Nov. 4, 1914).

2.
The purpose of the trip was to seek news of the *Alaska* or to meet a team from it and help it with food or transportation, while at the same time picking up reconnaissance information of the coastal region between Bernard Harbour and Cape Lyon (Chipman, 1913-16, Nov. 17, 1914), some 225 miles away, prior to mapping it topographically and geologically in the spring of 1915.

3.
Naqitoq was the 6-year old only son (not daughter) of Akhiatak and Niq (Jenness, 1922a, p. 68). See also the correct reference to the boy Naqitoq in diary entry of Sept. 28, 1914.

4.
The author, at some later time, pencilled "No" at this point in his diary, negating this observation about the trousers.

5.
For the occasion Cox baked a fine chocolate cake, Chipman brought forth a big box of cigars, Johansen presented O'Neill with a book, and "Jenness, with his usual unselfishness, gave him practically the only thing he had, and a thing he himself valued, a pipe made for him last spring by a native" (Oyaraq, on Barter Island). Then the four men played bridge (Chipman, 1913-16, Nov. 12, 1914).

6.
This decision may have been made because of the exhaustion of their supply of caribou meat on November 11. Thereafter until they got more caribou they obtained their protein from beans and peas (Chipman, 1913-16, Nov. 12, 1914).

7.
The comet Delavan, which the author mentioned on several previous days (Sept. 17, 26, and Oct. 15). This observation was 20 days later than the last heretofore recorded sighting.

8.
Trying to keep warm. The outside temperature, high winds, poor wood, and draftinesss of the house all contributed to its coldness. The inside temperature at 8 a.m. was 15° F (Chipman, 1913-16, Nov. 15, 1914).

9.
This two-word comment was added to his diary by the author at some later date, perhaps when he was writing *People of the Twilight* in the mid-1920's.

10.
Chipman intended to journey to Pierce Point to find out if Capt. Klengenberg, whom he hoped to find there, had any news of the *Alaska* (Chipman, 1913-16, Nov. 17, 1914).

11.
Cox, Johansen, and Palaiyak also started to build snowhouses for the dogs, which had suffered noticeably from exposure during the previous few days (Chipman, 1913-16, Nov. 17, 1914).

12.
Aksiatak's mother. Her physical characteristics and photograph are in Jenness (1923a, p. 26B and Plate X on p. 85B).

13.
This type of fish-spear, known as a leister, is described and illustrated in Jenness (1946, p. 111, and Fig. 134a on p. 112).

14.
They had 35 days' food supply, which Chipman detailed in his diary (1913-16, Nov. 18, 1914), and a team of seven dogs.

15.
They were, in fact, tent-bound at the west end of Cockburn Point, about 10 miles away (Chipman, 1913-16, Nov. 18-19, 1914).

16.
By 1914 nearly all Copper Eskimo harpoon heads were made of iron rather than bone or caribou antler (Jenness, 1946, p. 116).

17.
The author is referring to the collection of Eskimo artifacts Stefansson bought from Charles Brower, which the author studied in February 1914. These artifacts are in the collections of the Canadian Museum of Civilization, Hull, Quebec (see author's entry for Feb. 15, 1914, and footnote 4, Chapter 9).

18.
This Swedish book probably belonged to Johansen. Its full title is given in the references.

19.
Because of the limited distribution of musk-ox, musk-ox horn blubber-pounders were a special product of the central Arctic. They are described and illustrated in Jenness (1946, pp. 69-70).

20.
The author had small hands.

21.
There were two purposes for this arrangement: to study the natives in their own homes and to stop their regular visits to the station (Jenness, 1928a, p. 25).

22.
See map in back of Stefansson (1913a).

23.
My Life with the Eskimo (Stefansson, 1913a).

24.
See footnote 29, Chapter 21, regarding the caribou migration in 1914.

25.
In the Flaxman Island region, Northern Alaska.

26.
Ilavinirk was an Alaskan Eskimo hired at Fort McPherson by V. Stefansson in July 1908. Accompanied by his wife Mamayauk and 7-year old daughter Nogasak, he sailed west with Stefansson to Point Barrow on the *Karluk* after being picked up some 40 miles

west of Herschel Island. Ilavinirk and his family subsequently worked with Dr. Anderson and in 1909 adopted Palaiyak. Ilavinirk later took care of Stefansson's base camp at Langton Bay. In 1915-16 he accompanied RNWMP Inspector C.D. La Nauze across Great Bear Lake and down the Coppermine River, acting as interpreter during the search for and subsequent interrogation of the murderers of two French Roman Catholic priests. He remained with the police after the two suspects were apprehended and accompanied them up the Mackenzie River in 1917 to Edmonton, where he was one of the two court interpreters during the trial of the two Coronation Gulf natives (see Epilogue re Uloqsaq and Sinisiaq).

27.
This report must have been among H. Beuchat's personal books and journals and thus accessible to the author at Bernard Harbour.

Chapter 24. – First Encounter with Victoria Island Eskimos

1.
Hitqoq, age 40, was the young brother of Iguaq; his physical characteristics and picture are given in Jenness (1923a, p. B9 and Plate VI on p. 77B). Hogaluk, age about 14, was Hitqoq's nephew (Jenness, 1922a, p. 68).

2.
Back to Expedition headquarters, for the sled and dog-team were needed there.

3.
At Nulahugyuk Creek, 3 miles to the south, where Aksiatak and a few of his kin were residing (Jenness, 1922a, p. 68).

4.
This photograph is not listed in the author's 1913-16 CMC collection and must have been discarded as unsatisfactory. (See author's entry for Jan. 22, 1915 re photograph development.)

5.
This snow-hut is described in detail in Jenness (1922a, p. 64).

6.
A description and diagram of Aksiatak's two-roomed snow dwelling at the fishing creek (*Nulahugyuk*) are given in Jenness (1922a, pp. 68-70) and Fig. 19, p. 70). Another double hut at this locality is illustrated in the same report (Fig. 18, p. 69).

7.
Two photographs each of Iguaq (CMC Photo Nos. 37213 and 37214, taken by G.H. Wilkins) and Hitqoq (also taken by Wilkins but not listed) appear in Jenness (1923a, pp. 85B and 77B respectively). Iguaq, age 45, was Hitqoq's widowed sister and Aksiatak's mother.

8.
They asked questions about the author's country, clothes, and food (Jenness, 1928a, p. 25) and told him about a large tribe of natives assembling on the south shore of Victoria Island.

9.
Two photographs each of Aksiatak and his wife Niq, taken by G.H. Wilkins, appear in Jenness (1923a, pp. 73B and 87B, CMC Photo Nos. 51602, 51603, and 51604, 51605 respectively). Physical characteristics of both are given in Jenness (1923a, pp. 8B and 26B).

10.
The house measurements are given in Jenness (1922a, p. 70).

11.
This story was either "The Magic Bear" or "The Raven," both of which appear in Jenness (1924a, p. 42A).

12.
This photograph is not listed in the author's 1913-16 CMC collection and must have been discarded as unsatisfactory. From November 24 to 28 the author wrote his notes in pencil. His third sentence on Nov. 24 was written over part of the second sentence, probably because of insufficient lighting, and except for the words "fox-traps" and "Hitqoq and Hogaluk" is unreadable. The illegible third sentence has therefore been omitted here.

13.
Here as elsewhere in this diary the author's reference to 'Bernard Harbour' meant the small enclosed bay west of Chantry Island, not the larger embayment so-named on modern maps.

14.
A small group of Eskimo who wandered in summer about southern Victoria Island. The author was here using a spelling variant of V. Stefansson's term *Puiplirgmiut* (see Stefansson, 1913a, pp. 266-273). By December 1 (just a week later), he started spelling the word *Puivlirmiut*.

15.
The author has the word "read" at this point, obviously in error.

16.
"In ...an old book about Greenland" (Jenness, 1928a, p. 26). This may have been the Swenander volume (see footnote 18, Chapter 23).

17.
The author later spelled it *Ukallit* (Jenness, 1922a, p. 26); Chipman and Cox (1924, p. 40B) listed the word as *Ukulit*, defined it as a collective [Eskimo] name for the [three] Liston and Sutton Islands, and gave its translation as "Arctic hare." Dr. Anderson (1913-16, Dec. 30, 1914) spelled it *Okallit* and indicated it was the village on the Liston and Sutton Islands, that is, the winter snowhouses of the various groups of natives assembled there at that time.

18.
Probably Harkness Island, the smallest of the three islands in the group.

19.
Nuvuk, on the south side of Clouston Bay, is shown as a prominent peninsula on Map 1 in Jenness (1922a, p. 126). It was the locality from where the *Puivlirmiut* crossed the strait from Victoria Island to the Liston and Sutton Islands for their winter sealing. *Nuvuk* means "Point" and was used also for Cape Krusenstern (Jenness, 1922a, p. 17).

20.
Twelve snow-huts (Jenness, 1928a, p. 27).

21.
Forsyth Bay. The snowhouses were all two-roomed or in pairs with common passages, in a single line along the face of a low ridge (Jenness, 1922a, p. 76).

22.
Commonly translated as "white man"; also spelled *kabloona* (de Poncins, 1941), *kabluna* (Thibert, 1969, p. 44), and *kraslouna* (Malhaurie, 1956, p. 39).

23.
The author wanted a separate snow-hut where he could be undisturbed to write his notes (Jenness, 1928a, p. 28). He described the one built for him in detail elsewhere (Jenness, 1922a, p. 64).

24.
During this and subsequent times spent with the *Puivlirmiut* the author measured 21 men and 11 women (Jenness, 1923a, pp. 20B-23B, 30B-31B, 35B-36B).

25.
The author traded knives, files, and other articles for Eskimo stone lamps and pots, musk-ox horn ladles, and garments of sealskin and caribou fur (Jenness, 1928a, pp. 29-30).

26.
Haviuyaq was Akhiatak's cousin. Age 25, brother of the 45-year old Taptuna, Haviuyaq's facial features are described in Jenness (1923a, p. 20B), those of his 26-year old wife Itoqanna [Itoqana] in the same report (p. 30B).

27.
A double house with an attached offshoot house, described and illustrated in Jenness (1922a, p. 67 and Fig. 22).

28.
He had probably obtained this gun by trading with Capt. Joseph Bernard two years earlier, when the latter wintered in the harbour now given his name.

29.
A small group of Eskimos reportedly living some 60 miles to the west, near Cape Kendall.

30.
The author had by that time traded all his goods and had acquired a sled load of Eskimo items to take back to Bernard Harbour to pack for the National Museum in Ottawa (Jenness, 1928a, p. 30).

31.
Partly from curiousity to see the white men's things at the station and partly to have the first choice at trading (Jenness, 1928a, p. 30).

32.
Half a dozen families lived outside of Minto Inlet near Banks Island during the winter of 1914-15 (Jenness, 1922a, p. 41).

33.
Chantry Island, where the *Noahognirmiut* had assembled (Jenness, 1922a, p. 110).

34.
To return to Victoria Island for more trading with the *Puivlirmiut.*

35.
This, though mainly a children's book, was one of the many Arctic books in the Expedition's collection at Bernard Harbour.

36.
Chantry Island.

37.
Jenness (1928a, p. 31) identifies her as "Light" and comments on her charm as a hostess.

38.
To the Liston and Sutton Islands.

39.
One of the Expedition's dogs.

40.
Ahuttokullugmiut (= Akulliakattangmiut) were the Eskimos around Stapylton Bay (see Jenness, 1922a, p. 34).

41.
The tattoo pattern is probably one of the ones pictured in Fig. 45 in Jenness (1946, p. 53).

42.
Liston and Sutton Islands.

43.
Ayallik's house is described and this figure is partly reproduced in Jenness (1922a, p. 65 and Fig. 13).

44.
Putulik, "the place with the hole" (Chipman and Cox, 1924, p. 40B) is Sutton Island.

45.
The author gives a more detailed account of snow-hut construction in Jenness (1922a, pp. 59-61).

46.
A detailed description of the table and its supporting strut is given in Jenness (1922a, p. 61). A typical table and a table strut are illustrated in Jenness (1946, Figs. 61 and 57 respectively).

47.
To revisit, study, and trade with the *Puivlirmiut* on the south shore of Victoria Island.

48.
Qamiñgoq's 12-year old son.

49.
Akhiatak and his family moved across the strait to the *Puivlirmiut* settlement at Forsyth Bay partly for the sake of company (he was related to Haviuyaq; see entry for Dec. 12, 1914), but mainly because he was short of food and the *Puivlirmiut* had an abundance of caribou meat and fish (Jenness, 1922a, p. 67).

50.
It was at the same locality as on his earlier visit (Nov. 29) (Jenness, 1928a, p. 35).

51.
Called "Snow-Knife" in Jenness (1928a, p. 36).

52.
November 30 - December 2.

53.
These will be among the many cat's cradles described in Jenness (1924b).

54.
Lest evil befell them (Jenness, 1922a, p. 184).

55.
"It would violate one of their rigid taboos to finish the sewing on the sea-ice" (Jenness, 1928a, pp. 35-36).

56.
Pyrrhic; a war-dance, in armour, of the ancient Greeks.

57.
This confrontation, more serious than described here, is reported in more detail in Jenness (1928a, pp. 37-39).

58.
A small group of Eskimos farther southeast near Lady Franklin Point, Victoria Island, mentioned by Stefansson (1913a, p. 159).

59.
For more details on this event see Jenness (1922a, p. 95).

60.
To start seal hunting on the ice, since most of the women had completed their winter sewing (Jenness, 1928a, p. 39).

61.
Out on the ice, southward towards a low promontory en route to the Liston and Sutton Islands (Jenness, 1928a, p. 39).

62.
At the C.A.E. headquarters in Camden Bay the previous April 16 (see author's entry for that date).

63.
This Iguaq was Wikiaq's 60-year old father (Jenness, 1923a, p. 22B), not Akhiatak's mother, who had the same name.

64.
Kimiryuak River, which flows into Forsyth Bay (Jenness, 1922a, pp. 14, 35).

65.
When he wintered in 1912-13 in the harbour now bearing his name.

66.
This religious taboo is discussed in Jenness (1922a, pp. 183-184).

67.
The new settlement was located on the ice but only a few yards out from shore, for it was not yet safe to camp farther out (Jenness, 1928a, p. 40).

68.
This was much easier than carrying their possessions out through the long passageways. Such openings could be easily repaired if the houses were reoccupied, but the Eskimos seldom returned to their former houses (Jenness, 1928a, pp. 39-40). The author later photographed this type of activity at Bernard Harbour (CMC Photo Nos. 37013, 37017).

69.
The author later identified the waters flowing into the bottom of Forsyth Bay as the Kimiryuak River (Jenness, 1922a, p. 14). Chipman and Cox (1924, p. 41B) spelled it *Kimilyuak.*

70.
Haviuyaq had two younger brothers, Utuallu, age about 16, and Haugak, age about 8 (Jenness, 1922a, p. 67). The latter was evidently overlooked here.

71.
Akhiatak arranged with Haviuyaq that their two snow-huts should share an entrance, with but short passages leading to their respective abodes. Haviuyaq's was the larger, for it was to house more people. A ground plan of the joined snow-huts appears in Jenness (1922a, Fig. 17, p. 68). This settlement, located behind a sandspit, had two-roomed or paired houses arranged in an irregular line and a lone single house 100 yards away (Jenness, 1922a, p. 76).

72.
Since Akhiatak's father Taptuna was Haviuyaq's elder brother (Jenness, 1923a, pp. 9B, 20B), it would appear that Akhiatak was Haviuyaq's nephew rather than cousin, as the author states both here and on December 13, though Akhiatak was 30 years old, Haviuyaq only 25.

73.
Nuvok or *Nuvuk* (Jenness, 1922a, p. 26), which may have been the point now identified as Nuvuk Point just south of Rymer Point, though the location shown on Map 1 in Jenness, 1922a, p. 126, looks much farther south, was a day's journey to the Liston and Sutton Islands for the *Puivlik* Eskimos. By starting from *Nuvuk* they avoided the risk of having to camp on the ice far from land when they trekked to the islands in December (Jenness, 1922a, p. 26).

74.
This relationship may not be correct, for the author later wrote that Ikpukkuaq's only brother had died 6 years earlier (Jenness, 1928a, p. 126).

75.
The music chanted by a fresh young voice like Qanajuq's was not unpleasing, but becomes very monotonous in chorus. [D.J.]

76.
He tied a strip of deerskin round Scotty's neck at the same time, just why I do not know, but fancy it was to propitiate the dog. [D.J.]

77.
Although not identified individually, these string games are undoubtedly included among the many attributed to the Copper Eskimos in Jenness (1924b).

78.
Two of these snow-huts, which were close together but opened in different directions, are described and illustrated in Jenness (1922a, pp. 66-67, Fig. 15).

79.
In Forsyth Bay.

80.
The *Nagyuktomiut* lived around Lady Franklin Point on the south shore of Victoria Island; the *Umingmuktomiut* (*Umingmaktomiut*) lived on the east side of Bathurst Inlet (Jenness, 1922a, pp. 36, 39).

81.
The author was staying in Haviuyaq's house.

82.
Eleven- and ten-year old daughters of Wikkiaq and Huputaun respectively. A fine photograph of Alunaq (or Alunak), taken at Bernard Harbour in July 1916 by J.J. O'Neill (CMC Photo No. 38614), is included in a set of 24 Arctic prints *Inuit Traditional Life Series* (Department of Information, Government of the Northwest Territories, Yellowknife, N.W.T., Canada).

83.
Haviraun died 4 months later and was buried near Cape Lambert (Jenness, 1922a, p. 175 and Fig. 54). G.H. Wilkins took nine photographs of Haviraun's corpse on June 15, 1915 (CMC Photo Nos. 50936-50940,

51556, 37163, 37168, and 37169). Figure 54 in Jenness (1922a, p. 175) is CMC Photo No. 50939.

84.
About 3 miles from *Putulik* (Sutton Island) (see diary entry of Dec. 31, 1914).

85.
Qamiñgoq, a shaman, and Kallun were Ayallik's kinsmen (Jenness, 1922a, p. 68).

86.
Eskimo people dwelling at *Umingmak*, the high land on the east side of Bathurst Inlet (Jenness, 1922a, p. 39). At the time of the author's studies around Coronation Gulf the musk-ox were found east of the Coppermine River and in the northern part of Victoria Island (Jenness, 1922a, p. 15).

87.
The trip from *Putulik* (Sutton Island) to Bernard Harbour could usually be made in 5 hours (Jenness, 1928a, p. 42). This trip had taken more than 6 hours.

88.
On this expedition to Victoria Island the author had purchased caribou meat for his colleagues, seal meat for the dogs, and artifacts for the National Museum in Ottawa, for which he paid with steel knives, iron pots, other metal goods, and ammunition (Jenness, 1928a, p. 38).

89.
The reader may find this list of fox-trappings puzzling when members of the scientific party were under strict orders from the government to refrain from trapping for personal gain. However, though they had brought adequate food with them for their own needs, they still needed to supply meat for their many dogs. They had been assured by both Capt. J. Bernard and V. Stefansson that the southern migration of the caribou in early fall would pass nearby and supply them with all the meat they needed. Much of their dog pemmican, therefore, had been sent north with Wilkins on the *Mary Sachs*, from Herschel Island in August 1914, for the use of Stefansson's Northern Party. The late freeze-up of Dolphin and Union Strait in the fall of 1914 resulted in the diversion eastward of the caribou, and they did not migrate south past Bernard Harbour as expected. This left the men at Bernard Harbour having to spend much time seeking food for their dogs. The author had obtained meat for

the dogs through trades with the Eskimos on several occasions in the past weeks, but during his absence his colleagues at Bernard Harbour had been forced to trap foxes, the only mammals readily available to them for dog-food.

Chapter 25. – Christmas, Trading, and Trip to Victoria Island

1.
These are dance songs Nos. 116 and 119, reproduced in Roberts and Jenness (1925, pp. 346 and 350).

2.
The Expedition had among its considerable collection of books the 29-volumes of the 11th Edition (1911) *Encyclopedia Britannica*. The set was retained by Dr. Anderson after the completion of the Expedition and is now in the Library, CMN. Some copies bear the stamp "Library of Canadian Arctic Expedition, 1913." The painting article is in vol. 20, pp. 459-519; Johansen's father, Viggo Johansen, is mentioned on pp. 515-516 as "one of the best Danish landscape painters..." and "with his gentle dreaminess,...the best representative of modern Danish home-life."

3.
It was a little later than 10 a.m. because Dr. Anderson noted that his party passed the west end of Cockburn Point at 9:25 a.m. and reached the station at 12:30 p.m. (Anderson, 1913-16, Dec. 25, 1914), and Chipman wrote that they arrived at 12:45 p.m. (Chipman, 1913-16, Dec. 25, 1914).

4.
The *Herman* had reached Herschel Island on August 9, three days after the arrival there of the author and the *Mary Sachs* (see author's entry for August 9, 1914).

5.
While the author recounts Dr. Anderson's news here, the latter was recounting in his daily notes some of the author's news, mentioning that the Eskimos the author had visited on Victoria Island had killed many caribou, especially near Simpson Bay, using mainly bows and arrows for want of ammunition for their various guns (which they had obtained two years earlier from Capt. J. Bernard: a .45-70 Winchester, a .303 Savage, and some .30-30's and .44's). These Eskimos had some musk-ox skins obtained by trade from the *Umingmuklogmiut* who hunted in southern Victoria Island and some polar-bear skins obtained from the *Kanghiryuarmiut* of Prince Albert Sound (Anderson, 1913-16, Dec. 25, 1914).

6.
The meeting place was on the second peninsula west of the station where Cox had his traps (Chipman, 1913-16, Dec. 25, 1914). The first that the men at the station knew of their return was when Cox reappeared at the western entrance of the harbour with Dr. Anderson and three men from the *Alaska* and also Chipman and O'Neill (Jenness, 1928a, p. 44). Chipman and O'Neill had encountered Dr. Anderson's party on Dec. 10 near Keats Point (Chipman, 1913-16, Dec. 10, 1914).

7.
Each man received about a dozen sheets sent care of Dr. Anderson from Mrs. Anderson (Chipman, 1913-16, Dec. 25, 1914).

8.
Caribou meat, dehydrated potatoes, canned peas, rice pudding, and a small bottle of wine supplied by Dr. Anderson (Jenness, 1928a, p. 44). Chipman noted that as their return was unexpected no special menu was prepared for Christmas day, and Christmas was therefore a quiet affair rather than the celebration of the previous year. Furthermore, he added, Johansen was cook that day. Nevertheless, they did manage to have Christmas cake, a box of candy, two boxes of H & P biscuits, and cigars (Chipman, 1913-16, Dec. 25, 1914).

9.
The author later wrote "a Christmas cake presented to us eighteen months before by some friends in British Columbia" (Jenness, 1928a, p. 44-45). It was probably from Mrs. E.O.S. Scholefield, wife of the B.C. Provincial librarian and archivist; the latter helped the author greatly in May 1913. It might, however, have been from Mrs. S.J. Schofield, wife of a geologist with the Geological Survey of Canada, who worked in British Columbia and would have known Chipman and Cox, and perhaps Malloch.

10.
Eikie and Palaiyak.

11.
The store room was converted into a kitchen, with bunks for Aarnout Castel and

the cook Sullivan (see January 6), and with a dining table (Chipman, 1913-16, Feb. 2, 1915). The main part of the house was then reserved for the six members of the scientific staff (Jenness, 1928a, p. 45).

12.
Sutton Island, the northeasternmost of the three islands in the Liston and Sutton Islands. The Eskimo settlement, augmented by the *Puivlirmiut* from Victoria Island, now consisted of some 30 families in 25 snow-huts and was located on the ice a few yards from the island (Jenness, 1928a, pp. 45, 49).

13.
Ikpukkuaq and his wife Taqtu were among this group. Referring to the latter Dr. Anderson noted "The oldest woman, who was a very loud and voluble talker, was the only one who had seen me before (in June 1911, when Captain Joe Bernard and I visited a camp near Gray's Bay, about 100 miles east of [the] mouth of Coppermine River). She said that her husband at that time (named [Nerialaq; see D. Jenness diary entry for June 30, 1915]) had since died and she now has another husband Ikpukhrak [sic], a middle-aged man with a fair bunch of chin whiskers" (Anderson, 1913-16, Dec. 30, 1914).

14.
The Expedition members had expected to lay in a good stock of meat during the annual caribou migration, but when the caribou failed to appear the author bartered with the Victoria Island Eskimos for meat, for they had shot many caribou on the south shore of that island. He obtained in this manner over 500 lbs of caribou meat (Chipman, 1913-16, Feb. 2, 1915) at this time. The author also conducted a considerable amount of trading for Eskimo utensils and clothing on December 30 and 31 (see Appendix 3).

15.
Palaiyak served as both assistant and interpreter (Jenness, 1928a, p. 45).

16.
The settlement consisted of about 30 families (see footnote 12, this chapter).

17.
Dr. Anderson intended to take out the semi-annual reports he and his scientific colleagues had prepared on their activities, as well as their personal mail and requests for provisions and equipment to be shipped to them via Herschel Island in the summer of 1915. He also wanted to give the dogs a good work-out prior to the planned spring activities. Palaiyak was needed to shoot caribou en route to supply fresh meat for both men and dogs on the trip. The distance to Fort Norman was more than 500 miles.

18.
A group of some 40 Eskimos reported to live in the basin of Rae River (Jenness, 1922a, p. 36).

19.
Spelled *Ahungahungak* (the southern island) in Chipman and Cox (1924, p. 40B); this is Liston Island, the largest of the three Liston and Sutton Islands.

20.
This snow-hut is described and illustrated in Jenness (1922a, pp. 70-71 and Fig. 20).

21.
The significance of this statement is clarified by a footnote in Jenness (1922a, p. 203). The man who had just died had been unable to complete the opening stage of a cat's-cradle figure faster than the spirit and suffered the dire consequences of the defeat. This seance is also described in Jenness (1928a, pp. 51- 52).

22.
November 28, 1914. Kaullu (or Kaulluaq) was the 30-year old daughter of the *Puivlik* Kilgavik (Jenness, 1923a, p. 30B). She was photographed in May 1915 by G.H. Wilkins (CMC Photo No. 50914), who spelled her name Kaudlak, about the time she was briefly married to Billy Natkusiak (Jenness, 1922a, p. 159).

23.
Stefansson brought the Indians of Great Bear Lake and the Copper Eskimos together for trading purposes in 1910 (Jenness, 1922a, p. 47).

24.
To the tree line, to get the wood.

25. Dwellers of the southeastern part of Victoria Island.

26.
To Bernard Harbour with a sled-load of meat and specimens.

27.
Some if not all of this Eskimo clothing was for the use of the scientists, "made-to-order" items, and consisted of deerskin socks, long and short mittens, sealskin slippers, deerskin pants, a deerskin coat, and a pair of sealskin boots (Anderson, 1913-16, Jan. 4, 1915).

28.
The dog by that name, not Wikkiaq's daughter Alunaq.

29.
Spelled *Illuvilik* in Chipman and Cox (1924, p. 40B), it is called Harkness Island on modern topographic maps. The most westerly island, however, is Liston Island.

30.
Sutton Island. It is probable that the author's compass (assuming that he had one) was inadequately adjusted for the strong effect of the north magnetic pole, for Sutton is the most northeasterly of the three Liston and Sutton Islands, but Harkness Island (*Illuvilik*) is the most northerly. (Magnetic north is shown as 52° 45' east of true north at Bernard Harbour on an ink tracing Dr. Anderson made in 1916 of Cox's topographic map of the harbour.)

31.
The author meant .45-70, because a .55-70 gun did not exist. Four .45-70 guns with supporting ammunition had been ordered by the Expedition but had not been received at that time; they were on the *Alaska* when it reached Bernard Harbour September 6, 1915.

32.
The author later typed on several sheets of 5 x 8 inch paper lists of the items he traded and the articles he obtained from the natives between January 5 and January 15, 1915 (Appendix 3).

33.
These two seances are also described in Jenness (1922a, pp. 203-204).

34.
The author comments elsewhere that hysteria and religion went closely hand in hand among the Arctic peoples, especially during the long dark winter months (Jenness, 1928a, p. 52).

35.
To visit the *Haneragmiut* ("People of the land on the other side") some 40 miles to the

west (Jenness, 1928a, pp. 52, 54, 55). The author had completed his head measurements of all the adults in the settlement near *Putulik* and wanted to take the measurements on another group for comparison with those groups he had measured. The several small groups had originally been identified by Stefansson (1913a), and the author was seeking to establish whether or not they showed valid physical anthropological differences.

36.
The *Akulliakuttugmiut* (*Akulliakattangmiut*) lived around Stapylton Bay. Late in December 1914 they crossed Dolphin and Union Strait to the south shore of Victoria Island, where they united briefly at *Ingnerin* (Jenness, 1922a, pp. 23-24) [Innirit Pt.] with three families of *Haneragmiut* and were living in 11 snow-huts when the author reached their settlement. Later (in March) they moved south to the middle of the strait (Jenness, 1922a, p. 33). By the summer of 1915 the *Haneragmiut* had ceased to exist as a separate group (Jenness, 1922a, p. 34).

37.
This arrangement was a means of ensuring safe travel for Akhiatak and the author among people they did not know. While Itoqunna (Haviuyaq's wife - "Mrs. Snow-knife") was with him, Niq (Akhiatak's wife – "Mrs. Wealthy") was residing with Haviuyaq. This incident of wife exchange is discussed philosophically in Jenness (1928a, pp. 53-54). Itoqunna (or Itoqana) was about 26 years old, Niq 25 (Jenness, 1923a, pp. 26B, 30B).

38.
He had informed them that he had a wife back in his own country. Actually, he did not meet the woman he married until the fall of 1916, after he left the Arctic and went to work at the headquarters of the Geological Survey in Ottawa, Canada. The offer troubled him appreciably at the time, though he later understood better the reason for it, writing "in the eyes of the Copper Eskimos celibacy in either sex is a contemptible condition" (Jenness, 1922a, p. 158). He evidently discussed the incident with Chipman a short while later, for the latter reported that the Eskimos thought it a good joke when Jenness on two separate occasions refused to share his sleeping bag with an Eskimo woman, though "Jenness did not appreciate the joke" (Chipman, 1913-16, Feb. 2, 1915).

39.
Measurements of the heads, height, and weights of six males and six females from this group are given in Jenness (1923a, pp. 7B-8B, 24B-25B, and pp. 35B-36B).

40.
There was no need to stay longer on this trip, for these natives would soon migrate east to join the others in the Liston and Sutton Islands. And though "A stranger in an Eskimo tribe was a potential enemy and could be killed at sight," he had been introduced formally to these people and would be accepted among them the next time he met them (Jenness, 1928a, pp. 53-55).

41.
Later called Kila and Lucy; she was an orphaned girl of about 14 years. Two photographs of her taken by G.H. Wilkins in the spring of 1916 at Bernard Harbour (CMC Photo Nos. 51250-51251) are reproduced in Jenness (1922a, p. 267, Plate IX). During the next 15 years she had many strange experiences, before settling down as the wife of a prospector and trapper named Bill Storr, her eighth husband, at the west end of Coronation Gulf (Finnie, 1940, pp. 85-93; Finnie's photograph of her, taken about 1931, appears on p. 87 in his book).

42.
It was inadvisable to berate them at this time when he was so dependent on them for his own survival.

43.
An amusing description of the problems this group of three men and three women had fitting into an undersized snow-hut is given in Jenness (1928a, p. 56).

44.
The direction from *Iñnerin* (Innirit Pt.) to *Ukullik* (the nearest point of which is Sutton Island) is almost southeast, not east-northeast as the author states. The author's compass was probably not properly corrected for the strong local effect of the north magnetic pole. (The magnetic declination in 1916 was 52° 45' E; see footnote 30, this chapter). Modern topographic maps of this region carry the statement "The daily change of the North Magnetic Pole causes the magnetic compass to be very erratic in this area."

45.
Chipman and Cox (1924, p. 40B) list these three features as *Ingnerit* (pyrite), *Tulugak* (raven), and *Tipfiktok*. The first appears to be the locality now called Innerit Point; they described *Tulugak* as "a cape 20 miles east of Cape Hamilton" and *Tipfiktok* as a "hill on the coast 20 miles east of Ingnerit." Chipman undoubtedly checked these names and locations with the author and with Dr. Anderson before his report was published, for he worked in the same Victoria Memorial Museum building as they did.

46.
Ignerin appears to have been a cliff-shoreline prominence about 12 miles west of Falaise Bay (Jenness, 1922a, pp. 23-24). It is the place marked "Cliffs about 80 feet" on Rae's 1852 map (Chipman and Cox (1924, p. 40B) and probably the locality marked 'Innirit Point' on the Horton River topographic map (Canada, 1976).

47.
Sutton Island (*Putulik*).

48.
This was a two-page pencilled note, dated January 8, 1915, from *Ukullik*, asking Dr. Anderson to have Eikie bring the big sled to take back the caribou, seal meat, and clothing he had bought for the station. It was brought to Dr. Anderson by Huputaun on January 11th (Anderson, 1913-16, Jan. 11, 1915). The original note is in the Jenness file (Anderson papers, CMN).

49.
While the author was away visiting the *Haneragmiut*, Palaiyak stayed with the Eskimos at *Putulik* to net seals to supply food for the dogs at Bernard Harbour.

50.
The whereabouts of this book is not known.

51.
Rae River Eskimos at the west end of Coronation Gulf.

52.
For a more detailed account see Jenness (1928a, p. 61).

53.
Spelled *Kikiaktaryuak* in Chipman and Cox (1924, p. 40B).

54.
This is a curious statement, perhaps reflecting language misinterpretation, because later Jenness (1928a, p. 132) wrote that her first husband had vanished without leaving a trace in the hills west of Lake of Dancing

(i.e. Numichoin), Victoria Island. Taqtuk married Ikpukkuaq after he divorced his first wife Kitiksik (Jenness, 1922a, p. 161). Dr. Anderson had first met Taqtuk in 1911 (see footnote 13, this chapter.)

55.
Sewing kit.

56.
An Edison recording phonograph (see Fig. 184). The author recorded some 150 Eskimo songs during the next 1 1/2 years (Jenness, 1928a, pp. 57-58). Many of these are reproduced in written form in Roberts and Jenness (1925).

57.
A total of 13 songs recorded by Haquñaq (Haquñgaq) during the period January 1915 - June 1916, and 12 by Qanajuq have been reproduced in Roberts and Jenness (1925). Song No. 74 in that publication is the only one attributed to Haquñgaq's father, Kaiyorunna, so is probably the one recorded on this date.

58.
They took with them Qanajuq (called Sculpin — the English equivalent — in Jenness (1928a, p. 57)), and nicknamed Jennie by the scientists at the station because of her attachment to the author. The 12-year old daughter of Taqtuk, Ikpukkuaq's wife, by Taqtuk's previous marriage (Jenness, 1922a, p. 167), she was popular with the men because of her frank smile, merry laughter, and pleasant behaviour (Jenness, 1928a, pp. 57-58).

59.
A plan of this double snow-hut and the nocturnal arrangement of its dwellers is shown in Jenness (1922a, Fig. 20, p. 71).

60.
The items exchanged on this date are listed in Appendix 3.

61.
This trade was not included on the list in Appendix 3.

62.
Dr. Anderson and Castel were making the journey to take out mail and reports (see footnote 17, this chapter). Dr. Anderson had intended to leave before January 12, then by January 20, and expected to return in about two months. Chipman lists several of Dr. Anderson's preparations, commenting on how they were being undertaken (Chipman, 1913-16, Feb. 2, 1915).

63.
This report was prepared for Dr. Anderson to take to Fort Norman to mail to Ottawa but came back to Bernard Harbour with Dr. Anderson. It, or a modified version of it, was included in a longer report prepared in early August 1915 and left by Wilkins with the Royal North-West Mounted Police at Herschel Island for mailing to Ottawa. It was published in 1916 (O'Neill, 1916, pp. 237-239).

64.
Dr. Anderson made every effort to send full progress reports to Ottawa several times a year. Although neither of his two attempts to reach Fort Norman (in February 1915 and 1916) was successful, he did succeed in getting reports to Ottawa by other routes in time for their publication in the Summary Reports of the Geological Survey for 1914, 1915, and 1916, with additional accounts in the annual reports of the Department of the Naval Service for fiscal years ending March 1914, 1915, 1916, and 1917.

65.
They are reproduced as Dance Songs Nos. 135-137 in Roberts and Jenness (1925, pp. 385-390). No. 136 is reproduced in the version Eikie (Añutisiak) recorded it and in the author's version written about November 19, 1913. A third version, harmonized, appears as "Song of Asetsak" in Jenness (1922c, pp. 381-382) and as "Jimmy's Song" in Jenness (1957, p. 105).

66.
The author means "near the fishing lake," because Asecaq did not go to the fishing lake (Teshekpuk Lake) during the few days Stefansson's little party stayed nearby (October 5-8, 1913) while en route to Barrow.

67.
Now known as the Isthmus of Panama, between Central and South America. One cannot help but wonder if this story derives from tales of early British navigators and/or later whalers who sailed around the tip of South America to reach Bering Sea. Eikie, being from Point Hope, could have encountered such tales there.

68.
Liston Island, the southwesternmost, largest, and closest of the three islands to Bernard Harbour, is 12 miles distant. Viewed from

the station in Bernard Harbour, it would have obscured the other two islands.

69.
The author probably meant 11:30 a.m.

70.
December 10.

Chapter 26. – Journey up the Coppermine

1.
Dr. Anderson had enough food for himself and Castel for 60 days (he expected to make the 500-mile trip to Fort Norman in a month), and there was a 14-day supply for the other three men, plus 30-day food supply for the dogs. Dr. Anderson listed the food supplies taken on the trip (Anderson, 1913-16, Jan. 31, 1915). He had the Expedition's best team of dogs (Chipman, 1913-16, Feb. 2, 1915) and expected to be back to Bernard Harbour early in April (Chipman, 1913-16, Mar. 1, 1915).

2.
Dr. Anderson listed the items on each load. According to his calculations, the large toboggan with six dogs held 488 lbs, the small one with seven dogs 555 lbs. Part of the previous day had been spent weighing the equipment in order to equalize the loads (Anderson, 1913-16, Feb. 1, 1915).

3.
They also carried an ordinary A-shaped tent (Fig. 144) for the use of the author, Johansen, and Palaiyak on their return trip, after they had transported equipment and food supplies for Dr. Anderson and Aarnout Castel up the Coppermine River as far as the tree line. Their equipment included two wood stoves, two Primus stoves, five rifles and five pairs of snow shoes, sleeping-gear, and bags of spare clothing (Jenness, 1928a, p. 64).

4.
John Cox found the cliff to be 80 feet high when he measured it a month later (Anderson, 1913-16, Feb. 3, 1915).

5.
Close to the short portage across the neck of Cape Krusenstern, just north of Mount Barrow (Anderson, 1913-16, Feb. 3, 1915).

6.
Sir John Richardson explored east from the Mackenzie River to the Coppermine River in 1826 as a member of Sir John Franklin's second expedition and again in 1848, when he and Dr. John Rae were searching for Franklin. Dr. Anderson photographed the cairn (CMC Photo No. 38764), which was on a barren terraced beach a little northwest of Cape Krusenstern (Anderson, 1913-16, June 5, 1916). It no longer exists.

7.
Locker Point. It was named by Richardson in 1826 after Edward H. Locker, Secretary to the Royal Hospital at Greenwich, England (White, 1910, p. 396), but mistakenly labelled Pt. Lockyer on Rae's map (1852), from which the author and Dr. Anderson obtained the incorrect name. The point was not identified on the British Admiralty chart used by the Canadian Arctic Expedition.

8.
West to the mainland (Anderson, 1913-16, Feb. 6, 1915).

9.
Kigirktaryuk Island.

10.
They were using the Admiralty Chart or John Rae's map for locating themselves along this section of coastline. From their text descriptions, however, it is probable that they camped in the small bay southwest of what is now Gurling Point, east of Richardson Bay and about 7 miles east of the mouth of Richardson River. Dr. Anderson (1913-16) referred to Back or Backs Inlet on February 7, a name appearing on both old maps but now changed to Richardson Bay. On Rae's map the name Richardson Bay appears in the large bay immediately west of the mouth of the Coppermine River.

11.
Dr. Anderson, by distracting his companions with droll stories of his past college, war, and Arctic experiences, managed to take possession of and enjoy the joint marrow of most of the caribou leg bones that evening (Jenness, 1928a, pp. 65-66).

12.
Sir John Richardson (1851).

13.
They cached about 175 lbs of caribou meat here (Anderson, 1913-16, Feb. 9, 1915) for Dr. Anderson and Castel on their return journey (Jenness, 1928a, p. 65).

14.
Johansen photographed these clay banks when he and the author were heading back down the Coppermine River on February 21, 1915 (CMC Photo No. 42253).

15.
At a stony point on the west bank (Anderson, 1913-16, Feb. 9, 1915).

16.
Dr. Anderson photographed the dead wolf in front of the camp on February 10 (CMC Photo Nos. 39130, 39131) and later reported the incident to Ottawa (Anderson, 1916a, p. 225). This unusual incident was described and discussed in detail 70 years later (Jenness, 1985, 1989).

17.
The site was on the east side of the river (Anderson, 1913-16, Feb. 11, 1915). Stefansson, Billy Natkusiak, Tannaumirk, and Pannigabluk stopped there briefly while en route to Great Bear Lake in July 1910 (Stefansson, 1913a, p. 211).

18.
On February 11. On the same day he saw six wolves systematically hunting caribou about a mile from the campsite (Anderson, 1913-16, Feb. 11, 1915).

19.
The author's use of right bank and left bank in this day's entry is confusing but coincides with that in Dr. Anderson's diary. Both men were referring to the banks of the river when looking north, as indicated by reference in Dr. Anderson's diary (1913-16, Feb. 12, 1915) to the locations of patches of trees.

20.
The camp was near Sandstone Rapids, about 40 miles from the mouth of the Coppermine River and nearly 100 miles from the northeast corner of Great Bear Lake (Jenness, 1928a, p. 69).

21.
One of Johansen's purposes in making this trip was to try to determine why all the bigger trees in the spruce groves along the stream valleys at the northern tree limit were dead, a problem that had baffled travellers

on the river since the days of Richardson (in the 1820's). Johansen discovered that three or four species of beetles were responsible for the destruction of the trees and the southward recession of the tree-line (Jenness, 1928a, pp. 70 71).

22.
It was essential to obtain fresh meat regularly because three men and twelve dogs could consume an entire caribou in one day (Jenness, 1928a, p. 71).

23.
The little party stayed two days at this locality to permit Johansen to collect an adequate supply of biological specimens (Jenness, 1928a, p. 72). While there, Johansen photographed their camp in the white spruce grove (CMC Photo Nos. 42248, 42249, and 42250).

24.
Saccharine.

25.
CMC Photo No. 42254. These snow-huts had been erected by some Eskimos returning from the Dismal Lakes early in the winter (Jenness, 1928a, p. 66).

26.
These consisted of one species each of *Leda* and *Cardium* and three of *Macoma*, all marine Pleistocene molluscs from Collecting station 5284, west side of Coppermine River, 5 miles from mouth, clay bank, 3-15 feet above river (O'Neill, 1924, pp. 30A, 32A). *Macoma calcarea* specimens from this area have been radiocarbon dated at 9880 years (St. Onge, 1987, p. 27).

27.
These directions cannot be taken literally, if one seeks to plot the author's route, because of the strong influence of the north magnetic pole on his compass.

28.
Probably Seven Mile Island.

29.
Kulliksak or *Kullikshak* ("a place formerly inhabited now uninhabited") is the second island south of Locker Point (Chipman and Cox, 1924, p. 37B). It may be one of the Berens Islands.

30.
There were 21 to 23 snow-huts, 5 of them double, and 70 to 80 Eskimos in this settle-

ment in the Duke of York Archipelago (Jenness, 1922a, pp. 37, 76).

31.
This snow-hut is described and illustrated in Jenness (1922a, p. 66).

32.
This was Uloksak or Uloqsaq (called "Knife" in Jenness (1928a, p. 75)), a 30-year old member of the *Kilusiktok* group (Jenness, 1923a, p. B15, 67B). He was reputedly the most powerful medicine-man in that part of the country (Jenness, 1928a, p. 75).

33.
Cosmo D. Melvill and John Hornby were English game-hunters who came down the Mackenzie River with Stefansson and Dr. Anderson in 1908. They lived on or near Great Bear Lake from 1908 to 1911, and Stefansson visited them there on more than one occasion (Stefansson, 1913a, pp. 216, 220, 223, 236). Melvill returned to England in 1911; Hornby remained alone until 1914, when Melvill re-joined him. Dr. Anderson hoped to encounter them on his trip to Fort Norman at this time.

34.
These include CMC Photo Nos. 37008 and 37024, and probably also 37211 and 37212.

35.
These items had been pillaged by Uloksak and his kinsmen in the summer of 1914 from the cabin of two Belgian Oblate missionaries, Fathers Rouvier and Le Roux, on the Dismal Lakes, after their murder on the Coppermine River in 1913. Several other nearby families also held property of the two priests, for Palaiyak observed a cassock and crucifix in another hut (Jenness, 1922a, p. 77).

36.
Five double houses (Jenness, 1922a, p. 76).

37.
Uloksak. (See footnote 32, this chapter.)

38.
This game is described briefly in Jenness (1922a, p. 218).

39.
In 1848 Eskimos ferried Richardson and Rae and their exploration party across the mouth of the Rae River (Jenness, 1922a, p. 29). Rae returned to Coronation Gulf in 1851.

40.
Details about these eight groups of Eskimos are in Jenness (1922a, pp. 32-43).

41.
These Eskimos had heard through someone at or near Great Bear Lake that a big ship was coming into their region in 1914 and one of them had recently travelled west to Cape Krusenstern looking for it. There he discovered the trail made by Dr. Anderson's party early in February 1915. When the author reached their village they were preparing to follow that trail westward in search of the ship, hoping for a renewal of trading like they had enjoyed with Capt. J. Bernard in 1911 (Chipman, 1913-16, Mar. 1, 1915). On learning that the ship was within 80 miles the entire village prepared for go there (Jenness, 1928a, p. 80).

42.
The author took at least seven photographs of various facets of this migration. They are CMC Photo Nos. 37026, 37027, 37028, 37033, 37034, 37103, and 37104.

43.
Locker Point (see footnote 7, this chapter).

44.
The next sentence almost duplicates one that appears two sentences later starting with "A little baby..." so has been omitted here.

45.
He was pulling a heavily laden small sled; his two wives and six dogs pulled his larger sled (Jenness, 1928a, p. 80).

46.
The whereabouts of this notebook is unknown.

47.
A young wife warmed water in her mouth, then poured it on her husband's bearskin mitten, which he rubbed along the sled runner while she warmed some more. Re-icing the sled runners in this manner took 1/2 hour or more (Jenness, 1922a, pp. 118-119).

48.
Now known as Pasley Cove.

49.
To warn the men there of the impending arrival of the large group of Eskimos (Jenness, 1928a, pp. 81-82).

50.
Their previous settlement of 33 snow-huts on the shore of *Ilavillik* (Harkness Island,

the smallest of the Liston and Sutton Islands) was about 5 hours distant.

Chapter 27. – Trading Farther Afield

1.
The author's photographs apparently taken on this date include CMC Photo Nos. 37010, 37011, 37012, 37013, 37020, 37029, and 37054, but see entry of March 5 re his pictures being lightstruck.

2.
Chipman confirmed this observation, writing "...to attempt to work is useless. At night they jam in until one can only retire to the bunk, as much out of the way as possible. I usually sleep through it and then read when they have gone" (Chipman, 1913-16, Mar. 8-14, 1915).

3.
By this time more than 100 Eskimos had built snow-huts within 50 yards of the station (Jenness, 1922a, p. 83).

4.
They were camped near *Putulik* (Sutton Island).

5.
The author had warned the Eskimos that unless the fox-trap was returned sickness would befall the thief (Chipman, 1913-16, Mar. 1-7, 1915).

6.
"Jenness has filled several bags [with clothing] for specimens, we have outfitted ourselves and put a bag away for stock" (Chipman, 1913-16, Mar. 1-7, 1915). See Appendix 3 for tradings.

7.
Some of the Eskimos openly accused the author of murdering their companion, even though he had been more than 100 miles away at the time the man died; consequently Uloqsaq's seance was actually a form of murder trial. The author was well aware of the seriousness of the charge, for the Eskimo penalty for murder was assassination. More detailed descriptions of the seance are given in Jenness (1922a, pp. 207-209, and 1928a, pp. 85-89).

8.
The author spoke in French (and Latin) so that the cook (Cockney) would not under-

stand, for he did not want the cook to "ruin the little drama by some false move" (Jenness, 1928a, p. 87).

9.
Some of the Eskimos had learned this kind of dance at Great Bear Lake. Uloqsaq had one of his wives dance it, a "white man's" reel, with Cockney (Jenness, 1928a, p. 88).

10.
The author obtained a great deal of clothing and footgear on this date, mainly in exchange for ammunition. The items purchased on March 3, 4, and 5, and the goods traded for them, are listed in Appendix 3. Trading conditions were ideal, for the author could enjoy the "comfort of home" while trading and could store the traded goods on the site. Conditions were less than ideal for his fellow scientists, but they too found ways to keep the visiting Eskimos entertained (Jenness, 1928a, p. 84).

11.
At least one photograph (Fig. 146) was not as defective as suggested here (see also footnote 1, this chapter).

12.
This settlement was on the ice, west of the Liston and Sutton Islands.

13.
Chipman and O'Neill were clean shaven, while Johansen wore an 'imperial' beard (Jenness, 1928a, pp. 84-85).

14.
The author's 29th birthday had been February 10th, the day the wolf attacked him on the Coppermine River.

15.
These Eskimo names are given in Jenness (1922a, pp. 15-18).

16.
The author evidently 'lost a day' between March 7th and 11th, the entry here entitled Wednesday appearing in the diary as Tuesday March 8th, Tuesday March 9th, and Wed. March 10th, with only one Tuesday and the 8th and 9th crossed out.

17.
They were camped along the small beach slightly downhill and some 50 yards from the Expedition house (Jenness, 1928a, p. 83).

18.
This may be Song No. 100, recorded by a Coppermine River man (Roberts and Jenness, 1925, p. 317), which Jenness says was "intended mainly to produce an abundance of seals" (Roberts and Jenness, 1925, p. 14).

19.
The Eskimos were given blocks of matches for singing into the phonograph (see Appendix 3).

20.
Two songs by Uloqsaq recorded by the author appear in Roberts and Jenness (1925, pp. 241 and 289). Two other songs (pp. 78 and 205), are by another Uloqsaq (probably Uloqsaq II, who was later found guilty of murder). The author recorded 37 other songs by Coppermine River Eskimos, all of which are reproduced in this same publication.

21.
To go to Ikpukkuaq's, at *Putulik* (Sutton Island).

22.
Akhiatak had been wrestling with another man in the dance house (Jenness, 1922a, p. 171).

23.
These probably include CMC Photo Nos. 37019, 37109, and 36934.

24.
Ikpukkuaq was to be provided with a .44 Winchester rifle and ammunition, which he would be permitted to keep, together with an Expedition tent and other things if he served the author faithfully and returned with him in the autumn (Anderson, 1916a, p. 230).

25.
Ikpukkuaq's adopted son.

26.
Songs Nos. 56 and 70 in Roberts and Jenness (1925, pp. 223-225 and 254-256). See also Appendix 5.

27.
Song No. 71 in Roberts and Jenness (1925, pp. 257-258).

28.
They were to go west as far as the southwestern part of Darnley Bay in order to connect with the previous surveys at Cape Parry peninsula and carry the survey eastward (Anderson, 1916a, p. 231) and expected to return about the first of June (Chipman, 1913-16, Mar. 17, 1915). A list of the supplies they took with them is in the Canadian Arctic Expedition - Record (1913-16, p. 126).

29.
Because the *Alaska* had been unable to return to Bernard Harbour from Herschel Island the previous September there was insufficient coal for their stoves, so they had to seek driftwood along the shoreline from time to time.

30.
From just east of *Putulik*. Frequent changes of location were dictated by the limited supply of seals, the only food supply for both Eskimos and their dogs during the winter.

31.
Arnauyuk, later known as Kila and Lucy, married Aiyalligak a few months later; he divorced her the following winter (1915-16) and she returned to live with Ikpukkuaq. Within a month she was married again to a young divorced man, Ikpukkuaq's adopted son Qiqpuk (whose first wife Haquñgaq had become the third wife of the shaman Uloqsaq). Qiqpuk divorced Arnauyuk after a fortnight, and she later married an Eskimo from the Mackenzie River delta and left the region (Jenness, 1922a, p. 160; see Plate IX, p. 267, for a photograph of Kila). Some of her subsequent experiences are recounted in Finnie (1940, pp. 85-93). (See also footnote 41, Chapter 25.)

32.
There were six people in the snowhouse, not seven as would seem the case here. The author slept between Ikpukkuaq and the young boy Haugak, not between Ikpukkuaq and Higilaq. Higilaq was the second name of Taqtu, Ikpukkuaq's wife, a name she commenced using (without explanation) about this time (Jenness, 1922a, p. 167). Haugak was Haviron's son, now adopted by Ikpukkuaq (Jenness, 1922a, pp. 160-161, and Fig. 32, p. 99).

33.
A brief description and plan-view of the three united snow-huts about 15 miles north-

west of the Liston and Sutton Islands is given in Jenness (1922a, pp. 71-72 and Fig. 21).

34.
CMC Photo No. 37019 (Fig. 147).

35.
The author gave Ikpukkuaq six boxes of .44 cartridges in exchange for four boxes of .303 Savage and ten boxes of .30-30 Winchester ammunition, and twelve .44 cartridges for a dancing cap (see Appendix 3).

36.
These were in advance of the supplies issued to the author on April 11, 1915, and included 400-500 lbs of rice, pemmican, sugar, and coal oil, which would be stored for safety (less likely to be stolen) with native supplies on the south shore of Victoria Island (Anderson, 1913-16, Apr. 13, 1915).

37.
Cox surveyed the coast from the winter base to Locker Point on this trip. The author had volunteered to assist him for at least 10 days (Anderson, 1913-16, Mar. 30, 1915), while Aarnout Castel was away (Anderson, 1916a, p. 228),

38.
The supplies they took on the trip are listed in Canadian Arctic Expedition Record - 1913-16, p. 126.

39.
The author traded primers, lead, and gun powder for the stone lamp (see Appendix 3, Mar. 25, 1915).

40.
Cox's latitude and longitude for Cape Lambert were 68°29'05" N and 114°10'00" W (Chipman and Cox, 1924, p. 36B). The base mark was at Bernard Harbour; it in turn was based on the established location of a monument at the Canada-Alaska boundary.

41.
Aneraq was the 50-year old father of the shaman Uloqhaq; some of the Southern Party members gave him the nickname 'Cardinal Richelieu' (Chipman, 1913-16, Mar. 1-7, 1915).

42.
Now Locker Point; Eskimo name *Tikirak* (Chipman and Cox, 1924, p. 37B)

43.
Cox's readings were 68°17'34" N. Lat. and 114°00'21" W. Long. (Chipman and Cox, 1924, p. 36B).

44.
Dr. Anderson and Castel were coming from near Cape Hearne, which is to the southwest. Their encounter was at about 5 p.m. Cox had completed the shoreline survey to that point from Bernard Harbour (Anderson, 1913-16, Mar. 30, 1915).

45.
Dr. Anderson had expected to meet white men at Great Bear Lake, for several (including John Hornby and C.D. Melvill) had lived there in previous winters, and he could have given them the outgoing mail for Fort Norman. By the time he and Castel finally reached Dease River in early March, however, it was too late for him to continue towards Fort Norman and still be able to return in time to organize the scientific work for the spring and summer (Jenness, 1928a, p. 91).

46.
Some 25 lbs rice were also cached here. Soon afterwards both pemmican and rice were stolen by two old Coppermine River Eskimos (Anauyuk and Kongiun) according to a report on April 16 from another native, one known as "the Handshaker" (Canadian Arctic Expedition - Record, 1913-16, p. 126).

47.
With the return of Castel, Cox had access to a dog team and the assistant he needed for his topographical work, so the author was free to take his own dog team and join the Eskimos who were going to Victoria Island for the summer. He and Cox, therefore, terminated their survey and returned to the station with Dr. Anderson and Castel (Jenness, 1928a, p. 92).

48.
Cox planned to complete his topographic survey southeast to the Rae River, thence up that river to its source and from there overland back to Bernard Harbour. On the return of Chipman and O'Neill, who were surveying the coast west to Darnley Bay, Cox would join them in surveying east from the mouth of Rae River to the eastern end of Coronation Gulf. The author intended to leave with Ikpukkuaq and his family to cross

over to Victoria Island hunting and travelling with them and meeting Eskimos from Prince Albert Sound, until the straits froze up again in the fall and he could return, probably in November (Jenness, 1922a, p. 192). Dr. Anderson was preparing to take provisions west for Chipman and O'Neill, and mail to Baillie Island, from whence it would be taken on the *Alaska* to Herschel Island when navigation was again possible (Anderson, 1913-16, Apr. 21, 1915).

Chapter 28. – To Victoria Island

1.
The *Puivlik* natives were living in spring tents about 15 miles northwest of the Liston and Sutton Islands (Jenness, 1922a, p. 125).

2.
The Expedition used ice from a lake a mile to the south for much of its supply of drinking water (Johansen, 1922, p. 16N).

3.
The south shore of Victoria Island near Read Island.

4.
This direction was uncorrected for local magnetic declination. It was later corrected to north by east (Jenness, 1922a, p. 127).

5.
The meat was cached at Penny Bay, about 60 miles to the northwest (Jenness, 1922a, p. 127).

6.
A settlement of snow-huts near *Ignerin* built by the *Akulliakattak* natives earlier in the winter when they crossed from Cape Bexley to begin sealing (Jenness, 1922a, p. 127).

7.
They had not taken a tent with them (Jenness, 1922a, p. 127) and were still as far out from shore as when they started (Jenness, 1928a, p. 95).

8.
This height is close. The most recent topographic map (Canada, 1982) has the 200 ft contour close to shore here.

9.
Cape Pullen is the peninsula Rae (1852) had named Point Pullen; the author later identified it as Cape Kendall (Jenness, 1928a, p. 95), the name shown on the early British Admiralty chart No. 2443. It is now known as Cape Ernest Kendall.

10.
British Admiralty Chart No. 2443, which the author must have had with him.

11.
Without oil or wood they had no means of cooking or even melting snow or ice to drink.

12.
The author later spelled it *Ingnerin* (Jenness, 1922a, p. 23) but it appears as *Ignerin* on Map 1 (p. 126) in the same publication. It is listed as *Ingnerit* in Chipman and Cox (1924, p. 40B), where it is defined as "Place marked, 'Cliffs about 80 feet' on Rae's map. ('Pyrite' because pyrite, used for striking fire, is found here.)" It is shown as 'Innirit Point' on a modern topographic map (Canada, 1976).

13.
The author may have meant two nights previous, for he had no means of heating ice or snow to get water the night before.

14.
Lacking any means of cooking, the author tried to melt some snow in a cup by putting it against his body but had limited success (Jenness, 1928a, p. 98).

15.
The north side of Dolphin and Union Strait.

16.
April 15. It must have been cached at a site away from their present route.

17.
CMC Photo No. 37023 shows the dogs dragging two seals, with the seal hunters far behind. The other photos taken at this time were probably CMC Nos. 37022, 37025, and 37037.

18.
On the south side of Dolphin and Union Strait.

19.
Probably conveying items to the landing site on Victoria Island, including Ikpukkuaq's summer tent (see entry for May 9).

20.
CMC Photo No. 37004. Other photos taken by the author on this day were CMC Nos. 37046 (heating snow for drinking water), 37092 (preparing to migrate), 37097 (loading a sled before migrating), and 37094 (a brief rest during migration).

21.
This was the transitional time of year for the Eskimos between seal hunting on the ice and caribou hunting and lake fishing on Victoria Island. As the annual migration of caribou from the mainland north to Victoria Island had not yet commenced, the Eskimos were still totally dependent on catching seals for their food, clothing, and fuel, and could well afford to linger here and there on the ice of Dolphin and Union Strait during their journey, wherever the seal hunting was rewarding.

22.
The author discusses this subject (childbirth) at more length in Jenness (1922a, pp. 164-165).

23.
CMC Photo No. 37098 shows the camp with drying clothes. Photo No. 37006 shows a similar scene. Other photos taken by the author probably on this date are Nos. 37043, 37061, and 37099.

24.
The heavy blubber pokes, each weighing between 300 and 400 lbs when full (and each family had two pokes), were being transported to a site on the south shore of Victoria Island to be stored there for fuel for the autumn (Jenness, 1928a, p. 105).

25.
The author had a small copy of Homer's *The Odyssey* with him for mental stimulation and reflection.

26.
The Odyssey consists of 24 'books', few of which exceed 20 pages in length.

27.
On Read Island the blubber pokes would be safe, carefully protected by stones from small animals and birds until the Eskimos returned in the autumn.

28.
Both rabbits and foxes left the coastal island before open water cut off their access to the shore (Jenness, 1928a, p. 106).

29.
See diary entries for December 11 and 12. Kimiryuak River flows into Forsyth Bay.

30.
To a site near the mouth of Okauyarvik Creek (Jenness, 1922a, p. 128). This was the usual starting point on Victoria Island for these Eskimos, for the hills immediately to the north were lower than at any other place to east or west (Jenness, 1928a, p. 110).

31.
These were items Ikpukkuaq had sent ahead to this locality a fortnight previous (Jenness, 1922a, p. 128).

32.
To enquire into the prospects of food during the summer (Jenness, 1922a, p. 128). This seance is described also in Jenness (1922a, pp. 211-212).

33.
Spelled *atatsiak* and meaning "mother's father?" (Jenness, 1922a, p. 211).

34.
Sixty miles to the north (Jenness, 1928a, p. 109). The more accurate maps available today indicate the minimum distance across Wollaston Peninsula to Prince Albert Sound is 70 miles, and the circuitous route these Eskimos would have taken would have exceeded that by many miles.

35.
Including the author there were 20 persons in all. They were the only human inhabitants that summer of the southwestern part of Victoria Island (Jenness, 1922a, p. 128).

36.
A Canadian-made sporting model, .280 calibre, 5-shot rifle, the powerful copper-nosed bullets of which were more effective than the bullets of the .44 Winchester. A military version of this rifle used by Canadian soldiers during World War I proved unsatisfactory and had to be replaced (Jenness, 1928a, p. 161).

37.
They lingered at this coastal site, *Okauyarvik* (which means "the Home of the Dryad" or "Dryad Harbour," after the flowering plant *Dryas integrifolia*) for a week, arranging to leave there all their winter equipment until their return in the autumn (Jenness, 1928a, p. 110). *Dryas integrifolia*, commonly known as Arctic avens and now the

floral symbol of the Northwest Territories, is a widely established species in the north, favouring calcareous habitats such as abound on southwestern Victoria Island (Svoboda, 1978, p. 205).

38.
They had been out hunting ptarmigan with their bows and arrows (Jenness, 1922a, p. 128).

39.
One of these photographs survived. It is CMC Photo No. 37031 (see Appendix 6).

40.
The author cached most of his provisions here, retaining on his sled for the journey north only a little rice, cocoa, tea, and corn-meal to ease the transition from his regular diet to the meat and fish diet he was facing. Left behind were pemmican tins, rice, oat-meal, hard-bread, and the balance of his supply of tea (Jenness, 1928a, p. 110).

41.
From modern maps one can determine that the azimuths for the two directions the author lists are approximately 204 and 206, indicating a magnetic variation uncorrected on his compass of about 54. At Bernard Harbour it was determined as 52° 45'E (O'Neill, 1924, map in pocket).

42.
The author's confusion over the location of Read Island, which one can infer from this statement, was the result of his reliance on Rae's (1852) map, on which Read Island (shown as Bcads Island) is much farther west than it should be.

43.
This statement appears to be reasonably cor-rect, for from Stefansson's account (1913a, pp. 271-278) he started from Forsyth Bay and may well have moved initially westward to *Okauyarvik.*

44.
Once the sealing season ended the Eskimos broke into small groups and moved regu-larly about southwestern Victoria Island throughout the summer months. There were no great salmon trout runs in the streams and rivers on the southwest coast of the is-land, so that Ikpukkuaq and his companions had to move inland to lakes where they could catch lake trout (Jenness, 1922a, p. 122).

45.
Each family had its own separate cache (Jenness, 1922a, p. 128).

46.
Tins of pemmican. Ikpukkuaq placed his kayak on top of the author's cache (Jenness, 1922a, p. 128). Few Copper Eskimos owned kayaks, this being one of only two the author saw around Dolphin and Union Strait, and *umiaks* were unknown to these people (Jenness, 1946, pp. 139-140).

Chapter 29. – Encounter with the 'Blond' Eskimos

1.
Ikpukkuaq cleaned away the snow to get at the bare ground (Jenness, 1922a, p. 128).

2.
Ikpukkuaq's possessions were on Avrunna's sled, his own sled having been left at the coast (Jenness, 1922a, p. 128).

3.
This is close to the western margin of a magnificent, west-oriented glacial drumlin field (see Fig. 172; also Figs. 1 and 3 in Sharpe, 1988).

4.
Lake Ekallugak, the "first lake in the Col-ville Hills." It was about 1/2 mile wide and contained two kinds of fish in abundance, lake trout and lake salmon (Jenness, 1928a, p. 112). The salmon, however, are not true salmon but salmon trout of the genus *Sal-velinus* (Jenness, 1922a, p. 15, footnote 1).

5.
Sometime during the day the author photo-graphed Ikpukkuaq fishing through the ice at Lake Ekallugak (CMC Photo No. 36971).

6.
This is Mount Bumpus, which rises to just over 1600 feet above sea level. It was named by V. Stefansson after Dr. Herman C. Bumpus, then Director of the American Museum of Natural History in New York (Stefansson, 1913a, p. 276), which had co-sponsored Stefansson's previous (1908-12) Arctic expedition. The Eskimo name for this prominent hill was *Wivyaurun* (Jenness, 1922a, p. 24). The author's distant photo-graph of it (CMC Photo No. 38603) from the south side of Lake Añmaloqtoq appears

in Jenness (1922a, Fig. 2, p. 24). This photograph is listed with O'Neill's photographs, but the author was the only Expedition member at this locality.

7.
Stefansson (1913a) saw these hills when he crossed Victoria Island in 1911 and named them after the American Museum of Natural History in New York. The name appears on a map in the back of his book. The 'range' is part of the Colville Mountains.

8.
A mistake; all the drainage is above ground, though the differences in level [are] often imperceptible. [D.J.]

9.
It was, in fact, Avrunna's sled with Ikpukkuaq's possessions on it, for the latter had cached his sled at the coast.

10.
The *turq* was used to chisel holes in the ice. Copper was preferred to iron because the tool often struck stones in the bottom of shallow lakes, and would chip if made of iron and be more difficult to repair (Jenness, 1922a, p. 153, footnote 1). One is illustrated in Jenness (1946, p. 113, Fig. 137).

11.
This scoop was called *ilaun* (Jenness, 1922a, p. 153).

12.
Also spelled *kattak* (Jenness, 1922a, p. 153).

13.
The sealskin bag was called *ungellak* (Jenness, 1922a, p. 153).

14.
Spelled Ammalurtuq and shown as 259 metres (850 feet) above sea level on the Horton River (1:1,000,000) topographic map (Canada, 1976).

15.
Tiriaq (*tiriaq*) is a tundra weasel (Anderson, 1913, p. 496).

16.
This was *Dryas integrifolia* (called *oqauyaq* or *okauyak* by the Eskimos)(Jenness, 1922a, p. 98), a member of the rose family rather than a heather. This was the first time this season that Taqtu was able to cook over an *okauyak* fire; previously she had cooked with seal oil and a stone lamp (Jenness,

1922a, p. 130). CMC Photo No. 36972, taken by the author, shows Ikpukkuaq's adopted young son Haugak carrying a large bundle of the plant for the family's fuel supply (Fig. 32 in Jenness, 1922a, p. 99).

17.
It was the finest specimen the author saw on Victoria Island (Jenness, 1928a, p. 116).

18.
It was smaller than the lake they had just left, but lay near the watershed of north- and south-flowing drainage and was encircled by larger lakes that provided good fishing until mid-summer. The author later called it Lake of Dancing (Jenness, 1928a, p. 116). From descriptive clues in the diary, I have concluded that this lake is the small, deep, U-shaped lake (with the open part of the 'U' facing west), about 1 mile west of the southwestern side of Lake Añmaloqtoq (see Fig. 165). Also spelled NumiXoni (diary) and Numikhoin (Jenness, 1922a, p. 130).

19.
From Prince Albert Sound.

20.
This seance is described more fully in Jenness (1922a, p. 194; also 1928a, p. 117). Later Taqtu's companions stated as fact that she had been transformed into a wolf during the seance (Jenness, 1922a, p. 194).

21.
The author used this name (or the alternative spelling Tahiryuaq) for the large island-dotted lake (now called Lake Quunnguq (Canada, 1976)) some 20 miles northeast of Lake Añmaloqtoq (Ammalurtuq), which he called Big Lake in Jenness (1928a, p. 117). Lake Tahiryuaq, on a modern topographic map (Canada, 1976) lies about 28 miles north of the east end of Prince Albert Sound, roughly where Stefansson (1913a, map inside back cover) had shown it. However, there were in this region two lakes with this name known to the author's Eskimo companions, in addition to the one north of Prince Albert Sound, which they had not seen; the one with which they were most familiar was the one for which they were headed (Jenness, 1922a, p. 34).

22.
Tuhajoq and his wife were too old and Haugaq (Ikpukkuaq's adopted son) was too young to make unnecessary journeys. They stayed behind to look after the dried meat (Jenness, 1922a, p. 131; 1928a, p. 118).

23.
The author's sled had steel runners (Jenness, 1922a, p. 131).

24.
Dr. Anderson (1919a) questioned this identification in a letter to the author 4 years later, after the latter had sent him some notes on animal and bird life on Victoria Island. In those notes the author suggested this animal might have been a shrew. This was unlikely, replied Dr. Anderson, and suggested it might have been a mouse. The author replied (Jenness, 1919) that the Dr. was probably right and added that the Eskimos had called it *kilagmiutak* (which means lemming according to an entry in his diary dated July 5, 1915). As the author had captured lemmings for Dr. Anderson at Barter Island and Bernard Harbour (see Appendix 4C and footnote 6, Chapter 18) he must have known the animal he saw on Victoria Island was not a lemming. On the other hand Dr. Anderson was probably aware that mice were unknown on the Arctic coast, having been excited about capturing one at Herschel Island, farther north than he had found any previously; he concluded that it had come north down the Mackenzie in a box of supplies for the Southern Party (Anderson, 1913-16, August 6, 1914). The discovery of a mouse, albeit no longer alive, on Victoria Island, would have aroused much interest, therefore, but unfortunately the creature was not available to Dr. Anderson for accurate identification. It may have been a tundra or red-backed vole.

25.
Some of the Eskimos had no shelter at all (Jenness, 1922a, p. 131), as shown in two photographs by the author (CMC Photo Nos. 36984 and 37003).

26.
On his primus stove.

27.
This seance is described in Jenness (1922a, p. 212).

28.
The author did not supply a number here.

29.
It empties into Prince Albert Sound just south of what is now called Linaluk Island. Stefansson (1913a) had labelled it Uallinaluk Island on his map, but had shown it and the Nalluarjuk (he spelled it Nalluaryuk) River in their appropriate locations.

30.
The author must have had a copy of Stefansson's (1913a) map on which all of these features are shown.

31.
For another description of this incident see Jenness (1928a, pp. 120-121).

32.
This seance is further described in Jenness (1922a, p. 194, 212; 1928a, p. 119).

33.
This lake was 'famous' because it lay near the watershed on the Eskimos' route to Prince Albert Sound and was surrounded by good fishing lakes (Jenness, 1928a, p. 116).

34.
The author was not surprised by Ikpukkuaq's disability, after seeing him chasing fish in ice-cold water up to his hips (see diary entry for July 19, 1915).

35.
The *Mary Sachs* at this time was hauled up on a beach just east of Cape Kellett on the southwest coast of Banks Island (Stefansson, 1921, pp. 266-273) and exercised no influence whatsoever upon the movements of the small Eskimo population the author refers to. Most of the *Kanghirjuarmiut* had gone northeast of Prince Albert Sound for the summer (see diary entry for June 2, 1915).

36.
The first to spot their arrival was Milukkatuk. Qanayuq then ran forward to meet them and assure them of a friendly reception (Jenness, 1928a, p. 121a). Others followed suit, and the author photographed their meeting and the unloading of the newcomers' sled (CMC Photo Nos. 36996 and 36986 respectively).

37.
A minor confusion exists over the names of Kunana's wife and child, for elsewhere (Jenness, 1922a, p. 131) the author listed the wife as Allikammik, but gave facial details for Nateksina, who is listed as a 40-year old female from Prince Albert Sound (Jenness, 1923a, p. B29). The diary entry here appears correct.

38.
Nilgak, age 35, his wife Utuaiyok, also age 35, and their 11-year old son Akoaksiun.

Nilgak was crippled (Jenness, 1922a, p. 131).

39.
At this point the author wrote in his diary "(see notebook for full details)." Unfortunately the whereabouts of this notebook is unknown, but a few more details of this first encounter are given in Jenness (1922a, p. 131). It had been expected that 30 or 40 strangers (*Tormiats* as he called them) would turn up at this meeting place, but the author learned that most had gone far to the northeast, and it was not possible to follow them by sled at that season (Jenness, 1928a, p. 121). The newcomers joined their skin tent to that of the earlier visitors to make a double tent (Fig. 159).

40.
The trading was chiefly between the two groups of natives (Jenness, 1922a, p. 132).

41.
Descriptions of the dance-house and dances are given in Jenness (1922a, pp. 69, 112, 224-227). The author photographed the visitors dressing for the dance (Fig. 160 and CMC Photo No. 36981, which appears as Fig. 42 in Jenness, 1922a, p. 132).

42.
The names referred to here are on a map in the back of Stefansson's (1913a) book and on British Admiralty Chart No. 2443.

43.
As the *Tormiats* had little experience with 'white men' they showed much interest in the author, watching all that he did with curiosity and concern, perhaps half expecting him to turn into a monster (Jenness, 1928a, p. 123).

44.
A small band of Eskimos living on the south side of Victoria Island opposite Kent Peninsula (Cambridge Bay area, see Appendix 2).

45.
Measurements and other data on the three men (Kunana, Nilgak, and Imeraq) and two women (Utuaiyoq and Nateksina) are presented in Jenness (1923a, pp. 18B-B19, B29, B35-36B). Jenness also photographed Kunana and Nilgak (CMC Photo No. 36967; see Plate IVB in Jenness, 1922a, p. 257). Though he saw only these few representatives of Stefansson's so-called 'Blond Eskimos', the author was satisfied that they resembled his travelling companions so closely in physical features, language, and customs that he need not seek out others. To visit, observe, and examine these northern people had been one of the prime purposes of his seven-month trip to Victoria Island (Jenness, 1928a, p. 129).

46.
The name Allikumiq appears three times here in the diary, evidently in error (see footnote 37, this chapter). Allikumiq (or Allikumik) was Nateksina's adopted child (see diary entry for June 1, 1915).

47.
The whereabouts of this notebook is not known.

48.
This impulsive display of affection and its effect on Taqtu brought about the abrupt termination of the meeting with the *Kanghirjuarmiut* and the return of Ikpukkuaq's people to Lake Numichoin (Jenness, 1928a, pp. 124-126).

Chapter 30. – Lake Numichoin

1.
She was one of eight shamans in Dolphin and Union Strait during the winter of 1914-15, gaining her powers after the death of her father, who was also a shaman (Jenness, 1922a, p. 192).

2.
This seance is described more fully in Jenness (1922a, p. 212).

3.
Ikpuk's brother died near Lake Numichoin. This was [the] cause of his weeping. [D.J.]

His bleached bones lay on the crest of a nearby knoll. Ikpuk's eldest brother, he had died 3 years (Jenness, 1922a, p. 177) or perhaps 6 years before (Jenness, 1928a, p. 126). The author later met another older brother Ayallik (see diary entry for July 2, 1916).

4.
Previous observations (footnotes 4 and 41, Chapter 28) suggest that his compass was not corrected for the local magnetic declination of about 54°, so his real direction was more likely west-southwest. Indeed, all of the author's inland directions between May

15 and August 1 may need 50°-52° correction for magnetic declination. After August 1 he could ascertain his direction with reference to the south shore of Victoria Island. His distances between lakes are nearly correct, however, as shown by examining modern topographic maps.

5.
Lake Tahirjuaq (now identified as Lake Quunnguq (Canada, 1976)) lies northeast of Lake Numichoin, another indication that the author's compass was not corrected for the local magnetic declination.

6.
This specimen, now identified as a black-bellied plover, is No. 9950 in the National Bird Collection, CMN. Its Eskimo name *qealiauq* (or *kealiauk*) imitates the bird's cry (Jenness, 1919).

7.
Spelled Añmaloqtoq in the diary, Angmaloktok in Jenness (1922a, p. 132), Ammalurtuq on the Horton River topographic map (Canada, 1976), and called "Ever-Frozen Lake" in Jenness (1928a, pp. 127). This last name was apt, for the lake was still frozen on the 12th of July 1989, when I flew over it.

8.
During this brief stop the author climbed a nearby hill to examine the surrounding countryside and described it as singularly flat and depressing (Jenness, 1928a, p. 127).

9.
Named "Parted-Hair" in Jenness (1928a, pp. 127-128).

10.
They severely rebuked Tucik outside the author's tent that evening. Tucik's wife, Mikineroq, later sought amends by offering the author a large trout, but her offer was declined. The attitude of Tucik towards the author improved markedly thereafter, and he later became quite helpful (Jenness, 1928a, p. 128).

11.
This could be any of several small lakes about 3 miles west of Lake Numichoin.

12.
Tied to large stones the dogs could only look on with mournful eyes as the author and his Eskimo companions ate each night (Jenness, 1928a, p. 131).

13.
The author wrote "turnstone" here at some later date, probably after he had shown the specimen to Dr. Anderson at Bernard Harbour in the fall. The bird was a ruddy turnstone and is specimen No. 9951 in the National Bird Collection, CNM.

14.
See footnote 3, this chapter. Ikpukkuaq's eldest brother was Nerialaq, who may have been Higilaq's first husband and father of Avrunna and Jennie.

15.
By this time the females were producing their young and staying isolated while the bulls were wandering singly or in small groups (Jenness, 1928a, p. 130).

16.
Her concern stemmed from two personal matters: (1) her first husband had disappeared without a trace in the hills to the west of this camp many years before (Jenness, 1928a, p. 131-132) and her father had also disappeared without a trace while hunting (Jenness, 1922a, p. 177), and she was concerned lest the same fate befall the author; and (2) she and Ikpukkuaq had to bring the author back safely to the station at Bernard Harbour to receive the payment promised them for taking him to Victoria Island for the summer.

17.
A note on the inside back cover of volume three of this diary lists Homer under the heading "Books from Home." It is probable, therefore, that this copy of Homer's *The Odyssey*, which was in Greek, was one he had received from his home on August 6, 1914, when he was at Herschel Island. He had developed a special love for this book during his early college days in New Zealand, when in the summer of 1906 he had been invited to read (and translate from Greek) *The Odyssey* each Friday evening with Professor G.W. von Zedlitz, his Latin and Greek professor at Victoria University College, Wellington, New Zealand (Jenness, 1963). Years later, from the war front in France, he wrote Professor von Zedlitz of how much comfort he frequently derived from reading passages in this book while he was in the Arctic (Jenness, 1917).

18.
This was a horned lark, now specimen No. 9953 in the National Bird Collection, CMN.

19.
The seance she subsequently held is described in more detail in Jenness (1922a, pp. 213-214).

20.
A Lapland longspur, now specimen No. 9954, National Bird Collection, CMN.

21.
About this date Taqtu's second name, Higilaq, gradually was used more and more, and by the following year she was seldom called Taqtu (Jenness, 1922a, p. 167). The reason for the change was never ascertained.

22.
One can sympathize with Higilaq's position. The author's light sealskin boots could not be mended easily for want of replacement sealskin, and she knew that caribou skins would be scarce until the weather warmed up and the mosquitoes drove the caribou near again (Jenness, 1928a, p. 131).

23.
A tundra weasel. Many of the Copper Eskimos wore a weasel skin suspended from the back of the coat as a charm against sickness or for luck in hunting (Anderson, 1913, p. 523).

24.
This included skins, sinew, spare clothing, tools, and implements (Jenness, 1922a, p. 133).

25.
Higilaq told the author that two shades had entered the *atigi* and asked him who they were. When he suggested at random the name "Charlie," the gathered natives identified it with a white man they had heard about (possibly Capt. Charles Klengenberg). The second shade, he suggested, might be "Joseph." When both shades were driven out all returned to normal (Jenness, 1922a, p. 214).

Chapter 31. – A Nomadic Fishing Life

1.
Two of the *Kanghirjuarmiut*, Nilgak and his wife Utuaiyok, taught Ikpukkuaq's people one of their songs, which Avrunna later sang into the author's recording machine at Bernard Harbour (Song No. 51 in Roberts and Jenness, 1925, p. 212; Jenness, 1922a, p. 132, footnote 1).

2.
This was the usual name for all of the Eskimos who gathered for the winter's sealing at the west end of Coronation Gulf (Jenness, 1922a, p. 36).

3.
Arctic hare, still carrying its white winter coat (Jenness, 1928a, p.135). Though superficially resembling a rabbit, the Arctic hare is quite a different species. There are no rabbits in the Arctic.

4.
They buried the heads and limbs in the snow to collect the next day (Jenness, 1928a, p. 136).

5.
Avrunna was hunting with Ikpukkuaq's rifle at the time (Jenness, 1922a, p. 133).

6.
The *kaksuak* is a red-throated loon (*Gavia stellata*), whereas the *mallere* is a Pacific loon (*Gavia pacifica*) (Anderson, 1913, pp. 456-457).

7.
The author photographed Qanajuq and her cousin Kehullik making pebble houses on this occasion (CMC Photo No. 37038; see also Fig. 63 in Jenness, 1922a, p. 220).

8.
The *tullik* is the yellow-billed loon (*Gavia adamsi*) Anderson (1913, p. 456).

9.
These migration directions were reported also in Jenness (1922a, p. 133), but later the author (Jenness, 1928a, p. 136) stated that Uqalluk (Chatterbox) and his family went north, Tuhayok (the Listener) and his family south, and Ikpukkuaq and his family east, magnetic declination having been allowed for.

10.
One of these may have been of young Haugaq carrying a bundle of *Dryas* (CMC Photo No. 36972; see also Jenness, 1922a, Fig. 32).

11.
To Lake Sagsagiak (Jenness, 1922a, p. 133), whose location can only be approximated.

12.
The diary states 10 p.m. here but the context indicates it was morning.

13.
The author went into the higher land to the southeast to get a better view of the country and perhaps to see some geological exposures (Jenness, 1928a, p. 138).

14.
For before the mist came on she collected a little *okauyak* [D.J.].

15.
This divination by lifting is reported in Jenness (1922a, pp. 214, 217; 1928a. p. 139). Higilaq was confident that all would return when the fog lifted but was afraid her daughter Qanajuq would be very cold and miserable (Jenness, 1922a, p. 134; 1928a, p. 139).

16.
The diary has *Dryas octopetala* as the name of the plant; the author corrected the species name in his later writings.

17.
At Lake Kullaluk, about 4 miles to the east (Jenness, 1922a, p. 134), which was T-shaped and larger than most of the lakes nearby (Jenness, 1928a, p. 141).

18.
The large lake northeast of Lake Añmaloqtoq where they met the *Kanghirjuarmiut* the previous month. It was a well known meeting place of the *Puivlik* natives from southern Victoria Island and the *Kanghirjuat*

from Prince Albert Sound (Jenness, 1922a, p. 24).

19.
The rest of the meat was left for Higilaq to bring in later (Jenness, 1922a, p. 134).

20.
A third story, concerning a giant approaching *Putulik* (Sutton Island) but landing on *Ahunga-hungak* (Liston Island) is told in Jenness (1928a, pp. 142-143).

21.
The first of these stories is No. 58 "The Snow-bunting and her Husband," the second one probably No. 53 "The Wolf" (Second version) in Jenness (1924a, pp. 75A and 74A).

22.
One of Aesop's didactic fables.

23.
Probably purple saxifrage (*Saxifraga oppositifolia*), but possibly moss campion (*Silene acaulis*) (Dr. S. Edlund, Geological Survey of Canada, verbal communication, May 24, 1988).

24.
At Lake Sagsagiak.

25.
The hook was a polar-bear tooth. The author discusses this change in fishing methods in more detail in Jenness (1928a, pp. 144-145), and fishing equipment and methods of the Copper Eskimos in Jenness (1922a, pp. 152-156).

26.
Two fishing spears, the trident and the double gaff (Jenness, 1922a, p. 103)

Chapter 32. – Malnutrition

1.
The *North Star* was to take the two topographers (Chipman and Cox) and the geologist (O'Neill) to their summer work area.

2.
'Chamber pot'.

3.
The author explains elsewhere that the only places he could escape the swarms of mosquitoes were inside his tent, which had a fine netting in its doorway, and well out on

the ice still covering the lakes (Jenness, 1928a, pp. 146-147).

4.
That camp was on the northwest side of Lake Añmaloqtoq (see diary entry for June 19).

5.
The author later changed this to north of *Kauwaqtoq* (Jenness, 1922a, p. 134), thereby correcting for magnetic declination.

6.
Ikpuk decided to return to this lake because the ice on the smaller lakes was melting appreciably around their shores and it was increasingly difficult to get onto the middle of the ice to fish. Lake Añmaloqtoq (Lake Ever-Frozen) was so named because its large size kept it ice-bound much of the summer (Jenness, 1928a, p. 147).

7.
Forget-me-nots are rare on Victoria Island; the plants seen by the author may have been rock jasmine or Arctic bladder pod (Dr. S. Edlund, Geological Survey of Canada, verbal communication, May 25, 1988). The primrose-like flowers were the blossoms of the *oyauraq* (*Dryas integrifolia*) plants (which the author recognised on July 20; see diary entry for that date).

8.
This divination is described also in Jenness (1922a, pp. 214-215).

9.
Higilaq (Icehouse) was not surprised that her actions did not cure him because "Eskimo remedies had no efficacy with white men" (Jenness, 1928a, p. 149).

10.
They were fed.

11.
The author was taught this technique at this lake because the usual Eskimo method of drawing up the line, wrist over wrist, invariably tangled the long line needed in this lake to catch the deeper lying trout. Sometimes, however, the fish struck the ice near the surface and were knocked free of the barbless hook. To offset this Ikpuk would slow down to a walk when he thought the end of the line was near the surface (Jenness, 1928a, pp. 147-148).

12.
Red-throated loon (*Gavia stellata*) (Anderson, 1913, p. 457).

13.
The diary entry here is Milukattuk, which is obviously an error.

14.
They moved to *Kauwaqtoq* (Jenness, 1922a, p. 135), at the northwest corner of Lake Añmaloqtoq.

15.
The author complained in this manner in his diary only during those few weeks in July and August 1915 when he experienced considerable illness and misery.

16.
His thermometer was cached at *Okauyarvik* on the south coast.

17.
A few miles to the east, on the northeast side of Lake Añmaloqtoq.

18.
This incident, like the complaining he recorded the previous day, was also a reflection of the author's physical misery at the time. Under normal circumstances he would have tolerated the dog's misbehaviour, for he was fond of his dogs, as earlier comments in his diary indicate. These displays of temper during his illness are almost the only ones recorded in this 3-year chronology of the author's activities.

19.
It was the only lake in the neighbourhood still completely ice-bound (Jenness, 1922a, p. 136).

20.
The net had been set out in a nearby shallow lake on July 19.

21.
One of the "etc." caught for Johansen on this date was later identified as a new species of two-winged fly, to which the name *Diamesia artica* was given (Malloch, 1919, p. 37C), obviously after its collector.

22.
The *Hibbert Journal* was a quarterly review of religion, theology, and philosophy, published between 1902 and 1968 by George Allen and Unwin Ltd., London, England. The author would have known of it from his Oxford University days.

23.
This essay, entitled *The Eskimos of N. Alaska — A study in the effect of civilization* fills 12 handwritten pages at the end of the diary (volume 3). At the top of the first page the author jotted these instructions to himself "Look up Murdoch, Barrow Eskimos, Collinson, Dease & Simpson, Stefansson [sic], Schultz, Revenue Cutter Corwin, U.S.

Govt. Census, Petitot." These were probably all items he was able to check in the Expedition's collection of books on his return to Bernard Harbour. It is an indication of his scientific dedication, mental concentration, and his literary creativeness that even while suffering greatly from illness and deprivation he produced an essay that he later published (Jenness, 1918) almost word for word as he originally wrote it, differing only by the addition of several headings and a few insignificant editorial changes.

24.
The fur on the caribou was by now in its prime, the Eskimos had sufficient dried fish for the early winter (the period between the end of the fall migration of the caribou and the start of the winter sealing), and the fishing season was ending. Ikpuk had intended to spend the rest of the summer in the hills to the northeast, hunting caribou, but there was little fuel there, and because of the author's digestive trouble with uncooked food, it was decided that they would move closer to the coast where they could obtain *Dryas* and willows for fuel and could hunt caribou (Jenness, 1928a, p. 150).

25.
Lake Añmaloqtoq.

26.
The author had cached a few ounces of malted milk and 3 lbs of dog pemmican on June 18. The pemmican was brown with age, having been packaged for the Hudson's Bay Company perhaps 40 years earlier, and consisted of dried beef crushed to powder, and bone fragments. Mixed into a paste with cold water, however, the author found it more digestible than the half-dried fish and more palatable then the saltless boiled fish. For the next week he therefore ate nothing but the dog pemmican (Jenness, 1928a, pp. 149-150).

27.
These notes were apparently written in another notebook whose whereabouts is not known. The author did, however, publish several articles on Papua several years later, some or all of which may have been initiated at this time.

28.
This comment appears to reflect his concern over the extent of his commitment to the Oxford University individuals who had sponsored much of his one-man Papuan expedition in 1911-12.

29.
Milukattuk's facial features are reported in Jenness (1923a, p. B25 and 36B. See also p. B39 footnote 4 re the hair.)

30.
These may have included two photos of Avrunna mending his bow (CMC Photo Nos. 36926 and 37058 (Fig. 170)). Photo No. 36926 is reproduced in Jenness (1922a, p. 135, Fig. 43).

31.
This seance is described in some detail in Jenness (1922a, p. 207).

32.
The melting of the ice in the many small lakes brought a halt to fishing by the Eskimos, for they could catch few fish from the shorelines and had no means of making boats in this treeless land to fish on the lakes.

33.
A description of the play activities of Qanajuq and Haugak at Lake Kullalluk in early July is given in Jenness (1928a, p. 141). Other games played by the Eskimo children are discussed in Jenness (1922a, pp. 218-220).

Chapter 33. – Packing West in Search of Caribou

1.
This was at a point where the Colville Hills merged gently into the plain to their south (Jenness, 1928a, p. 153).

2.
This might be the 'stone house' mentioned by Stefansson (1913a, p. 274 and photograph facing p. 174).

3.
Ikpuk brought back only the skins of the two caribou. Higilaq and Qanajuq promptly dressed and departed with dogs and packlines to bring back the meat (Jenness, 1928a, p. 154).

4.
About 4 miles to the west (Jenness, 1922a, p. 136).

5.
This may have been *Potentilla rubricaulis*, the only member of the Rosaceae family known to have been collected by the author (Porsild, 1955, p. 149). It is identified by Field No. 574 in the National Herbarium Collection in Ottawa. Porsild's report reveals that the author collected at least four dozen plants during his 1915 adventure on Victoria Island, and most of these are in the National Herbarium Collection. Some and perhaps all of the other flowers he collected on August 3rd may be in that collection. Unfortunately the labels on most of his specimens list only the month of collection. (See Appendix 4D).

6.
The whereabouts of these notes is not known. However, the information they included may have been used later in one or other of his publications pertaining to Papua (Jenness, 1920; 1923b; 1967b; Jenness and Ballantyne, 1920, 1928).

7.
Ikpuk had a headache this evening -- stayed too long in the water when bathing I fancy. Taqtu questioned the *qila* (my *atigi*), found Qiñaloqunna's dead wife was *ugroqto*-ing, soothed her with fair words till she promised to be 'good'. [D.J.]

8.
The author later described this incident and discussed briefly the topics of cleanliness and body odours (Jenness, 1928a, p. 155).

9.
The *North Star* on this date was ice-bound at Bernard Harbour (Anderson, 1913-1916, Aug. 4-9, 1915) and outside the Eskimo's line of sight. The *Alaska* left Baillie Island for Herschel Island on July 13, where it remained until August 22 (Anderson 1913-1916, Nov. 9, 1915), hence also was beyond view from Victoria Island. The vessel seen by the Eskimos on this occasion may have been either the *Gladiator* (F. Wolki, master), which arrived at Herschel Island on August 4, or the *Polar Bear* (Louis Lane, Captain), which headed east from Herschel Island for Banks Island on August 3 (Anderson 1913-1916, Nov. 9, 1915).

10.
The rice was carried by the author's largest dog and was damaged soon after when the dog plunged into a deep pool (Jenness, 1928a, p. 156).

11.
Packing westward about 4 miles north of the coast (Jenness, 1922a, p. 136). The author's directions during most of the next few weeks are reliable for he had the coastline to guide him and was not dependent on his magnetic compass for directions as when he was inland.

12.
They had not seen these people since June 27.

13.
The other Eskimos had bows and arrows.

14.
They howled like wolves (Jenness, 1922a, p. 137).

15.
Probably Epiullik (or Ipiullik) Creek, which empties into the sea at Ipiullik Point (Canada, 1976), a few miles south of the author's location.

16.
Many of these ridges are short oval-shaped glacial drumlins, oriented in a west-trending band 6 to 8 miles wide (Sharpe, 1988, p. 272). They have been rounded by post-glacial marine erosion.

17.
The author collected the following freshwater snails (gastropods) from lakes, reportedly on August 8 but perhaps on this date, near Point Williams (now Williams Point): *Lymnaea vahli* and *Valvata lewisii* (F. Johansen *in* Dall, 1919, p. 25A).

18.
This divination is discussed briefly in Jenness (1922a, p. 215).

19.
The author used Greek 'phi's' where I have used 'f's' in this word. He later corrected the name for this prominent hill to *Tiphiktoq* on September 11, and later spelled it *Tipfiktok* (Jenness, 1922a, p. 137).

20.
Avrunna and his wife had hunted with the author's .22 automatic rifle 2 or 3 miles inland from the author's route (Jenness, 1922a, p. 137).

21.
The author collected post-glacial marine shells from a mud formation at one locality

between the Colville Hills and the southwest coast: Station 5285. Three species were present: *Macoma inconspicua, Mya truncata,* and *Saxicava pholadis* (O'Neill, 1924, p. 31A). None were recovered from elevations above 300 feet, nor west of about the locality where the author was on this date.

22.
Umingmuktor is the region around Point Everitt on the east side of Bathurst Inlet (Anderson, 1918, p. 48). The author knew that these men planned to use the *North Star* to investigate Coronation Gulf as far east as Bathurst Inlet, Chipman and Cox mapping the topography, O'Neill the geology, and Dr. Anderson collecting mammals and birds. Cox and O'Neill had gone east in early June with an *umiak* and sled. Johansen remained behind in charge of the Bernard Harbour facilities.

23.
These four had separated from Ikpuk's party in the middle of June (Jenness, 1922a, p. 137).

24.
The only occasion during the entire summer when all of the adults bathed (Jenness, 1922a, p. 137), although Ikpuk, Avrunna, and Milukattuk had bathed on August 3.

25.
The author probably had seen the Tarn River, which flows into the Garonne River near Toulouse in southern France, during one of his vacations while he was a student at Oxford University (1908-1911).

26.
The author, on this date, collected *Mertensia Drummondi* (now *M. lanceolata* var. *Drummondi*), a member of the Boraginaceae (Forget-me-not) family, for Frits Johansen. It is Field No. 410 (Porsild, 1955, p. 175) and Museum Spec. No. 94313 in the National Herbarium Collection in Ottawa. The previous day he had collected *Senecio atropurpureus*, one of the Compositae (Daisy) family (Field No. 329a, Porsild, 1955, p. 187) and now Museum Spec. No. 109956 in the same collection.

27.
Kiahiqtorvik (*Kiahiktorvik* or *Kiasiktorvik*) was the Eskimo name for the broad sandy plain (Jenness, 1922a, p. 137). It appears as a markedly light-coloured feature on the vertical RCAF aerial photographs of the area.

28.
A more vivid picture of this hunt can be found in Jenness (1928a, pp. 159-161).

29.
The author later recounted that his gun failed twice during this hunt and added that the tendency of the Ross rifle to fail to fire with the least bit of sand resulted in considerable bitterness in the early months of World War I and led to the re-arming of Canadian troops with British-built Lee-Enfield rifles (Jenness, 1928a, p. 161).

30.
It is wind-blown material from a glaciomarine delta deposited by a westerly flowing stream at an ice margin about 10,000 years ago (Sharpe, 1988, p. 267; Sharpe, 1989, Map-unit 6).

31.
About a dozen flowers collected by the author in August 1915, without specific collection dates, are in the National Herbarium Collection in Ottawa (see Appendix 4D). He may have collected one or more of these on this date. He had a plant press with him.

32.
They explained that the weather was unsuitable for travel, they had more meat than they could carry, and the hides needed to be scraped and dried. More likely they needed a few days to recuperate from their journey (Jenness, 1928a, pp. 161-162).

33.
The construction of the bows was at fault (Jenness, 1928a, pp. 162-163).

34.
Ikpuk's sketch is reproduced in Jenness (1922a, p. 151).

35.
This incident, on June 4, 1915, involved Nateksina rather than Allikumik (see footnote 37, Chapter 29). Higilaq's annoyance at the time brought about the shortening of the visit with the Prince Albert Sound Eskimos (Jenness, 1928a, pp. 125-126).

36.
The author later corrected these directions, stating that the two bands continued moving westward. Ikpuk, Avrunna, Tuhayok, and their families and the author followed a route 3 to 4 miles inland, the others farther inland (Jenness, 1922a, p. 138).

37.
Later called Lake Tasieluk (Jenness, 1922a, p. 138), which I believe is the unnamed lake 12 miles east of Cape Hamilton, the elevation of which is 325 feet (Canada, 1982). The author found time on this day to collect a variety of snapdragon (*Pedicularis capitata*, Scrophulariaceae family) for Johansen, which is Museum Spec. No. 97439 in the National Herbarium Collection in Ottawa (see Appendix 4D). He also collected a freshwater snail *Aplexa* from "a pond inland from Point Williams" (Johansen *in* Dall, 1919, p. 25A) on this date; the pond may have been Lake Tasieluk.

38.
Dr. Anderson (1913, p. 470) had reported earlier that the Eskimo name for this bird was *tatigiak*, but perhaps he was recording the dialect from Wales, Alaska, where the name of the brown crane is *tatiggaq* (Jenness, 1928b, p. 117).

39.
The author later spelled this Eskimo name Mt. Anovidli (p. 515), also *Annorillit* (Jenness, 1922a, p. 23), then *Annoridlit* ("the windy place") in a list of place names that had his approval (Chipman and Cox, 1924, p. 40B and footnote on p. 37B).

40.
The distance to the Kugaluk River from the lake fitting the dimensions given for Lake Tahialuk is closer to 16 miles. On his return from the Kugaluk River on September 5, the author again states his distance as 8 miles. These are the only places in his diary where his stated distances differ significantly from those between his camp locations as I have determined them through my study of the air photographs and topographic maps. The location of Lake Tahialuk can be questioned, but there is no lake within 8 miles east of the place where the author crossed the Kugaluk River (just below the S-shaped bend) that fits the dimensions for the lake given by him on August 16.

41.
These were eaten raw, though willow and the heather-like shrub *Dryas integrifolia* for fuel were plentiful (Jenness, 1922a, p. 138).

42.
Kilak (Jenness, 1922a, p. 180), *qilak* (Jenness, 1928b, p. 66).

43.
Shades of the dead. Some of the Eskimos thought that lightning was caused by a being named Asiranna shooting his arrows (Jenness, 1922a, p. 180). This is the only mention of lightning (a rare phenomenon in the Arctic) in this diary.

44.
The author meant Point Pullen (Jenness, 1922a, p. 23), the name shown on Rae's (1852) map for the rocky promontory on the west side of Lady Richardson Bay. Reported here as *Hinieluk* (the Copper Eskimos often use 'h' where the Mackenzie delta Eskimos use 's'), he later called it *Sinieluk* (Jenness, 1922a, p. 23), and it is now known as Singialuk Peninsula (Canada, 1978, 1982). The northwestern end of the peninsula is known today as Cape Ernest Kendall (Canada, 1978, 1982).

45.
This locality, which the author later called Bad Creek (Jenness, 1928a, p. 162) [now the Kugaluk River], was some 25 miles west of the sand plain.

46.
She had been left behind because she was not a good traveller (Jenness, 1928a, p. 159). (See also footnote 22, Chapter 29.)

47.
Spelled *Attautsikkiak* in Jenness (1922a, p. 23) and Chipman and Cox (1924, p. 40B).

48.
Shown on Rae's (1852) map as "Cliffs about 80 feet" this bluff was named by the Eskimos after the seagulls (*nauyat*) that made it their haunt (Jenness, 1922a, p. 23). It is now called Naoyat Cliff (Canada, 1982).

49.
Kikiaktaryuak, a name also used for Chantry Island (Chipman and Cox, 1924, p. 40B), is now known as Bell Island (Canada, 1982), as it was named by Rae in 1851. Capt. Joseph Bernard had reported the ruins of stone cairns and three old wood-framed sod huts on this island, evidence of the former presence of western natives there (Jenness, 1922a, pp. 50-51), and Stefansson had built a stone cairn on the southwest corner of the island, leaving in it a record of his journey across Victoria Island in 1911. Capt. Klengenberg had wintered with his ship the *Olga* behind Bell Island in 1905-06 (Stefansson, 1913a, p. 306).

50.
Gibson (1920) recorded the following butterflies collected by the author on this date: *Anarta leucocycia*, 4 specimens of *Lygris destinata*, 2 specimens of *Psychophora sabini*, and *Aspilates orciferaria*. Three days earlier he had also collected a *Titanio* specimen. These were placed in the National Collection of Insects in Ottawa. The "other insects" he collected on August 18, 1915, included a Diptera and a Coleoptera: *Scataphaga furcata* (Malloch, 1919, p. 81C) and *Amara brunnipennis* (Fall, 1919, p. 16E)

51.
Ikpuk carried the author's notebooks and plant press; the author had left his other books at Lake Numichoin (see entry for October 17).

52.
Kunuamnak, a group of large blocks of diabase visible for miles, on the forward slope of Mount Kingmiktorvik (Jenness, 1922a, p. 138; 1928a, p. 163); its approximate locality is shown on the author's sketch maps (see Figs. 173 and 174).

53.
During the winter of 1913-14 (Jenness, 1922a, p. 23), a few months before he encountered the Expedition at Baillie Island.

54.
Spelled *Qiñmiktorvik* prior to this point in the diary and also on August 30; spelled *Kingmiktorvik* hereafter in the diary and in Jenness (1922a, p. 23). It means "The place where caches of fish were made" (Chipman and Cox, 1924, p. 40B). At 500+ feet above sea level, it is not quite as high a feature as *Annorillit* (Mount Arrowsmith), which is 600+ feet (Canada, 1982).

55.
The river is now known to be about 100 miles long.

56.
Ikpuk improvised a comical song about the author's adventures with the wolf on the Coppermine River the previous year (Jenness, 1922a, p. 164). Unfortunately it was neither written down nor recorded on a phonograph disk.

57.
The author later described this direction as north (Jenness, 1922a, p. 138), presumably correcting for declination, for they could no longer see the shore to provide their direction. They needed to obtain more caribou in the hills behind Cape Baring before starting back east (Jenness, 1928a, p. 164).

58.
The author was totally unaware at that time of the war in Europe. As events subsequently unfolded his desire to return to New Zealand was not fulfilled until the spring of 1919, after he had spent many months in action in France with the Canadian Army.

59.
This was the first caribou Tuhayok had shot all summer (Jenness, 1922a, p. 138).

60.
She ripped out the stitches in the morning to use the skin as a coat, then stitched it up again at night for Kannayuk's use (Jenness, 1922a, p. 138). The author later described Higilaq's appearance in the make-do garment, writing that with her portly figure draped in the sleeping robe she waddled along with the rolling gait of a bear (Jenness, 1928a, p. 164).

61.
This direction was later corrected to north (Jenness, 1922a, p. 138).

62.
The task of cooking for the entire party fell on Higilaq because the only other woman in the group (Milukattuk) spent her time hunting and sewing for her husband Avrunna (Jenness, 1922a, p. 138).

63.
North (Jenness, 1922a, p. 139).

64.
The whole episode of the bears was worthy of April Fool's Day. Higilaq has exceptionally keen sight, though like many women she does not wear snow-goggles in spring. I couldn't induce her to stay in camp — she wanted to see the bears killed. Ikpuk, Avrunna, and others speared a bear near here some years ago. They fastened their knives to the end of stout poles. Ikpuk's knife broke in the bear, and it scratched him in the leg, but was killed before it could damage him severely. [D.J.]

65.
North (Jenness, 1922a, p. 139).

66.
Bwaidoga was a Mission Station established in the southeast corner of Goodenough Island, Papua, New Guinea, in 1898 by the Methodist Church of Australasia. The author's sister May was married to the missionary there. Following his graduation from the University of Oxford the author spent 1911-12 studying the natives in that part of Papua (Jenness and Ballantyne, 1920).

67.
A 3 1/2 page expanded narrative of the swans and polar bears entitled "An Eskimo Bear-hunt" follows the August 25th entry in the diary. Much of it appears in Jenness (1928a, pp. 164-169).

68.
About 4 miles north (Jenness, 1922a, p. 139).

69.
Losing half their original weight in the process (Jenness, 1922a, p. 139).

70.
The author did not identify these mountains. He wrote then stroked out the name 'Smoky' before 'Mts.', perhaps momentarily thinking of the Smoking Hills, but these are in Franklin Bay, well beyond his view. The promontory he saw was probably the cliffs west of Clifton Point, some 60 miles away. The "very high land" would then have been the Melville Hills farther south, which rise to an elevation of about 2500 feet.

71.
Clerk Island was thought to be a high island 10 or 12 miles north of the mainland (Richardson *in* Franklin, 1828, p. 247). Capt. S.F. Cottle claimed to have landed on the island, but no other persons prior to this time had seen it, and Chipman and Cox (1924, p. 20B) concluded the island was non existent.

72.
As recorded in this diary, Ikpuk's party of twenty, including the author, killed 167 caribou on Victoria Island between early May and early November. Of these the author shot 72.

73.
On August 4, 1915.

Chapter 34. – Packing East

1.
It was a lake rather than a lagoon (Jenness, 1922a, p. 139).

2.
The author collected two species of freshwater snails here: *Aplexa hypnorum* and *Lymnaea vahli*. The Copper Eskimo name for the *Lymnaea* gastropod is *siuterkok*, which is derived from the word for ears (Johansen *in* Dall, 1919, p. 25A; in a footnote on the same page Dr. Anderson added that in the Mackenzie Eskimo dialect any spiral mollusc was called *siutukayuk*).

3.
The author used two Greek 'phi's' where I have used 'ff' in this word. (See also footnote 22, this chapter.)

4.
Now identified as Innirit Point (Canada, 1976).

5.
Recent glacial studies of this region would seem to bear out the author's observation. Sharpe (1988, p. 263) has reported deglaciation at Cape Baring, some 30 miles north-west of the mouth of the Kugaluk River, as 10,700 years ago, based on the age there of post-glacial marine shells such as the author collected, whereas other marine shells obtained east of the Wollaston Peninsula dated only 9710 years ago. The author collected three species of Pleistocene marine molluscs from a mud formation somewhere between the Colville Hills and the southwest coast of Victoria Island (O'Neill, 1924, p. 31A). They must have been collected farther east than his location on August 31. A coloured map of the glacial and post-glacial (Quaternary) geology of the Wollaston Peninsula has recently been published (Sharpe, 1989).

6.
Caribou antler (Jenness, 1922a, p. 139). Avrunna's sled runner was the plank he and Ikpuk recovered at the coast on August 30.

7.
He then planed and smoothed the poles with his hunting knife to make fish-spears. The care he expended on the task and his great joy at its successful completion helped the author realize how severely his companions were handicapped through the scarcity of

wood in their country (Jenness, 1928a, p. 170).

8.
Lake trout (Jenness, 1922a, p. 139).

9.
The author did not record when and where Ikpuk obtained this hoop nor how he was able to split it.

10.
Kava is the root of the Polynesian plant *Piper methysticum* and also the intoxicating beverage prepared from it by maceration.

11.
The gorge is 4 miles above the mouth of the river (O'Neill, 1924, p. 52A) and is S-shaped (Jenness, 1928a, p. 171).

12.
For lake trout (Jenness, 1922a, p. 139).

13.
The pyrite is obtained from a gravel beach at the mouth of the gorge. The author's Eskimo companions gathered several lumps of pyrite to keep for starting their fires (Jenness, 1922a, p. 139; 1928a, p. 171). The dolomite through which the gorge cuts is unfossiliferous but of Silurian age (O'Neill, 1924, p. 52A).

14.
Both women and children also collected the seeds of the cotton-grass (*Eriophorum*) from a nearby meadow, which they stuffed into small bags made from a strange assortment of materials: worn-out stockings of squirrel or caribou fur, membranes lining the hearts of the polar bears they had recently killed, and pouches made from the webbed feet of red-throated loons. The cotton-grass would supply both tinder and wicks for their oil lamps. The bags were stuffed into the dog-packs for transporting (Jenness, 1928a, p. 171-172). Elsewhere the author (1922a, pp. 108-109) discusses the Eskimos' use of pyrite, cotton-grass, dry grass, and moss roots for producing fire.

15.
Annorillit or Mount Arrowsmith (Jenness, 1922a, p. 23). This was closer to 16 miles from Kugaluk (see footnote 40, Chapter 33).

16.
Spelled Lake Tahialuk on August 15 and 16.

17.
The Teriglu from Port Clarence assisted the author on Barter Island in June 1914.

18.
Each man had, in addition to his usual load, several green (i.e. 'undried') caribou skins; Ikpuk and Avrunna carried the heavy bear-skins, and Higilaq in addition to her usual load about 15 lbs of tallow boiled down from the caribou pot. The author was also carrying the plant press in which he kept the plants he had collected for Johansen; it had by this time attained a thickness of 6 inches (Jenness, 1928a, p. 172).

19.
The author's Eskimo companions re-proached him for stealing the dead woman's shelter. His actions would have been accept-able if he had replaced the tent poles (which were broken) with miniature poles (Jenness, 1928a, p. 173).

20.
The author's youngest sister in New Zea-land.

21.
Urinated.

22.
The author previously mentioned this fea-ture on August 8, when he passed it heading west, and on August 31. He later spelled it *Tipfiktok* and stated it was near where Link-later Island was shown on the old British Admiralty chart 2443 (Jenness, 1922a, p. 25). Linklater Island is now shown 3 miles northwest of Read Island (Canada, 1978). *Tipfiktok* is about 4 miles north of Falaise Bay, has a lake about 1 1/2 miles long by 1 mile wide on its south side, and is 24 miles west-northwest of the mouth of Okauyarvik Creek.

23.
Later spelled *Tunungeok* (Jenness, 1922a, p. 140).

24.
Later spelled *Epiullik* (Jenness, 1922a, p. 141). Now called Ipiullik Point (Canada, 1978). The ice on Lake Tunungeok was al-ready 3 inches thick (Jenness, 1922a, p. 140).

25.
Only two snow buntings were seen. They are the first migrating birds to arrive in the

spring and the last to depart in the fall (Jenness, 1928a, p. 173).

26.
The caribou's annual southward migration would take place over a period of 3 or 4 weeks (Jenness, 1928a, p. 173).

27.
Nagjuktok was either all of the islands off the south shore of Victoria Island northwest of the Jamieson Islands and between 111° and 113°W, or the south portion of Victoria Island between about Lady Franklin Point and the Richardson Islands. The author was unable to determine which area was the correct designation (Jenness, 1922a, pp. 36-37). Recently I was informed by a resident of Coppermine that it referred to the Richardson Islands region (Rosemarie Avrana Meyok, written communication, July 1989). *Ninnitak* (or *Nennitak*) was the Copper Eskimo name for the region "behind Cape Bathurst" (Jenness, 1922a, p. 39).

28.
The *Alaska* reached Bernard Harbour on September 5, from Herschel Island, and remained there. The *North Star* was ice-bound at Bernard Harbour until August 9, when it sailed east with Dr. Anderson and Chipman, who dropped off at Cape Barrow in Coronation Gulf on August 12. Wilkins then headed west with the *North Star* (Anderson, 1913-16, Aug. 12, 1915). It reached Banks Island on August 16 and was winter-bound in ice on the west side of that island by the end of August (Wilkins, 1918, pp. 68-69). Thus neither ship was within the author's view on this date. What he saw was the motor schooner *El Sueno*, which had brought supplies to Bernard Harbour from Herschel Island on September 7, at Stefansson's request, then sailed along the southwest shore of Victoria Island searching for caribou before heading west from Bernard Harbour on September 17 (Anderson, 1913-16, Nov. 9, 1915). It wintered at Pierce Point (see Jenness diary entry Apr. 24, 1916).

29.
The author later called it "Dryad Harbour." It was about 12 miles to the east (Jenness, 1928a, p. 174).

30.
At *Epiullik* (Jenness, 1928a, p. 174).

31.
Their tent was erected on a level patch of ground in a dip in the rolling plain behind *Okauyarvik* (Dryad Harbour) (Jenness, 1928a, p. 175). They could obtain drinking water from the lake (Jenness, 1922a, p. 140).

32.
These supplies had been cached there on August 4.

33.
Stefansson's 'stone house' was close to the shore of Simpson Bay (Stefansson, 1913a, pp. 274-275; photo p. 174).

34.
Later corrected to the plural form *tallut* (Jenness, 1922a, p. 148, 149).

35.
These berries are so uncommon and scattered that the wandering Eskimos seldom bother to pick them. They were Alpine bearberry (*Arctostaphylos alpina*) (Jenness, 1922a. p. 97).

36.
The Copper Eskimo word for a young caribou bull is *mikatukkaaq* (Rosemarie Avrana Meyok, Coppermine, written communication, July 1989).

37.
That part of Victoria Island near Lady Franklin Point.

38.
Bearded seal.

39.
From *Epiullik* (Jenness, 1922a, p. 141).

40.
The seals were easy to shoot at this time but very difficult to recover (Jenness, 1928a, p. 177).

41.
Singular: *kanayuq* = sculpin. This was also the name of Higilaq's 12-year old daughter Jennie, though the author spelled it Kanneyuk and several other ways (see Appendix 1).

42.
A *turk* was an iron or copper chisel mounted on a long stout wooden pole, and was a

standard part of the native fisherman's equipment (Jenness, 1922a, p. 153).

43.
Foul language (Oxford University Press, 1971, p. 216)

44.
The quiet was broken by occasional sobs from Kullaq, whose husband had disciplined her by tearing her *atigi* from top to bottom (Jenness, 1928a, p. 183).

45.
The word in parentheses here is not readily identified, but it looks like *'skotus'* or *'stertus'*.

46.
The *Nennitagmiut* inhabited the west side of Bathurst Inlet. The *Arkilininmiut* inhabited the Arkilinik or Thelon River district and had supplied some of the Copper Eskimos with guns, ammunition, knives, and other metal implements in exchange for skins of caribou, musk-ox, and foxes (Jenness, 1922a, pp. 39, 48). The Thelon River natives obtained their guns etc. from whalers in the Chesterfield Inlet area, Hudson Bay (Hanbury, 1904).

47.
A more detailed account of Ikpuk's efforts in catching these seals is given in Jenness (1928a, p. 177).

48.
Telluraq was one of the two trouble makers, but there was unrest among all of the dogs (Jenness, 1928a, pp. 180-181).

49.
Hanbury (1904, p. 171) described the insertion of a louse in the eye of a Copper Eskimo woman to eradicate a growth on the eyeball, not as a cure for snow-blindness. Hanbury's book must have been among those in the Expedition's library at Bernard Harbour.

50.
The sclerotis is the white of the eyeball. Ikpuk's two 'remedies' are mentioned in Jenness (1922a, p. 171).

51.
As a bearded seal weighs several hundred pounds it is more than a match for a man.

52.
To fish again in the many lakes near Lake Numichoin, since the caribou were no longer available to meet their daily food needs, and also to gather up the items cached there in the summer (Jenness, 1922a, p. 141) for the author's return to Bernard Harbour.

Chapter 35. – Return to Bernard Harbour

1.
This confined accommodation is described in more detail in Jenness (1928a, pp. 184-185).

2.
The caches included dried meat, dried fish, the author's sled and big spring tent, and his camera and books (Jenness, 1928a, p. 185).

3.
This was a serious blow to Ikpuk and Higilaq, for the latter had intended to use the white-bellied hides to make finely ornamented costumes for the winter dances. The author consoled her by promising to purchase other hides for her when the tribes reassembled at the sealing grounds (Jenness, 1928a, p. 185).

4.
Soil. The author photographed both Ikpuk and Avrunna applying mud to their sled runners (CMC Photo Nos. 37087, 37090).

5.
Hanbury (1904, p. 80) described the thawing of mud or peat in the iglu (or hut), mixing with water until it became a stiff paste, then plastering the sled runners with about 2 inches thickness. When this froze it was smoothed, and water was poured on it to form a layer of ice. The thin ice layer permitted the sled to slide easily over crushed snow, but wore off easily and had to be renewed frequently. Hanbury also observed that the iced mud surface was best in very cold weather, but unsatisfactory when the weather turned mild, and that metal under

the runners was useless in cold weather. Finnie (1940, p. 117) made similar remarks about the use of mud-covered vs metal sled runners. The author's sled had metal runners.

6.
This was a general name for all western Coronation Gulf Eskimos (Jenness, 1922a, p. 18, footnote 2).

7.
The name *Pallik* (the author spelled it *Pallirk* in his diary) is applied to both the Rae River and the region around it (Jenness, 1922a, p. 18, footnote 1).

8.
In the spring of 1910 Stefansson met and photographed Ekallukpuk (or Ekalukpik) at a small Eskimo settlement at the mouth of the Rae River. Ekalukpik told him that as a boy of about six he had met white men who wanted to cross the river. His story coincided with the account of Richardson and Rae crossing the river in 1848 (Stefansson, 1913a, p. 207, photo facing p. 206), not 1852 as the author stated here.

9.
The author had read up to Book 20 of the 24 books in *The Odyssey* by June 10, then evidently cached the book when he left Lake Numichoin. One gets an indication of his feelings for this classic work from a letter written from the World War I front lines in France (Jenness, 1917) "I brought *The Odyssey* over with me, and though I have almost no opportunities for reading proper, yet even to turn over the pages of this old book is a comfort. I remember how often in the Arctic — on a more than usually hard day's march — I would find old Odysseus' words repeating themselves over and over again in my brain — but always in English — 'Courage, my heart, thou hast endured worse things'."

10.
Also spelled *Kauwaqtoq.* It is at the northwest corner of Lake Añmaloqtoq.

11.
aniu: snow intended for some specific purpose, e.g. for melting, building a wall (Jenness, 1928b, p. 18).

12.
East by south (Jenness, 1922a, p. 191) after correction for magnetic north.

13.
Lake Kigiaktallik, the source of Okauyarvik Creek (Jenness, 1922a, p. 141), which empties into Simpson Bay at *Okauyarvik,* or 'Dryad Harbour'.

14.
Pihhuaq (Pissuak) and his family were still at *Epiullik* (Jenness, 1922a, p. 141) so this was Okalluk, Tusayok, and Tucik and their families.

15.
The author had cod-lines with his equipment (Jenness, 1928a, p. 185).

16.
The author photographed the camp, which was on the margin of the lake (Jenness, 1922a, p. 141 and Fig. 44, p. 142; CMC Photo No. 37005).

17. From one or more caches near Lake Numichoin.

18.
The author describes the surfacing of the runners in more detail in Jenness (1928a, p. 186). He also photographed the re-icing activities (CMC Photo Nos. 36987 (Fig. 177), 36988).

19.
The author reflected philosphically on the relative leadership abilities of Telluraq and Jumbo in Jenness (1928a, pp. 180-181).

20.
These notes were evidently written in another notebook, the whereabouts of which is not known.

21.
Quite possibly Telluraq's matted coat of long frizzy hair made him invulnerable to every adversary (Jenness, 1928a, p. 180).

22.
The author photographed Oqalluk's fall tent at this locality (CMC Photo No. 37055).

23.
The author's identification was correct (Jenness, 1928b, p. 87). The black brant was called *Niglirnaluk* and *Niglirknak* by the Mackenzie and Alaskan Eskimos respectively (Anderson, 1913, p. 469).

24.
For more on Eskimo superstitions concerning string figures, see Jenness (1924b, pp. 181B-183B).

25.
Read Island (Jenness, 1922a, p. 142).

26.
The sealing season commenced at the end of November. Once the Eskimos moved out on the ice they could sew no more until the sun reappeared at the end of January (Jenness, 1928a, p. 189).

27.
Using Ikpuk's ice chisel (*turq* or *turk*) she chipped the block out of a nearby lake (Jenness, 1922a, p. 142).

28.
The author attributed the monotony of life during the transitional period between the end of the fishing and caribou-hunting season and the start of the sealing season as the reason for the general restlessness and temper flare-ups of both individuals and dogs (Jenness, 1928a, p. 180, 189-190).

29.
This journey was never made, owing to two unexpected factors. First, the winter of 1915-16 was unusually cold and unsuitable for traversing the Wollaston Peninsula; and secondly, Wilkin's news of Stefansson's activities meant that the Eskimos the author hoped to visit would probably have migrated to Stefansson's base camp, well beyond reasonable reach, and could then be examined by Stefansson. The cached pemmican was brought back to the station on January 5, 1916.

30.
He took three photographs on this occasion: CMC Photo Nos. 38527, 38528 (see Fig. 182), and 38529.

31.
For a brief statement on the examination of this hair and that of four other Copper

Eskimos, see Jenness (1923a, p. B39, footnote 4).

32.
The same six families that assembled near this site the previous May 7. The various members are listed in Jenness (1922a, p. 128).

33.
Inirnerin is an adult caribou; the word for a yearling is *nukatukak*, which the author mistakenly used for a 2- to 3-year old caribou in his diary entry of July 3, 1916. This error was drawn to my attention by Rosemarie Avrana Meyok, Coppermine, July 1989.

34.
The author was prepared to make the 40-mile journey alone, but both Ikpuk and Higilaq insisted that Ikpuk see him safely back to the station (Jenness, 1928a, p. 191).

35.
These may have been boxes of pemmican for the author's intended journey to Prince Albert Sound. The island was probably Linklater Island.

36.
The author probably means *Illuvillik* (Chipman and Cox, 1924, p. 40B), which was Liston Island.

37.
Her name was Nogasak, and she is pictured with her brother in Stefansson (1913a, facing p. 268).

38.
Patsy Klengenberg was a 15-year old with hunting and sailing experience, whom Dr. Anderson had hired to serve as the author's interpreter for the next three-quarters of a year. He appears in several pictures taken by members of the Expedition, notably the one with his family at Baillie Island taken by the author (Fig. 208).

Chapter 36. – Quiet Time Around Bernard Harbour

1.
A great many newspapers had come with the mail from Herschel Island during the summer (Jenness, 1928a, p. 193).

2.
The diary has blank spaces on both sides of the word "Eskimo" here so the number of dogs is unknown. The author did not save Stefansson's letter.

3.
Ambrose's wife Unalina accompanied them. They were to bring back the author's specimens and cached caribou meat (Anderson, 1913-16, Nov. 12, 1915). Ambrose Agnavigak, a Herschel Island native, his wife, and their little daughter Annie arrived on the *Alaska* in September (Anderson, 1913-16, Nov. 9, 1915); Ambrose had been hired by Stefansson as a helper, his wife as seamstress for the Southern Party.

4.
The other two wives were Kukilukkak and Koptana. A photograph of Uloksak and his three wives, taken by John Cox (CMC Photo No. 39690), appears in Jenness (1922a, Plate VIIIC, p. 265).

5.
Sweeney's party had left the station on November 4 to look for Dr. Anderson and the Geological Survey men, who had failed to return when expected (see diary entry of November 8).

6.
Named Teddy Bear Island in 1958 to remember Capt. Joseph Bernard's little schooner *Teddy Bear*, the first vessel to winter in the harbour (in 1911-12).

7.
One of the eight shamans (three women and five men) in Dolphin and Union Strait during the previous winter (Jenness, 1922a, p. 195).

8.
Over the course of the next few months the author spent many hours teaching Patsy how to read and write in English, the results of which proved greatly beneficial to Patsy in later years when he was a trader in Coronation Gulf.

9.
The same exchange occurred again sometime during the following month, even though Milukattuk was in the late stages of pregnancy. Later she said that neither she nor her husband Avrunna had wanted to have any dealings with Uloksak but dared not refuse him because he was a shaman (Jenness, 1922a, p. 86).

10.
After the December 18 entry the author recorded the following: Kugluglu is Kanneyuk's other name. [D.J.]

11.
Also spelled *Akilinnik*, this is the Thelon River (Jenness, 1922a, p. 48). In this reference the author has used the term *Pallik* for both the region embracing the Rae River at the west end of Coronation Gulf (p. 18) and for natives from the southwest hinterland of Hudson Bay (p. 48).

12.
Also spelt *Saningaiyok*, this is the Backs River (Jenness, 1922a, p. 49). The author discusses the inhabitants of the regions south of Coronation Gulf on pages 48-49 in this reference.

13.
This may have been Baker Lake, at the mouth of which the tide from Hudson Bay rises 6-8 feet (Hanbury, 1904, p. 48).

14.
J.E. Hoff, hired by Stefansson at Herschel Island from the *Ruby* in the summer of 1915 to serve as chief engineer on the *Alaska* (Stefansson, 1921, p. 392).

15.
They even had a small Christmas tree, brought in from "a long way away" for the occasion, as well as paper flowers, and assorted gifts were laid out on the table (Jenness, 1916b).

16.
The seven songs were sung by Atqaq, a Thelon River native man, Qaqcovina, a Hudson Bay native man, and Tamoxiuna, a Bathurst Inlet native woman. They are Nos. 126-132 in Roberts and Jenness (1925, pp. 361-380).

17.
Ciss (or Sis) was the wife of the native Mike (Chipman, 1913-16, Nov. 30, 1915). She apparently came to Bernard Harbour on the *Alaska* in September 1915, for she had been left at Herschel Island in August 1914 (see diary entry for Aug. 10).

Chapter 37. – Folk-lore and Folk Songs

1.
This sentence has a line drawn through it in the diary.

2.
Items traded on this day and on subsequent trading days until April 18 are given in Appendix 3.

3.
This is one of four stories credited to Higilaq in Jenness (1924a).

4.
This is one of the twelve stories by Ikpukkuaq presented in Jenness (1924a).

5.
Three of Uloksak's shamanistic stories are given in Jenness (1922a, pp. 196, 199, and 200).

6.
These were some of the thirteen stories told by Uloksak (Uloqsaq), which appear in Jenness (1924a).

7.
Milukattuk's two stories are No. 54 and 72b in Jenness (1924a).

8.
The author's use of 'Tusayok' here for Higilaq's brother Tuhayok (as well as Kesullik for Kehullik and Pissuaq for Pihhuaq the next day) may reflect the influence of his young interpreter Patsy Klengenberg, whose dialect was a western one in which the 's' sound replaces the 'h' sound of the Copper Eskimos.

9.
The prohibition on sewing applied to a woman whose husband or brother was ill, and the additional prohibition on eating seal's liver or kidney was inflicted on Higilaq because of her second name Taqtu (kidney) (Jenness, 1922a, p. 173).

10.
The author probably refers to *Illuvillik*, which is Liston Island. However, as its highest point is just above 250 feet and that of Sutton Island just over 200 feet (Canada, 1971), he may have meant Harkness Island, whose maximum elevation is approximately 142 feet (Canada, 1971).

11.
These seances, including one by Agluak prior to Kuniluk's, are discussed in Jenness (1922a, pp. 204-205).

12.
Uloksak had suggested to the rather simpleminded Kinordluk that he should leave his rifle outside his hut. Uloksak had also been heard to say that it was absurd for an old man like Kinordluk to possess a rifle when he did not know how to use it. And no other member of the little community would have had the nerve to steal such a valuable item (Jenness, 1922a, p. 232).

13.
The rifle was the .44 taken apart by Ikpuk on June 21, 1915, on Victoria Island and incompletely reassembled by the author at the time. It had been sold to Kinordluk but a few weeks before. Further details on this incident are given in Jenness (1922a, p. 232).

14.
They were taking with them the scientists' semi-annual reports for the Geological Survey and for the Department of the Naval Service as well as personal mail. These they intended to turn over to Inspector La Nauze of the RNWMP, who they knew was at Fort Confidence on Great Bear Lake (Chipman, 1913-16, Nov. 30, 1915), with the expectation that someone at the Fort would take the mail on to Fort Norman, from whence it would ultimately reach Edmonton and beyond.

15.
This seance is described in Jenness (1922a, pp. 206-207).

16.
The author recorded three dance songs by the wife Niptanaciak, which are songs Nos. 25, 46 (3 versions), and 47 in Roberts and Jenness (1925) and one dance song and four incantations by her husband Nanneroak, which are songs Nos. 13, 86, 87, 89, and 102 in Roberts and Jenness (1925). (See Appendix 5.)

17.
Mistakenly labelled February 8th in the diary.

18.
Mistakenly labelled February 9th in the diary.

Chapter 38. – Visiting the Eskimos in Coronation Gulf

1.
This was a male Eskimo, not Higilaq's daughter Kanneyuk.

2.
Kaulluaq was the widow who had been offered to the author to look after him the previous year and then to Palaiyak (see diary entry for Jan. 2-3, 1915).

3.
The word 'left' is inserted as an afterthought in both places in this sentence; possibly one of them should have been 'right.'

4.
The inland district between Tree River and Bathurst Inlet was called *Pingangnaktok* (Jenness, 1922a, p. 21, footnote 3).

5.
A general name used for all of the natives who spent the winter on the ice off Bathurst Inlet (Jenness, 1922a, p. 39).

6.
The author took some ten photographs on this and the following day or two, mainly of the settlement on the ice, snowhouses etc. (See Appendix 7 and Fig. 187.)

7.
The word used by the author was 'chinnies', which is in neither the Oxford English Dictionary nor Webster's 3rd International Dictionary and appears to be either a coined word or a slang term for 'chinks.'

8.
The Expedition's library must have included a copy of one or both of Sir John Franklin's books on his two journeys into the Arctic (Franklin, 1824, 1828). Dr. Anderson took three photographs of this stone monument (CMC Photo Nos. 38748, 38749, and 38750), one of which (No. 38750) is Fig. 188. According to Anderson (1913-16, Sept. 30, 1915) the carefully built cairn was constructed by Peter Warren Dease and Thomas Simpson in 1839 during their third expedition along the Arctic coast; it is located on top of a stony point about 1 mile east of a high diabase bluff east of Port Epworth.

9.
The author refers to British Admiralty Chart 2443 of 1859, as the islands are not shown on Rae's map (1852) chart of Coronation Gulf.

10.
The word, meaning 'wing', refers to the two most westerly of the Jameson Islands. It is spelt *Huluklok* in Chipman and Cox (1924, p. 39B).

11.
In 1910-1911.

12.
Trade details are recorded in Appendix 3. Measurements of the natives are recorded in Jenness (1923a).

13.
The natives dwelling in the region around a small river called the Kilusiktok that flows into the southeast corner of Arctic Sound in Bathurst Inlet were given the same name (Jenness, 1922a, pp. 22, 39). Natives inland between Tree River and Bathurst Inlet bore the name of their district (*Piññannaktok* or *Pingangnaktok* (Jenness, 1922a, p. 21)). *Igloryuallik* is one of the Barry Islands, north of Aglak Island in Bathurst Inlet, *Igluhugyuk* is Hepburn Island, also in Coronation Gulf, and *Nagjuktok* (or *Nagyugtok*) may have been all the islands off the south coast of Victoria Island between 113° W. and 111° W (Jenness, 1922a, p. 36), now the Miles Islands (Canada, 1978), or the Richardson Islands farther east (Rosemarie Avrana Meyok, Coppermine, personal communication, 1989).

14.
See footnote 8, this chapter, for a different explanation.

15.
Iperviksaq, also spelled *Epeaviksuak* ("a hitching post" because of its appearance at a distance) is an island to the east of *Satualik*, which is an island about 17 miles east of Cape Krusenstern. It may be one of the islands in the Nanukton (or Nannuktun) Islands at the west end of the Duke of York Archipelago. Nannuktun or *Nanuktok* ("place where a polar bear was killed") is a group of islands northeast of *Satualik* (Chipman and Cox, 1924, pp.37B-38B).

16.
Pauneraqtoq or *Pauneraktok* ("it has berries") is the name for the first islands south of Locker Point (Chipman and Cox, 1924, p. 37B), probably the Black Berry Islands.

17.
The author drew this sketch (reproduced in Fig. 190) in the front of volume 3 of his diary.

18.
The temperature we learned the following day was -36° and we were going almost dead into a fairly strong rather gusty breeze. [D.J.]

Chapter 39. – Thievery and a Search for Johansen

1.
Kilusiktok was the native name given to a small river and surrounding country at the southeastern corner of Arctic Sound in Bathurst Inlet (Jenness, 1922a, p. 39).

2.
CMC Photo No. 36935.

3.
The author elsewhere described the recording session and the contents of the recordings in detail (Jenness, 1922a, pp. 209-211).

4.
The author photographed Mr. Girling with a group of natives on this occasion (Fig. 191; CMC Photo No. 36956).

5.
This seance is described in more detail in Jenness (1922a, pp. 215-216).

6.
Chipman expressed concern over Johansen's failure to return to the station by the scheduled day then added "Jenness with his usual willingness to be the goat of odd trips started out after him on the 10th" (Chipman, 1913-16, April 12, 1916).

7.
This was the last major trading recorded by the author (see Appendix 3).

8.
The map was made in 1851 (Rae, 1852).

9.
A typed copy of Johansen's note, six small pages long, was paper-clipped to the entry of April 7th in Jenness' diary. It is reproduced at the end of this chapter. The whereabouts of the original note is not known.

10.
Chipman made no mention in his diary of this conflict with Johansen on the latter's return but did comment that the topographic sketch maps and information Johansen had made on southern Victoria Island and brought back with him were useless (Chipman, 1913-16, April 12, 1916). According to Anderson (1913-16, April 11, 1916) Johansen could have returned on schedule but having some food left over "thought he would improve the time by 'exploring' the Kimeryuak River, which comes out in Forsyth Bay." He added that Johansen was peeved that Dr. Anderson had let Jenness go after him "as he thought he was capable of looking after himself." We have no record of Johansen's on the incident.

11.
Johansen collected specimens of *Halysites, Favosites,* and other fossils on the east ends of both Sutton and Liston Islands (see lists in O'Neill, 1924, p. 26A)

12.
The word 'pyrites,' in D. Jenness' handwriting, appears in the margin at the start of this line.

Chapter 40. – West with Girling

1.
Puivlik was that part of Wollaston Peninsula east of Innerit Point (Jenness, 1922a, p. 24), the same region they were in with the author the previous year.

2.
Girling needed to return to his vessel, 150 miles to the west, to be ready to sail it to

Bernard Harbour as soon as the ice broke up in the strait. As he was going alone and had no dog or sled, the author volunteered to accompany him with a sled and dog-team; the trip would also give the author the opportunity to search the coast-line for the ruins of ancient habitations (Jenness, 1928a, pp. 227-228.)

3.
This geological observation indicates the author's recognition that post-glacial marine seas had invaded the land in this region. That event, now known to have occurred within the past 10,000 years, left a trail of elevated beach or terrace deposits from Cape Parry, where there has been no up-warping, eastward to Coppermine, where the terraces are now found some 450 feet above sea level. Comparable elevated terraces abound in southwestern Victoria Island.

4.
Dr. Anderson took two photographs (CMC Photo Nos. 38760, 38761) of the gasoline schooner *Atkoon* of Collingwood on March 15, 1916, when he was en route to the Croker River with Chipman. The schooner had been built at Collingwood, Ontario, and sent down the Mackenzie River in 1914. It was driven ashore at this locality in September 1915 while en route to Bernard Harbour. Refloated in August 1916 it set off for Bernard Harbour, only to run aground 28 miles eastward, where it had to be unloaded. Somehow the vessel then caught fire and was totally destroyed. Girling returned to Fort McPherson to report the loss of his little schooner, and his assistants Merritt and Hoare packed the salvaged supplies the remaining 65 or more miles to Bernard Harbour.

5.
In August 1915 Stefansson arranged with Alexander Allan, captain of the *El Sueno*, a small motor schooner, to take supplies destined for the Southern Party to Bernard Harbour (Stefansson, 1921, pp. 392-393).

6.
Pausanna was a Christian Eskimo from Barrow, Alaska (Jenness, 1928a, p. 211), who had been influenced by the missionaries like the Eskimos the author knew in Harrison

Bay and refrained from carrying out routine work on Sunday.

7.
These were probably voles rather than mice. (See footnote 24, Chapter 29.)

8.
See Appendix 4E.

9.
The author later published three stories told him by Pausanna (Jenness, 1924a, pp. 32A-33A, 65A-66A), the two mentioned here probably being the shorter ones on pp. 32A-33A.

10.
D'Arcy Arden, a northern explorer and traveller, lived from 1914 to 1916 on Dease River at the northeast end of Great Bear Lake (Jenness, 1922a, p. 20). He brought to Fort Norman the news that some Coronation Gulf Eskimos were in possession of belongings of two missing Roman Catholic priests, the Reverend Fathers Rouvier and Le Roux, and agreed to guide Inspector La Nauze of the RNWMP to Dease Bay on Great Bear Lake, where the priests had made a base. Accompanied also by Constable Wight and the Eskimo translator Ilavinirk (who had worked with both Stefansson and Dr. Anderson between 1908 and 1912) they set out from Fort Norman in July 1915, wintered at Dease River, and continued their journey to Coronation Gulf in the spring of 1916 (La Nauze, 1918).

11.
Corporal Bruce had been sent in August 1915 east on the *Alaska* from Herschel Island, where he was stationed, to meet Inspector La Nauze in Coronation Gulf (La Nauze, 1918, p. 319). He had wintered at Bernard Harbour with the members of the C.A.E. Southern Party.

Chapter 41. – Murder Charges

1.
The Kugauyaq (Kugaryuak) River is the second small river east of the Coppermine River. The name means "River, not very large, not very small" (Chipman and Cox, 1924, p. 38B). Dr. Anderson (1913-16, Oct. 31, 1915) noted that there were two Kugaryuak Rivers between the Coppermine and Tree Rivers. The larger of these enters Coronation Gulf about 25 miles west of Port Epworth; the smaller empties into the Gulf

about 18 miles east of the Coppermine River. Capt. Joseph Bernard wintered inside the mouth of this latter river in 1910-11 with his schooner *Teddy Bear*, which drew only about 6 feet of water (Anderson, 1918, p. 57).

2.
I have been unable to find any explanation among the author's publications and letters for this statement.

3.
In a six-page letter to the Commissioner, Royal North-West Mounted Police, Regina, written on July 18, while on board the *Alaska* en route to Herschel Island, the author (Jenness, 1916a) urged the Canadian Government, through the RNWMP, to rigidly control the movement of white men into the regions occupied by the Copper Eskimo, lest their diseases and ways decimate the native population. This letter was forwarded from the Commissioner in Regina to the Comptroller of the RNWMP in Ottawa in September 1916 but was already too late, for the influx of traders and trappers from the west into the Coronation Gulf region had by then taken place.

4.
This prediction proved all too true. Within 20 years influenza, tuberculosis, and measles had struck in the Coronation Gulf region, killing many of the Eskimos known to the author.

5.
Ten years passed before the police (by then renamed the Royal Canadian Mounted Police) established a post at Bernard Harbour, and several more before they established one at Coppermine.

6.
These include some if not all of the following CMC Photo Nos. 36953, 36954, 36958,

36959, 36960, 36961, 36968, 36973, and 36974.

7.
A blank space appears at this point in the diary where the author intended to insert a mileage figure.

8.
Viscount Melville Sound.

9.
This map, which appears to be a tracing, with Dr. Anderson's writing, of Chipman and Cox's original map, was discovered among Dr. Anderson's maps in the Library of the CMN in 1988. It is the only known map showing the safe route to enter the little harbour used by the Canadian Arctic Expedition and gives credence to the original restriction of the name Bernard Harbour to that little bay. It also shows the location of the C.A.E. house and has the name Uluksak Island for the feature now called Cox Island (Canada, 1971). This map, extended southwards for several miles and eastward to include Chantry Island, was reproduced in O'Neill (1924). On it the name Bernard Harbour was applied for the first time to the entire embayment behind Chantry Island. The whereabouts of the original map is unknown.

Chapter 42. – Journey to the Stone Hut

1.
Nulahugyuk Creek ("the place with a covering of snow or ice"), which issues from a large fishing lake named *Hingittok* or *Hingiktok* about 6 miles south of Bernard Harbour (Jenness, 1922a, p. 16; Chipman and Cox, 1924, p. 40B). A detailed account of the fishing activities is given in Jenness (1922a, pp. 156-157).

2.
The author's nine photographs of the fishing activities are CMC Photo Nos. 37076-37084; Wilkins' seventeen photographs are CMC Photo Nos. 51182-51193, 51653-51657. Wilkins also took several minutes of moving pictures of the fishing activities, a copy of which is housed at the National Archives of Canada, Ottawa.

3.
Kogluktuaryuk Creek, which flows from a large lake of the same name lying a few

miles inland from Cape Lambert (Jenness, 1922a, p. 17).

4.
In July 1989 I found three rows of stones across this creek in almost the same locations as those in 1916. A small wooden cabin now on the east bank of the stream nearby belongs to Higilaq's grandson (Jennie's son) Aime Ahegona, who lives in Coppermine.

5.
Noahognik Creek, issuing from one of the many lakes 2 or 3 miles inland (Jenness, 1922a, p. 17). The author photographed the little Eskimo camp and the inhabitants returning from spearing fish in the creek (CMC Photo Nos. 37073, 37074).

6.
Also spelled *Kikigarnak* (Jenness, 1922a, p. 17; Chipman and Cox, 1924, p. 37B). It is a

high cliff ridge about 5 miles west of Locker Point (Anderson, 1913-16, June 4, 1916).

7.
It was erected perhaps as an observation post over the surrounding countryside (Jenness, 1922a, p. 17).

8.
The author took six photographs of the stone house and surroundings (CMC Photo Nos. 37066-37067, 37069-37071, 37101). The house had been discovered in November 1915 by Corporal Bruce, who revisited it with Dr. Anderson in February 1916, at which time Dr. Anderson photographed it (CMC Photo Nos. 38753-38756). It is 7 feet high, 6 feet in diameter at the base. In July 1989, I found the stone hut exactly as shown in the author's photographs, not a stone shifted from place. However, there was no sign of the nearby stone pillar and shelter mentioned by the author. A stone cairn 5 feet high and judged to be of fairly recent origin now lies some 200 feet to the north.

9.
Nukatukak means yearling. See footnote 33, Chapter 35.

10.
Toqalluaq appears in the author's CMC Photo No. 36977, taken earlier at Bernard Harbour. His seance is described and he is shown in another picture by the author (Jen-

ness, 1922a, p. 207 and Fig. 59, p. 206, which is CMC Photo No. 36953).

11.
This was the only bull-roarer the author saw during his two years in the Coronation Gulf region. It was a small and crudely made children's toy (Fig. 184 in Jenness, 1946, p. 143).

12.
Voles or lemming.

13.
Here the author photographed stone markers pointing to a place in the lake where holes could be dug through the ice for fishing (CMC Photo No. 37075).

14.
In his report O'Neill (1924, p. 71A) concluded that the Bathurst Inlet deposits (where he found the greatest abundance of copper in the Coronation Gulf region) probably were an important reserve of copper ore, but they were not sufficiently attractive under conditions of accessibility, transportation, and demand at that time to warrant the expense of proving and development. A flurry of prospecting interest occurred in the late 1920's and early 1930's when aircraft first reached the region, but it soon waned, and the copper deposits remain unexploited to this day.

Chapter 43. – Return to the Outside World

1.
Higilaq's daughter Kanneyuk (Jennie) and Ikpuk's adopted daughter Arnauyuk (Kila); the latter, after two brief marriages, had rejoined Ikpuk's family shortly after the author's return from Victoria Island. The two girls were jokingly referred to, among the Expedition members, as the author's 'children' (see diary entry for January 14th, 1916). They were photographed together in costume by Wilkins on July 11, 1916 at Bernard Harbour (CMC Photo Nos. 51250, 51251; see Jenness, 1922a, p. 267, Plates IX A and B). (See also Fig. 201.)

2.
The author took five photographs of the loading and departure of the *Alaska* (CMC Photo Nos. 37180, 37182-37185). Wilkins then photographed the author bidding farewell to his Eskimo family shortly before the departure (CMC Photo No. 51277). (See

Fig. 203.) On board were 26 people (11 white men and 15 Eskimos) and 24 dogs. Four dogs, including two of the author's, were given to Ikpuk (Anderson, 1913-16, July 13, 1916).

3.
A problem with the engine delayed the departure by about an hour. Wilkins and Jenness waited on shore while it was fixed, for Wilkins was to film the *Alaska*'s departure. Finally the ship got under way, the 'apparent' departure was filmed, and the two rowed to the ship, which halted and took them on board (Wilkins, 1913-16, July 14-23, 1916).

4.
The creek where the author started his Victoria Island traverses in May 1915, and where he ended them in November 1915.

5.
The implements were a copper fish spear, musk-ox horn cup, and sealing tools (Anderson, 1913-16, July 21, 1916).

6.
Cox got an observation time sight with transit, then built a small stone cairn on the site (Anderson 1913-16, July 24, 1914).

7.
During their wait Dr. Anderson photographed the author on the deck of the *Alaska* (CMC Photo No. 39209 and Fig. 206) as did also Wilkins (CMC Photo Nos. 51291 and 51292). Dr. Anderson also took care of a nasty incident when a nearly full-grown pup suddenly went crazy, snapping at men and dogs alike, and was frothing at the mouth. The Dr. managed somehow to untie it and throw it overboard, without injury to himself, whereupon it swam ashore and disappeared (Anderson, 1913-16, July 24, 1916).

8.
Patsy was due $300 for his 15 months service; he was paid in guns, ammunition, and stores (Anderson, 1913-16, July 26, 1916).

9.
The Arctic fox fur is white in winter or a greyish blue to pale beige, which is called 'blue' (Lopez, 1986, p. 238).

10.
In 1986 the Canadian Museum of Civilization (formerly the National Museum) unearthed a handsomely decorated Eskimo parka from its cold storage room, with the name D. Jenness attached. Its appearance indicated it was of Western Arctic design, not Copper Eskimo, and its decorations are almost identical with those on the parka (*atigi*) worn by Etna Klengenberg in the author's photograph taken on this date (see Fig. 207). As parka designs were highly individualistic, it is reasonable to suggest that this parka was made by Mrs. Klengenberg, an Alaskan Eskimo (or by her daughter Etna, an equally skilled seamstress) and presented to the author at this time as her gift in appreciation for the author's teaching of her son.

11.
Eikie (later known as Ikey Bolt) and Etna Klengenberg were reportedly married soon afterwards by "Father Frabsole or Fraisole" (MacInnes, 1932, p. 274). This was probably Father Frapsauce, the first Roman Catholic priest along the central Arctic coast. The register book at St. Andrews Mission, Coppermine (which I saw in July 1989) also records their marriage on August 29, 1924, at Bernard Harbour, performed by G.E. Merritt, the Church of England missionary there.

12.
The author photographed Capt. Klengenberg and his family sometime during the day (CMC Photo No. 36912; see Fig. 206).

13.
Stefansson (1921, p. 40) shows an elderly Eskimo wearing labrets like those observed by the author.

14.
Dr. Anderson took three photographs of the polar bear (CMC Photo Nos. 39469-39471).

15.
William George Phillips, then post manager at Fort McPherson. The post established in August 1916 by the Hudson's Bay Company at Bernard Harbour was initially named Fort Bacon, after Fur Trade Commissioner N.H. Bacon. It was later renamed Fort Thomson in 1920 after another Fur Trade Commissioner, then in 1925 Bernard Harbour. The post was abandoned in 1932.

16.
The two Eskimo prisoners (Sinnisiak and Uloksak) left the *Alaska* at this time along with Inspector La Nauze and Corporal Bruce. They remained at Herschel Island until the following spring then were escorted to Edmonton, Alberta, by way of the Mackenzie River. In August 1917, at Calgary they were found guilty of murder and sentenced to death, but their sentences were commuted to life imprisonment at Fort Resolution and within two years they were freed and returned to Coronation Gulf (Moyles, 1979).

17.
Inspector La Nauze found orders awaiting him that he was to remain in charge of the Herschel Island detachment for the next year (Anderson, 1913-16, July 28, 1916).

18.
All headings in the diary from this date onwards are incorrectly entered as July instead of August.

19.
Also known as Eunice, she was the wife of Daniel Sweeney. Her married sister, Laura, and Laura's husband were living there with

her husband (Wilkins, 1913-16, p. 77 after July 14-23, 1916).

20.
While there they picked up a box from Aiyakuk (the author's assistant on Barter Island in 1914), which contained a number of bird skins for Dr. Anderson and archaeological specimens collected by Aiyakuk on Barter Island in the summer of 1915 for the author. Dr. Anderson also received two notes from Aiyakuk at Herschel Island (Anderson, 1913-16, August 3, 1916). The archaeological specimens are noted at the end of Jenness (1914j).

21.
Cox and Wilkins went ashore to get a time sight with transit at the International Boundary (141° W. Longitude) (Anderson, 1913-16, August 4, 1916).

22.
The *Alaska* had gone inside the offshore islands through what is now called the Newport Entrance, east of Karluk Island, and ran aground on the landward side of Cross Island, in the same region Stefansson had wanted Captain Bartlett to take the much larger *Karluk* three years earlier. While there they saw the *Herman* (also a much larger vessel than the *Alaska*) about 1/2 mile outside Cross Island in the ice. Sweeney said that the flag flown by the *Herman* signalled it had mail for them, but the dory lowered by the *Alaska* was unable to reach the other vessel because of ice conditions (Anderson, 1913-16, August 5, 1916).

23.
Dr. Anderson explained that they needed to have the decks of the *Alaska* cleared in preparation for the open water and heavy weather they could expect en route to Nome (Anderson, 1913-16, August 8, 1916). He had kept the skin *umiak*, two sleds, two dog teams, and a considerable reserve of provisions on board the *Alaska* until they reached Barrow in case they had become ice-bound and had to leave the ship (Anderson, 1916b, p. 14).

24.
These are now lodged in the archaeological collections of the Canadian Museum of Civilization, Hull, Quebec.

25.
The author is referring to his journey into the Arctic in 1913.

26.
Able-bodied seamen.

27.
This was Reverend T.M. Hoare, resident missionary at Point Hope for several years. He and a retired old whaler, "Little Joe" Whitfield, had come on board the *Alaska* to visit the Expedition members (Anderson, 1913-16, Aug. 10, 1916). Rev. Hoare was shot and killed by a young school teacher a few years later (Brower, 1944?, p. 210). He was not related to the William Hoare who came to Bernard Harbour with Rev. H. Girling in 1916.

28.
Sweeney wanted to follow the shore around Kotzebue Sound because of the condition of the *Alaska*, but the others persuaded him to cut across. By the time they reached Cape Prince of Wales they were in a rolling stormy sea (Wilkins, 1913-16, p. 78).

29.
After a change of wind (Wilkins, 1913-16, p. 79).

30.
With about 20 fathoms of chain (Wilkins, 1913-16, p. 79).

31.
En route to Nome on this day they passed Capt. J. Bernard's schooner *Teddy Bear* being towed to Nome by the *Arctic*, a sister ship to the *Alaska* (Wilkins, 1913-16, p. 79). The *Teddy Bear* had broken its rudder in Kotzebue Sound. Capt. Bernard was on his way north for a two-year trading stint and had some mail for the C.A.E. members (Anderson, 1913-16, Aug. 15, 1916), the most recent mail they had received. Capt. Bernard finally reached Coronation Gulf in late September 1916, and wintered at the mouth of the Kugaryuak River, where he had wintered in 1910-11. The next two winters he spent in a bay on the southeast side of Victoria Island, then returned to winter 1919-20 again at the Kugaryuak River (Jenness, 1922a, pp. 243-244), after abandoning plans of returning to his home in Prince Edward Island via the Northeast Passage. He ultimately sailed his schooner *Teddy Bear* into Nome, Alaska, late in 1920, with three tons of furs and ethnological and mineral specimens (*Ottawa Citizen*, Dec. 23, 1920).

32.

The *Alaska* reached Sledge Island late in the evening of August 14 and anchored there so as to arrive in Nome during the day. Leaving the island very early next morning it reached Nome about 4:30 a.m., where after inspection by the United States health officers, its men were permitted to go ashore to arrange the unloading and shipment of the cargo and the disposal of the vessel (Anderson, 1913-16, Aug. 15, 1916). The medical officer in Nome at that time was Dr. Daniel S. Neuman, an authority on archaeology, ethnology, and the status of many Indian, Eskimo, and Aleut groups (according to the inscription he wrote in a little medical book he presented to Dr. Anderson in August 1913, a book now in the Anderson collection of the library, Canadian Museum of Nature, Ottawa).

Epilogue

1.

A large, open, flat-bottomed barge, used in unloading and loading ships wherever shallow water prevents these from coming into shore. Several Expedition members were photographed by Dr. Anderson on the lighter just before being loaded on the ship (CMC Photo Nos. 39341, 39342).

References

Abbreviations

ASC-CMC:	Archaeological Survey of Canada, Canadian Museum of Civilization, Hull, Quebec, Canada
CCFCS-CMC:	Canadian Centre for Folk Culture Studies, Canadian Museum of Civilization, Hull, Quebec, Canada
CES-CMC:	Canadian Ethnology Survey, Canadian Museum of Civilization, Hull, Quebec, Canada
CMN:	Zoology Division, Canadian Museum of Nature Ottawa, Ontario, Canada
NAC:	National Archives of Canada, Ottawa, Ontario, Canada

Allen, A.J. 1978. A whaler & trader in the Arctic, 1895 to 1944. Alaska Northwest Publishing Company, Anchorage, Alaska, 213 p.

Anderson, R.M. 1913. Report on the natural history collections of the Expedition, pp. 436-527. *In*: Stefansson, V. My life with the Eskimo. The MacMillan Company, New York.

Anderson, R.M. 1913-1916. Field Notes. Canadian Arctic Expedition Records. Original, 8 vols. in Anderson papers, CMN.

Anderson, R.M. 1915. Canadian Arctic Expedition, 1913-14. *In*: Summary Report of the Geological Survey, Department of Mines, for the Calendar Year 1914, pp. 163-166.

Anderson, R.M. 1916a. Canadian Arctic Expedition, 1915. *In*: Summary Report of the Geological Survey, Department of Mines in the Calendar Year 1915, pp. 220-236.

Anderson, R.M. 1916b. Report to the Deputy Minister, Department of Mines (Geological Survey), Ottawa, 18th January 1916, 11 p. Copy in Geological Survey file, Anderson papers, CMN.

Anderson, R.M. 1917. Recent explorations on the Canadian Arctic coast. Geographical Review, Vol. 4, No. 4, pp. 241-266.

Anderson, R.M. 1918. Canadian Arctic Expedition. Report of the Department of the Naval Service for the fiscal year ending March 31, 1917, pp. 22-64.

Anderson, R.M. 1919a. Letter to D. Jenness, August 22, 1919, 1 p. Copy in Jenness file, Anderson papers, CMN.

Anderson, R.M. 1919b or later. The Canadian Arctic Expedition, 1913-1918. Unpublished manuscript, incomplete, 22 typed pages. History of CAE file, Anderson papers, CMN.

Anderson, R.M. 1920. Memorandum dated September 29, 1920 to G.J. Desbarats, Department of the Naval Service, 10 p. Copy in Desbarats file, Anderson papers, CMN.

Anderson, R.M. 1921. Letter to G.J. Desbarats, March 21, 1921, 2 p. Copy in Desbarats file, Anderson papers, CMN.

Anderson, R.M. 1924. Letter to Dr. Charles Camsell, Deputy Minister of Mines, January 21, 1924, 9 p. Copy in Camsell file, Anderson papers, CMN.

Baker, A.W. 1919. Mallophaga of the Canadian Arctic Expedition, 1913-18. Report of the Canadian Arctic Expedition 1913-18, Vol. 3, Insects, Part D, pp. 3D-9D.

Bartlett, R.A. 1915. Diary of Captain Bartlett. Report of the Department of the Naval Service for the Fiscal Year ending March 31, 1915, Sessional Paper No. 38, Ottawa, pp. 22-54.

Bartlett, R.A. and Hale, R.T. 1916. The last voyage of the *Karluk*, flagship of Vilhjalmar Stefansson's Canadian Arctic Expedition of 1913-16. McClelland, Goodrich & Stewart, Publishers, Toronto, Ont., 329 p.

Bethune-Johnson, D., Conner, D.C.G., and Elias, D. 1986. Our Arctic way of life — the Copper Inuit. Prentice-Hall Canada Inc., Scarborough, Ont., 70 p.

Beuchat, Henri. 1913a. Letter to E. Sapir, July 15, 1913, 2 p. Original in Sapir Collection, CES-CMC.

Beuchat, Henri. 1913b. Letter to M. Barbeau, July 15, 1913, 3 p. Original in Barbeau Collection, B-Mc-2159, CCFCS-CMC.

Boas, F. 1901. I. The Eskimo of Baffin Land and Hudson Bay. From notes collected by Capt. George Comer, Capt. James S. Mutch, and Rev. E.J. Peck. Bulletin of the American Museum of Natural History, Vol. XV, pp. 1-373.

Boas, F. 1907. II. Second report on the Eskimo of Baffin Land and Hudson Bay. From notes collected by Capt. George Comer, Capt. James S. Mutch, and Rev. E.J. Peck. Bulletin of the American Museum of Natural History, Vol. XV, Part II, pp. 374-570.

Bockstoce, John R. 1977. Steam whaling in the Western Arctic. Old Dartmouth Historical Society, New Bedford, Mass., 127 p.

Bockstoce, John R. 1986. Whales, ice, and men. The history of whaling in the Western Arctic. University of Washington Press, Seattle, Washington, U.S.A., 400 p.

Bockstoce, John R. (Editor). 1988a. The journal of Rochfort Maguire, 1852-1854. The Hakluyt Society, London, 2 vol., 584 p.

Bockstoce, John R. 1988b. Arctic voyages of the motor-cutter *Belvedere*, 1983-87. Polar Record, Vol. 24 (150), pp. 231-234.

Brock, R.W. 1913. Letter to Dr. R.M. Anderson, November 22, 1913, 1 p. Copy in Geological Survey (Orders and Letters from) file, Anderson papers, CMN.

Brower, Charles. 1914. Letter to The Director, Victoria Memorial Museum, Ottawa, July 1914, 1 p. Copy on file MS.83-2129, ASC-CMC.

Brower, Charles D. 1944(?) Fifty years below zero - A lifetime of adventure in the far north. Robert Hale Limited, London, 254 p.

Burroughs Wellcome and Co. (U.S.A. Inc.) 1934. The romance of exploration and emergency first-aid from Stanley to Byrd. New York, 160 p.

Cameron, John, and Ritchie, S.G. 1923. Osteology and dentition of the western and central Eskimos. Report of the Canadian Arctic Expedition 1913-18, Vol. 12, The Copper Eskimos, Part C, 67 p.

Canada. 1971. Bernard Harbour, District of Mackenzie. Topographic map, Energy, Mines and Resources, Ottawa, scale 1:50,000.

Canada. 1976. Horton River NR-9/10/11/12. Topographic map, Energy, Mines and Resources, Ottawa, scale 1:1,000,000.

Canada. 1978. Dolphin and Union Strait (N.T.S. No. 87 S.W. and 87 S.E.). Topographic map, Energy, Mines and Resources, Ottawa, scale 1:500,000.

Canada. 1982. Penny Bay, Northwest Territories. Topographic map, Energy, Mines and Resources, Ottawa, scale 1:250,000.

Canadian Arctic Expedition. 1913-16. Trade list of D. Jenness. Box 3, File 1, ASC-CMC.

Canadian Arctic Expedition - Record. 1913-16. "Alaska Store Book." Unpublished record book, Box 3, File 6, ASC-CMC.

Childs, H.E., Jr. 1958. Letter to D. Jenness, August 4, 1958, 1 p. Photocopy in D. Jenness papers, File MG30 B89, NAC.

Chipman, K.G. 1913. Letter to W.H. Boyd, July 18, 1913, 10 p. Original in Chipman papers, File MG30 B66, NAC.

Chipman, K.G. 1913-16. Arctic diary. 3 volumes. Chipman papers, File MG30 B66, NAC.

Chipman, K.G. 1914a. Letter to W.H. Boyd, January 6, 1914, 4 p. Copy in Chipman papers, File MG30 B66, NAC.

Chipman, K.G. 1914b. Letter to O.E. LeRoy, April 30, 1914, 10 p. Copy in Chipman papers, File MG 30 B-66, PAC.

Chipman, K.G. and Cox, J.R. 1924. Geographical notes on the Arctic Coast of Canada. Report of the Canadian Arctic Expedition 1913-18, Vol. 11, Geology and geography. Part B, 57 p.

Cook, Fred. 1918. Report No. 14 of the Editorial Committee (on Government Publications), February 15, 1918. *In* Reports of the Editorial Committee, P.C. 484, pp. 22-24, King's Printer, Ottawa.

Dall, W.H. 1919. The Mollusca of the Arctic Coast of America collected by the Canadian Arctic Expedition west from Bathurst Inlet, with an Appended Report on the Collection of Pleistocene Fossil Mollusca. Report of the Canadian Arctic Expedition 1913-18, Vol. 8: Mollusks, Echinoderms, Coelenterates, etc., Part A, pp. 3A-29A.

Desbarats, G.J. 1913. Letter of Instructions [to all members of the Canadian Arctic Expedition] dated May 29, 1913, 5 p. Copy in Naval Service (Orders and Letters from) file, Anderson papers, CMN.

Desbarats, G.J. 1914a. Letter to V. Stefansson, April 30, 1914, 1 p. Copy in Naval Service (Orders and Letters from) file, Anderson papers, CMN.

Desbarats, G.J. 1914b. Letter to V. Stefansson, April 30, 1914, 1 p. Copy in Naval Service (Orders and Letters from) file, Anderson papers, CMN.

Desbarats, G.J. 1914c. Letter to V. Stefansson, May 5, 1914, 5 p. Copy in Naval Service (Orders and Letters from) file, Anderson papers, CMN.

Desbarats. G.J. 1919. Letter to Fred Cook, Chairman of the Editorial Committee on Governmental Publications, February 26, 1919, 1 p. Copy in Desbarats, G.J. file - C.A.E. Reports, Anderson papers, CMN.

Diubaldo, R.J. 1978. Stefansson and the Canadian Arctic. McGill-Queen's University Press, Montreal, 274 p.

Emerton, J.H. 1919. The spiders collected by the Canadian Arctic Expedition, 1913-18. Report of the Canadian Arctic Expedition 1913-18, Vol. 3, Insects, Part H, pp. 3H-9H.

Encyclopaedia Britannica. 1911. (11th edition). Painting. Vol. 20, pp. 459-519.

Encyclopaedia Britannica. 1956. Atalanta. Vol. 2, p. 595.

Encyclopaedia Britannica. 1982. (15th edition). Amundsen, R. Vol. 13, p. 258.

Fall, H.C. 1919. Family Carabidae. Report of the Canadian Arctic Expedition 1913-1918, vol. 3, Insects, Part E, Coleoptera, pp. 14E-16E.

Finnie, R. 1940. Lure of the North. David McKay Company, New York, 227 p.

Finnie, R. 1978. Stefansson's unsolved mystery. North, Nov.-Dec. issue, pp. 2-7.

Franklin, Sir John. 1824. Narrative of a journey to the shores of the Polar Sea in the years 1819-20-21-22. 3rd Edition. John Murray, London. (Vol. 1), 370 p., (Vol. 2), 399 p.

Franklin, Sir John. 1828. Narrative of a second expedition to the shores of the Polar Sea. John Murray, London. Reprinted in 1971 by Charles E. Tuttle Company, Rutland, Vermont, 320 p. plus Appendix of 157 p.

Gadacz, Rene R. 1985. Eskimo. *In*: The Canadian Encyclopedia, Vol. 1, Hurtig Publishers, Edmonton, Alberta, pp. 590-591.

Garst, S. 1948. Scotty Allan, King of the dog-team drivers. Wells Gardner, Darton & Co., Ltd., Redhill, Surrey, 198 p.

Geological Survey of Canada. 1915. Summary Report of the Geological Survey, Department of Mines, for the calendar year 1914. King's Printer, Ottawa, 209 p.

Gibson, Arthur. 1920. The Lepidoptera collected by the Canadian Arctic Expedition, 1913-18. Report of the Canadian Arctic Expedition, 1913-18, Vol. 3, Insects, Part I, 57 p.

Goddard, Ives. 1984. Synonymy. *In*: Handbook of North American Indians, Vol. 5: Arctic (David Damas, Volume Editor). Smithsonian Institution, Washington, pp. 5-7.

Godfrey, Earl. 1966. The birds of Canada. National Museum of Canada, Bulletin 203, 428 p.

Hall, Edwin S., Jr. 1987. A land full of people, a long time ago; An analysis of three archaeology sites in the vicinity of Kaktovik, Northern Alaska. Edwin Hall and Associates, Brockport, N.Y., Technical Memorandum No. 24, 360 p.

Hanbury, David T. 1904. Sport and travel in the northland of Canada. Edward Arnold, London, 319 p.

Hewitt, C.G. 1919. Letter to Mr. R.G. McConnell, Deputy Minister of Mines, February 27, 1919, 3 p. Signed copy in Arctic Biological Committee file, Anderson papers, CMN.

Hunt, William R. 1986. Stef, a biography of Vilhjalmur Stefansson, Canadian Arctic Explorer. University of British Columbia Press, Vancouver, B.C., 317 p.

Irving, Laurence. 1958. On the naming of birds by Eskimos. Anthropological Papers of the University of Alaska, Vol. 6, No. 2, pp. 61-78.

Jenness, D. 1913a. Letter to Dr. E. Sapir, June 10, 1913, 2 p. Original in Jenness Letters, Sapir Correspondence, CES-CMC.

Jenness, D. 1913b. Letter to Mr. Henry Balfour, July 3 and 17, 1913, 9 p. Original in Pitt Rivers Museum, Oxford University, England. Photocopy in Jenness papers, MG30 B89, NAC.

Jenness, D. 1913c. Letter to Marius Barbeau, July 7-11, 1913, 3 p. Original in Jenness correspondence, Barbeau papers, CCFCS-CMC.

Jenness, D. 1913d. Letter to Professor R.R. Marett, July 7-11, 1913, 3 p. Original in Bodleian Library, University of Oxford, England. Committee for Anthropology papers, File # Ms.UDC/C/2/4.

Jenness, D. 1913e. Letter to Professor W. von Zedlitz, October 16, 1913, 4 p. Original in the Hocken Library, University of Otago, Dunedin, New Zealand. Photocopy in Jenness papers, MG30 B89, NAC.

Jenness, D. 1913f. Letter to Professor R.R. Marett, October 17, 1913, 4 p. Original in Bodleian Library, University of Oxford, England. Committee for Anthropology papers, File # Ms.UDC/C/2/4.

Jenness, D. 1913g. Letter to Dr. E. Sapir, October 26, 1913, 4 p. Original in Jenness Letters, Sapir Correspondence, CES-CMC.

Jenness, D. 1913h. Letter to Dr. E. Sapir, December 2, 1913, 4 p. Original in Jenness Letters, Sapir Correspondence, CES-CMC.

Jenness, D. 1914a. Letter to 'Arctician', February 2, 1914, 2 p. B. McConnell Correspondence File, Stefansson Collection, Baker Library, Dartmouth College, Hanover, New Hampshire, U.S.A.

Jenness, D. 1914b. Letter to Dr. E. Sapir, February 27, 1914, 4 p. Original in Jenness Letters, Sapir Correspondence, CES-CMC.

Jenness, D. 1914c. Letter to Dr. E. Sapir, May 30, 1914, 4 p. Original in Jenness Letters, Sapir Correspondence, CES-CMC.

Jenness, D. 1914d. Letter to Dr. E. Sapir, July 30, 1914, 2 p. Original in Jenness Letters, Sapir Correspondence, CES-CMC.

Jenness, D. 1914e. Letter to Professor G.W. von Zedlitz, June 29, 1914, 5 p. Original in the Hocken Library, University of Otago, Dunedin, New Zealand. Photocopy in Jenness papers, MG30 B89, NAC.

Jenness, D. 1914f. Letter to Dr. R.M. Anderson, June 17, 1914, 3 p. with zoological notes dated June 1 to 5. Original in Jenness file, Anderson papers, CMN.

Jenness, D. 1914g. Letter to Professor R.R. Marett, August 2, 1914, 5 p. Original in Bodleian Library, University of Oxford, England. Committee for Anthropology papers, File # Ms.UDC/C/2/4.

Jenness, D. 1914h. Letter to Marius Barbeau, August 10, 1914, 1 p. Original in Jenness Correspondence, Barbeau papers, CCFCS-CMC.

Jenness, D. 1914i. List of "Stores brought from Martin Point to Barter Is." Original 5"x8" page *in*: Canadian Arctic Expedition - Record "Alaska Store Book," 1913-16. C.A.E. files, D. Jenness, Box 3, file 1, ASC-CMC.

Jenness, D. 1914j. Archaeological notes on Eskimo ruins at Barter Island on the Arctic Coast of Alaska, excavated by D. Jenness, 1914. Unpublished manuscript No. 85, 106 p., ASC-CMC.

Jenness, D. 1916a. Letter to the Commissioner, Royal North West Mounted Police, Regina Saskatchewan, July 18, 1916, 6 p. RG85, Vol. 571, File 244, NAC.

Jenness, D. 1916b. Letter to Mrs. Hart (Victoria, B.C.), December 19, 1916, 3 p. Original in Jenness Letters, Stefansson Collection, Baker Library, Dartmouth College, Hanover, New Hampshire, U.S.A.

Jenness, D. 1917. Letter to Professor G.W. von Zedlitz, December 21, 1917, 6 p. Original in the von Zedlitz papers, Hocken Library, University of Otago, Dunedin, New Zealand. Photocopy in Jenness papers, MG30 B89, PAC.

Jenness, D. 1918. The Eskimos of Northern Alaska: A study in the effect of civilization. Geographical Review, Vol. 5, pp. 89-101.

Jenness, D. 1919a. Letter to V. Stefansson, February 20, 1919, 3 p. Original in Jenness Letters, Stefansson Collection, Baker Library, Dartmouth College, Hanover, New Hampshire, U.S.A.

Jenness, D. 1919b. Letter to Dr. R.M. Anderson, August 24, 1919 (incorrectly dated 1915), 1 p. Original in Jenness file, Anderson papers, CMN.

Jenness, D. 1920. Papuan cat's cradles. Journal of the Royal Anthropological Institute, Vol. 50, pp. 299-326.

Jenness, D. 1922a. The Life of the Copper Eskimos. Report of the Canadian Arctic Expedition 1913-18, Vol. 12, The Copper Eskimos, Part A, 277 p.

Jenness, D. 1922b. Eskimo art. Geographical Review, vol. 12, pp. 161-174.

Jenness, D. 1922c. Eskimo music in Northern Alaska. The Musical Quarterly, Vol. 8, pp. 377-383.

Jenness, D. 1923a. Physical characteristics of the Copper Eskimos. Report of the Canadian Arctic Expedition, 1913-18, Vol. 12, The Copper Eskimos. Part B, 89 p.

Jenness, D. 1923b. The play hour in New Guinea — Telling of the pastimes of the youngsters under tropic skies. The Christian Herald, January 27, 1923, pp. 68, 78.

Jenness, D. 1924a. Myths and traditions from Northern Alaska, the Mackenzie Delta, and Coronation Gulf. Report of the Canadian Arctic Expedition 1913-18, Vol. 13, Eskimo folk-lore, Part A, 90 p.

Jenness, D. 1924b. Eskimo string figures. Report of the Canadian Arctic Expedition 1913-18, Vol. 13, Eskimo folk-lore, Part B, 192 p.

Jenness, D. 1925. A new Eskimo culture in Hudson Bay. Geographical Review, Vol. 15, no. 3, pp. 428-437.

Jenness, D. 1928a. The people of the twilight. The MacMillan Co., New York, N.Y., 247 p. Reprinted (softcover) 1959, with author's 1958 Epilogue, University of Chicago Press, 251 p.

Jenness, D. 1928b. Comparative vocabulary of the Western Eskimo dialects. Report of the Canadian Arctic Expedition, 1913-18, Vol. 15, Eskimo language and technology, Part A, 134 p.

Jenness, D. 1931. Letter to V. Stefansson, July 23, 1931, 1 p. Original in Jenness letters, Stefansson Collection, Baker Library, Dartmouth College, Hanover, N.H., U.S.A.

Jenness, D. 1946. Material culture of the Copper Eskimo. Report of the Canadian Arctic Expedition 1913-18, Vol. 16, 148 p.

Jenness, D. 1957. Dawn in Arctic Alaska. University of Minnesota Press, 222 pp. Reprinted (softcover) 1985, University of Chicago Press, 222 p.

Jenness, D. 1962. Eskimo administration: I. Alaska. Arctic Institute of North America, Technical Paper No. 10, 64 p.

Jenness, D. 1963. Tribute to Professor G.W. von Zedlitz. Appendix B *in*: G.W. von Zedlitz. The search for a country. Latimer, Trend & Co., Plymouth, England, 161-162 p.

Jenness, D. 1964. Eskimo administration: II. Canada. Arctic Institute of North America, Technical Paper No. 14, 186 p.

Jenness, D. 1965. Eskimo administration: III. Labrador. Arctic Institute of North America, Technical Paper No. 16, 94 p.

Jenness, D. 1967a. Eskimo administration: IV. Greenland. Arctic Institute of North America, Technical Paper No. 19, 176 p.

Jenness, D. 1967b. Ascent of Mount Madawana, Goodenough Island (New Guinea). Canadian Geographical Journal, Vol. 74, pp. 100-108.

Jenness, D. 1968a. Eskimo administration: V. Analysis and reflections. Arctic Institute of North America, Technical Paper No. 21, 72 p.

Jenness, D. 1968b. Letter to Dr. Geert van den Steenhoven, Sept. 18, 1968, 2 p. Photocopy in Jenness papers, MG30 B89, NAC.

Jenness, D. and Ballantyne, A. 1920. The Northern d'Entrecasteaux. Clarendon Press, Oxford, 219 p.

Jenness, D. and Ballantyne, A. 1928. Language, mythology, and songs of Bwaidoga, Goodenough Island, S.E. Papua. Memoirs of the Polynesian Society, Vol. 88, Thomas Avery and Sons Ltd., New Plymouth, New Zealand, 270 p.

Jenness, S.E. 1985. Arctic wolf attacks scientist - a unique Canadian incident. Arctic, Vol. 38, pp. 129-132.

Jenness, S.E. 1989. Letter to the Editor. Arctic, Vol. 42, p. 297.

Johansen, F. 1913-16. Arctic diary. Photocopy in Johansen papers (in Danish with English translation), MG30 B165, NAC.

Johansen, F. 1921. Insect life on the western Arctic coast of America. Report of the Canadian Arctic Expedition 1913-18, Vol. 3, Insects, Part K, pp. 3K-61K.

Johansen, F. 1922a. Life of some Arctic lagoons, lakes and ponds. Report of the Canadian Arctic Expedition 1913-18, Vol. 7, Crustacea of the American Arctic, Part N, 31 p.

Johansen, F. 1922b. Euphyllopoda. Report of the Canadian Arctic Expedition 1913-18, Vol. 7, Crustacea of the American Arctic, Part G, pp. 4G-34G.

Johansen, F. 1924. General observations on the vegetation. Report of the Canadian Arctic Expedition 1913-18, Vol. 5, Botany, Part C, pp. 3C-85C.

La Nauze, C.D. 1918. A police patrol in the North-West Territories of Canada. The Geographical Journal, Vol. 51, No. 5, pp. 316-323.

Le Bourdais, D.M. 1963. Stefansson, Ambassador of the North. Harvest House, Montreal, 204 p.

Leffingwell, E. de K. 1919. The Canning River region, Northern Alaska. United States Geological Survey Professional Paper 109, 251 p.

Leng, C.W. 1919. The Rhynchophora (except Ipidae). Report of the Canadian Arctic Expedition 1913-1918, Vol. 3, Insects, Part E, pp. 19E-21E.

LeRoy, O.E. 1914. Memo to R.G. McConnell, Deputy Minister of Mines, October 3, 1914, 2 p. Copy in LeRoy file, Anderson papers, CMN.

Lopez, Barry. 1986. Arctic dreams: Imagination and desire in a northern landscape. Bantam Books Inc., New York, 417 p.

Macbeth, Madge. 1923. Daring Captain Joe and his *Teddy Bear*. Toronto Star Weekly, April 7.

MacGillivray, A.D. 1919. The saw-flies (Tenthredinoidea) collected by the Canadian Arctic Expedition, 1913-18. Report of the Canadian Arctic Expedition 1913-1918, Vol. 3, Insects, Part G., Hymenoptera and plant galls, pp. 3G-l9G.

MacInnes, T. (Editor) 1932. Klengenberg of the Arctic, an autobiography. J. Cape, London, Toronto, 360 p.

Malhaurie, Jean. 1956. The last king of Thule; a year among the Polar Eskimos of Greenland. Crowell, New York, 295 p.

Malloch, J. R. 1919. The Diptera collected by the Canadian Arctic Expedition 1913-18 (excluding Lipulidae and Culicidae). Report of the Canadian Arctic Expedition 1913-18, Vol. 3, Insects, Part C, pp. 34C-90C.

Mamen, Bjarne. 1913-14. Diary of the Canadian Arctic Expedition. Typed copy of translation (from Norwegian) by Prof. M. Malte of diary June 17, 1913 – May 23, 1914. Mamen file, Anderson papers, CMN.

Marett, R.R. 1913. Letter to Marius Barbeau, January 26, 1913, 4 p. Original in Marett correspondence, Barbeau papers, CCFCS-CMC.

Mauss, M. and Beuchat, Henri. 1906. Essai sur les variations saisonnieres des societes eskimos. L'Annee sociologique, 9ieme annee, 1904-05, pp. 39-132.

McConnell, B.M. (Editor) 1913. Karluk Chronicle (a daily typewritten newsletter), June 18 - July 7, 1913. Copies in McConnell file, Stefansson Collection, Baker Library, Dartmouth College, Hanover, New Hampshire, U.S.A.

McConnell, B. M. 1913-14. Arctic Diary. Original in Stefansson Collection, Baker Library, Dartmouth College, Hanover, New Hampshire, U.S.A.

McConnell, B.M. 1915. The rescue of the "Karluk" survivors. Harper's Magazine, Vol. CXXX, No. 777, pp. 349-360.

McKinlay, W.L. 1913-1914. Arctic diary, July 25, 1913 - Sept. 6, 1914. Typed copy certified correct by W.L. McKinlay. January 5, 1927, in McKinlay papers, MG30 B25, NAC.

McKinlay, W.L. 1976. *Karluk*, the great untold story of Arctic exploration. Weidenfeld and Nicolson, London, England, 170 p.

Mikkelsen, E. 1955. Mirage in the Arctic. Rupert Hart-Davis, London, 216 p.

Moyles, R.G. 1979. British law and Arctic men. Western Producer Prairie Books, Saskatoon, Saskatchewan, 93 p .

Murdoch, J. 1888. Ethnological results of the Point Barrow Expedition, 1881-1883. 9th Annual Report of the Bureau of Ethnology to the Secretary of the Smithsonian Institution, 1887-88, by J.W. Powell, Director, pp. 19-441.

Noice, Harold. 1924. With Stefansson in the Arctic. George G. Harrap Co. Ltd., London, 270 p.

Nuttall, G.H.F. 1919. Report on *Pediculus* collected from Eskimos. Report of the Canadian Arctic Expedition 1913-1918, Vol. 3, Insects, Part D, p. 11D.

O'Neill, J.J. 1913-16. Arctic diary. Original notebooks and typescript copy. O'Neill papers, MG30 B171, NAC.

O'Neill, J.J. 1916. Geological reports, Canadian Arctic Expedition 1915. Summary Report of the Geological Survey, Department of Mines, for the Calendar year 1915, pp. 236-241.

O'Neill, J.J. 1924. The geology of the Arctic Coast of Canada west of the Kent Peninsula. Report of the Canadian Arctic Expedition 1913-18, Vol. 11, Geology and Geography, Part A, 107 p.

Orth, D.J. 1967. Dictionary of Alaska place names. United States Geological Survey Professional Paper 567, 1084 p.

Oxford University Press. 1971. The compact edition of the Oxford English Dictionary. 2 Vols., 4116 p.

Peary, R.E. 1904. Snowland folk. F.A. Stokes Co., New York, 97 p.

Poncins, Gontran de. 1941. Kabloona. Reynal and Hitchcock Inc., New York, 339 p.

Porsild, E. 1955. The vascular plants of the Western Canadian Arctic Archipelago. Canada, Department of Northern Affairs and National Resources, Museum Bulletin No. 135, 226 p.

Rasmussen, Knud. 1927. Across Arctic America - Narrative of the Fifth Thule Expedition. G.P. Putnam's Sons, New York, 388 p.

Rae, Dr. John. 1852. Journey from Gt. Bear Lake to Wollaston Land, and Exploration along the South and East Coast of Victoria Land. Journal of the Royal Geographical Society, Vol. 22, pp. 73-81.

Richardson, Sir John. 1851. Arctic searching expedition: a journal of a boat voyage through Rupert's Land and the Arctic Sea in search of the Discovery ships under the command of Sir John Franklin. Longman, Brown, Green, and Longmans, London, 413 p. (Vol. 1), 426 pp. (Vol. 2).

Roberts, Helen R. and Jenness, D. 1925. Songs of the Copper Eskimos. Report of the Canadian Arctic Expedition, 1913-18, Vol. 14, 506 p.

RNWMP. 1918. Report of the Royal Northwest Mounted Police for the year ended September 30, 1917, 27 p.

Sapir, E. 1913a. Telegram (Canadian Pacific Railway Co.) dated February 28, 1913 to D. Jenness, Lower Hutt, New Zealand, 1 p. Copy in Jenness Letters, Sapir Correspondence, CES-CMC.

Sapir, E. 1913b. Letter to D. Jenness, March 6, 1913, 3 p. Copy in Jenness Letters, Sapir Correspondence, CES-CMC.

Sapir, E. 1913c. Letter to D. Jenness, May 28, 1913, 2 p. Copy in Jenness Letters, Sapir Correspondence, CES-CMC.

Schrader, F.C. 1904. A reconnaissance in northern Alaska in 1901. United States Geological Survey Professional Paper 20, 139 p.

Sharpe, D. 1988. Late Glacial landforms of Wollaston Peninsula, Victoria Island, Northwest Territories: product of ice-marginal retreat, surge, and mass stagnation. Canadian Journal of Earth Sciences, Vol. 25, pp. 262-279.

Sharpe, D. 1989. Surficial geology, Wollaston Peninsula (Victoria Island), District of Franklin, Northwest Territories. Geological Survey of Canada, Map 1650A, scale 1:250,000.

Sherman, Jr., J.D. 1919. Family Dytiscidae. Report of the Canadian Arctic Expedition 1913-18, Vol. 3, Insects, Part E, Coleoptera, pp. 18E-19E.

Sladen, F.W.L. 1919. The wasps and bees collected by the Canadian Arctic Expedition 1913-18. Report of the Canadian Arctic Expedition 1913-1918, Vol. 3, Insects, Part G, Hymenoptera and plant galls, pp. 25G-35G.

Spearman, Grant, Etalook, Arctic John, and Riley, Louisa M. 1985. Preliminary report of the Ulumiut traditional land use inventory. Edwin Hall and Associates, Brockport, N.Y., 33 p.

Sperry, J.R. 1983. Ikey Angotisiak Bolt (1894-1981) — Arctic Profile. Arctic, Vol. 36, pp. 218-219.

Sperry, J.R. 1987. Letter to the editor. "Eskimo" - a term of dignity or derogation? Arctic, Vol. 40, p. 364.

St. Onge, D.A. 1987. Quaternary geology and geomorphology of the lower Coppermine River valley, District of Mackenzie, N.W.T. XIIth INQUA Congress Field Excursion A-22, National Research Council of Canada, Publication 27060, 32 p.

Stefansson, V. 1913a. My life with the Eskimo. The MacMillan Company, New York, N.Y., 527 p.

Stefansson, V. 1913b. Religious beliefs of the Eskimo. Harper's Magazine, Vol. CXXVII, November 1913, pp. 869-878.

Stefansson, V. 1913c. Cable from London to Dr. R.M. Anderson, New York, March 27-28, 1913, 1 p. Original in Stefansson Correspondence file, Anderson papers, CMN.

Stefansson, V. 1914a. The Stefansson-Anderson Arctic Expedition of the American Museum: Preliminary Ethnological Report. Anthropological Papers of the American Museum of Natural History, Vol. XIV, Part 1, 395 p.

Stefansson, V. 1914b. The Stefansson-Anderson Arctic Expedition. Anthropological Papers of the American Museum of Natural History, Vol. XIV, Part 2, pp. 397-457.

Stefansson, V. 1914c. Prehistoric and present commerce among the Arctic Coast Eskimo. Geological Survey of Canada, Anthropological Series No. 3, Museum Bulletin No. 6, 29 p.

Stefansson, V. 1914d. Letter to Dr. R.M. Anderson, April 8, 1914, 4 p. Copy in Local Arctic Correspondence file, Anderson papers, CMN.

Stefansson, V. 1920. Letter to G.J.Desbarats, Department of the Naval Service, September 7, 1920, 2 p. Copy in Desbarats file, Anderson papers, CMN.

Stefansson, V. 1921. The friendly Arctic. The MacMillan Company, New York, N.Y., 784 p.

Stefansson, V. 1944 (?) Introduction. *In* Charles D. Brower. (1944?) Fifty years below zero. Robert Hale Limited, London, pp. v-vi.

Stuck, Archbishop Hudson. 1918a. A journey round the whole Arctic coast of Alaska. Geographical Journal, Vol. 52, pp. 267-268.

Stuck, Archbishop Hudson. 1918b. A winter circuit of our Arctic coast; a narrative of a journey with dog-sleds around the entire coast of Alaska. Charles Scribner's Sons, New York, 347 p.

Svoboda, Josef. 1978. Plants of the High Arctic: How do they manage? Chapter 20 *in* Living explorers of the Canadian Arctic (Shirley Milligan and Walter Kupsch, Eds.). Outcrop Publishers, Yellowknife, N.W.T., Canada, pp. 194-225.

Swenander, Carl Gustof. 1906. Harpun Kastspil - og Lansspetsar fran Vastgronland. Svenska Vetenskapsakademiens Handlingen, Vol. 40, no. 3, Wiksell, Uppsala, Sweden, 45 p.

Taylor, W.E., Jr. 1972. An archaeological survey between Cape Parry and Cambridge Bay, N.W.T., Canada in 1963. Archaeological Survey of Canada Mercury Series Paper No. 1, 106 p.

Thibert, A. 1969. English-Eskimo dictionary, Eskimo-English (Revised Edition). Canadian Research Centre for Anthropology, Saint Paul University, Ottawa, Ontario, 173 p.

Thomas, Lowell. 1961. Sir Hubert Wilkins, his world of adventure. McGraw-Hill Book Co., Inc., New York, N.Y., 296 p.

Webster, J.H. 1987. Arctic adventure. G.C. and H.C. Enterprises Ltd., Box 1000, Ridgetown, Ontario, 131 p.

White, James. 1910. Ninth Report of the Geographic Board of Canada. Part IV. Place Names — Northern Canada, pp. 231-455.

Wilkins, G.H. 1913-16. Arctic diary. Original in Stefansson Collection, Baker Library, Dartmouth College, Hanover, New Hampshire, U.S.A.

Wilkins, G.H. 1914. Letter to Dr. R.M. Anderson, April 19, 1914, 2 p. Original in Wilkins file, Anderson papers, CMN.

Wilkins, G.H. 1918. Report of George H. Wilkins on the topographical and geographical work carried out by him in connection with the Canadian Arctic Expedition. Report of the Department of the Naval Service for the fiscal year ending March 31, 1917, pp. 65-70.

Williams, R.S. 1921. Mosses of the Canadian Arctic Expedition, 1913-18. Report of the Canadian Arctic Expedition 1913-18, Vol. 4, Botany, Part E, pp. 3E-15E.

Index

A

D

E

F

I

J

K

L

M

N

O

P

Q

R

S

T

U

V

W

Y